ENGLAND
IN
PARTICULAR

ENGLAND IN PARTICULAR

A CELEBRATION OF
THE *commonplace*,
THE *local*, THE *vernacular*
AND THE *distinctive*.

SUE CLIFFORD & ANGELA KING
WITH GAIL VINES, DARREN GIDDINGS & KATE O'FARRELL
FOR COMMON GROUND

HODDER &
STOUGHTON

Common Ground is a charity (no. 326335) and has been grateful
for grant support from the Cobb Trust, Countryside Agency,
Defra Environmental Action Fund, the John Ellerman Foundation,
the Garfield Weston Foundation, the Headley Trust, the Tedworth
Charitable Trust, the Lyndhurst Settlement, and many others.

First published in Great Britain in 2006 by Hodder & Stoughton
A division of Hodder Headline

A CIP catalogue record for this title is available from
the British Library

ISBN 9780340826164

Illustration Art Director: David Holmes

Typeset in Garamond, Gill Sans and Trade Gothic

Designed by SMITH
Victoria Forrest, Karl Shanahan

Printed and bound by L.E.G.O. SpA, Vicenza, Italy

The paper used to manufacture this book has been sourced from
a Forest Stewardship Council accredited paper mill in Sweden.

Hodder & Stoughton Ltd
A division of Hodder Headline
338 Euston Road
London NW1 3BH

C O N T E N T S

For Barbara Bender, Roger Deakin,
Robin Grove-White, Fraser Harrison,
Robert Hutchison, Richard Mabey,
Rupert Nabarro, Common Ground trustees
past and present, and David Holmes,
honorary art director since 1985,
with love & thanks.

Gold Hill, Shaftesbury, Dorset.

CELEBRATING LOCAL DISTINCTIVENESS

This book is about the extraordinary richness of our everyday surroundings; the landscapes, buildings, people and wildlife that give meaning to the places we know.

It is about the commonplace; for us to value it, a creature does not have to be endangered, a building does not have to be monumental, a prospect does not have to be breathtaking. A place may not even be 'ours' for us to feel attached to it. We just need to know something of it; it has to mean something to us.

Everywhere is somewhere. What makes each place unique is the conspiracy of nature and culture; the accumulation of story upon history upon natural history.

At Common Ground we have forged the idea of *local distinctiveness* to embody this concept. It is a dynamic thing, constantly evolving as places change – it is not about preserving the status quo, creating a frozen moment – and it includes the invisible as well as the visible: symbols, festivals and legends stand alongside hedgerows, hills and houses.

Rather than a gazetteer of places, we have focused on aspects of locality – archaeology, architecture, landscape, language, food, folklore, events, engineering – that interact with one another at the level of the street, the neighbourhood, the parish. We offer a way of looking that has universal potential, but is best done on an intimate scale.

Why A to Z? The alphabet helps us to break some conventions; it liberates us from classifying things, from following history as an arrow through time, from organising hierarchies. It shuffles and juxtaposes in ways that surprise. This can change what we see, make things we take for granted seem new to us; it may encourage us into action. We hope this book helps you to look at your own place, to see it through new eyes, to cherish it and to take it into your own hands.

LAND AS CULTURE

The land is our great creation. Underpinned by nature, it is a physical thing and an invisible web. It is held together by stone walls and swallows, Northumbrian smallpipes and Swaledale sheep, Devon lanes and Fenland skies, Diwali and 'obby 'osses, round barrows and cooling towers, high streets and Ham stone, dew ponds and dialects. Sometimes we forget that our everyday surroundings are nature's greatest store, history's biggest library. The filigree of rich understandings between people and the land is not about scenery. It takes us below the surface, to where the land might reflect back to us purpose and belonging.

The land harbours thousands of stories that have never been written down: tales of daily lives and struggles to find water, win stone, grow food, help neighbours, fight enemies, hold back tides, survive disease.

The land and its secrets are both robust and vulnerable. After surviving for four thousand years, subtle aspects of a farm's history can be all but erased in one afternoon of deep ploughing. The alignment of a new bypass, which may help a village to breathe again, can cause a stream to be banished, culverted, burying the very reason why the village established itself there. The stealing of a market-place to make a car park in the centre of town may deny people a place to meet and shop, to exchange news and gossip, to mark the seasons with festivals.

Stories are the currency of ordinary history. Small details spark the telling – a line of trees, the shape of a roof, the name of a street. They help us to share knowledge of what makes a place. We are all familiar with our own fragments of geography: places where we live, work, visit. We mostly take them for granted, but their significance lies in their very ordinariness to us.

Differentiating the ordinary demands close observation, cherishing the locally typical, allowing professional expertise and indigenous knowledge to inform one another. A greater care for local distinctiveness could help us to reinvigorate our sense of domestic attachment.

L O C A L I T Y

Scale is important, as is the question of who defines it. We are talking of a fineness of grain – the neighbourhood, the locality, the parish, the housing estate, the village, the suburb, perhaps even the street, as defined by those who live and work and play there. These are the areas to which people feel they belong, or which they have chosen and are claiming anew.

At Common Ground we are concerned not with regional diversity but with *local* distinctiveness. When things are looked at on a larger scale, sensitivity is lost. People become 'the public'; streets and fields become 'sites'; woods and streams become 'natural resources'. These abstractions render professionals forgetful of lives, livelihoods and places. 'Regions' are generally defined from the outside in; they are about form and function; they are academic, institutional or political creations. Locality needs to be defined from the inside.

The Chaos theorist Benoît Mandelbrot asked '*How long is the coast of Britain?*', asserting that any answer would be dependent upon the distance from which the measurement was taken. Someone measuring from a satellite map would give a much smaller figure than someone walking every inlet. For a snail every pebble would add to the length. The gauge matters.

While we have made the world smaller with trains, boats, planes, cars and elevators, we still have to pace most of our activities to our own size and our own walking. It is at this scale and speed that we see and savour most.

D I S T I N C T I V E N E S S

Distinctiveness is not the same as diversity, for it involves much more than variety. Strict edges rarely exist between places, other than at the coast or where there is a dramatic change in geology. One place ends gradually, as another begins. In biology the place where two ecosystems overlap – the ecotone – supports a variety of species that is often richer than in the habitats it buffers. Similarly, in a town, some streets may be dominated by small Indian shops and others by big chain stores, but the area of greatest fascination may well be the back lanes where they meet.

Geologists are excited by unconformity; archaeologists tell the time by reading the overlaps – parish boundaries lining up along a Roman road, which itself cuts across older field systems. Buildings may offer a 'confliction' of styles, histories and materials, but together they make this place.

CHANGE & DIFFERENCE

Local distinctiveness is not served well by simple preservation of the status quo; like nature it needs flux, but that is not to say that some things will not persist for a long time.

Just as nature is always experimenting, a locality, too, must be open to change, permeable to new people, ideas, buildings, plantings. But change may enrich or it may deplete, and richness is under siege. Mass production, fashion, increased mobility and forceful promotion of corporate identity have brought us uniform shop fronts, farm buildings, factories, forests and front doors. Intensive farming has created a bland, unfriendly countryside. New estates offer the 'Cheviot' or the 'Mayfair' house in any part of England.

The differences that places show are just the first glimpse of richness. Little things (detail) and clues to previous lives and landscapes (patina) may be the very things that breathe significance into the streets or fields. So much surveying, fact-gathering, analysis and policy-making leaves out the very things that make us love a place.

DETAIL

We can pick out a face in a football crowd, see a tiny bird high up in a tree of a hundred thousand leaves, place a beer by its taste and sneeze at things we cannot even smell. Detail informs our lives. Whatever our work or pleasures, our attention and affections are held by small complications and intricacies. We thrive on gossip, the delicacy of flowers, the differences between bricks and concrete.

In Australia vast areas may seem to look the same, but the cultured eye sees minute detail. Water can be found from the subtlest constellation of clues, stories cling to small marks on rocks, and the slightest rise can be a landmark for miles.

We are emotional, subjective beings with memories and imagination; we are provoked to reverie by the smallest of things. We often know and feel things for which words cannot be found, despite having one of the richest languages in the world. We have a much greater capacity to see than we have to describe. Hence people sense when something has gone from their local scene, but cannot articulate it. It could be summer silence where swifts once filled the sky; it could be the displacement of a family firm by a chain store.

Just as Thomas Hardy talks of divining the shape of a mountain in the dark by the absence of stars, we recognise where we are through many different cues, and often we sense what is there through something else. Ecologists use the term 'indicator species': dog's mercury suggests ancient woodland. Geologists (following aboriginal practice) recognise the presence of certain minerals by the plants growing above the ground: sandwort is known as leadwort in Derbyshire, Lancashire and Cheshire. Pollution and lichen experts read sulphur dioxide in the absence of *Lobaria pulmonaria* and *Usnea articulata*. We can see the winter salt line along roadsides in Huntingdonshire by the summer flowering of sea spurrey. A Warwickshire gate lets us know subliminally that we are not in Gloucestershire.

The invisible often has to be 'seen' through the visible. Original attempts to map climate had to rely upon patterns read from vegetation. Only when wind and temperature could be monitored by scattered weather stations and at altitude did scientists find evidence of what people already knew. The earlier fall of leaves at the bottom of a small valley murmurs 'frost pocket'. The field persisting at the centre of a village whispers 'festival'.

History is often pieced together by detective work from footprints and stories. There is much non-verbal communication between us and a place we know. As well as responding to the obvious, we identify signs, clues, traces, suggestions, intimations, and they gather further richness through juxtaposition. Colours look different according to their neighbours. We need the nourishment of detail – in things as ordinary as rumples in a field, the shape of a gable end, seasonal goods in the market – to stimulate our senses.

P A T I N A

Places remain vital through absorption and reinvention. In Northamptonshire compare a deep-ploughed field of a hundred acres with ten fields of ten acres. Read the richness in the latter – perhaps medieval ridge and furrow overlaid with Enclosure hedgerows, never ploughed or strewn with herbicide or fertiliser. Go to the East End of London and compare a sixties, seventies or eighties estate with the Huguenot buildings, bagel shops and Bangladeshi restaurants of Brick Lane and the mosque in an old synagogue that was once a chapel. Local distinctiveness must be about history continuing through the present, not about the past.

The crude sacrifices made by comprehensive and rapid change demean us. We can add without brutalism. Dynamism and vitality should be great allies of local distinctiveness. Attempts to arrest both progress and decay in a Cotswold village or in culturally diverse Leicester risk the danger of creating a frozen moment, the real place and people having sunk below waves of preciousness or poverty. We must hold on to most of the old while demanding the best of the new.

A U T H E N T I C I T Y

Why is it important that Wensleydale cheese continues to be made in this valley and not the next? Among the economic reasons, there is also an understanding that the cows and sheep of this place, eating grass in this valley, with expertise built here over generations, combine to create a food that reflects and reinforces identity. Its production brings dignity and pride to the place, since the people who make it are experts, as are the people who grow the grass to feed the animals. At its best the place that is created and sustained by this activity is one in which mixed grass, wildflowers and barns have real jobs, as do the people.

The French have made a profession out of the particular: *terroir* carries kudos, binding together identity, place and quality. *Appellation contrôlée* ensures that the place of origin is known and important. Trace elements can make the difference between good and better, and the educated nose can tell.

A Somerset hedge laid in a Midland pattern, a Bakewell pudding made with almond essence, *Far from the Madding Crowd* filmed in France: these things fall short. We are deprived by the ersatz, the kitsch, the substitute.

The packaging of history as 'heritage' to create brands, such as 'Brontë Country', degrades cultural complexity. It should be perfectly possible to reinforce the medieval 'feel' of York, the Orwell connections in Wigan, Lancashire, without reducing places to stage sets, someone's idea of the past, tourist destinations, one-dimensional and unsatisfying. Local distinctiveness is not necessarily about beauty, but it must be about truth.

I D E N T I T Y

The unusual, the special, the idiosyncratic or the rare may be important factors in giving a place a sense of itself – the fortifications, the football team, the fritillaries, the fair. But identity is not bound up only in the symbolism of features and festivals. It is the commonplace that defines – the locally abundant plants, the specific wall-building methods, the accents and dialects – the context that exerts the binding force.

Cottages exhibit vernacular responses to climate, materials and need. The identity of Georgian houses great and small lies in their recognisable similarity of form, function and façade, based upon proportional rules. But they are never the same. Their differences lie in their relations to the land and to one another, their places in the social hierarchy, their original tasks (workers' houses in Barnsbury, north London; aristocratic residences in the Royal Crescent, Bath), their materials (grey-gold limestone in Stamford, Lincolnshire; red brick in Nottinghamshire). While all leaves do the same basic jobs, they have developed drip tips, hairs and so on to adapt to local conditions. The demands of photosynthesis and family evolution do not sacrifice individuation. All species produce different kinds of leaves, and leaves vary on the same tree.

IMAGINATION & HUMANITY

It is salutary to recall that 'utopia' means 'nowhere'. The philosophising that builds the ideal usually imagines that nothing has been there before, and that life and culture will thereafter evolve no further.

Knowledge, new ideas and wisdom must be shared. The tumbleweed expertise of the professional, learnt and practised elsewhere; the fresh cultural eye of the incomer; the local wisdom of the indigene, amassed through generations: all have different apects of perception to offer.

This implies a radical shift in the way in which we plan and prognosticate, towards a more responsive, detailed way of changing things.

The forces of homogenisation rob us of both tangible and invisible things that have meaning to us; they erase the fragments from which we piece together stories of nature and history; they stunt our sensibilities and starve our imaginations. And, as Gaston Bachelard has said, '*if we cannot imagine, we cannot foresee*'. Our interest in local distinctiveness incorporates a profound concern for our common future.

Nature will endure whatever our actions bring. It is we who are in danger. We deprive ourselves of a rich life. We need to live better with the world, and it is our ordinary actions that will be our salvation or our downfall. To ground ourselves, understand our place, find meaning and take steps to cherish and enrich our own patch of land demands that we change our ways, share our knowledge, get involved. We have to know what is of real value to us, where we are, and find new ways of belonging.

Sue Clifford & Angela King
Shaftesbury, Dorset
January 2006

Fight for **AUTHENTICITY** and integrity. Keep places lived in, worked in and real.

Demand the **BEST** of the new.

CHANGE things for the better, not for the sake of it!!

Let the **CHARACTER** of the people and place *express* itself. Challenge corporate identity before it kills our high streets. Give local shops precedence.

Value the **COMMONPLACE**. Our cultural landscapes are our *ordinary* history and *everyday* nature intertwined.

Let **CONTINUITY** show. Decay is an important process. Don't tidy things up so much that the layers of history and reclamation by nature are obliterated.

Defend **DETAIL**. Respond to the local and to the *vernacular*. No new building or development need be bland or brash.

Local **DIALECT** should be spoken, heard and seen.

EATING should be a *creative* act. *Buy local* and seasonal.

We need **ENCHANTMENT**, clear streams as well as clean water in our *daily lives*.

ENHANCE the natural features – rivers and brooks, hills and valleys, woods and heaths. Never let a stream be culverted, out of sight and open to abuse.

Take the place's **FINGERPRINT**. Forget words such as resource, site, customers and public. Abstractions lead us astray. Think and talk about places and people.

Get to know your **GHOSTS**. The hidden and unseen *stories and legends* are as important as the visible.

GROUND yourself, *attachment* is the first step to changing the world.

Don't fossilise places. **HISTORY** is a continuing process, not just the past. *Celebrate* time, place and the *seasons* with feasts and festivals.

Work for local **IDENTITY**. *Oppose* monoculture in our fields, parks, gardens and buildings. Resist formulaic designs and automatic ordering from pattern books which homogenise and deplete.

Our IMAGINATION needs diversity and *variegation*. We need standards, not standardisation.

JETTISON your car whenever you can and go by public transport. Places are for people and nature. Cars detach us from places and unwittingly cause their destruction.

Know your place. Facts and surveys are not the same as **KNOWLEDGE** and *wisdom*. Itinerant expertise needs to meet with aboriginal, *place-based* knowledge so that we can make the best of both worlds.

The **LAND** is sacred in many cultures. Why have we put a protective noose around the spectacular and the special and left the rest? *All* of our *surroundings* are important to someone.

xiv

Buy things that are **LOCALLY DISTINCTIVE** and locally made – such as food and souvenirs. Resist the things that can be found anywhere.

Bring the countryside to the town. Keep the fruit, vegetable and local produce **MARKETS** open and alive. We should be able to buy Norfolk Biffins in Norwich and Laxton's Superb in Bedford.

Places carry **MEANING** in their associations and symbolisms. Don't plough through *significance*, it cannot be re-created. The well or tree may be the reason why a place is where it is.

Let **NATURE** in. Encourage the plants that want to grow in your locality. You'll find a succession of good and diverse neighbours that bring *richness* to your doorstep.

NAMES carry resonances and *secrets.* Respect *local names* and add new ones with care. It is not **good** enough to call a new estate 'Badger's Mead' when the badgers have been destroyed.

Champion the **ORDINARY** and the *everyday.*

Get to know your place intimately. Search out **PARTICULARITY** and **PATINA**, add new layers of interest.

QUALITY cannot be quantified. You know when **something** is *important to you* – make subjective and emotional arguments. Don't be put off because professionals have marginalised all the things *they can't count.* Make them listen and look.

REMEMBER the depth of people's *attachment to places.* Do not undermine local pride and rootedness with insensitive change.

REVEAL the geology. Use the *brick and stone* of the **locality.** Reinforce the colour, patterns, texture, craftsmanship and work of the place.

Get things in proportion and in **SCALE**. Every place has its own distinctive *dimensions.*

Personality often resides in **SUBTLETY** and idiosyncrasy. *Look* closely and look often.

THWART the urbanisation of the countryside. Fight the kerbstones and other roadside paraphernalia.

USE old buildings again. Find new functions for them. *Accretion* is better than demolition.

VALUE your own *values.* Democracy thrives on discussion about things that matter to us. Let the experts in on your terms.

Slow down. Wisdom comes through **WALKING**, talking and listening. Exile **XENOPHOBIA**, which fossilises places and peoples. Welcome cultural diversity and *vive la différence.*

Make an alphabet of **YOUR** own place. Work to reinforce local distinctiveness. *Play your part,* celebrate your differences.

Introduce **ZEITGEIST** to *genius loci.* Don't let the signs of the times destroy the power of the place.

ZONING and segregation *kill places.* If industry is bad enough to be hidden, should it exist at all?

The Historic Counties are used throughout this book. Rather than following the administrative units overlain in 1965 and 1974, as well as later tinkering, we have done our best to follow the bounds laid down a thousand years ago or more.

We have followed the admirable gazetteer produced by the Association of British Counties (ABC), which champions the historic counties: *'ABC contends that Britain needs a fixed popular geography, one divorced from the ever-changing names and areas of local government [and], instead, rooted in history, public understanding and commonly held notions of cultural identity.'*

Inevitably we have found it difficult.

We admit to inconsistency over London, favouring the name of the capital over Middlesex and the other counties that border the Thames. Other cities big and small confounded us, too – Liverpool may have been just one parish for a long time but now it covers a wider area; the urban agglomerations of Birmingham, Manchester, Newcastle and Gateshead, and those of Yorkshire, spread and subsume.

Some of the valleys and moors, rivers and small places may have evaded our intentions, but our heart is in the geographical use of historic meaning, not least because it is often visible in the land and heard in names and speech patterns. The longevity of identity is impressive, and it is to this identity, of course, that older references, from books and maps to paintings and poetry, relate.

Where the ABC gazetteer could not help us, we ran to old maps, particularly to a late and wonderful find – *The Illustrated Road Book of England and Wales* (AA, 1958) – and the *Reader's Digest Complete Atlas of the British Isles* (1965), which has a massive place index.

Please see 'Counties' in the text for a fuller description of the historic counties.

'What do you consider the largest map that would be really useful?'
'About six inches to the mile.'
'Only six inches!' exclaimed Mein Herr. 'We very soon got to six yards to the mile. Then we tried a hundred yards to the mile. And then came the grandest idea of all! We actually made a map of the country, on the scale of a mile to the mile!'
'Have you used it much?' I enquired.
'It has never been spread out yet,' said Mein Herr: 'the farmers objected: they said it would cover the whole country, and shut out the sunlight! So we now use the country itself, as its own map, and I assure you it does nearly as well.'

Lewis Carroll, from *Sylvie and Bruno Concluded*

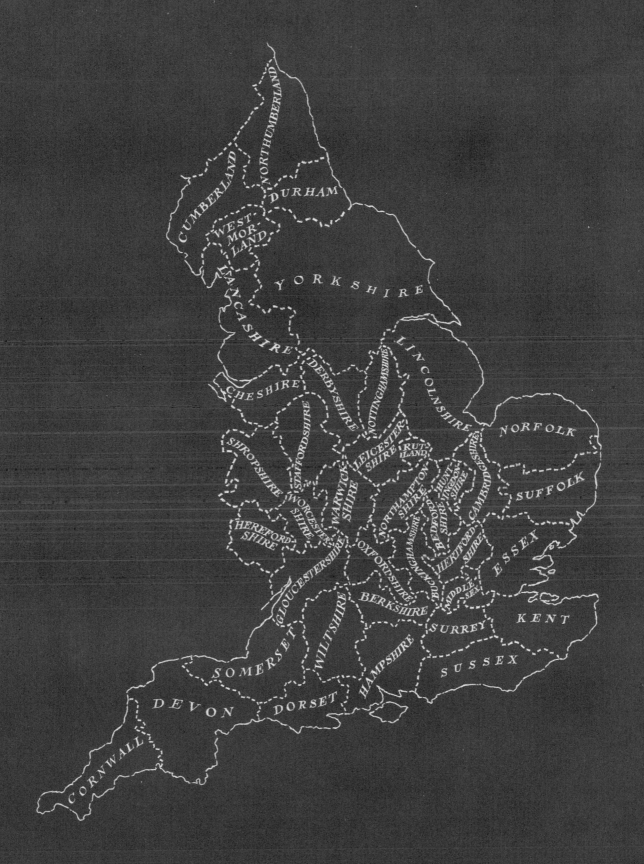

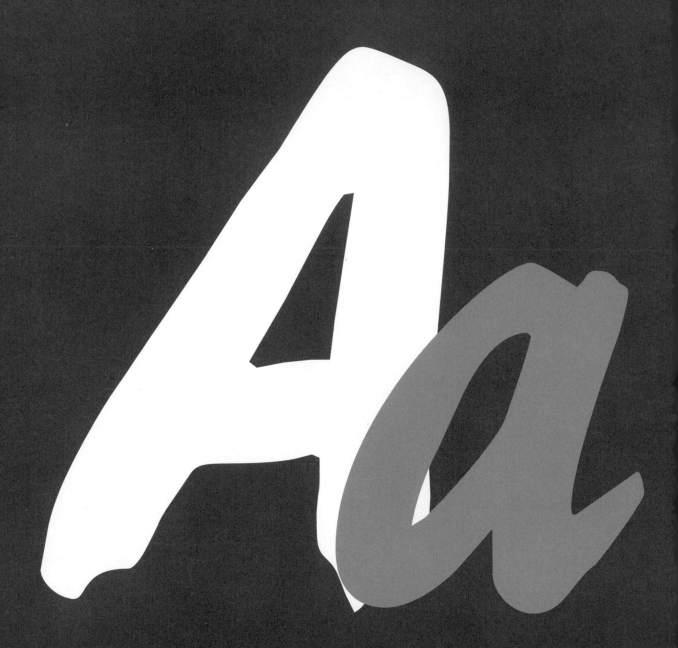

Ashley Script, Ashley Havinden, 1955.

A B B E Y S

Only the foundations remain of Shaftesbury Abbey, once the most powerful in the land, founded by King Alfred for his daughter Aethelgifu in 888. Such was the fate of many abbeys during Henry VIII's dissolution of the monasteries from 1536 to 1540. Monks and nuns were hanged or dispersed, the buildings were stripped of their valuables and their stone removed for local use. Remote abbeys, such as Muchelney on the Somerset Levels, mostly escaped self-interested recycling and remain evocative ruins.

An abbey was governed by an abbess or abbot according to the principles of a particular religious order. The nuns or monks that lived within its walls – Augustinians, austere Carthusians, reforming Cistercians, sparse Cluniacs, white-robed Benedictines, black-clothed Dominicans or grey-shrouded Franciscans – gave us erudite writings and beautiful manuscripts. Many travelled around mainland Europe, and their works introduced new plants, technologies and ideas, economic drive, social focus – they changed the face of the land. New abbeys were founded around the time of the Crusades in the twelfth century, when feudal lords, seeking prayers for their souls, endowed monastic orders with extensive lands. Priories were usually smaller than abbeys, to which they were subservient.

Across England hundreds of abbeys, deconsecrated during the Dissolution and sold to loyal subjects, are now visible as remnant towers or high-windowed wings of handsome houses built from abbey stones, as at Newstead, Nottinghamshire and Titchfield, Hampshire. A few abbeys survive – the citizens of Tewkesbury, Gloucestershire raised £453 to buy St Mary the Virgin as their parish church from Henry VIII.

The French Revolution drove monks back into an England where Catholicism was tolerated rather than welcomed. The Benedictines founded Ampleforth Abbey in Yorkshire in 1802 and continue to run a farm, orchard and school there. The Cistercians built a new abbey at Mount St Bernard in Charnwood Forest, Leicestershire in 1835, designed by Pugin.

Fountains Abbey, built among springs in the isolated valley of the river Skell in North Yorkshire, became the top Cistercian abbey in England with eight subservient houses by the twelfth century. Its fortunes rose with sheep and fell with Henry. Pillaged to build the Elizabethan Fountains Hall, it was later valued for its gothic picturesqueness and became part of the elaborate landscaped grounds of Studley Royal in the 1740s. Now in the hands of the National Trust, it draws more than a quarter of a million visitors a year.

See also CATHEDRALS, CHURCHES, COMMONS, DOVECOTES, LAWN, LEAD MINES, MONASTERIES, PONDS, SHEEP, SPRINGS, TITHE BARNS.

ABBOTS BROMLEY HORN DANCE

This could be '*the oldest surviving ceremony in Britain*', according to Charles Kightly. The dance and music certainly evoke eerie feelings of mystery and arouse elusive, deep-rooted memories that are at once unsettling and reassuring.

The age, purpose and meaning of the ceremony are not known. It could be pre-Christian; it has been performed on and off for perhaps a thousand years, although it was first recorded in Dr Robert Plot's *Natural History of Staffordshire* in 1686. One set of the horns has been carbon dated to around AD 1000.

The ceremony takes place in the Staffordshire village of Abbots Bromley (on the edge of Needwood Forest) on Wakes Monday, the old village feast day, which is the Monday following the first Sunday after 4 September. After a blessing by the vicar in St Nicholas's Church, six pairs of ancient reindeer antlers mounted on deer heads made of wood are taken down and dusted, together with a hobby-

3

horse and a bow and arrow. Most of the performers come from local families, some tracing their participation for four hundred years.

The six Deer Men, a Man-Woman (a man in women's clothes, called Maid Marion, with a wooden ladle and stick), a Hobby Horse with snapping jaws, a Bowman (a boy with a bow and arrow) and a Fool are accompanied by a boy with a triangle and a melodeon player. The dance starts at the vicarage and then moves to the butter cross and through the village to other houses, inns and farms.

Over and over again a simple dance is performed around the parish – a perambulation of about ten miles. With much weaving, backing and advancing, the climax evokes the drama of opposing stags, with the other players snapping jaws and tapping bow against arrow, stick against ladle to the beat of the music.

See also BEATING THE BOUNDS, FAIRS & FAIRGROUNDS, MORRIS DANCING, MUMMING PLAYS, 'OBBY 'OSSES, SAINTS.

A C C E N T S

Say 'bath' and it is evident whether you grew up in the north or south of England or are of a certain social class. Everyone speaks with an accent. Simply by the way we pronounce words many of us reveal our place of origin, our educational background, how new we are to the language, how much we have moved around, what sort of job we do, what television we watch, our age.

The English used to be more preoccupied with accents than they are now, but drop an h, say 'foo' rather than 'few', or 'init' at the end of sentences, and people may treat you differently. People from the West Country can still be teased for their slower speech delivery; those from Essex because of their 'glo'al' stops. In Brixton, south London, people from different Caribbean islands rib each other about the subtleties of their pidgin and creole.

Language changes so quickly that it picks up new trends within a single generation. There is nothing novel in this: '*certaynnly our language now used varyeth ferre from that whiche was used and spoken whan I was borne . . . And that comyn Englysshe that is spoken in one shyre varyeth from a nother*', William Caxton moaned in 1490; tectonic shifts had been pushing the language away from Anglo-Saxon and seasoning it with French words.

The very richness of our language relies upon its ability to absorb not only new words from inventions, discoveries and many lands, but also to drift in pronunciation. There is no doubt that our regional and local accents have suffered from Victorian snobbish notions of correct speaking, which became the received pronunciation (RP) of the early BBC, and that now our mobility and connectedness are erasing differences. But new patterns are being observed and new accents are emerging in urban areas, while broad variability is persisting. Aiden Turner-Bishop revels in the persistence of difference: '*If you travel on the train from Ormskirk to Liverpool you can hear the local accent become more Scouse as people board the train. In Ormskirk, the accent is clearly Lancashire, or "woolyback", as Liverpudlians call us. By Maghull or Aintree, the Scouse accent is clear and lively.*'

Children at school will pick up the local accent, no matter where their parents come from. And young people seem to be converging in their street talk, as mobile phones, radio, television and music are linking them as never before. Since the 1950s the rolled 'r' (especially after a vowel, as in 'further') has been sacrificed by the young because of its country connotations; it is now fading in all but the most westerly and rural places.

Meanwhile, pressing outwards from London, Essex and the south coast, the substitution of 'w' for 'l' (as in 'goal' and 'sail') reaches to Swindon, Norwich and Coventry. At the same time a school in Tower Hamlets, east London may have thirty languages in a single classroom, and the Globe Theatre on the opposite bank of the Thames is putting back the 'growled r' in attempts at delivering Shakespeare in its original Warwickshire form. But an accent remains a kind of badge, another expression of identity. Regional and local accents anchor us to one or more places that have affected our lives. Try 'who put the bus on the grass up the hill' and remember where you came from, my lovely.

See also DIALECTS, GREETINGS.

A E G I R S

An aegir (also spelt eagre or huger) is a bore – a wave driven by a high rising tide travelling up a narrowing and shallowing estuary. The name is occasionally used in relation to the bores on the Severn and Wye, and those around the Solway Firth and Morecambe Bay, for example on the river Kent. On the east of the country the Humber and Ouse present the right conditions, but the name especially clings to the river Trent, which narrows sufficiently to create a tidal surge as far as Averham in Nottinghamshire, whose name means 'at the floods'.

According to Christina Hole, '*Swedish legend says that the old gods took refuge in the rivers when Christian priests drove them from the land, and one at least survives to this day in the rushing Aegir of the Trent . . . The Trent in its upper reaches runs through the heart of the Danelagh, and the Jotun Aegir is still at home amongst the descendants of his former worshippers.*' Hole suggests a time before legend, when human sacrifice was made to the river. People still say the Trent claims three lives a year and, before the high steps down to the river were incarcerated in the defence wall, children in Gainsborough, Lincolnshire, 27 miles from where the Trent flows into the Humber, occasionally were lost as the bore swept upstream.

The Environment Agency says that the best time to see the Trent aegir is *'after a long period of dry weather. It usually appears during high spring tides, but the scouring action of winter floods and above average water levels in the river can reduce its size considerably.'* It gives time predictions for Gainsborough and Owston Ferry in Lincolnshire and West Stockwith, Nottinghamshire. But some suggest Littleborough, Nottinghamshire as the best vantage point.

See also BEACHES, BORES, COUNTIES, EELS, FOLKTALES, STAIRS, TIDES.

AGRICULTURAL SHOWS

Born in the crucible of experiment and improvement in the late eighteenth century and the agricultural depression in the early nineteenth century, agricultural societies and shows spread from county to county with a push from the National Board of Agriculture. Early shows pitted local landowners, farmers and inventors against one another for the titles of best clod-cruncher and pulveriser, two-horse harvest wagon, turnip cutter or field gate; in the mid-nineteenth century those who did the work did the innovating.

The Cornwall Agricultural Society founded in 1793 promoted plough matches and competitive animal gatherings across the county. By 1829 the 'shew fair' came to rest at Truro as the (Royal in 1848) Cornwall Show; the following year three hundred sheep were entered in competition. Finally locating at Wadebridge in 1961, the only breaks were in 1866 for Cattle Plague and 2001 for foot-and-mouth disease.

From the earliest Newark and Nottingham County Show, which has its origins in the Newark May Fair, to the biggest one-day show at Bakewell, Derbyshire and the still-local Manifold Show nearby, agricultural shows mark the season and the place. The show field is a year-round reminder. No signs mark the smaller shows, just subtle clues for those who recognise them: a double gate, a short stretch of hardcore, an odd wooden fence containing an inner field, a well-laid hedge.

The bigger county shows have purchased their own fields, created buildings and conference centres, nice asphalt roads, permanent show rings – and now the smaller shows are following. They have lost the plot – everything that has gone wrong with agriculture is in evidence at the Royal Showground, Stoneleigh in Warwickshire, which has become an industrial estate.

For the insider the day is about encounters, winning and losing, reaffirmations. The 'outsider' to farming is struck by otherworldliness: avoiding the cow pats, sinking fingers into a sheep's perfectly clipped back, seeing an egg appear from a clucking hen, comparing Devon Red with Gloucester cattle, feeling the ground shake to horses' hooves, catching the bull's eye in the Grand Parade. Marquees lend a glow to jams and cakes, flowers and perfect vegetables competitively made and grown for this moment. With smallholders' rabbits and chickens, the 'at heel' terriers and lurchers, waistcoats and white coats, pushchairs and tight jodhpurs, trilbys and vice-president tags, the whole 'country' spectrum jostles.

No prizes for knowing what dominates the Alwinton Border Shepherd's Show in Northumberland. At the Nidderdale Show in Yorkshire competitive classes in drystone walling and dressed walking sticks are included, and at the Bellingham Show in Northumberland, wrestling. These smaller shows still tell of local culture and offer authenticity lost from the industrial gatherings.

If you want to understand England and the depth of its variegation, you could do worse than map out your summer in visits to small agricultural shows. Let us pray with Philip Larkin that this indefinable *'. . . something they share/That breaks ancestrally each year into/Regenerated union. Let it always be there.'*

See also CATTLE, CROPS, DOGS, DRYSTONE WALLS, FAIRS & FAIRGROUNDS, FELL RUNNING, FIELDS, GATES, GOOSEBERRIES, HEDGES, HORSES & PONIES, ONIONS, PIGS, POULTRY, PRIDDY SHEEP FAIR, SCARECROWS, SHEEP, SHEEP-DOGS, SHIRE HORSES, SUFFOLK PUNCHES, TERRIERS, WATER-MEADOWS, WRESTLING.

5

AIRFIELDS

Like kites, the earliest planes needed a good run into the wind to help them lift off. Popham airstrip in Hampshire remains typical of the smallest take-off and landing place, literally a field with a telltale windsock. It now sports a

Gillingham & Shaftesbury Show, Dorset.

long, open-fronted shed shading a line of propellers and further ranks outside parked with colourful canvas coats.

In a hundred years more than 1,700 airfields have been developed in Britain. Some have grown into monsters, such as Gatwick (a racecourse in Sussex) and Heathrow (named after a hall in Middlesex). But many were surplus to requirements after both world wars and are remembered simply as 'Aerodrome Field', as in Elloughton, Yorkshire. Mown grass runways continued to be used until the 1940s, when heavier aircraft heralded the use of concrete.

In *The Landscape of War*, historian William Foot describes the huge impact of the Second World War military airfields. *'About 450 airfields, some occupying up to 800 acres, were built in Britain during the war and many of those already existing were enlarged and given concrete runways, amounting to the greatest single construction feat in Britain's history. Over 300,000 acres were gobbled up in the process, much of them prime farming land . . . The impact of these airfields on rural landscapes that had seen little change since the advent of the railways was like the building of so many new towns.'* Many were built in the south and eastern counties, usefully flat, to face the enemy across the North Sea; RAF airfields formed a defensive circle of seven fighter stations around London with now-familiar names including Biggin Hill and Northolt.

After the war, one in three military airfields was put to new use or returned to its former use. Areas of uncanny flatness without hedgerows or trees may be all that remains. On the edge of a flat arable field just outside Selsey, Sussex, a simple plaque on a plinth says *'RAF Selsey 1943-1945. From these fields spitfires & typhoons provided cover for the allied invasion forces on D-Day 1944. English, Belgian, French & New Zealand squadrons were based here.'*

Elsewhere bomb craters, concrete pillboxes, old gun emplacements, Nissen huts and hangers still survive, used for farming, horticulture and industry. The control tower stands out with its angled windows and all-round vision. The beautiful Art Deco terminal building at Shoreham, Sussex contrasts with the impressive tall octagonal brick and glass control tower at the former airport of Speke, Liverpool, where the terminal building is now a hotel.

Few early hangars survive. The most dramatic are the pair built in 1917 and 1928 from corrugated steel to house airships at Cardington, Bedfordshire, which loom over the flat landscape.

See also COMMONS, CORRUGATED IRON, HARES, HEATHLAND, PILLBOXES, RACECOURSES.

A L B I O N

This elusive old name for Britain may derive from *albus*, Latin for white. Many commentators mention this through time and it is both plausible and beguiling. This island is bounded to the south by high chalk cliffs kept constantly bright and white by rockfalls into the sea, and coasting seafarers making their way from the Mediterranean would easily recognise it from the description.

Others make Celtic claim – Albio, Alba or Alban(y), a name for all the islands of Great Britain or of parts of it (Scotland is sometimes cast as Alban).

One clutch of explanations has the giant Albion, son of Poseidon/Neptune, ruling the land for 44 years followed by his giant sons. Given that one old name for Stonehenge, Wiltshire is the Giant's Ring, it is easy to see how such stories might have gained currency. The giants, it seems, were displaced by a Trojan called Brutus; the land then was named after him, hence Britain.

Another story claims that Albia was the eldest of fifty daughters of a Syrian King. After killing all their husbands on their wedding night they were put aboard ship and left to the winds, which brought them to these shores, where they settled down. A parallel tale has 33 daughters of Diocletian, the Roman emperor, doing the same.

Ptolemy mentions the name in Greek (Alouion, AD 127) as does Pliny later in Latin (Albion). Bede picks it up in the eighth century, simply saying *'Britain, formerly known as Albion'*. Michael Drayton, in his epic *Poly-Olbion* of 1613, claims Albion as a Christian martyr from Rome, the first in Britain. Now poetry keeps the name alive, together with pubs and proud football teams, such as Brighton and Hove Albion. West Bromwich Albion (founded in 1879) notably was the first British team to welcome a high-profile triumverate of black players: Laurie Cunningham, Cyrille Regis and Brendan Baston – new giants for the 1980s.

The control tower, RAF Crosby-on-Eden, Carlisle, Cumberland. Haven Brow and the other Seven Sisters cliffs, Sussex.

The name Albion, as invoked by Peter Ackroyd, often devolves to England, seeming less territorial than poetical: '*Today, like those fading memorials, Albion is not so much a name as the echo of a name.*'

See also CHALK, FOOTBALL, GIANTS, ISLANDS, NORFOLK WHERRIES, SHIPPING FORECAST, STANDING STONES, WHITE CLIFFS.

A L D E R

Alders love water; through meadows they sinuously map the route of their companion streams. Many have been lost to land drainage and intensifying agriculture. Now a new threat, phytophthora – a fungus that invades the stems and roots of *Alnus glutinosa*, noticed first in 1993 – is spreading and threatening to change those river scenes already much diminished by our actions.

The favourite haunts of the alder are wet woods and plashy fens; they were abundant in the damp aftermath of the ice ages. In the West and North, where the rain really rains, they are still more widespread, whereas in the South and East they cling to the watersides and marshland. From the female catkin (known as black knobs in Derbyshire, where they are sought by well dressers) the minute seeds drop into water equipped with two floats that aid their journey to a nearby shore.

Uncommon now are whole woods of alder – alder carr – with their tangled and buttressed root systems that can stand substantial periods of inundation. But in East Anglia, around the Broads and in the wettest bits of Breckland, the alder remains a dominant tree.

In the New Forest, Hampshire, until the late nineteenth century, the alder was planted and coppiced to burn charcoal for use in the gunpowder mills; also in the Tillingbourne valley in the Surrey Hills. It is still prized for slow-burn charcoal making, being so wet. In London, along the Wandle, Brent and Lea rivers, lingering alders bear witness to their use by Dunn's of Kentish Town and other hat makers for their shaped blocks.

In the late eighteenth century alder was planted along rivers in Lancashire to help stabilise the banks, and was used by travelling bands of clog makers and chair makers, who took advantage of the pink-brown mahogany colour the wood attained after cutting. It can reach sixty feet in height, although it is uncommon to find single-stemmed old trees, as the alder was so much in demand for poles, dyes, boat making and pole-lathe work of all kinds. Like elms, alders were hollowed to make early water distribution pipes. They survive indefinitely in water – the remnants of ancient jetties show that their builders knew this well.

The wetter, woodier past is remembered in Old English place-names, such as Aldercar in Derbyshire, and Aldershot and Alresford in Hampshire. You can add field and farm names, including ellers, ollers, owlers (Yorkshire) and aul (Herefordshire).

Andrew Fraser says '*up in Shropshire, they are known as wallers. In the centre of Worcestershire, they are called arles and quite a number of wet woodlands along the valley of the Severn are named after it, e.g. Clifton Arles. Further south, they are called allers.*'

See also ANCIENT TREES, ASH, BEECH, BIRCH, BLACK POPLAR, BLACKTHORN, BOATS, ELM, FIELD MAPLE, HAWTHORN, HAZEL, HOLLY, HOLM OAK, HORNBEAM, HORSE CHESTNUT, JUNIPER, LANDMARK TREES, LIME, LONDON PLANE, MONKEY-PUZZLE, OAK, ORCHARDS, PEARS, POPLAR, RIVERS, ROWAN, ROYAL FORESTS, SCOTS PINE, SWEET CHESTNUT, SYCAMORE, WALNUT, WATER-MILLS, WELL DRESSING, WHITEBEAM, WILLOW, WINDSOR & COUNTRY CHAIRS, WOODS, YEW.

A L E X A N D E R S

Migrants making their way inland, alexanders suddenly make an impact in April, when they fill coastal verges with their shiny, dark green leaves and umbelliferous yellow tops, looking healthy and happy at four feet tall.

You can't miss them around Lulworth, Dorset, where they ambush old boats. Near Watchet, Somerset they follow smugglers' footsteps towards Exmoor; in Norfolk they often refuse domestication inland but clamber exuberantly around the cliffs.

Probably introduced from the Mediterranean by the Romans as a vegetable, they were cultivated in monastery gardens and are still sometimes found nearby. A staple of cottage gardens, they go by the local names of angelica in East Anglia and wild celery on the Isle of Wight. Sometimes known as Parsley of Alexandria, they have become naturalised where they feel happiest, near to the southern coasts. Every part of the aromatic plant can be used, its roots being favoured by fishermen to augment soups.

See also BLUEBELLS, CLIFFS, COASTS, GARDENS, GORSE, GRASSY TRIANGLES, GREEN LANES, LANES, MONASTERIES, RAMSONS, VERGES, WILDFLOWERS.

A L L E Y S

Between buildings or hedge and fence, the narrow walkway, wide enough for a person but not much more, is a reminder of the importance of permeability in the old parts of city, town and village.

Some alleys are public routes, others more private, as in Arab towns. Many travel under or through buildings (some as 'entries' through to the back yards of terraced houses); slopes may be negotiated by steps. They follow memories of old ownerships and rights of way that are now intimate short cuts for the cognoscenti. Such is their intricacy and particularity that many carry local names.

7

'In Hull (where my parents come from) they say ten foot – these connect the front of the house to your own back garden, between one house and the next. Great places for playing ball', Rosie Cross says. She goes on: 'Here in Teesdale we use the word wynd (and it is in many addresses), pronounced "weend" – this is an alley or windy narrow lane.'

Marylebone Passage at the back of Oxford Street, London survived the relentless pressure of building and is a relic of a well-used footpath all the way from St Giles in the Fields in Covent Garden to St Mary's. More intimate courts, yards and passages may have survived but lost their sky to the upper floors of buildings, as often happens in York – Coffee Yard, St Crux Passage to Whip-ma-whop-ma-gate and ways to and from The Shambles.

In Dorset, as Chris Slade observes, 'a drong is a narrow way between hedges, fences or walls. It appears on maps (and in the OED) as I have spelt it, but I have only heard it pronounced "drawn".' This lengthened sound, with a swallowed end, is how it would rhyme in William Barnes's nineteenth-century dialect poem 'The Turnstile':

> On Steän-cliff road, within the drong,
> Up where, as v'ok do pass along,
> The turnen stile, a painted white,
> Do sheen by day an' show by night.

While snicket sometimes appears in dictionaries as a northern dialect word describing a passage between buildings or fences, other well-used local terms are more elusive. 'Twitchel is used in Derbyshire to mean a narrow footpath between houses or running alongside fields', says Daphne Anson of Hunstanton, Norfolk. 'It is of a width that can carry two people, say, side by side; could possibly give room for a horse, although it is not officially a bridle path; and certainly nowadays can accommodate a bicycle. It is open to everyone. Sometimes it is defined by hedges, though in places these may be replaced by a fence.'

Around Nottingham, heading in different directions out of the city, you might find twitchel, ginnel or jitty used, a reminder of the simmering of cultures here during the so-called Dark Ages. Further north you will find more commonly gennel or gunnal, all with a hard 'g'. A passage between walls in Beverley, east Yorkshire is a racket.

Richard Barton says: 'I was brought up in Sussex, and the name we used was twitten for an alleyway behind some shops.

I was in Hamburg, Germany some years ago and the name for a similar alleyway or small street is Twiet in Plattdeutsch, or Low German, which is still spoken in that part of Germany. Twiet rhymes with street.' The oldest area of Brighton, Sussex, bordered by North, East and West streets, is called the Lanes, which is full of twittens. The narrow cobbled alleys are bordered by mainly eighteenth- and nineteenth-century buildings on a medieval street pattern, having been rebuilt more than once after ravages by the French and the sea (South Street has been found under beach shingle). These are no longer back alleys: tourists and locals linger in the antiques and clothes shops, cafés and pubs.

On the Isle of Portland, Dorset, an ope is a narrow passage between houses or walls that opens towards the sea. Margaret Somerville explains: 'We have come up with seven "openings to the sea", lanes particular to Chiswell, where the sea when it overtops the length of the beach can drain freely into Chiswell High Street then flow north into the Mere. It has been said that smugglers of old could quickly carry off their brandy and fishermen could bring their boats down them for safety, and in sunny weather wives would use them to carry their washing up onto the beach, where it would be laid out on the hot shingle to dry in the sun . . . The name of the wide ope beside the Chinese restaurant today defies identification, but may be called Lerret Ope. [The last] has been named No Ope by the present residents.'

Stow-on-the-Wold, Gloucestershire, with its ancient fairs, has alleys called the Tures, through which sheep were driven into the Market Square. Ilfracombe, Devon has its lanes; Bruton, Somerset its bartons; Lowestoft, Suffolk its scores. Liverpool has jiggers or jowlers; Hertfordshire has drokes; Great Yarmouth, Norfolk and Saffron Walden, Essex have rows. But in Chester The Rows are medieval shopping arcades at first-floor level, reached by steps from the street.

Northumberland calls slender ways chares (cerr is Old English for narrow place or bend). In Newcastle, of the 21 chares that led out over the old piers as the waterfront pushed into the Tyne in the early 1800s, just a few survived the great fire of 1853 – notably The Chare, Manor, Prudhoe, Plummer and Broad Chares. Pudding Chare recalls not sweetmeats but Pow Dene, the small ravine and its stream now hidden below the pavement. With its deeply incised river, Newcastle also has many stepped alleys, such as Tuthill, Castle and Croft Stairs. In London the many stairs between buildings edging the Thames are remnants of working access to the river.

Whitby in Yorkshire developed on steep slopes dropping down to the river Esk, so steps and stairs are common – Salt Pan Well Steps, Cliff Steps and Chair Stairs (Jacob's Ladder to earlier generations). The town still has more than eighty named yards. They trace the narrow burgage plots or tofts (old freehold ownership patterns) at right angles to the street and give access to the dense infill of Georgian and Victorian

8

houses. Arguments Yard (you can imagine: in the nineteenth century they were packed tight with families and had little sanitation) and many others are gone. Specific to Whitby are ghauts: explanations of the word are contested. The Oxford English Dictionary takes Hindi as the source, from *ghat* (mountain), morphing to a mountain pass and then a narrow way leading down to the river. Alan Whitworth offers a more domestic link: the word is locally pronounced as 'goat', an archaic name for stepping-stones, although lost are Tin Ghaut (T'Inn – the inn), Fish Ghaut and Collier's Ghaut, once leading to the water's edge. In Rochdale the name gauk may be related.

In Shrewsbury, where tourists enjoy exploring the convoluted and often stepped 'shuts' that ramify through the medieval town (Grope Lane, Coffee House Passage, St Julian's Steps, Castle Court), arguments rage about rights of way, gating and closure. The concern stemming from weekend wildness presumably was often revisited during the past thousand years, since one explanation of the name suggests that these lean lanes were closed at night.

See also ARCADES, BACK LANES, DENES, DIALECTS, FOOTPATHS, GREEN LANES, PORTLAND LERRETS, SHOPS, STAIRS, TERRACED HOUSES.

A L L O T M E N T S

Seen from the train, allotments, plotted and pieced, welcome you to a city. The original railway companies rented patches to their workers on swathes of land extra to requirements and many persist, despite the diesel fumes. Most allotments are owned by local authorities, having emerged in the nineteenth century as part of the movement to entice working people towards temperance and wholesome food-growing in the city. In the country, much earlier, they were vital to help agricultural workers survive when machines or economic fluctuation took their livelihoods.

Allotments' roots lie in struggles around loss of common land and ancient rights and the ruthless land-grabbing of enclosure. During Elizabeth I's reign, as common land was taken, commoners, if they were lucky, were given allotments of land near their tenanted cottages as part of their wages.

There were other beginnings. In 1605 Hunger Hill, Nottingham was rented in plots to burgesses, freemen and their widows; by the 1920s there were 540 hedged pleasure-garden plots. Cultivation of parts of the common of Town Moor in Newcastle began in the 1770s. Guinea Gardens, named after the yearly rent, were set up for the middle classes in Birmingham, Coventry and Sheffield from the eighteenth century, for recreation as well as food production.

These contrasted with allotments set up to help people supplement meagre wages or survive. Great Somerford, Wiltshire was the first Inclosure Act to ensure that land was made available for the labouring poor in 1806, but it was not until 1845 that the General Inclosure Act demanded that 'field gardens' must be set aside as a condition of enclosure. In 1887 the Allotment Act demanded that local authorities provide such land if there was demand.

Now, typically, an allotment may be paced out, thirty strides by ten, and may cost you from 25 pence to 85 pounds a year, but its functions and faces are wonderfully variable. Allotments offer a lateral look into the personalities of places: orderly lines of erect cabbages and huge leeks may await inspection, fruit trees may or may not be allowed, water-catching devices and idiosyncratic sheds may dominate, formal paths separate the bean rows, particular languages may babble together and sounds of children delight the senses.

The North holds on to its pigeon lofts; Nottingham's detached pleasure gardens, with their 'front doors' through hedges and their summerhouses, are Grade II* listed by English Heritage; Birmingham still has its high-hedged Guinea Gardens (also listed), now a multicultural paradise. Bristol has its 'leisure gardens'; Bolton, Lancashire its Food Plot organic and wildlife allotments (with crèche), including Nai Zingani (New Life) at Great Lever for Bangladeshi women. Welbeck Road allotments in Long Eaton, Derbyshire have a clubhouse and community polytunnel.

Roses have a history in Nottingham; chrysanthemums in Yorkshire. In the cool and damp of north-east England, competitive leek growing has its devotees. In Barnet, London you may learn how to grow and cook peppers in the Greek way from your neighbour. At Uplands in Handsworth, four miles from the centre of Birmingham, you may discuss the cultivation of coriander, dhania, Egyptian onions, methis and mooli with people whose gardening and cooking cultures draw on England, Ireland, Wales, Poland, Ukraine, various Caribbean islands, South Asia and further afield.

Pressure is rising for local authorities to sell land holdings (which belong to the people) in the face of demand for

9

housing, which greatly increases the price per acre. Of the one and a half million plots that helped Britain through the Second World War, the number has dwindled to only 297,000 in England.

See also BEACH HUTS, COMMONS, CORRUGATED IRON, COTTAGE GARDENS, GARDENS, GOOSEBERRIES, LEEKS, ONIONS, PIGEON LOFTS.

A L M S H O U S E S

Most almshouses are beautifully built, elegantly proportioned and worth seeking out, but you almost always notice them anyway. At the time of building most would have been on the edge of town. This was convenient for travellers, far enough out for disease not to spread and where less expensive land was found. They were supported by charitable gifts or alms. Many are built next to churches.

Small-scale composed units, different from the organically grown vernacular around them, almshouses were planned in rows or quadrangles, sometimes with tall chimneys, often with many arched doors, graced with cupola, clock or sundial over the central door. There is no meanness about them – they seem to have been built to last, with great attention to detail, usually from local materials. Typically they offer a few homes '*for the maintenance of six ancient Men and five Women*', each with a separate entrance, but some are grand and extensive buildings. The Royal Hospital at Chelsea, for example, was designed for King Charles II by Christopher Wren to house five hundred old soldiers, and still fulfils its original function.

Almshouses were first intended for anyone who needed temporary shelter: the poor, sick and elderly or travellers and pilgrims. Perhaps founded by the Knights Hospitallers of St John of Jerusalem, crusaders who protected the roads to the Holy Land, they were known as hospitals, sometimes abbreviated to Spitals or Spital Houses, Lazar Houses (associated with lepers), Maisons-Dieu (God's houses), Bedehouses (where the inhabitants were expected to pray) and almshouses. By the fifteenth to sixteenth centuries they were refuges, where the needy, including retired seamen, soldiers and workers, could live permanently and eat and pray communally – the first examples of social housing.

St Mary's Hospital in Chichester, Sussex, constructed in the early thirteenth century, is still used for the same purpose seven hundred years later. The Hospital of St Cross has been offering sheltered accommodation since 1136 on the Itchen water meadows at the edge of Winchester, Hampshire. Centred round a Norman church, part-quadrangles of two-storey buildings dating from the fourteenth and fifteenth centuries complete a scene of tranquillity attended by a distinguished array of high stone chimneys '*built tall to improve the draught*'. Now 25 men above the age of sixty live in one-bedroom quarters here and are still seen in gowns of black or red doing duties in the church or working a little towards their keep.

Responsibility for city and village almshouses originally set up by churches and monasteries was lost during the Dissolution; some were taken up by secular societies, industrialists and rich patrons. There may be a thousand remaining, some of them four hundred years old. Others are being built now. In Devon the Wakefield Almshouse Charitable Trust won awards in the 1990s for the design of its new homes and conversions in Totnes.

See also CATHEDRALS, FLAGS, SYCAMORE.

A M M O N I T E S

It would be strange if the presence of tiny snail-like and great bicycle-wheel coils of stone had not nourished stories in our inquisitive ancestors. Across the south of England, it was known that fairies who had been bad were turned into snakes and then into stone. 'Snakestones' in Whitby, Yorkshire and 'conger eels' on the Isle of Portland, Dorset were just some of the names given to fossils of extinct molluscs. The Egyptians, Greeks and Romans recognised rams' horns in these stones and, preoccupied as they were with sacred symbols, associated them with the god Amon.

Local tales give insights into a time before appreciation of the organic origin of petrified fauna and flora informed the discipline of geology. St Hilda took a novel approach when clearing the land to build a new convent in seventh-century Whitby, Yorkshire. The story goes that:

> *Of thousand snakes, each one*
> *Was changed into a coil of stone*
> *When holy Hilda pray'd*
>
> Sir Walter Scott, from *Marmion*

Indeed it is a great delight to wander the beaches of Yorkshire and come across a fist-sized nodule that can be broken open to reveal a perfect golden snake with its matching imprint. These creatures seemingly curling around their own tail do not possess a 'head'; this omission was rectified by local carvers, who added the necessary eyes and mouth for early tourists. *Hildoceras bifrons* – named for St Hilda – was a favourite for this. Today, three coiled shapes lie together in Whitby's coat of arms.

St Keyna, who gives her name to Keynsham, Bristol (Radio Luxembourg fans will remember the spelling), is reputed to have petrified serpents long before St Hilda. What links the two is the geological formation of the Lias, from northern Yorkshire to Lincoln, Northampton, the Cotswolds, Somerset and down to Dorset.

The flat bedrock along the beach from Lyme Regis to Charmouth in Dorset entices with small and huge whorls smoothed by the relentless waves. It is also notable for fossil hunters. After every storm, since at least Georgian times, seekers of stones have followed attentively the sifting work of gravity and the sea. Here are found hundreds of different ammonites, sometimes glinting gold, vacuum-packed in iron pyrites. Mary Anning, the knowledgeable amateur palaeontologist and professional fossil seller, could distinguish two hundred in the early nineteenth century.

The scientific importance lies in finding ammonites in situ. Their rapid evolution, as they changed in size, shape, patterned striations and sutures, has been fundamental in giving us an idea of the sequence of events in the ebb and flow of the early Jurassic seas. Proto ammonites enter the stage in Carboniferous times (as goniatites), but it is in the Jurassic and Cretaceous that they reach their zenith and then extinction, together with the dinosaurs.

These free-swimming molluscs immigrated in numbers as the seas invaded. Their capacity to keep on changing made them the perfect time-tellers. The sheer profusion and variety of these coiled stones intrigued nascent geologists, who began to recognise that they could use specific species to correlate and date the sequence of sedimentary beds. They have helped to demonstrate nuances in the theory of evolution. The remarkable sequence of ammonites discovered in Southerham Grey Pit, near Lewes, Sussex, has recently enabled geologists to unravel the history of the early Lower Chalk as a greenhouse climate became established on earth, perhaps ninety million years ago.

Titanites giganteus from the Whit Bed on the Isle of Portland, Dorset reaches one metre in diameter; you can see them embedded into the walls of houses and gardens in Easton and Southwell. In Sussex they present a rustic counterpoint to the Regency reproductions of Lewes and Brighton. A builder called Amon Wilds so rejoiced in his given name that, on discovering the 'ammonite order' created by London architect George Dance – who decorated his Shakespeare Gallery on Pall Mall (1789) with ammonite motifs – he set about topping his own columns with elegant coils. The façade of 166 High Street in Lewes, and Brighton's Oriental Place, Hanover Crescent and Montpelier Crescent,

still demonstrate his work and that of his son in the early nineteenth century.

See also BEACHES, BEACHCOMBING, BUILDING STONES, CLIFFS, DUDLEY LOCUSTS, FOLKTALES, QUARRIES, SAINTS, WALLS.

ANCIENT TREES

Just as rocks keep a deep memory of the evolution of the earth, trees also compress history into their very being. That weight of knowledge is visible in old trees and it is part of England's special heritage to have more ancient trees than anywhere north of the Mediterranean except Greece.

We share with the Greeks, south Asians and many other cultures an appreciation and awe of ancient trees. They are full of enigma, capable in deciduous forms of apparent death and resurrection. They are the biggest beings we know; they stay rooted to the spot and in offering permanence, longevity and grace they often organise the spirit of the place around them and are the reason why some places are where they are. They are the repository of memory.

These trees tell us of continuity and give us a glimpse of the old wild wood and ancient wood pasture. In cultural and ecological terms they are extraordinary. Oliver Rackham shook us by saying that *'ten thousand oaks of 100 years old are not a substitute for one 500-year-old oak'*.

Ancient trees are at the centre of their own ecological web. Some trees have lived so long that they harbour an extensive array of lichens and fungi as well as insects and microflora, some unique to themselves. Enormous and complex communities of symbiotic mycorrhizal root fungi are being discovered in the surrounding soil. The ancient oaks of the Wyre Forest in Shropshire and Worcestershire have become as Galapagan islands. In Herefordshire, those *'Old Men of Moccas Park'*, deferentially described by Francis Kilvert in his diary as *'those grey, gnarled, low-browed, knock-kneed, bowed, bent, huge, strange, long-armed, deformed, hunchbacked, misshapen oak men that stand waiting and watching century after century'*, have a far greater conservation status than as simple trees. The world population of the beetle *Hypebaeus flavipes* lives in just six Moccas Park oaks. The oaks and beeches of Windsor Great Park and Forest make that area the richest in northern Europe for invertebrates (two thousand species) and for fungi (one thousand species and counting). For bats and birds these trees offer habitation and food throughout the year.

Dendrologists can read a tree. Through the size and disposition of the rings laid down, one for each year, in its wood, they can tell something of the precipitation, the load of hungry insects and the level of happiness or distress of the growing organism. Real senility is easily apparent, but a measure of gnarledness translates with difficulty into specific age. Trees become more stable with time, they

hollow naturally and become shorter but bulkier, and this natural engineering means that their annual rings cannot be counted.

Each tree is different. John White from the Forestry Commission has worked out a rule of thumb just for the Windsor oaks: a tree that is eighty inches in diameter at breast height with a girth of twenty feet and eight inches is around 433 years old; 120 inches in diameter with a girth of thirty feet eleven inches is 924 years old. Some of the oldest Windsor oaks are certainly more than a thousand years old.

Sitting inside the yew at Much Marcle, Herefordshire you feel the weight of centuries. It is thought to be fifteen hundred years old. Allen Meredith, whose yew work has sparked much investigation, thinks it may be five thousand years old; others have suggested nine thousand years.

The longevity stimulated by frequent cutting has meant that coppiced and pollarded trees number among our oldest. In Bradfield Woods, Suffolk an ash stool reaching 18½ feet across may be one thousand years old, and one small-leafed lime in Silk Wood, Westonbirt, Gloucestershire, 48 feet across, is thought to be six thousand years old.

These rich characters may have been nurtured by consistency of ownership – some areas of wood pasture have been in and out of the same family for a thousand years; most are in old deer parks or hunting forests, where stag-headed trees, humans and deer seem to merge:

> *There is an old tale goes, that Herne the Hunter,*
> *Sometimes a keeper here in Windsor Forest,*
> *Doth all the winter time, at still midnight,*
> *Walk round about an oak, with great ragged horns . . .*

William Shakespeare, from *The Merry Wives of Windsor*

In other places old trees have been retained to lend stature to a new park. Certain trees mark boundaries that date back to Saxon times. Some areas of land have never lost their status as commons, although few have enjoyed good woodmanship latterly, such as Epping Forest, Essex and Burnham Beeches, Buckinghamshire, where beech pollards may be four hundred years old.

Ted Green, an enthusiastic champion of ancient trees, who works as conservation consultant to Windsor Great Forest, is keen to understand the nine hundred mainly oak pollards that are more than five hundred years old. He wants to help them age and '*grow downwards*' – losing height, hollowing, putting on breadth and gravitas. They are being released from the pressing companionship of other trees. Haloes are cut around the ancients, since oak does not like to touch its neighbours, and more room to stretch is visibly reinvigorating even the oldest. Care is being taken not to expose the trees too much, because a sunburnt trunk begins to 'cook'. Preventing compaction above the roots helps them too, as fencing off the Major Oak in Sherwood Forest, Nottinghamshire from admirers has shown. Some trees are being selected to become successors to the ancients and their inhabitants and are being planted or left to grow nearby. Close observation and learning from countries where traditions remain unbroken is unlocking some of the secrets that were once everyday working wisdom in England.

Ironically, while wood folk who pollard and coppice have prolonged the lives of trees, foresters have been some of their worst enemies. The tunnel vision of those trained for timber growing during the twentieth century has defined 'over mature' trees as a waste of space. It is only in the past decade that the industry has begun to appreciate and champion their importance.

12

Dog Oak, Kentchurch, Herefordshire.

Any old tree is worth the space it occupies, whether a three-hundred-year-old sycamore or pear, a 150-year-old birch or a thousand-year-old yew. Giving names to these old characters endows them with some protection, but they should have the same conservation status as cathedrals and ancient monuments.

See also ALBION, ASH, BEECH, BLACK POPLAR, BLUEBELLS, COMMONS, CROSSROADS, ELM, FERNS, FOLKTALES, GREEN MAN, GROVELY RIGHTS DAY, HENGES & STONE CIRCLES, HORNBEAM, HORSE CHESTNUT, LICHENS, LIME, LONDON PLANE, MIDSUMMER DAY, MISTLETOE, MONKEY-PUZZLE, OAK, ORCHARDS, PARKLAND, PEARS, RAMSONS, ROBIN HOOD, ROWAN, ROYAL FORESTS, SCOTS PINE, SWEET CHESTNUT, SYCAMORE, WALNUT, WILLOW, WOODS, YEW.

A N T Y - T U M P S

Late in the evening, with the low sun highlighting the hedgerows, a flock of shadows catches the eye. The field is full of hummocky anthills. Often beginning their life as molehills, these were a common feature of the countryside, but as long ago as 1794 they were considered a nuisance and were often ploughed in or spread over the ground as top soil. Now they are becoming rare, but the landscapes they enrich and the microcosms they enfold are curious and fascinating. In Herefordshire they are called anty-tumps.

The anthill is a nest containing many underground passages and chambers. The yellow ant, *Lasius flavus*, makes low mounds that are added to each year; they can reach eighteen inches or so in height. They can still be found on the downs and in fields that have been grazed for hundreds of years and probably never ploughed. At Roche Court Down and Porton Down in Wiltshire there are about three million anthills, built by some 35 billion yellow ants; some may be more than one hundred years old. They offer beautifully sifted, dry soil and support distinctive flora, such as thyme-leaved sandwort, wall speedwell, common mouse-ear, wild thyme and common rock rose; as many as 68 plant species on the chalk of southern England '*have an affinity for ant-hills*', according to C.J. Smith.

The butterflies belonging to the group Lycaenidae, such as the green hairstreak, Adonis blue and chalkhill blue, have strange and symbiotic associations with the red ant (*Myrmica sabuleti*) or black ant (*Lasius alienus*), passing part of their larval stages in the nest and/or hibernating under the protection of the ants.

The wood ant thrives under cover of conifers and makes substantial heaps of needles, leaves and twigs two to three feet in height. Not places to play king of the castle, since angry half-inch ants squirt formic acid, memorable also for its smell (the heaps were known as pismires), for example among the resinous pines of Bournemouth in Hampshire.

See also CHALK, DOWNLAND, FIELDS, GORSE, WALLFLOWERS, WOODS.

A P P L E   D A Y

Traditions have to begin somewhere and Apple Day, now regarded as a part of the festive calendar, began on 21 October 1990. Common Ground took over the Piazza at Covent Garden in London for a demonstration of the importance of the apple to our culture, landscape and wildlife.

Apple Day, and its herald All Fruits Eve, was conceived as an annual celebration to link the fruit we eat with the people who grow it and the places they make in the process. The apple, with its powerful symbolism, rich poetry and extraordinary variety, was chosen to stand for all, though its success has prompted Damson Day in Westmorland, Plum Day in Pershore, Worcestershire, Pear Day at Cannon Hall Museum, Yorkshire and more.

The apple is a wonderful emblem of diversity. In Britain we have grown more than two thousand varieties and hundreds more cider apples. The Carlisle Codlin, Crawley Beauty, Devonshire Quarrendon and Worcester Pearmain tell of the place of origin; Ashmead's Kernel, Cox's Orange Pippin, Laxton's Superb, Peasgood's Nonsuch and Charles Ross tell of the people who developed and raised them, and their stories provide a further expression of the place – memorable, repeatable.

We wanted to create a popular festival, a date in the calendar, to alert people to our heritage of fruit, to broaden their knowledge and to inspire action. We wanted to stimulate initiatives promoting the importance of our relationship with the land and the links between local production and ecological care, social customs and culture. By giving people reasons to value and conserve them we aimed to prevent further extinction of varieties and loss of traditional orchards. We intended to excite the creation of new produce and sales linked to places and to build solidarity across the country, connecting people who had similar interests. And we wanted to encourage people to make their own links with locality, to broaden the celebration of and care for the cultural landscape.

We brought together forty stallholders with integrity and passion at Covent Garden – originally the Convent Garden, which included an orchard – a place that had been London's prime market for fruit and vegetables, although it had seen no fruit for sixteen years. Stallholders who had different connections with the apple were chosen from across the country: organic growers; the WI, with chutneys, jellies and pies; a school from north London using its orchard as a classroom; nurserymen dispensing advice as well as trees; bee keepers; juice makers; cider makers with presses; photographs of orchards; and a hundred varieties of apples to taste and talk about. Apple 'doctors' and identifiers worked non-stop all day.

The intention was to encourage others to take the idea on and Apple Day has multiplied; at six hundred events in

13

1999 we gave up counting. It has been celebrated in village halls, the Houses of Parliament, school meals services, museums, nurseries, allotments, bakers' shops, restaurants, doctors' surgeries, arts centres, agricultural and horticultural colleges, botanic gardens and community orchards; by farmers, fruit growers, cider makers, juice producers, English Heritage, the National Trust, the WI, the Wildlife Trusts and the Soil Association, as well as by families and friends at home. Some are domestic parties; some attract thousands of people.

Each year the demand for apple identification grows. In Cornwall, Red Rollo, White Quarantine and other varieties thought to have become extinct have 'turned up' at the county-run Apple Day in Truro. Following Common Ground's *Apple Map*, a first attempt at a county gazetteer of varieties, county versions have been researched; some counties are producing their own *pomonas* – annotated variety lists. Cheshire, Gloucestershire, Devon and Hertfordshire are among the counties creating 'mother orchards' of all the county apples.

The success of Apple Day in Bath after two years gave the organisers courage to try out broader markets on the surrounding weekends – this was the start in 1997 of the countrywide reinvention of direct-selling farmers' markets.

14   *See also* ANCIENT TREES, APPLES, APRICOTS, CHERRIES, CIDER & CIDER ORCHARDS, COBNUTS, DAMSONS, FOOD, HAZEL, HONEY & BEES, LICHENS, MISTLETOE, ORCHARDS, PEARS, PLUMS, WASSAILING.

A P P L E S

You could eat a different kind of apple every day for more than six years and still not come to the end of the list we can grow in Britain. An amazing two thousand varieties of dessert and cooking apples have been cultivated in this country, as well as hundreds of cider apples, which are specific to the West.

Apples do well across the country partly because we have loved them. In Victorian times gardeners and nurserymen worked hard to dabble and cross-pollinate, discover and graft, to bring on a wonderful inheritance of new varieties.

We may rejoice in our own assertions that we grow the best apples in the world, but the truth is that they arrived here from the Tien-Shan mountains, which now find themselves on the border between China and Kazakhstan. They accompanied traders along the Silk Road to the Balkans and then came via the Romans and others to our shores.

But it is we who have sifted and sorted the novel saplings and their fruits to find varieties that suit us and the places where they grow. Every apple pip offers a new shuffle of the genetic pack; varieties flourishing by the motorway, wildings from thrown-out apple cores, may hold as much

taste and goodness, or even economic promise, as a new variety from a research establishment.

Many apples are traceable to their orchards, woods, hedges and gardens of origin. Since a variety can be perpetuated only by grafting a twig onto a rootstock, or the tree being left to grow up again after it has fallen, our relationship with it keeps it alive. Unless we value it for its flavour, natural goodness, hardiness, heritage importance or beauty it will disappear. Currently the few varieties that add most to the national economy dominate and hundreds of others are simply slipping away unnoticed.

Without the benefit of cold storage, the season for apples starts in July, with Emneth Early, Gladstone, Beauty of Bath, Laxton's Early Crimson and Discovery, and continues until spring with May Queen. The early varieties have short shelf lives, but the later ones, such as Blenheim Orange and Annie Elizabeth, can be stored in mouse-proof cool sheds or garage roofs into May. The Hambledon Deux Ans is reputed to last for two years. Chastise yourself then, when you take from the superstore shelf Golden Delicious from France, Idared from the US or Granny Smith from Australia during our long season.

The Pitmaston Pine from Worcestershire fits into the smallest hand; it is a delicate yellow, its juicy flesh paler lemon. Compare this elegant little dessert apple with Peasgood's Nonsuch, a giant apple from Lincolnshire, or Reverend Wilks from Middlesex, with its bright white flesh and greasy-feeling skin, which is pale and creamy with a few red stripes.

Laid out along a table for comparison on Apple Day (21 October), apples take the breath away with their variety, colour, aroma and presence. Tasting and identifying them requires all the skills of the wine connoisseur. In Devon, the Save our Orchards group has compiled a list of nearly two hundred apples with a close Devon association, such as Devonshire Quarrendon, Fair Maid of Devon, Killerton Sharp and Whimple Queen. June Small of Charlton Orchards in Somerset has identified 156 Somerset apple varieties, many of which have links with particular villages, towns or parts of the county, such as Yarlington Mill and Bridgwater Pippin.

The trees have their preferences. D'Arcy Spice is suited to the dryness of Essex. Blenheim Orange is said to grow best on the stone brash and calcareous soil of Oxfordshire, within a few miles of Woodstock, where one Mr Kempster first grew it. Such was the word-of-mouth reputation of Kempster's Pippin (even before it was taken on by the big house and renamed), that coaches would stop to allow people to glimpse the tree and graft wood was frequently stolen over the garden wall at night.

A tree that should carry Mary Ann Brailsford's name was planted by her as a pip in Southwell, Nottinghamshire at the start of the nineteenth century. This is the mother of

all Bramleys, named after the man who inherited the tree. Every apple pie made with Bramley apples comes from a tree that originated as a graft, or a graft of a graft, from this single tree. Battered by nearly two hundred years of falling over and starting again, the original tree can still produce a ton of fruit and has recently given grafts to reinvigorate the stock.

Isaac Newton's revelations are celebrated at his home, Woolsthorpe Manor in Lincolnshire. The orchard still contains the variety of the tree that he sat beneath when the apple dropped, now known as Isaac Newton's Tree or the Gravity Tree. Richard Cox, a retired brewer from Bermondsey, east London, whiled away his hours cross-pollinating trees in his garden at Colnbrook, Buckinghamshire (the place has found itself variously in Middlesex, Surrey and Berkshire). The Cox's Orange Pippin is just one of the varieties he created. He died in 1845 before it achieved popular recognition in the 1880s.

There was great activity and competition to introduce new varieties in the nineteenth century, spurred on by Royal Horticultural Society certificates and economic fortune. Thomas Laxton of Bedford and his family after him were some of the most successful plant breeders in the world, producing varieties such as Lord Lambourne, Laxton's Fortune, Laxton's Superb and Barnack Beauty/Orange. At Park Wood Community Orchard on Brick Hill Drive in Bedford, 230 varieties of apple, pear, fig, damson, plum, medlar, quince and walnut have been planted by local residents and Bedford Borough Council in their memory.

Variety comes on other levels: a single Ribston Pippin (a Yorkshire forbear of the Cox) has more vitamin C than a pound of Golden Delicious. In the Tamar valley on the Devon/Cornwall border there are apple trees with aerial roots. Recipes for cider cake vary from village to village in the West Country, where there are cider gravies, peas cooked in cider and Squab Pie, which pairs pigeon with apple.

In Devon, apple cake is made with apple purée, cinnamon and raisins and in Dorset with chopped cooking apple and currants; in Somerset the chopped apple is combined with cinnamon and mixed spice. In Cornwall the cake may resemble the French *tarte Tatin*.

The hundreds of customs and games that we have created around the apple echo the importance it has had in our lives. Almost every farm, from Northumberland to Cornwall, had its orchards; labourers were paid in cider. City folk travelled to pick fruit in the Garden of England and the orchards of Herefordshire. Costermongers' (apple sellers) cries rang out in street markets, and greengrocers put out baths of water for games of duck apple at Hallowe'en, known as Dookie Apple Night in Newcastle and Duck Apple Night in Liverpool. In Mobberley, Cheshire and other places, Crabbing the Parson was practised, crab apples pelted at the incumbent on the local saint's day. Griggling, a'scraggling, souling, pothering and ponking, a' cattin, going a gooding, clemening, worsting, howling and youling and taking round the calennig are just some of the local traditions.

It takes time for customs to differentiate themselves, just as an intricate landscape demonstrates the deep relationship that we and nature have developed over hundreds of years. The rich repertoire of apple games and customs links season, produce and locality, yet we are in danger of forgetting what they mean because we have ceased to value our apples and orchards. They are the more vulnerable since some are peculiar to a single place.

Within the landscape fruit trees flavour the locality. The individual geographies and histories of apples are not merely interesting, they are fragments of knowledge from which a future can be made. They may amount to the same thing, but gene banks, biodiversity and endemism do not have the same ring as Keswick Codlin, Teesdale Nonpareil, Cornish Gilliflower, Kentish Fillbasket, Lady Henniker, Roundway Magnum Bonum, Stoke Edith Pippin and Yorkshire Greening . . . nor do they carry the cultural depth of Ten Commandments and Slack ma Girdle.

See also ANCIENT TREES, APPLE DAY, APRICOTS, AVALON, CHERRIES, CIDER & CIDER ORCHARDS, COBNUTS, DAMSONS, DEVIL, FOOD, FROST & FROST HOLLOWS, HAZEL, HONEY & BEES, LICHENS, MIDSUMMER DAY, MISTLETOE, ORCHARDS, PEARS, PLUMS.

15

A P R I C O T S

Apricots used to be grown much more widely in England than they are now. In the nineteenth century they were planted against south- or west-facing walls in kitchen gardens or in glasshouses and were particularly valued for sweet and savoury dishes. But climatic shifts are bringing warmer weather, and in 2005 the first commercial apricot harvest was achieved in Kent.

In Aynho, Northamptonshire, the apricot was a way of life; it still grows against houses in the village. As long ago as 1616, to encourage the production of more fruit, the lord of the manor of Aynho gave his tenants apricot trees to plant against the warm chimney breasts of their cottages, in the hope that future rents could be paid in the fruit. The Cartwright family continued to replace dead trees up until the 1950s.

The idea spread locally. In Kidlington-on-the-Green over the border in Oxfordshire, cultivation was so successful that six thousand dozen apricots were sent to Covent Garden in 1839. Ruth Ward notes that the *Gardener's Chronicle* of 1851 described the Woodstock area: '*Every cottage in every village has its apricot tree which, in a good season, will pay the rent. All the finest fruit is sent to London, and "Kidlington Apricots" are well known in Covent Garden, and command a higher price than those from other parts of England.*'

The most popular variety grown in England today is Moor Park. It was planted from a (peach apricot) stone by Admiral Lord Anson in 1760 at Moor Park, near Watford, Hertfordshire – now a golf-course, where the apricots are being replanted.

See *also* APPLES, BUILDING STONES, CHERRIES, DAMSONS, GOLF-COURSES, PEARS, PLUMS.

A Q U E D U C T S

The ancient *qanats* of Persia still lead water underground by gravity from mountains to desiccated plains. The ever-inventive Romans would later develop the aqueduct, an artificial way to lead (*ducere*) water (*aqua*) from rivers and springs to where it was needed for drinking and irrigation. Perhaps the Duke of Bridgewater, on the Grand Tour in the mid-eighteenth century, saw in the grand Roman stone aqueducts – as at Segovia in Spain – the solution to an engineering problem: how to keep his new industrial canal level as it crossed valleys and natural waterways between Worsley in Lancashire and Manchester. He commissioned an aqueduct for Worsley Colliery and one to take his eponymous canal over the river at Barton upon Irwell. This latter was designed and built by James Brindley; when opened in 1761 it was a '*wonder of the age*', one newspaper correspondent enthusing two years later about Brindley's '*navigable canal in the air*'. Once the Manchester Ship canal began to take advantage of the route along the Irwell, Brindley's aqueduct was an obstacle to large shipping. Edward Leader Williams's imaginative solution was a swing aqueduct, its 235-foot span remaining full of water as it swung open to let ships pass. Opened in 1893, it is rarely called upon to swing now.

John Rennie brought the then-fashionable classical style to bear on aqueduct building, conferring a new elegance. In 1797 he used five arches of local millstone grit to span six hundred feet across and 62 feet above the

Lune valley at Lancaster. Rennie was not always so keen on local materials. Moving to the Kennet and Avon canal in Wiltshire and Somerset (where 'Hucky Duck' is the local dialect for aqueduct), he was obliged by the shareholders to build aqueducts at Avoncliff and Dundas in Bath stone – he preferred brick.

Further north Benjamin Outram built the first cast-iron aqueduct on the Derby canal. It opened in February 1796. Thomas Telford, who probably originated the idea of using cast iron, completed one at Longdon upon Tern in Shropshire a month later. Anthony Burton described it in 2002 as looking '*like a prototype, with a rather crude trough carried on spindly iron supports*'.

Today more than seventy large and many smaller canal aqueducts survive on English waterways, a number of them still on navigable routes. Huddersfield Narrow canal has five, including the Saddleworth aqueduct across the river Tame. The branches of the Grand Union have seven. The Bridgewater canal can still boast twelve, all navigable.

Not all aqueducts – or, indeed, canals – have been so lucky. The remnants of the Cromford canal west of Nottingham have been lovingly resurrected as a waterway to Langley Mill, but the aqueduct at Bullbridge was destroyed in 1968 so that a road could be widened.

See *also* BEATING THE BOUNDS, BRIDGES, CANALS, LANDMARKS, RESERVOIRS, RIVERS, VIADUCTS.

A R B O R   D A Y

Until 2 September 1995 you would come round the bend at Aston-on-Clun in Shropshire and see before you a crotchety, old, hollow, pollarded tree filled with poles carrying flags from across the world. The male black poplar which fell on that day stood at the meeting of four ways and was – is – the

Barton aqueduct, Bridgewater canal crossing Manchester Ship canal.

focus of a unique ceremony. Such is the importance of the tree to this place that a cutting from the 250- to 300-year-old fallen one had already been planted.

The people of the village know 29 May as Arbor Day (the American and others are different and much later inventions). Perhaps it is coincidental that it was on this day in 1660 that Charles II triumphantly re-entered London at the end of the Civil War. He declared a public holiday – Oak Apple Day – since commemorated by the wearing of a sprig of oak in memory of the tree at Boscobel, Shropshire in which the king successfully hid after defeat at the battle of Worcester. At this moment of Restoration, maypoles were once more allowed and appeared in the south of Shropshire, together with bell-ringing and bonfires. Oak Apple Day ceased to be a public holiday in 1859, and the wearing of oak has virtually disappeared except by the Chelsea Pensioners, army veterans who reside in the hospital Charles II founded in 1682.

According to one story, the Brides Tree, as the black poplar is also known, first held flags in its branches in 1786 to celebrate the wedding of John Marston to Mary Carter. She is said to have admired the flags so much that she gave a guinea for the custom to continue annually (it is now paid for by Hopesay Parish Council). On Arbor Day each year the flags are ceremoniously taken down and replaced, and a wedding procession to the tree is re-enacted. Festivities continue in a local field and include Morris dancing with the Shropshire Bedlams and Martha Rhoden's Tuppenny Dish – active in these parts since 1975.

Perhaps something much older is continued, developed from the custom of hanging rags on trees (known as Clootie trees) around healing wells, or a throwback to the use of prayer flags in the worship of St Brigit or St Bride, a Celtic goddess of fertility – offering another reason for the tree's alternative name.

The little replacement tree cannot carry fifteen-foot poles and full-sized flags for St George, Patrick, David and Andrew as well as Australia, New Zealand, USA, Canada and the Union Flag – they are held by posts around the tree waiting for it to grow into them.

See also ALMSHOUSES, BELLS & BELL-RINGING, BLACK POPLAR, BONFIRE NIGHT, CASTLETON GARLAND DAY, FLAGS, GROVELY RIGHTS DAY, MAYPOLES, OAK, TREE DRESSING DAY.

A R C A D E S

In 1990 a roof was completed over the length of Queen Victoria Street in Leeds. Brian Clarke's brilliantly coloured stained glass adds a new dimension to the resurgent reputation of the city and its unsurpassed shopping arcades. The area, now known as the Victoria Quarter, was first flamboyantly regenerated from a labyrinth of slaughter-houses and butchers' shops as the twentieth century began.

Inspired by Paris and, later, Italian cities, glassed-over arcades were seeping into English city life (the aristocratic Burlington Arcade in London opened in 1819) before Leeds built its first arcades towards the end of the nineteenth century. Four remain of the original eight.

Thornton's Arcade (1878) and Queen's Arcade (1889) were both designed by music hall architects and constructed where inn yards linked one street with another. The former was once Old Talbot Inn Yard, only fifteen feet wide, which joined Briggate with Lands Lane. The grand County Arcade, with its domes and mosaics, has been lavishly restored, having slipped into a decline that had left only six original shop fronts out of fifty. The Cross Arcade, birthplace of Marks and Spencer's Penny Bazaar in 1904, was redeveloped in the 1990s to house the Harvey Nichols department store. The glass and steel entrance adds a fresh face to Briggate.

Elsewhere, compressing much into a little space to increase the commercial prospects of a city achieved elegance: in Lancashire, Accrington's Victorian Arcade (1896) is built over the river Hyndburn; Birmingham's Great Western Arcade (1875) is constructed over the railway; the Barton Arcade (1871) in Manchester is three storeys high.

There is another sort of arcade; the proportions are still grand but the feeling is of a noble cloister, since here buildings reach over the pavement and are supported by columns or arches that offer slats of shade and light. Inigo Jones's seventeenth-century Covent Garden in London was the earliest, based upon Palladio's Italian architecture. At the end of the twentieth century it has been joined by modern arcades at the back of the Royal Opera House, which finally complete the piazza. From Marlborough in Wiltshire to Saltburn in Yorkshire arcaded shops front the street and shelter shoppers from rain and sun.

See also ALLEYS, CAFÉS, MARKETS, QUARTERS, SHOPS.

17

A R C H E S

Arches sculpted by weather and waves around our shores show great fortitude despite attack from every side. Perhaps this is what draws us to them; easily described, unambiguous points of reference, they are obvious landmarks for seafarers.

Bat's Head in Dorset has a fledgling arch, but the beautiful Durdle Door stands at the other end of the bay, west of Lulworth Cove. Linked to the mainland, this great gothic portal through Portland and Purbeck stone frames views of the sea. The isolated rocks of the Bull, Blind Cow, Cow and Calf are part of the same line of heaved limestone and foretell the fate of the arch.

Thurlestone Rock stands solitary in Bigbury Bay, Devon. Only when you walk to either end of the sands are you surprised and delighted by the realisation that this is a huge archway in the sea. The hard conglomerate mass is mentioned by name as a boundary marker in a Saxon charter dated 845, its resilience echoed in the local saying '*brave every shock like Thurlestone Rock*'. The rock is more than thirty feet high and the hole twenty feet; in 1864 it was said that '*the noise made by the wind rushing through the archway is sometimes heard many miles away, and when it is perceptible at Kingsbridge it is regarded as the forerunner of storms of rain*'.

The word thirl – occasionally used in north-country dialect for gate or hole – deriving from Old English *thyrhil* or Old High German *durhhil*, meaning pierced, is evident in both of these names. Etymological evidence alone suggests that these names are more than a thousand years old.

Older names exist. In Cornwall, Enys Dodman, an arch in obdurate granite, stands in the angry sea off Land's End; it has counterparts by Gribba Point and Carn Vellan. Enys, or ynys, means 'island' in Cornish, as in Welsh.

The kittiwakes make much of the challenge at Bempton Cliffs in Yorkshire, flying through the limestone arches like First World War aces. Blackhall Rocks include an arch visible at low tide along the Durham coast. Less resilient has proved the wonderfully stolid-looking limestone arch of Marsden Rock, County Durham. Several choirs gathered one hundred feet up on its top in 1903 to give an early rock concert; in 1911 there was a big rockfall, and over the years

pieces have toppled; but in 1996 it lost its bridge to gravity. The totemic power of the arch was then further tamed as the smaller buttress was removed by blasting to make it 'safe', leaving just one square stack. This remodelling by nature and man has had an impact on local people – the silhouette they grew up with has been stolen.

At the western tip of the Isle of Wight, an arch split from the mainland in 1815, isolating another stack as part of the Needles. In Freshwater Bay, Arch Rock remains in name only; it fell in 1992. Back in Dorset, quarrying took the White Hole, a natural gateway near Portland Bill, in the 1870s, leaving a remnant known as Pulpit Rock.

Waves, searching every crevice often with explosive force, soon trace a weak line or bedding plane in a cliff face. In areas where geology has been much contorted, fracturing and cracking leave faults and joints often parallel and at right angles to one another; these are the perfect conditions for the formation of caves, possibly followed by arches.

Joining forces with the sea, aerial bombardment by rain, frost and wind ensures that arches are short-lived in geological time, the 'bridge' always vulnerable to gravity. The sequence runs from cave to arch to stack to heap to dispersal by the sea, but in between these rocks are endowed with personalities, stories and significance.

See also BUILDING STONES, CHALK, CLIFFS, COASTS, DIALECTS, GRANITE, LIMESTONE, SEA CAVES, STACKS.

ARTISTS' COLONIES & SCHOOLS

The group we know as the Norwich School painted their beautiful medieval city and the extensive flatnesses of East Anglia at the start of the nineteenth century. John Sell Cotman sought national recognition, but John Crome remained around the banks of the river Yare, rooted in the landscape, once declaring to his pupils: '*This is our Academy.*' His invention of the Norwich Society of Artists in 1803, the first provincial group to be formed, was instrumental in galvanising a movement with learning and expression at its heart. This was born out of the city's own tradition of dissent and the welcoming of 'Strangers' seeking refuge from hostility across the North Sea. The gatherings were progressive, the painting innovative, despite conservative patronage and the turbulence of war – the focus on familiar landscapes offering reassurance while classical rules and subjects were routed. Their legacy is a rich vein of works by pupils, acolytes and masters, from Cotman's *Mousehold*

Durdle Door, Dorset; Thurlestone Rock, Bigbury Bay, Devon.

Heath to Crome's *Moonrise on the Yare*, portraying fragments of Norwich, including its abbeys, mills, markets and river traffic.

London always attracted and harboured artists of all kinds. Different quarters have had their associations, such as Holland Park with its Royal Academicians. The alchemy of the aristocracy and upper middle classes – linking fashion and power – created an art market that Bond Street and the Academy still pursues.

Chelsea carried the banner for Bohemian living and expression (Rossetti, Whistler). Fitzroy Square waved no particular flag until the Slade School of Art two blocks east gained a progressive name at the turn of the twentieth century (Sickert, Gore, Augustus John). Camden emerged as the home of the avant-garde, until it progressed uphill to Hampstead with Sickert at its prow. In the decade before the Second World War, artists, architects and commentators, including Naum Gabo, Walter Gropius, Barbara Hepworth, Piet Mondrian, Henry Moore, Paul Nash, Ben Nicholson and Roland Penrose, although never forming a school, came together in Hampstead, nourishing local life and world art in an unprecedented way.

In the 1980s the East End was said to have ten thousand artists within a couple of miles of Old Street. Young architects and artists, like pioneering species, colonised down-at-heel, interesting corners in which to cheaply live and work. In the late 1960s Bridget Riley, Peter Sedgley and others inspired the creation of SPACE, an organisation to find and administer working places for artists. Their pioneering work began among the ghosts of vacated St Katherine's Dock beside Tower Bridge. Newly graduating artists, desperate for space in which to create their bigger canvases and constructions, created ACME in 1972 to organise access to short-lease properties. Some campaigned unsuccessfully against the inevitable property developers, who began to see potential and profit spreading through the Wapping warehouses during the 1970s.

In 1975 the focus was moving towards Hackney, east London, particularly Beck Road, which became a haven for living and work as well as a crucible for the politics of housing. Many artists still live there. By the 1990s the scene had moved to Hoxton. Exhibitions and happenings invested these parts of the East End with New British Art glamour and brought people to places they never would have explored.

In parallel other artists left the city. The Ruralists, including Ann and Graham Arnold, Peter Blake, David Inshaw and Annie and Graham Ovenden, flourished as a group in Somerset in the 1970s. One hundred years earlier the Manchester School, following Joshua Anderson Hague, avoided the industrial engine of the city by taking frequent expeditions to north Wales, where they explored Impressionism.

The cosmopolitan nature of coastal settlements, however small, the light – a gift from the sea, cheap accommodation and the character of their huddled dwellings attracted those seeking a life free from social constraint. Staithes, a tiny fishing village in Yorkshire, drew towards the end of the 1800s the Northern Impressionists, excited by the naturalistic painting activities found in fashionable Brittany, France. Around the 1880s at Newlyn in Cornwall, Stanhope Forbes, Frank Bramley, Thomas Cooper Gotch, Norman Garstin and later Laura and Harold Knight settled, seeking the same experience of *en plein air* painting.

To the north of the peninsula, St Ives had been home to artists since the 1870s. But it was with potters Bernard Leach and Shoji Hamada that a new phase began in the 1920s. By the start of the Second World War, Adrian Stokes, Ben Nicholson, Barbara Hepworth and Naum Gabo had moved here. Peter Lanyon was native born. Roger Hilton, Terry Frost and Patrick Heron arrived after the war. With the exquisite light particular to the Cornish coast, the sensuality of the land-forms, the Celtic heritage and standing stones, the local surroundings seeped into their work, together with the currents of modernist thought that were washing around the world.

Further enrichment was at work. No doubt given courage by the painting culture in the town, a Devonian seaman called Alfred Wallis began, at the age of 75, to paint ships and harbour using boat paint on scraps of board. His naïve eye and flattened perspectives palpably influenced Nicholson and others, though he died in poverty in the war.

St Ives artists survived through sales to tourists; now the town owes them a great economic debt as visitors come to see the places where they worked. With post-modernism has come the Tate Gallery St Ives, opened in 1993. Its very presence is part of the artists' legacy. It maintains the momentum begun in 1895 by Passmore Edwards's innovative benefaction of the Orion Art Gallery in Newlyn.

19

Positively remote from the metropolis, with nourishment brought for centuries by sea, Cornwall, with its palette of ancient rocks, wild weather, beguiling light, deep identity and tough lives, continues to feed the imagination.

See also CAFÉS, COASTS, GASHOLDERS, HARBOURS, QUARTERS, TERRACED HOUSES.

A   S   H

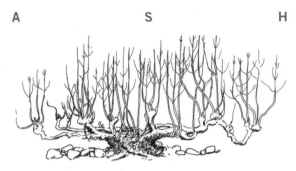

In Bradfield Woods, Suffolk there are rings of ash, each being the coppice stool of a single tree, reaching 18½ feet in diameter. Oliver Rackham believes that these have been cut and recut for a thousand years; the woods have been documented, as part of the estate of Bury St Edmunds Abbey, since 1252.

Although most ash will die within 180 to two hundred years, Rackham asserts that cutting at ground level on a rotational basis can allow it to live indefinitely – a singular example of humanity and nature working together. We have used the leaves for feeding animals, the poles for turning, the wood for furniture and burning. Its resilience and shock absorbency made it ideal for hammer and axe handles, oars, shepherd's crooks, hockey sticks, sledges, coaches, early cars and the finest ladders. Morgan still makes cars using ash for the chassis. In Northumberland the frames of crab and lobster pots (creeves) are made from local ash and hazel.

It is one of our most common trees, as a glance at the numerous place-names containing *ash* or *ask* in any gazetteer will tell: Ashby de la Launde in Lincolnshire, Long Ashton in Somerset, Askam in Lancashire, Askrigg in Yorkshire, Knotty Ash in Lancashire. Reaching heights of 140 feet, unhindered by air pollution, it thrives in city parks. Enjoying the lack of competition for light, it is a frequent hedgerow tree, often covering for lost elms. Ash also makes fine woodlands: by itself on the steep slopes of the Derbyshire Dales; with oak on the Herefordshire borders; and on chalky boulder clay in the east, where it also lives with maple and hazel, accompanied by the richest of woodland ground flora.

Monyash in Derbyshire means 'many an ash', and certainly the valley ash woods as well as roadside trees in the White Peak and Yorkshire pick out the Carboniferous

limestone; further east the north–south sliver of magnesian limestone from County Durham to Nottinghamshire also favours ash. The Cumbrian woods of Arnside and Silverdale, dominated by ash with birch, speak again of limestone. Ash is common in the Jurassic limy Cotswolds and the Carboniferous limy Mendips, where the oldest ash tree in Europe is said to be found at Clapton in Somerset – 29 feet in girth, it is of no age compared with the coppice stools in Suffolk. We have a wealth of ash woods with bluebells, such as Hayley Wood in Cambridgeshire, which are rare elsewhere in Europe.

Looking out for the first tree to leaf in spring is one of the ancient and best-known forecasting tools: '*Oak before ash, we're in for a splash, ash before oak, we're in for a soak.*' The latter may never happen again. The oak relies on warmth, the ash on light; our climate has changed sufficiently in the past two decades to bring the oak into leaf before the ash every year – it is now ten days ahead.

See also ABBEYS, ALDER, ANCIENT TREES, ASH, BEECH, BIRCH, BLACK POPLAR, BLACKTHORN, BLUEBELLS, ELM, FIELD MAPLE, HAWTHORN, HAZEL, HOLLY, HOLM OAK, HORNBEAM, HORSE CHESTNUT, JUNIPER, LANDMARK TREES, LIME, LONDON PLANE, MONKEY-PUZZLE, OAK, ORCHARDS, PEARS, POPLAR, ROWAN, ROYAL FORESTS, SCOTS PINE, SWEET CHESTNUT, SYCAMORE, WALNUT, WHITEBEAM, WILLOW, WOODS, YEW.

A S P A R A G U S

Cultivated asparagus comes from southern Europe, perhaps introduced here in the sixteenth century. Within a hundred years, 'sparrow-grass' was being grown around London, in places such as Deptford, Mortlake, Fulham, Isleworth and Gravesend. One enterprising shop became famous for its Battersea bundles. Before Victoria came to the throne, more asparagus was grown in this country than any other.

Now its main centres of cultivation are the South East, the Cambridgeshire Fens, the well-drained sandy soils around Thetford in Norfolk and the Vale of Evesham, Worcestershire, where asparagus was first planted between rows of plum trees. A wild, native subspecies grows along the sea cliffs of Cornwall, and a small island off Kynance Cove is named after the plant.

In the 1930s, the Vale of Evesham was the centre of asparagus growing with an asparagus show, an asparagus day and an asparagus week. People with gardens along main roads sold it from wooden stalls. At the beginning of the Second World War, asparagus growers were made by the Ministry of Food to plough up their beds to grow other crops; after the war asparagus growing never gained its pre-eminence.

Two asparagus events still take place in the area. In 1967, Buster Mustoe, a publican in Badsey, Worcestershire,

20

changed the name of his pub from the Royal Oak to the Round of Gras (after the name of the bundles sent to market) to reflect his enthusiasm for the vegetable. As well as serving more than a ton of asparagus during the six-week season, he also collected asparagus memorabilia, such as special serving dishes. New landlords have carried on the tradition. Meanwhile, the Fleece Inn at Bretforton still holds an annual asparagus auction on the Sunday of the last bank-holiday weekend in May, when some of the highest-quality bundles are sold.

Formby, Lancashire was famous for its asparagus. Around 250 acres were cultivated by 1900; eighty years later this had dwindled by ninety per cent. The sand-dunes provided perfect conditions – they were levelled to create little fields with ridges and hedges, which can still be picked out. In 2005 Formby held its first Asparagus Feast, accompanied by poetry and readings spanning two thousand years. Reg Yorke reports that '*we consumed four hundred spears on the night of 20 May! We are thinking of doing it again next year.*'

One farm in Worcestershire is growing sixty varieties to see which do best. The asparagus is doubly welcome because it is the first vegetable of the summer, traditionally emerging from 1 May for about six weeks. But in 2003, because of a warm March, harvesting began in the first week of April.

See also COASTS, COVES, INNS, ISLANDS, MARKET GARDENS, PUBS, SAND-DUNES.

A V A L O N 21

Avalon may mean island of apples, and/or it may refer to a 'pointed rock', perhaps that of Glastonbury Tor, a numinous island-hill visible for many miles across the watery levels of Somerset – summer land.

Afall means apple tree in modern Welsh, *afal* means apple, evolving through the Celtic and Medieval Welsh *aballa*. *Ynys avallach* appears in Welsh texts and is taken to mean the isle of apples, but, in medieval times, it was also taken as the isle of a ruler called Avallach, who lived there with his daughters, one of whom was Morgan. It seems the tales wandered and returned changed. Breton storytellers understood it as a place-name and translocated the story to either Avaellon or Avallon in France, where Morgan, a water spirit, was substituted for Modron, the Welsh goddess daughter of Aballach.

The name Avalon is referred to in the *History of the Kings of the Britons* in the 1130s. But it is not fixed in space, and Desmond Hawkins said of the writer: '*That old spell binder, Geoffrey of Monmouth, who either preserved or fathered the early Celtic legends of Arthur and his company, has much to answer for – and some reason for pride in the power of his pen.*' After a life of wisdom, glory and ups-and-downs, it is told that, following a great battle, Arthur is brought to the Isle of Avalon by nine faery sisters, where he dies.

Not until the thirteenth century are Glastonbury and Avalon named together, although the stories of Arthur had

Glastonbury Tor, Somerset.

echoed around Glastonbury since Henry II encouraged the monks to search for the great king's grave a few years after their abbey had lost everything in a fire. The monks discovered not only the supposed remains of Arthur and his wife in 1191, but also the remains of St Dunstan and a manuscript of St Patrick. Dunstan had made this the prime shrine of the tenth century and the wealthiest abbey in newly emergent England. The monks learned much about promotion and power from him, turning to myth-making to help rebuild the attraction of the abbey.

The abbey's power was broken vehemently by Henry VIII, and from 1539 to the mid-nineteenth century little attention seems to have been paid to the place, save to quarry its walls and visit for antiquarian scholarship. But as the Victorians quested for their own identity, they rediscovered the mysteries of the Dark Ages and reinvigorated the myths through literature, such as Tennyson's *Morte D'Arthur* in 1842, and the paintings of the pre-Raphaelites.

In 1907 the site of the abbey was purchased by the Church of England; by the 1920s the New Avalonians had moved in – mystical poetry and art had found a home. Since the 1960s this aspect of the place has been reinforced; it has become a kind of New-Age homeland, relaxed and welcoming, full of purple and crystals, mystical shops and courses, events and explorations.

New pilgrims of all kinds journey here; ley lines meet here; it is a powerful place. Avalon, Arthur and the Holy Grail is just one of the legends that draws them. The potent myth – or is it a story? – of Arthur and his grave, where the tissue between this and the other world still seems so thin, laps around the Christian and pagan, ancient and modern fragments of Glastonbury with ease.

See also ABBEYS, ALBION, APPLES, GLASTONBURY FESTIVAL, HILLS, ISLANDS, JACK AND JILL, RHYNES, TORS.

A V E N U E S

A 1914 watercolour by Heywood Sumner entitled *A Bird's Eye View of Badbury Rings Looking South* wonderfully shows the avenue of beeches that snakes for two miles on either side of the B3082 on the western approach to Kingston Lacy park in Dorset. It was planted by William Bankes in 1835, a tree for each day of the year: 365 on one side and 366 on the other – an extra one for leap year.

Looking at them from the ground, the beeches arch over the road, forming a dark, comforting tunnel, so when you emerge from beneath them you are amazed by the brightness of the light. J.H. Wilks described it as '*one of the longest natural tunnels known*'. With its thick foliage, the beech, more than any other species of tree, is best at creating tunnels. A much shorter avenue of oak trees at Pamphill nearby is reminiscent of an airy cathedral.

The longest avenue in Europe is at Clumber Park in Nottinghamshire. Two double rows of limes stretching three miles were planted in 1838 by the fifth Duke of Newcastle as the entrance to Clumber House, now demolished. Common limes were fashionable trees to plant in avenues because they are relatively quick-growing and tolerant of pruning.

John Evelyn, who advocated the planting of trees along the approaches to country houses in the 1660s, recommended lime, elm, sycamore, plane and horse chestnut avenues, the latter being in vogue in France at the time.

Avenue planting soon got out of hand and, in addition to the entrance avenue, they extended and radiated like stars from the house in all directions. By 1700, four thousand avenue trees had been planted at Hampton Court, Middlesex. Badminton House in Gloucestershire had avenues criss-crossing the land like runways at a modern international airport, and at Boughton in Northamptonshire, 72 miles of elm and lime avenues were created between 1684 and 1705. Every grand house had to have them.

Then a new fashion blew in. Landscape designer Capability Brown, critical of the formality of avenues, advocated a more naturalistic way of planting trees in the 1750s to 1780s. Many avenues were cut down.

The Chestnut Avenue at Bushy Park, Middlesex is the most celebrated in the country, designed by Sir Christopher Wren as a mile-long carriage drive for William III from Teddington to Hampton Court Palace. It is flanked on both sides by four rows of limes and a single row of horse chestnuts, which, planted in 1690, are still magnificent. Many of the original trees are flourishing, tall and robust. They make a splendid backdrop to the annual Chestnut Sunday parade and picnic on the nearest Sunday to 11 May, when the white candelabras are in full flower.

See also ANCIENT TREES, ASH, BEECH, BLACK POPLAR, CATHEDRALS, ELM, HORNBEAM, HORSE CHESTNUT, LANDMARK TREES, LIME, LONDON PLANE, MONKEY-PUZZLE, OAK, ORCHARDS, ROWAN, SCOTS PINE, SWEET CHESTNUT, SYCAMORE, WALNUT, WEATHER, WILLOW, WOODS, YEW.

22

Baskerville Roman/Italic, John Baskerville, 1757.

BACK LANES

As terraced houses spread around industrial areas in the nineteenth century, particularly in northern cities, many were planned with back lanes. These proved splendid football and courting grounds and allowed access to the rear of the terraces, which also enabled night soil to be collected from privies at the bottoms of the gardens.

The Open Spaces Society is fighting battles of principle to ensure that in Manchester and Rotherham, Yorkshire, for example, back lanes and ginnels are not gated and taken out of the public domain or privatised in the name of crime prevention. Salford, Lancashire has even produced an *Alleygaters' Guide*. Arguments about closing these old urban rights of way are accompanied by observations that crime is committed by people, not alleys; indeed, if more people walked them, there would be fewer incidences of anti-social behaviour.

See also ALLEYS, TERRACED HOUSES.

BADGERS

Hans Helweg

Some of us are privileged to live among ancient beasts; at nights in Shaftesbury, Dorset you may even see them nosing along the High Street. Their poor eyesight means you can get quite close before they smell you or notice a movement, lift their skirts and scuttle off down an alley. Despite a bumbling appearance, badgers move fast, are agile and able to climb quite high walls. They are familiar to us as bit-part characters in *The Wind in the Willows* and Rupert Bear stories, wise and dependable with their bold, black-and-white-striped heads and heavy, blue roan bodies.

Although foxes and other creatures defer to them, badgers are secretive and careful, because for hundreds of years they have been persecuted. Since they were given protection by the 1973 Badgers Act, their numbers have increased. But they are still hunted for baiting by dogs and fifty thousand are found dead on our roads each year – you know if you are in badger country from the corpses.

Rare in upland areas, badgers are widespread in lowland England, particularly in the South West and the Welsh Borders. The big exception is East Anglia, where populations have not recovered from persecution by gamekeepers. In places such as Broxted in Essex and Brockenhurst in Hampshire, the Old English name *brock* lives on, and in Dorset they have a beer named after them. They have been with us for half a million years, and the same species is found all the way to Vladivostok.

Living together in extended families, badgers are creatures of habit. Their paths are centuries old and undisturbed setts can be as complex as medieval cities. Ernest Neal described the largest he had seen in the Brendon Hills, Somerset extending over nineteen hundred square yards with eighty entrances, and in Gloucestershire one large sett had 94 tunnels totalling a thousand feet in length, reaching nearly seven feet in depth. During the years the badgers had extracted 25 tons of soil.

They prefer fields and woods to high streets. Intensive farming practices, housing developments, road schemes and ungenerous gardeners threaten them. Badger groups are also attempting to stop illegal live-catching, as well as killing and culling, taking place because badgers are unfortunate enough to catch the same TB as cattle.

25

> . . . *But far more ancient and dark*
> *The Combe looks since they killed the badger there,*
> *Dug him out and gave him to the hounds,*
> *That most ancient Briton of English beasts*

Edward Thomas, from 'The Combe'

See also BEER, CATTLE, DOGS.

BAKEWELL PUDDING

Not, as Philip Harben put it, '*to be confused with the heretical, commercial Bakewell Tart*', the pudding that put this Peak District market town on the map of European culinary heritage is still the subject of controversy about its secret recipe and origins.

History, though misty, suggests a mistake in the kitchens of one of the town's coaching inns in the mid-nineteenth century. Mrs Greaves, too busy to be in the kitchen herself that day, told the cook to finish the meal with a rich jam tart made by mixing beaten egg and melted butter into the pastry. Surprised by the guests' emphatic praise for the pudding, Mrs G cross-examined the cook, who admitted her error. After making puff pastry spread with jam, she'd remembered the mixture of beaten eggs and melted butter and simply poured it over the top. So a new dish arrived, bringing fame for the Rutland Arms, which still produces these oval puddings for visitors.

Mason and Brown beg to differ, tracing the earliest written recipe to Eliza Acton in 1845. This northern dish, already famous in Derbyshire, topped candied fruit and jams with a rich mix of egg yolk, sugar, butter and almond liqueur, with no pastry base. By 1861 Mrs Beeton had added puff pastry and a layer of jam overlain by a custard made with ground almonds.

See also CAKES, FOOD, PUDDINGS.

B A N D S T A N D S

Bexhill's seafront has a new bandstand, completed in 2002. It can be moved around on its small wheels in front of the marine lines of the De La Warr Pavilion, that unparalleled monument to modernism on the Sussex coast. Against the backdrop of Mendelsohn and Chermayeff's lauded 1930s pleasure palace, the little mobile bandstand, by architect Niall McLaughlin and engineers Price and Myers, holds its own. It seems like a fragment of white sail, pinned down but billowing in the wind.

Most bandstands date from Victorian times. With public health and welfare, temperance and social control on their minds, city fathers opted for the creation of city parks and seaside pleasure grounds, in which the bandstand provided a vehicle for both passive diversion and active endeavour.

Many have an oriental feel. Elegant cast-iron posts and railings stand on circular or octagonal plinths, supporting slightly upturned low-pitched roofs with delicate lanterns and filigree ironwork. Some were particular to their place; in the South West some were thatched.

The first bandstand was built in the newly laid out Dartmouth Park in West Bromwich, Staffordshire, close to the iron foundries, in 1887. Some were designed by well-known architects: Francis Fowke, architect for the Albert Hall in London, designed bandstands for the Royal Horticultural Society in Kensington, London – one still functions after removal to Clapham Common. They soon became so popular that iron makers began to create standard patterns.

With reviving interest in the urban park, bandstands are being resurrected once more, such as the colourful and ornate bandstand in Newcastle's Exhibition Park and the fine cast-iron bandstand on the Quomps in Christchurch, Hampshire.

See also BRASS BANDS, PARKS, PROMENADES, QUOMPS, THATCH.

B A N K   B A R N S

Taking advantage of the slope, most bank barns are built along the sides of hills, enabling easy access to two floors. The top storey is used for threshing and for storing corn, straw and hay – large double doors on the hillside allow carts to enter, and a winnowing door for ventilation lies directly opposite. Below, shippons (closed cow houses) and/or space for horses and carts open onto the farmyard. Trap doors allow feed and bedding to be dropped down to the animals.

In Cornwall they are known as chall barns. Brunskill, who introduced the American term bank barn, talked of their typicality in parts of Lancashire, Cumberland and Westmorland. '*At least four hundred are known and there well might be two or three times that number still surviving. The bank barn is the predominant type of farm building in most parts of the Lake Counties, especially in the west and south west.*' Bank barns orientated the other way, with gable ends set into the hill, are found in the South Hams in Devon.

See also BARNS, BRICKS, CIDER & CIDER ORCHARDS, COB, GIN HOUSES, THATCH.

B A R N S

Built to last using local materials, the barn was usually the most substantial and important building in the farmyard. The storage of grain, straw and hay through the winter demanded, still demands, ingenuity and care. Bulky produce has to be accessible while being kept aired,

26

The Quomps, Christchurch, Hampshire; mobile bandstand, Bexhill-on-Sea, Sussex.

Neolithic long barrows *'are among the earliest monuments found in England'*, Barbara Bender says. *'At a time when people were still moving around the landscape, herding animals, but also still very dependent on hunting and gathering, they began to mark the landscape. On the one hand, there were hill-top enclosures, which seem to have been meeting places, and places for feasting and rituals. On the other, they built long mounds. They often seem to have been set close to well-known, well-worn ridgeway paths. They may have served to mark the territories used by herding communities, and they may have been seen as ancestral places – the places of the old ones.'*

At Belas Knap, south of Winchcombe in Gloucestershire, the remains of nearly forty people were found. But Paul Ashbee suggested that *'long barrows, the long houses of the dead, should be regarded as shrines rather than mausolea.'*

Every barrow is different in shape and size, orientation and position. Not confined to the highest ground, they lie on slopes, spurs and along river valleys, sometimes in pairs. With a heartland in Dorset, long barrows reaching nearly five hundred feet, with ditches to each side, are still being discovered in south and central England. In Cornwall, on the hills, ridges and slopes of West Penwith, rounded cairns of stones covered with earth, up to seventy feet across, harbour internal chambers. More than four hundred of them have been found on the Isles of Scilly in big clusters.

By the Bronze Age round barrows were favoured, a pattern carried on by the Romans (although it was Ordnance Survey maps that gave us the Latin name tumulus). Gatherings of up to thirty round barrows in cemeteries are sometimes found across the country, but Wessex is the centre, from Priddy Nine Barrows in Somerset to Lambourn Seven Barrows in Berkshire. Several round barrow cemeteries are constructed close to much earlier long barrows around Stonehenge. Very often on higher ground and in sight of the great stones, the biggest surprise is that some of the largest round barrows to the east were not only constructed from chalk but were kept white.

Of the square Iron Age barrows dating from the sixth to the first century BC, nine out of ten are clustered in the East Riding of Yorkshire. The Saxons, before turning to Christian burial, clustered their dead in cemeteries of up to three hundred round barrows, from ten to forty feet in diameter; they preferred the crests of hills or spurs. Many ancient barrows in Dorset were used for Saxon burials, lying as they do on the boundaries, a favoured place for pagan burial, which continued in use for 'outsiders'.

Many ancient burial mounds have been lost under the plough. Some found new uses: Belas Knap means beacon mound; at Gally Hills, Surrey nearby barrows have done service as gallows mounds and latterly as golf bunkers; on the Lincolnshire Wolds, one still supports a Cold War concrete lookout. With endless evidence of

27

uncontaminated and uneaten. Before modern materials and access to electricity, high holes were built into walls for ventilation. In Staffordshire brick barns have chequered patterns of holes left by absent bricks; elsewhere arrow slits are typical. There are triangular holes in Cotswold stone barns and square ones in the Yorkshire Dales, to allow owls to enter to keep down rodents.

The variety of building styles owes much to available materials. Barns are characterised by their expansive pitched roofs and large double doors on the long side of the building to enable the comings and goings of loaded carts. The doors are positioned so that, when open, they catch the prevailing wind, blowing away dust and chaff as threshing and winnowing take place inside.

The barn is satisfying, being simple in form and built for the job, while responding to the demands of locality. Examples range from timber-framed and clad with tile roofs in Kent, to stone-built in Yorkshire, with many varieties around and between.

Some barns are finding new agricultural uses, coyly hiding colourful grain silos; others are full of farm machinery. A few have been carefully made into houses, more have been demeaned by insensitive conversion. The loss of access to barns does not help the beleaguered barn owl, and the decline of barns and barn owls is eroding the particularity of farmyard and field.

See also BRICKS, BUILDING STONES, CIDER & CIDER ORCHARDS, COB, CORRUGATED IRON, FARMS & FARMSTEADS, FIELD BARNS, FIELDS, GIN HOUSES, THATCH, TITHE BARNS.

B A R R O W S

A giant buried in a silver coffin is said to lie at Firle Beacon in Sussex. It is easy to see how a huge, low mound up to 394 feet long might get the name of Giant's Grave.

plunder and great damage caused by twentieth-century ploughing, it should not surprise us that stories are told of associated restless ghosts, goblins, soldiers and even of singing barrows.

See also ALBION, BEACON FIRES, BOUNDARIES, CAIRNS, COMMONS, EARTH STATIONS, EARTHWORKS, FOLKTALES, GALLOPS, GIANTS, HAUNTED PLACES, QUOITS II, STANDING STONES, WHITE HORSES.

BASKING SHARKS

28 From April to September, around the south-west peninsula, especially Cornwall, the world's second-largest fish can be seen feeding alone or in groups of a dozen or so. Growing as big as coaches, 35 feet long, basking sharks gently follow the plankton, swimming with their vast mouths open like windsocks, straining water through their special gills.

They congregate where the meeting of water fronts stirs up nutrients from the seabed and fuels a plankton bloom – off Lundy Island in the Bristol Channel, for instance. Occasional sightings are recorded on the north-east and north-west coasts, too. Recent research reveals that we have one of the world's largest populations off our shores, but it is moving northwards, following the plankton as the seas get warmer.

Despite protection up to twelve miles offshore, populations have declined by half in the past twenty years. Like so many other sea creatures, the basking shark is being seriously overfished – its six-foot dorsal fin is a delicacy in Chinese cuisine and its liver produces valuable oil.

See also BOATS, COASTS, ISLANDS, TIDES.

BASTLES

In Northumberland bastle houses are the oldest vernacular buildings. These defensible farmhouses, which look like heavy, steep-roofed barns, were built during the peak of border feuding, or reiving, between England and Scotland from the mid-sixteenth to mid-seventeenth centuries. *'They were intended more for the defence of small tenant farmers and their possessions'*, Richard Sim says. *'Such small, thick-walled farmhouses characteristically had both ground-floor and first-floor doorways. The lower led into a basement, where animals and supplies could be secured . . . an upper, first floor could be reached by a ladder, which could afterwards be pulled up, making it impossible for raiders to reach the living quarters.'*

Built from huge blocks of Carboniferous sandstone, bastles are found in a twenty-mile band all along the border, unique to this part of the country. In Cumberland they were timber floored, but in Northumberland, barrel-vaulted floors are also found. They occur in pairs and groups and would have been among buildings with no defences. The style continued once there was no need for defence, with thinner walls and more first-floor windows.

'There are well over a hundred Bastle houses remaining, but Haltwhistle has more . . . than any other English town', Richard Sim says. *'There is a cluster of defensible buildings on the Main Street, five bastles . . . and one tower.'* He adds: *'The origin of the term Bastle is unknown, but thought to be derived from the French prison fortress, Bastille.'*

Good examples in the Northumberland hills are at Black Middens and Gatehouse North Bastle in the parish of Tarset, and Woodhouses in the parish of Harbottle, but most are roofless and ruined. Mary Herdman from Wall names the bastles, changed over time, but still lived in around the green: Greenhead House, St Oswald's Cottages, Stable Cottage, possibly Town Farmhouse and more.

See also BARNS, BUILDING STONES, CASTLES, CATTLE, PELE TOWERS, SHEEP.

BATTLEFIELDS

Seven miles from Hastings, east Sussex the famous moment of the last conquest of England was fought out. The Bayeux Tapestry shows King Harold being struck in the right eye by an arrow '*near the hoar apple-tree and the Sandlake stream*', a mile from Telham Hill, A.H. Burne wrote.

William's conquest changed everything: the Duke of Normandy brought his court, his language, his administrative system and his leisure pursuits. In the place hereafter to be known as Battle, he ordered an abbey to be built with the high altar on the spot where Harold died. This became one of the most prosperous and powerful Benedictine abbeys in the country before it was demolished during the Dissolution. The town continues to attract pilgrims, tourists seeking to understand something momentous from a thousand years ago or to watch the dramatic reconstruction of the Battle of Hastings each October.

Re-enactments are also frequently played out at Stamford Bridge in Yorkshire, Shrewsbury, Bosworth Field in Leicestershire, Flodden in Northumberland, Edgehill in Warwickshire, Marston Moor in Yorkshire, Naseby in Northamptonshire and Sedgemoor in Somerset, although the exact locations of battles may be disputed by historians. Where little overt physical evidence of old battles remains – bones, cannon-balls, spearheads lingering beneath the soil – the hills, rivers and marshes described in accounts of these conflicts may be read from field and place-names, such as Bloody Meadow and Crown Hill.

With the death of Richard III on Bosworth Field in 1485, the Plantagenets were defeated, the Wars of the Roses lost and won and the Tudor dynasty initiated. Although the exact location of Bosworth is contested, a visitor centre claims the place near Sutton Cheney in Leicestershire. Close by, landmarks such as Richard's Bog, Dickon's Nook (a barrow), Richard's Field, Ambion (one tree) Hill and Crown Hill at Stoke Golding – where Lord Stanley crowned Henry VII – help us to re-enact the scenes of battle. Now, on a grey day out of the tourist season, with the light dying, the slow flap of Richard's standard on Ambion Hill lends an air of melancholy. To settle the question of geography, new research is exploring marshes a mile away and an unexcavated mound eight miles away at Atherstone, Warwickshire, where local stories and chronicles claim were heaped thousands of Yorkist and Lancastrian dead.

Piper's Hill, Branxton Hill, Twizell Bridge, the river Till, Ford Castle's St James's Tower, Flodden Edge, Pallin's Burn and Branx Brig are strategic landmarks in north Northumberland, where King James IV of Scotland and up to ten thousand of his men, including many of the nobility, fell in battle against the English at the 'Fatal Field of Flodden' in 1513. In this place, bloody hand-to-hand warfare ended (muskets and advanced battlefield manoeuvres were to follow) and the fate of Scotland as a separate nation was sealed, ensuring that this moment stays alive in the hearts of Scots. Nearly four hundred years later, in 1910, a memorial granite cross was erected on Piper's Hill. Each August the battle and its consequences are remembered; a lone piper plays as a cavalcade makes its way up Branxton Hill.

More than 220 battlefields need to be understood as graveyards and historical records as well as conserved to let our imaginations understand something of the scenes. In Gloucestershire in 1999, the Tewkesbury Battlefield Society successfully campaigned to prevent Gaston Field being built upon. Despite such pressures, battlefields do not have any legal protection, although 43 were selected by English Heritage for the Register of Historic Battlefields in 1995. They remain deeply significant, ancient or modern. The Battle of Britain and other fights in the sky during the Second World War have left their memories – Beaford in Devon is not alone in having a Bomber Field, where a stray German pilot came down.

See also ABBEYS, AIRFIELDS, FIELDS, WHITE HORSES.

BAWMING THE THORN

Up with fresh garlands this Mid-summer morn,
Up with red ribbons on Appleton Thorn,
Come lasses and lads to the Thorn Tree today,
To bawm it, and shout as ye bawm it!

This is the chorus to a song composed by R.E. Egerton-Warburton in the nineteenth century for local children to sing as they danced around the old hawthorn tree in the village of Appleton Thorn in Cheshire. This hawthorn, significant enough to add its name to the village, is *Crataegus monogyna* 'biflora' – it flowers twice a year, in spring and at Christmas or thereabouts. It is known as the Holy Thorn of Glastonbury: legend suggests that the original grew in Somerset from the staff of Joseph of Arimathea, who visited after the Crucifixion. A Norman Knight, coming back from fighting in the Holy Land, brought a cutting from Glastonbury to Appleton in thanks for his safe return.

The ancient custom of bawming the Thorn is unique to this village. The ceremonious adorning of the tree with ribbons, garlands and flags on St Peter's Day, 29 June, was discontinued because of rowdiness in Victorian times. It was revived in the 1930s, when children danced around the tree carrying bouquets of flowers, which they then hung on the railings surrounding the tree, and sang the bawming song, followed by tea and sports.

A much-loved thorn tree planted in 1880 blew down in 1965, and the sapling that replaced it also soon died. An unusually high number of deaths and broken marriages were blamed on the lack of a Holy Thorn in the village, so

29

another cutting from the original Glastonbury Thorn – a purported successor from the original still grows in the grounds of the ruins of Glastonbury Abbey – was planted in 1967, when the ceremony was again revived. In 1992 two saplings were planted – one in the church and one in the schoolyard.

So long as this thorn tree o'ershadows the ground,
May sweethearts to bawm it in plenty be found;
And a thousand years hence, when 'tis withered and dead,
May there stand here a thorn to be bawmed in its stead.

See *also* ANCIENT TREES, ARBOR DAY, HAWTHORN, TREE DRESSING DAY.

BEACHCOMBING

It is hard to resist the pull of the beach as the tide recedes, always bringing something new from nature or from the flotsam and jetsam of humanity. In the West Country, the locals call it 'wrecking'. They are more likely to make the effort after a storm. Flotsam derives from the Anglo-Saxon word meaning 'to float', while jetsam defines things thrown from a boat, perhaps to lighten it in stormy conditions (from the French *jeter* – 'to throw'). In Cornwall they call them scummow.

Cornish people and those from the Isles of Scilly have a history of lifesaving against the odds and avid retrieval of artefacts following storms and wrecks. The offshore rocks have long snagged nets and keels, barrels of brandy and rum; chests of wares from far-off places embellish many a story. Now it is more likely to be polystyrene, doomed to wander the seas forever, and bright yellow, red and blue plastics, together with driftwood, that liven up the strand line after a storm.

We can mourn organisms that have been ripped from their moorings or simply flung too high on the beach to return, but they fascinate natural historians. From Northumberland, Phil Gates described the carnage in his 'Country Diary' for the *Guardian*. '*Warkworth beach: the high tide and stormy seas had left tangled piles of kelp, torn from the seabed, all down the beach . . . delicate hydroid colonies, sea squirts, sponges, whelks, hermit crabs and piles of sand mason worm cases.*' But, he added, '*the principal casualties were the starfish*', which cannot live out of water. Many of the prominent women naturalists of the early nineteenth century, such as Margaret Gatty, were seaweed collectors.

Along the coast near Lyme Regis, Dorset, geology buffs arrive in droves after word of big storms and rockfalls to seek out fossils emergent from their long sleep. The southern beaches of the Isle of Wight yield crunchies

– smoothed vertebrae of dinosaurs; elephant bones are found on Norfolk's Overstrand; and on the edge of Northumberland, around Holy Island, St Cuthbert's beads – segments of crinoidal fossils – can be gleaned from the sand.

The glister of iron pyrites on the edge of rounded pebbles on the east Yorkshire coast may promise an embedded ammonite. From here to Essex, but particularly from Cromer in Norfolk to Felixstowe in Suffolk, you might get lucky after a big storm to find pieces of amber along the high-water mark, especially among the frondy seaweeds that are good at sweeping the sea floor. Amber is so light that it is flung high up the beach, perhaps having been loosened from submarine rock layers or having taken a long ride all the way from the Baltic.

The age and mixture of rocks around the south-west peninsula make for sparkling natural finds. Cornish diamonds (rock crystal – a sort of quartz) are quite widely scattered, while rare green and red serpentine is particular to Kynance Cove. From Penzance to Marazion, gems of agate, amethyst, citrine, carnelian and jasper are found. 'Plymouth limestone' and black glassy pieces are actually smelter's slag on the beaches around Penpol, possibly from ship's ballast. Along the Durham coast, once black with coal waste, it now requires concentration to turn up a fair piece of coal, while on the north side of Morecambe Bay, near Ulverston, Lancashire, the Town Beck chews on slag heaps that make for a milky tide.

In the past beachcombing supplemented income and kept families in fuel. In Dickensian London young children and women, called mudlarks, worked the Thames foreshore for anything they could sell, from lost coal to copper and old rope. Now anyone can walk the foreshore, but no one is allowed to dig without a Port of London Authority Permit. It is not easy to join the Society of Thames Mudlarks, who have permission to metal-detect and dig between the Tower and the Houses of Parliament.

Washed up whales and sturgeon, as Royal Fish, were claimed by the reigning monarch, although now the Natural History Museum has first refusal for whales. Objects that fall off ships must be declared to the Receiver of Wreck.

See *also* AMMONITES, BEACHES, CHALK, COASTLINE, COASTS, JET, PIT TIPS, SAND-DUNES, SHINGLE, STARFISH, TIDES, WEATHER, WHITE CLIFFS.

BEACHES

Beaches attract us with the exhilaration of the freedom of 'the common'. But 55 per cent of the littoral zone is owned by estates, local authorities, statutory bodies, government departments and business interests that control large areas for energy production, oil refining and so on. The Crown owns the rest, although it leases some to ports and wildlife organisations.

One day a beach may have a simple, falling profile, for example along Yorkshire's Holderness coast. The next it may have giant terraces redrawn by storm waves. Breakwaters erected to slow longshore drift make for exciting walking along the shore, with sand piled high up to one side and a big drop down to pools on the other, as at Clacton in Essex.

Chesil Beach in Dorset is a geological wonder of the world. A tombolo linking the mainland with the Isle of Portland, it stretches for eighteen miles, rising eastwards to forty feet in height. Along its length the pebbles are so predictably sifted that local fishermen can read their whereabouts in them: at Abbotsbury they are smaller than a Fisherman's Friend lozenge, while at Chiswell a single pebble is bigger than the hand. Thousands of little terns nest among the pebbles. It is dangerous for them, and illegal for walkers to wander here between 1 May and 31 August.

Winter walking is nowhere better than on the crunchy East Anglian stretches of shingle at Scolt Head, Blakeney Point and Orford Ness, with skeins of geese flying noisily above, or along the south coast, for example at The Crumbles, Sussex and Dungeness, Kent, with the groynes adding to the distractions at Selsey, Sussex. But there are scant amounts of shingle in the north.

Pure white sand may be of ground coral – calcium rich and useful in farming. But most sand is dominated by pure quartz; it will frost glass when blasted by the wind. Among the colours in a handful of sand the other constituent seen most easily is mica – shiny dark flakes, light in weight, that stick to the skin. Alum Bay on the Isle of Wight is famed for the many discrete sand colours created by erosion of the vertically tipped rocks.

Sara Hudston compares the sands in the Isles of Scilly, Cornwall. '*Scilly sand is white, palest palomino when wet, and full of sparkling mica. It varies in grade from island to island. St Agnes, the western-most inhabited place, has gritty sand that scrunches underfoot like coarse glass. Tresco's long flanks are heaped with fine powder. Bryher sand has the texture of table salt and St Martin's beaches are packed hard and clean. On St Mary's, sand from Porth Mellon was once considered so superior that parcels of it were sent as presents to the Mainland to blot the wet ink on letters and documents.*'

Dramatic cliffs at Staithes and Robin Hood's Bay in Yorkshire are the backdrop for wave-cut platforms over flat-bedded rocks revealed on the falling tide. In Somerset, at Kilve Pill, the oil shale strata are slightly tilted, offering a complex of tiers with necklaces of pools in which the locals once went 'glatting' for conger eels.

Small sandy coves offer a joyous combination of security and prospect. Polzeath Beach in north Cornwall has it all: soft, clean sand, splendid safe surf, cliffs, island, rock and sand pools, as well as simple facilities. The popularity of Bournemouth beach is due to sunshine and soft, clean sands, while Brighton draws the crowds because it is fashionable despite the pebbles.

Meanwhile, in the centre of London on a warm summer night, the river police may be heard shouting ashore that the tide is coming in and the Reclaim the Beach party begins to wind down. Between the Oxo Tower and the South Bank complex is a beach, contested for many years – this land is jealously championed by local people, despite the riverward push of shoreline development. Many have memories of relaxing on the beach created between 1934 and 1964 in front of the Tower of London. The rising tide of pollution and drownings eventually led to its being abandoned. But the great and positive story of the clean-up of the Thames may bring more made beaches, as in Berlin and Paris.

Sharing the beach with birds is a pleasure compounded by seasonal variations. The scurry of the rushing turnstone upending flotsam along the strand line, ridding us of sand-hoppers; the more considered actions of the oystercatcher probing for molluscs; a long-beaked curlew stretching a leg; these are not seen everywhere. The query 'Any stuff about?' as you pass someone with binoculars might bring you 'loads of avocets' on the Norfolk coast or in Northumberland 'the Arctic terns are back'.

31

Dawlish Warren, Devon.

B E A C H H U T S

The prudish nature of Victorian bathing has left us a colourful legacy – the beach hut is a descendant of the wheeled bathing machines from which daringly clad men and women stepped down for a dip in the sea. Reminiscent also of simple bungalows, '*the verandah style probably owes much to the British Empire . . . India and the Caribbean*', says Tim Baber. There is also a great tradition in mainland Europe of the summerhouse or dacha.

Along parts of the coast, rag-tag gatherings of railway carriages, boats that have 'dunsailin', fishing huts and shacks link the land and the sea. Yorkshire, Cornwall, Essex and Devon all have their beach-hut fraternities. They bring twinges of jealousy to those who pass by the carefree domestic scenes featuring cups of tea and deckchairs, snoozing magazine readers and liberated tots with buckets and spades.

At Selsey, west Sussex, shingle-side plots originally squatted by makeshift buildings now support permanent brick and concrete. There are glimpses of old railway carriages; one has 'No Smoking' etched into its wood-framed windows.

Some beach huts cluster in wild corners, untamed, undesigned. But ranks of beach huts tend to be municipally owned and standardised, always in demand for hire by the season or the day. Where privately owned, rigidity of plot size and restrictive bylaws have not stifled the imagination. The variety and richness of decks and shutters, gable ends and roof lines, stilts and varnish make for seaside splendour even in winter.

Tim Baber's family owned a beach hut at Mudeford, Hampshire for more than fifty years. It was well equipped: '*A small solar panel fitted on the asphalt roof powered a laptop for the newspaper, a small television and a cassette player. Over the years almost any twelve-volt appliance invaded the place.*' It stands among a double line of 350 others, making

a splash of colour and a zigzag of roofs along a sand spit that gives owners a dual outlook, inland over Christchurch Harbour and seaward towards the Needles. The sadness is that they have become real estate – Werere or Lazy Days may change hands for £140,000, even where the threat of rising sea levels is almost palpable and insecurity is only a storm away.

Local authority ownership should prevent the excesses of buying and selling, but controlled huts tend to regimentation and most allow no sleeping overnight. Some look like stable blocks for thin horses, as at Porthminster Beach in Cornwall, or like beach garages with padlocks, as at Hove, east Sussex. Further east at Bexhill-on-Sea, they range from pointed roofed sheds to flat-roofed minimalist concrete, lively and colourful when occupied but unrelentingly white and introspective when not. Bournemouth owners have splashed theirs with primary colours. Along Shoebury beach in Essex every hut is different in size, shape and colour.

New lines of beach huts have been built during the past few years. The East Riding of Yorkshire retained Bauman Lyons Architects to refurbish Bridlington's South Foreshore Promenade. Working with the artist Bruce McLean they created a café, shops, boat slipways, paddling pool and viewing terrace linked by the mile-long promenade. Sculptures, water channels and a solar-heated shower add new dimensions to the seaside atmosphere, as do the robust, asymmetrically gabled beach huts, which have to be booked a year in advance.

At Whitstable, Kent, on the West Beach Promenade, double rows of former fishermen's huts have their own gardens. Some, two storeys high, are clearly lived in – old, black-painted lobster-pot and net sheds. Some of the huts at Southwold in Suffolk are like colonial bungalows for children. Others, still with gables to the sea and open balconies, are painted from a palette of deep blues, pinks and soft yellows normally seen only in sweet shops; some have carved fretwork gables and name boards – Dog Watch,

32

Wells-next-the-Sea, Norfolk; Bournemouth, Dorset.

Harry's Bar, Spunyarns. With ten steps leading up to a terrace, sometimes sideways on, the huts at Wells-next-the-Sea, Norfolk stand on stilts like welcoming bird boxes.

Kathryn Ferry has been studying beach huts. *'What particularly struck me as I travelled around the coast was the diversity of beach hut shapes and sizes within very small areas. For example, beside the flat expanse of Lincolnshire sands between Mablethorpe and Sandilands, the difference in ownership as well as the relative property prices on the land behind has caused a surprising variety of styles . . . From flat-roofed concrete boxes and square, double-fronted chalets painted in blocks of glossy red, blue and green for hire at Mablethorpe, one can walk along the promenade past a line of Oriental-looking huts towards Sutton-on-Sea. These are among my favourite huts. Built of pre-cast concrete they have corrugated asbestos roofs in a sort of Chinese pagoda style. I appreciate that they don't sound too promising, but en masse they are superb. Further along on the Bohemia Promenade, this type gives way to private wooden huts with verandas and traditional seaside names, while towards the posher end of Sandilands, the emphasis is on a sea view, with the huts ranged gable to gable with large windows that glint in the sun.'*

See also BUNGALOWS, COASTS, DAGS, DEEZES, FLOODS, PROMENADES, SHINGLE, TIDES.

BEACON FIRES

Fires have probably been lit on hilltops since pre-Christian times all over Europe, especially at Midsummer's Eve, in celebration and to strengthen the waning powers of the sun. Warning of invasion could be transmitted by the use of fire signals from one vantage point to another – a controlled form of 'spreading like wildfire'.

We know beacons were in use in 1242 from the place-name Wardleigh in Devon ('ward' first referred to a lookout, then to a guiding fire) and from the Close Rolls of 1377, which refer to some beacons in Essex and Kent. But the main period of construction was by the Tudors from 1539, primarily from the Thames estuary to Land's End, to prepare against invasion by the French. In 1588 beacons were lit on the Cornish coast when the Spanish Armada was sighted. They were used later during the Napoleonic wars, but the fires were replaced by a more complicated system of signalling – the equivalent of Native American smoke signals. The last beacons were built in the 1740s.

The first beacons probably would have been simple bonfires – on Bonfire Hill in Burnley, Lancashire, for example. Later, more sophisticated pole beacons were constructed, made from a square post with an iron fire basket or cresset at the top, containing a pot of pitch and flax or peat, supported by four posts. It could be reached by rungs through the pole or by a ladder. At strategic places,

such as on the Isle of Wight, there may sometimes have been as many as three baskets together, signalling varying degrees of danger.

On the Blackdown Hills, which straddle Somerset and Devon, a beehive-shaped hut built of local chert stone, with a circular opening in the domed roof, survives. From Devon, Margaret Bromwich says: *'We call it loosely Culmstock Beacon, but we may mean the hill, the fire, or the edifice . . . It seems that our fire beacon is unique now, although others remain in fragments at Shute Hill in Axminster and Harpford . . . Recently experts have told us that they have discovered postholes in the floor of the structure, indicating how it was used: it protected and supported iron stakes upholding an ironwork basket, in which tinder and logs would burn easily with a good up-draught. Tar-soaked pitch, gorse and coal were likely to have been pushed into the basket, too – if it was ever lit.'*

Church towers were used in the absence of hills; an example still exists in Richmond, Yorkshire, and St Giles's Church in Norwich has a fire basket on top of its western tower. Elsewhere churches helped with coastal navigation.

Beacon sites can be found at the top of many prominent hills – for example the Herefordshire and Worcestershire Beacons in the Malverns and Ivinghoe Beacon in the Chilterns – as part of links in a chain. But most were created along the south coast and the Scottish borders. There are 25 beacons in Dorset, found on hilltop ancient monuments. Along the Sussex Downs, Firle Beacon (commemorated by the composer George Butterworth) and Ditchling Beacon are situated on barrows. Dunkery Beacon on Exmoor stands at 1,705 feet, and Selworthy Beacon in Somerset at 1,013 feet. The hauling of wood to these places was no mean feat; sometimes small plantations were maintained nearby for fuel.

The magic of seeing a chain of hilltop fires is so potent that we have re-created them as part of non-military celebrations, from Queen Victoria's diamond jubilee in 1897 and the coronation of Queen Elizabeth II in 1953 to the turn of the new millennium in 2000.

See also BARROWS, BEACONS (COASTAL), BONFIRE NIGHT, HILLS, LANDMARKS, MIDSUMMER DAY.

33

Culmstock Beacon, Blackdown Hills, Somerset.

BEACONS (COASTAL)

'One thousand poor fishermen in open boats, not daring to near the shore, with a hard gale from ENE and raining in sluices, till a large coal light was raised on Beadnell Point, when nearly one hundred boats run in and all got safe, to the inexpressible joy of their numerous poor families.'

John Wood recounted this incident in 1828 to Trinity House, and was thereafter permitted to show a light on Beadnell Point, or Ebb's Neuk, in Northumberland for the herring season from 25 July to Michaelmas. Church towers standing proud of flat land were also used for beacon fires or lanterns: at the fifteenth-century church of St Nicholas (patron saint of seafarers) in Blakeney, Norfolk an extra tower was built in the north-east corner for this purpose.

Coastal beacons come in many guises. Although help for seafarers night and day is now dominated by the Global Positioning System (GPS) and radar, there is still a need for workaday 'road signs' to aid navigation into harbour. In Whitby, Yorkshire two cylinders, red and green for starboard and port, stand on wooden legs at the end of the jetties on either side of the harbour entrance. Day marks – big obelisks or triangles of stone, sometimes striped in red or black and white – mark in idiosyncratic form the entrance to creek or harbour. At Walton on the Naze in Essex stands a brick tower once nearly ninety feet high. At Heugh Hill on Holy Island, Northumberland the steel 'Black Beacon' shines a light at night and carries a red triangle as day mark; its partner Guile Point Light Beacon has a solar-powered light.

The simplest of fixed beacons are attached to buildings or driven into sand, mud or rock, and stand in the sea with a distinctive top mark attached to them. These silhouettes demarcate navigable channels or note hazards. Selsey Bill in Sussex is edged by poles topped with triangles enclosing vertical bars to note the ends of groynes lost under the high tide. In Hampshire, the Channel Pilot says: *'to approach the entrance to Lymington river in the deepest water, bring Jack-in-the-basket beacon in line with the Lymington church'.* The striped pole topped by an iron cage and a light sports

34

its name, as do other beacons in the harbour – Tar Barrel Post, Cocked Hat, Bag of Halfpence – reinforcing the other-worldliness of the language of the littoral.

See also BEACON FIRES, BOATS, CHURCHES, HARBOURS, LANDMARKS, LIGHTHOUSES, SEA-MARKS.

BEATING THE BOUNDS

The traditional day for beating the bounds of the parish was Holy Thursday, Ascension Day, forty days after Easter. It fell on the last of the Rogation Days – also called Cross Days, Gang Days or Grass Days in different places – the four days from the fifth Sunday after Easter (which itself falls on the Sunday after the first full moon following the vernal equinox).

Rogationtide, an ancient festival to invoke a blessing on fields, stock and folk, emerged after a sequence of natural disasters in fifth-century France. By the eighth century in England it involved parishioners 'ganging' (walking) after the Cross around the edge of the parish. This helped everyone to remember the boundaries before maps were commonplace. Along the way prominent trees – Gospel Oaks – often became places for preaching.

The locations of various landmarks – stones, streams, hedges and ponds – were impressed upon children by ducking them in water, ritually beating them and then giving them a treat. In the twenty-first century anyone shopping on Ascension Day at Marks and Spencer in Oxford will see dignitaries and followers hitting a floor plaque with sticks, a formal reminder of the parish bounds of St Michael in the Northgate.

The Enclosures of the eighteenth and nineteenth centuries, which 'fixed' so many common lands into fields and bounds, killed many of the perambulations. But where they do survive they prove a sociable way of exploring. Afterwards you may be offered ganging beer and Rammalation biscuits, as they did at Aveton Gifford, Devon to celebrate the completion of their Parish Map in 1992.

In Rochester, Kent a boat is required every year to carry the Mayor of Medway, who holds the title of Admiral of the River, to trace the boundary down the centre of the estuary. His counterpart in the City of London does the same in the Thames. Every seventh year in Richmond, Yorkshire in September halberdiers and sergeants-at-mace lead an eighteen-mile perambulation and watch the water bailiff stride out into the river Swale.

In Cumberland and Northumberland it is still customary to Ride the Marches on horseback, as the parishes are large. At Berwick-upon-Tweed they have ridden the bounds on May Day annually since the reign of Henry VIII – in 2003 at least eighty riders followed Chief Marshal Alison Borthwick along a fifteen-mile stretch of Lamberton Moor.

Jack in the Basket: Lymington Harbour, Hampshire. Top marks: Lymington Harbour, Hampshire; Selsey Bill, Sussex.

Hodgson's *History of Northumberland* has the grand jury walking the boundaries of Morpeth and leaving a detailed description on 3 April 1758, including: '*and along by Watty's-hole, and so into the Standers and through the garden in the same, walked over the water called Bowls-green Steps to the bounder Stones*'. Today the Riding of the Bounds takes four hours, ending in the late afternoon with the St Mark's Day Races on Morpeth Common.

See also BEER, BISCUITS, BOUNDARIES, BOUNDARY STONES, COMMONS, LANDMARKS, MAY DAY, MIDSUMMER DAY, RIVERS.

B E C K S

Where the Norse and Danish settled throughout the North, the language remembers them in small, often fast-flowing streams (*bekkr* is Old Norse). Ekwall suggests that the use of beck is common in Cumberland, Westmorland, Yorkshire, Lancashire and Lincolnshire, and 'fairly numerous' in Derbyshire and Nottinghamshire.

Norman Nicholson captures the slow flow of rock in the turbulent words of water tumbling through the rainy and steep Cumbrian hills.

> *Motionless to the eye,*
> *Wide cataracts of rock*
> *Pour off the fellside,*
> *Throw up a spume*
> *Of gravel and scree*
> *To eddy and sink*
> *In the blink of a lifetime.*

Norman Nicholson, from 'Beck'

See also BOURNES. BRIDGES. BROOKS. BURNS. CHALK STREAMS. DIALECTS. FLOODS, FOOD, FOOTBRIDGES, FORDS, FRESHWATER FISH, GHYLLS, KENNELS, OTTERS, RHYNES, RIVER NAMES, SOUGHS, SPRINGS, STEPPING-STONES, SWIMMING PLACES, WATERFALLS, WELL DRESSING, WINTERBOURNES.

B E E B O L E S

Before the mid-nineteenth century, when they began to be kept in wooden hives, honey bees were housed in woven wicker and, later, coiled straw baskets called skeps, often made by thatchers. They were placed in gardens and orchards on low wooden stands and, although their tops were covered with straw hats, known as hackles, added protection from the elements was needed.

Recessed into garden walls at least two to three feet from the ground, bee boles are usually rectangular niches, sometimes arched at the top. Occasionally located in house walls, they are seldom found outside Britain and Ireland, most dating from the seventeenth and eighteenth centuries. Sally Francis from Norfolk writes: '*We have six brick arched structures in a south-facing stretch of an old garden wall.*'

A wall could have from one to thirty bee boles, in a row or placed on top of one another. Each usually held one skep, sometimes three. In Cumberland and Westmorland most bee boles measured fifteen to thirty inches high by seventeen or more inches wide, with a slate projecting out at the top to keep off the rain and one on the bottom to provide a landing platform for the bees – a characteristic also found in Devon and Cornwall. They are found in drystone and mortared walls of the local stone. In Kent they are smaller and mainly built into brick walls.

Of the 855 sets of bee boles recorded between 1953 and 1983 by the International Bee Research Association, most are in Cumberland and Westmorland, which has 105. Yorkshire has 102 and Devon 101. Local names for bee boles noted by A.M. Foster include '*bee holes . . . bee niches (Derbyshire), bee walls (Gloucestershire), bee houses (Yorkshire), bee boxes (Kent) and bee garths*'. In Lancashire alone Penelope Walker and Eva Crane document names varying from bee stacks near Grizedale, bee shells at Finisthwaite, bee holes around Blawith and bee houses near High Nibthwaite.

Bee keeping is an ancient art, and wicker skeps could have been used here for two thousand years. Many boles are associated with monasteries, which used beeswax for making candles and honey for sweetening and making mead. The land that belonged to Furness Abbey in Lancashire has most bee-keeping structures. Clusters also occur in places where bee skeps needed extra shelter from bitter east winds or from the rain, such as in Cumberland, the Pennines, Devon, east Yorkshire and parts of Kent.

Bee shelters are less permanent structures, often leaning against a wall, with a roof and shelves for the skeps, but fewer of these have survived. A unique, thirty-foot-long stone bee shelter containing 33 boles was found in a dilapidated state in Nailsworth, Gloucestershire in 1957 and moved to Hartpury churchyard, where it is being renovated.

See also BUILDING STONES, COTTAGE GARDENS, DRYSTONE WALLS, HONEY & BEES, ORCHARDS.

B E E C H

Ivor Gurney betrays his Cotswold stamping grounds in whispering that '*Beech woods have given me truest secrets*' in his 1922-25 poem 'Song of Autumn'. Swathes of beech woods dominate the steep slopes between Birdlip and Dursley in Gloucestershire, big trees forming a continuous canopy to the exclusion of other trees and bushes, but

35

favouring low-growing rarities, such as helleborines, bird's-nest orchid and common wintergreen. Beech is most loyal to oolitic limestone and to the chalk land of the south.

With a pollen record reaching back eight thousand years, beech is native to the south, but has been planted and naturalised elsewhere, such as the Blackdown Hills in Somerset, in the Culmhead beech avenues and along the ridge tops, and in Devon, where the wide beech hedge banks lend character to the fields and lanes, particularly on Exmoor. Here, and in the Quantocks, Somerset, many of these hedges, planted to mark out nineteenth-century enclosures, have long been left unlaid and form summer dark and dappled tunnels over the lanes.

Landmark trees are common, telling where roads meet; some mark isolated farms. Hilltop clumps sculpted by the prevailing wind offer orientation points. In the Lincolnshire Wolds, beech trees dating from the enclosures line wide drove roads. On chalkland spurs, ancient graves, standing up as barrows, are topped by groups of beeches. Up and down the Pennines, beech was planted as shelter belt for farm and field, always doing best on limestone.

The Wealden industries of iron making and glass making used beech, while many eighteenth-century stately houses were surrounded by plantations. The beech hangers of Hampshire and Sussex cling to the chalk scarps, much like the woods of the Cotswold edge, and beech woods are a badge of identity for the Chilterns. The woodland canopy is often so dense, preventing eighty per cent of the light penetrating to the ground, that little grows here and the woods are easy to navigate. The furniture trade has long favoured the beech, and around High Wycombe, Buckinghamshire, wandering bodgers would set up seasonal camp and turn beech for the legs, stretchers and back spindles of Windsor chairs.

London must have been an important market for the furniture makers, just as it was hungry for firewood and but a short journey down the Thames. Many pollarded and coppiced beeches fed this trade from medieval times, but because of the importation of coal from the North East, some ancient pollards have stood unworked for one or two centuries. The largest assembly in the world still stands at Burnham Beeches, Buckinghamshire (on gravelly sands, it should be noted), acquired by the Corporation of the City of London in 1880 to protect it from development. Some of its pollarded beeches are five hundred years old and the quest now is to relearn the nuances of this ancient art in order to prolong their lives.

The ageing pollards of the New Forest, Hampshire and their offspring still provide tons of beech mast in a good year, and rights of pannage allow pigs to compete with wood mice, squirrels, rooks and bramblings. The seed production is often exceptional after a hot summer, which is also the time to see the most intense colours in the turning leaves.

See also ALDER, ANCIENT TREES, ASH, AVENUES, BIRCH, BLACK POPLAR, BLACKTHORN, CLUMPS, EDIBLE DORMOUSE, ELM, FIELD MAPLE, HAWTHORN, HAZEL, HEDGES, HOLLY, HOLM OAK, HORNBEAM, HORSE CHESTNUT, JUNIPER, LANDMARK TREES, LIME, LONDON PLANE, MONKEY-PUZZLE, OAK, ORCHARDS, PEARS, POPLAR, ROWAN, ROYAL FORESTS, SCOTS PINE, SWEET CHESTNUT, SYCAMORE, WALNUT, WHITEBEAM, WILLOW, WINDSOR & COUNTRY CHAIRS, WOODS, YEW.

B E E R

Before the nineteenth century many places – Derby, Dorchester, Windsor and Nottingham were just a few – produced distinctive beers. This diversity may have been linked to the type of herb used for flavouring – willow bark, cloves, juniper, sage or even ground oyster shells – but water quality was also crucial. Ideal water for beer has high calcium and magnesium content, high sulphate concentration and low presence of sodium, bicarbonate, potassium and chloride. The water of Burton upon Trent, Staffordshire, long regarded as the best, has a very high sulphate count – 638 parts per million.

Although beer became big business, regional brews and village brewers persisted. Celebrations prompted their own brews, such as 'cuckoo ales' for the first signs of summer. The name Spingo is now entirely associated with the beer produced for several hundred years at the small brewery attached to the Blue Anchor pub in Helston, Cornwall, and especially enjoyed at the Furry Dance in May, but the word historically implied strong beer.

Variety can still be found. Ronald Atkins in 1997 noted generally that English bitters tend to be *'sharper in the South East; maltier in the South West; sweeter in the Midlands; then becoming hoppier as you go north . . . The more bitter bitters are found in south-east England and, in particular, parts of Lancashire and Yorkshire.'*

Beers come in many guises. IPA (India Pale Ale) was brewed originally with an unusually high hop content so that it would mellow in the time taken to export it to troops in the far corners of the then British Empire. Full-flavoured dark beers, such as porters and stouts, have come in and out of favour over the centuries; now Irish Guinness dominates.

Brown ales, one of the oldest English beers, still appear, traditionally brewed from brown malt smoked over a fire of hornbeam, oak or beech. Manns is the best known of the few to survive, sweet, with old South London associations but now produced at Burtonwood in Lancashire. Other brewers, including Harveys of east Sussex, produce examples as well. The North East is particularly associated with the name brown ale, but although Newcastle Brown (first brewed in 1927) has a special place in people's hearts, it and other north-eastern browns, such as Samuel Smith's Nut Brown Ale, are quite different, stronger drinks. Mild, once an English pub staple, had all but vanished, but it is beginning to make a slow return thanks to a growing band of enthusiasts.

From the mid-twentieth century, the large beer producers became global concerns and quality, variety and authenticity suffered. Sales of continental-style lagers doubled between 1965 and 1969 and have continued to supplant the home-grown beers. But resistance was growing: the Society for the Preservation of Beers from the Wood appeared, succeeded in the early 1970s by the Campaign for Real Ale, which remains busy campaigning for beers made with care. It has been instrumental in creating an environment in which smaller-scale micro-breweries, producing up to fifteen thousand barrels a year, can begin to compete with mass producers.

Their scale encourages brewing with attention to detail, using local resources and aimed often exclusively at a local market. Abbey Ales in Bath offers its beers only to pubs within a twenty-mile radius of the brewery. Beers from micro-breweries often have colourful names with local resonances: Riggwelter (Black Sheep, Yorkshire); Old Tongham Tasty (Hog's Back, Surrey); Freeminer (Cinderford, Forest of Dean, Gloucestershire). Some go one better: Stonehenge Ales's Sign of Spring (Netheravon, Wiltshire) is green.

Legislation once gave small producers a foothold in markets such as 'tied' pubs, where tenancy conditions often restrict 'guest' beers. Unfortunately this legislation was repealed in 2003. Although this could have a negative impact, the number of micro-breweries continues healthily to grow: 34 new ones were listed in the 2004 edition of the *Good Beer Guide*.

See also BEECH, BREWERIES, CROPS, CUCKOOS & CUCKOO POUNDS, HOPS, HOP-GARDENS & HOP-YARDS, HORNBEAM, JUNIPER, OAK, OYSTERS, PUBS, RIVERS, SPRINGS, WILLOW.

BELLS & BELL-RINGING

'Treble – going – gone' marks the start of something we take for granted, the sonorous sounds of churchbells. Yet nowhere else has developed such complex, tuneful ringing, save occasional churches in other English-speaking lands.

A ring of bells, together with the sound box of the tower, makes a complex musical instrument. In Europe the bell is still rung through ninety to 180 degrees. But the Reformation here led to a new, evolutionary path. Within the emergent Church of England successful experiments using wheels and levers meant that much more control could be exerted over the bell. Being rung round the whole circle enabled the bell to use its full voice and it could be

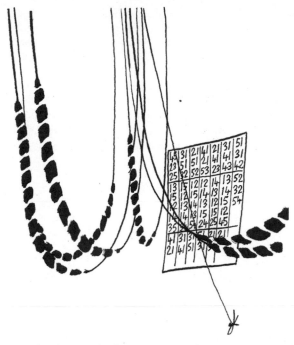

started and stopped at bottom or top. This capacity to 'set the bell' led to the perfection of change ringing.

Joseph Strutt explained: '*Ringing of rounds; that is, sounding every bell in succession, from the least [the treble] to the greatest [the tenor], and repeating the operation, produces no variety . . . becomes tiresome: for which reason the ringing of changes has been introduced, wherein the succession of the bells is shifted continually, and by this means a varied combination of different sounds, exceedingly pleasant to the ear, is readily produced.*'

Many still agree. Across most of the country you will hear 'method' or 'scientific' ringing, which builds upon the mathematical explorations (by Richard Duckworth and Fabian Stedman) of *Tintinnalogia* in 1668 and *Campanalogia* in 1677. Their computations revealed that with twelve bells 479,001,600 unrepeated changes could be rung.

Since then hundreds of 'methods' have been elaborated, distinguished by names such as Stedman Doubles, Grandsire Triples and Bob Major. The number of bells is intimated in the title: Doubles means five bells; Minor, six; Triples, seven; Major, eight; Cators, nine; Royal, ten; Cinques, eleven; and Maximus, twelve. Changes such as London Surprise and Double Norwich Court Bob Major suggest where they were first perfected.

In the West Country the dialect varies. The styles of round ringing in Cornwall and call change ringing in Devon demand swift and crisp striking. The different way of raising the bells means that the concatenation of sound starts immediately. Here, too, is the greatest concentration of churches with more than five bells: Somerset has 337, Devon 372. Compare this with 49 in Cumberland and Westmorland and sixteen in Northumberland (at the end of the twentieth century there were some 5,338 across England). While not all put in the same hours of practice as the Ancient Society of College Youths, a London society ringing since 1637, across the country societies of bell-ringers travel to ring bells for enjoyment and competition. On Dartmoor, Devon in 2004 and 2005 listening walks, recordings and celebrations of change ringing in all of the towers with five or more bells were initiated by Andy Stevens with Aune Head Arts.

Bells, rung to mark the time of day, times of prayer, events in the church calendar, rites of passage and festivities, from horse fairs to Pancake Day, have invisibly impressed themselves on many generations. The Curfew Bell sounded at eight or nine in the evening and is still rung in Chester, Stratford-upon-Avon in Warwickshire, Berwick-upon-Tweed in Northumberland and Chertsey in Surrey. The Morning Bell summoned labourers to work. This has proved contentious recently in Beaminster, Dorset, where through the summer the bell is still rung one hundred times just before 07.45, having shifted twice previously from 5am to 7am. One holidaymaker wrote in a visitors' book: *please ring Quasimodo's neck!*

The start of the year is traditionally marked by the ringing of bells. Margaret Baker in 1974 wrote of the Vale of Aylesbury in Buckinghamshire: '*Typifying the English tradition, one tower after another takes up the chain of sound, bell-music floating full and clear over the sleeping farms on the wind, tangling in branches of moonlit elms moving against the winter sky. Sometimes a muffled peal is first for the death of the old year, then as the last stroke of midnight dies away, the bells break into a merry open peal to welcome the new year.*'

Bells may be used for warning. Between 1940 and 1945 every bell tower was silenced, for use only in case of invasion. To ring out a celebration of the fiftieth anniversary of VE Day in 1995 carried that poignant reminder; at Wool in Dorset they took a minute longer to ring 5,040 Grandsire Doubles than their predecessors in 1945 – Philip Tocock conducted on both occasions. Many people of Lincolnshire carry terrifying memories of being woken by the frantic ringing of bells to alert them to the rising floods of 1953.

Few parts of the country lie outside a 'sound parish'. The 'bongs', as media folk call them, are broadcast by the BBC World Service across the globe, making Big Ben the most famous of bells – the more to surprise you when you hear them really ring out over the traffic in Westminster and on the Thames. Being born within the sound of London's Bow Bells (St Mary-le-Bow, Cheapside) traditionally marked the Cockney. On Highgate Hill, Dick and his cat

were called back to the City on hearing Bow Bells call out: '*Turn again, Whittington, thrice Lord Mayor of London.*'

Bells have power, they hold people in their protection. Henry VIII knew well what he was about when he silenced Roman Catholic church bells; they remained without voice for three hundred years. Commentary on the stealing of church bells in nineteenth-century France suggests the seismic rocking of a community's sense of identity and belonging. Echoes of these kinds of fears persist in English legend. A bell, being stolen from Knowlton church in Dorset by the people of Sturminster Marshall, was dropped or hidden in the river Stour as they crossed White Mill Bridge. Salvaging it proved impossible, as it continuously slipped back into the river, where it supposedly remains. Elsewhere the devil is implicated in similar stories.

Memory or legend, both die hard. An earthquake is said to have devoured the whole village of Raleigh in Nottinghamshire and, until the nineteenth century, it was said that bells could be heard below the ground. Stories from Yarmouth in Norfolk and Tintagel in Cornwall tell of ringing being heard through the waves after boats carrying bells were lost at sea. The sound of bells haunts the sea off Selsey in Sussex, Whitby in Yorkshire and the Suffolk coast, where nine churches have slipped into the sea, together with the whole port of Dunwich, since medieval times.

See also BESTIARY, CHURCHES, DEVIL, DIALECTS, FLOODS, INNS, LOST VILLAGES, PANCAKE DAY, PUBS.

B E S T I A R Y

'*Please, would you tell me,*' said Alice, a little timidly
. . . '*why your cat grins like that?*'
'*It's a Cheshire cat,*' said the Duchess, '*and that's why.*'

Lewis Carroll, from *Alice in Wonderland*

If only the explanation were so precise. The Cheshire Cat is first mentioned in writing by the satirist Peter Pindar (John Wolcot) before 1801. Some suggest it comes from a family coat of arms or medieval carving. Lewis Carroll lived his first decade in the county and gave us the fading smile as a signpost to Alice's wanderings through Wonderland, where the cat '*vanished quite slowly, beginning with the end of the tail, and ending with the grin, which remained some time after the rest of it had gone*'. Some say that Cheshire cheese was moulded to resemble a grinning cat, but Dorothy Hartley reminds us that '*a Cheshire cat was an old cheese measure*'.

In Alnwick the pride of the Dukes of Northumberland are celebrated in the Percy Lions, which stand with their tails stiff and horizontal on bridges and monuments. The lions guarding Nelson's Column in Trafalgar Square, London sit quietly to have their photographs taken, their symbolism changing as time passes. For one generation their proximity to the South African Embassy evoked the fight against apartheid and the moral heroism of the other Nelson – Mandela.

The big cat in all its forms has a stronghold not only in heraldic terms but in myth and story, and perhaps in reality. The Isle of Wight puma, Wrangaton Lion, Mendips Monster, Hade Edge Panther and Lindsey Leopard all hit the headlines recently, and fear of the Beast of Bodmin Moor must in part stem from folk memory. Since the early 1980s more than sixty such beasts have been reported, dead sheep have been cited, paw prints identified, video films offered, yet all but the tabloid press remain sceptical.

In 1910 the eighteen-inch-high bronze sculpture of a mongrel dog sitting above a drinking fountain and trough disappeared from Latchmere Recreation Ground in Battersea, south London. A protest against animal experiments, the sculpture had focused fury for seven years, including the Brown Dog Riots of 1907. Anti-vivisectionists, municipal socialists, suffragettes and trade unionists found common cause against the 'anti doggers' – the academic medical fraternity and the 'Brown Dog League' (students from University College London, where live experiments had sparked the controversy). The borough council removed the fountain secretly in the night. Battersea was shocked and protests moved to Trafalgar Square and the High Court, but the loss of the focus and the power of the Establishment dampened the whole affair. In 1985 a new brown dog by Nicola Hicks was unveiled a short walk away in Battersea Park, and the Battersea Dogs' Home, originally set up to rescue stray dogs from the hands of the vivisectionists, still shelters abandoned animals.

In Somerset, at Queen Camel, the Church of St Barnabas has 35 bosses of carved beasts, from camel to merman, pelican to siren, unicorn, phoenix and eagle, each with a symbolic role. The Church of St Swithun at Wickham, Berkshire sports eight enormous elephants above the north

aisle. These were preferred by the patron over the angels suggested by the architect; he returned with four of them from an exhibition in Paris in the 1840s.

Memorial, mythical or made up, unnamed beasts and heraldic creatures populate our streets, buildings and culture, from grotesques serving as waterspouts (gargoyles), to griffins, wyverns and basilisks that might breathe death or kill with a look.

See also BLACK DOGS, CHEESE, COUNTIES, DRAGONS, FERAL ANIMALS, GARGOYLES & GROTESQUES, UNLUCKY WORDS.

B I R C H

The Queen of the Forest is an elegant tree; its silver bark and airy foliage gives it a regal quality by day and an eerie presence by night. *Betula pendula* (the silver birch) and *Betula pubescens* (the white or downy birch) are both native. They rarely grow as single or hedgerow trees, being more at home as part of extending woodland. Among the hardiest and most versatile of trees, they may be found anywhere.

Pollen analysis shows birch were among the first invaders after the ice receded, and still birch is a pioneer, growing first and fast from tiny wind-blown seeds that find foothold where others cannot penetrate. With an open sky and ample rain the minute seeds germinate and grow quickly.

Huge old birches live with the ancient oaks of Windsor Forest, but generally the birch is short-lived, surviving but eighty to 120 years and rotting down quickly to make good soil in which others may succeed it. Paradoxically it is also one of the commonest trees in ancient woodland, a companion particularly of oak, hornbeam, chestnut and beech and swiftly covering any clearings resulting from storm damage, fire or timber felling. On burnt heath, disused railway sidings, forest clearings and old pit heaps, its presence is an indicator of change.

Like the sycamore it has been too successful for its own good, historically treated as a weed by foresters, who only recently have seen its potential. Yet birch besoms were commonly used for beating out small forest fires and used in ironworks for brushing away slag from the hot metal. We import birch ply for furniture and much as pulp for paper.

The birch has a long history in Nottinghamshire. The lone surviving area of the original Sherwood Forest, Birkland translates from the Scandinavian as 'birch grove'. Oliver Rackham shows that this was ancient wood, not heathland like the rest of the forest. Stands of birch live with ancient oaks on the Bunter sandstone. By contrast, Holme Fen in Huntingdonshire supports a pure wood of birch on a raised mire.

Birkenhead in Cheshire means 'headland covered with birch', while Birchanger, Essex suggests 'birch slope'. The Lancashire cotton industry is still visible in the many-

39

The Percy Lion, Alnwick, Northumberland.

stemmed trees around the Lake District – coppiced relics of the cotton reel and bobbin trade.

Birch has gathered a rich fauna of its own in these islands, visible through the activities of the great tit, blue tit, coal tit and long-tailed tit, which forage in its branches. *Amanita muscaria*, the toadstool also known as fly agaric or pixie's seat, feeds on birch roots. It is a beautiful but dangerous companion – its large, white-spotted red cap warning us of its poisonous nature.

See also ALDER, ANCIENT TREES, ASH, BEECH, BLACK POPLAR, BLACKTHORN, ELM, FIELD MAPLE, FOLKTALES, HAWTHORN, HAZEL, HEATHLAND, HOLLY, HOLM OAK, HORNBEAM, HORSE CHESTNUT, JUNIPER, LANDMARK TREES, LIME, LONDON PLANE, MONKEY-PUZZLE, OAK, ORCHARDS, PARKLAND, PEARS, PIT TIPS, POPLAR, ROBIN HOOD, ROWAN, ROYAL FORESTS, SCOTS PINE, SWEET CHESTNUT, SYCAMORE, WALNUT, WHITEBEAM, WILLOW, WOODS, YEW.

B I S C U I T S

Neither cakes nor breads, these thin, dry, crisp patties of baked flour and water (or milk) have developed many delectable flavours and inventive textures. Yorkshire's parkin is better known as a dense cake, but can vary in texture to a thin, hard, oatmeal biscuit flavoured with ginger. Brittle, lemon- (or sometimes rosewater-) perfumed Shrewsbury biscuits from Shropshire have been around since the sixteenth century.

Some had a worthy purpose and (perhaps inevitable) blandness. Bath Olivers were invented as an aid to digestion for visitors to the spa by a certain Dr Oliver during the seventeenth century. Sally Francis points out that *'traditional Norfolk recipes use local produce, and there are influences from the Low Countries and Normandy, as a result of immigration. An example of Dutch influence is rusks; rusks or hollow biscuits called Norfolk Nobs are made by a bakery in Wymondham.'* Dorset Knobs are solid and named after a popular button produced in the county during the eighteenth century; they are still made by Moore's of Morcombelake.

Shortbread is sweeter and its varieties are many. Goosnargh cakes are flavoured with caraway. Rich in the butter produced around Preston in Lancashire, they are now eaten all year round instead of the traditional Whitsuntide. Easter biscuits – round, fluted shortbreads with currants and sometimes peel – are a tradition in the South West.

Lincoln biscuits, patterned with raised dots but unclaimed by the city, are also based on shortbread. Lincolnshire takes more pride in pale gold Grantham gingerbread. Grasmere gingerbread biscuits from Westmorland combined local oats with spices, rum and unrefined sugar from nearby ports that traded with the Caribbean. They may be square or rectangular, very thin and chewy or crumbly topped. A thicker gingerbread is produced for the rush-bearing ceremony on St Oswald's Day (5 August). Lancashire's Ormskirk ginger-

bread is a strongly spiced round biscuit, while Market Drayton gingerbread from Shropshire – made in crisp fingers, ridged lengthways and traditionally flavoured with cinnamon and Jamaican or Indian ginger – is best dunked in a glass of port. Gingerbread is still made in the town using an old, hand-operated African Biscuit Machine.

Gingerbreads were once sold at fairs as a legacy of our medieval enthusiasm for newly available spices. Now 'fairings' are available at any time. Nottingham Goose Fair has sadly lost its round gingerbread with a hole, but perhaps the biscuits sold by travelling fair workers were reinvented in the places they left behind, as the long, pale, hexagonal gingerbreads with peel from Ashbourne, Derbyshire, or spicy Cornish fairings, Norfolk Fair Buttons, Barnstaple Fair gingerbreads or Norfolk gingers.

See also CAKES, DRAGONS, EASTER CUSTOMS, FAIRS & FAIRGROUNDS, FOOD, RUSH-BEARING, SPAS, STAFFORDSHIRE OATCAKES.

BLACK & WHITE BUILDINGS

The Staple Inn stands where Gray's Inn Road meets High Holborn. It was built eighty years before the Great Fire and stands as a reminder that the city of London and many other towns were once dominated by timber-framed buildings. The extravagantly patterned black (timber) and white (plaster) façade demonstrates not only the attractiveness but also the structural strength and longevity of wood.

Large areas did not paint the wood black and plaster white, for example Essex, which retains the most timber-framed houses; the Weald and Suffolk also have many towns and villages that flaunt their oak frames from the fifteenth and sixteenth centuries. The buildings often have overhanging (jetted) upper floors with curved braces and thin upright timbers placed closely together, with tall, narrow, softly coloured panels – limewashed plaster, wattle and daub, carved wood, brick noggin, or flint – in between; the timbers, having been left untreated, are silvery and patinated.

40

Although this close studding is also found in the west Midlands, the predominant pattern here is of panels that are square and painted white, the more dramatic against tarred and heavy timber. Perhaps the westerly rainfall provoked the need for more protection, but the tar was not available until the nineteenth century. The postcard villages of Eardisland, Pembridge and Weobley in Herefordshire are starkly black and white, and the effect continues through Warwickshire, Shropshire, Worcestershire, Cheshire and adjoining counties, with outliers in Yorkshire and the South.

Fashion developed during the seventeenth century and bigger houses began to indulge in ever more complex black-and-white decoration, with stars, herringbone and diamond patterning. Little Moreton Hall in Cheshire offers a heady crescendo of carving, pattern and paint.

A few groups of surviving medieval timber churches are found in counties such as Hampshire, Essex, Cheshire and Shropshire, where the fifteenth-century St Peter at Melverley, with its little square-panelled spire, has walls with massive double-height studs that give less width to the white paint than the timbers.

Somewhere along the way, half-timbering, though a far cry from Anne Hathaway's cottage, entered the canon in suburban semi-detached and detached houses, the stuff of nostalgia bastardised by builders' dreams.

See also CHURCHES, COTTAGES, DOVECOTES, EARTH PIGMENTS, FLINT, PARGETING.

B L A C K   D O G S

Tales of phantom beasts, many less than benign, cling to lanes, old gibbets, gateways, crossroads, fording places and bridges – all places where our forbears perceived the divide between our world and the supernatural world to be at its weakest.

Some emanating from Dartmoor tell of blue light, thunder and wind accompanying the appearance of a giant dog with long hair and blazing eyes, which portends death or disaster. Sir Arthur Conan Doyle must have heard a good few while walking with his friend Bertram Fletcher Robinson across the moor, gathering material for *The Hound of the Baskervilles* in 1901. In particular Wistman's Wood, with its gnarled oaks and tangled tales, was believed to shelter a whole pack of black dogs known as the Wish Hounds (local name for the Wild Hunt). Both words may derive from wisht – dialect for uncanny.

Attempts to build a bridge over the river Monnow led Jack O'Kent, a squire of legends in Herefordshire, into a deal with the devil, who agreed to help if he would own the first to pass. When the bridge was made Jack cunningly threw a bone over it, and the devil gained but a dog. The pub sign by the bridge between Kentchurch and Grosmont shows a great dark beast on its way to the other side.

In Suffolk, the Black Dog of Bungay – Old Shuck – appeared in the church on 4 August 1577, '*a dog as they might discerne it, of a black colour; at the sight wherof, togither with the fearful flashes of fire which then were seene, moved such admiration in the minds of the assemblie that they thought doomes day was already come. This black dog, or the divel in such likeness, running all along down the body of the church . . . passed between two persons . . . wrung the necks of them bothe at one instant clene backward, insomuch that even at a moment where they kneeled, they strangely dyed.*' On the same day, at Blythburgh, Suffolk, he left his claw marks on the church door. In Lancashire Shuck is called Trash or Skriker.

The hills of Church Stretton, Shropshire are haunted by a Barguest, a shape-shifting dog thought to be Edric Wilde, a resistance leader of the eleventh century. A huge hairy dog with fiery eyes that sometimes drags a clanking chain haunts the deep Troller's Gill near Appletreewick, Yorkshire.

Not all spectral canines are fearsome. Margaret Bromwich of Culmstock, Devon tells of the '*Black Dog of Higher Cross, who ran alongside walkers keeping them company*'. Lost travellers on Birdlip Hill, Gloucestershire were fortunate to be offered guidance by a black dog.

See also BESTIARY, BRIDGES, CROSSROADS, DEVIL, FOLKTALES, FORDS, GHYLLS, LANES, WEATHER-VANES.

41

BLACKPOOL ROCK

Pink, minty rock with the name of a place running through it shouts seaside town, Blackpool in particular.

Made by boiling, cooling and pulling sugar, lettered rock may have been invented in the 1850s by a London confectioner and street vendor, who developed a technique for incorporating words into the sticks – his eclectic messages included 'Do you love me?', 'Lord Mayor's Day' and 'Sir Robert Peel'. But it was Ben Bullock, a miner and confectioner from Dewsbury, Yorkshire, who, while on holiday in Blackpool in 1887, conceived the idea of rock that spelled out the name of the town – 'the perfect edible souvenir', as Laura Mason described it. Blackpool rock caught on, business blossomed, and Bullock was soon selling to other coastal towns.

In 1902 a sugar boiler who had worked for Bullock started his own rock factory in Blackpool. This marked the beginning of a thriving trade, with the opening of many factories and shops. In the 1930s, when the mills in nearby towns closed for the annual Wakes Weeks, Blackpool was full to the brim with holidaymakers and the factories worked to capacity, with itinerant sellers plying the beaches and streets.

During the Second World War, sugar rationing and loss of workers hit the factories. Women ran some of them: *They did all the boiling, lettering and "rolling the lump", making smaller batches so they could handle the weight*', Margaret Race wrote. Although prices rocketed, the rock remained as popular as ever. In the post-war years of sweet rationing, a thousand people patiently would form long queues to buy their holiday souvenirs.

According to Race, the 1950s were the '*boom time*', with up to fifty factories making the traditional sticks (mainly pink with red letters, but also multicoloured) as well as cat-faced lollipops and other rock novelties. Although the 1960s brought purchase tax on sweets, innovations, such as the move from wax paper to cellophane as a wrapping, enabled the factories to remain open and continue production all year round. In the late 1980s one to two thousand tons, made by seventeen producers, were sold every year in Blackpool alone.

Despite its cheapness, rock is largely handmade, and the sugar boilers are skilled operators – it takes five years to become '*completely competent*'. To make it, strips of red toffee are formed into letter shapes and wrapped around white sugar to form a very fat tube – about five feet long and up to twelve inches in diameter. This is rolled, spun and then stretched and stretched into thirty-foot strings, which are cut into bars.

Now rock is sold worldwide and has lost some of its cachet as the memory of a holiday. But if you go to the seaside you can't help buying some.

See also BEACHES, CONFECTIONERY, CROPS, PIERS, PROMENADES.

BLACK POPLAR

A giant, casually leaning, knobbly tree with undisciplined branches and talkative leaves, the black poplar seems to have slipped away without our realising it, despite its hugeness – it can reach one hundred feet. In medieval times it was as common as oak and ash; now it is regarded as our rarest native timber tree. In 2001 recorded trees numbered 6,750 in England, of which only six hundred were females. The tree is thought to be even rarer in mainland Europe.

With the draining of many of our flood plains, the black poplar finds it hard to set seed. But Oliver Rackham reminded us of the whole subgenus's ability to '*grow on unstable river gravels, and it is their business to be uprooted by spates and to root again from the fallen trunks. Our black poplars are evidently the last shadow of the vanished flood-plain wildwood.*' Fallen trunks and branches will root – but this has long been regarded as an untidiness.

More recently found as a farmland (but not woodland) tree, growing south of the Lune (Lancashire) and Humber estuaries, numbers do persist in Cheshire, Derbyshire, Dorset, Gloucestershire and Sussex. Old pollards of black poplar are found in East Anglia and Worcestershire. The Arbor Tree in Aston-on-Clun, Shropshire is newly planted after its aged parent fell in 1995. On farmland in Roydon, Essex there is a unique assemblage of thirty female trees. In Poplar, London – the name was first recorded in 1327 – one tree hangs on, while Hackney has a fair number.

But the stronghold is on the damp soils of the Vale of Aylesbury in Buckinghamshire, with something like 2,400 trees. Around Long Marston and Astrope, for example, Fiona Cooper suggests *they were planted as boundary markers, and were probably chosen because the vale is a wet area, the poplars are a thirsty species . . . planting is needed as suitable germination conditions no longer exist.*

Under the name of the Manchester poplar, the tree has been leading a double life; excluded from surveys because of its urban plantings, it adds perhaps six thousand trees to the total from playing fields, old factory sites, parks and streets around Manchester and its sister towns. Fiona Cooper has pieced together a history: *In 1913, £2,500 was spent restoring Philips Park and replacing lost trees with black poplar, apparently chosen because of its tolerance to air pollution and its ease of propagation . . . around 25,000 were grown in 1915 alone . . . No females were planted in the city, because of the unpopularity of the fluffy seed, although females can be found around Cheshire and Lancashire. The name Manchester poplar appears to have evolved in the late 1920s and 1930s . . . before this the tree was known locally as the Blackley poplar, after an area north of the city where possibly the tree grew naturally.*

Ironically, just as we have begun to value their importance, many of these trees in the north and east of the city have become susceptible to a pathogenic fungus, first noticed in 2001. Manchester City Council has felled all of its street black poplars. In 2004, with no treatment for poplar scab in sight, the felling of all the black poplars across Greater Manchester was being mooted, and fears for the country's entire population were growing. Almost seven hundred trees had been felled by August 2004, with many more programmed, but the Royal Botanic Gardens at Kew has donated a hundred female trees to the Red Rose Community Forest near Manchester, *to help safeguard the future of the species in the city*.

See also ALDER, ANCIENT TREES, ARBOR DAY, ASH, BEECH, BIRCH, BLACKTHORN, BOUNDARIES, CROSSROADS, ELM, FIELD MAPLE, FOLKTALES, HAWTHORN, HAZEL, HOLLY, HOLM OAK, HORNBEAM, HORSE CHESTNUT, JUNIPER, LANDMARK TREES, LIME, LONDON PLANE, MIDSUMMER DAY, MONKEY-PUZZLE, NURSERIES, OAK, ORCHARDS, PARKLAND, POPLAR, RIVERS, ROBIN HOOD, ROWAN, ROYAL FORESTS, SCOTS PINE, SWEET CHESTNUT, SYCAMORE, WALNUT, WHITEBEAM, WILLOW, WOODS, YEW.

B L A C K T H O R N

The blackthorn is widespread. It can grow up to twenty feet tall, making impenetrable hedges; if unchecked it spreads out by suckering to form dense thickets. The white blossom, which shines out against dark, leafless branches, is one of the welcome signs of spring, flowering after the sallow and a few weeks before the hawthorn in March/April, usually during a particularly cold spell – a 'blackthorn winter'. The blossom is so thick that the tree can look as though it has been covered in snow, and is an important early source of nectar for bees, hoverflies and many kinds of beetle.

The tree's long, pointed thorns are vicious, with a reputation for being sharp enough to puncture a tractor tyre. The unspectacular leaves are also attractive to many insects, including about one hundred species of moth and, in particular, the Black Hairstreak butterfly, which is dependent on the abundant supplies of blackthorn found in coppiced woods on the east Midlands clays.

It is probably an ancestor of our garden plums. The small, round stone fruits, like blue-black grapes covered in yeast bloom, are usually known as sloes, but also Heg-pegs in Gloucestershire, Slags in Oxfordshire and Winter Kecksies on the Isle of Wight. Their beauty belies their taste, described by William Cobbett as *astringent beyond the powers of alum*; they are commonly picked after the first frost to add taste and a rich plum colour to the warming drink sloe gin.

In 2003, after a long, hot summer, the sloes were unusually big and prolific in the hedgerows of Dorset; some could even be eaten without the face automatically gurning. In the Iron Age people found a way to enjoy the fruit – there is evidence of its large-scale use.

From November to January, sloes are eaten by the visiting thrush, fieldfare and redwing and by our own song thrush, mistle thrush and blackbird. Hawfinches are the only birds with beaks strong enough to crack the stones.

See also ALDER, ANCIENT TREES, ARBOR DAY, ASH, BEECH, BIRCH, BLACK POPLAR, BOUNDARIES, CRAB FAIR, ELM, FIELD MAPLE, FOLKTALES, HAWTHORN, HAZEL, HEDGES, HOLLY, HOLM OAK, HORNBEAM, HORSE CHESTNUT, JUNIPER, LANDMARK TREES, LIME, LONDON PLANE, MIDSUMMER DAY, MONKEY-PUZZLE, NURSERIES, OAK, ORCHARDS, PARKLAND, PEARS, PLUMS, POPLAR, RIVERS, ROWAN, ROYAL FORESTS, SCOTS PINE, SWEET CHESTNUT, SYCAMORE, WALNUT, WHITEBEAM, WILLOW, WOODS, YEW.

B L O W   H O L E S

Where weaker rock has given in to the harrying of the sea occasional roof collapses into wave-filled caves create constricted holes capable of exciting sound, water and air effects. The shape of the cave, the state of the tide and the depth of the swell compresses the air and the water to create and destroy these small wonders.

Game Victorian tourists were lured to hold out letters to be grabbed by air suction above the Devil's Letter Box in Kynance Cove, Cornwall, and wetly watch as great spouts of water were blown like whale breaths from the Devil's Bellows on Asparagus Island. The Blowing Hole of Porth Island puts on a display that can be seen from Newquay. The Lion's Den appeared near the Lizard Lighthouse in 1847 after the roof of a cave fell in.

43

With roar or gulp these 'gloops' fed the imagination of those who named them. Rumble Churn in Northumberland has been silenced by a rockfall, but the churn on Inner Farne Island can still steam up to a hundred feet in stormy weather. Near Flamborough Head in Yorkshire, Pigeon Hole contains the boiling sea.

See also ASPARAGUS, CLIFFS, COASTS, DEVIL, DEW PONDS, DOWNLAND, DRAGONS, ISLANDS, STACKS, WELLS.

BLUEBELLS

'No woodland scene has the power to move the heart more than a bluebell wood in May', Peter Marren reminded us. In spring, the floor of a bluebell wood becomes a carpet, a lake, a sea of azure, as the massed blooms merge and shimmer like a pool of water.

Only ramsons (wild garlic) have the same capacity as bluebells to take possession of whole woods. But bluebells outdo them, providing one of the most glorious spectacles in the botanical world. 'No other country has them on so large a scale', said ecologist Oliver Rackham. Spring is their season because bluebells are shade evaders, seizing the chance to grow and flower before the trees sprout leaves and when more than a third of the sun's rays can still reach the woodland floor. Numbers multiply where recent thinning or coppicing has let in more light.

Rejecting the extremes of both dry and waterlogged soils, bluebells flourish among all manner of trees, on moderately acid, sandy loams as well as in clay woods and chalky hangers. Among the best, photographer Bob Gibbons reckons, are West Woods in Wiltshire, Hayley Wood in Cambridgeshire, Tortoiseshell Wood in Lincolnshire and the woodlands along the Ribble valley east of Preston in Lancashire. Bluebells even thrive on Atlantic coastal cliffs, beside the ruins of Tintagel Castle in Cornwall, for instance. The hedge banks and deep-set

lanes of Devon delight with the good companions of bluebell, red campion and stitchwort.

On the eastern side of England especially they have long been taken as a sign of old, undisturbed woods, with bluebells in hedgerows or bracken testifying to woods that have disappeared. Persistent plants, they shade out wildflower competitors through sheer force of numbers, and stockpile poisonous glycosides that deter foraging animals. As a result, some bluebell carpets, as Marren observed, 'may be unfathomably old, waxing and waning according to the vicissitudes of light, climate and woodmanship, but essentially changing little'.

Bumblebees appreciate their nectar, advertised by the blooms' spicy, balsamic perfume. The Elizabethan herbalist Gerard knew it as the English Jacinth, or Blue Harebell, and reckoned the flowers had 'a ſtrong sweet smell, somewhat ſtuffing the head'. The pear-shaped bulbs once generated starch to stiffen Elizabethan ruffs, while the flower stalks exuded a versatile glue used for binding books or fixing feathers on arrows.

Wildflowers with a rich folklore, names include Granfer Griggles and Goosey Ganders, shared with the early purple orchid. West Country bluebells have long been away with the fairies: local names include fairy cap in Wiltshire, fairy bells and fairy thimbles in Somerset and fairy cup, fairy ringers and ding-dongs in Dorset.

See also ANCIENT TREES, BEER, DAFFODILS, GORSE, HAZEL, OAK, RAMSONS, ROYAL FORESTS, SMELLS.

BLUE JOHN

Unique to Treak Cliff Hill near Castleton in Derbyshire, this semi-precious stone, bleu-jaune, is a fluorspar stained during crystallisation by hydrocarbons, which impart sometimes yellow but mainly deep blue or regal purple bands. Nero is said to have had a Blue John vase, but it became particularly sought after by the French for ormolu (gilded bronze) work and by the aristocracy in England during the past three centuries. Within the county Kedleston Hall has chimney-pieces inlaid with Blue John and Chatsworth House has a great vase. But it looks its best au naturel, secret as protruding veins in the caverns and then cut and simply polished as a geological wonder.

The Treak Cliff, Old Tor and Blue John Mines have all been exploited, and fluorspar was mined relentlessly here during the Great War, so much Blue John must have been lost. It is still mined in the winter, and small pieces, fashioned locally, make their way around the world. The name alone has inspired attention; Conan Doyle indulged himself in a tale called The Terror of the Blue John Gap.

See also BUILDING STONES, CAVES, CLIFFS, COES, GORGES, LEAD MINES, LIMESTONE, QUARRIES, SEA CAVES, TUNNELS.

Haddon Hill Wood, East Knoyle, Wiltshire.

BLUE VINNEY BOAT RACE

Made '*by the wives of dairymen*', according to Patrick Rance, this cheese was produced in Dorset in the eighteenth and nineteenth centuries, from milk left after the cream had been skimmed off and which contained a blue mould (*vinew* is the Old English word for mould). It is thought that the blue mould came by chance at first, as the cheese was '*produced in a dairy often rich enough in natural mould spores to produce a blue cheese without more ado*', Rance continued. It was made until the 1930s, after which production was sporadic and secretive.

In the 1980s Blue Vinney made a comeback. It is now being produced by the Dorset Blue Cheese Company at Waybridge Farm in Stock Gaylard near Sturminster Newton, under the label of Dorset Blue Vinny. A penicillin mould is added to produce the distinctive blue-green veins. It is drier and crumblier than Stilton and low in fat, with a fairly strong taste. Dorset Blue Cheese has gained a Protected Geographical Indication for its Blue Vinny, meaning that at least one stage of its production must take place in Dorset.

Other English blue cheeses are proliferating. To the traditional Stilton we can now add Blue Cheshire, Buxton Blue, Beenleigh Blue (sheep's milk), Brendon Blue (goat's milk), Chalk Hill Blue (goat), Harbourne Blue (goat), Belvoir Blue, Coleford Blue (sheep), Devon Blue, Blue Wensleydale, Shropshire Blue, Somerset Blue and Yorkshire Blue (sheep), all telling of their places of origin.

See also CATTLE, CHEDDAR CHEESE, CHEESE, DOUBLE GLOUCESTER, FAIRS & FAIRGROUNDS, FIELDS, FOOD, STILTON, WENSLEYDALE CHEESE.

On a Saturday near the spring solstice the Light Blues and Dark Blues do battle along the Thames and the mantra of familiar landmarks is chanted over the airwaves.

The tidal reaches of the river Thames have been awash with boats for centuries. In the early 1700s there were more than forty thousand licensed watermen operating between Chelsea and Windsor, and many of them raced each other for fun or money.

A century later, competitive rowing was taking place at Oxford and Cambridge Universities, and public schools, such as Eton and Westminster, had begun to row. The first race between Oxford and Cambridge took place in 1829, when Christopher Wordsworth of Trinity College challenged Oxford, via his friend Charles Merivale, to a rowing contest at Henley, Oxfordshire. In 1839 this became an annual event, the start moving to Putney, west London in 1845 so that more spectators could watch.

The two crews (eights) each comprise eight top oarsmen from Cambridge (Light Blues) and Oxford (Dark Blues), each with one oar, facing backwards towards the coxswain (cox), who steers the boat from the stern. The long, slender boat is also known as an eight. There are few rules: each boat must allow the other enough water to manoeuvre and both boats must pass through the centre arches of Hammersmith and Barnes bridges.

The four-and-a-quarter-mile race from Putney to Mortlake typically lasts around eighteen minutes. About a quarter of a million spectators line the banks, hards and bridges, cycle along the towpath and frequent the dozen

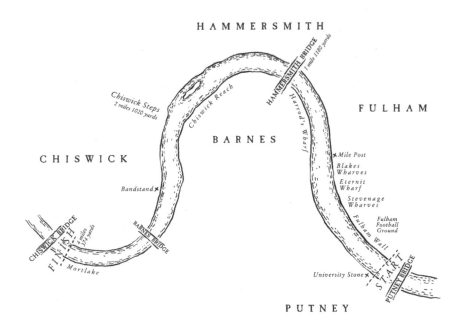

or so pubs along the route, such as the Duke's Head at Putney and Blue Anchor at Hammersmith, which serves a special Boat Race barbecue. The crews are followed by a flotilla of small boats, including the umpire in a launch shouting instructions through a megaphone. About four hundred million people around the world take a partisan view via television.

Apart from inter-varsity rivalry and personal allegiances, one of the excitements is the possibility that a boat will sink in choppy water, as Cambridge did in 1859 and 1978. Cambridge holds the course record of sixteen minutes and nineteen seconds, set in 1998, and won the 150th race in 2004. Oxford beat them in 2005, but still trail by 72 to 78.

See also BOATS, BRIDGES, CORNISH GIGS, EYOTS, FOOD, HARDS, PUBS, RIVERS, STAIRS.

B O A T S

With such a varied coastline and rivers that make their way through diverse geology, it is inevitable that we should have perfected a wide range of inland and inshore boats for fishing and trading.

The first clue to the identification of a wooden boat lies in the method of joining the planks. Clinker-built boats rely on a small overlap of the timbers, a pattern that seems to have Viking origins and historically is found all the way from Berwick-upon-Tweed, Northumberland to Bournemouth, Hampshire. Originating in the Mediterranean, carvel-built boats rely on the abutting of timbers, giving a smooth finish to the hull; this way of building was practised from Purbeck, Dorset to the Solway Firth, Cumberland.

Eric McKee's wonderful *Working Boats of Britain* meticulously celebrates the diversity and aptness of our working wooden boats. He analysed the coastline by landscape, seascape, tidal range, fetch and degree of exposure to the wind and looked at the influence of surroundings, work and boatmen. In exploring the structures of boats, he observed that *'though one has to separate out the component elements, like climate, tide, fish, timber, and so on, for discussion, in reality they are interlocked in various mixtures peculiar to particular places'*.

One is drawn by the names, telling of their place of origin and work, such as Aldeburgh sprat boat, Hastings lugger, Norfolk wherry, Parrett flatner, Portland lerret, St Ives pilchard driver, Thames sailing barge and Whitstable oyster dredger.

All manner of nuances are noted by fishermen, boat builders and students, but even in the 1970s they agreed with McKee that variation, long honed, was diminishing: *'Boat building in wood is declining in favour of other materials such as metal, cement and petrochemicals, which have no local character.'* Later he conceded that *'as working*

boat designs move towards more general-purpose craft, their variety must decrease'.

See also BEACHES, COASTLINE, COASTS, COBLES, CORNISH GIGS, FISH & CHIPS, FLATNERS, FRESHWATER FISH, HARBOURS, NOBBIES, NORFOLK WHERRIES, OYSTERS, PIERS, PORTLAND LERRETS, SEA FISH, SEA TRACTOR, SHIPPING FORECAST, THAMES SAILING BARGES, TIDES.

B O L L A R D S

You would think that you were in London when you read the inscriptions on the bollards: 'St Anne's Soho', 'St Martin-in-the-Fields', 'St James Clerkenwell', 'City of London' and 'City of Westminster'. But no, this is Dorset. Swanage revels in the activities of one George Burt and his uncle, John Mowlem, founder of the contracting dynasty. In winning a contract to pave the streets of the capital, they decided to re-use its defunct artefacts and loaded boats with architectural salvage. Thanks to the 'King of Swanage', as Thomas Hardy called him, the town is known for its early nineteenth-century cast-iron bollards, lamp-posts and other booty carrying their original inscriptions.

Originating as wooden posts placed to protect pedestrians and footways from horse-drawn carriages, bollards developed in London in the eighteenth century. By 1815 old and obsolete cannons had found a new use, and their success as bollards led to demand for purpose-made 'street furniture' in new designs. The cannon shape developed and the identity of different parishes was soon being marked by posts with four, six or eight sides, inscribed with names and coats of arms.

Urban refurbishment schemes in the past fifty years have gone to town with imitation cast-iron cannon-shaped bollards and pre-cast concrete varieties. Now they come in tropical hardwoods (why?), cast polymer and steel core coated with polyurethane in every shape imaginable.

The *Dartmoor National Park Design Guide* recommends granite or timber as the most suitable material. Shunning pattern-book street furniture, the city of Chester commissioned its own bollards and street lighting for the Rows in the 1990s. In Liverpool's Chinatown, bollards with diminishing tops are painted in red and green for prosperity; the message is reinforced with *Jixiang*, meaning 'good luck', written down the side of each bollard in Chinese characters.

In Bakewell handsome angular stoops are fashioned in millstone grit; Barry Joyce pointed out that *'Derbyshire folk are perfectly familiar with the word stoop, which is still in use to describe a post or bollard'*. The shaped metal bollards designed by Antony Gormley on Bellenden Road, Peckham, which he has nicknamed *'the penis, the egg, the peg and the snowman'*, make this part of south London the more memorable.

See also BUS SHELTERS, CHINATOWNS, COBBLES, FENCES, KERBSTONES, PAVEMENTS.

BONFIRE NIGHT

At the end of October, at dusk, with the full moon on the eve of Samhain – the moment of 'summer's end' and New Year – Celtic peoples gathered on open ground and hilltops to light fires to purify and protect the land. This was a moment for remembering the dead. David Keys wrote that human sacrifice would have been a common 'bribe' to keep evil spirits at bay, and he suggested that *today – symbolically – those human sacrifices still take place. Guy Fawkes Night absorbed the bonfire ceremony which until the early nineteenth century used to be a major feature of Hallowe'en . . . For some two thousand years, effigies have replaced human sacrifices.'*

The Christianising of the calendar, including All Hallows Eve, never quite supplanted the power of the things that had long guided the year. The proximity of Hallowe'en and Bonfire Night is no coincidence – powerful politics and clever marketing seem to have welded the two. After Guy Fawkes and his Catholic band were foiled in their attempt to blow up Protestant Parliament on 5 November 1605, an Act was passed decreeing an annual public holiday. Official celebrations gained in popularity; long after the threat of 'Popery' vanished, this persistence, together with enthusiasm for bonfires, has continued to amaze governments and historians.

All across England it is still acceptable for small children to wander the streets at this time of year, carrying a dressed, stuffed dummy and demanding a 'penny for the guy'. In back gardens and city parks firework displays and bonfires draw small and large groups. In Nottinghamshire and Yorkshire, bonfire or plot toffee is made to eat around the fire. In Morecambe, Lancashire they make cinder toffee. Bonfire parkin was popular in Yorkshire, but now the more ubiquitous bangers are roasted in bonfires and potatoes baked in the embers.

In Lewes, Sussex the burning of effigies is a long-held tradition. Each of five Bonfire Societies, representing different parts of the town, burns its own Guy; some still parade Pope Paul V, but every year the focus is on different contemporary figures. In the early evening parades of up to six hundred 'bonfire boys and girls' carry out their own ceremonies, before joining the mile-long Grand United Procession together with Bonfire Societies from other parts of Sussex and up to a hundred thousand onlookers.

Giant effigies are stuffed full of fireworks to be ignited by the bonfires. Massive firework tableaux, five flaming tar barrels carried on poles (which end up in the river Ouse), five mock archbishops and other clergy, exotic costumes and hundreds of flaming torches that turn the streets into rivers of fire, make this a night to remember. The local brewery, Harveys, even creates a special Bonfire Boy Ale each year.

In the reign of Queen Mary, who was determined to restore Catholicism, Sussex was steadfastly Protestant; seventeen Protestants were martyred, burnt at the stake, in Lewes between 1555 and 1557. The Gunpowder Plot reinforced local anti-papist views and the people took up the bonfire celebrations of 5 November with driven enthusiasm. By the mid-nineteenth century some Guy Fawkes Night celebrations had become too rowdy for Victorian sensibilities and in Lewes, where they let off their own home-made squibs – Lewes Rousers, there were heated clashes with the police and threats to ban the event.

This lead to the formation of the Bonfire Societies in 1853 to calm things down and organise counter-tactics, such as disguise – blackened faces were used to hide identities from the police. Over time the costumes have become more elaborate and each Society has adopted different modes of dress. The striped 'smuggler's' guernsey, with white trousers and a knitted cap, has been the 'uniform' of the Bonfire Societies since 1847, when a Bonfire Boy so attired was arrested; each Society has adopted its own colours.

There are about thirty Bonfire Societies in Sussex and one in Edenbridge, Kent, which compete with one other to make the best display and raise money for charity. Each visits the others' events, so the season starts early, in August.

The oldest Society – the Battel Bonfire Boyes – was formed in 1646 and '*is proud to have the oldest guy in the world*'. Its bonfire night has recently been moved from its ancient place in front of the Battle Abbey gateway to the battlefield, much to the sadness of local people.

In the West Country, especially Somerset, these autumn bonfire celebrations have transformed into carnivals, with tableaux lit by thousands of light bulbs carried on huge lorries or pulled by tractors. Bridgwater still has its squibs,

47

and Hatherleigh and Ottery St Mary in Devon have held on to their older flaming tar-barrel customs. In Allendale Town, Northumberland they light them at New Year.

See also BEACON FIRES, BEER, CARNIVALS, CONFECTIONERY, GANSEYS, HALLOWE'EN, HILLS, MIDSUMMER DAY, MUMMING PLAYS, NOTTING HILL CARNIVAL, PARKS, POTATOES, TAR BARREL ROLLING.

B O R E S

48

A bore (from the Old Scandinavian *bara*, meaning wave or billow) raises both exhilaration and fear in the heart as the full incoming force of a spring tide squeezed by narrowing riverbanks and a shallowing riverbed meets the outflowing water of a large river. They happen in several of our estuaries, the Solway in Cumberland, the rivers flowing into Morecambe Bay in Lancashire, and the Trent in Nottinghamshire and Lincolnshire, where it is more likely referred to by the alternative name aegir.

The river Severn creates one of the most spectacular bores in the world. With a tidal range reaching fifty feet, second only to the 'Silver Dragon' of the Qiantang river in eastern China, the Bristol Channel in addition offers a narrowing funnel to the incoming tide. Close to the spring and autumn equinoxes, the spring tides are at their highest. Five-star bores are possible around the end of March and early in October, with lesser bores expected twice a day on four or five days every month, around the full moon. With a speed of ten miles per hour the wave front may reach six and a half feet; it achieved nearly ten feet at Stonebench, Gloucestershire on 15 October 1966.

Near Framilode, where the river is still quite wide, the 2003 spring bore was around three feet high – you could see it coming, quickly covering the exposed sandbars and propelling waiting canoeists upstream. Then came the noise – agitated lapping of waves against a sturdy defence wall.

Suddenly the river was full of water, bringing up torn-out trees and other debris.

Most people congregate at Minsterworth, Stonebench and Over Bridge, where public access is easy. At bends in the river, the bore swooshes up and over the outside curves, sometimes engulfing cars on the road. Catherine Fisher captured a more benign mood, describing the river spilling its banks: *'slopping into the wellingtons of watchers, swamping the nests of coots, splashing binoculars'.*

This is a harsh environment for plants and animals, with two tidal changes every day and huge surges twice on sixty days of the year. The elver run was one of the wonders of the world, breathtaking in the sight and sheer quantity of tiny eels catching a ride and dealing with the ebb. Although the numbers are nothing like they were, this is still the time when elver fishermen take their catch.

Others use the natural energy to their advantage. F.W. Rowbotham recorded that *'Severnside men of Minsterworth, Elmore Back and lower down in my earlier years would take their boats, ride out the bore and let the flood stream carry them to Gloucester; they would do their shopping and drift home on the ebb'.*

The sport of bore surfing is made the more thrilling and dangerous by the unpredictability of the surge. It has a longer history than one may expect, as Rowbotham recalled: *'at 10.30am on 21st July 1955, Colonel Churchill swam from the bank below Stonebench with his surfboard . . . as the fair sized bore approached, the Colonel placed his board beneath him and began to swim upstream. Moments later the leading slope of the bore slid under him and he started planing forward.'* The members of the Severn Bore Riders Club are inspired by such pioneers. Dave Lawson holds the world distance surfing record: on 29 August 1996 he rode the bore for forty minutes, covering 5.7 miles.

See also AEGIRS, BEACHES, EELS, RIVERS, TIDES.

B O U N D A R I E S

Bounds beaten every year, lines on a map or shades of subtle change in the land – the traces of a thousand or more years are still recognisable and, in many places, the historian, the archaeologist and the ecologist can demonstrate their persistence through ancient banks and walls, names and corners, stones and flora.

Natural features, such as ridges and rivers, were often used as lines on the land. Rivers could cause havoc by shifting their course – maps often reveal a boundary quite out of step with the meandering of a river or stream that has moved on.

Without landmarks to mark the edge of territory, ancient overlords frequently resorted to the digging of ditches, the creation of great banks and the erection of stones.

The Fosse Way, running straight from the Devon coast to the Humber, is an ancient track. It was singled out when the Romans first invaded for the building of a high, fortified road (foss alludes to the ditches) for the fast deployment of forces; for years this doubled as a frontier. As with Hadrian's Wall on the England/Scotland border, an important political boundary was being defined, at least for a while. Taking advantage of the great natural cliff of the Whin Sill, Hadrian's Wall also marks the collision of two ancient continents.

Domestic territorialising has a long history. On Dartmoor, above one thousand feet, a huge system of Bronze Age walls, or reaves, contours around hills, separating uphill from downhill land, and marches along watersheds – some seem to mark individual farms. Elsewhere, ancient relict banks have been found, some still working as field edges in Nottinghamshire, Berkshire and Suffolk.

Many banks and stones used for parish boundaries date at least from Roman times in Dorset, Wiltshire and elsewhere. Ecclesiastical parish boundaries, creating territories based on the church, priest and the payment of tithes, emerged mainly during the Dark Ages. In Northamptonshire the map still shows the continuing importance of Roman Watling Street, which marks the edge of 25 parishes.

Variation in the shapes of parishes gives clues about the working of the land. The long, thin parish typical of the Yorkshire Dales, taking in the river's edge and flat valley land then soaring uphill to the watershed, demonstrates the usefulness of having access to water as well as winter and summer grazing. In Norfolk eleven parishes converge on a series of meres at Rymer Point.

Some human earthworks have long histories as landmarks that serve as points of change or contact. Wormelow Tump in Herefordshire is a barrow where three parishes and six roads meet, and was a meeting place for people in the Domesday Wormelow Hundred, too.

Some sunken lanes began life as important boundary ditches dug out with banks on either side in Saxon times: Hoskins described Armourwood Lane in east Devon, which may date from the seventh century, marking the edge of the lands of Exeter Abbey. Medieval monasteries extended their ranges until they met on the Pennine hills – miles of walls still pick out the once-contested boundaries between the lands of Fountains, Salley and Bolton Abbeys on Malham Moor, Yorkshire.

The counties emerged from the Norman administrative system, but most of the country already had its shires or provinces. Less stable sub-divisions, such as hundreds in the South or wards and wapentakes in the North, tend to be the province of historians, although memories of leets persist in East Anglia, as do the rapes of Chichester, Arundel, Bramber, Lewes, Pevensey and Hastings in Sussex; in Kent the lathes or lests include Sutton-at-Hone and Sheppey.

In the flux of industrialisation and expanding populations the Victorians began to invent new municipal units, but still the historic county and parish endured. After 1889 the civil parish emerged as the smallest theatre of democracy. Based upon the ecclesiastical parish for the most part, it has since evolved, with boundary changes and amalgamations. But the old boundaries are still remembered, as John Field pointed out. *'Names alluding to boundary land include No Man's Land, Ball Close and Mear Oak Close. The rogation ceremonies provide a good selection of names, e.g. Amen Corner, Luke Stone and Epistle Field.'*

Within the city it is more difficult to envisage old boundaries, unless walls and buildings survive, but there are clues. The Lord Mayor of London is taken by boat to the centre of the Thames each year to beat the bounds. On Hampstead Heath oaks that have marked the boundary for hundreds of years stand alongside younger boundary stones – a kind of belt-and-braces approach. Other edges can be read. Gillian Tindall's seminal work on London's Kentish Town, *The Fields Beneath*, demonstrated how old field and estate boundaries continue to be etched in the curve and disposition of the streets.

New lines are wrought. In 2003 the Orthodox Jews of Golders Green, north London celebrated the creation of the first *eruv* in this country. This mostly invisible line is linked by poles and wire to make an enclosure of more than six square miles, which enables observant Jews to pursue otherwise prohibited activities on the Sabbath.

See also BARROWS, BEATING THE BOUNDS, BEER, BOUNDARY STONES, CHURCHES, COMMONS, COUNTIES, DIALECTS, FIELD PATTERNS, FIELDS, GREEN LANES, HOLLOW WAYS, LANDMARKS, LANDMARK TREES, NOMANSLAND, NORTH, PARISH MAPS, PLACE-NAMES, PONDS, RIVERS, SHIPPING FORECAST, STANDING STONES, WAYSIDE & BOUNDARY CROSSES.

BOUNDARY STONES

Sometimes an imposing natural feature, a landmark in its own right, magnetically draws a boundary towards it, as at Navelin Stone on Cleator Moor, Cumberland. Elsewhere great or small stones were positioned where the edge was deemed to be, to emphasise territorial claim. At Breocke, Cornwall the parish boundary was described in the seventeenth century to include *'a place called in the Cornish Tongue Mene Gurta which signifieth in English – a Staie Stone where a Stone Standeth (for a bound betweene land of our parishe and land of St Wen) of a huge bignes'*. 'Stone' marked on an Ordnance Survey map, always worth investigation, often has an ancient functional role.

Great stones marked with crosses were erected in 1279 to bound the contested lands between Salley and Fountains Abbeys above Wharfedale in Yorkshire. On Dartmoor there are inscribed granite stones from the nineteenth century edging the parish of Ilsington, Devon – one is marked 'Old Jack'. Handsomely paired and lettered boundary stones give the names of adjoining parishes, such as at Clapham/Austwick in the Craven district of Yorkshire. In the centre of the small river Cole near Coleshill stands a stone with 'Berks' carved into one side. In this instance it is not the river but the county that has moved away: this is currently the administrative boundary of Oxfordshire/Wiltshire.

In the Lugg Meadows in Herefordshire, the possibly pre-Saxon strips are marked with more than a hundred mere, or dole, stones – mere derives from *maere*, meaning boundary in Old English, and dole refers to the demarcation of land doled out. Many of these had become lost or covered during the centuries.

But local activists began conservation work on the meadows in the early 1990s and some stones began to turn up. After a discussion on national radio, Anthea Brian was contacted by someone with '*a load of stones about to be built into a wall twenty miles away, and we were able to buy them back. Two more were advertised in the local paper, but when the owner . . . heard the Nature Trust wanted to buy them . . . he gave them to us.*' One set of stones, marked 'CB 1833', had been used to mark out charity land to '*support ten poor maids*'. The Herefordshire Nature Trust has erected a set of stones marked HNT 1994 to mark its strips.

Horrabridge in Devon once marked the junction of three parishes; *hore* (Old English) implies boundary and may be found as horestones and harepath.

See also BEATING THE BOUNDS, BOUNDARIES, LANDMARKS, WAYSIDE & BOUNDARY CROSSES.

B O U R N E S

In the South, especially Kent, Surrey and Wiltshire, bourne is still used to describe an intermittent stream. Deriving from *burna*, the Old English for stream or brook, it is also found as a relic of old river names, lingering in place-names, such as Sittingbourne, Kent and Lambourn, Berkshire. *Burna* must have been in general use across England, as burn still dominates in the North East.

See also BECKS, BROOKS, BURNS, DIALECTS, FORDS, RIVERS, WINTERBOURNES.

B O W L I N G   G R E E N S

Behind a fence at the edge of the park or discreetly tucked behind houses, neat white figures sedately bend and roll dark balls across a small square of green so tightly cut and edged it is hard to imagine that it is growing grass.

Grass grows well in England, but bowling greens need the most exquisite of tight turf. One option, Cumberland turf – the predominant species being slender creeping red fescue and bentgrass – begins life resisting twice-daily washing by the sea. Cut from the salt marshes, for example on the Solway coast, it needs almost barber-like management to produce playing surfaces that look as smooth as billiard tables, otherwise the latent seeds of sea pink, sea milkwort and buck's-horn plantain begin to make fools of the groundsmen.

But any bowls player knows that even grass cut so short has a nap, since it reaches for the sun, upward and slightly south. And in the South, lawn bowls is played on a flat green measuring forty yards square, enclosed by a ditch a couple of inches deep and a foot wide, bounded by an angled bank. The game is played from one end to the other and then reversed. In the North and the Midlands you are more likely to find crown greens, which, rather than being level, rise slightly in the centre and are played from all directions, with more open rules. Many crown greens were created as taverns were built, and still the most famous tournaments take place in Blackpool – the Waterloo and the Talbot are both named after hotels, although the latter, when sponsored, is now held at the Raikes Hall Hotel.

Around the Tyne a kind of wild straight-line bowls is played along country lanes or over moorland, the winner covering the distance with the least number of throws.

Although he '*cannot by any means ascertain the time of its introduction*', Joseph Strutt traced the pastime of bowling back to the thirteenth century from a manuscript in the Royal Library. Lewes, Sussex claims a green laid just after the Norman Conquest on the jousting ground of the castle, and Southampton has a green built originally in 1187 and still holds a tournament to celebrate its frequent use from 1299. We all know what Sir Francis Drake was doing on Plymouth Hoe as the Armada approached on 19 July 1588, and indeed bowls is more popular now as a seaside diversion than when the Spanish threatened.

See also BLACKPOOL ROCK, ESTUARIES, LINKS, SALT MARSHES, SHEEP, TIDES.

B R A S S   B A N D S

Brass bands were well established in England by the start of the twentieth century. As Vic and Sheila Gammon note, many already thought them '*the musical expression of the spirit of the English people*'. The movement originated in the 1840s and 1850s in the creativity of church bands that were expelled from playing at religious services, and from village and town bands encouraged by the availability of relatively cheap and improved valved instruments. By the 1850s most villages, mines and mills, especially in the North, had bands, providing people who had hard and monotonous jobs with an opportunity to learn and express themselves together.

Their heartland was in the coalfield and textile areas of Durham, Lancashire, Leicestershire, Nottinghamshire, Northumberland and Yorkshire, but by the 1870s bands had been formed in every part of the country. For example, as Vic and Sheila Gammon observe, '*the "forest" communities of north Sussex, Horsham, Crawley, Horsted Keynes, Nutley, Fairwarp, Turners Hill, West Hoathly and East Grinstead were veritable hothouses of band activity in the later nineteenth century*'.

The bands were influenced by the Salvation Army and military bands; discipline was strict and they aimed for the highest standards and technical excellence.

The Belle Vue contests in Manchester (now the British Open Championships) from 1853 were to become the focus of the entire brass band movement. Their purpose was to raise standards and they led to fierce competitiveness, bands vying with one another to play test pieces with most proficiency. One result was a loss of regional variation, musical expression being suppressed by the rigid standardisation imposed.

The band from Besses o' th' Barn near Whitefield, Manchester, formed in 1821, became all brass in 1853 and by the end of the century had won everything. In the village of Queensbury, between Bradford and Halifax in Yorkshire, John Foster built a cotton mill on land known as Black Dike and, in 1855, created the Black Dyke Mills Band. It became one of the most accomplished and best-known bands, winning thousands of pounds in prize money each year as well as making records.

In Yorkshire the Grimethorpe Colliery Band, formed in 1917, came into prominence when Elgar Howarth became its conductor and commissioned new pieces from Harrison Birtwistle and Hans Werner Henze. It touched the nation's hearts when it won the National Brass Band Championships five days after the closure of the pit in 1992; after providing the soundtrack for the 1995 film *Brassed Off*, it toured Australia, New Zealand and Japan.

There was great local pride in the bands. In the early 1900s followers in the Yorkshire Dales would walk long distances to the railway station to greet their bands returning from national contests. Then, as Arthur Raistrick reported, '*the whole crowd marched down to the river bridge to hear the band play its test piece, where we firmly believed the water, the woods, and the surrounding hills gave a resonance and setting far superior to anything the Crystal Palace or any other place could supply*'. So much did they want to hear their music in its own setting, they used to have contests by the Hardraw Force waterfall in Wensleydale, with the '*cliffs acting as a sounding board*'. Since 1989 contests have been held there again.

The brass band became an essential part of such civil ceremonies as fêtes, fairs and festivals, and an institution in

city parks and seaside resorts. In its heyday it became more important than the events it came to support – 33 special trains were put on for a band contest in Skegness in 1937. Park bandstands proliferated in Victorian Britain to keep the players out of the rain. There was also much marching. From the 1870s brass bands were associated with trades union demonstrations and May Day celebrations.

Percy Fletcher's tone poem *Labour and Love*, which was used as the test piece in the National Brass Band Festival thirteenth championships in 1913, marked a landmark in the history of brass band music, attracting an audience of more than a hundred thousand people. This was the first of many original pieces commissioned from leading composers, including Holst, Elgar, Vaughan Williams and Sir Michael Tippett, which built a more radical repertoire and brought recognition from the classical music establishment.

At the turn of the twentieth century there were about forty thousand bands. Now about nine hundred are associated with the British Federation of Brass Bands, twenty of which are in the top championship league. Brass bands have become accepted as part of our serious music culture, with full-time degree courses in brass band musicianship. The Grimethorpe Colliery Band was the first of its kind to become an ensemble-in-residence at the Royal College of Music, London.

Many small towns rely on their silver and brass bands to lift the carnival and agricultural show or to calm the memorial service with marches, hymns, classical and contemporary music, maintaining the dignity of places in changing times.

See also BANDSTANDS, CARNIVALS, MINES, MUSIC, WATERFALLS.

51

B R E A D

In the mid-nineteenth century, the harvest loaf, resembling a wheatsheaf, was made from the last sheaf in the field and became the centrepiece of the harvest festival service. Even in 1954 Dorothy Hartley could write: '*Nearly all counties of England have their own special type of bread.*' Yorkshire breakfast bread, made with flour, salt, yeast, one pint of milk and sugar, and Newcastle bread, brown with caraway seeds, were among them. But much has changed since then. We may have a variety of shapes – the cottage loaf, cob, Coburg, chapel, pot or sandwich – but they are not specific to place and many taste much the same. We have many names for the same thing, such as baps, plain teacakes, bread cakes, basin cakes and softies.

Joanna Blythman comments on the loss of the loaf's significance: '*This is a logical conclusion of the general devaluation of bread which has taken root in Britain since the early Sixties when the infamous Chorley-wood, or "no time" bread, process took a grip. It's an entirely industrial system, reliant on flour "improved" with chemicals and the substitution of high-speed mixing for the lengthy bulk fermentation of dough which characterises traditional bread. It can produce a cooled, sliced and wrapped loaf in three-and-a-half hours. Since bread became push-button and devoid of character, it is easy to see why it lost the respect and status it deserves, and why price became the only relevant issue.*' Chorleywood, Hertfordshire, where the process was invented, is forever associated with the production of bland, sliced, wrapped bread. With the particularity of the bread went the richness of the fields; home-grown soft wheats were abandoned in favour of North American hard wheats, which can withstand the rough treatment of the steel rollers used in large-scale baking that crush the life out of the grain.

As Auden would have it, '*a culture is no better than its woods*', and Felicity Lawrence notes that John Lister, who runs Shipton Mill in the Cotswolds, '*believes a country's bread is a barometer of its culture*'. It is in part to do with scale and near monopoly, she goes on. '*By 2003 eleven factory baking companies were making 81 per cent of the nine million*

or so loaves we eat each day . . . two giants . . . produce two thirds of British bread.'

The homogenisation and denaturing of bread would be a sad story had our choice not been enriched by new breads – bagels, baguettes, chapatis, ciabatta, naan, pitta, roti, tortillas – made by local and small craft bakers who have settled here from many parts of the world. The Flour Advisory Bureau says we produce more than two hundred kinds of bread in the UK. In London you can find pitta bakers in Kentish Town, the Beigel Bake in Brick Lane and Polish rye-bread bakers in Park Royal. In Southall, Middlesex you can watch the making and cooking of Asian breads in tandoor ovens through the restaurant windows. As Neal Ascherson reminds us, '*we are in the grip of processes which are not complementary but contradictory . . . Local distinctiveness appears to be at once both declining and recovering.*' Unfortunately we also make and import mass-produced versions of many so-called 'speciality breads', sacrificing for speed the authenticity of traditional techniques and ingredients and the subtleties of taste and texture.

Some small bakers and millers are experimenting with different flours to enhance flavour and are using single-variety wheat flour instead of the usual grists (blends). They are rediscovering, as with apples, that some of the older varieties have the character that the new, higher-yielding kinds have lost. At Cann Mills in Dorset, Michael Stoate is stone-grinding Maris Widgeon, '*a low-yielding, labour-intensive variety; it's not easy to cultivate, but it has that rare thing – character . . . It allows us to retain the wheat germ . . . in the steel-roller process, they take it out because of its high oil content.*' In 1994, Andrew Whitley grew a crop of Maris Widgeon on his allotment in Stoke Newington, London and ground it in a hand mill. He went on to use it in his Village Bakery in Melmerby, Cumberland, with resounding success. An increasing number of artisan bakers are beginning to use locally grown flour. The Trescowthick Craft Bakery near Newquay, Cornwall grows its own wheat to make flour.

Smiths, a long-established bakery in Shaftesbury, Dorset, was challenged by Common Ground to make a special loaf for the annual Gold Hill Fair in 2004. Peter Smith created a sweet breakfast loaf that, to allow it to be torn easily, is deeply indented to resemble the cobbles on Gold Hill. This photogenic street is known for another kind of loaf, itself with a long history. The famous Ridley Scott-directed television advertisement in which a small boy wheels his bike, with its basket full of bread, up the steep hill, to the accompaniment of Dvořák's New World Symphony, was made in 1973 to promote the Hovis loaf, invented by Richard 'Stoney' Smith in 1886. First called 'hominis vis' (strength of man) and then shortened to Hovis, it reintroduced wheatgerm to the British loaf.

See also BISCUITS, BUNS, CAKES, COBBLES, CROPS, FOOD, HARVEST FESTIVALS.

Cottage loaf.

B R E W E R I E S

Brewing, originally a domestic craft, has been big business since the eighteenth century. Large breweries appeared where abundant water – liquor – was available, especially water with the right chemical balance to make good beer. The water at Burton upon Trent, Staffordshire, with its high calcium sulphate content, became the marque. Strangeways brewery in Manchester and Jennings in Cumberland still use water from nearby wells.

Until developments in chemistry liberated brewers from geographical dependence, water was at the centre of the process. Mill, malting and brewery were usually found in sensible proximity in the self-contained world before rail and tarmac – in Hertford, local rivers supplied McMullens brewery and powered the Sele Roller Mill, where the barley grains were processed.

Coal-fired boilers and steam power became essential to industrial breweries, for boiling the hot liquor with barley malt to make wort. This, and the spiriting away of carbon dioxide produced during the fermentation process, explains the tall chimneys that are a feature of the buildings. The landmark chimney of the Strangeways brewery is still in use, but now it acts as a ventilator for the gas heating. By the mid-nineteenth century, tower breweries had emerged as the favoured design, tall structures in which brewing progressed systematically from top to bottom. McMullens in Hertford and the Highgate Brewery in Walsall, Staffordshire are notable survivors.

Breweries often command attention, even if they no longer fulfil their original function – the distinctive Hardy and Hansons building on the edge of Nottingham is one example. Samuel Whitbread's eighteenth-century brewery in London's Chiswell Street, a wonder of the city in its day, is now a conference centre.

Many brewers remain deeply associated with the place they operate from, such as Adnams of Southwold, Suffolk

and, in Wiltshire, Wadworths of Devizes (which still delivers locally by horse-hauled dray) and Arkells of Swindon. To this day a family concern, Elgood and Sons of Wisbech, Cambridgeshire has brewed in the same place since 1795.

Since the mid-twentieth century many small breweries have been devoured by multinational companies, familiar local names incongruously transplanted elsewhere. Banks and Ansells beers no longer emanate from Birmingham or indeed anywhere in the Midlands.

Even Burton has seen the demise of some of its best-known products at the hands of globalisers. The town's riverbanks have been dominated by the brewing industry since the eighteenth century; its yeast by-products also gave us Marmite. Many of the town's public buildings were presented to the town by rich brewers, such as the Bass family, who had brewed there since 1777. The Bass brewery in Burton is still the country's largest, but its American owners have re-branded it: '*It seems that Coors have tried their best to eradicate all traces of the existence of Bass in the town*', Toni Parker says.

A refreshingly different story is emerging in Wiltshire. Barley grown on the Ramsbury estate is brewed in a rebuilt farm building nearby, and then malted in Warminster. Ramsbury Flintnapper and Kennet Valley are beers of the avant-garde. Other modern micro-breweries might be an anonymous garage, a unit on an industrial estate or tucked into the back of a pub. Many redundant old brewery buildings, when not converted into homes, offices and shops, have been given new life by their smaller-scale successors; the Phoenix brewery in Heywood, Manchester is a former nineteenth-century Bass brewery.

See also BEER, GIN, HOPS, HOP-GARDENS & HOP-YARDS, MALTINGS, PUBS, RIVERS, SHIRE HORSES, SPRINGS.

53

B R I C K S

Bricks are heavy; the cost of moving them soon exceeds the cost of making them. So, for centuries, they were made literally where a building was to grow – itinerant brick makers in Suffolk, for example, dug clay and made bricks on demand and on location. Roman knowledge having withered, the idea of using brick had been reintroduced to England in medieval times, with knowledge from the Low Countries, to East Anglia and east Yorkshire, where stone is rare. In 1547 half the brick buildings of England were found in Essex, Suffolk and Norfolk.

Water transport liberated the brick from its place of origin, with coasting boats and then canal barges beginning to influence the geography of building. Terrifying fires, especially the Great Fire of London, gave bricks a ready market as legal demands grew to make the city a less combustible place.

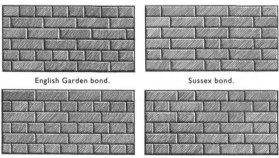

English Garden bond.

Sussex bond.

0%
1–19%
20–49%
50%+

English bond.

Flemish bond.

Gradually bricks invaded traditional stone localities as they became cheaper, but until the Second World War most bricks travelled less than thirty miles. The really profound change came with road transportation and the swallowing of small brick works by large companies. Produced in vast quantities from fewer and fewer sources, standardised bricks have lost their local attachments.

Made in small quantities, brick reinforces locality. Its animated patterns and mellow colours, based on local geology, create a wonderfully variegated map, readable on many levels. Handmade bricks offer textured richness, the impurities in the clay giving colour and personality, intensified by a few tricks of the trade. As Penny Berry wrote: '*Iron produces a red brick; chalk or lime will give a cream or yellow shade; manganese a purple colour. The temperature to which the bricks are fired will also influence the colour; each clay has its own maturing temperature beyond which it will warp or melt, but within its firing range generally the higher the temperature the darker the colour.*' Introduced sands, salts and metallic oxides give further texture and colour.

There are many reds, from the aggressive Accrington Bloods of Lancashire to Leicester's rich orange-red and Southampton's terracotta. The soft reds of the Georgian farms and townhouses of south and east Nottinghamshire and much of Leicestershire, made from Keuper Marl, contrast with the deeper reds of the Victorian buildings on the exposed Coal Measures. As the Industrial Revolution progressed, the exploitation of iron-rich shales spread across the Midlands and north of England. Alec Clifton-Taylor did not like the result: '*Accrington . . . has the dubious distinction of having made some of the most durable and visually disagreeable bricks in the country. By the end of the nineteenth century bricks of a quite relentless redness were being made in many other places.*'

The Carboniferous also gives us Staffordshire Blues made from Etruria Marl, named after a town in the Potteries. They are useful for damp-proofing and engineering tasks, being dense and strong. Their solid blue-grey colour is achieved as oxygen is reduced during firing. Similar bricks are made in County Durham, Wigan in Lancashire and Almondsbury in Gloucestershire.

The wood-fired kilns of Sussex included the old Ashburnham Estate works, which supplied bricks between Burwash, Hollington and Eastbourne for houses and bridges during the Victorian expansion. Kim Leslie explained: '*The sand-faced Ashburnham reds [are] distinguished by their rich red colour (revealing their iron content), and by the burnt grey ends of those whose heads had been exposed to the direct fire . . . In the nineteenth century and earlier these grey headers were worked into patterns*' – as in Ashburnham Place and Forge Lodge on the estate.

Now two companies make most of England's bricks, under many brand names. The seeds of homogenisation

54

London changed colour as it grew and spread. The yellow-brown stock bricks that had built Georgian London from clay beneath its own foundations were succeeded by hard, brighter yellow bricks from coastal brick works in Suffolk and Kent, transported up-river on stumpies or brickies – kinds of Thames sailing barge.

In the nineteenth century the railway companies brought colour from across the country. Liverpool Street Station was constructed with bricks from Lowestoft, Suffolk. The great yellow-brick arches of King's Cross Station (1851) were joined in 1873 by George Gilbert Scott's Gothic St Pancras Station and Grand Hotel, with their bright red Gripper's Patent bricks from Nottinghamshire, founding county of the Midland Railway.

English Garden bond.

Sussex bond.

English bond.

Flemish bond.

were sown with the expansion of the London Brick Company; some claim that one-third of England's brick houses are made from its bricks. Sixteen million 'Londons' a day were produced at the height of post-war redevelopment in the 1960s.

Flettons (originally from Fletton in Huntingdonshire) were common bricks for the unseen parts of buildings, but their use externally gave us boring red relieved only by paler 'kiss marks' resulting from their touching one another in the kiln. Now sand-blasting and mineral additives offer different colours and surface effects, producing cheap bricks that purport to suit local conditions. Given this increasing sophistication, it is sad and bad that so many of the nation's bricks are flettons, made from the lower Oxford clay of Bedfordshire, Huntingdonshire and Cambridgeshire and transported the length of the country by road.

Some small brick works hang on and are busy with demands from the conservation industry. Peter Minter at the Bulmer Brick and Tile Company near Sudbury, Suffolk boasts sixty different sizes of mellow, red facing bricks made from London Bed clay, and women workers make the '*squints, bullnose and plinths, purpose made copings, crowsteps, mullions, jambs and moulded terracotta from a selection of some three thousand special moulds*'.

Bricks are laid in courses and bound together with (ideally) lime mortar – which gives a wall the invaluable capacity to move a little without cracking – or cement, which is rigid. They are not laid directly one above another but overlapped for strength and stability. During laying, patterns are made, some simply for show – these 'bonds' make a big difference to the texture of a building, as does the colour and thickness of the pointing.

Flemish bond describes a simple pattern of header, stretcher, header, stretcher – the long side of the brick alternating with the short side. English bond alternates a whole course of headers with a whole course of stretchers – this is stronger but demands more bricks, increasing expense. The most common variant is English Garden bond, which is cheaper, with several courses of stretchers to a course of headers, which hold the wall together. All kinds of variations on these are possible: header bond, stretcher bond, Monk bond, Rat Trap, quarter bonding, Quetta. Chequered and diaper-patterned brickwork is achieved using blues or vitrified headers. Local patterns make a difference in modest buildings by protruding bricks in dentilations or dog-tooth patterns just below the eaves, reminiscent of the ends of rafters.

Anthea Brian found that regional as well as historical differences exist in the distribution of brick bonds: '*Some bonds proved to be very regional, for example English Garden bond in the north; Sussex bond, Monk bond and Flemish Stretcher bond in the Midlands. English bond was more* universal, often in very old brickwork or railway buildings and suchlike. Flemish bond was used for show on the fronts of houses everywhere, but in East Anglia it was almost the only bond used at all. Occasionally an architect does something different, without any respect for the local bond. In Norwich the Town or County Hall is probably the only brick building in the whole county to be built in English Garden bond.'

The invention of cavity walls brought the now ubiquitous stretcher bond, which has become the universal pattern used in house building and for cladding big structures, reducing the chances of poetry of any kind.

See also CHIMNEYS, CRINKLE-CRANKLE WALLS, HAUNTED PLACES, LIME-KILNS, SMELLS, TERRACED HOUSES, THAMES SAILING BARGES, VIADUCTS.

B R I D G E S

The place-names of Stockbridge in Hampshire and Trowbridge in Wiltshire both refer to tree-trunk bridges. Many town names reveal early crossing points – Brigg, Lincolnshire; Bridge and Tunbridge Wells, Kent; Bridgwater, Somerset; Sawbridgeworth, Hertfordshire; Knightsbridge, London.

The oldest surviving timber-framed bridge links Herefordshire with Brecon downstream of Hay-on-Wye. Early stone bridges used large slabs of stone resting on stone piers, such as the ancient clapper bridge across the river Barle at Tarr Steps in Somerset. Some claim these are more than two thousand years old; others date them from the early Middle Ages. Packhorse bridges, usually small, arched bridges, are characterised by low parapets designed not to obstruct the horses' panniers. They were common on trade routes; examples can be seen at Wycoller, Lancashire and Moulton, Suffolk.

More sophisticated stone bridges were built abundantly in the thirteenth century. The river Skell at Fountains Abbey, Yorkshire is crossed by probably the oldest arched

55

bridge in England. Thirteenth- to fourteenth-century bridges can be recognised by their pointed arches and by the V-shaped extensions over the cutwaters for pedestrian refuges. These were superseded by flatter ribbed arches in the fourteenth and fifteenth centuries and semi-circular arches in the eighteenth century.

Bridge building and maintenance was often instigated by churches or monasteries, leading to the inclusion of small chapels, oratories or chantries for the blessing of travellers. One such on the Chantry Bridge at Bradford-on-Avon, Wiltshire was replaced in the seventeenth century by an elegant domed lock-up. During the Reformation the symbolic cross was removed from many medieval bridges.

Bridges were often places for public events, from executions to festivals. Some had water mills, hermitages or sheep dips attached. Robert Adam's Pulteney Bridge in Bath, built in 1770, is one of the few remaining bridges to have shops on both sides of it.

While styles varied with designers and builders, they had to be modified by the needs and conditions of their locations. In Yorkshire, in the early eighteenth century, Daniel Defoe observed '*the Nyd, smaller then the Wharfe,*

but furiously rapid, and very dangerous to pass in many places, especially upon sudden rains. Notwithstanding, such lofty high built bridges are as not to be seen over such small rivers in any other place.'

The eighteenth-century bridge over the river Swale at Richmond, Yorkshire is built from local Carboniferous sandstone. In the eastern counties bridges were built with timber and then brick; Mayton Bridge, eight miles north of Norwich, has four centred brick arches. By the sixteenth to seventeenth centuries many bridges were being strengthened and widened to cope with increased traffic. In the late eighteenth century the masonry arch was being challenged, and Wordsworth was filled with regret that '*these monuments of the skill of our ancestors, and of that happy instinct by which consummate beauty was produced, are disappearing fast*'.

The construction in 1779 of the cast-iron bridge across the Severn at Coalbrookdale, Shropshire triggered a revolution in civil engineering. So important that the place was named after it, this high and elegant structure is almost two hundred feet long. Today its use is restricted to pedestrians; the abutments have needed attention since 1784.

As the nineteenth century progressed, engineers such as Telford and Brunel pushed the designs and techniques of iron construction. The spectacular Clifton Suspension Bridge that spans the Avon Gorge is claimed by the city of Bristol as its symbol; designed by Brunel, it was completed after his death in 1864.

One hundred years later, across the fiercest of estuaries, the nearby Severn Bridge was opened. For a while the world's longest bridge, this arched suspension bridge with two towers and inclined suspension cables was slender, graceful and daring. Engineers building bridges from the Bosphorus to the Humber followed the lessons of its technical innovations, although its Grade I-listed structure had to be strengthened in the 1980s.

Crossing the Tyne is always exciting, the silhouettes of the bridges instantly identifying the city. The importance

Landacre Bridge, river Barle, Somerset; the Iron Bridge, river Severn, Coalbrookdale, Shropshire.

of shipping has meant that Newcastle's bridges must allow boats to pass beneath, so they are high or they move. The elegance and ingenuity of the new Millennium Bridge has enabled it to eclipse in public affection the Tyne Bridge of 1928, Robert Stephenson's High Level Bridge of 1849 and the Newcastle Swing Bridge of 1876. Any small bridge may have the same importance in its place.

See also BUILDING STONES, DROVE ROADS, FOOTBRIDGES, FORDS, HORSES & PONIES, LANDMARKS, RIVERS, SHEEP-WASHES, STEPPING-STONES.

BRITANNIA COCO-NUT DANCERS

On Easter Saturday since 1857, eight men with blackened faces have appeared on the streets of Bacup in Lancashire wearing white hats, short skirts over breeches and white stockings, to dance in black clogs around the town. From the Travellers' Rest on the Rochdale Road, accompanied by the local silver band, they do their onerous dances from one boundary to another all day.

Local story has it that Cornish miners following jobs in the North brought with them dances learned from sailors or Moorish pirates. These spread through Rossendale but are now unique to Bacup, passed on by surviving members of the Tunstead Mill Troupe, which has roots in the nineteenth century, to workers from the Britannia Cotton mill. Blackened faces are a common disguise in folk custom, protection from recognition by evil spirits – or perhaps employer.

Among the seven dances performed there are five flamboyant garland dances and two energetic leaping-nut, or coconut, dances. These make full use of the cotton bobbins attached to hands, waists and knees, clacked together to add to the percussion of iron-shod clogs upon the road.

See also BOUNDARIES, BRASS BANDS, FURRY DANCE, MORRIS DANCING.

BROADS

They may look natural, but the broads of east Norfolk and north-east Suffolk are inundated peat diggings dating from the thirteenth and fourteenth centuries. Peat was used for fuel in this area of sparse woodland and, from Norwich to Great Yarmouth – then the second most populous area of the country, demand for fuel was high. A general rise in sea level and a huge surge from the North Sea in 1287 may have forced tidal water up the rivers and into many of the peat diggings.

Situated in the valleys of the Bure, Ant, Thurne, Yare and Waveney, the forty to fifty broads, some a mile wide and ten feet deep, lie alongside the rivers. The baulks, narrow walls of peat that acted as walkways for the peat diggers, stand up as small islands. Oliver Rackham estimated that about nine hundred million cubic feet of peat would have been extracted to form these broads. He observed that they do not have their own Anglo-Saxon or Norse names, but are '*called after parishes, people, fens etc*', such as Filby, Hickling, Hoveton, affirming their later creation.

Until the coming of the railways, the rivers and linked broads were important trade routes. Norfolk wherries, with their single black sails, and smaller, square-sailed keel boats carried goods, such as textiles, coal, bricks, tiles, timber and grain. The riparian landscape was populated by boatyards, inns, bridges and later drainage windmills – mainly brick tower mills with moveable wooden caps and four wooden sails covered with canvas.

Over time, the broads are silting up; expanses of reed beds traditionally cut for thatching roofs have trapped the sediment. Alder carrs have formed, bordered by fens and reclaimed grazing marshes.

Some broads are tidal, and the nearly two thousand acres of broads, rivers, fens, ditches and ponds vary in their levels of salinity and acidity, creating a huge range of habitats. They are important for over-wintering wildfowl and reed bed-dwelling birds, such as the bittern and bearded tit, as well as dragonflies, butterflies (the Swallowtail is peculiar to these parts), yellow water lily, water violet, water plantain and water soldier. Twenty-five species of freshwater fish, including eels, are found in the Broads, making it a popular place for angling.

Boating on the navigable waterways became fashionable in the late eighteenth century and more accessible with the construction of railway links in the 1840s. Its growing popularity was boosted by George Christopher Davies, who wrote *The Handbook to the Rivers and Broads of Norfolk and Suffolk* in the 1880s. But when sailing, pleasure boats and wherries gave way to hired motor cruisers in the early 1920s, the banks and reed beds began to suffer erosion from the wash. Water was polluted by boat fuel, agricultural run-off and sewage, resulting in a huge loss of

57

wildlife diversity. In 1989 The Broads Authority was set up to stop the rot. Now grants are available for boat owners to convert from diesel to electric propulsion to reduce noise and pollution. The threat of further inundation as climate change causes rising sea levels will alter this landscape again, as nature and man play each other in an ebbing and flowing game.

See also ALDER, ARTISTS' COLONIES & SCHOOLS, BOATS, BRIDGES, EELS, FENS, FLOODS, FRESHWATER FISH, GRAZING MARSHES, INNS, LAKES, NORFOLK WHERRIES, REED BEDS, RIVERS, SALT MARSHES, THATCH, TIDES, WINDMILLS.

B R O O K S

Common throughout most of England, this Old English word for stream (*broc*) is rarely used in the north parts of Lancashire and Yorkshire, or in Cumberland, Westmorland Northumberland and Durham.

'The Song of the Brook' by Alfred Lord Tennyson is said to describe one of the upper streams of the river Lymn, which runs near Bag Enderby and Somerby in Lincolnshire – an area full of 'bys and 'thorpes.

> *By thirty hills I hurry down,*
> *Or slip between the ridges,*
> *By twenty thorpes, a little town,*
> *And half a hundred bridges.*
> *Till last by Philip's farm I flow*
> *To join the brimming river,*
> *For men may come and men may go,*
> *But I go on for ever.*

See also BECKS, BOURNES, BURNS, CHALK STREAMS, DIALECTS, FORDS, PLACE-NAMES, RHYNES, RIVER NAMES, RIVERS, SOUGHS, WINTERBOURNES.

B R U S S E L S   S P R O U T S

In Britain we grow and eat more Brussels sprouts than anywhere else in Europe. We even export them to Brussels. These brassicas originated in the Middle East and were brought to England by Flemish refugees via the Low Countries, where they were considered a delicacy. They have been grown here for about 150 years, thriving in our mild climate.

Lincolnshire produces more than half, and about fifteen per cent come from Bedfordshire. John Hargreaves said: '*The A1, the old London road, as it passed from Baldock through Biggleswade and Sandy to Duloe and St Neots, was once known in the trade as "The Brussels Trail". And as blown sprouts were heeled into the ground when pickers rejected them, to decay and put precious nitrogen back into the soil, it was said "and by the smell you shall know it".*'

Around Sandy, Bedfordshire, market gardeners and farmers grow Brussels sprouts as part of a four-crop rotation, with corn, sugar beet and potatoes. Before the advent of the railways, market gardeners had to get the crop by horse and cart to London in one day, returning with manure from London's stables. When the railways arrived, the London and North Eastern Railway brought back the manure from the 'shit sidings' at King's Cross to Biggleswade and Sandy.

Before mechanical harvesting, pickers would go through a field four times, picking the ripe sprouts from the bottom of the stems and working upwards. The tops would be cut for eating like spring cabbage. Now the plants are mainly cut and stripped mechanically. Although sprouts are available from October to March, most are eaten over Christmas.

Bob Taylor, managing director of the Bedfordshire Growers, recalled the old, late-maturing local varieties, such as the Bedfordshire Monach, Bedfordshire Prize and Bedford Fillbasket, with their light green, large 'fluffy' sprouts and subtle flavour, which thrived on the heavy boulder-clay soil. Growers would save their own seed, but now most of it comes from the Netherlands.

In October 2002 Chipping Campden in Gloucestershire hosted the first annual British Sprout Festival in an attempt to revive the vegetable's soggy reputation. Fifteen restaurants in the town added unusual sprout dishes to their menus and walks were organised through the sprout fields.

See also ASPARAGUS, CROPS, MARKET GARDENS, POTATOES, RAILWAYS, SMELLS, WATERCRESS BEDS.

B U I L D I N G   S T O N E S

Collyweston lies at the northern end of Northamptonshire. The village has given its name to a palamino-coloured, oolitic, lime-rich building stone, used traditionally in local roofing because, like slate, it splits easily. The buildings are of a single hue, and these huge, thin slabs lend a different scale, grain and robustness to the cottages. Blisworth limestone, honey coloured with more obvious shelly fragments, is used in the Northamptonshire buildings of Oundle and Cranford as well as its home village. Through the centre of the county run bright orange sandstones and dark rusty ironstones, which, in buildings, are sometimes patterned with pale courses of Blisworth limestone.

Jurassic Northamptonshire is not alone in being a colourful county. The richly varied geology of England has left us a legacy of vernacular buildings fashioned out of stone comfortable in its own surroundings. To look at them is to see into the ground, for it was unusual until water and rail transport developed that stone would be moved far from its place of origin.

You can travel the country in an alphabet of English stone: St Bees Head Red, Shap Pink Granite, Sherborne

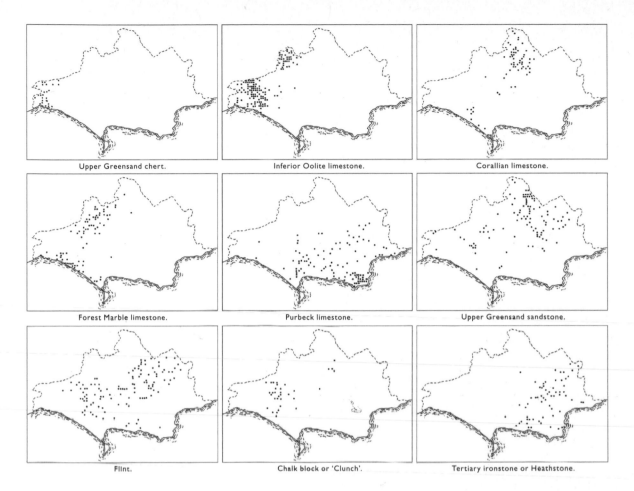

Upper Greensand chert.

Inferior Oolite limestone.

Corallian limestone.

Forest Marble limestone.

Purbeck limestone.

Upper Greensand sandstone.

Flint.

Chalk block or 'Clunch'.

Tertiary ironstone or Heathstone.

59

Stone, Snettisham Carstone (Gingerbread), Somerset Marble, Storeton Stone, Stamford Limestone, Stancliffe Sandstone, Stanton Buff Gritstone, Surrey Stone, Sussex Sandstone, Swale Dale Fossil, Swithland Slate. Travelling from Leeds to Brighton you would cross most of our sedimentary rocks, while from the Humber to Bridport in Dorset you could remain simply on oolitic limestone. But both journeys would offer wonderfully different buildings because even the same rock series vary.

To find granites and assorted metamorphic rocks you have to go to the rugged moors and cliffs of Devon and Cornwall and the mountains of the Lake District. But there are surprises everywhere. Britons invented geology, perhaps because England and its neighbours Scotland and Wales boast the richest compact range of rocks in the world.

Used early for fortification and important buildings, unworked or rubble stones became commonplace in simpler constructions, while more sophisticated buildings were clad in ashlar with a dressed surface. From the found granite used to build Iron Age houses at Chysauster in Cornwall, to the polished Shap granite columns along Piccadilly in London, the way stone is treated gives it different looks and capabilities.

Things appropriate for town may not feel at home in the country, where more depends on appropriate use, local knowledge, sensitive design and siting. It is, of course, possible to build 'out of place' buildings with local stone, but less likely. Local stone is more quickly colonised by endemic lichens and mosses, which add patina more quickly. The integrity of Kendal in Westmorland owes much to the stone of its old buildings; the town is known as 'the auld grey town', dominated as it is by the Carboniferous limestone from Kendal Fell.

London, built on clay, became hungry for stone very early and its situation on the river made it relatively easy to satisfy demand – the White Tower (the Tower of London) was built of stone shipped from Caen in northern France almost a thousand years ago. St Paul's Cathedral, built at the end of the seventeenth century, demonstrates that trade in stone stretched from the Baltic to Greece. But, together with the other London churches built by Wren, it also created a new fashion for Portland stone in civic architecture.

Distribution of stone used in buildings, Dorset.

Blessed with proximity to the sea and hence a boat ride from the Thames, the quarries of the Isle of Portland in Dorset provided the bulk of the material for the great work. Even in the late twentieth century, highly fossiliferous roach beds from Portland were used to face the choir school next door. From the old Palatine, Midland and Lloyds banks in Manchester to the Shire Hall in Nottingham, Portland stone changed the face of our cities. On Portland itself the vernacular revels in it: small and large houses (including their roofs), field and town walls (some with ammonite ornament), kerbstones; even the roads have gutters of stone.

Beyond Portland, Dorset has an abundance of choice geology. Jo Thomas writes: '*Each century has provided a market for building stone, but apart from on the isles of Portland and Purbeck, quarrying activity has been on a small scale, often carried out by farm labourers . . . Churches, houses and farm buildings have been repaired or wholly rebuilt many times as stone weathered away, fashions changed or populations expanded. The tenants of a parish were given the right to draw stone whenever they required it for repairs. The best quality stone has survived the weather, and the mason's style of work often gives a clue to the age of parts of a building, which in turn can suggest when the quarries were being worked. A medieval wall looks totally different from a Victorian one, but the Victorian quarry can be seen on a map, whereas a medieval one would be hard to find.*'

Local names offer insights into colours and textures. Snettisham 'gingerbread' from the lower greensand in Norfolk is a dark, tasty brown; Gooseberry Beds are named after the shape of the fossil *Terebratula sphaeroidalis* in the oolite around Sherborne, Dorset, and Penny Earth in Bedfordshire after the *Ostrea hebridica* fossils in the marls. Less transparent, in Essendine, Rutland, the limestone is called Bullymong, which draws on the old word for sowing peas, oats and vetches for animal feed – a perfect description for a mixed-up white, marly limestone full of fossils. Budleigh Buns were once taken from the beach at Budleigh Salterton, Devon and are still used in the distinctive walls around the town. These bap-shaped quartzite stones are rounded by jostling in water. It is illegal to take them from

the beach, but the quarries in the Budleigh Salterton Pebble Beds, stretching north from the town to the Somerset border, produce them for decorative walls and cobbles.

See also BARNS, BREAD, BRICKS, BRIDGES, BUNS, CAIRNS, CASTLES, CHALK, CHURCHES, COBBLES, CORRUGATED IRON, COTTAGES, DRYSTONE WALLS, FLINT, GABLES, GRANITE, GRAVESTONES, GREENSAND, HIGH STREETS, IRONSTONE, KERBSTONES, LIME-KILNS, MILLSTONE GRIT, PAVEMENTS, PLACE-NAMES, PUDDINGSTONE, QUARRIES, SCULPTURES, SHINERS, TUNNELS, UNLUCKY WORDS, VACCARY WALLS, WAYSIDE & BOUNDARY CROSSES.

BUNGALOWS

It is hard to imagine that the acres of single-storey homes on small plots close to, say, the Sussex coast, or strung out along roads on the outskirts of towns, should have any connection with Bangladesh.

Bangla means 'of or belonging to Bengal', and a *banggolo* was a peasant's rectangular dwelling with a simple thatched roof. As early as the 1650s the East India Company started setting up factories in Bengal, and temporary homes called *bunguloues* were built for the European merchants. In the 1800s travel and reports of life in India increased, and the idea of living in a 'bungalow' in an Indian hill station began to inspire people around the world.

Two architects, John Taylor and John Seddon, built the first 'bungalow settlement' in Birchington, Kent in 1870, to provide a '*new specialised recreational house by the sea*'. These luxurious houses were for upper middle classes wanting to enjoy the healthy air of the coast, with nine to eleven bedrooms on large plots. Each single-storey home had a low belvedere tower, large verandahs, brick and flint

West Wittering, Sussex.

walls and a tiled roof, as well as a private tunnel bored through the chalk cliffs up to the garden. They sold for eighteen hundred pounds, to be used for part of the year and rented for the remainder.

As interest in seaside resorts grew, old railway carriages (first used by fishermen to store nets) were brought to places such as Selsey Bill in Sussex as weekend retreats for Londoners. By 1902, two hundred bungalows with 66-foot frontages had been built and rented out on the beach between Shoreham and Lancing in Sussex, later to become known as Bungalow Town. Positioned on railway sleepers with white-painted weatherboard walls and corrugated-iron roofs, they were hired out or sold for twenty pounds. They appeared at Heacham in Norfolk, Selsey in Sussex and Moreton in the Wirral, Cheshire.

By the 1880s reinvented bungalows were offered in catalogues for export all over the world. At Felpham, near Bognor, Sussex, a row of superior bungalows on cast-iron stilts with large verandahs and flat roofs were obviously not intended for our shores.

Agricultural depression, which started in the 1870s and continued during the inter-war years, drove farmers to sell bits of cheap land for development, and scattered across the South East are makeshift landscapes developed by families with bungalow and garden or smallholding. Essex still has many acres of plot lands – fields split into plots of perhaps twenty feet by a hundred feet, sold to East Enders from the 1890s. At Pitsea and Laindon in Essex the land could be bought for five pounds and bungalows self-built for less than fifty in the 1920s.

Between the wars real expansion took place as the motor car and electric trains out of London created 'Metroland', in John Betjeman's word. In suburbs, such as Upminster, Hornchurch, Rainham, Uxbridge and Hayes, bungalows were mushrooming, often aided by generous government grants for people to build their own.

There was a huge expansion of bungalows by the sea, especially along the coastal strips of Lancashire and Yorkshire and those of Hampshire and Sussex – many for the retired. A bungalow development of 415 acres at Peacehaven, between Newhaven and Rottingdean in Sussex, became the focus for frustrated objectors. For Clough Williams-Ellis, 'the intrusive impertinence of the bungalow knows no bounds'. The Council for the Preservation of Rural England was 'appalled by the rash of squalid little bungalows which disfigures even remote beauty spots', built with alien materials that did not blend into the landscape, but the great need for housing had precedence. The Town and Country Planning Act of 1932 at last addressed the worries about bungalow spread and ribbon development along roads, giving local authorities powers to regulate the size, height, 'design and external appearance of buildings'.

In the 1950s bungalows grew in size, providing more than the usual two bedrooms, sitting room, bathroom and kitchen. Later, in more prosperous areas, they erred towards the hacienda type, no doubt influenced by holidays in Spain. And images of Australian homes, minus the swimming pools and eucalypts, fed back into our suburban scene.

The bungalow culture of the twentieth century reflects the emerging passion of the English for owning their own plot of land – their own castle – and doing with it whatever they like.

See also BEACH HUTS, CORRUGATED IRON, COUNCIL HOUSES, DEEZES, FLOODS, LOST VILLAGES, TERRACED HOUSES.

B U N S

'Bath buns, hot cross buns, spice buns, penny buns, Chelsea buns, currant buns – all these "small, soft, plump, sweet, fermented" cakes are English institutions', wrote Elizabeth David, quoting John Kirkland. Some are enjoyed across the country, such as spiralled Chelsea buns and Yorkshire tea cakes, made with yeast (unlike their Lancashire counterparts) and flavoured with spices and currants. Others are still primarily local specialities, such as Isle of Wight doughnuts, made in Newport, filled with jam and sultanas, or Sally Lunns from Bath, flavoured with lemon peel and eaten hot with butter or clotted cream.

Another of that city's specialities, the Bath bun, is distinctive for its topping of nib sugar, hard little sugar chips. Like others, they were topped with caraway seed comfits until the later nineteenth century, when simpler, cheaper recipes prevailed with mass production, particularly after the London Bath bun was created for sale at the Great Exhibition of 1851. Whitby lemon buns, square or round with thick, lemon icing, may owe their popularity to the success of Whitby, north Yorkshire as a tourist resort since the nineteenth century.

Hot cross buns are defined by time, not place, eaten during Holy Week, though increasingly over a longer period each year. Kightly noted that they were attributed with *'quasi-magical powers'*, associated with the cross, which some say links them to the communion wafers marked with a cross and consecrated on Good Friday. Their origins may go back much further, the crossed bun perhaps representing the four quarters of the moon, or the sun and our four seasons.

Cornish saffron buns were traditionally eaten with clotted cream on Good Friday, although they are now on sale all year. The persistence of saffron in Cornish recipes, while its use declined elsewhere (including in Saffron Walden, Essex), may be because it continued to be grown there until the nineteenth century.

61

Buns hold such a place in our affections and prove so useful in description that we use the word in other contexts. Budleigh Buns are sensuously rounded flattened stones found around Budleigh Salterton, Devon, where they are much used in walls. Hampshire Buns are cottages with voluptuous thatch, while, in the south-east corner of the New Forest, Hampshire, Fawley Bun is the name given to little cushions of woodland moss that roll unattached in the manner of tumbleweed. Echinoid fossils are sometimes called buns. In those places where it is dangerous to say 'ra**it', bun, bunny, batty, bunk and other words are used, although originally bun was a name for the red squirrel.

See also BISCUITS, BREAD, BUILDING STONES, CAKES, COTTAGES, DRYSTONE WALLS, EASTER CUSTOMS, FOOD, MOSSES, UNLUCKY WORDS.

BURNING BARTLE

In West Witton, Yorkshire a rather brutal enactment of the killing of an effigy takes place on the Saturday night following St Bartholomew's Day (24 August).

Bartle, a larger-than-life straw, wool and cloth figure with eyes lit by light bulbs, appears from a doorway carried by its two creators and is paraded around the Wensleydale village to peer into windows and open doors. When he pauses, a poem is chanted by a third man:

> *At Penhill Crags he tore his rags*
> *At Hunter's Thorn he blew his horn*
> *At Capplebank Stee he had the misfortune to brak' his knee*
> *At Grassgill Beck he brak' his neck*
> *At Wadham's End he couldn't fend*
> *At Grassgill End we'll mak' his end*
> *Shout, boys, shout!*

This is followed by cheers of 'Hip, Hip', further cheers and the taking of a swig of whatever is to hand.

On reaching the lane Grassgill End Bartle is stabbed, soaked with paraffin and set alight. Sometimes fireworks explode out of his body and the onlookers sing.

It is not known who Bartle was – perhaps a persistent pig stealer or the bad Giant of Pen Hill, or St Bartholomew of the local church on whose day the ceremony originally took place. Kightly recalled a local theory that Bartle was a plaster replica of the saint, paraded on his saint's day and kept in the church during the Middle Ages. At the Reformation, when the Protestants were destroying such things, the locals tried to carry him away for safe keeping but were seen and pursued across Pen Hill. Parts of his body were broken at Capplebank and the other places mentioned in the poem until he was finally burnt at Grassgill End.

See also BONFIRE NIGHT, GIANTS, MIDSUMMER DAY, SAINTS, TAR BARREL ROLLING.

62

BURNS

Within the dialects of Kent, Surrey and Wiltshire, burn or bourne is sometimes used to describe an occasional stream, whereas in Northumberland (Pow Burn, Long Nanny Burn) and Durham this Old English word is virtually the only one used for a permanent stream. Brook, from the Old English *broc*, ousted its use further south, although it occurs in the similar form of bourne in river and place-names, such as Duntisbourne Rouse in Gloucestershire and Easebourne in Sussex.

See also BECKS, BOURNES, BROOKS, CHALK STREAMS, DIALECTS, FORDS, RHYNES, RIVER NAMES, RIVERS, SOUGHS, WINTERBOURNES.

BUSES

For London the red double-decker bus remains an icon. Until the national bus network was deregulated in the 1980s, every region had colours distinguishing its buses from its neighbour's. Blue buses were run by the Midland General and red ones by Trent in different parts of Derbyshire and Nottinghamshire; there were greens in Nottingham city, Bristol and Kent; blue in Great Yarmouth, Norfolk; yellow on Tyneside. Before nationalisation in 1968, numerous independent companies formed a loose national network. Most were small operations rooted in communities and closely associated with them, such as Silver Star

Routemaster, London.

around Salisbury in Wiltshire or Delaine's, which still operates its blue and silver buses around Peterborough, Northamptonshire.

Locality was felt through the small companies. The colours often attracted strong allegiances, as Aiden Turner-Bishop from Preston explains: *Each of the northern boroughs had its own corporation transport department (there are a few left). If you travelled from, say, Rochdale to Bolton, you went from white and blue (Rochdale), lime green and yellow (Bury) to maroon and cream (Bolton). Salford was proudly green – with no exterior advertisements – to rival Manchester's red.*

'*Some smaller companies are/were clearly identified with their areas. "The Delaine" still runs stylish blue and silver buses from Peterborough to Bourne. The two tones of green of J. Fishwick & Sons of Leyland, Lancashire were specified in the founder's will, and the company still uses them out of respect for his wishes.*

'*In Winchester, Hampshire the King Alfred company sold out some years ago, but such is the local regard that each New Year's Day all the available preserved King Alfred buses (green and cream) run in the city, providing a free service. This means that, at least for one day a year, Winchester is properly King Alfred territory.*

'*Accrington Corporation (and latterly Hyndburn Borough) buses were painted a distinctive navy blue, crimson and black. The black is said to have commemorated the Accrington Pals, more than 250 of whom were killed in one day on the Somme. They are still very much remembered in Accrington. The buses were sold off to Stagecoach when the company went bust, but now local private operators have recycled the livery, since it is so strongly identified with the town. A similar thing has happened in Halifax, where the Halifax Joint Committee Company (actually a family firm) is painting its buses in the green and orange colours of Halifax Corporation.*

'*The application of corporate liveries, such as the turquoise and "Cotswold stone" of Arriva, has meant the loss of some famous colours: the green and cream of Maidstone & District (Kent on wheels); the dark red and cream of Colchester*

Corporation; and the green of Crosville, Cheshire. All gone, yet so evocative of their districts.

'*There's a fashion now for some of the groups to revive much-loved liveries on single buses for PR purposes: Travel West Midland has buses painted in Walsall's turquoise blue; there are also West Bromwich's two tones of blue, Birmingham's smart navy and cream and Coventry's maroon and cream.*

'*In the last thirty or forty years we've lost the crimson of Ribble – very "northern", the red of West Yorkshire Road Car, the two-tone green of Aldershot & District in Hampshire and Surrey, and the green of Bristol Omnibuses. That's why the remaining distinctive liveries are so important for some towns and counties.*'

London's red buses have been running since 1907. The most famous design, the much-loved Routemaster, celebrated its fiftieth anniversary in 2004, when more than a third of the nearly three thousand built were still operating. Sadly 2005 saw most of them permanently retired, a few retained for 'heritage' routes. The open rear platform failed to meet modern safety standards and was hopeless for wheelchair access.

London's single livery has been lost since deregulation, a globally known identity thrown away – strange in an increasingly market-orientated world.

A combination of pressure from enthusiasts, public support and commercial shrewdness has led to several smaller concerns reverting to famous liveries. Black Prince of Leeds uses the old corporation green, the blue and cream has come back to Hull. And on a Vintage Bus Running Day you might even find yourself on a Bristol K6A from 1945 or a 1950 Leyland PS1, a reminder of the original pride in the place of manufacture.

See also BUS SHELTERS, LONDON TAXIS, ROADS.

BUS SHELTERS

On the A350, north of Chippenham in Wiltshire, a new stone shelter offers a cosy resort. In Devon a thatched shelter of cob was built in Down St Mary in 1978 and another in Starcross in 1989. Westcott in Surrey has its thatched shelter. Oxfordshire asserts that its Chiltern shelters should continue to be of timber '*with clay tile or wooden shingle roofs*'. These are a responsible change from the pattern-book efforts of manufacturers whose glass and steel boxes are often paid for by advertising companies.

There is a history of design and care. Dating from the times of trams, Northampton has two fine, curvaceous, patterned cast-iron shelters from the 1920s, complete with cast-iron dags, now retired. In 1937 the architect Edwin Lutyens built two handsome timber bus shelters on the A1 in Stannington, Northumberland; they have arched windows and are painted white.

63

Recent public transport initiatives have brought a new generation of interesting bus shelters to cities. London is building shelters lit by photovoltaic power. Six landmark 'super shelters', which sing to you and tell you stories, were inaugurated along the Manchester Road in Bradford in 2002. Designed by the architects Bauman Lyons, with the help of performance artists, these dynamic glass and red steel structures have wind turbines on elegant poles to generate energy for heating the seats.

See also BUSES, CABMEN'S SHELTERS, DAGS, PROMENADES, WIND FARMS.

64

BUTTS

It is common to find fields and new cul-de-sacs called The Butts or Butts Close, especially near churches. They are where archery was practised on Sundays and holidays. Glebe and town land was often used for compulsory archery practice between the reigns of Henry I and Elizabeth I, indeed until the longbow gave way to the handgun. Often low mounds of earth remain, against which the targets were placed. Other field names include Archery Ground in Trimingham, Norfolk and Robin Hoods Butts in Cuddington, Cheshire.

Field names also record where jousting was practised, such as Justing Lands in Ecclesfield, Yorkshire. The Little Quintern Field in Chetton, Shropshire is a reminder of the medieval practice of quintain, at which knights showed off their horsemanship skills by riding at full tilt to lance a target at the top of a pole, avoiding a sandbag that would swing round to knock them off their mount. One quintain, or tilting pole, still remains on the village green at Offham in Kent.

See also FIELD NAMES, GAMES, ROBIN HOOD, VILLAGE GREENS.

Caslon Roman/Italic, William Caslon, 1725.

CABMEN'S SHELTERS

'Timber framed, tongue and groove timber panels; felt clad timber roof. 7 bays by 3 bays. Entrance to centre of north side. Windows to upper wall in second, fourth and sixth bays. Stump of fleche to roof. Decorative rafter ends to eaves. Cabmen's shelter 1888. Kensington Road London SW7.' So reads the Grade II listing entry for this little green box, taking up no more road space than a Hackney carriage and horse.

Starting in Liverpool and Birmingham and spreading across the country, the creation of places for cabbies to pause began in the 1870s. After years of sitting and working in all weathers most drivers suffered rheumatic and bronchial complaints, and the aspiration was to make life easier.

In Hitchin, Hertfordshire and Ripon, Yorkshire odd examples can still be found. The latter, made in Norwich in 1911, stands now in the market square; it has been restored a few times and still sports a beech shingle roof.

In London, the Cabmen's Shelters Fund was established to create shelters within a six-mile radius of Charing Cross. Of the 61 erected between 1875 and 1914, thirteen remain.

At Warwick Avenue taxis quietly stand outside while their drivers exchange news and imbibe tea to smells of bacon that waft out through the louvres and sliding windows. On the north-west corner of Russell Square the renovated hut stands on blocks getting used to its new surroundings, having been relocated due to the pedestrianisation of Leicester Square. Reminiscent of an aristocratic beach hut or dacha, the fretted roofline of the box in Temple Place by the Embankment flaunts finials and a louvred roof lantern.

See also BEACH HUTS, BUSES, DAGS, LONDON TAXIS.

CAFÉS

Alfredo's closed and people thought that would be the end of it. Grade II listing for an Art Deco café with a late 1940s interior surely wouldn't stand up to any developer's notion of progress. But after a long time dark the lights once again shine bright through windows still edged with chrome on the Essex Road, north London. A new entrepreneur, with 'S&M' – sausage and mash – above the door, is nurturing the good old English-Italian caff. Ingredients include Formica, leatherette, linoleum, tiles, Vitrolite and world-weary wood, but telltale clues to the new millennium are also chalked on the boards: sausages listed by provenance and content, including '*Vegetarian: Mushroom*'.

Transport cafés, cringing behind big lorries beside the A1 or the A5, were rare stops for cars. Every one was different, but welcoming, full of condensation and backchat, each with its own regulars. They were inhabited by garrulous guys with muscular arms, who ate bacon, eggs, fried bread, sausage, tomatoes, beans and slice upon slice of white bread and butter with pint-sized white mugs of tea.

These mud-splattered island lodges in holey asphalt seem to have been ousted by motorway service stations, which attract trucks from many nations, their drivers getting by on bland food in bland surroundings. Could they be anywhere? No, sadly, only here; in France there would be *Les Routiers* signs to look out for, indicating family-run services with food so good it's worth a detour. An exception is Tebay Motorway Services on the M6 near Orton in Westmorland, where food is home-made – much sourced locally – the views are big and calming and the buildings are made from local stone and slate.

One former transport caff at Stonebridge on the North Circular Road, London has moved on from its 1938 beginnings. Bombed and rebuilt, used as a filling station, bookmakers, office building and tyre depot, its Art Deco lines are as smart as ever. After thirty years the Ace Café reopened in 2000 in homage to rock and roll. Fifty years before it had begun to attract Teds, rockers and Ton-up Boys – amazingly twelve thousand of them and their bikes turned up to a reunion in 1994. Now the car park is dominated by motorbikes, new and big ones, proud with leathered riders. The jukebox satisfies further the nostalgia and you can eat breakfast all day. We have bikers to thank for many more such places, such as Squire's Café Bar on the A162 at Sherburn in Elmet, Yorkshire. Its new premises seat seven hundred, with a bike park to match.

We have made the café our own, but we do have to thank the French and the Italian communities for staying with us, their knowledge of real coffee hissed and whispered through the espresso machine. Morelli's, with its pink Formica and neon, remains a beacon above Viking Bay in Broadstairs, Kent.

The fashion for coffee travelled from the east to Constantinople and Venice in the late 1500s. Through the 1650s establishments opened in Oxford and London, later in Exeter, Plymouth and Bristol, and the coffee house became news exchange, business centre, political meeting

67

ACE CAFE LONDON

From the Black Cat in Street, Somerset, to the 49 Club in Nottingham, a new culture was on the prowl, listening, looking and buying for itself. The 2i's in Soho famously nurtured Tommy Steele, Adam Faith and disappeared. E Pellicci in Bethnal Green, east London fed the Kray brothers and lives on. Classic cafés evolved from places fomenting sedition in the seventeenth and eighteenth centuries into imagined stables of evil in the 1950s and 1960s.

They now fight for their individual lives among the tide of sofa-strewn coffee chains and pavement tables. While the classic café conservationists may care less about food than interior design, writer Iain Sinclair demands good food and good position. He prefers what he calls 'bastard' cafés, constantly reworked or mutated with bits from all times. Darren Giddings remembers Café Pop in Manchester – 'veg, vinyl album sleeves, retro kitsch' – and Rumbletums in the Shiels Road, Newcastle – 'big portions and cheap'. Workmen, too, in the wholesale veg market or near the docks, rest in the authentic greasy spoon, surrounded by the smell of frying and the sounds of the city.

See also CABMEN'S SHELTERS, FARMS & FARMSTEADS, FISH & CHIPS, HIGH STREETS, MARKETS, PIGS, POTATOES, POULTRY, QUARTERS, SHOPS, STATIONS.

CAIRNS

At the summit of large hills and mountains, a pile of stones commemorates the achievement of reaching the top or acts as a waymark, informal trig point, memorial, boundary mark or beacon. Many are just small mounds of stones, a gathering of whatever is to hand, but some are landmarks in their own right.

On the Yorkshire/Westmorland border, on a hill overlooking the Vale of Eden, a line of stone cairns on the skyline 'stand like sentries on a rampart at the northern edge of the Yorkshire Dales'. The Nine Standards Rigg inspired artist Andy Goldsworthy, who lived in Brough in his early twenties: 'I could look across at Hartley Fell, and see the Nine Standards . . . They have all been added to and taken away from by visitors over the years, and this change adds to their life; they have "grown" there over a long time, where the stone is plentiful and suitable. What is really interesting was the way that they affected the valley, the way they dominated the valley . . . The ones on the top act for me like sentinels, they look like a group of people and there is a protective side to them.' They proved seminal, Andy says: 'I have made cones all over the world and they are like markers to my travels.'

Describing his walks in the Lake District, Alfred Wainwright commented on the many cairns at the summits. At the top of Hopegill Head he noticed thirty to forty swifts wheeling round the cairn and then round his head as he drew nearer: 'This was the only time I came within

place, indeed the precursor to the London club, with no women allowed. At around the same time cafés also began serving sherbet, chocolate from Mexico and tea from India and China; tobacco smoking might be acceptable. In the City, Edward Lloyd's coffee house was a place for shipping news, and business burgeoned with the emergence of marine underwriting and the Lloyd's List.

In Covent Garden the poet John Dryden held court at Will's in Russell Street. By the end of the seventeenth century more than two thousand coffee houses were to be found in London. The temperance movement revisited the 'coffee tavern' in the 1880s, and in Edwardian London the Bohemian set were lured to coffee houses in Soho and elsewhere, run by Turks, Greeks, Arabs and Italians, who were often former prisoners of war.

By the end of the 1940s the first milk bars had appeared in Fleet Street and Soho, which became once more the focus of immigrant activity, with espresso bars and the Gaggia machine, newly capable of making froth. The beatnik and the CND campaigner mingled in The Troubadour on London's Old Brompton Road, which still draws cosmopolitan poetry and music aficionados. The modern coffee bar appeared just in time to greet the 'teenager', rock'n'roll and the jukebox. For many this is the defining moment of the authentic, classic coffee bar.

five yards of a summit cairn yet was unable to reach it: that short distance was made untenable by the diving swifts, but I was near enough to see the pile of stones was covered by flying ants and that I was disturbing a feast. On other occasions I have found colonies of winged ants on summit cairns but unattended by predators, and once on the top of Caw in the Duddon Valley I found the cairn completely plastered with ladybirds, the stones appearing to be stained a bright red. These migrating flights of insects seem to have a liking for coming to rest at summit cairns, bless their little hearts, just as I have.' Like us, migratory birds and insects use cairns as navigational aids.

Blawearie cairns on Bewick Moor in Northumberland have a different history: a jet and shale necklace, a flint knife and a food vessel were found within them. Archaeologists know cairns as round mounds of stone dating from the Bronze Age and accommodating a single burial, though there may be one or more secondary burials placed in the mound at later dates. Barbara Bender adds that *'these burials were complete and were often accompanied by fine beakers, archery equipment and gold ornaments. Clearly the most important people were placed below the mounds.'* In the South West, ring cairns are widely found on the moors; a fine example exists at Cheriton Ridge on Exmoor.

Gough's Memorial of 1890 on the top of Helvellyn is one of many cairns built in memory of the dead. An engraved stone slab backed by rough stones, it recounts how Gough's dog stayed faithfully beside his master three months after he had died close to the summit. Whatever their origin, however old or new, we can agree with Wainwright that *'To pull down a summit cairn is a sacrilege'*.

See also ANTY-TUMPS, BARROWS, BEACON FIRES, EARTHWORKS, FLINT, JET, LANDMARKS, STANDING STONES.

C A K E S

Know where you are from the lardy cake, varying from rectangular in Oxfordshire to a loose spiral in Gloucestershire. Bakers along the same street might contest the origin, recipes and shapes of local specialities, but they may well use ingredients of the locality. The crocus has a long history of cultivation in Cornwall, producing the saffron used in the county's dense yellow saffron cakes and buns. Walsingham's hives traditionally provided the honey for Norfolk honey cake, while the mixture for the cider cakes of Herefordshire, Gloucestershire and Oxfordshire is raised by local cider reacting with bicarbonate of soda. Apple cakes thrive in orchard-rich areas. Those of Somerset and Devon differ from those of Dorset by containing cinnamon or other spices.

Special occasions call for special cakes. Parkin from Yorkshire, a dense, sticky gingerbread made with coarse oatmeal and black treacle, is associated with Bonfire Night. At Christmas, it might also contain fruit and peel, sometimes with coriander, cloves and caraway seeds. Jam puffs may have evolved from Coventry God cakes, triangular (as a symbol of the Holy Trinity), mincemeat-filled puff pastries, once given by godparents on the Twelfth Day of Christmas (in Warwickshire a God cake is also a grassy triangle where old roads meet). The Southwell galette is for Nottinghamshire's Twelfth Night celebrations: layers of mincemeat, local Bramley apples and apricot jam with a pastry lattice, finished off with cream and hazelnuts.

Fruit cakes crop up in most places, such as Lincolnshire's plum loaf and dough cake, Oxford fruit cake and Suffolk harvest cake. Fat Rascals originated in Yorkshire simply as cakes containing dried fruit, but are now often decorated with a face of almonds and halved glacé cherries. Black cake from Cornwall gets its name from its high content of currants and dark brown sugar. Simnel cakes, rich fruit cakes made with currants, spices and almonds, were star-shaped in Devizes, Wiltshire, round and flat in Bury, Lancashire, and decorated with eleven balls of almond paste (representing the faithful apostles) in Shrewsbury. These were once popular gifts during Lent.

The delight of local cakes is as much in their names and resonances as in their tastes and smells. Singin' Hinnie from Northumberland is so called for the sound it makes as it heats on the griddle. Lincolnshire dripping cake is a spicy, fruited cake sliced from a square tin and buttered. Heavy cake, or Fugga, from Cornwall also uses dripping, with butter, cream, peel and currants.

See also APPLES, BAKEWELL PUDDING, BISCUITS, BONFIRE NIGHT, BREAD, BUNS, DRAGONS, ECCLES CAKES, FAIRS & FAIRGROUNDS, FOOD, GRASSY TRIANGLES, GREETINGS, PUDDINGS.

69

Nine Standards Rigg, near Kirkby Stephen, Westmorland.

CANALS

Where there are no rivers, they have been created, ever since the Romans linked the Trent and Witham rivers in Lincolnshire by the Fossdyke. The 'cut', or canal, came to prominence in the mid-eighteenth century, built for moving inland coal to industrial centres and ports. Merseyside and Manchester benefited, and other trades followed: pottery on the Trent and Mersey; copper at Tavistock in Devon. Canals came to Shrewsbury, Coventry and Birmingham, which had 159 miles of them by 1898 – many are still in use. The military built a canal from Sussex to Kent, for troop movements, supplies and to create an obstacle for invaders.

A new linear particularity was laid across the country, in new byways (towpaths), bridges and buildings constructed from newly accessible materials. Round houses were built for employees on the Thames and Severn; barrel-roofed cottages and delicate split bridges lined the Stratford-upon-Avon in Warwickshire; ornate classical lodges appeared on the Gloucester and Sharpness. The Kennet and Avon wharf at Devizes, Wiltshire brought fashionable Bath stone for the town's new buildings. The Grand Union, linking London with the Midlands, was the most extensive network in the country, its unique features including Lombardy poplars and pollarded willows along its towpaths, as well as mooring bollards, pumping stations and mileposts. Where buildings were required and the right clay could be found, local brick works appeared. At Foxton, Leicestershire a brick works was the starting point for a small community that developed to service canal travellers.

Canal people decorated everything – their narrow boats, with bold lettering and floral decorations, and their domestic ware, with brightly coloured paintings, mainly of roses and castles on dark backgrounds. At Cut End, Measham in Derbyshire glazed brown Measham Teapots (known as 'barge teapots'), with moulded and glazed decorations and a miniature teapot on the lid as a handle, were made until 1939.

The canal network decayed once the railways took their trade. Some were completely overbuilt, others changed their nature. Part of the Wiltshire and Berkshire canal is now Swindon's shopping precinct The Parade. Their revival for leisure purposes during the twentieth century sprang from enthusiasts' zeal. Linton Lock in Yorkshire was among the earliest restoration projects in 1949. By 1962 there were two thousand miles of network, which British Waterways was created to manage.

Many remain sleepy and tranquil; wildlife has returned both to disused and restored stretches of cut. Water voles have reappeared; there have been otters on the Pocklington canal in Yorkshire. Some are the focus of festivals, boat galas and town fairs, such as Skipton and Standedge in Yorkshire, Foxton Locks in Leicestershire and Gas Street Basin in Birmingham. In 2001 the Association of Inland Navigation Authorities proposed a number of projects to revive and make links between canals. These would bring a new cohesion to the network, but also cause ecological concern if they were to move and mix water on a serious scale between catchments.

See also AQUEDUCTS, BRICKS, INNS, LOCKS, MILESTONES, PUBS, TUNNELS, WAREHOUSES.

CARNIVALS

Old and new daylight processions punctuate the year in many cities, towns and villages – the Spalding Flower Parade in early May, Weymouth's Water Carnival in June and Hastings's Old Town Carnival in August. But the West Country blares through the autumn with illuminated night-time carnivals, each a remarkable show of floats that travel competitive 'circuits', from the North Cornwall Carnival to the Wessex Grand Prix, raising money for their participants and for charity.

Carnival clubs, such as the Gremlins, Gorgons, Lime Kilns, Marketeers and Masqueraders, in towns from Launceston, Cornwall to Wincanton, Somerset, work all year long behind the locked doors of barns and sheds – the Revellers in Motcombe, Dorset welcome members with skills in design, costume making, float building, electrics, engineering, welding, painting and carpentry. When they emerge, the results may be mounted on a sixty-foot trailer hauled by a tractor or truck, plus a towed generator. The 'cart', as it is called locally, is dominated by light and music way above fairground brightness and loudness. There may be moving parts; the lights may flow, oscillate or stammer; people might remain still in tableaux or dance and move – there are various carnival trophies to compete for.

One lone girl
And 17,000 light bulbs
Dancing the night away
Up front on the Vagabond's cart

James Crowden, from 'Carnival Girl'

Canal ware.

It is 7pm and dark, the glow in the sky suggests a big town, but the colour is white, not orange, and the town is small. Walking along the mile of growling vehicles waiting for the off at Shepton Mallet, Somerset is almost the best way to see both the domesticity and the otherness of the whole affair. Ladders are held vertical by big fellows as the 'sparks' trots up to fix a group of delinquent flashing bulbs. At the roadside neat black waste sacks brim with empty light-bulb boxes. Suddenly all the lights go out and you remember that you are walking by fields and odd houses outside a town. Lights back on, the caravan lurches forward into the main street and the music is squeezed by the buildings into a cacophony, throwing out excerpts of recognisable rock and pop songs as each bright world passes by. Ancient Egypt, jungle scenes, the Wild West, treasure islands, disco and calypso, starships and Sinbad parade with perfect composure. Between the floats, costumed masqueraders stroll, fool and chat and open-backed vans, shaped to catch coins, invite philanthropy.

The brashness of these occasions excites and overwhelms. The crescendo in Bridgwater, Somerset on the closest Thursday or Friday to 5 November now attracts crowds of 150,000. The two-hour procession of spectacular floats is just part of the almost riotous night, which ends with a unique display of squibbing along the High Street (windows boarded). One hundred or more squibs tied to wooden 'coshes' are simultaneously lit to provide waterfalls of golden sparks. Originally Bridgwater Squibs would end with a loud bang, but no longer.

This very particular carnival claims a history born of 1605 and celebrations following the failure of the Gunpowder Plot. It is first written about in the 1860s, with torch-lit processions and wild bonfires. Just before the Great War, lighting by car battery arrived; now each mobile generator may provide thirty thousand bulbs with electricity. From torches and bonfires to electric light, the link with Samhain, the Celtic autumn fire festival celebrating the new year, seems too close to ignore.

See also BONFIRE NIGHT, DIWALI, MELAS, NOTTING HILL CARNIVAL, TAR BARREL ROLLING.

C A R O L S

The Festival of Nine Lessons and Carols from King's College, Cambridge, held before Christmas since 1918, is today, thanks to radio and television, a celebration that everyone can enjoy. But carols are for participating in. They were originally dancing songs for saints' days, direct and exuberant; some fragments have passed through folk tradition since Chaucer's time. Now, up and down the country, local church and chapel choirs are in more formal voice while impromptu groups sing outside people's houses, collecting money for their favourite charities.

In areas where nonconformist faiths are still strong, the carols have some of the joyfulness and vigour of the early 'caroles'. In Sheffield and North Derbyshire, in towns and villages such as Castleton, Coal Aston, Dungworth, Eyam, Foolow and Hathersage, there is a tradition from the nineteenth century of carol singing in pubs and around villages at Christmas time. Each of the villages has its own repertoire of carols and ways of singing them. As well as the more familiar standard repertoire, including 'O Come, All Ye Faithful', local carols that have been handed down orally for generations are sung with gusto. The well-known song 'On Ilkley Moor Baht 'at' is sung to a tune originally written for 'While Shepherds Watched', which, by the way, is regularly sung to many other tunes (such as 'Liverpool', 'Pentonville' and 'Old Foster'.

'One of the chief characteristics of many of the tunes is the pattern known as "fuguing" – a kind of call-and-answer repetition towards the end of the verses, where the bass line answers the melody, and usually builds up a fair head of steam. "Mount Moriah", "Old Foster" and "Egypt" are just three popular and spectacular examples', says Barry Callaghan.

At the Royal Hotel in Dungworth, near Sheffield, the organist leads the singing. Carols written by local people with titles relating to nearby places, such as 'Spout Cottage', 'Stannington', 'Bradfield' and 'Harwell', are embellished with instrumental interludes, known as symphonies, played between the verses. Some carollers sing unaccompanied, such as at the Fountain in Ingbirchworth and at the Black Bull in Ecclesfield.

Village carolling in Beeston, Nottinghamshire is thought to have been brought by weavers from Yorkshire, who came to work in the hosiery trade around 1800. The Methodist Carol Choir sings its own local carols around the town every Christmas Eve.

Cornwall is another stronghold of Methodism, and in Padstow, Troon and other towns and villages in the west and centre of the county, there has been a tradition since 1890 of *a cappella* perambulatory carolling before Christmas. Carols such as 'Sound, sound, your instruments of joy', composed by former tin miner Thomas Merrit from Illogan, are at their best sung unaccompanied. Some of these village folk carols, especially traditional Cornish ones, were written down by Davies Gilbert and William Sandys in the 1820s and 1830s. More recently, Ian Russell of Village Carols in Sheffield has documented, recorded and championed them.

In the West Country, the tradition of west gallery music is kept alive by groups such as the Stanchester Quire and Mellstock Band. Thomas Hardy, whose father and grandfather played in church bands, wrote affectionately about them in *Under the Greenwood Tree*. These bands, comprising local men, were encouraged after the Restoration, and galleries aping the minstrels' galleries of grand houses were built in the west ends of churches to accommodate them and the choirs. Their lively playing and singing was frowned on by the Victorians, who replaced them with large piped organs. Many of the dispossessed musicians were attracted to the exuberant music of the nonconformists and swelled their ranks. Lancashire, too, had its west gallery choirs: in Rossendale the Larks of Dean Quire were influential in the hundred years before 1850. They have risen again, taking the name in 1994.

The history of the carol and of folk tradition is so tainted with old and more recent puritanical attempts to tidy it up, or indeed suppress it, that it has taken great effort to liberate it. Its continuing existence owes much to villagers themselves, to folk song and annual broadsheets. As the nineteenth century came to a close and Cecil Sharp began to collect folk songs, he sparked off a search for fading knowledge, of which Percy Dearmer remarked in 1928: '*only just in time . . . to this we owe the recovery of one lost carol tune after another . . . It is a thrilling history, full of significance. Something transparently pure and truthful, clean and merry as the sunshine, has been recovered from under the crust of artificiality which had hidden it.*'

There is still much to do. It took the bringing together of people to celebrate the local distinctiveness of their village – Landkey in north Devon – to give some of the older women courage to reveal, sing and teach local carols to young members of the community.

See also BRASS BANDS, CHAPELS, MUSIC, PUBS.

C A S T L E S

Tudor castles replaced Norman castles, which replaced Saxon castles, which replaced Roman *castra*, which replaced prehistoric hill-forts. But the age of castles as we know them – grand stone edifices dominating their surroundings – came with the Normans after 1066. They were not defending against invaders, rather making a statement of conquest. They cowed the English and glowered out from the Marches towards the untameable Welsh. Barnard Castle in County Durham, Windsor in Berkshire and Warwick took advantage of commanding natural positions. These castles were there to threaten and intimidate, extract taxes and service – military and domestic. Feared and hated though they were, their links with the locality were symbiotic, the service of the one being rewarded with the economic and military benefits of the other. Often new communities grew around them. The concentric layout of Devizes, Wiltshire was dictated by the castle; a street called the Brittox originates from the *bretesque*, the stockade that flanked the castle approach.

Initially wooden palisades or baileys on top of man-made mounds or *motte*, Norman castles quickly adopted stone where it was readily available, as at Launceston in Cornwall and Totnes in Devon. Although wood was still used in enormous quantity, some castles demonstrated their wealth and power dramatically in stone, which was sometimes shipped in from the quarries of Caen in Normandy. The riverside quarries at Barnack in Northamptonshire, Reigate in Surrey and Maidstone in Kent prospered.

Colchester Castle used the Roman bricks and stones from the handy ruins, as well as Caen ashlar, Kentish ragstone and dressed stone from Barnack or Reigate. Red sandstone from local quarries was used at Acton Burnell, Shropshire. Baconsthorpe Castle in Norfolk has East Anglian knapped flintwork, and the raw materials of Bolton Castle in Yorkshire came from nearby Greets Quarry. Windsor, Berkshire acquired stone from further afield, from quarries in Totternhoe, Bedfordshire. In the East, from the fifteenth century, locally made bricks were utilised; Caister Castle, Norfolk has them, and at Tattershall, Lincolnshire nearly a million bricks were required, made of local clay from Edlington Moor.

Nikolaus Pevsner called Northumberland '*the castle county of England*'; Paul Johnson gave a similar honour to the North Riding of Yorkshire. Certainly the Northern defences have a scale and ruggedness that are hard to match. Richmond, Yorkshire was built to '*dominate the entrance to*

Bamburgh Castle, Northumberland.

Swaledale'; Bamburgh, Northumberland seems the perfect castle and occupies an impressive natural vantage point, where the Whin Sill runs out to the sea. Dunstanburgh nearby is proving to be one of the most remarkable of castles; research is revealing that it was built to be approached from the sea.

The expression '*an Englishman's home is his castle*' was first quoted by Sir Edward Coke in 1623, demonstrating that the purpose of the castle was shifting away from the purely defensive. As their military use declined, many became financial liabilities, left to ruination. Oliver Cromwell consolidated their demise, smashing places where his enemies might fortify themselves. Overgrown and forlorn, castles became symbols of lost chivalry to the Romantics from the late seventeenth century.

A spate of 'sham' castles and new houses in fantasy castle style appeared. Nineteenth-century Gothic inspiration prompted the building of Eastnor Castle in Herefordshire, its stones brought by pack mule from the Forest of Dean at great expense. Even in the twentieth century the romance of the castle wouldn't die: Sir Edwin Lutyens designed the mock medieval Castle Drogo, built of granite on the edge of Dartmoor between 1910 and 1930.

See also BRICKS, BUILDING STONES, DESERTED VILLAGES, FORTIFICATIONS, GAPS, HILL-FORTS, LANDMARKS, MARTELLO TOWERS, PARK GATE LODGES, PILLBOXES, RUINS.

CASTLETON GARLAND DAY

This ceremony, which seems to have roots in May Day and connections with Jack in the Green and beating the bounds festivities, takes place in the village of Castleton, Derbyshire on Oak Apple Day, 29 May (or 28 May if the 29th falls on a Sunday).

Ostensibly the ceremony celebrates Charles II's restoration to the throne in 1660; his successful escape by hiding in the Boscobel Oak is remembered, as people wear oak leaves and hoist branches of oak up the church towers. Castleton shares this and a number of features with the Great Wishford Oak Apple Day in Wiltshire. Kightly observed that '*so closely identified were Maying and the Restoration*', celebrations no longer being suppressed, that '*in many places the May Day festivities were transferred to Oak Apple Day*'.

But in Castleton the 'Garland' rather than the oak bough takes centre stage. Each year one of six pubs takes it in turn to make the Garland on the morning of the ceremony. A three-foot-high, bell-shaped frame is covered in garden and wildflowers and topped by a posy of special flowers called 'the Queen'.

At about six in the evening the Garland King and his Lady, dressed in clothes of the Stuart period, mount white horses and ride around the parish boundary, stopping at the pub that has made the Garland. This is put over the head and body of the King so that only his legs are visible – like Rochester's Jack in the Green. The silver band strikes up the 'Garland Tune' and leads a procession around the village. It is followed by young girls dressed in white, carrying flowers and coloured ribbons, then by the King and his consort. At each pub the group stops for drinks and the girls dance.

The King and Lady ride alone to the churchyard gate, where the Garland, minus the Queen, is removed and hoisted onto one of the eight pinnacles of the tower of St Edmund's Church, the remainder having been decorated with oak boughs, where it is left for a week.

Final celebrations take place on the village green, where the girls dance around the maypole. The King places the Queen on the war memorial in the market-place and the 'Last Post' is played.

See also ARBOR DAY, BRASS BANDS, CHURCHES, FOLKTALES, GROVELY RIGHTS DAY, MAY DAY, MAYPOLES, MUSIC, OAK, VILLAGE GREENS, WHITE HORSES.

C A T H E D R A L S

Cathedrals,
Luxury liners laden with souls,
Holding to the East their hulls of stone.

W.H. Auden, from 'Here on the cropped grass of the narrow ridge I stand'

Cathedrals are the grandest manifestations of church architecture. Most dominate their place even now: Ely is known as 'the ship of the Fens', visible on its isle of eels from miles around, intended to send a tremble through the resistant Saxons. Durham and Lincoln stand high on their hills. They were meant to tower over the skyline of their cities, for to have a cathedral is to be a city.

The *cathedra* is the throne/seat of the bishop; the souls of all in the diocese are in his care. The cathedral is the place for the formal worship of God through meditation and prayer. But in addition to hosting the liturgy, William the Conqueror set them up as centres of administration. In England, unlike France, they stand in their closes, powerful and separate.

William razed the Saxon cathedrals, creating his own pattern and his own bishops and administrators within centres of population. At Hexham in Northumberland the church stands on an extant Saxon cathedral crypt. York Minster and Worcester Cathedral conceal ancient foundations expunged by Norman power.

Each was built from east to west, over generations as finances allowed and itinerant masons were available. Even before they were finished, fashion may have moved on,

73

and during the centuries extension and restoration has accumulated further styles. The focus and longevity of faithful endeavour, as well as the emergent scale and unique beauty, sculpted identity on city dwellers and pilgrims, too. Nothing like these houses of God had been seen before and, despite all of the engineering, design and material feats our generation knows, they still take the breath away. The medieval pattern has proved so resilient that it shines through even in the twentieth-century cathedrals of Coventry and Guildford.

The stone stair to the chapterhouse and the scissor arches in Wells, the soaring spire of Salisbury, the watery crypt of Winchester, the leaves and green men of Southwell, the flint of St Albans, the steps of Canterbury, the medieval stained glass of York, the floor at Ely, the giant patterned pillars and inbuilt secrets of Durham, the Perpendicular fan-vaulting of Bath Abbey – each offers indelible fragments as well as landmark images. In medieval times each had its saints or relics to draw the crowds and income – marketing was clever, it had to be. Pilgrims, then as now, exchanged coins for comfort and awe.

Norwich succeeded in building the tallest of towers, completed in the mid-twelfth century, but the Normans had yet to perfect the tower; many fell and the higher structures are often later additions. Their overall durability has depended upon the quality of the mostly local stone, with the New Red Sandstone buildings of Carlisle, Chester, Lichfield and Worcester faring worse than cathedrals built of oolitic and magnesian limestone, such as Gloucester, Oxford, Peterborough and York. Caen stone from Normandy came by boat for Canterbury. Limestone from the Isle of Portland was shipped in to build Wren's Baroque St Paul's after the Great Fire of London. That cathedral still makes its presence felt, though it has long been eclipsed as the sole focus of the skyline.

Durham deserves special mention. This Romanesque building, its nave completed in 1133, stands in a spectacular position high on the rock of an incised meander in the river Wear. Its rib-vaulting set the standard and was linked here for the first time with the pointed arch and the flying buttress. The ancient patterns of spiral and chevron cut into its huge columns remain fresh and provocative.

The Gothic style aspired to fill buildings with spiritual light. Exeter's luminous interior glories in thirty ribbed columns, often likened to trees, supporting fan-vaulting along more than one hundred metres of roof.

Coventry Cathedral suffered badly during bombing in 1940. The actual and symbolic importance of rebuilding from the ruins, bringing together the best designers and artists in the land, gave us a glimpse of the pride of building the original.

These extraordinary buildings have made and judged history for a millennium, from nation-shaking murder to a

city's fire, from Catholicism to Protestantism/Anglicanism, from medieval to post-modern England. Their cloisters and closes, and the final flourish of the Gothic – the Perpendicular style – distinguish them from the cathedrals of mainland Europe, and each offers a unique sedimentation of styles and stories.

See also ABBEYS, BELLS & BELL-RINGING, BUILDING STONES, CHAPELS, CHURCHES, EARTHQUAKES, EAST, EELS, GREEN MAN, LANDMARKS, MONASTERIES, MOSQUES, RUINS, SYNAGOGUES, TEMPLES.

C A T T L E

Within just 365 acres of Northumberland, 'the Lord's Wild Beasts' have roamed since the thirteenth century. White, with red hair on their ears and chin, black noses and upward-curving horns, Chillingham cattle are unique, their DNA pure since early times. The wild or feral herd numbers forty to sixty, with as many bulls as cows, and it follows strict social codes. A dominant 'king' bull fights for supremacy about every four years, which is just the length of time it takes for heifers to mature to breeding age, ensuring the bull never breeds with its offspring. They have seen much in seven hundred years in this place, and are so wild they were not even rustled by the border reivers.

White Park cattle, like the cattle of Chillingham Park, may be remnants of the wild herds of pre-Norman England. Chartleys in Staffordshire have downward-curving horns, black points, including ears and nose, and seductive black eyelashes. Most of these traits are shared by the British White, although it is naturally hornless (polled). These old breeds calve easily and will do so for a decade and a half.

Beyond the estate pale, cattle were bred over centuries to stand up to weather and make the most of the land. Their names differentiate them by county of origin. Herefords are easily recognised by their 'points of special and peculiar interest . . . the face and forward part of the back and mane, as well as the throat, belly, inside and lower parts of the legs, and the tip of the tail, are white, the greater part of the body red or brown, varying from a light to a dark shade, and . . . well covered with soft glossy hair, having a tendency to curl'. They have given much to the global gene pool. Most of us know them better from cowboy movies than from our own fields; indeed, numbers of traditional Herefords have dwindled so severely in England that they are regarded as endangered.

Ted Tims has championed Sussex cattle all his life. '[They] are descended from the red cattle that inhabited the dense forests of the Weald at the time of the Norman conquest. For generations prior to the nineteenth century their primary use was as draught animals. They were broken to the yoke by the age of three years and used for ploughing and carting for three or four years being then fattened for the butcher at six or seven . . . They existed in large numbers in the agricultural counties of

Devon.

Longhorn.

Old Gloucester.

Hereford.

75

south-east England and were not affected by the introduction of other breeds . . . The beef seldom leaves the district in which the animals are reared.'

The relative isolation of the West Country gave Devon cattle local dominance for a long time, and red cattle travelled out with the earliest American settlers. Some believe Devon cattle can be traced back to aboriginal stock; other stories have them arriving with Phoenician tin traders. The North Devon or Red Ruby is celebrated in a plaque at Molland. Here James Quartly at Champson Farm in the early eighteenth century developed the breed to withstand moorland exposure and rain and provide meat and milk (and cream).

By the early twentieth century it had made its way widely across the world. But at the end of the century it had to be rediscovered as the best breed to deal with and thrive on north Devon's marshy culm grassland. With longer intestines than most, the Red Ruby can digest the harsh grasses. The bigger South Devon was developed (perhaps by crossing with Channel Island cattle) as a milch cow, better suited to the lower meadows of the South Hams.

The Gloucester – mahogany brown and distinctively marked with a white underbelly and white finching, or

streaking, along the length of its spine and tail – is most likely still to be found along the Severn in its home county. Its milk, with a high content of small fat globules, makes the best Double Gloucester cheese. In 1972, Charles Martell, recognising the vulnerability of the breed, which then numbered only 68 in the world, began buying them and building his own herd near Dymock. He also began to champion the breed by leading a revival of real cheese – he makes Single and Double Gloucester cheeses from his cattle at different times of the year. The numbers of the breed are now up to seven hundred, of which Martell has a modest 25 (together with 98 varieties of Gloucestershire apples, some Gloucester Old Spot pigs and county chickens and ducks).

Robert Bakewell and his followers in the Midlands made much of the Longhorn, which had originated in Yorkshire around the Craven district, perhaps introduced by the Romans. Its distinctively flamboyant horns rendered this big breed useless for intensive rearing, despite its gentle nature. Luckily this handsome red roan or brindled animal is gaining favour as a producer of lean meat and an excellent conservation grazer. In Epping Forest, Windsor Great Park, the Bollin valley in Cheshire and the National Forest in Leicestershire, groups of Longhorns are grazing down the bracken and brambles among ancient trees, helping once more to maintain open parkland.

Out of Lincoln Red stock came the successful Shorthorns, originally bred by the Colling brothers in Ketton, near Darlington, County Durham, from four cows and a bull they found in Haughton Le Skerne. In the early 1800s they had established how to breed to maintain characteristics specific to a herd.

From the earliest times of genetic experiment, animals were being interbred. But in the last half of the twentieth century, incoming cattle varieties from the European mainland and further afield have dominated to such an extent, and artificial feeding conditions developed so far, that animals have been separated from the land and we have forgotten the qualities and strengths of our local breeds. Rather than cattle that do well in response to local conditions, we have favoured beasts bred specifically to produce the largest quantity of cheap meat or milk.

With farming practices changing so dramatically, breeds were lost in the twentieth century, including the Sheeted Somerset, with its white cummerbund. The Rare Breeds Survival Trust's priority list of endangered breeds in 2005 included the Gloucester, White Park, Beef Shorthorn, Red Poll, Chillingham, Lincoln Red and Traditional Hereford.

76   *See also* AGRICULTURAL SHOWS, APPLES, BASTLES, CHEESE, DOUBLE GLOUCESTER, DROVE ROADS, MARKETS, PARKLAND, PELE TOWERS, PIGS, SHEEP.

C A V E S

If you sat at the entrance of Thor's Cave in Staffordshire and looked out over the intimate valley of the Manifold, you would be echoing a posture practised for thousands of years: home and refuge behind you, prospect before you. Kent's Cavern in south Devon sits two hundred feet above sea level and half a mile from the present shoreline. Its complex of chambers has yielded evidence of habitation from half a million years ago and a 31,000-year-old human jawbone, the oldest remnant of modern man in Europe.

The discovery of twelve-thousand-year-old wall engravings, depicting an ibex and possible birds of prey, in April 2003 in the magnesian limestone caves of Creswell Crags on the Nottingham/Derby border, was the most northerly find of Ice-Age cave art in the world. The caves and valley were already renowned for palaeolithic artefacts and fossil mammals, including woolly rhinoceros and mammoth, but the ibex has never been known in Britain. It is another pointer to the great mobility of our ancient forbears, who seem exuberantly to have painted underground and open-air surfaces in similar genre, from Portugal to Creswell Crags to the Urals.

Some of the Cheddar Caves have been on the tourist circuit for hundreds of years. Set in the wonder of a 450-foot-deep gorge cut originally by a rushing Ice-Age river, many of the caverns have been explored. Gough's and Cox's Caves are open to visitors, who delight in grand deposits with names such as the Frozen River, the Rainbow Room, the Peal of Bells, the Marble Curtain and the Ladye Chapel, whose pools reflect great stalactites and stalagmites. The Cheddar Yeo emerges as a full river low down the gorge.

Lime-rich stone offers the greatest treasury of natural subterranean caverns. Limestone seduces water underground into streams and torrents, which gouge and drip, giving us the spectacular caverns and potholes of Derbyshire, Yorkshire and the Mendips in Somerset, as well as Kent and Devon.

Speleology is a dangerous pastime, but the sheer exhilaration of coming across fabulous rock formations or a new passage drives people on. In Yorkshire the name Jingle or Jingling Pot/Caves recurs in Wharfedale, Swaledale, Chapel-le-dale and Kingsdale, as does Hell Hole in Teesdale, Wharfedale and Whitewell. Rumbling Hole and Boggart's Roaring Holes are some of the more suggestive names. Gaping Ghyll on Ingleborough describes itself; from the moor to the bottom of Flood Entrance Pot is a drop of 450 feet, and you can seriously wander the passages for three and a half miles. Every cave and pot is different. Simpson's Pot in Kingsdale attracts the note: '*Any cuts in this pot require attention as they invariably turn septic.*'

Thyrsts and hobthyrsts, threatening giants of our Norse forbears (hence Thor's Cave and its alternate name of Hob Hurst's House), boggarts (ghosts) and witches frequented the depths. Hermits found quiet and sanctuary, as at the fourteenth-century Cratcliffe Hermitage on the ancient Portway by Robin Hood's Stride, Winster in Derbyshire, which has a high relief crucifix carved into the wall. Others, too, led the troglodytic life. At Wolverley and Drakelow near Kidderminster the cave houses were lived in until the 1950s; indeed, Mr Kempe did not move out until 1974.

Take a drink in The Trip to Jerusalem, Nottingham and you can sit in tiny rooms cut into rock and look up high into the gloom of a fissure. The twelfth-century inn is built into the great block of Sherwood Sandstone upon which the castle stands. No drips here.

See also BLUE JOHN, CHEDDAR CHEESE, GORGES, HAUNTED PLACES, LIMESTONE, MINES, QUARRIES, SEA CAVES, TUNNELS.

C E M E T E R I E S

Our relationship with the dead says much about our culture. Where we place their remains tells us more, from the barrows of the Bronze Age, Saxon burials, plague pits and nonconformist burial grounds to the great necropolises of the Victorians. Early modern-style cemeteries, such as the Rosary in Norwich, appeared when churchyards and crypts in expanding communities became dangerously full. Publicly funded cemeteries were established in the 1850s, the first being St Bartholomew's in Exeter, Devon. Design was influenced by formal layouts, as suggested by John Claudius Loudon in an 1843 guide. Level cemeteries were enhanced with winding paths and trees, but sloping ground was favoured for effect and for the benefits of well-drained land and airy aspect.

Victorian cemeteries are often impressive as landmarks in suburbia. Arnos Vale in Bristol is designed along the lines of a Greek necropolis lost in a hilly Arcadia, and is now cared for by an active trust. The large Victorian cemeteries surrounding London served different parts of the city: fashionable Highgate and Abney Park for the north, Tower Hamlets the east, West Norwood and Nunhead the south, Brompton and Kensal Green the west. Different denominations and religions are accommodated: Greek and Caribbean in New Southgate, north London; Italian Catholic and Parsee in Brookwood, near Woking, Surrey. Many of London's Quaker burial grounds are now gardens, including Bunhill Fields, where the Friends founder George Fox is interred. Their burial ground at Idle, Yorkshire seems empty; a stone bench around the inside of the wall offers seating for outdoor meetings. In the new Gardens of Peace Muslim Cemetery in Ilford, Essex, the graves are orientated towards Mecca, each marked by a stone and a sapling.

The enormous loss of life in the First and Second World Wars prompted the building of simple, formal military cemeteries. In Cambridge, the American services' cemetery has regimental headstones in concentric circles on flat ground. Its British counterpart at Aldershot, Hampshire is on hilly ground with differing family-selected stones. Many German servicemen buried in English church-yards were moved to the German Military Cemetery on Cannock Chase, Staffordshire after its creation in 1962. Hundreds of Polish airmen are buried at Newark-on-Trent, Nottinghamshire, having flown to their deaths from its surrounding airfields.

Old cemeteries are increasingly recognised as important open spaces and natural habitats. Some, such as Bisley Road in Stroud, Gloucestershire, have become Local Nature Reserves. Towards the end of the twentieth century a demand for non-religious and more environmentally sensitive burial prompted the creation of green burial grounds where a tree replaces a headstone. By 2002 there were around 140, and the number is growing.

See also BARROWS, CHURCHYARDS, HILLS, MOSQUES, QUAKER MEETING-HOUSES, QUARRIES, RIVERS, RUINS, STATIONS, TEMPLES, YEW.

77

Undercliffe Cemetery, Bradford, Yorkshire.

C H A L K

By the end of the Cretaceous the great dynasties of dinosaurs, ammonites and many others were gone. But the swathes of green marked on geological maps across the south and east of England, with a northern continuation through Lincolnshire and east Yorkshire, marks a time of dying on a truly vast scale. In some cultures white is a sign of mourning, but here we are looking at actual graveyards, for, as Richard Fortey wrote: '*Chalk is fossils . . . organisms in their trillions. Its whiteness, its purity, is the pure calcite manufactured by animals and plants, and here unsullied by sediments from other sources.*'

While not all chalk dates from the late Cretaceous, The Chalk, as it is known, was laid down in great phases at this time reaching depths of a thousand to 1,300 feet. Along the south coast the bastions of the White Cliffs of Dover, the Seven Sisters, the Needles and Old Harry are emblems of England. Where the sea erodes at their feet they are kept glistening, formidable and beautiful, as Neil Featherstone comments: '*Haven Brow and the other Seven Sisters cliffs to the east of the Cuckmere valley looking towards the Birling Gap are unprotected from coastal erosion . . . [they] become undercut on a regular basis ensuring that they remain white in appearance (although when covered in snow they are in fact quite grey). The cliffs at Dover are by and large protected by sea defences and are covered in vegetation.*'

Where the chalk is folded or tilted it faces up to the weather, standing out as rolling downs and heart-soaring vales or steep scarps and long dip slopes. As the sun falls low in the sky or drought parches the tops, a drama of marks is revealed: sheep tracks running parallel with the contours; thousands of ant hills; hollow ways; long ditches and round mounds; terraces, sometimes level, sometimes climbing – lynchets – casting bold, sharp, angular patterns. Spurs, with the rounded contours that mark the edge of the chalk, plunging sometimes one or two

hundred feet, are the sort you could fly from in dreams. The deep, steep-sided, flat-bottomed valleys enclose one in secret and tranquil places. Some are so dramatic they have attracted 'explanatory' names, such as the Devil's Punch Bowl in Surrey. This is one of the iconic landscapes – Frank Newbould's Second World War poster offered the South Downs as a backdrop to the call '*Your Britain, Fight for it now . . .*'

Sixty years on our chalklands are among the most ruined landscapes in the country, farmers drenching them with herbicides and fertilisers and ploughing out the history of several millennia.

On Salisbury Plain, which makes up sixty per cent of the county of Wiltshire, the horizontally bedded chalk gives long, open views with undulations on the scale of an ocean swell. V.S. Naipaul walked near Stonehenge as he attempted to '*shed the nerves of being a stranger in England . . . daily I walked in the wide grassy way between the flint slopes, past chalk valleys rubbled white and looking sometimes like a Himalayan valley strewn in midsummer with old gritted snow*'.

Chalk is porous, permeable like a sponge. This makes for many dry valleys, where water will only run when the rain has filled every pore – sporadic springs and winter-bournes emerge, following the weather with a time lag. Within the chalk, water is naturally purified and stored. The great aquifer fed by the North and South Downs has given London cheaply potable water for generations. The fountains of Trafalgar Square once erupted under artesian pressure from the head of water that was released from the hidden bowl of chalk sandwiched by impermeable clay beneath the city.

Chalk gives us hard water – furred kettles and scum around the bath – but it is good for our bones and bodies. Water companies are now encouraging the movement of water between catchments to the extent that the particularity of geology experienced through water from the tap is being lost.

Being so soft, chalk makes an easily worked building material, but it must be protected from above and below, giving us those beguiling garden walls with little roofs of tile or thatch. Where it is quite hard, as at Uffington in Berkshire, Totternhoe in Bedfordshire and Melbourn in Cambridgeshire, small houses and even churches may be built of clunch – smooth, white blocks. The absence of more durable materials meant that the roofs were made of straw thatch.

Chalk varies from its pure white massive state. In Norfolk the red-and-white-banded cliffs at Hunstanton are red with iron from brachiopod fossils. At Beer in Devon the cliffs are a light cream in colour. Stone quarried above the town hardens in the air and Adela Wright noted that '*at Broadhembury, which is on the high*

Chalk micro-fossils.

ground between Honiton and Exeter, the Beer Stone grows a red lichen and where red lichen grows this Stone weathers best'. The great Yorkshire cliffs at Flamborough Head are of chalk hardened by secondary deposits of calcium carbonate, which makes it more like limestone. The sea seeks out weaknesses along jointing, creating caves, coves and isolated stacks.

The chalk gives up some of its secrets after drought, crop marks often giving the first suggestion of long-lost habitation and activity. Archaeological digs and building sites that have been left bare glow eerily in the darkness. 'Dorset Milestones' were cairns of chalk to see your way by along the ridgeways.

Chalk is the moon's Stone; the skeleton is native to its soil. It looks anaemic, but has submerged the type-sites of successive cultures. Stone, bronze, iron: all are assimilated to its nature; and the hill-forts follow its curves.

Jeremy Hooker, from 'Matrix'

See also ALBION, AMMONITES, ANTY-TUMPS, BARROWS, BEECH, BUILDING STONES, CAVES, CHALK STREAMS, COB, DEW PONDS, DOWNLAND, EXMOOR PONIES, FLINT, GLOW-WORMS, HENGES & STONE CIRCLES, HILL FIGURES, HILL-FORTS, HOLLOW WAYS, JUNIPER, LIME-KILNS, LOST VILLAGES, LYNCHETS, OLD MAN'S BEARD, PANTILES, RACECOURSES, SEA CAVES, SHEEP, SPRINGS, STACKS, THATCH, TURF MAZES, WHITE HORSES, WINTERBOURNES, YEW.

CHALK STREAMS

It is a bold claim, but it was made by Barbara Young and Andy Brown, chief executives of the Environment Agency and English Nature. '*There are 161 chalk rivers and streams across England – more than in any other country in the world . . .*' With their clear, cool water and unique panoply of animal and plant life, they are like no other places in the land.

The closely observed painting by Millais of Ophelia floating in the '*glassy Stream*' evokes the complexity of nature with extreme care. Great drifts of water crowfoot and starwort offer hiding places for brown trout, while watercress and lesser water parsnip thrive along the edges. The gentle, stable flow and gravelly bottom ensure good anchorage for a host of aquatic plants.

Fed from underground chalk aquifers with a constant temperature of eleven degrees Celsius, the streams are charged with calcium, enabling freshwater shrimps, crayfish and water snails to build carapace and shell. They are also rich in dissolved plant nutrients: nitrates, phosphates and potassium. Mayflies feed trout and salmon, which in turn are sought by anglers equipped with their own, man-made flies. Other fish join in the feast: the grayling, with a penchant for freshwater shrimp;

and the bullhead, or miller's thumb, with its flattened head, which forages and hides among the stones. Otters, water voles and water shrews, together with mink, relish life in these streams, too, while kingfishers make nests in their banks.

The most famous chalk streams, especially to anglers, arise from Salisbury Plain in Wiltshire and the Hampshire Downs, running south to the Solent as the rivers Avon, Test, Itchen and Meon. But chalk streams also reach north to the Kennet and Lambourn, and further west, to the Frome in Dorset. In the Yorkshire Wolds above Beverley they are rich in trout, feeding the river Hull, which on reaching flat land changes personality dramatically as it crosses to enter the Humber and name a town on the way. In East Anglia they feed the upper reaches of the Nar. These streams are Sites of Special Scientific Interest, designated by English Nature for their rich wildlife. The Itchen and Hampshire Avon, with its sea- and brook lampreys and Desmoulin's whorl snail, are ranked among the best natural places in Europe.

Over many centuries, these streams and rivers have been exploited by entrepreneurs, to drive mills, keep a network of canals afloat, warm and fertilise water meadows. Watercress beds change the landscape in some valley bottoms, where springs are exploited for their purity and even temperature.

Weed cutting by scythe is a traditional technique used to control flooding and improve game fishing – plants growing in profusion slow down the water and can be beneficial for some creatures, but if they trap silt and cover bare gravel they inhibit salmon and trout spawning. But cutting is now often done mechanically from boats, and the scale, frequency and impact are detrimental to the complex cycles of plant growth. For a century or more the dominant water crowfoot has been cut once or twice a year, to control flooding and to make fishing easier. But over the past decade or more, it has often been in short supply, as have aquatic flies, with their evocative common names: mayfly; iron blue; sedge or caddis fly; large dark, medium and blue-winged olive. Anglers talk of 'chalk stream malaise' to describe the decline they notice. The Environment Agency has concluded that the likely culprits are low flow rates and pollution from intensive agriculture, fish farms and sewage.

To the chagrin of local people in Hertfordshire and Kent, some streams, notably the Misbourne in the Chilterns, completely ran dry in the 1990s due to over-exploitation – in many places abstraction from chalk aquifers is progressing at such a rate that rain replenishment cannot keep up, especially in years of drought.

See also BECKS, BOURNES, BROOKS, BURNS, CHALK, DIALECTS, DOWNLAND, FORDS, GHYLLS, RHYNES, RIVERS, SOUGHS, WATERCRESS BEDS, WATER-MEADOWS, WINTERBOURNES.

79

THE CHANNEL

Claimed on these shores as the English Channel, but La Manche to the French, the Channel is an ancient riverbed that has evolved into an ever-changing sea. Linking the North Sea and the Atlantic Ocean, this unpredictable waterway has been central to our evolution. Both barrier and vital corridor, the Channel is replete with contradictions. When travel by water was easier than by land (or air), it united more than it divided, yet remained a source of patriotic pride as a barrier.

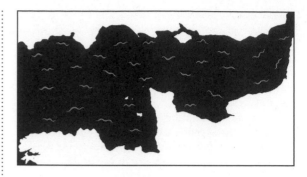

Invasion, or the threat of it, has long been central to the Channel's symbolic life. Pompey dismissed the Channel as an insignificant mud-flat, Napoleon considered it a '*ditch to be jumped*'. To Shakespeare, however, in the wake of the defeat of the Spanish Armada, it was '*a moat defensive to a house*'. Small yachts and oil tankers treat it with respect. Today it is probably the busiest shipping channel in the world, with ferries running like buses between French and English ports and crossing through traffic from the Baltic and Atlantic. Underneath lies a multitude of telecommunications cables, the oldest dating from the Victorian era, and a rail tunnel – the world's longest undersea construction, completed in 1993 after a century of debate and trial borings.

'*England's white cliffs are more conspicuous from France than is the French shore from Britain*', wrote Michael Bonavia, a railway man who directed an abortive attempt to build a tunnel under the Channel in the 1970s. '*In fine weather, Dover's residents, however, can enjoy reading the time of day through a telescope focussed on the town hall clock in Calais.*'

Covering some thirty thousand square miles and a hundred miles at its widest at Finisterre, the Channel is at its narrowest just 21 miles from France, at the Strait of Dover, stretching from Dungeness to South Foreland in Kent. In the Strait, the water is shallow, 220 feet at most. Yet unique tidal streams, strong winds and heavy sea fogs that arise with disconcerting suddenness can make navigating the Channel a challenge. Between November and February, winds of force seven or eight can be expected on up to fifteen days a month, accentuating the short, steep waves so dreaded by travellers. Humps in the seabed add to the hazards – the Varne bank, midway between Cap Gris Nez and Dover, for instance, lies thirty feet below the surface at high tide and is marked by a lightship.

The Channel was cut by a massive European river system, the Greater Seine, as it flowed west into the Atlantic. But at various times during the past few thousand years, as the climate in the middle Pleistocene fluctuated between warm and cold spells, a ridge of chalk joined England to the continental landmass, enabling migrants – human and non-human – to recolonise the land when ice retreated. The first humans are believed to have walked here some half a million years ago, dated from fossil fauna and flint hand-axes recently discovered at Boxgrove in west Sussex.

The last important cold period was at its height thirteen thousand years ago, when a sheet of ice three-quarters of a mile thick sat over Scotland and north-west England. As the climate warmed over a few thousand years, hunter-gatherers crossed the North Sea and the Channel, still dry because of low sea levels. But as more ice melted, the landmass began to recover from the weight, rising in Scotland and the South East but tilting into the sea in the South West. Britain became an island again perhaps five thousand years ago.

The Channel west of the Solent remains distinctly different from its eastern reaches in Kent and Sussex, where medieval harbours, at Rye and Winchelsea, for instance, were stranded by a retreating coastline. Ports in the west, meanwhile, such as Southampton, Portsmouth, Dartmouth and Plymouth, prospered, especially as trade with the Americas developed.

Long the domain of fishermen, the Channel is now being dredged for sand and gravel to meet rising demand for concrete to build roads and houses in the South East. Plans are under way to mine some two hundred million tons from the Median Deep, midway between the Sussex coast and northern France. Such substantial damage to the sea-bed will harm fisheries, other marine life and archaeology, which is entering a new phase. English Heritage has begun an exciting three-dimensional survey of territorial waters in the Channel and North Sea, which might show ancient settlements and throw light on artefacts that are occasionally brought up in nets.

See also ALBION, CHALK, CHINES, CLOCKS, COASTLINE, COASTS, ESTUARIES, FLOODS, FOG & MIST, FORTIFICATIONS, FRETS, HARBOURS, ISLANDS, LIGHTHOUSES, LOST VILLAGES, RIAS, RIVERS, SEA FISH, SHIPPING FORECAST, WEATHER, WHITE CLIFFS.

CHAPELS

Chapels are easily recognised as a building type despite their local and regional variations and changes in their architectural styles over the years.

Widely dispersed but most prevalent in poorer mining and industrial areas, where nonconformists or dissenters flourished, many have been altered, fallen into disuse or been demolished. Recognition of their cultural, social, historical and architectural merit has been slow in coming. Their earlier proliferation has led us to take them for granted. But English Heritage now believes that they '*represent one of the most threatened building types in England*', particularly in rural areas.

Following the Toleration Act of 1689, there was a rush of chapel building before 1700. Almost two and a half thousand chapels, known as meeting-houses, were registered. Early surviving examples are modest externally and could be mistaken for domestic buildings except for their large windows.

The South West, and in particular west and central Cornwall, has been a stronghold of nonconformity, especially Methodism, since 1743. By 1851 Methodism had become the dominant religion and chapels had become '*a prominent feature of the Cornish landscape*', according to the Cornwall Archaeological Unit. The buildings vary from small roadside chapels seating fifty, made by local builders from local materials, such as cob and thatch, stone and slate, to the imposing architect-designed buildings of the larger towns – Camborne, Penzance, Redruth, St Just and Truro – which can accommodate hundreds.

The early town chapels are the most elegant, with their granite ashlar classical pediments, tall, round-headed windows and doors with fanlights, and double tiers of large (often sash) windows with clear glass on the side walls. Porches were often added later, indeed, most chapels have been repeatedly enlarged and altered to meet changing needs. Many built after 1850 were influenced by the Gothic revival and resemble Victorian Anglican churches with spires.

The simple exteriors of the earlier buildings hide wonderful spaces and beautiful interiors, many of which are modelled on London's City Road Chapel of 1778.

Wooden galleries along the side walls and west end are supported by wooden columns and fixed pews in the centre, with the pulpit as the focal point (later replaced by a rostrum) in front of the communion table. Many smaller chapels did not have a gallery and were paid for by pew rents – stained or varnished boxed pews with doors were placed in the centre of the chapel, later replaced with pitch-pine pews. Medium-sized chapels often had a gallery at one end, while in the larger ones it could be shaped like a horseshoe or oval.

Wesley's favourite chapel was the Octagon chapel in Norwich, built for the Presbyterians in 1754. He described it as '*perhaps the most elegant one [meeting-house] in Europe*'. The Methodist chapels at Yarm (1763) and Heptonstall (1764) in Yorkshire are also octagonal.

Chapels built by the Presbyterians, Independents, Unitarians, Baptists, Bible Christians, Methodists and their recombinations are similar in style, while the meeting-houses of the Quakers have an elegant austerity of their own.

The Methodists were the most prolific chapel builders. They built them where there was a need, unencumbered by parochial boundaries. In Cornwall nearly a thousand were built, 275 of which survive in use now; 106 of these are listed, but listing does not guarantee their survival. Many have been converted to houses. For local people the importance may lie in their familiarity in the street scene. The main aim of English Heritage and others is to conserve the chapels that retain most of their original features and fittings and to find new uses for the rest.

Champion of the unfashionable, John Betjeman wrote in 1952 of his love of nonconformist chapels, '*the true architecture of the people . . . despised by architects, ignored by guide books, too briefly mentioned by directories, these variegated conventicles are witnesses of the taste of industrial Britain*'.

See also CHURCHES, MOSQUES, QUAKER MEETING-HOUSES, SYNAGOGUES, TEMPLES, TIN TABERNACLES.

81

Tredizzick, Cornwall; New Road, Upper Tean, Staffordshire.

CHEDDAR CHEESE

If you go to Cheddar Gorge in Somerset you can once more buy a locally made Cheddar cheese. Authentic traditional foods made in the place they are named after are not easy to come by in England, and no doubt the tourists buy some to take away (we did). This is how Cheddar cheese originally got its reputation and name – people who came to see this extraordinary limestone gorge, and later the caves, ate the local cheese at inns and hostelries.

Cheese making in Cheddar has a long tradition. A local story relates that long ago milk was stored in the caves, and there was great excitement when it was found in its more solid (and delicious) form. The lush pastures of the West Country are ideal for dairy cattle, and hard cheese made in Somerset, Devon and Dorset took on the name of Cheddar.

Cheddar was being made in Tudor England, if not before. By the seventeenth century, cheeses were made co-operatively by farmers with small daily yields of cow's milk, which led to the creation of cheeses as big as ninety to 120 pounds in weight. These could take from two to five years to mature, resulting in a fine, close texture, described by Defoe as '*the best cheese that England affords*'.

The cheese was a luxury in the seventeenth and eighteenth centuries, but was already being sold to London market buyers and others at important regional fairs, such as Bridgwater Fair in Somerset, St Giles's Fair in Winchester and Weyhill Fair in Hampshire.

Methods were greatly improved in the nineteenth century by influential cheese makers Joseph Harding, T.C. Candy and Henry Cannon, and were practised in a school for cheese making founded by the Bath and West Southern Counties Society in 1890. The First World War signalled the beginning of a hard time for the producers – many small farmers gave up cheese making, while the manufacture of block cheese by farms and large creameries increased. Rigid grading of hard cheese by the Ministry of Food reduced local diversity by favouring the '*harder, drier, uniform type*', said Patrick Rance, a passionate advocate of traditional British farmhouse cheeses. In 1939 only 333 farms in the South West were making Cheddar and by 1988 this had reduced to 25, eleven of which were using traditional methods.

In his *Great British Cheese Book*, Rance said Somerset's traditional cheese was still '*England's greatest cheese gift to*

the world', but went on to say that authentic handmade farmhouse Cheddar had become very rare. This was in 1982, and now, thanks to him and the Specialist Cheesemakers' Association, handmade Cheddar and other local and regional cheeses are making a gradual comeback.

Currently, according to Neal's Yard Dairy, which sells and promotes specialist cheeses from all over the country in its London shops, there are only ten farms in the West Country making traditional Cheddar. Predominantly they use their own milk, sometimes unpasteurised, with old-fashioned starters and traditional cheddaring (cutting and turning) processes. Their Cheddars have a cylindrical shape and are wrapped in cloth 'bandages' to allow them to breathe as they mature.

The name Cheddar cheese has no protection. The cat was let out of the bag long ago by British colonists, who made their own versions of the cheese wherever they went. According to Rance, '*the honourable name of Cheddar has been given away to all the world, and is now equated in its home country with mouse-trap fodder*'.

Cheese making has come full circle: Wookey Caves, a stone's throw from Cheddar's underground cathedrals, is being used once again to store locally made Cheddar at a constant temperature.

See also BESTIARY, BLUE VINNEY, CATTLE, CAVES, CHEESE, DOUBLE GLOUCESTER, FAIRS & FAIRGROUNDS, FIELDS, FOOD, GORGES, SHEEP, STILTON, WENSLEYDALE CHEESE.

CHEESE

'*Our really fine cheeses are lost to England*', Dorothy Hartley wrote in 1954. She would be delighted to find that there has since been a renaissance in English cheese making. Now roughly fifteen per cent of all home-produced cheeses are from small-scale makers, who are putting the taste and goodness back into one of our favourite foods and forging a new reputation for local cheeses.

Making cheese is one of the things we have done really well. England's lush pastures produced fine dairy cows, and cheese makers made good use of the milk produced at different times of the year and of the subtle differences between morning and evening milkings. As Dorothy Hartley explained, '*All milk varies during the year, and in most of the individual cheeses there was some definite seasonal reason for the excellence of the cheese. For example a*

Mary Holbrook's Mendip, Tyning, Tymsboro, Emlett and Little Rydings, Somerset.

'moorland" cheese was only made in spring, when the winter, hay-fed cattle went out and grazed the scented alder and new grass on the mountains.'

By the eighteenth century the characteristics of cheeses made in different parts of the country were recognised. Our most famous cheeses became known in the trade as territorials – Cheshire, Cheddar, Derby, Double Gloucester, Lancashire, Leicester, Stilton, Wensleydale. Small-scale cheese making flourished and annual cheese fairs were part of the calendar.

According to Dorothy Hartley, 'the end of individual localised cheese came with the development of motor transport. Milk collecting became easy, so the makers in the large cheese centres took over the small local trade, and closed down the local cheese-making, and in about fifty years over fifty different types of English cheese had ceased to exist! The milk marketing scheme completed what was already begun.'

Made in factories, or creameries, from the 1870s, the territorials began to lose their distinctive tastes and some could not be told apart. By the turn of the twentieth century we were importing 'cheddar' from Canada and New Zealand. Many cheese makers gave up before or after the First World War.

At the outbreak of the Second World War, the remaining 1,600 small cheese farms were still producing nearly a quarter of the country's cheese. But in order to conserve resources the Ministry of Food decreed that only hard cheeses should be made. According to cheese enthusiast Patrick Rance, 'all the soft cheeses were written off'. During and after the war even more cheese makers quit. To make matters more difficult, cheese was rationed until 1954.

When Patrick Rance was researching his book on British cheeses in 1982 he found our traditional cheeses close to extinction. We were buying soft cheese from France and plastic-wrapped supermarket block cheese that lacked character, and the pasteurisation of milk 'brought about a standardisation'.

The Specialist Cheesemakers' Association was formed in 1989 in response to the Ministry of Agriculture's proposed ban on selling cheese made from raw milk. There has since been a resurgence in cheese handmade by small producers, boosted by the annual British Cheese Festival, the hard work of creative protagonists.

Randolph Hodgson started making and then selling cheese from Neal's Yard Dairy in Covent Garden, London in 1979. He recalls that 'one day a sweaty little piece of cheese, tightly wrapped in cling film, arrived in the post. Hilary Charnley had sent us some of her handmade Devon Garland. The cheese tasted good, but more exciting still was the thought that there was a real person, not a machine, producing this cheese.' He goes on: 'Farm cheese is almost always made on the farm itself. This makes a difference not only because milk from different pastures has special flavours, but because using

milk from just one farm enables the cheese makers to have much closer control over the quality of that milk.'

According to Devon cheese seller Guy Garrett, impetus came from the introduction of milk quotas. 'When farmers saw that they weren't going to have a market for all of their milk, they were prompted to diversify . . . Some started making ice-cream, some started making butter, and some, prompted by the invasion of French cheeses, started making cheese. Devon is a tremendous milk-producing area, so it had one of the biggest problems in terms of excess milk. That's what really made the whole thing take off.' Even in Cornwall, not a county renowned for its cheeses, sixty varieties are being made, such as Cornish Brie, Cornish Smoke, Nanterrow, St Endellion, Stithians Special, Tintagel Organic and Tresco.

Now at the British Cheese Awards there are about 750 British cheeses on show, many of which are soft ewe's- and goat's-milk cheeses. New cheeses, such as Lincolnshire Poacher, Cornish Yarg, Norfolk White Lady, Yorkshire Blue and Sussex Yeoman, may become the new territorials.

See also BLUE VINNEY, CATTLE, CHEDDAR CHEESE, DOUBLE GLOUCESTER, FAIRS & FAIRGROUNDS, FIELDS, FOOD, STILTON, WENSLEYDALE CHEESE.

C H E E S E   R O L L I N G

Chasing a cheese down a precipitous one-in-two slope has taken place for hundreds of years on the common at Cooper's Hill in Brockworth, Gloucestershire, even during the Second World War, when cheese was rationed. Cheese rolling was part of the Whitsun Monday Wake, together with other bizarre sports that were suppressed by the Victorians for being too boisterous. Since 1967 the event has been held on Spring Bank Holiday Monday.

Its origin is thought to be connected with ensuring that local people maintained their rights to graze the common. But it has recently been discovered that cheese rolling used to take place on Midsummer Day, so originally it may have

Kirkham's Lancashire.

been linked to an attempt to capture the waning sun, as midsummer bonfires were purported to do.

At noon the participants gather at the summit of the hill around the maypole, which has a cockerel on its top. The Master of Ceremonies, wearing a white coat and top hat tied with ribbons, hands the thick-crusted, wheel-shaped, seven-pound Double Gloucester cheese to the Starter, or Roller. At the count of three the Starter sends it rolling down the two-hundred-yard hill; on the count of four the brave (foolhardy) chasers, all men, tumble after it. Many sustain broken limbs and bruised heads and are administered to by a rescue team, Rapid UK. Whoever catches the cheese or reaches the bottom first may keep the cheese. After three men's races, a women's race follows, then several uphill races for children. All of this is watched by four thousand or so spectators located behind safety fences, some of whom no doubt end up in the nearby pub in Shurdington, The Cheese Rollers.

Cheese rolling used to be more widespread. Thomas Hughes describes it as one of the games that accompanied the scouring of the Uffington White Horse in the eighteenth century, in which a cheese was rolled down a hill known as the Horse's Manger.

Three cheeses are blessed and rolled three times anti-clockwise around the church at Randwick, near Stroud in Gloucestershire, on the first Sunday in May, an old custom revived in 1972. One is carried to the village green and eaten, the others are kept for the Randwick Wap Fair on the following Saturday, when they are chased down the steep slopes of Well Leaze.

See also CATTLE, COMMONS, DOUBLE GLOUCESTER, FAIRS & FAIRGROUNDS, GAMES, MAYPOLES, MIDSUMMER DAY, WEATHER-VANES, WHITE HORSES.

C H E R R I E S

Those fortunate enough to have seen the magnificent sixty-foot-tall cherry tree orchards in springtime in Kent will never forget them – blossom as far as the eye could see. Now if cherries are grown at all in Kent they are likely to be grafted onto dwarf rootstock, and their impact is small. With the tall trees, Rebecca Hubbard wrote, have gone the special '50-foot stale (rung) ladder', which tapered

towards the top, the 'cherriers (pickers) with "ladder skills" for harvesting' and the Romney sheep that used to graze beneath their forty-foot-wide canopies. Going, too, are the old Kent varieties – Amber Heart, Goodnestone Black, Ham Green Black, Kentish Red (with transparent juice), Malling Black Eagle, Newington Late Black, Rock Heart, Rodmersham Seedling, Sutton's Purple, Webb's Black and Wye Morello (grown for Kentish cherry brandy) – together with cherry ale, cherry wine, cherry fritters and cherry pie.

Dudley Stamp, in his land use survey of 1943, recorded that 'about 20 well-known kinds of eating cherries are grown in Kent, and they differ in dates of ripening as much as in other ways'. Cherry expert Norman Grubb said six years later that 'The best cherry orchards are always found on the deep brick earths' and that the heart of cherry cultivation was Kent, on the brick earths around Sittingbourne and Faversham, but also in parts of Berkshire, Buckinghamshire and Hertfordshire.

In south-west Hertfordshire cherries and apples were the main crop. Caroon and Small Black were the main varieties grown because, according to Arthur Young in 1804, 'the Kentish will not thrive here at all'. A relict cherry orchard in Croxley Green has been saved as a Community Orchard and replanted with local Croome (Caroon) and Hertfordshire Black cherries, plums and apples. In Buckinghamshire, Prestwood Black cherries, known locally as 'chuggies', and Caroons were collected for Cherry Pie Sunday, the first in August. Fairs have recently been revived at Seer Green in Buckinghamshire (Cherry Pie Fair) and at Stowmarket (Suffolk Cherry Fair).

Grafted onto wild cherry seedlings found in woods in the Tamar valley in Devon and Cornwall, mazzards, such as Burcombe and Birchenhayes, were often named after the farms where they were first grown. According to Virginia Spiers, Mary Martin and James Evans, who have been recording and replanting local varieties, mazzards grew on the Devonshire bank and in the sheltered valleys among the apple orchards and market gardens on the Cornish side. Paddle steamers from Plymouth would bring day trippers up the Tamar to see the spectacular springtime blossom. As Virginia Spiers recalls: 'Such was the celebration of the cherry that Pentillie estate, downriver from Cotehele, held an annual cherry feast, when huge cherry pies were cooked for local children . . . This festival has recently been re-established at St Mellion.' One magnificent orchard of tall trees remains at Bohetherick.

Only a few of the mazzard greens remain; for more than four

hundred years they produced Big Dun, Small Dun, Green Stem Black and Bottlers around the north Devon villages of Landkey, Swimbridge and Harford. One story has it that scions were brought over, mainly from France, by the Huguenots fleeing persecution. In Landkey a new Millennium Mazzard Green has ensured the continuity of these local fruits.

The Wyre Forest in Shropshire was a centre of cherry cultivation and, in *A Shropshire Lad*, A.E. Housman reminded us that the wild cherry, much appreciated by bees and birds, lit up the woods, too:

> *Loveliest of trees, the cherry now*
> *Is hung with bloom along the bough,*
> *And stands about the woodland ride*
> *Wearing white for Eastertide.*

After a big decline, which started in the 1950s, cherry growing may be making a comeback with new, disease-resistant varieties and dwarf trees that can be grown under polytunnels to prevent the fruits from splitting after rain. But the soul and the splendour is virtually lost from the landscape. The tall trees offered places for camping and picnicking, under-grazing by sheep and chickens, inter-cropping by daffodils or soft fruit – a multiple use of the land that dwarf trees cannot supply.

See also ANCIENT TREES, APPLE DAY, APPLES, APRICOTS, COBNUTS, DAMSONS, FOOD, FROST & FROST HOLLOWS, HAZEL, HONEY & BEES, LICHENS, MIDSUMMER DAY, MISTLETOE, NURSERIES, ORCHARDS, PEARS, PLUMS.

C H E R T

Chert is solid silicate, a hard rock similar to flint, though it is less predictable to knap. It is found not in chalk but in Carboniferous limestone, mainly in the Pennines from Derbyshire to Lancashire and Yorkshire. Around Bakewell in the White Peak, the most extensive use of 'hornstone' has been in the manufacture of ceramics: extracted from Holme Hall, Holme Bank and Pretoria mines, it was used in the bone-grinding mills for bone china and as a whitening agent for earthenware.

Chert varies a great deal in colour and texture. Sometimes occurring together in bands, white chert betrays granular quartz, whereas black chert is finely crystalline. Neolithic and Beaker people made arrowheads from priz* black chert mined around Bakewell.

In the Blackdown Hills of east Devon and south Somerset, chert-stone houses and boundary walls catch the eye; the small, knobbly, yellow-brown buildings, edged with brick or with Hamstone, cluster around Whitestaunton and Higher Wambrook.

See also BUILDING STONES, CHALK, FLINT, GREENSAND, LIMESTONE.

CHESHIRE RAILINGS

Hedges were replaced by one hundred and ten miles of iron railings at Cheshire road junctions and dangerous corners in 1929 to give better sightlines. At a time when motor transport was increasing it was a county councillor who suggested these simple iron railings to improve road safety. Effort is now going into restoring the eighty-odd miles that remain. Where they are not rusting away they are painted white, and around Bosley, every fifth upright and the bottom of the five rungs is painted black. Curved over and in towards the field at the top, they are also called hurdle fences.

Still known as Cheshire railings, they can be found on the bends of roads in other parts of the country; around Braceborough in Lincolnshire, attempts have been made to encourage the local authority to re-erect and paint them.

See also DRYSTONE WALLS, HEDGES, RAILINGS.

CHIMNEYS

Britain is said to have the most beautiful chimneys in the world. The amazing craftsmanship of elaborate Tudor spiral, fluted, hexagonal, tall brick and terracotta chimney stacks, with zigzag, chevron and diamond patterns, can still be seen on grand houses, especially in the South East. They were followed in Victorian times by Gothic Revival imitations.

Their vernacular cousins are even more interesting, since they represent generations of fine-tuning. The resulting regional and local differences and huge range of stacks and pots often reflect the difficulties of mastering the vagaries of the wind rather than architectural vanity.

The London roll, Quaker pot, fluted beehive, beaded cannon-head, tulip, bottle pot, rook, castle, tallboy and

85

crown pot are just a few of the different types of chimney pot mentioned in the National Clayware Federation's catalogue of 1964, which listed nearly five hundred. It included 102 varieties of plain round chimney pot, sixty square pots, 54 octagonal and 147 ornamental round ones. They were (and some still are) made by firms such as Doulton's, near Tamworth in Staffordshire, and Kinson Pottery of Parkstone in Dorset. Measham in Derbyshire is underlain by clays that make fine chimney pots, ranging from Lancashire bishop to Lady Broughton, horned cap and tea can with lid.

There is variety, too, in positioning. Large external chimneys on the long sides of houses are found in Devon, Cornwall, Exmoor and the north Somerset coast, whereas brick chimneys were built in the centre of timber-framed buildings in Suffolk and the South East to support the wooden structures. In north-east Norfolk the chimney is usually placed in the gable end, as it is in the Cotswolds. Thatched roofs required careful building of tall stone or brick chimneys to keep sparks from the reed or straw. The tall, round, stone chimney is a feature of the South West. A booklet, *Building on Exmoor*, published by Somerset County Council for two shillings and sixpence, stated that '*The vale lands of the Moor near the coast are noteworthy for their round chimney stacks and this method of construction went with round masonry gateposts and round masonry columns for the linhays of the farms.*'

Enthusiast and collector Valentine Fletcher, who has written one of the few monographs on chimneys, claims that arriving blindfolded he could '*tell you what region we are in by a look at the nearest vernacular chimneys or chimney pots*'. He believes the Lake District is '*the region which has probably the most striking chimney arrangements of all in Great Britain*'. They were first admired by Wordsworth: '*Nor will the singular beauty of the chimneys escape the eye of the attentive traveller. Sometimes a low chimney, almost upon a level with the roof, is overlaid with a slate, supported upon four slender pillars, to prevent the wind from driving the smoke down the chimney. Others are of a quadrangular shape, rising one or two feet above the roof; which low square is often surmounted by a tall cylinder, giving to the cottage chimney the most beautiful shape in which it is ever seen. Nor will it be too fanciful or refined to remark, that there is a pleasing harmony between a tall chimney of this circular form, and the living column of smoke, ascending from it through the still air.*'

Other distinctive types noted by Fletcher in the Lake District include '*four slates peaked at the tops, surmounted by a slate and kept in position by a big stone*' and '*two slanting slates meeting together over a chimney-hole*'. He goes on: '*The stone areas of Yorkshire, Lancashire and Derbyshire are characterised by modest solid stacks with good copings, and baked fireclay chimney pots*', whereas '*splendid seventeenth-*

century stepped and buttressed chimneys may be seen from Halifax in the West Riding to Coxwold in the East Riding.

'*In the Midland clay belt*', he continues, '*one notices chiefly the plain brick stacks, often very tall, bearing buff or red pots. These are mainly gable stacks. The prominent chimney pots are the Bishop and the square pot.*' Also distinctive, he says, are the '*old black pots of Norfolk*' and the '*fine rust-red pots and many tallboys of outsize dimensions*' in the Reading area. The '*proud Fareham Reds, banded near the top with white ornamentation . . . [are] perhaps the handsomest chimney pot in Britain*'. The magnificent tallboys of London and Reading, reaching seven and a half feet, were installed to outreach the tall buildings close by.

Reuse is better than recycling, and salvaged pots can be found, for example, at Longport in the Potteries, Staffordshire, where Cherished Chimneys also has a small chimney pot museum.

Few new houses are built with working chimneys, but they have non-functional ones to break up the roofline. Apart from their obvious function, chimneys provide ventilation and homes for jackdaws, which drop sticks down the pot until they become lodged and stable. Chimneys on new buildings could be designed specially for them and other birds.

Cowls, designed to increase or minimise draughts, add further interest. Brighton has an array; more are found on the Kent coast. Huge, revolving, brightly coloured cowls excite the eye on the new BedZed buildings in Sutton, Surrey. At the Earth Centre near Conisbrough, Yorkshire they will turn in the lightest wind to help with air circulation and heat exchange. Perhaps a new generation of rotating cowls will begin to take the place of the traditional chimney in the 'carbon neutral' world we must invent.

See also ALMSHOUSES, BRICKS, BUILDING STONES, COTTAGES, GABLES, INDUSTRIAL CHIMNEYS, SLATES.

From top left, clockwise: Lake District; Essex Tudor; Nottingham; South Hams, Devon.

C H I N A T O W N S

At the beginning of the twentieth century around five hundred Chinese people were resident in England. A century later there were more than one hundred thousand in London alone. Migration began in the seventeenth century, steadily increasing from the eighteenth, prompted by the work of the East India Company and, later, the English-engineered opium wars. Initially, Chinese settlers provided services for their country's sailors passing through the docks, but over time their laundries and, later (especially after the Second World War), restaurants and takeaways, became widely known and appreciated.

Limehouse Causeway in east London had a self-supporting Chinese community by the 1880s, with shops, restaurants and seamen's hostels. Life was fraught with abuse, and their clubs and fongs (meeting places) offered sanctuary. Trade decline and bombing during the 1930s and 1940s changed the area's nature, but places such as the Young Friends in Pennyfields survive, succeeding the Good Friends and Old Friends in Mandarin Street. Street names – Canton, Nankin, Pekin and Ming Streets – recall this strand of social history.

Post-war Soho provided homes for the dispossessed: today's Chinatown is in and around Gerrard Street ('the Imperial City' to the Chinese), where the clatter of mah-jong tiles and the rhythms of languages, smells and colours create a potent atmosphere.

The first Chinatown to be known as such was in Liverpool rather than London. Chinese settlement around the docks began in the 1830s, but, as in London, its inhabitants were displaced by wartime bombs. Subsequently the Chinatown formed around Nelson Street and George Square, announced by six bronze lions on podia. Manchester opened its first Chinese restaurant in 1948; Birmingham in 1959. Both cities now have established Chinatowns, the former gathered around Faulkner Street, the latter in Snow Hill. Newcastle upon Tyne's is the most recent, growing on Stowell Street from 1982.

Chinatowns are communities rather than simply retail centres or tourist attractions, the focus of many social projects. Festivals are organised and Chinese New Year celebrations draw significant crowds. Chinatowns adopt Chinese references and imagery in design, architecture, street furniture and script, and have their individual grand gestures: three Cantonese-inscribed steel gateways in London; Imperial Arches in Manchester and Liverpool; and Birmingham's seven-storey granite pagoda.

See also CHINESE NEW YEAR, DRAGONS, FOOD.

C H I N E S

In past times landing contraband and smuggling it inland must have been easier under the cover of the steep, woody ravines through soft, sandy cliffs that are peculiar to the Dorset, Hampshire and Isle of Wight coasts. Chines were eroded by short, small streams after the Ice Age and made more precarious by clay slides. In Poole and Bournemouth they are more domesticated, filled since Victorian times

Imperial Arch, Liverpool.

Flaghead Chine Canford Cliffs Chine Branksome Chine Branksome Dene Chine Alum Chine Middle Chine Great Durley Chine Little Durley Chine Bournemouth Pier

W   E

with rhododendrons and pines. John Betjeman captured their spirit: '*Walk the asphalt paths of Branksome Chine/ In resin scented air like strong Greek wine.*'

There are nineteen chines on the southern side of the Isle of Wight; a dozen between Shanklin and Freshwater, with names such as Shippards, Cowlease, Ladder, Blackgang and Shanklin, which has a dramatic forty-foot waterfall. From the air some look like little rifts, others are great clefts, yawning gaps, exactly what the word *cinan* meant in Saxon. On the ground they are exciting, small-scale landscapes, some grazed, some wooded, rumpled with landslips, always changing, perfect for exploring. At Mackerel Rail people stood lookout on the cliff top for fish, shouts going down to the beach for the boat to encircle the shoal with a seine net, which could be pulled in to the shore. In 1758 a 63-foot whale was marooned here and the name changed to Whale Chine. The chine itself is changing; recent landslips have cut off steps to the beach.

These southerly secret valleys are often the first landfall for migrating birds in spring, affording them shelter and food before they travel on. Butterflies also find them, and sea pink, bird's-foot trefoil and rock sea spurrey tempt other visitors, too.

See also CLIFFS, DENES, LANDSLIPS.

CHINESE NEW YEAR

Festivities last for fifteen days, starting on the eve of the new moon on the last day of the twelfth lunar month and ending with the full moon. The dates therefore vary from late January to mid-February. The celebration is for the arrival of spring and the beginning of the agricultural year.

Each of the twelve years of the lunar calendar is named after an animal, the twelve that came at the bidding of Buddha before he departed from earth, including the rat, dragon, snake and monkey. The nature of the beast that rules the year are thought to influence its character and those of the people born in that year: '*The year of the Ox is reckoned to demand hard work from everybody*', Ian McAuley wrote.

Preparations for the holiday involve a thorough cleaning of the house, the paying of outstanding financial debts and the buying of new clothes and food. Scrolls of red paper bearing poetic couplets wishing good luck, health and prosperity are hung on doors and windows.

New Year's Eve dinner is the highlight of the festivities, when families get together to remember their ancestors and feast on traditional foods. Many of these are eaten because of the sound of their names. According to James Kell, fish is eaten because the word for fish – *yu* – also means luck. Dumplings – *jiaozi* – are popular because the word can sound like 'replacement' – of the old with the new. Red clothes are worn to frighten the legendary monster Nian (also the word for 'year'), who '*came out for his supper on the last day of the lunar year and gobbled people up . . . Fire, red cloth and the crack of a whip*' were the most successful ways of keeping him at bay. So firecrackers are set off at the beginning of the meal and at midnight, together with fireworks.

On New Year's Day relatives, friends and neighbours are visited and gifts exchanged. Traditionally, married couples pass on their luck and give children and single adults money in decorated red envelopes – a custom known as *Hung Boa* ('red packet').

In Newcastle, Manchester, Birmingham, Liverpool and London, street celebrations are held in Chinatown on the Sunday nearest to New Year's Day. Loud music from gongs, cymbals and drums, accompanied by firecrackers, heralds the Lion (or dragon), whose famous dances frighten evil away and bring good luck.

The Lion, with its enormous papier-mâché head, gaping mouth and long, sinuous body, which is animated by performers hidden beneath a bright cloth, dances down the streets, stopping to snap at and collect the lettuce leaves and attached money that are hung down from the first-storey windows or doors of houses, shops and restaurants. This traditional custom, called *Choi Cheng*, or 'picking the green', involves the lion in chewing and spitting out the leaves (which signifies future abundance), then taking the red packet of money in its mouth, bringing luck to the household or business.

The celebrations end with a Festival of Lanterns on the fifteenth day, when lanterns are hung in houses, rice dumplings eaten and the last of the fireworks exploded.

See also BESTIARY, BONFIRE NIGHT, DIWALI, DRAGONS, EASTER CUSTOMS, MELAS, MOON, 'OBBY 'OSSES.

88

CHOUGHS

In England the chough lives more in our imagination, folklore and heraldry than in reality. If you are fortunate enough to see one of these striking black, red-legged, red-billed members of the crow family, you are likely to be on the cliffs of Cornwall. As a result of persecution they had deserted the coasts of Sussex, Kent, Hampshire, the Isle of Wight, Somerset, Northumberland and north-west England by the end of the nineteenth century.

Even in Cornwall their numbers are few. They have been strongly associated with the county and with Arthurian legends – it is said that the soul of King Arthur migrated into a chough. There are many Cornish names for the bird – Cornish chough, Cornish daw, Cornish jack, Cornish jay, Cornish kae, killigrew and Market Jew crow (after the old name for Marazion, where they congregated). It appears on the county's coat of arms and in the Duchy of Cornwall's emblem.

The chough, pronounced 'chuff', stopped breeding in Cornish cliff-top caves and deserted buildings in 1952, but individual birds were seen performing their amazing aerial manoeuvres, riding the updraughts, until 1974. Then they left, as the cliff-top ecology changed, mainly due to changes in agriculture.

The birds need a short grass sward so that their long, curved bills can probe for insect larvae. Ten years of improving the habitat for the chough along parts of Cornwall's coastline, by reintroducing cattle-grazing right up to the cliff edge, has encouraged the bird to return to breed on the Lizard peninsula. First sighted in summer 2001, a breeding pair hatched three broods of four chicks in three years, watched around the clock to keep egg collectors at bay.

Since 1380 the chough has also featured on the City of Canterbury's coat of arms and three choughs appear on Thomas à Becket's arms. It was a Royalist symbol during the Civil War, which may explain The Three Choughs as a pub name, for example in Blandford Forum, Dorset.

See also CLIFFS, ROOKERIES, ZAWNS.

CHURCHES

We take our parish churches for granted, yet they mark out the country and the city in remarkable ways. Built to command respect and awe and draw the eye to the heavens, they are impressive even now, to the extent that they form literal landmarks for mariners and migrating birds. The tiered contours of St Bride's spire in Fleet Street provokes any London taxi driver worth 'The Knowledge' to comment on how it inspired the shape of the wedding cake. Breedon church is vulnerable above the quarry face in Leicestershire; Great Salkeld in Cumberland is simple and sturdy. St Mary the Virgin in Shrewsbury is lit with windows of five centuries of stained glass, and we agree with Simon Jenkins that Christchurch Priory in Hampshire is, simply, sensational.

Christianity had spread through urban Roman Britain, but it took another wave of influence from the reconstructed continental church, from the late sixth century, to establish Christianity across England. Pre-Christian practices and Celtic sensibilities nevertheless continued to play an important role. Churches are orientated towards the east. Those dedicated to St Michael are invariably on significant hills that can catch the rising of the sun, a legacy of Egypt, Osiris and the Coptic church – think of St Michael's Mount in Cornwall and the skyline around Glastonbury in Somerset. Churches devoted to St Mary, the mother of Christ, are often situated beside springs.

Many believe that the positioning of churches owed much to an intention to take over the power of the pre-Christian sites, to insinuate and absorb. The yew trees at Darley Dale in Derbyshire and at Clun in Shropshire may pre-date their stone companions by two thousand years. Ruined Knowlton in Dorset sits quietly in the centre of a circular neolithic earthwork, and the church at Rudston, Yorkshire, keeps company with a prehistoric monolith nearly twenty feet in height.

Although some churches were built to stand alone – such as those of the Charnwood Forest in Leicestershire – following the enclosure of 1830, there are many isolated churches that tell of the contraction, desertion and mobility of settlements over the centuries.

Early worship was outside beside a stone cross or in small wooden buildings. The minsters were the mother churches, centres of evangelism; their names linger in the towns – Wimborne Minster in Dorset, Kidderminster in Worcestershire. Later came the churches built by Saxon lords – Escomb in County Durham is a rare survivor. By 1066 most people could walk to a church and some were within the sound of church bells and sight of a tower. The close pattern of parishes and church sites was laid.

Rebuilding took place at many churches with the coming of the Normans and again as the wool, worsted

(in the East) and broadcloth (in the South West) trades of the fourteenth and fifteenth centuries, and later economic booms, offered money and energy for refashioning. Then, in 1539, England broke with the Church of Rome and English churches fragmented into yet further idioms. Victorian generosity founded new chapels and churches, but the overzealous 'restoration' of Tewkesbury Abbey in Gloucestershire prompted William Morris to create the Society for the Protection of Ancient Buildings, because all the accretions of intervening ages were being wiped away in a misguided attempt to recapture someone's idea of the purity of the original.

Once the centralised cultural grip of the Middle Ages began to diminish, the building of a church was an expression as much of wealth and building skills as it was of the glory of God. With the interest in bells came the need for height and the unparalleled flowering of one of England's greatest wonders – the parish church with tower or spire.

Towers predominate, although spires, with myriad variations, have a heartland in the east Midlands. Yorkshire, with a tradition of towers, has one of the most elegant spires, in Patrington. Simple gabled towers, mostly of the thirteenth and fourteenth centuries, looking like tall, medieval square silos with pitched roofs, are found along a line linking Somerset and south Lincolnshire. They coincide with the Lias limestone, poorer for agriculture and wealth generation and hence associated with plainer building techniques – the simplicity of Fingest church is a real prize in its now opulent Buckinghamshire village.

So near and yet so different, polygonal towers, influenced by continental Europe and dating from the twelfth to sixteenth centuries, march along the line of fine building stone from Norfolk, through Ely and Peterborough, to Somerset. Christopher Wren picked up the style in some of his London churches a century later.

The timber towers of Worcestershire, often separate from the nave, as at Pirton and Warndon, delight with simplicity and pattern. The annual rings in the timbers of the freestanding bell tower at Yarpole, Herefordshire tell us that the oaks were cut in 1195, setting a local style seen again in Pembridge, Bosbury and Richard's Castle. At Greensted-juxta-Ongar in Essex stands the oldest of wooden churches. Its nave is lined with split oak and it has a white, weather-boarded tower.

Somerset's large, elegant towers have elaborate pinnacles at each top corner and fine parapets. There is variety across the county, from Mells in the Mendips to Bishops Lydeard (with a red sandstone tower) in the Quantocks, and variation within and between. Here the silhouettes of the Perpendicular towers are ornamented by carvings of mythical birds and beasts, locally called hunky punks. Some leaning steeples persist, as at St Peter's in Barnstaple, Devon, Temple Church in Bristol and the famed twisted spire at Chesterfield in Derbyshire.

Lichenologists love stone churches; more than a third of all lichens present in Britain have been recorded on church and in graveyard. Their great age has allowed these very slow-growing plants to spread undisturbed for centuries. Leaky pipes and gutters, while foreshortening the church's life, increase the range of species – typically thirty to forty species may be found. The mix and age of the stone and the church's east–west orientation offer a variety of habitats, particularly in the contrast offered by north- and south-facing roofs and walls. Some lichens are so precise in their needs that they tell of the invisible variation in stone. In Northamptonshire, *Hypocenomyce scalaris* will grow only on the local sandy ironstone, and Sulgrave church demonstrates colourful patina, with yellow lichens at the top of the tower, white lichens on the string course,

90

many-coloured communities on south-facing walls and grey-green communities on the north side.

The simple broached and crooked stone spire of St Enodoc leans into the dunes by the beach at Daymer Bay, Cornwall. In the eighteenth and nineteenth centuries sand overwhelmed the church, to the extent that the locals called it the 'sinkininny church' and the vicar was lowered in through the roof once a year to maintain its consecration. Lovingly cleared and renovated by careful Victorians, it is enfolded now by sand-holding tamarisk, that candy-floss-pink flowering tree that softly coats our warmer coasts. It is fitting that John Betjeman, who so idiosyncratically celebrated the richness of our building heritage, lies here, bringing others to a favourite corner of England.

Around two thousand churches and chapels have been made redundant during recent years; some now house apartments, art centres, places of work or leisure. The church may or may not still be at the religious centre of its parish, but it often forms the aesthetic focus and performs a spiritual role. It behoves all who care for the embodied history in each one to think creatively about the future of these exquisite buildings in a secular society.

See also BEACON FIRES, BELLS & BELL-RINGING, BLACK DOGS, BOUNDARIES, BUILDING STONES, CATHEDRALS, CHAPELS, CHURCHYARDS, DESERTED VILLAGES, DEVIL, DRAGONS, GARGOYLES & GROTESQUES, GRAVESTONES, GREEN MAN, HILLS, ISLANDS, LANDMARKS, LOST VILLAGES, MIDSUMMER DAY, MOSQUES, PARISH MAPS, ROUND-TOWERED CHURCHES, SAINTS, SLATES, SYNAGOGUES, TEMPLES, WAYSIDE & BOUNDARY CROSSES, YEW.

C H U R C H Y A R D S

Churchyards are often ancient – much older than the church – some beside yew trees, sacred springs or ancient burial grounds. They may breathe antiquity and peaceful solemnity now, but they have not always been like this. In medieval England they would have been busy, noisy places, the focal point of the community.

Missionaries sent by Pope Gregory to England around 600 were instructed not to destroy existing sacred sites but to absorb and assimilate them into the Christian faith. In some places, notably Knowlton Circles in Dorset, churches were built among prehistoric earthworks. Evidence may remain in the circular shape of the churchyard, as at Ozleworth in Gloucestershire. In Cornwall, ancient, raised, often oval, burial grounds, indicating hundreds of years of burials before a church was built, are

known as lans – the parishes of Lanhydrock and Lanivet reveal the existence of these features in their names.

Ancient, venerated standing stones had crosses inscribed into them. Elsewhere wooden, then stone, crosses were erected to mark burial places before the first wooden churches were built. Hundreds of beautiful churchyard crosses survive in Cornwall, some of great antiquity, but these granite crosses are not so intricately carved as some crosses found in the North, such as the seventh/eighth-century sandstone Bewcastle cross in Cumberland, with complicated carved knotwork featuring figures and birds.

In 752 permission was given by Rome to create grave-yards around churches, because people passing the dead on their way to church would be more likely to pray for their souls. The four cardinal points were marked with crosses. The earliest burials were on the south side. The poor had to chance it in the sunless north, regarded as '*open to the activity of demons*', Geoffrey Grigson wrote.

Preaching crosses, around which people gathered to hear visiting missionaries and priests, were erected. Medieval crosses are characterised by their tall, often intricately carved, tapering shafts, set into large socket stones surrounded by three or four steps. Many were destroyed at the Reformation but rebuilt during the Celtic revival in the 1800s.

During the tenth century churchyards began to be enveloped by walls, banks, hedges and fences, enclosing what became known as God's Acre, although churchyards are of varying sizes and shapes. During the Middle Ages, markets, fairs and games took place in churchyards. There was space for these activities then, as headstones and tombs were not erected until the eighteenth and nineteenth centuries. Oliver Rackham estimated that '*the average country churchyard contains at least ten thousand bodies*' – one reason why the ground level of the churchyard tends to rise well above the surrounding land.

Some rural churchyards have lych gates – covered gateways – dating from about 1470, to give coffin bearers a chance to catch their breath while waiting for the priest.

91

Damerham, Hampshire.

Some have coffin stones and benches, mostly Victorian but built in a medieval manner. Aymer Vallence, writing in 1920, said: '*The distribution of lych gates in various districts is most unequal. Thus nearly every one of the 24 churches of the Deanery of Woodleigh, Devonshire, is said to possess a lych gate . . . [in] Troutbeck, Westmorland . . . there are, or were, no less than three stone lych gates to one and the same churchyard.*'

At St Margaret's in Warnham, west Sussex, a growing lych gate made from topiaried one-hundred-year-old yews makes a magnificent entrance to the church. Yews were often planted by the lych gate.

There is nothing to beat the spreading English yew allowed to grow unfettered. It seems more at home than the fastigiate Irish yew, which became funereally fashionable in Victorian times. Richard Mabey reflected on the '*remarkable and probably unique association [yews] have with ancient churches*' in England and Wales, something not replicated anywhere else in the Western world.

Stiles or gates leading from the churchyard into a field are particularly appealing. At Mells in Somerset, a grass path behind St Andrew's Church, flanked by an avenue of clipped and trained yews designed by Sir Edwin Lutyens, leads into a field through what must have been a stile, now replaced with a wrought-iron gate; just outside it stands a small, simple, rounded wooden cross. A rusty kissing gate leads from the churchyard at Bigbury in the South Hams of Devon into a wheat field; it contrasts with the smart, wrought-iron entrance gate with stone pillars topped with orbs of stone, which leads to the dog-leg lane.

Churchyards harbour a rich array of wild animals and plants. During hundreds of years a regular form of management and, in recent times, we trust, no applications of fertilisers, herbicides and pesticides, have allowed wild plants and creatures to flourish. In spring, Damerham churchyard in Hampshire is a sea of snowdrops; in Kempley, Gloucestershire wild daffodils brave the bitter winds.

Large expanses of local stone make churches and churchyards a sanctuary for six hundred species (a third) of Britain's lichens. Boundary walls, headstones and chest tombs are enriched by their yellow rosettes and grey-green crusts. The lived-in look of many old churchyards owes much to the use of local stone for gravestones, which the indigenous lichens inhabit quickly. One hundred and fifty species of lichens have been found on the stone and trees in the churchyard at Mickleham, Surrey.

Bats are more likely to roost in the roof of the porch than in the noisy and windy belfry. People put up wire mesh doors to prevent them and also birds from nesting there. St Francis would surely find imaginative ways of offering these beleaguered creatures sanctuary.

See also BARROWS, BELLS & BELL-RINGING, BUILDING STONES, CEMETERIES, CHURCHES, CLIPPING THE CHURCH, DAFFODILS, GRAVESTONES, LICHENS, SPRINGS, STANDING STONES, STILES, YEW.

CIDER & CIDER ORCHARDS

With more than four hundred varieties of cider apple, many named after the place where they arose, one expects variation in the drink and in the landscape. The heyday of cider making was in the 1650s to 1750s, when much of Devon, Somerset, Gloucestershire, Herefordshire, Shropshire and Worcestershire were covered in orchards. Thirty- to forty-foot-tall cider-apple trees (and, in the last three counties, perry-pear trees) were spaced thirty to forty feet apart so that grass could grow under them, allowing stock to graze. What a magnificent sight they must have been en masse.

Some of these traditional orchards survive in the main cider-making areas because they are home to many things: grazing sheep, cattle and pigs (in Gloucestershire, the Gloucester Old Spot is known as the orchard pig); chickens; beehives; mistletoe; and overnight campers. Fruit wood is also much sought after by musical instrument makers.

Modern bush orchards, widely planted from the 1970s, with the first branches reaching just two to three feet from the ground, have a planting density of 160 to 240 trees per acre (rather than forty to sixty per acre in a traditional orchard). They may achieve a greater tonnage per acre but suffer and perpetrate all the problems of monoculture. These orchards look much like vineyards, arranged in long lines of bare earth.

Traditional orchards are shady wood pastures, green always visible through the widely spaced rank and file, blowsy in spring and filigree in winter. In the Somerset Levels spring floods demonstrate people's real knowledge of the land, when old houses, church and orchard stand dry on subtle island slopes.

In Sussex, Norfolk and Suffolk, cider is made in the 'eastern tradition', with eating or 'cull' (culinary) apples, not considered the 'proper job' in the wetter climate of the South and West, where cider-apple trees flourish. Each cider maker creates a unique blend of flavours; over the years, counties and localities have developed preferences. '*Bittersweets became the most popular in Somerset but pure sharps and sweets predominated in the southern part of the county near the Devon border*', Liz Copas writes in *A Somerset Pomona*. '*A different kind of sweet apple became the favoured taste in the eastern part from Wincanton to Shepton Mallet.*' Joan Morgan notes that '*Devonshire had become known for its sweet ciders as a result of the planting of pure "sweets", such as Sweet Alford, Sweet Blenheim, Northwood, Slack-ma girdle and Sweet Coppin.*'

These assorted tastes can be found in today's farmhouse ciders. Somerset and Herefordshire county councils have produced maps showing the juice- and cider makers that sell direct from farm shops, and CAMRA publishes a *Good Cider Guide* listing producers, pubs and outlets.

In the hop-growing areas of Herefordshire, the trough mill, made from old red sandstone (granite in Devon), where apples were first crushed using horse power, was housed in the kell (oast-house). In Somerset, where the local limestone reacted with the acid, stone troughs are uncommon. Where there was no suitable stone, wooden troughs and grindstones were used, or the Ingenio apple mill invented by John Worlidge in the 1670s.

In other counties, cider making might take place in the threshing barn, which had enough head room to accommodate the screw press. This squeezed the pulp through horse hair or straw 'cheeses' to produce juice, which fermented in oak barrels for about six months. The leftover pomace was spread along the hedgerows and left, to see if germinating pips would turn into promising new varieties (these seedlings are known as gribbles in Somerset). In Herefordshire it is enchanting to see occasional apple trees in the hedge shining with winter red or yellow apples. Some of the best cider apples, including Redstreak, Foxwhelp and Yarlington Mill, are wildings – discovered rather than bred.

Cider has a long and distinguished history. It was made in *pomaria* in monasteries as long ago as the 1200s. High-quality cider has been imbibed from beautiful engraved glasses and regarded as superior to the best wines. It was taken on ships to prevent scurvy and became a popular drink in villages and cities when water was not to be trusted. Workers were paid in cider as part of their wages, a practice that extended to farm labourers in cider-making areas until the Truck Act of 1887 made it illegal.

There have been many attempts to improve the quality of cider and to find new varieties. In the 1640s in Herefordshire, Lord Scudamore experimented with fermentation in bottles, resulting in a sparkling apple 'champagne'. Impressed by the quality of Norman ciders, he advocated the planting of Redstreak. It became so popular that John Evelyn remarked: '*all Herefordshire has become, in a manner, but one entire orchard*'.

Another Herefordshire fruit breeder, Thomas Andrew Knight, wrote a *Treatise on Cider* in 1797 and the *Pomona Herefordiensis* in 1811. Dr Robert Hogg was commissioned by the Woolhope Naturalists' Field Club to survey the orchards, resulting in the *Herefordshire Pomona 1876-85* and the distribution of hundreds of Foxwhelp and Skyrme's Kernel (and Taynton Squash pear) to fruit growers in the county. The 1903 National Fruit and Cider Institute became, in 1912, the Long Ashton Research Station near Bristol. Much work was instigated on varieties and orchard management, which favoured intensive bush orchards to enable mechanical harvesting. It was closed in 1985.

From the late 1870s cider began to be made on a larger scale in small factories by firms such as Gaymers and Whiteways. Now two giants remain, controlling more than eighty per cent of the market. When quality is sacrificed to quantity, it usually signals a downturn. Whereas real cider is the pure, fermented juice of apples, cider made on an industrial scale and sold in kegs is carbonated and contains apple concentrate (often imported), water, sugar, yeast and other additives. Simply using apples alone does not guarantee superiority: scrumpy, the memorable if not

93

desirable rough, strong, home-made cider, has left a bad reputation, which sophisticated artisan cider makers are now routing.

The big manufacturers buy apple concentrate on the world market and locally may buy only from farms contracted to them. Hundreds of small orchards become vulnerable. In the South Hams of Devon, Orchard Link has been set up to help find markets for small growers; it has a mobile mill and press to enable growers to make their own juice and cider. Elsewhere, the New Street Ciderists in Berkshire show what can be done by gathering apples from gardens and producing cider in a garage for domestic consumption.

A new wave of single-variety and organic ciders have reinvigorated the retail scene, together with an English distillation to rival Calvados – made in Hereford as King Offa in 1987, it has been produced by Julian Temperley as Somerset Royal Cider Brandy near Kingsbury Episcopi since 1992.

See also APPLE DAY, APPLES, MISTLETOE, OAST-HOUSES & KELLS, ORCHARDS, PEARS, WASSAILING.

C I N E M A S

94   The ghosts of old cinemas inhabit almost every small town and city high street. Look closely at the bingo hall, carpet warehouse or nightclub and you may recognise parts of the façade of an early twentieth-century picture house. In Eastwood, Nottinghamshire, Woolworths inhabits the old Empire, the Rex having disappeared under a rambling traffic roundabout.

The first purpose-built cinemas were erected in 1909. The Electric (1910) in Portobello Road, London is the oldest operating cinema in the country; after varying fortunes it underwent refurbishment at the start of this century. The Phoenix in London first opened its doors as the East Finchley Picturedrome in 1910. Recent work on the Cottage Road Cinema in Leeds has brought to light the stonework and decorated plaster that graced its frontage when it opened in 1912 as the Headingley Picture House.

Many of the early cinemas were combined with ballrooms, restaurants and cafés. A familiar feature was a domed structure on the roof, which ventilated the auditorium before the invention of air conditioning. The fantasy promised by the cinema was reflected in the names: Apollo, Astoria, Dreamland, Gaumont, Orpheus, Plaza, Picturedrome, Regal.

With the advent of the talkies, huge atmospheric auditoria were built to emulate exotic outdoor scenes with sunsets and twinkling stars, magical places for the new storytelling. Louis Barfe has written of the early cinema experience: '*The newer, larger, wired-for-sound cinemas often had vast stages and fully-equipped fly towers, along with an organ . . . The major locations also employed a large orchestra. With all of this on offer, it was a short step to putting live shows on to complement the films. The result was called "cine variety".*' This was the diet served at cinemas such as the four Astorias, which opened in London between 1929 and 1930. Many will recall the rainbow-lit Wurlitzer triumphantly emerging from the orchestra pit with its organ soloist, a transmogrified memory of the pianist who accompanied the old 'silents'.

The Odeons of the 1930s, with their avant-garde style influenced by North American and German cinema architecture, created an exciting new genre. Masterminded by Oscar Deutsch with architects such as Harry W. Weedon, more than a hundred new cinemas were built in fewer than ten years. Odeon, taken from a name for Greek amphitheatres, was also used in France and Italy, but for Deutsch it meant 'Oscar Deutsch Entertains Our Nation'. These Odeons were streamlined buildings, often with rounded corners and tall slab or fin towers, with generous use of cream-glazed terracotta (faïence) tiling and contrasting red brick. The bright red Odeon sign became one of the first iconic logos – placed in a prominent place on the fin it could be seen from great distances, especially when the new neon lighting was embraced, outlining the building in the dark.

The cinema was at the height of popularity in the late 1930s. In 1939 there were nearly five thousand in Britain. The war changed things. After it ended, a lack of money, and the rise of television during the 1950s and 1960s, led to the industry's collapse, with huge numbers of cinemas closing.

The Odeon, Sutton Coldfield, Warwickshire.

Some cinemas found new lives as music venues, notably in London the Hammersmith Apollo, formerly the Odeon, and the Brixton Academy, once the Astoria. Others have become bingo halls or theme pubs. Finsbury Park Astoria in London is a church, and *'there is a swimming pool-sized baptismal font on the stage where the Astoria Girls did their high-kicks'*, Louis Barfe wrote.

Most cities have at least one art-house cinema, often with an integral café and bookshop. The popularity of Indian cinema is spreading, subtitles making it more accessible. Posters for South Asian films are layers thick in Bethnal Green, east London. At the other side of the capital, the Southall Liberty cinema owes much to Mr Surjit Pandher, who, following a serious fire, has transformed this Grade II*-listed confection of Chinese temple filled with Art Deco colour back into a picture palace – the Himalaya Palace, for Bollywood and Hollywood movies. It is a landmark, with a tiered pagoda roof, dragons inside and out, sumptuous in its detail. The Rex in Berkhamsted, Hertfordshire, a refurbished Art Deco cinema complete with cocktail tables, offers a meal and drinks while you watch the film.

Despite the flagship restorations, magnificent cinema buildings of the golden age are still neglected; journalist Eric George created the Cinema Theatre Association in 1967 out of concern for them. At the turn of the millennium English Heritage asked which cinemas we loved most. As a result 32 buildings were listed anew and eight were upgraded in importance. The Granada in Tooting, south London, currently Gala Bingo, is the first cinema to receive Grade I status.

See also CONFECTIONERY, DRAGONS, FILM LOCATIONS, SUNBURSTS.

C L I F F S

'The cliff coasts of Great Britain should be reckoned one of the country's most treasured possessions, they are of every variety and form, including the great chalk promontories of Flamborough Head and Beachy Head, the granite masses of Land's End, the sandstones of St Bee's Head . . . the newer limestones, sandstones and clays of Dorset, and the glacial cliffs of Holderness and Norfolk', J.A. Steers wrote.

Cliffs offer the closest thing we have to wilderness in England, for here nature is in charge and there is little we can do to halt the inexorable processes of sea and tempest. About a fifth of England's coastline – some 750 miles – consists of cliff. Here an extraordinary array of the earth's ancient history is exposed to view: layered, tilted, folded, faulted rock forms of many kinds stand not only in vertical faces but as natural sculptures, from pillars, stacks and buttresses to arches and caves.

Most of our cliffs range from 150 to three hundred feet in height. Boulby Cliff on the Yorkshire coast is our highest length of coastline, layers of Liassic shales and sandstones and boulder clay rising to 650 feet. Hard-rock cliffs that are nearly vertical, and hence tricky for humans, provide relatively safe breeding places for seabirds, although in the past people found ways to harvest these colonies. In the nineteenth century climbers, or 'climmers', took thousands of seabird eggs from nests along the Yorkshire coast at Bempton Cliffs.

Flamborough Head and Bempton Cliffs support England's only, and Britain's biggest, mainland gannet colony, as well as one of the largest kittiwake colonies in the North Atlantic. The sandstone cliffs of St Bees Head on the Cumbrian coast host England's only breeding colonies of black guillemots, as well as fulmars, kittiwakes, razorbills, cormorants, puffins and shags.

Plants also enjoy the freedom cliffs offer from grazing and competition. Ledges and crevices provide opportunities for hardy plants, such as rock sea-spurry and rock samphire, as well as lichens. But they have had to learn to live with wind and sea spray. The magnesian limestone cliffs at Hart Warren in County Durham support eight species of orchid, as well as moonwort, grass-of-Parnassus and bird's-eye primrose. The Lizard in Cornwall has an international reputation for its distinctive flora growing on serpentine rock.

The botanical diversity of all these cliffs is put to good use by butterflies, such as the chalkhill blue, holly blue, Lulworth skipper along the Dorset coast, and Glanville fritillary, confined to the disturbed cliff-face vegetation of the Isle of Wight. Short-tailed voles thrive on ungrazed cliff slopes and bats colonise caves and clefts along the mixed cliffs of Dorset: greater horseshoe, Beckstein's, Daubenteon's, Naterer's, whiskered and the very rare mouse-eared bat are all found there. On broken cliffs, adders, common lizards and slow-worms make a home, while the now rare sand lizard persists on soft, sandy, south-facing cliffs around Bournemouth.

Modern geology was forged in part by men and women who scoured the crumbling cliffs of Dorset, spurred by finds of long-extinct life forms in the rocks later defined as Jurassic, with exposures growing steadily older towards the west. Local fossil hunters still find prime specimens of ancient marine reptiles below these cliffs; they are on sale at fossil shops in Lyme Regis and Charmouth.

Many places offer particular views of the earth's crust, highly prized by geologists. Thanks to its cliff face, Kimmeridge Bay in Dorset gives its name to a particular period of geological time: rocks deposited anywhere in the world between 145 and 154 million years ago are said to be of Kimmeridgian age. Dinosaurs, such as iguanodon, turn up on the soft cliffs of the Isle of Wight, drawing a modest tourist trade. From the London clay in Essex and Kent, fossil shark's teeth spill out onto the beach.

95

Sea cliffs have been quarried in the past – near Whitby in Yorkshire for alum; Portland in Dorset for its prized building stone. In north Cornwall at Barrett's Zawn, slate was drawn through a now-collapsed tunnel to be loaded onto boats.

Between Flamborough Head and the Thames estuary stretches our flattest coastline, but there are cliffs of banded red chalk at Hunstanton, Norfolk and low cliffs of Pleistocene sand, gravels and boulder clay near Cromer and along the Holderness coast in Yorkshire.

Soft cliffs formed of shale or boulder clay slump as they erode, and the mosaic of habitats is readily colonised by plants. Only 160 miles remain free from coastal defences. Once stabilised, naturally or artificially, the natural mosaic of habitats is destroyed, as scrub takes over and nearby beaches, starved of sediment, start to disappear. During the past century, sea defences have probably reduced the flow of sediment from cliffs to coastal beaches by as much as fifty per cent. Current conservation wisdom is erring on the side of nature: increasingly cliffs are being left to retreat.

See also ALBION, AMMONITES, ARCHES, CHALK, CHINES, CHOUGHS, COASTGUARD COTTAGES, COASTLINE, COASTS, COVES, DENES, DEVIL, DRAGONS, ESTUARIES, FERNS, FLINT, GIANTS, LANDSLIPS, LIGHTHOUSES, LOST VILLAGES, RIAS, ROCKS, SALT MARSHES, SEA CAVES, STACKS, WATERFALLS, WHITE CLIFFS, ZAWNS.

CLINTS & GRIKES

Limestone pavements are at their most glorious around Malham in Yorkshire, among the best examples of glacio-karst scenery in the world. Exquisitely adapted plants find rootholds in the grikes (cracks) between clints (bare slabs). Derived from Old Danish, these north-country names describe a unique landscape within a landscape, a kind of deeply etched crazy paving with fantastical patterns of fissures and stony slabs and lumps. Over thousands of years, rain has regularly doused these rocks with a mildly acidic solution, steadily eroding any crack.

Strange botanical bedfellows are typical of the territory. Woodland anemones and bluebells, for instance, turn up in shady grikes; large fissures may house a lime-loving ash tree. The limestone pavement on Souther Scales to the north of Ingleborough boasts a wealth of mosses and ferns, such as green spleenwort, which share the grikes with herb-Robert, dog's mercury, herb-Paris and baneberry. The Craven door snail and the rock snail are at home here.

Many areas of limestone pavement have been seriously damaged by quarrying to supply weathered stones for garden rockeries, a fashion fuelled by Edwardian plant collector and gardener Reginald Farrer of Ingleborough Hall.

See also BUILDING STONES, DALES, FERNS, GARDENS, LIMESTONE, MOSSES, WALLS, WILDFLOWERS.

CLIPPING THE CHURCH

Originally held on Shrove Tuesday, the clipping ceremony often takes place on the feast day associated with the saint to whom a church is dedicated; at Guiseley parish church in Yorkshire it falls on St Oswald's Day, 5 August. Other examples include Burbage and Wirksworth in Derbyshire and Edgmond in Shropshire.

While Painswick in Gloucestershire is well known for its churchyard containing 99 yews, the clipping ceremony, as with all the others, involves not the trees but 'embracing' St Mary's Church. On the first Sunday after 19 September, the Feast of the Nativity of St Mary, hundreds of school-children encircle the church, hold hands and move forwards and back three times while singing the 'Clipping Hymn'. If you find a small china dog sold in the patisseries of Painswick on Clipping Day, it is because, at a former feast, 'puppy dog pies' were sold. The people of Painswick were quick to turn bad press to their advantage, subsequently putting ornaments in the pies instead.

See also CHURCHES, CHURCHYARDS, PUDDINGS, SAINTS, YEW.

CLOCKS

Clocks have ticked and tocked on churches from the twelfth century, and later on town halls, barracks, factories and shops. Salisbury Cathedral has perhaps the oldest surviving mechanical clock in the world, from 1386. Churches at Cookham, Berkshire and St Leonard-at-the-Hythe, Essex have early chiming clocks, but Claughton in Lancashire claims the oldest working bell, founded in 1296. Rye church in Sussex has the earliest clock still working in its original location, a gift from Elizabeth I in 1515.

Two styles predominated: 'turret' clocks on high walls and towers, and 'bracket' clocks projecting out from them. The latter became popular on jewellers' shops, and a fine bracket clock juts from almshouses at Longbridge Deverill, Wiltshire. St Peter's Church in Colchester, Essex was weakened by an 1844 earthquake and its clock moved to a bracket on the side of the tower. Clocks' distinctive decorations led to affectionate familiarity – St Martin-le-Grand Church in York was a bombing casualty in 1942, but its remains include a clock topped with a small naval figure known as Little Admiral. Greenwich Mean Time was introduced in the 1840s to bring meaning to railway timetables, but some towns, including Norwich and Portsmouth, resisted standardisation until 1880. The station clock was a necessity, and as the modern working day evolved, the accuracy and ubiquity of public clocks became essential. Pragmatism and pride joined philanthropy, and the grand new classic and gothic buildings – town halls, such as Burslem and Leeds, and Leicester Corn

Exchange – were invariably crowned by a monumental clock. Sir Charles Barry wanted Halifax town hall to have *a Clock which could be seen from all parts of the Town, to mark the time both by night as well as by day*'. Bolton town hall boasted one of the country's largest, with twelve-foot-diameter dials.

The largest of all was E.J. Dent and Lord Grimthorpe's clock for the Houses of Parliament in Westminster. Born turbulently from designers' rivalries and technical exasperations, work began on the clock in 1854. Two years later the hour bell cracked. Sir Benjamin Hall at the Ministry of Works commissioned another, and consequently his name adhered to it. Big Ben, weighing more than thirteen tons, is the most famous bell in the world, thanks to the BBC's World Service.

The Victorians jumped at numerous excuses for clock building. Victoria's Jubilees of 1887 and 1897 prompted a spate, with examples appearing in Brighton, Grimston in Norfolk and Cricklade in Wiltshire. Floral clocks made their debuts in public parks.

New public clocks still appear. Astronomical clocks advanced in the twentieth century. York Minster has one, made in 1955, which displays planetary movements as observed by airmen. Sculptural engineer and cartoonist Tim Hunkin has built several public clocks, including a water clock for Neal's Yard, London in 1982 and one on a recycling theme, which, since 2001, has had a permanent home on Southwold pier in Suffolk.

See also CATHEDRALS, CHURCHES, CRICKET, EARTHQUAKES, EAST, FACTORIES, JACK OF THE CLOCKS, MONUMENTS, PIERS, SCULPTURES, SHOPS, STATIONS, TOWN HALLS & GUILD-HALLS.

Charles Street, Leicester.

C L O U D S

'Mackerel sky and mare's tails, make lofty ships carry low sails.' Seafarers know their clouds, and so do farmers. *'When clouds appear like rocks and towers, the earth's refreshed by frequent showers.'* Descriptive names and chronic observation are part of the weather lore that drives English bus-stop conversation and universal weather forecasting.

Strange to say, a full lexicon of cloud names does not seem to have come down to us – lamb's wool sky, mackerel sky, mare's tails, overcast, rain cloud, stacken cloud, thunder cloud and wane cloud are about the extent of it. That is, until 1802, when Luke Howard named the clouds. He had closely observed their shapes and altitude for years, and, filled with the light of Linnaeus, classified their patterns and gave them Latin names. The success of this venture permeates meteorology: what Howard did was to help us see the invisible – to begin to understand the atmosphere.

In 2002 he was remembered; his old house in Tottenham, north London now carries a blue plaque. At the time his fame went wide. Goethe lauded him in four poems: *'As clouds ascend, are folded, scatter, fall,/Let the world think of thee who taught it all.'* Shelley, too, was moved to precision in 'The Cloud', and he offers in almost riddle form a fine evocation of the water cycle:

I am the daughter of earth and water,
And the nursling of the sky;
I pass through the pores of the ocean and shores;
I change, but I cannot die.

John Constable's sketchbooks of 1821/2 are filled with exquisite observations of clouds over London. From the fields off Prospect Walk on Hampstead Heath he painted more than a hundred studies of *'noble clouds and effects of light'*, the notes and dates giving us a diary of two summers, his close observation built upon a childhood of intimacy with a Suffolk windmill and hence the Suffolk sky. His paintings of Weymouth Bay from the Dorset coast demonstrate something we have all done, which is to watch the weather going or coming.

Sometimes clouds redefine the landscape. Edward Burra's painting *Near Whitby, Yorkshire, 1972* has a road, edged by plunging moorland slopes, running into numinous mist-cum-cloud. Memorable are the days when hills become islands and new shorelines seem to edge the valley of the Trent seen from Charnwood, Leicestershire, when cloud sinks into the bottoms and leaves the high places to gloat in the sun.

There are repeated local rhymes that warn of weather to come. *'If Simonside has her nightcap on in the morning, it's sure to rain'* is one saying from Cambo in Northumberland,

97

while in Devon they say, '*When Hall Down wears a hat/ Let Kenton beware of a skat*' (shower).

One can become mesmerised by clouds: by high, wispy cirrus made more from ice crystals than water vapour; lower duvets of stratus; heaped cumulus – flat-bottomed, discrete and fluffy, suggesting settled weather – or cumulo-nimbus, big and billowing, threatening rain. Seen from a plane they make their own fabulous landscapes and, from the ground, what you will:

Hamlet. *Do you see yonder cloud that's almost in shape of a camel?*
Polonius. *By th' mass, and 'tis like a camel, indeed.*
Ham. *Methinks it is like a weasel.*
Pol. *It is backed like a weasel.*
Ham. *Or like a whale?*
Pol. *Very like a whale . . .*

William Shakespeare, from *Hamlet*

See also ARTISTS' COLONIES & SCHOOLS, BUS SHELTERS, FOG & MIST, FRETS, SHIPPING FORECAST, WEATHER, WHALES, DOLPHINS & PORPOISES.

C L U M P S

Clumps, or 'plumps', were first planted in deer parks in the early 1700s as landscape features, for fox coverts and shooting birds. It was a natural progression that they should move to the tops of hills, where they could be seen from the windows of grand houses taking the view into their own domain.

Above the towns of Abingdon and Wallingford in Berkshire Duncan Mackay placed Wittenham Clumps as '*sentinels of the Chiltern Hills and guardians of the Goring Gap*'. These beech trees, planted in the 1700s, stand tall on the tops of two round chalk hills known locally as the Berkshire Bubs or Mother Dunch's Buttocks. Known instead to the Ordnance Survey by their Celtic name – the Sinodun Hills –

Round Hill and Castle Hill, topped by a hill-fort, marked the territories of the Iron-Age tribes of the Catuvellauni and the Atrebati. Surveying a wide sweep, Wittenham Clumps became well known from the paintings of Paul Nash.

There is a tradition of planting beech clumps on the hilltops of Somerset, too. One of the most magnificent, the Seven Sisters on Cothelstone Hill in the Quantocks, can be seen against the skyline from the Vale of Taunton Deane. On 21 June, the Taunton Deane Morris Men 'Dance up the Sun' under the trees.

The distinctive shape of the wind-blown beeches on Win Green on the Wiltshire/Dorset border guides people home for thirty miles; nearby, above the Blackmore Vale, the many-legged beech clump above Zig-Zag Hill is known as The Caterpillar.

Beeches were not the only trees planted. A clump of Scots pines was planted as a war memorial on a hill near Alfoxton in the Quantocks, and at Maiden Bradley on the Somerset/Wiltshire border there is a prominent hilltop copse of Scots pines, called Kate's Bench Clump. The thin clump of Scots pines at the top of the conical Colmer's Hill near Symondsbury, Dorset stands darkly against the rusty bracken.

Visible for miles in every direction, May Hill, on the border of Gloucestershire and Herefordshire, is distinguishable because of its hilltop pines, planted in 1887 to celebrate Queen Victoria's Golden Jubilee. For many years John Masefield saw them as '*a man ploughing with a yoked team*'. In the Ashdown Forest in Sussex, a knoll of pine trees planted in 1816 on Gills Lap was sometimes referred to as Camel's Clump, because, Roger Penn wrote, '*two of its trees seemed from a distance to be shaped like a camel*'.

Sometimes one or two trees pierce the sky, such as the single sycamore on Higher Burrow near Kingsbury Episcopi, Somerset – wonderfully graced, when you climb to it, by a swing. Often, they sprout out of old barrows and, if they are on the skyline, as at Bincombe above Weymouth, Dorset, they resemble planted clumps.

Far from the farmsteads and settlements in the dales of the north Pennines, there are occasional isolated tree clumps, such as the Kirkarrion clump on a barrow where Lunedale meets Teesdale. There is one known as Elephant Trees near the watershed south of Stanhope, County Durham.

Hilltop trees are vulnerable to wind, but it is amazing how resilient they are. Some of the two-hundred-

Colmer's Hill, Symondsbury, Dorset.

year-old beech trees in the Chantonbury Ring on the Sussex Downs fell in the storm of 1987 and have been replanted. So have those at Wittenham Clumps, by the Northmoor Trust.

For some, the clumps serve as more than landmarks – as they did for Paul Nash. Alfred Watkins included clumps as pivotal points in his ley lines, and they are often a location for celebrating the summer solstice. It doesn't seem to matter if the trees planted on the clumps are not locally typical. The silhouette identifies the place.

See also BARROWS, BEECH, HILL-FORTS, HILLS, LANDMARKS, MAY DAY, MORRIS DANCING, SCOTS PINE, SYCAMORE, YEW, ZIGZAGS.

COAL MINING

If anything changed the face of England, it was coal. Its economic impact, together with the heavy industry and the steam engines it fuelled, spanned the country. Its environmental footprint is still visible, often in places far away from the mines, in blackened buildings and melanistic moths half a century after the passing of the Clean Air Acts. The consequences of burning fossil fuels are now recognised in changing climate and unpredictable weather across the world.

The abiding changes came in instant villages, people migrating in not only to work underground but to labour in the brick kilns, the iron and steel mills and in the making of railways, canals and reservoirs. A landscape of pit tips was the result of questing for what Sid Chaplin called *'precious twenty inches of coal in a wilderness of stone'*.

> *They came near to the colliery. It stood quite still and black amongst the corn fields, its immense heap of slag seen rising almost from the oats.*
> *'What a pity there is a coal-pit here where it is so pretty!' said Clara.*
> *'Do you think so?' he answered. 'You see, I am so used to it I should miss it. No; I like the pits here and there. I like the rows of trucks, and the headstocks, and the steam in the daytime and the lights at night.'*

D.H. Lawrence, from *Sons and Lovers*

Growing up in the coalfields was as much about fields as coal in Nottinghamshire, as well as parts of Durham, Northumberland, Cumberland, Lancashire, Cheshire, Shropshire, Staffordshire, Gloucestershire, Warwickshire, Yorkshire, Derbyshire, Leicestershire, Kent and Somerset, even during much of the twentieth century. It was the inexorable growth of heavy industry, transportation and settlements that made the big, visible changes.

Pithead gear, wheels and superstructure graced the old pits. For many that silhouette of working wheels and wires against the sky will be the abiding memory, nothing visible now save the occasional sad pit wheel forever stuck in a bed of concrete.

Coal for making gas, for the railways, for domestic use and general industrial use fell dramatically between 1958 and 1968 and continued to fall. County Durham had 128 working mines in 1947, 34 in 1970. Now it has none: they say you can buy a village for peanuts, if you can cope with the ghosts. The Nottingham field once had thirty collieries; the remaining three are vulnerable.

Coal is a beautiful rock, sometimes with fossils, like shadows, of fern-like leaves from the vast forests of the Carboniferous. We laughingly called them 'Moorgreen brights', with their healthy shine and stepped fractures, from the colliery at the bottom of the fields at Moorgreen, beside Eastwood in Nottinghamshire. There were stories of pregnant women chewing on coal and tiny children playing at cooking nutty slack in the oven. Strange how so many of us who grew up with coal fires, subsidence and the sound of shot-firing deep below us, who have windowsills filled with pebbles from beaches and screes, have not a single piece of coal. We never gave it a second thought – how the commonplace becomes rare.

When economic policy and vindictiveness decimated the mines in the 1980s, we turned around and found that within months the headgear was dismantled, the railway lines and sheds removed, applications for open-cast mining fought, lost or won. All trace of the endeavour was wiped away, bar the great spoil heaps, subsidence and the ragged culture holding on.

The Forest of Dean stands alone as having a tradition of Free Miners. Because their forbears helped Edward I undermine the fortifications at Berwick-upon-Tweed in the fourteenth century, any man born within the Forest of Dean, above the age of 21 and with a year of mining behind him, can 'without tax or hindrance' dig for coal. Terminology is unique and mining practices are archaic. The mines themselves are called gales, seams are delfs, dipples are inclined roads. Miners lie in the seams and work the longwall faces by hand. With an ageing workforce and the closure of the Forest's only maternity hospital, in the Hundred of St Briavels, this tradition is endangered. Some mines have reverted to the Crown, but in 2003 Monument, Phoenix and Hamblins Yorkley are still in production.

With a long history of self-education, miners now share their knowledge, memories and activism in the great wormholes of the World Wide Web. Despite huge reserves under Snaith, Pollerton, Thorne and Hatfield in Yorkshire, between York and Durham, and in Oxfordshire, some argue that we are seeing the last days of coal.

See also BRASS BANDS, DENES, DIALECTS, INDUSTRIAL CHIMNEYS, IRONSTONE, LEAD MINES, MINES, PIGEON LOFTS, PIT TIPS.

99

COASTGUARD COTTAGES

The view is stupendous, out over the sea and the coast for miles and miles. The circumstance is isolated, but a single wall embracing a terrace of houses with tall chimneys and their gardens make a little world somehow safe from the raiding wind. With their towers or lighthouses, these were literal lookout points, places where the sea was scanned night and day for invasion fleets, boats in peril and smugglers who had made it past the customs boats.

The Preventative Water Guard was formed in 1809, superseded by the Coast Guard in 1822. Coastguards were posted away from their home towns to prevent collusion with smugglers, so the coastguard stations had to be built with living quarters to accommodate single and married officers. By 1839 more than four and a half thousand coastguards were in service.

An iconic image of Sussex, reproduced on countless postcards and tourist brochures, shows the sea, the white cliffs of the Seven Sisters and a row of gleaming white coastguard cottages in the foreground. These dwellings, perilously perched on the cliff above Cuckmere Haven, may now be private retreats for wealthy urbanites, yet they domesticate the wild landscape. Up the coast at Birling Gap, another lonely outpost with magnificent views across the Channel is fighting for its existence. Built in 1878, the eight cottages are being allowed to crumble into the voracious sea; at least two have been demolished for safety's sake. The National Trust, which has taken on many coastguard cottages, is following a policy of allowing natural realignment, despite local opposition.

See also THE CHANNEL, CLIFFS, COASTLINE, COASTS, LIGHTHOUSES, LOST VILLAGES, STACKS, WHITE CLIFFS.

COASTLINE

What is this coast? Horizon. Strand
With no beginning and no end,
A line, rewritten hour by hour,
The tale we tell about ourselves.

Katrina Porteous, from *Turning the Tide*

The shape of Britain is defined by the sea, but England has never been an island. Few of us can picture other than Britain, with the high head of Scotland, bulging gut of East Anglia, dragging cloak of Cornwall and Wales. Isolated, England seems unfinished where it marches with Wales and Scotland. The shift in shape is hard to come to terms with; part edged by sea, part bound by land.

While the political redrawing of boundaries goes on, the real work of flux is practised by the sea, making and breaking the rocks, plotting and piecing the edges, creating the richest of natural moats, chivvying and harrying anything 'man made'.

The geological past has seen massive alterations. Ancient tectonic territory crunching, along a line from Berwick-upon-Tweed to the Solway Firth, affirms that we are floating in a sea of deep and solid rock slowed by the grating together of bits of the landmasses of Gondwana and Laurentia some four hundred million years ago. A few hundred thousand years ago the ebbing and flowing of ice chased people away, and only eight and a half thousand years ago we were northern Europe's bulwark to the Atlantic, being joined by land across what became the North Sea and the Channel. People, beasts and plants moved across this land bridge as the tundra and ice withdrew to the north. But from that defining moment,

100

Dunwich Heath, Suffolk.

when the sea broke through, only things that could swim or fly, float on sea or wind or make boats could make it to our shores. Some things stopped coming until we carried them.

Jonathan Raban quoted Hilaire Belloc: '*Nowhere does England take on personality so strongly as from the sea.*' Raban wrote of '*the high excitement of making a landfall as the coastline across the water slowly thickens and takes shape . . . The land surfaces lazily out of the sea, first grey and indistinct, then flecked with hazy colour, then decorated with a sudden scatter of sharpening details – a broad scoop of chalky cliff, a striped beacon like a stick of candy, a continuous waterfall of slate roofs down the slope of a valley.*'

This is a small land both made vulnerable and protected by the sea. Most of us would have shared John Clare's childhood notion of space, imagining 'that the world's end was at the 'orizon and that a day's journey was able to find it'. Our view of the world would hardly have been shaped by maps until the nineteenth century, with the coming of the Ordnance Survey and universal education. Two hundred years later the assertion of our neighbouring countries and the contraction of the state requires a perceptive reworking of who we are and where we live. How long will it take to know our new skin – the outline of England?

See also ALBION, BOATS, BOUNDARIES, THE CHANNEL, COASTS, COUNTIES, SHIPPING FORECAST, UNLUCKY WORDS, WHITE CLIFFS.

C O A S T S

England's diverse and dynamic coastline stretches some five thousand miles. Taken twelve miles out to sea – the limits of British sovereignty – it covers seventy thousand square miles, nearly the size of England's total land area.

Every foreshore is unique. '*There is an atmosphere which only the sea can produce, a nautical tang, a seaside flavour*', Kenneth Lindley wrote in 1967. '*Every mile of coast, every square foot of beach has its own character. Most of it exerts its own peculiar attraction. Nothing like it can be found inland.*'

Sand, carried by currents and blown by the wind, varies from beach to beach. Walk a few feet along a natural shingle coast and the nature of the pebbles changes. Forensic study shows that the precise mix of tiny rock grains and minute shell fragments found in one place is never repeated in another.

Shingle makes up about a third of the coastline, with many shingle banks occurring in the South and South East, the largest at Dungeness in Kent. Vegetated shingle banks are scarce in Europe and this is one of six large examples in

England. At Foulness in Essex are the largest shell banks in the country; these so-called sub-fossil accumulations form part of one of the largest inter-tidal flats in Britain. Seven species of birds visit in internationally important numbers and there are breeding colonies of little, common and sandwich terns.

Our many offshore islands and sandbanks, big and small, provide refuges for birds and sea mammals. The Farne Islands in Northumberland are famous for their grey seals and nesting bird colonies. Hilbre, Roa, Foulney, Walney and Piel Islands, the Isle of Wight, Lundy, Steepholme, Flatholme, Bryher, Samson, Tresco, St Martin's, St Mary's, St Agnes, Holy Island, Coquet Island, St Mary's Island, Read's Island, Brownsea Island, Burgh Island, St Michael's Mount and many more add length and richness to our coastline.

Our estuaries are '*unrivalled anywhere in Europe for their diversity and, in wild life terms, are quite outstanding*', Andrew Cooper wrote. Vital for industry and shipping, sixteen million people live around them. After Sydney, Australia, Poole Harbour is the world's second-largest natural harbour. The river Severn has the second-highest tidal range. Rias, a particular and beautiful feature of the south-west coasts, are drowned river valleys. Morecambe Bay, the Wash and the Thames estuary have three of our most extensive salt marshes, important places for wading birds, where vast expanses of sand are uncovered at low tide. Coastal lagoons sound exotic, but we have more than a hundred around the English coast, notably the Fleet behind Chesil Bank in Dorset.

101

There are fine sand-dune systems at Braunton Burrows in Devon, Ainsdale in Lancashire and on Lindisfarne and at Ross Links, Northumberland. At Studland on the Isle of Purbeck you may come across naturists, whereas at Ainsdale, in the slacks, you may find (at night) a running toad with a yellow stripe down its back. Known as the natterjack, it is called locally Southport nightingale and Bootle organ, owing to its nocturnal chorusing.

The rocky shores of Cornwall, built of solid granite, resist the force of the sea, but crevices and pools abound on soft shores of slate or shale. The easily eroded mudstone cliffs of Dorset still reveal fossil ichthyosaurs and plesiosaurs, reptiles that swam in the Jurassic sea. As soft cliffs disintegrate they release stones and finer sediment, which travel along the coast during the relentless process known as longshore drift, providing raw material to build salt marshes, sandy beaches, dunes and shingle.

Chalk shores, at Flamborough in Yorkshire, Hunstanton in Norfolk and, most spectacularly, along much of the coasts of Kent, Sussex, Dorset and the Isle of Wight, are rare in Europe; England lays claim to nearly two-thirds of the continent's coastal chalk. Soft, and liable to crumble away from the cliffs, chalk supports a distinctive array of plants and animals, including molluscs, sponges that can bore into the rock, and green seaweeds found on no other type of rock.

All along the coast, attempts to control these natural forces have led to unforeseen and unwanted consequences, ultimately starving beaches of replenishing sand, sediment or pebbles, or leaving them more vulnerable to erosion. The remnants of the fishing village of Hallsands in south Devon stand as a monument to the folly of interfering with the sea. Once, the village was protected by a large pebble ridge, but it was destroyed by a January storm in 1917 after more than half a million tons of sand and gravel had been dredged offshore to extend the naval dockyards at Plymouth.

It is now known that extracting sand and gravel from beaches results in more wave energy reaching sea cliffs or sea defences, undermining them. Inappropriate coastal defences and the dredging of shipping channels have starved estuaries of sediment. Solid coastal defences can deflect wave energy back, eroding sediment and causing a beach to disappear. Removing sea walls to allow salt marsh and mud-flats to adopt their natural form will start to compensate for some of the losses.

Divers in the cold English sea visit a world as important and colourful as any tropical reef, populated by corals, kelp forests and a seabed teeming with some forty thousand species. Rocky landscapes hide under the sea as well, particularly around the Farne Islands in the North East. Diversity in England's underwater life is heightened by the presence of colder northern waters that give way to warmer southern ones. Transition zones lie at Flamborough Head in the North Sea and along the English Channel, although this is changing with global warming. Species with demanding requirements choose their place along the continuum.

For instance, a beautiful coral called the pink sea fan, more typically a denizen of Mediterranean waters, is found only off the coast of south-west England, while the cold-water-loving bottlebrush hydroid sticks to the east coast, venturing no further south than Flamborough Head. The health of these species, together with that of the cold-water herring in the North Sea and the pilchard off Cornwall, is being monitored as climate change affects sea temperatures. We are learning about the richness around us just as it is diminishing through our own actions.

Lundy Island in Devon is England's first official 'no-take zone', with support from local fishermen. A little more than a square mile has been set aside to create a refuge for fish, shellfish and corals, such as the pink sea fan. But elsewhere, fishermen using beam trawls and scallop dredges damage large areas of the seabed. Even rocky coasts can now be harvested with so-called rock-hopper trawls. Further disturbance comes from large-scale marine sand and gravel extraction, mostly off East Anglia, Kent and Sussex – each year 23 million tons are removed from the seabed.

In the open sea off England's coasts, basking sharks follow the plankton bloom. Leatherback turtles swim in warmer English waters in search of their jellyfish prey, but often fatally take plastic bags by mistake, or drown after becoming tangled in lobster- and crab-pot lines. Dolphins hunt in the English Channel, where a large number of their deaths have been linked to pelagic trawling for bass. In the North Sea, harbour porpoises are killed by mid-water trawls. The mammals are dying at a rate estimated to result in their decline and eventual loss from our waters. Worse, scientists believe that the North Sea's ecosystem is on the brink of collapse.

Thirty per cent of us live within six miles of the coast, and every year half the population visits at least once. When a Lewes doctor, Richard Russell, published his '*dissertation concerning the use of sea water in diseases of the glands*' in 1750, he helped to spark the development of Brighton as a bathing resort, attracting the patronage of the aristocracy. Beachcombing and sea bathing developed as respectable middle-class pursuits in the Victorian era, combining healthful exercise with morally improving nature studies. Piers and well-lit promenades along the sea, at Southend-on-Sea in Essex and Blackpool in Lancashire, attracted thousands by day and night. By the 1880s the Great Eastern Railway Company was offering Londoners cheap weekend returns to Cromer and Yarmouth on the Norfolk coast.

Our love affair with the sea extends cautiously to its bounty: kippers from Craster, Northumberland; cod landed at Grimsby, Lincolnshire; mackerel from Brixham, Devon. But the dramatic loss of fish from our waters is changing the lives of people and settlements that have lived and died by the sea.

See also AMMONITES, ARCHES, ASPARAGUS, BANDSTANDS, BASKING SHARKS, BEACHCOMBING, BEACHES, BEACONS (COASTAL), BLOW HOLES, BOATS, CAVES, CLIFFS, FERRIES, FLINT, FUNICULAR RAILWAYS, HARBOURS, HOTELS, ISLANDS, LAGOONS, LIGHTHOUSES, LOST VILLAGES, MARTELLO TOWERS, PIERS, PROMENADES, RIAS, SALT MARSHES, SAND-DUNES, SEA FISH, SHELLFISH, SHINGLE, SHIPPING FORECAST, SMELLS, STACKS, SWIMMING PLACES, TIDES, WATERFALLS, WHALES, DOLPHINS & PORPOISES, WHITE CLIFFS, ZAWNS.

Selsey, Sussex.

C O B

Those curvaceous walls with little thatched roofs are made of cob, or clunch. This now undervalued material comes from the earth, and the soft lines it allows in building create houses and barns that are comfortable to live in and sit comfortably in their own landscapes.

Mud is widely available, it insulates well, is cheap and easy to use. Every region, indeed, every farm, had its own recipe, according to chalk, clay, sand and soil type and tradition. This vernacular method of construction is the most popular in the world. It was commonly used here until Victorian times, although parts of the West Country, East Anglia and Lincolnshire were and still are the strongholds. Today the method is enjoying a belated renaissance in the canon of eco-friendly practices.

The key to success, apart from the good fortune of living on perfect clay, is 'a good hat and boots' – protection from the rain and rising damp. Built on stone footings, the base of cob walls is often painted in black tar, to keep rats out and stop the erosive splash from vehicles. Always the roofs hang a good way over the thick walls; they are frequently of thatch but may be of tile, slate or corrugated iron.

Cob is a word of the West. Here, mud and straw were first mixed by cattle to enhance elasticity and binding. In the dunland (Culm Measures) and redland (New Red Sandstone) of Devon, and in northern Cornwall, layer upon horizontal layer would be built up and trodden into place. They would be built on plinths of stone or pebbles. Later the sides would be sculpted smooth, with doorways, windows and corners cut out and rounded. They would be left the colour of earth or covered in plaster or limewash of cream or pink.

Devon has the most medieval earth buildings of any county, and they are most prolific in the north and east. Here combed wheat-straw thatching makes for hipped roofs, often with external stone or brick chimneys; sometimes they have round, projecting oven backs. Walls and farm buildings, as well as houses, may end up with roofs of corrugated iron – without these many more would have been lost. In 'A View of their Parish by the People of Winkleigh', they reported that *the village is mostly colour-washed render, in traditionally pale colours, and most new buildings follow this theme . . . In some places cob is unrendered, like the gable end of Hillmans, and the corner of Court Walk. Cob has different colours indicating different mixes . . . Curved corners, non-vertical walls and irregular rendering, like at Church Cottage, are also features of the older buildings.'*

Townhouses up to twenty feet tall were being constructed by the nineteenth century, just as Victorian sensibilities began to frown on mud. During the twentieth century cob building virtually ceased; today it is being reinvented with little access to continuous tradition.

The word dob was used in Hampshire. In the New Forest many cottages of clay were reinforced with heather on heath stone plinths. Dabbs, dabbins, clay daubins or biggins describe the clay buildings south of the Solway in Cumberland – and the method of construction. Here the boulder clay or estuarine clays, layered with straw, produce orange and yellow walls respectively. Originally they were roofed in turf; now many are being lost, although corrugated iron is saving some from decay.

In East Anglia's midlands clay lump is commonplace, sometimes called cob lump or clay bat. Glacial boulder clay with couch grass or straw, trodden by horse or cattle, was made into big blocks in wooden frames and, when dried in the sun like adobe, built up with puddled clay. On footings of flint or later brick, they were covered with renders to protect from frost and wet. Often the materials used – coal tar, lime, yellow or red ochre (ruddle) – produced strong colours: yellow brown dominated in Norfolk, with Suffolk Pink to the south. Sometimes clay was built up between shutters (then removed) to make thin walls, peculiar to the great estates.

East Lindsey in Lincolnshire shares mud and stud walls, in which timber frames act as skeletons, with the coasts of the Netherlands, Scandinavia and eastern Scotland, but nowhere else in England.

Chalk cob with an admixture of clay was used to build the model village of Milton Abbas in Dorset and recurs across the chalk belt of the South, from Farnham and Briantspuddle in Dorset to Upavon in Wiltshire. Around Aylesbury in Buckinghamshire a clayey chalk or white earth occurs naturally, known locally as wychert or wichert. Haddenham is a village defined by tall, pale yellow wychert walls, rubble based and topped by tiles.

See also BUS SHELTERS, CHALK, CORRUGATED IRON, COTTAGES, EARTH PIGMENTS, FLINT, PARGETING, SLATES, SOILS, THATCH, WALLS.

C O B B L E S

Cobblestones still pave footways in many villages and towns and give solid foundations to modern roads under the tarmac. Buffeted by water, in rivers or the sea, these fragments of rock have had their rough edges worn away. Rolled back and forth on the seashore, many have become smooth and almost perfectly spherical, although stones with an inbuilt penchant for splitting in one particular direction assume different shapes – schists and slates, for example, tend to become disc-shaped and are used on end. Strictly speaking, a cobble must have a diameter greater than two and a half inches but less than ten inches; anything smaller is a pebble, larger is a boulder.

People used local stone where they could, and sensitive highway authorities try to follow suit, sometimes using them as suggestive barriers to discourage people from crossing or getting too close. In Devon, they are often used where other towns might have pavements; East Budleigh, for example, has cobbles – they change direction to announce front doors and lanes, but are otherwise set at right angles to the road. Newton Poppleford's name records that fords were often cobbled, although there is now a bridge over the river Otter. Popple is a local word for cobbles, and they follow the river to the sea and form a great bank on the shore. They are used as much to make walls as they are to create firm ground in Budleigh Salterton, where they are known as Budleigh Buns.

In villages and towns along the South Downs, cobble-stones are nodules of flint, taken originally from shingle beaches. Durable local sandstone forms a more comfortable surface at Richmond, Yorkshire; sandstone cobbles are water-worn into flat shapes with well-rounded edges, and can be split. Paviors traditionally graded the stones for size, and set them into a bed of lime mortar.

From the streams of the Lake District they are known as beck-stones; from the beach around Bootle, Lancashire they are called cobble-ducks, and may be used for building as well as road laying. Flint cobbles from the sea were called 'petrified kidneys' in Lewes, Sussex; they made gutters in the middle of the road and were a cheap building material, as they were for houses in Cromer and Cley, Norfolk. From one of eleven houses in Steart, Somerset, Joanna Haxby reports that *at the mouth of the river Parrett . . . our houses and the field boundaries are built of beach cobbles bound with lime mortar*.

Setts are made rather than found. Hewn from durable granite, but sometimes of basalt and gneiss, they were cut by hand into oblong or square cubes. The Victorians filled city streets and docks with them, shipping them in from Aberdeenshire, Cornwall, Lundy Island and the Charnwood Forest, Leicestershire. Dhustone, a basalt that splits easily both vertically and horizontally, continues to be quarried from the Clee Hills in Shropshire, but is no longer used for setts.

Most mews in London still show their setts and they are often revealed in the gutters of streets. Occasionally, as in Endell Street, Covent Garden, a glimpse of wooden blocks is revealed through the tarmac. They were used to quieten the sound of horses and carriages beside hospitals and the houses of the wealthy.

Cobbles and setts are now sought after for restoration projects. In 2001, loss of domestic traditional skills meant that Portuguese workers were employed to lay new cobbles, imported from northern Italy, in the streets of Blackburn, one of many northern towns stereotyped by its cobbles until it was covered by asphalt in the 1950s.

See also BEACHCOMBING, BECKS, BUILDING STONES, FLINT, FORDS, KENNELS, KERBSTONES, MEWS, PAVEMENTS, RIVERS.

Under a big, rectangular, dipping lug sail the coble sends a Viking reverberation down the spine. Indeed, in north Northumberland it is popularly understood that the Norse longship informs the design of this inshore fishing boat.

From Humber to Tweed graceful cobles work directly from the beach, where a gaggle of salt-rusted tractors lie waiting to haul them up the sand. The boat is narrow fore and aft, but is shallow and wide-bellied to withstand the rigours of landing on the sand. It is clinker-built for lightness, with strength to launch into crashing waves and stand up to the intense squalls and storms of the North Sea.

Bill Smailes from Craster described the nuances of making this boat to Katrina Porteous: '. . . *if you go and order a coble, you give them the length of the ram plank and they build it from that. The ram plank is the bottom centre one that runs from just forrard of the engine, aft to the centre bottom of the stern. That plank is generally 22 to 24 feet in length. If it is 26 feet you will get a big, clumsy coble, impossible to work with on a beach.*' He goes on to describe the long timbers of larch that are copper-nailed and riveted, then the inside frame: '*oak or elm is used up the side, and they are cut from crooked pieces of tree grown roughly to that shape naturally. They are much stronger than if they had been artificially shaped. These pieces take a lot of fitting, and it takes a craftsman to do it. I hope it won't all be lost.*'

All the coastal villages had a fleet, often painted in a middle shade of blue, with fine Roman lettering. A few fishermen still work out of Beadnell in these traditional boats, now fitted with engines. In Yorkshire, where the pronunciation has shifted from 'ceoble' to 'cobble', the coastal conditions have varied sufficiently for small shifts in design. Some are double ended for launching into waves, as at Redcar, where they were differentiated as 'cockton'.

Although a few are being built, all by eye rather than formally designed, each year the numbers of these beautiful boats dwindles. The Filey coble, for example, fell in numbers from 190 to seventeen in the hundred years to 1984; by 2000 there were just five. As a demand of decommissioning, simply to prove to the government that the boat is no longer being used for fishing, they are burnt on the beach.

See also BEACHES, BOATS, CORNISH GIGS, FLATNERS, HARBOURS, NOBBIES, NORFOLK WHERRIES, PIERS, PORTLAND LERRETS, SEA FISH, SEA TRACTOR, THAMES SAILING BARGES, TIDES.

C O B N U T S

A 'cob' was a plump nut used in a game called coblenut (perhaps a precursor of conkers), played by children in the sixteenth century, so cobnuts came to be known as the fruit of the wild hazel tree. The first cultivated nuts, probably from Turkey, were known as filberts or fullbeards, which have long frilly husks, to differentiate them from the wild hazels that have rounder nuts and shorter husks.

The commercial growing of hazelnuts was established in Kent by the late eighteenth century. Several hundred acres of White Filbert grew around Maidstone, sometimes interplanted with hops, apple or cherry trees. In the 1830s a new variety was introduced by a Mr Lambert from Goudhurst. First called Lambert's Filbert, it was so widely grown that it became known as the Kentish Cob.

Kent, especially the ragstone between Sevenoaks and Ashford, remains the heartland of cultivation in England. The trees, which grow in orchards, or 'plats', were thinned and trained into a bowl shape, with about eight branches growing outwards and upwards to a height of about six feet. This allowed plenty of light to get to the shoots. Suckers, known as wands or spawn, were removed annually and the soil between the rows dug to kill the nut weevil larvae.

As with hop-picking, itinerant workers were joined by Londoners. The first picking, or 'firsting', is in mid- to late August, when the husks and nuts are still green, fresh and juicy. A month later, when they are ripe and have lost some moisture but their taste has become concentrated, the 'seconding' takes place, and eventually the 'thirding' includes anything that is left. The nuts were put into wicker baskets called kipsies and then into round baskets, or 'sieves', holding *about 28 pounds of green nuts or forty pounds of ripe ones*', as Meg Game remembered. They were sent off on special carts, known as fruit-vans, to the station, to be sold at the London markets of Borough, Spitalfields, Farringdon and Covent Garden. Rags, waste from wool mills, goose and turkey feathers and horse dung from London stables came back on the return journey to manure the crop.

The peak of cobnut production was before the First World War, when more than seven thousand acres were under cultivation, some in Worcestershire but mostly in Kent. By 1990 the acreage had plummeted to 250 in Kent. Cheaper imports, aided by better means of storage and transport, undercut the industry, and less labour-intensive crops helped by artificial fertilisers took the cobnuts' place. An important source of protein and a way of life were slipping away.

Since 1990, when the Kentish Cobnuts Association was formed, the acreage has increased in the villages around Plaxtol and Ightham. At Meg Game's plat in Ightham, Turkish residents from Hackney and Lewisham in east London come each year to pick this favourite food and taste the freedom of the country. Other nut lovers, less appreciated by the growers, include nuthatches, great tits, grey squirrels and the dormouse, which eats them when the shells are still soft, leaving a telltale round hole in the shell. Bluebells and primroses thrive where the trees are less intensively managed. The catkins have other names, including aglets, blowings, kentice and gull.

See also HAZEL, HOPS, HOP-GARDENS & HOP-YARDS, MARKET GARDENS, ORCHARDS.

C O E S

These limestone buildings, smaller than barns, mark lead mines in Derbyshire. Sometimes they were built right over the shaft, and contained a windlass or stowe to lower miners down and to lift lead ore to the surface. Miners kept their gear and clothes here.

The Parish Map of Bonsall recalls the freedom to mine anywhere beyond church ground, house or garden, and the harsh punishment for theft:

By cuſtom olde in Wirksworth Wapentake
if any of this nation find a rake or sign
or leading to the same; may set
in any ground & there lead oar may get
they may make crosses, holes and set their ſtowes
sink shafts, build lodges cottages or coes
but churches houses gardens all are free from this ſtrange
cuſtom of the minery
for ſtealing oar twice from the minery the thief that's taken
fined twice shall be, but the third time, that he commits such
theft, shall have a knife ſtuck through his hand to th' haft
into the ſtowe & there till death shall ſtand, or loose himself
by cutting loose his hand
and shall foreswear the franchise of the mine
& always lose his freedom from that time.

Ground pock-marked with slumping shafts may be dangerous now, so mines are capped with concrete and stone. In Yorkshire and further north little stone field shelters are called bields.

See also BARNS, BUILDING STONES, CHIMNEYS, DEW PONDS, DRYSTONE WALLS, GRUFFY GROUND, HORSES & PONIES, LEAD MINES, LIMESTONE, PARISH MAPS, SOUGHS, ZIGZAGS.

C O M M O N S

Raggle-taggle open land with a wild, unkempt look may spring to mind, but the variety of common land ranges from thousands of mountain-top acres in the Lake District to slivers of roadside in Herefordshire. Each contributes to the feel of the place. The 'Strays' of York are now used for town recreation rather than grazing. Northamptonshire has virtually no common land, whereas great expanses of unenclosed common cover the uplands of the northern counties, as well as Bodmin Moor in Cornwall and Dartmoor in Devon.

The name describes not the land but the rights over it. Common rights are of great antiquity, perhaps pre-dating private property, remnants from a time before the Normans made land-grabbing the sport of kings, courtiers and church. From town fairground to unfenced heath, 'the common' is shorthand for something made complicated by time, change and struggle. For centuries commons have been areas of land over which the specific rights of local people have persisted over someone else's 'soil'. These rights made the difference between starvation and survival.

Commons are still owned by a lord of the manor, who now may be a local authority, and it is only since the Countryside and Rights of Way Act 2000 came into force that the right to walk on registered common land has been open to all. The Open Spaces Society has been campaigning for this for more than a century.

Apart from new-won access to air and exercise, the range of rights is manifold. The most widespread are to estovers (pollarded branches, underwood for fencing, bracken and gorse for bedding); housebote (bigger timbers for repair or building); pannage (running pigs under woodland to take fallen acorns and beechmast); pasture (stock grazing); piscary (fishing); turbary (peat digging for fuel); and the right of common in the soil (sand, gravel and stone). They are matched by rigorous rules, such as the stinting or regulation of stock numbers or grazing hours, set by the commoners or by court leet. The landholder usually retains rights of minerals and shooting and may or may not share some of the common rights.

In 1963 Dudley Stamp computed that of England's 1,055,000 acres of common land, two-thirds lay in the upland moors and fells of Durham, Cumberland, Lancashire, Northumberland, Yorkshire and Westmorland, and that of the lowland commons nearly half lay within fifty miles of London. It was around that time that commons registration began. Now we seem only to have 370,000 hectares (914,307 acres). Yes, we changed measurement systems in between, but this is not a European conspiracy. Many commons were simply not registered: to Dorset's shame, for example, a large number simply faded away.

The Surrey heaths have a long history of recreational use, with more common land owned by local authorities than any other county. This reflects pioneering work done by the Commons Preservation Society and the National Trust. Chobham Heath, busy with human toil since the Stone Age, is now criss-crossed by pipelines, aerial lines, railway lines and the M3, as well as footpaths and bridleways. Here the Bagshot Sands, rendered even less fertile by the removal of trees as early as Neolithic times, are typical of manorial 'waste' – land marginal to cultivation.

In Dorset's Blackmore Vale, wayside common land borders roads now metalled but once so soggy that wide swathes were left for carts to find their own way through. Cut for hay, left for nature or occasional use by travellers and Romani, some were squatted long ago and have thin cottages with stretched gardens along the roadside.

The lack of commons in the midland counties dates from the century following 1750 and reflects the greater success here of landowners enclosing the land for agriculture. Today, farming is changing again, and its fluctuating patterns are echoed in the look and ecology of the land. Many lowland heath commons suffer from under-grazing, while upland commons may be over-grazed; both threaten vulnerable fauna and flora.

'Commons left free in the rude rags of nature', as John Clare had them, may have been on the poorest land, and this is what makes them ecologically rich. Mellis Green, a mile long and 174 acres, is the biggest grazing common in Suffolk. It is a nature reserve: 158 recorded species of flowering plants, many butterflies, owls, skylarks, kingfishers, water voles and pigmy shrews are all desirable neighbours. But the Suffolk Wildlife Trust, to whom the lord of the manorship was given in 1989, spent the early part of the new millennium hassling house owners around the green for amounts of money for vehicular access rights across the common to their houses, some of which are hundreds of years old. Roger Deakin, a resident, says in doing this 'the Suffolk Wildlife Trust may have surrendered the moral authority it needs to safeguard the vulnerable historic landscape'; the people who edge the common ought to be its chief allies.

Survival of commons requires people to work together to practice appropriate farming, wildlife and recreational activities. English Nature is busy learning how in the Yorkshire Dales, where scars, screes and limestone pavement offer varied calcareous habitats, with plants such as bloody cranesbill and bird's-eye primrose among the grassland, mire and juniper shrub, enjoyed by the northern brown argus butterfly and birds such as curlew and wheatear. Agreements with grazier commoners have already seen the re-emergence of juniper on Moughton Common.

Every common has its own story to tell, of great struggles in different centuries between lords of the manor and commoners. The Town Moor in Newcastle, where travellers and showmen arrive in late June for the great fair, the Hoppings, is owned by the city council. The commoners carry the title Freemen of the City and have grazing rights over some of the 350 acres. As the city grew this expanse was maintained as open land because the commoners fought for their rights. The struggles never end. Town Moor has been made to accommodate formal recreation and sports grounds, parks and allotments, although the Friends of Town Moor have successfully countered the relocation of the Newcastle United Football Club from St James' Park.

Lord Thomas Maryon Wilson tried for half a century from 1818 to enclose Hampstead Heath. He took such quantities of sand as to change the shape of the land and tried repeatedly to introduce Acts of Parliament to build. The commoners were, however, men of means and connections, resisting at every turn. After his death the land was bought by the Metropolitan Board of Works, to which it added Parliament Hill in 1889. By 1924, with the addition of Kenwood, the Heath reached eight hundred acres. It is just one of the jewels in the capital city's crown of commons, many safeguarded by the Metropolitan Commons Act of 1866, which prevented enclosure of land within a fifteen-mile radius of Charing Cross. It is now managed by the Corporation of London, as is the greatest of the Essex commons, Epping Forest – five thousand acres of ancient pollarded hornbeams and oaks preserved by the Epping Forest Act *'for the enjoyment, in perpetuity, by the citizens of London'*.

Having been a place for army training in the First World War, then bought by the old Borough of Newbury in 1939 for recreation, Greenham and Crookham Commons in Berkshire were requisitioned for the war effort. In 1941 an airfield was built and after the war the Air Ministry let it to the US Air Force. In the early 1980s this became the focus of a protest against cruise missiles and nuclear war. Women from across the country created a peace camp, lived here, penetrated the base, danced on missile silos and created a vortex of (dis)enchantment.

Who stole the Goose off the Common?
Who stole the Common off the Goose?
Who stole the land for airfields?
Who turned the scientists loose?

Dennis Gould, from 'Greenham Common Blues'

Feminists, anarchists, pacifists, ecologists, Buddhists and Quakers joined a long roll call of civil disobedience to prevent a final extinguishing of rights and to win back the common for the people. By 8 April 2000, the perimeter fence had been completely removed – seventeen years after hundreds of women had been arrested for cutting down five of its nine miles. The Greenham and Crookham Commons Act was passed in 2002, guiding restoration, conservation and rights for public access to this place of ecological, cultural and historical significance.

The concrete from the runway, the longest in Europe, has been crushed and used to build a local school. Some has remained and been grassed over – the contrast with the indigenous acid soils produces an unexpected mix of flora. The brooding missile silos, clustered and grassed over like giant barrows, still crouch behind wire, and barn owls have moved in. Walking here with the smell of gorse, the sounds of larks, the sight of a hare, the laughter of children and the pounding of jogging feet, anyone now can be part of the process of reclaiming this place, despite its ghosts, for nature and people.

See also ALLOTMENTS, BARROWS, BEACHES, BEECH, BOUNDARIES, COMMUNICATION & RADIO MASTS, FAIRS & FAIRGROUNDS, FELLS, GALLOPS, GORSE, HILLS, HORNBEAM, LANDMARK TREES, LEAD MINES, RACECOURSES, VILLAGE GREENS.

COMMUNICATION & RADIO MASTS

Guglielmo Marconi sent the first radio signals across water from Flatholm Island in the Severn estuary to Wales in 1897, and from Alum Bay on the Isle of Wight. For longer-range experiments he proceeded to Cornwall and in 1901 sent the first radio signal across the Atlantic from Poldhu. The masts are long gone, but a memorial obelisk stands on the cliffs.

Radio and, from 1936, television have always needed dramatic masts for the sending and receiving of information. Early television came from the BBC at Alexandra Palace in north London, its mast immortalised by the television newsreel's titles. Regional affiliations still cling to independent television transmission aerials, such as Rowridge on the Isle of Wight, Holme Moss in Yorkshire and Caradon Hill in Cornwall. Winter Hill near Horwich serves viewers in Lancashire and the Wirral, and is a visible part of North West identity. Manchester band A Certain

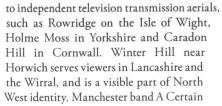

Emley Moor ITV mast, Yorkshire.

107

Ratio recorded a song about it in 1980. Emley Moor, near Kirkburton in Yorkshire, is the country's tallest self-supporting mast, the third in that location, and has been suggested for listing.

London's Post Office Tower was built between 1961 and 1965 to beam telephone messages across the city. At 620 feet tall, it remains one of the city's most recognisable orientation points.

Since the 1980s, the increasing use of mobile telephones has prompted the erection of many masts. The debate about proliferation is fuelled by fears of proximity to microwaves and laughable attempts to disguise masts in incongruous artificial trees, such as the giant 'conifer' on the high road near Blandford Forum in Dorset. The clean lines of water towers and tall buildings are being lost to sprouting aerials, and city skylines are also changing – at least one decapitated church spire in Camden, London has become hirsute.

See also BEACONS (COASTAL), CHURCHES, EARTH STATIONS, FILM LOCATIONS, FOLLIES, INDUSTRIAL CHIMNEYS, LANDMARKS, OBELISKS, SOUND MIRRORS, TOWER BLOCKS, WATER-TOWERS.

CONFECTIONERY

108

In George Orwell's *Coming Up for Air* George Bowling remembers how he used to pass the sweet shop. It had '*a peculiar fascination for children. Even when we had no money, we'd go that way so as to glue our noses against the window . . . Most of the sweets were four ounces a penny.*' Each generation of children has its favourite assortment of sweets, but today the corner sweet shop is rarer.

After the austerity of the war, regional association with sweets was dying. Pontefract is known for its pomfret cakes because liquorice was grown there, but most sweet manufacture had no geographical imperatives, apart from proximity to docks and sugar refineries. Many of the early confectioners were grocers, apothecaries, traders or pastry cooks who fell into sweet making.

Until the 1960s, Fisherman's Friends menthol lozenges were sold only in and around Fleetwood in Lancashire. They were first made in liquid form in the 1860s by James Lofthouse, a pharmacist who sought to help the local '*fishermen working in the extreme conditions of the Icelandic deep-sea fishing grounds*', according to the story told on the packet. The popularity of these liquorice, menthol, eucalyptus and capsicum tablets, still made in Fleetwood, has spread across the country.

Kendal Mint Cakes, written about in the 1700s, are made from sugar and water, heated until dissolved, cooked, cooled, flavoured with peppermint oil and left to crystallise. They have been wrapped and sold in slabs in Kendal, Westmorland since 1868; four companies still make them

there. In Northumberland, pink-striped, pepperminty boiled sweets are made and sold in tins – '*Cowe's genuine original celebrated Berwick Cockles . . . entirely different from imitations*'. Toffees made by Molly Bushell in the late 1700s, when Everton was a village overlooking the picturesque Mersey, gained a reputation; soon people came from all over Lancashire to buy her soothing sweets. Generations later, the football team is known as the Toffees and 'Molly Bushell', or 'Mother Noblett', as she became, dispenses Everton mints to the fans at home games.

Chocolate bars have been the nation's favourite sweet for many years. The largest English chocolate companies were started by three Quakers – Rowntree, Fry and Cadbury – who were debarred from going into the professions. Cadbury's at Bournville, south of Birmingham, was built as a model factory and town; it is now a tourist attraction. The distinctive smells from the Terry's (closed in 2005 after 250 years) and Rowntree's factories in York and the cocoa mill in Hull, Yorkshire are both loved and hated.

Only a few firms make sweets by hand. According to Nicholas Whittaker, Britain's ten thousand sweet makers had been reduced to 580 in 1956 and a mere eighty by 1998. Shops selling traditional sweets have opened in Bath and in Haworth, Yorkshire, for example, the latter selling local specialities, such as a Yorkshire version of sherbert, called Kali, 21 types of liquorice and thirteen kinds of toffee.

Different occasions bring their sweets: candy floss and toffee apples at the fair, rock and ice-cream at the beach, Turkish Delight and marrons glacés for Christmas, chocolate eggs for Easter and fruit pastilles on a long car journey. Brittle bonfire toffee is still enjoyed in the North on 5 November and toffee apples at Hallowe'en. Since 1990 they have been a favourite addition to Apple Day celebrations.

See also APPLE DAY, BISCUITS, BLACKPOOL ROCK, BONFIRE NIGHT, EASTER CUSTOMS, FOOD, FOOTBALL, HALLOWE'EN, LIQUORICE, SMELLS.

COOLING TOWERS

What a magnificent presence they have, these great chess castles gathering beside rivers as if for communal ablutions. They steam away water and heat generated by the making of electricity from coal.

A plume of cloud can pinpoint Ratcliffe on Soar; from thirty miles away the cluster of towers becomes visible. Soft, steamy sculptures emerging from the curved concrete shapes catch the colours of the setting sun or tell of the wind's direction. You may pass virtually underneath them on the train into Nottingham; up close they are hugely and gloriously dripping.

The Trent valley once had even more coal-fired power stations, all with their gaggle of towers, taking advantage of the nearby mines, the railways and the river's volume. From the flat Lincolnshire edge near Gainsborough they stand against the sky, and from high in the Charnwood Forest in Leicestershire they spread out before you. High Marnham, Staythorpe and Drakelow are little places made big with sculptural towers. Sulphur dioxide and nitrogen oxide are unacceptable pollutants from coal burning, expelled invisibly from a tall chimney; the cooling towers emit only steam. What a waste of energy – no wonder the old Battersea power station in London was conscripted to heat the whole of Pimlico. Along the Trent, populations of fish bloom near the warmer outflows; populations of anglers, too.

Cooling towers are landmarks bold enough for giants. The towers of Sheerness power station are visible far from the Essex coast. In Berkshire Didcot's towers dominate views across the Thames valley and from Wittenham Clumps. Close to the towers a (once) mobile-home village has settled.

The undistinguished newish houses of Camblesforth, near Selby in Yorkshire, are given landmark status by the twelve cooling towers of Drax power station, the biggest in Europe. The squat, reddish towers tucked into the Ironbridge gorge beside the river Severn in Shropshire are like another species, enfolded by verdant and clinging hills.

Perhaps during the next twenty years these structures will disappear, taking their functional beauty into the history photographs. The dismantling of the single tower beside the M6 in Birmingham proved disorientating. Drivers on the A1, however, wrestling with strong winds on 1 November 1965, must have thought the world was ending as three of the eight cooling towers collapsed at Ferrybridge in Yorkshire. It was concluded that they were grouped badly, enhancing the wind's effect to the extent that all were damaged.

See also CATHEDRALS, CLUMPS, COAL MINING, FRESHWATER FISH, GRAVEL PITS, LANDMARKS, RIVERS, WINDS.

C O R N   D O L L I E S

Cambridgeshire has the handbell; Durham, the chandelier; Essex, the collar turret; Northamptonshire, the horns; Staffordshire, the knot; and Suffolk, the horseshoe. Each county has its corn dollies, and there are many more local specialities – the Topsham cross from Devon; the Luston ring from Herefordshire; the Vale of Pickering chalice from Yorkshire. Local names include Maiden Cross, Crook, Apple, Boat, Turnip, Crown, Clayack; Mare in the Midlands, Mell Doll in Yorkshire, Kern baba in Northumberland and Neck in the South West. In the North they were dressed like dolls. Any shape is permissible, providing it contains some ears of corn.

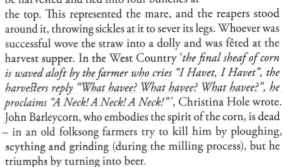

Ceremonies took place on each farm to celebrate the cutting of the last sheaf of corn. These took a number of forms, such as 'Crying the Neck' in Devon and 'Crying the Mare' in Herefordshire, where a patch of corn was left in the last field to be harvested and tied into four bunches at the top. This represented the mare, and the reapers stood around it, throwing sickles at it to sever its legs. Whoever was successful wove the straw into a dolly and was fêted at the harvest supper. In the West Country *'the final sheaf of corn is waved aloft by the farmer who cries "I Havet, I Havet", the harvesters reply "What havee? What havee? What havee?", he proclaims "A Neck! A Neck! A Neck!"'*, Christina Hole wrote. John Barleycorn, who embodies the spirit of the corn, is dead – in an old folksong farmers try to kill him by ploughing, scything and grinding (during the milling process), but he triumphs by turning into beer.

The making of the corn dolly using straw from the last sheaf was to ensure that the spirit of the corn lived on until spring. It was made in the field by plaiting the straw into intricate shapes, usually by men who had learned the craft from their fathers, and brought back ceremonially with the last load. It was hung in the farmhouse until the spring, when it was taken back into the fields so that the spirit of the corn could return to the earth. Then it was stored again in the farmhouse until the next harvest.

Of all the grain crops, wheat straw was preferred because it was easiest to plait – old varieties with long and hollow stems, such as Maris Widgeon, Maris Huntsman, Flamingo, Eclipse, Squarehead Master and Capelle, were used. Today these old varieties are grown in small quantities especially for straw work.

Mechanisation in the nineteenth century made the straw unworkable and the custom waned. However, a life-size lion and unicorn representing the Royal Arms, made in straw plaits by Fred Mizen for the 1851 Great Exhibition, revived interest in straw work. The Victorian invention of the harvest festival brought the practice of hanging plaited straw harvest crosses in churches, together with fruit, vegetables and bread.

See also CROPS, HARVEST FESTIVALS, THATCH.

109

CORNISH GIGS

As a vessel returning from the Americas or Australia entered Cornish waters she would be met by gigs racing out from the Isles of Scilly or the mainland. The winning gig would get the work of piloting the vessel through the treacherous seas. Built for speed and manoeuvrability, pilot gigs are light, narrow, clinker-built boats, around 32 feet long and four feet, nine inches or more across the beam. Powered by six oars, they risk the sea in all weathers and can reach speeds of nine knots. Stories are told of further use as lifeboats and for long-distance visits to France for contraband.

This tradition of hard competition is now matched in the thriving sport of pilot-gig racing. Originating in Cornwall and the Isles of Scilly, it has increased in popularity since the 1980s and is beginning to spread along the south coast and across the world. More than forty clubs gather for competition from March to October, with exciting and colourful races for men, women, youths and veterans. The World Championship gig races draw teams from as far away as Australia, America, The Faroes, France and Holland.

The oldest boats date from the early nineteenth century. The Newquay, for example, built in 1812, is still raced from its home harbour, and the Treffry, dating from 1838, is used as the design blueprint for speed and fitness in these waters. A revival of boat building has been sparked, with small-leaved Cornish elm, *Ulmus stricta*, being used for planking and silver spruce replacing ash for the eighteen-foot oars.

See also ASH, BEACHES, BOATS, THE CHANNEL, CLIFFS, COASTS, COBLES, ELM, FLATNERS, HARBOURS, ISLANDS, NOBBIES, NORFOLK WHERRIES, PORTLAND LERRETS, SEA FISH, THAMES SAILING BARGES, TIDES, ZAWNS.

CORNISH PASTIES

 The Cornish pasty is a meal in itself. It was invented to fit into a pocket and be eaten without a knife or fork. These are the qualities that made it the staple diet of Cornish tin- and copper-mine workers, blacksmiths and engineers in the first half of the nineteenth century.

The traditional Cornish pasty is made with thick, short-crust pastry and filled with raw chopped onions, potatoes, swedes (known in Cornwall as turnips), skirt or chuck steak and seasoning. The pastry is rolled to about a quarter of an inch thick and cut into round, plate-sized portions; the filling is put onto one half and the rest of the pastry folded over, the edges dampened and crimped with fingers and thumb. Some prefer to place the filling in the centre of the pastry and have the 'seam' at the top. Initials might be carved into one corner. It is glazed with egg or milk, a slit is made on the top to let out steam, and it is baked in a hot oven for about twenty minutes and then at a lower temperature for a further forty.

There used to be many variations on the fillings – beef and potatoes, fish, pork, cheese and onion, egg and bacon, rabbit, whatever was to hand. Some combined savoury and sweet ingredients, the pudding half of apple, jam or treacle separated by an internal portion of pastry, to be washed down with sweet tea – this is reminiscent of the Bedfordshire clanger.

The pasty became known as 'Cornish' in Victorian times by visitors to the county. Now three million pasties are made in Cornwall every week, although ninety per cent are sold outside the county. Their makers are trying to get European Protected Geographical Indication status, so that only pasties made in Cornwall can be called by that name.

See also APPLES, CAFÉS, CAKES, CHEESE, FOOD, MINES, ONIONS, POTATOES, PUDDINGS.

CORRUGATED IRON

It may be thought that sheets of galvanised corrugated iron would make for standardised buildings. Far from it. The material has not had a homogenising influence, mainly because it lends itself to small-scale, self-build enterprises that respond to a precise, functional need. The result is simplicity, locally tempered and idiosyncratic. Painted colours often carry or create local resonances – red, black, white, grey – while deterioration leads to the soft, rusty, patinated walls and roofs that feel such a part of the landscape.

From its early days in the 1820s, popularity increased for 'the galvanise' well into the twentieth century. Invented here, it went from catalogues to all corners of the world. Here it was used for substitute roofing, especially for thatch, and for small buildings of all kinds because of its cheapness and ease of use. Perhaps for these same reasons it has not been highly valued, but it has admirers. Terms of endearment range from 'furrowed iron' and 'wriggly tin' to 'the corrugated'. It has been used for fishermen's huts, isolation hospitals, air-raid shelters, stations, museums, mobile shepherd's huts, schools, shops, stores, houses, pavilions, churches and chapels. All kinds of agricultural uses persist, including the black Dutch barns that stand in fields.

Many are just hanging on, some lovingly valued, like Bob Shepherd's Garage at Little Somerford in Somerset, festooned with flowers. There are large examples, too, such as the old Ministry of Supply wartime food stores, preserved at Buckinghamshire Railway Centre, and the massive covered slips at Chatham Dockyard in Kent. Many curvaceous Nissen huts have been turned to new uses.

Various corners of the country carry memories of 'tin towns', transient settlements built to house workers. In the

Derbyshire Peak District, for example, navvies who built dams for the Derwent Valley Water Board were housed from 1901 to 1914 at Birchinlee, once a town of two and a half thousand people.

Peter Beacham writes of his love of the material in Devon. '*Only when we focus more sharply on the individual buildings of the farmstead might we realise we have naturally absorbed into this palette of harmonious perfection some rusted roofs of corrugated iron . . . Officialdom, at least in the form of the Ministry of Agriculture, has proved reluctant to accept its unpretentious virtues for the repair of traditional buildings. There is an indisputable case for its widespread use not only in the conservation of existing structures but in their sympathetic extension and sometimes at least for the wholly new.*'

A supporter at English Heritage writes: '*I have always thought that corrugated iron is one of the most valuable conservation materials ever invented: it has probably saved more historic buildings than anything else.*'

See also AIRFIELDS, ALLOTMENTS, BARNS, CHAPELS, CHURCHES, HOPS, HOP-GARDENS & HOP-YARDS, MOSQUES, QUAKER MEETING-HOUSES, RESERVOIRS, SYNAGOGUES, TEMPLES, TIN TABERNACLES, VILLAGE HALLS.

COTTAGE GARDENS

The most successful cottage gardens are unpretentious, honest, working gardens, exuberant collections of plants crammed harmoniously together into small spaces. The garden and the cottage seem as one, growing out of the ground together.

The first cottage gardens would not have had much room for decorative plants, although some flowers had symbolic and protective roles. Gardens had to provide for the family – pigs, chickens and other livestock would have shared the space, together with the plants grown to feed them. Cabbages, broad beans, carrots, kale, leeks, onions, parsnips, marrowfat peas, potatoes (from the eighteenth century) and turnips were the staple vegetables grown, supplemented by fruit – apples, damsons, cherries, gooseberries – and herbs for medicinal use and flavouring – borage, chives, dill, garlic, horseradish, fennel, hyssop, mint, rosemary, sage, sorrel and thyme. Many herbs and flowers were brought in from the wild, such as dog roses, foxglove, heartsease, wild geranium, herb Robert, honeysuckle, old man's beard and wild strawberries. The garden was protected by a hawthorn hedge, wattle fence or stone wall.

Plants were exchanged; herbs and fruit trees were salvaged from abandoned monasteries. Some, such as meadowsweet, wormwood and rue, were selected for their fragrance when dried – for strewing on the floor – or, like cowslips, tansy and sage, for distilling into perfumes. Sweet violets were used in cooking for sweetening. Over the years, more plants became available, many from the gardeners who worked at the big houses, who had access to specimens brought from overseas by plant collectors.

In the early 1800s, John Claudius Loudon wrote: '*A florist's society is established in almost every town and village in the northern districts . . . Derbyshire miners raised pansies, Lancashire cotton workers auriculas, Sheffield workers polyanthus, colliers of Northumberland and Durham pinks. Norwich was noted for its carnations, Manchester for its gooseberries, and Spitalfields in London was famous especially for its auriculas and tulips.*' The anemone, hyacinth and hollyhock were also popular florists' flowers. The hollyhock, with its back to the cottage wall, is the archetypal English cottage garden plant; it may have been collected by Crusaders from the other end of the Mediterranean.

The cottage in Helpston, Northamptonshire that belonged to the parents of the poet John Clare cost forty shillings in rent, which was paid for by '*an old apple tree in the garden*'. In Aynho, the apricot fulfilled this function.

Philanthropists built model villages for their workers in the picturesque or romantic style, such as Blaise Hamlet near Bristol, designed by John Nash in 1809. The thatched and tile-roofed buildings with tall, ornate chimneys had cottage gardens with wicket gates and rose archways over the paths, an image popularised by the painters of the time and still in currency today on birthday cards – an aspiration of a secure and quiet life.

In the mid-nineteenth century, with the growing popularity of glasshouses in which to grow exotic and less hardy flowers, the growing of annuals for carpet bedding became fashionable; hardy perennials and cottage gardens fell out of favour. The provision of allotments in the late 1800s meant that more space could be given to growing flowers around the house.

111

Steeple Aston, Oxfordshire.

William Robinson advocated a more naturalistic form of gardening. He hated the geometric flowerbeds and formal carpet bedding he saw in Victorian parks and gardens. Gertrude Jekyll said: '*I have learnt from the little cottage gardens that help to make our English wayside the prettiest in the temperate world. One can hardly go into the smallest cottage garden without learning or observing something new.*' The gardens she designed for the affluent offered swathes of colour reminiscent of the French impressionist painters.

Garden writer Margery Fish, distressed at the disappearance of the old cultivars of cottage garden plants, started to create a garden at East Lambrook in Somerset in 1938, which combined old cultivars with new varieties. She strove for an informal effect, wanting to '*produce in a garden what nature does outside, but with cultivated plants*'. Her influential books made people realise the need to conserve garden plants.

Vita Sackville-West's stylish garden at Sissinghurst, Kent, influenced by Jekyll and Robinson, with its sophisticated white enclave, draws more crowds than any other National Trust property. Naturalistic planting has become fashionable, and ecological imperatives have revived interest in cottage-style gardening. Gardens with close-packed hardy perennials need less energy in production and less water than bedding plants and close-shaven, weed-free lawns. The cottager's knowledgeable and homely way of mixing up flowers and vegetables is now called companion planting – a natural way of reducing the build-up of pests and diseases.

See also ALLOTMENTS, APPLES, APRICOTS, CHERRIES, COBNUTS, COTTAGES, COUNCIL HOUSES, DOG ROSES, GARDENS, GOOSEBERRIES, LAWN, OLD MAN'S BEARD, RUSH-BEARING, TOPIARY.

C O T T A G E S

The dark, smoky, damp and overcrowded cottage, originally the home of the poor peasant, labourer or miner and his extended family, offered simple shelter and sometimes a place to work. Building materials came from nearby, some to be used time and again. William Wordsworth opened our eyes to these buildings: '*these humble dwellings remind the*

contemplative spectator of a production of Nature, and may (using a strong expression) rather be said to have grown than to have been erected; – to have risen, by an instinct of their own, out of the native rock – so little is there in them of formality, such is their wildness and beauty'.

The cottage is much loved for its honesty, simplicity and truth to locality. Its drawbacks have had money and technical sophistication poured upon them, making it comfortable now to let the cottage evoke a time of 'harmony with the land' for which we long to return (never having to suffer its realities). It is telling that the two most popular house names are The Cottage and Rose Cottage. Other attractions lie in its adaptability. Its stories are felt, age is seen to have gathered, and longevity, back beyond even an eighteenth-century exterior, may be hidden behind additions and adaptations.

Cottages, farmhouses and farm buildings, more than any other building types, bring stone and earth to life and demonstrate all kinds of local nuances learned from

From top, clockwise: Kingston, Devon; Liverton Mines, Yorkshire; Cowden, Kent; Skirmett, Buckinghamshire; north Pennines.

112

experience of the place by craftsmen and builders. In turn, the flavour of the locality is heightened. The legacy of variation demonstrates the richness of geological sequences and rising economic fortunes to be read in periods of rapid building and the extending use of local stone, brick or earth. That is, until the 1850s, when mass production and the railways brought cheaper and more uniform bricks and Welsh slate to all but the most inaccessible parts.

Cottages had sprung up along spring lines, around village greens, by mineral workings and woodland edges. If you could put up a building on common land in one night, with a bit of thatch on it in Devon, or just a smoking chimney by dawn in Herefordshire and Shropshire, then you earned squatters' rights to stay.

Where large pieces of timber were available, early one-room cottages were made either with cruck frames, resembling a big A, with walls of wattle and daub in the West Midlands and the North, or with a box frame, more frequently found in southern and eastern England. Cottages with thick, unbaked earth walls or cob, protected by plaster and limewash and a thatched roof of reeds, straw, gorse, bracken, heather, brushwood or turf, with overhanging eaves, were common in the South West, East Anglia and parts of the Midlands.

By the end of the 1600s, cottages were being built of locally quarried uncut (rubble) stone if it was available. Bricks appeared in cottages in the 1700s, usually handmade locally – the range of size, shape and colour has contributed to subtle differences in and between places. Brick noggin (an infilling of bricks often placed in a herringbone pattern), if it could be afforded, began to replace wattle and daub or cob. At the same time, clay tiles and pantiles began to oust thatch in some areas.

The shape and mass of cottages vary. Some are hard-edged and precise, such as the long rows of single-storey stone and slate cottages in Northumberland, built by landowners to house their workers. In the Derbyshire and Yorkshire sand and gritstone areas, the workability of the stone makes for solid lintels, window and door surrounds and the little shoulders or 'kneelers' protruding from the gable parapet. Cottages sharing walls were common, as they were cheaper to build and kept each other warm or cool.

Others appear sculpted and are situated less rigidly, face or gable to the road, their plasticity deriving from softer materials of cob or thatch. Peter Mason wrote: '*The most commonly occurring small house type in Hampshire is the thatched, one-and-a-half-storeyed building, often called a "bun-cottage".*' John and Jane Penoyre observed: '*With eyebrows of thatch over the half-dormers and their soft, brown, rounded outlines curving down over their half-hipped ends, the cottages seem more roof than wall, an effect heightened by the technique, logical in a moulded material, of extending the thatch downwards to cover the porch.*'

Homeworking was once commonplace – jewellery in Birmingham, saddlery in Walsall and silk in Leek, Staffordshire. 'Cottage industry' could make demands on the shapes of buildings. Weavers' windows betray the need for extra light in upstairs rooms, as in Saddleworth and Thurlstone in Yorkshire and Macclesfield in Cheshire. Plate glass for windows became available for labourers' cottages in the 1800s, replacing small panes of bottle glass in lead casings.

Cottages built for lock keepers and level-crossing lookouts are visibly tied to their time, task and place, even though other evidence may be long gone. Enlightened philanthropists built estate and model villages in the eighteenth and nineteenth centuries, some with exaggerated rustic charm, known as cottage orné. The Victorian picturesque and Gothic Revival brought romantic cottages with tall chimneys, intricate tiling, thatched roofs with low eaves, dormer windows and carved barge-boards – more for the squire to savour than for the incumbent.

During the past decade a new generation of cottages has begun to appear. At Osmington and Corfe in west Dorset, South Creake in Norfolk and Bishop's Mead in Chelmsford, Essex, builders are leaning on the vernacular, but with the market in mind. A new generation of people, some working from home, is buying two-storey buildings, sometimes helping to keep small quarries open and local craftsmanship alive, while embracing new, energy-conscious technologies.

113

See also ALMSHOUSES, BARNS, BLACK & WHITE BUILDINGS, BRICKS, BUILDING STONES, BUNGALOWS, CANALS, CHIMNEYS, COASTGUARD COTTAGES, COB, COMMONS, COTTAGE GARDENS, EARTH PIGMENTS, FARMS & FARMSTEADS, FLINT, PANTILES, PARGETING, RAILWAYS, SHINGLES, SLATES, TERRACED HOUSES, THATCH, TILES, TOLL-HOUSES, VILLAGES, WEATHER-BOARDING.

COUNCIL HOUSES

From rows of semi-detached houses to 'dwelling units' in concrete blocks, the council house comes in many guises. Few have made any gesture to locality. In the bigger council estates, you might hardly know which county or city you were in; the houses are often the same and streets hard to distinguish. Residents orientate themselves with intimate knowledge, but a stranger may find few landmarks.

Civic duty and optimism fired the house building of the twentieth century. Cynicism and cost-cutting ended it. Most villages and towns have at least one row of council houses, such as Church Road in Sherington, Buckinghamshire, or the odd couple of semi-detached examples forming the main body of a country hamlet. The earliest ones are of simple and dependable design, almost like a child's drawing. From the heart of a town or village they radiate outwards

along the approach roads or fill the shape of a single field. Those nearest to the centre, built before or after the First World War, are likely to have good-sized front gardens and vegetable plots at the rear.

In the 1920s and 1930s, improved transport links from overcrowded London pushed large estates out into the Home Counties. They were adjoined to existing villages and towns, such as Bexley, Sevenoaks and Woking, whose characters changed forever. Maps of Aspley, Bilborough and Broxtowe in Nottingham show the circles and crescents of 1930s municipal housing.

The well-built brick semi-detached houses of the late 1940s were housing minister Aneurin Bevan's dream, finally to honour the promise of the previous world war to provide 'homes fit for heroes'. Idealism and utopian boldness demanded quality mass housing, but it caused a financial crisis and desperation led to quick and cheap solutions: some 'prefabs' intended to last a decade are still extant and proudly maintained, like the semi-prefabricated estate at Twerton, Bath. The houses of the next thirty years showed a marked decline, those of the 1960s and 1970s, some filled with architectural idealism, all too often turned into alienating, vaguely modernist estates of frightening alleys, graffiti and smelly stairs. Many lasted only two to three decades: the condensation-ridden flats and houses of Portsdown Park in Cosham, Hampshire were demolished in 1987. Places like this gave council housing a bad name, although when the government of the 1980s gave tenants the opportunity to buy their houses, the sturdier inter-war and Bevan houses were snapped up.

The tower block was the council's other weapon in its housing armoury. International architects, such as Le Corbusier and Mies van der Rohe, had utopian visions of living units in the sky, served by every amenity. The Alton estates in Roehampton, south-west London tried to live up to these ideals. Park Hill in Sheffield is Grade II*-listed, but loathed by its occupants. Newcastle's Byker estate, a 1970s design, worked hard to keep families and communities together, but generates mixed feelings. The same city's Killingworth estate was award-winning and influential in the 1960s; thirty years later it was demolished. Lack of maintenance, of responsive and sympathetic management and simple bad building wore it out. With the collapse of Ronan Point in east London in 1968, confidence in high-rise building fell. But it became clear that the good design, security and cleanliness achieved when tower blocks were sold into private hands made them desirable. All along, the need was for money and quality.

Perhaps the greatest failure of twentieth century municipal housing was in not involving people, not generating and maintaining community. Still, many small-scale groups of original social housing are quietly loved by tenant or recent owner and add their story to the locality.

See also ALLOTMENTS, BUNGALOWS, GARDENS, PREFABS, TERRACED HOUSES.

C O U N T I E S

In 1974 Avon, Cleveland, Cumbria, Merseyside, Humberside, South Yorkshire and the West Midlands stared back at us from administrative maps. Greater London had appeared in 1965. Rutland, Huntingdonshire, Westmorland, East Yorkshire and Middlesex – '*that most hardly used of all counties*', as Betjeman put it – seemed to evaporate, and other parts of the familiar jigsaw changed shape. But many of us had not moved an inch and the unsettling truth became clear two decades later, when things changed again – these were just passing clouds. Our 'real' counties, 39 shapes, historic bounds of cultural life and identity, had never gone away.

The Association of British Counties has persuaded us of the usefulness of discerning between counties (historic counties), administrative counties and ceremonial counties (the domain of the Lord Lieutenant, which in Derbyshire, for example, includes the City of Derby). All are constructs, but the historic counties tell us about deep identity, having earned credibility through continued use over a thousand years or more. Kent is the oldest entity to be recorded, first in 55 BC, the land of the Cantii tribe, whose name could come from Celtic *canto*, an edge or rim (geographically appropriate), or from *caint* – 'open country'.

As Oxford and Cambridge blues compete along the Thames, reference to the Middlesex side and the Surrey side reminds us of the historic configuration, the boundary between the people of the Middle Saxons and the people of Suthrige – the region south of the Thames. Rivers and hills are often taken as borders and boundaries. But there are traces of old political rivalries, too, some of which may reach back to Celtic times.

As Norman Davies writes: '*The transformation of the chaotic patchwork of statelets into a map containing fewer but much larger and more integrated political cultural units was the work of half a millennium. It was not a foregone conclusion. Through a thousand military conflicts, marriages, mergers and mishaps, the teeming territories of the fifth century amalgamated in the course of two hundred years to form a dozen rival kingdoms. After two hundred years more, the kingdoms of the seventh century had been still further reduced, leaving two distinct zones – one predominantly Celtic, the other exclusively Germanic.*'

In the Germanic zone, smaller units – Saxon *scirs* (shires) and Norse *jarldoms* (earldoms) under the Danelaw – appear in written documents: for example, East Seaxe (Essex) in 604; Beaurrucsir (Berkshire), referring to a wooded hill, in 860; Scrobbesbyrigscir (Shropshire) – the shire of Shrewsbury, Latin Civitas Scrobbensis, 'the city around the scrub folk' – in 1006.

The counties of England emerged out of the Norman administrative system, based in most of the country on these shires or provinces, arranged around kings, upon peoples and obligations of providing soldiers and taxes. The lands of the middle, south and east Saxons were governed as the shires of Middlesex, Sussex and Essex; the 'folk of the north and south' were resolved into the shires of Norfolk and Suffolk. Wessex under Alfred had long been divided into smaller *scirs*. The Celts were confined by the Saxons to the 'land of the foreigners' – Kerno, kern-wealh or Cornwall. Northumbria and Yorkshire were already defined and the Mercian midlands had been divided in the tenth century. As he drew the country together, all William the Conqueror had left to delineate were Durham, Cumberland, Westmorland, Lancashire and Rutland, with his counts at their helm.

And so the county remained for centuries, persisting for the most part through the Victorian invention of a new administrative system with

elected members, but with cities now jostling for power. Closer to our time, years of debate over what to put where was resolved by a change of government in 1970. The Conservatives recoiled from radical rewriting of administrative boundaries and settled for a partial and inconsistent rejigging. In 1974, when new two-tier structures and unitary authorities appeared, people felt their counties had been dismembered.

Lancastrians were upset by the inclusion of Lancashire, North of the Sands, in Cumbria. Confusion persists. In criticising Common Ground's england-in-particular.info website, gazetteer Michael Dutson was more restrained than some: '*Lancastrians are proud of their county and its achievements and we do get a little miffed with people who fail to recognise the seven-hundred-plus-year-old county of Lancashire in preference to a county that existed for only fourteen years.*'

Steve Sherdley kept up the pressure and told us about Lancashire Day. '*People have assumed*

The historic counties.

115

that Lancashire places have "moved", so that Southport is now thought of as Merseyside, Hawkshead is thought of as Cumbrian, Wigan Greater Manchester and Warrington Cheshire, etc.' The celebrations on 27 November remember 1295, when the first elected representatives of the county entered King Edward I's Model Parliament. Chris Dowson adds that red roses are worn and proclamations are read by town criers '*from the Furness Fells to the River Mersey, from the Irish Sea coast to the Pennines*'.

It is likely that administrative counties will be changed again as regions begin to assert their power and attempt to market themselves. It will fall to those who keep writing Middlesex on their letters, strong followings of friends, such as for Huntingdonshire, Lancashire and the smallest county for which we all have an underdog kind of fondness – Rutland – to demonstrate ways of maintaining their presence in the twenty-first century.

See also BEATING THE BOUNDS, BOAT RACE, BOUNDARIES, BOUNDARY STONES, DIALECTS, EASTER CUSTOMS, NOMANSLAND, NORTH, PLACE-NAMES, RIVERS, SHIRE HORSES.

C O V E S

A small wonder of the world, Lulworth in Dorset is the dream cove. It takes you straight to adventures with George, Anne, Julian, Dick and Timmy, solving mysteries involving '*Brandy for the Parson, 'Baccy for the Clerk*'. The land almost completely embraces the water; from the land the glimpse of the open sea is overwhelmed by the intimacy and security of the bay.

This is the geomorphological archetype: hard rock broken through, enabling the sea to scoop out soft rock behind. Portland limestone stands fast on the seaward side, but once breached, the Purbeck limestone and Wealden Beds are more quickly eroded. There are bonuses close by – the Lulworth Crumple (rocks visibly folded) at Stair Hole; the Fossil Forest at Durdle Door. At Lulworth, the grass-topped white cliffs are crossed by white footpaths and little terraces of sheep tracks. From on high the picture of a safe haven is complete and the reasons for settlement obvious to the eye.

No doubt mariners along the north Cornwall coast learn quickly to distinguish Hells Mouth from Hudder Cove, and coastal footpath walkers head back to sandy Porthmeor and Treen Coves, Veor Cove or Pendour. Piskies Cove and Folly Cove beg further investigation. Cornwall shows well the difference between an open bay and a cove – a tiny inlet, often lined with sand, part of a complicated, varied coastline. Redshin Cove, just south of Berwick-upon-Tweed in Northumberland, is one of the very few in the north of England.

See also ARCHES, BEACHES, BOATS, CAVES, CHALK, CLIFFS, COASTS, ISLANDS, SHINGLE, STACKS, WHITE CLIFFS, ZAWNS, ZIGZAGS.

C R A B   F A I R

Since 1267 a Crab Fair has been held in the old mining town of Egremont, Cumberland at Michaelmas. It takes its name from the small, hard, sour crab apples traditionally distributed to the villagers by the lord of the manor, for which people had to 'scrabble' as he threw them from his horse. Originally he had scattered money. Crab apples, a wild ancestor of our cultivated varieties, are an odd substitute for money, as they are not even palatable to birds until February; because they were inedible they were mainly used as missiles. Now the fair takes place on the nearest Saturday to 18 September, and cultivated apples have replaced the wild ones.

The fair is known also for traditional sports, such as street races, Cumberland wrestling, cycling races, terrier racing, hound trails and climbing the greasy pole, which is erected in the main street. In the evening there are contests for the best sentimental, comic and hunting songs, and a pipe-smoking match.

The most bizarre event, surely linked to the sourness of the crab apple, is the annual World Champion Gurning Competition held in the Market Hall. Gurning contests were a popular event at country fairs, especially in Cumberland and Westmorland. Competitors have to put their heads through a braffin, or horse collar, and pull '*the ugliest face possible*', wrote Norman Nicholson. Charles Kightly suggested that being able to remove one's teeth aided the mobility of the mouth to extreme distortion.

See also AGRICULTURAL SHOWS, APPLES, BOUNDARIES, FAIRS & FAIRGROUNDS, FELL RUNNING, HOUND TRAILING, WRESTLING.

C R E A M   T E A S

Cream teas are an invention and speciality of the West Country. More than a century ago, clotted cream, produced from cow's milk with a high butter-fat content, was being

116

made near Ilfracombe in Devon and sold in small glass pots locally and further afield. Traditionally it was made by heating or 'scalding' unpasteurised milk in an enamel pan in a bain-marie for a couple of hours. It would thicken to the consistency of soft butter and form a golden crust, and then be skimmed off. This process enables cream to last for about two weeks rather than two days.

In Devon the cream is thickly spread onto the halves of a warm scone and topped with strawberry (or other) jam, accompanied by a pot of tea. White bread rolls called splits are often used in preference to scones in Cornwall. They, or scones, are buttered hot first, then spread with jam with the cream placed on top.

See also BREAD, CAKES, CATTLE, CHEESE, CORNISH PASTIES, FOOD, STRAWBERRIES.

C R I C K E T

For some, village cricket is the epitome of Englishness and, for most of us, a chanced-upon game on the green is hard to pass by. In the mind's eye you remember only untainted summer days, with white flannels against the fading green of the manicured pitch and the sound of leather on willow. The timeless nature of this seemingly languid game slows the heartbeat of those not bound up in its intimate competitiveness. It carries the weight of English 'fair play' and aspiring selflessness – '*Give of Your Best for the sake of Giving & not for what You can get out of the Game for Yourself (Major Villiers)*', reads the elegant sign in Saltwood Cricket Club's wooden pavilion, which overlooks sixty Sunday matches a year in the Kent Village League.

Cricket is said to have evolved on the chalk downs of southern England, where, according to *The Oxford Companion to Sports and Games*, '*on the short, downland grass, a ball of rag or wool, literally bowled – all along the ground*

– would run truly'. The wicket gate of the sheepfold was the wicket and the shepherd's crook the bat.

The common and village green were the obvious homes for early cricket, with the inn providing food and a place to change. Many still provide this function, such as the Cricketer's Arms in Seacroft, Leeds, The Cricketers in Ockley, Surrey and the Hit or Miss in Penn Street, Buckinghamshire. While county cricket struggles to draw audiences, the amateur leagues often hold their own.

The most famous amateur pitch is at Broadhalfpenny Down in Hampshire, where modern cricket began at the home of the Hambledon Cricket Club between 1750 and 1787, and where the Bat and Ball inn served as the pavilion. It was on these pitches that the social barriers between the squire and the tradesmen were broken. They were the forerunners of modern hallowed grounds – Lord's, Edgbaston, Headingley, Trent Bridge and so on.

Not everyone can have their own pitch and eleven as Sir Paul Getty did, but people do play country-house cricket. The pitch at Little Bredy in Dorset seems lost in time. The 22-yard-long cricket square, one tenth of a furlong, recalls the width of a medieval strip or acre. Slightly less closely cropped grass extends 75 yards to the boundary.

In cities things are changing. The back lanes of Yorkshire resound with tennis balls and cricket bats, but Asian clubs, such as Batley and Mount, play on poorly maintained council-owned grounds and face prejudice.

Cricket pavilions are remarkable in their own right. The smaller varieties maintain something of the colonial about them: simple wooden bungalows with verandahs, tiled or thatched according to locality. The Sedgwick House pavilion in Cumberland has a fine corrugated-iron roof; the Gargrave pavilion is roofed in local Yorkshire stone tiles and overlooks the best pitch in the Craven area. On one of the earliest Parish Maps, the people of Uplyme in Devon charted the cricket pavilion as a loved local icon. The more

117

Hurstbourne Priors, Hampshire.

elaborate two-storey buildings, with shaded verandah and balcony, often sport a clock and, of course, the idiosyncratic scoreboard.

They could never be upstaged by the great test pitches, such as Lord's, with its new architecture: Grand Stand, Mound Stand and Stirling Prize-winning Media Centre. City grounds have great presence – the combination of gasometer and stands at the Oval in Kennington, London; the generosity of the ground in the centre of Bath, into which you can look as you walk along the high North Parade Road; the test match roar from Trent Bridge, which moves even Nottingham Forest fans.

See also BACK LANES, BUNGALOWS, CLOCKS, CORRUGATED IRON, GASHOLDERS, INNS, PARISH MAPS, PUBS, THATCH, TILES, VILLAGE GREENS, WEATHER, WILLOW.

CRINKLE-CRANKLE WALLS

Serpentine walls often surround the kitchen gardens of large houses. The curves, like corrugations, give the wall strength and enable it to be built high but only a brick thick. The recesses provide extra shelter and warmth for trained fruit trees and increase the wall's beauty with the effects of shadows.

118

Most crinkle-crankle, or ribbon, walls are found in Suffolk and are late Georgian. Norman Scarfe found 45 in the county and 26 elsewhere. The best example, and the longest in the world, surrounds Easton Park, where the now-demolished seat of the Duke of Hamilton, Easton Hall, once stood. It was built by French prisoners of war at the turn of the nineteenth century; French bricklayers excelled and were much sought-after by wealthy landowners.

A beautiful eight- to ten-foot, lichen-encrusted, hundred-year-old crinkle-crankle wall encloses the kitchen garden at Dean's Court in Wimborne, Dorset; others can be seen at Heveningham Hall in Suffolk and Egginton and Hopton Halls in Derbyshire.

See also BRICKS, CORRUGATED IRON, VACCARY WALLS, WALLS.

CROP CIRCLES

The recorded history of the crop circle is a twentieth-century one, the phenomenon first coming to a mass audience after 1978 (though there were earlier circles reported in 1976), when round depressions were observed in a cornfield at Headbourne Worthy, Hampshire. The crops were flattened neatly in a clockwise swirl, with stems bent but unbroken. From 1980, each year has seen fields subject to the mysterious appearance of these enigmatic features, displaying gradually more ambitious and perplexing designs. They resist all attempts to explain them – as soon as a reasonable solution is postulated, a more complex group of pictograms appears to contradict it. By 1986, the wheel-like form began to turn.

And acquired a rim . . .
And spun the rim into the space
around it to make a ring . . .
And showed itself capable of the anti-clockwise

Ralph Noyes, from *The Crop Circle Enigma*

Although they have been found in small numbers across the world, and in England as far south west as Penzance in Cornwall and as far north east as Middlesbrough in Yorkshire, most have been found in what has become known as the Wessex triangle, an area bounded by Winchester in Hampshire, Avebury and Warminster in Wiltshire. The Barge Inn, alongside the Kennet and Avon in Honeystreet, Wiltshire, has become a busy centre for crop circle enthusiasts.

There is a shrewd, almost calculated quality about the air of mystery that surrounds crop circles. They began to appear at a time when pre-millennial tensions were equal (however differently motivated) to those of a thousand years earlier. They nodded in the direction of Celtic art and created a new cod-Keltic genre of their own. They tapped into imagery that connected with the mythology

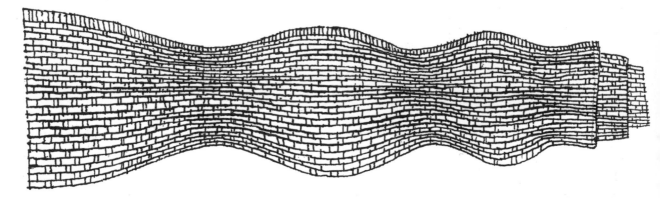

Easton, Suffolk.

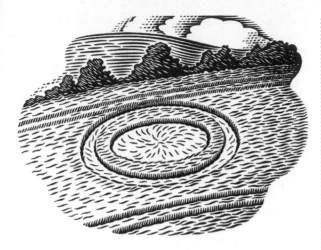

C R O P S

Crops colour the countryside, from the over-bright greens of ryegrass on 'improved' pastures to the pale blue of flax and shocking yellow of oilseed rape. Crops also tell our story: archaeology and historical records reveal the drift from working with nature towards domination by monocultures, fertilisers, herbicides and pesticides.

The North and West grow most of our oats, a rarity now, although the grain is increasing in popularity as healthy fodder for humans as well as horses. Wheat has doubled its acreage since the 1970s and commands more than forty per cent of arable land in the UK. Barley, second in popularity, occupies about a quarter. Oilseed rape stands in third place with some eight per cent.

There are colourful surprises. Lupins, in white, blue or yellow, are gaining ground as a livestock feed that fixes nitrogen in the soil. Just a few acres of delphiniums in Pershore, Worcestershire, grown for confetti, make a big impression when they are in flower, with candyfloss stripes of pinks, whites, purples and pale blues. Likewise, in Norfolk and Kent, lavender fields and the occasional presence of borage surprise and please at blossom time.

East of a line drawn from Berwick-upon-Tweed to the Isle of Wight, conditions are semi-arid, with surprisingly little precipitation – less than thirty inches. Arable farming is traditionally pursued where annual rainfall is between 15 and 35 inches. Further west and in the hills, grain generally gives way to grass, the biggest crop of all, as the climate grows wetter or soils become more impoverished.

One great zone of dairying runs from the Vale of Gloucester southwards to Cornwall; another from Lancashire to Shropshire, through Cheshire, where more than forty per cent of agricultural land is devoted to milk production. Dairy cows also venture into higher altitudes, in the uplands of east Lancashire and on the limestone plateau of Derbyshire. Traditional mixed farming, increasingly rare, is most likely to persist south of Birmingham and north of the arable zone in Yorkshire, Durham and Northumberland.

East Anglia is famous for its quick-frozen peas, mustard fields and barley barons – big landowners who have made grant fortunes with thousands of acres put down to cereals. North Norfolk produces the greatest malting barley. Premium varieties for beer making and whisky, including Golden Promise and Maris Otter, thrive in light, sandy soils over chalk; mild winters and summer sea mists mellow the crop, bestowing delicate flavours.

Colman's mustard mill and silos at Carrow, Norfolk are the result of two centuries of breeding, growing and refining mustard. Another East Anglian and Lincolnshire speciality, sugar beet, needs a warm, dry climate; the crop was introduced in the early twentieth century, with the first sugar-refining factory built in 1912 at Cantley, Norfolk.

of the land: the magic of fairies and witches, who could conjure whirlwinds and fly on straws and danced in circles. Children are still warned not to step into lighter patches of grass, known as fairy circles – folklore has those who do spirited away by the fairy dance, a single night passing for them while many years elapse in the real world.

From fairies the leap is not too great to the mischievous natural spirit Puck, and his archetypes – the Irish pooka, Welsh pwca and European kornbock. The mythology could be informing the circles, or perhaps the reverse is the case. There are certainly historical references to things that might be crop circles. Robert Plot drew and described geometrically flattened crops in Staffordshire in 1686. J. Rand Capron wrote of similar occurrences in the journal *Nature* in 1880. Then there is the famous woodcut of the Hertfordshire 'Mowing Devil' of 1678, showing a black, horned creature scything a field of crops into a flat oval – although this may owe more to political pamphleteering than a genuine phenomenon.

It is almost futile to ask 'what are they?' or 'where do they come from?', as everyone has an opinion and no one a solution – such is the joy of a mystery. Scientists probe whirlwinds, rare effects of magnetism or 'plasma vortices'. Conspiracy theorists blame the military, whose baleful and often clandestine presence in Wiltshire and Hampshire has always led to the posing of questions. Some point to the planet itself as the source, others look to the stars.

They may well be human constructs of some sort, either elegant pranks or scientifically rigorous. Certainly they are not 'hoaxes', a word that denies credit to a skilled circle-maker, whether a man with a plank and a piece of string, a scientist operating a satellite, a soldier in a helicopter or, indeed, whoever is at the controls of a passing flying saucer. Legendary physicist Richard Feynman perhaps came close to the answer when he said '*I hope that you can accept Nature as She is – absurd*'.

See *also* CORN DOLLIES, CROPS, FIELDS, WEATHER, WINDS.

Potatoes thrive in the fertile fenlands of Lincolnshire. Celery, too, enjoys the rich, black peat. Carrots grown in East Anglia and Lincolnshire under plastic and straw can supply a crop more than fifty weeks of the year. Brussels sprout production thrives in Bedfordshire and Lincolnshire. Hothouse tomatoes soak up the sunlight in greenhouses at Runcton, Sussex; indeed, more than eighty per cent of the UK crop is grown in the west Sussex plain.

In seven hundred years, from medieval times to the Second World War, yields of wheat gradually increased about fivefold. Since the war, yields have more than trebled again, while barley and oats have more than doubled. The consequences for both farm workers and wildlife have been devastating: intensifying crop production has resulted in a profound reduction in the diversity of wild animals and plants. Knowledge and care cannot be achieved by machines; the legacy of monoculture and economic overdrive has changed our countryside and our culture. And although positive changes are increasingly happening, it would be so much harder now for John Clare to say '*I found the poems in the fields and only wrote them down*'.

See also APPLES, BARNS, BEER, BREAD, BRUSSELS SPROUTS, CATTLE, CHALK STREAMS, CROP CIRCLES, DAFFODILS, DRYSTONE WALLS, FARMS & FARMSTEADS, FIELD BARNS, FIELDS, FRETS, FRITILLARY MEADOWS, FROST & FROST HOLLOWS, GLOW-WORMS, HAY MEADOWS, HEDGES, HOPS, HOP-GARDENS & HOP-YARDS, INGS, LAVENDER, LEEKS, MARKET GARDENS, ONIONS, ORCHARDS, PEARS, PIGS, POTATOES, RHUBARB, RIVERS, SHEEP, SMELLS, THATCH, WEATHER, WILDFLOWERS.

C R O S S R O A D S

A cross within a circle in the oldest Egyptian hieroglyphs means 'city'; it represents the meeting of four roads within the walls or moat. In many cultures the crossroads is a place where magic is strong – in the old European cultures the intersection of ways might harbour fairies, restless souls, ghosts, the devil.

The Roman name was *quadrifurcus*, four-forked. A crossing on their ambitious road system was a significant point: the Fosse Way and Watling Street meet at High Cross in Leicestershire, where a much later monument, dating from 1712, announces that the roads '*extend to the uttermost boundaries of Britain*'. Over time, *quadrifurcus* contracted to *carfax*, hence Carfax Street in Oxford. The word 'cross' to describe the four-armed shape came to England from the Latin *crucis*, and began to be used to describe anything with that form.

In 1546 Gardiner wrote: '*I do the office of a hande, at a crosse, to saye this is the ryght waye.*' Fingerposts were known as Cross-in-the-hands. The word 'cross-road' had to wait until 1719 to make its way into print, in Gardner's *Pocket Guide to the English Traveller*.

Gallows Gate near Fowlmere in Cambridgeshire was a crossroads; sixty skeletons, some Anglo-Saxon, testify to their unnatural deaths. The remote crossroads was often the place where the gibbet stood. Here, too, was the final resting place of suicides, deprived of the sanctity of the churchyard. Perhaps the physical cross was offered as an act of kindness or protection, or maybe it was to punish the already tormented soul with a cruel directionlessness, and to protect the living – if the crossroads was at the parish boundary, the soul would be left in limbo.

Thick Hollins Crossroads on the old packhorse route from the rivers Colne to Don is marked by a stoop dated 1761. It reads Marsden 4 miles, Penistone 11 miles, Holmfirth 2 miles. Difficult as it must have been to achieve, this Yorkshire stone has suffered turning round, as many rural crossroads signs do – a modern form of the confusion of souls. In Devon the names of the crossroads are written on the signposts – Couples Corner, Five Wyches Cross. In Dorset, Shave Cross tells of the place where pilgrims shaved their heads on the way to St Catherine's Chapel. Four Lane Ends will be well known to those travelling on Tyneside buses.

The Fosse Way through Leicestershire and Warwickshire provided a direct, though leisurely, route across country; it remained gated as recently as the 1960s. Now, as the B4455 and B4114, it has staggered junctions with chequered hoardings to slow you down. In the name of road safety many crossroads have been replaced by roundabouts.

See also BLACK DOGS, BOUNDARIES, BUSES, FINGERPOSTS, GRASSY TRIANGLES, HAUNTED PLACES, MILESTONES, ROADS, ROUNDABOUTS.

CUCKOOS & CUCKOO POUNDS

Envoy of spring, symbol of optimism, the call of the cuckoo evokes pangs of memory and anticipation – of bright days of warmth, growth and green. Though ephemeral and rarely seen, the cuckoo's importance to us lives in literature, songs and stories, many of which are particular to place.

It is the song of the bird that we respond to. It is named after its call and it sounds different in different places, as Wordsworth noted: '*There is also an imaginative influence in the voice of the cuckoo, when that voice has taken possession of a deep mountain valley, very different from anything which can be excited by the same sound in a flat country.*'

April is littered with Cuckoo Days and Fairs to hail '*the merry cuckoo, messenger of spring*', as Edmund Spenser described it, migrating from sub-Saharan Africa. One of the best places to see their first landfall is the Isles of Scilly. On Bryher, a place of few trees, cuckoos in numbers landed before our eyes on the rocks and, although palpably exhausted, still engaged one another in noisy squabbles of the male kind.

The travelling cuckoo was thought to come to the Wareham Fair around 6 April, to '*buy himself a pair of breeches*', and to the Beaulieu Fair in Hampshire nine days later, '*to buy him a great coat*', Jeremy Harte wrote. First Cuckoo Day is 14 April in Sussex, where a tale of Heathfield Fair depicts an old woman releasing the cuckoo from her basket, whereupon '*he flies up England carrying warmer days with him*'. It is said the bird is expected in Cheshire on the fifteenth, Worcestershire on the twentieth and Yorkshire on the twenty-first. Traditional, too, is the report of the first cuckoo on the letters pages of *The Times*, announcing the arrival of spring.

A Cuckoo Feast, sometimes called a Crowder Feast, survives in Towednack, Cornwall on the Sunday nearest to 28 April. It stems from the local legend about a farmer who invited some friends to warm themselves by his fire on a cold spring day. He put a hollow log onto the fire and a cuckoo flew out; the weather changed to become warm.

Around 27 April, Marsden Cuckoo Day recalls the story of the people of Marsden in Yorkshire, who, knowing that as the cuckoo arrived so did the spring and summer, built a wall around it to prolong its stay. But the cuckoo flew out of the top, the people lamenting '*it were nobbut just wun course too low!*' Every year on May Bank Holiday Monday they 'dress the cuckoos' – giant cuckoos that are displayed around the village – put on a Cuckoo Play and have a Cuckoo Ball. Not far away, Austwick is known as Cuckoo Town after a similar legend. Such stories persist here and there across the country, probably dispersed by chap-books and part of the rich history of tales about silly villagers.

In Borrowdale, Cumberland the local word for the bird is gowk, also a word for fool – '*By gow! If we'd nobbut laid another line o' stanes atop, we'd a copped 'im.*' The tale, retold by Jennifer Westwood, is echoed in Wareham, Dorset and Gotham, Nottinghamshire, where the Wise Men stood around a bush with a cuckoo in it to try to prevent it from flying away. A hilltop bush a mile south of Gotham was known as the Cuckoo Bush in 1864; Cuckoo Bush Farm still exists, as does the Cuckoo Bush pub in the village.

Named cuckoo pounds can be found in at least eight places in Dorset. The Cuckoo Pen at Corfe Castle comprises an old circular rampart containing a few trees. At Langton Matravers the Cuckoo Pound 'is a small plantation of stunted trees surrounded by a dry stone wall', Jeremy Harte wrote. He concluded that in Dorset the name was given to eighteenth-century tree plantations on earthworks.

According to Dorset author and historian Rodney Legg, '*most parishes in south-east Dorset have their Cuckoo Pen or Cuckoo Pound, attaching to small and often wooded enclosures*'. He suggested one reason for their name is that cuckoos were once thought to hibernate in hollow trees, and as their first calls were often heard coming from copses in spring it followed that they must have overwintered there. Another

is that these enclosures were originally stock pounds for bullocks and hogs rounded up for the Wareham Cuckoo Fair, and that once they had lost their use, cuckoo fair pounds became known as cuckoo pounds.

John Field found about 24 cuckoo pens in Oxfordshire, more than twelve in Gloucestershire and more in other counties, '*particularly in central and southern England*'. He described them as being often '*plantations of trees on the summits of hills [which] may be survivals of groves or other ritual sites, left uncleared and protected by the trees to prevent desecration*'.

Wing, Rutland has a Cuckoo Inn, as does Hamptworth, Wiltshire, on the edge of the New Forest. They may carry a memory of a nineteenth-century tradition of celebrating the arrival of spring by downing tools when the first call was heard, and 'wetting the cuckoo' with new cuckoo ale in the pub for the rest of the day. This was especially prevalent among colliers in Shropshire. A different version of this story, which persisted until the 1930s in Hoffleet Stow, Lincolnshire, tells that people would go to the wood where the cuckoo was calling, with a barrel of ale to drink '*the health of the cuckoo with the new cuckoo ale*'. This custom is surely ripe for revival, to help both the cuckoo and local beer.

It is not surprising that the cuckoo has so many tales attached to it, for it is an extraordinary bird. The males arrive first, having flown for thousands of miles, announcing their return with the familiar call. The females follow a few days later and signal to the males with a bubbling call. Much is made of the date of arrival, between 17 and 23 April in southern England and between 1 and 7 May in northern Scotland. But equally fascinating is the observation that most adult cuckoos breeding in the Fens leave Britain in the second week in July, often on the same day – 10 July.

The drastic decline in cuckoo numbers during the past thirty years may be attributable to the decrease in numbers of meadow pipits and dunnocks, in whose nests they may lay, or a shortage of their favourite food: hairy caterpillars. Climate change may be a factor – the hairy caterpillars may have pupated by the time their predators arrive.

See also BEER, CLUMPS, FAIRS & FAIRGROUNDS, FENS, MAY DAY, NICKNAMES, PUBS.

121

C Y C L I N G

In 1869, an order for hundreds of velocipedes, an early two-wheeled machine developed across the Channel, came to Britain because it could not be fulfilled in France. They were made by the Coventry Machinist Company, diversifying from the manufacture of sewing machines. James Starley refined the design into the Penny Farthing, and his nephew created the Rover safety bicycle, with even-sized wheels, brakes and gears. Within twenty years, the Midlands was known as the cycle capital of the world, with companies such as Humber, Coventry Eagle, Swift and Triumph.

Originating in 1878, the British Cycling Federation governs cycling sports, such as track racing, time trials and cross-country or downhill mountain biking. For more leisurely pursuits, local branches of the Cyclists' Touring Club, founded the same year, organise group tours, still stopping off at their usual cafés, hotels and pubs en route. Some retain the once-common CTC plaques of a wheel spoked with three wings, welcoming and perhaps giving special rates to cyclists. There is one on the wall approaching the Coach and Horses in Longborough, Gloucestershire and at the Sykes House in Askrigg, Yorkshire.

The bicycle sheds around most factories until the 1960s were huge. At ten past four, the thousands of workers cycling away from the bus and lorry plants in Leyland, Lancashire appeared as a stream.

In 2002 Nottingham's heart skipped a beat. Raleigh closed. It was founded in and named after Raleigh Street, Nottingham by Frank Bowden in 1890. The factory complex between Faraday Road and Triumph Road (Cycle Road and Dunlop Avenue are also nearby) has been demolished and redeveloped as Nottingham University's Jubilee Campus, leaving little trace of the buildings that employed a workforce of thousands, once part of the identity of the city. A building on Ilkeston Road with a bicycle sculpture outside is named Sillitoe Court, in honour of Alan Sillitoe, author of *Saturday Night and Sunday Morning*, who worked at the age of 14 in the Raleigh factory. The biggest monument to this company lies not so much in the cycles made now in the Far East, but

in the pride of the thousands of people who worked here over a century and in the millions of us whose first bike was a Raleigh.

In addition to hazardous busy roads, cyclists can now use ten thousand miles of routes on the National Cycle Network created by Sustrans, the charity that promotes cycling and sustainable transport. Some, especially along disused railway routes, are enlivened with sculptures.

In Britain we are near the bottom of the European cycle users' list. Three per cent of employed people cycle to work (2001); add to this two per cent of secondary school journeys and it is evident that we do not compare well with Holland, with around thirty per cent. Cycling in flat areas is all very well, but battling against the wind in east Yorkshire is a very lonely business and cities are never flat. London has an active cycling fraternity, boosted in the 1990s by the flourishing of cycle couriers. The congestion charge in central London has made it an easier and safer place, at least for a while.

Cyclists add to the atmosphere of a place. Most notable are the oldest university towns, with their upright black bikes with baskets leaned against railings or being ridden flamboyantly from college to library or pub. Red cycles from Mike's Bikes are commonly hired by tourists in Cambridge, and Betjeman's picture of '*churches stacked with bicycles outside*' on a stroll to the Eastgate of a '*marmalade Oxford*' in *Summoned by Bells* is still part of the scene.

See also BOWLING GREENS, CAFÉS, CANALS, CUCKOOS & CUCKOO POUNDS, DRAGONS, FORDS, PUBS, ROADS, SCULPTURES.

122

Doric Bold, Walter Tracy, 1973.

DAFFODILS

Once experienced, an expanse of wild daffodils does *'flash upon that inward eye'*, as when William and Dorothy Wordsworth came upon a host of them along the shores of Ullswater in the Lake District in 1802. At Graveteye Manor in Sussex, William Robinson planted thousands of wild and cultivated varieties in the late nineteenth century: *'A very delightful feature of the Narcissus meadow gardening is the way great groups follow each other in the fields. When the Star narcissi begin to fade a little in their beauty the Poets follow, and as I write this paper we have the most beautiful picture I have ever seen in cultivation.'*

Daffodils are one of the most popular garden and municipal plants, perhaps because their cheerful forms signal the end of winter. The Royal Horticultural Society's Classified List and International Register contains about eight thousand cultivated varieties.

Lincolnshire produces most of the country's daffodils and, in spring, great swathes of white, yellow and orange cross the land around Spalding.

Where Cornwall meets Devon in the warm Tamar valley more than a thousand people were employed in the nineteenth and early twentieth centuries, growing strawberries and early daffodils for the cut-flower market – the earlier the pricier. Only one grower, in St Dominick, Cornwall, still produces daffodils on a large scale. At Cotehele House near Saltash in Cornwall the National Trust is gathering a permanent collection of the estimated four hundred varieties that were grown in the 'little gardens', as the smallholdings were called, thanks to Virginia Spiers, who has campaigned for many years to save them. They include the Double Whites and those raised by the du Plessis brothers, such as Tamar Fire and Noss Mayo, and are celebrated on a special day in mid-March. Further along the Cornish coast, where tiny relict fields cling to the cliffs, odd daffodils reveal their old economic use.

Daffodils are still grown on the Isles of Scilly between November and May, although by only fifty growers in 2003.

Rough granite walls demarcate the tiny enclosures where the bulbs were once grown. Old strip fields are hedged against the wind by high euonymus hedges on Bryher, tamarisk on St Agnes and euonymus, pittosporum and escallonia around Middle Town on St Martin's. Many of the old varieties have naturalised around the edges of fields and provide an important genetic memory bank. The mild climate enables non-hardy varieties of the tazetta type, such as the deliciously scented 'Grand Soleil d'Or' and 'Paper White', to be grown.

Fashion has been drawn towards cultivating the big and the blowsy, and how depressing it is to see village, town and farm opting for over-sized varieties to welcome you to their places. The fine wild daffodil (*Narcissus pseudonarcissus*) has become increasingly rare. In the late sixteenth century Gerard wrote that wild daffodils were growing almost everywhere throughout England, thousands picked for cut flowers. Agricultural intensification, field drainage and a failure to value this dainty, pale yellow flower has led to its demise. In Ambergate, Derbyshire Joanne Jones says *'there is an abundance of wild narcissi . . . this small area of woodland is now under threat from adjacent properties, which do not appear to value its beauty. It should become a protected area.'*

But how exciting it is to come upon the elegant wildflowers self-set along the central reservation and sides of the M50 in Gloucestershire, where they are known as Lent lilies. Nearby people search out the places where they still flourish: you can do a ten-mile walk from Dymock and Four Oaks to Kempley, through fields and orchards where clusters of flowers are dotted among the sheep; daffodil teas are served in village halls during March and April. Daffodil walks are organised by groups such as the Wildlife Trusts in Dunsford Wood in Devon, Ashdown Forest in west Sussex, Lesnes Abbey Wood in Kent, Butley Woods in Suffolk and Farndale in the Dove valley, Yorkshire. In the Lake District at Glencoyne Bay (also known as Wordsworth Point), the daffodils are conserved as 'a historic feature of Ullswater' by the National Trust and there is a Daffodil Hotline.

See *also* BLUEBELLS, DRYSTONE WALLS, LAKES, LANDSLIPS, MARKET GARDENS, RAMSONS.

125

DAGS

Simple fretted teeth ornamenting the underside of platform canopies on railway stations, dags seem to have no function save aesthetically to complete a simple building. The detail varies on different routes and even stations along the same route, large or small.

But there is something about dags that is reminiscent of the patterns on old Russian wooden churches and houses, which cast rain and snow as well as intricate shadows. All had meanings; perhaps much has been lost in translation,

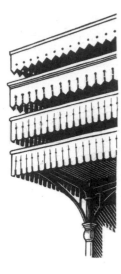

for now we see only decoration in the etched awnings of stations, beach huts, cabmen's shelters and the barge-boards of Victorian houses.

Nigel Wikeley and John Middleton observed that '*some patterns were more economical than others*' and that '*decorative valencing . . . was not without functional value in its day. The shaping of the boards helped to keep the lower edges dry and in varying degrees the cutting and piercing increased natural light and ventilation inside the canopy and assisted the escape of steam . . . it seems reasonable to suggest that many lines had their individual styles when first constructed and that these became mixed when extensions and alterations were carried out at later periods.*' Many date from 1860 to 1900.

Once you have noticed them, their absence really rancours, especially where they have been ruthlessly sawn off; so, too, does the crude box-edging on the metal canopies of the homogeneous, systems-built stations of the 1960s.

126

See also BEACH HUTS, CABMEN'S SHELTERS, RAILWAYS, STATIONS.

D A L E S

We understand 'dale' as a word of the North; it derives from *dalom*, a deep or low place, from old Germanic languages reinforced by Norse. It is found from Dovedale in Derbyshire to Coquetdale in Northumberland; its heartland straddles the 'backbone of England'.

Airedale, Patterdale, Wensleydale . . . a torrent of dogs, sheep and cheeses reminds us that each of the deep valleys of the Yorkshire Pennines were different worlds. Some are narrow, some more open, linked along their length by river and road and separated by steep hills and wild moors, offering sufficient isolation to reinforce small divergences of culture and quite different identities. Each landscape is different: Littondale is intimate and contained, but with expansive views from the clints and grikes beside the high pass at the head of the valley; Swaledale has a wider valley floor and an exquisite scatter of field barns among the stone-walled hay meadows.

But they may contain similar elements: patterns of limestone or gritstone walls ascending steep valley sides to thin out at the open moors; high, dry valleys with limestone scree or water tumbling over flat-bedded rock; spouts, becks, gills and groughs; caves; old mineral workings; sycamore clumps; green and flower-rich meadows; gritstone-topped field barns catching the light on their gable ends; small stone settlements and dignified market towns; viaducts and quarries; and words on maps that show just how long people have been farming and mining here. Arkengarthdale means 'the valley of Arkil's enclosure', *garth* being Old Norse for enclosure.

Hardraw Force in Wensleydale takes a single thundering bound onto the softer Yoredale shales, while Kisdon Force on the Swale hops and skips from ledge to ledge. But it was ice that first gouged out these deep dales and then left water to finish the job.

The Derbyshire Dales, including Lathkill Dale and Dovedale, are more intimate and particular to the limestone, their winding ways deeply incised, partly because of the rock type but also because the streams were rejuvenated by dramatic uplifts of this bit of land in the recent geological past, reinforced by the melt-waters of receding ice. Long-abandoned caves look out over intricately carved dales, some of which may have resulted from roof collapses in caverns originally etched by underground waters. Some, like Gratton Dale, are dry, while in its winding valley next to Dovedale the river Manifold in Staffordshire continues to play hide and seek, disappearing below Darfur Crags and reappearing at the Boil Holes – extraordinary upwellings below a small cliff in what are now the grounds of Ilam Hall.

See also BARNS, BECKS, BRASS BANDS, BRIDGES, CAVES, CHEESE, CLINTS & GRIKES, DOGS, FIELD BARNS, GHYLLS, GRUFFY GROUND, HAY MEADOWS, LYNCHETS, NOMANSLAND, QUARRIES, SHEEP, SPRINGS, SYCAMORE, TERRIERS, VIADUCTS, WATERFALLS.

D A M S O N S

Depending on your eye the damson makes a scrawny shrub or a tree of Japanese elegance, unpredictable in its leanings, which for a brief moment in spring flowers white and frothy, like the sloe, turning hedgerow to cappuccino. This moment lights up the Lyth valley in Cumbria, where damsons march with the stone walls or stand together in loose half orchards at field edges. In Shropshire, too, because of their unpredictable harvest, the trees are placed in hedgerows to fruit at will.

One of our under-sung fruits, a relative of the plum, the 'damascene' may have been introduced from Damascus by returning crusaders. Damsons have certainly been grown and sold in Westmorland since the early 1700s. The fruit is widely cultivated across Europe, but here we have selectively bred it, watching for the sweeter or bigger fruiting seedlings, such as the Farleigh damson found by James Crittenden in Kent in the early nineteenth century.

The Westmorland prune predominates in the Lyth valley; it has a stronger taste and is used by the Mason's Arms at Cartmel Fell to flavour its distinctive beer. The Worcester damson is bigger, and in years of abundance the county's roadsides offer treasures of boxes, tables and heaps for sale or the taking. In Market Drayton, Shropshire the Godstone Hall Hotel hosts a damson feast at the end of September, one continuing memory of the great fair held there until the 1930s.

Shropshire, Staffordshire and Cheshire sent fruit for use in dyeing to Lancashire and Yorkshire mills (they gave their colour to khaki fatigues) and to the nearer potteries, but most damsons were stored over winter as jam or damson cheese. Beyond domestic use in pies and crumbles, ice-cream and preserves, the purple-black fruits, bloomed with wild yeast and quite acid with shades of astringency, make the finest of commercial jams.

See also APPLES, APRICOTS, BLACKTHORN, CHERRIES, CIDER & CIDER ORCHARDS, COBNUTS, HAZEL, HEDGES, ORCHARDS, PEARS, PIES, PLUMS, SWEET CHESTNUT, WALNUT.

D A W N   C H O R U S

The sound of birds singing together at the break of day in spring is one of the wonders of the natural world. Many more sing then than at any other time of the day or year.

In the city the blackbird and robin may sing in the night, but in darker places either will wake the others before the sun rises. Birds in the South West begin their singing earlier in the year but easterly birds get up before them. The sun rises over Suffolk (Lowestoft, 05.15) 37 minutes before Cornwall (Penzance 05.52) on 4 May, where in 2003, in the Kensey valley outside Launceston, the sequence went

as follows: robin (04.52), tawny owl (on his way to bed?), blackbird, pheasant, cockerel, wren (05.07 and getting light), blackcap, woodpigeon, jay, magpie, chaffinch, crow, mistle thrush, chiffchaff, great spotted woodpecker, green woodpecker and finally blue tit and great tit (05.38). The robin sang for fifty minutes.

Apart from the joy of singing, it is observed that male birds are probably establishing their territory and attracting a mate (the sedge warbler and the pied flycatcher stop singing after pairing). But why sing at dawn? Theories abound. Song, or rather lack of it, may reveal a vacant territory after a night death. In the cold of first light fewer insects are about, so why not warble?

Some places resound with more song than others. River birds sing less than birds of the woodland edge; the sedge warbler arriving from Africa in mid-April hardly draws breath before jazzing up its trills and rhythm changes. You will hear as much in Highgate and Queen's Woods, north London as you will in open farmland. And mature suburban gardens emulate woodland edge, so you may be able to lie in bed and have the best of both worlds. But effort will repay. A visit to a woodland before dawn breaks in May will impress both place and nature on the memory. On a dawn chorus walk at Leighton Moss, Lancashire you may hear the booming of the bittern; at Gibraltar Point, Lincolnshire you are more likely to hear the skylark, the 'peewit' of the lapwing or the incessant call of the cuckoo; on the Roundshaw Downs in the London borough of Sutton resound the songs of the whitethroat, blackcap and chiffchaff.

The chiffchaff calls its name, the wren hammers out 56 notes in 5.2 seconds, the chaffinch sings more than four hundred songs in an hour, the song thrush hones its song year by year by repeating each phrase three times. All in concert with greenfinch, goldfinch, dunnock, linnet, blackcap, willow warbler, blackbird, robin, pheasant, wood pigeon, blue tit and great tit.

In the city robin and blackbird dominate but the starling may sit on your balcony and, with feathers a-tremble, try out his mimicry – mobile phones have interested him recently. Research shows that traffic noise is taking its toll on birds, some not finding mates; the great tit is singing at higher frequencies among the sounds of the city just to be heard.

Anyone with a clear memory will recall rightly that the dawn chorus was much more intense a generation ago before we were assailed by the problems captured so vividly by Rachel Carson in *Silent Spring*. In March 1999 the Royal Society for the Protection of Birds reported that 27 million birds have simply vanished in a quarter of a century. We have four million fewer blackbirds, half the song thrushes and two-thirds of the mistle thrushes; linnets are down by one-third and yellowhammers by half. One of the reasons is loss of habitat; another is profligate use of pesticides and herbicides in garden and on farm. At this rate we shall be left with a little bit of bread and no birds.

See also ROBINS, SKYLARKS, STARLINGS.

D E E Z E S

On the shingle beach – the Stade – at Hastings in Sussex a unique collection of three-storey weather-boarded huts squeeze together in front of the high sandstone cliffs.

Used to store fishing nets, rope and other tackle, they are known locally as deezes, a dialect word suggesting herring were originally dried here. The 45 remaining tarred sheds, some dating back to the sixteenth and seventeenth centuries, are constructed with diagonal bracing, the upper floors reached from inside by ladders nailed to the walls. Each storey has an exterior door that opens outwards. Many deezes have been lost to fire but some have been rebuilt. They once extended much further along the beach, and were raised up on posts so the sea could wash beneath them. They may have Norse origins or connections with Spain via shipwrecked sailors.

In 1588 fishermen were charged a farthing a foot to lease land on Stonebeach, as it was known then. In the 1830s new council regulations stipulated that the huts should be no larger than eight foot square.

The Old Hastings Preservation Society has worked for thirty years to conserve these zany buildings for the fishermen – about forty boats still fish from here. Now they are a tourist attraction and no doubt the pressure will be on to turn them into pied-à-terres – as has happened to the old fishermen's huts at Whitstable, Kent. In Yorkshire flocks of green fishermen's huts were common from Redcar to Skinningrove, and the Northumberland coast has not only kipper smokeries but also old, upturned boats, tarred and doored for gear storage.

See also BEACHES, BEACH HUTS, BOATS, HARBOURS, KIPPERS, SEA FISH, SHINGLE.

D E N E S

Occasionally found further south, 'dene' is commonly used in Durham, Tyneside and Yorkshire to describe a deeply incised valley, often running out to the coast, filled with semi-natural ancient woodland. Katrina Porteous, in her poem 'Roads', catches the feeling: '*The dene is a green road the red fox travels.*' These are rich places.

In County Durham glacial melt-water bit deep into the rock: Hawthorn Dene cuts a gorge fifty metres deep and supports magnesian limestone grassland and eight species of orchid as well as oak, ash, elm, large-leafed lime and yew underlain by snowdrops. Castle Eden Dene is etched first through boulder clay, making some thirty-metre cliffs along its four miles. The juxtaposition gives a mosaic of alkaline and acid soils on which more than 450 species of plant have been counted, including wild garlic followed by bluebells. Pedunculate oak and ash dominate the woodland, enjoyed by the increasingly rare red squirrel. Beech and rhododendron have been planted and sycamore has invited itself. The northern brown Argus butterfly is known as the Castle Eden Argus.

Chellow Dene in Bradford, Yorkshire has two reservoirs in the wooded valley much loved by birdwatchers and walkers. The steep denes with their streams running into the river Tyne – although some have been filled in – are perfect havens of peace and play for the people of Newcastle. Jesmond Dene (given to the citizens of the city in 1883), Sugley Dene and Walbottle Dene, like their coastal counterparts, have remnants of ancient woodland.

See also ALDER, ASH, BEECH, BLUEBELLS, CHINES, HAWTHORN, HAZEL, OAK, RAMSONS, RED FOXES, RED SQUIRRELS, ROWAN, SYCAMORE, WILDFLOWERS, WOODS, YEW.

DESERTED VILLAGES

Thousands of settlements have lived and died in our landscape. An isolated church, a field name or a colour change in the soil may all signal their passing.

The moors of Devon, Cornwall and the Pennines and the chalk downs of the South betray signs of prehistoric settlements. Perhaps 33 villages were cleared to transform the New Forest into a hunting paradise for William I, some later to be resettled. On the foundation of Revesby Abbey in Lincolnshire the villages of Revesbia, Schictlesbia and Thoresbi were expunged in 1143; the Cistercians wanted solitude.

The weakening manorial hold on peasants, aided by the Black Death in 1348, brought about changes in tenure and attitudes that altered the face of England. Within a hundred years the land in the 'champion' areas (dominated by the open-field system) from Dorset to Norfolk and up to eastern Northumberland was being cleared for grazing. In Warwickshire, Leicestershire, Buckinghamshire and Northamptonshire particularly, Tom Williamson and Liz Bellamy noted that this *'produced many of the deserted medieval villages of England, rather than the fatal impact of the plague. The earthworks, house platforms, traces of roads and fragments of churches that we see today are monuments to a change in the balance of power in the land.'* Enclosure brought more change, and the trend for creating parkland around country houses, which reached its height in the eighteenth century, caused whole villages to be moved. Traces of settlement can still be seen among old field systems, as at Berrington Park in Herefordshire.

There have been more recent losses. Tyneham in Dorset and Imber in Wiltshire were taken for 'defence purposes' during the Second World War. Part of the army's Salisbury Plain ranges, Imber is now a ghost town – the church hangs on, with the manor house and a couple of ruined cottages, supplemented by recent black-eyed houses with a Balkan look that are used for street-combat exercises. Recently even Imber has been abandoned, for a bespoke village at the other side of the plain called FIBUA – 'fighting in built-up areas'. In County Durham whole villages were put up for sale as the mines closed in the 1960s, 1970s and 1980s. Leasingthorne was demolished in 1969.

After twenty years of research The Deserted Medieval Village Group gave up counting in 1977, when, at more than three thousand and rising, it became clear that deserted villages were a common feature of our land. Any shadows cast on winter mornings or evenings are worth investigation, and every year sees more traces being recognised.

Perhaps more damage has been done to remnants during the past half-century by intensive farming than in all previous history, and development is pressing too hard on the land. The ghosts of these places and their stories are worth cherishing and understanding, if only to shake us from the complacent notion that once somewhere is born it will simply persist.

See also ABBEYS, COAL MINING, FIELD PATTERNS, FIELDS, FLOODS, HAUNTED PLACES, LOST VILLAGES, MONASTERIES, PARKLAND, RIDGE & FURROW, VILLAGES.

D E V I L

Old Nick has a lot to answer for. His name is associated with many places and he appears as protagonist or antagonist in many often long and complex tales to explain drama in the landscape.

The Agglestone (Holy Stone) in south Dorset is also called the Devil's Nightcap. The story, recounted by Charles Warne at the end of the nineteenth century, goes this way: *'The country people say of it that his Satanic majesty (who is often a very important personage in these capricious freaks) was one day sitting on the Needles Rock, Isle of Wight, whence, espying Corfe Castle in the distance, he took the cap from his head and threw it across the sea, with the intent of demolishing that structure. But it would appear that he overestimated his powers of jactation, for the missile fell short of its mark; and there it stands today on Studland Heath, a monument of disappointed malice, a wonder to the peasantry, and a theme of antiquarian conjecture.'*

Similar stories abound, especially to explain big stones or heaps of rocks, ancient earthworks and even lines of hills. In Somerset the devil dropped an apronful of stones on the Blackdown Hills before he could reach Wellington church; the result is an acre of stones called the Devil's Lapful and five barrows called the Devil's Glove. Cheddar Gorge in Somerset was dug by the devil to spoil the Mendip Hills; his first spadeful landed in the Bristol Channel as the Isles of Steep Holm and Flat Holm.

The Devil's Spadeful (an outcrop of sandstone at Kidderminster, Worcestershire) resulted from the devil giving up diversion of the Severn to drown the over-pious town of Bewdley. He decided that it was too far, having met a wily cobbler carrying many shoes, who told him that in walking from the town he had worn them all out.

The Devil's Ditch is found near Byard's Leap in Lincolnshire and in Norfolk between the heaths of East Harling and Garboldisham; the Devil's Dyke in Hertford beside Wheathampstead and at Brighton, Sussex. The latter town, it seems, was so full of good people that the devil, to rid himself of them, began to gouge a great dyke to let in the sea. He had to do it in a single night, but an old woman heard him, provoked a cock into crowing and illuminated an inflated pig's bladder. The devil imagined the sun was rising and fled, leaving the job unfinished. One result of his frenetic digging was a great clod that fell to make Chanctonbury Ring.

It is easy to see how mariners might have named the Devil's Bank in the river Mersey and told how he built Filey Brigg off the Yorkshire coast to catch unwary sailors.

Michael Scott, a magician with many stories to his name on both sides of the England/Scotland border, is sometimes called the Devil's Piper. In Northumberland, as Mitchell Scott, he is known in many of the villages; he accompanied the devil in making Hadrian's Wall. He assured the burgesses of Morpeth that if a certain man ran from the shore without looking back the sea would follow him and bring tidal water and hence good trade to the town. The man's nerve failed and the town remains five miles above the tidal reach of the Wansbeck.

See also BELLS & BELL-RINGING, BLACK DOGS, BRIDGES, DOWNLAND, DRAGONS, EARTHWORKS, FOLKTALES, GIANTS, GORGES, HOLLOW WAYS, ISLANDS, MILLSTONE GRIT, QUOITS II, RIVERS, SAINTS, SHIPPING FORECAST, STACKS, STANDING STONES, TURNING THE DEVIL'S STONE.

D E W P O N D S

The earth's eyes, these fine, saucer-shaped ponds were built on the tops of chalk hills, in defiance of local hydrology. With great skill and ingenuity, land famed for its drainage was made to hold water.

There is an art to making dew ponds. As late as the 1930s small teams of professional men would still travel distances to mend and re-line or dig new dew ponds above the spring lines on chalk and limestone uplands, where sheep and cattle needed water.

Many of these large, shallow ponds were probably first built in the seventeenth or eighteenth centuries and lined with puddled clay to make them watertight. A few are much older; archaeologist David Rudling confirms that clay-lined dew ponds are known to date from the Bronze Age in Sussex, for example at Blackpatch on the South Downs. Refurbished during the centuries, such ponds may lie in auspicious spots. A boundary description in a Saxon land charter of 825 AD mentioned a pond called Oxenmere, still visible on Milk Hill behind the White Horse of Alton Barnes in Wiltshire.

The South Downs, especially the Sussex Downs, are often regarded as the traditional home of the dew pond, and two of the finest specimens can be seen on Chanctonbury Ring and Ditchling Beacon. But they are also found on the chalk of the Yorkshire and Lincolnshire Wolds, the limestone around Flamborough Head in Yorkshire and the White Peak in Derbyshire.

A strange fascination with how water got into these ponds seized the popular imagination in the late nineteenth and early twentieth centuries, when prolonged debates on the subject appeared on the letters pages of *The Times*. To discover the truth, the Royal Society funded Edward Martin to conduct a series of painstaking experiments on Clayton Downs above Brighton. The inescapable conclusion in his 1915 book, *Dewponds*, was that the bulk of the water came from rain.

Today most survive only as ghostly, weedy depressions. The alloy troughs that have replaced them are not much use to wildlife. Writing in 1927, Barclay Wills admired the linnets and finches that he had watched drinking and

bathing in Sussex dew ponds, and he might have seen rabbits, hares, foxes and badgers, too. In recent years, conservation groups on the South Downs have restored a few ponds by installing plastic linings. Free of predatory fish, revitalised dew ponds can be havens for newts, frogs and water beetles, providing watering holes for many more wild creatures.

In Derbyshire some of the two and a half thousand dew ponds known to have been in the White Peak in the nineteenth century are being remade, with the help of English Nature, by clay puddling or with liners overlain by original soil and stone. The chosen ponds, for example in Lathkill Dale, are within hauling distance of working dew ponds, which have populations of great crested newts.

See also BADGERS, BEACON FIRES, BLOW HOLES, BOUNDARIES, CATTLE, CHALK, DOWNLAND, EARTHWORKS, HARES, LIMESTONE, PONDS, RED FOXES, SHEEP.

D I A L E C T S

From place to place, even street to street, the living language, our greatest shared creation, relies on us for constant reinvention. Pronunciation gives us different accents, but dialect is about vocabulary and how we formulate sentences.

We need to communicate, that is what language is for. Standard English is a dialect that most of us use for writing (but not for txt msgs) and perhaps fifteen per cent of us speak. The rest, including users of sign language, betray strong or weak geographical, social and cultural dialects.

Our way of speaking is the result of at least 1,500 years' decanting: parts of the country have inherited fragments from ancient indigenous languages and bits of Latin, which were overwhelmed by incoming Germanic speakers. Vikings overlaid their Old Norse speech patterns in the North and East, while Alfred protected the culture and language of Old English in Wessex and the mid lands. But the uneasy peace hardly had settled when the Normans arrived – once Norsemen themselves but now bringing Old French and, as conquerors, not interested in going native. The scene was set for the still-common stereotypes of 'correct' speech (of the victors) and 'country bumpkin' language of the vanquished Anglo-Saxons; also for the divergence of North and South. Oblivious to the language and convention of the court, the many and varying working languages of England emerged as a kind of feral continuum.

Law and parliament persisted in using French until 1362, after which the anti-French feeling in a court dispossessed of its continental lands inspired the emergence of English literature. Chaucer, Langland and the author of *Sir Gawain and the Green Knight* all wrote in different dialects from the mid lands. Two and a half centuries later Richard Carew was commenting that '*all write English alike*' despite '*the diversitie of our Dialects*'. When dialect eventually re-emerged

130

as a literary style in the eighteenth and nineteenth centuries – William Barnes being the most notable practitioner – it had become self-conscious and a symbol, however well-intentioned, of a political, social or cultural imperative to save and preserve, or as a vanguard against oppressive homogeneity. Cornish, a language related to Welsh and Breton, was killed, but it has been resurrected: in 2004 around three and a half thousand people spoke it.

Words and ways of speaking have been drawn in through trade, colonisation, necessity (new technology, scientific exploration and materials) and cultural exchange and have been lost as agriculture, industry and social intercourse have changed. Leaving the land and settling in cities forced dialects to mingle, but we still know our Brummies from our Scousers. Geordie twang stands apart from its neighbours with Dutch words probably gathered during trading and working together at sea, denoting everything from whaling to smuggling. Canny lass, meaning fine girl, seems to derive from the Dutch *cant*, meaning neat, for example.

Likewise, with migration in the Middle Ages – Norwich had whole communities of Spanish Jews, French, Dutch and Danes – and later from the old colonies, words, spellings and rhythms were bartered. As people crowded into London from across the country, and world, they added their patter to the Cockney everyone had spoken, bar those at court. Jews fleeing from mainland Europe left spiels and shemozzles; Romany *palare* offered mush (mouth), pal and dukes (hands). In 2004 Tower Hamlets in east London had 78 languages spoken in its schools, with countless dialects; 62 per cent of pupils were bilingual. Benjamin Zephaniah's dialect was forged in Handsworth, Birmingham and Jamaica.

In Southall and Brixton in London, with their big Indian, Pakistani and Caribbean communities, street language is constantly remaking its own sounds and patterns. Coached by black, urban America, through music, television and direct contact in the early twenty-first century, new words flare up so briefly in youth parlance that by the time they have entered da house they have lost their original power.

The rich progression of our language could have been arrested by arbiters who would have dictated accent and dialect. A great unifying force came with the publishing of the King James Bible in 1611; people who could not write or read now heard a lingua franca closer to their own speech than Latin. But still the language remained open and somehow the variety persisted, regardless of the 'correct' grammar and pronunciation perpetuated through the court and the professions for generations and through schools since mass education began in 1870.

Since people first gathered around radio sets in the early 1920s, the BBC was a great advocate of Received Pronunciation. Few regional dialects were heard in broadcasting, indeed they were frowned on. The colourful and inventive language brought here from the US through film and television liberated us into recognising the richness of our own. Increasingly anything goes.

See also ACCENTS, ALLEYS, FIELD NAMES, GREETINGS, GYPSIES, NICKNAMES, PLACE-NAMES, UNLUCKY WORDS, YAN TAN TETHERA, ZAWNS.

D I W A L I

The night of the new moon in the month of Karttika (October/November) marks the Hindu New Year. It is a time of 'spring cleaning' and for the start of festivities. Deepavali is from Sanskrit and means a row of lights. The Festival of Lights, Diwali/Divali, celebrated by Hindus, Jains and Sikhs across the country, spills out from domestic confines in places from Southall and Ealing in west London to the Lancashire and Yorkshire textile towns.

It has become a great social spectacle in Leicester. The five-day festivities start in Belgrave and Melton Roads with the turning on of the Diwali lights, thousands of them kept on as Christmas decorations in the city. Inside and outside houses lights burn and thirty thousand people gather to see the shops decorated with divas – earthenware lamps – and lights, to eat the seasonal foods, to admire the *rangoli* patterns created out of coloured sand or rice powder on the thresholds of the nineteenth-century terraced houses nearby, and for traditional dancing, music and fireworks. On Diwali 'Day', thousands more come to see the grand firework and laser display at Cossington Street recreation ground.

For the Jains Diwali is a day for fasting, meditation and lighting lights for Mahavira's entry to nirvana (527 BC). For Sikhs the celebration is for the freeing of Guru Hargobind Sahib and, through his intervention, 52 Hindu kings, by the Mughal emperor Jahengir (AD 1577), and the laying of the foundations of the city of Amritsar. The god Kali is worshipped by Bengalis, who hold this as the night of the ancestors, whose souls are guided by lights on long poles. For Hindus Diwali marks, among other things, the coronation of Rama, the conquest of good over evil, light over dark and the start of the new season with the planting of winter crops and the opening of fresh accounts. Divas lit in houses entice the goddess Lakshmi to stay and bring prosperity and good fortune. New clothes are worn, gifts and sweets made from nuts flavoured with spices and sweetened with coconut and condensed milk are exchanged and special foods prepared, such as neuris (samosas with spiced coconut) and aharsi, special sweet rice biscuits.

See also BONFIRE NIGHT, CAKES, CARNIVALS, CHINESE NEW YEAR, CONFECTIONERY, MAY DAY.

DOG ROSES

The most common of our fourteen native wild roses, its root is said to have cured a soldier of the Praetorian Guard, who was bitten by a rabid dog, hence its name. *Rosa canina*'s scented single white or delicate pink flower and bright red hips are often out of reach, as it likes to climb high into the canopies of trees.

Wild roses may have been overshadowed by cultivated ones, but their very charm lies in finding them in the places where they want to grow. Wayside hedgerows and motorway verges in May and June are always enlivened by the elegant white/pink tangle.

The curator of the Cambridge Botanic Garden in the 1870s wrote: '*We all allow the Roses of the florist to be without rival among flowers of the garden, and we can but admit that wild Roses are perhaps the most lovely of flowers of the field. But there are numbers of the wildings, and all beautiful, and some of surpassing charm. We want to see them more often grown in our gardens.*'

Other wild roses of the hedgerows are the Burnet or Scotch rose – its creamy white, sweet-smelling flower is the first to open in May; the white-flowered field rose, smelling of honey; the pink-flowered downy rose, with soft, hairy leaves; and the sweet briar or Eglantine, which has a fragrant, deep pink flower and leaves that, when rubbed, smell of apples.

Crimson bedeguar galls formed by the larvae of the gall wasp, known as robin's pincushions, are often found on roses. Local names include robin redbreast's cushion in Sussex, briar boss in Shropshire, briar-ball in Northamptonshire and mossy gall in Wiltshire. They were used to cure whooping cough, toothache and rheumatism and as a charm to prevent flogging. It is difficult to believe that five hundred tons of rose hips were collected from hedgerows during 1943; the equivalent in vitamin C content to 25 million oranges.

The cultivated rose is often drawn upon as a symbol of England, but for many of us Rupert Brooke offered the truer spirit: '*unkempt about those hedges blows/An English unofficial rose*'.

See also COTTAGE GARDENS, GREEN LANES, HEDGES, LANES, ROADS, VERGES, WILDFLOWERS.

DOGS

Over thousands of years domestic dogs have been bred to serve particular needs – many originally practical, some despicable – including herding and droving, baiting, hunting, flushing, retrieving, treadmill working, carrying, cart pulling and racing. More recently they have been used as message carriers, assistance dogs for the blind and deaf, rescue dogs, mine detectors, drug sniffers, guard dogs and, increasingly, as companions.

The collection of stuffed dogs at the museum in Tring, Hertfordshire includes all kinds of dogs from Pekinese to Irish wolf hounds and demonstrates the fickleness of fashion and the constant flux of interbreeding. Today indigenous breeds are being neglected and exotic dogs, such as the Shih tzu and Lhasa apso, are gaining favour. Only 82 Sussex spaniel puppies were registered with the Kennel Club in 2003, compared with 35,000 Labradors, and there is no canine equivalent to the Rare Breeds Survival Trust to ensure their future.

See also BLACK DOGS, CAIRNS, GUN DOGS, HOUNDS, HOUND TRAILING, MUSEUMS, SHEEP-DOGS, TERRIERS.

DOUBLE GLOUCESTER

There are records of Double Gloucester cheese being made as long ago as 1594. Originally made in many parts of the shire it became concentrated in the Vale of Berkeley on the east side of the river Severn.

Two kinds of cheese were made: Single and Double Gloucester, both shaped like a wheel or millstone. There are several theories about the differences between the two. According to the English Country Cheese Council, '*the Single was known as "Haymaking" cheese because it was produced from early season milk. As it matured quickly, it was light in colour. In contrast, Double Gloucester used to come from late season milk, and as it was slower in maturing, became darker.*' Patrick Rance described Single Gloucester as being made from '*the cream of only one milking*', whereas Double was made '*either of cream from the overnight milking added to the whole morning milk, or the whole overnight milking ripened to start the whole morning milk when added to it*'. It may simply be that the Double is twice as big as the Single.

In taste, Single Gloucester is light and creamy with a subtle flavour, whereas Double Gloucester is rich and tangy with a firm, dense, smooth texture. In the eighteenth century, cheese merchants persuaded the makers to add a red dye, such as carrot or beetroot juice, to make Double Gloucester look more distinctive. Annatto is used today, giving the cheese an orange-red colour.

Both cheeses were made from the rich milk of handsome Gloucester cattle. In 1779 it was estimated that the Gloucester cattle, together with the Longhorn and Shorthorn herds, were producing eight thousand tons of cheese a season. The rooms where the cheeses were left to mature are still discernible in the tall old farmhouses – Rance counted 350 of them in 1982. They are situated above the bedrooms under the eaves and had wooden dormer vents instead of windows.

The cheeses were sold at cheese fairs at Berkeley, Lechlade, Stow-on-the-Wold and at Barton Fair, Gloucester – the important one, held at Michaelmas and in spring. By 1875 Gloucester cheese started to be made in factories and '*creameries employed agents to go round farm sales and buy and destroy farm cheese-dairy equipment, to reduce the capacity of farmhouse cheesemaking*', Rance wrote. Gloucester cheese making declined until the 1950s, when it was revived by the creamery at Sturminster Newton, Dorset.

In the 1970s, to save Gloucester cattle from extinction (there were only 45 animals left in 1974), Charles Martell started making this cheese in the traditional way at his farm near Dymock, Gloucestershire. Now the number of Gloucester cattle has risen to seven hundred and both Single and Double Gloucesters are made by a handful of craft makers, including Martell. The rest is factory made and of a different quality.

See also APPLES, CATTLE, CHEESE, CHEESE ROLLING, FARMS & FARMSTEADS, MARKETS.

D O V E C O T E S

Sitting between church and farm buildings a circular, windowless stone building draws the eye, looking a little like a fortified windmill that has never had sails, narrowing towards the top. Inside, the three-foot-thick walls are lined with twenty tiers of 33 ledges. Above the small door is inscribed '*In the year 1326 Brother Richard built this columbarium*'. This corner of Garway, Herefordshire maintains a medieval air.

Dovecotes may have been brought here in Roman times, but they were certainly built by the Normans to supply fresh meat all year round, since the lack of grass meant few livestock could be overwintered.

Their interiors neatly replicate the natural nesting places of the domestic pigeon, whose ancestor, the rock dove, bred colonially in dark sea caves. Three-quarters of these early buildings were circular, mostly detached, and were built from whatever local materials were to hand. With the appearance of brick in the sixteenth century styles began to converge, though in the seventeenth and eighteenth centuries polygonal and square-plan buildings increased in number, with small cupolas or louvres so the birds could enter and leave. Pigeons were used as quarry for falconry and in the nineteenth century for shooting matches.

The largest surviving dovecote at Culham Manor, Oxfordshire provided nesting holes for three thousand pairs of pigeons, which mate for life. The young pigeons – squabs – were eaten before they were fully fledged at four weeks old; eggs and old birds were also taken for dishes such as jugged pigeon. A potence, a kind of revolving gallows with ladders, enabled the gathering of the eggs and squabs.

The manure was used as fertiliser and was also much prized for the manufacture of saltpetre, used to make gunpowder. From the mid-sixteenth to mid-seventeenth centuries, dovecotes were located near gunpowder mills, as along the Tillingbourne valley in Surrey.

Only the lord of the manor had the right to build a dovecote until the seventeenth century, when he could permit tenants to build them, too. They huddled close to the manor, monastery or farm and this intimacy still lends richness to the landscape.

After a golden age between 1650 and 1800 the introduction of the turnip started the decline. Now farm animals could be fed over the winter, and with the price of corn rising during the Napoleonic wars, fewer pigeons could be afforded. It became common to keep a few pigeons in the gable ends of barns or in the loft, where square holes are still occasionally in evidence.

Of the estimated 26,000 dovecotes, pigeon-houses, columbaria or culver-houses in the seventeenth century, around two thousand survive, a few in National Trust and English Heritage ownership, such as at Gunby Hall near Spilsby, Lincolnshire and Conisbrough Castle, Yorkshire.

At Norton sub Hamdon in Somerset a circular Ham stone building with a steep roof topped by an elegant cupola, small buttresses giving it an ecclesiastical look, sits inside the churchyard. A sixteenth-century octagonal brick dovecote is marooned among office blocks in the centre of Shrewsbury, Shropshire. At Embleton, Northumberland the medieval domed 'ducket' is of stone. Elsewhere the materials may range from weather-boarding in Kent to flint and brick in Wiltshire and wattle and daub or granite in different corners of Devon.

In the north east of Herefordshire 'magpie' dovecotes – square, timber-framed, painted black and white – such as that at Luntley Court are about as different as they

133

could possibly be from the ancient stone columbarium of Garway in the south west of the county.

See also BARNS, BLACK & WHITE BUILDINGS, CROPS, FARMS & FARMSTEADS, MONASTERIES, PIGEON LOFTS.

DOWNLAND

The old man's beard tells you when you are entering chalk country. This indigenous clematis appears like magic in the scruffy hedgerows, and in summer that triangle of grass where three roads meet on the way up and over to Cerne Abbas whispers welcome with chicory blue as the sky. Dorset is blessed with bold chalk and quiet indicators of its presence, too.

Many plants favour the thin soil, mainly grassland species that have evolved with the close-grazing sheep and rabbits. A huge number of plants jostle for light among the short, dry, springy turf – a rich complexity most gardeners would die for, and which, when ploughed out and sprayed with fertilisers, is reduced to one or two chosen crops and a handful of tough and tall arable grasses against which the rest cannot compete. On the Berkshire Downs and at Epsom, Surrey, where the turf is world famous for training and horse racing, it is the tougher grasses that are managed for, not the original sward.

In the early 1900s W.H. Hudson observed: '*It may be fancy, or the effect of contrast, but it has always seemed to me that just as the air is purer and fresher on these chalk heights than on the earth below, and as the water is of a more crystal purity, and the sky perhaps bluer, so do all colours and all sounds have a purity and vividness and intensity beyond that of other places. I see it in the yellows of hawkweed, rock-rose, and bird's-foot-trefoil, in the innumerable specks of brilliant colour – blue and white and rose – of milk-wort and squinancy-wort, and in the large flowers of the dwarf thistle, glowing purple in its green setting; and I hear it in every bird-sound, in the trivial songs of yellow-hammer and corn-bunting, and of dunnock and wren and whitethroat.*'

Less than a hundred thousand acres of chalk downland remain unharmed. Forty-seven per cent of Wiltshire's downland was ploughed between 1937 and 1971 and half of Dorset's rich downland turf was ploughed up between the 1950s and 1990s. The largest area of undisturbed chalk grassland is on land owned by the Ministry of Defence on Salisbury Plain, where fifteen kinds of orchid grow. Fragments survive on ancient hill-forts and hilltop barrows, where the earliest pioneers started to cut down the trees that covered the chalk.

The parts that remain are precious. Ancient mounds constructed by yellow ants, covered in wild thyme and common rockrose, pick out the land that has never been ploughed, and on summer nights female glow-worms advertise their presence with a pale, yellow-green light, having fed on snails dependent on the calcium for their shells. The downland flora offers sustenance to many butterflies and moths. The buzz and whirr of insects is one of the magical aspects of the downland in summer. Bees, grasshoppers and crickets contribute to this summer symphony, with skylarks adding a '*silver chain of sound*' as George Meredith says, '*chanting an everlasting melody*', in Hudson's words.

Juniper, with its blue-green needles, was once the characteristic shrub of the downs; it is now rare with a stronghold at Porton Down, Wiltshire. Dark yew woods stare back from Kingley Vale, Sussex and Hambledon Hill, Dorset. Box makes a stand on its very own Hill in Surrey. But most of us accept that beech is the tree of the chalk. Beech woods hang on the steep scarps of the Chilterns, ancient pollards linger at Burnham Beeches, Buckinghamshire, and in hilltop clumps it is shaved by the wind.

Dew ponds to water the animals on the tops linger as hollows, and many of the springs near the bottoms are dry, as the water table is drawn ever downwards.

The ebb and flow of farming economics can be read as the plough takes more or less of the downland. Government grants made it more profitable for farmers to grow barley and wheat. With the ploughing of the precious turf went traditional breeds of downland sheep and the wisdom of the shepherd. While cereals dominate the farmed chalk of Hampshire and Wiltshire, grants are now given for setting land aside from cropping and for conservation. Where grassland survives but sheep-grazing patterns have diminished, the stronger grasses have gained dominance. On the Sussex Downs herds of displaced, hard-mouthed Exmoor ponies are blazing a new trail, eating out tor grass to encourage back forty species of downland flora.

See also ALBION, ANTY-TUMPS, BARROWS, BEECH, CHALK, CHALK STREAMS, CLUMPS, COB, DEW PONDS, EXMOOR PONIES, FLINT, GALLOPS, GLOW-WORMS, HENGES & STONE CIRCLES, HILL FIGURES, HILL-FORTS, JUNIPER, LIME-KILNS, LOST VILLAGES, LYNCHETS, OLD MAN'S BEARD, RACECOURSES, SEA CAVES, SHEEP, SKYLARKS, STACKS, TURF MAZES, WHITE CLIFFS, WHITE HORSES, WINTERBOURNES, YEW.

134

Upper Bache Farm, Kimbolton, Herefordshire.

D R A G O N S

Stories help us to memorise and indeed visualise places. Cultures remaining closer to the land than ours tell stories to help find their way about, to know dangers, to know themselves and where they came from. Most dragon tales are geographically connected, sometimes to a roundish hill or mound, sometimes to water.

At Drakelow, the 'dragon's mound', in south Derbyshire the reference is to a dragon protecting a treasure in a burial mound; the same story adhering to Wormelow Tump in Herefordshire reminds us that dragons were often referred to as worms. When the constellation of Draco (the dragon) dominated the sky, midsummer bonfires burnt bones to keep them at bay. With the Old English word for dragon being *draca*, there are also fields that carry memories: Drakestones in Stinchcombe, Gloucestershire; Drakelows in Thornton Hough, Cheshire.

Treasure-guarding stories carry echoes of Norse and Germanic myth. Thor attempts to destroy a vast serpent coiled about the whole world. In the great poem *Beowolf* the interwoven stories of Germanic tribes also involve a dragon roused by a thief. Seamus Heaney translates from the Anglo-Saxon:

> *The hoard guardian*
> *scorched the ground as he scoured and hunted*
> *for the trespasser who had troubled his sleep.*
> *Hot and savage, he kept circling and circling*
> *the outside of the mound.*

On the Yorkshire coast the waves crash and break against a ridge of flattish rocks; Heather Elvidge from Muston tells one story about how Filey Brigg came to be. A troublesome dragon in those parts made a hero out of Billy Biter, whose wife was eaten by the beast, followed by the parkin she had made. *'There was so much that its teeth became stuck together. So the dragon set off down the Ravine to the sea, where it began to wash the sticky stuff from its mouth . . . Billy and his neighbours . . . set up such a din with pots and pokers that the dragon was afraid to come ashore, so it had to stay in the sea, where it drowned . . . it eventually turned to stone and it is still there to this day, stretching out into the sea.'*

Dragons, the devil and Satan seem interchangeable in old texts. *'Better to reign in hell than serve in heaven'* – Milton puts these words into the mouth of Satan as he leaves heaven with the Fallen Angels. Hell is a place of fire. The Bible (Revelation xii, 7-10) describes it thus: *'And there was war in Heaven: Michael and his angels fought against the dragon . . . And the great dragon was cast out, that old serpent, called the Devil, and Satan, which deceiveth the whole world.'* Epstein's

sculpture of St Michael on Coventry Cathedral has Satan beneath his feet; elsewhere, as at the church in St Bees, Cumberland, the dragon lies at his feet. Of the six hundred churches dedicated to St Michael, remarkable ones are found near or on rounded hills – Mere in Wiltshire, St Michael's Mount in Cornwall. Was the dragon already known there, or was he a construct of the new religion?

St George, of course, is England's champion dragon slayer; we share him as patron saint with Catalonia, Georgia, Greece, Lithuania, Palestine, Portugal, Genoa, Venice and more. A soldier turned evangelist, who died a terrible death in AD 303, his association with dragons appears in medieval times, when he saves a maiden from a dragon to gain thousands of souls for the Christian faith. His role locally is now more associated with socialising and quenching thirst, the George and Dragon being a favourite pub name.

Dragons also had a hard time from knights, prodigal sons and adventuring princes, who never gained sainthood. The best known is the Lambton Worm from Lambton Castle, County Durham.

Of the Knucker Hole near Lyminster, Sussex and its dragon, Jacqueline Simpson wrote: *'It is a pond locally reputed to be bottomless, though in fact it is about thirty feet deep, and it is fed from below by a strong underground source, so that it never freezes over, nor does the water level ever vary, even in an intense drought like that of 1976. At one time there were several such . . . all known as "Knucker Holes" or "Nickery Holes" . . . it is derived from an Anglo-Saxon word, nicor, which means "water monster" and occurs in Beowolf.'* The place-name, therefore, tells us that the story has been long in the telling. In a long and convoluted tale including much rampaging, a 'gert pudden' of flour and water seems to have played a part in the downfall of the Knucker.

Few of our dragons live to tell their own tales, so foul of mouth and habit they are portrayed, but the Chinese dragon, the Lung, is a noble, protective beast. It is particularly associated with rain, rivers and water-holes and brings good fortune. Two

Filey Brigg, Yorkshire.

135

hundred dragons adorn the Chinese Archway in Liverpool, built to welcome the New Year of the Dragon in AD 2000. More dragons, always a symbol of power, stand guard at the entrance to Chinatown in Manchester on a Ming Dynasty Imperial Arch – each with feet of five talons. Commonplace dragons have only four.

See also AMMONITES, BARROWS, CAKES, CHINATOWNS, CHINESE NEW YEAR, CHURCHES, CYCLING, DEVIL, FLAGS, GIANTS, HILLS, MIDSUMMER DAY, 'OBBY 'OSSES, PLACE-NAMES, PONDS, PUB SIGNS, SAINTS.

D R O V E   R O A D S

To this day painted on the Drover's House in Stockbridge, Hampshire, '*Gwair tymherus porfa flasus cwrw de a gwal cysurus*' offered to Welsh drovers good pasture, tasty beer and a cosy place to sleep. The driving of cattle, sheep, pigs and poultry by foot across long distances ended only with the coming of the railways in the nineteenth century. Drovers not only came from as far as Wales but also across the Cheviot Hills from Scotland.

They came along the Driving Road to Gearstones at Ribblehead, Cumberland. They came along the Maiden Way from Hadrian's Wall to Kirkby Thore, Westmorland, and down the Hambleton Drove between Durham and York. They dallied at the great trading fairs across Yorkshire and Lancashire and Horham St Faith in Norfolk, Chilham in Kent and Brentwood in Essex. The main destination was London's Smithfield and Cheapside markets. In 1600 around thirty thousand animals were being annually 'drifted' from Wales alone. The trade was already ancient: across East Anglia the Icknield Way's name preserves an old word for oxen, via the Iceni tribe, who lived along it.

Drovers brought news, gossip and money; the Black Ox was the symbol of one of their banks, later crucial in the development of Lloyds, the Ox evolving into the black horse. They have marked permanently the places through which they passed: Drover House, Northumberland; Sheephouse Barn and Guiting Power in Gloucestershire. Oxway, rothern, neat, droveden, shieling . . . all speak of drovers.

In East Anglia droves were also called lokes. Across the country cattle might rest in halts, booths or lairages. Trespassing animals were held in a pinfold until errant drovers paid a fine. A field called Penny Piece or Halfpenny might be their night-time resting place, the name stating the price; Halfpenny Lane travels from the Berkshire Downs to Cholsey, Berkshire. Drover inns proliferated, such as the Drover's Rest at Monkhill, Cumberland and The Shepherd and Dog at Langham, Essex. The Bull and Last in Dartmouth Park, north London was the penultimate stop for northern drovers, perhaps referring to the last trough.

There are more physical reminders. Thirsk, Yorkshire has an old milestone showing a drover with his sheep. Lines of well-worn stemming stones are sometimes set into the ground across droves, 'traffic calming' measures for cattle hastening downhill. Forges lined the routes to make the crescent-shaped cattle shoes for the long walk. Yew trees marked the routes in Hampshire. A few Scots pines implied hospitality to Highland drovers.

See also CATTLE, DOGS, FAIRS & FAIRGROUNDS, GREEN LANES, HEDGES, INNS, LANDMARK TREES, MILESTONES, PINFOLDS, ROADS, SCOTS PINE, SHEEP, TOLL-HOUSES, VERGES, YEW.

D R U M L I N S

The nearest most of us will come to swimming with whales is to find ourselves in a swarm of drumlins. People of a southerly disposition are surprised, first because the South has nothing like this and secondly because the topography is so smooth and intimate. Drumlins are elongated hillocks several hundred metres long and perhaps fifty metres high, often found in clusters. In Newsholme, in the Craven area of Yorkshire, each was just the right size for a field – Greenber, Lingber and Pearsber.

These droppings are enigmatic; lots of theories revolve around the movement of glacial ice and the internal sculpting of till. They tell you by their shape that ice moulded them, leaving a blunt front end and a streamlined tail. They are found on the way from places where great sheets of ice scraped away rock and on the way to where boulder clay was dumped more or less evenly.

Drumburgh Castle on the south side of the Solway Firth in Cumberland is lifted from the water on the back of a huge drumlin. Anyone travelling the smaller roads of the Eden valley in Cumberland, the Tweed valley in Northumberland, the Lune estuary and Bowland Fells in Lancashire or in Holderness, Yorkshire will note the endless ups and downs, made the more memorable if pedalling. An easier view can be had from the Settle to Carlisle railway between Horton in Ribblesdale and Ribblehead, where it seems pod after pod of whales has gathered.

See also BASKING SHARKS, BRICKS, CASTLES, VIADUCTS, WHALES, DOLPHINS & PORPOISES.

D R Y S T O N E   W A L L S

Something of the identity of England is bound together by drystone walls: the hard work they betray, the geology they divulge, the patterns they make. They were built at different times in more than twenty, mostly upland, counties. Cornwall, Cumberland, Derbyshire, Westmorland and Yorkshire have more than half of the total, with the latter

having the greatest length. The craft skills needed to make walls solid and safe, using no binding material, vary in time and place, as do the shapes of the fields enclosed. Together they reflect the way we have controlled the land, embodying a common wealth and an unwritten history often still awaiting translation.

Clearing the land of stones in order to work it challenged early settlers. Enclosure seems a by-product in West Penwith, where, at the furthest end of Cornwall, the density of drystone walls is at its greatest. Here, in the Iron Age and Romano-British times, enormous granite boulders, known as grounders, were built to and levelled off by smaller stones to make hundreds of small, irregular fields.

By contrast, straight walls made with quarried, flattish, hand-sized stones neatly mark out and show off the oolitic limestone swell of the Cotswolds. They were mostly created at the times of Parliamentary enclosure between 1760 and 1825. The rectilinear patterns suggest more recent enclosure of land, whereas sinuous walls tend to be very old.

Since their main task is to hold animals in or out, they need to be robust against climbing sheep, scratching cattle and pushing horses. Shelter against wind and snow also proves useful. Some were built to encircle mine shafts or to resolve ownership. The disputatious Yorkshire abbeys of Bolton, Fountains and Salley finally built walls along the Pennine tops in medieval times to mark their territories. Built and built again these still remind us of the early value of Malham Moor for sheep farming and mining.

Geology offers or denies the possibility of stone walling. In lowland England the sudden appearance of walls instead of hedgerows or ditches usually gives away the underlying Jurassic limestone, as at North Rauceby in Lincolnshire, or volcanic intrusions, as in Leicestershire's Charnwood Forest, where hills are crossed by walls of dark boulders.

The culture of drystone walling is intricate. The county council in Cornwall specifies stone hedges where roads are widened, but there is an increasing tendency, even in western granite areas, to face them with cheaper northern slate, which is made to a herringbone pattern of 'Jack and Jills'. In Yorkshire the 'magpie' walls around the Craven Fault require a local touch.

The flavours are picked up in the words. Cripple holes allow the passage of sheep – they may go by the name of hogg holes or sheep creeps, smout holes or sheep smooses. Across Yorkshire the word used varies from lunkie, smoot and creep hole to thirl. Water smoots are built over simple stone lintels to allow streams to pass under them.

The walls of Wharfedale in Yorkshire are more simply built than those of Wensleydale, which have neat rows of through stones that protrude from each side. Dales sometimes developed their own style as roving gangs earned their living or followed specifications demanded by the Enclosure Awards.

137

Volcanic rock, Wasdale, Cumberland; Dartmoor granite, Devon; millstone grit, Whaley Bridge, Derbyshire; Cotswolds limestone, Sherborne estate, Gloucestershire.

In the High Peak of Derbyshire, whatever the geology, walls have three rows of through stones. Around Coniston in Lancashire and Ambleside in Westmorland solid slate is often used vertically, like gravestones standing shoulder to shoulder, to enclose the fields. In the Duddon valley at Far Kiln Bank you can look up to a nine-foot-high Cyclopean wall comprising huge boulders at its base finished by smaller ones.

At the other end of the country you can see through the seemingly haphazard walls that shamble across the Isles of Scilly. The ill-fitting angular granite is but a single stone deep; some islanders explain that this was to allow rapid removal and rebuilding if they had to launch or land boats in odd places because of a tempestuous sea.

The conditions of sun and shade, exposure and shelter on the opposing sides of walls make for interesting differences. Slate fences are hard and rather mean, except to lichens, but most walls attract lichens, ferns and mosses, stonecrop and saxifrage. Limestone flora is always richer, but the walls of the South West have warmth and longer days on their side. Cornish walls, found mainly on high ground, harbour wall pennywort, stonecrop, wild thyme, polypody fern, spleenworts and dry stone mosses, yellow crustose and grey-green foliose lichens, dog's tooth lichen and more.

The imposing Cornish hedge bank, with its earth centre and battered stone facings, is often so profusely lived upon that it is hard see the stones. Depending on exposure it offers a feast of plants: gorse, blackthorn, hawthorn, heather, bilberry, roses, Atlantic ivy, brambles and honeysuckle, and possibly oak, ash, elm, sycamore, holly, elder and hazel growing along the top. Among the concave stones, thrift, sea campion and kidney vetch might be found on the coast, or, inland, bluebell, red campion, foxglove, fumitory, hawkweeds, woundworts, common violet, toadflaxes and many more. Ferns might include hart's tongue, male fern, broad buckler, black spleenwort and soft shield fern. In Cumberland, where the river Ehen meets the sea south of St Bees Head, roughly stone-faced earth banks, called kefts, support gorse or hawthorn hedges.

Snails love all kinds of walls, as do spiders and glow-worms. The wall butterfly, like many of its fellows, enjoys soaking up solar energy on a warm wall. Small mammals, such as mice and voles, abound, so the adder, stoat, weasel and little owl find drystone walls perfect for hunting, as well as cover. Wheatear, perhaps intending to fly on to the Lake District, catch their breath on the Purbeck walls of Dorset. When they reach their summer grounds they will use the walls as highways, lookouts and feeding places. Walls make good nesting places for redstarts and spotted flycatchers, as well as wrens, blue tits, great tits and sparrows.

The ebb and flow of fortunes in farming has reached a giddy pitch during the past half-century. Ever bigger machinery demands wide access gates and turning circles, to the extent that many walls have been removed, the stone sold. Road construction and development eat away walls, while fashions in gardening provoke stealthy removal and sales. Neglect and clambering walkers bring further threat. A survey of the condition of drystone walls still standing in 1994 found that *nearly half the country's walls were ruinous, derelict or not stockproof*; a further 38 per cent were showing serious signs of advancing or potential deterioration. Nine per cent were stock-proof and just four per cent were in excellent condition. Out of seventy thousand miles, that does not amount to much.

See also ABBEYS, ARCHES, BECKS, BOUNDARIES, BUILDING STONES, CAIRNS, CRINKLE-CRANKLE WALLS, FERNS, FIELDS, GATES, GLOW-WORMS, GORSE, HEDGES, LICHENS, PINFOLDS, ROCKS, SHEEP-FOLDS, SHINERS, STILES, VACCARY WALLS, WILDFLOWERS.

DUDLEY LOCUSTS

Where the Wenlock limestones surface at Dudley, Worcestershire they contain more than six hundred species of marine invertebrates, some of which are *among the most perfectly preserved Silurian fossils in the world*, according to English Nature. One four-hundred-million-year-old fossil, a trilobite, *Calymene blumenbachii*, was dug from the town's Wren's Nest quarries in such numbers that it was used as the symbol of the limestone mining industry in Victorian times, and was given the nickname Dudley Locust or Dudley Bug. It measures about nine centimetres, its hard carapace in three segments intricately replaced by stone. Trilobites were small arthropods that scavenged for food on the sea floor.

It is an emblem of the town, sitting in the centre of the coat of arms under the keep of Dudley Castle, with an anchor and miner's Davy lamp on either side, above a salamander in flames (the emblem of the smith).

Wren's Nest, surrounded by suburbs, was established as the first National Nature Reserve for Geology in 1956. Fossils from the quarry can be found at Dudley Museum and collections all over the world.

See also AMMONITES, BUILDING STONES, LIMESTONE, MUSEUMS, QUARRIES.

138

Ee

Egiziano Bold, Vincent Figgins, 1815.

EARTH PIGMENTS

Colour has always enlivened our surroundings and been put to ritual or workaday uses, from the vegetable bases of weld and woad to animal sources, such as ox blood. Mineral or earth pigments range from haematite (red ochre) to kaolin (white china clay). Staining their surroundings with iron, chalybeate springs were often endowed with spiritual significance.

The river Umber runs through the long, narrow valley inhabited by Combe Martin in Devon. Here, until the 1880s, rotted Devonian limestone was quarried for pigments rich in iron and manganese to produce umber and deep brown burnt umber. Clay, full of carbon, from the nearby Culm Measures was used to produce Bideford black for cheap blacking paint.

In the Forest of Dean, Gloucestershire free miners still search out ochre pigments in the Clearwell Caves among the iron ores, as they have for more than seven thousand years. Red ochre seems to have been in demand for ancient ritual purposes, but a panoply of colours, from yellow and orange to red and brown and rare purple, continues to be mined by hand for use in natural and allergy-free paints. In the Mendips in Somerset remnants of pits last dug in the 1950s for ochre, iron and lead can be found on Banwell Hill and Sandford Hill.

Reddle, raddle or ruddle, red iron oxide mixed with clay, enabled millers to test their millstones for even grinding. Shepherds still use dye to mark their sheep, and to follow the progress of the ram in serving the ewes – a small bag of dye is strapped to his chest, leaving telltale colour on their behinds.

Thomas Hardy noted in *The Return of the Native*: 'Reddle *spreads its lively hues over everything it lights on, and stamps unmistakably, as with the mark of Cain, any person who has handled it half an hour . . . Reddlemen of the old school are now but seldom seen. Since the introduction of railways Wessex farmers have managed to do without these Mephistophelian visitants, and the bright pigment so largely used by shepherds in preparing sheep for the fair is obtained by other routes. Even those who yet survive are losing the poetry of existence which characterized them when the pursuit of the trade meant periodical journeys to the pit whence the material was dug, a regular camping out from month to month, except in the depth of winter.'*

Field names recall such activities: Riddle Pot in Kendal, Westmorland; Raddle Pit in Braithwell, Riddle Pits in Hepworth, Ochre Hole in Fixby and Far Ochres in Knapton, all in Yorkshire; Ocre Mead in Chigwell St James, Essex; Ochre Ground in Forest Hill, Oxfordshire; and Radling in Wootton, Surrey.

Mineral lime and water has given us white farmhouses in villages, and cities too. They are widespread, although sadly now coated with unsympathetic white paints that require less frequent renewal. Umber, ochre and other pigments were sometimes added to limewash to become part of the local scene.

Cambridge whites and Kentish reds had their place. Cornwall and Devon used whites and pinks. Essex, Hertfordshire and Suffolk are distinguished by their plastered and pargeted buildings in a range of colours. Suffolk pink used to be derived from a robust red ochre; now it tends to a pale wash. Colours have drifted over time. In Dedham Vale on the Essex/Suffolk border, the magenta pinks and blues, and brilliant whites instead of gentle whitewash, are considered less harmonious by conservationists than locally derived natural pigments.

See also CAVES, COB, COTTAGES, LIME-KILNS, MILLSTONE GRIT, MINES, PARGETING, RIVERS, SOILS, SPRINGS.

EARTHQUAKES

Three to four hundred earthquakes are detected each year in England, of which about twenty are felt by people. Monitored by the British Geological Survey, most occur between lines linking the dots of Penzance and Holyhead, Carlisle, Doncaster, Leicester and the Bristol Channel. The head of Wensleydale in Yorkshire has suffered the most small but significant earthquakes, in 1768, 1780, 1871, 1933 and 1970. Shropshire and Herefordshire experienced big ones in 1863, 1896, 1926 and 1990. The South East tends to be quiet, although the most damaging earthquake in four hundred years happened around Colchester, Essex in 1884, when turrets, parapets, chimneys and walls fell, as well as part of the church steeple (4.6 Richter scale). From Chichester in Sussex to Dover in Kent activity in the 1830s was matched in 1963 and 1970.

The biggest earthquake, measuring 6.1 on the Richter scale, had its epicentre on the Dogger Bank in the North Sea on 7 June 1931 and was registered by ships at sea. In Filey, Yorkshire the church spire rotated and elsewhere plaster cracked and chimneys were damaged, with cliffs falling at Flamborough Head and Mundesley in Norfolk.

Structural geology gives no clues as to the likely pattern of events. We are fortunate that, because the serious tectonic activity around the mid-Atlantic Ridge and the pushing from Africa are sufficiently distant, the shaking earth is restricted in its effect here. Nevertheless engineering projects include hazard analyses to take seismic activity into account in England.

Despite our perception that England is a quiet place beyond volcanic and seismic afflictions, the people of Warwick (23 September 2000), Melton Mowbray in Leicestershire (28 October 2001), Dudley in the west Midlands (22 September 2002) and Manchester (10 and 11 March 2003) told the

141

British Geological Survey otherwise: '*there was a very loud bang*', '*a rumbling noise like thunder*', '*the whole building wobbled*', '*felt a jolt as if the house had dropped an inch*', '*items fell from shelves*', '*woke me from a deep sleep*', '*felt ripples in my water bed*', '*pet parrots went mad*'. A telephone conversation with Lizzie Kessler in Shrewsbury on 2 April 1990 was interrupted as the house moved and cracked. The quake, centred on Bishop's Castle in Shropshire, measured 5.1.

Vivid recollection accompanies the experience of natural phenomena. Schoolgirls at a swimming class in the Victoria Baths, Nottingham on the afternoon of 11 February 1957 were excited when a great wave rolled down the pool and took minutes to calm. The wireless later reinforced the unsettling truth – the earth had moved.

See also LANDSLIPS, WEATHER, WINDS.

EARTH STATIONS

Farms of giant, man-made mushrooms, such as those at Martlesham in Suffolk or Madley in Herefordshire, send and receive thousands of signals from all over the globe every day. As recently as 1962 the landscape-dominating Goonhilly Downs Earth Station on the Lizard in Cornwall was required to receive the first single flickering and unstable black-and-white television picture from America.

Well-placed to receive signals from across oceans, Cornwall has had a pioneering role in radio and telecommunications since Marconi's early radio experiments at Poldhu on the Lizard. In the century that has followed, Goonhilly has seen the first live television sent to America, the first programmes received from Australia and the first colour programmes sent and received from other continents.

The station consists of about sixty satellite-tracking dishes on a plateau of serpentine rock with a 360-degree horizon, free from radio interference. It made a hero of the Telstar satellite in the 1960s (and made it a pop star, too, thanks to Joe Meek and the Tornados' chart-topping single of the same name). In 1967 The Beatles sang 'All You Need Is Love' to the world through Goonhilly's dishes, part of a grand international satellite link-up for television called 'Our World'. In 1969 it was the conduit through which the images of the moon landing poured. Such is the speed of change that, by the early 1970s, Arthur, as the main dish was called (they have all picked up Arthurian allusions), was obsolete. It was declared a Grade II-listed building in 2003 and, although still in full operation, is a popular tourist attraction.

The landscape historian W.G. Hoskins was uncharacteristically enthusiastic. '*Goonhilly is one of the most marvellous sites in England. What caps it all is the way that as you approach these immense saucers there are circular barrows – the burial mounds of Bronze Age men. It is the combination of these burial mounds four thousand years old and Goonhilly Earth Station which is to me a magnificent conjunction of the ancient world and the future. Goonhilly is obviously not just scenery: it is pure landscape and as deeply moving as any landscape fashioned a thousand or so years ago. Goonhilly at sunset, with no man in sight, silently listening all the time to the most remote signals. It is a scene that would have inspired Thomas Hardy.*'

Not all communications stations are so 'cuddly'. The giant golf balls, or radomes, at Menwith Hill near Harrogate, Yorkshire belong to an RAF base where the US National Security Agency allegedly carries out secret listening activity. Three similar golf balls – at their most surreal during the great snows of 1962/3 – used to mark the site of the early-warning system at RAF Fylingdales on the eastern edge of the North York Moors. Since they were flattened in 1987, an even more ominous monolith has appeared in their place.

See also BARROWS, COMMUNICATION & RADIO MASTS, LANDMARKS, MOORLAND.

EARTHWORKS

One story goes that Six Hills Barrows in Hertfordshire is the result of the devil pitching earth at Stevenage. Our forbears spent much creative energy explaining the works of those who went before. Now archaeology is revealing more and more about the subtle clues around us. Everywhere secretes its own stories; mundane rumples in the ground may prove the key to new understanding of a locality.

The more we know, the more we see the traces of activity of ancient peoples, often ploughed over or built upon so that we have overlooked the earth moved to make amphitheatres, banks, graves, barrows, camps, dykes, fishponds, fortifications, henges, mining pits and mounds, monumental hills, mottes, plague pits, ring ditches, salt workings and warrens. Nature may have reclaimed abandoned villages and remnants of farming and monastic activity, which show up when the shadows are long or drought dries out the ground.

It is difficult to miss the astonishing Silbury Hill, the largest constructed prehistoric mound in Europe. Built in the first half of the third millennium BC near Avebury in Wiltshire, it is contemporary with the early stages of Stonehenge and is thought to have had a ritual purpose.

More modest, Perran Round at Rose in Cornwall gives example to the richness of meaning gathered by these ancient places. Roger Glanville, part of the local history group that helped in its restoration, wrote in 1984 that it was *'originally constructed during the Iron Age as a fortified farm . . . During the Middle Ages the Round was adapted and used as a Plen an guary or open-air theatre for the enactment of Cornish miracle plays . . . the Round was used for many years as a preaching pit . . . as well as for children's Tea Treats and occasional village fêtes.'* It has also been used for Cornish wrestling and for the Gorsedd of the Bards of Cornwall. By 2003 the Round was badly overgrown and the cycle of care and new use was beginning again.

See also BARROWS, BOUNDARIES, CHURCHES, DESERTED VILLAGES, DEVIL, FIELDS, FLINT, FOLKTALES, FORTIFICATIONS, GREEN LANES, HAUNTED PLACES, HENGES & STONE CIRCLES, HILL-FORTS, HOLLOW WAYS, LEAD MINES, LYNCHETS, MONASTERIES, PIT TIPS, PONDS, QUARRIES, RIDGE & FURROW, ROADS, RUINS, WARRENS, WRESTLING.

E A S T

But, look, the morn in russet mantle clad,
Walks o'er the dew of yon high eastern hill.

William Shakespeare, from *Hamlet*

Above all 'east' invokes the dawn, the breaking of a new day, the return of the sun. In this guise it is the most charismatic of the cardinal points. Perhaps our mainly urban lives, with lessening experience of the dawn, have diminished our interest, yet it draws our attention at the significant points of the year – the solstices – when Stonehenge in Wiltshire attracts a serious following.

It is in England that east begins – Greenwich in south-east London is bisected by the imaginary line of zero longitude, the Prime Meridian, where east and west begin their separate journeys across the globe.

It is from the east that we 'orientate' ourselves. The Latin *oriens* means the rising sun. 'East' seems to grow through Old High German *ostar*, meaning to the east. Eostra was the goddess of the dawn; dawn in Greek is *eos*;

and further east still *usas* in Sanskrit means dawn. Most of the building blocks of our history and culture arrived from the east, from the mainland of Europe and out of Asia.

Our churches are built east–west, their altar to the rising sun. At the top of spire or tower their weather-vanes tell the wind direction but often also signify the importance of the east, with a proud cockerel first to catch the sun. Christian bodies are laid with heads towards the east; archaeologists read ancient burials from their orientation.

Geographically the east suggests less rainfall, less humidity and lower wind speeds. But the flatnesses of Yorkshire's Holderness, Lincolnshire and East Anglia have a reputation for searching winds, withering in their treatment of field workers, rude in their penetration of badly fitting windows, dangerous to windmills and the devil to cycle against.

Graham Swift, in *Waterland*, wrote *'some say that the Wash, that gaping wound in the backbone of Britain, is not formed by the effects of tides and rivers and geology, but it is simply the first bite the East Wind takes out of the defenceless shoreline with its ice-whetted incisors'*.

In *The Compleat Angler* Izaac Walton repeated the observation: *'When the wind is in the east 'tis good for neither man nor beast.'* He would also have known the adage *'fish bite the least with wind in the east'*. Easy to turn your back on, but people who have grown up on the eastern side of the country find the dry air difficult to live without – less than 25 inches of rainfall in a year is technically semi-arid, despite the Fenland drains.

See also BRICKS, BROADS, CHURCHES, DIALECTS, FENS, FEN SKATING, MAY DAY, NORTH, PLACE-NAMES, SHIPPING FORECAST, WEATHER-VANES.

E A S T E R   C U S T O M S

Eostre, goddess of dawn and spring, gave her name to Easter. Although we seem to know little about her, she was clearly an important pagan deity. Tied to the first Sunday following the first full moon after the vernal equinox, this 'moveable feast' falls between 21 March and 25 April. It is one of the most important festivals in the Christian calendar.

The common practice of giving Easter eggs may seem a recent commercial enterprise, but in many parts of the world eggs have been used in spring to celebrate the continuity of life for thousands of years. Early Christians adopted them to symbolise Christ's resurrection.

Pre-dating the introduction of chocolate eggs in the mid-1800s, chicken, duck and goose eggs are still hard-boiled and painted or dyed using vegetable dyes, such as onion skins, gorse, spinach leaves and the petals of the pasque flower. In Lancashire and elsewhere children with blackened faces, coats turned inside out and decked with ribbons, would beg for eggs, or money to buy them, by

143

singing pace-egging songs. The decorated eggs would be put on display on windowsills until egg-rolling time.

Paste (*Pasch/Pasque* means Easter in Scots/French) or pace egging, the rolling of eggs down a steep slope, is mysterious. It was probably a solar rite, a rite of spring or a custom associated with divination. Eventually the sport accrued the Christian explanation of symbolising the rolling away of the stone from Christ's tomb.

Egg rolling is prevalent in the north of England, particularly in Cheshire and Lancashire, and for a long time the event at Avenham Park in Preston, Lancashire has attracted hundreds of participants on Easter Monday. The practice has been revived recently by the Middleton Pace Eggers near Manchester, who roll eggs down the hill by the parish church, and by the Lanchester Wildlife Group in County Durham, which discovered that a steep field close to the village was called Paste Egg Field. The landholder was so enthusiastic that he mowed a special 'bouling sward' to help the eggs on their way. Usually the egg that rolls the furthest still intact is the winner. Before the Second World War, the competition would have been followed by an orgy of eating squashed eggs, washed down with beer. Recently oranges have been rolled as well.

The Pace Egg play is peculiar to cotton Lancashire, including Manchester, around Lancaster and Furness in the north. Spread by broadside songs and ballads, chapbooks and strolling players of the eighteenth century, this mumming play is unusual for being held at Easter. The plays increased in popularity in the second half of the nineteenth century and took different forms in different places. By the turn of the twentieth century Rochdale was the only place where the plays continued, performed by the children of Rochdale Municipal High School from 1930 to 1987. Since the 1960s they have been revived in places such as Stockport, Lancaster, Furness, Middleton and Bury. The Middleton Pace Eggers perform on Easter Monday in and outside various pubs in Rhodes and Middleton, whereas the Bury Pace Eggers give about thirty performances during the week before Good Friday. Easter Saturday is also when the Britannia Coco-nut Dancers of Bacup make their appearance.

Easter, like Shrovetide, was a traditional time for games. A kind of mass participation football called Uppies and Downies is still played on Good Friday, Easter Tuesday and the following Saturday at Workington in Cumberland. The Hare Pie Scramble at Hallaton, Leicestershire takes place on Easter Monday. The hare, considered by Eostre as a sacred animal, was thought to have been the provider of Easter eggs, and children would search for them in their gardens. The Easter bunny, an American import, has now usurped it.

Hot cross buns are traditionally eaten on Good Friday, and increasingly now, weeks before. In the Herefordshire villages of Hentland, Kings Caple and Sellack, flat, round biscuits known as Pax cakes are passed round the congregation by the vicar on Palm Sunday. Depicting the Lamb of God and the words 'peace and good neighbourhood', they were made originally to pacify quarrelling parishioners. In Sidmouth, Devon, bags containing a bun and a chocolate egg are given to children on Good Friday at Bedford Lawn. On Easter Monday at the old workhouse in Biddenden, Kent, widows and pensioners are given bread, cheese and tea, known as the Biddenden Dole, while visitors receive a biscuit called a Biddenden cake, stamped with a picture of the legendary Siamese twins or Biddenden Maids, who left land to the parish to pay a yearly dole to the needy in the 1100s.

One traditional Easter pudding is still eaten in the north Pennines and, in 1971, an annual competition for the best one was instigated at Hebden Bridge, Yorkshire. Known as dock pudding, it includes the leaves of the common bistort, a pretty plant of damp meadows that has local names, such as Easter Ledges and Passion Dock, which indicate it was originally eaten in the last two weeks of Lent. There are many local recipes for dock pudding: one is to boil the leaves of bistort, nettle and dandelion, then chop and mix with boiled barley and a chopped hard-boiled egg, heat, then press into a pudding basin and serve with bacon.

See also BISCUITS, BRITANNIA COCO-NUT DANCERS, BUNS, CAKES, GAMES, GORSE, HARE PIE SCRAMBLE, HARES, MOON, MUMMING PLAYS, POULTRY, PUDDINGS, WILDFLOWERS.

ECCLES CAKES

Competing stories agree that Eccles cakes were banned for their associations. Some say that the Puritans in 1650 saw pagan promise in the bulging richness of the Eccles cake; others record that they were part of Wakes Week in Eccles, Lancashire, which was banned in 1877 because of 'riotous' behaviour. Despite this they continued to be made locally. By 1818 they were already being exported.

Philip Harben, the 1950s television chef, remembered that his wife grew up in Eccles and, despite the tradition

Pace Egg Rolling, Lanchester, County Durham.

of secrecy, offered the recipe of her grandmother. He noted that *'they are little round envelopes of puff paste filled to bursting with a mixture of currants and sugar . . . Rum as a matter of fact, makes an excellent addition . . . but the result is not a true and authentic Eccles Cake, for the real thing contains nowt but currants and sugar.'* Eccles cakes are identifiable by their round shape and the three slits in the top layer of pastry that show the rich, dark filling. Make it into an oval and you will have created a Banbury cake, *'best eaten gently warmed'*, as the label advises, in Oxfordshire. They, too, were once sold on fair days but are now baked all year.

See also CAKES, FAIRS & FAIRGROUNDS.

EDIBLE DORMOUSE

In a 25-mile radius around Tring in Hertfordshire people enjoy the company of an animal that is not commonly found elsewhere in the country.

In 1902 the Hon. Walter Rothschild released some small, plump dormice on his estate at Tring Park. Twice the size of our native dormouse, they were a favourite dish of the Romans, who fattened them up in large earthenware jars called *gliaria*. Here, they thrived in the fields, deciduous woods and conifer plantations and multiplied. They soon became a nuisance, causing damage to thatch and grain crops and prompting a campaign to exterminate them.

Eradication was presumed to have been successful until the glis glis (as they are commonly known) were spotted again in 1925, and since then they have slowly expanded their range. In 1988 they could be found from Potters Bar in the east to High Wycombe in the south and Bledlow Ridge in the west. (Some sightings have been made outside this area, latterly in north Dorset, probably a result of people catching them in their attics and releasing them some distance away.)

Recent research in Italy has explained why the edible dormouse has expanded its range so slowly – approximately four miles a year. The creatures breed only in years when there are ample supplies of beech mast. The production of mast is variable, and perhaps abundant once every three years, but glis glis can predict a good harvest, apparently, according to Andrea Pilastro, detecting *'a specific chemical in the beech flower buds, signalling a good year for nuts'*.

Edible dormice are not easy to see, even if you live with them. You may hear them scuttling about the attic at night, and worry about their penchant for chewing electric wires, but they are normally off at dusk into the tree-tops to feed, and they hibernate for six months in winter. They look rather like small, fat squirrels, but with bushier tails and dark rings around their eyes.

See also BEECH, FERAL ANIMALS, RED SQUIRRELS.

EELS

Jellied eels are a speciality of London's East End, sold from street stalls and in Essex coastal towns, such as Leigh-on-Sea and Southend. The eels are chopped and baked with onions, thyme, parsley and vinegar – the jelly is a strong, challenging green. Londoners also created the eel pie, no longer made, giving its name to an island in the Thames that was once a noted jazz venue. While the demand for jellied eels has been dwindling, smoked eel has gained popularity.

For hundreds of years eels have been the staple fare of people living near rivers – especially the Thames, the Severn in Gloucestershire, the rivers of the Somerset Levels and the Fens of East Anglia. Elver cake was eaten throughout the country. The elvers were cooked with herbs, maybe with onion and bacon fat, put *'into a dish, and pressed down till set and cold'*, Dorothy Hartley wrote. The cake was then turned out and cut into slices. Keynsham in Somerset was known for a version of elver cake that was like a Cornish pasty.

An annual elver-eating contest was held on Easter Monday on Frampton Green in Gloucestershire until 1994, when it became unaffordable. In 2002 Eric Miller from Gloucester told us: *'Today I saw a number of cars with "elver nets" on top, the drivers were off to fish for the elver that arrives in the river Severn at this time of the year after a long journey from the Sargasso Sea. It reminds me of the days when we could go to our local elver man and buy a pint of elvers from a tin bath in the front garden for the princely sum of 6 old pence. Today they are sold to elver stations in the country for nearly £40 a kilo. I really miss my annual feed of elvers with eggs stirred in and served with rashers of thick streaky bacon – alas no more to be, they are all exported. Ah, I can smell them now just thinking about it. How times have changed.'*

England must have been heaven on earth for eels before we started straightening and dredging our muddy rivers, blocking them with sluices and draining our extensive marshlands and moors. Medieval and recent records show an abuse of abundance – fifteen thousand eels for Henry

145

III's feast to celebrate St Edward's Day in October 1257. In Ely (isle of eels) the monks paid their annual tithes to the Cathedral with thirty thousand eels. In living memory catches have been so large that they have been used for animal feed and fertiliser.

Young elvers once gathered in their millions in our estuaries in March. They drift on the currents for three years across four thousand miles of the Atlantic until the smell of 'their' river compels them. They wait for the spring tides to carry them upstream – the Severn Bore proves particularly useful. Then they travel up to the headwaters, where they lie low for perhaps fifteen years in muddy drains and ditches, feeding at night, shunning the light. At the onset of winter some mature 'silver eels' start their breeding journey home. They travel on wet, stormy, moonless nights, moving over ground, across watersheds, to the big river and south to the Sargasso Sea.

Eels are caught as they leave our rivers, elvers as they enter. In Aveton Gifford in Devon the children know places where the tiny transparent glass eels cling around pebbles but disperse immediately a finger probes.

The elver run up the river Severn is a phenomenon of nature. Fifty years ago Dorothy Hartley described it as being like a 'mass of jelly swimming in the water; it consists of millions of elvers' looking like 'transparent spaghetti'. They have probably been caught for many hundreds of years, but it wasn't legal to sell or even catch them until the Elver Act of 1876 legitimised it. Before the Thames became too polluted to sustain them, the elver run was known as the eel fare, and Londoners helped themselves to the bounty. In 1832 it was 'calculated that up to 1,800 elvers were passing each minute at Kingston on Thames', Tom Fort relates.

In the autumn, returning silver eels are caught in fyke nets (in which otters can also drown unless the nets are equipped with special guards – four drowned in Dorset in 2002) and in racks or grids erected near water-mills on the tributaries of the Thames and other rivers. In the Fens, Roger Deakin wrote, they are 'caught in wing-nets, stretched across the river'. But they are also caught throughout the year, at one time with stick spears and in 'v-shaped weirs known as kiddles', according to Tom Fort; in long, woven willow traps known as hives or grigs in the Fens; or with babs – balls of worms – on a willow rod and line.

But eel fishing may have to cease if we are to save the species. It is sad that as the Thames is becoming ever cleaner, eel populations are critically low across England. Charles Dickens's son wrote in the *Dictionary of the Thames* in 1880 that 'eels have greatly fallen off in individual size and collective numbers in late years'. Figures show that around the Severn estuary catches fell from about fifty tons in the 1980s to ten tons in 2002. In 2004 the Environment Agency reported a population crash to just one per cent of the numbers of twenty years ago.

Many believe the overfishing of elvers plays its part – they are air-freighted to eel farms in China and other faraway places, to the detriment of our own rivers and people, as well as the bitterns, herons and otters that would feed on them. In writing of the river Parrett in Somerset, James Crowden concluded 'we are in effect selling the future for a pittance, a future stock that can never be replaced'. Like the bison and cod, once so numerous that we never thought we could make inroads into their populations, the eel is slipping out of our lives.

See also BORES, EYOTS, FENS, FLATNERS, FRESHWATER FISH, LEVELS, RHYNES, RIVERS, SEA FISH.

ELEANOR CROSSES

Twelve Gothic shrines were ordered to be made by Edward I in memory of his wife, Eleanor of Castile (Infanta de Castile), who died in 1290. A cross was built at each place where her body rested on its journey from Harby in Nottinghamshire to Westminster Abbey.

Three survive – in Geddington and Hardingstone in Northamptonshire and at Waltham Cross in Hertfordshire. The final shrine, at Charing Cross, is a nineteenth-century replica of the original and is the 'centre' of London for mileage computations.

See also BESTIARY, CHURCHYARDS, MARKET CROSSES, ROADS, WAYSIDE & BOUNDARY CROSSES.

ELM

Familiar from the paintings of Constable and maintained in the mind's eye of people with memories stretching back to the 1960s, the English elm, *Ulmus procera*, 'came to be regarded as the quintessence of the English landscape', R.H. Richens wrote. This tall, billowing, elegantly asymmetrical tree had the widest distribution of all the elms, favouring the fertile valleys of the South and Midlands but reaching as far north as Yorkshire and west to Plymouth and the Welsh borders. Its ability to spread by suckering offered a free and easy way for early farmers to enclose stock; whole valleys or parishes had hedgerows of what was essentially a single tree.

It seems ironic that a species that appears 'to perpetuate' itself 'for ever unless carefully eradicated', as Oliver Rackham put it, should be so reduced over the centuries by waves of disease. In the past few decades Dutch elm disease has killed 25 to 30 million, more than three-quarters of England's elms. With them has gone the large tortoiseshell butterfly, now extinct here. An organism that has worked out how never to die is, nevertheless, vulnerable to our ignorance. Many dying trunks were removed – indeed, the practice was encouraged – but we now know that the roots keep on regenerating, surviving the repeated attacks of elm bark beetles, which carry the microscopic fungus that spreads to prevent the tree from taking up water. In time, these elms may become resistant to infection, or learn to live with it, and survive us all.

From the Middle Ages the English elm was one of the commonest hedgerow trees, frequent in Anglo-Saxon place-names, such as Elmscott and Elmhurst. The wood was used for piling under bridges, groynes and keels, as weather-boarding for farm buildings, seats of Windsor-type chairs, coffins for the poor (the wood being plentiful and cheap), and bored as pipes for water. In some places the trees were pollarded and the leaves used as fodder.

On the advice of John Evelyn, Charles II planted six thousand elms at Greenwich in the 1600s, starting a fashion for elms in parks and as avenue trees. By the 1720s landscape gardeners Wise and Bridgeman had planted 23,000 elms and limes along gravel walks in Kensington

Gardens in London, making elms, as Susan Lasdun wrote, '*the most commonly planted tree in England*'.

Several kinds of elm are indigenous. The narrow-leaved elm can be found in East Anglia, eastern Kent and the east Midlands, and the Cornish elm, with its skirts of epicormic shoots, west of Plymouth. On the Isles of Scilly, free from Dutch elm disease, the Countryside Agency observed that '*the lines of wind-sculpted, lichen-encrusted trees*' stand out. The narrow-leaved elm is variable, appearing in many local forms. In the 1950s and 1960s Richens studied elms in old boundary hedgerows in Essex – '*holy ground for the elm systematist*'. He found the most complex assemblage of elms in Europe, some different in each parish, such as the Farnham elm, Chigwell elm, Little Hallingbury elm and Latton elm. Owen Johnson, talking of Sussex, said '*Ulmus minor, the smooth-leaved elm, has a regional variant which is one of the commonest native trees along the southern edge of the Weald from Glynde to Rye*'.

One thousand English and Dutch elms were planted around the Level in Brighton in 1845. By 1995, 180 had survived the disease and continue to be actively cared for. But it was the English elms running along the hedgerows of the Ouse and Cuckmere valleys that local people were most concerned to save. In 1973 the far-sighted East Sussex county council and 34 local councils created a cordon sanitaire south of the Downs between Eastbourne and Shoreham, pruning, felling and injecting diseased trees in the control area. Thousands of elms were lost but some were saved, including 'Lofty' in Preston Park. Those that survive constitute the only population of mature English elm trees in the world.

Elms that propagate from seed include the large, spreading Wych elm, which occurs in mixed woodland but is also a hedgerow tree. Its homeland is the North – the Yorkshire wolds and Pennine dales – but it can also be found on the escarpments of the Chilterns, the Cotswolds, the Mendips and Herefordshire. Although it is less susceptible to the disease, many have been lost.

See also ALDER, ANCIENT TREES, ASH, AVENUES, BEECH, BIRCH, BLACK POPLAR, BLACKTHORN, FIELD MAPLE, HAWTHORN, HAZEL, HEDGES, HOLLY, HOLM OAK, HORNBEAM, HORSE CHESTNUT, JUNIPER, LANDMARK TREES, LICHENS, LIME, LONDON PLANE, MONKEY-PUZZLE, OAK, ORCHARDS, PARKLAND, PEARS, POPLAR, ROWAN, ROYAL FORESTS, SCOTS PINE, SWEET CHESTNUT, SYCAMORE, WALNUT, WHITEBEAM, WILLOW, WINDSOR & COUNTRY CHAIRS, WOODS, YEW.

147

ENGINE HOUSES

In Cornwall and parts of the Pennines lonely stone towers, like fortified dwellings with solid chimneys, mark the skyline. These ruined buildings once housed steam engines, which drew water or hauled waste rock from mines, sometimes breaking up ore for smelting.

Dartmoor, Bodmin Moor, Redruth, Penwith and the Isles of Scilly have been trading tin for thousands of years, but demand drove the mines deeper and the problem of pumping water from the shafts increased. Steam pumps, developed by Thomas Newcomen in the early eighteenth century, provided the solution. The wetter the area, the bigger the engine and the engine house; the clay sites, killas, were the wettest.

Engine houses are atmospheric signs of Cornwall, from East Kit Hill just over its border with Devon to the steep cliffs of Botallack facing the Atlantic. They stand over capped shafts of tin, copper, lead, silver and arsenic mines, and survive because of their robust construction. Windows are small and arched to keep the structures strong. Massive beam engines were fixed into the masonry – winding was whimsey to the Cornish, and engines for this purpose consequently were called whim engines. Huge granite blocks were used for the foundations, the rest of the building was in local stone. When active they were whitewashed, with red-painted woodwork, and kept fastidiously clean.

148

The chimney is usually circular in section, incorporated into the corner of the building for strength, as at South Crofty, with its squat, strong stack. At Hawkes engine house in Killifreth the chimney is tall and almost delicate. Sometimes stacks are separate, as at Ventonwyn, East Wheal Rose and Tregurtha Downs (now a private house), with its elegant tapering stacks.

Even engine houses sited on the exposed coast remain. Wheal Coates has two, one above the other, on cliffs overlooking a white sandy beach; at Botallack engine houses sit low on the cliffs.

See also BASTLES, BLUE JOHN, BUILDING STONES, CHIMNEYS, COAL MINING, COES, GRUFFY GROUND, LANDMARKS, SOUGHS, ZIGZAGS.

ESTUARIES

We may associate the Tyne with fine bridges and a once-defining ship-building industry, the Tees with a twinkling and smelly chemical complex, the Humber with industry and latterly great fishing fleets, the Wash with open skies, the Thames with trade and commerce, the Blackwater with sailing, the Severn with its bore, the Mersey with songs and Morecambe Bay with a voracious running tide, but all of them are distinguished by being complex places in constant flux. These were the Saxon and Viking motorways, offering fast access inland. Where deep water is available, as in Southampton Water in Hampshire, they remain the points of entry for the heavy liquids that drive our economy.

Created where rivers run into the sea, our estuaries are tidal, offering a mosaic of challenges and opportunities for us and for wildlife. Some offer deep water, others are edged by salt marshes and rich mud-flats. They provide vital nurseries for many inshore marine fish, such as flounder, golden grey and thin-lipped mullets, sea trout and sea lamprey. Morecambe Bay, the Humber, Maplin Sands, the Ribble and Dee estuaries are key feeding grounds for wildfowl and waders, offering worms, shrimps and shellfish.

Likewise the Wash, fed by the rivers Nene, Ouse, Welland and Witham, extends over sand- and mud banks carved by intricately branching channels to more than 250 square miles, despite the massive drainage of the Fens. It supports huge populations of invertebrates and, in the south, brittle-stars and starfish. Eel grass is concentrated around the mouth of the Welland, where widgeon, teal, shelduck and mallard dominate. Enteromorpha, a type of algae, grows on the Wash flats, with huge flocks of knot, dunlin, curlew and oystercatcher as well as redshank, sanderling, bar-tailed godwit and grey and ringed plovers. Migrants add to the numbers. The sandbanks of the Nene, Ouse and Welland mouths attract common seals in quantity and some grey seals, too. In the South West, at the Exe estuary, spoonbills and avocets are among the annual visitors.

St Agnes Head, Cornwall.

Including the four shared with Scotland and Wales, England has 81 estuaries. They form our largest coastal habitat, one-fifth of Europe's Atlantic and North Sea tidal inlets. About a third of the estuarine surface has become dry land since Roman times, and much that remains is under pressure from port developments and industrial expansion. Chemicals and waste released into rivers accumulate in the estuarine sediment, risking long-lasting contamination. Rising sea levels compound the problems. For all these reasons, estuaries are among our most threatened maritime habitats.

See also BOAT RACE, BOATS, BORES, COASTLINE, COASTS, EAST, HARBOURS, RIAS, RIVERS, SALT MARSHES, SHIPPING FORECAST, STARFISH, TIDES.

E X M O O R   P O N I E S

Around 21,000 years ago, with ice or tundra covering the country, the re-establishment of plants and animals had to wait until the permafrost receded. Some time during the succeeding oscillations of climate, colonisation by trees and the disappearance of the land bridge linking us to mainland Europe (between eight and five thousand years ago), a group of animals made themselves at home on the open moors that are the source of the Exe.

Isolated, the forbears of the Exmoor pony evolved and now persist as one of the world's most ancient breeds, somehow surviving man's predations and interferences. They are small, 11.2 to 13.1 hands high, with double-thickness coats that keep out the cold and wet. They

are consistent in colour and marking – shades of brown with darker points and characteristic pale muzzle and eye surrounds. They are round, with extensive and efficient digestive systems carried on strong legs and feet that work well in wet and rocky conditions.

Exmoor, an exposed area of wild, high moorland on the border of Devon and Somerset, faces the winds of the Atlantic, which bring penetrating rain, snow and cold as well as hot, sunny days. From the eleventh century it was a royal forest – a hunting ground – but with no woods at all within its bounds. Any management of the ponies tended to be based upon the principle that nature had the best design and introducing other blood led to dilution of hardiness. But the moor was sold in 1818 to an industrialist bent on productivity. He bred the ponies to the extent that they could no longer survive the harsh conditions. Luckily the retiring Warden of the moor, Sir Thomas Acland, took thirty ponies and some of the surrounding farmers bought a few – to them we owe the continuance of the line. Many families are still breeding Exmoors and, on Winsford Hill, the descendants of Acland's herd are run, still carrying the Anchor brand mark.

The Second World War also nearly saw their end. Indiscriminate target practice and rustling for meat left barely fifty animals. Mary Etherington inspired other Exmoor farmers and they began a careful programme of breeding.

Only a small number of animals remain, with few bloodlines. So, although they are off the critical list, the Rare Breeds Survival Trust classes them as endangered. About two hundred feral Exmoor ponies still graze the

149

moor, and across the world as few as twelve hundred exist. The Exmoor Pony Society oversees gatherings in October and November, where the year's youngsters are selected and branded. An annual stallion parade is held in Exford in early May.

Their continued presence on the moor is important; the place and the animal have evolved together for perhaps as long as there has been grass on Exmoor. They do not simply excite us as 'wild' creatures, they are, in some sense, the place itself. Full of stamina and strength, their lives were intertwined with those who made their living on the moor. They have been used for shepherding, driving, riding, agriculture and postal delivery.

But their future lies in finding new roles; in addition to tourism, driving and riding they are earning their keep in other ways. Although it means small, free-living herds working in other places, one promising task performed with relish is that of conserving grassland habitat, such as the Sussex Downs and Askham Bog in Yorkshire. Exmoors are very good at eating tough herbage – tor grass, thistles, invasive scrub – that crowds out delicate wildflowers. There is a positive symmetry in one highly endangered creature building its own survival on the saving of others.

See also CATTLE, THE CHANNEL, DOWNLAND, FELL PONIES, FELLS, GALLOPS, HORSE FAIRS, HORSES & PONIES, HOUNDS, LONDON TAXIS, MOORLAND, NEW FOREST PONIES, PIGS, POINT TO POINT, POULTRY, RACECOURSES, SHEEP, SHIRE HORSES, SUFFOLK PUNCHES, WHITE HORSES.

150

E Y O T S

Pronounced 'eight', alternatively spelt ait, an eyot is a small island, usually in a river. Connected is the 'ey' in Canvey and Sheppey, which already suggests island, as does the 'ea' in Brightlingsea and also the 'y' in Lundy and Ely. Pixey Mead in Oxfordshire is a meadow on Pic's island.

The languid Thames abounds in little, low-lying, tree-covered eyots, some the size of a rowing boat yet still supporting semi-natural vegetation, providing refuge for wildfowl and water life. Isleworth Ait has a small sycamore wood with hawthorn, holly and elder; Lot's Ait has an ash, crack willow and elder wood.

Eyots are frequently used for bridge crossings or weir making and boat bypasses. Elsewhere, in splitting the stream, they offended river engineers, who regarded anything impeding flow as a problem. Island dwellers are more sanguine. Houses on stilts on Rod Eyot by Henley in Oxfordshire tell of winter flooding. The Chiswick Ait in west London is familiar as the one the Boat Race goes by. Eel Pie Island sounds delicious, and indeed the dish was served in the inns along the Thames; jazz buffs will recall the music scene there that drew young rock-and-rollers, too, in the mid-twentieth century. Perhaps eel pie hides an older

'ey' name, the superfluous word 'island' added by those who did not understand the Old English or Norse.

The eyot fringed with willow, silver birch and alder that Mole and Rat came across in *The Wind in the Willows* was their ideal destination. '*"This is the place of my song-dream, the place the music played to me," whispered the Rat, as if in a trance. "Here, in this holy place, here if anywhere, surely we shall find Him!"*'

See also ALDER, BIRCH, BOAT RACE, EELS, FLOODS, HERONRIES, ISLANDS, SYCAMORE, WILLOW.

Ff

Fashion Compressed. Alan Meeks, 1986.

F A C T O R I E S

Factories can be landmarks, memories of a society that once lived on its capacity to make things. Built to last, most have outlived their original purpose and have been reinvented for residential use, such as Typhoo Wharf in Birmingham and the workshops of Nottingham's lace market. Others have become shopping centres or, in the case of the Victorian lead works on Anchor Square in Bristol, restaurants. Some have preserved a little of their original industriousness by becoming warrens of small businesses: Dubarry Soap and Perfumery Manufactory in Hove, Sussex is one such, and at Glovers Yard in Brighton – formerly Cornelia James's glove factory – artists and craftspeople live, work and trade.

Many places that seem to say 'factory' remain only as shells, and some are shells of administrative buildings rather than works. The only surviving remnant of Huntley and Palmer's biscuit factory in Reading, Berkshire is the old workers' recreation club headquarters. It still bears the name of the company, once so important that Reading was known as Biscuit Town, its prison the Biscuit Factory and its football team the Biscuit Men.

Dramatic Art Deco factories often stand alongside main roads, such as the colourful 1930s Hoover Factory on Western Avenue in Perivale, Middlesex, Kayser-Bondor in Baldock, Hertfordshire and the Wills Tobacco Factory in Newcastle upon Tyne (now also a shell, filled with expensive apartments and fortunate to have survived). After the Second World War factories became austere concrete monoliths, but in time there came more dramatic statements, such as the bold blue 1982 Herman Miller building on the outskirts of Chippenham, Wiltshire, certainly a landmark, if not yet entirely embraced.

Others expanded on an unprecedented scale. The JCB factory beside Rocester in Staffordshire is as big as the whole village, its grey-green reflection in the lake adding to its bulk. The car plant on the old South Marston airfield in Swindon, Wiltshire is bigger still, and although largely hidden from view it has made a real impact by becoming (unofficially at least) a place-name, appearing as Honda on road signs, maps and roundabout names.

New design does not have to be loud, deferential or replicate the old. The Mellors cutlery factory in Hathersage, Derbyshire, built in 1990, pleases both architects and residents. Its roundness reminds us of the built form it replaced – a gasholder – offering continuity. Its size and use of local stone are comprehensible, they do not detract from the feel of the place, instead adding a new dynamism.

Thanks to the vision and persistence of architects and developers, such as Urban Splash, the imaginative reuse of old factories, mainly for residences, is causing momentous change in formerly deteriorating parts of Manchester and Birmingham. At least a thousand more workers are employed now in small businesses than worked originally in the beautifully refurbished Bryant and May match factory in Garston, Liverpool, a beacon of regeneration.

See also AIRFIELDS, BISCUITS, BUILDING STONES, FOOTBALL, GASHOLDERS, SMELLS, WAREHOUSES.

153

F A I R S & F A I R G R O U N D S

Feria meant holiday to the Romans, and Charles Kightly reminded us that '*Every village in Britain has or had its own special yearly festival, generally celebrated on or about the feast day of the patron saint to whom its parish church is dedicated. This is known as "the Feast" in north eastern England, Yorkshire and the south and east midlands; as "the revel" in parts of the south west; and in the north west and the north and west midlands as "the Wake" – from the medieval custom of "waking" or keeping vigil at the church on the night before the great day.*' A result of the Reformation was to decree that all parishes hold their wakes on the first Sunday in October, but as Kightly pointed out, '*this enactment was simply ignored in most places . . . English feasts stuck as close as possible to the proper saint's day, even (or indeed especially) if the saint commemorated was an obscure and local one.*' Even with the change of calendar in 1752 the feasts often remained fixed to the old day.

The right to hold a fair or market was through long use or a charter sought from the King. Once it was established the freedom to trade at the town fair was given to anyone and everyone, bringing income for the lord of the manor, Church and Crown. In 1110 a charter for an eight-day Easter fair was granted by Henry I to the Abbot of Ramsey for St Ives in Huntingdonshire; since his feast day is 24 April, there may have been a local 'waking' here already. Brough (Hill) Fair in Westmorland may have been active since Roman times.

Whereas markets were frequent and domestic affairs, jealously controlled by powerful guilds for local benefit, fairs were part of the wider calendar. They positively welcomed non-indigenous, often international traders. Scarborough Fair used to last a rumbustious 45 days, drawing French, Spanish, Italian, Baltic and Mediterranean traders in wines, iron, gold, amber, silk and spices, who would return home with cloth, grain, foods and drinks.

Fairs were dominated by trade in animals, with drovers sometimes bringing cattle, sheep, geese, pigs and horses long distances. But local specialisms abounded: Birmingham had its Onion Fair; Great Yarmouth in Norfolk its Herring Fair; Norwich its Rush Fair. Coventry still has its Crock Fair; Whitstable in Kent its Oyster Festival; Priddy in Somerset its Sheep Fair. Lee Gap in Yorkshire clings on to its First and Latter Lee horse fairs; Egremont in Cumberland its Crab (apple) Fair. There are reinvented damson, hop and cherry fairs; Winchester in Hampshire has a new Hat Fair and Soham in Cambridgeshire a Pumpkin Fair.

As industry and cities expanded, and fluidity increased in agriculture, communications and demographics, feasts, festivals and fairs changed; some grew. Animal trading was sometimes lost and pleasure fairs, more like those we know today, began to evolve. Efforts to quieten the exuberance led to organised 'processions of witness' – the Manchester Whit Walks, Walking Day in Warrington, Lancashire and the Club Walks in the Welsh Marches. Feasts sometimes became more demure fêtes, and time away – holidays – began to develop.

During Wakes Weeks in Yorkshire, Lancashire, Cheshire and Staffordshire factories and mills preferred to close down (and catch up with maintenance) rather than support the aftermath of excess. Workers might stay in Blackpool rather than at home, sobering towards the end of a week, or two, without pay.

Victorian preoccupations with temperance, modesty and work forced many fairs out of existence. But from the innovations of travelling entertainers, storytellers, trinket sellers, prize fighters, musicians and jugglers, and the introduction of food- and game-stalls and man-powered fairground rides, the funfairs we enjoy today evolved. The arrival of steam brought great swing boats, gallopers and organs. With electricity came lights. The rides have grown in stature, as have the lorries that pull them – Colchesters – which carry the name of the place where they were built by John E. Mills.

With the fair came exotic foods, including pomegranates and coconuts. Biscuits, especially gingerbreads, originally sold as fairings, have their regional variations. In Devon, Widecombe Fair offered gingerbread and spiced ale; Norwich had gingerbread 'husbands and wives'. Tradition suggested when certain foods would be eaten, as Christina Hole described: '*Weaverham Wakes [in Cheshire] were held in the spring, on Quinquagesima Sunday, and the menu for the three days was fig pie on Sunday, furmenty on Monday, and pancakes on Tuesday.*'

The prejudice that follows fairs has pushed many of them from old fairgrounds, market-places and town centres, places that they have earned more right to visit during hundreds of years than have shop chains. Fair fields and show grounds are a special part of any town. Some have deep histories. Above Wakefield, Yorkshire the fair sets up on old Heath Common; in Cambridge on Midsummer Common, around 24 June. At Epsom in Surrey around Derby Day, the fair used to be within the racecourse – now it is in the car park, a typical move.

154

Dorset Steam Fair, Tarrant Hinton, Dorset.

Nottingham boasts the biggest of all – the Goose Fair, held over three days from the first Thursday in October. With 150 children's rides, more than sixty adult rides and 550 stalls, this is a mammoth show that has lost its connection with geese. The other great rivals are The Hoppings (the Northumberland word for fair), which has been held since 1882 on the Town Moor in Newcastle, and Yorkshire's Hull Fair.

More than four and half thousand fairground families ply the roads; every family has its own circuit, so every town has a unique mêlée. King's Lynn Mart opens the traditional showmen's year.

New fairs are born. Not yet forty, one of the most successful is the Dorset Steam Fair, which takes over six hundred acres of downland between Salisbury and Blandford and surrounds itself with encampments for several days. Its enormity, breadth and bustle offer an unrivalled day out. At night the noise of a hundred fairground organs and fifty showman's engines, creating the power and light for the old fairground rides, brings spectacle to Cranborne Chase. Demonstrations and dancing, cider and traditional ales, the mingling of people and steam, give a real taste of the activity and excitement of old gatherings.

See also BISCUITS, BLACKPOOL ROCK, BURNING BARTLE, CATTLE, CHEESE, CHERRIES, CHURCHES, COMMONS, CRAB FAIR, DAMSONS, DROVE ROADS, FOOD, FURRY DANCE, HOPS, HOP-GARDENS & HOP-YARDS, HORSE FAIRS, MARKET CROSSES, MIDSUMMER DAY, PIGS, PRIDDY SHEEP FAIR, SAINTS, SHEEP.

F A M I L Y   N A M E S

A family name is a medieval convenience. It is also called a surname, which has a French air, its roots in the new Norman administration of the eleventh century. A century passed before any serious adoption of hereditary family names began to take place, firstly among the aristocracy and then, by the end of the fourteenth century, with ordinary people, starting in the South as administration was centralised. The names might indicate where a person came from or to which duke they owed allegiance. The Normans called themselves Paris, Lyon and Beaumont. England had the likes of William of Malmesbury and Julian of Norwich. Names such as York represented more a banner to march under than a place to originate from.

Names could refer to notable physical characteristics – Large, Redhead, Strong – or indicate whether you were Good, Noble or Sweet. They also helped the clerks know what you did. These administrators were likely to be the ones who assigned the names in the first place, to differentiate John the Baker from John the Farmer, and John of the Hill from John of the Woods. The most common appellation was Smith, from the Anglo-Saxon *smitan*, to strike. This was one of the earliest specialist trades and the name is international. But at first these names were not fixed; they could shift several times during a lifetime.

The Society of Genealogists notes that only a *'very small number of . . . British families can be traced to the person who first used the surnames.'* The names we have today are often the result of the caprice of whichever priest or registrar wrote down the name of a newborn child and his family, when there was no formal guidance in such matters and widespread illiteracy. This was the case up to the nineteenth century.

Because names refer to a place of origin or to a trade that might be closely associated with a locality, they can help to define a place. Philip J. Dance notes that even in the early twenty-first century there were numerous Gobles, Edneys and Cawtes in the Portsmouth area and fewer elsewhere. Ling and Greengrass cling to East Anglia; Chalk and Down are names of the South.

Cornwall has names relating to places, and to things that were part of everyday life when the names were formed: rock piles, bogs, heaths and marshes, old places, buildings and farms (Hendra and Hendry), valleys, the sea and a hint of the tin mine. Many have terminal points, ends, headlands and promontories encapsulated in the prefix Pen (Pengelly, end of a grove; Penrose, of a moor). Others have Ros, meaning moor (Roscarrock, Rosevear), or the almost ubiquitous Tre, a farm or homestead (Tremayne is by a stone; Trevorrow by a track). Islands restrict family-name distribution yet further. Each of the Isles of Scilly has long-persisting families: Bond and Ellis on St Martin's, Jenkins on Bryher, Hicks on St Agnes and Woodcock on Samson.

Despite the best efforts of the Industrial Revolution and mass transport there are still Grundys in Lancashire, Charltons and Robsons on footballing Tyneside. Melvyn Bragg points to his childhood in Cumberland and the ghosts of naming Old Danish-style: *'At my own school there were Johnsons, Pattisons, Robsons, Harrisons, Rawlinsons, Watsons, Nicholsons, Gibsons, Dickinsons, Hudsons, Hewitsons, Stevensons. And it is still true today that despite the centuries of people moving around these comparatively small islands, there are still markedly more shop names, "Harrison", "Johnson", "Wilkinson", more sons, than in any other part of the country.'* Many people tend to move no further than the nearest big town, then return to their roots. Family ties remain strong.

With more than half a million bearers, Smith is still the most common family name in England, according to Office of National Statistics data gathered from the 2001 census. When Nigel Kneale wrote the television adventures of Professor Quatermass in the 1950s, there were *'still a few in the phone book'*. One was a London market trader, the name perhaps originating from the military quartermaster. In 2001 only 27 remained. In London more than 95 per cent of the names in the UK can be found.

155

The use of places in family names is not quite so common as might be expected, trades (Turner, Taylor, Wright) and patronyms (Wilson, Robinson) taking the honours. In the top one hundred most widespread names, only Barnes, Wells and Walton seem to indicate an English place. And of those only the last might be a genuine memory, either of Walton itself or a recollection in the Anglo-Saxon tongue of a settlement of the Welsh – the native Romanised-Britons they ousted. The surname London rates 3,508th, Birmingham 4,975th, Bristol 13,134th. As a name, Norwich, at 85,116th, languishes far below even the abandoned Wiltshire village of Imber, which was surname to 380 people in 2001.

Names continue to appear from overseas – the 24th most common surname in England in 2001 was Patel, and between numbers 50 and 100 were found Khan, Hussain, Begum, Ali, Ahmed and Singh. Many cling to particular areas and bring new life to that most public of family-name statements – the shop sign. The coming of chain stores and superstores in the twentieth century has rapidly pecked away at the little shop with the family name above the door. We can but hope that the enterprise of families with roots in Asia and the Mediterranean continues to revitalise it, as has happened in communities such as the Kingsland Road in north-east London and 'the Curry Mile' along the Wilmslow Road in Manchester.

See also DIALECTS, GRAVESTONES, ISLANDS, JACK AND JILL.

FARMS & FARMSTEADS

There are lanes in Cornwall that take you on such intimate journeys through farmyards that you feel like an intruder. Scattered settlement characterises the South West and is discernible in Essex, the Weald of Kent and the Lake District. In the Somerset Levels and the Fens farms often clustered on islands of dry ground; in the North, around a defendable village green. Elsewhere people gathered cheek-by-jowl in villages, as in the Midlands, with gables to the street, surrounded by open fields, until enclosure came. Some old farmsteads may have occupied the same ground since Norman times and perhaps long before. The more we learn, the more longevity we read in the landscape. As people sought shelter, warmth and water, the buildings often seem to have grown out of the land, inclining, as H.J. Massingham would say, to the will of the geology.

Pastoral farming in the higher lands was always a lonelier task; farms in the Pennines and the Lakes are still isolated, although the collection of buildings may give them the air of a tiny hamlet. Elsewhere isolation usually tells of assarting – the clearing of woodland or moor – survival of pestilence, or enclosure.

Much rebuilding dates from 1570 to 1640, a little later in the North, as economic prosperity and European fashion drove changes from the wealthier South East. While these traditional buildings may have been superseded, many still populate their land with confidence: the granite long houses stepping down Dartmoor slopes (with house at the top end, a cross passage and animals on the down side); the Peak Forest laithe houses, with barn and byre all under the same roof; the fortified farmhouses of Cornwall; and bastles, with living quarters above animals, built for defence along the Scottish border.

It is unusual in the East and South East to find the house attached to the farm buildings. The Yorkshire Dales are populated with field barns, called laithes, far from the village farmhouses. Where the buildings are separate there are still examples in Lancashire of barns combining cow house and threshing space, and bank barns making use of slopes. The working buildings tend to remain unadorned and might be gathered around a courtyard, be built in parallel, make a U or L shape, or have been organically collected over time.

Laithe house, near Todmorden, Yorkshire.

Perhaps a third of farms disappeared in the late eighteenth century. Old buildings became workers' cottages or smallholdings, and in the areas of enclosure from the Midlands to Dorset between 1750 and 1850 dispersed farms were built in the middle of new holdings. Model farms were established by the bigger landlords during the eighteenth and nineteenth centuries to demonstrate evolving good practice. Quadrangles, paved yards and octagonal dairies brought a new formality, and in the early twentieth century model farms developed hygiene practices and mechanisation. Farms that were hitherto mixed began to separate out, with dairying, beef and sheep concentrated in the wetter West and the hills, and the East and South growing more grain.

English Heritage says that '*Traditional farm buildings are by far the most numerous type of historic structure in the countryside.*' Many have been adapted to new uses or saved by corrugated iron. To the distinctive combinations of farmhouse, barns, work sheds, animal houses and hemmel or linhay (open-fronted cattle shelters), the last century has added the Dutch barn, silo, silage pit and drying kiln, all homogenising in their large scale, materials and ubiquitous colours. Old buildings ill-fitted to modern use have been replaced or converted into workshops or homes. Many farmers have found sale with planning permission a way of supporting farm income, and the coherence of the farmyard has been lost.

Where it persists, the integrity of the farmstead remains one of the touchstones of local distinctiveness. The white-washed farmhouse of Lakeland is rare to see in bare-stone north Yorkshire; the black-and-white, timber-rich buildings of Shropshire, bricks of Nottinghamshire, weather-board in Kent and white- or pink-painted cob in Devon reflect and create the vernacular, together with the disposition of the buildings. As English Heritage says, '*the historic farm buildings of the countryside present a particularly acute dilemma . . . large-scale dereliction of buildings or, equally, the wholesale, poorly informed or ill-conceived conversion of surplus buildings could irrevocably damage important and*

irreplaceable historic assets . . . impair valued landscapes and damage their appeal for locals and visitors.'

Yet they need a function to survive, and so do farmers. The number of holdings is fast diminishing and with them much knowledge. Farms should not be factories, they are the unique and varied expression of long relationships with the land. Farming by GPS has nothing to do with wisdom, and much of value to the locality is lost as global practice and economics override familiarity.

Farming for local consumption can, on the other hand, reinforce direct contact with the surrounding community, decrease remoteness, spread knowledge, understanding and responsibility and bring environmental and welfare benefits, since transport is minimised. As European grant systems change from supporting production to encouraging conservation, there may be a chance for local distinctiveness to reassert itself.

See also AGRICULTURAL SHOWS, BANK BARNS, BARNS, BASTLES, BEE BOLES, BLACK & WHITE BUILDINGS, BUILDING STONES, CATTLE, CHEESE, CHESHIRE RAILINGS, CORN DOLLIES, CORRUGATED IRON, COTTAGES, CROPS, DOGS, DOVECOTES, DRYSTONE WALLS, FENCES, FIELD BARNS, FIELD NAMES, FIELD PATTERNS, FIELDS, FOOTPATHS, FROST & FROST HOLLOWS, GATES, GIN HOUSES, GRAZING MARSHES, HAY MEADOWS, HEDGES, HORSES & PONIES, MOATS, OAST-HOUSES & KELLS, ORCHARDS, PELE TOWERS, SHEEP, SHEEP-DOGS, TITHE BARNS.

157

FELL PONIES

From the west side of the Pennines this is the equivalent of the Dales pony, though smaller. They were drove animals with a long, fast stride, carrying sixteen-stone panniers of lead down to the coast. They stand around 13.2 hands and overall black is the favoured colour, although dark bay, grey or dun are also found. Like Dales ponies they have long manes and feathers around their heels.

Their history is bound up with Picts, reivers and smugglers, as well as Cistercian monks, who favoured greys. Because of their versatility and hardiness, they are now used as shepherds' ponies and for competitive riding, driving and trekking. They are great trotters, and helped to breed the Hackney pony in the nineteenth century.

They are classed as 'endangered' by the Rare Breeds Survival Trust. Fewer and fewer range over the Lakeland and Howgill fells, with too few male bloodlines and currently only around 250 breeding mares surviving on common land that is diminishing because of army and leisure activities. Ponies are taken off the hills in the autumn when the foals are separated, kept by owners until the mares are covered and then put back on the hill. There is a show and sale in October.

See also EXMOOR PONIES, GREEN LANES, HORSE FAIRS, HORSES & PONIES, NEW FOREST PONIES, POINT TO POINT, SHIRE HORSES, SUFFOLK PUNCHES.

Devonshire long house, near Widecombe in the Moor, Devon.

FELL RUNNING

Lakeland, the Yorkshire Dales and the Peak District are this sport's home grounds. The runners take on the fells in leaps and bounds in a punishing uphill struggle to the summit followed by a headlong descent. As well as having strength and stamina, the best runners read the ground, knowing scree and which grasses and mosses might give way to soft, wet ground causing a twisted ankle or worse. The history of fell racing lists some remarkable athletes, many of whom have been sheep farmers, used to the tough conditions and prepared for the hard graft of their sport. Perhaps the most famous, Joss Naylor, farmed sheep on the high fells of Wasdale, Cumberland.

Runners from athletic clubs in the North began to set up fell races in the mid-twentieth century, including 'challenges' involving a series of races and peaks, which have become so internationally popular that competitor numbers must be limited to avoid environmental damage. Races are now run far and wide, from Cornwall to Northumberland, where the Hill-forts and Headaches Race takes place at Rothbury.

The Bob Graham Round is a gruelling 72 miles, with 42 peaks around Keswick, Cumberland, including Scafell Pike, Helvellyn, Bowfell and Wasdale, to be run in 24 hours. It was first completed by Bob Graham in 1932 and not repeated for almost a quarter of a century. Lamb's Leg, Kinder Downfall and Mount Famine are among more than forty fell races just around Hayfield, Manchester during the year. Hundreds more are run across the Lake District. Borrowdale has a seventeen-mile race taking in Scafell Pike, Great Gable and Honister Pass – the nine miles around Fairfield Horseshoe takes the runners about an hour and a half over eight summits.

Fell running may have begun competitively between shepherds or mountain guides, with races becoming incorporated into fairs, agricultural shows and sports days. In the Lake District, Ambleside Sports falls on the Thursday before the first Monday in August; Ennerdale Show is on the last Wednesday in August; the Buttermere Shepherds Meet and Wasdale Show are in October. The famous Grasmere Sports includes the Senior Guide's Race, a short, fast contest (twelve minutes), the most important of them all. In Derbyshire, Hope village holds an annual fell race during its Wakes Week, which begins with well dressing on the nearest Saturday to St Peter's Day.

In the Yorkshire Dales Burnsall Feast Sports is a smaller affair. There have been games and sports on the Green here since at least Elizabethan times. According to Leonard Horton, the show's president in 2004, *'As a spectacle, the scene has no equal. The bridge parapet is thronged with spectators, the green a hive of activity.'* This, the oldest short-distance fell race, dates from 1870. Its origins are said to be in the Red Lion pub, where, for a bet, a local man called Tom Young, known as Weston, agreed to run the proposed course that night, naked.

Always the Saturday after the first Sunday after St Wilfred's Day (the patron saint of the village church), the day begins with the placing of a flag at the half-way point, on a cairn atop Burnsall Fell, a task fulfilled each year by members of the Fitton family. The day is opened by the Skipton Brass Band. While spectators enjoy the festivities, competitors from the local sporting community, joined by athletes from across the country and the world, contemplate the challenge ahead: an arduous race up to the summit and a breakneck run down the rocky slope from the cairn to the finish line, a descent achieved in a legendary two minutes, 42 seconds by the gamekeeper Ernest Dalzell in 1910.

See also BRASS BANDS, DALES, FAIRS & FAIRGROUNDS, FELLS, FLAGS, HOUND TRAILING, MOUNTAIN HARES, PUBS, SAINTS, VILLAGE GREENS, WELL DRESSING.

FELLS

The Vikings must have found it easy to settle in the Cumberland and Westmorland hills, coming from Norway around the tenth century. They gave the name 'fell' to the high hills of the Lake District. The name persists in other regions peopled by the Norse: Hare Appletree Fell and Tarnbrook Fell in Lancashire, for instance, and Mickle Fell, Durham's highest point. Though bleak, these hills are fruitful, too: Bleaberry Fell near Keswick takes its name from the beautiful bilberry, still collected in early August to make jams, jellies and wine and known locally as bleaberry, blueberry, whortleberry and wimberry.

The fells of the Lake District are the most mountainous of England's uplands. Scafell Pike, our highest mountain, is 3,206 feet above sea level. Such knobbly, bony, gnarled peaks are the legacy of a long period of ice and weathering

Borrowdale, Cumberland.

of hard volcanic rock, eruptions caused by the collision of two primeval tectonic plates five hundred million years ago. Rainfall is at its highest here, too: the central mountain area around Scafell enjoys an annual average of more than 150 inches.

These steep, craggy slopes shed cascades of loose scree that can deter even experienced rock climbers. The highest mountain tops are often barren fields of boulders coated with moss and lichen, sheltering diminutive dwarf willows and junipers alongside ancient club-mosses, whose ancestors are almost as old as the hills themselves. Much of the high ground is covered with a thin, acid soil; heavily grazed, it supports little more than closely cropped grassland. Yet on the fells above Haweswater and Derwentwater, where the mineral content of the soil is richer, a diverse flora flourishes, including alpine lady's mantle. Much of the mountain flora now survives only on steep ledges, cliffs, gills and gullies: purple saxifrage tenaciously thrives in the depths of Piers Gill on Scafell Pike. The damp, flower-rich ledges of Honister Crags, sporting wood cranesbill, globeflower, goldenrod, marsh hawksbeard and wild angelica, are celebrated as the hanging gardens of Lakeland.

Buzzards, peregrines, ravens and ring ouzel all breed in the high fells dotted with heather moor and bog. In recent years at least one pair of golden eagles has arrived from the Scottish Highlands, the only English representatives of their species. Mountain ringlet butterflies breed only on the Lakeland high ground as well.

On the north Pennine moors, as the geology changes from central Lakeland, a distinctly different flora thrives on lower-lying limestone fells. Cronkley Fell and Widdybank Fell are famed for their rich limestone flora and a natural juniper grove that stretches over three hundred acres. The plants are an unusual mix of arctic alpines, survivors of cooler times after the last ice age, and more southern species. Some are found nowhere else, including alpine foxtail grass, marsh saxifrage, alpine forget-me-not and spring gentian.

Hundreds of wading birds, including lapwing, oystercatcher, curlew, golden plover, snipe and redshank, breed on Widdybank Fell. Around Alston, where lead mining has released copper, zinc and chromium into the soil, unusual plants, such as spring sandwort and alpine pennycress, grow, able to cope with high levels of heavy metals that are toxic to us.

The stark and dangerous yet beautiful landscape of Lakeland has long been the haunt of fell walkers, foremost among them Alfred Wainwright. Born in Blackburn in 1907, he moved to his beloved Lakes in 1941. Between 1952 and 1966 he compiled seven guidebooks to the Lakeland Fells, illustrated with his own drawings. They have become classic guides to these mountains, almost outdoing the Wordsworths'.

Rock climbing on the Lakeland Fells reached its golden age in the late nineteenth century, when young men keen to improve their mountaineering skills for summer climbs in the Alps spent Christmas and Easter breaks scaling the fells, from their base at the Wastwater Hotel in Wasdale. One young climber, Fred Botterill, took the lead in 1903 on a steep slab on Scafell, which now bears his name.

See also CAIRNS, DROVE ROADS, FELL PONIES, FELL RUNNING, HILLS, HOLLOW WAYS, HOUND TRAILING, JUNIPER, LEAD MINES, MOORLAND, ROADS, WINDS.

F E N C E S

The humble fence can have a significant impact, defining enclosure, unifying patterns in the landscape and revealing a little of the workings of a place. White picket fences around a garden are rare in drystone wall country, yet chestnut paling can be seen set within the stone-fenced fields parallel with the A40 as it crosses the Cotswold tops – its task is to cause snow to drift before it reaches the road. Since 1905, one of the main uses for small cleft chestnut has been in this pale-and-wire fencing. Used liberally as a temporary barrier, it is still sent all over the country in large quantities from the South East, where the tree is common. Chestnut is durable out of doors, it cleaves readily and is used for fence posts as well as the hefty cleft-chestnut post-and-rail fencing unique to the Weald, the most wooded part of England. It is undergoing a small resurgence as people recognise its importance visually, ecologically and economically.

Before the invention of uniform barbed wire (devil's rope) at the turn of the twentieth century, fences had affinity with their place. Thinnings of oak and coppiced chestnut were put to use in their immediate locality. Cleft-oak post and rails, made without nails, once enclosed farm stock and woodlands in the New Forest, Midlands and Cheshire plain. It is stronger than round or sawn rails and lasts for about forty years. Gertrude Jekyll, writing in the early 1900s, stated her preference for '*stout old oak post and rail*', which she saw as '*the true fence of the country, and a thing of actual beauty in the free play of line of the rails and the slight inequality of the posts . . . A wooden fence of sawn timber must always be a stiff and soulless thing; but for these fences the posts are simply shaped with the adze and side-axe from the butts of tree trunks of a suitable size, or of larger trunks quartered, and the rails are also of oak, quartered by rending with the wedge, driven by the axe.*' She could not understand why iron railings were used in places where there was plenty of woodland, which was being wasted. The same argument still applies – woodland needs to be worked. Hazel hurdling is again being made for garden privacy and wind-breaks, as well as for temporary sheep pens, giving a new life to hazel coppice and the bluebells beneath.

159

There is nothing more mean and monotonous than municipal wire-mesh fences with concrete posts – at the very least a hedge offers cover and food for wildlife. So different but equally unattached to local materials, elegant black iron railings signal the possibility of herds of deer as they edge parks and country estates. They are still made by local blacksmiths, with flat bar verticals and round rails, the spaces between them diminishing towards the bottom. The use of railings at blind corners along roads has spread out from Cheshire since the early 1930s.

See also BLUEBELLS, CHESHIRE RAILINGS, DRYSTONE WALLS, GATES, HAZEL, HEDGES, OAK, PARKLAND, RAILINGS, STILES, SWEET CHESTNUT.

F E N S

Many plashy places or low-lying marshes are called fens. The Fens straddle Lincolnshire, Cambridgeshire, Norfolk and Suffolk, the 'Holy Land of the English', where the Angles settled in the Dark Ages. At home on water rather than in towns, they thrived here. This is a *'country of space, a place where two-thirds of your field of vision is sky'*, Rex Sly says. Woods might line odd roads and estates, but, other than the orchards around Wisbech, this is a flat, sky-heavy, tree-starved land, its long roads disciplined by stern, steep ditches marching straight then turning through ninety degrees, as well as roddons – ghosts of old rivers evident in meanders of raised silt. Ely is one of few island places where dry footings made for town growth.

There are two shades of fen: the rich silt of the tulip and daffodil fields of the north, around Spalding, and the Black Fens of the south, between March, Breckland, Cambridge and Peterborough, with their light-swallowing peaty earth and mineral-rich skirt land. Its sometimes brutal difference has been eulogised in music (by Ralph Vaughan Williams) and words (John Masefield's verse, Graham Swift's prose and Caryl Churchill's drama). Here be monsters, such as Beowulf's grim Grendel, the hell-hound Black Shuck, the marsh gas Will o' the Wisp and Jack o' Lantern.

Even the people were once cast as monstrous, self-contained and suspicious, called Breedlings and Fen Tigers. They spoke their own words for important things. Bankers made banks rather than money. Streams and drains became leams, becks, lodes, eaus. Witches added to an atmosphere that attracted both saints, such as Guthlac of Crowland, and criminals.

Drainage projects were promoted from the Middle Ages to tame a wild region and make it productive. Four million acres needed draining. Pioneers are recalled by their channels: Morton's Leam, Sam's Cut, Moore's Drain, Bevill's Leam, Popham's Eau. Inevitably the schemes lined pockets elsewhere, and local protest grew. For Oliver Cromwell of Ely it was an early step towards civil war.

Today cereals, celery and sugar beet are produced despite fen blows (blizzards of eroded topsoil) and peat shrinkage, which leaves buildings' foundations high and dry above ground. Potatoes, onions (pickling onions in Southery) and carrots (around Chatteris) are widespread. Bulbs became

160

Celery harvesting, Little Downham, Cambridgeshire.

popular in the nineteenth century and are celebrated in May by South Holland churches' flower festivals and Spalding's Flower Parade. Wicken Fen has been a nature reserve since 1899, famous for its swallowtail butterflies, milk parsley and fen violet. The ambitious and exciting Great Fen Project and others are re-creating 25,000 acres of wetland, which includes the joining and enlarging of Wood Walton Fen and Holme Fen nature reserves between Huntingdon and Peterborough.

See also AEGIRS, BLACK DOGS, BOATS, BORES, BUILDING STONES, CATHEDRALS, COASTLINE, CROPS, DAFFODILS, EELS, EYOTS, FEN SKATING, FIELDS, FLINT, FLOODS, GREEN LANES, ISLANDS, LEVELS, MOSSLAND, NICKNAMES, POTATOES, SALT MARSHES, TIDES.

FEN SKATING

This sport depends on substantial periods of freezing weather to make it possible. Its ephemeral nature is what some find attractive, but it must be frustrating to have to wait years for a long cold snap. The last speed-skating championships were held in the winter of 1996/7.

People have skated along the miles of waterways in the Fens for centuries, first using sharpened animal bones, called pattens, attached to the bottom of their shoes. Skates with metal blades are thought to have been brought over by the Dutch labourers who worked on Vermuyden's drainage schemes in the seventeenth century; adapted by the Fenmen to have curved blades at the front, they were known as fen runners. It was much quicker to travel on the ice than on land, using the rivers and drains as thoroughfares, and people thought nothing of skating thirty or so miles in a day.

The first recorded speed-skating event took place on the Fens in 1763 over a fifteen-mile course. Two barrels were placed at each end of a long run and there was much skill in rounding them at great speed. Farm labourers laid off during bitter weather became skilled at speed skating, and readily took part in races with generous prizes of food, known as 'bread and meat' races. In 1821 John Gittan sped over a two-mile course in two minutes, 53 seconds. These

speed merchants gained notoriety and were given affectionate nicknames, such as William 'Turkey' Smart and George 'Fish' Smart. They took part in races abroad and often came home the winners.

The National Skating Association was set up in 1879. It allows skating championships to take place only '*when entire fens at Welney, Bury and Whittlesey in Cambs freeze safely enough to carry racers*'. Then, a sudden transformation of the landscape takes place, as inveterate skater Roger Deakin describes: '*The great fenland sport is as evanescent as the ice itself. As soon as there's ice thick enough, the normally deserted Ouse washes from Welney to Earith can still wake up to a sudden throng of skaters and spectators, and word goes round somehow that the Fenland Championships are on: held whenever, and wherever, the weather permits.*'

Robin Page, another fen-skating enthusiast, describes this special experience: '*with the ice-edged wind on your cheeks, the sound of metal on frozen water, and the call of fenland's winter birds – lapwing, golden plover, widgeon and wild whooper swans – it gives communion with nature that no other activity can give in urban, overcrowded Britain*'.

See also BROADS, EAST, FENS, FROST & FROST HOLLOWS, ICE SKATING IN THE OPEN AIR, LAKES, TARNS, WEATHER, WINDS.

FERAL ANIMALS

While it is a pleasure to see more animals in this country, which is relatively impoverished compared with the mainland of Europe, many unplanned introductions have had unforeseen and detrimental consequences. Grey squirrels, which were deliberately introduced in the 1870s, have ousted the red in many places.

Rabbits were brought over by the Normans in the twelfth century and kept in warrens; pigeons, descended from native rock doves that were domesticated and bred in dovecotes, have reverted to the wild. In the past fifty years most exotic animals that have survived or flourished in our countryside have been deliberately released or have escaped from fur farms, zoos or private collections.

On the south-east edge of the Peak District reported sightings of marsupials would be greeted with jovial taunts. But for four or five decades following their release from Swythamley Hall during the Second World War, secretive red-necked wallabies survived in the woods around the Roaches, near Leek in Staffordshire. Five animals multiplied to perhaps fifty by 1962. Since then their numbers have dwindled and there have been no sightings for some time. There have been releases of wallabies in Ashdown Forest, Sussex and near Teignmouth in Devon, but they have not flourished.

The American mink has been the most successful interloper, having escaped from fur farms since the 1920s and

more recently released by animal rights activists. It did not start breeding in the wild until the 1950s but now inhabits most of our rivers and streams. At one time it was thought to be a threat to otters.

Another American escapee is the signal crayfish. Larger than our native white-clawed crayfish, which was common in chalk streams and other rivers, it has been bred here since the 1980s and inevitably has escaped into streams and rivers. Unfortunately it carries a fungus (to which it is immune) that kills our now-rare native crayfish – attempts are being made to eradicate it from the wild.

A number of exotic deer species have become established in our countryside. Fallow deer were first re-introduced by the Normans and by the mid-seventeenth century they were roaming in perhaps seven hundred deer parks. These attractive animals, with their large, flattened antlers and white spots on pale brown coats, had been present here until the last ice age. They have made their way back into the wild near old or current deer parks and are quite common in the South.

Sika deer were first imported from Japan by Viscount Powerscourt for his deer park near Dublin in 1857, but they bred so well he gave some to his friends with deer parks, such as Melbury Park in Dorset. Some escaped, even those put on Brownsea Island – they swam to the mainland. Sika are found along the south coast from east Devon to the New Forest. They can be seen on the south-east side of the London-to-Bournemouth railway line – fallow deer live across the tracks. Other small populations can be found in Cumbria, Lancashire and Northamptonshire.

The Chinese or Reeves' muntjac was brought to Woburn Park, Bedfordshire in 1894 and escaped, spreading slowly into the surrounding counties of Berkshire, Buckinghamshire and Hertfordshire and beyond into East Anglia, Oxfordshire and Warwickshire. The size of a wire-haired terrier, with

small tusks growing from the buck's upper jaws, it inhabits woodland and hedgerows. Woburn Park was also responsible for Chinese water deer, which escaped from there and other parks during the Second World War. The densest populations are around the Norfolk Broads and the Fens, which offer cover and extensive reed beds. They are slightly bigger than the muntjacs, and the bucks have distinctive and rather frightening retractable canine tusks, although they do little damage to trees or crops.

Hunted to extinction here in the sixteenth century, wild boars began to be farmed for their meat in the 1980s. Some having made their way into the wild, there are thought to be several hundred feral animals in the wooded parts of Kent, Sussex, Dorset and Herefordshire. They are secretive, nocturnal animals and hard to spot, but can be aggressive when protecting their young.

People living in and around the Isle of Thanet in Kent, around south London, along the Thames valley and those driving on the M25 south of Heathrow take the long-tailed, yellow-green, ring-necked parakeets for granted. These escapees have been around for thirty years, surviving cold winters (they hail from the Himalayan foothills) with the help of food put out in gardens. Chris Butler, who runs Oxford University's Project Parakeet, counted 2,764 birds in trees at the Esher rugby club in the winter of 2001. Other big winter roosts are at Lewisham cemetery, Reigate railway station and Reigate Heath, where people love to watch them gathering at dusk. By 2002 Butler estimated that the population had increased to 5,700.

There are many alleged sightings of big cats that have escaped or been released from captivity, but little hard evidence. The Isle of Wight Puma, Beast of Bodmin Moor, Wrangaton Lion, Mendips Monster, Hade Edge Panther, Fen Tiger and Lindsey Leopard have all made headlines. A few small cats and lynx have been shot or run over, but the remainder, if they are out there, are adept at avoiding us. The British Big Cats Society is undertaking research.

Another type of feral cat is the uncared-for domestic moggie. It tends to form small colonies in towns, especially in ports. In Portsmouth's naval dockyard a colony of about two hundred animals was studied by Jane Dards during three years from 1975. She found that numbers remained stable, which indicated that there could be some form of social self-regulation of numbers. In rural areas many farmyard cats kept to get rid of rats are semi-feral. The black-and-white cats of Fitzroy Square in London were fed for years by local people. One story is that they were Phoenician stowaways, which may have jumped ship thousands of years ago.

Two breeds of goat and sheep, recognised for their ability to graze difficult terrain, are being used by conservation groups. The herd of rare British native feral goats that loom out of the mist in the Valley of Rocks near Lynmouth in north Devon seem attuned to their place and are breeding

Valley of Rocks, near Lynmouth, Devon.

well. Goats were recorded here at the time of the Domesday Book, but they are likely to have grazed this valley since neolithic times. The present stock came from the College Valley herd in Northumberland in 1976, the original herd having been removed and replaced with domestic white goats that did not survive the harsh winters. Some have been taken from here to Lundy Island off the Devon coast and Bonchurch Down on the Isle of Wight. Yeavering Bell in Northumberland takes its name from *Ad Gefrin*, meaning 'of the wild goats'; they still eke out an existence here.

There are a hundred or so feral Soay sheep in England, on Lundy Island off the north Devon coast (introduced in 1927) and on Holy Island in Northumberland. Soay may be descendants of the first domesticated sheep brought to Britain in 5000 BC. With curled horns and brown/tan fleece, they are our oldest and most primitive breed of sheep, able to survive on the sparsest vegetation.

See also CATTLE, CHALK STREAMS, DOVECOTES, EDIBLE DORMOUSE, OTTERS, PARKLAND, PIGEON LOFTS, RIVERS, SHEEP.

F E R N S

The slow unfurling of a fern's frond, like a butterfly's proboscis, is one of the wonders of spring. Collected and cultivated by the Victorians, and favoured for their elegant symmetry by today's gardeners, ferns are among the most enduring of ancient life forms. They first evolved in moist Carboniferous forests more than three hundred million years ago, long before flowering plants appeared on the scene. Fossil ferns discovered in coal seams bear an uncanny resemblance to species alive today.

Moist, shady places are ferns' stronghold. Woods are one of their chief refuges, and the richest are the wettest in the North and West. Moist air supports filmy ferns surviving in rock crevices on the Devonshire tors, while on old harbour walls in the South West, Chris Page noted that the sea spleenwort makes the most of '*wavebreak spray*'.

The most abundant and unmistakable of the forty or so species is bracken, also known as ferny brake or common fern. It blankets acres of open woodland, commons and neglected pasture, with a preference for acid soils. Smallholders still cut bracken for dry bedding for livestock.

Root crops, such as swedes and turnips, benefited from a bracken mulch. Large fronds formed a durable thatch; it provided fuel for heating ovens and a packing material for fragile goods or fruit. Burnt, it provided a source of potash for making soap and glass. Recently peat-free garden compost with '*a natural high potash bracken-based soil conditioner*' has been developed by Dalefoot Farm in Cumberland.

Many ferns thrive only in relatively undisturbed places, such as ravines and gullies. Walls also harbour ferns; wall

rue prefers old walls built with traditional lime mortar. The polypody prefers the tops of walls, and many Lakeland stone walls are crowned with its distinctive dense growths. It also grows on the mossy bark of woodland oaks, especially in the North and West, and in rock clefts, old wells, mines and caverns.

Another common fern is the hart's tongue, with its distinctive long, wavy fronds. It luxuriates in damp woods, sunken lanes, hedges, stream banks, ditches, cliffs, limestone pavements, rocky fissures and even in caves beside tungsten light bulbs. Archaeologists use it to tell tales in areas that are low in lime – a flourishing of hart's tongue signifies lime mortar and often an absent mill.

Some of the most magnificent ferns, with long, arching fronds, are creatures of damp acid wood: the common male fern, the graceful, fragile-looking lady fern and the broad buckler fern. The stately royal fern, one of our largest, can reach nine feet in height and is the longest-lived and most sought-after of ferns. It prefers acidic conditions, such as wet woodland bogs, wet heaths and fens in East Anglia and Cornwall.

See also ALLEYS, CAVES, CLINTS & GRIKES, DRYSTONE WALLS, GARDENS, GORGES, HOLLOW WAYS, THATCH, TORS, WALLS, WOODS.

F E R R I E S   163

The ferryman at Symonds Yat, Herefordshire pulls the punt across the Wye by rope. Tiring but effective in quiet waters, this is one step up from the simple rowing boat that crosses the river Blyth from Walberswick to Southwold in Suffolk. One of the several ferries that crossed the Severn

in Shropshire survives at Hampton Loade, its name recalling the Old English for ford or river crossing. It is a two-minute, fifty-pence journey, joining the east and west banks and the cottages beside them. The small wooden passenger ferry is moved or restrained by pulley along a chain, the ferryman or -woman using the rudder to make it move sideways across the river. It was threatened with closure, but a grant has not only ensured its survival, but created a new boat, maintaining an important link for residents, cyclists and walkers.

Rivers unite and divide; many used to be highways. The river Derwent, which marks the boundary between east and west Yorkshire, was once criss-crossed by small ferries, many run by farms and cottages on a request basis. Clues abound, such as tracks or footpaths leading to the water's edge, and pubs at the end of lanes with rivers as their only neighbours.

Car ferries add an extra dimension to a journey and give one a chance to savour the place. In Norfolk a small, brightly coloured car ferry crosses the river Yare at Reedham, linking both sides of the B1140. Pull's ferry operates on the river Wensum in Norwich; James Pull spent 46 years as ferryman here in the nineteenth century. The village of Bawdsey Manor on the river Deben in Norfolk is linked to Felixstowe by ferry across the estuary in summer. In Cornwall the road drops steeply down beside Daphne du Maurier's old house to the ferry, which travels every day of the week across the ria from the village of Bodinnick to Fowey, allowing cars to avoid a twelve-mile detour via the nearest bridge at Lostwithiel. Fowey is also linked to

the 'other side' by a small motorised passenger ferry, which goes to the village of Polruan.

Only some large river crossings have been replaced by road links, such as the great Severn and Humber bridges. The latter is a couple of miles downstream from where the Romans embarked and disembarked, at Winteringham on the south side and Brough (Petuaria) on the north side of the estuary.

Some stretches of water retain their boat crossings in places where high-clearance bridges would be needed to allow large ships to enter the docks. At Poole harbour in Dorset the ferry runs along underwater cables across the demandingly tidal Swash Channel between the two sandy peninsulas of Sandbanks and Shell Bay. Any perched herring gull is always called Charlie, and the resident ghost of a former skipper is said to switch lights on and off, although the *Bramble Bush Bay* is the fourth ferry to date.

In slowing us down ferries remind us what formidable barriers rivers and tidal waters can be, and they help to accentuate the differences between one side and the other. 'Ferry 'cross the Mersey' is still a familiar sight. Two passenger services link Liverpool and the Wirral peninsula, although cars use two tunnels – the Kingsway and the Queensway; the latter's completion in 1934 was celebrated with a walk-through of eighty thousand people. A ferry has crossed the Tyne between North and South Shields since at least 1377, and the two present ferries continue every half-hour – the *Pride of the Tyne* was built at the Swan Hunter yard in its last years. Yellow passenger ferries bustle around in Bristol, including the *Independence*, a shallow-draughted launch that once took passengers ashore from ships in the Severn.

The longest ferry journey in England is from Penzance in Cornwall to the Isles of Scilly. It takes two hours and forty minutes, making it further than some of the services from the Kent ports to mainland Europe. Walkers on the South West Coast Path join locals at St Mawes in Cornwall, where a small ferry crosses to St Anthony Head in Falmouth Bay, and at the South Hams in Devon, where foot passengers can cross the river Yealm between Noss Mayo, Newton Ferrers and Warren Point. Another boat crosses the Avon from Bantham slipway to Cockleridge Ham.

These small excitements are much preferable to the extended car-park experiences of the cross-Channel services. But the many ferries that still work provide more than pleasure: without them the plashy places and islands would have fewer visitors and little cargo, and many river communities would be parted by water.

See also BEACONS (COASTAL), BOATS, BRIDGES, THE CHANNEL, COASTS, ESTUARIES, FENS, HARBOURS, INNS, ISLANDS, PIERS, PUBS, RIAS, RIVERS, SALT MARSHES, SEA TRACTOR, TIDES.

164

Fowey to Bodinnick ferry, river Fowey, Cornwall.

FIELD BARNS

In lowland England it is unusual to see isolated stone barns, but throughout the northern Pennines these scattered buildings, roofed in slabs of gritstone or Lake District slate, were built in the hundred years from the 1750s as the uplands were enclosed. In the valleys of the Lake District they are found in hay meadows, edged by neat drystone walls, and they enable the farmers to store the hay near to where it was cut.

Part of the glory of the Yorkshire Dales landscape lies in the intricacy of drystone-walled fields studded with stone field barns, known here as laithes. Around sixty of these byre/barns cluster within a half a mile's radius of Muker in Swaledale. Sometimes the laithes are built into the slopes. Hay is stored above, taking perhaps three-quarters of the space, and cattle overwintered below, with manure spread back on the adjoining fields – a simple, integrated system.

The barns in Wensleydale have courses of projecting stones in the walls, testifying to their method of construction – rubble-filled inner and outer walls held together by big through stones. Typically the roof will be of stone flags, which reduce in size nearer to the crest. As farming demands change, these robust buildings have been seeking new uses: Ellergill barn in Littondale has gained awards for its sensitive conversion to a bunkhouse barn that welcomes walkers overnight. But with perhaps six thousand such barns in the Dales, most of which are off the beaten track, creative thinking is needed to give them continuity.

The pale limestone field barns around Castleton in Derbyshire show a great array of lichens on their slab roofs. The villagers of Bonsall suggest that '*historically, as most farming was not a full-time occupation, farmers often lived within the village and walked to their fields each day, rather than constructing farmhouses on the Moor. The large number of stone barns in the fields around Bonsall were used to store agricultural tools and supplies and are a distinctive feature of the area.*' In other parts of Derbyshire and Staffordshire they can be found at lower altitudes. In Devon Peter Child

notes that, although the reason is not clear, '*in the South Hams there is a fairly regular occurrence of substantial corn barns standing alone in the fields*'.

See also BANK BARNS, BARNS, BRICKS, CHEESE, CIDER & CIDER ORCHARDS, COB, COES, DALES, FARMS & FARMSTEADS, FIELDS, GIN HOUSES, SLATES, THATCH, TITHE BARNS.

FIELD MAPLE

Acer campestre is sometimes called field maple, but originally was just maple, from the Old English *mapulder*. Long admired by craftsmen for its hard, fine-grained wood, ideal for turning, it is one of about a dozen trees that have shaped our native woodlands during the past twelve thousand years. It often teams up with ash and hazel to create woodlands that harbour more wildflowers than any other kind. More than one hundred species of lichen have been recorded on its nutrient-rich, furrowed bark, and its leaves feed several species of rare moths, including the maple pug, the maple mocha and the plumed prominent.

This sturdy, beautiful tree is most common in woods and hedges on clayey or calcareous soils in the South, East and Midlands, where it is often a sign of ancient lineage. During the past two hundred years at least, the tree has seldom been planted.

The maple has given its name to many towns and villages, including Mapplewell in Yorkshire, Maperton in Somerset, Mappowder in Dorset, Mappledore in Wiltshire, Mapledurham in Oxfordshire and Maplestead in Essex. Intriguingly these Anglo-Saxon place-names correspond well with the maple's present distribution. The tree is mentioned as a boundary landmark in Anglo-Saxon charters. Carvings of its leaves dominate the forest of foliage in the Chapter House at Southwell Minster in Nottinghamshire.

Sometimes coppiced, or small, given a chance it will grow into a substantial tree, with small, delicate, pinkish leaves in spring that turn yellow in autumn, standing out in the hedgerows after the nights turn cold. The tallest living specimen is probably the 78-foot maple in Mote Park, Maidstone, Kent, while the oldest tree may be a hollow, pollarded maple on the boundary of the churchyard at Downham in Essex, with a girth of fourteen feet.

Anglo-Saxon and medieval craftsmen favoured the wood for musical instruments – harps made with maple wood were unearthed in a Saxon burial excavated at Taplow in Buckinghamshire and at the Sutton Hoo ship burial in Suffolk. High-quality drinking or wassailing bowls called mazers, which were filled with hot ale and passed around, were also made of the wood. Corpus Christi College in Cambridge treasures its swan mazer, described in a fourteenth-century inventory, which is made of fine silver and maple with an exquisite feathery grain.

165

Local names include maplin tree in Gloucestershire, whitty bush in Shropshire, cat oak in Yorkshire, oak or dog oak in Somerset and Nottinghamshire, and oak apple in Devon – the leaves of maples were often used in place of oak in Oak Apple Day celebrations. Near its climatic limit in England, it fails to fruit some years; many trees become male in resting years. When it does fruit, it forms distinctive seeds, or keys, known as boots-and-shoes in Somerset, hasketts in Dorset, kitty-keys in Yorkshire and shacklers in Devon. The seeds wait until the second spring to germinate, unless they are found first by elusive hawfinches, which can crack open the hard keys with their strong beaks.

See also ALDER, ANCIENT TREES, ARBOR DAY, ASH, BEECH, BIRCH, BLACK POPLAR, BLACKTHORN, CATHEDRALS, ELM, HAWTHORN, HAZEL, HEDGES, HOLLY, HOLM OAK, HORNBEAM, HORSE CHESTNUT, JUNIPER, LANDMARK TREES, LICHENS, LIME, LONDON PLANE, MONKEY-PUZZLE, OAK, ORCHARDS, PEARS, PLACE-NAMES, POPLAR, ROWAN, ROYAL FORESTS, SCOTS PINE, SWEET CHESTNUT, SYCAMORE, WALNUT, WASSAILING, WHITEBEAM, WILLOW, WOODS, YEW.

FIELD NAMES

acre allotment assart balk/baulk bank/bong/bonk bench bottom brae breach breck broad brunt land butt carr cauel close croft/croat/croud/crowd daymath/demath dole dote/doat eddish enclosure fields eng erg ersh etch fit flat fold furlong furrow garſton garth grounds goar/gore hale/ball half ham hatch haugh haw hay/hey heads/headland hectare herne/hirn hide/hyde hields hold holme hop hoppet hyrne infield ings inhams inhook inland inning innge intack iron jack laigh land lag ſtream land langate lawn lea/lee lease/leaze/leys leasow ley leyn linch field loon/loond/loont lot mead meadow nook open field outfield oxgang paddock park paſture patch peak pen pightle/pingle/pingot pike plank plack/pleck/plock plash plat/plot pre prey quarter ray/roe rood royd runrig sarch/sarts screed seloin severals shoot shot shovel broad sick/sitch/sutch slade slaight sleight sling slip slough spot ſtart/ſtert/ſtort ſtitch ſtong ſtrip swathe thwaite tye tining water meadow wong

John Field, from *Field Names: A Dictionary*

Every field has a name; many are precise in their descriptions if we can translate them from, say, Old English or Old Norse. Names may be descriptive of prominent features – soil, animals, vegetation – or tell of landholders or events. Some are traceable over hundreds of years; some have changed repeatedly as the fields have altered in size, use or ownership.

Farmers know their field names and they can be found in title deeds, on the tithe maps of the 1840s held in county record offices or on individual farm maps. The old sources are particularly rich, since no reductive or mishearing surveyor has simplified things, as happened with place-names on Ordnance Survey maps. Land agents and some farm managers are sacrificing names for numbers – Field 1, Field 2, Field 3 – demanded by agricultural census returns. This not only denies the memories of hard work and long local knowledge, but breaks the chain of clues about the potential of the land.

There is not much historically revealing or descriptive about fields as numbers, commodities or production units, whereas the following are rich in hints, suggesting what grew in or inhabited the land: Batterdocks (buttercups), Blue Button Field (devil's-bit scabious), Havadrill Bank (a slope on which daffodils grew), Vierny Field (fern-covered), Toad Pipe Meadow (horsetail), Asker Meadow (lizards) and Custard Stiles (steep land frequented by cushats, wood pigeons). They also offer ideas for the future. Can corncockles be persuaded to grow again in Cockle Close, frogs to return to Frog Hall or hedgehogs to Urchins Dumble?

Field names might also give clues to geology and soil conditions: Checkers (light and dark patches of soil), Catsbrain (brain-shaped fossils on outcrops of oolitic limestone), Chisley Field (land from which gravel was obtained). Often whimsical names are given to land a long way from the farm (World's End or Zululand) and to poor land (Hard Bargain or Starvation Hill). Indications of past activities linger in seemingly straightforward names: Blackland in Oxfordshire, Black Field in Wiltshire, Black Miles in Leicestershire and Black Helm in Rutland have discoloured soils that have yielded finds, some dating back to the Roman occupation. Archaeologists use place- and field names to discover the past.

Moot fields are places where local assemblies settled lawsuits in Anglo-Saxon times and, later, where parish meetings were held. They often contained conspicuous landmarks, such as barrows – as at Mobberley and Mutlow in Cheshire – or stones – Staine in Cambridgeshire and Mottistone on the Isle of Wight. Mot Close in Thurlaston, Leicestershire and Mott Lands in Kingsley, Hampshire still survive.

Until recently fields have been a common focus for seasonal festivities, especially at harvest time: Banquetting Field in Henley, Fair Ground in Northmoor and Summer Leazows in Rollright, all in Oxfordshire; Dancing Plain in Alresford, Hampshire; May Day Meer in Over Haddon, Derbyshire; Maypole Meadow in Newnham and Midsummer Leys in Willersey, Gloucestershire; St John's Field in Walkern, Hertfordshire. Continuing use for annual celebrations may save the land from development.

Parish Maps produced during the past twenty years have set people researching their local field names and charting them. Some landholders are etching field names onto their farm gates for passers-by to muse upon.

166

We have many words to denote enclosures: acre, allotment, assart, balk, breach, butt, carr, close, croft, dole, garth, ham, hide, leys, paddock, pightle, slade, strip and wong are just a few. Many adhere to a particular area. Tye, which used to mean 'an outlying common', is found only in the South. Tyning or tining suggests a fenced enclosure and is found in midland and western counties.

See also DRYSTONE WALLS, EASTER CUSTOMS, FAIRS & FAIRGROUNDS, FAMILY NAMES, FIELD PATTERNS, FIELDS, GATES, GROVELY RIGHTS DAY, HEDGES, HOUSE NAMES, MAY DAY, MIDSUMMER DAY, PARISH MAPS, PLACE-NAMES, RIVER NAMES.

FIELD PATTERNS

In north Cornwall, where the parishes of St Ives and St Just meet the sea, as many as two hundred fields to the square kilometre betray a rugged landscape long worked. In East Anglia it is possible to find lands unfenced to the far horizon.

Dark shadows striate a hillside, simple terraces reminiscent of a Mediterranean vineyard but grazed by cattle or sheep. Strip lynchets, like dry, grassy cascades, dominate groups of hillside fields from Wharfedale in Yorkshire to the cliffs at Worth Matravers in Dorset. The treads and risers of these flamboyant staircases originate from medieval times, but in some places lynchets mark prehistoric farming.

Side by side, or one on top of the other, field patterns date from different periods yet jostle on the stage we inhabit today. Fields are living history, cultural landscapes to be read. Farmers first worked some of them four thousand years ago and, although many are disappearing under development and deep ploughing, the patterns await deciphering.

So they drained it long and crossways in
the lavish Roman style –
Still we find among the river-drift their
flakes of ancient tile,
And in drouthy middle August, when the
bones of meadows show,
We can trace the lines they followed
sixteen hundred years ago.

Rudyard Kipling, from 'The Land'

Relict Roman fields are rare, but on the silt lands of the Fens around March in Cambridgeshire and on Martin Down in Hampshire the bones are visible.

A wide stripe from Dorset to Durham, Sussex to Norfolk, known by agricultural historians as the Central Province, was dominated by huge open fields created in medieval times, each tended strip by strip. In Braunton in Devon, Haxey in Lincolnshire, Soham in Cambridgeshire and at the tip of the

Isle of Portland in Dorset, vestiges of the great open fields can be seen. At Laxton in north Nottinghamshire there is a fascinating survival of the system, although the undulations of ridge-and-furrow strips have long been ploughed flat.

This swathe of country is now the landscape of enclosure, which brought dramatic change to the look, feel and working of the land. Common fields were taken in by landholders during a century of Acts of Parliament gathering pace from 1750. These shadowed agricultural reform, imprisoning more and more land behind fences and hedges, to be farmed scientifically using new equipment and grazed by selectively bred cattle and sheep. The Enclosures brought *'large nucleated settlements and distinctive field systems, in sharp contrast to other parts of England where much older enclosed field systems and dispersed patterns of farmstead and hamlet form the historical character of the landscape'*, David Hall writes. Typically geometry dominates, with regular squarish fields, wide-verged straight and dog-leg roads and angular hedges – formal, but not as elegant as the Georgian houses that were appearing at the same time. The manifold losses were mourned by John Clare in his native Northamptonshire:

Inclosure came and trampled on the grave
Of labour's rights and left the poor a slave . . .
Fence now meets fence in owners' little bounds
Of field and meadow large as garden grounds
In little parcels little minds to please
With men and flocks imprisoned ill at ease

John Clare, from 'The Mores'

Illegal enclosure and squatting also saw the erosion of much common land. In Dorset heathland was being bounded by banks and, just to the north in the Blackmore Vale, twenty Acts of Parliament legitimised the enclosure

167

and removal of woodland. In Lancashire, Chat Moss was drained and made into fields, as was much of the Somerset Levels and the Fens.

The word 'field' implies containment, and their shapes have given the landscape enthusiast much to explore. Christopher Taylor summarised: '*In Devon we find small irregularly shaped fields bounded by large banks, which are often surmounted by huge thick hedges. In Sussex the rolling downlands are a sea of arable land, divided occasionally by wire-mesh fences. Over much of the east Midlands the most common types of fields are those of rigidly geometric form defined by hedges, largely of hawthorn, with occasional trees. Over the fenlands of eastern England there is an infinite variety of field shapes and sizes, each bounded by narrow and usually straight drainage ditches. Farther north in Westmorland and Cumberland the small stone-walled paddocks, or strip-shaped fields on the sides of the dales, give way to vast areas delineated by apparently endless walls.*'

Reading the fields demands an eye for superimposition, a nose for tracing layer upon layer of activity, and not only in the countryside. Christchurch Meadow still hangs on in the middle of Oxford, but every city and town carries some memory of *The Fields Beneath*, Gillian Tindall's evocative title for an exploration of the history of Kentish Town in north London. She shows the old field boundaries predisposing housing expansion to follow street by street.

Since the Second World War and our entry into the European Union, fields have grown to accommodate big machines and escalating economic expectations. Stone walls and hedges have been removed, sadly not liberating the land as Clare might have wished, but rendering it less readable, less rich in nature and less welcoming.

See also BATTLEFIELDS, BOUNDARIES, CATTLE, CROPS, DESERTED VILLAGES, DRYSTONE WALLS, FENCES, FENS, FIELD BARNS, FIELD NAMES, FIELDS, FRITILLARY MEADOWS, GATES, HARES, HAXEY HOOD GAME, HAY MEADOWS, HEDGES, INGS, IRONSTONE, LYNCHETS, PARKLAND, PIT TIPS, RIDGE & FURROW, SHEEP, SKYLARKS, WATER-MEADOWS, WILDFLOWERS.

F I E L D S

Having carved ourselves out of the wild woods, creating clearings that we called fields, we have spent millennia balancing nature and culture to create rich patterns that are perhaps *the* defining feature of the English landscape. The heart leaps, after time away, as the green patchwork comes into view from a plane: '*Landscape plotted and pieced – fold, fallow and plough*', as Gerard Manley Hopkins had it. The eye feasts on centuries of hard work, somehow surviving among changes in technology, economy and culture.

The sun-devouring black peat stretching to the horizon, cut by clean straight ditches, in the Lincolnshire Fens contrasts with the rich green grasslands drained by

rhynes, edged with pollarded willows, on the Somerset Levels. The orderly Enclosure fields of Otmoor in Oxfordshire reminded Lewis Carroll of a chessboard; the vast production hectares of Suffolk are (wrongly) likened to prairies.

Remnants of neolithic farming are found from Dartmoor and the chalklands of Wessex to Northumberland. Iron-Age or Roman angularity persists in the Dengie peninsula in Essex. Terraces or lynchets, like giants' steps, medieval ridge and furrow and water-meadows, increasingly common in the southern chalk vales in the seventeenth and eighteenth centuries, are all at their most revealing when the sun casts telling shadows. The flower-studded hay meadows of Swaledale, edged by elegant parallel limestone walls running up the valley sides, are a world away from the irregular small fields, penned in by bulky hedge banks, of Cornwall.

Fields full of history are often the richest for nature. In mid-west Nottinghamshire around 1950 some of the first fields taken for opencast coal mining were reinstated – remade – for farming. It is salutary to look at them after half a century of wearing in. The real giveaways are the uncanny absence of trees, the plain hawthorn hedges containing hardly a wild rose, and the ground veering wildly with the weather between rock hard and cloying clay. There is something else, difficult to put your finger on: a general sense of uniformity, an uneasy dullness.

Hedgerows, banks, drystone walls, ditches, streams and rivers may be stock-proof barriers or territory markers that have been in use for centuries. Clearing fields of rocks and constructing stone walls often went hand in hand, as at Penwith in Cornwall and Wasdale Head in Cumberland, but the results are not the same. Trees in hedges are important for creating shelter and shade for livestock and wildlife, and providing fodder, food and other materials. Necessity, idiosyncrasy and generations of cultural experience and knowledge of locality led to different styles of working, adding to the identity of each place.

The sumptuous red soil of the Devon hills, the white plough of the Dorset Downs and the black soils of the Coal Measures in south Yorkshire are the extremes that surprise visitors, but a single field may have a range of soils, slopes and aspects. The thing most of us love about the English countryside is the collision of history with geography visible to the eye. The names of fields tell their stories, too, as do the words given to types of fields and enclosures, from assart to wong.

The depth of history read by those who work the fields increases their intimacy with the land:

The farmer ploughs up coins in the wet-earth-time,
He sees them on the topple of crests gleam,
Or run down furrow; and halts and does let them lie
Like a small black island in brown immensity,
Till his wonder is ceased, and his great hand picks up
the penny.
Red pottery easy discovered, no searching needed . . .
One wonders what farms were like, no searching needed

Ivor Gurney, from 'Up There'

Now agronomists use satellites to help them read what farmers and labourers spent generations getting to know, the subtle nuances of the land, but their aspiration is to smooth out these differences. So much of modern technology, especially the gigantic machines, has led to the homogenising of the land. Fields have in some parts of East Anglia all but disappeared. With the shift from production per acre to production per man, causing a huge reduction of the workforce, we have lost close knowledge and care. The cry was that these were factory floors, not fields, and for the last decades of the twentieth century losses to archaeology, ecology and culture have been devastating.

Age and patina feed the senses. The land around us is our creation; it can tell us stories that have never been written down. The saddest thing is to watch a farmer deep-ploughing away the traces of his own history and spraying away the creatures and plants that have accompanied those before him in the making of the place.

See also BATTLEFIELDS, BOUNDARIES, CATTLE, CHALK, CROPS, DOWNLAND, DRYSTONE WALLS, FENCES, FENS, FIELD BARNS, FIELD NAMES, FIELD PATTERNS, FRITILLARY MEADOWS, GATES, GRAZING MARSHES, HARES, HAY MEADOWS, HEDGES, INGS, IRONSTONE, LEVELS, LYNCHETS, PARKLAND, PIT TIPS, RIDGE & FURROW, SHEEP, SKYLARKS, WATER-MEADOWS, WILDFLOWERS.

FILM LOCATIONS

People make special journeys to Carnforth Station in Lancashire simply to see where Celia Johnson met Trevor Howard in *Brief Encounter*, released in 1945. Standing on the Cobb at Lyme Regis in Dorset gives one a wistful link to *The French Lieutenant's Woman*, etched in the memory from the 1981 film of the book by John Fowles, who lived in the town. The Tyneside of Mike Hodges' brutal gangster movie *Get Carter* is so iconic that there has been a long-standing push-pull between Gateshead residents and film and architectural enthusiasts over whether the multi-storey car park featured in the 1971 film, designed by 'brutalist' architect Owen Luder, should be demolished. New meaning is endowed upon the real by the unreal, sometimes adding glamour, sometimes not.

The landscapes and buildings of England are much in demand by film makers, whether due to their appropriateness (Knebworth House, Hertfordshire was chosen as Harry Potter's Hogwarts school because of its domes and gargoyles) or practicality (it is easier to take James Bond to a factory in Swindon than a Far Eastern refinery).

In theory the profession of finding film locations should be perfectly attuned to the idea of local distinctiveness, and when all the details are right the depth of authenticity helps the film to sing. *Brighton Rock* (1947) is most definitely situated in Brighton; Inspector Morse and Oxford were synonymous. But often there are incongruities that leave an unfocused discomfort – Thomas Hardy filmed in France because the small fields and hedges of Dorset had been sacrificed to agribusiness. London has become a filmic cypher. All too often it tends towards a ubiquitous backdrop in which the Houses of Parliament, St Paul's Cathedral, Nelson's Column, Buckingham Palace and now the London Eye can be seen from every apartment window and the number 73 bus passes things never previously on its route.

Once a valley or even a street has become familiar through television and film it becomes a tourist attraction. There is something absurd here, as quite frequently the locations represent somewhere else. Gold Hill in Shaftesbury, Dorset is still known as the 'Yorkshire' hill up which the Hovis boy pushed his bicycle for Ridley Scott's 1970s commercial. Bath's Georgian architecture is repeatedly Victorian London. *Chariots of Fire* (1981) used Bebington Oval on Merseyside for the Paris Olympic Stadium.

Famous film studios have immortalised certain places, such as Elstree in Hertfordshire – not one but four studios, near to the metropolis but free from its smog. Two of its studios have gone. The earliest, dating from 1914, now houses

169

The Cobb, Lyme Regis, Dorset.

Albert Square, the BBC's permanent set for *Eastenders*. The other survivor, after a long campaign by local people in the 1980s, was sold to Hertsmere Borough Council, which continues to run it as a going concern.

Of the twenty studios local to London in the 1930s only a handful survive, but the names Beaconsfield, Denham, Bushey and Welwyn evoke memories. Pinewood, once home to James Bond and the Carry On team, has merged with Shepperton, continuing to service international blockbusters. Even that most quintessentially English of studios, Ealing, has recently become active again after years belonging to the BBC.

The big business of film making, and our success at certain aspects of it, has prompted the building of new studios. The three hundred thousand square feet of Leavesden in Hertfordshire, once a Rolls Royce aerodrome, is where Harry Potter's on-screen magic is conjured up. Bristol basks in the success of Aardman Animations, which brought home an Oscar for its beautifully observed *Wallace and Gromit*, sons of a lost Yorkshire.

See also BREAD, BUSES, ELM, MONUMENTS, STATIONS.

F I N G E R P O S T S

At the hill-top by the fingerpost;
The Smoke of the traveller's joy is puffed
Over hawthorn berry and hazel tuft.
I read the sign. Which way shall I go?

Edward Thomas, from 'The Sign-Post'

Fingerposts, or '*posts with hands*', as the great traveller Celia Fiennes called them in 1698, cling to lanes and side roads,

offering guidance. The oldest may offer quarters and eighths as well as whole miles left to travel. Lively representations of hands, some with the attitude of the '*ferocious flying glove*' (a character coined by The Beatles), point the way. The fine local landmark in Pelsall, Staffordshire sports a lamp on top as well as two assertive pointing hands.

Before 1964, when the Worboys Committee demanded their replacement by standardised signs, fingerposts varied considerably from place to place. This particularity lingers here and there. Somerset has retained about twelve hundred cast-iron fingerposts. The most common is a round white post with a pyramid-shaped finial bearing 'SCC' on its four faces. Forty-two different sorts of road sign were counted in Devon in 1988, which included six kinds of finial – pyramid, ring-shaped, pear-shaped, onion-shaped, acorn and crown. Guidance from the Department of Transport now recognises that '*the wide variety of surviving regional and local designs helps to reinforce local distinctiveness, maintaining a sense of continuity in a rapidly changing environment*'. It supports the conservation of surviving fingerposts and permits the replacement of traditional fingerposts that '*match the original style and upper case font*' on minor roads.

The standard early post is made of wood or cast iron, usually painted white or striped in black and white, with a circular finial or ring top. In parts of Essex the name of the parish was marked, and there are examples of finials in the shape of a half-moon or, more often, a small, conical top, painted black.

East Sussex has maintained sturdy oak, in octagonal white posts topped by small, black, eight-sided 'pies'. The direction signs, or guide arms, have scalloped ends. Replacements are faithfully following the old models. You know when you have crossed into west Sussex because the shorter posts are of cast iron, painted black and white with

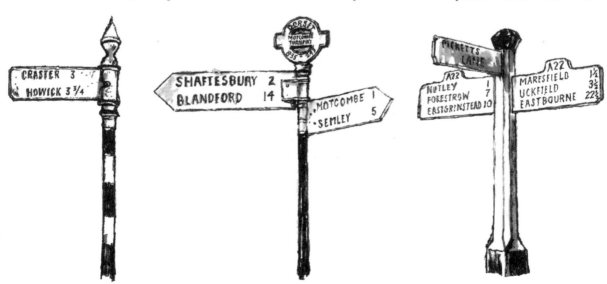

Northumberland; Dorset; Sussex.

moveable arms; the narrow-ringed finial is painted white, edged with black and a simple 'WSCC'. Newer versions show the county crest in the centre of the finial and the name of the place underneath.

In Northumberland the elegant metal posts topped with a pointed acorn in a cup are being freshly painted grey, with black letters on white for the directional arms. There is a fine one at Ancroft on the A6111, while one on the A6354, indicating 'Shallacres 2¾' and 'Tiptoe 1¾', awaits renovation.

West Yorkshire, Dorset and north Berkshire have some fingerposts with grid references; the Ministry of Transport commissioned them in 1930 as an experiment. Wartime saw a general removal of all signs to confuse the enemy (and the visitor – a rural sport still practised, together with the realigning of swivelling metal signs). In Dorset, cast-iron fingerposts are topped with a metal ring bearing 'Dorset' and the grid reference, often with a crossbar for the place-name. There are also two red posts – near Bloxworth on the A31 and north of Sherborne on the B3145 – about which there is much debate.

New 'traditional' posts are beginning to appear. In the New Forest cast-metal posts have white-ringed finials with 'Hampshire' at the top and the place-name below; two ponies are depicted in the centre of the ring.

In Devon 'maintenance free' signs are replacing the old wooden ones, on which the county's logo is shown on a small triangular finial and the name of the crossroads – Couples Corner, Five Wyches Cross, Cold East Cross – is written vertically on the white post, evoking stories and offering clues in the tangle of Devon lanes. A photograph taken by James Ravilious before 1999 shows an old, leaning fingerpost at Chawleigh Week Cross. It has a chunky, chamfered white wooden post and rounded direction signs with decorative fretwork underneath. The black letters are large and raised. Obviously handmade, it speaks of craftsmanship and reminds us that we have mislaid something that was good.

See also CROSSROADS, FOOTPATHS, GRASSY TRIANGLES, MILESTONES, NEW FOREST PONIES, ROADS, VERGES.

FISH & CHIPS

The British devoured around three hundred million portions in 1999, sixty thousand tonnes of fish and half a million potatoes – more than ten per cent of all the potatoes eaten in the country in a year.

As with so many things we hold to be specially English, fish and chips is just another example of historic cultural weaving. Potatoes, of course, came from the Americas with Sir Walter Raleigh. The Belgians claim the invention of the chip – even though they famously eat it with mayonnaise – but it is as likely that the French first cut potatoes into thin pieces and fried them as *pommes frites*. During the next two hundred years chips became popular in England, sold in Irish 'potato shops'.

In 1860 Joseph Malin opened a shop in Cleveland Street, Bow, east London, combining Franco-Belgic-Irish chips with fish fried in a style popularised by Portuguese Jews. From there the 'traditional' fish and chip shop evolved. Trade boomed as the new steam ships increased fishing productivity and the railways took advantage of developments in ice storage, bringing fresher fish from Grimsby, Fleetwood, Hull and Scotland to London.

As industrial workers gained a little disposable income, fish and chips became a staple, one of the few meals that working people could afford to buy ready-cooked and ready to eat. This was true well into the 1950s. Harry Ramsden opened the first sit-down chip restaurant in a hut at Guiseley near Leeds in 1928. Different regions had their preferences: hake in Lancashire, haddock in Yorkshire, dogfish or rock salmon in the North East. Laurie Fricker reports that in Glastonbury, Somerset you can have fish and chips served with cider.

Once paid holidays became the norm, industrial workers went to the seaside resorts and wanted the food they could buy at home. The resorts met demand by becoming increasingly synonymous with fried fish. To this day, according to statistics compiled by the National Federation of Fish Friers (NFFF), more than a third of the population '*believes that Blackpool serves the best fish and chips in the country*'. Food writer Tony Mudd is clear: '*the seaside is the best place to eat fish and chips. The fish is likely to have come straight from the sea, and the smell of chips will add to that holiday feeling.*' Among his favourites are the fish shop in Aldeburgh, Suffolk, Bill's Fish Bar in Cullercoats, Northumberland and Maddy's

171

Chippy and Restaurant in Ilfracombe, Devon, where a fish and chip meal can be followed by apple and blackberry pie with custard.

Cod is by far the most popular fish, taking more than 61 per cent of the chip-shop market, with haddock, plaice and whiting trailing behind. Some places, such as Seniors in Blackpool, offer more unusual varieties, including skate, John Dory, red snapper and black bream. These figures could be overturned, however, if the dramatic depletion of cod stocks around our shores during recent decades is not addressed. Its disappearance from chip-shop menus might be as much a necessary measure for saving it as a symptom of its decline.

For the chips, potatoes with a low-sugar, high-starch content are preferable. Maris Piper has been a favourite since its introduction in 1964, but Record is the industry standard. Crown, Cara, Dunbar Standard, Kestrel, Desiree, Pentland Squire, Pentland Dells and Idaho Russets have all been suggested as good chip spuds. James Leith summed up the type of potato essential for chipping: '*largish tuber, a high dry-matter content (that means it soaks up less oil) and a pale golden-finished colour*'.

At their peak in the 1920s, there were around 35,000 chip shops in Britain. In 2004 there were still nearly 8,600, far outstripping the seemingly ubiquitous burger bar by eight to one. The NFFF rewards the best with an annual award; recent winners have included the Brownsover Fish Bar in Rugby, Warwickshire, Bizzie Lizzies in Skipton, Yorkshire, The Halfway Fish Bar in Poole, Dorset and the Elite Fish Bar in Ruskington, Lincolnshire.

See also BOATS, CAFÉS, FOOD, POTATOES, SEA FISH.

F L A G S

Bold red on a white background, England's flag is the cross of St George. Possibly a Turkish soldier, his cross was first recorded as England's national flag in 1277. When the fifteenth-century reformation abolished extraneous saints'

banners, his took centre stage. Anglican churches fly it and some places raise it on St George's Day. In Mere, Wiltshire, for example, it flies from a flagpole that towers over the town on a landmark hill.

The patriotic appearance of St George's flags on vans, hanging out of windows and on people's faces to mark sporting occasions at the beginning of this century has helped to shake off lingering connections with extreme right-wing politics. The singer Billy Bragg, long associated with anti-racism and anti-fascism, has, with many others, welcomed its reclamation.

It is part of a movement of assertion that is separating out the Union flag (Union Jack when flown from a ship's bow on the jack-staff), a combination of English, Scots and Irish flags assembled between 1606 and 1801. Wales and Cornwall, in particular, were regarded as part of an indivisible English realm and denied the right to distinct identity. Strong and lively independence movements changed that, flags reinforcing their cases. Cornwall's flag is as defiant as it is geographically defining, the cross of St Piran, patron saint of tin miners – a white cross on a stark black background.

Like a groundswell of separatism slowly bubbling up, other former kingdoms and shires have taken Cornwall's example. East Anglia has a St George Cross with a central

blue shield containing three gold coins. The mid lands kingdom of Mercia traditionally used a gold saltire on blue. A new one proposed in 2001 adopts blue, wavy-edged blocks to represent its bordering rivers, Humber and Thames. Essex's flag shows three *seaxes*, the swords from which the Saxons took their name. Northumberland county council's flag was inspired by the purple and gold banner that Bede described at St Oswald's tomb.

Yorkshire has long used a white Yorkist rose against a blue background. Many of these sprang up in Sproxton during 2003, after a local farmer fell foul of planning regulations by flying a particularly sizeable example. Michael Faul designed a new flag, combining the St George Cross with the white rose. Lancashire, however, has never used its red rose on a flag.

Wareham, Dorset. From top left, clockwise: Cornwall; Yorkshire; Northumberland; Essex.

Increasing numbers of counties have used flags to help reinforce identity in flux since the 1950s. The restoration of Rutland in 1997 after 23 years in the administrative wilderness was marked by a new green flag showing a golden horseshoe in a ring of acorns, relating to an ancient right of local barons to take a horseshoe from visitors.

See also DRAGONS, FOOTBALL, HORSES & PONIES, SAINTS, WEATHER-VANES.

F L A S H E S

Flooded wetlands resulting from subsidence following brine extraction in Cheshire and coal mining in Lancashire are called flashes. In Yorkshire the local word is ing.

See also BROADS, COAL MINING, DEW PONDS, FENS, FIELDS, GRAZING MARSHES, GREEN LANES, HAY MEADOWS, HERONRIES, INGS, LAKES, MOORLAND, MOSSES, MOSSLAND, PEAT, PONDS, RIVERS, SALT MARSHES, WATER-MEADOWS.

F L A T N E R S

'Flatties' were home-built double-ended boats with flat bottoms. Particular versions plied the rivers and shoreline of Somerset, including sixteen- to twenty-foot turf boats, carrying peat to market on the river Brue, and withy boats, which ferried osiers through the rhynes of the Levels, along the Tone and the Parrett. Rare now, they were clinker-built or simply constructed of flat elm boards, and pulled or propelled by pole, paddle or outboard engine.

The Parrett flatner is a farmer's fishing boat used to work the river and estuary – dip netting for salmon brought useful extra income. Close to twenty feet long, it relies on oars to take it with the tide upstream, its narrow, gently bowed hull being easily pushed down muddy riverbanks at low tide. Using an angled rudder and a dagger board to steady it, it can be sailed, too.

The 'little flat bottomed boats bravely fishing out in the bay' noted by Samuel Taylor Coleridge in the early 1800s would have been Watchet flatties. Launched over the rocky foreshore, they were double planked on the bottom for protection. With jib-headed sail and simple sprit they would go fetching or fishing for sprats and mackerel in the sea. Regarded as obsolete fifty years ago, the first of a new generation is now moored in the harbour, while a collection of old flatties resides in the nearby Watchet Boat Museum, run by Friends of the Flatner. The last remaining Weston-super-Mare flatner rests here; at 23 feet long it used to round the isles of Steep Holm and Flat Holm, carrying pleasure trippers in summer and fish in winter.

See also BOATS, COBLES, CORNISH GIGS, EELS, FRESHWATER FISH, NOBBIES, NORFOLK WHERRIES, PORTLAND LERRETS, THAMES SAILING BARGES.

F L I N T

Follow the plough on the downs of the South and in the boulder clays of the East, or kick along miles of shingle beaches, and you will find yourself picking up flints.

Counting the pebbles of Dungeness, 98 per cent of which are flints, could take a while: the debris of the southern chalk cliffs (Beachy Head is striped with bands of flint nodules) that has fetched up here covers 28 square miles and reaches sixty feet deep.

The amorphous remains of marine creatures and debris from Cretaceous seas, flints may, in some places, have fossils of sponges and sea urchins embedded within them. They are found in layers in the Upper and Middle Chalk and, stolen by ice, they are secreted in boulder clay. Lumpy, rounded and often bone-like, they inspired Henry Moore. Some flints take on bizarre branching shapes, like fingers or stag's horns. Here the burrows of ancient crabs and lobsters, invaded by sponge-derived silica, have been turned to stone.

Flint is almost pure silica, but any impurities give different colours. 'Some are blue with the texture of resin, the trap of a primeval shadow', Jeremy Hooker wrote. White flint is found only in parts of Lincolnshire. Phil Harding notes that Bullhead flint 'is distinctive (derived from flint beds stained by overlying Thanet Sand in Kent and Essex – it has a green outside with an underlying orange rind) but Bullhead flint is also present in Reading Beds in Berkshire and Dorset'.

Four and a half thousand years ago people were mining 57 feet below Norfolk at Grimes Graves near Thetford, where more than four hundred pits are evident. This, one of Europe's earliest industrial centres, was the unique source of beautiful black flint, which was expertly fashioned into axe heads for tree felling, as well as saws, knives, scrapers and arrowheads. It makes for a pocked and poignant landscape redolent of twentieth-century wars, for which flint laid some groundwork.

To knap flint (knappen means to crack in Dutch and German) requires skilled hands. Judicious strikes produce flakes for blades and gun flints. Through the Middle Ages, and again in the seventeenth to twentieth centuries at Lingheath and Brandon in Suffolk, flint was being mined and fashioned to make the spark to set off gunpowder; Brandon blacks are still prized for flintlock guns.

But flint plays more than a walk-on part in our history and landscape. It is a significant building stone, for example in Norfolk churches, Hertfordshire walls, Wiltshire houses and Sussex barns. Later flint tended to be used for domestic building, with freestone and brick taking on the grander roles.

Neolithic flint tool.

In Norfolk, conservation architects can tell where they are by the type of flint: brown field flints eroded from the chalk around Fakenham; black flint around Thetford and Swaffham; chalk-covered grey flints north of North Walsham; light grey around Holt; rounded beach flints near Wells-next-the-Sea, Sheringham and Cromer.

While they do not exist on the chalk wolds of Yorkshire and Lincolnshire, flint buildings once predominated beyond the towns in Berkshire and Hampshire. From Norfolk, Suffolk, north Essex, through the Chilterns and across the southern chalk counties, Adela Wright notes that *'flint buildings in these areas are said to be more numerous than anywhere else in the world'*.

Stephen Hart lists 54 kinds of flint work in East Anglia, including eight varieties of flushwork. This invention of fourteenth-century masons uses knapped flint and freestone to produce flat, vertical surfaces in ever-more intricate patterns, giving 250 years of innovative decoration to the churches. Beautiful flushwork can also be seen at St John the Evangelist in West Meon, Hampshire, where the panels of exquisitely knapped, small-squared flint were crafted by women for the new church, completed in 1846. In some places diaper work offers patterns of bricks among the flint. In Hampshire buildings are banded with flint and brick; elsewhere, including Wilton and the Wylye valley in Wiltshire, they are built in chequerboard style with stone blocks between.

In the Chilterns, where about a third of domestic buildings have some flint, differences are noted: banded flint work is found only in the south west, while the eastern scarp closer to the Vale of Aylesbury exhibits more thatch and flint. Boundary walls of flint are well scattered, and barns often have flint bases. More examples of knapped flint are found close to chalk quarries, since the unweathered black and white flints are easier to work. From Maidenhead in Berkshire to High Wycombe in Buckinghamshire, the old Great Western Railway had knapped-flint stations.

See also BEACHES, BUILDING STONES, CHALK, CHURCHES, COASTLINE, COASTS, ROUND-TOWERED CHURCHES, SHINGLE, STATIONS, WHITE CLIFFS.

F L O O D S

Upton upon Severn in Worcestershire has a series of small, diamond-shaped markers on the wall around the churchyard, easily missed as you walk up the steep street away from the river. The dates and heights of the metal plates recollect serious floods. Upstream, in the county town, a stone wall beside the Severn has carved dates far above the heads of onlookers. The memory of floods never fades from those who have experienced the unchallengeable right of a river or stream to revisit any parts of the valley it has made. In Boscastle, which suffered

terrible floods in 2004, explanations never dwell on the fact that the valley in which this Cornish village sits was carved by such incidents.

Likewise Lynmouth, Devon, which became a world cause on 15 August 1952. Exmoor had soaked up a month of rainfall. The rocks, peat and streams were full, and then came a day of incessant rain. *'About 8.30pm there occurred one of those catastrophes of nature – a cloudburst . . . Five inches in one single hour . . . over nine inches in twenty four hours. Nine inches! More than three months' normal fall.'* Two rivers entered the steep-sided valley above the town. *'Onwards and downwards the boiling torrent raced with a velocity of twenty miles per hour. Bridges, debris, carcasses of sheep, fowls, dogs and cows, and later scores of motor-cars, were gathered into its maw.'* Eric R. Delderfield's illustrated book, *The Lynmouth Flood Disaster*, evokes the terror and havoc that only the force of nature can bring. Twenty people died; four were never found.

Six months later an even greater tragedy struck, this time on the east coast. On the night of 31 January 1953 a deep depression over the North Sea, sufficient to perturb sea levels, brought big winds and huge waves. By sad coincidence it was also the time of high tide, and sea water rushed through sea defences and natural coastline all the way from the Humber estuary to Deal in Kent. More than three hundred people were lost, 24,000 houses flooded, with massive damage to towns, villages and farmland. Both sides of the North Sea experienced storm surge levels more than six to seven feet higher than normal. For the Low Countries it was worse.

In Cleethorpes, Lincolnshire, fifteen hundred houses were flooded. Wells-next-the-Sea in Norfolk found a three-hundred-ton coaster on its quay; hundreds of caravans disappeared from Hunstanton. Frinton in Essex lost all its beach huts; Herne Bay in Kent lost its pier. Canvey Island was completely inundated, 58 people died. Five per cent of the people of Jaywick in Essex were drowned. At Ingoldmells in Lincolnshire the sand-dunes simply disappeared. People remember the darkness, clambering into roof spaces or clinging to roofs, hearing the church bells over the gale.

In mid-October 2000, after a wet summer, Lewes, Robertsbridge and Yalding went under water. Sussex and Kent had received six inches of rain. Later that month three inches of rain fell in 24 hours across the South, accompanied by strong gales. The soil, already waterlogged, was unable to absorb any more and flooding became inevitable. Early warning systems and good communications meant that lives were not lost, but the level of disbelief was widespread. In good humour Harveys of Lewes produced bottles of Ouse Booze, an ale made after the brewery flooded on 12 October.

Flooding is just one of many natural states for a river. Floodplains are their overspill areas, acting as sponges. They are created over millennia as rivers move across their valleys. Enriched by silt deposited during flooding and with a high water table, they are good for farming and for wading birds and waterfowl. Overgrazing and removing woods from hills, as well as building too close to rivers and across floodplains, stops infiltration and increases the speed of run-off, causing erosion in the hills and flooding downstream.

Ironically, drainage is also a problem. Much of Fenland has been drained, to the extent that rivers stand high above the land, rendering it vulnerable. The view from the train crossing Somerset can bring on a bout of sea-sickness when the Levels are flooded. Winter wheat, which is sown in September, leaving the ground bare all winter, can increase water run-off by between ten and one hundred times more than from a field of grass. And the very flatness of floodplains attracts development – the worst scenario.

With sea levels rising, land levels falling and the volatility of the weather increasing, mathematical odds are moving in the wrong direction. The Met Office's Hadley Centre for Climate Change predicts that the risk to lives and property will increase tenfold during this century. Some of the most expensive real estate in England lies along our coasts and estuaries. The Essex estuaries have protection: Colne Barrier, Fobbing Horse Barrier, East Haven Barrier and Benfleet Barrier. Along the Thames at Eel Pie Island there is discussion about raising houses on stilts, which works upriver at Rod Eyot near Henley, Oxfordshire.

The Thames Barrier, a shimmering wonder, is a necessity. In the first week of 2003 it was closed fourteen times, a record – on one occasion water levels in the estuary rose four feet above average for only the third time in 120 years. The barrier saved 26 tube stations, as well as Chiswick, Fulham, Westminster and Docklands, from flooding. It is built to withstand a one-in-a-thousand-year flood.

The Environment Agency now 'manages flood risk' rather than defending against floods. Until we wholeheartedly reduce our use of carbon fuels, accept more holistic planning of water catchments, stop building on floodplains and embrace upland care and floodplain forests, we shall continue to intensify the problems.

Every culture has its flood myths. Our generation has global warming and rising sea levels. They are redrawing the coastline of England.

See also ALDER, BELLS & BELL-RINGING, BORES, BOURNES, BRIDGES, CLOUDS, COASTLINE, EAST, EELS, ESTUARIES, EYOTS, FENS, FLASHES, FOOTBRIDGES, FORDS, FRETS, FROST & FROST HOLLOWS, INGS, ISLANDS, SALT MARSHES, SAND-DUNES, SHIPPING FORECAST, STEPPING-STONES, TIDES, WEATHER, WINDMILLS, WINDS, WINTERBOURNES.

FOG & MIST

Clouds sometimes have to learn how to fly. They sit quite quiet or swirl a little, but keep contact with the ground. Mist is simply water droplets, too small to fall, impeding the view. It evokes a more benign, poetic outlook than fog, which is denser, cutting visibility to below a thousand metres. Inland fog is more likely in autumn and winter, especially after cold, clear nights. Sea fogs happen most often in spring and summer, when warmer air over a cooler sea brings the water vapour down to the dew point.

Fog changes our view of the world, literally and psychologically. Looking out from our hill town of Shaftesbury, it is not unusual to catch an early mist in Dorset's Blackmore Vale; on sharp winter's mornings this may lap like a sea around the 'islands' of Duncliffe, Melbury and Hambledon and at the 'shores' of Bulbarrow and far Rampisham.

Sometimes the clouds sit on the hilltops and threaten Marnhull and the other river Stour villages with rain:

If Duncliffe Wood be fair and clear,
You Stour Boys need have no fear.
But if Duncliffe Wood do wear its cap,
You Marn'll folk watch out for that.

In Sussex it runs: '*When Firle Hill and Long Man has a cap, We in the valley gets a drap.*' In Devon and Cornwall a wet hill fog goes by the name of mizzle. The Trent valley is naturally one of the foggiest places in England and this, together with the chemical reaction of fog with coal smoke, caused exceptionally severe smogs in the 1950s and 1960s.

Coal was understood to cause air pollution even in the thirteenth century. By 1661 John Evelyn had written in *Fumifugium* of the '*Hellish and dismal cloud of sea-coale*' that shrouded London and recommended banning trades that used it from the city. By 1800 a murky miasma along the Thames was known as a London Particular:

I asked him whether there was a great fire anywhere? For the streets were so full of dense brown smoke that scarcely anything was to be seen.
'O dear no, miss,' he said. 'This is a London particular.'
I had never heard of such a thing.
'A fog, miss,' said the young gentleman.
'O indeed!' said I.

Charles Dickens, from *Bleak House*

Its tendency to hug the docks was necessary to the plot of many a Sherlock Holmes mystery. By the mid-twentieth century this had evolved into the full pea-souper, tasting, as well as appearing, thick and greeny yellow. It killed people. The Great Smog in London, trapped by an inversion that lasted from 5 to 9 December 1952, led directly to the Clean Air Act of 1956 after at least four thousand people died. In the early 1960s east Londoners received thirty per cent less sunshine in winter than those who lived in the countryside around; now they receive about the same. While smogs seem to have been contained, many oil-derived pollutants make today's city air just as dangerous, but less visibly so.

If fog on land is disorientating and dangerous, imagine fog at sea, resting on the waves. The long, low moans of the diaphone foghorn on the lighthouse at Portland Bill, Dorset, sounding night and day, are viscerally registered. The Humber in fog used to be full of sounds, including the whoop-whoop-whoop of small boats seeming to dare the big vessels to play tag. '*You don't hear foghorns very often now, as all the boats have radar*', Katrina Porteous writes of Northumberland. '*I loved the mournful sound of the one on Longstone. Further down the coast (on Coquet Island off Amble) there was "the Coquet Gun". The old men used to speak of "a thick" coming in. They seemed to use this word both for summer and winter fog, and both as a noun and an adjective. They used some lovely metaphors: thick as tar, thick as a hedge, thick as glaur (mud).*' In the North East, rook or roaky fogs tend to be thick, perhaps related to one of the nicknames for Edinburgh, Auld Reekie.

In the economical litany of the Shipping Forecast, after sea area, wind direction/speed and precipitation, comes visibility: '*moderate with fog patches, becoming good*'; or, the best punctuation of all, simply '*good*'.

See also CLOUDS, COASTS, FRETS, LIGHTHOUSES, RIVERS, SHIPPING FORECAST, WEATHER, WINDS.

F O L K T A L E S

People tell tales as a way of transmitting histories and moral lessons, whether of Robin Hood or James Bond, King Arthur or Dr Who – who knows what richness the layering of time and human imagination will bolt on to recently minted characters? Religious tenets have been mythologised: the devil is in rocks, chasms, earthworks, roads and hills. Comic premises disguise harder truths. The people of Hartlepool, Yorkshire are ridiculed for hanging a monkey they believed was a French spy during the Napoleonic wars. In a similar Scots story the monkey was the only survivor of a shipwreck, and the villagers couldn't claim salvage rights while it lived. Perhaps the Hartlepool residents were no more innocent than the Moonrakers of Bishops Cannings, Wiltshire, a band of smugglers who feigned idiocy to protect contraband goods hidden in a pond – they told excisemen that they were trying to retrieve the big, round cheese they could see – the moon's reflection.

Folktales can make a germ of truth miraculous to fit social and moral needs. Saxon landowner Godgifu transmuted over time to Coventry's Lady Godiva, a paragon of moral rectitude. King Arthur, the best example of an obscure historic footnote catapulted into grand fiction, was perhaps a sixth-century Romano-British statesman. A symbol of resistance against invading Saxons, he was later an inspiration for Normans developing a national identity and, later still, a romantic hero for soul-searching Victorians. His origins, history and remains are claimed from Cornwall to the Scottish borders and further. Rocks near Tintagel, Cornwall are his cups and saucers; an earthwork near Rowtor, Derbyshire was his hall; his well was at Walltown, Northumberland. Robin Hood was a peasant hero, given Establishment trappings when unrest in the underclasses made him dangerous.

Tales adhere to prodigious and unusual people, such as Moses Carter of Histon, Cambridgeshire – the Histon Giant of the mid-1800s, who stood seven feet tall. They may explain natural processes or pass on knowledge of the natural world or farming – John Barleycorn's ballad is an allegory for crop cultivation. Stories of river spirits, such as Jenny Greenteeth, claiming lives were valuable warnings. In Devon: '*Dart, Dart, cruel Dart, every year thou claimst a heart.*'

Wayland's Smithy, Berkshire.

These tales are not just 'ours', their themes manifest themselves in stories worldwide. Cultural interchange brings Norse heroes to Wayland's Smithy, the burial mound on the Ridgeway near Uffington, Berkshire, associated with the mythical blacksmith Weland. His 'saga' is typical of tales in which fantastic heroes overcome adversity to reach enlightenment and triumph – although Weland's victory was bleak. Sagas were told by bards, poetic chroniclers whose praise or sarcasm could build or wreck reputations. The Welsh revived and embellished their bardic traditions in the eighteenth century. Attempts to do the same in England have too often faltered.

Despite global themes, innumerable stories protect local interests. The survival of cider making in Devon depends on the outcome of a battle on Culmstock Bridge between an evil brewer called Frankan and a Devon cider maker. If Frankan wins, Margaret Bromwich tells us, the devil will blight cider apples with frost.

See also ALBION, AVALON, BARROWS, BESTIARY, CHINESE NEW YEAR, CHURCHES, CIDER & CIDER ORCHARDS, DEVIL, DRAGONS, FIELD NAMES, GIANTS, HAUNTED PLACES, JACK AND JILL, MIDSUMMER DAY, MOON, NICKNAMES, 'OBBY 'OSSES, ORCHARDS, PONDS, PUB SIGNS, RIVERS, ROBIN HOOD, SAINTS.

F O L L I E S

'Folly' implies a lightness of spirit in intent as well as an essential absurdity and pointlessness. England's overseas trade from the seventeenth century brought wealth to build and buy enormous houses with extensive grounds, and exotic ideas to inform them. This, and a classical vogue, resulted in estates full of folly buildings, either systematically illustrating classical mythologies, as at Stourhead in Wiltshire, or self-consciously harking back to idealistic rusticity, as at Stowe in Buckinghamshire. Buildings appeared in Oriental, Asian, Moorish and Egyptian styles, rendered uniquely English in the translation. The Egyptian House in Penzance, Cornwall says more about nineteenth-century English culture and taste than it does about Egypt. Romantic ideals of English history were plundered, too, with mock stone circles and sham castles.

Thomas Tresham's Triangular Lodge at Rushton, Northamptonshire is among the earliest recognisable follies, but Tresham's inspiration was religious, the building's proportions and ornaments corresponding to the Holy Trinity. A folly should be a structure devoid of utility: you can't live in it, it's not defensive, it doesn't help you navigate. It can help you, possibly, better to see the view, or, as an eye catcher, it can become the view. Surrey has more towers than most. Cumberland, Northumberland and Durham's follies are overwhelmingly Gothic.

The inexplicable group at Barwick Park near Yeovil in Somerset might result from nineteenth-century landowner George Messiter's bid to remedy unemployment in the glove industry. One, a rugged stone arch topped by a round tower with a conical spire and a statue of Mercury, is the retreat of Jack the Treacle Eater.

It is difficult to imagine getting planning permission now for a folly in the grand tradition – Lord Berners had enough trouble with Faringdon tower in Oxfordshire in 1935 – but they do still appear on a small scale. Many older ones have fallen or are in disrepair. The eighteenth-century Horton Tower in Dorset now hosts hidden mobile telephone masts. Enthusiasts established the Folly Fellowship in the 1980s to record, discuss, visit and, where possible, protect the country's 'rogue architecture'.

See also BUILDING STONES, CAVES, FOLKTALES, FORTIFICATIONS, LANDMARKS, MONUMENTS, OBELISKS, QUARRIES, WATER-TOWERS.

F O O D

With every apple we eat we make a landscape . . . somewhere. The relationship between our food, our surroundings and our culture is in our hands and increasingly it is recognised that economics falls short of measuring the value to us of eating food produced locally and organically.

An orchard demonstrates the complexities. When we stop eating English apples, or the price falls on the world market, orchards in England are grubbed out. The loss of an orchard, especially a well-established, traditional tall-tree orchard, is not a simple loss to the local economy and landscape. An old orchard sustains a complex web of wildlife and holds together a cat's-cradle of cultural richness. It may have varieties of fruit particular to the locality, each with its own stories and uses. Recipes will have been developed, perhaps cider or damson beer typical of nowhere else, and buildings for storage and production. Customs, wassailing, songs and festive gatherings reinforce community. Hard but social work shares and deepens the wisdom gathered over generations of pruning, grafting, dabbling and discerning about slope, soil and season – as with the olive groves, cork oak fields and vineyards of mainland Europe.

Keeping knowledge working, changing and celebrated in the place is both ecologically safer, ethically transparent and culturally more robust than leaving production to monocultures and mills two continents away, trusting that people are well treated and hoping that at home institutions will maintain seed banks and museums of rare breeds. How powerful then, to eat bread made from locally produced organic flour, stone milled using the energy of water from the stream in the valley. Organic production should ensure that the fields are sufficiently edged with flowers to satisfy butterflies, bees and birds; that the river is not over-enriched with nitrate run-off; that energy use, transportation costs and pollution are minimised; that the local economy is boosted, people know where things come from and the farmer, miller and baker know to whom they are responsible.

As far as local distinctiveness is concerned, quality is built upon authenticity. Charles Martell has been the champion of Gloucestershire apples, perry pears, cattle, pigs and poultry for more than thirty years. Others are now following his lead. Jane Powell from the Green Shop in Bisley, Gloucestershire told us of a new cheese being created in order to make viable the expansion of the endangered Gloucester cattle herd and to maintain the particularity of Cotswold grassland. It will carry the typicality of the area in its flavours, which may vary with the changing seasons. New wisdom will emerge, stone walls be rebuilt and the traditional hay meadows shine with flowers, sustaining all manner of wildlife.

The partaking of something of the place in the place is paradoxically one of the most memorable ways of taking it home: a Rum Nicky in Cumberland; strawberries around Cheddar in Somerset; Eccles cakes in Eccles, Lancashire; water from St Anne's Well in Buxton, Derbyshire; Craster kippers in Craster, Northumberland; York ham in York; Isle of Wight doughnuts on the Isle of Wight or Cromer crabs in Cromer, Norfolk.

The French have made a philosophy out of the particular: *terroir* is all. The significance of land, soil and tradition is conveyed by the term *appellation contrôlée*, which ties together identity, authenticity, quality and place. This has informed the European Union's legal protection for food: if its quality or characteristics are essentially due to a geographical area, it may gain a PDO – Protected Designation of Origin; if from a traditional recipe or a reputation associated with a place it may be awarded a PGI – Protected Geographical Indication – or be granted a certificate of special character (CSC).

Food, its production, trading, preparation and consumption, is integral to our way of life. Two centuries of urbanisation strained our links with the land, and the austerity imposed by thirteen years of wartime and post-war rationing was followed by a yearning for the unseasonal, the colourful and the exotic. Lured by food writers, such as Elizabeth David, and by foreign travel, we began to appreciate and even cook peasant, popular and demanding dishes from mainland Europe. Increasing cultural diversity, the spread of Chinese and Indian restaurants, the appearance of Caribbean foods in city markets and the ubiquity of American culture all beckoned, so that we became easy game for both experiment and laziness, television chefs and fast-food chains. Our changing mix of cultures has given us a new national dish – chicken tikka masala, an Indian confection for British tastes. But as the new millennium proceeds we are moving on to ever more exotic foods, from Thailand, Japan and Indonesia.

We can mourn the state of our seas with the crash in fish stocks, and the state of our fields after decades of chemical abuse, the loss of our will to cook and the stranglehold of the superstores. But between the cracks of these homogenising and depleting forces food in England is reinventing itself. Awakened local and regional pride in produce is seeing a resurgence of traditional recipes and the embracing of newly introduced foods. Vineyards are coming of age, new cheeses are being born, pubs are creating their own micro-breweries, Westmorland damsons are valued again, Cornish clotted cream has a PDO, Whitstable oysters a PGI. Farmers' markets are popularising direct sales and reminding us what market towns can be like. Jamaica patties are available at the bakers in Shaftesbury, Sichuan food in Manchester, sushi in Swindon.

As Billy Bragg puts it:

My breakfast was half English and so am I you know
I had a plate of Marmite soldiers washed down with
a cappuccino
And I have a veggie curry about once a week
The next day I'll fry it up as bubble and squeak
Cos my appetite's half English and I'm half English too

See also APPLE DAY, APPLES, APRICOTS, ASPARAGUS, BAKEWELL PUDDING, BEER, BISCUITS, BREAD, BUNS, CAFÉS, CAKES, CATTLE, CHEESE, CHEESE ROLLING, CHERRIES, CHINESE NEW YEAR, CIDER & CIDER ORCHARDS, COBNUTS, CONFECTIONERY, CORNISH PASTIES, CRAB FAIR, CREAM TEAS, DAMSONS, DIWALI, DOVECOTES, DRAGONS, EASTER CUSTOMS, ECCLES CAKES, EDIBLE DORMOUSE, EELS, FAIRS & FAIRGROUNDS, FIELDS, FISH & CHIPS, FRESHWATER FISH, GARDENS, GIN, GOOSEBERRIES, HALLOWE'EN, HARE PIE SCRAMBLE, HARES, HAY MEADOWS, HOPS, HOP-GARDENS & HOP-YARDS, JUNIPER, KIPPERS, LIQUORICE, MALTINGS, ORCHARDS, PIGS, PUDDINGS, RHUBARB, SEA FISH, SHEEP, SHELLFISH, SPRINGS, STAFFORDSHIRE OATCAKES, WASSAILING, WATERCRESS BEDS.

FOOTBALL

Football's attraction is its simplicity: where there is a ball, there is a game. In England it is ancient, but the word didn't appear until the 1400s – and then usually because the activity was being banned. Medieval football tended towards the carnage of Shrove Tuesday games, the 'Ur-football' still practised annually in Ashbourne in Derbyshire, Atherstone in Warwickshire and St Columb Major in Cornwall, perhaps echoing sun-worshipping rituals or old means of settling border disputes. In Alnwick, Northumberland and in Chester the ball represents an enemy's severed head.

Modern football evolved in the 1800s, moving to school and university, church and Sunday school, trade and industry. Aston Villa of Birmingham and Fulham of London were Methodist church and Sunday school teams respectively. Staff from the Woolwich Royal Arsenal (Nottingham Forest helped them with an old set of strips) and Crystal Palace in London had teams. Railwaymen formed Manchester United and the members of Millwall, east London were jam factory workers. Teams' nicknames reflect local trade: Yeovil Town in Somerset is the Glovers; Fleetwood Town in Lancashire the Fishermen.

Early teams played on farm fields, meadows and cricket pitches. Bolton Wanderers moved from field to field, hence the name. The Football Association and League formed in the late nineteenth century, greater crowds came and dedicated grounds became essential. Many famous names were established from the 1890s: Goodison Park, Maine Road, Hillsborough, Elland Road, St James' Park, Old Trafford and, of course, Wembley, with its once-iconic twin towers, demolished in 2003.

Unfortunately the big business that is modern football can sacrifice the sanctity of the old for the commercial demands of the new. Roger Herman noted ruefully the cynicism that replaced Sunderland's 1898 Roker Park with the Stadium of Light a century later, with the team (traditionally the Mackems) 'rebranded' The Black Cats, a name with no connection to locality or even the team colours (red and white).

Many disillusioned fans are returning to the grass-roots play of amateur and semi-professional non-league football, often driven by enthusiasts who care passionately about football and its place in their community. Simon Steele tells of the resurrection of Leamington Spa's team, associated with the Midlands motor industry and called The Brakes. Its Warwickshire ground was sold in the 1980s and became a housing estate called, woefully, Brakes Mead. The hard work of supporters brought the team back with a new ground in 2000.

The essential spirit of football is perhaps found in parks, waste ground, beaches, alleys and cul-de-sacs, between goal posts in inner cities and remote backwaters, ragged nets on neglected recreation grounds or painted on garage doors. These spaces are as important to football lovers as professional grounds. In Swindon, Wiltshire Steve Cann's 'field of dreams' is Ferndale School Field, where, in the 1960s, 'a generation of pre-teens spending its free time kicking a ball around' could be found. Inevitably those places stick in the memory.

See also BISCUITS, BOUNDARIES, CHAPELS, CHURCHES, FIELDS, FLAGS, GAMES, NICKNAMES, PARKS, ROOKERIES, SHROVETIDE GAMES.

FOOTBRIDGES

Thomas Hardy in *The Mayor of Casterbridge* describes that moment of contemplation above the middle of a stream: '*These bridges had speaking countenances. Every projection in each was worn down to obtuseness partly . . . by friction from generations of loungers, whose toes and heels had from year to year made restless movements against these parapets, as they stood there meditating on the aspects of affairs.*' The river Frome takes a gentle swing around Dorchester (Casterbridge), and many little bridges cross it. Further downstream at Moreton the river is shallow and wide – an old fording place. The hundred-yard-long bridge isn't particularly attractive, made of concrete with metal rails, but the setting lends it magic. You can see the tiny fry gathering around the piers and darting off like shape-shifting clouds as a horse and rider lazily amble across the ford. In the adjoining catchment of the Stour, the stone-piered Colber Bridge at Sturminster Newton has simple horizontal iron railings, while between Canford and Wimborne the footpath crosses the river by a narrow but sophisticated suspension bridge.

Where shallow streams run beside roads through sleepy villages, small footbridges have been built for access. Often they are straightforward beam bridges of stone or single arches, but in Mere, Wiltshire, where a row of gardens backs onto the shallow Shreen Water, bridge after bridge has its own personality; some have elaborate railings with

179

cross bracing. At Otterton in Devon simple flat stones lie on beams to link roadway with footpath and houses. Packhorse bridges and bridges beside fords (known as clams in the South West) have found a lasting use by walkers; in Milldale, Derbyshire, a stone bridge sturdily spans the river Dove.

The celebrated Millennium Bridge over the Tyne in Newcastle is one of a new generation of urban footbridges. Opened in 2001, the newest of seven, the 'Blinking Eye' is the world's first tilting bridge. To let ships pass underneath the entire structure pivots 45 degrees to form a gateway fifty metres high. Each opening and closing takes just four minutes; it is so finely balanced that the energy required costs £3.60. Designed by Wilkinson Eyre Architects for Gateshead council, this is the only purpose-built bridge for pedestrians and cyclists across the Tyne (it links two cross-country riverside cycle ways), and the first opening bridge to be built across the Tyne for a hundred years.

See also BRIDGES, BUILDING STONES, CHALK STREAMS, CYCLING, DROVE ROADS, FOOTPATHS, FORDS, HORSES & PONIES, KENNELS, RIVERS, SHEEP-WASHES, STEPPING-STONES.

F O O T P A T H S

The path is the oldest mark we ever made upon the land, history written in a single line. A link with all the feet that have trodden there gives significance to all those tracks

that strike out across moors, linking village with village and valley with valley – lanes for coffins, smugglers, lovers, pilgrims, salt traders, drovers, lead and stone carriers, school-children and churchgoers.

Our pattern of footpaths both illustrates and symbolises rights of passage created by generations of ordinary people going about their business. That they are to be cherished simply for their common-place qualities and because they are

everywhere may seem odd, but the intricate network of paths provides a vital link with the land. The path was born long before land was 'owned'.

A route 'padded' down by frequent use became, in the Anglo-Saxon tongue, a *paeth*. Morpeth in Northumberland means, sombrely, 'murder path'. Northern England has a colourful litany of words for paths, especially those going up hills: bar, bargh, borstal, bostal, burstel, peth. Bostel crops up in Sussex, too. Norfolk might instead have a loke. Derbyshire paths can be racks, as at Wreakes Lane in Dronfield. The Bonsall Parish Map shows paved paths criss-crossing the fields to link different parts of the village with each other, connecting one squeeze stile to another.

Around Strelley and Cossall in Nottinghamshire remnants of stone causeways known as monk's or pilgrim's paths may be part of the fourteenth-century monastic trade network. In the Fens people hardly left footprints; they used poles to vault ditches – in Friesland, Holland this is still a springtime sport. In Lancashire and Yorkshire the laborious and heavy work that went into making packhorse ways has left us with beautiful slabs, causeys, stone trods or flag paths. These routes, worn down by two to three hundred years of packhorse hooves, now enable dry walking, for example across the moors above Slack and Heptonstall.

The Countryside Agency suggests we have 120,000 miles of public rights of way. But walking along a 'right of way' is different from striking out across country. There have been tensions at every turn. John Ruskin wrote in 1885 to the *Pall Mall Gazette*: '*Sir – Will you kindly help me to direct general attention to the mischief now continually done by new landowners in the closing of our mountain footpaths? . . . Of all the small, mean, and wicked things a landlord can do, shutting his footpath is the nastiest.*' Ewan MacColl recalls a time in the aftermath of the Industrial Revolution when weekly the people of the northern cities broke free from the looms, steelworks and mines:

I'm a rambler, I'm a rambler, from Manchester way
I get all my pleasure the hard, moorland way.
I may be a wage slave on Monday,
But I am a free man on Sunday . . .

From 'The Manchester Rambler'

It was on a Sunday that the Kinder Scout Mass Trespass took place, on 24 April 1932. This brave gathering of hundreds of people from Manchester and Sheffield on the 2,088-foot peak in Derbyshire, despite the presence of gamekeepers who lined up to stop them, was a high point in the movement towards broad access to open country that is only now being achieved. The Hayfield and Kinder Scout Ancient Footpaths Association had sought a 'right to

181

roam' since 1876. After the original trespass, ten thousand people assembled in the nearby Winnats Pass, an ancient salt way, for rallies to support the creation of national parks. Out of these actions came the Peak District National Park in 1951, the first of many, and, after persistent work by the Ramblers' Association and others, the Countryside and Rights of Way Act in 2000.

New recreational paths have to be mapped out and negotiated, linking old and new rights of way. It is not an easy task. Creating a right of way along the route of Hadrian's Wall demanded sensitive discussion with seven hundred landholders, many highly sceptical of the notion of access for all. Farmers and archaeologists imagined disturbance and loss. It took nearly twenty years to traverse the legal and diplomatic minefield: Hadrian's Wall Path was opened in 2003 with many new stiles, fourteen new footbridges – some in the weathered steel of industrial Tyneside – and turf protection for ancient buildings. A march along this now civil path might take three days in two-thousand-year-old footprints along the 84 miles from Wallsend, Northumberland to the Firth of Solway, Cumberland.

Disused railway lines and river and canal towpaths, where open, provide easy access for the wheelchair-bound and pram pushers – the Tissington Trail following the old Ashbourne to Buxton line in Derbyshire has thirteen miles of flat walking. The real heroes of countryside and town are the unsung paths, the twitchels, dog walks and ambling ways. But problems still abound – perhaps a third of footpaths are obstructed by barbed wire, broken bridges or padlocked gates.

Herefordshire is rich in footpaths; Lincolnshire has far fewer. This may be a result of extensive as opposed to intensive farming and the loss of hedgerows, but it must also reflect the power of large landowners in the East. An area full of footpaths is in part a memorial to the hard work of local people to keep the rights alive.

See also ABBEYS, ALLEYS, BARROWS, BEACON FIRES, BEATING THE BOUNDS, BOUNDARIES, COASTS, DROVE ROADS, DRYSTONE WALLS, FELLS, FOOTBRIDGES, FORDS, GREEN LANES, HEDGES, HILLS, HOLLOW WAYS, LANES, MONASTERIES, MOORLAND, PARISH MAPS, ROADS, STILES, WAYSIDE & BOUNDARY CROSSES, ZIGZAGS.

F O R D S

You need courage to start the journey of nearly a mile when the river Tarrant in north Dorset takes to the road. Tarrant may mean 'trespasser' (from the Celtic), but of course the road is in the river's bed. A ford is really about crossing a

stream, and the depth gauge beside a water splash, and sign saying 'Deep' or even 'Unsuitable for Motors', has to be taken seriously.

The parish of Bekesbourne-with-Patrixbourne has three fords (called Splash Bottom, Old Palace Ford and the Recreation Ground Ford), all in regular use on the Nailbourne river in Kent. Jill Thomas, Parish Clerk, tells us that this *is an intermittent chalk stream so in some years the fords are dry, but when they are full they are great fun to splash through. All three fords have an adjacent footbridge. One is an ugly concrete and metal affair, but the others are brick arches of ancient origin. One carries a keystone from the eighteenth century. In the 2001 floods the fords were impassable for more than three months. Cars often underestimate the depth and get stuck and our village church is cut off. In 1995 a bride arrived for her wedding in an old car delivered on a low loader.*

Fords have been so important from the earliest times that they are the commonest topographical place-name. Oxford, Hertford, Hereford and Stratford have grown, but there are many more: in Devon the Domesday Book mentions 480 places named for their fords or wades. On the coastal path around the South Hams you are invited to walk through the river Erme at low tide or face a great detour around the valley.

This was always the dilemma: to chance the short or go the long way round – originally even the biggest of rivers had to be crossed at fords. Romans paved some fords with slabs, as at Kempston in Bedfordshire and Iden Green in Kent. Stamford in Lincolnshire and Stoneyford on the Erewash in Derbyshire; Slaggyford in Northumberland and Mudford in Somerset; Chalford (meaning chalk) in Gloucestershire – all suggest the conditions of crossing; some have been cobbled. Efford tells of a way passable at low tide, as at North Efford by Aveton Gifford (Giffard was a family name) in south Devon. Here, three-quarters of a mile of road disappears twice a day and, despite the guiding black-and-white stakes, is not negotiable.

Penrith means the chief or hill ford, with *ritu* being the British word for ford. Geoffrey Grigson found more than seventy such place-names (including rit, red, ret) in Cornwall. In Cumberland, Westmorland and the north of Yorkshire the Norse word *vath* appears, as in Sandwath, Dubwath and possibly implicated in the name Solway.

You may sit with a warming drink at the village bakery and watch vehicles negotiate the ford in Hovingham, north Yorkshire. At Rolleston on Dove in Staffordshire a sometimes-deeper-than-you-think ford gives endless amusement to locals as overbearing four-by-four drivers run out of machismo in the middle.

Nearly a hundred fords were banished underground in Devon in the fifteen years after 1949; our tendency is to concrete or culvert anything that occasionally inconveniences us. In cases where a dry crossing is vital, the best plans maintain the useable ford in parallel. In Hampshire, on the edge of Brockenhurst, there is a surprising ford within the busy suburban scene – it should be a model. Elsewhere Edward Grimsdale and the Buckingham Society have been trying to save their ford. *'Buckingham's ford was an ancient way across the river Ouse; these days the Old Ford is too deep to cross. It is recalled in Ford Street; on each side there is a concrete slope to tempt those looking for a short cut. Nearby Ford Meadow is the home of Buckingham Town Football Team. Competition between the New Inn (frequented by the gas workers) and The Woolpack (the farmer's choice) was played out in a tug of war match across the ford, a tradition that exists on a haphazard basis to this day. Now the Environment Agency has decreed that such scenes must not, will not, be repeated. Our ford will be confined behind Flood Gates. The shallow, dreamy and breamy reach of the Ouse must be walled up, channelled into a narrow rapid. Another of England's diminishing collection of fords, once the poor man's bridge, will be lost.'*

Fords determined the routes of roads, the positions of settlements; where they persist they remind us of the intimate ups and downs of the land. Association with stepping-stones and small bridges adds to their significance. Brief though our encounters with these fast-disappearing ancient crossings may be, they make us want to play and they remind us to be aware of the route of the stream. However inconvenient, their sheer presence is worth it. They shine in the memory.

See also BOURNES, BRIDGES, CHALK STREAMS, FLOODS, FOOTBRIDGES, ISLANDS, PARISH MAPS, QUICKSAND, ROADS, STEPPING-STONES, TIDES, WINTERBOURNES.

F O R G E S

Most places had their worker in iron. Under the dense shade of a horse chestnut or lime, the modest forge was often situated on the edge of the old part of a village or town. Frequently right on the road, with easy access for horses and space for deliveries of fuel and iron, the buildings are usually simple, one-storey constructions in the local vernacular. Relict double doors and a substantial chimney may offer a clue to a lost smithy.

James Crowden says: '*The slow evolution of the forge into a garage happened in the thirties and forties as tractors came in. At harvest time repairing a reaper-binder or helping a traction engine out was essential. The role of the village blacksmith should not be underrated. They literally held the community together and produced window frames, locks, handles and all manner of metal work. Without good shoeing there were no active horses to pull the ploughs.*

'*My own house in Winsham, Somerset is called Forge House. It was a blacksmith's house for more than a hundred years. Mr Churchill lived here with his family. His son Ned took the forge over but slowly the work changed from shoeing horses to repairing farm machinery, cars and then tractors. They were skilled smiths and in the thirties they made decorative main gates for Forde Abbey. The forge itself was situated in a long, low building next to the road, and several people today remember, as children, being sent in riding cart-horses bareback to be shod, then being put back up there and sent on home. The forge stopped being worked in the 1960s and the garage work took over.*'

Blacksmiths were crucial for keeping horses at work on the road and also for providing a huge range of goods, from defensive to decorative ironwork. Most would turn their hands to anything as well as shoeing horses, although some were specialist farriers. Large estates or farms would employ their own blacksmiths, and Felbridge, Surrey, on the London to Brighton road, had at least five forges in the mid-nineteenth century, when blacksmiths were most in demand.

There are still many jobs for blacksmiths, from the creation of railings and gates to village signs and weather-vanes, and, of course, the shoeing of horses – nowadays blacksmiths often have mobile forges and travel to shoe. The repetitive ringing of hammer on red metal, the sound of the bellows, the smell of bone burning as hot shoe is tested to shape of hoof, and the hiss of hot metal plunged into cooling water are no longer part of the language of the street.

See also GARAGES, GRAVESTONES, GYPSIES, HORSE CHESTNUT, HORSES & PONIES, LIME, RACECOURSES.

F O R T I F I C A T I O N S

Repeated conflict in history and prehistory has stamped itself on downland horizons, vulnerable coastlines and contested borders. The fortifications of the Iron Age, the Romano-British and the Saxons speak of internal struggles; those of the Tudors, the Napoleonic and twentieth-century wars of survival against threat from overseas. The dramatic British hill-forts, such as Maiden Castle in Dorset, set themselves against the Roman invaders but failed in the face of dynamic new continental warfare.

The Romans used a network of forts for policing their territories: a line across East Anglia quelled resistance there. Hadrian's Wall was their north-western frontier, a boundary made permanent by its namesake emperor in the AD 120s. Stretching from Newcastle upon Tyne in the East to Bowness-on-Solway in the West, it follows the Whin Sill, its hard face set against the north, tracing a line where two great tectonic

Hadrian's Wall and the Great Whin Sill, Northumberland.

183

plates once collided. Along the wall, place-names reflect its presence: Wallsend, Heddon-on-the-Wall, Wall, Walwick, Banks. Forts stood at intervals, such as Housesteads and the recently restored Segedunum at Wallsend. Every Roman mile saw a milecastle, and between a turret, as at Brunton, depicted on the Parish Map of Wall, Northumberland.

The Romans were finally threatened by Germanic tribes arriving on the South and East coasts: the Saxon Shore. At least eleven defensive forts were built, from Brancaster, Norfolk to Portchester, Hampshire, but they failed to stop the Saxons, who, six hundred years later under Alfred, were under attack themselves, from the Danes. Alfred's forts were thrown up using fortification methods that prehistoric hill-fort builders would have known.

England's Norman conquerors faced more troubles at home than abroad, but international relations declined and invasion threats returned. In the sixteenth century Henry VIII built a line of coastal bulwarks, blockhouses and artillery device forts in the South East, the Solent and Cornwall. Castles by name, though much less elaborate, the latter were compact, like a tiered cake, with a solely military purpose.

Other invasion fears came and passed. The great terror of the early nineteenth century was the French emperor Napoleon Bonaparte. Forts defended against an invasion that never came, from the small but hardy Martello towers to the extensive works at Dover: the Citadel, North Centre Bastion and Drop Redoubt. The Mersey was defended, too; the imposing red sandstone gate of Liscard Battery survives where Magazine Brow meets Fort Street. Many extraordinary Napoleonic forts and Palmerston Follies, around Portsmouth, for example, outlived their original purpose to be used into the twentieth century. Fort Amherst, built in 1756 to defend Chatham and the Medway in Kent, was still in use during the Second World War. Others moved into decommissioned retirement. The angular defensive banks and moats of the extensive seventeenth-century Tilbury Fort on the Thames are now protected by English Heritage.

See also BASTLES, BRIDGES, CASTLES, HILL-FORTS, LANDMARKS, MARTELLO TOWERS, PELE TOWERS, PILLBOXES, SEA FORTS.

FRESHWATER FISH

Most rivers would have evolved their own varieties of fish if their populations had become isolated. In 1653 Izaac Walton wrote of several kinds of trout, *'which differ in their bigness, and shape, and spots, and colour'*. He described the habits of a little trout called a Samlet in the Thames at Windsor, one named after Fordidge (nowadays Fordwich) in Kent, an Amerley (Amberley) trout from Sussex and a Bull trout in Northumberland. Today, truly wild brown trout can be found only in the upper reaches of a few rivers.

Before our interference, rivers in the East naturally had a few more fish species, relict populations from a time when the Thames was a tributary of the Rhine, such as the barbel, burbot (now extinct), silver bream and spined loach. The river Lymm in Lincolnshire boasts fourteen different species of fish.

Freshwater fish tend to occupy different sections or zones of a river, from the source to the mouth. In the hills or uplands, where most rivers emerge and the water is shallow, fast, cold and clear, only small trout, bullheads and a few minnows can survive. Below this, where there are deeper pools and some aquatic plants, grayling, trout and minnows can be found, and salmon may come up to spawn. Where the young river widens out the barbel zone begins. Chub, dace, roach, pike, perch and eel live here as well. The bream zone comprises the mature, lowland, slow-flowing part of the river and includes also barbel, roach, carp, tench, pike,

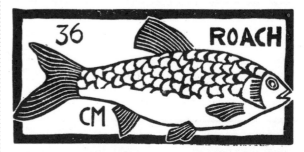

Fish of the Stour.

184

perch and eel. The thin-lipped and thick-lipped mullet, bass, flounder and sea trout frequent the tidal waters and estuaries. Twaite shad are returning to the Severn and Thames estuaries after many years of absence.

The homogenisation of fish species in rivers has come about not only because of pollution and the destruction of natural systems, such as meanders and washlands, but also from introductions, the translocation of species from one river to another, and restocking. The assemblages of fish in our rivers were much more distinctive before widespread stocking for angling and the removal of competitive species – ten million fish are bred to stock more than three thousand locations in England and Wales each year.

Populations of the 'king of fish', the Atlantic salmon, are seriously depleted in English rivers. The reasons for its demise are not understood, but global warming could be a factor, affecting its feeding grounds off Greenland. Other possible causes are netting in the North Sea, the effects of agricultural run-off, the silting up of spawning grounds, the impact of salmon farms, and low water at spawning times, when they need to swim upstream. Salmon occur in about 43 rivers in England, the majority in the North, South West and South. Serious declines are in the chalk rivers, such as the Test, Itchen and Hampshire Avon, but salmon are making a comeback in rivers that have recently been cleaned up, such as the Mersey, Tyne and Stour in the Midlands.

Recreational fishing, England's most popular pastime, is divided into two camps: angling or coarse fishing and game or fly-fishing. Jeremy Paxman explained: *'Pursuing fish is to return to the wilderness. The magic of fishing is something to do with the primeval challenge of our hunting ancestry; something to do with peace and solitude and utter concentration upon the unimportant, with time to watch the world turning around you.'* Trout and salmon, considered harder to catch, are lured by artificial flies. Perhaps we should be paying more attention to actual aquatic flies, which have declined by more than 75 per cent since the Second World War.

The fishing rights to most stretches of river, canal and lake are owned or leased by angling clubs, hotels and institutions. Fishermen know well the geography of their rivers; every stretch and pool has its name. Henry Williamson described them in *Tarka the Otter*: Junction Pool, Tunnel Pool, Dark Pool, Mouse Hole Pool.

Game fish traditionally were killed to be eaten, but now bylaws demand that any salmon and sea trout caught between specific dates are returned because of their growing scarcity. Most coarse fish are weighed and returned; some coarse fishermen do not know or care what the species are, it is the weight they are interested in, for competitive reasons. In France coarse fish are eaten, but they do not seem to suit the English palate any more.

See also CANALS, CHALK STREAMS, EELS, ESTUARIES, FLATNERS, FLOODS, LAKES, MOATS, PONDS, RIVERS, SEA FISH, WINTERBOURNES.

F R E T S

In Yorkshire, Durham and Northumberland the fret is a summer mist that occurs at the coast with moist air brought in on an easterly wind (and sometimes the tide). It is a frustrating phenomenon, being sometimes just tens of feet thick and a few hundred yards wide while just over the hill the day is beautiful. Villagers in Staithes, Yorkshire, with the arts group Blaize, captured its stealth:

From Eight Bells and Gun Gutter
Broom Hill and Lining Garth
Beck Side and Laverick Doorstones
Old Stubble to Barber's Yard
Up Slippery Hill to the Barras
Through Dog Loup up from the Staithe
The fret's creeping in from the harbour
As the tide brings it on the wave

The Scots call it the haar; in Scarborough, Yorkshire people know it as the sea roke. Local people and meteorologists have noticed that during the past twenty years frets have become less frequent because of the decrease in summer easterly winds, but the summer of 2004 seemed to bring a resurgence.

In north Norfolk the summer fret creates the best conditions for growing premium barley for malting. On the Isle of Wight the fret will occasionally creep in from the sea while cloud sits on the downs, leaving in between an extraordinary stratum of clear air with a view of both.

See also ALLEYS, BEER, CLOUDS, COASTS, CROPS, FOG & MIST, LIGHTHOUSES, SHIPPING FORECAST, WEATHER, WINDS.

F R I T I L L A R Y   M E A D O W S

Passing through Ducklington in Oxfordshire on a Sunday in the second half of April, you will wonder what all the fuss is about. The normally quiet village centre is packed, there is hardly a seat in the pub and the church hall is full of people taking tea. People travel to Ducklington from all over the country to see one of our most beautiful and rare flowers – the snake's head fritillary. Yet many villages have a memory of indulging in this way before wetland habitats were subjected to great pressure during the Ploughing for Victory campaign of the last war and further drainage for agriculture. This has reduced the flower to just a handful of places, such as Magdalen College Meadow in Oxford, North Meadow in Cricklade, Wiltshire, Lugg Meadow in Herefordshire and Framsden in Suffolk.

The flower is held in particular affection by local people, who, with the visitors, like to wander, head down, across the damp meadow admiring the purple and sometimes white

By contrast, the 108-acre North Meadow in Cricklade is a vast, open field, often flooded in winter. Here these dainty flowers grow in their millions – 75 per cent of the UK population. They are the last vestiges of what was once a commonplace plant of river valleys and attract five to six thousand people a year.

Gerard Manley Hopkins wrote in 1864 that the flower owes the name 'snake's head' to its *mottling and scaly look*. Local names include chequered lily in Somerset, dead men's bells in Shropshire, drooping bell of Sodom in Dorset, frockup in Buckinghamshire, Oaksey lily in Wiltshire, snake's-head lily in Buckinghamshire and Oxfordshire, Turk's head in Warwickshire and weeping widow in Northamptonshire and Staffordshire.

See also BELLS & BELL-RINGING, DAFFODILS, FIELDS, HAY MEADOWS, INGS, MAY DAY, MORRIS DANCING.

FROST & FROST HOLLOWS

While cities are well known as 'heat islands' (London is warmer than the country around on average by up to two degrees Celsius), locally there are memorable cold places. The Rickmansworth frost hollow has some notoriety: in December 1935 it took and still holds the UK record for the lowest average over a month – minus eight degrees. On 29 August 1936, in this corner of the Hertfordshire Chilterns, the temperature rose from 1.1 degrees to 29.4 degrees in nine hours.

Because cold air follows gravity, moving like water, whether in the deep coombes of the Chilterns, in the Weald of Sussex and Kent or between the drumlins in the Eden valley in Westmorland, frost hollows are common where the flow is impeded or slowed sufficiently to make pools of cold air. A railway or road embankment, even a garden wall, might act as a dam.

Houghall in the Wear valley near Durham boasts a frost hollow where temperatures have been known to plummet to minus six degrees in March. The drier the air, the more rapid the night-time cooling, so sandy regions are particularly prone to frost. A hollow in Breckland at Santon Downham on the Norfolk/Suffolk border has recorded air temperatures of minus 7.7 degrees in May.

During the intense frost of December 1784 Gilbert White and his friends were struggling to make sense of their thermometer readings. What worried White was that the high ground largely escaped the freezing temperatures he experienced near his house in Selborne, Hampshire. He assumed that his thermometer must be faulty. The explanation came in 1814, when Dr William Wells demonstrated that in the absence of wind, cold air, being heavier, sinks and collects in the hollows. On many a calm, clear night, an English valley is chillier than a hilltop up to as high as

186

blooms on Fritillary Sunday, the one day of the year when access to the field is permitted. Tea towels can be bought, together with mugs and pots of cultivated fritillaries. There is an exhibition, and the vicar will take pleasure in showing you the fritillary represented in the stained-glass vestry window, the carvings on the pews and pulpits, and the wedding dress displayed in the church that is embroidered with images of the flower.

The meadow in which the flowers grow is leased to a local farmer, who manages it for hay. Cutting the grass after the flowers have seeded guarantees the continuation of the flower, the event and a singular aspect of identity. Those who enjoy Morris dancing should note the purple and yellow ribbons on the sleeves of the dancers, which represent the purple of the fritillaries as well as the yellow of the dandelions, which are their neighbours. The women's team similarly sports purple breeches and waistcoats.

Up the road in the middle of Oxford, tantalisingly out of reach behind iron railings, the fritillaries in Magdalen Meadow are one of the most impressive floral sights in the country. With the density of the purple hanging heads against the fresh green of the grass, a backdrop of church and bells, it is easy to see why many make an annual pilgrimage, which each year becomes earlier than the traditional May Day.

2,600 feet. This can happen during any season but especially in early autumn and late spring.

Blackening of an oak's spring leaves is a sure sign of a frost pocket. In the Cotswolds trees on the slopes come into leaf much earlier than those in cold gardens below. Vineyards and orchards do better on slopes. Tall-tree orchards may keep their blossom as frost moves under their canopy, while dwarf trees may lose theirs and can even impede the flow.

In lowland England frosts are likely between November and April, but even in the South West James Crowden notes that '*The three nights cider makers most worry about are May 19, 20, 21. Indeed so serious is the problem . . . that folklore has stories in both Devon and Cornwall that the Devil did deals with certain brewers of beer, who sold their souls for three nights of late frost.*' One old saying goes: '*Till Culmstock Fair be come and gone, there mid be apples and mid be none*' – this Devon fair was held on 21 May.

Districts near the coast are less liable to frost, as warmer sea breezes drift inland. The further north and the higher you go the longer the season of frosts (apart from the anomalies of frost hollows).

Virginia Woolf in *Orlando* vividly imagined the atmosphere of the last of the great Thames frost fairs in February 1814. About twice a century the air remained cold enough for perhaps four weeks, and the nineteen arches of London Bridge impeded the progress of increasing numbers of ice floes. Once frozen solid it quickly became fashionable to promenade. It is said that the watermen, having lost their income, would open stalls to sell food and drink and pull people by horse in their boats. Skating and music, dancing and games, fires and roasts added to the fairground appeal. Since the building of the new London Bridge in 1831 with only five arches, and its twentieth-century successor, the changing climate, the heat island and the faster flow of the river have not been able to conspire to create such a spontaneous festival. Perhaps we need a Ministry of Frost.

See also BRIDGES, CIDER & CIDER ORCHARDS, DEVIL, EAST, FAIRS & FAIRGROUNDS, FEN SKATING, FOG & MIST, FOLKTALES, FRETS, ICE SKATING IN THE OPEN AIR, JACK AND JILL, MARKET GARDENS, NORTH, ORCHARDS, RIVERS, VINEYARDS, WEATHER, WINDS.

FUNICULAR RAILWAYS

Synonymous with 'cliff railways', as they are usually raised and lowered up and down an incline by cable (*funis* is Latin for rope), funicular railways appeared in the new seaside resorts in the nineteenth century. The earliest were on the rocky cliffs of Scarborough and Saltburn in Yorkshire. The latter, still working, extended to a pier at the foot of the cliff to make direct connections with pleasure boats. Scarborough's opened at South Cliff in 1884 and is still running, from the foreshore up 284 feet to the Esplanade.

Although many now run on electricity and diesel, such as the West Cliff lift at Hastings in Sussex, Scarborough's still depends on the water-balance principle. Both cars incorporate a water tank. Filling the tank of the car at the top makes it descend, pulling the lower one up. The lowered car discharges its load, while water is added at the top to continue the cycle.

The idea quickly spread. The famous railway linking Lynton and Lynmouth in Devon – the longest in the country – also uses the water-balance process. Without the funicular the two communities would still be wedged apart, the only link being a steeply twisting road. Southend in Essex and Torquay in Devon have them; Bournemouth in Hampshire has three; Folkestone in Kent, sadly, retains only one of three, although it has four tracks.

Inland, the Shipley Glen Tramway in Yorkshire gives visitors to Saltaire a lift up to the moors above, and Bridgnorth's Castle Hill tramway in Shropshire has ferried passengers between High and Low Town since 1891.

The last of the 'classic era' funicular railways to be built in England was at Fisherman's Walk in Pokesdown, Bournemouth, which is still active; since the 1980s several have appeared in theme parks.

See also BEACHES, BRIDGES, CLIFFS, DAGS, PIERS, STATIONS, TOLL-HOUSES.

187

FURRY DANCE

One of our oldest traditions, the Furry Dance takes place in the old stannary town of Helston on the Lizard peninsula in Cornwall on 8 May (or the Saturday before if the 8th falls on a Sunday or Monday).

It may be an ancient May Day festival, as the town band plays the Furry Dance music in the streets on 1 May, the week before, and 'Furry' derives from the Cornish *fer*, from the Latin *feria*, meaning fair. At some time the event became Christianised and the date was moved to the town's patron saint's day – the feast of the Apparition of St Michael the Archangel.

There are many stories about why these celebrations take place. One is that during a fight between St Michael and the devil, the devil took a stone from Hell's mouth and threw it at his adversary, who was hiding on St Michael's Mount. The stone missed by nine miles, landing in the yard of the Angel Hotel (the west wall still incorporates a large boulder). The people of the town danced for joy in the streets – and have done so ever since.

Houses and public buildings are decked with bunting, foliage and flowers on this communal celebration of the arrival of spring. At six in the morning the bells of St Michael's Church ring in the day. Originally there were separate dances for different strata of society, now they are organised by age. The first of the four dances takes place at seven and is for young couples.

At half past eight, the lads who are to take part in the Hal-an-Tow Maying procession, revived by the Old Cornwall Society in 1930, return from the woods and, waving branches of sycamore, stop at strategic places to sing a song, whose chorus goes:

> *Hal-an-Tow, jolly rumble, O!*
> *For we are up as soon as any day, O!*
> *And for to fetch the Summer home,*
> *The Summer and the May, O,*
> *For Summer is a come, O,*
> *And winter is a gone, O.*

The song, welcoming summer and recalling Robin Hood, the Spanish Armada, St George, St Michael and Aunt Mary Moses, is thought to be Elizabethan, with parts of the chorus from a fifteenth-century sea shanty from Bristol. '*The whole song seems to be a local version – and a rare survivor – of those which accompanied the "Robin Hood" May games once played from Cornwall to southern Scotland*', Charles Kightly wrote; he suggested Aunt Mary Moses could either be Maid Marion or the Virgin Mary, since *mowse* is Cornish for maid and virgin.

Next it is the turn of the hundreds of schoolchildren to dance, dressed in white with lilies of the valley in their buttonholes (symbols of May Day in France and Germany).

The main dance at midday is by invitation only. The town band strikes up (it plays the Furry Dance tune hundreds of times during the day) and the dancers emerge from the Guildhall. Dressed in top hats and morning suits or long summer dresses and hats, around 150 couples take part in the processional Morris dance along the street. They thread their way in and out of the houses and shops, attempting

to enter and leave by different doors to bring, in Christina Hole's words, '*the luck of Summer to the owners and tenants, and drive out the darkness of winter*'.

The last dance, at around five, is for young couples again, but by the end of the evening, Hole enthused, '*the whole town seems to be dancing*'. They are fuelled, no doubt, by a pint or two of Spingo, brewed at the Blue Anchor Inn, and Helston pudding, a kind of light Christmas pudding traditionally eaten on this day with Cornish clotted cream.

Spectators often comment on the dignity of the occasion, which remains fresh and true to itself. Locals say it is their most special day of the year.

See also BEER, DEVIL, FOOD, GROVELY RIGHTS DAY, MAY DAY, MORRIS DANCING, PUDDINGS, ROBIN HOOD, ROCKS, SYCAMORE, TURNING THE DEVIL'S STONE.

Helston, Cornwall.

Gill Sans Regular/Bold Italic, Eric Gill, 1929.

G A B L E S

Close to the Scots border, some stone farmhouses have gables that step down from the ridge. These crow-stepped gables are notable in East Anglia, too, though in brick, as are the curvaceous outlines of 'Dutch' gables, both owing much to Flemish connections, which were closer than those of the English hinterland for many centuries. Most are old, dating from the sixteenth to eighteenth centuries; standing in parallel or gable-end to the street, they interrupt the rhythm and catch the eye. They are found in the Trent valley and in Kent, too. In Nottinghamshire and Lincolnshire, as well as East Anglia, there are also gables with tumbled brickwork, patterns at right angles to the roof slope, which serve to tie the edge in; these again suggest connections with the Low Countries.

The steep and often compound gables that have such presence in the Cotswolds have high windows, the more ostentatious are edged by a smooth, stone, sliding parapet, with a chimney or finial on top. In the Pennines and the North York Moors the gable ends are finished at the eaves by kneelers – more or less ornate stone 'ears', which visually hold the parapet in place.

See also BANK BARNS, BRICKS, BUILDING STONES, CORRUGATED IRON, COTTAGES, DRYSTONE WALLS, FIELD BARNS, PANTILES, QUARRIES, SHINERS, THATCH, VILLAGES.

G A L L O P S

The expansive feel of Newmarket owes much to those wide, eastern skies and the perfect gallops around the town. Where Suffolk and Cambridgeshire meet, Newmarket Heath recorded its first horse race in 1622, but it was Charles II and his bawdy court that built the foundations.

The formalisation of racing began in a coffee house in the mid-1700s; now the Jockey Club owns two and a half thousand acres of land around the town. There are two racecourses, the Rowley Mile and the July Course. The July Course follows the line of the ancient earthwork of the Devil's Dyke, which leaves one wondering for just how long horses have been pitted against one another in this place. The National Stud is here; 75 trainers, yards and horse fitness centres fill the locality. The white rails of the racecourses stand out, and the proliferation of big trees in the stud fencing offers shelter and shade.

But the thrill of the place is in the horses, more than two thousand of them. Lindy Wale observes: 'It struck me that in Newmarket vehicles wait for the horses, whereas in most other towns the horse would defer to the traffic. And the chattering of the jockeys as they ride along is very social.' Foals stretch their long legs in paddocks with their mothers, strings of horses exercise in the early morning on New Winter Ground Canter, Yearling Canter, Back of the Flat or New Turf Gallops. The sound of horses on the gallops raises the blood pressure, but it is somehow a domestic affair, the jockeys still bantering at full speed.

The thick, A-shaped hedges that line the roads into town fill the air with the scent of privet in June, but 'bushes' here refer to white markers that line the gallops, which are moved to conserve the quality of the turf, although there is some wood fibre for all-weather use. Access to the gallops is open to people walking except when the riders are out from dawn to 1pm on Monday to Saturday. Special crossing places over the roads, and horse walks through the town, on the inner side of the pavements and with a small hedge to separate walkers, emphasise where you are and what is king.

With increasing sophistication more owners sought good ground for training their horses and, in the 1830s, fashion drew some of the fraternity to the Wiltshire and Berkshire Downs. Here the extensive gallops curve and play with the rise and fall of the chalk hills, gashes in the turf being echoed in the long stretches of white rails.

Middleham Gallops, nearly a thousand feet up on the High Moor above Wensleydale, Yorkshire, offers the drama of exposure to wind, mists and stunning views as well as strings of horses being put through their paces. Further east, Malton in the Howardian Hills and the chalk wolds provide excellent gallops. In Bishop Burton the pub is called the Altisdora after the locally trained winner of the 1813 St Leger.

It is not all heath, moor, wold and down. Birkdale Sands in Lancashire famously built the stamina of Red Rum, who won the Grand National at nearby Aintree three times.

See also BEACHES, CAFÉS, DOWNLAND, EARTHWORKS, FOG & MIST, HEATHLAND, HORSES & PONIES, MOORLAND, POINT TO POINT, PUBS, RACECOURSES, WINDS.

191

G A M E S

More than two hundred teams were playing stoolball in Sussex in 1990 and it is still going strong, mainly as a women's game. Sussex schools also compete in girl's junior and senior tournaments. First recorded in 1450, stoolball has been described as one of the ancestors of rounders, baseball and cricket. It was popular across the country in the seventeenth century, but is now confined to Sussex, east Hampshire, west Kent and Surrey. The rules are similar to those of cricket, but wickets – square boards mounted on stakes, sixteen yards apart – replace the stumps and the wooden bats are

short-handled and round-headed. Because the ball is thrown underarm and does not bounce (as in rounders and baseball), the game can be played on any reasonable turf. Two teams of eleven take it in turns to bat and field; overs are of eight balls and centuries are scored by making fifty runs.

In Somerset a number of freestanding, very high walls are vestiges of the game of fives, popular there in the eighteenth century. At the Anchor Inn, Combwich, a fine, flat-topped, twenty-foot-wide and thirty-foot-high brick wall has buttresses on either side, as has the wall at the pub in Bishops Lydeard. At South Petherton and Shepton Beauchamp two similar giant, freestanding fives walls of local stone with arched tops look like the remains of a grand building, but were built by former inns where there was local enthusiasm for the game.

Fives was usually played with gloved hands (the name may come from 'a bunch of fives') and was played by striking a small, hard ball against the wall, using the ledges and buttresses as bouncing-off places to try to prevent the opponent (either a single player or a pair) from returning the ball. (Fives may have evolved from the Basque *pelota* or from the French game of *jeu de paume*, and has similarities with squash and real tennis.) Before inns or the gentry built special fives walls, the game was played against any available wall – usually a church tower. At Martock church, niches in the buttresses show where players repeatedly climbed up to

retrieve their balls from the roof. Damage to windows and masonry made the game unpopular with the clergy, who did their utmost to ban it.

In the 1850s, as fives was losing its appeal in the villages and towns of Somerset and elsewhere, it was being taken up by the public schools of Eton, Rugby and Winchester, which each continue to play a variety of fives. At Eton it was played at first against the chapel wall '*among the strange collection of ledges, steps, and drain holes*', according to the *Oxford Companion to Sports and Games*, and now takes place in a three-walled court based on the chapel wall, with a ledge along the front wall and 'pepperbox' (irregular buttress) at the end of the left-hand wall. The Winchester fives courts are not quite rectangular, with a projecting buttress on the left-hand wall, whereas the Rugby court is rectangular, measuring 28 by eighteen feet with a wooden board across the front wall.

See *also* BOAT RACE, BOWLING GREENS, BUTTS, CHEESE ROLLING, CRICKET, FEN SKATING, HARE PIE SCRAMBLE, HAXEY HOOD GAME, ICE SKATING IN THE OPEN AIR, INNS, PUB GAMES, RACECOURSES, SHROVETIDE GAMES, WRESTLING.

G A N S E Y S

Guernsey and Jersey are well known for their cattle, but have no history of sheep farming. So how did they give us the blue woollen sweaters and generic names of gansey and jersey? Apparently Sir Walter Raleigh, Governor of Jersey in the early 1600s, initiated links between Newfoundland and the islands, which built a trade of building ships and making garments for seamen on imported wool. Guernseys are typically deep blue, while jerseys may be of other colours, too.

Seamen and especially fishermen around the north-east coast of England had a tradition of wearing sealskin that was gradually superseded by thick, knitted ganseys, which are virtually waterproof. The patterns belonging to different fishing families have passed down through generations. A book published by Tyne and Wear County Council Museums explains: '*They were knitted by eye, without a written pattern. Many of the designs incorporated in them had symbolic meaning. It is sometimes maintained that patterns were unique to particular villages or that it was possible to identify the origin of a drowned fisherman from the pattern of his gansey. While it was true that a fisherman's wife might be able to identify her own work, patterns were not unique, but were passed between villages, especially through marriage.*'

The comings and goings of Scots fishermen also ensured that patterns informed one another up and down the east coast. Many had the initials of the wearer knitted in. The stitches or *masks* (a Viking/Norwegian word) have particular names: zigzags were named after the steep paths winding up the cliffs; marriage lines or 'ups and downs' were a double zigzag; rope/cable, net or herring masks were stitches used in Flamborough,

192

Marbles championship, Tinsley Green, Sussex; fives wall at The Fleur-de-Lis, Stoke sub Hamdon, Somerset.

Yorkshire; double and single moss stitches were called sand and shingle; a double plait was print o'the hoof – like hoof marks in the sand; triple sea wave came from Northumberland; rig and fur, from Runswick Bay and Staithes in Yorkshire, was named after ridge and furrow fields.

Not until Gladys Thompson started to 'collect' the patterns in the 1930s were they written down. '*When I first remember Filey, every doorway in the old town held a knitter, in a black or coloured sunbonnet, with their needles flicking in and out so quickly it was impossible to follow their movements.*' Although some patterns are known by town or village, from Whitby, Scarborough and Staithes in Yorkshire to Craster in Northumberland, others carry the knitter's name – Mrs Foster from Withernsea, Betty Martin from Filey, Miss Ester Rutter from Seahouses, Mrs Rowe from Newbiggin.

Worked on five needles with the sleeves included, ganseys have no seams. Most of the ganseys of Yorkshire, Durham and Northumberland are dark blue, but in Amble on the river Coquet in Northumberland different colours are worn: grey for summer, blue for winter and black on Sundays and for funerals.

The tradition is dying, some say because the knitters can no longer get 'wassit' or fivefold (ply) double worsted of the quality needed.

See also BOATS, COBLES, RIDGE & FURROW, SEA FISH, SHEEP, ZIGZAGS.

G A P S

While the wind and weather diffuse through the Cheshire Gap, Watford Gap is the place we confuse with Watford (just north of London) and hence the start of all things North. As a service station on the M1 it is less memorable. In fact, *the* Watford Gap, a pass near the Northamptonshire village of Watford, has been the focus of transport communications for generations. The northern line of the Grand Union canal was built through here in 1814, the London and Birmingham Railway (now the West Coast Main Line) in 1838 and the motorway in 1959. They were all following Watling Street, now the A5, laid out by Roman surveyors, who were probably tidying up an even older way that took the easiest and flattest route for man and beast. The hills here may be hardly noticeable to the car, but the canal clambers through seven locks and jostles with rail, road and motorway

to squeeze between Watford and Welton Lower Farm. This is the watershed between the river catchments of the Avon/Severn and the Nene/Ouse.

The Goring Gap in Oxfordshire is guarded by the Sinodun Hills, topped by Wittenham Clumps. The Dorsetshire Gap seems a much more tranquil place. At this secret spot in the centre of the county four sunken ways meet below Nettlecombe Tout (tout is a lookout). Their status now is bridleway, and on horse or on foot you feel yourself stepping among ancestors.

See also CAFÉS, CANALS, CLUMPS, FOOTPATHS, HILLS, NORTH, RAILWAYS, RIVERS, ROADS.

G A R A G E S

Of the fifteen thousand or so motor garages in Britain at the beginning of the twenty-first century, few are independently owned with roots in the community. Many originated as blacksmiths swung from repairing farm equipment to cars, and where there were cars, there was a demand for petrol. The Forge at Condover in Shropshire is one such: an early seventeenth-century timber-framed building that became a petrol station later in life.

Petrol originally was bought by the can from ironmongers and pharmacies (it was a treatment for head lice). The first roadside pumps didn't appear until Shrewsbury adopted one in the 1910s (the town also had one of the earliest garages in around 1900). The first station proper, at Aldermaston in Berkshire, was introduced in 1920 by the Automobile Association for its members. The Store Street garage is London's oldest; evolved from the Duke of Bedford's Bloomsbury mews, it continues as a petrol station.

Paul Barker suggests that '*the petrol station is the last prop of local life. It's the village shop; here you can glance at the Sunday paper . . . while edging towards the milk fridge. The sale of petrol seems marginal.*' Tintagel in Cornwall once had five filling stations. Since the closure of Fry's in 2000, it has had none: '*Another victory for the supermarkets, another tragic loss for village life*', David Flowers writes.

Modern-style petrol stations and canopies appeared in the 1960s, increasingly with self-service pumps. Offering fuel separately from the selling and maintenance of vehicles marked a shift, the petrol companies competing for and exerting power.

Some old-style independent stations still operate. Weston's Cider runs a distinguished corrugated-iron garage at Much Marcle in Herefordshire. Potter Brothers at Rowgate in Kirkby Stephen, Westmorland was described by Simon de Burton in 2004 as having been '*caught in a time warp for more than fifty years*'. Petrol station design expert Helen Jones singles out Clovelly Cross filling station in Devon, designed in 1930 by Bideford architects Orphoot and Whiting, and

193

'an independently owned 1928 station in Colyford . . . built in the style of a Devon cottage'. In 2003 local people fought off plans to redevelop the Grade II-listed G. and T. Motors in Newbury, Berkshire. Other garages have taken on new uses. One on the A442 in Staffordshire is now a farm shop, complete with canopy. In Northwich, Cheshire a black-and-white 1920s building is now a café-bar; above the door is the word 'garage' in stained glass.

The corrugated-iron Shepherd's Garage in Little Somerford continues to serve the community and carry off prizes in north Wiltshire's flower festival. But most garages today are workaday affairs, under the arches of a city viaduct or in a new metal shed on an industrial estate, or along the main road with rows of gleaming vehicles displaying prices on their windscreens.

The Holbrook Garage in Bisley, Gloucestershire offers many surprises. This was the first in the UK to sell blended biodiesel in 2002; bioethanol will come soon. But Roger Budgeon has been pioneering sustainability for more than two decades: '*The new car workshop, built in 1994, is a surprisingly clean and pleasant environment. It has lots of natural light, a rainwater collection system for flushing loos and pressure-washing of cars, solar and wind systems for heating water and producing electricity, and is cosy in winter due to good insulation and heating by waste oil.*' The garage demonstrates and trials these systems, which it also sells from the forecourt Green Shop.

See also AIRFIELDS, BEACH HUTS, BLACK POPLAR, BUNGALOWS, CIDER & CIDER ORCHARDS, CORRUGATED IRON, FORGES, MEWS, ROADS, SHOPS.

GARDENS

Gardening is about domesticating the green, originally to grow food, medicinal and useful plants and some for aesthetic pleasure. Few of us garden for self-sufficiency, and along the spectrum of gardeners there is a defining watershed between those who want to work with nature and those who want to dominate, or even extinguish it.

Old cottage gardens expressed much of their place; wild plants were brought in from the surrounding fields and lanes, cuttings were swapped and seedlings shared. There were local and regional differences in the kinds of plants grown, perhaps some had been imported for monastic gardens or could cope easily with salt spray. People relied on plants that did well in their places and differentiation was amplified.

Currently, rather than capitalising on what grows best, we presume to grow anything we fancy, whatever the soil, climate or setting, whatever the age and style of the house or history in the land. Generations of knowledge of plant cultivation has become diluted, gardens and plants have become ever more to do with fashion and hence time, rather than place. Propelled by the television show, book and magazine explosion, antipodean tree ferns, water 'features', patios, decking, gravels and boulders and 'low maintenance' planting are pushing aside the postage stamp lawn and the edging border that has dominated for decades. Today's gardens are often even more formal, there is less neighbourly plant swapping and more quick fixes from the garden centre. Christopher Alexander noted that the more artificial 'have none of the quality which brings a garden to life – the quality of a wilderness, tamed, still wild, but cultivated enough to be in harmony with the buildings which surround it and the people who move in it'.

We shall all be challenged as we have to take a more responsible attitude towards water conservation, ravaging the flora of other continents and using herbicides and pesticides. Perhaps the fetish for demanding annual bedding plants and showing off with rare exotics will pass. If the gardener's imperative was to sustain nature rather than subdue it, to understand and take advantage of local potential, the mix of wildlife and the coherence of locality would be much increased.

William Robinson wrote in 1883 that '*we should not so much follow an idea because we have seen it carried out somewhere else, but rather seek things that suit the ground*'. It is the predominant plants – the ones that find the soil, aspect and microclimate to their liking – that characterise places;

the locally typical that give the real colour, seldom the rare. These may be indigenous or introduced: campanula along the pavements of Dartmouth Park in London, primroses on Devon banks, fine ferns in the Lake District. When the garden writer Mary Keen moved into her new Cotswold garden, one of her first projects was to remove '*a bank of heather and hypericum more reminiscent of Scotland or Surrey than Gloucestershire*'.

Cultivated plants are as much to do with people as with nature. We have influenced their distribution as well as their shapes, sizes and colours. Britain has produced many inventive amateur and professional gardeners and plantsmen and -women. Celebrating them and their plant progeny in the places where they lived and worked creates new richness. Plants came to us along the Silk Road, the Baltic and Mediterranean Sea ways, as well as from Europe for thousands of years before the Victorian plant hunters plundered the world. Many exotic plants have naturalised here, from the apple to the wallflower, the sweet chestnut to the buddleia.

People, too, have naturalised here, bringing with them plants and tastes that have extended and reinvigorated our gardens and palates. Many an allotment as well as garden echoes the tastes of Turk and Bengali, Jamaican and Somali. In Notting Hill, London the chances are high of finding a balcony or basement splash of bright colour tended by a Caribbean enthusiast.

Geology is irrevocably local. Gardens with walls of local stone not only reveal the underlying rock but also display local walling techniques. The pale Carboniferous limestone walls of the south-east Derbyshire villages of Carsington and Brassington, covered with aubretia in spring, or the valerian-topped oolitic limestone walls of Milborne Port in Somerset, conspire to tell you where you are. These are precious assets made the more valuable since the closure of small local quarries and the high cost of stone means that they will not be replaced.

Many of the mellow brick boundary walls in Great Bowden, Leicestershire still have the traditional coping; the Sussex and Kent Weald has its chestnut paling fences; Bournemouth abounds in rhododendron and laurel hedges; fuchsia hedges prove hardy in Cornwall; privet binds the housing estates of north-west Nottingham; holly hedges hold together Osmaston in Derbyshire – all add to the identity of these places. Front gardens in particular can be so generous to the street.

The most significant plants for any place are mature trees. The Scots and maritime pines first planted by the Victorians in the 1800s in Bournemouth and Poole bestow a unique identity. The fruit trees planted when Hampstead Garden Suburb was built in north London offer a blowsy display in spring and a great crop of fruit in autumn. Chris Bray of Worcestershire county council said '*the survival of the black pear will help to retain the county's identity*', as the council made the Worcester black pear available for garden planting.

Watching new development pace across any area one is struck by the lack of care for what is already prospering, from trees to topsoil – most are simply removed and the gardens seen as commodities rather than our link with nature. This is a far cry from the approach advocated by John Brookes: '*the way ahead is to take a closer look at the garden within its setting, to study the natural plant associations which create that setting and to learn from them*'.

Allowing the locality to express itself through the plants and their inclinations to live together with you is not to allow nature to take its own course – that would no longer be a garden – but to move towards a more subtle mixing of nature and culture. Derek Jarman's garden on Dungeness, with its found sculptures and sparse, drought-loving plants, expresses wonderfully the empathy of the gardener with this great shingle bank on the south coast of Kent.

See also ALLOTMENTS, APPLES, APRICOTS, BRICKS, CHERRIES, COBNUTS, COTTAGE GARDENS, COTTAGES, DOG ROSES, DRYSTONE WALLS, FENCES, FLINT, GOOSEBERRIES, HEDGES, LAWN, TOPIARY, WEM SWEET PEA SHOW.

GARGOYLES & GROTESQUES

195

Crouch we and leer from our quoin of the guttering,
And rain in our jowls goes a-gurgling and spluttering

Clive Sansom, from 'Gargoyles'

Gargoyles are waterspouts, '*projecting gutter stones*', according to Geoffrey Grigson. Their purpose is to drain and eject rain from the large lead roofs of churches, cathedrals and other important buildings, far enough away to keep the walls and foundations dry. The name comes from the French *gargouille*, meaning 'throat'.

From the twelfth and thirteenth centuries it became fashionable for church masons to decorate their buildings with carvings, symbols for mainly illiterate congregations. Monsters and grotesques were made to frighten people into obedience; demons guarded the church from bad spirits.

The fertile imagination of the English is exemplified in the gargoyle and non-functional grotesque. Some are terrifying monsters, the stuff of nightmares – half man/half dog, lion or dragon. Others are vulgar or humorous representations of local people, perhaps poking fun at pompous clergy or officials. Some have lead gutter spouts issuing from their open mouths to make the water shoot out further.

A huge sandstone fish, sturgeon-like, leans out precariously, mouth agape, from the tower of St Mary's Church at Stogumber in Somerset. A dozen or so towns and villages in south and south-west Somerset – from Long Sutton,

Langport and Curry Mallet to Westonzoyland and Middlezoy near Bridgwater – are known for their tall, fifteenth- and early sixteenth-century church towers, embellished by an extraordinary array of grotesques, known locally as hunky punks. Peter Poyntz Wright suggests: '*This term has probably developed from older English usage and the two words "hunkers" and "punchy". Hunkers means squatting on the haunches, and punchy means short or squat characterised by a short thick set body and short legs. Both these meanings fit very closely the style and appearance of the hunky punks.*'

These stone carvings were made for aesthetic rather than functional reasons. Leaning out precariously from the centre and corners, as if leaping for freedom, they add interest to and break up the lines of these Perpendicular towers. The carvings are mainly of imaginative, mythological animals, some influenced by heraldry or folklore: half lions, dragons, goats, boars, dogs, cockerels, basilisks and griffins, with wide-open mouths, pointed or castellated teeth and puffed-out chests. A number of the carvings are of a dragon with a stone in its mouth, apparently a depiction of a local story about a menacing dragon that was killed by someone who threw a stone down its throat. Many of these carvings, especially those carved from Ham stone, are badly weathered, and imagination is needed to decipher their extraordinary sky-high silhouettes.

St Peter's Church at Winchcombe, on the edge of the Cotswolds in Gloucestershire, is famous for its gathering of forty gargoyles, known locally as Winchcombe Worthies. These are carvings of people around at the time when the church was being built in the 1460s – one is an unhappy-looking fellow with wings and a top hat.

The Oxford colleges and churches abound with fine medieval carvings, but few true gargoyles remain, since their function was replaced by the modern drainpipe. In his tour of Oxford's gargoyles and grotesques, John Blackwood has found that eleven have disappeared from the front of All Souls College since 1675, but there are some '*hybrids, figures which take water from the guttering and pass it into the head of the drainpipe beneath*'.

This must have happened in other places, or the carvings worn away by acid rain and the ravages of time to the extent that the fine detail has been lost. The masons in Oxford have an ongoing programme of restoring and creating new grotesques and heads, many of which depict their colleagues and bosses.

See also BESTIARY, BUILDING STONES, CHURCHES, DRAGONS, GREEN MAN, SUFFOLK PUNCHES.

GASHOLDERS

Gas had arrived to light the streets and homes of the capital by 1812, when the London Gas Light and Coke Company was founded. The gas was stored in pressurised tanks, or gasholders – the word is now used synonymously with gasometers.

The 270-foot towers (one has 'LHR' painted on it in large letters so that pilots stay on track for Heathrow Airport) with metal tracery sprang up in the Victorian era. They come in three distinct types: guide frame, in which a gas-tight container rises and falls under pressure along vertical runners in a cylindrical water tank; spiral, where the guiding rails coil up the side of the tank so that effectively it screws itself up and down; and waterless or tankless, which eschews the containing water tank in favour of a cylinder and piston method of keeping the gas under pressure. Many were very small, leaving us Gasworks Lanes in Ashford, Kent and Bourton-on-the-Water, Gloucestershire.

The manufacture of coal gas by the carbonisation of coal had all but ceased by the early 1970s. Many gasholders were retained for temporary storage of North Sea natural gas, but cheaper and more efficient methods ensured their eventual redundancy. They became symbols of a past age, sometimes reviled as eyesores, sometimes admired.

Michael Lancaster praised sensitive paintwork: '*Rust helps with the job of colouring gas-holders, producing interesting combinations. Very occasionally they are carefully painted in bands of analogous hue in ascending order of lightness; sometimes they are painted green in the misguided impression that they will be lost in the landscape. But usually they are painted a light greenish-grey which makes them remarkably inconspicuous in the town.*' Later, due to the

· Hunky punk, Staple Fitzpaine, Somerset; St Peter's Church, Winchcombe, Gloucester. Kennington Oval, London.

impetus of the garden festival, the gasholders of Gateshead in County Durham were brightly painted.

The gasholder beside the Oval cricket ground is an international television star, part of the London skyline and a local landmark. So, too, were the beautifully intricate set of three behind St Pancras Station in London, memorable in their red and black livery against the sunset. Two have been dismembered and stored, reputedly to be re-erected after the building of the new Eurostar rail-link terminus.

In 2002 there were only 22 listed examples of Victorian gasholders – for example in Kirkby Stephen in Westmorland, Great Yarmouth in Norfolk, Sunderland in County Durham, Fulham in west London and Carlisle in Cumberland. The others are an easy target for developers, frequently in a deteriorating state of repair on decaying 'brownfield' sites, where the hand of regeneration might be poised to strike at any moment with no feel for the quiddity of the place. Rarely, demolition is followed by echoes of what has gone before, such as the round buildings of the Tate at St Ives in Cornwall and the Mellors cutlery factory in Hathersage, Derbyshire.

Stuart Burroughs, curator of the Museum of Bath at Work in Bath, Somerset, is one of an increasing number who believe that the guiding frames that hold the rising bell of the holders could be retained and used to support temporary or permanent structures. At least one of Bath's redundant examples is being considered for retention, offering identity to the redevelopment scheme for the former industrial district by the river.

See also COOLING TOWERS, CRICKET, EARTH PIGMENTS, INDUSTRIAL CHIMNEYS, LANDMARKS.

G A T E S

The wooden field gate, with its gateposts and detail, offers a small working text of vernacular engineering, with a long history and a previously insistent geography. The demanding alternative in woodless parts, still in use on the Isles of Scilly, is to fill up the hole with piled stones and remove them every time you need access.

In the gritstone of the Forest of Bowland in Lancashire the gate 'stoops' and wall copings are carved with sophisticated parallel grooves. At Appleton-le-Moors in Yorkshire dark balls on the tops of the gateposts are known locally as the devil's eyes. Sturdy gateposts of red sandstone guard the fields of the Carndurnock peninsula in Cumberland. In the mountains of Borrowdale, Cumberland you may see the remains of tall, slender slate posts, with five or six holes through which poles could be fitted. In Yorkshire, in the Dales and around Halifax, slip gates worked on a similar principle – on one side of the gap the stone posts have holes, on the opposite side inverted L-shaped slots. In Nidderdale they are called stang stoops.

One simple and effective form of hinging to make a gate swing open and closed can still be seen occasionally in the walls of Westmorland and Cumberland. The vertical pole of the gate sits in holed stones, top and bottom, enabling it to turn; slate makes it easy. Some have traced this method to the Etruscans and Egyptians. In 1898 Joseph Wright followed this ancient hinging method in the words har, harl, haur, haw and her, through Scotland, Northumberland, Durham, Cumberland, Yorkshire and Lancashire and as far south as Somerset, Wiltshire and Hampshire. The heavy hinge-end vertical is still often called the arle-, arr-, hartree-, hur- or harr-end of the gate. So dialect remains a conduit of culture as much as the gates themselves; our history follows us in words as well as artefacts.

Gates with bars closer together near the ground tell of sheep and lambs, sturdy higher gates of cattle and horses. They had to be strong and were made to last sixty to a hundred years. Oak is still the favoured wood, combining durability with lightness, followed by ash, Scots pine or larch, depending on locality. Cleft oak gates must have been common and they persist in oak-rich counties, such as Sussex, but mostly the less durable sawn oak has beaten its forbear in popularity for ease of making. In the Weald of Kent and Sussex, sweet chestnut is much used. The Sussex heave-gate is a simple cleft oak or chestnut lift gate with a diminutive fence of verticals along the bottom. Hazel hurdles are sometimes still used to fill a gap.

We can speculate that gates, like hedges and walls, had been perfected locally over hundreds of years. The gate pattern that now predominates usually has five bars, closer together at the bottom, and is braced by a wide V crossed by an inverted V. Some claim an Oxfordshire beginning, some believe it originated in East Anglia. In Devon and parts of Cornwall gates have perhaps five or six bars, two verticals and a diagonal brace from the top bar at the harr-end to the bottom of the first vertical. Most have tall harr-ends with the brace starting high above the top bar. In Berkshire, Surrey

197

and Buckinghamshire you may see gates that have a top bar thickened at the harr-end, with a brace that flies diagonally up from the bottom of the harr-end.

Gloucestershire gates had beautifully carved harr-ends and elegant ironwork. Much pride went into their making – they were to be read by your great-grandchildren, after all. Anthea Brian reports that initials and dates have been found discreetly carved into the hinge sides of estate gates in her part of Herefordshire. In the nineteenth century overlarge O, W and M were used more as brand than brace. Y for Yeatman is still in use throughout the estate at Stock Gaylard in Dorset, more interesting for the fact that 'gyeat' is how the locals would say 'gate', as in William Barnes's poem 'The geate a-vallen to' – straight from the Old English *geat*. Names such as Yate, Yately, Woodyates, Donyatt and Leziate all suggest gate. Gate itself may mean 'gate', unless its root is Danish, as in York and Nottingham, where it means 'street'.

There is resurgent interest in the particularity of gate patterns. After all, this is a subtle way to tell people where they are. Common Ground has tried to persuade landowning agencies, such as the Forestry Commission and local authorities, to research, encourage and commission local patterns. We want to be able to say, with Moreland: '*In some parts of the country it would be possible to locate oneself pretty exactly by a study of the design of local gates.*'

Once you have noticed these small signatures, you cannot help looking in the hope that particularity and local knowledge, woodland and jobs are still tied together through this simplest of forms. It is clear from the range of gates still being made that it is possible to achieve standards without standardisation.

See also DEVIL, FENCES, FIELDS, FOOTPATHS, HEDGES, HOLLOW WAYS, OAK, RHYNES, ROADS, STILES, SWEET CHESTNUT, WALLS, WAYSIDE & BOUNDARY CROSSES.

G H Y L L S

Surprisingly this word is at home in the deep valleys of the greensand in the Sussex Weald, although it is an Old Norse word with a hard 'g'. Meaning a ravine or a deep and narrow valley with a stream, it is most often used in the North West. Perhaps its most extreme example by name, Hell Gill lies near the Pennine watershed, and the beck that inhabits it is the border of Yorkshire and Westmorland. 'Hell' here might imply 'hidden', but Roger Deakin's experience, recounted in *Waterlog*, suggests otherwise: '*The torrent continually sought to sweep me with it, and so I slithered and climbed down Hell Gill's dim, glistening sides, through a succession of cold baths, in one long primal scream.*' He described the gorge as being like '*a pothole whose roof has cracked open sixty feet or more above. It plunges almost vertically down the hillside for four hundred yards in a continuous series of waterfalls dropping into overflowing pools of hollowed limestone.*'

Sometimes it crops up in place-names, such as Gaisgill, Reagill and Sleagill in Westmorland. But it is mostly called into topographical use, though often reduced to stream names, perhaps by the original Ordnance Surveyors, as in Great Gill, Washer Gill and Raygill Sike – all of which feed the upper Ure – Gunnerside Gill above the Swale and Hebden Gill, all in Yorkshire.

Further memorable usage is in Gaping Ghyll, the pothole below Ingleborough, Yorkshire, which is more than 350 feet deep and, reputedly, could harbour York Minster. In Dorset, Devon and Somerset the words gwyle, goil and goyle have a similar ring. Chris Slade says that in Dorset '*all the ones I have seen are small, steep-sided, wooded valleys. Probably it has the same root as gully.*'

See also BECKS, BOURNES, BROOKS, BURNS, CHALK STREAMS, CHINES, DENES, DIALECTS, FORDS, GREENSAND, LIMESTONE, RHYNES, RIVER NAMES, RIVERS, SOUGHS, WATERFALLS, WINTERBOURNES.

G I A N T S

At Porthleven in Cornwall a fifty-ton erratic boulder, dropped by a passing iceberg in the Pleistocene, is known as the Giant's Rock. While we employ science to explain our topography, our forbears used legend, folktale and story to endow places with significance or embed places in their memory. Hills in particular must have been sacred, since only the emergent Christian could have been responsible for associating the devil with so many pointed hills, ancient earthworks or heaps of stone. Some of the stories are retold in different locations in a way that suggests they were translocated rather than derived from the land. These explanations often have alternative tales involving giants.

The giant Gorm, Ruth Tongue recounted, '*one day was wandering across England carrying a nice sizeable hill on his*

198

spade. Why he had dug it up he had forgotten, and what he meant to do with it . . . he didn't quite know.' What seems to have happened then is that he tripped off the end of the Cotswolds and dropped the spadeful, which became Maes Knoll in Somerset. In leaning on his spade he made the Wansdyke, and in running away from a challenge by the Lord of Avon he fell and drowned in the Bristol Channel, forming the islands of Steep Holm and Flat Holm. Other tales claim that these islands are the work of the devil. The same confusion occurs in Cornwall – *'One day the devil having nothing to do/Built a great hedge from Lerryn to Looe'* – yet this feature bears the name of the Giant's Hedge. In Somerset it is said that giants emerge from thousand-year-old willow trees.

Giants' graves are found countrywide. For example, the four hog-back stones in Penrith churchyard, Cumberland mark the grave of Ewan Caeserius, a fifth-century killer of

monsters and wild boars. Near Topcliffe in Yorkshire a giant terrorised the country for humans, whose bones he ground to make his bread at Dalton Mill. A young lad called Jack, a long-kept prisoner, finally outwitted the giant by putting out his single eye, then escaping, wrapped in the fur of the giant's dog. The giant soon died and the great mound near the mill is his tomb.

With all of these tall stories it was inevitable that someone such as Jack the giant killer would emerge. In Cornwall, off the coast at Marazion, he slayed a giant called Cormoran, whose wife, terrified, dropped the rock she was carrying, which, falling from her apron, made St Michael's Mount. In Norfolk it was Tom Hickathrift, a young man more than eight feet tall, who, wielding a cart axle and wheel as an improvised sword and shield, rid the marshes between Ely and Wisbech of a demanding giant.

Giants, it is said, populated Albion when Brutus, fleeing from Troy, landed here; his champion Corineus fought

and slayed the leader of the giants (some say his name was Gogmagog, some say that Gog and Magog survived). Brutus gave his name to Britain, Corineus to Cornwall, and New Troy was established – we know it now as London. The parade for the Lord Mayor's Show is headed by the giants Gog and Magog, the guardians of the City. There are formidable carvings of them by David Evans in the Guildhall in the City of London, dating from 1953. During the early sixteenth century, municipal records reveal that people were paid eight pence to keep cut and clean the giant figure of Gogmagog on Plymouth Hoe. The Gog Magog hills south of Cambridge attract speculation that there were carved giants at Wandlebury Camp, based upon the name and medieval tales.

As with the extraordinary hill figures of the Cerne Giant in Dorset and the Long Man of Wilmington in Sussex, the thrill these presences offer is in their very enigma, and the challenge is to keep faith with the locality in passing on the intertwining tales – fantastical and academic. Giants are figures in the land; visible or not, they particularise the place.

See also ALBION, BARROWS, BLACK DOGS, BONFIRE NIGHT, BOUNDARIES, CARNIVALS, CHALK, DEVIL, DRAGONS, EARTHWORKS, FOLKTALES, HAUNTED PLACES, HEDGES, HILL FIGURES, HILL-FORTS, HILLS, HOLLY, MAY DAY, MIDSUMMER DAY, NOTTING HILL CARNIVAL, OAK, 'OBBY 'OSSES, PARGETING, ROCKS, STACKS, STANDING STONES.

199

GIN

The original Dutch courage, geneva (from the French *genièvre*, meaning juniper), was sold by chemists for tropical fevers, stomach and gall bladder problems in Holland in the early seventeenth century. It was introduced to the British during the Thirty Years War.

More than two hundred years ago, the makers of gin for the Royal Navy (at 57 per cent proof) were attracted by the softness and purity of the water of Plymouth, and so proud were they of the clarity and purity of their product that they were the first company to use clear glass bottles. Plymouth Gin is still made in the old Dominican monastery, Black Friars, and is the only gin to hold a Protected Designation of Origin, singling it out as being made within the town with the soft water from Burrator reservoir on Dartmoor. The blend of botanicals includes juniper berry, peel of orange and lemon, coriander seed, cardamom, angelica and orris root, which give a unique aroma and taste when the grain is distilled for a second time. This is the original base for a dry martini – no doubt Agent 007 would expect it, Ian Fleming apparently did.

At the end of the seventeenth century Londoners were already drinking a half-million gallons of gin when the raising of beer taxes made it the cheapest way of getting *'drunk for a penny, dead drunk for tuppence'*. The year before 1751, when

the Tippling Act demanded quality and closed the small gin shops, eleven million gallons were consumed in the capital. In the same year William Hogarth's etchings of the desperate scenes of excess in Gin Lane were contrasted with the generally wholesome and busy Beer Street. Not until the nineteenth century did it become known as mother's ruin, and gin palaces appeared, perhaps five thousand of them by the middle of the century in London, together with the Temperance movement.

Gins had been made all over England in the eighteenth century, but just Plymouth and London have maintained their production. London Dry Gin is still made by Gordon's, which in 1769 located itself at Clerkenwell to use the pure water of the Clerk's Well. In England it is sold in a green bottle and is usually drunk with ice and tonic water – a combination that evolved in India as a way of taking bitter quinine to keep malaria at bay.

See also BEER, FOOD, JUNIPER, SPRINGS, WELLS.

G I N H O U S E S

A cone or half-circle of roof on top of a rounded wall attached to the barn usually gives away the presence of a gin house. Pity the poor animals trudging round and round all day to power an engine, threshing machine or cider press.

Anne Lawson describes one of two stone-and-slate sheds in Milburn, Westmorland as an '*engine house where a horse was used to turn a centre post, which drove machinery in the barn behind. I believe our "gin cases" are particular to this area.*' Indeed they are more prevalent, because in 1784 a horse-powered threshing machine was invented here. Its use did spread to other parts of the country, especially the North East. In Northumberland, perhaps powered by four horses, they went by the name of gin gangs or wheel houses, and sometimes stone pillars supported the roof, leaving the sides open.

They also made their way to the South West, where, Peter Child said, '*The form of the buildings is very varied, semi-circular, polygonal or rectangular in plan, completely open-sided on piers, or with varying numbers and sizes of openings. Stone and slate houses are commonest, but they occur in brick and cob or with simple wooden posts and with tiled or thatched roofs.*'

A completely round brick-and-thatch horse-mill house survives at Winterborne Whitechurch in Dorset, standing alone away from the main barn. These variously named horse-engine houses, round houses, horse gins and horse-mill houses often survive as sheds, although horses were replaced by steam power during the second half of the nineteenth century. In the Peak District gin circles sometimes remain where horses once powered the winding engines for lead mines.

See also BANK BARNS, BARNS, BRICKS, CIDER & CIDER ORCHARDS, COB, ENGINE HOUSES, FARMS & FARMSTEADS, FIELD BARNS, GRUFFY GROUND, LEAD MINES, SLATES, THATCH, TITHE BARNS.

GLASTONBURY FESTIVAL

Michael Eavis was at the Bath Blues Festival with his wife in 1970 when an idea struck him. David Holmes and his family, who were on holiday at Eavis's farm in Somerset, remember casually being asked if a festival on the farm bringing rock musicians together with a sort of fair might work. That year Marc Bolan and Quintessence played at Worthy Farm to 1,500 people. David Bowie was signed up for 1971, and the festival was born.

The weekend after the summer solstice has been the regular date since the second festival, called the Glastonbury Fayre. Eavis's intention to '*embrace a medieval tradition of music, dance, poetry, theatre, lights and spontaneous entertainment*' brought 24,000 people by 1981. Women remember the nightmare of the loos, but the continuing spirit of the 1960s, the relaxed atmosphere, the warmth of so many young people together enjoying the open air and the music seem more palpable than the mud.

Festivals elsewhere came and went. Because Glastonbury is not run for profit – from the beginning money went to

Allerford, Somerset.

CND, later also Greenpeace and Oxfam – and because many local people and groups help it to run smoothly, it has a different atmosphere. This has been amplified since 1984, when a corner called the Green Fields started. Promoting green issues, harnessing wind and solar power and demonstrating that people have to clear up their own debris brings ethics down to earth.

Kate O'Farrell remembers festivals, now attracting a hundred thousand people, in the 1990s and early 2000s. '*The place becomes like a town, anything can happen, but there's the excitement of being part of something ephemeral that will soon be packed up and put away. And there's also a real sense of where you are; this couldn't be just anywhere. Camping in the Green Fields there is grass beneath your feet and you can look up past the fence to greener fields and trees. Looking out you can see Glastonbury Tor. Light shows stretch far into the distance across the heads of the crowd . . . [there is] yoga, massage, dance, music, sculpture, woodturning, solar and wind power, gardening and, of course, food: Manic Organic or Henry's Beard Café for breakfast, Tiny Tea Tent for a sit down and a dose of calm reality, fresh lemonade and watermelon stalls for the hot days, the Cider Bus and Burrow Hill Cider.*' Glastonbury is loved for the experience of freedom, even if only for a few days.

See also AVALON, CIDER & CIDER ORCHARDS, COUNTIES, FAIRS & FAIRGROUNDS, FIELDS, MIDSUMMER DAY, MUSIC.

G L O W - W O R M S

'*The Gloworm is a sort of catterpillar insect*', John Clare explained in the early to mid-1800s, '*and thousands of them may be seen on Casterton Cowpasture on a summer night they appear as if a drop of dew hung at their tails which had been set on fire by the fairys for the purpose of a lanthorn*'. No such concentrations of glow-worms exist now anywhere in England, never mind just down the lane in Northamptonshire.

As with the flash of the kingfisher, you always remember where you have seen glow-worms. And an evening walk on a moonless, warm summer evening has one scanning the edge of tall grass and springy downland turf, hedge bottom along the lanes or disused railway lines, for the pinpricks of pale greenish light. These magical little signals from female glow-worms, actually small flightless beetles that look like grubs, are searchlights for males, who take flight after dark in search of mates. The light is a kind of bioluminescence, produced by a chain of chemical reactions and emitted from the last three segments of the female's body.

After mating the female lays her '*pale luminous yellow*' eggs, as John Tyler described them, on the undersides of leaves and on grass stems, then dies. Adults live only for two or so weeks; the bulk of their lives, about three years, is spent as larvae, sucking the juices from small slugs and snails.

Glow-worms are now mainly found in southern England and on the chalk, where snails are most numerous, although they do occur in other parts of the country. They appear to be declining, probably because of the destruction of their habitat and difficulty of the flightless female to colonise new areas. But an additional problem could be the proliferation of street lighting, which may prevent the male from seeing the female's glow.

For the past few years glow-worm walks have been organised by wildlife groups and the National Trust. In 1991 a colony of glow-worms was saved from destruction by the laying of a gas pipeline in Barrowden, Rutland. Villagers negotiated the re-routing of the pipeline around the glow-worms' hedgerow home.

See also CHALK, DOWNLAND, GREEN LANES, HEDGES, HOLLOW WAYS, LANES.

G O L F - C O U R S E S

In Scotland and Northumberland the sheep-grazed turf and blowouts of seaside sand-dunes are known as links. North of the border, golf had been played for centuries before the courses using the natural links at Leith beside Edinburgh (established in 1744) and St Andrews in Fife (1754) were formalised. Near London golf was being played in Blackheath on the common in 1608, but courses away from the links and the sea were seen as poor substitutes.

Designers have tried to replicate the sand-dunes, short turf and pine trees natural to these places across Britain and the world, creating artificial landscapes jarring with their local surroundings. The more successful have incorporated the character of in situ chalk downland, heathland, woodland, earthworks or water systems into their schemes. One golf-course at Taunton, Somerset is blessed with the undulations of old opencast calamine workings.

Lytham on the Lancashire coast, with its memorable tingle of blowing sand, despite the best efforts of the 'starr grass', has a long history of 'the rage of sand'; its inhabitants are even known as 'sandgrown 'uns'. With the building of the adjacent new town of St Annes, Lytham seized the time and, in 1886, founded the Lytham and St Anne's Club. Despite having to shift, not because of sand but pushed by rapacious developers, it created a new course. Now along the Sefton coast, between the Mersey and Ribble estuaries, golf-courses take up a quarter (approximately twelve hundred acres) of the largest sand-dune system in England.

While this has changed the nature of the place, the golf-courses have checked the spread of housing and many of the dry dunes and seasonally flooded slacks have been retained, providing valuable habitats. Parts of the Royal Birkdale course and others have been designated as Sites of Special Scientific Interest, conserving plants, such as grass-of-Parnassus, dune

201

helleborine, Baltic rush, Isle of Man cabbage and fourteen willow hybrids, and eight reptiles and amphibians, including important colonies of natterjack toads and sand lizards. The Royal St George's on the Sandwich Links in Kent and the Temple Golf Club in Berkshire are home to many species of orchid. The course at Ludlow, Shropshire sits amid gorse, encircled by the racecourse.

With great expansion in the 1980s and 1990s, golf-courses have gobbled up one per cent of the land in Britain. The change of use from field to golf-course has caused many problems and increased the over-use of herbicides, pesticides and water. But there is a small groundswell of interest in the importance of reference to locality, of replacing the bright green grass with local species and the use of local soil instead of sand for bunkers. Extending this approach to embrace a kind of 'wild golf', with sympathetic design of new clubhouses, hotels and executive houses, could prove exemplary. There are tremendous opportunities to create courses that accentuate the surrounding landscape, improving habitats and offering glimpses of history in the land, giving them an immediate and unique identity. Only the tees, fairways and putting greens are intensively used; the roughs, comprising perhaps forty per cent or more of an eighteen-hole course, can be relatively undisturbed.

See also BEACHES, LAWN, LEAD MINES, LINKS, NATTERJACK TOADS, NICKNAMES, SAND-DUNES.

202

G O O S E B E R R I E S

The gooseberry is a 'cottager's' plant, sown by seed and cross-fertilised down the generations of gardeners to produce bigger and better varieties – green, red, white, yellow, oval, round, hairy and smooth.

Widely grown in gardens and market gardens around London since the 1700s, they were used when green to make a sauce for fish (a perfect accompaniment to oily mackerel), pork, duck or goose and, when ripe, for tarts. Cooked in pies, eaten raw and used for making sparkling wine equal to the Champagne of the day, in 1697 John Worlidge remarked that they had the closest resemblance to grapes of any English fruit.

In the 1750s the weavers of Lancashire founded the gooseberry clubs and shows, which soon spread to Cheshire, Derbyshire, Staffordshire, Yorkshire and Nottinghamshire. Dave Smith, a gooseberry collector and historian from Lancashire, remembers: *'Annually for 150 years, a hundred to two hundred club meetings and shows were held, in the convivial atmosphere of the public house. The sole aim was to produce the heaviest berry on Show Day, when the berry would be carefully weighed to half a grain (Troy). In 1852 a "London" became the first 2oz berry. The prizes were often curious, ranging from copper pans and kettles, bags of manure, or soot, even a pistol.'*

More than 2,500 varieties were raised during this time, and many of the most successful were introduced at the shows, such as Mr Hartshorn's ruby red Lancashire Lad in 1824, Crompton's large, yellow Careless, and Greenhaulgh's large, oval, yellow-green Leveller in 1851. They are still available from nurseries today.

Commercial production was boosted by the abolition of sugar tax in 1874. Together with strawberries and plums, gooseberries were grown extensively for jam and for pectin in jam making and the confectionery trade. Careless, Lancashire Lad, Crown Bob and Whinham's Industry were planted between the Bramley apple trees around Wisbech in Cambridgeshire. In Sussex, Leveller grows particularly well around Chailey and Newick. The production of artificial pectin and reduction in jam consumption led to a decline in commercial gooseberry growing.

Most of the seven remaining gooseberry shows take place in mid-Cheshire at the end of July and beginning of August. One show survives at Egton Bridge, Yorkshire in early August. The gooseberry 'trees' are pruned, pampered and cajoled into perfect ripeness. Timing is of the essence – the fruit must be at its heaviest but not burst before the show. Some trees are partly covered over by 'pens' to protect them from too much rain or sun; some are fed with special concoctions, secrets passed down.

The first gooseberry pie of the year is traditionally eaten at Whitsun. Raised gooseberry pies were a feature of Whitsun fairs, such as the Mansfield Fair in Nottinghamshire. Oldbury-on-Severn in Gloucestershire still has its gooseberry tarts, although they are really pies, best *'eaten from the hand'*, according to Laura Mason and Catherine Brown. At the Castleton Garland Day in Derbyshire on 29 May an old poem sung by the villagers reveals that 'feberry loaf', or gooseberry pie, was one of the festive foods consumed on the day. Feaberry, fabes, feabs, feaps and thapes were local names for the fruit in Yorkshire, Lancashire, Leicestershire, Derbyshire, Cheshire, Shropshire, Warwickshire, East Anglia and parts of southern England. In the north east of Northumberland the word grozer, a corruption of the French *groseille* (red currant), was often used. Goosegog, goosegob and goosebob are still common in some parts of the country.

A commercial nursery in Yorkshire specialising in fruit has 45 varieties of gooseberry in its catalogue – perhaps things are looking up for the gooseberry and more will be available, as Edward Bunyard suggested, for *'ambulant consumption'*.

See also AGRICULTURAL SHOWS, ALLOTMENTS, CASTLETON GARLAND DAY, GARDENS, GREEN MAN, STRAWBERRIES.

Lancashire Lad.

G O R G E S

Dramatic, in-facing cliffs, separated by a narrow sliver of sky, characterise the gorge, just as a steep V-shape denotes the smaller ravine, chine or dene. We have a few serious gorges in England, mostly in limestone country, sculpted by melt-waters and roof falls at the end of the Ice Age. One of the most spectacular is the Avon Gorge, spanned by Brunel's suspension bridge at Clifton, after the river has meandered in an ever-steepening valley from Bradford and Bath to Bristol. In nearby Somerset's Mendip Hills, the famous winding Cheddar Gorge, more than three hundred feet deep and edged by caves, is arguably the largest. Here, lime-loving plants flourish, including the rare and beautiful Cheddar pink and Cheddar bedstraw. Nearby the diminutive Ebbor Gorge is just big enough to squeeze through on foot, noted for its silver-washed fritillary butterflies and nettle-leaved bell flowers.

To the north, in the limestone of the Pennines, gorges abound. Astonishing in its narrowness and splendour, inhabited by a misfit beck, the gorge below Gordale Scar in the Yorkshire Dales has a waterfall at its mouth. Two centuries ago this colossal cleft attracted visitors keen to feel awe and terror in the presence of its vast, inhuman dimensions. This *'sublime'* experience was promoted by Edmund Burke, who, in 1757, challenged the notion that 'beautiful' was the highest form of aesthetic emotion. In 1814 John Ward tried to capture the sublime on canvas in a painting of the Scar that, at almost fourteen feet by eleven, is the largest landscape in London's Tate Britain. To accentuate the sense of human insignificance in the face of primeval nature, Ward exaggerated the looming heights and rocky overhangs and filled the sky with vast, rolling clouds. By the early nineteenth century the view was one of the most celebrated in the country.

Narrow gorges small and large offer moist, sheltered spots beloved by lowly plants. In Teesdale the river Tees rushes through a narrow gorge just fifty feet wide for half a mile or so downstream from Eggleston Abbey bridge. '*The gorge is perpetually humid and shaded for much of the day, even in high summer, so its banks are draped with emerald-green ivy, mosses and hart's tongue fern fronds*', Phil Gates writes. '*Fungi and lichens seem to take on greater luminosity in these damp, dimly lit surroundings. On dead twigs patches of coral spot fungus covered the decaying wood with glowing orangey-pink pustules of elemental intensity. A lemon-yellow slime mould on a tree stump, cadmium yellow witches' butter, and encrustations of yellowy-green Xanthoria lichen could have been splashes from a painter's palette.*'

See also BRIDGES, CAVES, CHINES, CLINTS & GRIKES, DENES, FERNS, GHYLLS, HOLLOW WAYS, LAKES, LIMESTONE, MOSSES, OAK, RIVER NAMES, RIVERS, TEXTILE MILLS, WATERFALLS, XANADU.

G O R S E

Vast expanses of spiny, golden, sweet-smelling gorse glow like sunshine. No wonder the plant finds favour as a cure for '*hopelessness and despair*', according to the makers of Bach Flower Remedies. The Pre-Raphaelites loved to paint it, and the Swedish naturalist Linnaeus fell down on his knees and wept for joy when he saw the swathes of gorse in flower on Putney Heath.

The presence of gorse often indicates poor or acid soil; it grows on commons, open ground, scrub and lowland heaths, often among heather in most, if not all, counties. Because it grows in such profusion it is one of our most significant 'landscape' plants – this rapid coloniser was planted alongside the first motorways in the 1960s.

Three species grow here. The most widespread, common gorse (*Ulex europaeus*) grows larger, has longer spines and bigger flowers. April is the month when it comes into full bloom. Western gorse (*Ulex gallii*) flowers in the autumn in the South and West, where it flourishes on the heath-lands and in Cornish hedges. Dwarf gorse (*Ulex minor*), with smaller and more numerous spines, flowers from July to November. Its strongholds lie in the South and East in places such as the Dorset heaths, the New Forest, Ashdown Forest and on the commons of Sussex, Surrey and parts of East Anglia.

Gorse is often called furze in the South and whin, from the Old Norse, in the North. '*Derivatives include Gorsey, Gorsty, Gossy, Whinny, Furzey and Furzen*', resulting in field names such as Gorsty Field, Gossy Close, Fuzzardy, the Fuzzens and Fuzzy Ground, John Field wrote. Many

203

place-names describe the abundance of gorse: Furze Green in Norfolk; Furzebrook in Dorset; Furzley in Hampshire; Whin Lane End in Lancashire; Whinney Hill in Yorkshire. A hill near Hastings in Sussex is called Firehills by local people because of the brilliance of the gorse.

A valuable commodity, its use was strictly controlled on the commons. On the heaths around Verwood in Dorset, furze, or fuzz, burning at a high temperature, was used by brick-makers, potters and bakers. Since it is widely said that *'kissing is in season when the gorse is in flower'*, Cornwall is the place to be or to avoid – gorse flowers here all year round and fuzz was harvested extensively for fuel before the era of coal.

Gorse provided valuable fodder; the young shoots are palatable and nutritious and branches were crushed in special gorse or cider mills to tenderise their spines for feeding to horses and cattle. It was used to stop damp rising up into a haystack, in field drains to help under-draining, as temporary shelters for cattle, for warren walls and as fox coverts. Gorse flowers are still boiled to dye Easter eggs, fermented for wine, and the wood fashioned into walking sticks.

In 1994 The Vuz Dance was revived in Great Torrington, Devon. Once part of its May Day festivities, gorse, or vuz, celebrated the link between the town and the surrounding commons, where it was collected. Shop fronts in the town square were decorated with gorse, and gorse faggots were tied onto hazel poles around which a complicated dance was woven.

Much decried as a nuisance since exploitation lapsed, gorse stands are a favourite habitat of birds, such as the Furzeling (Dartford warbler) and Gorsechat (Stonechat).

See also ANTY-TUMPS, CIDER & CIDER ORCHARDS, COMMONS, DRYSTONE WALLS, EASTER CUSTOMS, HEATHLAND, HEDGES, WARRENS.

G R A F F I T I

'RIBS', 'WABAZO', 'BLONDIE', 'KOF', 'BASHA', 'DRED' – these were a few of the readable 'sprints', or spray paints, on parapets and buildings along the line into London's Waterloo Station in 2004. This gateway to the city was at that moment silver edged, with constantly reworked *'part sign and part language'*, as Peter Ackroyd describes it, evolving before our eyes. Among the miscellany of signs, the graffiti boys and girls dare to flaunt their parishes with flamboyant tags, demonstrations of prowess in dangerous places. As Ackroyd writes, *'It is a way of asserting individuality, perhaps, but it becomes immediately part of the anonymous texture of London; in that sense graffiti are a vivid token of human existence in the city.'*

Although the train-borne audience is huge, the target audience is small. Iain Sinclair pointed out that *'Spraycan bandits, like monks labouring on a Book of Hours, hold to their patch, refining their art by infinite acts of repetition . . .*

The tag represents a corporate identity; not so much a gang as a studio or "school of". Battles are not territorial; the climate here is clubbish, mildly hallucinogenic.'

The great legs of the Westway are marked with tags as high as the reach of someone on someone's shoulders. These youth-invented ritual expressions of bravado are very different from overtly provocative and political demands, which include the anti-Establishment, anti-racism daubs of the 1960s and 1970s as well as overt racism.

A stencilled sign in Marylebone Road invited *'By order National Highways Agency this wall is a designated graffiti area.'* Banksy, widely admired for his high-quality stencil work – thoughtful, humorous, unsettling – is active in London, Bristol and elsewhere. He says: *'The irony is that despite having to scuttle around at night like Jack the Ripper with a marker pen, writing graffiti is about the most honest way you can be an artist. It takes no money to do it, you don't need an education to understand it, there's no admission fee and bus stops are far more interesting and useful places to have pictures than museums . . . Graffiti has been used to start revolutions, stop wars and generally is the voice of the people who aren't listened to. Graffiti is one of the few tools you have if you have almost nothing.'*

Three decades before him Heathcote Williams had been busy provoking our thoughts – *'Corrugated iron is the character armour of the council'* appeared on metal carapaces around 'development', as well as *'Come Back Rachman all is forgiven'* on boarded-up buildings in Lancaster Road, London and *'Squat Now while stocks last'*. One of Williams's favourites, emblematic of the 1960s, lit up Basing Street for years: *'The road of excess leads to the palace of wisdom'*, from William Blake.

Low-grade, high-density graffiti clusters around the poorer parts of any city, and many find that the busier the walls are the less safe they feel. There is much aggressive fascism and racism manifest that should make us all feel insecure. But this is countered by the countless exhortations for us to think – *'Rock against Racism'*, *'Get out of Iraq'*, even *'Free the Tamworth Two'*. Some are more personal: at least one bridge in the East End still sports an exclamation widely scrawled in the 1970s – *'George Davis is innocent'*. So much for ephemera.

Contours of language, concern and prejudice can be drawn across London and many other cities using graffiti as the guide. It is evident that cities are the laboratories, but rashes do break out in small towns, suburbs and even villages, raising alarm.

Nothing lingers in the mind better than irony and philosophical humour – one favourite, seen on the repeatedly repainted white wall of the Conservative Club in Kentish Town, London in the 1980s, was *'Your Karma has just run over my Dogma'*.

See also ALLEYS, CORRUGATED IRON, PIGS, STATIONS, TOWER BLOCKS.

G R A N I T E

One of the world's toughest natural building stones, granite is ancient magma, slowly cooled underground to form hard crystals of felspar and quartz, peppered with flakes of glittery mica, silvery white or black. The precise recipe varied from place to place, giving each granite now exposed a distinctive look. The overall tint is dominated by the felspar, which can be red, pink, white or grey and sometimes slightly greenish.

The Lake District is famed for its beautiful granites – the stone of Shap Fell, for instance, bears huge pink felspar crystals that make fine ornamental polished slabs. Further south, exposed islands of granite at Charnwood Forest are quarried at Mountsorrel, near Leicester. Granite shapes the grandest and wildest landscapes of south-west England, too, from Devon to Land's End, Lundy and the Isles of Scilly. Dartmoor, the largest granite massif south of the Scottish Highlands, is scattered with tors and granite blocks (clitter) or moorstones, the stuff of prehistoric megalithic monuments and field walls, bridges, troughs, gateposts and stiles. On the shingle beach at Start Bay are granite pebbles, brought down from Dartmoor by the river Dart.

Granite tramways still visible from Haytor quarries on Dartmoor carried off stone to build London Bridge. The quarries between Bodmin Moor and Land's End once supplied the usually light silver-grey stone for the lighthouses that dot the coast; miniature lighthouses of polished local granite were sold as souvenirs. Granites in Devon, Cornwall and the Lakes also famously contain veins or lodes of valuable minerals – tin, copper, silver, lead, even uranium – inciting mining enterprises, some dating from prehistoric times.

See also BUILDING STONES, COBBLES, ENGINE HOUSES, KAOLIN, KERBSTONES, LEAD MINES, QUARRIES, STANDING STONES.

GRASSY TRIANGLES

As horses and carts, farm animals and vehicles and carriages and cars turned left or right over the years, a wide splay often formed at the junctions of country roads. Between the turning curves, undisturbed by traffic, grassy triangles were often left untouched when the roads were first metalled.

Here, sometimes a tree and certainly a small nature reserve flourishes, the wildflowers escaping the drift of herbicides and fertilisers from neighbouring fields. A favourite triangle lies near Buckland Newton in Dorset; it contains a small stand of sky-blue chicory in the summer, telling travellers they are on the chalk.

Crowned by finger- or direction posts, these are small places in the scheme of things, but their loss diminishes both locality and journeys.

Dee Tracey, writing about Warwickshire's triangular '*jam puffs*', recalls that the '*delightful islands of grass, which are so distinctive at the junction of two to three narrow, winding, obviously old, country roads*' are also known as God cakes.

See also CAKES, FIELDS, FINGERPOSTS, ROADS, WILDFLOWERS.

G R A V E L   P I T S

Regions heavily quarried for their gravel and sand become rich in lakes formed from the disused wet pits. Thanks to the post-war boom in fishing and boating, gravel pits that might have been filled with rubbish have been retained as recreational lakes, along the coastal plain south of Chichester in Sussex, for instance, and in London's green belt. In the dry Cotswolds in the upper Thames valley more than three and a half thousand acres of open water in different pits are used for sailing, nature conservation (little egrets are recent residents) and clusters of new second homes.

South west of Nottingham, Attenborough Gravel Pits lies between the river Trent and the railway land. Here, wetland and marsh birds make use of a mixture of wood, scrub and reed beds. It is also home to two rather local diving beetles, who feast on tadpoles and small fish in the old pits. At Holme Pierrepont, downstream, the gravel pits have been modelled to form world-class rowing courses. Woolly mammoth fossils, skulls, tusks and teeth are often found, as at Watermead Country Park near Syston, Leicestershire.

In the Nene valley, Northamptonshire the gravel pits have been colonised by otters, who find safe haven on the islands. Especially in southern England, the great crested grebe has found a sufficient foothold in gravel pits to enable it to recolonise areas from which it has long been absent, having been almost exterminated by exploitation for feathers in the late nineteenth century.

See also BOUNDARIES, BRICKS, BROADS, BUILDING STONES, DEW PONDS, FELL RUNNING, FELLS, LAKES, LOST VILLAGES, MOATS, PONDS, REED BEDS, RESERVOIRS, TARNS.

205

GRAVESTONES

Graveyards are monuments to stone as much as souls. The early chest tombs and headstones scattered among the yew trees and grass tend, like the church, to be wrought from local material. They are geological reserves in their own right. Few inscribed memorials date before 1700. Important and rich people were buried inside the church and, when space ran out, they were buried on an east–west axis on the south side of the churchyard. The graves of the poor were marked by a simple wooden cross or by small head- and foot-stones.

Some of the most interesting chest tombs are in the Cotswolds, made from the local golden limestone. Bale, or shroud, tombs differ from the simpler rectangular, hollow, box-shaped tombs (the body is buried beneath) by having curved, diagonally grooved tops, resembling the corded bale of wool in which the body was wrapped or the metal hearse in which it was carried. Good examples can be found in the churchyards of Asthall, Broadwell, Burford and Windrush. The yew-filled churchyard in Painswick is also known for its Georgian memorials, including pedestal tombs, which are like tall stone plinths topped with urns. These, and the round 'tea-caddy' pedestal tombs, display the local masons' skill.

Graveyard monuments tend to get increasingly grotesque with size. Mausoleums predominate in Yorkshire, and there is a kind of table tomb – a flat slab of stone raised by stone supports in the corners – found north of the Humber, for example in Haworth and Keighley, Yorkshire. Victorian sarcophagi have infiltrated parish churchyards, but most big monuments found their homes in the cemeteries built around towns and cities to relieve congested graveyards.

The more common and affordable headstones differ in materials and styles all over the country. Unyielding West Country granite is less elaborately carved than the Ham Hill stone (limestone) of Somerset or the sandstone memorials of the Forest of Dean. The shapes differ – according to the stone available, local wealth and fashion and the style of the stone-mason – from simple curved tops to one main curve bounded by two smaller ones, ripple tops, angular tops and many more. In the North they were often laid flat on the ground.

In places without good local supplies stone was brought in. Stone from Northamptonshire and Rutland came to the Fenlands by water. Portland stone from Dorset was transported by sea to London. They were used to replace graveboards (dead-boards, bed-boards, sheep-boards, leaping-

boards) – inscribed wooden boards suspended from posts, a few of which still exist in Surrey and East Anglia.

In Suffolk occasional chest tombs were made of brick, and in Heathfield, Sussex Jonathan Harmer made terracotta plaques that were attached to headstones in the early 1800s, as at Mayfield and Herstmonceux.

The early iron foundries of the Weald produced decorative cast-iron grave slabs, small Celtic crosses and headstones. Dating from 1537 to 1711, they can still be seen in some churchyards, such as Wadhurst and East Grinstead in Sussex. This custom continued in the iron-smelting areas of the Severn valley. The presence of cast-iron pedestal tombs in churchyards usually indicates that there was an iron foundry nearby; there is a fine one painted white with black lettering at Madeley near Coalbrookdale in Shropshire. In limestone areas brass plaques overcame the problem of eroding lettering. Some fine examples remain at Painswick.

In the 1730s slate became fashionable, especially grey-blue Swithland slate from the Charnwood area of Leicestershire. Its sawn, polished surfaces could take fine engraving and low relief carving. The intricate work of local craftsmen, such as William Charles of Wymeswold – identified by his winged hourglass trademark – can be found in most of the church-yards of Leicestershire and surrounding counties. By 1887 the Leicestershire slate quarries had closed, superseded by cheaper Welsh slate that was shipped to Liverpool and then by canal all over the country.

Slate headstones are also common in Cornwall and parts of Devon, quarried from Delabole and other smaller quarries in the two counties. Around Polyphant, Cornwall, the dove-grey stone of the same name graces the churchyards and is visible in the church towers, too. Many headstones in mid- and north Cornwall have delightful naïve carvings of winged heads, known as Cornish Angels, similar to the more sophisticated Belvoir Angels on the gravestones in St Mary's churchyard in Wymeswold, Leicestershire and those at Fingest church in Buckinghamshire.

Symbolically butterflies and winged heads represented the soul on its journey to heaven. A snake eating its tail signified eternity; the skull and crossbones, death. The occupation of the deceased might be illustrated, or the cause of death, such as shipwreck, a collapsing bridge or falling tree. On some early headstones a letter is endearingly placed above a word to correct the spelling.

Away from home, how out of place Italian white marble or polished granite looks in our country churchyards. Local stone enables lichens to colonise and mellow the headstone; these slow-growing, ancient plants are part of the richness of the churchyard. One tea-caddy tomb in Kirkland, Cumberland, carved in 1789 from red sandstone, is thought to accommodate 47 species of lichen.

See also BUILDING STONES, CEMETERIES, CHURCHES, CHURCHYARDS, FAMILY NAMES, FERNS, GRANITE, LICHENS, QUARRIES, SLATES, YEW.

St Mary de Castro, Leicester; St Mary's Church, Baldock, Hertfordshire; St George's Church, Crowhurst, Surrey; St Mary's Church, Swaffham Prior, Cambridgeshire.

GRAZING MARSHES

Marshes remain shifting, uncertain, often forbidding places. In Dickens's *Great Expectations*, Pip describes the moment he became aware that '*the dark flat wilderness beyond the churchyard, intersected with dikes and mounds and gates, with scattered cattle feeding on it, was the marshes; and that the low leaden line beyond was the river; and that the distant savage lair from which the wind was rushing was the sea*'.

Most often along the coast, marshes are watery lands, drained and defined by networks of dykes and protected from flooding by earthen walls or embankments. On rich clay and silt soils, rather than the peat-based fens, they offer valuable agricultural land, providing good pasture or even arable land. Here the dykes may have been first dug in late Saxon or medieval times. Reclamation from the sea has been achieved over centuries and plagued by setbacks, as land was lost as well as gained.

Marshes are a feature of the South and East and include the marshland of Lincolnshire, the Essex marshes, the Suffolk Sandlings and, in the Norfolk Broads, the wide expanse of the Halvergate marshes. Once a great estuary into which the rivers Bure, Yare and Waveney flowed, they are cut off from sight or sound of the sea and peppered with the ruins of brick tower mills, drainage schemes dating from the eighteenth century. Pollarded willows, cut low to withstand the wind, form close-set lines along the roads.

The marshes of north Kent still have a wild, windy and remote air, despite the oil refineries, paper mills and power stations on the skyline. In south Kent lies Romney Marsh, a vast stretch of windswept flatland scattered with houses and villages. Arable fields sometimes run up to the sea wall. Traces remain of the dense network of medieval dykes, and surrounding fields each amount to just two or three acres.

In Cumberland, along the Solway Firth, coastal grassland, known as merse, is dominated by bents and fescues, with autumn hawkbit, soft rush, Yorkshire fog and white clover. It provides fine grazing for sheep and is often colonised by gorse, altering the open character of the landscape.

Inland, grazing marshes once extended along many lowland rivers. In Sussex they are known as brooks, such as the Lewes Brooks and Malling Brooks in the Ouse valley, and Pulborough Brooks, now a Royal Society for the Protection of Birds reserve, on the Arun.

The intensification of coastal developments and agriculture has significantly reduced grazing marshland, now estimated to stand at less than half a million acres. Two-thirds of the Essex marshland and half of Romney Marsh were lost as grazing marsh between the 1930s and the 1980s. What remains is drying out and suffering nutrient overload from fertilisers. Only some twelve thousand acres of unimproved grassland remain, with a spread of native plant species and wetland breeding birds, such as lapwing, snipe and curlew, as well as overwintering flocks of Bewick's and whooper swans.

See also BOWLING GREENS, CATTLE, FENS, GORSE, GREEN LANES, INGS, LEVELS, MOSSLAND, PEAT, RHYNES, RIVERS, SALT MARSHES, SHEEP, TIDES.

GREEN LANES

Green lanes, unmetalled tracks, have somehow escaped the changes demanded by motor transport. Owned by many different farmers and landholders, some are just wide enough for a cart; others, fifty feet wide, are bounded by banks, hedges, ditches or drystone walls. They include ancient tracks and more recent unmade roads. The Ridgeway, running from Dorset to the Chilterns, and other ridgeways of the chalk country often follow watersheds. Some are tellingly known as summerways.

'*Every lane has its history*', W.G. Hoskins wrote. '*It is not there by accident, and every twist it makes once had some historical meaning which we can decipher today, but not often.*' Tracks from the coast, some for carrying exotic contraband; routes for moving livestock or droving to markets near and far; roads for miners, traders and soldiers; paths between abbeys and pilgrims' ways: all tell stories within the landscape. In the northern Pennines they may still be called thrufts; in Lincolnshire gatterams. Grundles suggest a gravelled surface, common in East Anglia.

The passage of animals to market, some walking from Scotland or Cornwall to London, is suggested by half-penny and farthing fields (where stock could be kept overnight), inns called the Drover's or the Shepherd's Rest, or a handful of Scots pines on the horizon. Parts of long-distance routes, such as the Ridgeway and Icknield Way, have large sections that are unmetalled. Valerie Belsey described the situation, when timber, for example, was hauled very simply without wheels: '*The resulting erosion . . . by the sledges led these primitive hauliers to create parallel tracks, such as on the Icknield Way at Goring.*'

An old packhorse route over Salter Fell in the Forest of Bowland, Lancashire was hailed by Alfred Wainwright as '*possibly the finest moorland walk in England*'. Salt, the great preserver of meat and fish, was transported far and wide by lines of laden horses. From the seventeenth century, from the underground sources in Cheshire, Staffordshire and Worcestershire, salt ways fanned out from Nantwich, Northwich, Middlewich, Baswich, Shirleywich and Droitwich. Some can be located by names, such as Salters fords, lanes and bridges. The suffix 'wich' had taken on the implied meaning of brine workings in the Dark Ages.

Trackways crossed the Lincolnshire Wolds east–west to take salt inland. Long before the mining of rock salt and the Roman roads that enabled quicker distribution, salt had been evaporated from sea water all around the coast,

207

in some cases for thousands of years. Middle and late Bronze-Age salt production has been found at Fenn Creek by South Woodham Ferrers and Mucking in Essex, and the names Eastwick, Bridgewick and Landwick also suggest old workings. The turf causeways from the sea's edge across the Essex marshes are raised slightly above the surrounding land; many link the 'red hills' – grassy mounds that are relics of salt evaporation methods – enabling sheep to get to higher ground at the highest tides.

In south Devon the medieval system of tracks was even more intricate than today's roads. Abbots Way links Buckfastleigh and Buckfast Abbeys, but many connect moor with coast, offering breathtaking views of the sea. A survey by Valerie Belsey, begun in 1983, identified 191 green lanes covering 450 miles of the county, many overgrown and unlinked. South Hams district council has begun restoration, with the help of landholders and volunteers. A deeply incised and wooded lane near Mothecombe is not untypical, but often they are more open, with high hedge banks and grassy tracks that are excellent for wildflowers, birds and butterflies.

Walkers share these quiet lanes, not only with infrequent and indigenous farm traffic but also with cyclists, horse riders and, increasingly, motorbikes and four-by-four vehicles, claiming 'once a highway always a highway'. Some of the lanes are even more churned up than they would have been after bad weather and hundreds of cattle in the early nineteenth century. The impact and conflict in some lanes of the Yorkshire Dales, Lake District and Hampshire has led to vehicles being experimentally banned. David Gardiner, while chairman of the Green Lanes Environmental Action Movement, observed: '*The condition of the Ridgeway is nothing short of a disgrace and it's getting worse and worse so it is no longer a pleasure to walk. This ancient road is up to six thousand years old. It is surrounded by ancient monuments but I have seen four-by-fours using an Iron Age burial mound as a ramp to perform stunts.*'

208

Horton Scar Lane, Ribblesdale, Yorkshire.

See also BEECH, DROVE ROADS, DRYSTONE WALLS, FAIRS & FAIRGROUNDS, FOOTPATHS, GYPSIES, HEDGES, HOLLOW WAYS, HORSES & PONIES, LANES, RACECOURSES, ROADS, SCOTS PINE, TIDES, WAYSIDE & BOUNDARY CROSSES.

GREEN MAN

May morning sees many a leafy fellow shambling across hillsides and shaking through streets. From Rochester in Kent to Knutsford in Cheshire the Green Man, deciduous dancer, still eludes explanation. In his festive form he seems to be a harbinger of spring, a celebration of regeneration. Right across the country you may come across him in other guises, from leafy faces carved into cloisters to local plays, or as the Green George, a relative of our patron saint. Elsewhere, across Mexico, through Japan, in India and through Europe, the beleafed one keeps reappearing. He has been our cultural companion for a long time and carries ancient resonances.

In her seminal essay botanist Kathleen Basford wrote of *The Green Man* as '*foliate head*', from first-century appearances across the Roman Empire to the '*demons and spectres of the demon wood*' in the churches of the early Middle Ages. But she located in the thirteenth to fifteenth centuries '*the era of the Green Man*' in Christian imagery, as did William Anderson in *The Rise of the Gothic*.

Sometimes terrifying, often benign, he can be seen in many old churches, as a leafy mask or with tendrils and leaves emerging from his mouth, on roof bosses, corbels, capitals, tympanums, tombstones, misericords and bench ends, in choir stalls, cloisters and over doorways. The thirteenth-century Southwell Minster, in Sherwood Forest in Nottinghamshire, is resplendent with foliage, so special that it moved Nikolaus Pevsner to write *The Leaves of Southwell*. In the chapterhouse alone, the carved stones, dominated by maple, oak and hawthorn, are made the more dynamic by an array of nine green men, arresting characters with somehow recognisable faces. In the Minsters of Beverley and York, carvers portrayed him prolifically.

More than sixty green men populate Exeter Cathedral. Indeed his presence in almost every church in Devon might point to continuing attempts by the church to draw tree worshippers towards Christianity, either by demonising their gods or by giving them a place in the church's 'pantheon' of images. Next door in Somerset, stone foliate heads are generously augmented by green men carved in wooden bench ends. The naïve styles, often with bared teeth, belie great craftsmanship and imagination, as at Bishops Lydeard and Lyng, where whole figures, some women, are intertwined with bines or whole trees and stylised leaves and fruits. Often they resemble ivy and berries, or is it vines and grapes, which might link him to the masked and horned god of Old Europe, later Dionysos of the Greeks and Bacchus of the Romans?

The Green Knight, a giant of a man, bursts onto the scene in the fourteenth century (or rather into the written record) by gatecrashing the New Year's banquet at Camelot:

> *Men gaped at the hue of him*
> *Ingrained in garb and mien*
> *A fellow fiercely grim,*
> *And all a glittering green.*

From *Sir Gawain and the Green Knight*

As originally told in the dialect of Cheshire, Lancashire and Staffordshire, the tale involves the Green Knight challenging the revellers to cut off his head. Sir Gawain accommodates him but is then bound to journey to find the Green Chapel at the next New Year, to offer his own head, as the now headless Green Knight demands. This is a fantastical tale of destiny and temptation, but unmistakably offers imagery of death and renewal associated with the turning of the year.

There are stories of leaf children in Norfolk, and a handful of green women exist across Europe, but the Green Man dominates. Roy Judge warned us all against assumption, however, for he found no Green Man in the origins of Jack in the Green, who emerged in chimney sweeps' attempts to raise money on May Day in the streets in the late 1700s. Yet those who have resurrected Jack for May Day celebrations in both Hastings, Sussex and Rochester, Kent see him thus.

Green men took to the streets long before this. In 1578 a line in a play runs: '*Two men, apparrelled, lyke greene men at the mayors feast, with clubbes of fyre worke.*' Brandon Centerwall tells of post-medieval London and Chester green men, who were path-clearers and entertainers brandishing torches and fireworks at the Lord Mayor's pageant. He also explores the role of the wild man and the Green Man in pub signs. There is evidence of green men getting a laugh by acting the drunkard, which explains a pub in London's East End called the Green Man and Still – although the sign in the 1980s was of a wizard-like fellow with a glass distilling flask. The Reformation stamped on pagan imagery to the extent that leafy or ivy-clad characters brandishing knobbly sticks were replaced by the sign of an axe-carrying woodsman and Robin Hood – these signs continue to hang above our pubs, although a wider variety has appeared.

In *The Tree*, John Fowles reminded us that '*One of the oldest and most diffused bodies of myth and folklore has accreted round the idea of the man in the trees. In all his manifestations, as a dryad, as stagheaded Herne, as outlaw, he possesses the characteristic of elusiveness, a power of "melting" into the trees, and I am certain the attraction of the myth is so profound and universal because it is constantly "played" inside every individual consciousness.*'

As a historical presence the Green Man is enigmatic; as a future force he offers a positive face. The leaf stands for the

magical transformation of energy from the sun, something that we in our super-sophistication cannot achieve. The tree in its deciduous forms symbolises the cycle of death and rebirth, re-enacted each year as leaves fall and grow again. The Green Man has emerged in our time as a symbol of reconnection with nature, of regeneration and hope.

See also ANCIENT TREES, CASTLETON GARLAND DAY, CATHEDRALS, CHURCHES, GARGOYLES & GROTESQUES, GROVELY RIGHTS DAY, HENGES & STONE CIRCLES, HILL FIGURES, MAY DAY, OAK, PARKLAND, PUB SIGNS, ROBIN HOOD, SAINTS, STRAW BEAR DAY.

209

G R E E N S A N D

Born as geology was emerging, the name is a compound mistake; the Greensand is the name given to an age, but the rocks it comprises are not often green and include limestones. Here and there, however, greensand is green sandstone.

Deposited by the Cretaceous seas, the Greensand is overshadowed by and marches with the Chalk. A thin line, only a few miles wide at its greatest, it circles the Weald from Eastbourne, Sussex to Folkestone, Kent and, having made curvaceous sweeps from north of the Wash down to Abbotsbury, Dorset, it enjoys a little freestyle flirting with Dorset, Devon and Somerset.

Between the Upper and Lower Greensand lies Gault clay, which sometimes causes land to slide, as along the Lympne scarp in Kent. The Greensand itself parts and changes as the ancient seas saw fit. So here and there it includes ragstone, a sequence of blue limestone strata, hard and useful, called 'little diamonds' and 'square rock' by the quarrymen around Maidstone, Kent. Commercial hazel plats follow the ragstone. In Bedfordshire and Cambridgeshire the Greensand becomes brown carstone, so rich in iron that in Norfolk it is known as gingerbread. In Surrey it is soft and sandy firestone, similar to malmstone, a grey or white, limy sandstone, which was quarried from Farnham to Selborne in Hampshire.

Resistant rocks in the Greensand stand up in ridges and in Surrey are typically crossed by many sunken lanes – deep and winding, they lend a real intimacy to the heavily wooded or heathered hills.

Despite its presence in the landscape and the many small quarries used for local building, the Greensand is not highly regarded for building stones, since they do not wear well. Wren, in his conservation job for Westminster Abbey in 1713, lamented on '*the unhappy Choice of Materials, the Stone is decayed four Inches deep, and falls off perpetually in great scales . . . This Stone takes in Water, which, being frozen, scales off, whereas good Stone gathers a Crust, and defends itself.*' This Reigate stone and limy sandstone mined from the Surrey hillsides was used in many churches on the clays around London, for Southwark Cathedral and the original London Bridge in 1176. The Hythe Beds are less easy to cut in all directions but form better building materials in browns, greens and yellows. This includes the iron-rich Bargate stone, used by Lutyens in some of his houses – *the stone of south-west Surrey, quarried around Guildford and Godalming*. It is often set off by galleting, the little jewels of brown ironstone set in the mortar around the stones. In Lincolnshire Spilsby sandstone has been used for churches in the vicinity of Horncastle. Alec Clifton-Taylor noted regretfully that if '*they had more Strength, these Lincolnshire churches would be amongst the most beguiling of all English greensand buildings*'.

Glauconite is a green hydrous silicate of iron; it suggests a shallow marine origin and open to the air it tends to rust. But in some places it does hold the green seen in the village buildings of south Lincolnshire – the church at Burgh le Marsh is browny green. In Shaftesbury, Dorset, which stands high on its greensand spur, the buildings really are of greenstone, giving the high street a distinguished air sadly marred by the rendering of some of the buildings. A small quarry has recently re-opened to supply stone for local conservation and new building. Although the oldest building, St Peter's Church in the high street, shows the signs that Wren described, it will outlast most of the buildings now being erected.

See also BUILDING STONES, CHALK, CHURCHES, COBBLES, COBNUTS, DOWNLAND, DRYSTONE WALLS, HOLLOW WAYS, IRONSTONE, LANDSLIPS, ORCHARDS.

GREETINGS

'Aye up, mi duck'. In Nottinghamshire and Derbyshire local people rarely say 'hello' or 'hi'. 'Aye up, yowth' and occasionally still 'Aye up, serry' (possibly from sirrah) are also heard, and there is a version of 'how are you' or 'how do you do' – 'Aa do?' – that may be accompanied by a tick of the head to the side. Sometimes just the action suffices. 'Awreet, mon?' (Newcastle), 'Ah do' or 'Ow do' (North and West), 'Ow bis?' (West) and 'Oroyt, moyte' (Birmingham) all suggest a question, but do not necessarily expect an answer, save the same: 'alright'.

Tom Rawling captures the rhythm in his poem 'The Old Showfield', recalling the Ennerdale Show in Cumberland. '"*How do?", "How ista?", "What's thi fettle?",/"Champion", "Middlin", "Nut sa Bad".*'

Cockneys were saying 'wotcher' in the sixteenth century – what cheer? Possibly this came with coals from Newcastle, where they still say 'Whaat cheor?' as well as 'Hulloo, hinnie', pet or petal. 'Ello, my dear' takes over in the West Country, and further south west 'Ello, my lover', contrasting with 'Yo' in Brixton and 'Wassup' in Caribbean/city/youth slang. East Enders might call you cock, cobber, chum, darlin', dear, guvna, luv, mate; in the eastern counties it might be bor. It all depends on who you are speaking to and your intimacy with them.

See also ACCENTS, DIALECTS, UNLUCKY WORDS.

GROVELY RIGHTS DAY

'*Grovely Grovely Grovely and All Grovely/Unity is Strength.*' The lines scrolled across the Royal Oak's pub sign, which depicts four women dancing in a circle holding bundles of wood, suggests that there is more to the quiet village of Great Wishford, six miles west of Salisbury in Wiltshire, than first meets the eye.

On 29 May the villagers 'claim' their ancient rights to collect wood from nearby Grovely Wood, once part of a royal forest. This used to take place between Maundy Thursday and Whit Monday, but was transferred after the Restoration to Oak Apple Day – a public holiday, on which people were invited to celebrate Charles II's escape from the Roundheads by hiding in the 'Royal' oak at Boscobel in Shropshire.

A strange set of customs has persisted and evolved over hundreds of years. At four in the morning the Midnight Band, a gang of rowdy individuals banging dustbin lids, blowing trumpets off-key and shouting '*Grovely, Grovely, Grovely and All Grovely*', wakes up the villagers and will only leave when a house has 'shown a light'. At dawn villagers walk up to the wood to collect branches of oak, no thicker than a man's forearm, and bring them back 'by strength of people' – hand carts only, no horses. Some are hung above their front doors. One large oak branch is cut, decorated with ribbons and hoisted to the top of the church tower. This 'marriage bough' is supposed to bring luck to the year's newlyweds.

Part of the claiming ceremony has to be made at the altar of Salisbury Cathedral. At nine-thirty a coach leaves for Salisbury – at one time the villagers would have danced the whole way – where four women dressed in Victorian costume and carrying 'nitches' of wood (the ones on the pub sign) dance on the Cathedral Green, surrounded by people carrying a large white banner. They are all led to the high altar, where the Rector of Great Wishford reads out pertinent passages from a Charter dating back to 1603. Then the villagers make their 'shout' of '*Grovely, Grovely, Grovely and All Grovely*'.

Back in Great Wishford, after lunch in a marquee in Oak Apple Field, participants in the procession gather at Town End under an oak tree. Wearing sprigs of oak leaves, they are led by a man carrying the Union flag and followed by the May Queen, children from Wishford School and decorated carts. Also in the procession are Amesbury town band – sitting on straw bales on a tractor-pulled trailer – the four dancing women, carrying their white banner with '*Grovely! Grovely!*' etc written in green, and members of the Oak Apple Club, founded in 1892, carrying a banner and boughs of oak. The solemnity of this walking forest is quite moving. Spectators follow it through the main street and past the water meadows to the bridge over the river Wylye. The main procession continues for a while to turn round, but those carrying oak boughs pause at the bridge, the parish boundary.

On the return a skirmish is played out: teenagers who have been lurking among the gravestones in the high ground of the church emerge with water bombs and pelt one of the passing groups, the Red Barrows (dressed in early flying gear and pushing painted wheelbarrows, some with biplane wings), who retaliate with glee.

The main festivities take place in Oak Apple Field. By a handsome wooden tithe barn on staddle stones, in front of their banner, the four women perform their dances with their 'nitches', accompanied by a man playing the concertina. This is followed by another 'shout'. Then the morris dancers take over, children dance around the maypole and the fun of the fair begins.

See also ARBOR DAY, BOUNDARIES, CASTLETON GARLAND DAY, MAY DAY, MORRIS DANCING, OAK.

G R U F F Y   G R O U N D

The turmoil left behind by old surface mining, offering niches for plants and creeping creatures, is called gruffy ground in the Mendips and is prevalent around Lamb's Lair, Rowberrow, Shipham and the Yoxter Ranges. Frances Neale described how the grooves or gruffies came about: '*The prospective miner, having applied for a licence to dig on the common of his chosen minery, made a hole and stood waist deep in it. He then threw his "hack", the small and efficient miner's pickaxe, as far as he could in either direction . . . The line between his throws constituted his claim. In this way he dug his surface mine as a long trench, with spoil piled alongside, or tipped back into the trench at intervals. Such small scale, individual workings can be discovered all over central Mendip.*'

Passing a pub called the Miner's Arms is usually a clue to nearby old workings. The Somerset miners were seeking lead,

and the diggings, dumpings, collapsed shafts, leats (water channels) and buddle dams (separation ponds) stretch out in long lines along the rakes. Some of these can be traced back two thousand years, the last mine closing at the start of the twentieth century, leaving much to ponder around Charterhouse and Priddy Pools.

In Derbyshire, Yorkshire and as far as Westmorland, groughs are deep, sinuous, water-worn channels across peat, which walkers in the Dark Peak around Kinder and Bleaklow find exhausting and disorientating.

See also BLUE JOHN, BUILDING STONES, COAL MINING, COES, DEW PONDS, ENGINE HOUSES, FLINT, FOOTPATHS, HORSES & PONIES, INDUSTRIAL CHIMNEYS, LEAD MINES, LIMESTONE, MINES, MOORLAND, PIT TIPS, SOUGHS, ZIGZAGS.

G U N   D O G S

The favourite dogs of the English were bred as gun dogs – the Labrador retriever, cocker spaniel, golden retriever and English springer spaniel head the list. Some are associated with particular places as well as defining an aspect of Englishness.

Spaniels came from Spain. They have been with us for about five hundred years and have been bred for finding and flushing out game birds. The English cocker was originally bred as a woodcock-er. It is slightly smaller than the springer, with long, floppy ears. The English springer, which makes game birds 'spring' from the ground, is longer in the leg.

Apart from the diminutive King Charles and Cavalier King Charles spaniels, there are three other varieties. The field spaniel, originally similar to the cocker, was recognised as a separate breed in 1892, after which it was bred to become longer and heavier. The Sussex spaniel is also a heavier animal, with a dark gold-coloured coat. During the French Revolution, a number of spaniels were presented to the Duke of Newcastle for safekeeping by the Duke of Noailles. They were named after his seat in Nottinghamshire – Clumber spaniels are thick-set animals with basset hounds and St Bernards in their ancestry.

The English setter, now becoming rare, was bred from a spaniel by Edward Laverack in Ash, Shropshire in the 1870s. Like a pointer, a setter will indicate the location of a bird, but it crouches down, or 'sets', rather than 'points'. Pointers, which came from Spain in the early 1700s, find game and then freeze or 'point' with a foreleg raised.

St John's water dogs retrieved fishing nets along the coast of Newfoundland and were brought back by fishermen to Poole in Dorset. In the 1850s the Earl of Malmesbury crossed them with spaniels to produce the country's most successful gun dog and family pet – the Labrador retriever. Like golden retrievers, they have a natural instinct to take things in the mouth without harming them. Lord Tweedmouth is largely responsible for breeding the golden retriever, which

211

is descended from the Caucasian sheep-dog. There are only three breeders left in the UK of the third in the group – the curly-coated retriever – and the flat-coated retriever is also dwindling in popularity.

See also BLACK DOGS, DOGS, FIELDS, HOUNDS, HOUND TRAILING, MOORLAND, SHEEP-DOGS, TERRIERS.

G Y P S I E S

Perhaps a thousand years ago, warriors from the Indus valley in India began a working diaspora, which brought them to England in the 1500s. By this time their trades were as metal workers and smiths, showmen and entertainers. Their language still carries Sanskrit/Hindi dialect enriched by Persian, Greek, Romanian and Slav, and the preference of many is to be known as Roma.

Some have kept an understanding of the land and the usefulness of nature. Those patches of horse-radish (originating from near Asia) along road verges and at grassy triangles are thought by some to be the conscious plantings of Gypsies, revisited on their travels. The horse chestnut, hailing from the Balkans, is used as a medicine and a food. Jeff Cloves explored a theory that the tree was brought here by Roma in the early sixteenth century. The relationship between the tree and the smith's trade was well established by 1862, as H.W. Longfellow observed: '*Under a spreading chestnut tree, the village smithy stands*'.

The *vardo*, or horse-drawn caravan, ousted bender tents in the early nineteenth century, but before itself being eclipsed by modern trailers it had time to diverge into Bowtops, Burtons and Readings. The carvings of horses, birds and fruit and bright patterns that characterise them is strangely reminiscent of the flamboyantly painted lorries that ply the high passes of Afghanistan and India now, matched here by the vitality of fairground colours. Ostentation is still found in the cut-glass windows and chrome of the motor-pulled caravans more prevalent today.

With seasonal work based on hop, fruit and vegetable picking, Herefordshire, Kent and the Fens had a long tradition of attracting the same Roma families year after year. Still along wide verges and old road remnants they stake out washing lines and appear at home. The reduction in demand for seasonal labour and continual harassment has led many to settle recently around towns, although their contribution to the culture of London's East End is long established.

Roma have borne much prejudice during the five centuries that they have travelled our roads. '*My mother said/I never should/Play with the gypsies in the wood*', the old skipping song ran. Dislike of the unlike is amplified perhaps by envy of what appears to be the freedom of the road and the romance of the unattached. Or, rather, the deeply attached, being of the land rather than part of the scenery. John Clare gently captured both prejudice and understanding in the eighteenth century, calling Gypsies a '*quiet, pilfering, unprotected race*'.

From the late 1960s onwards their image was further tarnished in the eyes of the Establishment by the appearance of bands of hippies in old ambulances, buses and vans, usually young people disillusioned by capitalism and inspired by ecology. Not having the internal social structure of the Roma, these new travellers were neither traders nor jobbing workers and so gained the resentment of both house dwellers and the established travelling community, which often found itself blamed when 'new-age' travellers left mess and disruption in their wake.

With the lure of Stonehenge at the solstice and the Big Green Gathering in Somerset, social interaction continues as a lively part of new travellers' lives. For Roma, too, gatherings of all kinds are full of exuberance, music and colour, with boisterous weddings and the great horse fairs, such as at Appleby-in-Westmorland and Stow-on-the-Wold in Gloucestershire.

More than 325 'official' traveller sites exist, provided by local authorities. To our continuing shame they tend to be surrounded by industry, on land next to dumps or squeezed between transport routes, such as the one within the junction of the London Westway/M40 with the road to Shepherd's Bush. Revoking the 1968 obligation on local authorities to provide sites, in 1994 the Criminal Justice and Public Order Act encouraged those who had settled '*to move from caravan sites into both private and public sector housing*'. This laid the foundation for ongoing disputes between travellers, villagers and local authorities.

This was singularly to ignore the traditions and social requirements of communities that had been travelling for centuries. Many Roma are born and die in their vans, and when they die the caravan is burned. Some Roma commented: '*Live in houses? We would go round the bend looking at walls all the time*'; '*They would be taking away all our culture.*' Councils must now help travellers to locate appropriate sites. Given the resilience of the race, despite slavery, pogroms and everyday abrasion, the hope is that their many cultures will persist, to bring richness to our fairs, lanes, neighbourhoods and language.

One New Year's Day, around 1990, along a ridgeway in Wiltshire, snow brushing the milestones and the hedges, a *vardo*, cart and two coloured ponies stood, tied out in the freezing grass. A family were sitting around a fire, in the open, painting big wooden pegs bright red. It is a scene Thomas Hardy might have described. But there was no romance in it – the continuity and integrity of their lives left a humbling glimpse of the persistence of culture.

See also CANALS, DIALECTS, FAIRS & FAIRGROUNDS, FENS, FORGES, GLASTONBURY FESTIVAL, GRASSY TRIANGLES, GREEN LANES, HENGES & STONE CIRCLES, HOPS, HOP-GARDENS & HOP-YARDS, HORSE CHESTNUT, HORSE FAIRS, ORCHARDS, WILDFLOWERS.

Horley Old Style, Robert Norton, 1977.

HALF-YEAR BIRDS

It was Izaac Walton who called the swallows '*half-year birds*', suggesting that they are '*not seen to fly in England for six months in the year, but about Michaelmas leave us for a hotter climate*'. Spring would not be the same without the arrival of these migrants, some having survived a perilous 3,700-mile journey from South Africa and Namibia to be here.

We did not know where they went until 1913, when a female swallow that had been ringed in Staffordshire in 1911 was discovered in Natal, South Africa. Bird ringing was developed by a Dane, Hans Cornelius Mortensen, in 1899 and started in England in 1910. It was taken over by the British Trust for Ornithology in 1937, which has masterminded it ever since. Now three-quarters of a million birds are ringed in Britain and Ireland each year by thousands of trained volunteers, making possible our understanding of the movements and behaviour of many species.

Bird observatories around the coast, including Portland in Dorset, Dungeness and Sandwich Bay in Kent, Landguard in Suffolk, Holme in Norfolk, Gibraltar Point and Spurn Point in Lincolnshire, Filey Brigg in Yorkshire and Walney in Lancashire, keep detailed records of arrivals and departures. In 2003 the first swallows flew over the Portland Bird Observatory on 29 March; the house-martins followed on 8 April and the swifts on 23 April. They are all 'site-faithful', returning to the same nesting areas, sometimes the same nests, each year. We look out for the swift, house-martin and, particularly, the swallow to announce the official arrival of spring. They intimately live with us, in or under the house or barn roof.

Swallows prefer the farmyard, nesting in dark places, such as cow and pig sheds, with restricted access points to avoid the predation of magpies. The bowl-shaped nest, often placed on a ledge, is made of mud and grass bound with saliva; this takes many hours, so the same nest is used year after year. Swallows are more likely to nest where cattle and horses are grazing, presumably because of the insects associated with them and the fields they graze – they are abandoning the cow-less arable farms of East Anglia for the pastures of the West and the hills. They seem much rarer now; when you visit places by rivers, lakes or reservoirs, their aerial virtuosity as they skim low over the water to feed and drink, makes one feel sad at one's own local loss.

House-martins also make the incredible journey to and from sub-Saharan Africa, although it is not known exactly where. In spring they return to their old mud nests under bridges and the eaves of houses, painstakingly built on north- and east-facing walls. They often form loose colonies, their twitterings as they swoop up to their nests and the chirruping of fledglings bringing joy to any street. The availability of wet mud for nest-building is a constraining factor; it needs to be within 650 feet. Their nests need conservation status often more than our houses. New buildings seem rarely to create the eaves necessary to attract these summer friends, and over-tidy people destroy nests.

Swifts also travel from south of the Sahara. The only time they settle is when they are rearing their young. They are the last to arrive (late April/May) and the first to leave (middle to end of July). These city slickers have over-sized scimitar wings, sculpted to cut the air; noisy, risk-taking, assertive birds, their aerial courtship displays tell us that summer really has arrived. Near Hampstead Heath in north London the adolescents screech as they play 'wall of death' games along the streets in training for the longest of hauls. Their enthusiastic noises have given them local names, such as devil bird in west Yorkshire, devil's screecher in Devon, devil screamer in Hampshire and Yorkshire and, in Berkshire, simply devil.

In London, East Anglia and the warmer South East there are concentrations of swifts, although people notice there are fewer. The tower of Oxford University's Natural History Museum has held a swift colony for at least fifty years, recorded by ornithologist David Lack. About a hundred swifts return each year to nest in the ventilation holes and visitors to the museum can watch the young in their nests via a television monitor. Research on these swifts revealed that they '*keep the selfsame hole from year to year*', as John Clare put it, the occupants screaming at prospecting birds. When the eggs have hatched, the adults collect aerial plankton – a daily catch of a million insects by the whole colony over Oxford.

Swifts like to nest in church towers, under ill-fitting tiled or slate roofs or under the eaves of buildings more than sixteen feet high, gaining access through very small holes. Chris Mead argued for access for swifts to buildings: '*the problem is [that] the PVC soffits that are being put around eaves prevent swifts from reaching the wall plate, where the brickwork meets the roof. This can be remedied by a small hole being cut in the soffit where it meets the wall.*'

Nest boxes are available for all three species. Glasgow and Edinburgh councils demand that all new developments should be bird-friendly, especially with regard to swifts; in Amsterdam, Holland it has been made illegal to re-roof unless access for swifts is retained. As well as places to nest, all three species need ample supplies of insects, which seem to be fast diminishing in our drained, sanitised, overdeveloped land.

Meanwhile, we rejoice at the arrival of other visitors: the chiffchaff, echoing along a lane; the spotted flycatcher,

215

jaunty in its acrobatic endeavours to catch breakfast; the black redstart, searching for insects among the urban rubble it takes to be scree and on the new 'green roofs' specially made to welcome it in Deptford, south London. Wheatear and sandwich tern, grasshopper warbler and common sandpiper, tree pipit and whinchat – all return to 'their' places, our places.

Then there are the winter wanderers. The swooping groups of redwings seeking out holly berries, the field-fares scouring the meadow, the starlings from Saxony and Scandinavia, and the geese, hours of skeins marking out the Wash, the Severn estuary, Morecambe Bay and the Tees.

Their arrivals and departures signify much more than temporal landmarks. In 'Season Songs' Ted Hughes wrote of swifts: *'They've made it again,/Which means the globe's still working.'*

See also BEACHES, CUCKOOS & CUCKOO POUNDS, SKYLARKS, STARLINGS, TIDES.

H A L L O W E ' E N

The connection between the Celtic festival of Samhain and Spalding's pumpkin festival may seem tenuous, but traditions do not stand still. Samhain would have been marked by fires on the day of the autumn full moon. This was the start of the new year, the moment of the death of summer and the onset of winter; Beltane, our May Day, marked the start of summer. The Christian calendar tied All Hallows Eve – Hallowe'en – to 31 October, All Saints'/Hallows Day to 1 November and All Souls' Day to 2 November. Pumpkins, meanwhile, did not arrive here until the sixteenth century – now two million each year are grown at Spalding, Lincolnshire, the 'pumpkin capital' of England, which celebrates at the end of October.

For the Celts the day began at sunset, hence the 'eve' is still celebrated as the start of the festival; this in-between time was fraught with danger. This was a moment when the dead were able to commune with the living, some to play havoc with us. Perhaps human sacrifices were made to appease them, and remnants of this ritual have been stolen into our Bonfire Night celebrations on or near 5 November, with the burning of effigies of Guy Fawkes and others.

This is a time when ghosts, hobgoblins, witches, fairies and demons are abroad, and one ploy persists to frighten

the spirits away. Heads with scary faces are made from hollowed-out and carved turnips and swedes, lit by candles from inside and carried as lanterns on poles or long wires. In many places these have been supplanted by the much-bigger pumpkins. Guisers – mummers who wore blackened faces or masks and costumes to curdle the blood a little – calling at houses for money have been replaced by children dressing up as witches or with frightening masks, asking for sweets or playing the American game of trick or treat (which origi-nated in Scotland).

At Hallowe'en it is possible to see into the future, or so it was thought. It was known as Nut Crack Night in the Cheviots, where nuts were used in divination games. Two nuts, representing a man and a woman, were put into the embers of a fire. If they simmered together, a happy marriage was predicted; if they hissed and spat, the marriage was doomed. If a person wanted to discover where their future partner lived, apple pips were consulted. In Lancashire you would move in a circle, squeezing a pip between finger and thumb. When the pip jumped it would suggest the direction in which to look.

Pippin, pippin, paradise,
Tell me where my true love lies:
East, West, North or South,
Pulling Brig or Cockermouth.

In Yorkshire this is Mischief Night – pranks are played. In Nottinghamshire it was the prime time for knocking on doors and running away. Hallowe'en games, always more popular in the North, are played and special food eaten. Tony Hopkins remembered *'bobbing for apples, eating treacle scones hanging from a clothes pulley, and finding coins wrapped in mashed potato'*. Charms, such as rings, wishbones and other totems of divination, were also hidden in dishes of mashed potato, and in some places 'mash of nine sorts' (of vegetables) was used.

On the last Thursday in October, children in Hinton St George, Somerset carry punkies, mangel-wurzel or pumpkin lanterns around the streets while chanting the 'Punky Night Song' and collecting money for charity. This custom is supposed to have originated long ago, when the women of the village, worried about the absence of their husbands, who had gone to Chiselborough Fair, went out to look for them, carrying punkies. Now there are competi-tions for the best-decorated punkie, and the Punky King and Queen are crowned. Christina Hole thought that this custom was likely to have come out of the Hallowe'en guisers' ritual, while Ronald Hutton reminded us that punkies, or spunkies, are *'the common name for the balls of ignited marsh gas sometimes seen upon the Levels'*.

See also APPLE DAY, BONFIRE NIGHT, CONFECTIONERY, HAUNTED PLACES, TAR BARREL ROLLING.

HARBOURS

Where sheltered havens do not naturally exist, we have conspired to build them. The shapes of harbours tell us much about the need for protection from winds and waves, tidal movements, the volatility of rivers and the problems of silting and longshore drift.

The rias of the South West offer natural anchorage out of the Atlantic weather, but elsewhere breakwaters, piers and quays create shelter, famously at Lyme Regis in Dorset, with its protective arm of the Cobb. Small stone harbours nestle into coves along the rocky coasts of Devon and Cornwall. The fishing village of Mevagissey in Cornwall has an inner and an outer harbour, both embraced by walls. The harbours of Shoreham, Sussex and Great Yarmouth, Norfolk, which take advantage of long, deflected estuaries, need constant dredging. Staithes, Yorkshire cowers into the steep ravine behind its breakwaters and, like so many small harbours, it dries at low tide. By contrast, Whitehaven in Cumberland offers 25 acres of water behind lock gates.

Small harbours continue their decline as fishing and trading patterns change. Leisure boating and tourism are moving in. At Brighton the artificial harbour at Black Rock is one of the biggest marina developments in Europe.

See also BOATS, FERRIES, LOST VILLAGES, RIAS, SHIPPING FORECAST, TIDES, WAREHOUSES.

HARDS

A hard, often simply and anciently constructed, is a firm edge of stone, gravel or concrete along a river or seaside foreshore. Small ferries, boat builders, fishermen and commercial adventurers all need small-scale landing and launching places, together with myriad recreation seekers, from dinghy sailors to anglers, who want to reach the water. But rights of access to the edges of rivers and the sea have dwindled, together with those of our footpaths and commons.

Hithes, staithes, quays, steps and stairs all offer possibilities. Along the Hampshire coast the county council has identified seventy public slipways or hards and nine beach launching areas. The Bursledon Rights of Way Group is fighting for continued access to the river Hamble, where commercial activity has given way to recreational use and encroachment by developers presses. Similarly, along the river Thames, Kim Wilkie has counted more than forty slipways from Hampton to Isleworth and many more landing stages.

See also AEGIRS, ALLEYS, BEACHES, BOAT RACE, BOATS, BORES, COMMONS, EYOTS, FOOTPATHS, ISLANDS, PIERS, QUICKSAND, RIVERS, SAND-DUNES, SEA TRACTOR, SHELLFISH, STAIRS, TIDES.

217

HARE PIE SCRAMBLE

No boundaries and few rules govern the mass-participation contest waged in the village of Hallaton, Leicestershire on Easter Monday, which shares elements with Shrovetide Football and the Haxey Hood Game.

Although the origins of the hare pie scramble and bottle-kicking are unknown, the rector of Hallaton has paid for the making of two hare pies and provision of ales and penny loaves for the Easter Monday celebrations since 1771 – a condition imposed with the gift of a piece of land.

In the morning an enormous 'hare' pie (made with beef) is blessed in the church and, after lunch, the rector distributes parts of it by the church gates. People then gather in the Market Square by the conical butter cross, where the loaves are thrown to onlookers and ribbons are tied onto three wooden, iron-hooped 'field bottles' – small barrels originally used by farm workers for their midday refreshment.

The villagers regroup outside The Fox Inn and follow a group of characters: a green-robed man carrying a pole surmounted by a bronze hare; women bearing a basket of bread rolls and the rest of the hare pie; men wearing rugby shirts holding up the bottles, two of which contain beer. Accompanied by a band, all make their way to a small rise in a field known as Hare Pie Bank. The rest of the hare pie is scattered and scrambled for.

From top, left to right: Mevagissey, Cornwall; Dover, Kent; Whitehaven, Cumberland; Lowestoft, Suffolk; Blyth, Northumberland; Shoreham, Sussex.

Then, two teams of any number from Hallaton and Medbourne attempt to carry the bottles over the Hallaton stream or Medbourne hedge, a mile apart on either side of the Bank. One of the full bottles is thrown up into the air three times; on the third throw a mass of bodies launches towards it. Each team tries to manoeuvre the bottle towards its end in a series of moving loose scrums that may last an hour or so. After a 'goal' has been scored, the second bottle is used and, if there is a tie, the third, empty barrel. The winning team drinks the contents of the bottles (at least) by the butter cross and, more often than not, one of the victors manages to sit on top of it.

See also FOOTBALL, HARES, HAXEY HOOD GAME, MARKET CROSSES, OBELISKS, SHROVETIDE GAMES.

H A R E S

The hare, the hare-kin,
Old Big-bum, Old Bouchart,
The hare-ling, the frisky one,
Old turpin, the fast traveller,
The way-beater, the white-spotted one,
The lurker in ditches, the filthy beast,
Old Wimount, the coward,
The slinker-away, the nibbler
The one it's bad luck to meet, the white-livered,
The scutter, the fellow in the dew,
The grass nibbler, Old Goibert,
The one who doesn't go straight home, the traitor,
The friendless one, the cat of the wood . . .
The hare's mazes . . .
The dew-beater, the dew-hopper,
The sitter on its form, the hopper in the grass . . .
The stag of the cabbages, the cropper of herbage . . .
The animal that all men scorn,
The animal that no one dares name . . .

This is but the start of a list of 'Names of the Hare in English', a late thirteenth-century poem from Shropshire. It offers 77 different names for the hare, many of them derogatory, supposedly for the hunter to recite. The hare was one of the taboo animals of ancient Britain; even her name (many thought all were female) should not be spoken, hence the alternatives.

The mountain hare is native. While some believe that the brown hare has been here since the Iron Age, it is more likely that it was brought here two thousand years ago and has pushed the mountain hare into the hills.

Hares were believed to bring good and bad luck: if a fisherman in the North East met one on the way to work, he went home. Elsewhere to encounter one may be lucky, unless it is white. In Cornwall a white hare presaged storms.

The hare was a symbol of spring's fertility in ancient Egypt and later in Europe as well, where it became associated with the goddess Eostre and, more recently, with Easter customs. An old game was to search for eggs laid by the Easter Hare, which became displaced by North America's preference for the Easter Bunny.

George Ewart Evans and David Thomson's exposition *The Leaping Hare* says: '*a Claydon (Suffolk) woman told us she used to say Hares, Hares before going to bed on the last day of the month, and Rabbits, Rabbits, when she got up in the morning. But this is a very common custom. The connection of the hare with the moon and therefore with the monthly cycle needs no further comment.*' Many legends and rich folklore link the hare with the moon, the supernatural, fertility, spring, fire and witches. It was commonly held that witches would transform themselves into hares.

The number of hares shot on farms and by organised drives on estates, usually in February, was estimated at two to three hundred thousand per year by the Burns Report in 2000. Once widespread, hares have declined in numbers since the 1960s, owing to the intensification of farming, increased use of agrichemicals and the move from cutting hay to earlier silage – the cutters kill the leverets, which stay in their forms (nests) among the growing crop. Hares are now most likely to be seen on the arable farms of Cambridgeshire, Norfolk and Suffolk or on aerodromes. They are taken by foxes and buzzards and poached by gangs of men with lurchers.

Hares can be differentiated from rabbits by their larger size, extraordinary amber eyes, longer ears with black tips and large, powerful hind legs. They can reach speeds of 45 miles per hour over short distances and can change direction suddenly, which helps them to evade predators – this is called the maze. This agility has been both their saving and their downfall: man has enjoyed the spectacle of pitting dogs against hares for sport. Before the Hunting Act 2004 made it illegal, hares were hunted by one hundred packs of beagles, basset hounds (on foot) and harriers (on horseback) and by about 24 hare-coursing clubs (using greyhounds and whippets). The annual Waterloo Cup at Great Altcar, near Southport, Lancashire, a three-day hare-coursing event, attracted ten thousand spectators in 2003.

Lines from William Blake's 'Auguries of Innocence' are brought to mind – *'Each outcry of the hunted hare/A fibre of the brain does tear'* – and from *The Dog Beneath the Skin* by W.H. Auden: *'Happy the hare at morning, for she cannot read/The Hunter's waking thoughts . . .'*

The hare's unusually gregarious springtime behaviour of chasing and 'fighting' is a ritual of the mating season. A dominant male (buck or jack) will chase and drive away others who come close to the female (doe or jill) he is guarding. Boxing, while they stand on their hind legs, usually takes place between a doe and a buck whose advances are premature.

See also AIRFIELDS, EASTER CUSTOMS, FOLKTALES, HORSES & PONIES, HOUNDS, MOUNTAIN HARES, RED FOXES, THREE HARES, UNLUCKY WORDS.

HARVEST FESTIVALS

Harvest Home was the culmination of the agricultural year; the crop was gathered in and the farmer could repay his workers with food, drink and entertainment. According to Charles Kightly, these harvest suppers were known as the Horkey in eastern England, Mell Supper in northern England and Harvest Frolic in the West Country. To quieten these rowdy, and often drunken, occasions, the Victorians introduced church services to bless the crops, based on blessing the Lammas, or first loaf, in August. Today flowers and foliage welcome parishioners, who bring tins of beans and pineapples, with some local fruits and vegetables, to be blessed. Special harvest loaves resembling wheatsheafs are sometimes baked.

Harvest festival in the church of St Martin-in-the-Fields by Trafalgar Square in London sees London's costermongers, the Pearly Kings and Queens, process in their elaborate costumes of black velvet covered with patterns of pearl buttons to give thanks for the abundance of fruits and vegetables that they sell in London's streets. At Richmond, north Yorkshire, the ceremony of First Fruits takes place in September.

Many faiths hold their own harvest blessings. Succoth, the Jewish Feast of Tabernacles, is a reminder of forty years in the wilderness journeying from Egypt to Israel. Sukkots – little shelters – are made and hung with fruits and vegetables. Vaisakhi, an ancient Punjabi harvest festival, is celebrated in April by fifty thousand or more Sikhs in Southall, west London.

See also BREAD, CORN DOLLIES.

HAUNTED PLACES

Anywhere that people have lived is haunted in some way, by physical legacies, memories and associations. The British Tourist Office estimates that these 'Ghostly Islands' have perhaps ten thousand recorded hauntings.

No surprise, then, that England is the land of the Gothic ghost story. Montague Rhodes James, whose supernatural tales have never been out of print, was born in Goodnestone, Kent in 1862. Kent also boasts the 'most haunted village', Pluckley, with nearly thirty ghosts. The residents dread Hallowe'en, not for its hauntings but for the crowds of drunken ghost-hunters who cause more havoc than poltergeists. Derby, by contrast, revels in its haunted heritage, with 159 hauntings (beating rival York's 126).

Ghosts can have regional varieties. Lancashire has its boggart, which becomes a barguest or a bogle in Northumberland. Boggart Hole Clough on the fringes of Manchester recalls one, as does Hollinhey Clough at Towneley Hall near Burnley, where holly trees (hollins) were planted to keep one happy. The names might derive from the Germanic *burgh-gaist* (town ghost) or *berg-geist* (mountain ghost). Northumberland and Durham have silkies, silk-clad spirits that have left their mark on Silky's Bridge near Stamfordham and a tree known as Silky's Chair at Belsay. In Yorkshire you might see a waft or waff, but you won't live long to tell the tale – they take on your image in order to destroy you.

219

Churches, cemeteries and churchyards are perhaps obvious places to suffer hauntings, with castles and old manor houses a close second. Berry Pomeroy in Devon claims the banner of most haunted castle in England, and castles from Scarborough in Yorkshire to Bamburgh in Northumberland, Burgh in Norfolk to Scotney in Kent, and Wardour in Wiltshire to Tintagel in Cornwall, all have stories.

The East is permeated by Old Norse beliefs and fears. Perhaps the god Woden drove his wild hunt across the fens, kick-starting countless tales of phantom horses, riders and coaches (of the horse-drawn kind rather than some other-worldly Leyland Leopard). Near Welwyn in Hertfordshire, White Horse Lane is haunted by the eponymous horse, albeit headless. It is illustrated on the pub sign at nearby Burnham Green.

Places once hunted are also haunted: Herne the Hunter's legends centre on Windsor Forest; the Forest of Bowland in Lancashire was 'witch-country'. The trees themselves attract associations, from the churchyard yew to the Great Melton Beech in Norfolk, where a maternal ghost nurses her child at midnight. The Midlands has its haunted battlefields, notably Edgehill, and the celebrity of highwayman Dick Turpin on Watling Street and at Woughton on the Green in Buckinghamshire. The West is haunted by legends of its heroes: Francis Drake in Devon; King Arthur and Merlin at Tintagel, Cornwall.

The vicar of Chiseldon, Wiltshire in 1864 reported a strange phenomenon that had been observed near a line of elms, trees known in country lore as *'bad, sinister trees'*, according to Ted Walker, perhaps because of their use in coffin making. These elms played host to a ghostly *'sack of water'*; Katy Jordan suggests this is an example of the 'Boneless', an amorphous shape that can also be found in the folklore of Somerset and Oxford. The Oxford Boneless was described chillingly as *'a shapeless Summat as slides behind and alongside in the dark night'*. Crowborough in Sussex ventures a step further, as Jennifer Westwood explained: *'Jarvis Brook Road was haunted by a bag of soot, which on certain nights would chase people.'*

See also BLACK DOGS, BRICKS, BRIDGES, CASTLES, CEMETERIES, CHURCHES, CHURCHYARDS, CROSSROADS, ELM, FINGERPOSTS, FOLKTALES, HALLOWE'EN, HOLLY, HOTELS, INNS, LANDMARK TREES, PUBS, RIVERS, ROADS, YEW.

H A W T H O R N

Named for its fearsome spines and bright red autumnal fruit – hags or haws, relished by bank voles and blackbirds alike – these stout, hardy trees grace hedgerows throughout the land on every soil. As solitary trees, hawthorns have long marked boundaries and significant landmarks, winning mentions in Anglo-Saxon charters. The Salcombe Regis

Thorn near Sidmouth in Devon probably marks the spot of an ancient open-air meeting place, as does the Hethel Old Thor, or Witch of Hethel, in Norfolk, cited in a thirteenth-century document. The hawthorn spinny on Goonhilly Downs in Cornwall, which still thrives, was noted in records of AD 977.

Long accorded supernatural powers – some say a 'thorn cult' thrived in pre-Christian times – the hawthorn still symbolises the change from spring to summer. The tender young leaves, nibbled by adventurous children, were once a famine food, inspiring the ironic name bread-and-cheese tree. It is also known as the whitethorn, quick, quick-thorn, thorn-bush, mother-die and, most often, the may, after the month in which its abundant white flowers, with their stale, sweet scent, burst into bloom. The tree has long been linked to sex and fertility and especially to licentious May Day celebrations, used to make garlands for maypole dancers, Jacks in the Green and Green Georges. It is a plant to be kept outside – bad luck or a death in the family follows it indoors.

Like any magic, hawthorn can harm as well as protect, and prohibitions and warnings abound. Yet the tree has entered churches, sprouting from the mouth of many a Green Man; in Southwell Minster master carvers wreathed their heads in hawthorn leaves, together with other magical plants: oak, ivy, cinquefoil, buttercup and maple. Sacred thorns stood by sacred water sources – holy wells, as they became.

Joseph of Arimathea is said to have come to Glastonbury after Christ's death, carrying a staff of thorn. His staff rested on the ground, and there grew a tree with special powers – the Glastonbury thorn flowers in winter, at Christmas and again in May. Cuttings of this variety (*Crataegus monogyna* 'Biflora') still grow in the abbey ruins and at Appleton Thorn in Cheshire. Closely related is the Midland thorn (*C. laevigata*), sometimes called the woodland thorn, with plum-like leaves and two-seeded haws. Less common, it is most often found on clay soils in central and southern England, where it can be an indicator of old woodland.

See also ABBEYS, ALDER, ANCIENT TREES, ASH, BAWMING THE THORN, BEECH, BIRCH, BLACK POPLAR, BLACKTHORN, CATHEDRALS, CHURCHES, EARTH STATIONS, ELM, FIELD MAPLE, GREEN MAN, HAZEL, HEDGES, HOLLY, HOLM OAK, HORNBEAM, HORSE CHESTNUT, JUNIPER, LANDMARK TREES, LIME, LONDON PLANE, MAY DAY, MONKEY-PUZZLE, OAK, ORCHARDS, PEARS, POPLAR, ROWAN, ROYAL FORESTS, SCOTS PINE, SWEET CHESTNUT, SYCAMORE, WALNUT, WELLS, WHITEBEAM, WILLOW, WOODS, YEW.

H A X E Y   H O O D   G A M E

This game has a prelude almost too extraordinary to recount. No wonder its origins are obscure and it only happens once a year.

220

It takes place on the afternoon of 6 January (or the day before if the 6th is a Sunday) in Haxey and Westwoodside in north Lincolnshire. After a tour of the pubs, the bells of Haxey church begin to ring. The Fool, Lord of the Hood and Chief Boggan lead the procession towards the church, while everyone sings the Hood Song. The Fool, reminiscent of a court jester, has a black-and-red-smeared face and wears a red shirt and white trousers with red patches. He carries the Hood, which is a two-foot-long cylinder of rolled-up rope covered in leather. The Lord of the Hood wears a scarlet coat and top hat full of flowers and feathers, and carries a staff made from thirteen willow wands bound thirteen times. Behind them are the Chief Boggan, also in a scarlet coat and similar top hat, and his twelve Boggans, wearing red shirts.

The Fool attempts to escape, but is quickly caught by the Boggans and mounts the Mowbray Stone, the base of an ancient cross by the church wall. He makes a speech

that always includes the words 'Hoose age n' hoose, toon agen' toon/If tha' meets a man, nok 'im doon/But doant 'ot 'im', and 'mysteriously' states, as Christina Hole added, 'that two bullocks and a half have been killed, but the other half had to be left running about the field, and can be fetched if it is wanted'. At the same time a small fire is lit beside him, a custom known as 'smoking the Fool', which is a tamer version of a former practice.

The Lord of the Hood leads the participants and spectators to Upperthorpe Hill on the boundary of the two villages. What follows is a kind of free-for-all rugby game – the aim is to get the Hood to the Carpenter's Arms at Westwoodside or the King's Arms, Duke William Hotel or The Loco at Haxey. The Hood cannot be thrown forwards, carried or kicked, but is pushed or pulled along.

For the first hour or so, the youngsters try to get any of twelve sack 'hoods', or 'dummies', past the Boggans, who

have formed a wide ring around the crowd, to one of the pubs. Then the Lord of the Hood throws up the leather Hood, also known as the Sway Hood, and a large Sway (scrum) forms around it as each team tries to push it towards their pub. A hundred or so people may be in the Sway at any one time, and it may take a few hours to reach the desired goal, demolishing walls and trampling crops and cars in the process. The winning landlord puts the Hood on display for the coming year and celebrates victory by offering drinks on the house.

See also BELLS & BELL-RINGING, FOOTBALL, HARE PIE SCRAMBLE, NICKNAMES, SHROVETIDE GAMES.

HAY MEADOWS

'The flower-rich hay meadow is a masterpiece of the pastoral arts. Like the great cathedrals, its construction has taken a century or more. Like them it is the handiwork of generations of unknown craftspeople.' Graham Harvey is describing fields cut in summer for winter fodder and later grazed, a fine example of how we and nature together can make useful, beautiful and ecologically rich places.

Richard Jefferies, writing in the 1880s about his early Wiltshire life, tussled with the drudgery of toil but couldn't stop himself evoking the depth of pleasure to be found. 'I used to stand by the mower and follow the scythe sweeping down thousands of the broad flowered daisies, the knotted knapweeds, the blue scabious, the yellow rattles, sweeping so close and true that nothing escaped; and yet, although I had seen so many hundreds of each, although I had lifted armfuls day after day, still they were fresh. They never lost their newness, and even now each time I gather a wild flower it feels a new thing.'

Hay was needed in quantity to feed plough oxen, horses and other stock over winter. Not long ago the hay meadow was the most common type of field in the lowlands. But a mere five per cent have escaped agricultural intensification. The 1980s seem to have been the decade of escalating loss – in just six years Dorset lost sixty per cent of its best flower meadows.

The typical regime was of annual cutting after mid-July, then grazing on and off until April, resulting in perhaps as many as 150 different grasses and flowers in one meadow. Cutting for silage comes too early, and cutting the hay before mid-July gives no time for flowers and grasses to set their seeds, ground-nesting birds to fledge or myriad insects to go through their life cycles. Traditional hay meadows are 'unimproved' in the sense that they have received only light dressings of farmyard manure and occasional liming. Artificial fertiliser positively encourages fewer species of stronger, coarse grasses, such as perennial rye grass and crested dog's-tail, which out-compete and severely reduce the abundance of flowering plants.

221

Graham Harvey describes some of their variety. '*In northern England the neutral hay meadows, which are concentrated in the valley grasslands and river banks of the Pennine dales of Swaledale, Wharfedale and Teesdale, have their own special glory. Here the dominant grass is the early flowering sweet vernal grass, Anthoxanthum odoratum, whose dried leaves impart the smell of new-mown hay to a winter cattle yard. Wood crane's-bill, Geranium sylvaticum, with its lobed leaves and purple flowers, is the second characteristic species.*'

He continues: '*Like the southern hay meadows, those of the north have their own particular floral gems. Among them are the powerfully aromatic perennial spignel, Meum athamanticum, and a trio of rarer variants of the common lady's mantle, Alchemilla vulgaris, with its small yellow-green flowers.*'

These are some of the richest surviving hay meadows, but they cover less than two and a half thousand acres now. In the lowlands, most of the remaining hay meadows are in river floodplains, where the flowers are joined by ragged robin and marsh marigold. Examples include the Derwent Ings in the Vale of York and the Lammas meadows along the river Lugg in Herefordshire.

Goldfinches come in search of the seeds of thistles and knapweeds; twites and linnets eat the seeds of the sorrel and dandelions; kestrels and barn owls hunt for long-tailed field mice, bank voles, field voles and shrews. The burnet moth and meadow brown, marbled white and orange-tip butterflies flutter in places variously inhabited by glow-worms, meadow grasshoppers, bush crickets, meadow ants, craneflies, hares and rabbits.

How did we let these wonderful places slip through our fingers, once so common and now so rare? Every country parish, and a few city ones, too, should resolve to have its own hay meadow to enjoy the richness and the hard but social work.

See also ANTY-TUMPS, BARNS, CATTLE, DALES, DRYSTONE WALLS, FIELD BARNS, FIELDS, FRITILLARY MEADOWS, GLOW-WORMS, INGS, RIVERS, SHEEP.

H A Z E L

The magnificent hazels of Spittlemoor Coppice in Hatfield Forest, Essex may hint at how great stands of hazel once dominated the land – hazel was among the first trees to colonise as the Ice Age came to an end. Gradually, however, taller, warmth-loving trees, such as pine, elm, oak and lime, moved in and hazel lost its pre-eminence. The diminutive trees found a new home along edges of oak and ash forests and in the understorey.

Nuthatches and jays, red squirrels, wild boars and beavers, which sometimes store whole branches of hazel, helped to ensure that the species was widely distributed.

Hazel may even have travelled back here in the company of prehistoric settlers, who found a staple food in its nutritious seeds – hazel is the only British wild tree that produces edible nuts (walnuts and chestnuts arrived centuries later). Humans soon learned that the tree responds well to regular cutting, sprouting a crown of sturdy shoots from its stump. This created the industry, sixty centuries old, of hazel coppice.

In the medieval economy, hazel was a vital resource, and pre-Conquest charters frequently cited landmark hazel groves, hazel hedges and solitary trees. The fifth commonest tree in Anglo-Saxon place-names – remembered in Haslemere, Surrey, for instance, and Nuthampstead, Hertfordshire – the tree has a wealth of local names, from cibbedy-cut in Cornwall to hasketts in Dorset. Its versatile wood is exceptionally useful, able to be twisted and bent without breaking. Scores of applications include wattle-and-daub for houses, woven hurdles as fences – especially vital for folding sheep on the downs – spars for thatching, pea and bean sticks, faggots for fuel, poles for walking sticks and crooks, rods for fish traps, stakes for hedging and split poles for basket work and barrel hoops.

The once-common dormouse, the hazel dormouse, relies on the nuts and shelter offered by dense hazel coppice. During the past century or so its numbers have fallen dramatically, in step with the precipitous decline of hazel coppice. As the harvest lost its commercial value, men stopped cutting the hazel stools regularly and in rotation, every dozen years or so. If neglected for more than forty years, hazel stools rapidly die; according to Oliver Rackham hazel is now the most threatened of common trees, apart from elm, partly due to damage by grey squirrels.

In 1945 there were just 114,000 acres of hazel coppice surviving in Britain; more than a quarter of these were in Hampshire. But now only a fraction survives, mostly as derelict, overgrown hazel stools shaded out by standard trees. Traditional management with regular coppicing persists in a few woods, however, thanks to renewed interest in hurdles for garden fences and spars for thatching. Particularly on nature reserves, a revival of the ancient art of coppicing is benefiting both hazel and the varied wildlife that depends on it: hazel supports 106 plant-eating insects and gall mites. In spring, in lighter clearings, bluebells, red campion, white windflowers and yellow primroses cover the woodland floor.

A magical tree, hazel was reputed to be supernaturally protected from destruction and was the proper source of wands and divining rods. Symbols of fertility and plenty, its nuts were carried to ward off rheumatism; two nuts on a single stalk, a loady nut in Devon, could cure toothache. To Christianise the pagan tree, its nuts were claimed by a

Benedictine saint, Filbeard or Filbert – his saint's day is 22 August, just when the nuts begin to ripen. Two months later, 31 October is not only Hallowe'en but also Nut Crack Night. In the north of England, two nuts placed side by side in the fire divine the future of a couple: if the nuts jump, the pairing will be short-lived.

In medieval times gathering nuts in season became part of the labour owed by peasants to their overlord; by 1826 nutting was a social occasion. Larger, cultivated varieties of hazelnut, Lambert's Filbert or Kent Cob, are grown in plats in Kent.

See also BLACK & WHITE BUILDINGS, BONFIRE NIGHT, COBNUTS, FERAL ANIMALS, FOLKTALES, HALLOWE'EN, ORCHARDS, PINFOLDS, SHEEP-FOLDS, WOODS.

H E A T H L A N D

The classic lowland heath – Thomas Hardy's '*blasted heath*' – shimmers in summer under a warm sun and buzzes with bees as yellow gorse blooms scent the air with coconut. In autumn, heathers send up spikes of delicate pink, mauve or purple flowers – common heather or ling, bell heather, cross-leaved heath, Dorset heath and Cornish heath are five species, each with their own character. Five thousand species of invertebrate make a home here, including silver-studded blue butterflies, green tiger beetles and slave-making ants.

Formed thousands of years ago by the felling and burning of forest, heaths were long prized by rural communities as common grazing land for cattle and ponies. The commoners also cut gorse, bracken and heather for fodder, fuel, bedding and thatch. During the past two centuries the lion's share has been lost to agriculture, forestry, golf-courses, quarrying, roads and housing estates. But England still holds a fifth of the world's lowland heath, about 89,000 acres.

On a global scale heathland is an unusual habitat. Strongholds remain in Dorset, east Devon, the Lizard Peninsula in Cornwall, Breckland and the Suffolk Sandlings in East Anglia, and in Surrey and Hampshire. The largest patch of surviving heath in the Midlands is Cannock Chase, with upland cowberry and crowberry, as well as lowland bell heather and a rare bilberry known as the Cannock Chase berry.

Exmoor ponies, Highland cattle, feral goats and Soay sheep graze heaths managed as nature reserves to benefit their rich and distinctive fauna. For example, the night-singing field cricket inhabits Lord's Piece near Fittleworth in west Sussex, while the Dartford warbler is named after a heath in Kent but has its stronghold in the south Dorset and Hampshire heaths. Smooth snakes, adders and sand lizards relish the open sand; stonechats perch on top of gorse. Nightjars feed on the abundant moths – emperor, oak eggar, common heath, ling pug – while hobbies (small falcons) dive on the dragonflies, especially on the wet heathland of Thursley Common and on Esher and Oxshott Commons in Surrey.

Lullington Heath on the South Downs in east Sussex is a rare example of chalk heath, where acid soils overlay alkaline chalk. It supports a unique mixture of heathers and tormentil among chalk-loving plants, such as thyme and salad burnet, and a rich complement of butterflies, including dark green fritillary, green hairstreak, grayling and grizzled skipper.

See also COMMONS, GOLF-COURSES, GORSE, HORSES & PONIES, MOORLAND, ROUNDABOUTS, SANDSTONES, SHEEP, THATCH.

H E D G E S

'*If we never win a Test match again, we shall still have the world's finest hedges!*', Edmund Blunden exclaimed in 1935. '*Their white and red may, their bramble-roses, their wild-apple bloom, their honeysuckles, their traveller's joy, have been the spring of the year to most of us more inseparably than any other aspect of the season.*'

Sad to say, since 1950, more than half of our hedgerows have been ripped up – condemned as old-fashioned relics that shaded crops, sheltered vermin, wasted space and got in the way of farm machinery. For years the government paid farmers to bulldoze them out of existence. At last, in the 1990s, agri-environment schemes began to encourage care for those that remained and the planting of new ones. In 1997 the Hedgerows Regulations made it illegal to remove most countryside hedgerows without planning permission. But hedges continue to be lost through neglect and bad management.

Those that survive are utterly various, legacies of diverse soil and climate and agricultural histories. A few are remnants of lost woods: at Shelley in Suffolk one unusual roadside hedge of woodland trees – small-leaved lime and service – is all that remains of the eighteenth-century Withers Wood. Most are planted; nowhere else has plotted and pieced its land in the same way. '*Hedges are good for intimacy, an enhanced sense of locality*', Adam Nicolson wrote. '*That closeness of hedge-texture, the way in which they reflect and embody the nature of the particular place, is why they have such a hold on the English imagination.*'

The starkest contrast is between the 'champion' fields of the clay vales of the Midlands and the 'bosky', long-enclosed countryside of the South West. In the Midlands, where fields are large and regular in shape, hedges are typically thin,

223

Dorset heath (*Erica ciliaris*).

Cumberland hedge bank.

Devon hedge bank.

Midlands.

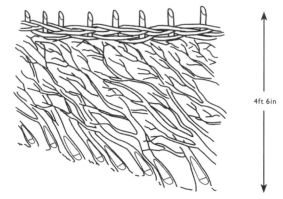

4ft 6in

Staffordshire.

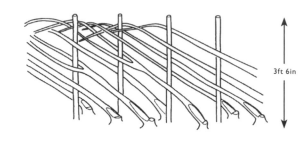

3ft 6in

Yorkshire.

224

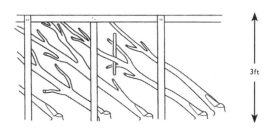

3ft

South of England.

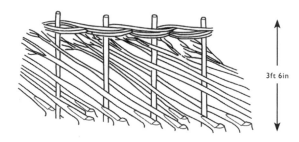

3ft 6in

quickset (hawthorn), straight with right-angled corners, '*all very tidy – and dull*', opined the great landscape historian W.G. Hoskins. '*It is an artificial and comparatively modern landscape, and that is what is wrong with it, what makes it so unsatisfying, so unappealing to anybody born in the far west, beyond the Somerset plain.*'

The Midlands hedges were planned and planted only two hundred years ago, as common fields were parcelled out to landholders and enclosed. By contrast, in the ancient landscape of the South West, small, irregular fields are '*shut in by massive hedge-banks which are often faced with great blocks of native stone; and on top of these hedge-banks tall trees – sycamore, oak, ash and elm – grow freely*', Hoskins wrote. '*The hedge-banks are high and massive because they had to keep wild animals away from the stock – or give shelter to stock and crops – especially in Cornwall and west Devon where the salt Atlantic winds stunt even the trees.*' On Cornwall's Land's

End peninsula, hedge banks that carry hardly any shrubs have been dated to the Bronze Age, ranking them among the world's oldest artefacts still in use.

Hedges still mark ancient boundaries, between manors, parishes or larger estates, in many parts of the country. Saxon settlers called the hedge *haga*, derived from their name for the hawthorn fruit. In some places the hedge gave its name to the land it enclosed: Haigh in south Yorkshire and Manchester; Hagley in Herefordshire; Northaw in Hertfordshire; Thornhaugh in Northamptonshire.

If hedges imposed order and ownership on an evolving landscape, they also provided a valuable resource, especially as woodland declined during the medieval period. Hedge trees – oak, ash and elm – were often pollarded to produce a crop of fuel wood every decade or so. This practice also lengthened a tree's life; many ancient trees were once pollards in hedges. Hornbeam is popular in the South East, its hard wood valued for flails and mill machinery. On Exmoor beech standards tower above the beech hedges planted when the moor was enclosed in the nineteenth century.

Hedges provided fodder for livestock. Elm was a favourite 'leafy hay' in the Midlands, and many hedges composed entirely of elm are found on the south Essex plain and on the Dengie peninsula, as well as in parts of Kent, Suffolk and Worcestershire. Holly-rich hedges are plentiful in and around the Pennines and in parts of the South East – holly is stock-proof, tolerant of grazing, provides excellent winter forage for sheep and can thrive on poor, sandy soils. Kent still has a few tall hedges, once up to twenty feet tall, designed to shelter fields full of hops; alder is the preferred tall hedge for sheltering commercial orchards. Alder and willow are used in wet river valleys in Sussex, while buckthorn does well on chalky soils in Essex and Hertfordshire.

Crab, hazel, field maple, buckthorn, elder, dogwood, guelder rose, privet, wayfaring tree, sallow, bramble and a variety of roses – dog, burnet, field, sweet briar – all find their way into hedges. After hawthorn, the sloe, or black-thorn, is the most popular woody hedging plant. Like elm it is a suckering species, creating wide, dense hedges.

Lilac is a familiar feature of hedges on the sand soils of coastal Suffolk, while in parts of the South West fuchsias hedge small fields. On windswept Cornish coasts salt-tolerant tamarisk comes into its own. Hedges of gorse dot the New Forest. 'Deal rows' – lines of Scots pine – still grow in Breckland and on the Suffolk Sandlings in East Anglia; on the Elveden estate in Breckland these trees are still maintained as true hedges.

Fruit trees feature in old hedgerows, too. There are cherries in Norfolk, cider apples in Herefordshire, damsons in the Lyth valley, Westmorland and in Shropshire, too, with goose-berries and spindle near the villages of Shelve, Pennerley and Stiperstones, where squatters enclosed wasteland with hedges rich in fruit. Bullace, a wild plum, often partners crab apple in fruit hedges in Kent, Cheshire and Staffordshire, where it also supplied a dye for carpets or leather.

Hedgerows now form one of the last refuges for woodland and grassland species banished by development and intensive agriculture. Six hundred species of plant, 65 species of bird and twenty species of mammal have been recorded living in hedges. Some forty types of butterfly – two-thirds of the British list – depend on hedgerows, including the brimstone, green-veined white, comma, small tortoiseshell, peacock and hedge brown, or gatekeeper. Orange-tipped butterflies feed on cuckoo flowers at the roots, while the rare brown hairstreak spends its days in the tops of hedges. The hawthorn shield bug, dozens of bees and hoverflies and many of Britain's forty species of ladybird depend upon them – all in all, fifteen hundred species of insect rely on hedgerows, making them in turn a bonanza for insectivorous birds and bats.

In autumn and winter great flocks of fieldfares and redwings descend to raid the berries; bullfinches, black-birds and mistle thrushes also exploit these natural harvests for vital cold-weather food. Many species find shelter and nesting places, including tree sparrows, dunnocks or hedge sparrows, wrens, robins, blackbirds, whitethroats, linnets, yellowhammers and turtle doves.

Grey partridge, rabbits, wood mice, field voles, bank voles and common and pygmy shrews make homes among the roots, attracting sparrowhawks, barn owls, little owls, kestrels and stoats to hunt along the hedge lines. Adders and grass snakes favour dry, sunny hedge banks, where badgers may sometimes dig setts, their spoil heaps soon colonised by elder. Hazel hedges can harbour the enigmatic dormouse. Hedges link hospitable enclaves across bleak agricultural landscapes.

Hedges are kept dense and stock-proof by plashing, or laying, in winter every few years. Techniques vary – more than a dozen local styles have evolved, reflecting the varied nature and role of hedges. The key is to cut the stems of the main shrubs three-quarters of the way through, bend them downwards and overlap. Come spring the bent stems sprout a thick fence of vertical growth. In the Midlands style of plashing, the hedge is severely cut back; the remaining shoots and branches, known as pleachers, are bent and woven around stakes of ash or hazel (stabbers) spaced at intervals. The bushy, or 'brush', side of each shrub faces the field, to protect new growth from browsing livestock; a ditch protects the other side. The result is a strong, thick hedge that should be able to withstand the weight of a bullock leaning against it.

In Bedfordshire it was common practice to lay each side in turn, with a few years' gap, to make sure that the hedge remained stock-proof. In Leicestershire hedge-laying produced very tall, thick growth – called bullfinches – to keep beef cattle in. By contrast the hedges of the South West tend to be laid lower and more densely, because they enclose sheep, which are better at getting through small gaps. In the South the often ditchless hedge is 'double-brushed', with spiky brushwood protruding on either side to render it stock-proof. A new style of laying, called Motorway, has been devised: pleachers are laid in the direction of traffic flow to minimise damage from vehicles crashing through the hedge.

Cutting tools, such as the slasher and billhook, once displayed regional diversity, too; their use required great skill and the whole process was labour intensive. Today, most agricultural hedges are flailed with mechanical hedge cutters, adding to their degradation and often denying wild creatures a winter food source.

In Edmund Blunden's day the hedger and ditcher had already become rarer, but the hedge 'will last some time yet', he predicted in 1935. 'And when there are no more English *hedges, and the expedient of barbed wire has carried the day everywhere, "Then shall the realm of Albion/Be brought to great confusion".*

See also ALBION, ALDER, ANCIENT TREES, APPLES, ASH, BEECH, BLACK POPLAR, BLACKTHORN, BOUNDARIES, CATTLE, DAMSONS, DOG ROSES, DRYSTONE WALLS, ELM, FIELD MAPLE, FIELDS, GATES, GOOSEBERRIES, GORSE, HAWTHORN, HAZEL, HOLLY, HORNBEAM, HORSE CHESTNUT, LIME, OLD MAN'S BEARD, ORCHARDS, PARKLAND, ROWAN, SCOTS PINE, SHEEP, SWEET CHESTNUT, SYCAMORE, WILLOW, WOODS, YEW.

HENGES & STONE CIRCLES

Henges are known only in Britain. Built in the late neolithic and early Bronze Age, they consist of a roughly circular or oval bank with one or more ditches and originally timber, mainly oak, structures. They tend to be earlier in Scotland. English Heritage counts 273 possible henge monuments across England, but fewer examples are known in the South East and in the Welsh Marches. In 1984 the traces of a wood henge were revealed by drought in Devon, an area abounding in names such as King's Nympton, George Nympton, Nymet Tracey, Broadnymett, Nichols Nymet, Nymetwood and Nymphayes – nymet means sacred place.

Our preoccupations have tended to be with mountains, but these sacred places are usually associated with more subtle topography, often found near rivers and springs. On the chalk downs, the banks and ditches of henges are thought to have gleamed white, making striking forms in the land. Contained by the rivers Ure and Swale, evidence of six henges has been found near Ripon, north Yorkshire. Three have survived plough damage, standing in a row half a mile apart at Thornborough. The bank of the central henge was capped with gypsum, white like the chalk of the South.

In Wiltshire, Avebury is dominated by a henge nearly a third of a mile in diameter; the high bank once stood 56 feet tall. Inside, two circles of stones are enclosed by a wide circle of bulbous stones, much desecrated and plundered. An avenue of standing stones strides off for a mile and a half towards 'the sanctuary' – more stone circles on Overton Hill. Within the security of the great bank, roads cross and a settlement has grown up; the Red Lion pub is a busy stopping place in a unique village that has a heightened sense of the juxtaposing millennia.

Stonehenge is thought of more for its magnificent stone triliths and stone circle than its earthen bank and ditch. The henge was the first of five built in the area between 3100 and 2300 BC; the stones were erected in 2100 to 2000 BC. But long before, in the eighth millennium BC, the earliest hunter-gatherers kept returning to this place. In the Stonehenge car park three post holes are of this age. In line with them is a pit, which archaeologist Tim Darvill believes to have been where a tree stood. The stones of Stonehenge are remarkable in many ways: whoever built the circle were workers in wood – the mortice and tenon jointing is unnecessary in stone. At Coneybury Hill to the south east, a henge once embraced a circle of timbers, as did Woodhenge to the north east, the concentric post holes now marked with concrete.

The projected submerging of the A303 and other roads and the liberation of Stonehenge into the highly charged landscape of burial mounds, cursus and standing stones will bring a new understanding of the whole area.

Stonehenge, Wiltshire.

226

In Cornwall standing and toppled stones form a circle in the Stripple Stones henge on Hawk's Tor, Bodmin Moor; many of the original stones are missing. The Hurlers, near Minions, form three close circles – tradition says these are men turned to stone for playing games on a Sunday. The Merry Maidens near Newlyn and the two Pipers nearby were also petrified for Lord's Day follies. Similar stories gather in Cumberland around Long Meg (twelve feet tall) and her Daughters – once seventy stones, now 59 – a witches coven turned to stone by an astrologer, Michael of Kelso, at the end of the twelfth century.

At Stanton Drew in Somerset a whole wedding party was caught dancing to the devil's music. In Northumberland the Duddo Four Stones stand forever as a memorial to men who gathered turnips on the Sabbath. The Rollright Stones on the Oxfordshire/Warwickshire border include the Whispering Knights – a close group of leaning megaliths, the King's Men – a wide circle of very weathered stones, and the eight-foot-tall King Stone. Among the many tales told is that they were petrified after an encounter with a witch. These stones have been much plundered for small chips for good luck, and this was a place for gathering on Midsummer's Eve.

Circular banks, circles of stones, lines of stones, revealed stones – these enigmatic places are full of secrets. Having persisted for perhaps four to five thousand years, whatever the interpretations of their meaning and the many voices that seek to speak on their behalf, we all have a deep responsibility to let them be.

See also BARROWS, BOUNDARIES, CHALK, CHURCHES, DESERTED VILLAGES, DEVIL, EARTHWORKS, FIELDS, FLINT, FORTIFICATIONS, GIANTS, HAUNTED PLACES, HILL-FORTS, HOLLOW WAYS, LYNCHETS, MIDSUMMER DAY, OBELISKS, QUARRIES, ROADS, STANDING STONES.

H E R O N R I E S

Grey herons may hunt on their own, but they breed in colonies, choosing the same trees year after year, refurbishing their nests each season. Heronries are wonderfully noisy and smelly places. According to Arthur Tansley, the stinging nettle is particularly luxuriant under herons' nests in Norfolk, '*where it obtains heavy supplies of combined nitrogen*'.

The oldest heronry is thought to be in a deer park by Chilham Castle in Chilham, Kent, first recorded in 1293. Locally it is predicted '*if the herons do not return to nest there by St Valentine's Day each year, unspecified but dire misfortunes will befall the castle's owners*'. Surely an ancestral place such as this, used for more than seven hundred years, should be listed – as buildings are.

Heronries have been recorded systematically since 1928, when the Heronries Census was initiated by the British

Trust for Ornithology. It is the longest-running bird-breeding season monitoring scheme in the world. More than four hundred colonies have been counted in Britain, and the population is steadily increasing after a crash during the cold winter of 1962/3. Currently there are about ten thousand breeding pairs.

Recently threatened by a proposed airport at nearby Cliffe, the largest heronry is at Northward Hill wood near Gravesend in Kent, containing 160 pairs. There are sixteen heronries across London, each averaging thirteen nests. All are in trees on islands in lakes and reservoirs, except one on rafts. Herons took up residence in Battersea Park in 1990 and today there are 27 nests. One pair nested in Regent's Park in 1968, but the wind blew down their nest – now they are back.

The nest is made of a platform of sticks collected by the males and arranged by the females in February. Eggs are laid between then and May, and the young are fed by both parents for a couple of months. Adults may travel twelve miles or so in search of food. In flight, herons have a look of the pterodactyl, with their six-foot wingspan, neck drawn back and legs trailing behind them. They will fly over suburban gardens prospecting for frogspawn, goldfish and prized koi carp, much to the exasperation of fish fanciers. They usually frequent marshy places, rivers and estuaries ('*haunts of coot and hern*', as Tennyson wrote), where they will stand motionless for a long time and suddenly stab at a small fish, frog, eel or water vole.

They were eaten, too, as were two other members of the heron family – cranes and bitterns. In the Middle Ages herons were, like swans, protected royal birds, but were used in falconry as a favourite prey of peregrines. Heronries were prized assets and noted on land deeds. Place-names such as Cranborne in Dorset and Cranbourne in Hampshire refer to the crane; after they became extinct in this country at the end of the seventeenth century (they have recently returned to the Broads), herons often took the name.

Common in the Norfolk and Suffolk Broads, herons are sometimes referred to as harnsers; other old names include hernsaw, hernser, heronshaw and handsaw. Shakespeare's

Hamlet claims: '*I am but mad north-north-west: when the wind is southerly I know a hawk from a handsaw.*'

Since 1993 little egrets – small, pure white herons – have been attracted by our warming climate. Recently they have begun to breed here and, in southern England, they are making their nests among the grey herons. In the Calder valley near Wakefield, Yorkshire two white storks appeared to be making a nest between the motorway and a housing estate in 2004, the first recorded attempt since 1416.

See also EELS, ESTUARIES, FRESHWATER FISH, ROOKERIES.

HIGH STREETS

High Street, Fore Street, Main Street – these names imply importance and in some places appeared as the street gained status. 'The High' in Oxford was Eastgate Street before the seventeenth century. There are 34 High Streets in greater Manchester and 236 across London. Some have a prefix, as in Peckham and Kensington (which many people know as High Street Ken).

Fore Street is a noticeable street sign from Somerset (Taunton, Chard) to Cornwall (Newquay, St Austell). In Kingsbridge and Budleigh Salterton in Devon, Fore Street leads straight down to the quay or sea. This tends to be *the* commercial street, although the larger places may have a High Street or a King Street, too. Sometimes the suggestion is that Fore Streets lie before or in front of something; in Exeter the High Street becomes Fore Street at the city wall.

Main Street is more direct and tends to the North, as in Grange-over-Sands and Blackburn in Lancashire, Haworth and Bingley in Yorkshire.

High Streets should be the commercial and convivial focus at a town's heart, and some certainly have magnetism. But it has been sad to watch the erasing of small businesses and elegant shop fronts as chain stores and plastic fascias have pushed their way even into small towns. As independent shops with local family names are ousted, individuality is forfeited.

Bravo to the politicians and council officers who have given pedestrians priority with high-quality, locally distinctive paving and very slow traffic, and to those who have demanded that the big shop chains defer to the town.

See also ARCADES, BUILDING STONES, COBBLES, FAMILY NAMES, MARKETS, PAVEMENTS, ROADS, SHOPS.

HILL FIGURES

Chalk offers steep slopes and, just a few inches below the grass, a bright white surface. Since peoples in the Bronze Age had the idea and the artistry to carve the White Horse near Uffington in Berkshire, others have followed.

Above Cerne Abbas in Dorset significance clings to a figure carved into the land. For something that is merely an absence of turf the figure raises more than questions. At 180 feet tall, the outline is of more than a man. It is of his manhood, too, 26 feet of it, lovingly tamped with new chalk every few years. For how long he has been the focus of May-morning incidents, prudery, laddish and girly convulsions, no one has agreed upon.

Locals say here lies the sheep-stealing giant pinned down and slain by their forbears, his outline traced as at the scene of a crime. But maybe this is an ancient sacred figure that generated the tales of giants walking the Downs. Is he a symbol of fertility or regeneration? There is something of the Green Man about him: is his club indicative of the Holly Knight, waiting to do battle with the Oak King, the story of death and resurrection, time endlessly rolling round?

Perhaps it is Hercules, a Romano-British refugee from the Mediterranean sun? Or could this fearsome frown on the brow of the hill be to frighten Civil War soldiers, signifying the ferocity and flaunting the superiority of the Club Risers (labourers and others who banded together to protect their crops in this part of the world)? Perhaps simply what we have here is Billboard Willie, a great poster announcing cudgel games at Revels Farm, over the hill. He is first mentioned in 1694 in church warden's accounts mentioning the expenditure of '*3s od*' for '*repaireing of the Giant*'.

He must, like the Cheshire cat, have faded and brightened, but the secret of his perpetuation is not in his own magic, it is in the hands of the people of this place. His story, however long, could be recorded as a document of social decision-making; he only exists because people here have wanted him and have worked to keep him.

In Sussex another enigmatic figure stands on the Downs. An outline with arms raised, holding a stave in each, the Long Man of Wilmington faces north on Windover Hill. One of the tallest carved figures in the world at 226 feet high, he is laid out on a 28-degree slope. The earliest drawing

The Long Man of Wilmington, Sussex.

228

of 1704 makes him seem fatter; some sketches have him holding spears, some scyth and rake. By 1873/4, reduced to rumples in the ground, he was 'redrawn' in bricks and then again in 1891. These were painted green during the Second World War. After various acts of vandalism the outline was again picked out, this time in concrete blocks, in 1969. He is not averse to political gestures – during a particularly grey time in politics in the early 1990s he was seen briefly wearing Y-fronts as people protested against the route of a motorway nearby.

Above the Long Man are barrows and neolithic flint mines, a Romano-British road/ridgeway and quarries. Theories and stories relating to his origins and meanings are as numerous as with the Cerne Giant; a few are very similar. Some believe him to be holding open the gates of heaven for the Spring as the Norse god Baldur; some see him as a prehistoric surveyor. In 2003 Martin Bell from Reading University established an age for the Long Man, by studying pottery, flint and brick shards, changes in the populations of land snails and by dating when soil was last open to the light. To his surprise (he was expecting at least an Anglo-Saxon origin) this evidence suggested the sixteenth or seventeenth century – the time of turmoil around the Reformation, Civil War and Restoration.

In these figures we have paradox: fragility, yet defiant persistence. While they carry memory, they are not things of the past. They are continuing history, they exist now, they belong to us here. If we don't remake their significance for ourselves they will not endure. The land is our most elaborate storyboard. That we cannot precisely read the compression of history or translate the contradictions leaves room for us all to join in the telling: layers of meaning, tangles of ambiguity, overlays of possibility, a great weaving of significance. Adding to the depth of knowledge should never narrow our imagination – this is what created the Giant and the Long Man in the first place. Many giants populate our land, but only rarely can we see them.

See also ALBION, BARROWS, BESTIARY, CHALK, DOWNLAND, FLINT, FOLKTALES, GIANTS, GREEN MAN, HILL-FORTS, MAY DAY, ROADS, TURF MAZES, WELLS, WHITE HORSES.

H I L L - F O R T S

When the late sun catches the great whaleback of Hambledon Hill in Dorset, the complications of its earthworks, so much part of today's landscape, are thrown into high relief. Line after line of elaborate ditches circumnavigate the hill's top – long ago creating a place of safety, further defended by stockades, they now provide walkers and sheep with snug places out of the sou'westerly gales. Large and complex ramparts are typical of central England and the West; east of the Hampshire Avon single ramparts predominate.

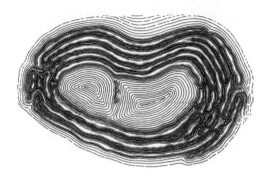

Although some date from the Bronze Age and many have evidence of more ancient use, hill-forts were mostly built between the sixth century BC and the first century AD, perhaps offering a display of power by the elite of competing tribes, as well as practical protection. They proved no match for the Romans, but their frequent location overlooking major river valleys suggests that they may earlier have acted as centres for controlling trade.

There are clusters of hill-forts in the Marches, where typically a promontory with a steep slope or cliff for protection might be used, as in the large fort of Croft Ambrey overlooking the Lugg valley near Leominster, Herefordshire. It has a single rampart, except on its north-western side, where there is a one-in-two drop (and views as far as the Black Mountains). Examples in the South West are usually of small but often striking forts, as at Cow Castle, standing on a round hill overlooking the valley of the river Barle near Simonsbath, Somerset. In the South Downs and the Chilterns many are overgrown with trees. In the Pennines and Northumberland ramparts are often of stone, sometimes now turf-covered. Old Bewick in Northumberland has two forts side by side with multiple ramparts; stones incised with cup-and-ring marks peculiar to this area stand in the adjacent field. Yeavering Bell in the Cheviots is the largest northern hill-fort, its single rampart built in stone around the hill's contours.

Society in the East and its defence must have been organised differently – there are few hill-forts in east Yorkshire, Lincolnshire, East Anglia and east Kent, although they continue to be found. The promontory fort at Roulston Scar near Thirsk on the edge of the North York Moors was discovered in 2001.

Sometimes they loom over a town or village, as Caer Caradoc does over Church Stretton in Shropshire. Their positions on hilltops, escarpments and spurs were about seeing and being seen. They still are sizeable landmarks, almost but not quite part of the natural landscape. West Wycombe church in Buckinghamshire is a landmark itself, standing in a small hill-fort now hidden by trees. Caesar's Camp finds itself part of a golf-course on Wimbledon Common in south London. Many hill-forts were used as

229

lookout posts for enemy aircraft during the Second World War, and some keep their structures, such as the pillbox inside Old Bewick. Economics has won over wonder at Breedon on the Hill, Leicestershire, where half of an extraordinary hill and hill-fort has been quarried away – the high village church protects the remaining enclosure.

Their influence on local communities remains, folklore often associating them with malevolent forces. Sally Francis from Norfolk remembers hearing a story about the ploughed-out hill-fort at Bloodgate Hill, South Creake. *'It is said there was once a battle here, and the fallen warriors' blood turned to stone when it hit the ground. This was told to me by a school friend, who lived nearby, and I can remember playing in the field gateway with her and there being a lot of tiny red flints, which aren't very common, in the field. So it's a story to explain the red flints.'*

See also BARROWS, CHALK, DEVIL, DIALECTS, DRAGONS, FELL RUNNING, FLINT, FOLKTALES, FORTIFICATIONS, GIANTS, HILLS, PILLBOXES, QUARRIES, SEA FORTS, STANDING STONES, WHITE HORSES.

HILLS

The enormous number of English place-names that refer to hills, high places, summits and mounds – whether in native Briton, Latin, Saxon, Welsh or Norse – demonstrates the importance of hills as sacred places, landmarks, beacons, places to meet (moots, like Mutlow, near Cambridge) or places to settle. British and Welsh words for hills and heights gave us Brent, Cannock, Creech, Pennard, Vobster, Malvern, Lydeard and Bredon. The Anglo-Saxons brought the *dun* of Swindon, Abingdon and Ashdown and added their own words to pre-extant ones to get bilingual hybrids. The name Pennard Hill in Somerset means Hillhill Hill: *pen* is Welsh; *ard* is a form of Gaelic.

230

Cumberland and Westmorland stand tall, overtopping hills with mountains, pikes, crags and fells. Millstone grit forms jagged edges in the Pennines, where tors stand out as natural sculptures with names such as 'Dancing Bear' and 'Hen Cloud'. Northumberland shares the Cheviots but faces off the Scots with the great resilient rocks of the Whin Sill, underpinning Hadrian's Wall and staring north.

Margaret Gelling, who has studied place-names and landscape, says that *'the Old English topographical vocabulary is at its most discriminating in the classification of hills and ridges, and this aspect of study can afford great pleasure to the informed observer. Here, most of all, we are seeing what the Anglo-Saxon settlers saw.'*

There are knolls and knowes, tumps and cops, ridges, edges and banks. Some hills have astonishing names – Thorpe Cloud, Roseberry Topping, Clougha Pike, Brown Clee, Hard Knott, The Yelds. Above Bovey Tracey in Devon, and Ilkley and Pickering in Yorkshire, there are moors. From Littlehampton, Sussex, you go up into the Downs, and from Market Rasen, Lincolnshire, the Wolds. The Howgills, between the Lakes and the Yorkshire Dales, are fells, but the Cheviots, Chilterns, Clent, Quantocks and Malverns are hills.

Many hills are topped by burial places, prehistoric barrows or the hillside cemeteries of the nineteenth century. The striking combination of abrupt hill with church on top suggests a place of some pre-Christian significance. These churches are generally dedicated to St Michael, as at Brent Tor in Devon, Breedon on the Hill in Leicestershire, Glastonbury and Burrator in Somerset. Our taming of these high places extended to their use as triangulation points for the Ordnance Survey; the concrete 'trig points' mark the tops of many inter-visible hills.

Hills have proved useful as places of defence, and hill-forts and castles have accentuated their impregnability

Malvern Hills, Worcestershire.

– Nottingham Castle fortified a great bluff overlooking the Trent. Some we have refashioned; Tegg's Nose at Rainow, Cheshire is one of many bearing the scars of quarrying – hills have long been plundered for building stone, minerals and fuel.

Chosen for their conspicuousness, hills can be good places to rally a community, for warning beacons and as lookouts. Tout or toot hills were places where people kept watch. Hambury Tout and Worbarrow Tout are high points on Dorset's coastal cliffs. At Tout on the Isle of Portland people watched out for the landing of smuggled goods.

St Catherine's Hill just outside Winchester, Hampshire overlooked a prodigious twentieth-century struggle, its quiet and poise lost to the building of the M3 straight through Twyford Down. On St George's Hill in Surrey people gather still to remember the Diggers, who for nearly half a year in 1649 staunchly attempted to change the world. Gerrard Winstanley said: '*if thou dost not act, thou dost nothing . . . I took my spade and went and broke ground upon George-hill in Surrey, thereby declaring freedome to the Creation, and that the earth must be set free from entanglements of Lords and Landlords, and that it shall become a common Treasury for all.*' They were violently evicted, though demonstrating against poverty and hunger, and continue to inspire.

Scutchamer Knob near the Hendreds in Oxfordshire speaks of the festivities and fairs of cloth workers (a 'scutcher' was used to beat out soaked and softened flax). Today a kite gathering enlivens the ridge beside Barbury Castle near Swindon once a month. Adventurous people parascend, paraglide and hang-glide across the country from White Sheet Hill in Wiltshire or Ingleborough in the Yorkshire Dales. Heading uphill, motor and bike enthusiasts seek out sections for racing, although on made roads these are mostly on private property, such as the Gurston Down Hillclimb in Wiltshire and Harewood Speed Hillclimb in Yorkshire.

Edward Elgar lived in Worcestershire and eulogised the Malverns, which stand up so strikingly above the Vale of the Severn. One hundred and fifty years earlier, Celia Fiennes, traveller and diarist, had called this '*the English Alps*'. Ralph Vaughan Williams titled one of his pieces of music *Wenlock Edge*, although it was at Leith Hill, Surrey and not in Shropshire where he started a music festival. Perhaps one of the most evocative of lines in English poetry is from *A Shropshire Lad*, in which A.E. Housman asks: '*What are those blue remembered hills . . .?*'

See also BARROWS, BEACON FIRES, BONFIRE NIGHT, CAIRNS, CEMETERIES, CHEESE ROLLING, CHURCHES, CLUMPS, COMMONS, DOUBLE GLOUCESTER, DOWNLAND, DRAGONS, FELL RUNNING, FELLS, FOLKTALES, FORTIFICATIONS, HILL-FORTS, JACK AND JILL, LANDMARKS, MIDSUMMER DAY, MOORLAND, NORTHUMBRIAN SMALLPIPES, PANCAKE DAY, SAINTS, TORS.

HOLLOW WAYS

The idea that generations of feet and hooves and wheels could literally carve a hollow way should humble us. Oliver Rackham cited 38 mentions of *hola weg*, hollow ways and hollow paths, in Anglo-Saxon charters. These and the names Holway and Holloway, as in the Holloway Road, north London, are likely to signify extremely ancient routes.

Geologist Hugh Prudden explains the likely processes as he surveys the Nynehead holloway in south-west Somerset, cut through the Permo-Triassic Otter Sandstone. '*The holloway presents a paradox: the walls are strong enough to maintain vertical sides and yet erosion has created the deep cutting! The sand's grains are held together with a cement of calcium carbonate and tend not to get waterlogged; hence the sides are less likely to slump, which would happen if they were composed of clay. On the other hand, carts and feet of animals would have pounded the sandstone in the days before tarmac was laid; the loosened sand grains would then have been swept down the steep slope when there was heavy rainfall.*'

Yellow hollow ways are peculiar to the area just north of Yeovil, Somerset, marking the approach to the town – cliffs of glowing sandstone with lines of 'doggers', protruding harder stones, useful handholds for the climber.

The beauty of the long, winding hollow ways through the older greensand of the Surrey hills is hard to beat. The tangle of tree and hedge roots and the tunnel effect created by the trees adds to the intimacy of long use. It is easy to feel at home here. Even the out-of-scale four-by-four drivers sometimes attempt a more polite pace; the worry is that rat running will lead to demands for widening.

The naturalist Gilbert White, describing the land around Selborne in Hampshire in the eighteenth century, wrote: '*Among the singularities of this place the two rocky hollow lanes, the one to Alton, and the other to the forest, deserve our attention. These roads, running through the malm lands are, by the traffic of ages, and the fretting of water, worn down through the first stratum of our freestone, and partly through the second;*

231

so that they look more like water-courses than roads . . . In many places they are reduced sixteen or eighteen feet beneath the level of the fields; and after floods, and in frosts, exhibit very grotesque and wild appearances, from the tangled roots that are twisted among the strata, and from the torrents rushing down their broken sides; and especially when those cascades are frozen into icicles hanging in all the fanciful shapes of frost-work. These rugged gloomy scenes affright the ladies when they peep down into them from the paths above, and make timid horsemen shudder while they ride along them; but delight the naturalist with their various botany, and particularly with their curious filices with which they abound.' Malmstone is a Hampshire and Sussex term for the hard Upper Greensand, and filices an early word for ferns. These shady caverns may be lined with hart's tongue, shiny cranesbill and moschatel, and, in very small corners in the South, Cornish moneywort clings to permanently dripping walls.

In the Weald the zigzag routes up the scarp faces are called bostels. Medieval local drove roads certainly, but perhaps prehistoric peoples found this the easiest way to climb the slopes. East of Plaxtol Spout, Kent, beyond the hamlet of Roughway, a sunken lane full of bluebells in the spring strikes towards a route thought to have been used in the Bronze Age. On the Isle of Wight the eroded sunken trackways are known as shutes. Occasionally these protected ways are the result of travellers taking advantage of a natural ravine; in East Anglia these are called grundles.

Alfred Watkins suggested that some hollow ways were etched as prehistoric notches to give sightlines to and from fords and hill passes. He gives examples in Herefordshire, such as Holme Lacy, where a hollow way leads straight to an old crossing of the Wye.

See also ALLEYS, BOUNDARIES, BRIDGES, CHINES, COBBLES, DENES, DOWNLAND, DROVE ROADS, FAIRS & FAIRGROUNDS, FELL PONIES, FERNS, FOLKTALES, FOOTPATHS, GAPS, GREEN LANES, GREENSAND, GYPSIES, HEDGES, MILESTONES, SANDSTONES, ZIGZAGS.

232

H O L L Y

A much-loved evergreen tree with prickly leaves and scarlet berries, in winter the holly outranks: '*the first tree in the greenwood, it was the holly*' the 'Sans Day Carol' proclaims. Cuttings brought in on Christmas Eve once protected homes from fire, lightning, witches and fairy folk. With pagan roots in Roman Saturnalia, holly was Christianised in carols that linked its red berries to the blood of Christ. But traces of the ancient Holly Boy and Ivy Girl, personifying the battle of the sexes, persist in old songs, where the prickly holly sometimes triumphs over the clinging ivy: '*Of all the trees that are in the wood, the holly bears the crown.*'

Spared by farmers, since bad luck would surely follow, it is today the commonest hedgerow tree in the vast arable

plains of East Anglia. In east Sussex holly trees are left to stop witches running along the hedge tops. Hollies are widely protected as boundary markers, long growing and easily identified, with lingering resonances that link cutting down with bad luck. Perhaps the evergreen tree was a symbol of life; the Green Knight is depicted holding a holly bush as a club, and some see the Cerne Abbas Giant's club as knobbly holly.

Able to withstand grazing and cutting, hollies can form a virtually impenetrable living wall. Holly-rich hedges thrive in south-east Suffolk, especially the Shotley peninsula; around Woburn and Ampthill in Bedfordshire; and on the Chiltern dipslope in Hertfordshire, clustered round Sarratt and Chipperfield. Holly hedges are also a notable feature in counties bordering the Pennines.

Remarkably tolerant of shade, hollies survive in the understorey of oak and beech woods, slowly growing up to sixteen feet, but poised to shoot up should a gap appear. Woods rich in hollies are rarely found outside Britain. Vulnerable to prolonged frost, the trees do best in damper, warmer parts of the South and West, or near coasts in the East.

The importance of the tree to Hulver in Suffolk is shown in the village sign; the original name, Holieverd, means 'green holly'. At Staverton Park in the Suffolk Sandlings squat pollard oaks festooned with moss and ferns are joined by hollies contorted into fantastic shapes. This '*jungle of monstrous hollies*', as Peter Marren described it, known as the Thicks, is the legacy of regular pollarding over 250 years up to 1850. The upper branches of the hollies were lopped off to provide winter fodder for livestock. Young saplings and the upper branches are particularly palatable; the trees produce prickly leaves only on their lower branches, to the height reached by cattle or deer.

Magnificent groves of old pollard hollies, once exploited in a similar way, survive at the north end of the Stiperstones in Shropshire, where crofters grazed their sheep and cattle. It is one of the few remaining examples of such holly-dominated wood pasture, known as hollins, and is perhaps the oldest stand of holly in Europe; some trees could be four hundred years old.

Another ancient and unique holly wood is the amazing stand of windswept holly bushes, no more than thirteen feet tall but with girths of up to 56 feet, rooted on the bare shingle at Holmstone Beach in Dungeness, Kent. Just a few acres in extent, the wood could be very old: *holm* derives from the Anglo-Saxon name for holly, and a royal charter of 741 alludes to a wood on the shingle roughly in its present position. The wood, which once housed a heronry, was old when the celebrated traveller John Leland mentioned it in his *Itinerary* of 1539.

In the Hamps and Manifold valleys in Staffordshire, old pedunculate and sessile oaks consort with holly in a classic partnership. Also in the west Midlands, a relict wood pasture, carved out of a royal forest at Sutton Park, supports sessile oaks and a luxuriant riot of holly that rivals the famous holly groves of the New Forest.

See also ANCIENT TREES, ASH, BEECH, BLACK POPLAR, BOUNDARIES, ELM, FIELDS, GIANTS, GREEN MAN, HAWTHORN, HAZEL, HERONRIES, HILL FIGURES, HORNBEAM, HORSE CHESTNUT, LIME, OAK, PARKLAND, ROWAN, ROYAL FORESTS, SCOTS PINE, SHINGLE, SWEET CHESTNUT, SYCAMORE, WILLOW, WOODS, YEW.

H O L M   O A K

This evergreen oak, a native of Mediterranean climes, has greyish green leaves that resemble a spineless holly – holm is an old name for holly. Introduced to England around 1580, probably from Corsica and Italy, the tree became fashionable in the early eighteenth century, when it started to be widely planted as an ornamental tree.

On the Holkham estate in north Norfolk, prized individual specimens thrive in the parkland. In villages nearby, single specimen evergreen oaks are commonplace in the gardens of rectories, halls and substantial farmhouses. According to Sally Francis, these trees arrived in the neighbourhood '*via a very interesting route; its acorns were the eighteenth century's equivalent of the polystyrene packaging chip and were used to pack antiquities brought back from Italy during Grand Tours*'.

Despite their southern origin, these trees have thrived along the coast. They can tolerate strong winds, as well as alkaline soils and low rainfall, and their waxy leaves resist salt burn from sea spray. In Bournemouth, Hampshire stands of holm oaks planted as wind-breaks against the sea winds add to the exotic holiday atmosphere. Cold causes

problems; the fine holm oaks below the Cotswold edge at Toddington, Gloucestershire suffered badly in the prolonged and deep freeze of 1981/2.

The biggest holm oak wood luxuriates on the Isle of Wight's crumbling south coast. On St Boniface Down above Ventnor, on one of the mildest and sunniest banks, thousands of holm oaks have spread up the slopes, perhaps with the aid of acorn-burying jackdaws and jays. '*The first trees are said to have been sown as acorns about a century ago by a local man who always carried a pocket full of them on his walks across the downs*', Peter Marren wrote. '*The wood is almost impenetrable and you risk your neck scrambling down over the slippery carpet of leaves. The evergreen shade and deep leaf litter produce a hostile environment for woodland plants, but already a few tough pioneers, such as clematis and wild madder, are appearing, along with other exotic escapes from the Mediterranean, such as Turkey oak, walnut and Laurustinus . . . It will be interesting to see how this, our own "Mediterranean wood", will develop in the future, assuming of course that people can be persuaded to leave it alone.*'

See also HOLLY, NURSERIES, OAK, PARKLAND.

H O N E Y   &   B E E S

Honey is a wild food, and a quintessentially local one, made by social bees from flowers within a few miles of their home. So bee keepers have long sought to shape the nature of the end product by siting their hives near good sources of nectar and honey. Heather blossom makes one of the world's finest honeys, with a unique jelly-like texture and fragrance that is highly prized. Over millennia bee keepers have taken their bees up to the moors and fells and to lowland heaths in late summer and early autumn, as the bell heather and ling come into flower. Flower-rich meadows are appealing, too: honey rich in clover smells of caramel and has a buttery taste.

Old, traditional orchards, with their abundant wild-flowers, are perfect places for bees – the fruit blossom itself is rich in nectar and pollen, intended to entice pollinating insects. In Kent, bee keepers are paid to move their hives into commercial orchards in spring to boost fruit yield. Bees are vital to farmers and horticulturalists, but ironically much modern practice has made life difficult for the insect. The spread of the parasite mite *Varroa* infected five thousand apiaries between 1992 and 2002.

One bee keeper takes his hives to the nature reserve at Dungeness, where his bees forage on the shingle flora in summer, rather than the ubiquitous oilseed rape which makes a bland honey that is prone to crystallisation. Another commercial crop, borage, or starflower, grown for the pharmaceutical industry, also produces a rather undistinguished honey, said to be thin, sweet and rather watery.

233

Hives can thrive in towns and cities: on London rooftops or in the botanic gardens at Cambridge and Kew, bees make the most of the cultivated blooms. These days, town honeys can be more interesting than country ones – a hive perched in a lime tree beside the Beehive Inn in Grantham, Lincolnshire has produced honey since 1830.

See also BEE BOLES, FELLS, HEATHLAND, MOORLAND, ORCHARDS.

HOPS, HOP-GARDENS & HOP-YARDS

A forest of poles the height of three men, supporting a cat's-cradle of wires, is an extraordinary scene with no parallels in English agriculture. It is hard to imagine the landscape in the main growing areas of Kent, Sussex, Herefordshire and Worcestershire at the peak of hop-growing in the 1870s, when nearly 72,000 acres were under cultivation.

The hop is a native wild plant of hedgerows and scrub, but it was not until Flemish weavers settling in the Weald and east Kent in the 1520s introduced new varieties of hops, together with cultivation and brewing techniques, that hop-growing developed.

The alluvial loams and plentiful supplies of chestnut for coppicing – for poles, wood and the charcoal used in drying – together with an abundance of prosperous farmers, who could risk the initial high capital outlay, made the Weald of Kent the *Mother of Hop grounds*, according to Daniel Defoe in the 1720s. In Kent they are known as hop-gardens; in the west Midlands hop-yards. Kilns for drying the hops, with their distinctive conical, or sometimes square, roofs and wooden cowls, are known as oast-houses in the South East and kells in Worcestershire and Herefordshire.

Each clockwise-climbing plant has a productive life of about twenty years. Traditionally sixteen-foot-high poles were erected near to each plant and taken down each year. These supported a framework of wires and coir strings, constructed by stringers walking on high stilts, for the fast-growing bines to climb. Today the strings are unhooked and the bines stripped from them.

At the beginning of September the aromatic cones of the female plant are ripe for picking. Many hands were needed, and it became traditional for families from London's East End, Gypsies, itinerant workers and local residents to spend three to four weeks 'hopping' in Kent and Sussex. In the west Midlands they came from the Black Country and south Wales. The hoppers were badly paid and provided with little in the way of shelter, but after the First World War hopper-huts in Kent, 'bunk' houses near Oyster Hill, Ledbury, Herefordshire, and 'tin towns' in the Teme valley were provided. Families looked forward to their 'holidays' in the country and meeting old friends, even though the work was hard. The hop-picking machine first used in the west Midlands after the Second World War put paid to these seasonal activities. To keep the memories alive, Swale Borough Council organises an annual International Hop Festival in Faversham, Kent at the end of August.

At first hops were used because they prolonged the life of beer. Their alpha acids impart bitterness and their volatile oils give flavour and aroma. Each variety has unique qualities that give beers their range of tastes. In 1790 a plant nurtured by Mr Golding of Roughway in Kent became one of the most revered varieties. Now Goldings refers to a group developed from the original, including Cobbs, Canterbury Golding and Eastwell Golding. Richard Fuggle of Brenchley, Kent noticed a plant that had potential growing in Horsmonden in 1861; by the 1950s Fuggle accounted for nearly eighty per cent of the hop acreage. Its decline in popularity was due to the demise of darker beers, but Fuggle and Goldings are being grown again for single-variety and wheat beers. New varieties less susceptible to pests and diseases are also being bred.

By 2003 the acreage of hops in the UK had fallen to 3,600 acres on only 79 farms, mainly in Kent, east Sussex, the Teme valley and the Hereford-Ledbury-Bromyard triangle in Herefordshire and Worcestershire. But this acreage is further diminishing as more farmers in the South shift their allegiance to lavender and other herbs for the burgeoning market in essential oils, a response to a global market flooded with hops from America and China.

See also BEER, CORRUGATED IRON, GYPSIES, HORSE CHESTNUT, LAVENDER, MARKET GARDENS, OAST-HOUSES & KELLS, ORCHARDS.

H O R N B E A M

The hornbeam is also known as hardbeam. It has the hardest wood of any tree in Europe – it blunts carpenters' tools. It was used for cogs in mills, screws, skittles and skittle balls, piano keys and hammers and to make charcoal for gunpowder mills. Billiard cues and drumsticks are among its current uses.

John Hunter described enormous Essex pollards as having *'thrown buttresses to support the weight of the "groves" of upward-growing branches springing from their overloaded crowns'*. These exquisite pollarded hornbeams reside at Bush End Plain in Hatfield Forest, where pollarding was resumed by the National Trust in 1976 after extensive research by Oliver Rackham. He pointed out that the South East is the home of the tree, and that it is *'the commonest woodland tree throughout south Essex, Hertfordshire and the*

London area'. Pure stands of hornbeam in Epping Forest, Hatfield and Hainault Forests in Essex have usually been coppiced or pollarded; until the 1870s branches were cut by commoners with lopping rights for fuel. Hornbeam faggots, together with beech, fuelled the bakers' ovens, fires and furnaces of medieval and Tudor London. The tree also grows around Harleston on the Norfolk/Suffolk border, around Ipswich, on the North Downs of Kent and in the hedgerows of Sussex.

In its natural state the hornbeam can be confused with beech, as its form, leaves and grey bark are similar. On close inspection the leaves are more serrated, and in summer distinctive green bracts surround the seeds, eventually acting as sails to fly them to less shaded ground. Where there are hornbeams there are hawfinches; the seeds provide the bulk of their autumn and winter food.

See also ALDER, ASH, BEECH, BLACK POPLAR, ELM, HAWTHORN, HAZEL, HORSE CHESTNUT, MONKEY-PUZZLE, OAK, ROWAN, SCOTS PINE, SWEET CHESTNUT, SYCAMORE, WHITEBEAM, WILLOW, WOODS, YEW.

HORSE CHESTNUT

Introduced to England from the Balkans about four hundred years ago, this showy tree was originally deemed rather coarse in comparison with the sweet chestnut, with its edible nuts – 'horse' is said to be pejorative. But the Turks call it horse chestnut, too, using its aescin-rich conkers to treat their steeds (pharmaceutical companies are taking note). The association with the smithy – usually sited beneath a horse chestnut or lime on the edge of the village – may come in part from this, but also the horse chestnut casts a deep shade, useful in hot summers to the extent that anyone finding horse chestnut and lime planted near a considerable bump in the ground should try searching for an ice-house.

This bold pyramid of a tree won praise from the artist Samuel Palmer, the Pre-Raphaelites and Tennyson, too, and was soon highly fashionable. By the eighteenth century great avenues had been planted around stately homes and grand houses, such as Windsor Castle, Berkshire and in Bushy Park, north of Hampton Court, Middlesex, where 11 May or thereabouts is celebrated as Chestnut Sunday.

A popular tree in towns and parks since mid-Victorian times, it is admired for its sticky buds, cut for vases, and its spectacularly large, lobed leaves – among the first to unfurl in spring. It flowers early, too, with 'candles' of pink and white blossoms. In autumn the conkers arrive. Freed from their hard, green, spiny cases, these shiny seeds make perfect gaming material, threaded on strings and crashed together. The winner is the chestnut that demolishes the greatest number of its fellows, and there is much lore about this: 'conkers' comes from conqueror, the original name for the game when it was played with cobnuts.

Quite when the game arose is unclear, but it has been popular among schoolchildren from at least the 1850s. Children undergo some kind of chemical change in the autumn, seeking out the tree and pounding the lower branches with sticks to force the seeds to fall to the ground. Alas, in recent years, concerns about safety have led a few local authorities to pollard or even cut down trees – Norwich, to its shame, entertained such notions. Some schools have banned the game; one headmaster requires competitors to wear safety goggles.

The World Conker Championships on the second Sunday in October take place in Rothschild's model village of Ashton, Northamptonshire, with its mile-long avenue of horse chestnuts. It began in 1965, when a fishing trip was rained off. Disappointed, the group began a serious game of conkers, raiding the trees on the village green. Now the village is thronged. King Conker, the chief adjudicator, wearing a necklace and skirt of stringed conkers (one for each year of his reign) and hat covered in them, keeps a sharp eye out for malpractice among the crowds in a very English manner (the strict rules now govern the game countrywide). The Conker Club has mapped all of the horse chestnuts in the parish, maintaining an eye on their condition.

A leaf-mining moth newly arrived from Macedonia has begun to infest the trees, while a virulent fungal disease, known as bleeding canker, is also making inroads. First reported in the UK in the 1970s, the disease may be on the increase as mild winters and wetter springs encourage its spread.

See also AVENUES, COBNUTS, FORGES, GYPSIES, HORSES & PONIES, VILLAGE GREENS.

HORSE FAIRS

Before the combustion engine there were millions of horses and many markets. Horse fairs dealt in work horses, carriage horses, fine ponies and 'soldiers' (horses for the army), some attracting buyers from across Europe, such as the great fair at Howden in Yorkshire.

Eight hundred years of tradition embedded Brigg Fair into the locality. That was until this Lincolnshire town, named after its bridge, drove the travelling community away in the 1970s, after the right to sell horses was gained by a local auction company. In 1993 the Brigg and District Community Association agreed to re-organise things and travellers were encouraged to return. By the turn of the millennium more than twenty thousand visitors joined them in the centre of the town to see a hundred horses traded and enjoy a range of entertainments. With the loss of the traditional ground to a superstore, and the outbreak of foot-and-mouth disease in 2001, the fair floundered further, exacerbated by official intransigence over the '*problem over*

235

where to have the horses'. With hard work and care the eight-hundredth anniversary in 2004 located itself by the railway station. Tom Glossop opened the day by singing 'Brigg Fair' (Delius's music is based upon a Gypsy song). Now, perhaps, the place can begin to enjoy this unpredictable side of its identity once more.

Two other fairs are around eight centuries old. Lee Gap Fair at West Ardsley near Wakefield in Yorkshire once extended over three weeks and three days. Now it happens on just two days: First and Latter Lee, 24 August (St Bartholomew's Day) and 17 September. In London, close to the Great North Road, Barnet Fair is held in early September. London cabbies used to buy their horses here; now they seek ponies for their children.

The people of Widecombe in the Moor, Devon have had the foresight to buy a field for their fair, which rides on the back of a song that most of us somehow know because of '*Uncle Tom Cobbley and all/All along, down along, out along lea*' – although we may be less familiar with '*When the wind whistles cold on the moor of a night/Tom Pearce's old mare doth appear ghastly white*'. The September day has nothing of the bustle of past times, but an old grey mare does make an appearance and Dartmoor ponies are offered for sale, together with other livestock and produce; there are craft demonstrations, tugs o' war and a race from hill to fair.

Priddy Sheep Fair fills the big triangle of a Somerset village green to overflowing with pens of sheep and stalls and jostling people. The farmers and the Roma revel in each other's company under the trees to one side of the green, where horses, mainly black and white, change hands. Gloucestershire's Stow Fair was one of the biggest markets, also dealing mainly in sheep when the Cotswolds was at its richest. It continues as a gathering centred on horses. Its meeting ground has been under threat and it is currently held in fields between Stow-on-the-Wold and Maugersbury on the Thursdays nearest to 12 May and 24 October.

Early June sees a transformation in Appleby-in-Westmorland, which hosts our greatest one-day gathering of Roma, lasting at least a week. Since 1685 (James II's charter) every kind of vehicle, from the *vardo* to the cut-glass caravan, as well as new and traditional bender tents, have camped on Fair Hill. The river Eden is a magnet for the washing and swimming of horses, which are then run, driven or ridden, often at quite a pace, through the town. All manner of dealing, socialising, entertaining, fortune-telling and bargaining – for glass and china, tools, bright buckets, harnesses and saddles – goes on through the day, which ends with trotting races in the meadow. Many coloured ponies – black and white, brown and white – demonstrate their paces; robust and showy, they are used for drawing sulkies, carts and loads, for riding and for selling, as well as holding together a dispersed community. Although there have been attempts to end it, most recently in 1965, Appleby

Horse Fair endures. This and other fairs that have resisted dilution and tidying give us the most intriguing glimpses into continuity.

See also FAIRS & FAIRGROUNDS, FIELDS, GYPSIES, HAY MEADOWS, HORSES & PONIES, MARKETS, MUSIC, PRIDDY SHEEP FAIR, SHEEP.

HORSES & PONIES

We are alone in the world in having so many indigenous horses in such a small space. The mountain and moorland ponies have evolved separately, interacting with their specific habitats over long periods of time, making them able to cope with the fullest extremes of weather, to thrive on poorer grasses and to remain strong and sure-footed in hilly and difficult terrain. The Exmoor pony is thought to have walked here before we were severed from mainland Europe, before the Old Stone Age. The Dartmoor, the New Forest, the Dales and Fells ponies of the north Pennines have ancient roots. But we have lost the Cushendale, Devonshire Pack Horse, Goonhilly, Lincolnshire Trotter, Lincolnshire Fen and Longmynd ponies.

We also have big working horses – the Cleveland Bay, the Suffolk Punch and the Shire – as well as the Hackney for driving and the English Thoroughbred for racing and riding. Over the centuries farmers and traders have selectively bred varieties of horse, cattle, sheep and pig to make the best of local conditions and achieve the work of the area and the time.

For horses and ponies the future now is for riding and driving, jumping and racing, and there is a growing use of heavy horses in woodland and forestry work; they are more manoeuvrable and damage the ground far less than machinery.

See also AGRICULTURAL SHOWS, CATTLE, THE CHANNEL, DOWNLAND, EXMOOR PONIES, FELL PONIES, FELLS, FERAL ANIMALS, GALLOPS, HORSE FAIRS, HOUNDS, LONDON TAXIS, MOORLAND, NEW FOREST PONIES, PIGS, POINT TO POINT, POULTRY, RACECOURSES, SHEEP, SHIRE HORSES, SUFFOLK PUNCHES, WHITE HORSES.

Cleveland Bay, Yorkshire.

H O T E L S

Those 'taking the waters' at seventeenth-century spas and seaside resorts required accommodation more refined than roadside inns. Hotels were founded, the word evolving from *hostel* (French) and suggesting a mansion. A century later railway companies were providing accommodation at termini, some extremely lavish – the Midland Grand Hotel, which dominates St Pancras Station in London, is the *marque*. Railway hotels (some carrying the old company name) may remain, even if the line or station is long gone.

Railways encouraged seaside holidays, and Devon saw sophisticated resorts spring up, such as Sidmouth, Teignmouth and Torquay, all sporting fashionable new hotels with grandiose names – Imperial, Belmont, Grand, Royal Beacon. Scarborough in Yorkshire, with both chalybeate spring and railway, was a prime location. Its landmark Grand Hotel, with four towers said to represent the seasons, was built in 1867 in yellow and red brick. The nineteenth century was the era of the monolithic cliff-top hotel, such as the Headland alongside Newquay's Fistral Beach, Cornwall.

Hotels rarely followed the vernacular, instead flaunting the modern and cosmopolitan. The marine architecture of the 1930s is particularly evocative. The curving Midland Grand on Morecambe Bay, Lancashire opened to great acclaim in 1933. One of England's finest Art Deco buildings, it is now in a state of disrepair.

London inevitably has the big names – Claridges, with origins dating back to 1812, Savoy, Ritz, Dorchester and, more discreetly, Brown's. The Regent Palace was built in 1915 as a 'people's palace', with cheap but grand rooms. In the late twentieth century international hotel chains began to take hold, starting with the American Hilton group, whose 1960s high-rise was regarded as a brash imposition. In corporate thinking standards of comfort require standardised facilities, and new city and airport hotels purposefully deny any sense of place.

But the rise of the boutique hotel is bringing a new vibrancy to the scene. In London, at the exclusive St Martin's Lane Hotel, designer Philippe Starck has used light as a magnet for the fashionable, while One Aldwych has a health club, sauna, steam rooms and a pool with underwater music. Their impact on the street is one of discreet opulence, a far cry from the early hotels. It is to small hotels that we now look for particularity, comfortable but different and serving finely cooked local dishes and locally sourced food.

See also BRICKS, COASTS, FERRIES, FILM LOCATIONS, FOOD, INNS, LANDMARKS, PUB SIGNS, SPAS.

H O U N D S

Hunting with their eyes more than their noses, the greyhound, lurcher and whippet are known as sight, or gaze, hounds. The greyhound is an ancient breed that originated in the east and arrived here with the Romans via Greece. Refined over the years, it was much valued by the nobility for hunting deer and later foxes, and for coursing and racing. Greyhound racing was popular in the Black Country before the advent in the 1920s of big-time track racing, in which greyhounds chase a dummy hare on a rail around a circular course. Although the sport has lost some of its allure, the 33 tracks that remain command more than twenty per cent of betting in the UK.

The agile whippet, sometimes called the poor man's greyhound, was bred by miners and mill workers in northern England for the 'sport' of rabbit coursing and then for track racing, especially in Lancashire and the Black Country. At first the dogs ran towards rags shaken by their owners at the end of a two-hundred-yard track. Champion sprinters could cover the ground in twelve seconds. D. Brian Plummer recalled that, in the 1930s, during a depression that deeply harmed the leather-, chain- and nail-making industries of Walsall and the adjacent districts, *'there was a whippet or a bull terrier in every other house – and even if kids weren't fed right, dogs were'*. In 2004 a whippet won the coveted Best in Show award at Crufts.

'One of the chief auxiliaries of the poacher', Arthur Croxton Smith wrote, *'is that clever rascal, the Lurcher, a compound of Sheepdog and Greyhound, with the brains of one and the speed of the other.'* The lurcher was described in a statute in Queen Anne's time, but the breed probably goes back further. Slightly smaller than a greyhound, its parentage isn't known – some suggest Bedlington terrier, deerhound, Border collie and greyhound origins. Despite being looked down upon as poachers' dogs and not recognised by the Kennel Club, lurchers became fashionable in the 1970s.

237

Grand Hotel, Scarborough, Yorkshire.

Dogs with good noses, or scent hounds, had been bred for centuries for hunting in royal forests and deer parks. During the Civil War many deer park pales were vandalised by the Roundheads and, by the eighteenth century, foxhunting had emerged as a fashionable cross-country sport; gradually the foxhound was bred to improve its hunting skills. *'At one time the shape and size of individuals varied across Great Britain'*, explained Croxton Smith. *'Hounds from Yorkshire were the fastest, while those from Staffordshire were larger and slower with deeper voices. Today, most English Foxhounds share a similar shape and personality.'*

The lighter fell foxhound from the hill country of Cumberland and Westmorland still has *'hare feet (rather than the round cat feet), which are more suitable for clambering up rocks and working in rough hills'*, Croxton Smith wrote. From the fell foxhound, the trail hound has been bred less for stamina than speed to race across country following a laid scent.

King John was reputed to own the first pack of otter hounds in the thirteenth century. These large, shaggy dogs with webbed feet have an ability to follow a trail in water. In *Tarka the Otter* Henry Williamson described Dewdrop, the only true otter hound in the pack (unlike Deadlock, who had *'the blood of Talbots'* in his veins – bloodhound and mastiff), as having *'long fawn-coloured hair . . . curly with wet'*. The otter hound was a declining breed before otter hunting was banned in England in 1978. Now the breed is being preserved by the Otterhound Club.

See also BLACK DOGS, DOGS, GUN DOGS, HOUND TRAILING, RED FOXES, ROYAL FORESTS, SHEEP-DOGS, TERRIERS.

HOUND TRAILING

Over the fields and fells of Cumberland, Westmorland, Northumberland and surrounding counties, hounds compete against one another to follow a pre-laid scent of aniseed or paraffin. The hounds used in these races have been bred for speed and will leave any foxhound, bred for stamina, far behind. With betting in full swing and yelps of highly strung dogs against a backdrop of wild hills, hound trailing makes for a great day out.

A race may take half an hour; excitement builds as the hounds make their way across the face of the fells and as they turn for home. There is nothing like seeing them strain all sinews towards the bloody treats at the finish as they speed towards their owners' cries and the shouting crowds.

The Hound Trailing Association was founded in 1906 when hound trailing was part of sports and agricultural shows. By the 1940s there would be trails almost every day in summer and autumn somewhere in the region; the industrial and mining areas were the main focus. Norman Nicholson caught the essence of it: *'the hound, running a trail, does seem to lead an independent life. It has no jockey, no man wagging a flag before it or driving an electric hare. It goes off on its own, has a look around the country, and comes back again, and the winning hounds seem to have a real idea of what they are doing. Sometimes, of course, they don't come back.'* He continued: *'For many, however, the main interest in the trails is not the dogs but the men. Here bookie, miner, shipyard- and steelworker, shopkeeper and clerk mix with farmer, farm labourer and squire. The unnatural antagonism between town and country, industry and agriculture is forgotten, and both acknowledge what they owe to the same tradition.'*

See also BLACK DOGS, CAIRNS, DOGS, GUN DOGS, HOUNDS, SHEEP-DOGS, TERRIERS.

HOUSE NAMES

The most popular house name is The Cottage, followed by Rose Cottage (115,000 in the UK) and The Bungalow. Distinguishing names were hardly needed when the bungalow was the sole example in its place.

Between Poole, Dorset and Bournemouth, Hampshire a number of houses are called The Shieling (summer grazing places). Presumably they were named by Scots or north-country expatriates, retiring with romantic reminders of home. According to Joyce Miles, transferred place-names are the most common: from the 1850s Cheltenham and Exeter had house names such as *'Bath Cottage, Chester House, Thanet Villa, Malvern Lodge and Exmouth Cottage'*, which say something of past mobility.

Names may reflect a feature of the locality. Trees are popular – Orchard House has recently risen from twelfth to fifth place. Oaklands, Yew Tree Cottage, The Beeches, Apple Tree Cottage, Pear Tree House and Cherry Orchard are high on the list of house names kept by the Halifax Building Society. The Elms was quite a frequent name, but its decreasing popularity has mirrored the tree's decline.

A house called The Rookery is likely to be large and old. Local wild animals inspire names such as Badger's Hollow and Foxhanger. With so many chapels, barns, post offices, forges, village schools and police houses falling out of use, it is not surprising that many of these, recently converted, are reflected in house names usually prefixed by The Old . . . Some owners of new houses have researched the names of the fields they were built on, such as The Pennings, Cat Leap and Belly Flatt Cottage.

The English passion for a good outlook is reflected in names such as Prospect Villa, South View, Sea View, Sunny View, Belle View and Bona Vista – no doubt a good selling point for bed and breakfast operators.

See also BUNGALOWS, COTTAGES, ELM, FAMILY NAMES, ROOKERIES, SUNBURSTS, WILDFLOWERS.

Johnston Regular, Edward Johnston, 1916.

ICE SKATING IN THE OPEN AIR

John Evelyn and Samuel Pepys often noted in their diaries that the Thames was frozen over. On 9 January 1684 the weather was treacherously cold. John Evelyn *'went across the Thames on the ice, now become so thick as to bear not only streets of booths, in which they roasted meat, and had divers shops of wares, quite across as in a town, but coaches, carts and horses passed over'.*

On 24 January: *'Coaches plied from Westminster to the Temple, and from several other stairs to and fro, as in the streets, sleds, sliding with skates, a bull-baiting, horse and coach-races . . . so that it seemed to be a bacchanalian triumph, or carnival on the water.'* These frost fairs took place *'once or twice every century until 1831'*, when *'the removal of Old London Bridge allowed the river above it to flow too fast to freeze solid'*, and the 'Little Ice Age' of the sixteenth to eighteenth centuries, which had gripped Europe and given Brueghel much inspiration, had slipped away.

Skating on the lakes and tarns of the Lake District, such as Rydal Water, Ratherheath Tarn, Tarn Hows, Derwent Water and Windermere, used to happen much more frequently than it does today. In his 'Country Diary' columns for the *Guardian*, A. Harry Griffin described how in the cold winter of 1929 the railways ran excursions from London and other cities to the 'Lakeland ice carnival', where *'there seemed as many people on and around the "toe" of Windermere as on a busy summer's day in Blackpool. And not only crowds of people on the ice but many cars parked on it, and roaring hot braziers as well.'* He recalled how he *'left the Lakeside crowds and skated northwards, completely alone, up the lake for two or three miles, with so far as I could see, the whole black ice of Windermere to myself. A happy memory of carefree winters that perhaps won't be repeated in these days of global warming.'*

The usually sleepy town of Sturminster Newton on the river Stour in Dorset has been transformed by the freezing of the river. In 1891, according to Rodney Legg, *'skating was indulged in by the light of Chinese and other lanterns, and many of the persons were attired in fancy costume. The band played selections of music, and the scene was a most lively one.'*

The ornamental lake in front of Nottingham University is rigged with lights and opens to skaters when the weather gives a hand. Following New York, London offers a small circle of ice among the office towers of Broadgate and the courtyard of Somerset House, both of which throng day and night with delighted learners and cool customers. But nothing can beat the excitement of wild skating. Since the 1950s land drainage schemes have meant that many of the safe places for skating – flood meadows – are no longer available.

See also FENS, FEN SKATING, FROST & FROST HOLLOWS, LAKES, TARNS, WEATHER.

INDUSTRIAL CHIMNEYS

The need for draw, to increase the heat in furnaces, and the resulting roar and smoke would have been nothing new to the iron smelters of the Weald and the Shropshire valleys, and the lead and silver smelters of the Northumberland moors. In the seventeenth to nineteenth centuries the limestone hills were alive with sturdy, sprouting chimneys. The four-sided example at Stone Edge, south-west of Chesterfield, Derbyshire, lays claim to the title of oldest standing industrial chimney in the world, and the extraordinary smelt mill flue above Grassington in Yorkshire, now collapsing in parts, lies on the ground for hundreds of yards up the hill before becoming a vertical stack. There are also atmospheric ruins of tin-mine engine houses in Cornwall.

Eighteenth-century steam technology necessitated chimneys for mills and mines. Smitham chimney in East Harptree, Somerset stands testament to Mendip's lead mining. The Cotswold woollen industry threw up chimneys, especially around Stroud and Nailsworth in Gloucestershire. The chimney at Bliss Tweed Mill in Chipping Norton, Oxfordshire has Tuscan stylings. In Lancashire and the Midlands they were built of brick; L.S. Lowry made an industry out of painting them. Thirty years after his death, Manchester has only four. Quieted survivors make powerful landmarks: Dixon's chimney, standing three hundred feet above Carlisle in Cumberland; India Mill in Darwen, Lancashire, red-brick and elaborately Italianate; Lister's Pride, towering over Bradford, Yorkshire since 1871. Above Hebden Bridge in Yorkshire there are feral stacks lost among trees.

Chimneys illuminate a rich spread of industry, marking water pumps (Ware, Hertfordshire), gunpowder mills (Powdermills, Dartmoor; the Tillingbourne valley, Surrey), tar works (Crew's Hole, Bristol), brass mills (Saltford, Bath) and dye works (the never-used Wainhouse's Folly in Halifax, Yorkshire, now a prospect tower). They impress themselves onto a scene by their

incongruity. The Candlestick above Whitehaven in Cumberland is a shipping landmark, and the small one at Jenny Brown's Point near Silverdale, Lancashire may have been a beacon.

The tall cement works chimneys in Castleton, Derbyshire and Westbury, Wiltshire offer white-plumed orientation points. Middlesbrough's chemical works in Yorkshire and Fawley's oil refinery in Hampshire both repel and fascinate with skylines of metal and fire, the latter a surreal sight across the New Forest heathland. Similarly, from Gowy Meadows nature reserve at Ellesmere Port in Cheshire, the stacks of Stanlow refinery glower – once the subject of a song by Orchestral Manoeuvres in the Dark.

Power-station chimneys are not as well loved as their cooling-tower neighbours or industrial forbears, but there are aristocrats: the quartet of stacks, disused since 1983, on Battersea's famously extinct power station are important to south London's skyline.

See also BRICKS, COOLING TOWERS, ENGINE HOUSES, IRONSTONE, LANDMARKS, LEAD MINES.

I N G S

This Old Norse name is given to flood lands, mainly in the north of Lincolnshire and the south of Yorkshire, where Pete Bowler points out a further extension of the word: '*The Ings, a local name for a flooded depression, usually caused by mining subsidence, are part of the flood management of the River Dearne. They provide safety valves, holding capacity alongside the river to take off high storm flows. They are also havens for wild life.*' The Derwent Ings, the collective name for Wheldrake, Duffield, Aughton, Bubwith and East Cottingwith Ings, south-east of York in the Lower Derwent

valley between Wheldrake and Bubwith, are awash with lady's smock, marsh marigolds, great burnet, meadowsweet and pepper saxifrage. In the summer they are cut for hay and, when flooded in winter, they provide feeding grounds for wildfowl, including Bewick's swans, wigeon, teal, pintail, mallard and shoveller. A part of Hull is named Sutton Ings, clustering around a long lake in East Park. Across the estuary around Barton-upon-Humber, Lincolnshire old clay workings cling to the south bank for five miles. Squarish and drowned, they are a reminder of the brick- and tile-making industries of the nineteenth century; the most westerly are now a nature reserve called Far Ings.

Riparian fields are often subject to flooding, especially in winter – or they used to be. Since the 1960s river engineering works have lowered water tables for cereals and improved pasture. Banks have been straightened to force water to run away as fast as possible, drying the fields and making them less supportive of wildlife, especially birds that need high water tables, such as snipe, redshank and curlew, which have declined drastically in number.

Millions of pounds are now being spent undoing all the expensive work spearheaded by the Ministry of Agriculture. Low-lying areas by rivers are once more being recognised as natural washlands; created for the river's own use and, at the same time, enriching the land with silt, they are areas where excess water can be safely stored so that towns and villages downstream do not get flooded.

There are few fields bordering rivers that have not been drained, ploughed and re-seeded. Of those that remain untouched, many are old Lammas meadows (divided into strips under different ownership and cut for hay) and are inundated for a couple of months each winter.

The Ouse Washes in Cambridgeshire and Norfolk; Port Meadow along the Thames in Oxfordshire; North Meadow

242

in Cricklade, Wiltshire; and much of the Somerset Levels: all are now special examples of a once-common landscape lost to drainage and fertilisers.

See also BROADS, FENS, FIELDS, FLASHES, FRITILLARY MEADOWS, GRAZING MARSHES, GREEN LANES, HAY MEADOWS, LEVELS, MOORLAND, MOSSES, MOSSLAND, PEAT, PONDS, RIVERS, SALT MARSHES, WATER-MEADOWS.

I N N S

'*There is nothing which has yet been contrived by man by which so much happiness is produced as by a good tavern or inn*', Dr Johnson once eulogised. In the 1940s Thomas Burke could still write about the institution being '*as familiar in the national consciousness as the oak and the ash and the village green and the church spire*'.

The decline of the inn in its traditional sense – as a place where a weary traveller could obtain food, drink and accommodation – has been swift. Railway hotels stole trade, and then cars contracted the distance between places and lessened the need for overnight stops. Holidaymakers wanted more, so inns evolved into hotels, such as the White Hart in Lewes, Sussex and the Lygon Arms in Broadway, Worcestershire. Other drivers just wanted a pub lunch, an evening meal or a quiet pint. Such was the change in aspect of the old coaching inns that John Black ruefully observed in 1974 that they often could be recognised by '*the forbidding "No Coaches" sign outside*'.

The buildings that survive tell of former glories. Marlborough College, Wiltshire was once an inn. The Ship in Mere, Wiltshire and the George in Stamford, Lincolnshire still boast their arched entrances and large cobbled court-yards. The Talbot in Oundle, Northamptonshire has iron railings designed to protect the walls from carriage wheels. The New Inn in Gloucester and New Inn in Salisbury, Wiltshire date from as recently as the Middle Ages.

Many of the earliest inn users were pilgrims, plying the roads to Canterbury and Dover in Kent and Winchester in Hampshire. There is a Pilgrim's Rest in Battle, Sussex, and the Maison Dieu hostel in Dover is now the town hall. Geoffrey Chaucer's famous Canterbury pilgrims set off from the Tabard at Southwark, London, which was demolished in 1874. In 2003 its passing was marked by the unveiling of a blue plaque in Chaucer's honour.

Beyond Chaucer, literature is frequently enriched by colourful inns: *Tom Jones*, *Lavengro*, *Silas Marner*, *Middlemarch*, the works of Dickens and G.K. Chesterton's *The Flying Inn*. The reality of the inn could be livelier than the fiction, with characters as unsavoury as the Jarmans of the Crane (now the Ostrich) in Colnbrook, Buckinghamshire, who murdered their guests in a vat of boiling ale.

Where not built for the church, inns may have been related to the lords of the manor, such as the Gloucester Arms in Penrith, Cumberland. Others were for the benefit of workers: labourers on the New Bedford River (the Hundred Foot Drain) in Cambridgeshire stayed in The Anchor at Sutton Gault. In nearby Lincolnshire the Leagate Inn at Coningsby was a 'guide house', where safe passage across the Fens was arranged. Inns called the Ferry, their foundations on dry land, served as a pausing point for those in wait for a river or estuary crossing.

Inns were always closely linked to roads. The toll cottage opposite the Spaniards Inn in Hampstead, north-west London is a fair indicator of the symbiotic relationship between the two. Further north, inns were essential to the packhorse and coaching routes across desolate and often snow-filled passes. The Tan Hill Inn in Yorkshire is the highest, but the Kirkstone Pass Inn in Cumberland is equally remote, waiting at the top of a road known bleakly as The Struggle. The stagecoach was defeated by this road, passengers having to get out and walk to the inn along the most troublesome section. Ye Horns Inn in Goosnargh, Lancashire was a popular stopping-off point for packhorse trains.

Places where people from far and near could meet one another, it is not surprising that inns always had an important place in the community, whether for gossip or trade. Many inns carry particularity in their styles and building materials, some became known for their food: the landlord of the Bell Inn at Stilton, Huntingdonshire offered cheese to travellers on the London coach.

See also ABBEYS, ALMSHOUSES, ASPARAGUS, BAKEWELL PUDDING, BEER, BLACK & WHITE BUILDINGS, CIDER & CIDER ORCHARDS, COBBLES, CRICKET, FERRIES, GOOSEBERRIES, HOTELS, MARKET GARDENS, MORRIS DANCING, MUMMING PLAYS, PEARS, PLUMS, PUB GAMES, PUBS, PUB SIGNS, ROADS, STILTON, TOLL-HOUSES, TOWN HALLS & GUILD-HALLS, WASSAILING.

243

The White Swan, Pickering, Yorkshire.

IRONSTONE

Any rock with a high iron content may be called ironstone. It appears in the Jurassic rocks, mysteriously formed among sediments on the seabed, often as ooliths (tiny orbs) with shelly layers. Some forms are sandy, some calcareous, the iron content creating ferruginous sandstone or limestone rocks ranging from orange to rusty dark brown, darkening upon contact with the air.

The ironstone buildings of north Oxfordshire, Northamptonshire, Leicestershire, Rutland and Kesteven have beguiled many observers. Alec Clifton-Taylor extolled the Hornton ironstone from the Oxfordshire/Warwickshire border, with its mixed shades of brown and green. In Little Harrowden, Northamptonshire striped cottages mix limestone with 'bastard stone', a calcareous ironstone no good for iron making; Pevsner enjoyed it in Rothwell church, '*singularly beautiful in its tawny colour*'.

Iron Acton in the Cotswolds betrays hard work, and Ironstone Country is the name given to the Wychwood Forest area in Oxfordshire. Carstone is a dark brown ironstone found in Kent, Surrey and Sussex; splinters are used to great effect in stone buildings as contrasting lines of beads between blocks, a decoration known as galleting. Carstone is called gingerbread around Snettisham, Norfolk. In the Lincolnshire Wolds, around Nettleton and Claxby, ironstone is a rich ochre.

The Weald of Kent and Sussex, the Forest of Dean, the Black Country and Shropshire all have long histories of iron winning; to this the coalfields added steel making. In the Rockingham Forest, Northamptonshire iron ore has been smelted sporadically since at least Roman times. But it took the extension of the rail network to remind the Victorians how much richness lay beneath the surface, revealed in the railway cuttings.

In the 1930s Corby and Kettering in Northamptonshire began to expand as new steelworks exploited one of the biggest ironstone fields in the world. This was an opencast operation, and the enormous walking machines were bigger than any dinosaur. They caused most excitement when they took to open country. In 1974 a walking dragline called Sundew, weighing more than 1,400 tons, took nine months to amble thirteen miles from Rutland to its new job in Corby. The extensive holes were restored to agriculture and may now need a local eye and knowledge to pick them out, although a long quarry face (gullet) or steep slope may give them away.

The Frodingham ironstone fed the iron and steel industry in north Lincolnshire. North and east of Scunthorpe the derelict opencast working at Yarborough Gullet is more than one and a half miles long. Some of the worked-out gullets are 130 feet deep. These have become valuable for waste disposal, but some have been protected as flooding and reclamation

244

by nature have created fine wildlife habitats, such as Risby Warren and Dragonby Ponds; some have splendid geological sections, as at Yorkshire East Gullet.

Ironstone mining started along the coast of Yorkshire in the late 1840s. More than eighty mines opened from the cliff land (Cleveland) to Rosedale. The many mining villages, with their allotments and pigeon lofts, are virtually all that is left of this vibrant industry, save the great steel mills at Skinningrove, which sit on top of the windswept cliffs surrounded by fields. When the Carlin How and Loftus mines closed in 1958, the Kilton Beck began to rust. For four decades the polluted, iron-rich water flowed a dramatic orange through Skinningrove and out to sea. Now an experimental project attempting to catalyse the iron from the water is creating new problems for the villagers – how to use the precipitated iron? If it works, another will follow.

See *also* ALLOTMENTS, BECKS, BRIDGES, BUILDING STONES, CHALK, CHURCHES, COAL MINING, COBBLES, CORRUGATED IRON, COTTAGES, DRYSTONE WALLS, FLINT, GRANITE, GRAVESTONES, GREENSAND, LIMESTONE, MILLSTONE GRIT, MINES, PIGEON LOFTS, PLACE-NAMES, PUDDINGSTONE, QUARRIES, RIVERS, TUNNELS, WARRENS.

ISLANDS

Although we add the words 'island' or 'isle' to Brownsea, Hilbre, Horsey, Mersea, Northey, Osea, Osney, Scilly, Sheppey and Walney, they are already implied in the Old English *eg* or Old Norse *ey*. Even in land-bound Canvey in Essex, Ely in Cambridgeshire and Muchelney in Somerset, memories of plashy beginnings are embedded in the name.

Lundy means puffin island in Old Norse. Although only half a mile by three, it stands a proud granite beacon at four hundred feet high, with room for birds, flowers and lichens – the puffins for which it was named are few now. Its position in the Bristol Channel means that the pirate, the wrecker and the lighthouse (actually two) have a history here, but its modern role is as a retreat, bird colony, tourist haven and sheep farm. It is surrounded by the pioneering marine nature reserve of Europe, and more than a square mile of sea has also been designated the UK's first No Take Zone, meaning that no living thing can be fished or dredged-for here.

Around the island there are fine rocky reefs of coral and sponge, as well as magnificent kelp forests, with visiting basking sharks, resident seals and laid-back lobsters. The Lundy cabbage is unique to the island and plays sole host to a couple of flea beetles and a weevil found nowhere else. The meat of the Soay sheep that maintain the herbage is marketed with a Lundy label; there is also a Lundy stamp for your postcard home from this little piece of land, which was once owned, notwithstanding names such as the Devil's Slide and Devil's Limekiln, by the Heaven family, who bought it with money gained from Jamaican estates when the slaves were emancipated.

Tiny Steep Holm and Flat Holm, limestone outliers of the Mendips – one steep, one flat – lie further into the Bristol Channel. Holm is an Old Norse word for island.

The Isle of Wight is a giant in comparison, 23 by 13 miles. Flashing its chalk cliffs to the east and west, it enlivens the horizon from Portsmouth and Bournemouth. This island stands in the way of water striving to ebb and flow north and south, east and west, creating a unique double tide that is felt along the nearby coasts of Hampshire and Dorset. It interferes with the wind, too, making the Solent challenging for sailing.

The Isles of Scilly in Cornwall are made of defiant ancient granite confronting a ravaging ocean, an archipelago of rocks and lands so resilient that gales with a fetch of thousands of miles and ships at full throttle barely seem to graze their edges. Far out of sight of other land, the elements rule here. Yet things do change. Only four thousand years ago this was made up of fewer, bigger islands; sea level was lower and the tilting of the whole mass had not accelerated. Now the main islands are surrounded by drowned prehistoric fields and villages, as well as rocks and wrecks, hundreds of them – there are at least thirteen broken ships on the Crim Rocks to the west, and islets have warning names, such as Hellweathers, Roaring Ledge, Steeple Rock, The Hats and Ragged Island. Geoffrey Grigson apprehended it: *'The islands are raw and original in the whole, humanised only in the detail. The detail is rich, curious, coloured, varied and variegated . . . but it is the original which governs, the human which is incidental.'*

Hilbre, Little Hilbre and Little Eye form a broken rampart of long, low sandstone islands edging the Wirral in Cheshire, surrounded by miles of red tidal sands. The patterns of lugworm casts and rippled sand texture the hour-long walk across at low tide. Sea spleenwort and rock sea-lavender may be rare, but most surprising is to find bluebells among the thrift in early spring. The marshes and mud-flats, sands and sea make this a rich place for birds, resident and migrating, which in turn make this a place of birdwatchers and ringers; the bird observatory has been here since 1957.

The Great Whin Sill marches across the northern edge of England, standing in a high cliff as it meets the sea below Bamburgh castle in Northumberland. It reappears a couple of miles out as the dark Farne Islands, 28 pieces of dolerite, some disappearing under the tide, the larger being coated in boulder clay and peaty soil. Puffins normally breed here in serious numbers, together with kittiwakes, guillemots and shags among the thirteen species that nest on different islands, but, as at Coquet Island further south, breeding is now erratic. Scientists fear a catastrophic fall in numbers as a result of rising temperature in the North Sea: it has increased by two degrees Celsius in twenty years, and sand eels are following plankton further north as the sea warms.

Coquet Island, off Amble in Northumberland, is for the birds. It has a lighthouse built on a monastic outpost of Tynemouth Priory. St Cuthbert spent time here as well as living in solitude on Inner Farne, where he tried to stop the plundering of the eider duck – it has since locally been named after him as Cuddy's duck. Both he and St Aidan before him were also associated with Lindisfarne, or Holy Island, making it a place of pilgrimage and retreat for 1,300 years. The most pious still cross the tidal causeway on foot, overtaken by drivers careful to note the tide tables.

Islands that can be reached at low tide have a certain magic. St Nicholas at Wade in Kent stands beside the old wading place to the Isle of Thanet, and just to the north is Plumpudding Island. St Michael's Mount in Cornwall rises three hundred feet, with a zigzag track to a medieval priory, fortified church, cottages and shops. This high-tide island, a dramatic landmark all along the south Cornish coast, is reached by boat or causeway from Marazion. On the north coast Tintagel, with its tales of Merlin and King Arthur, has become an island since the sea severed its natural arch.

See also ALEXANDERS, ARCHES, AVALON, BEACHES, BOATS, CASTLES, THE CHANNEL, CHINES, CHURCHES, CLIFFS, CLOUDS, COASTLINE, COASTS, CORNISH GIGS, DAFFODILS, DENES, DEVIL, DRYSTONE WALLS, EYOTS, FENS, FERRIES, FLOODS, FOG & MIST, FRETS, GARDENS, GRAZING MARSHES, HARBOURS, HILLS, INGS, LANDMARKS, LEVELS, LICHENS, LIGHTHOUSES, PIERS, PILLBOXES, RIAS, SAINTS, SAND-DUNES, SEA FORTS, SEA TRACTOR, SHEEP, SHINGLE, SHIPPING FORECAST, STACKS, TIDES, TUNNELS, ZIGZAGS.

245

Staple Island, the Farnes, Northumberland.

JACK AND JILL

The hill referred to in the Jack and Jill rhyme is in Kilmersdon, a village midway between Bath and Wells in Somerset. The story goes that in the reign of Henry VIII, Jack and Jill, a married couple, were collecting their daily pail of water from the well (strangely up the hill) when a boulder from the quarry at Bad Stone, later known as Batson, rolled down and killed Jack. Jill, who was pregnant, died soon after giving birth to her son. The surname Gilson means Jill's son and, according to the village's website, 'there are more Gilsons in the area than in the whole of Manchester, Birmingham and Liverpool combined'.

Visitors to the village may not know its connections with the nursery rhyme, but a discreet sign recently carved in low relief on a wall directs one to the hill. This is an example of small-scale public art at its best. 'Milestones', with fragments of the rhyme carved into them, lead the way along the path up the hill, renamed Jack and Jill Hill, to the restored well, which sits by the primary school at the top. The rhyme is cut into big slabs of slate attached to the school wall, and Jack and Jill with their pail are depicted on the metal entrance gates.

Little Jack Horner, who was caught with his thumb in a pie, lived not far away in Mells. He was steward to the last abbot of Glastonbury. His real name was Tom, but 'Jack' might refer to his knavishness in allegedly stealing the deeds to the Manor of Mells, which were hidden in a pie together with the deeds to eleven other manors – a gift from the ill-fated abbot to the King at the Dissolution. Tom Horner's descendants, who are convinced we have the wrong man, still live in Mells.

It is difficult to find reason in some of our nursery rhymes. 'Humpty Dumpty' seems particularly hard to crack. Some argue that the rhyme refers to a cannon positioned on the city walls close to St Mary's-at-the-Wall Church in Colchester, Essex, which was used by the Royalists in the Civil War to defend the city during the siege of 1648. According to Jean Harrowven, Humpty Dumpty was a wooden war machine, used by Charles I to gain the City of Gloucester from the Roundheads. While being rolled downhill and across the river, it was irretrievably broken – 'all the king's horses and all the king's men' could do nothing.

Banbury Museum coyly notes that 'By today's standards the words of many early rhymes seem strikingly unsuitable for those of tender years', in a leaflet that struggles not to mention the possible sexual connotations in this Oxfordshire rhyme:

> Ride a cock-horse to Banbury Cross,
> To see a fine lady upon a white horse;
> Rings on her fingers and bells on her toes,
> And she shall have music wherever she goes.

This is an old verse, but it was first published in 1744 and more widely between 1784 and 1877 in chap-books for children; over the years the words have changed. There were three crosses in Banbury in the Middle Ages – White Cross, Bread Cross and High or Market Cross – all of which were destroyed by the Puritans in about 1600. The cross that stands now at Horse Fair, built in 1859, is not the cross in the rhyme.

There is much dispute as to the identity of the 'fine lady'. Celia Fiennes, who travelled the country on horseback in 1697, is one suggestion; Lady Godiva, another. Others believe she was an earth goddess and part of a pagan spring ritual. A cock-horse means a 'high-spirited horse', according to The Oxford Dictionary of Nursery Rhymes, a child's hobby-horse and the name given to an additional horse harnessed to pull coaches up steep hills.

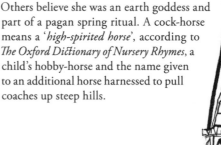

Banbury is now riding on the rhyme. In June 2000 an annual celebration of hobby-horse and animal-disguise customs was initiated and has started to draw jovial beasts from across the country.

See also FAMILY NAMES, FOLKTALES, HILLS, HORSES & PONIES, MARKET CROSSES, NEW MILESTONES, 'OBBY 'OSSES, SCULPTURES, WELLS.

JACK OF THE CLOCKS

Automated clock jacks have attracted tourists since the Middle Ages. People made detours to see two metal giants clubbing the bells at St Dunstan's-in-the-West on Fleet Street, London. Abinger Hammer in Surrey, renowned for iron forging, has a jack that takes a hammer to its bell. Jacks also strike the times in Exeter (on a decorated clock at St Mary Steps Church, known as Matthew the Miller), Oxford and at Wells Cathedral, where Jack Blandiver strikes bells at the hours and quarters with his hammer and heels from his sentry box.

Automata art is not quite dead. Weston-super-Mare's Sovereign shopping centre has stylised military bandsmen appearing at regular intervals, accompanied by music. They were made in the 1990s by John Smith and Sons of Derby, who have been building clocks since the eighteenth century and are responsible for a number of new ones – at Birmingham's Market Hall and on the waterfront at Gosport in Hampshire, set into a steel pyramid.

See also BELLS & BELL-RINGING, CATHEDRALS, CHURCHES, CLOCKS.

JET

Akin to coal, though much lighter in weight, jet is a fossilised wood from a Jurassic relative of the monkey-puzzle tree. Like amber, a tree resin, it is easily shaped and polished and feels warm to the touch. Rubbed on wool or silk it soon picks up a static electrical charge. The intensity of its blackness is also remarkable. These must be some of the reasons why it was highly prized by prehistoric people – jet beads have been found in high-status Bronze-Age burials near the Sussex coast.

The best hard jet in England comes from around Whitby in north Yorkshire, where miners soon learned that a particular sort of ammonite fossil was a reliable indicator of jet-bearing rock. In its heyday in the 1870s the industry employed three hundred men, including craftsmen who carved the jet into the elaborate ornaments and mourning jewellery beloved of the Victorians. Today the seaside resort supports a thriving market in both antique jet and new craftwork, with stiff competition to find rough jet in the cliffs or on the beach after winter storms.

See also AMMONITES, BEACHCOMBING, BEACHES, MONKEY-PUZZLE.

JUNIPER

'At a distance it may be mistaken for a furze-bush, being not unlike that plant in size, colour, and manner of growth. Seen nearer, it is brighter green than the furze; the topmost slender sprays, gracefully curved at their tips, are tinged with red; and where the foliage is thick there is a bluish tint on the green that is like a bloom. In some lights, especially in the early mornings, when the level sunbeams strike on the bushes, wet with dew or melting hoar-frost, this blueness gives the plant a rare, delicate, changeful beauty . . .' W.H. Hudson loved this *'handsome'* shrub and its variety of form. Writing in the 1920s he noticed even then that juniper was disappearing, *'simply because the great landowners have not thought proper to preserve it'*.

Juniper was once widespread on the chalk of the South, hence Juniper Hill in Oxfordshire, the birthplace of the writer Flora Thompson, and on the Surrey Downs. H.J. Massingham wrote: *'You know by experience that juniper is the only nurseling of the true chalk downs, with the possible exception of yew.'* It is now rare on the chalk, as well as on heaths and moorland, where it also grows, destroyed by ploughing and burning. It cannot survive being shaded out by trees, or overgrazing, which prevents its seedlings from growing.

The largest concentration of junipers – about eighteen thousand bushes – is on the Ministry of Defence land at Porton Down in Wiltshire, where it supports more than a hundred different types of insect, some of which live exclusively on it.

On very different soils and situations, juniper also grows on the fells of Upper Teesdale and on the valley sides in the Lake District. Here, and at other places where relict populations hang on, attempts are being made to allow the juniper, one of our three native conifers, to regenerate – something it seems reluctant to do.

247

Its blue-black berries, used in cooking, were once collected here to add flavouring to gin (the spirit was first known as geneva, from the French *genièvre*, meaning juniper), but today these come from eastern Europe.

See also CHALK, DOWNLAND, FROST & FROST HOLLOWS, GIN, GORSE, YEW.

K A O L I N

Around the granite moors of the South West, especially near St Austell, is the biggest of the few workable deposits of kaolin or china clay on earth. The landscape produced is otherworldly. Unless there is a mist, from most of the tops of west Cornwall you can see the hallmark white, circular, pointed heaps of quartz sand (only fifteen per cent of the rock yields kaolin). The nearer you get the more likely you are to catch a glimpse of the huge white working holes, up to four hundred feet deep, and the milky blue-green pools left after mining – water plays a big part in both the mining of the clay and the refining of kaolin.

To the west of St Austell near the river Fal, with pits at Treviscoe and Wheal Remfry, for example, is an area quarried specifically for china stone – this has gone only part way towards kaolin and is used to make high-quality porcelain. A third of china clay production is also for this purpose; other uses are in paints, rubber, plastics, building materials, agriculture, cotton 'bleaching', pharmaceuticals and chemicals. More than 45 per cent goes to the paper industry for bulking and for coating high-quality paper. But the market is changing, with substitutes and increasing competition from Brazil.

Concrete blocks are made from some of the waste, which includes quartz, granite, slates or killas and other overburden. The heaps and holes from three centuries of working define this area, with a unique succession of plants that colonise the inhospitable niches.

The Eden Project brings plants from across the world into ground-breaking architecture settled into an old kaolin pit more than two hundred feet deep and the size of 35 football pitches. The brief was to '*create a spectacular theatre in which to tell the story of human dependence on plants*'. The biomes, designed by Nicholas Grimshaw and Partners, are giant, freeform greenhouses harbouring tropical and temperate plants.

All kinds of relict workings of the 'white industry' enrich the landscape. In Devon, at Crownhill Down on the south-west edge of Dartmoor, the fascinating lines of low, parallel, vertical stones, each course laid a little lower to promote the settling out of water-borne debris, are overgrown nineteenth-century mica traps. Three active pits on Lee Moor still work around the edge of the Dartmoor granite.

See also GRANITE, LANDMARKS, POTTERY, QUARRIES, SLATES.

K E N N E L S

A town or village with a stream running down the street has a special attraction. Between the footway and the main road in Otterton, east Devon a wide waterway runs, with small bridges frequently crossing its shallow concrete bed. In July 2004 the stream had no water in it after a dry spell, as often occurs; it floods sometimes, too. Bob Butler, who runs Otterton Mill, tells of a local custom: '*You are not considered to be truly "local" unless you are fully immersed in the Brook (willingly or not) on your birthday.*'

At East Budleigh, nearby, the Budleigh Brook trickles its way down the main street in a walled channel, running where the pavement should be and as wide as it would have been; its bed is part cobbled with Budleigh buns. Small stone-and-brick arched footbridges cross over to the cottages and shops beside it.

Further along the coast at Beer fast-running water is confined in a narrow and deep stone channel less than two feet wide between the pavement and Fore Street. Self-seeded pink and white daisies cling to its sides, outshining the gaudy flowers in silly planters that straddle the stream alongside occasional bridges for the faint-hearted. Spanning the kennel, which was used to flush away night soil and fish tailings, are two elegant stone conduits with roofs, topped with orbs, which brought clean piped water from above the town, an early gift from Lady Rolle.

In 1903 Arthur L. Salmon wrote of two Cornish streams: '*The main street of Helston is rendered musical and clean by rills of water running perpetually down its gutters, as at Truro.*' Today there are '*streams running down either side of Wendron Street, Church Street and Coinage Street. In earlier times these kept the gutters clean but today only add to the charm of Helston*', according to the town's website. In Frome, Somerset, down the middle of Cheap Street, water from the spring above speeds downhill in a narrow channel, which shoppers simply step across.

Cornish Alp, St Austell, Cornwall.

Brian Human tells us that *'In Cambridge the street streams running down either side of Trumpington Street and St Andrew's Street are called Hobson's Conduit. They originally carried Cambridge's first clean water supply from the Nine Wells, which lie to the south of the City, and date from around 1794.'* Now these runnels are turned on only in summer.

The culverting of streams and kennels has resulted in many a large and small settlement losing the memory of its connection with nature, often its very reason for being just where it is.

See also CHALK STREAMS, COBBLES, DROVE ROADS, FOOTBRIDGES, HIGH STREETS, MARKETS, NICKNAMES, RIVERS, WELL DRESSING, WELLS, WINTERBOURNES.

KERBSTONES

Two familiar stories come from different ends of the country but echo the same cry for perpetuation of detail and quality in situ. Residents of Wallsend, Northumberland wrote to a local newspaper in 2003: *'We are writing to express our disgust at the removal of the original kerbstones from our back lanes and the manner in which it was done. No consultation. No explanation. Ugly tarmac casually slapped down in their place and the fact that the stones are to go to another "more deserving area". There is pride in the small things of quality in Wallsend, but soon there'll be nothing to be proud of, if our council continues to act in this disgraceful manner.'*

In Bradford-on-Avon, Wiltshire a town councillor told us in 2001 that he had *'found a stone wall demolished and a very wide new pavement being installed. Noticing concrete kerb-stones being installed with original stone kerbstones discarded, I asked if they could be rescued.'*

Once an area is designated as deserving of conservation, the remainder is not lavished with such care. Simple things, such as kerbstones and flags, long a part of a neighbourhood, are often traded down to off-the-peg concrete then lost, sold privately or removed to a conservation area.

Poole in Dorset is notable in parts of its coniferous suburbs for grass running into the road; in many rural settlements this is also valued. In Bonsall, Derbyshire, according to the village design statement, *'The absence of pavements and kerbstones is characteristic of the village.'* In Great Bowden, Leicestershire the village design statement observes that *'Around the Green and on some other streets the road kerbs are still the attractive granite, which assists in retaining the link with bygone times. Along Sutton and Knights End Roads the verges are without kerbs; to maintain their rural character they need to be kept that way.'*

Civic societies strive to remind municipal authorities to value the particularity of a village or town's old kerbstones and prevent the unnecessary imposition of kerbs that suburbanise the countryside.

Most early roads and streets were mud, at best simply strewn with gravel and sand from the local gravel pit; a differentiated paved footway rarely existed. Road surfaces in the city might be of rough stones or cobbles with a kennel or drain running down the middle, and possibly a stone flag pavement on either side.

The development of new estates, such as Bedford and Belgravia in London, led to a raising of standards. The Westminster Paving Act of 1762 gave responsibility for the condition of roads to Paving Commissioners, who could 'impose a rate' to fund street improvements. It demanded stone kerbs, replacement of central drains with kerbside gutters and raising the pavement above the road surface to make walking a safer and drier experience. A precedent was set for other London estates, towns and cities, and many towns were paved in the late 1700s.

Coastal quarries began to do well – Purbeck stone was even specified to replace pebbles in some London streets by the 1762 Act. Granite was sought, being durable, impervious to water and aesthetically pleasing. Trade developed around the coast, much came from Aberdeen quarries to London, and coastal towns without their own hard rock found themselves kerbed with granite from Cornwall, Dartmoor, Lundy and the Lake District. As the canals extended and the railways came, rock from Charnwood Forest began to travel out of Leicestershire.

In Kentish Town, north London the kerbstones are edged with pink granite, white granite and diorite, filled

249

with dark enclosures known by quarrymen as heathens and to geologists as xenoliths and enclaves. Geologist Eric Robinson describes a small section of the Mile End Road in east London: '*the thin kerbstones offer us blue and veined Channel Island diorites, speckled Cornish Granite, dull red Mountsorrel Granite, and a few dark grey Aberdeenshire Granite lengths*'.

In many places distinctiveness is a result of quality rather than localness, although in Loughborough, Leicestershire '*the old pink kerbstones made of local granite from Mountsorrel show the chisel marks of the quarrying instruments*', according to a local website. In Derbyshire, Barry Joyce pointed out that '*The old causeys (pavements) are under threat . . . each area had its own tradition of paving, based on locally available materials.*' In The Dale in Wirksworth limestone paving is still edged by limestone kerbs from Dale Quarry up the road. There are examples in Norfolk of the use of brick where the local material is not hard enough. In Bridgnorth, Shropshire the pavements are of hard yellow engineering bricks with the gutters in big blue tiles.

See also ALLEYS, BOLLARDS, BUILDING STONES, COBBLES, GRANITE, KENNELS, PAVEMENTS, QUARRIES, RAISED PAVEMENTS, ROADS.

K I P P E R S

250

No kipper ever swam in the seas. Kippering is a curing and smoking process, which transforms a humble herring into something that cookery writer Jane Grigson justly described as '*one of this country's worthy contributions to fine food*'.

The English kipper is a product of the North East. John Woodger of Seahouses in Northumberland is credited with the invention of kippered herring in the 1840s, although it is a far from positive identification. The word itself seems to derive from the Dutch *küpper*, 'to spawn', and refers to the end-of-season salmon, which was not wasted if it was split and smoked. The North East has always been emotionally closer to the Netherlands and Scandinavia, where herrings are practically a staple (even Ikea's food halls demonstrate it). Woodger marketed the 'Newcastle kipper' in the markets of London and, thanks to railways and fridges, they are coming still.

Think of them and two places immediately spring to mind: Craster in Northumberland, where the Robson family's smokery has been hard at work since the 1850s; and Whitby in Yorkshire, where the Gothic associations with Bram Stoker are only enhanced by the conjoining in the narrow Victorian streets of the sea mist and the aromatic smoke from Willy Fortune's smokehouse.

Further south in Norfolk, Great Yarmouth's connection with the fish was so important (although its main stock-in-trade was the bloater – whole, salted, cold-smoked herring – rather than the kipper) that three herrings appear on the town's coat of arms. Woodger extended his empire to Yarmouth to use local fish and, as in North Shields, utilised the talents of Scots women, who migrated with the trade and became known as 'herring lassies'.

The kippering process is straightforward. Herrings are split and gutted, cleaned, salted, then hung on wooden poles or 'tenter-sticks' from metal hooks. For these authentic smokeries there are no dyes or impatiently speedy throughput. At Robson's the kippers are hung for up to fourteen hours above fires of whitewood shavings topped with oak sawdust. Fortune's smokes them for up to thirty hours, then sells them in pairs.

In spite of occasional threats from would-be legislators, there are still a few other producers using traditional methods, including Swallows of Seahouses. Like the others they have to rely on Scottish and Icelandic herring, the fish being peculiarly fickle geographically. The shoals of the nineteenth century, in Bill Weeks's words, '*would turn the sea's surface to quicksilver*'. But the herrings vanished as mysteriously as they came and, inevitably, took the local trade with them. The last were landed at Whitby in the 1970s. North Sea herring fishing was banned in 1977 in the hope that the stocks would be re-established.

See also BOATS, EELS, FOOD, GANSEYS, SEA FISH.

LCD, Alan Birch, 1981.

L A G O O N S

Of the hundred lagoons around the English coast, a quarter are in Hampshire, but the largest is in Dorset. Here, the Fleet shelters behind Chesil Bank and is home to the largest mute swan colony in the UK. The name 'fleet' recurs along the Essex coast, as in Broad, Besom, Mersea and Tollesbury Fleets. Suffolk has many little rivers more or less frustrated in their approach to the sea by sandbars; here they are called broads. Just south of Kessingland lie Benacre, Covehithe and Easton Broads.

Lagoons vary in salinity; some are tidal. The shingle bar at Slapton Ley in south Devon holds back a virtually freshwater lake. The reeds here welcome clouds of roosting starlings in winter. Most lagoons attract different waders and wildfowl, but less mobile creatures have to be special-ised to cope with an uncertain saline content. Delicate stoneworts, the lagoon sand shrimp and the starlet sea anemone may be found. The trembling sea mat is found in only one Cornish lagoon – Swanpool, near Falmouth.

See also BROADS, COASTS, LAKES, SHINGLE, STARLINGS, SWAN UPPING, TARNS.

L A K E S

In England's North West some sixteen lakes, mostly long and narrow in shape, give their name to an upland region roughly thirty miles by twenty miles. These great, limpid mirrors of fell, scree and sky, their basins carved out by glaciers, radiate from the central dome of the Lake District and its ancient volcanic core. That main branch of modern tourism – the holiday as a journey back to nature in search of solace and sustenance – had its origins in this land of spectacular lakes.

Lakeland has not always attracted travellers. Daniel Defoe, touring in the early eighteenth century, judged it to be barren, wild, useless and frightening. By the 1770s and 1780s, however, a tourist boom was under way, fostered by the publication of a welter of guides for visitors, even before William Wordsworth was born. His own *Guide to the Lakes*, published in 1810 and reprinted many times, sold far more copies in his lifetime than did any volume of poetry.

These lakes have also intrigued biologists intent on cataloguing and categorising. Each lake's ecology is shaped by its setting. Esthwaite and Windermere, for instance, nestled in the softer slates of south Lakeland, are eutrophic, rich in nutrients from the soil and from sewage and farm run-off. Wast Water and Ennerdale, by contrast, are nutrient-poor oligotrophic lakes, lying in the hard Borrowdale volcanic rocks in the main mountain masses.

In East Anglia Langmere, Ringmere and Fenmere in Breckland, connected to the deep chalk water-table below, fluctuate in depth and breadth dramatically over months to the extent that they drown their surrounding trees. In Shropshire kettle holes were formed when great blocks of abandoned ice melted on the spot, leaving depressions that water filled. Crose Mere extends to 150 acres, while Sweat Mere is just more than an acre. In Cheshire, Oak Mere is another example, although some pools, known as flashes, have been amplified by subsidence caused by the dissolution of underlying salt beds. Coal, peat, sand, clay and gravel pits have made lakes. The Blue Pool in Dorset, created from old clay diggings, became famous for its remarkable colour, caused by clay particles suspended in the water, after Augustus John painted it in 1911.

On the estates of stately homes, ornamental lakes have multiplied since the eighteenth century, when Capability Brown reshaped landscapes at the royal palace at Kew, now the Royal Botanic Gardens. In the nineteenth century, as the health and wellbeing of urban populations became an issue, boating lakes appeared in Victorian parks.

Many of England's lakes now suffer nutrient enrich-ment from agricultural run-off and sewage, and are further damaged by the spread of invasive imported plants. Australian swamp stonecrop, for instance, has smothered indigenous vegetation in hundreds of ponds and small lakes. Carp and bream introduced for coarse fishing can make matters worse, by stirring up bottom sediment, increasing turbidity and releasing more nutrients.

See also BOUNDARIES, BROADS, DEW PONDS, FELL RUNNING, FELLS, FLASHES, GRAVEL PITS, LOST VILLAGES, MOATS, PONDS, REED BEDS, RESERVOIRS, TARNS.

253

L A N D M A R K S

The huge arc above Wembley stadium is visible across London from hills and a few floors up. The two towers it replaced, while remembered on signs here and there, are now history. Landmarks are about meaning, identity, visibility and orientation. The Liver Building remains an icon as well as an orientation point for Liverpool, as do Newcastle's bridges. Large-scale features play their part: the massive cranes at Tilbury, Essex, like creatures waiting at the water's edge; the sheaves of chimneys around the Bedfordshire brick fields; the white heaps around St Austell, Cornwall; Warwick Castle; Boston Stump, Lincolnshire. There are also natural landmarks: Bredon Hill, Worcestershire; the Wrekin, Shropshire. A church tower on top of Heanor Hill in Derbyshire, with Codnor monument and Crich Stand some 8 miles away, begins to build a grid of reference points as you move through the locality. And, at the finer grain, as you walk, small, personal, seasonal landmarks (perhaps a hawthorn in flower) add themselves to your Parish Map.

Some landmarks work at night: the glow of the London Eye; flares from the chemical works in Middlesbrough, Yorkshire; the concentration of lights and ghostly presence of Hinkley Point nuclear power station on the Somerset coast; the red light at the tip of Salisbury Cathedral.

Most of the pithead gear and the pointed heaps, so important in the coalfields, have vanished, as have the hundreds of chimneys in the industrial centres of Yorkshire and Lancashire. Gone but, like the giant 'golf balls' at Fylingdales, Yorkshire, still impressed on the mind's eye.

Introducing *The Old Straight Track*, John Mitchell pointed out that '*The revelation took place when Watkins was 65 years old. Riding across the hills near Bredwardine in his native county [Herefordshire], he pulled up his horse to look out over the landscape below. At that moment he became aware of a network of lines, standing out like glowing wires all over the surface of the country, intersecting at the sites of churches, old stones and other spots of traditional sanctity.*' Alfred Watkins knew the land intimately, and in offering the idea of ley lines, linking ancient places of meaning, he set a hare running through archaeology that continues to cause controversy. Perhaps his greatest gift to us is to demand that we look closely and at detail, while appreciating the wide picture; that we keep our curiosity high as well as our scepticism.

254

See also AQUEDUCTS, AVENUES, BEACON FIRES, BEACONS (COASTAL), BEATING THE BOUNDS, BOUNDARIES, BOUNDARY STONES, BRIDGES, CAIRNS, CASTLES, CATHEDRALS, CHURCHES, CLUMPS, COMMUNICATION & RADIO MASTS, COOLING TOWERS, EARTH STATIONS, ENGINE HOUSES, FOLLIES, FORTIFICATIONS, GASHOLDERS, HILLS, HOTELS, INDUSTRIAL CHIMNEYS, ISLANDS, KAOLIN, LANDMARK TREES, LIGHTHOUSES, MONASTERIES, MONUMENTS, OAST-HOUSES & KELLS, OBELISKS, PARISH MAPS, PELE TOWERS, PIERS, PIT TIPS, POTTERY, SEA-MARKS, STACKS, TORS, TOWER BLOCKS, VIADUCTS, WHITE CLIFFS, WHITE HORSES.

LANDMARK TREES

Many trees have been endowed with significance. The Meavy Oak, eight hundred years old, was where the people of this Dartmoor village gathered; the Tolpuddle Martyrs' sycamore in Dorset was the focus of an early agricultural workers' protest. Gospel oaks mark places of preaching on the parish boundary at Rogationtide; the Boscobel Oak in Shropshire is remembered for concealing Charles II.

On tithe maps and old estate maps, boundary trees are often marked individually: crab-apple and oak, for example, being long-lived, were appropriate for this purpose. Richard Mabey noted that '*The highly distinctive appearance of black poplars meant they were also employed as landmark trees. One ancient, weatherbeaten tree (c. 200 years old), in the Bourne Gutter near Berkhamsted (Hertfordshire), marks the intersection of parish, manor and county boundaries.*'

Trees were used not only to demarcate territory, but as visual signposts, different species or groupings having distinct meanings. Katrina Porteous says that '*Trees have always been important to north Northumberland fishermen. Individual trees or groups of trees (known as "plantin's") serve as landmarks for navigation (less important now due to the increased use of electronic navigational instruments). Some examples seen from Beadnell include Heiferlaw, Shepherd's Cottage Plantin', Beadnell Trees.*'

In the nineteenth century trees were often used as road signs. According to J.H. Wilks, an ash and sycamore were planted together at strategic points to warn of dangerous places. '*The combination became known as John and Mary, and was recognised as an old form of warning of crossroads or of a main road ahead.*' In north Devon two beech trees planted on either side of a farm lane are known as 'mother and father' trees. Male and female black poplars were planted close to one other for propagation, as were monkey-puzzles by the Victorians.

Yews line drove roads through Hampshire and are planted along a drove in Ashdown Forest, Sussex. Three yews signified accommodation for animals and people; two meant people only. A few Scots pines frequently advertised places where drovers/travellers could stay. Trees marking the start of turnpike roads were later replaced by toll-houses. At Boddington in Gloucestershire a hollow tree with a wainscoted interior, 54 feet in circumference at its base in the 1780s, is thought to have been used as a room for taking tolls.

'Mile trees' are depicted on early maps. A seventeenth-century map shows eight mile trees on the Racecourse Way in Wiltshire. William Stukeley described them further in

Beeches, near Beaford, Devon.

1723: along 'the road from Wilton to Shaftesbury, called the "Ten Mile Course" . . . a traveller is indebted to Lord Pembroke for reviving the Roman method of placing a numbered stone at every mile, and the living index of a tree to make it more observable'. The trees were limes, planted at around the same time as the milestones in 1700. A correspondent to *The Times* in November 1960 traced several of them, but none seems to have survived.

It would be refreshing to see more imaginative and meaningful tree planting in England. In 1993 Common Ground proposed a scheme called County Entrances, to encourage the planting of locally typical trees on roads at county boundaries, but at the time boundaries were under review – another good reason to mark the traditional counties that have stood the test of time.

See *also* CHURCHYARDS, CLUMPS, COUNTIES, DROVE ROADS, LANDMARKS, MILESTONES, OAK, SCOTS PINE, SYCAMORE, TOLL-HOUSES.

L A N D S L I P S

The pub sign for the Slip Tavern in Much Marcle, Herefordshire shows terrified agricultural workers running this way and that as the earth cracks beneath them. This 'wonder' happened in 1575 and is remembered in local stories that recount how a church and a herd of cattle were swallowed up.

Earth tremors sometimes trigger landslides. Rock fell from Kern Knotts on Great Gable in the Lakes following seismic activity in 1980, changing a well-used climb. But gravity, an excess of water and the presence of slippery, impermeable underlying rock are the usual reasons for landslips. They are more common than imagined and have shaped surprising places.

In Derbyshire the Shivering Mountain – Mam Tor – with what is left of a seventeen-hundred-foot-high, Iron-Age hill-fort, has a face sculpted by landslides to reveal horizontal layers of unstable sandstone and shale. Frequent movement meant that in 1977 the main road between Buxton and Sheffield was finally abandoned to all but walkers.

Occasionally terraces reveal that land has tilted as well as slid. The chines on the southern edge of the Isle of Wight are filled with ledges and rumples, while the cliffs at Colwell Bay deliver constant slides of mud and fossils to the beach. At Reeth Bay in 1799 a farm called Pitlands, with a hundred acres and some cottages, slid into the sea; in 1928 Windy Corner lost 120 thousand tons of rock; and in 1978 25 acres, including a length of road, disappeared. The Gault clay is known locally as blue slipper.

Dramatic stories persist of landslips along the coast between Charmouth and the mouth of the Axe on the Dorset/Devon border; indeed, the cliffs are still active.

Small rock falls and mudslides help reveal the geology: Mary Anning, the pioneer of fossil collecting in Lyme Regis, Dorset, observed that landslips were a godsend in her searches. Goat Island is the result of a spectacular slippage at Christmas 1839 between Bindon and Dowlands; a field fell sixty feet and, though rotated a little, was cropped the following August.

Barbara Bender says that '*sometimes, along the coast to the east and west of Branscombe in Devon, the landslides create unexpected environmental micro-niches in the undercliffs, which are particularly sheltered and warm. Tiny fields or cliff plats have been carved out of them, and here, in the late nineteenth and early part of the twentieth century, the earliest potatoes and daffodils were grown and then sent on their way to London.*'

East Yorkshire's Holderness coast has lost a mile of land to the sea in a thousand years; it is currently receding at a rate of four to seven feet per year. Satellite technology is being used to record movement around Filey Bay and Scarborough, where in the early 1990s the Holbeck Hall Hotel gained a national television audience for a week as it fell, room by room, 150 feet down the crumbling cliff.

See *also* AMMONITES, BELLS & BELL-RINGING, CHINES, CLIFFS, COASTS, LOST VILLAGES, LYNCHETS, PUB SIGNS, ROADS.

L A N E S

The memorable lanes feel embedded in the landscape: one-car narrow, mud- or sand-stained, brambles and flowers reaching in, trees arching over. Perhaps there is a ford, or gates that demand stopping and starting, allowing open views as you cross fields. Devon comes to mind; deep lanes winding their way, taking their time.

Lanes do a straightforward job of linking place with place, but, rarely following a beeline, they feel unplanned,

255

like tracks that have matured. What does Inner Ting Tong mean, that lane near Exmouth, Devon? Church Lane and Back Lane are common across the country, the destination just down the road. Lovers' lanes suggest intimacy, solitude; it doesn't matter where they go. Smugglers' lanes demand concealment, yet they should not ramble.

They may look good on calendars, but their real forte is in softly speaking their history. Pirates Lane in Weymouth, Dorset; Apple Lane in Frome, Somerset; Anglers Lane beside the ghost of the river Fleet in Kentish Town, north London; not to mention the hundreds of Mill Lanes and School Lanes – they all keep fragments of history alive. Some have fallen out of memory now, such as Deadman's Lane in Moorgreen, Nottinghamshire, its function as the coffin route to the church gone. It is ironic that lanes caught in the aspic of urban spread retain their title but not their function. Green Lanes in north London heads northwards for miles, desperate for verdure; there are 150 like-named roads in the capital.

John Clare once bemoaned: '*There once were lanes in natures freedom dropt*', before '*inclosure*' tyrannised the Midland scene. The 'new' lanes that were created with the new fields dog-leg between verges and hedges and have, through two hundred years, gained a freedom of sorts. But, like the tracks through the Fens, straight and to the vanishing point, they do not feel as much at home as the meandering sunken lane.

In Surrey there is talk of removing white lines from the sides and middle of narrow lanes to slow drivers down, even the possibility of encouraging grass to grow along the middle of single tracks – the beginning of putting vehicles in their place.

See also ALLEYS, BACK LANES, BOUNDARIES, BRIDGES, CROSSROADS, DESERTED VILLAGES, DOWNLAND, DROVE ROADS, DRYSTONE WALLS, FIELDS, FOOTBRIDGES, FOOTPATHS, FORDS, GALLOPS, GATES, GRASSY TRIANGLES, GREEN LANES, GYPSIES, HAUNTED PLACES, HEDGES, HOLLOW WAYS, LANDSLIPS, LOST VILLAGES, STEPPING-STONES, WAYSIDE & BOUNDARY CROSSES, WINTERBOURNES, ZIGZAGS.

L A V E N D E R

For a moment, the warm, sweet scent in the air takes you back to the arid hillsides of the Mediterranean, where aromatic herbs are at their happiest. But lavender has been grown at Caley Mill near Sandringham in Norfolk since 1935; now more than ninety acres of purple-blue bushy stripes hum with bees on the light, sandy soil.

Since the Romans brought it here it has been grown in monasteries and physic gardens for its essential oils and medicinal properties. By 1900 Mitcham, Carshalton and Wallington in Surrey were the heart of the world's lavender industry. The First World War saw the fields taken over

for food production, and later the London suburbs crept over them. Battersea power station was built on lavender fields; there are many Lavender Roads and Groves in the area, as well as Lavender Hill.

Always popular in cottage gardens, lavender gained status as a garden plant after Gertrude Jekyll designed informal plantings and drifts of colour set against drystone walls. One of the most popular varieties today is Munstead, raised by Jekyll in Surrey.

In 1996 the BioRegional Development Group, based in Wallington, Surrey, set out to bring back lavender to Carshalton. At Stanley Park Allotments three acres have been given over to them, raised and planted by inmates of Downview Prison. They are now run by a local community group. In 2003 twelve hundred small bottles of lavender oil were produced and sold locally. In Kent lavender for essential oils is replacing hops, changing the landscape in the process.

See also CROPS, DRYSTONE WALLS, GARDENS, HONEY & BEES, HOPS, HOP-GARDENS & HOP-YARDS.

L A W N

How English – the lawn. But the name seems to have arrived with the Normans. Launds, from Old French, were compartments in medieval parkland constantly open to deer. In the New Forest, William the Conqueror's hunting ground, bright green areas of sweet grasses are still known locally as lawns and are at their most beguiling as clearings in the woodland cropped short by all the grazers of the forest.

By 1538 a laund was defined as '*a place voyde of trees, as in a parke or forret*' (Thomas Elyot's dictionary). In 1791 Gilpin records the evolution of the word: '*The forest-lawn in itself is a mere field. It is only when adorned with the furniture of surrounding woods, that it produces its effect.*' This must have been the very effect desired by monastic builders in creating the cloister, with its quiet, sun-filled patch of green.

Grasses are good at growing despite constant grazing or cutting, because the sensitive growing tissues (meristems) are at ground level where the leaves emerge. Many are also practised at rising from the dead; once nature decides to move from drought to deluge, grasses will resuscitate of their own accord. With an equable climate, England has, until recent extremes of wet and dry, been famed for its grass-growing capabilities.

Far from the forest floor the lawn now defines Englishness for visitors. The taming and manicuring of grass has been a domestic obsession, a symbol of the dominance and control of man (for it is he) to the exclusion of nature, bar a handful of pliant but insubordinate grass species.

Englishness, with its arrogance and charm, was taking on the lawn as a symbol of pre-eminence even in the seventeenth century. Bowls (from *boules*) was being played not on the traditional French surface of clay or gravel but on greens, so that Samuel Pepys could venture the superiority of our bowling alleys (*allées*) over the French. Groundwork was laid even before *The English Husbandman* in 1613, in which Gervase Markham demanded preparation through weed and stone removal, followed by scalding water and the beating and treading of the ground, followed by the placing of upturned turfs. After these assaults, to persuade the grass to '*put forth small hairs*', the next trick was to '*dance upon with the feet*' so that '*finally it is made the sporting green plot for ladies and gentlemen to recreate their spirits in*'.

By the end of the seventeenth century Christ Church College, Oxford had its internal square of grass. But lawns were to become the foreground for views from the grand house, punctuated by the ha-ha, that surprise drop in level that kept out the beasts.

Then, in 1838, John Claudius Loudon saw the future. His book *The Suburban Gardener and Villa Companion* anticipated and, indeed, informed the idea of the lawn in prospect from the drawing-room window, with flower-beds and edged by shrubs. The lawn demanded intensive care – scything, raking, sweeping. But already, in 1830, the seeds had been sown for a labour-saving invention that would change everything.

The lawnmower was invented by Edward Budding and produced at the Phoenix Ironworks on the river Frome above Stroud in Gloucestershire. His imaginative leap, from solving textile-carding problems to creating an ambulatory machine that shaved the grass with moving blades against a still blade, is undersung. The cylinder lawnmower and its refined successors liberated the lawn into the Victorian park, the municipal bowling green, the football field. As early as 1850 Suttons was selling different seed mixes of fine grasses for many situations and dimensions.

The growing middle classes of the nineteenth and twentieth centuries could break with the need simply to grow food on their plots. The lawn became a symbol of house ownership, leisure and suburbia. It followed the seepage of bungalows, detached and semi-detached houses along roads and over fields. For many, its paradox of toil and liberation is remembered through the happy summer sound of clicking blades, the smell of new-mown grass and the sensuous pleasures of bare feet.

The front lawn tended to more competitive formality, with striped sward and sharp edges. War was waged on the worm, the weed, the wandering mole. Reginald Beale, in 1931, demanded '*fight the weeds year in and year out*' or '*they will win the battle*'; his hatred of the earthworm would have confounded Darwin, who understood its '*importance in the history of the world*'. In the last half of the twentieth century, aspiring to the ideal meant rising sales of pesticides and herbicides, excessive use of water (the sprinkler can use as much in an hour as a family of four uses in a day) and seeding or turfing with far fewer and different species of grass than would naturally grow in any place.

Currently the 'perfect front lawn', surrounded by bedding plants, is likely to comprise Herald creeping red fescue, William Chewing's fescue, Liprosa slender creeping red fescue and Highland brown top bent, with the more robust back lawn being of Livonna perennial ryegrass and Herald creeping red fescue, wherever you are. It must be among the most unecological of habitats, akin to intensively farmed agricultural land.

But the perfect lawn is losing some of its power. Tom Fort suggests that '*by 1989 more than one third of Britain's 16 million or so lawns were smaller than 38 square yards, and a mere tenth covered a hundred square yards or more*'. In the opening years of the twenty-first century many people have become armchair gardeners, happier to read and watch others tinker on television, unless they can afford a ride-on mower. Some prefer personal car parks to front lawns, and others favour the early philosophy of W.H. Hudson: '*I am not a lover of lawns. Rather would I see daisies in their thousands, ground ivy, hawkweed, and even the hated plantain with tall stems, and dandelions with splendid flowers and fairy down, than the too well-tended lawn.*' The worms would prefer that, too.

See also BOWLING GREENS, CRICKET, DESERTED VILLAGES, GARDENS, GOLF-COURSES, LINKS, PARKLAND, PARKS, ROYAL FORESTS.

257

L E A D   M I N E S

Much working history is visible in limestone country as the aftermath of delving for ores containing lead, silver, zinc and copper. At more than two thousand feet on Fountains Fell, collapsed bell pits are one glimpse of the extensive search for lead in the Craven and Askrigg areas of Yorkshire. The northern Pennines, the Peak District, the Lake District,

Abandoned rakes (possibly from Old Norse *rak*, meaning stripe or streak) may run for miles as they follow narrow veins of enriched rock, settled in the faults and joints of the limestone. In the south Pennines walls and sometimes trees follow the craters and heaps. Everyone knew that lead was toxic – the grasses growing over the old waste poisoned animals – so trees were planted to shade the grass, dissuading it from becoming lush. Miners were farmers, too. Tracks etched like parallel earthworks, or following standing stones across featureless moors, mark the trails of endless trains of packhorses heading for Chesterfield lead market. The 'lead road' took ore along the Romanised ridgeway to Sarum, Wiltshire and Southampton from Somerset.

The Romans lined the Great Bath in Bath with Mendip lead. Its malleability, water resistance, longevity and the simplicity of smelting made lead the prime conduit for water – hence plumbing and plumbers (*plumbum* is Latin for lead). It was also sought for coffin making and for roofing, in which it has not been surpassed, especially for church and cathedral. We use it still for shot, plumb lines, glazes, glass making, lead paint, red lead, white lead and in petrol, although in reducing quantities. Demand increases for its use in radiation insulation.

Rich ancient mining landscapes are continually lost to the process of hillocking – the reworking of old waste once seen as derelict land. And, since opencast is cheaper, vast open pits now mark workings that, like agriculture and dumping, continue voraciously to obliterate precious cultural history and identity.

See also BASTLES, BLUE JOHN, COAL MINING, COES, DALES, DEW PONDS, ENGINE HOUSES, FLINT, FOOTPATHS, GIN HOUSES, GREEN LANES, GRUFFY GROUND, HAUNTED PLACES, HOLLOW WAYS, HORSES & PONIES, INDUSTRIAL CHIMNEYS, IRONSTONE, LANES, LIMESTONE, MINES, PIT TIPS, SOUGHS, WILDFLOWERS, ZIGZAGS.

L E E K S

Since they were introduced by the Romans, leeks have been grown all over the country. Jane Grigson wrote: '*When Englishmen 1,400 years ago spoke of a vegetable patch, they called it leaćtun, leek-enclosure . . . They scattered England with leek-patch names – Leckhampstead, Latton, Leighton Buzzard.*'

In the North East the passion for cultivating giant leeks started with coal miners more than a century ago and is still popular with members of working men's clubs, horticultural clubs and societies. The best kind for showing is the pot leek, and the requirements for the perfect vegetable are exacting. Varieties such as the Jumbo, bred by ace Northumberland grower Paul Harrigan, have reached more than 130 cubic inches.

the Mendips in Somerset, Devon and Cornwall all have significant histories of surface and deep mining.

In Derbyshire, Matlockite, Cromfordite and Blue John, unique to Castleton, excite the geologist, who can recognise the presence of certain minerals by plants. Spring sandwort (*Minuatia verna*) is known as leadwort in Derbyshire, Lancashire and Cheshire. Other plants tolerant of heavy metals include the woodland lady fern, alpine pennycress, Pyrenean scurvy grass and mountain pansy, which exhibits its own particularity, being yellow in the Peak District and blue in the northern Pennines. The lead rakes host specific lichens and other rare plants, including frog orchid, fragrant orchid, maiden pink, autumn gentian and moonwort. Once lost, the complexity of these mosaics is gone forever.

In Derbyshire, Youlgreave means 'old working' – for the Saxons the place already had a history. Bole Hill suggests smelting. Magpie Mine by Sheldon ceased production only in the twentieth century and still boasts an engine house, fine round chimney and winding gear. But most remnants are more subtle: small beehive caps of stone over mine shafts, adits, tramways, old chimney foundations, head gear, gins, humps, flats and hollows, crushing circles, drains (soughs), ponds, dams and washing troughs (buddles), tangles of structures and debris.

Every year the World Leek and Onion Championships are held in the coal town of Ashington near the Northumbrian coast. The edible monsters on show will be admired but not eaten. After the show they will be replanted and used to propagate the next generation of prize winners.

See also AGRICULTURAL SHOWS, ASPARAGUS, BRUSSELS SPROUTS, GOOSEBERRIES, ONIONS, POTATOES.

L E T T E R B O X I N G

Rather like entrusting a letter to a bottle at sea, in 1854 a Dartmoor guide called James Perrott put his visiting card in a glass jar. He placed it in a bank at a remote place called Cranmere Pool near the source of the West Okement river, presumably hoping that someone would find it.

Intrepid walkers who came across Perrott's card added their own and, by 1888, the jar had been replaced by a tin box that could accommodate more. In 1905 two walkers put a visitors' book in the box, which attracted 1,741 signatures in three years. People began to enclose self-addressed and stamped postcards to be sent on by the next visitor from his home town.

Similar boxes appeared on Belstone Tor in 1894 and at Duck's Pool on South Moor in 1938, to commemorate the Dartmoor writer William Crossing. In 1976 fifteen letterboxes were included in a guide and their numbers proliferated. The Dartmoor National Park Authority proposed to ban the practice, since ancient cairns were being desecrated, but a campaign to save them, led by the *Western Morning News*, resulted in an agreed code of conduct.

The letterboxes at Duck's Pool and Cranmere Pool are made of stone and appear on Ordnance Survey maps. Most of the others – there are over 3,000 registered boxes and many more unrecorded ones – are secreted under stones, in hollows and caves, often discovered only with the help of cryptic clues or by word of mouth.

Letterbox hosts (anyone can place and register a box, as long as they maintain it) are beginning to make rubber stamps bearing emblems – a running fox for Fox Tor, an adder for Willtor Clitter, an engine house for Hooten Wheals – so that visitors can stamp their own books. A new folk art has arisen. New versions of the stamps may be put into boxes each year or for special occasions, and some boxes contain rewards (such as miniature bottles of whisky) for the first person who finds the new issue. Letterboxes

not only celebrate the wildlife and natural features of the moor, but also its industrial past, including peat digging, tin mining, glass making, quarrying and charcoal burning. Instead of signing the visitors' book, regular letterboxers, such as the Moorons and the Brixham Grasshoppers, use their own personal stamps.

In the early 1980s Godfrey Swinscow started the Dartmoor Letterboxes 100 Club for people who have visited more than a hundred boxes; it now has at least twelve thousand members. It publishes a catalogue of Dartmoor Letterboxes, with clues to their locations, twice a year.

See also TORS, WAYSIDE & BOUNDARY CROSSES.

L E V E L S

Levels are named for their utter flatness, water made. The term first appeared in the early seventeenth century, describing the levels in Yorkshire, embracing Hatfield Chase, and Bedford Level or the Great Level in the fens of East Anglia. The latter was the focus of an ambitious drainage scheme masterminded by the Dutch engineer Vermuyden.

In Sussex the Pevensey Levels are remains of once-extensive marshes tamed over many centuries, drained by a network of dykes that dissect rich grazing meadows and arable fields. The ditches are mostly six to ten feet wide and up to six feet deep, and in summer fill with sluggish waters enjoyed by a rich panoply of aquatic plants and invertebrates; the beetles are particularly celebrated. Embankments against the sea, built by the medieval abbots of Battle Abbey, are still prominent in the landscape; track-ways, known locally as trades, ran along their tops.

Also in Sussex, the Rother and the Pett Levels lie on the edge of a wide, marshy alluvial flat, formed as the rivers Rother, Tillingham and Brede deposited their silt in the bay after a shingle spit cut off the sea. Today the marshland is drained by sewers fringed by feathery reeds, creating open, desolate farmland with few roads or houses. Kent has the Sandwich Levels.

The land of the summer people, Somerset, has a wetland landscape like no other, covering 250 square miles. The land lies at or near sea level, yet higher ground is never far away in the varied forms of the Mendips, Quantocks, Blackdowns and Poldens. Scattered across the flatland are outcrops of rock that are home to ancient settlements: Chedzoy, Westonzoyland, Middlezoy and Othery, suggesting islands in the river Sowy. At Athelney, 'the prince's island', King Alfred and his men hid from the Danes in AD 878 on a two-acre rise of ground in the midst of Sedgemoor.

Glastonbury Tor is a landmark from every direction. The monks of the powerful abbey were ambitious hydraulic

259

engineers; they dug canals, shored up lakes and banks, and altered the course of the rivers Brue and Axe. Centuries later the ten-mile King's Sedgemoor Drain of 1791 and subsequent drainage schemes criss-crossed the landscape with an intricate network of ditches, called rhynes.

The Environment Agency manages a network of sluices and pumps that lift water into main arterial drains and embanked rivers. Without the pumps the levels and moors would stay flooded most of the year. Peat is dug in the Brue valley, while withy-growing for basketry centres on Sedgemoor. The willows also produce a good supply of artists' charcoal. On the edges of the Levels apple orchards give local cider makers a ready source of fermentable fruit, while dairy herds supply cheese makers.

The peat lands are home to a distinctive mix of wild plants and animals: southern marsh orchids, silver diving beetles, hairy dragonflies, otters and bitterns. With infinite patience grey herons watch for eels – together, these creatures are the presiding spirits of this strange and unfamiliar landscape.

See also ABBEYS, BOATS, BOWLING GREENS, BROADS, CATTLE, CHEESE, CHURCHES, CIDER & CIDER ORCHARDS, COASTLINE, EELS, EYOTS, FENS, FLOODS, GRAZING MARSHES, GREEN LANES, HERONRIES, INGS, ISLANDS, MOORLAND, MOSSES, MOSSLAND, ORCHARDS, OSIERS, OTTERS, PEAT, RHYNES, RIVERS, SALT MARSHES, SHEEP, TIDES, WILLOW.

260

L I B R A R I E S

Libraries began as exclusive places, the preserve of monks and lords, in religious establishments and private estates. Before the widespread adoption of printing, books were handwritten onto vellum manuscript, made from animal skins. Only the wealthy could afford to keep a library. Few commoners could read and, as the few books they might see in an ecclesiastical chained library (as in Hereford Cathedral) were in Latin, illiteracy among the masses was fated to continue. They were lost at the Dissolution of the Monasteries, university libraries supplanting them.

In 1653 the bequest of merchant Humphrey Chetham enabled the foundation of our oldest public reference library in Manchester. The concept of the subscription library began to spread. The Economical Library of 1797 in Kendal, Westmorland, and those provided by 'improving' organisations, such as Mechanics' Institutes, offered books at rates that workers might afford.

But public libraries continued to be endowed by wealthy patrons – most notably the industrialist Andrew Carnegie, who helped provide for 380 – until corporation-sponsored libraries began to appear from the middle of the nineteenth century. Some of the earliest of these were at Canterbury in Kent, Winchester in Hampshire and Ipswich in Suffolk.

Rural libraries flourished in the 1920s, followed by those in market towns and urban areas. The Carnegie Corporation continued to influence design, based on principles of centrality, access, light and low noise. The Belsize branch in north London is rectangular with a rounded end, like a Romanesque church.

Concrete modernism dominated the huge programme of rebuilding following the Second World War. For economy, simplicity prevailed. Libraries are often the last organisations to benefit from local council funds: Swindon's central library in Wiltshire still occupies a prefabricated building, nearly fifty years after its 'temporary' construction. Some places utilised existing buildings. In Box, Wiltshire the village library shares the Selwyn Hall, a 1960s community building. There are occasionally informal lending libraries in rural railway stations, and esoteric libraries exclusively known to long-distance lorry drivers.

Victorian library buildings often retain fine relief or engraved entrance signs. The colourful new Peckham Library in south London announces LIBRARY in huge letters on its roof; visitors tripled in the first year. Norwich's new Forum Library is a hangar-like, glass-ended building, offering cultural activities as well as local archives and computer and internet access. But the heart of the library is the book, with all of its capacity to engage and provoke, offer and demand. The closure of a library, such as the Passmore Edwards benefaction to Whitechapel in east London, known as 'the university of the ghetto', is a loss both to memory and imagination.

See also CATHEDRALS, CHINATOWNS, CLOCKS, PARISH MAPS, STATIONS, TOWN HALLS & GUILD-HALLS.

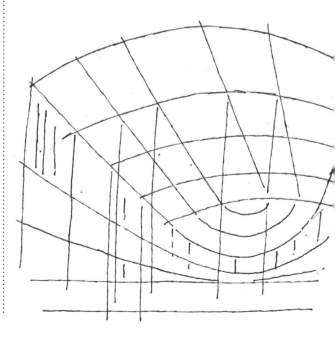

Millennium Library, Norwich.

L I C H E N S

'Air fit for lichens, water fit for trout', was ecologist Kenneth Mellanby's battle-cry in the 1960s. Once a source of dyes for wool, lichens – or, rather, the lack of them – are now famed as indicators of air pollution. Lichen diversity is greatest in the northern hills and in the West and South, and relatively poor elsewhere. But, as air quality improves, lichen species are recolonising places where they haven't been seen since the start of the Industrial Revolution.

Patches of colour – delicate shades of grey, green, yellow, orange, brown and purple – on roofs, walls, trees and gravestones mark the remarkable alliance between a fungus, one or more algae and/or cyanobacteria. Lichens can grow, albeit slowly, on almost any surface, and their size can sometimes date gravestones or walls. At Stonehenge and Avebury in Wiltshire some eighty sorts of lichen, perhaps thousands of years old, thrive on the sarsens. On walls, they can give away the nature of the stone: on acid rocks in the high lands, yellow 'map' lichens dominate, while limestone walls host a greyish lichen with a pitted surface (*Verrucaria baldensis*).

See also BUILDING STONES, DRYSTONE WALLS, GRAVESTONES, HENGES & STONE CIRCLES, LIMESTONE, MOSSES.

L I D O S

Poor fitness of conscripts in the First World War prompted a national drive for health improvement. Open-air swimming caught the public imagination and, from the 1920s, pools appeared from London to Ilkley in Yorkshire, including tidal pools, as at Shoalstone in Brixham, Devon and Walpole Bay at Cliftonville, Margate, Kent. These were rendered exotic by being called lidos, after the Italian word for beach and, more directly, referring to the municipal bathing area in Venice.

Often grandly set within Art Deco complexes, they proved expensive to maintain, and few survive. Many closed during the 1980s and 1990s, including those at Hackney in east London, Stoke-on-Trent in Staffordshire, New Brighton in Cheshire and Alfreton in Derbyshire. The Olympic-sized lido built using miners' contributions at Murton Colliery in Durham – once the only pool of its size between Sheffield and Edinburgh – was closed with the pit in 1991 and demolished because the council would not take it on.

Campaigns by local people and the Twentieth Century Society have led to increased recognition and funding. Brockwell near Brixton, south London, built in 1937, was rescued from near dereliction in the 1990s, as was Ilkley, with its Art Deco café, fountain and startling view over the moors. The tidal pools at Saltdean near Brighton in

Sussex and Penzance in Cornwall, with its grand terraces, are listed. Tinside at Plymouth was restored and re-opened as part of the city's waterfront regeneration in 2003. The three pools at Tunnels Beach in Ilfracombe, Devon are being restored, one at a time. A new drive for health and developing technology may yet see a resurgence of the much-loved outdoor pool.

See also BEACHES, CAFÉS, COAL MINING, COASTS, SURFING, SWIMMING PLACES, TIDES.

L I G H T H O U S E S

Lighthouses have saved ships and inspired us. John Constable, Eric Ravilious and Virginia Woolf responded to their melancholy and constancy. Benedict Mason's musical composition *Lighthouses of England and Wales* (1991) orchestrates the pulses from forty lights. '*See hoo she flashes an' fades in the hush/A' the dark an' the sea*', wrote Katrina Porteous of Longstone Light in Northumberland, the scene of Grace Darling's heroism in 1838.

These slender, tapering, blinking columns are rich with the draw of the sea, like the four that have successively stood at Eddystone, fourteen miles from Plymouth, Devon since 1698. They come in many shapes and sizes. A boxy white building underpins Bamburgh's lantern in Northumberland. Fleetwood's low light in Lancashire has ornate balconies above a classically pillared shelter. Watchet in Somerset has a small, red, hexagonal tower with a slate pagoda roof, rather like a tall pillar-box. Some are even inland: Weldon church in Northamptonshire doubled as a lighthouse guiding people through once treacherously dense woods.

Dover in Kent has its Roman Pharos ruins. Later the Church protected its trading interests by displaying warning lights on coastal chapels; some, like St Peter the Poor Fisherman in Revelstoke, Devon, were built solely for that purpose. St Nicholas at Ilfracombe in Devon is still illuminated. Local story has the fourteenth-century Pepper Pot (or Salt Cellar) at St Catherine's Point on the

261

Burnham-on-Sea, Somerset.

Isle of Wight built in penance after shipwrecked goods belonging to the Church were plundered.

Private ownership was the lucrative norm. Trinity House was formed to represent mariners' interests, building its first lighthouse at Lowestoft, Suffolk in 1609 and, over time, buying out the others. Sometimes the payments benefited the community. The Reverend David Davies was the driving force behind the wooden box on stilts that still stands at Burnham-on-Sea, Somerset. The funds received bought the town's bath house, esplanade and the hamlet of Daviesville.

Of the 72 active lighthouses in England in 2004, all are now automated and many have lost their voices. The last to have residents, until 1998, was North Foreland, Kent. Dungeness, Kent gained a sleek modern lighthouse in 1961, floodlit to be more visible to night shipping and migrating birds. The black-painted Old Light came up for sale in 2005 for £150,000. The Needles and Bishop Rock (Isles of Scilly) lights are now truncated by the addition of helicopter landing pads. Many, such as Lundy South, are solar-powered. Some, like the Gothic Belle Tout, near Beachy Head in Sussex, are private houses. Others, including Lundy Old Light and Trevose, near Padstow in Cornwall, have become holiday homes.

Lighthouses are usually white with black or red stripes to stand out against sky, land or cliffs. They have become local icons and tourist magnets. The Isles of Scilly council has incorporated Bishop Rock into its new island flag.

See also BEACONS (COASTAL), CHURCHES, COASTS, FLAGS, FLOODS, FOLLIES, ISLANDS, LANDMARKS, MONUMENTS, SHIPPING FORECAST, TIDES, WHITE CLIFFS.

L I M E

Our common lime is a hybrid of the native small-leaved and large-leaved limes. By the early 1600s it had become a fashionable tree, planted in avenues. In 1838 two double rows of common limes at Clumber Park, Nottinghamshire became the longest in Europe.

The tallest of our broad-leaved trees, it is often colonised by mistletoe, and was widely planted in deer parks, country estates, large gardens and village greens, and later in public parks. It does grow in the wild where both parents are present, for example in the Derbyshire Dales and the Wye valley, Gloucestershire, but it is an unusual tree to see in woodlands.

Limes are tolerant of heavy pruning, and lines of trees with pleached or interlocking branches are still lovingly cared for in churchyards and in streets. In avenues, the trees were often pollarded at the same height, but this was condemned as mutilation by Arthur Young and others in the eighteenth century and a more naturalistic way of growing trees prevailed.

The small-leaved lime, also known as the linden and, in Essex, the pry, was the commonest lowland tree in the country six thousand years ago. The names Lyndhurst and Linwood in Hampshire and Lynderswood in Essex probably derive from this. Richard Mabey described it as among '*the most beautiful and historic of all British native trees*'. Its distribution is now fragmented, and our cooler climate means it has been less able to propagate itself from seed, but it is able to spread by layering. One remarkable coppice stool near Westonbirt, Gloucestershire is 48 feet in diameter; estimated to be six thousand years old, it could be the oldest living organism in Britain. Small-leaved limes can also be found growing in woods or as pollards in hedgerows in a wide sash from Lincolnshire, Nottinghamshire and Norfolk to the Welsh borders and Somerset.

The large-leaved lime, although widely planted, is the rarest of the limes in its natural state. It is found in the Wye valley, south Pennines and north-east Yorkshire, and old coppice stools have been found on the north side of the South Downs, in steep-sided combes, mixed woodland and on boundary banks.

All three species of lime have distinctive heart-shaped leaves that vary in size and are loved by browsing animals and aphids, which cover them in sticky honeydew. The small, yellow flowers, with their sweet, heady smell, are

262

rich in nectar and much sought-after by insects and ourselves: we make soothing lime-flower tea and enjoy lime honey. Carvings by Grinling Gibbons in the Actors' Church in Covent Garden, London demonstrate the fine sculpting qualities of the pale yellow wood.

See also ALDER, ANCIENT TREES, ASH, AVENUES, BEECH, BIRCH, BLACK POPLAR, BLACKTHORN, BOUNDARIES, ELM, FIELD MAPLE, HAWTHORN, HAZEL, HOLLY, HOLM OAK, HONEY & BEES, HORNBEAM, HORSE CHESTNUT, JUNIPER, LANDMARK TREES, LONDON PLANE, MONKEY-PUZZLE, OAK, ORCHARDS, PEARS, POPLAR, ROWAN, ROYAL FORESTS, SCOTS PINE, SWEET CHESTNUT, SYCAMORE, WALNUT, WHITEBEAM, WILLOW, WOODS, YEW.

LIME-KILNS

Beside farms, woods and canals, on the coast, on limestone outcrops, lime-kilns can still occasionally be seen, in varying degrees of dilapidation. A small archway is evident in a circular or four-sided stone or brick building, open to the air. Sometimes they are pressed into hillsides and, where they survive more completely, they have a grotto-like romance.

They mark a foul-smelling, unhealthy industry. Lime, or quicklime, was an invaluable material for building, plastering, waterproofing and bleaching, latterly also used in agriculture and effluent treatment. It was even a medicine. The ash was used as flooring for the cottages of the poor. Roman kilns, as at Weekley, Northamptonshire, are the earliest to have been discovered.

The design might vary, but the principle elements remained the same for two millennia: an open top through which materials were dropped, a pot or bowl, beneath which the burning took place, and a draw hole leading into the pot to fan the flames. Into the pot went limestone and a cheap culm/coal; the two were heated to more than a thousand degrees Celsius and the quicklime extracted.

Where not used for building it was 'slaked' with water and spread over fields as a check to acid-heavy land lacking

chalk or limestone. This encouraged many farmers to establish field kilns of their own, built in many shapes, sizes and materials. Surrey and Sussex kilns had pots lined with brick inside walls of sandstone. Northumberland had turf-topped hollows, called sow kilns. Around Cotehele in Cornwall are several with half-arched entries. Dudley in Worcestershire had horseshoe kilns, Derbyshire 'pye' or 'pudding-pye' ones. The Yorkshire Dales and the Peak District have many lonely survivors.

Wherever the lime oasts (oast being another name for kiln) were, place-names stuck, such as Limehouse in London, Limehurst in Lancashire and Lye Woods in Somerset. Across the country, field names such as Old Kiln are a giveaway if you are looking to trace lost examples; names including furze (gorse) indicated the availability of material for burning.

Where lime is still burnt it is in steel rotary kilns, designed for the cement industry. Old kilns are scarce, but some are preserved. Mendip had a high density; forty could still be identified in 1984. Arnside and Silverdale Area of Outstanding Natural Beauty in Lancashire has thirty-six. Northumberland had a thriving lime industry, and there are fine kilns at Thorngrafton, on the coast at Beadnell and offshore on Holy Island.

Lime-burning in the old style might seem a trade we are well rid of, with its smells, smoke and dust. In 2003, however, the National Trust, English Heritage and the Society for the Protection of Ancient Buildings supported the re-opening of some lime works to produce authentic building materials for restoration projects. Their ultimate vision is the establishment of a number of small-scale kilns across the country.

See also CHALK, COAL MINING, FIELDS, GORSE, LIMESTONE, QUARRIES.

263

LIMESTONE

Peter's Stone is a coral reef knoll as big as a church between Wardlow and Litton in Derbyshire. It stands surrounded by cropped grass, framed in a streamless, cliffed valley. Three hundred and fifty million years ago fish flew by in a warm sea, which was nurturing what we know as Carboniferous limestone.

Later in the geological calendar more and different limestones were laid down in Permian and Jurassic times, and then swathes of chalk in Cretaceous seas. This has given us some dramatic landscapes, variegated building stones and fascinating settlements, although, as Richard Fortey wrote, '*Industry and large towns particularly avoid the Carboniferous Limestone. It has a propensity for wildness.*'

Chalk is porous; water seeps in everywhere. Oolitic limestone, with its well-cemented, microscopic, egg-like grains, tends to be more like chalk, but the other limestones are permeable, with cracks, joints and faults luring water downwards, eating at the stone as it goes. The Pennine reef limestone is cemented so tight with fossils and remains that the water finds it hard to penetrate, but more passively sedimented rocks, vulnerable to slightly acid rainfall, are easily etched into limestone pavements or clints and grikes and, over eons, into cave systems.

Great underground systems are found in the Carboniferous limestone around Cheddar in Somerset and in Derbyshire and Yorkshire. Here, too, are gorges – enormous at Cheddar and Matlock Bath, Derbyshire; narrow but awesome at Hell Gill, Yorkshire. Perhaps some are great collapsed caverns; their ice-melt streams are shrunken to little misfits or completely gone, leaving also the high, dry waterfall at Malham Cove, Yorkshire. The higher lands are dotted with swallets, swallow holes, sink holes, waterfalls into netherworlds, water disappearing and appearing as risings, springs. In between there is a world of dissolving and dripping, stalagtites and stalagmites, calciferous creativity to be chanced upon by cavers or worn down by the eyes of tourists.

From Nottingham to Catterick in Yorkshire a sliver of dolomitic limestone deposited in Permian times makes a bold stand to the east of the M1; Hardwick Hall looks out towards Sheffield from the scarp top. South of Darlington it spreads to reach Hartlepool and Sunderland. In it, magnesium as well as calcium is bound by carbonate. Its colour when fresh is between cream and custard, although it is coal-smoke-darkened in many villages and towns, which owe their coherence to this building stone.

The common thread on the surface is the dry valley, but they vary. The Carboniferous limestone Mendips fold gently, the oolitic Cotswolds roll. In deep Pennine valleys you can walk along sections of dry riverbeds, as in Lathkill Dale or the Manifold in Derbyshire and Staffordshire. The locations of villages and farms show where water is (or was) and, in the White Peak of Derbyshire, thanks for water are still given in well-dressing ceremonies in high villages.

Quarries abound. You can see where the houses and walls come from along the 'limestone belt' (as architects call the many-coloured Jurassic oolites) from Portland to Bath through the Cotswolds, Northamptonshire, Huntingdonshire, Rutland and Lincolnshire. Some stones are more likely to be reused, such as the honey-coloured Cotswold 'slates' – a fissile, 'flaggy' oolite – and, in the Carboniferous, the Yoredale 'slates' that roof the limestone cottages of north Yorkshire. The old buildings of Teesdale and Weardale in Durham and Northumberland are dominated by limestone from small holes nearby; lime-kilns also made their demands.

The metamorphosed sugar limestone of the north Pennines was heated by nearby igneous activity; its coarse crystals are on their way to true marble. In Portland and Purbeck in Dorset the various limestone beds are used in different ways; local masons and wallers have left a legacy of buildings, roofs and field walls of some substance. Stone was often quarried from the sea cliffs for easy shipment. Abandoned pillared caves at Tilly Whim and Whin Spit, with their square mouths, visibly pick out chosen strata. On Portland the quarries give up solid Whit Bed, for building and sculpture, and Roach Bed, full of fossils, for decorative cladding.

Limestone surrounds us in our cities, much from Portland, some from distant places. It is always a pleasure to bump into fossils: so-called Purbeck marble, full of shells, forms dark pillars and carvings inside many a church. On polished walls and floors, such as at London's Festival Hall, you can find the confused patterns of Hopton Wood crinoidal limestone from Wirksworth in Derbyshire. On the beach at Holy Island in Northumberland you can pick up St Cuthbert's beads, little coins of crinoid stems that tell you this is the sea fall of the Carboniferous limestone.

Buildings speak loudest when they tell stories of the rock beneath. The sympathy of buildings with landscape can be profound, as in Arkengarthdale and Littondale in Yorkshire. Bath stone from nearby Box, Wiltshire makes Bath, Somerset. Buxton, Derbyshire is wrought of limestone from down the road. Now the superquarries waste good stone in the making of cement and road stone. Aggregate for roads, runways, car parks, harbours and concrete is also dug from many Mendip quarries; Sandford and Dulcote Hills will halve in size. Which makes all the more poignant W.H. Auden's vision at the end of 'In Praise of Limestone':

> . . . but when I try to imagine a faultless love
> Or the life to come, what I hear is the murmur
> Of underground streams, what I see is a limestone landscape.

See also ALBION, ASH, BARNS, BLUE JOHN, BUILDING STONES, CAVES, CHALK, CLIFFS, CLINTS & GRIKES, COES, DEW PONDS, DOWNLAND, DRYSTONE WALLS, FERNS, FIELD PATTERNS, FORDS, GORGES, GREEN LANES, IRONSTONE, LEAD MINES, MILLSTONE GRIT, QUARRIES, SEA CAVES, SLATES, SOUGHS, TUNNELS, UNLUCKY WORDS, WATERFALLS, WELL DRESSING, WHITE CLIFFS.

L I N K S

The coastal sand-dunes found along the Northumberland coast are known as links. Where they are not held together by marram grass or sheep-trimmed turf, the wind will create natural bunkers, making it easy to see how they, or rather their Scottish counterparts, gave birth to golf.

Lindisfarne, Ross, Bamburgh, Beadnell, Embleton, Alnmouth and Warkworth all have extensive links. Newton

Links has for more than twenty years fallen under the gaze of Phil Gates, who says the dunes have *a wonderful natural economy – for example, the scarlet and black sexton beetles that serve as gravediggers for dead birds and mammals by excavating the sand under the corpse and then laying their eggs in the underground larder*'. With common blue, small copper and wall butterflies, harebells, lizards, dragonflies and all manner of sea and land birds, the links are just holding their own against modern golf-courses, which, in their attempt to emulate, only reduce the richness.

See also BEACHES, GOLF-COURSES, LAWN, NATTERJACK TOADS, NICKNAMES, SAND-DUNES.

LIQUORICE

Yorkshire pennies – shiny, black, liquorice pomfret cakes, stamped like seals – evolved because an apothecary added sugar to liquorice in 1760. Liquorice may have been first grown in Pontefract by monks, if it did not persist in local use from Roman rhizomes. The sandy soil suits the plant *Glycyrrhiza glabra*, its sweet roots burrowing deep and wide. It hails from the Middle East – the confluence of the Tigris and Euphrates is the long-standing centre of cultivation – and its medicinal uses have long been known. It is also sweeter by fifty times than cane sugar.

Mentioned by Layamon in the *Brut* in 1200, it later appears in *The Canterbury Tales*, in which Chaucer tells of one of its abiding uses: *first he chewed a grain of liquorice to charm his breath before he combed his hair*'.

Its association with Pontefract is first reported in 1600 in Camden's *Britannia* and thereafter it is repeatedly mentioned in gazetteers and local records. By 1794 a hundred acres were in production in gardens across the town. Men dug the roots and women and children packed them off to factories, where women dominated the production lines. There is just one liquorice hedge now left – juice is imported and seventeen factories have dwindled to two – but the rhizomes are sought for domestic use and reach high prices at the annual Liquorice Festival in July. The locals are proud of their premier product, but not so self-centred that they will not refer to it as 'the Spanish' or 'the Italian'.

Before it became exclusive to Pontefract, liquorice was grown around Brigg in Lincolnshire, Ely in Cambridgeshire, Mortlake, Mitcham and Barnes in Surrey, Knaresborough in Yorkshire and Worksop in Nottinghamshire (until 1775), where wild liquorice survived in the hedgerows until the last century. Spaw Sunday was celebrated in Calderdale,

Yorkshire in the 1800s with the drinking of health-giving spring water, sometimes with liquorice and sugar. Palm Sunday became known as Liquorice Day in west Yorkshire and Spanish Liquor Sunday on the annual walk through the Forest of Wychwood in Oxfordshire.

Liquorice is regaining favour, as twigs to chew, in the shapes of shoelaces and chewy pipes, and as allsorts – the mixture of ten pink, white, brown, orange and black delights that were invented after a bumbling Bassetts salesman dropped several boxes of samples onto the floor in front of a buyer in 1899.

See also CONFECTIONERY, FOOD, HEDGES, RHUBARB.

LOCKS

Engineering techniques were challenged as canals spread. Locks were an important step forward, an ingenious solution to the problem of moving a watercourse up and down a gradient. Primitive locks, known as pound locks, had developed on rivers in the later sixteenth century, probably as developments of the small, gated weirs provided by local water-mill owners. Bottisham Lode, a tributary of the Cam, still has an example (they were known variously as staunches, water gates, flash-locks and half-locks). Staircase locks are a notable feature of

265

Grand Union canal, Barrow upon Soar, Leicestershire.

the Leeds and Liverpool canal, culminating in the much-loved Bingley Five Rise Locks in Yorkshire. These, and the astonishing flight of 29 locks at Caen Hill in Devizes, Wiltshire, demonstrate the speed of sophistication of the lock-makers' art.

The impressive boat lift at Anderton, near Northwich in Cheshire, was designed to move boats between the Trent and Mersey canal and the river Weaver, by means of hydraulics. It was first completed in 1875, but an improved design superseded it in 1908 and was in use until 1982, when structural problems led to its closure. After a collaboration of public, private and voluntary organisations worked together to restore it, it was re-opened to traffic in March 2002.

Canals had a language of their own. The gates of locks are paddles, but on the Leeds and Liverpool canal they become cloughs. Oaks were planted near the locks, to be used when the gates would need replacing in fifty to a hundred years. This practice is being considered again in Lancashire.

See also AQUEDUCTS, CANALS, OAK, RIVERS, SWIMMING PLACES.

L O N D O N   P L A N E

This is London's tree. First planted more than three hundred years ago in the new squares and streets, these huge trees are only now in their prime; we do not know how long they can live. It proved an excellent choice of tree to plant: it can withstand the city's grime by shedding its bark; its glossy leaves douche well in the rain; it can survive in compacted soil. Accounting for half of central London's trees, it provides most welcome shade.

A hybrid between the oriental plane and the American plane, the tree has a preference for the South. The first, planted in Barnes, are now so huge that six people are

needed to circuit their girth. Those planted at the Bishop's Palace in Ely, Cambridgeshire in about 1650 are still going strong. A tree in the grounds of Passmores House in Essex, planted around 1721, has a girth of nearly 23 feet and is more than a hundred feet high.

In the hurricane of 16 October 1987 some London plane trees fell. It had never happened before. In Russell Square sad parents sat in stunned silence as happy children swarmed in the prostrate boughs. Sadly, some that re-grew from their base were sacrificed, as in front of Euston Station, to new plantings.

The plane trees in Berkeley Square are among London's jewels. Planted in 1789, some have incredibly fat boles and one tree has a huge, low limb at right angles to the ground. In Bath, Somerset one statuesque plane tree's boughs fill the aerial space in Abbey Green; people gravitate to it. It is loved, too, for its pale, 'dappled' trunk and its silhouette in winter, its fruit hanging like baubles.

See also ALDER, ASH, BEECH, BIRCH, BLACK POPLAR, ELM, HORNBEAM, HORSE CHESTNUT, LIME, MONKEY-PUZZLE, OAK, POPLAR, ROWAN, SCOTS PINE, SQUARES, SWEET CHESTNUT, SYCAMORE, WALNUT, WEATHER, WILLOW, WINDS, YEW.

L O N D O N   T A X I S

The Hackney coach (from the French *haquenée*, meaning horse for hire) first appeared on the streets of London in the 1620s. Its many transformations have included the Hansom cab (a cabriolet was an open tourer) and, in the 1950s, the Austin FX3, Wolseley Oxford and Beardmore Paramount Mark VII. Since then brief appearances have been made by the fibreglass Winchester and the Lucas electric cab. Having a bespoke vehicle for the job is unique in the world.

The cab reached its iconic moment in 1958 with the Austin FX4, perfectly poised to accompany the swinging sixties. Its ghost still dominates the London street scene. The orange sign on its roof now may read 'Taxi' rather than 'For Hire', and all but the driver's door handle has changed, but the last-of-the-line LTI Fairway of 1997 is, to most eyes, the FX4. Who would have guessed that the brief, in 1834, for space beside the driver to carry a bale of hay, as well as room for passengers with tall hats, would lead to this?

It is a treat to hop into a Fairway. Since 1997 the Metrocab Series III and the TX1 from London Taxis International have competed for sales to fleet operators and owner-drivers. They may offer more comfort, but they just don't have the 'jizz'. Royalty and businessmen run their own 'black cabs' and export numbers are buoyant.

Despite attempts by advertisers to colonise its every contour and even turn it pink, the old black taxi is part of London's identity. Marketing consultants would be

lies Milton; sandbanks now submerged off the Kent coast perhaps once supported fishermen's huts; St Enodoc's Church in Cornwall may be a remnant of a village overtaken by sand; Shotwick in Cheshire was lost, though the church remains, defended by reclaimed land of the Wirral.

Coastal villages are not the only casualties. In Gloucestershire the village of Charlton was flattened under Filton airfield, extended for the ill-fated Brabazon airliner in the late 1940s; reservoir building in Yorkshire claimed West End and Timble; Derwent and Ashopton were swallowed by the Ladybower Dam in Derbyshire, and Mardale by Haweswater in Westmorland. Low rainfall in 2003 revealed Mardale's streets and walls, adding to the distress of local people and the appeal for sightseers.

The Celtic lost land of Lyonesse had been written of by Richard Carew in the Survey of Cornwall 1602 as the birthplace of King Arthur. Camden's *Britannia* linked it with Lethowsow or the Seven Stones between the Isles of Scilly and Land's End. Local stories have echoes of the Breton tale of Kêr-Is, the Welsh story of Bottom Cantred and, indeed, Atlantis. The Isles of Scilly have themselves lost land and buildings since Roman times, when it is possible that isles were joined – partly submerged hut circles, walls and burial chambers attest to this. But story of Lyonesse – *'A land of old upheaven from the abyss/By fire, to sink into the abyss again'* (Tennyson) – recounts the loss of the City of Lions (Carlyon), much good land and 140 churches.

267

The sea will have its way and scientists are now acknowledging this by encouraging 'managed realignment'. In the process the north Norfolk coast, for example, will be constantly redrawn, with villages such as Bacton, Mundesley, Ostend and Walcott slipping away during the next century. The removal of millions of tons of aggregate from the seabed off the coast, to be sold to Holland and Belgium to shore up their own coastal defences, does not help and leaves residents apoplectic.

Tim O'Riordan, professor of environmental sciences at UEA, says: *'Building sea walls on a mobile and eroding coast is ultimately a waste of time and money. Where there are major communities and installations at stake we may have no other choice but to try to defend as best we can. Where there is a highly dynamic beach and rapidly eroding cliffs, such works may defend odd properties, but they destroy coastlines. A mobile seashore will protect more by letting nature replenish the beaches. I care about the fate of endangered villages, and am trying to use the new planning frameworks to create sustainable villages alongside redesigned coastlines, with the help of the residents and newcomers. This process will take ten to fifty years to complete, but new communities will evolve out of danger.'*

See also BELLS & BELL-RINGING, CHURCHES, COAL MINING, COASTLINE, COASTS, DESERTED VILLAGES, FIELDS, FLOODS, FOLKTALES, HAUNTED PLACES, HENGES & STONE CIRCLES, LANDSLIPS, MONASTERIES, PARKLAND, RIDGE & FURROW, RIVERS, SHIPPING FORECAST.

paid handsome sums to arrive at such a symbol, yet, like the Routemaster – London's red double-decker bus – it emerged from an evolutionary process to a moment of prolonged perfection.

See also BUSES, CABMEN'S SHELTERS, HORSES & PONIES.

LOST VILLAGES

On the east coast the sea has been eating soft land and settlements with relish. It transports debris along the coast and drops it, to make new land, fill in harbours and wreck ships. The Yorkshire coast of Holderness suffers losses of four to seven feet a year, with occasional lurches of twenty feet in a day. The cliffs may reach above eighty feet in height, but the boulder clay is no match for storm waves.

In 1786 one J. Tuke made a ghostly map of places *'washed away by the sea'* – Hartburn, Kilham, Hyde, Hornsea Burton, Aldbrough, ancient Withernsea and Frismarsh. Before him, in 1360, the *Liber Melsae* mentions the loss of Hotton, Northorpe, Dymitton and Out Newton. We can add Sunthorpe, the old port of Hornsea, Seathorne or Owthorne, and Atwick. The mobility of Spurn, a series of sand and shingle banks extending into the Humber estuary, has seen the loss of Ravensrodd, built in the mid-thirteenth century and lost within a hundred years.

In Suffolk, Dunwich was a busy market town at the start of the thirteenth century, failing by the end of it. House after house, church after church *'yielded to the impetuosity of the billows breaking against and undermining the foot of the precipices'*, a story told time after time in guide books. The port and ten churches have been lost. The succession of artists drawn to the drama included Turner, who captured the Church of All Saints, perched and vulnerable; it fell finally in 1912.

Stories, folktales, archaeological evidence and historical records mount up. Beyond the pier at Southend, Essex

L Y N C H E T S

As you leave the Square and Compass pub in Worth Matravers in Dorset and head for the sea cliffs, there are giant steps on the slopes of the West Man headland to your right and East Man to your left – we know them as strip lynchets. Some of the 'treads' here, the flat strips, are wide at nearly seventy feet; originally they were ploughed. The sloped 'risers', highlighted by the evening sun, are thought by David McOmish to have been used for grazing or hay-cropping. To the west, around Lulworth, about 570 acres of 'Celtic' fields survive, some cut by the receding cliffs. Evidence of field lynchets – irregular terraces, some with possible flint revetting on the steep slopes – is prehistoric. The shadows on the steep combe of Scratchy Bottom may have been cast for four thousand years.

While some lynchets may have ancient origins, reused or abandoned through the centuries, many are presumed to have been created in the twelfth and thirteenth centuries, when a high rural population created pressure on agricultural land. The strip lynchets may have been cut into hillsides by pick and shovel, widening occurring as a result of ploughing along the contours, forcing soil downslope.

Most strip lynchets survive in hilly areas of chalk and limestone, although not exclusively – some in Somerset are on clay. The sculptural sharpness of the lynchets in the chalk combes north of Mere, Wiltshire has created a landscape of considerable beauty. The Vale of Pewsey in Wiltshire is heavily lynchetted; the fact that its lowlands were marshy in the Saxon and medieval periods goes some way to explaining the need to cultivate the slopes, as at the Cannings, Allington and Urchfont. On the chalk of the Gog Magog hills south-east of Cambridge, and other parts of East Anglia, they are often reduced to faint traces. Much evidence of early field and strip lynchets on less steep ground has been ploughed out over centuries.

In the southern valleys of the Peak District in Derbyshire, flights of strip lynchets proliferate, as at Priestcliffe and west of Bakewell. In Wensleydale, Yorkshire, looking from Thornton Rust, the interplay of giant geological steps with strip lynchets and later walls makes for splendid sunset patterns.

Some systems of lynchets have been protected by the early creation of parkland, as at Studley Royal deer park on the Fountains estate near Ripon, Yorkshire. In Derbyshire, strip lynchets, together with ridge and furrow and older earthworks, are preserved in the park at Chatsworth.

See also DESERTED VILLAGES, DOWNLAND, EARTHWORKS, FIELD NAMES, FIELDS, LIMESTONE, PARKLAND, RIDGE & FURROW.

Mere, Wiltshire.

Mason Bold/Alternate Bold, Jonathan Barnbrook, 1992.

MALTINGS

Barley for brewing has to be 'malted' or germinated, then roasted to make malt. Before the era of multinational brewery corporations, making malt was the preserve of the independent maltster. He needed a bespoke building, with a large floor space where the barley could be laid out and kilns where the roasting could take place. This prompted the classic maltings shape: long, barn-like buildings with shallow roofs, square ventilation shafts for steam and smells and steeply pitched kiln chimneys.

The shape makes them easy to recognise. A cowhouse at Tumbler's Green near Stisted, Essex has the telltale cone of a roasting kiln. The large, oast-like roof of the Maltings apartments near Sheering in Epping Forest, Essex is a give-away. The old maltings at George Street in York, now a warehouse, is not so obvious, although its scale – long and three storeys high – is a clue.

Few survive as places where malt is produced, their commercial viability declining after the Second World War as commercial and specialist interests polarised. In the 1950s the brewers Whitbread had maltings at Dereham, Whittington and King's Lynn in Norfolk. None still operate. Where small-scale 'human' maltsters survive, they tend to serve micro-breweries and specialist brands. French and Jupps in Ware, Hertfordshire has survived as a museum, and its coloured malt is as much in demand by interna-tional beer brands as by small brewers. Tucker's in Newton Abbot, Devon, which first opened its doors in 1900, is now as much a tourist attraction as a producer. Warminster Maltings in Wiltshire continues to use traditional methods. It is ahead of the game. From 2006 it is also offering brewers *domain over their barley/malt supply*, so that beer can be traced all the way from specific farms and even fields with a *warranty of origin*.

The scale of the buildings has made them adaptable. When care is taken over regeneration projects, old maltings can become a striking and distinguished feature. Thanks in part to the composer Benjamin Britten, and his concert hall in a converted maltings at Snape in Suffolk – the main venue for the Aldeburgh Festival since 1966 – the very word 'maltings' has become almost synonymous with arts centres, conference venues and 'character apartment complexes'. Farnham's maltings in Surrey, which first appears in records in 1729, was saved from demolition in 1968 and developed into an independent arts centre. Gainsborough's in Lincolnshire is an art, crafts and antiques centre with a bistro, while in Northumberland, Berwick-upon-Tweed's maltings is a theatre.

See also BEER, CROPS, HOPS, HOP-GARDENS & HOP-YARDS, INDUSTRIAL CHIMNEYS, OAST-HOUSES & KELLS.

MANHOLE COVERS

Beneath your feet on most urban streets is a fascinating array of iron grate and manhole cover designs: grids of raised squares; parallelograms arranged in floral patterns; spokes radiating out from a central hub; chequers. Manhole covers have prompted everything from rubbings to an exhibition in 2001 called 'Quilts from Manhole Covers'.

271

Cast-iron covers, big enough for a man to climb through, appeared in the late eighteenth century for access down to some of the necessary aspects of urban life. The majority are round to stop them falling down the holes. Rectangular ones tend to indicate a shallower drain or hole. The newly industrialised towns, with their foundries, beat out the iron discs and oblongs, their places of origin given pride of place in raised letters. Nineteenth-century Derbyshire had iron ore and foundries in almost all of its towns: Chartres and Son made covers for the Melbourne Sanitary Board; Stanton originally for Stanton by Dale. Now Stanton Warriors are found everywhere. On a perambulation around Consett in Durham, Katrina Porteous found the

works of manufacturers from Durham, Sunderland, Bishop Auckland and Newcastle.

One Devon engineer pointed out that the roadside grates, once made locally for local conditions, are now the same across the county (and the country), and they do not do nearly as good a job in clearing water.

Smaller covers have a role. In nineteenth-century London Haywards of Union Street made the coal plates that punctuate pavements around Hampstead and Bloomsbury. They enabled coal to be directly shot into cellars beneath the pavement.

In the twenty-first century London is pioneering new cover design. As part of the regeneration of Deptford in the south east, a number of artists have been invited to contribute street furniture: Geoff Rigden is providing manhole covers made of bronze.

See also PAVEMENTS, ROADS.

MARKET CROSSES

Markets were often held in churchyards on Sundays until the practice was banned by Edward I in 1285. Markets moved to the centres of settlements and with them went the churchyard cross, which had become an important symbol of honesty. Although many suffered during the Reformation and later in the Civil War, the market cross continues as a rendezvous point in many towns and cities, with wide steps to sit on and wait for friends.

Some markets developed covered areas for selling goods, such as the poultry cross. The butter cross is the most common, a cool place; in Oakham, Rutland it is of eight sturdy oak posts supporting a roof of slates from nearby Collyweston. Some developed with a top floor for market administration. The solid seventeenth-century red sandstone Market House at Ross-on-Wye in Herefordshire stands on columns, in contrast to the black-and-white timber-framed buildings opposite; the market still gathers below. Swaffham's eighteenth-century Market House is a rotunda on Tuscan columns, reflecting the wealth of this town, built on the corn of north Norfolk.

See also ARCADES, CATTLE, CHEESE, CHURCHYARDS, COBBLES, COMMONS, DROVE ROADS, FAIRS & FAIRGROUNDS, HIGH STREETS, HORSE FAIRS, MARKETS, MIDSUMMER DAY, PAVEMENTS, POULTRY, ROADS, SHEEP, SHOPS, TOWN HALLS & GUILD-HALLS.

MARKET GARDENS

Market gardens, where vegetables and soft fruit for human consumption are intensively produced, evolved with towns and shifted outwards with urban expansion.

Vegetable growing was enhanced by the arrival of Flemish and Huguenot refugees in the 1560s, who practised their horticultural skills in Sandwich and Deal in Kent and at Norwich, Colchester and Yarmouth on the east coast. Some moved to London, settling in Battersea, Wandsworth and Bermondsey. Human waste was used on the land; from 1665 night soil was also shipped to market gardens along the Thames and to Kent from Dung Wharf near Puddle Dock in the City.

Market gardening was a profitable business. Fulham became known for its carrots, Battersea for its Battersea bundles of asparagus, grown around Nine Elms. In 1794 Peter Foot wrote of the north side of the Thames: '*Brompton, Kensington, Fulham, Hammersmith, Chiswick, Brentford, Isleworth and Twickenham are almost a garden and orchard of apple trees, pears, plums, cherries etc and in*

272

Market Cross, Wymondham, Norfolk; Butter Cross, Bungay, Suffolk.

rearing them nearly the same methods are followed. Isleworth is also celebrated for strawberries.' Basket makers along the Thames cut osiers and willows from the banks and eyots, such as Tagg's Island, to make pottles – tapered cones to hold half a pound of strawberries.

In the 1870s about one-seventh of all market gardens were in Middlesex, employing nearly fifteen thousand people and using six hundred greenhouses by 1900.

Nothing was wasted. First by cart, then by rail, huge amounts of horse manure went from the 'shit sidings' at King's Cross to Biggleswade and Sandy in Bedfordshire and Wisbech in Cambridgeshire. Some of Twickenham's fertility may have come from the large amounts of putrid fish sent from Billingsgate Market, as well as horse manure from the coaching inns along the Bath Road and barracks of Hounslow. Thousands of tons of Manchester's manure and night soil went out by barge via Muck Wharf, and by rail, to Rixton Moss, where potatoes and peas were first grown. From Birmingham, horse manure, soot, dried blood and bone-meal from the slaughterhouses, and leather waste and shoddy from the mills and factories, were sent by rail to the Vale of Evesham.

Kent, the Garden of England, is blessed with fertile soil, climate and good river links to London. The area between Gravesend and Dartford overtook west London as the prime market-gardening area and, in the 1840s, women and children came from the city to work during the 'podding season'. Now market gardens are found from Swanley to the Hoo Peninsula, where early potatoes, spring cabbage, peas and other vegetables are grown; students from Eastern Europe are among the workers now. The Isle of Thanet has been a centre of vegetable growing since a number of Scots started growing spring cabbage, cauliflower, broccoli and early potatoes there from the 1900s.

Linking Devon and Cornwall, the Tamar valley is an area where mild spring weather allows the cultivation of early crops. Virginia Spiers recalled the work of the industrious market gardeners: *'Over the years a greater variety of crops was grown, partly to counteract serious diseases arising from the mono-culture of strawberries. Fruit trees helped bind the soil and stop it washing downhill as well as increasing the diversity of crops and spread of tasks throughout the year: yellow daffodils and later white fragrant narcissi were picked in Spring, followed by strawberries and then cherries and apples. Small patches of vegetables and flowers, such as Devon violets, polyanthus, kaffir lilies and anemones, were fitted in and around the main crops so there was always something to be picked, bunched, packed and dispatched in boxes and chip baskets by road and rail to Covent Garden, the Midlands and Northern markets.'*

To the west of Birmingham the market gardens of the Vale of Evesham covered about twenty thousand acres in 1906, some containing glasshouses to raise tomatoes

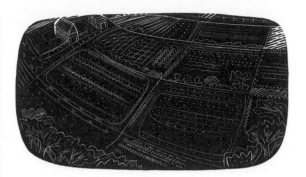

and other tender vegetables. Since the 1960s, however, government grants for cereals have caused a decline in fruit and vegetable production.

Now market gardeners and farmers are learning to be more inventive, growing specialist produce for niche and expanding markets, such as aubergines and peppers for restaurants and hotels. In south Huddersfield, Yorkshire, herbs such as coriander and fenugreek are being grown at the request of Punjabi families and Indian restaurants and sold at the wholesale market in Bradford.

Some growers are exploring methods of production that work well with nature. Tolhurst Organic Market Garden in Berkshire comprises a two-acre walled garden and sixteen acres of vegetables, rotated every seven years. It produces five hundred vegetable boxes a week. Legumes are grown for green manures, which are rich in nitrogen, allowing a closed 'stock-free' system that is not dependent on animal manures containing antibiotics.

Much can be grown in a few acres; it is labour that needs to be increased. The old methods point to the future: food fresher for travelling short distances, creating less pollution and traffic; use of organic waste products; direct feedback to growers. Perhaps we shall see an expansion around cities once more.

See also ALLOTMENTS, ASPARAGUS, BRUSSELS SPROUTS, CORRUGATED IRON, CROPS, EYOTS, GOOSEBERRIES, MARKETS, RIVERS, STRAWBERRIES.

M A R K E T S

Old English gave us the word *ceap* for market. This resonates in Chipping Warden in Northamptonshire and Chipping Hill in Essex; the road through Chipping Barnet in Hertfordshire discreetly widens. Cheapside and Cheap Street, as in Birmingham, Halifax in Yorkshire and Newbury in Berkshire, are the old market streets.

The market-place was the centre of town. Its position and shape reflects the importance of the buying and selling of animals, food, local and exotic goods. Marlborough's market street is the broadest in England, gently curved with a church at each end; its scale perhaps tells of the importance of sheep in Wiltshire's history. A simpler widening of the street can be seen in Ludlow, Shropshire, where competition for frontage made for typically narrow burgage plots extending back from the high street. In St Albans, Hertfordshire the triangular market-place evolved along the route of Watling Street, the Roman road; by the fourteenth century permanent shops lined the alleys and courtyards of Market Place and Chequer Street. Medieval makers and sellers clustered together and, gradually, patterns began to ossify. Shambles were built to house butchers and fishmongers, as in Worcester, York and Shepton Mallet, Somerset. Market crosses, especially butter crosses, sometimes provided cover for the wares.

By the middle of the nineteenth century cattle, sheep and other animals were less welcome in the high street because refined shops and shoppers found them unacceptable. King's Lynn in Norfolk had a separate cattle market from that for butter and vegetables, as did Wetherby in Yorkshire. Soon many livestock markets moved to the edge or another part of town. The railways, too, were changing the patterns of production and sale and many small markets began to fail. At the end of the twentieth century the remaining livestock markets began slipping faster out of town life, and in 2005 Tring in Hertfordshire lost one of the last Victorian ensembles to have survived.

274

But growing industrial towns, such as Burslem in Staffordshire and Accrington in Lancashire, were establishing markets. Corporations and councils acquired rights and built covered markets. The Market Hall in Bolton, Lancashire is an airy, Victorian cast-iron structure, now attached to a modern shopping arcade. Smithfield Market,

still active as a meat market in the City of London, has three and a half acres under a glass-and-iron roof. On Devon's north coast, Barnstaple's mid-nineteenth-century pannier market is open all week, with local producers setting up on the busiest days; the contemporary Butcher's Row, hosting fifteen butchers and two fishmongers, was built facing north to keep produce fresh. The Victorian Fish Market in Leicester, supported by a row of blue columns, is now home to shops. Next door the indoor market, built in the 1970s, is the biggest in Europe and, outside, stalls are bright with the colours and smells of Asian and Caribbean foods.

In east London Petticoat Lane, with its Jewish origins, works traditionally on Sundays. The Columbia Road flower market is ever more popular as a tourist detour, with its mix of stalls, shops and cafés. Walthamstow has the longest street market in London. A market started as youthful endeavour in the 1970s around Camden Lock, selling clothes, music and art goods, now drives the High Street. Borough Market in Southwark remains a wholesale vegetable market under a Victorian canopy. It has reinvented itself with weekly high-quality food stalls and provided a new home for the old Covent Garden cast-iron Floral Hall building.

The first farmers' markets held in Bath in 1997 began reconnecting us with good food produced close by, the birth of a countrywide movement offering fresh, local produce to an eager audience. Perhaps we can reinvent the market-place as the convivial heart of the town.

See also ARCADES, CATTLE, CHEESE, CHURCHYARDS, COBBLES, COMMONS, DROVE ROADS, FAIRS & FAIRGROUNDS, HIGH STREETS, HORSE FAIRS, MARKET CROSSES, MIDSUMMER DAY, PAVEMENTS, POULTRY, ROADS, SHEEP, SHOPS, TOWN HALLS & GUILD-HALLS.

Newgate market, York.

MARTELLO TOWERS

Martello towers are particular to the south and east coasts, built, all in a rush, between 1805 and 1812 to protect these shores from Napoleon's advances. Each was topped by a large gun, more terrifying to ships trying to land men than the one used in performances of Tchaikovsky's symphony. Inspired by a defensive tower that repulsed our navy at Mortella, Corsica, these small sea batteries were built mainly of brick and rendered, with walls up to thirteen feet thick towards the sea and five feet to landward. Some had dry moats. A door more than half-way up the thirty-feet-high battered walls was reached by a removable ladder.

Of the original 74 in the South, 29 can be found between Folkestone in Kent and Seaford in Sussex. They are elliptical in shape, compared with the slightly later ovoid plan of the eighteen (out of 27) up the coast of East Anglia, from St Osyth Stone in Essex to Aldeburgh in Suffolk, where a four-gun, quatrefoil tower survives. Three Redoubts, which were more complicated and carried ten guns, were built; two can still be seen at Eastbourne in Sussex and Dymchurch in Kent, the latter used by the army. A way beyond it is Martello tower number nineteen; raided finally by the sea in 1975, it lies in a scrambled heap, the most challenging of beach sculptures. Tower number fifteen, near Hythe in Kent, leans not far from number fourteen, both sturdy landmarks, for the moment. Elsewhere, towers are lived in or have become museums and cafés, having been sold by the Ministry of Defence for one pound or more.

See also BRICKS, BRIDGES, CASTLES, COASTS, FORTIFICATIONS, HILL-FORTS, PELE TOWERS, PILLBOXES, SCULPTURES, SEA FORTS.

MAY DAY

At one time 1 May was regarded as the most auspicious moment of the year, heralding summer and all that goes with it – supplies of food and warmth. The Celts celebrated Beltane with hilltop fires on 'Tan Hills', around which they danced 'sunwise'. On May Hill in Gloucestershire, morris dancers still greet the dawn, as they do on other high places.

Nature's fecundity was mirrored by human activities, such as 'bringing in the May', which involved young women and men going into the woods at midnight to collect branches, preferably in flower (not just hawthorn, but birch, sycamore in Cornwall and rowan in the North and West), which they brought back at dawn for decorating the outsides of their houses. (May Day was eleven days later in the Old Calendar, when more hawthorn blossom would have been out.) Wildflowers, especially yellow ones, such as marsh marigolds – 'the herb of Beltane', known as may blobs, may blubs or may bubbles – were woven into garlands. Cowslips were made into cowslip balls, and young women washed their faces in the dew.

Tall, straight trees were cut for maypoles. They were decorated with foliage and flowers and bound with coloured string, then raised on village greens, where dancers wove in and out of one another among much eating, drinking, tug-of-war and other games, archery, morris dancing, bawdiness and irreverence. At May Day celebrations in Fenchurch Street, London in 1557, a Lord and Lady of the May wearing *'scarfs, ribbands, and other fineries'*, according to Joseph Strutt, were elected to supervise the games. Robin Hood and his entourage, and St George and the dragon, were also often present at the feast. The Puritans frowned on the licentiousness of these occasions; by 1644 the erection of maypoles had been made illegal and all other May Day festivities were suppressed.

When Charles II returned to the throne on 29 May 1660 some places cleverly moved their May Day ceremonies to that date – this probably happened with Grovely Rights Day and Arbor Day – and others to Rogationtide. The events were more subdued than before and waned in popularity, until the Victorians created a notion of 'Merrie England', their sanitised version of history.

Today, many towns and villages crown their May queen. Some hold a May fair, such as Knutsford in Cheshire, Ludlow in Shropshire, Beaconsfield in Buckinghamshire and Hereford. Some erect maypoles for a day of festivities, including games and morris dancing, such as Barwick-in-Elmet in Yorkshire, Ickwell Green in Bedfordshire, Offenham in Worcestershire and Wellow in Nottinghamshire.

But some places are renowned for their May Day festivities. Two ancient 'obby 'oss beating the bounds ceremonies survive in Padstow in Cornwall and Minehead in Somerset. In Berwick-upon-Tweed and, less often, in Morpeth, Northumberland the bounds are ceremonially ridden.

Garlands were a central part of May Day ceremonies. Children used to make them and take them around houses, singing garland songs, to collect money. Garland Days still linger on in a few places. In Abbotsbury, Dorset it persists

275

on Old May Day, 13 May. Children carry three garlands through the village, collecting money as they go. Until the turn of the 1900s, Garland Day marked the opening of the mackerel season here, and a garland was hung on the prow of each boat. In memory of this a garland is still thrown out to sea.

Royal May Day in Knutsford, Cheshire is a Victorian reinvention of 1864, with Jack in the Green leading a procession through Knutsford, followed by the maypole, which is erected on Knutsford Heath and the May Queen crowned. A tradition unique to the town is 'sanding the streets': the story goes that in the eleventh century King Canute emptied sand from his shoes after fording the river (Knut's ford) in front of a newly married couple, wishing them '*happiness and as many children as there were grains of sand*', Charles Kightly wrote. Patterns of coloured sand are still made on the pavements outside the house of the May Queen and local brides.

London's chimney sweeps took 1 May for their festival. May was a slack time for sweeping chimneys and they used the holiday to raise money to keep them going. The parading of a Jack in the Green – a frame covered in leaves, under which a man can stand – together with music and dancing, was a way of legitimising begging. An old Sweeps festival was revived in the 1980s in Rochester, Kent, where the seven-foot-high Jack, a giant 'garland' of moving foliage, is woken at dawn on Bluebell Hill and accompanied by morris dancers and sweeps with blackened faces to Rochester, where they process through the streets. In Southwark, London, The Lions Part, a verse drama group, organises an annual pageant with traditional May games along the route. There are combat plays taken from the 1470s, which feature Robin Hood, '*quarter-staff, rapier, short sword fights with a great deal of word and horse-play*'. The aim is to reintroduce celebrations of the seasons on urban streets as a way of reconnecting with the natural world.

May Day was formally taken as International Workers' Day in 1889 after anarchists were hanged for campaigning for a reduction in factory working hours in North America (they were asking for an eight-hour day). Throughout the communist world it became a day to parade weapons and

armed forces. More recently it has been the lightning conductor for protest from the anti-capitalist movement; in London, Reclaim the Streets will be remembered for its guerrilla gardening in Parliament Square – emulating the original spirit of turning things upside down and reasserting the voice of the common people.

See also BEATING THE BOUNDS, BONFIRE NIGHT, CARNIVALS, CASTLETON GARLAND DAY, CHEESE ROLLING, CHINESE NEW YEAR, DAWN CHORUS, DIWALI, EASTER CUSTOMS, FURRY DANCE, GREEN MAN, HALLOWE'EN, HAWTHORN, MAYPOLES, MIDSUMMER DAY, MORRIS DANCING, 'OBBY 'OSSES, TAR BARREL ROLLING.

M A Y P O L E S

The earliest maypoles were cut from the forest. Philip Stubbes, writing in the 1580s, described it thus in *The Anatomie of Abuses*: '*their chiefest jewel they bring from thence is the Maiepole . . . their stinking idol rather, which they covered all over with flowers and hearbes, bound round with strings with variable colours, having two or three hundred men, women, and children following it with great devotion. And thus equipped it was reared with handkerchiefes and flagges streaming on the top, they strawe the ground round about it, they bind green boughs about it, they set up summer halles, bowers, and arbours hard by it, and then fall they to banquetting and feasting, to leaping and dauncing about it, as heathen people did at the dedication of their idols.*'

Seventy-odd years later maypoles were banned by the Puritans, but to celebrate the return of Charles II in 1660 a 134-foot-high maypole was brought up the Thames by boat and erected by the Church of St Mary-le-Strand, where it stood for fifty years before Sir Isaac Newton bought it to support his '*great telescope*' in Essex.

If the maypole arose from some form of tree worship, it is ironic that some of the most recent maypoles are no longer made from wood (wooden ones usually last for about 25 to thirty years). In Gloucestershire, Welford-on-Avon's seventy-foot-high maypole is made from the shaft of an aluminium ship's mast, and the huge maypole on the green at Wellow in Nottinghamshire is of steel.

In 1991 the new maypole at Burnsall, Yorkshire disappeared one night and an identical one appeared on the village green in nearby Thorpe. It is not the first time that Yorkshire's maypoles have been spirited away. In 1850, Gawthorpe's pole ended up in Chickenley.

Also in Yorkshire, Barwick-in-Elmet's pole is laced to a burglar alarm; reaching 86 feet, it is a landmark. A maypole has stood here for a thousand years; every third year, until 1999, it had been taken down on Easter Monday for painting '*white with a thin red and blue stripe running down and around it*', Homer Sykes wrote. Its four garlands renewed, the pole was carefully raised again on Whit Tuesday by a

Rochester, Kent.

hundred or so men, using ropes and ladders. Once the earth around it had been rammed down, a volunteer would shin up the pole to remove the supporting ropes and then up to the top to twirl the fox weather-vane. In 2002, however, the event was cancelled. The maypole committee, worried about personal liability and costs, suggested ending the tradition, replacing the wooden pole with an aluminium one. The motion was rejected, the villagers understanding what the committee failed to recognise – that community is held together by such ritual. Uncowed by insurance demands, a new committee ensured its continuance, albeit with hard hats and a crane, and in 2005 a new pole was erected.

The permanent maypole on Ickwell Green, Bedfordshire, which is topped with a crown, has a smart red-and-white spiral stripe, like a barber's pole; at Offenham, Worcestershire, it has red, white and blue stripes.

In the 1880s maypoles re-emerging after a period of suppression or disinterest had plaited ribbon streamers attached to them; the maypole dances we know today emanate from this time, when John Ruskin and John Faunthorpe at Whitelands College, and others, invented 'Merrie England'.

Maypole Lanes, Fields and Inns tell of lost traditions. But despite the spiralling insurance costs and our litigious

culture, new maypoles are going up. In 1996, in Dunchurch, Warwickshire, a wooden maypole painted with red, white and blue spirals was erected. In Otley, Yorkshire in 2004 a pole was raised on Cross Green, where previously maypoles had stood, only to be struck by lightning. A lightning conductor is now attached.

See also FAIRS & FAIRGROUNDS, GREEN MAN, MAY DAY, MORRIS DANCING, 'OBBY 'OSSES, VILLAGE GREENS, WEATHER-VANES.

M E L A S

277

Mela, from the Sanskrit for 'gathering', describes many different south Asian celebrations, religious fairs varying in size from small local 'marhais' to the Kumbha Mela (held every twelve years) when pilgrims make their way to four sacred places in northern India.

In England melas are often held in urban parks as summer festivals; all have a focus on local community involvement. They draw together rich cultural diversity and exuberance, particularly through music, dance and food. The Belgrave Mela in Leicester, held in Abbey Park, is one of the largest, together with Bradford Mela in Peel Park. Two stages were erected in the town centre for Oldham Mela in 2004, one for international Asian artists, the other for local groups. The recently established London Mela attracts tens of thousands of people to Gunnersbury Park in Ealing.

See also CARNIVALS, CHINESE NEW YEAR, DIWALI, NOTTING HILL CARNIVAL, PARKS.

M E W S

London has more mews than any other city. Often built behind large houses to form a back street of two-storey stable blocks with living quarters, many have been transformed from cramped and smelly dwellings for servants and horses to much sought-after residences or smart offices. 'Mews' derives from the Latin *mutare*, meaning 'to change'

– hawks belonging to the king were kept in cages at the Royal Mews when moulting. The meaning mutated to include stable blocks clustered around a yard.

The development from the seventeenth century of large blocks of London, for example the Bedford estate around the British Museum, the Westminster lands around Mayfair and Belgravia, the Portland and Portman estates of Marylebone, Bayswater and Kensington and the Holland and Ladbroke estates of Notting Hill, enabled planned development on an unprecedented scale. The large landowners risked nothing, offering long leases to speculative builders while accruing the ground rent and retaining ownership of the land and buildings for themselves. The personalities of the mews vary with each builder's aspirations and the fashions of the time, with the added overlays of the present.

Barbara Rosen and Wolfgang Zuckermann described a hierarchy of streets, the houses around the square being the grandest, with the mews behind. Where there are parallel streets, the mews form a back lane or a T- or L-shaped cul-de-sac inside the block, sometimes three to nine feet lower than the surrounding streets. In fashionable areas, such as Belgravia and Kensington, fine archways were '*cunningly set into principal street facades*', as at Cornwall Mews in South Kensington and Roberts Mews in Chelsea.

Many of the older mews buildings have flat Georgian frontages with a balustrade or parapet masking the roofline. They housed carriage and riding horses in stalls or loose boxes, a harness room and one or more carriages, yet many had frontages of 25 feet or less, dominated by hinged stable and carriage doors. The 'lavatory' was under the stairs (but adequate supplies of running water reached the Mayfair mews only in the 1890s). The hay or grain was often stored upstairs, as high doors and hoists suggest. The coachman and his family, grooms and other servants also lived above the horses. As well as being cramped, there were usually no back windows towards the big house and no side windows, so ventilation was poor.

The narrow mews streets were cobbled with granite setts, which sloped gently to a central drain or two side run-offs. There were smells and flies, since storing and getting rid of the tons of manure was a serious problem. It was sold to the market gardens surrounding London and as far away as Sandy in Bedfordshire and Chailey and Newick in Sussex. Not surprisingly the mortality rate in mews streets was higher than in other areas.

The domination of the streets by the horse and carriage began to wane in the second half of the nineteenth century. The London omnibus offered an alternative mode of transport from 1829, but many of the wealthy persisted with private transport, the car finally ousting horses from stable and street.

At the turn of the century many mews had become the run-down tenanted homes of the poor, but change started in Mayfair, where the prospect of a smart, yet affordable, address appealed. Many of the mews in the Bedford estate were demolished at the end of the nineteenth century for the expanding University College and hotels, and in other parts of London some disappeared in post-war developments. But many were included in conservation areas and began to be valued for their quiet positions and central locations.

See also ALLEYS, BUSES, COBBLES, GARAGES, HORSES & PONIES, LONDON TAXIS, MARKET GARDENS.

MIDSUMMER DAY

Midsummer belongs to the sun; 21 June is the summer solstice, when at Greenwich the sun rises at 3.48 GMT and sets at 20.20, giving us sixteen hours and 32 minutes of day length and even longer daylight – more or less the longest day. This has been known for thousands of years in the northern lands, where sunlight and heat fluctuate so dramatically.

Midsummer Day, though, is 24 June, and betrays the attempt by the Christian church to claim the power of existing activities. It is the feast day (actually the birth day, six months before that of Jesus) of St John the Baptist, herald of Christ, a heavyweight in the Christian pantheon – signifying what serious counterpoise was needed to the pagan rituals around the solstice.

Dancing, Robin Hood games and the lighting of bonfires on Midsummer Eve on the tops of particular hills was common in the areas settled by Angles, Saxons and Danes (it is still popular in Sweden and Hungary). Having clung on until the 1850s, fires finally disappeared from Cumberland, Derbyshire and Durham, but in Northumberland the Whalton Baal Fire (*baal* or *bel* means sun) is still lit on 4 July, Old Midsummer Eve, and villagers dance around it.

In Cornwall the Celts continued their rituals; a bonfire lit on Garrack Zans, the Holy Rock, at Escalls in Sennen was followed by fires in liminal places all over the west of the county on the eve of St John.

Tany'n cunys	*Now set the pyre*
Lemmyn gor uskys,	*At once on fire,*
May tewo an Tansys	*Let flame aspire*
Yn Hanow Dew!	*In God's high Name!*

As well as fires set to honour the sun and ritually add to its strength, there were fiery tar barrels, torches or flaming straw wheels. Even in the cities effort was made – before 1540 in London John Stow (quoted by Joseph Strutt) said that they made bonfires in the streets and '*everyman's door was shaded with green birch, long fennel, Saint John's wort, orpin, white lilies, and the like, ornamented with garlands of beautiful flowers. They, the citizens, had also lamps of*

glass with oil burning in them at night; and some of them hung out branches of iron, curiously wrought, containing hundreds of lamps lighted at once, which made a very splendid appearance.'

Dancing and games reinforced the purifying, strengthening, protecting role of the fires. As Shakespeare showed in *A Midsummer Night's Dream*, this is a time when the tissue between worlds is very thin, and St John's Wort was worn for protection. But many of the pre-Christian rituals so apparent around midsummer, despite the presence of St John, were asphyxiated by the Reformation and finally extinguished by the Victorians.

A dragon was paraded up and down the steep high street of Burford, Oxfordshire until perhaps the eighteenth century, and Strutt notes that fires were *'made to drive away the dragons and evil spirits hovering in the air . . . for "the dragons hattyd nothyng mor than the styncke of brenyng bonys"'*.

Places where bonfires were lit may still carry the names – John Field mentions St John's Ground in Shrewsbury St Chad, Shropshire and St John's Acre in Warter, Yorkshire. He also mentions that *'The cryptic St John and Half a St John, in Stanton St John (Oxon), has the earlier forms Syngett or Singett occurring in documents between 1522 and 1687, meaning "burnt (place)".'* Summer Gams in Horkstow, Lincolnshire recalls the field where summer games took place. Cambridge Fair is held on Midsummer Common and is the biggest of many traditional fairs taking place at this time.

In Penzance, Cornwall the revival of the Quay fair has brought showmen back into the midsummer festival, and local effort has brought about the reinvention of Golowan (gol Jowan – St John), which now attracts more than seventy thousand people. It began as a single day of community celebration called Mazey Day in the early 1990s, initiated by Stephen Hall and what became Golowan Community Arts. A mock Mayor of the Quay is elected by local people,

and the town is decorated with laurel leaves. On St John's Eve bonfires are lit once more around Penwith, Cornwall and, at the end of the festival, there is a great procession with folk song, dance and banners, made in the outlying parishes. The popular revival of the snake dance bonds people in an ancient ritual in the streets. As many as can hang on hold hands for the boisterous 'Threading the Needle', with Penglaz the 'obby 'oss and his teaser causing some havoc in their midst. Shouts of *'an eye, an eye'* demand that the lead pair lift their arms for all to bend under and keep on swirling and curling through the streets until spent.

See also BEACON FIRES, BEATING THE BOUNDS, BONFIRE NIGHT, DIWALI, DRAGONS, FAIRS & FAIRGROUNDS, GIANTS, HILLS, 'OBBY 'OSSES, ROBIN HOOD, RUSH-BEARING, WELL DRESSING, WILDFLOWERS.

279

MILESTONES

In telling the distance to two or more places, milestones pinpoint their own location precisely. They are small and functional, frequently made from local stone and carry a wealth of history and character in their shapes, letter forms and styles. Most have black lettering on whitewashed stone or cast iron. They have become small landmarks in their own right.

Every thousand paces along their new roads, the Romans placed cylindrical stones about six feet high; the few that survive have been removed to museums. In the early eighteenth century distance markers were reinvented by turnpike trusts. By 1773 the trusts were legally obliged to provide stones where these roads crossed parish boundaries, as well as mile markers, and in so doing they standardised miles. William Addison noted that *'Many of these early milestones served the dual purpose of milestone and mounting-block. In some districts they were called upping-stones. We find them across Dunsmore in Warwickshire.'*

Dorset county council researched the state of the county's milestones in 1980: '*The stones varied not only in shape but also in the type of stone used; in the south limestone was prevalent, while in the north some sandstone ones were found. The script also varied according to the Trust, from the ornate to the very plain.*' A single six-foot-high milestone made from Swithland slate can be seen where the old A42 entered Ashby de la Zouch in Leicestershire. Slate was also used in parts of the Lake District.

Distance and destination predominate; embellishment is rare. There are notable exceptions, such as the crescents on the Trinity Milestones, which represent the arms of Trinity College, Cambridge, paid for by bequest. On the A22 to Eastbourne there are a number of milestones known as the Sussex Bow Bells, indicating the distance from Bow Bells in London. On the A30 at Crows-an-Wra, at the junction with the road to St Buryan in Cornwall, stands an ancient granite stone cross. Beside it, a white-painted milestone is unique for the barley-sugar scroll down its sides; its lettering is different on both faces, there is a flourish around 'miles' and a pointing hand is outlined in black. In the 1990s Peter and Ruth Stenner of St Just found sixteen individual 'finger stones' in Penwith, which seemed to have been made by different craftsmen but all had the distinctive '*pointing finger of a carved hand*'. Milestones and direction posts are the place to look for the pointing hand – it varies from the naïve (on Derbyshire's Chesterfield Road) to the refined and embossed.

During the eighteenth century some milestones grew into grand obelisks, inspired by the fashion for Egyptology. One, at Ampthill in Bedfordshire, built in 1785 for the Earl of Ossory, gives the number of miles to London, Bedford and so on and has a lamp perched on its top. In the nineteenth century mileposts made from cast iron became predominant, especially in the west Midlands and North East.

Derbyshire bobbins – small, cylindrical mileposts on a short pole – can be found on the Ashford in the Water to Baslow road in Derbyshire, in Cheshire along the Buxton to Macclesfield road, and in Staffordshire. The 'open book' is another regional style of cast-iron milepost, of which there are about five variations. A fine example, dated 1833, survives at Stanthorne, Cheshire, along the A54. A cast-iron milepost at Thirsk, Yorkshire is unusual for its depiction of a sheep and lamb on one face and a shepherd on the other.

Milestones and mileposts have faced many hazards. Many were originally defaced by local people who resented having to pay for travel. During the Second World War many milestones were removed or buried, and some were never replaced. More recently they have been lost or destroyed during road widening, car accidents and pilfering. The highways authorities have responsibility for their upkeep, and some have been keen enough to get them listed, but they need local vigilance, with help from the Milestones Society.

See also CANALS, FINGERPOSTS, FOOTPATHS, LEAD MINES, MOORLAND, NEW MILESTONES, OBELISKS, ROADS, TOLL-HOUSES, WAYSIDE & BOUNDARY CROSSES.

MILLSTONE GRIT

In geological terms the Millstone Grit Series includes mudstones and siltstones, as well as sandstones. But the rock we know as millstone grit is hard and often so coarsely grained that you can see the bits of feldspar and quartz that once were gathered into sandbanks in Carboniferous seas. It stands up for itself, capping hills or providing broad shoulders, with the softer rocks etched in deep vales.

The landscapes of millstone grit present real drama. In the Forest of Bowland in Lancashire, Pendle Hill rises like a whale, recognisable from all angles. The whole area is of rounded hills, themselves sandpapered by ice, clothed in peat and heather moorland alternating with acid grassland – black moor and white moor. In Yorkshire Nidderdale exemplifies another face of gritstone, with giant steps evident on hillsides and crags on the tops, sometimes eroded to form sculpted tors, such as Raven Stones, Rowantree Crags, 'Jenny Twigg and her daughter Tib' and the most complicated gathering at Brimham Rocks.

In the Dark Peak of Derbyshire the high Kinder Scout grits make for miles of savagely exposed blanket bog, etched by intermittent stream channels or groughs. Here, ironically, the ground is also prone to erosion by the thousands who walk the Pennine Way, now having to negotiate their way past one another on a metre-wide flagstone path across this wild place. Just to the south and east there are craggy edges, long scarps facing to the west, which give the Dark Peak its look of durability.

Darkened gritstone is much used in building. Downham is representative of the villages in Bowland, all of which

Yorkshire; Cambridgeshire; Cheshire; Devon; Cornwall; Yorkshire; Yorkshire; Northumberland.

are held together by fine gritstone walls with worked copings and stoops (gateposts). Three 22-foot-high tapered monoliths – the Devil's Arrows – stand south of the river Ure near Boroughbridge in Yorkshire. They are thought to have been dragged here from Plumpton Rocks at Knaresborough around 2,700 BC, so resilient that after nearly five thousand years of weathering they have merely gained some vertical grooves.

The Derbyshire edges attract thousands of climbers. Stanage Edge is a favourite, with stupendous views, remarkable rock formations and colourful climbers' parties attempting some of the ten thousand possible climbs. Walkers, too, are drawn to walk the tops and below the faces, where there is added the excitement of finding heaps of old millstones, as under High Neb.

This stone was so important that it was named after the job for which we used it. Mills were everywhere, powered by water or wind, and each might have had several pairs of stones that needed to be re-cut or replaced. From the Middle Ages onwards mills ground anything from wheat for flour to beans for cattle feed; for this they needed grinding stones that were robust.

The best millstones, it was agreed for five hundred years, were of French burr stone (a chert found east of Paris), but war often rendered them inaccessible. Some must have been fashioned at Quernmore in Lancashire – quern is an old term for millstone – and some came from local quarries. But most came from the Peak, millstone grit 'greys' quarried from the edges. Domed millstones, six feet and six inches in diameter, were hauled to Bawtry and thence by barge to Hull, then shipped down the east coast into the Thames and beyond.

Below Gardom's Edge above Baslow, quarries, tracks and sheds linger in the landscape, with broken stones among the tree growth. Looking like the beaded stems of giant crinoids, the fossil 'lilies' of the nearby limestone, there are lines of abandoned, flat-edged millstones, four feet across, holding each other up on the slopes above Hathersage. Here they have lain for a hundred years. Stone is still quarried at Stanton and Birchover for building, lintels and gateposts, and, across the moors, it is possible to see the remains of worked boulders as well as quarries around the edges.

See also BRIDGES, BUILDING STONES, DEVIL, DRYSTONE WALLS, EARTH PIGMENTS, FARMS & FARMSTEADS, FIELD BARNS, FOOTPATHS, GATES, GRUFFY GROUND, LIMESTONE, MOORLAND, PELE TOWERS, ROCKS, SANDSTONES, SHEEP, STANDING STONES, TORS.

M I N E S

The Red Men of Cumbria were iron miners. Perhaps it comes as more of a surprise to know that there are histories of iron winning in Wiltshire. In Somerset you can see

Romano-British exploitation of iron ores on Exmoor and nineteenth-century delving in the Brendon Hills. The area of the Blackdowns that looks like a battleground is riddled with iron pits; similarly pocked places around Thetford in Norfolk are neolithic flint mines, and the craters of bell pits on Grassington Moor in Yorkshire were scrapings for lead ore.

In Sherwood Forest, Nottinghamshire a hundred nodding donkeys have quietly secured high-quality oil from beneath the sandstones since early in the Second World War. There was much local pride in the oddity of the Eakring oilfield until it was overshadowed by higher-profile discoveries and the beginning of gas and oil exploitation in the North Sea in the late 1960s.

Where and when coal was king, the outcrops on the surface were followed ever deeper underground, first from sloping adits, then from vertical shafts, until Yorkshire men were plummeting greater distances into the earth than could be achieved by climbing the mountains of the Lake District.

Mining for so many minerals – alum, ball clay, barytes, calcite, coal, fluorspar, fuller's earth, gold, gypsum, iron, kaolin, lead, potash, salt, silica sand, silver, tin, umber, zinc and more – has ebbed and flowed through every county. The memories linger in the culture, even where work ceased a long time ago, and, of course, in the landscape.

Unless, that is, it is stripped away. Surface mining is still part of the repertoire of the iron, fluorspar and barytes industries, and the threat of opencast working of shallow coal seams and pillars remains a continuing uncertainty for many ex-coal-mining communities. This strips away every valued scrap of history and nature in the landscape, replacing it, eventually, with bland, featureless fields or 'brown land' for industry.

281

Kit Hill, Tamar valley, Cornwall.

Spoil heaps and headgear were part of the scenery in all mining areas, and heated debate continues about their future. The surface traces of old mining tell us much about our predecessors. Indeed, there is a huge nostalgia for the mutual reliance of working underground and for the physical relics that prompt people to tell their stories.

Above ground a wider culture is still seeking a new handhold and identity. Pit ponies have long gone, the hay meadows that fed them, too, and the forests growing pit props are no longer planted. The reading rooms and libraries, chapels, allotments and pigeon lofts have lost their magnetism, their use and the pride in them has declined.

The number of Free Miners of the Forest of Dean is dwindling as they age, but also because they have to have been born in the Forest to acquire rights to mine, and the maternity hospital has moved. As Durham reclaims its beaches from a hundred years of coal-waste dumping, the deep mine that ramifies for some miles under the sea from Boulby in Yorkshire, producing potash for agricultural use and salt for winter roads, has a new role hosting the Dark Matter Collaboration – a consortium of astrophysicists and particle physicists searching for the non-luminous matter that makes up our galaxy, their experiments sheltered from cosmic rays nearly four thousand feet down.

Conrad Atkinson's Parish Maps for his home place of Cleator Moor, Cumberland in the 1980s echo with unwelcome words, such as caesium, uranium, ruthenium and strontium. They remind us of the invisible assets of a place just over the hill at Calder Hall/Windscale/Sellafield – the nuclear alternative to burning fossil fuel. Despite changes of name the problem of lingering radioactivity will continue to be identified with this place for several thousand years.

See also ALLOTMENTS, BLUE JOHN, BRASS BANDS, CHALK, COAL MINING, DIALECTS, EARTH PIGMENTS, FLINT, GASHOLDERS, GRAVEL PITS, GRUFFY GROUND, HORSES & PONIES, INDUSTRIAL CHIMNEYS, IRONSTONE, JET, LEAD MINES, LIBRARIES, LIMESTONE, PIGEON LOFTS, PIT TIPS, QUARRIES.

M I S T L E T O E

Golden mistletoe shines in weak February sunlight, surrounding the bare branches of the tall lime trees. River valleys, such as the Itchen in Hampshire, are one of the preferred places for mistletoe, and hybrid limes are one of the commonest hosts.

But the heartland of this semi-parasitic plant is the cider-apple and perry-pear orchards of Herefordshire,

Mistletoe, lime trees, Itchen valley, Hampshire.

Worcestershire, western Gloucestershire and Somerset. In some old cider orchards the mistletoe is encouraged for cutting for the Christmas market. On these lichen-encrusted trees there may be twenty or more clumps. But the grubbing up of traditional orchards is a threat to its distinctive contribution to these places, together with its cultural associations.

Ancient reverence for 'the golden bough', alive when all else seems dead, has bestowed mistletoe with magical powers, especially if found growing on an oak. The kissing bough has been known for its aphrodisiac properties.

At Christmas mistletoe becomes a locally valuable commodity. The market at Tenbury Wells in Worcestershire holds weekly auctions of English mistletoe from late November to early December. But the mistletoe sold in London markets tends to hail from northern France, where the custom of kissing under the mistletoe is less common.

See also APPLES, LIME, OAK, ORCHARDS, PEARS, POPLAR.

M O A T S

'Swimming in the moat behind my house in Suffolk, I can float right up to a frog or hang watching the great crested newts swim straight up out of the clear green depths through a subterranean Manhattan skyline of waterweed reaching up to the sunlight', Roger Deakin wrote. He is fortunate to live in the Waveney valley in Suffolk, where simple house moats are thick on the ground, but he is probably unusual in sharing it with nature and using it as an outdoor pool.

About six thousand moats have so far been recorded in the UK, making them one of the most common medieval monuments. Defence may have been the first motivation for this hard work, and the castles at Alnwick in Northumberland and Kenilworth in Warwickshire are stage-set fortresses, surrounded by water with a drawbridge for added protection.

Nunney Castle near Frome, Somerset comes near to perfection. Here water laps a small rectangular island, out of which rises a tall, ruined castle with four cylindrical towers. A terrace with short grass and vertical sides with revetted stone (apparently a later addition) surrounds the ruin. The perimeter grassy banks are, in turn, encased by a low stone wall. A simple wooden bridge has replaced the drawbridge, and the moat is fed by the Nunney Brook, which flows on through the village.

Many moats had more to do with monasteries, farms or houses, although security may have been the original motivation, as much from animals as humans. Many were constructed between 1250 and 1350, but some may have been dug in the mid-1100s, others as late as the early 1500s. There are few moated buildings in Devon and Cornwall, although there are fortified farms, and bastle

houses offered protection in Cumberland, Westmorland and Northumberland. But moats can be found in most parts of the lowlands, with concentrations in the Midlands, such as in north-west Warwickshire, and in north-east Hertfordshire, north-east Cambridgeshire, Huntingdonshire and Buckinghamshire. They abound in East Anglia, with more than 855 in Essex alone (especially north-west of the county) and hundreds in west Suffolk, Norfolk and Lincolnshire. Perhaps, as moats became less of a necessity, they became fashionable as status symbols.

Moats come in all shapes and sizes. They are usually about seven feet deep and ten to twenty feet wide. They can be fed naturally by springs or streams, or artificially by means of leats; one end may contain a dam to impound the water. On the heavy boulder clays of Essex and Suffolk moats may have been dug to aid drainage. A moat may completely surround an island, be bisected by a causeway or only part-circumscribe a building. It may be circular, oblong, rectangular or square and, occasionally, contain two islands. Circular moats are thought to be medieval and are seldom found north of the Humber. In Norfolk the spoil from the moat was often placed on the island to raise it up from the water, but this was rarely done in Cambridgeshire. The largest island is Caxton Pastures, Cambridgeshire, which extends to five acres.

Manor houses, granges, farmhouses, chapels, barns, dovecotes and windmills have all been found with moats – some islands may not have buildings on them, only a garden or orchard. Many are deserted. Roger Deakin recalled a favourite moated island of snowdrops, near Gissing in Norfolk: *'if there was once a house there, its timbers are long since rotted or plundered'*.

Oliver Rackham described moats as being distributed singly or in pairs, but occasionally there are clusters: *'East Hatley (Cambridgeshire) now has a moated church, moated tennis court, moated scrapyard, and others, at least twelve moats in all, and there are eight moats in the deserted village of Bottisham Park (Cambridgeshire).'*

Moats had other practical uses: enriched by night soil from the dwelling, carp and other fish were grown in them. In the latter Middle Ages moats were often extended, excavated or used as garden features. Now, as well as offering tranquil reflections of house or trees, they make excellent refuges for water voles, newts, frogs, toads and wild swimmers.

See also ABBEYS, BASTLES, CASTLES, DEW PONDS, FARMS & FARMSTEADS, FRESHWATER FISH, ISLANDS, MONASTERIES, PONDS, SWIMMING PLACES.

283

M O N A S T E R I E S

Monks probably sought isolation in Cornwall and Glastonbury, Somerset from the fifth century. By the seventh, there were communities from Canterbury in

Kent to Lindisfarne in Northumberland. Starting as retreats, they became missionary centres, the hearts of local economies, where travellers could rest, trade and exchange news. Monks and lay brothers were farmers, millers, miners, brewers and builders as well as scholars. The learning of Bede of Jarrow, the eighth-century chronicler, is still remembered at an academic lecture each May at the Jarrow church in Durham that was central to his monastic life.

Quickly recovering from Viking disruption, monasteries grew in scale and influence. The Augustinian order was the most widespread, especially in the Midlands and East Anglia. The most powerful house was Shaftesbury in Dorset, built by Alfred for his daughter in 888. Yorkshire's important houses – Guisborough, Whitby, Rievaulx – monopolised certain packhorse breeds, and Guisborough broke the pope's alum monopoly.

Twelfth-century monasteries dominated the landscape; they might incorporate barns, granaries, breweries, vineyards, bake-houses, orchards, mills, mines, forges, dovecotes, fish-ponds, cloth workshops and clothing factories, guesthouses and inns, as well as the monks' accommodation, study and religious buildings. Cleeve Abbey in Somerset has a remarkably complete set of domestic buildings, although the abbey church is gone. Estates spread well beyond their nominal borders, often to country farms called *grangia*, granges – such as Roystone Grange, Derbyshire, associated with Garendon Abbey in Leicestershire – as well as to quarries and mines.

Many became the hub around which towns formed, such as Ely in Cambridgeshire, Abingdon in Berkshire, Evesham in Worcestershire and Whitby in Yorkshire. Other towns derive from a monastic decision to create them: Kingsbridge in Devon and Burton upon Trent in Staffordshire. Throughout the country, place-names incorporate 'monks' or 'priors' or 'abbots', indicators of either a foundation or other monastic interest.

In 1536 monasteries were closed as religious institutions, their wealth redistributed to Henry VIII, their assets stripped, their buildings sold into secular ownership. Most survive only in fragments, here an abbey church retained for parish worship, there an abbot's palace becoming a lord's manor. Ruins and remains, such as those at Fountains, Rievaulx and Byland in Yorkshire and Cleeve in Somerset, have great drama. Yet these presences are eclipsed by the transformed landscapes of the various orders. The Cistercians' driving work ethic encouraged deforesting, canal building, marsh draining, pond digging, building. Villages were razed, river courses altered and leats led water to work. Earthworks reveal complex water distribution for mills, water-meadows and for the growing of fish. Immense industry went into changing the land, subduing it, exploiting it, as along the valley of the river

Arrow in Worcestershire around Bordesley Abbey and Kirkstead in Lincolnshire. Lead roofed the abbeys and cathedrals, made water conduits, and the monasteries of the Mendips and the Yorkshire Dales, diversifying to great effect, took lead ore from surface and underground veins. Hundreds of thousands of sheep changed upland and lowland vegetation in Yorkshire alone. The Carthusians, from La Grande Chartreuse, France, craved isolation; their foundations embedded themselves in place-names such as Hinton Charterhouse in Somerset, as did those of the austere Grandmontines at Grosmont, Yorkshire.

Revived or recently created monasteries still exist. Only Buckfast in Devon is in its medieval location. Our Lady of Hyning in Carnforth, Lancashire dates from 1974. Downside in Somerset and Ampleforth in Yorkshire run schools. The white-habited monks of Prinknash in Gloucestershire make pottery and incense. Other religions have also created retreats: Britain has about twenty Buddhist sanghas, including the Amaravati Monastery at Great Gaddesden in Hertfordshire and the Aruna Ratanagiri Monastery in Harnham, Northumberland.

See also ABBEYS, CATHEDRALS, CHURCHES, DESERTED VILLAGES, DOVECOTES, LANDMARKS, LEAD MINES, ROBIN HOOD, RUINS, SHEEP, TEMPLES, TITHE BARNS, TUNNELS.

MONKEY-PUZZLE

The monkey-puzzle tree is most often found in gardens once owned by wealthy Victorians. These exotic prickly pines, with hard, scale-like leaves rather than needles, were greatly prized, and people paid huge sums for them

Bicton, Devon.

– £25 for one tree in 1834. The enterprising nurseryman James Veitch from Exeter sent his own plant collector to South America to bring back seeds. Under his direction an impressive avenue was planted for the Rolle family at Bicton in Devon in 1844. Some of the original fifty trees were lost to storm damage, but have been replanted with seeds from the parent trees.

Monkey-puzzle trees grow very tall and lose their lower branches as they ascend, so they form a distinctive and unmistakable shape in the landscape. They have lost favour in recent years, but there are landmark trees that are much loved, such as the imposing specimen in the village of Wheddon Cross on Exmoor.

Forests of monkey-puzzle trees once stretched from Antarctica to Brazil; now a few remain in the Andes. In Chile the tree is close to extinction due to illegal logging and forest fires.

See also ALDER, ANCIENT TREES, ASH, BEECH, BIRCH, BLACK POPLAR, BLACKTHORN, ELM, FIELD MAPLE, HAWTHORN, HAZEL, HOLLY, HOLM OAK, HORNBEAM, HORSE CHESTNUT, JET, JUNIPER, LANDMARK TREES, LIME, LONDON PLANE, OAK, ORCHARDS, PEARS, POPLAR, ROWAN, ROYAL FORESTS, SCOTS PINE, SWEET CHESTNUT, SYCAMORE, WALNUT, WHITEBEAM, WILLOW, WOODS, YEW.

M O N U M E N T S

The Monument, a Portland stone column by Christopher Wren and Robert Hooke, marks a traumatic moment in London's history. In the year of 1666, '*on 2 September, at a distance eastward of this place of 202 feet . . . a fire broke out in dead of night*'. The plaque baldly states it; the column of 202 feet, with its golden flaming urn, symbolises the importance of continuing to remember.

Most monuments serve in remembrance of wars and battles. Edwin Lutyens's Cenotaph in Whitehall, London (1919) is poignantly echoed in domestic form in every town and village.

Monuments tend to be about power. The deeds of the Duke of Wellington and Admiral Nelson were the subject of innumerable tribute structures in the early nineteenth century, London's Trafalgar Square, with Nelson's Column, being the *marque*. Rodney Mace pointed out that '*to the mass of ordinary people . . . the square offers no bronze or granite memorial; yet it is they and their descendants, who in the course of time by the use of the site as a public forum have given it its real significance*'.

Meaning may be lost but monuments may continue as simple landmarks. Somerset has its 175-foot-high Wellington Monument (c. 1817), an obelisk that overlooks the Vale of Taunton Deane. Alnwick in Northumberland has the 83-foot-high Percy Tenantry Column, topped with its famous horizontal-tailed lion. The column is known

as Farmers' Folly: it was built by tenants of the Duke of Northumberland in thanks for a timely rent reduction in the early nineteenth century, but the Duke realised that if they could afford this monument, they could afford the higher rents, and he put them back up. The tenants then couldn't afford to finish the column, and the Duke himself had to pay for its completion.

See also BESTIARY, DEVIL, FOLLIES, LANDMARKS, LANDMARK TREES, LIGHTHOUSES, MARKET CROSSES, OBELISKS, SCULPTURES, WHITE HORSES.

M O O N

It is full moon in March and people along the tidal Trent await the aegir. At full moons between Easter and Lammas, off Colchester and Whitstable, the oysters are spatting (not fighting, but spawning). Our calendar, once driven by the sun and moon, still keeps the moveable feast of Easter on '*the first Sunday after the full moon which happens on or next following the 21st of March the Spring Equinox: and if the full moon happens upon a Sunday, Easter-day is the Sunday following*' (*Book of Common Prayer*); upon this date rest many others in the Christian panoply of festivals.

Sun day and Moon day are still part of our daily lives. Chinese New Year begins on the eve of the new moon on the last day of the twelfth lunar month, and ends fifteen

the heart of folktales, which have him as a light-fingered peasant making off with brushwood over his shoulder, as Shakespeare described in *A Midsummer Night's Dream*:

> *One must come in with a bush of thorns and a lantern,*
> *And say he comes to disfigure, or to present,*
> *The person of Moonshine.*

Moon daisy is an older name than ox-eye, and still goes by the name of moon flower or moon's eye in Somerset, moon penny in Cheshire and, simply, moons in Berkshire, Buckinghamshire, Cambridgeshire, Cheshire, Essex, Gloucestershire, Warwickshire, Wiltshire, Worcestershire and Yorkshire. Geoffrey Grigson reminded us that its time is midsummer and its other names link it with thunder and the sun.

The people of Wiltshire are known as Moonrakers, from a tale that echoes that of the Mad or Wise Men of Gotham, Nottinghamshire, who went fishing for the moon. Alice Oswald takes up the tale:

> *. . . and they threw the net,*
> *They steered away, they pulled the running cord,*
> *The net turned over like a purse, it rose*
> *Into the moon and through the moon and out;*
> *The moon broke up in pieces and came whole.*
> *Three times they cast the driftnet, saw the net*
> *Grope for a ghost and gather what it could*
> *And ropes of water reeve themselves away.*

Rolling cheeses downhill to send them off to market on their own, drowning eels, building cuckoo pounds, trying to catch the reflection of the moon . . . By all accounts the stories of the exploits of these loony villagers was sufficient to cause King John to give them a wide berth in his peregrinations, saving the village a great deal of effort and money.

See also AEGIRS, BORES, CHEESE ROLLING, CHINESE NEW YEAR, DIWALI, EASTER CUSTOMS, EELS, FIELD NAMES, FOLKTALES, MIDSUMMER DAY, NICKNAMES, OYSTERS, PUB SIGNS, TIDES.

days later with the full moon some time in January or February. Psalm 81 calls up the Jewish new year, Rosh Hashanah, in September: '*Sound the horn on the new moon.*' This is the annual celebration of the creation of the world, the day of judgment and the reinforcement of Israel's bond with God. The Hindu, Sikh and Jain new year is celebrated on the night of the new moon in the month of Karttika in October to November.

A glimpse of the full moon between the verticals of the city offers a rare reminder of one's link with the cosmos. People who live and work by the sea are attuned to the ebb and flow of the moon through the tides; at new and full moon come the higher spring tides, and at the mid-points of waxing and waning come the neap, or lower, tides.

Working or walking under the harvest moon in late September, one is struck by its brilliance, by the starkness of shadows and the brightness of badgers. Moonless and cloudless nights give us the full glory of the Milky Way, if we are lucky enough to live under pollution-free, dark skies.

As it becomes ever harder to find a really dark place to ponder the stars and the moon, fields with moon names offer their own attractions. The meanings of Moonshiney, Moon Mead, Moon Piece and Moon Field remain obscure, although some may be describing the shape, as in Half Moon. Moon Hill in Sussex perhaps describes a natural topographical crescent on the flank of the hill. It is possible that other things may be implied, as John Field pointed out in relation to Moonfield in Great and Little Munden in Hertfordshire: '*It may allude to a location favoured for moonlight activities, such as poaching.*'

Moonless nights were preferred for moving brandy. The Man in the Moon appears on many pub signs; he is at

M O O R L A N D

The dramatic force of brooding Heathcliff in Emily Brontë's *Wuthering Heights* owes much to the novel's setting on the bleak moor above Haworth, Yorkshire. For much of the year such land looks dark and lifeless, and anyone forced to make a living from it faced a life as dour and gritty as the stone underfoot.

Until the last century or so, travellers detested moors, signalling as they did the prospect of a hard day's ride liable even in summer to mists and drenching rain, always dogged by the risk of losing one's way; local guides were deemed essential. But by the 1850s the enthusiasm of the Brontës for moorland marked a sea change in popular perception; the Romantic movement was to see beauty, innocence and spiritual calm in these wild wastes.

Today moors are widely celebrated as spectacular walking country and even as desirable places to live. Dark in winter, the fresh green of young bracken in spring brightens the hillsides; the ferns have colonised many old intakes. In July and August, when the heather comes into flower, the moor becomes a stunning sea of purple. Emily Brontë summed up the transformation: *'In winter nothing more dreary, in summer nothing more divine.'*

In the north Pennines and Yorkshire Dales, ling, the most common heather, was once pulled up by its roots to make a durable thatch, and a few cottages near Bowes, Teesdale and at Hurst, Swaledale still boast a 'black' heather roof. On the moors, bilberry, cowberry and crowberry are also common in boggy patches, together with cross-leaved heath and bell heather, heath rush and cotton-grass.

The wildness of the moors is a paradox, for this once-wooded land was cleared by humans and kept open by grazing sheep and cattle. The moors offered valuable common land, exploited by farmers living in the valleys sometimes more than twenty miles away; the place-name elements 'scales' or 'scholes' (as with shieling in Northumberland and north of the border), or words ending in 'sett' or 'seat', highlight the sites of summer huts occupied by herdsmen. After the Norman conquest huge stretches of moorland were turned into royal or seigniorial forests; the whole of Dartmoor, for instance, was declared a forest under the jurisdiction of the Duchy of Cornwall.

In recent years moorland has been widely managed for private grouse shooting. The red grouse, found only in Britain and Ireland, feeds almost entirely on ling and is quintessentially a bird of the moor. Curlews, golden plovers, ring ouzels and lapwings also thrive. In places the merlin, our smallest falcon, still hunts for its favoured prey, the meadow pipit. The moors of the Peak District support populations of twite, merlin, red grouse, golden plover, dunlin and moorland-breeding short-eared owls, as well as adders, slow-worms and common lizards, which sun themselves on the drystone walls.

The South West has its moors, too, on flat, high plateaus of ancient rock, stripped of their cloying mantle of heavy clays. In Cornwall Bodmin Moor is still unenclosed by wall or fence, the haunt of cattle and ponies that belong to local farms with common grazing rights. Tons of granite quarried on the moor have gone to build farmhouses, churches, kerbstones, bridges, roads, lighthouses, docks and London's Embankment. Dartmoor, Devon is a vast expanse of moor stretching more than two hundred square miles, capped with tors. Bilberries, locally whortleberries or hurts, thrive alongside the boulders, basking in reflected heat. A welter

of hut circles, walls and barrows testifies to dense settlement by prehistoric people.

Further east Exmoor in Somerset is a tamer landscape, broken by roads, woods and farms. During recent centuries much of the moor has been converted to grassland. The biggest stretches of Exmoor's surviving moorland lie to the west, where hardy ponies and herds of wild red deer graze. Like much of England's moorland it is threatened by uncontrolled fires, and by encroaching bracken and rank grass, hastened by a decline in traditional cutting and grazing. Even more has been lost to enclosure and agricultural improvement, drainage and peat digging, mining, reservoirs, forestry plantations, new roads and urban expansion. The creation of National Parks, beginning with the Peak Park in 1951, together with the rise of the National Trust as a moorland landowner, has done much to slow the destruction of this distinctive landscape.

See also BARROWS, BLACK DOGS, BUILDING STONES, CAIRNS, DROVE ROADS, DRYSTONE WALLS, EARTH STATIONS, EXMOOR PONIES, FELLS, FERNS, FOOTPATHS, GRANITE, GREEN LANES, GRUFFY GROUND, HEATHLAND, HILLS, HOLLOW WAYS, HOUND TRAILING, LEAD MINES, LEVELS, LIGHTHOUSES, PEAT, ROADS, ROYAL FORESTS, THATCH, TORS, WAYSIDE & BOUNDARY CROSSES, WINDS.

MORRIS DANCING   287

Morris originally encompassed mumming plays – for which faces are also blackened in disguise – and the sword dancers of the North East, who originally hid behind their beards and hats. Many morris sides can trace their origins back to the 1600s, and the dance may have pre-Christian roots. They danced at festivals and to raise money. From the end of the Middle Ages women also took part, but were probably discouraged by the Victorians.

In the 1800s there were about 250 teams across the country, but half a century later their popularity began to decline. Cecil Sharp rediscovered morris dancing in 1899 by chance at Headington Quarry near Oxford, and largely through his efforts it became popular again. His advocacy of the Cotswold Morris (he recorded sixty of their dances) spread this version far beyond its traditional range, but gradually local idioms have reasserted themselves, with different costumes, dances and music.

The Cotswold Morris's heartland is north of Oxford, where they traditionally performed at Whitsun, but their reach extends across Oxfordshire to Gloucestershire, north Berkshire, Buckinghamshire, Bedfordshire, Northamptonshire and Warwickshire. They are the most visually quoted – six dancers in white costumes adorned with ribbons, bells around their knees and flowers in their hats, holding handkerchiefs or sticks to perform figures, accompanied by a fool.

In East Anglia the tradition of Molly dancing is focused on Plough Monday. Costumes are covered in ribbons and faces blackened. The 'Molly' is a man/woman character. The counties bordering Wales have a tradition of Border Morris, with costumes covered in strips of coloured rags and, again, blackened faces.

Clog dancing developed first in the industrial mill towns of Lancashire in the early nineteenth century and then spread across northern England. The fast, rhythmic movements may have been danced in time with the machinery of the cotton mills. This tradition is for solo dancers, but steps have been incorporated into the Sword and Rapper dances of the North East and the Processional Morris of the North West.

Processional Morris is mostly found around Lancashire, Cheshire and Derbyshire, associated with the Rush-bearing processions held at the end of the summer, also at Saddleworth in Yorkshire. The teams are large – eight to sixteen men make up many Derbyshire teams. Unlike Cotswold and Molly, but similar to Border Morris, North-West morris is often accompanied by a full band. Their costumes are elaborate, usually white with ribbons and coloured sashes, hats covered in flowers, and long beaded necklaces. Their iron-soled clogs help to tap out the rhythm of the figures, usually involving a polka step, and they twirl sticks braided in ribbon and rope.

In the last decades of the twentieth century John Kirkpatrick and the Shropshire Bedlams, and many other vibrant sides, brought new life to the Border Morris. Also in south Shropshire, Sue Harris and others gave tradition a kick and started a trend towards women's morris with Martha Rhoden's Tuppenny Dish, named after a local tale – one of their dances celebrates Martha's less than symmetrical pottery, 'All asiden'.

See also ABBOTS BROMLEY HORN DANCE, BEATING THE BOUNDS, BRITANNIA COCO-NUT DANCERS, DRAGONS, FURRY DANCE, GIANTS, MAY DAY, MINES, MUMMING PLAYS, MUSIC, 'OBBY 'OSSES, RUSH-BEARING, SAINTS, SWORD DANCING.

288

MOSQUES

A mosque or masjid is the essential place of worship for followers of Islam. The original was established by Prophet Muhammad in his courtyard at Medina, Saudi Arabia, with palms trees providing shade, and this pattern is sometimes reflected in subsequent designs, such as the Mezquita in Córdoba, Spain. There are more than a thousand mosques in England, where religious tolerance took centuries to achieve, and the original tendency was to convert buildings, such as the terraced house on Coventry Road, Birmingham, which became the Jami Mosque, or the Huguenot chapel off Brick Lane, London, now the Jamme Masjid.

Mosque buildings are designed to serve Islamic ritual. Five daily prayer sessions are announced by a call, where possible delivered from a minaret – tall, elegant towers, such as those on the East London Mosque on Whitechapel Road, dating from 1985. Washing fountains are provided for purification before prayers. Inside the main body of the building, pattern dominates, but nothing figurative – representation is discouraged. Muslims face the holy city of Mecca for prayer, focused internally on a wall, the Qibla, with a niche called the Mihrab. Mosques are aligned to accommodate this; the Jamia Mosque in Derby is at an angle to the street.

The striking and colourful Shah Jehan Mosque in Woking, Surrey was the first to be purpose built, in 1889. The architectural style resembles the Taj Mahal and Lahore's Badshahi Mosque, reflecting the Bhopal origin of the benefactor.

The London Central Mosque at Hanover Gate, Regent's Park was built in the late 1970s, where the Islamic Centre had been created in the 1940s to pay tribute to Indian soldiers killed in the Second World War. It lends further dignity to the gleaming white Regency terraces, adding its white angular form with great arched windows, curvaceous golden dome and singular minaret.

See also BELLS & BELL-RINGING, CEMETERIES, CHAPELS, CHURCHES, ROUND-TOWERED CHURCHES, SYNAGOGUES, TEMPLES.

M O S S E S

Mosses are at their most luxuriant and most various in the mild and rainy climes of the West Country and the Lake District, in woods and hedge banks and on old stone walls. In very wet places – swampy woods, peat bogs and moors – the landscape is often dominated by spongy-looking bog or sphagnum mosses, tinged with bright crimson or gold.

These bog mosses, largely responsible for the formation of peat, are remarkably absorbent, able to soak up many times their own weight in water. During both world wars, sphagnum moss was collected for the Red Cross and sent to the front, to pack the wounds of soldiers. Resistant to rot and mould, dried mosses were also valued as a packing material and as stuffing for mattresses and pillows. Gilbert White admired the little brushes that foresters made out of the stems of great golden maidenhair, or silk wood, ideal for dusting curtains and carpets.

Although mosses as a whole are adventuresome in their choice of habitat, individual species are often distinctly fussy, so much so that a bryologist could probably deduce where he or she was if allowed to peruse a sample of the local mosses. Excitement would be high on Drumburgh Moss, Cumberland, where a dozen or so species of bog moss grow.

Nineteenth-century weavers in Lancashire, who taught themselves botany – and shared the knowledge with their fellows in the back room of a local pub – often had a particular interest in mosses; perhaps their demanding work helped to give them an eye for detail and the patience to unravel the intricacies of these subtle life forms.

Moss is still gathered by licensed collectors for the florist trade, for wreaths in winter and hanging baskets in summer, from specific Forestry Commission lands. But unregulated collecting can cause problems.

See also BUNS, CAVES, FENS, FLASHES, FROST & FROST HOLLOWS, GRAZING MARSHES, HOLLOW WAYS, INGS, LICHENS, MINES, MOORLAND, MOSSLAND, PEAT, PONDS, RIVERS, SALT MARSHES, THATCH, WOODS.

M O S S L A N D

Moss, from the Old English mos, has always meant both the diminutive green plants and the places – bogs – where mosses grow in great abundance. In the North West, where mossland abounds, moss remains the common place-name for a bog, a usage that extends as far south as Shropshire.

Chartley Moss in Staffordshire is Britain's largest and best floating bog, or schwingmoor. As the glaciers retreated at the end of the Ice Age they scooped out holes and depressions, many of which remain as lakes or meres, particularly where Cheshire, Staffordshire and Shropshire meet. Smaller hollows were gradually swamped by bog vegetation and ultimately filled in. Floating bogs are a half-way house, sporting a floating raft of peat across the lake. Chartley's floating bog reached the bona fide peat bog stage some five thousand years ago; then subsidence linked to salt extraction underground created a new lake and a bog started to develop all over again, above the ancient peat deposits. In this fearsome habitat, acid enough at a pH of 3.8 to sprinkle on fish and chips, a host of specialist species makes a living. The bog moss is joined by the carnivorous sundew, and the bog rosemary and cranberry, at the south-eastern limit of their distribution in England. Sixteen species of dragonfly regularly breed in the pools, most famously the beautiful white-faced darter. Nearby lie Fenn's and Whixall Mosses, equally threatened by drying out and encroachment by Scots pines and birch.

At Leighton Moss in Lancashire old peat workings have been flooded to create a nature reserve that supports bitterns, marsh harriers, bearded tits and otters. It has been managed to retain a mixture of open water, reed beds, willow scrub and mixed fen carr, mirroring the stages in the evolution of mossland itself. Nearby, at Hawes Water, a rich fen flora thrives on the north of the marl lake. Elsewhere, most of the peaty mosslands along Morecambe Bay and the Lancashire coast have been stripped of their peat, or drained and reclaimed as flat, fertile farmland. Another chain of mosses – Chat Moss, Barton Moss, Trafford Moss, and more – between Liverpool and Manchester are now mosses in name only. Rixton Moss between Warrington and Irlam, brought into production in 1879, was growing a monoculture of iceberg lettuce in the 1980s.

Meanwhile, on the Solway coast, Glasson Moss, Bowness Common and Salta Moss survive as domes of peat and sphagnum moss rising ten feet above ground level, sprinkled with bog rosemary and cotton-grass, with its white flowers, and joined by cranberry, cross-leaved heath, heather and purple moor grass in the drier areas.

See also BROADS, FENS, FISH & CHIPS, FLASHES, GRAZING MARSHES, GREEN LANES, HERONRIES, INGS, LICHENS, MARKET GARDENS, MOORLAND, MOSSES, PEAT, PONDS, RIVERS, SALT MARSHES.

M O U N T A I N   H A R E S

Only in the Derbyshire Peak District might you be lucky enough to catch sight of a native mountain hare in England, most likely on a winter's evening before the snow has come, when its coat has turned white (with hints of blue in the undercoat). In spring its coat reverts to brown-grey, making it more like the brown hare, although smaller and with shorter ears. They are also less solitary, although not averse to bouts of spring-time boxing. On the heather moors, grassland and blanket bogs between a thousand and two thousand feet, small groups nibble away at the young heather shoots, grasses, rushes and bilberry.

Mountain hares were once widespread but survived only in the Highlands of Scotland. In the 1870s small numbers were translocated to various parts of England for game shooting, but only those in the Peak District and the Isle of Man have persisted. Since big losses in the cold winter of 1962/3, their numbers have slowly increased to more than nine hundred, but their small, isolated populations are still vulnerable. Severe winters, overgrazing by sheep, disturbance, poachers with lurchers and cars are their main enemies, and their vulnerability is increasing because of snowless winters, their white coats offering no camouflage.

See also EASTER CUSTOMS, HARES, HOUNDS, MOORLAND, THREE HARES, UNLUCKY WORDS, WARRENS.

290

M U M M I N G   P L A Y S

'In comes I', says Bold Slasher, and Saint or King George, the Turkish Knight or Black Prince of Paradise, Robin Hood, the Doctor/Toss Pot, Beelzebub, Father Christmas, Jack Finney or the King of Egypt, as each, among their fellows, 'takes the stage' – commonly the street. The extraordinary casts of mumming plays may include other bizarre mixes of characters.

The stories and parts have been passed on orally. Their origins are unknown; the earliest written texts do not appear until the early 1700s. Mumming plays could have been influenced by the 'drolls', short dramas shown in portable booths at medieval and later fairs, or by the plays of the strolling players performed in transportable theatres. They spread rapidly in chap-books, with titles such as *Alexander and the King of Egypt, A Mock Play as it is Acted by the Mummers Every Christmas*, which were printed around the 1750s and distributed by chapmen (itinerant buyers and sellers) on their travels across country and at fairs and markets.

Mumming plays were enacted between the end of October and Easter, and one purpose is clear – they were a means of raising money (a collection was always made afterwards). The Lancashire plays may have started with house visits,

performances taking place indoors before migrating outside. Eddie Cass observes that mumming plays *'survived relatively untouched through the period of the Industrial Revolution'*, through all the social upheavals of the time, forming part of our popular culture almost until the outbreak of the First World War.

Most mumming plays are performed at Christmas time. According to Cass, the hero-combat play is performed before Christmas and the sword play on Boxing Day or at the New Year. The exceptions are the Lincolnshire Plough or Stott Plays, which take place on Plough Monday (the first Monday after Twelfth Day, 6 January) and/or between Christmas Eve and Plough Monday. The Pace-Egg plays are performed at Easter, and the Cheshire Souling Plays occur on or near All Souls' Day, 2 November.

Although mumming plays share a central theme, they vary across the country. The most common is the hero-combat type, with a simple plot – two or more characters, such as St George, the hero, and Bold Slasher/the Turkish Knight, the villain, start the dialogue with boastful taunts that result in a fight. One of the two is killed or badly wounded, and is then 'lamented' by one of the others. A Doctor is called for; he claims he can cure everything (the audience was aware of the shortcomings of the quack doctor), and miraculously he revives him. A collection (quete) is taken.

This captures the action repeated five times by the Marshfield mummers, or Paper Boys, on Boxing Day in the main street of this handsome Gloucestershire town. In the square by the church, hymns are sung by the expectant throng before the crowd is parted by the entrance of the Paper Boys (men only). They are disguised in fringed hats and costumes completely covered by strips of yellowing newspaper (more recently coloured strips of paper have augmented the black and white, and one of the characters wears red). Their performance lasts for about ten minutes, and each player offers his own lines in his own style; it is almost a collage as opposed to an interplay of action. The final performance finds players and followers outside the pub.

The Soul-Caking plays of north-west Cheshire are distinguished by the addition of a hobby-horse or wild horse. In Antrobus, where the custom survives, the traditional St George hero-combat play is enlivened at the end by the entrance of the Wild Horse – Dicky Tatton – with his Driver (dressed as a huntsman). The horse is a scary beast made from a horse's skull painted shiny black, with eyes made from bottle tops, jaws that open and shut, and *'decorated with plumes, coloured ribbons and horse bells'*, according to Violet Alford, mounted on a short pole. He is worked by a man bent double under a black rug. The horse, described as being very old, which snaps and petrifies the audience, is the *'star attraction'*, according to Charles Kightly.

The plough plays are an example of the so-called wooing play, which was known in the east Midlands, Lincolnshire and parts of Leicestershire and Nottinghamshire. The plots differ from place to place, but the main theme is described by the Lincolnshire Folk Department: *'A Recruiting Sergeant is calling up the Farmer's Man. His Lady is not pleased and turns her attention towards the Fool. They agree to be married. Dame Jane appears carrying a baby. She claims that the Fool is the father. Beelzebub enters and knocks down Dame Jane dead. A Doctor is called who raises Dame Jane to life. The Plays are delivered in a mixture of song, verse and prose, with plentiful use of ad libs. There is sometimes dancing.'* The woman is always played by a man. These plays are associated with the custom of the pulling of a decorated plough around the villages by farm labourers, wearing clothes embellished with ribbons, as a means of collecting money.

The rarest of the mumming plays is the sword dance play of the North East, *'at the end of which all the dancers plaited their swords in a "Lock" round the victim's neck, and then, when the swords were withdrawn sharply, the death occurred'*, Alex Helm wrote. Kightly described how none of the dancers owns up to the killing – they each say *'"I'm sure it's none of I, that did this bloody act/It's he that follows me, that did it, for a fact".'* The victim eventually is brought to life by a Doctor.

The actors in mumming plays are known by different names in different parts of the country: Tipteerers in

Sussex/Surrey; Seven Champions in Kent; Soulers/Soulcakers in Cheshire; Guisers and Plough Jags in Lincolnshire; Jollyboys in Cumberland; Tosspotters in parts of Lancashire, North of the Sands; Pace-Eggers in Lancashire and parts of Yorkshire and Cheshire; Paper Boys in Marshfield, Gloucestershire.

Mummers' plays can be performed anywhere. There is no stage and few props, except for some swords or clubs and the Doctor's bag, containing hammers and saws and a bottle with magical contents. The cast usually forms a line, and the 'enterer in' introduces the players, who step forward to deliver their lines (rhymed couplets delivered in a dead-pan way) and step back again. There is little action, apart from the sword fight or combat.

Most of the characters in mumming plays are in disguise – it was easier to collect money if they were not recognised. In the Pace-Egg plays of Midgley, west Yorkshire most of the cast wore *'a red smock covered with rosettes . . . and an elaborate hat with a floral decoration'*, Eddie Cass writes. In Lancaster in the 1920s strips of wallpaper were attached to the Pace-Eggers' clothes (Storeys of Lancaster was one of the town's biggest firms). In other places coloured rags were used. Alternatively Pace-Eggers turned their coats inside out and blackened their faces with soot and grease; it was later that performers started to dress in character.

The simple line *'Give us your money and let us away'* belies the deep impression left by these direct performances.

See also ABBOTS BROMLEY HORN DANCE, BEATING THE BOUNDS, CHINESE NEW YEAR, DRAGONS, EASTER CUSTOMS, FAIRS & FAIRGROUNDS, FOLKTALES, GIANTS, JACK AND JILL, MAY DAY, MORRIS DANCING, 'OBBY 'OSSES, SAINTS, SWORD DANCING.

291

M U S E U M S

With antecedents in religious reliquaries and the rich man's cabinet of curiosities, the nation's leading museums garner valuable objects from almost anywhere. A treasured few, however, celebrate the riches of their locality – from jet in Whitby, Yorkshire to ceramics in Staffordshire, fishermen in Hastings, Sussex to lifeboatmen in Cromer, Norfolk. The museum in the village of Southwold on the Suffolk coast displays interesting things washed in by the tide alongside sprigs of wildflowers collected in season, while the writers' gallery in Dorset's county museum in Dorchester reveres the pens and paper that captured the words of Thomas Hardy, Sylvia Townsend Warner and the Powys brothers.

Local industries inspire specialist museums: shoes in Street, Somerset; coal mining in Salford, Lancashire; pencils in Keswick, Cumberland; mustard in Norwich; lawnmowers in Southport, Lancashire; beer in Burton upon Trent, Staffordshire; and colour in Bradford, Yorkshire, in an old wool warehouse that is now the headquarters of the

Marshfield Paper Boy, Gloucestershire.

Society of Dyers and Colourists. At Singleton in Sussex the Weald and Downland Open Air Museum rescues vernacular buildings and has built a glorious new one out of local materials. At Tring in Hertfordshire Walter Rothschild's natural history collection – with four thousand specimens on show, including stuffed pedigree dogs – bravely retains its Victorian character in an age of electronic images.

Industrial monuments dot the countryside, from the Ironbridge in Shropshire to Arkwright's water-powered cotton-spinning mill in Derbyshire. Local heroes are remembered, too: Mary Anning, Grace Darling, the Venerable Bede, Beatrix Potter and the Viking invaders are commemorated in museums in Lyme Regis in Dorset, Bamburgh in Northumberland, Jarrow in County Durham, Ambleside in Westmorland and York.

See also ABBEYS, AMMONITES, BATTLEFIELDS, BEACHES, BESTIARY, CASTLES, CATHEDRALS, CHURCHES, DOGS, LAWN, LIGHTHOUSES, MONUMENTS, OAST-HOUSES & KELLS, QUARRIES.

M U S I C

The landscape must take some credit for the emotional shape of our music, even at a remove, where it has shaped the culture in which music is made, in church, court or inn, concert or village hall, on the sea or in the fields. Victorian and Edwardian composers inspired by Cecil Sharp's researches loved folk song, but wanted to make it 'respectable'. Others drew the genius from places through their art and experiences rather than borrowing with an improver's zeal: Ralph Vaughan Williams in the Fens and Norfolk, John Ireland on the South Downs, Edward Elgar around the Malvern Hills, Benjamin Britten on the East Anglian coast, specifically Aldeburgh, Suffolk. Peter Maxwell Davies says that as a young man he heard the music he would write while walking in the Lakeland hills.

Music has come from around the world in diverse forms to settle on our festivities and localities. Songs connected with celebrations are not always from or about the place in question, but loyalty to them is strong and their power in helping to create spectacle is unquestioned. Our oldest ballads developed from Scandinavian traditions. The 'Hobby Horse Song' from Minehead's May Day celebrations in Somerset is an old tune variously known as 'Soldier's Joy', 'French Four' or 'King's Head'. 'On Ilkley Moor Baht 'at' puts Yorkshire words to a Kentish hymn tune. Old songs permeate celebrations, from the Haxey Hood Game in Lincolnshire to plough plays, each making them their own: 'Drink England Dry', 'John Barleycorn', 'Farmer's Boy'.

Often money, beer or apples are requested: Pace-Eggers and Cheshire Soulcakers *'hope you'll prove kind'*. Padstow's May Day celebrations in Cornwall begin with the 'Night Song', exhorting people to *'Rise up'* and *'Unite'* (a similar

Day Song continues the theme). The Furry Dance from Helston, Cornwall is not written down but passed on (don't mistake it for the wrongly sourced and mis-named 'Floral Dance' of 1948). Abbots Bromley's 'Horn Dance' is known after Wheelwright Robinson, the only resident of this Staffordshire village who could remember it in 1857. Morris has regional differences: Cotswold embraces both ancient tunes ('Trunkles') and music-hall ('Old Black Joe'); in the North West contemporary pop tunes might join their Victorian precursors as long as they adhere to the correct dance time.

Music might reflect the latent patterns of composers' native languages. The sound and register of the smallpipes prompts Northumberland's songs. Families for whom there is still an oral (and aural) tradition of music-making, such as the Coppers of Sussex, help to preserve the authenticity of songs sung about a place in that place. During the twentieth century, with its vast social changes, folk music persisted less in pubs and clubs and became the stuff of preservation societies, enthusiasts' groups and the concert platform.

Folk music went to America with early settlers, coming back transformed into country and western or mingled with black music as blues, then rock and pop. We reclaimed it for our own places, whether the Beatles' Liverpool or the Kinks' Waterloo. New-wave bands sang about real lives and places, from London to Liverpool, Swindon, Sheffield, Bristol and Manchester ('Madchester' in the early 1990s). Jamaican rhythms boomed out of Brixton, London. On returning with a new language, music high and low is increasingly at peace with itself. Billy Bragg is as comfortable singing of the A13 as Chuck Berry might be singing about Route 66.

See also BANDSTANDS, BELLS & BELL-RINGING, BRASS BANDS, BRITANNIA COCO-NUT DANCERS, CARNIVALS, CAROLS, CHURCHES, DIWALI, FIELDS, GROVELY RIGHTS DAY, INNS, MAYPOLES, MELAS, MORRIS DANCING, MUMMING PLAYS, NORTHUMBRIAN SMALLPIPES, NOTTING HILL CARNIVAL, 'OBBY 'OSSES, PUBS, VILLAGE HALLS, WASSAILING.

Nina Bold/Bold Italic, Matthew Carter, 2000.

NATTERJACK TOADS

The natterjack toad is the rarest of our amphibians, partly because of its exacting living demands, and we have not made its life easy. It is a creature of sand-dunes and sandy heaths, requiring temporary, seasonally flooded, shallow, unshaded pools in which to spawn, short turf in which to forage and sand to burrow in for hibernation. It spawns later than the common toad and frog, usually in April to June, when the pools have had a chance to warm up, and because of the danger of the pools drying out, the tadpoles develop more quickly than their amphibian cousins.

Night-time social croaking of the males is for the benefit of females at the spawning ponds in spring and can be heard a mile away on warm, still nights. On the Sefton coast, between the estuaries of the Ribble and the Mersey in Lancashire, the largest sand-dune system in England contains the greatest number of natterjack toads. They have probably lived here for nine and a half thousand years, which demands some respect. In 1838 they were noted as being 'in great abundance' in the dune systems around Ainsdale, where their vernacular names are Southport nightingale and Bootle organ. On the Surrey heathlands they were called the Thursley thrush. Other local names include Goldenbacks in Surrey, after their yellow stripe, Running Toad and Walking Toad in East Anglia, because of their running gait, and natterjack 'nadder' in Lincolnshire, from the Old English, meaning 'to crawl'.

The natterjack toad was locally abundant on the heathlands of Surrey, East Anglia, Dorset and Hampshire and the dune systems of the Lancashire, Lincolnshire and other sandy coasts before twentieth-century incursions. Now only isolated populations remain and, to help its survival, English Nature is translocating toads to suitable habitats.

See also COASTS, DAWN CHORUS, GOLF-COURSES, HEATHLAND, LINKS, PONDS, SAND-DUNES.

NEW FOREST PONIES

Wild horses were described in the area of the New Forest long before King William created his hunting lands after 1066. Surviving over the centuries, the current breed was much modified, to its detriment, at the end of the nineteenth century. The ponies are owned by commoners and still roam the sandy land, grazing the forest lawns and roadsides among heather and woodland. They are of strong constitution and show little shyness to people and vehicles, the forest being well inhabited and criss-crossed by roads – the ponies always have right of way. They tend to be gentle and sure-footed and are mainly brown or bay (although most colours are accepted, except black and white, cream or brown and white).

Four to six Agisters oversee the welfare of the ponies; they are employed by the Court of Verderers, which helps to manage the New Forest. The Court said in its 2001 report: '*Britain needs to ensure that the prime points of the feral breeds are retained, including their ability to thrive throughout the year in the area of their origin. The genetic reservoir contained within the New Forest, Exmoor, Dartmoor is as important to conserve as the historic landscape and buildings [that] enjoy national protection.*'

The New Forest pony is part of the ecology of the forest; it has evolved to do well with little. This fact has often been misunderstood. In 1765 and 1852 Arab stallions were offered to 'improve' the stock for the benefit of the commoners. Generally it was about satisfying aesthetic prejudices and it served to soften the palates of the ponies, which no longer browsed on gorse, a real staple in times of drought.

Ponies learn to stay in a particular area, called their 'haunt' (for Dartmoor ponies, the equivalent is 'leer'). 'Drifts' take place from August to October, when the feral ponies are rounded up and driven into pounds, where they are tail-marked to show the area of the forest they graze, branded, wormed and catalogued. Foals are parted from their mothers.

The annual breed and stallion show is held at the end of August near Brockenhurst, where a special sale yard at Beaulieu Road was rebuilt in 2002 with local timber fences, earth-floor holding pens and chopped heather to line the show ring. It deals with one thousand ponies in a year. The aspiration is to raise better animals in greater sympathy with their surroundings, building their reputation through a new regime of focused management and fewer, younger stallions.

For visitors to the New Forest there is an ancient frisson when one encounters ponies in deep woodland, on a sunlit lawn or asserting their right to languidly amble across road and along street.

See also CATTLE, THE CHANNEL, DOWNLAND, EXMOOR PONIES, FELL PONIES, FELLS, FERAL ANIMALS, GALLOPS, GORSE, HORSE FAIRS, HORSES & PONIES, HOUNDS, LAWN, LONDON TAXIS, MOORLAND, PIGS, POINT TO POINT, POULTRY, RACECOURSES, ROYAL FORESTS, SHEEP, SHIRE HORSES, SUFFOLK PUNCHES, WHITE HORSES.

295

NEW MILESTONES

Public art used to be the province of wealthy individuals, large companies or agencies. 'Men on plinths' were put in 'spaces' or 'sites', not places, for 'the public', not people – abstractions that allow arrogance in commissioner and artist. The New Milestones project was a pioneering venture by Common Ground to encourage local people to commission sculptors to celebrate their place.

Several sculptures in Dorset and north Yorkshire are the result of the pilot phase of the mid-1980s. The young sculptors who participated shared Common Ground's philosophy of wanting to release art from the gallery into the wild, to make work that has local significance and adds a new layer of meaning to places. They were willing to spend time with people, to try to crystallise their feelings about their surroundings. Works were commissioned by landowners, parish councils, farmers, local organisations and city tenants groups. And the experiment stimulated others to do it for themselves.

Sculptors have left significant works for local people and visitors to come across and reflect upon. In Dorset Peter Randall-Page's three 'Wayside Carvings' were positioned on a footpath set back from the coast as part of the Weld estate's desire to encourage people to walk to places beyond Lulworth Cove and Durdle Door. Peter made *something which would strike up a resonance with the surrounding landscape by making a distillation of certain aspects of it. This area of the Dorset coast is famous for its abundance of fossils – in fact the chalk cliffs beneath this downland are literally made up of tiny fossils and the nearby Purbeck limestone comprises the fossilised remains of the gastropods, bivalves and ammonites etc which once lived in an ancient sea. I liked the idea of making a kind of tribute to the ancient lives that now constitute our terra firma. I also wanted to incorporate something of the rhythms of the hills into the work – sweeping in broad, rounded curves, tightening and plunging into deep gullies.'* His 'three snails', carved from Purbeck marble, itself full of fossils, are set into drystone-walled niches about 150 feet apart. Like wayside shrines, they are dug into the field bank that runs along the footpath; they look as if they have always been there.

The most ambitious commission was on the Isle of Portland, a source of building stone for centuries. One of its settlements, Chiswell, decided to celebrate its safety from flooding following the completion of a multi-million-pound sea defence scheme. The Chesil Gallery and Portland town council decided to celebrate their renaissance with sculpture. John Maine was chosen and, following many discussions, he started work on a small triangle of sloping and slipping land at the point where the twenty-mile Chesil Beach reaches the island. It was criss-crossed by paths and used as a dumping ground, but John saw its potential, which the borough engineer welcomed as a way of stopping landslips.

The sculpture, 'Chiswell Earthworks', comprises five terraces, flowing waves undulating like the sea and making reference to the strip lynchets – stepped field systems – of Dorset. They are held back by drystone

'Chiswell Earthworks', Isle of Portland, Dorset.

walls representing the different Portland Beds in stratigraphical turn, each worked in their traditional ways. The lines of the footpaths have been respected, the walls dipping or stepping to let them through. The sculpture is a monument to geology and to the masons, a powerful exposition of cultural intimacy with the land. It has taken many years to complete and called upon the help of many, especially the indefatigable Margaret Somerville, owner of the Chesil Gallery, who managed to fight off predatory beach hut owners encroaching onto common land.

In Yorkshire, Cleveland Arts, with Steve Chettle and Skelton and Brotton parish council, commissioned Richard Farrington, who worked from British Steel's Skinningrove Works. In discussion with local people, three works evolved, all placed on the three-hundred-foot-high Huntcliff near Warsett Hill on the Cleveland Way. The 'Charm Bracelet', or 'Huntcliff Circle', frames the magnificent sea view. Hanging from a large steel circle are metal 'charms' of local significance: star, cat, pigeon, thunder god's hammer, egg pod of skate, belemnite, ring and a horse – the Cleveland Bay.

As Richard Cork said, *'we must never allow this process to happen indiscriminately. If the widespread dissemination of art beyond the gallery is initiated without any genuine awareness of the places involved, then the whole enterprise will be irretrievably betrayed by a flood of inferior work.'* Public art was emerging, bringing us inventive, important works associated with regeneration schemes. And, in parallel, the aspirations of the New Milestones project to stimulate high-quality, small-scale works of the imagination, commissioned and informed by local people, has asserted that localities have meaning to us and should demand our involvement.

See also COMMONS, DRYSTONE WALLS, JACK AND JILL, LYNCHETS, MONUMENTS, ORCHARDS, SCULPTURES, SHEEP-FOLDS.

N I C K N A M E S

There is a difference between Men of Kent and Kentish Men. It is the river Medway that divides them, as well as a history of resistance to William back in the eleventh century. Men of Kent, the westerners, still chide the Kentish Men, born to the east, for being less than brave. The shadows of difference may reach back further to the settling of the area by the Jutes, who created East and West Centingas. Until 1814 the two areas continued to be administered from Maidstone and Canterbury respectively.

That Cockneys are supposed to be born within the sound of Bow Bells is first mentioned in a dictionary of 1617; there are explanations linking the word with Cockaigne, that fabulous place. But it may come from the wider sixteenth-century use of the word 'cockney', meaning a townie or 'soft' city dweller.

Geordies also get called toonies by their country cousins. Geordy is a diminutive for George. Locals say this name was given to the people of Newcastle when they remained loyal to George II in 1745 against the Jacobites. Others point to the preference the local colliers had for the George Stephenson over the (Humphry) Davy lamp for use down the mine (Stephenson had invented it while working at Killingworth Colliery around 1815). Both pit men and collier boats carried this name along the Tyne. As pits closed inland in County Durham, men seeking work at Easington Colliery in the 1970s and 1980s were called woolly backs; the men from sheep country called their seaside counterparts cod heeds (fish heads).

Epithets can be very local. Even within the archipelago, Scillonians call the men from St Martin's ginnicks; St Agnes folk are called turks; Tresco, caterpillars; Bryher, thorns; St Mary's, bulldogs. They all hate reference to the Scilly Isles as opposed to the Isles of Scilly. In Northumberland people from Beadnell proudly say *'she's Beadlin'*, meaning 'she belongs here' while perpetuating the old name for the place.

Linda Briggs, visiting an aunt in a village in Leicestershire forty years ago, remembers being told *'you can't be a real Hemington pigtail until you've fallen in the brook'*. This recalls the possibility of becoming accepted in Market Lavington, Wiltshire if you fell in Broad well. Likewise, you can become an Aldbourne dabchick by taking a ritual ducking in the pond. Otherwise only a native of this Wiltshire village can be called a dabchick. The story goes that when an unidentified bird landed on the pond, the oldest resident was wheeled in a barrow three times around it before declaring that the bird was a dabchick. To the people of Ramsbury, just down the road, it is one of the most ordinary water birds. Teasing stories to make neighbours seem less than clever are common.

But stories fashioned to give those on the outside a sense that they are dealing with simpletons are often countered from the inside by the clever 'true' tale. Wiltshire folk carry the title of Moonrakers (first recorded 1787). Surprised by customs men on a clear, bright night while attempting to rake in brandy barrels secreted in the village pond, the locals explained how they were trying to catch the moon (or was it cheese?). The officials moved quickly on . . .

Stephen Pewsey offers the following examples of *blason populaire*: Bedfordshire bulldog, Cambridgeshire crane, Essex calf, Hampshire hog, Norfolk dumpling, Surrey capon, Yorkshire tyke, *'as well as more local terms, like Fen tigers and pork-bolters (people from Worthing)'*. But where did these jocular handles come from?

Islanders have easy claim to particular identity. Caulkheads born on the Isle of Wight distinguish

297

themselves from overners from the mainland. Portland lost its island status in 1839 with the completion of the bridge to mainland Dorset, but the identity and introspection of its people is still evident, although they no longer throw stones at kimberlins (unwelcome strangers).

See also CUCKOOS & CUCKOO POUNDS, FAMILY NAMES, FOLKTALES, FOOTBALL, GOLF-COURSES, ISLANDS, JACK AND JILL, KENNELS, MOON.

NOBBIES

Nobbies are found working the tidal waters from the Dee to the Solway Firth. They are carvel-built, of shallow draught, with a sharp bow adapted for negotiating shifting sands under sail or motor. The Morecambe Bay nobby was used for trawling for shrimp, although it is often called a prawner; it has a deck, open cockpit and often carried a stove, for boiling the catch while still fishing. Elegant under sail, it has been the inspiration for popular yacht designs; it now earns its keep as much from tourist trips as from shrimping.

See also BEACHES, BOATS, COBLES, CORNISH GIGS, FLATNERS, NORFOLK WHERRIES, PIERS, PORTLAND LERRETS, SEA FISH, SEA TRACTOR, SHELLFISH, THAMES SAILING BARGES, TIDES.

298

NOMANSLAND

Nomansland appears as a settlement name in Wiltshire, Hertfordshire and Devon, and, as a more intimate place-name, describes land on the edge of a parish, often common land.

No Man's Heath lies at the junction of the counties of Derbyshire, Leicestershire, Staffordshire and Warwickshire. Between north Yorkshire and County Durham, above Arkengarthdale, one area was sufficiently contested to be called The Disputes. No Man's is a community orchard purchased in the 1990s by the neighbouring parishes of Chartham Hatch and Harbledown in Kent. Each year on Apple Day they hold a tug-of-war across the parish boundary, proving that a boundary need not be a frontier.

See also BOUNDARIES, COMMONS, ORCHARDS.

NORFOLK WHERRIES

Wherries were found in the Tyne and the Thames (the goozieboat, for example, worked from Gravesend in Kent). Their size was dictated by the bridges, their shape by the nature of the work in hand, tempered by the personality of the watercourses. In their heyday, in the nineteenth century, both under sail and powered by steam, great numbers moved grain, coal, cement, chalk/marl, timber, tiles, bricks, iron and probably a fair amount of illegitimate cargo, too.

But the boat is native to the Norfolk Broads, its rivers and cuts. Oak and clinker-built, it is a wide, shallow-draughted boat with a keel. Big Norfolk wherries worked the lower river systems, such as the Yare, under a single gaff sail, originally black. Smaller, twenty-five-foot boats could extend their reach by lowering their masts to shoot the bridges and slipping their keels to sail well up-river.

Norfolk wherries no longer carry freight, but, modified with white sails, they still work as pleasure boats, giving tourists a view of life on the water and East Anglia a considerable income.

On their retirement, boats were often sunk to strengthen riverbanks, but these days interest is such that, among others, *Maud* has been raised from Ranworth Broad, where she had held up the banks for twenty years. After restoration she is once more cruising the waterways that she had worked since 1899. *Albion* is available to charter as the single surviving trading wherry carrying a black sail.

See also ALBION, BOATS, BROADS, COBLES, CORNISH GIGS, FLATNERS, NOBBIES, PORTLAND LERRETS, THAMES SAILING BARGES, WINDMILLS.

N O R T H

What does North mean? For many there are negative connotations of winter, cold, dark and far away. Even Tony Harrison asked himself:

> *God knows why of all the rooms I'd choose*
> *The dark one facing North for me to write,*
> *Liking as I do air, light and views,*
> *Though there's air in the North wind that rocks the light*

From 'Facing North'

It seems harder to travel with the pull of gravity against you, since north is upwards, the North point conventionally towards the top of the map. True North will take you straight along an imaginary line of longitude to the geographic North Pole, but Magnetic North (where the geomagnetic field pulls vertically into the earth) wanders and is already out of date by the time you buy your Ordnance Survey map. It was the Chinese who gave us navigation by the compass with the discovery that the rock we call magnetite would transfer its magic to a needle rubbed against it. The needle, pushed through cork and left to float on water, would always home to the north. On a clear night it was easier to set course out of sight of land by Polaris, the star that moves but sparingly above the North Pole, its constancy proving a true beacon.

While birds on migration do use visual and other physical cues, it is known that many of them also use the earth's magnetic field to head polewards and equatorwards. And, as winters fade in coldness, and plants, too, begin to migrate towards the pole, what then of the vestiges of our bluebell woods? This raises the question of where the north begins. The awesome visits of the aurora borealis playing in the night sky are a truly northern phenomenon, or are they? The homeland of the Northern Lights is sixty to seventy degrees north (Shetlands to Norway), occasionally dipping to the south: but in October 2003 people around Bristol were treated to a small display.

Compelled by an Irish sensibility, Louis MacNeice suggested '*The North begins inside*' and in the English context it is culturally hard to deny the power of that statement. You know if you are

from The North, even if people from further north would cast you as a southerner.

The stereotypes remain true – many people of the South have no idea of what lies beyond Watford (or the Watford Gap, as in common parlance it seems to have gravitated further up the M1). But they are cynically disposed towards 'it', perhaps a little afraid that in the wilds there may be dragons as well as short 'a's. Home of the north wind is where the sagas come from, although it is in the words more than the stories that the Old Norse stays with us. For the Danelaw does persist in the everyday, a north–south divide built on long cultural as well as physical differences. It is resident in people and how they speak: as Melvyn Bragg says, '*it is that Nordic element, always building on Old English but in the north clawing deep into the language, which lies at the core of the fundamental separation – so often noted – between north and south*'. Language and dialect, as well as accents, prove hard for southerners to understand.

But there is more. The north is associated with the devil. On the north side of the church you may find an undersized door; this was opened to let the devil out at times of communion and baptism. Poor people and suicides were buried on the dangerous north side of the churchyard. Ancient peoples facing the rising sun – *oriens* – at daybreak would have the north to their left hand, the sinister side.

Easy, then, for demonising. '*It was a town of machinery and tall chimneys, out of which interminable serpents of smoke trailed themselves for ever and ever, and never got uncoiled. It had a black canal in it, and a river that ran purple with ill-smelling dye, and vast piles of buildings full of windows where there was a rattling and a trembling all day long . . . It contained several large streets all very like one another, and many small streets still more like one another.*' Charles Dickens, writing of his fictional Coketown in *Hard Times* (1854), seems to derive much from the factual work of Friedrich Engels in Manchester in 1844. Engels's observations in *The Condition of the Working Class in England* could, to our shame, still be applied to places in most of our cities anywhere in the country now. But somehow the North has been saddled with a reputation based upon mining, heavy industry and mills, which has left its melanistic mark on the southern mind. This is the same North that connected water and coal and iron, that invented so many industrial processes and machines, which innovated, bringing together the steam

299

Alconbury, Cambridgeshire.

engine, the flanged wheel and the railway. It had the whole bag of tricks that drove the Industrial Revolution, including entrepreneurial and adventuring skills.

Despite one's experience of proud and self-knowing northerners, polls still show self-esteem lower the further north you go, with the exception of Yorkshire, where county identity is strong. It stands in opposition to The South, but the latter does not measure itself against the other. '*The North [is] where England tucks its shirt in its underpants. It's not all to do with Peter Snow's election map being mainly blue at the bottom and completely red at the top, although that comes into it*' – Simon Armitage began his own long, yet partial, list of the complications of Yorkshire.

The North is much bigger than that. It has the mountains, it has the wild places, the Venerable Bede, *Adam Bede*, *Wuthering Heights*, *Women in Love*, *Saturday Night and Sunday Morning*, *The Road to Wigan Pier*, *Room at the Top*, *Get Carter*, *Kes*, *Billy Elliot*, *Z Cars*, *Coronation Street*, *Our Friends in the North*, daffodils and steel ships, pigeon lofts and chrysanthemums, pit tips and tight communities, mining banners and poetic women, big industry in decline and football in the blood, more drama in the landscape, more directness in the people, more warmth in the welcome, more cold in the hills, moors and mushy peas, comedians and fishing, steel and songs.

300

See also ACCENTS, BLUEBELLS, CHURCHES, CHURCHYARDS, DIALECTS, EAST, FILM LOCATIONS, FOOTBRIDGES, INDUSTRIAL CHIMNEYS, LIMESTONE, MILLSTONE GRIT, MINES, PIT TIPS, SHIPPING FORECAST, WEATHER-VANES.

NORTHUMBRIAN SMALLPIPES

Northumbrian smallpipes are one of our few indigenous instruments, with a history of more than eight hundred years. Smaller and quieter than Scottish bagpipes, small-

pipes are not blown; instead, leather bellows worked under the arm feed the air bag. The melody is controlled by fingers over the holes of the chanter, a pipe connected to the bag. More pipes – drones – provide sonorous harmony. The resulting sound is mellow and intimate, but can step lively when combined with a fiddle. Rooted in hill farms and the shepherd's lonely craft, the pipes were embraced as a sign of an eroding cultural identity during the nineteenth-century industrialisation of Tyneside. In wartime they were used to inspire pride in North-Eastern regiments.

The melodies are often born of Northumberland's wild countryside. Great twentieth-century players, such as Billy Pigg, whose talents are preserved on numerous amateur recordings from the 1960s, composed hornpipes and airs named for Biddlestone and Billsmoor, Wallington, Tosson and Hindhope, adding to the lineage of folk tunes. There are Scottish as well as Irish influences (from immigrant workers), sometimes traditional songs being renamed for Northumberland: the Scottish jig 'Kenmure's Up and Awa'' became 'Hexham Races'.

Alistair Anderson and Folkworks have been at the heart of a working revival of interest in the playing of the small-pipes, the concertina and the traditional music of the North East among young people. The revival is provoking new forms and, although the passing of knowledge through the family has atrophied, the skills and songs are alive and well and developing through international exchange and even degree courses. Pipers and pipe bands are an important part of local festivities, such as the annual Northumbrian Gathering at Morpeth, where the Northumbrian Pipers' Society still meets regularly at the Chantry Pipe Museum. In 2004 Peter Maxwell Davies worked with celebrated piper Kathryn Tickell on a composition for Gateshead's new concert hall, the Sage.

See also AGRICULTURAL SHOWS, FOLKTALES, HILLS, MUSIC, ROCKS.

NOTTING HILL CARNIVAL

Given impetus by early Trinidadian immigrants, the Notting Hill Carnival now parades not only the rich range of Afro-Caribbean cultures but also players and masqueraders from Bangladesh and Brazil, Afghanistan and the Philippines, in the heart of north Kensington, London. They were building on a festival born of the Christian calendar, exported from France by slave owners to the Caribbean, liberated by African slaves and enriched by indentured labourers from India. Mingling and travelling has fomented enthusiasms and a strong identity.

Slavery allowed no exuberance, save for the moment before Lent, when slaves were allowed to entertain their masters with music and costume. With slavery legally renounced in 1833/4, carnival began to be claimed for

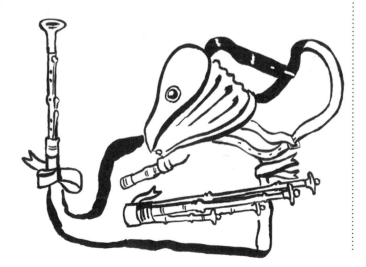

black celebration and satire, a simple demonstration of liberty and complex parody of slave owners, a symbolic and dignified show of freedom. Arriving in Britain after the Second World War, many having fought in it, new black Britons were shocked at the hostile environment – the place was literally much colder and the people less than welcoming. North Kensington was one of the few places in London to head for – it was here that Rachman made his money renting slum properties when no one else would rent to black people. In 1958 violence in Nottingham was followed by ugly scenes in Notting Hill; both places became synonymous with race riots inflamed by 'keep Britain white' groups.

So below the newly built Westway flyover around Golborne Road and Ladbroke Grove, a community struggled to find itself. In 1965 a politically astute, peripatetic West Indian Carnival, first held at St Pancras Town Hall in 1959 to build identity and belonging through culture, collided with a simple festival for the poor, ethnically diverse communities of Notting Hill, from English and Irish to Ukrainian, West Indian and African-born people.

Part of its role was to enable communities to demonstrate to their new neighbours and one another the richness of the variegated cultures, and to encourage groups from the different islands towards some solidarity through working together. It evolved into wire-work costumes and lorries carrying steel-pan bands, which would musically war with each other at the junctions along Portobello Road in the 1970s, later amplified through big sound systems. By 2005 many of the shops and restaurants are sensibly boarded up for the weekend, residents flee and the explosion of colours and sounds draws perhaps two million participants over the two days of the August Bank Holiday to watch, listen, dance, drink, eat and party. Second only in size to Rio's Mardi Gras, which keeps its pre-Lent timing, this is a phenomenon and an institution.

Carnival prefaces the time of no meat in the Christian calendar, a moment to 'use up' and celebrate before fasting for forty days. Many of England's carnivals have moved from Lent to the summer or autumn and most now simply celebrate, but Notting Hill also presents food in style. You may find yourself eating roasted corn husks, souse, peas and rice or jerk – chicken and pork run through with hot spices, a dish Jamaicans derived from native Carib-Arawak people.

The action centres on music and masquerade. Still part of Venetian Mardi Gras, in Notting Hill masquerade has evolved into mas – creative costumes with great structures of wire work, aluminium, cane or fibreglass. The mas bands, some up to five hundred strong, may use biblical themes, legend, fairytale or recent politics.

The costumes – the Kings and Queens being the most flamboyant – can reach fifteen feet tall, using carbon fishing rods to extend wings or giant ruffs of light, dyed or painted material, perhaps with plumes, mirrors and sequins. They are designed to sway with the rhythm of 'chipping', the dance step of carnival. Competition is still part of the parade, but now there are judges to decide on prize winners.

Added to this is static and moving music – Steelband (the instruments originally tempered from oil drums), Calypso (extemporised satirical ballads to syncopated music, which emerged in Trinidad and Tobago with echoes of the call and response of Dahomey work songs) and Soca (a fusion of soul and calypso produced out of Carnival itself). The excitement of high decibels, multiple rhythms, new choreography, fast-evolving black music and huge, bright and fantastic costumes has taken to the streets in St Paul's in Bristol, Preston, Manchester, Coventry, Birmingham, Nottingham and Leeds, too.

The active participants are the repository of authenticity, from the Trinidad and Tobago Carnival Club to the Paraiso Samba School. Two days' celebration means 363 days of focus, design, hard work and enjoyment, especially in June and July, with events and parties.

See also BEATING THE BOUNDS, BONFIRE NIGHT, CARNIVALS, MELAS, PANCAKE DAY.

N U R S E R I E S

The English excel at breeding plants as well as animals, and horticulture has a long, proud history. By 1533 Henry VIII's fruiterer, Richard Harris, was cultivating apple, cherry and

301

other fruit trees he had brought back from Europe, and in the 1680s the Brompton Park Nurseries was supplying big estates with trees for their expanding avenues.

Outside Devon County Hall in Exeter stands the Lucombe Oak, an evergreen oak first grown by William Lucombe at his nursery in St Thomas, Exeter from the 1720s. He was one of the first nurserymen to bring back plants from abroad, a precedent followed nearby by John Veitch and his son, who sent collectors to the Americas, Malaysia and Indonesia to find plants, such as orchids, berberis, escallonia, rhododendron and the seeds of Wellingtonia. The vast array of plants we find in our gardens today can mostly be traced back to these Victorian plantsmen.

The most prominent Victorian horticulturalist was Thomas Laxton (1830-93). A friend of Charles Darwin and follower of Thomas Andrew Knight, he was passionate about cross-breeding garden plants, as well as fruit and vegetables. In establishing his experimental nurseries near Bedford and Sandy in Bedfordshire in 1858, he pioneered selection and cross-breeding to improve commercial plants, keeping a meticulous diary for forty years.

His early work on peas brought huge advances and was followed by strawberries, where he made his greatest success, producing Traveller and Royal Sovereign, still considered by some to be the best-tasting variety ever grown. Potatoes, runner beans and cucumbers were all worked on, as well as the Laxton's No. 1 red currant, Laxton's Giant black currant and the Charles Darwin rose. His descendants were to add some remarkable apples between 1904 and 1921 – Laxton's Fortune, Laxton's Superb and Lord Lambourne. Laxton's seed merchants opened at 63 High Street, Bedford and traded until 1957. Park Wood Community Orchard at Black Hill Drive, Bedford contains many Laxton varieties, the nearest thing to a memorial. Laxton's land at Goldington Road was sold and built on.

Thomas Rivers and family of Sawbridgeworth in Hertfordshire bred some of the finest top fruit from the 1820s, such as Early Rivers, Late Transparent, Czar, Monarch and President plums and Conference pear – the latter our most popular garden pear variety of the twentieth century. The nursery was run by the Rivers family for 250 years until it closed in 1985. Much of the land was bought for the construction of the Thomas Rivers medical centre, a private hospital, and retirement homes. The remaining orchard of apples, cherries and plums has been restored by the Friends of Rivers Orchard.

Now plant breeding, including the old national research stations, has been taken over by commerce; new varieties are even branded and marketed with multi-million-pound promotions. Despite the proliferation of garden centres some true nurseries survive, where horticultural knowledge resides, but we have been slow in recognising the huge contribution that nurserymen and -women have made; their nurseries could be shrines on the gardeners' pilgrimage routes.

See also APPLES, GOOSEBERRIES, MARKET GARDENS, MONKEY-PUZZLE, OAK, ORCHARDS, PEARS, PLUMS, STRAWBERRIES.

Olympian Bold/Italic, Matthew Carter, 1970.

O

O   A   K

Those green-rob'd senators of mighty woods,
Tall oaks, branch-charmed by the earnest stars,
Dream, and so dream all night without a stir

John Keats, from *Hyperion*

We have an uncommon affection for old oaks. Our culture has held them in esteem for so long that we have forgotten why. But, as Peter Ackroyd writes, '*Oaks mean something to us and somehow the old oak stands for England.*'

Oaks are among our longest-lived trees. Pollarded, like most of the oaks in Old Windsor Forest (where they are known as dodders), their life span can be more than doubled to perhaps a thousand years – through just a handful of generations they link us to the time when plants were returning after the Ice Age. Our oldest oaks are considered to be the most important individual oaks of the species *Quercus robur* (pedunculate) and *Quercus petraea* (sessile) remaining on earth.

The word for oak shared across the Indo-European languages is something like dur – among its meanings are door and strong (durable). Our place-names remember it: Derwent, Darent and Dart all mean 'river abounding in oaks'. By the time we were speaking Old English, we were coining names such as Accrington – 'acorn farm'.

From the earliest times oaks made domestic craft for fishing, coasting and plying the inland waters, later ships for exploring, adventuring, fighting and defending (and slaving and marauding). They made the timber frames of stout houses, tithe barns and great halls. The roof of Westminster Hall dates back to 1399; some of its timbers may have annual rings that tell of rainfall in 1066.

There is evidence of the oak's sacredness to ancient peoples. Seahenge, four thousand years old, discovered in 1998 in the beach at Holme next the Sea, Norfolk, was constructed of a circle of oak timbers with a huge, upturned oak boss at its centre. Oaks fed our animals and provided tannin for treating leather; they stood as boundary markers, Gospel oaks and landmarks, and as symbol in parkland, literature, painting and poem. From the acorn a mighty oak may grow; with the oak, dependability and longevity are assured.

All over England places are immortalised by their famous trees: Bowthorpe Oak near Bourne in Lincolnshire, thought to be a thousand years old; Marton Oak in Cheshire, more than a thousand years old. On Oak Apple Day (29 May) Chelsea Pensioners still wear oak leaves in memory of Charles II's escape from capture by hiding in the Boscobel Oak in Shropshire. The Meavy Oak, though diminished, still commands this Dartmoor village. The top was kept clipped flat and, at festival time, a platform would be installed with tables and chairs for a dance and feast.

The Druids worshipped the spirit of the oak and the mistletoe that grew on it. Sir James Frazer wrote that '*the fuel of the midsummer fires is always oak . . . the month, which takes its name from Jupiter the oak-god, begins on June 10th and ends on July 7th. Midway comes St John's Day, June 24th, the day on which the oak-king was sacrificed and burned alive.*'

305

The Major Oak, Sherwood Forest, Nottinghamshire.

A recurrent theme in ancient tales is of the holly king and the oak king in an endless cycle of life and death.

Other stories play with the emblematic power of the oak. Robin Hood and Herne the Hunter both gain from the association. Old oaks tend to become stag-headed to conserve themselves, like Herne's Oak, described in *The Merry Wives of Windsor*, '*disguis'd, like Herne, with huge horns on his head*'. The lost tree at Yardley Chase in Castle Ashby, Northamptonshire receives tribute in 'Yardley Oak', William Cowper's 1791 poem: '*Time made thee what thou waſt – King of the woods;/And time hath made thee what thou art – a cave/For owls to rooſt in.*'

In stashing and forgetting autumn-picked acorns, it is to the jay that we owe most plantings. Sherwood Forest in Nottinghamshire, the New Forest in Hampshire, Cannock Chase in Staffordshire, the Forest of Dean in Gloucestershire and Savernake Forest in Wiltshire all have expanses of old oaks. In the latter they support more than a hundred epiphytic species; in Sherwood Forest at least a thousand species of beetle and spider and more than two hundred fungi are associated with old oaks. So many caterpillars feed on oak leaves it is amazing that the trees survive.

Both sessile and pedunculate oaks are widely distributed and hybridise. Sessile oaks tend to be found in the uplands of the North and West, and pedunculate oaks '*on base-rich soils in the south and eaſt*', according to Derek Ratcliffe.

Oak dominates our most common and widespread type of woodland. In the Midlands and the South a system of coppicing with standards was praƈtised. The oaks and other timber trees were left to grow tall, while the under-storey of hazel was coppiced in rotations of between seven and 24 years for hurdles and working wood. This let in light and encouraged woodland plants, such as bluebells, dog's mercury, ramsons, daffodils and primroses, to flourish in spring.

But in Wistman's Wood on Dartmoor, fenced off now from browsing animals, the pedunculate oaks are small and contorted. John Fowles captured their richness: '*Their dark branches grow to an extraordinary extent laterally; are endlessly angled, twiſted, raked, interlocked, and reach quite as much downwards as upwards . . . every lateral branch, fork, saddle of these aged dwarfs is densely clothed in other plants – not juſt the tough little polypodies of moſt deciduous woodlands, but large elegantly pluming male ferns; whortleberry beds, grasses, huge cushions of moss and feſtoons of lichen.*'

See also ALBION, ALDER, ANCIENT TREES, ASH, BEECH, BLACK & WHITE BUILDINGS, BLACK DOGS, BLACK POPLAR, BLACKTHORN, BLUEBELLS, CROSSROADS, DAFFODILS, ELM, FERNS, FOLKTALES, GREEN MAN, GROVELY RIGHTS DAY, HAWTHORN, HENGES & STONE CIRCLES, HORNBEAM, HORSE CHESTNUT, LICHENS, LIME, LONDON PLANE, MIDSUMMER DAY, MISTLETOE, MONKEY-PUZZLE, ORCHARDS, PARKLAND, RAMSONS, ROBIN HOOD, ROWAN, ROYAL FORESTS, SCOTS PINE, SWEET CHESTNUT, SYCAMORE, TEMPLES, WALNUT, WILLOW, WOODS, YEW.

OAST-HOUSES & KELLS

Hops are dried in these tall, steeply roofed kilns. Most were built in the 1800s and are of brick. At first they were square, but in the 1830s it was thought that circular kilns were more efficient at distributing and retaining heat. By the 1870s it was found that square ones were equally good. The brick-canopied furnace at ground level slowly dried the hops, which were laid out on horse-hair cloth on a slatted drying floor above. Revolving pointed wooden cowls (in the west Midlands) and flat-topped cowls painted white (in the South East) with horizontal wind vanes drew the air through.

The largest concentrations of oast-houses are in Kent and Sussex, and in Herefordshire and Worcestershire, where they are called kells. Those no longer used for hop culti-vation tend to have been converted into houses. Beltring in Kent had the largest concentration in the world, twenty magnificent oast-houses clustered around two buildings at Whitbread Hop Farm in the 1980s. Incredibly only five remain in what is now the Hop Farm Country Park.

See also BEER, HOPS, HOP-GARDENS & HOP-YARDS, LANDMARKS, MALTINGS.

'OBBY 'OSSES

Hobby-horses, for such is their refined title, could be ancient – they may have arrived with the Anglo-Saxons – but not until the fifteenth century do we find documentary evidence of their presence and aƈtivities. Two main 'breeds' exist: the tourney, or tournament, horse, in which a 'rider', often masked, protrudes above a skirted hoop that disguises not four but two legs; and the simpler mast, or pole, horse, in which a powerful head (sometimes a real horse's skull) sits on a pole with cloth concealing both pole and bearer.

In reviving the Hunting of the Earl of Rone, not performed between 1837 and the 1970s, Combe Martin in Devon has researched its own history and reinvented a powerful celebration. A hobby-horse and its company once more take a turn around the village on Ascension Day (now the first May bank holiday). The cast of charaƈters comprises the Earl of Rone in a mask, with ship's biscuits in a string around his neck; a large hobby-horse with mappers – snapping jaws; a live donkey, also with a biscuit collar; a Fool with a besom; and a troop of grenadier guards (sojers) in red coats with (sort of) muskets.

At eventide five hundred villagers swell the ranks. They are led up to Lady's Wood, where all hunt for the Earl of Rone. Shots are fired, the Earl is caught and ignominiously made to ride the donkey with his face to its tail. Journeying towards the sea, incidents occur – each time volleys are fired, guards are praised, drums are beaten, lamentations take place – and the Fool raises the Earl from wounds or death. As the sun sets the players and the crowd reach the shore and, with a great crescendo, things happen in the sea. In the early nineteenth century '*licence and drunkenness*' then began, which led a rector to have all the costumes burned; the ceremony was suppressed in 1837.

Scraps of history may be intertwined with ancient ritual. In 1607 the Earl of Tyrone, escaping from Ireland after insurrection, was washed ashore, perhaps here or in France. Skimmity riding, being made to ride a donkey backwards to the sound of pans being clashed together, is an old form of rough punishment. In Rome the October horse, drowned each October, wore biscuits to symbolise the end of harvest.

Hobby-horses and other beasts take centre stage in many ancient customs. The horse mask is played out in spring not only in a few corners of England but, as Violet Alford found, in Austria, the Czech Republic, France, Poland, Slovakia and Switzerland.

In Minehead, Somerset there is luck in greeting and paying the hobby-horse that ventures out on May Day. Minehead has even customised the calendar: Warning Eve or Show Night is the local name for 30 April, when the Sailor's Horse first appears. He dances to his own tune in the streets as drum and melodeon are played by the 'sailors', who attend him. Before six o'clock on May morning the Sailor's Horse bows three times to the rising sun, then starts on his way. Chasing children, prancing precariously near the water's edge by the harbour, seeing off the Town Horse with his Gullivers and the Dunster Horse, if they emerge, he seeks donations and sustenance all the way. He does not rest until after 3 May, with visits to nearby Dunster, Periton and Cher Steep and ceremonies at crossroads.

At the same time the equally robust Old Hoss and friends will be busy in Padstow on the north Cornish coast. At midnight all eighteen verses of the 'Night Song' are

sung to rouse particular residents from their beds. All is then quiet until eight in the morning, when two children's 'osses appear and dance for an hour. At ten o'clock on May morning the Blue Ribbon horse emerges. At midday (eleven o'clock British Summer Time) the Old Hoss gets up to celebrate the first day of summer. All day long 'Day Song' alternates with 'Night Song', both of which begin:

Unite and unite and let us all unite,
For summer is acome unto day,
And whither we are going we will all unite,
In the merry morning of May.

Black, light on his feet and bold with the ladies, the Old Hoss dances and rampages. Accompanied by the Teaser and mayers dressed in white, he corners and envelops girls with his skirts to much shrieking. From time to time he dies and is revived. All the while the sound of drums and accordions accompanies the songs, shouts and screams. In neighbouring streets Blue Ribbon goes about his business and, in the evening, they meet at the maypole, which is topped with larch and flowers, to dance before being stabled until the next year.

Padstow claims these traditions have possible connections with ancient Britons and four thousand years of settlement in their place. The Minehead custom may have grown out of beating the bounds, or repelling Viking attacks, or a shipwreck involving a drowned cow – academics and residents muse and disagree.

Hooden horses are particular to east Kent. A carved horse head with a noisy, articulated lower jaw is affixed to a pole hung with hessian, which hides the performer. He is accompanied by a carter, a rider and a betsy (man as woman), who join him in a short play performed for money before Christmas – a time when work was short. After virtually dying out, hoodening had a resurgence in the 1950s. A new white horse, Invicta (after Kent's emblem), appeared and has joined the East Kent Morris Men. More hooden horses have appeared and, in 1998, three appeared together in one play. They can be seen between Whitstable and Folkestone.

The Wild Horse (or Hodening Horse) appears in Cheshire on All Saints' and All Souls' Days at the start of November. In Antrobus he accompanies a souling (St George) play around the pubs with his driver, dressed as huntsman. In Richmond, Yorkshire, T'Owd 'Oss appears on Christmas and New Year's Eves; this tradition is secretly passed on through families. Old Tup (a ram with similar tendencies to the 'obby 'oss) occasionally emerges where Derbyshire, Nottinghamshire and Yorkshire meet.

In Oxfordshire a brand-new gathering is taking root. The Banbury Hobby Horse Festival honours a nursery rhyme and reinforces the identity of the place. At the end of June

307

Banbury welcomes many beasts to its streets to perform and dance, to race, to joust, to be admired. Accounts of the first few years suggest there is a lot of horsing about.

See also ABBOTS BROMLEY HORN DANCE, BEATING THE BOUNDS, BESTIARY, CHINESE NEW YEAR, CROSSROADS, DRAGONS, EASTER CUSTOMS, FOLKTALES, GIANTS, JACK AND JILL, MAY DAY, MORRIS DANCING, MUMMING PLAYS, SAINTS, SWORD DANCING.

OBELISKS

The Greek *obelos* was a cooking spit, and it was the Greeks who named the Egyptian, four-sided, tapering pillar *obeliskos* – little spit. In Egypt their tip, *pyramidion*, was of bronze to catch the sun, emblem of regeneration, first at dawn and last at dusk. The Romans took them to their capital and, more than fifteen hundred years later, the classical pretensions of artists and architects brought their images to England.

The early eighteenth century saw their first use as triumphal monuments. Nicholas Hawksmoor designed the earliest survivor (1702), the focal point of Ripon's Market Place in Yorkshire, made with stone from nearby Studley and topped with a copper horn. Then Sir John Vanbrugh included a ninety-foot-high obelisk in his dramatic Castle Howard development in Yorkshire in 1714, and after that no landscape was complete without one. In Richmond, Yorkshire an impressive obelisk surrounded by low steps

replaced the old market cross in 1771. It stands on a large reservoir that once supplied the town with drinking water.

Obelisks became landscape conceits. 'Mad' Jack Fuller was responsible for a number on his Sussex estate in the early 1800s, as well as the 65-foot-high Needle on Brightling Down. By the nineteenth century obelisks had become common public memorials made of faced brick (although the eighteenth-century iron founder extraordinaire John 'Iron Mad' Wilkinson, perhaps predictably, had an iron one erected at Lindale, Lancashire). Obelisks were used as milestones, at crossroads and as memorials, in polished granite, in Victorian cemeteries.

Georgian and Victorian obelisks had to compete with the 'authentic' item as ancient ones began to be stripped from their original locations and transplanted to English country houses and parks. Philae Needle came to Kingston Lacy, Dorset from Egypt in the 1820s. Jean François Champollion had used it, together with the Rosetta Stone, to solve the mystery of Egyptian hieroglyphs. Cleopatra's Needle started life in Egypt in the fifteenth century BC, but was given to the British in 1819 and finally established on the north bank of the Thames in 1878.

See also BATTLEFIELDS, CEMETERIES, FOLLIES, HILLS, LANDMARKS, MILESTONES, MONUMENTS, PARKLAND, PARKS, SEA-MARKS, STANDING STONES.

OLD MAN'S BEARD

This precise indicator of underlying lime has many names. Traveller's joy is an apt description, for *Clematis vitalba* climbs most happily through hedgerows and along railway embankments, enlivening them with its feathery seed heads, so conspicuous in autumn and winter. These are responsible for the name old man's beard; local variants include

Richmond, Yorkshire; Hallaton, Leicestershire.

grandfather's whiskers in Cornwall and Somerset, old man's woozard or maiden's hair in Buckinghamshire, father time in Somerset, hedge feathers in Yorkshire and tuzzy-muzzy in Gloucestershire.

See also CHALK, DOWNLAND.

O N I O N S

The onion is one of the oldest cultivated vegetables. It was very strong in taste, probably brought here by Romans to help conceal the saltiness of winter meat. According to Lawrence D. Hills, who knew his onions, a few strong-tasting varieties still survived in 1971, such as Up-to-Date, Oakey, James Long Keeping and Giant Zittau, which was *'reputed in the North to be capable of opening the garden gate with a single breath from the proud grower'*.

Commercial production now centres upon the Fens near Ely, Cambridgeshire. But acres of old varieties that we have lost or are losing were once grown around Bristol.

As with leeks, some people have a passion, especially in the North, for growing very large and heavy onions. Reaching more than ten pounds, they win prizes at onion fairs and festivals, such as at Harrogate and Dewsbury in Yorkshire and Ashington in Northumberland.

Onion Johnnies, almost an endangered species, still arrive here in July and August with strings of sweet pink onions (*oignons roses*), garlic and shallots draped over the handlebars of their black bicycles. They were given permission to sell without licences as a token of thanks, after the French rescued members of the British royal family from a shipwreck off Roscoff, Brittany in 1815. Until the disruption of the Second World War hundreds of farm workers made annual migrations across the Channel to sell their wares door to door. One Onion Johnnie, still sporting

his navy-blue beret, continues to park his bike in the centre of Shaftesbury, Dorset each year, but he is one of only twenty or so French farmers who continue the tradition.

See also AGRICULTURAL SHOWS, LEEKS, MARKET GARDENS, NURSERIES.

O R C H A R D S

Old orchards are the richest kind. Some have occupied the same land for centuries. The orchard at Bawdrip in Somerset has been traced on maps back to at least 1575. Yet the land was contested for seven years, with repeated applications and appeals for houses, despite local opposition. The continuity of land use makes for rich wildlife, long-told stories and a deeper sense of loss.

Orchards and individual fruit trees are found in every county, but the major commercial fruit-growing areas remain Cambridgeshire, Devon, Essex, Herefordshire, Kent, Somerset and Worcestershire. Kent grows eating and cooking apples, cherries, pears, plums and cobnuts; the eastern counties apples; the South West cider apples, perry pears and mazzards (cherries); the Vale of Evesham apples, plums and pears. Cherries were grown extensively in Hertfordshire and Berkshire, damsons in Cumberland and Westmorland, apples in Middlesex.

Orchards, with their tall, 'standard' trees, are important in the landscape. Current commercial orchards are of dense lines of small trees; some are so intensive they are more like vineyards. By contrast, standard cider apples were spaced on a thirty-foot grid, and the majestic cherries on the north Kent coast more than forty feet from one another. Tall perry pears were planted every sixty feet. Under them sheep might graze, sometimes flowers or soft fruit would be grown.

Orchards are like wood pasture, full of micro-habitats, their biodiversity no less rich for having been sustained through nurture by many hands. They tell the seasons frankly, flaunting blossom, dropping fruit, enticing creatures large and small, enjoying winter wassailing. They display an intricacy of particularity to place. In Westmorland, damson trees keep company with stone walls, in Shropshire they march along hedgerows, as do cherries in some parts of Norfolk. Giant cherry trees, sixty feet high, gather in (the few remaining) orchards around Faversham, Kent, while further south in the Weald, squat cobnut plats pick out the ragstone of the Greensand ridge.

Newly planted elder trees are remaking the landscape in Leicestershire and Surrey as the demand for elderflower cordial grows. Hereford, Somerset and Devon are renowned for their cider-apple orchards. Gloucestershire, despite losing three-quarters of its orchards since 1945, still has many kinds of perry pear. These huge, long-lived trees (they can reach 60 feet and 350 years) are so particular about their conditions that some varieties will not grow more than five miles

309

from where they arose; each parish produced its own single-variety perry or local blend.

Every farm and big garden had its own orchard of mixed fruit trees for domestic use, and farm labourers were often part-paid in cider. In Ryedale, Yorkshire George Morris discovered that on marriage a woman would move to her husband's farm, taking with her graft wood to add to the orchard, which would be her domain. Typically in apples alone there would be Yorkshire Cockpit, Green Balsam, Yorkshire Greening (also called Yorkshire Goose Sauce), Backhouse Flowery Town (with its pink flesh), Yorkshire Beauty, Keswick Codling, Warner's King, Lane's Prince Albert, Dog's Snout, Catshead, Burr Knot, Striped Beefing, Gravenstein, Lemon Pippin and Northern Greening.

Apparently the latter are often grubbed out now as people do not realise that their hard and sour early persona is transformed by Easter. The whaling ships making their way from Whitby in Yorkshire to the southern ocean would carry apples that took perhaps six months to mature, ensuring a supply of vitamin C against scurvy (long before oranges). Orchards around the Vale of York finally crashed in numbers when Rowntree began to use chemical pectin to set its fruit gums.

When we lose an orchard we sacrifice not simply a few old trees (bad enough, some would say), but we risk losing forever varieties particular to the locality, together with wildlife, songs, recipes, cider, festive gatherings, the look of the landscape and the wisdom gathered over generations about pruning and grafting, aspect and slope, soil and season, variety and use. We sever our links with the land.

Looked at from a different angle, if we lose real cider we lose the need for cider barrels, flagons, wassail bowls, mugs, tools, troughs, presses . . . people. We lose interest in artefacts and buildings often unique to their place. They are devalued, left to rot, mislaid, broken up, and with them fades the knowledge, the self-esteem and soon the varieties, the wildlife, and so on. Everything is dependent upon everything else; culture and nature, when so finely tuned, create a dynamic, intimately woven working world.

It would be wrong to assume that the city is bereft of orchards. Norwich, it was famously mused, '*was either a city in an orchard or an orchard in a city*'. In north London, in 1989, the Hampstead Garden Suburb Horticultural Society organised a great apple hunt to identify garden fruit trees planted by Dame Henrietta Barnett in 1899. More than forty varieties were rediscovered scattered across the front and back gardens, making an extensive orchard. Because fruit trees can be trained to take up little space, the idea of creating espaliers against walls in the smallest of city gaps is a feasible proposition, and there are now parks and allotments that await the fruits of newly planted small orchards.

Many old orchards are being lost to other forms of agriculture (since fruit is so cheap on the world market) and to building. Wiltshire has lost 95 per cent of its orchards since 1945, Devon ninety per cent since 1965. For many counties the loss is more than two-thirds. But much renewed interest in orchards has stemmed from recognising the links between variety and place. Community, city and school orchards are being created with varieties that are local to the parish, town and county, reinvigorating knowledge and keeping it practised in its locality.

See also ALLOTMENTS, ANCIENT TREES, APPLE DAY, APPLES, APRICOTS, AVALON, CHERRIES, CIDER & CIDER ORCHARDS, COBNUTS, DAMSONS, DEVIL, FOOD, FROST & FROST HOLLOWS, GREENSAND, HAZEL, HONEY & BEES, LICHENS, MIDSUMMER DAY, MISTLETOE, PEARS, PLUMS, WASSAILING.

O S I E R S

Small osier-beds were planted by rivers and other damp places all over the country; every village had its basket maker, and traditional local design flourished. In the 1800s willow began to be grown on a commercial scale in the valleys of the Thames, Kennet, Great Ouse, Cam, Soar, Trent, Stow and Welland. The main growing area is now concentrated on the Somerset Levels around Curry Moor and West Sedgemoor.

Some of the main species of willow grown for basketry are *Salix viminalis* (the osier), *Salix triandra* (almond-leaved willow) and *Salix purpurea* (purple willow). The wood is extraordinarily versatile. Combining lightness and strength, it has been put to hundreds of uses, including fish traps, cages, hurdles to contain animals, as a building material, for baskets, string, willow furniture, laundry baskets, picnic hampers and post-office baskets. During two world wars it was much in demand for mule panniers, shell cases, balloon baskets, for carrying pigeons and for panniers to drop supplies to the troops. The industry then declined due to competition from imported cheap baskets and, increasingly, from plastic substitutes.

Today willow-growing and basketry are in resurgence, thanks to a demand for natural materials and good craftsmanship. Three to four hundred acres are worked by a dozen families on the Somerset Levels. On this flat land, drained by rhynes and tidal rivers, you may see bundles of willow stacked up, waiting to be used or soaked; low, square, brick chimneys and buildings, which house withy boilers that are used to soften the wood for peeling; and the bright purples, greens, yellows and reds of:

The withy beds
Work horse of the Wetlands
Colonies of sallow and osier
Tall forests
Tremulous and vibrant

James Crowden, from 'In Time of Flood'

Small lengths of cut willow between eight and ten inches long, known as sets, are simply pushed into well-drained soil from mid-January (at a density of ten to twenty thousand per acre). The wands grow to about eight feet by the autumn and are cut near the ground in winter, sometimes mechanically. Willow sends up multiple shoots from the stump or stool for fifty years, withstanding long periods in floodwater.

The giant 'Willow Man' by Serena de la Hey, which runs alongside the M5 near Bridgwater, marks the Levels for drivers. Willows are being produced for artworks of all kinds, including living willow sculptures, high-quality charcoal sticks and spiling – using living willow hurdles to stabilise riverbanks. Willows coppiced on short rotations are increasingly being grown in any part of the country to produce biomass for 'clean energy'.

See also EYOTS, FENS, LEVELS, RHYNES, SCULPTURES, WILLOW.

O T T E R S

The otter has returned to the river Otter in Somerset/Devon after three decades of absence. It would seem obvious that otters should be there; Daniel Defoe in 1724 mentioned that the river was said to have got its name '*from the multitude of otters always found in that river*'. Otters were abundant on most lowland rivers when Defoe was alive; this must have been a phenomenon.

At home on land and in fresh and sea water, their main food is fish, preferably coarse fish, especially eels. They can travel great distances overland between watersheds.

Though seldom seen, having perforce learned to be nocturnal, out of man's way, otters swam into public consciousness when Henry Williamson wrote *Tarka the Otter* in 1927. Almost too harrowing to read, it paints a picture of what it was like to be an otter in north Devon, playing under the bridge at Bideford or being hunted by hounds led by '*Deadlock, the great pied hound with the belving tongue*'.

From being common on most watercourses, the otter faced near extinction by the 1970s, populations fading even in the South West and along the Welsh Marches.

Their story a cautionary tale in the dangers of hedonism, over-simplification and 'standard practice', otters declined in part because after the Second World War the most misguided period of land management ever, spearheaded by directives from the government, encouraged the straightening out of rivers and the clearing of bank-side vegetation. Wholesale land drainage schemes and the poisoning of the land by organochlorine pesticides also affected wildlife, especially the creatures at top of the food chain, such as otters and birds of prey.

Then there was otter hunting, formalised in 1796. Led by the Friends of the Earth Otter Campaign, many worked for a ban, which began on 1 January 1978, when the otter was added to the list of species protected under the 1975 Conservation of Wild Creatures and Wild Plants Act.

Once it was protected by law, conservationists turned their attention to improving the otter's habitat. In 1977 the Vincent Wildlife Trust set up the Otter Haven Project, which aimed to protect good stretches of river and work with riparian owners to improve other stretches, so that otters could have secure places in which to lie up and/or breed. Artificial holts and log piles are constructed in the absence of natural hollows under the roots of mature trees. Since then, with the help of the Otter Trust – which has, rightly or wrongly, released captive-bred animals into the wild – as well as the Environment Agency, English Nature, water authorities, Wildlife Trusts and many dedicated individuals, otters are gradually beginning to recolonise their old haunts.

This is a success story, although the effects of the now catastrophic decline in eel populations are yet to be seen. The obvious threat to otters these days is the car. Fifty-one otters were killed on roads in the South West alone in 2002, usually when rivers were flooded. Road underpasses are being made, but not quickly enough.

As part of Confluence, Common Ground's three-year exploration and celebration of the river Stour in Dorset (1998-2001), music *animateur* Helen Porter and poet Paul Hyland, together with many local people, created a moving choral work: 'Otter: Lutra lutra on the Stour'. These are Paul Hyland's lyrics for the final song to sing otters back to their waters of old:

Otter returns now, almost unnoticed,
beds down in holts, roots of trees or man-made,
reclaims its own liquid world – all the fast
sunlit currents, slow meanders in shade,
redundant mill-races, still pools, misplaced
rivulets – home for a species mislaid.

See also EELS, FRESHWATER FISH, HOUNDS, REED BEDS, RIVERS, WILLOW.

O Y S T E R S

Gin and gingerbread herald the start of the dredging season for the much-coveted oyster fishery near Colchester, Essex in September. The Mayor, Chief Executive and Town Sergeant, in civic robes, set out with forty guests on a sailing barge from Brightlingsea to the main oyster farming beds in the Pyefleet Channel by Mersea Island. The ancient Proclamation of 1256, which affirms Colchester's exclusive rights for time immemorial, is read and the fishery declared open. The Mayor drinks the Loyal Toast to the Queen with gin, followed by gingerbread, orders the first dredge to be made and has the honour of eating the first oyster. All are treated to an oyster lunch. A month later, on the eve of St Dennis's Day (21 October), four hundred guests indulge in an Oyster Feast at Colchester's Moot Hall.

Oyster fishing took place before the Romans built Colchester, where the Pyefleet Native thrived in the shallow creeks around the mouth of the Thames and in the estuaries of the rivers Colne, Crouch, Blackwater, Roach and along the Essex coast. The oysters were dredged – scraped off their beds – but conservation measures as early as 1577 prevented harvesting between Easter and Lammas, when the oysters were spawning (spatting). At its height in the 1860s the Colne Fishery produced about seven million oysters a year. Now the centre of the industry is Mersea Island, where Mersea Natives and Colchesters are sold from The Company Shed on the foreshore. Local fishermen are lobbying to get Protected Geographical Indication status for Colchesters.

Until the 1860s oysters were the food of the poor. But the once-thriving industry was ruined by overfishing, propelled by railway links to Billingsgate Market in London. Then came polluted rivers and disease. Imported oysters brought with them the slipper limpet, American oyster-drill and the barnacle from the antipodes, creatures that harm or destroy oyster beds. The severe winters of 1947 and 1963, floods and toxic anti-fouling paints all added to their demise. Oysters have become scarce, a delicacy for the rich.

Whitstable Oyster Festival and Blessing of the Waters takes place around St James's Day, 25 July. The first catch of the season is blessed and presented to the Mayor, then paraded through the town, accompanied by the civic party, Shire horses, dray and musicians, before being delivered to restaurants, pubs and cafés. There is music, oysters for sale, boats to board and trips on sailing barges. The Men of Kent and Kentish Men present the annual Blessing of the Waters ceremony on Reeves Beach, and the festival ends with fireworks over the sea.

Present-day cultivation takes place from Suffolk to Cornwall. Native oyster grounds are still found in the estuaries of the Thames, Solent, Helford and Fal – on the Fal the oysters are dredged by the world's last sail-powered fishing fleet and the boats race one another at the annual Falmouth Oyster Festival in October. But none of the grounds recovered from the winter of 1963, which killed 95 per cent of stocks. A closed season protects native oysters while spawning, spatfall, which happens with the full moons between 14 May and 4 August.

See also BISCUITS, BOATS, COASTS, GIN, MOON, NICKNAMES, SEA FISH, SHIRE HORSES.

Perpetua Italic/Bold, Eric Gill, 1928.

PANCAKE DAY

Traditionally pancakes were eaten on Shrove Tuesday, the day before Lent begins, to use up perishable foods, such as eggs and butter, before the period of abstinence.

In the morning the Shriving Bell would ring to call Christians to their pre-Lent confession. After the Reformation the bell signalled the beginning of festivities, becoming known as the Pancake Bell. In Daventry, Northamptonshire it was the Pan Burn Bell; in Maidstone, Kent the Fritter Bell; in Cheshire the Guttit Bell. It is still rung in Scarborough, Yorkshire and Olney, Buckinghamshire.

Olney is where the first pancake race is reputed to have been held in 1445; now it attracts  hundreds of onlookers. Only women who are aged over 18 (and have been resident for more than three months) are allowed to take part. Wearing skirt, apron and hat or scarf, holding pans out in front of them, they run 415 yards from the Bull Hotel in the Market Place down Church Lane, tossing their pancakes at least three times as they go. Other opponents race in Liberal, Kansas, US, having first challenged Olney in 1950. After the race, which lasts about 62 seconds, there is a Shriving Service in the parish church, where the frying pans are placed around the font.

At Westminster School in London there is a ceremonial Pancake Greeze, during which the cook tosses pancakes over a sixteen-foot beam and the boys try to catch them before they land. In Scarborough post-pancake skipping over long ropes takes place on Foreshore Road. There are tugs-of-war in Ludlow, Shropshire.

Claire Wagstaff tells us that '*In Toddington, Bedfordshire, there's a Norman motte and bailey mound called Conger Hill . . . it used to be that on Shrove Tuesday every year, when the Pancake Bell rang at midday (to let the housewives know to start cooking their pancakes), all the children in the village would run to Conger Hill and put their ears to the ground to listen. They would hear the sizzling of the witch in the hill cooking her pancakes. The local school used to take the children to do it, but has stopped now.*'

See also BELLS & BELL-RINGING, CASTLES, FOOD, SHROVETIDE GAMES.

PANTILES

Stacked up in composite heaps
Single Romans, Double Romans,
Triple Romans
Pan tiles, Finials, Triple Angulars,
Scallops, Clubs, Plain and Ziggurat
Weatherblock and Bargeboard
Waterbar and Hurricane, Fishscale and Homestead
Wineglass Paragon, Lockjaw and Marseille –
Acres of roof running wild, miles of tiles.

James Crowden, from 'Bridgwater Reclaimed'

Pantiles are a celebration of baked clay and the subtle range of colours it can produce. Unlike flat, plain tiles they are S-shaped to interlock. With local variations, they give a furrowed appearance to roofs, rippled with alternate lines of light and shade.

The traditional areas for pantiles are those that traded with Holland in the seventeenth and eighteenth centuries: predominantly along the east coast from the Thames estuary to Scotland, around Bridgwater in Somerset and up the Bristol Channel. Bridgwater exported wool to the Netherlands and brought pantiles back; in the early eighteenth century companies began to make their own bricks and pantiles from local clay. They were sent up the Severn as far as Gloucester, down the Bristol Avon to the Vale of Pewsey in Wiltshire, and up the river Parrett into Somerset, where they gradually replaced thatch.

On the east coast pantile making began at places such as Tilbury, Essex (by a firm owned by Daniel Defoe) and Barton-upon-Humber. They were shipped up the Humber and Trent into Lincolnshire and Nottinghamshire, and up the Welland, Nene and Ouse. The coast of Northumberland, the Tees valley, the North York Moors and the Vale of York are traditional pantile-roof areas, as is the coast edging Essex, Suffolk, Norfolk (and Cambridgeshire), where they vary in colour from red in north Norfolk to brown in the south.

Pantiles were readily accepted because, although larger, fewer were needed. They overlap at each side, whereas plain tiles have to be two to three deep to keep out the rain. Less weight meant fewer roof timbers and a reduction in labour costs. They also enabled the pitch of the roof to be as low as thirty degrees, although when replacing thatch they were laid on roofs as steep as 55 degrees.

315

The S-shaped are the most common, but shapes vary, from the Essex flat-and-roll to the Bridgwater flat-and-two-rolls and the '*small-scale double-S, which gives a much more even overall ripple to the roof*', described by John and Jane Penoyre.

Colours vary, from bright red in the Vale of York to brownish red in parts of Suffolk and a pale buff colour in Cambridgeshire. A speciality of Boston in Lincolnshire and north Norfolk, glazed black pantiles were imported into Hull in the seventeenth century from Holland – glazing gave them added strength and protection against frost. They were particularly admired by Richard Fortey, '*when they are combined with tar-washed sea cottages on the Norfolk coast*', and by the Penoyres, who wrote that the '*shiny, black-glazed pantiles . . . look extremely well on flint buildings*'. Alec Clifton-Taylor remarked: '*When they reflect the sky they often appear dark blue.*'

There are few companies making pantiles today. After the Second World War volume house-builders preferred concrete tiles. The last Somerset tile makers disappeared in the 1950s, creating a thriving second-hand market in Bridgwater double romans for older properties in Bristol and surrounding areas. Sandtoft, a firm of tile makers based in Yorkshire and Humberside, still produces handmade and machine-made tiles and traditional pantiles, including the Bridgwater double roman and single roman.

See also BRICKS, BUNS, CORRUGATED IRON, COTTAGES, FLINT, GABLES, HALF-YEAR BIRDS, SLATES, THATCH, TILES.

P A N T S

Alnwick, Northumberland is full of pants. St Michael's Pant, built in 1755 in the centre of town, is a prominent Gothic-style sandstone statue of a winged St Michael about to slay a dragon (although his lance is missing). He stands at the top of a tall pedestal and, to one side, at ground level, a square trough accepts water trickling from a lion's head. In Market Street a heavy Victorian domed drinking fountain supported by pink granite columns is surmounted by a glass lantern; a gift to the town in 1891, it is called Robertson's Pant. The Will Dickson Fountain, which replaced an old pant in Pottergate, has a glass lantern-top and a bath-shaped trough for horses. Sadly the fountain no longer works.

Pant is a Northumbrian term for a '*water supply that may, or may not, be continuous*', according to the county council, and many fine Victorian (or earlier) stone or cast-iron examples still stand in towns and on village greens. Elsewhere the parish pump, usually over a well, is the equivalent.

Without a water supply there would have been no settlement, but although the Romans manipulated flowing supplies it was not again until the nineteenth century that

generous benefactors made people's (women's) lives easier. Mary Herdman writes of the pant in Wall, Northumberland: '*Lt Col. Butler of Brunton House erected it for the village (in 1858), giving the villagers their first piped water supply . . . Previously the villagers had had to go to a spring up Spouty Lonnen, a lane to the south of the village. The pant stands centrally on the village green. It was fed from a reservoir on the fellside. The water was flowing until 1996, when a housing development was built on the line of the feed pipe and it was cut off. Before that, although it had been declared unfit for humans, it was often used to water horses . . . The parish council is endeavouring to have it functioning again.*'

Hollon Fountain in Morpeth, which stands in a prime position in the Market Place, where the market cross once stood, is a handsome, grey granite structure with a lantern at its top and four protruding drinking basins under rounded arches. The parish pump on the green at Dufton in Westmorland, built by the London Lead Company, a Quaker firm, was described by Brian Bailey as '*a striking stone structure with a ball finial at the top, all (but the ball) painted in that maroon colour which, for some unexplained reason, is very popular in the Pennine region*'.

Most of these elaborate Victorian monuments are no longer functioning. Their troughs are becoming filled at best with geraniums. Yet the sight and sound of running water is such a reminder of our dependence upon it, and animals and birds would welcome it. Should we allow them to crumble gracefully? Are the fountains in Rome allowed to run dry?

See also SPRINGS, VILLAGE GREENS, WELL DRESSING, WELLS.

P A R G E T I N G

Saffron Walden in Essex offers a standing festival of pargeting, the decorative low-relief plaster work on old timber-framed buildings. There are simple, delicate patterns with stylised fruits and flowers, such as the Saffron crocus, and bolder plaster carvings of birds and fruits, which are picked out by shadows and dust. One of the most charming examples of modelled parget work can be seen above the entrance to the former Sun Inn, where the figure of the Wisbech Giant with his club is separated by a cartwheel from local carter Tom Hickathrift, defending himself with the axle from his wagon.

Pargeting became fashionable in the sixteenth century. Adding ornament, and protecting the wattle-and-daub panels between the timber frames from the weather, its heartland was north-west Essex, south-west Suffolk, south Norfolk, east Hertfordshire, Cambridgeshire and Kent, where timber-framed houses and wealth were prevalent.

Simple, incised plaster work made by pressing templates into wet lime plaster or using implements, such as sticks or combs, to make fans, herringbones, scallops, chevrons, diamonds, squares and other patterns, started first and continued longest. Designs were usually made on the panels between the timbers, but decorative foliate friezes between the floors or under the eaves were also common. Adela Wright wrote that the plaster was often covered with limewash, 'tinted with earth pigments of a particular area: there were Suffolk pinks, apricots and buffs, Kentish reds and Cambridge whites'.

The more elaborate, raised parget work was hand-moulded by skilled masons or plasterers, or made with wooden or beeswax moulds, using soft lime plaster, sand, cow dung and animal fat, bound with animal hair. Designs became bolder and soon covered the complete frontage of buildings.

The small town of Clare in Suffolk has some good examples of pargeting from the seventeenth century, especially on the walls of the Ancient House Museum, the medieval priest's house, which displays a swirling floral design. Most of the original pargeting on its houses has been destroyed or covered with layers of limewash; what is left has been renewed by dedicated craftsmen.

Individual pargeters had unique styles and used different imagery and patterns according to local fashion. In Suffolk crowns, royal arms, Tudor roses and other badges are more frequently seen in traditional pargeting, as well as the Suffolk cable or rope pattern, whereas in Essex chevrons, fans and scrolls predominate.

Pargeting is still practised on a small scale in places such as Thaxted and Finchingfield in Essex, and it is beginning to appear in some newly built houses, as around Long Melford in Suffolk.

See also COTTAGES, EARTH PIGMENTS, GIANTS, LIME-KILNS.

P A R I S H   M A P S

Making a Parish Map begins with a question: What do you value here? Turning one another into experts in this way helps to liberate all kinds of quiet knowledge, as well as passion, about a place.

The Ordnance Survey has produced maps to many scales; in addition estate maps, tithe maps and road maps take us back hundreds of years. But Common Ground is interested in encouraging community renditions of attachment. We suggested that people define 'Parish' together in their own way – from a street or neighbourhood to an actual civil or ecclesiastical parish. And to liberate people's imaginations about what a map could be, we challenged eighteen artists and launched the project with a touring exhibition. After a decade we held a second exhibition at the Barbican, London, including Parish Maps from across the country and prompting many more. We have no idea how many hundreds have been made, but Kim Leslie from the West Sussex Record Office alone has encouraged more than a hundred as a way of celebrating the millennium. Despite the positively parochial focus, there are groups across Italy, in Lithuania, Romania, Australia, Canada, the US and beyond that are finding this an effective way of 'getting started'.

Helen Sadler wrote from Barrow upon Soar, Leicestershire in 1997: '*Not surprisingly the Map has not changed everyone's idea of whether or not Barrow is a great place to live. At least one family was disappointed by the lack of photographs of old and beautiful Barrow. But is it a coincidence that for the first time we held an official switching-on ceremony of the Christmas lights with community carol singing? Is it a coincidence that we are staging a village pantomime? That we are negotiating to buy an old forge and so bring it into the public domain? That a group of individuals were motivated enough to enter the Better Towns Competition. Our Map, perhaps, created a*

317

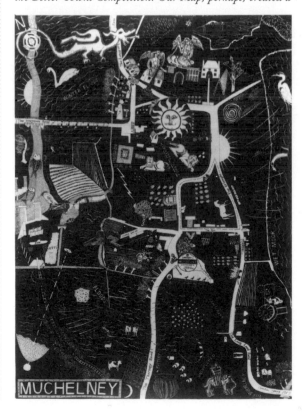

Muchelney, Somerset.

little hiatus into which a sense of pride and purpose can creep before we spill over the edge of the next millennium. It certainly proved to me that community spirit is not dead: it simply has to be approached in the right way.'

People in Elham, Kent created a painting eight feet long. They also checked out 56 footpaths and started conservation work on an old chalk pit and its rich flora. In Bristol, Vizability Arts drove a double-decker bus around for two weeks, luring people from different ethnic groups to climb aboard, tell their stories and add to the Map – an eight-foot-square batik to be hung in the community centre. The Map produced by the people of Thirsk in Yorkshire, with the help of textile artist Margaret Williams, is 26 feet long and hangs in the library. It has made sorties to public inquiries, giving people confidence in their own knowledge, values and sense of place. In Sunderland Museum a huge Map of the city made by a generation of schoolchildren hangs. The posters made by the people of Chideock in Dorset and Aveton Gifford in Devon have been sent all over the world, generating much income for their groups.

Parish Mapping is helping people to find, express and demonstrate their sense of identity and intimacy with their places. It has avoided the confining and repelling capacities of questionnaires, formal surveys and all the things that emerge when experts try to re-create people in their own image. So much surveying, measuring, fact-gathering, analysis and policy-making leaves out the very things that make a place significant to the people who know it well.

The great thing about making the Map yourselves is that you can choose what to put in and what to leave out. You can decide on how to gather and discuss the mix of natural history with buildings, or legends with livelihoods, select the scale at which you wish to work, what boundaries to impose, what materials, symbols, pictures, words to use and the place where the Map is to hang. You can move at your own pace, be diverted into clearing the old railway line, acting in a community play . . . because actually these are the point. Parish Map-making sets people off on a voyage of discovery about their locality, themselves and their potential within the physical, social and cultural arena.

It is the feel of a place that ultimately makes us happy to be there, makes us want to stay, work and play, to engage with it and one another. Social intervention in continually creating and re-creating particularity is not easy; it reminds us that communities are driven by tension as much as compassion, that the fluidity of insiders and outsiders needs constant bridge-building, that it is hard work to sustain enthusiasm and effort. But the power of creating a discourse between local people and professionals, of increasing social memory and involvement by charting significance, can reinvigorate a spirit of belonging and caring about what happens in the everyday world.

See also BEATING THE BOUNDS, BOUNDARIES, MUSEUMS, PLACE-NAMES.

PARK GATE LODGES

Park gate lodges were designed as entrances to country houses, parks and estates, to impress visitors and hint at the architectural splendours within. They were built to house the porter and his family, whose job was security and the opening and shutting of the gates.

Tim Mowl and Brian Earnshaw estimated that, as there were around a hundred parks per county, each averaging two lodges, there may be ten thousand *small houses ambitiously designed often by famous architects which reflect in concentrated form the changing architectural fashions of the last 250 years*'. They claimed that these buildings have not received the attention they deserve.

Park gate lodges flourished during the eighteenth and nineteenth centuries and encompassed neoclassical, neo-Gothic, cottage orné, Italianate and Arts and Crafts architectural idioms. Often a grander arched entrance fronted the main drive of the estate and a pair of pavilions protected the back entrance.

The pair of Jacobean gate lodges at Campden House in Chipping Campden, built by Sir Baptist Hicks in about 1613, was the forerunner of this familiar building type. Of Cotswold stone, with ogee-shaped roofs, they flanked an arched gateway. Lodges started to become fashionable after 1712; within a hundred years a pattern book dedicated to them had been published.

Lodge gatehouses and gateways range from modest classical 'boxes' (satirically described as dolls' houses for adults by Mowl and Earnshaw) influenced by Robert Adam to the impressive arches of William Kent's Worcester Lodge for Badminton House in Gloucestershire, built in 1750, with its flamboyant dining pavilion above the arch.

The paradox of designing a building for a working-class family while creating an imposing entrance combined '*a pretentious façade with a humble function*', Mowl and Earnshaw wrote. Humphry Repton observed in 1803 that

Campden House lodges, Chipping Campden, Gloucestershire.

the park-keeper's lodge was in danger of becoming a social scandal as a living unit. At Stowe in Buckinghamshire Thomas Pitt 'resolved the problem' of separate accommodation by hiding the living quarters within the piers of the Corinthian Arch.

By the late 1820s Gothic and classical styles were being joined by the cottage orné, in a quest for a kind of rustic simplicity said to be more appropriate for the English countryside than the Greek temple. A good example of this is Gaunt's Cottage at Hinton Martell in Dorset, which has been described as a 'tethered ombrello' – the mushroom-shaped thatch is draped over the house with deep, overhanging eaves, and the porches, held up by stilts, are also thatched.

Critics say that these cottages lack the formality that sets lodges apart from other buildings; this is also true of the mid-Victorian lodge, which is *often indistinguishable from the small suburban house with decorative features*, according to Mowl and Earnshaw. Nevertheless the more informal and modest lodges have a distinct charm, and can usually be recognised for the function they perform.

By the time the Arts and Crafts movement was in the ascendant, porters were provided with more spacious, comfortable accommodation. Lodges with decorative half-timbering by Lutyens, and with steep, tiled roofs by Voysey, together with those by other architects, are forerunners of the typical suburban house of the 1900s to 1940s.

Few lodges were built after 1939. Those that have not succumbed to road widening are often renovated and sold for hundreds of thousands of pounds – a far cry from their earlier role as home to the peasant at the gate.

See also ABBEYS, CASTLES, MONASTERIES, PARKLAND, TOWN GATES.

P A R K L A N D

A few deer parks existed before 1066. But it was the Normans who used their skills to create parks enclosed by ditches, banks and fences (pales) to contain the native red and roe deer and the fallow deer. The latter they introduced, with conies (rabbits), partridges and pheasants, for the table.

Woods, clumps and single trees, which provided shelter and shade for stock, were often pollarded for timber and surrounded by grassland.

During the reign of Edward I (1272-1307) there were more than three thousand deer parks; now one or two hundred. London's Royal Parks are the legacy of Henry VIII's passion for hunting. He owned more than two hundred deer parks all over the country. Many were destroyed during the Civil War, the deer killed or left to escape. The aristocracy turned its attention to another quarry – the fox – and the park became the view from the big house, with landscaped avenues, ha-has and lakes. Cattle and sheep grazed the grass and also browsed the well-spaced, full-canopied trees, giving them the distinctive browsing line characteristic of parkland trees today.

English Heritage estimated in 2005 that nearly half of England's historic parkland recorded in 1918 has since been lost – an area the size of Warwickshire. The surviving forty to eighty square miles of deer parks provide wood pasture that is not only beautiful but also contains a huge proportion of the country's ancient trees, enriched by and essential to the invertebrates, lichens and fungi that live on them. The wood pasture of Moccas Park in Herefordshire is grazed by fallow deer and dotted with trees, mainly oaks, of which Francis Kilvert wrote: '*They look as if they had been at the beginning and making of the world, and they will probably see its end.*' The violet click beetle, stag beetle and Moccas beetle are among the hundreds of insects living on them, and they support more than a hundred kinds of epiphytic lichen. Staverton Park, near Woodbridge in Suffolk, has some of the country's largest hollies, rowan and birches, as well as magnificent oaks.

See also ANCIENT TREES, LAWN, OAK, ROYAL FORESTS, WOODS.

P A R K S

Until the nineteenth century recreation happened in the streets, in the fields, on the commons or at fairgrounds, such as Newcastle's Town Moor or Oxford's Port Meadow. The Victorians tended to see these as debased places, where immoral things went on, and began to establish more edifying public parks for healthy exercise. Man could be enlightened by Art, and Nature tamed. Highly manicured, parks were partly about teaching nature and people 'good manners'. Battersea Park in London was built to supersede the wilder Battersea Field. Derby Arboretum, with its grand entrance lodge (now a photographic gallery and workshop), and Birkenhead Park in Cheshire were among the earliest municipal parks. The latter's grandeur inspired New York's Central Park. Seaside and spa towns also took on the park ideal, with promenade gardens.

These Victorian parks were typified by neat landscaping and elaborate fixtures, such as bandstands, fountains, aviaries – particularly ornate are those at Darwen in Lancashire and Penzance's Morrab Subtropical Garden in Cornwall – sculptures and statues, including Peter Pan in Kensington Gardens and the dinosaurs at Crystal Palace Park, both in London.

Towards the end of the twentieth century parks were seen as a burden – difficult and expensive to maintain, abused by drug pushers, unsafe and unsavoury. People had fled. With the cost-cutting Local Government Act in 1988 local authorities had to find the cheapest ways of looking after their open spaces, by putting jobs such as grounds maintenance out to 'compulsory competitive tendering'. Out went apprenticeships, groundsmen, park keepers and real gardeners; in came roving contract staff with no attachment to place, plants imported rather than grown internally. Knowledge and pride were lost, parks deteriorated in quality.

But those that held their traditions have not declined and maintain a special place in the hearts of people, as a green escape in town, a quiet retreat at lunchtime, for jogging, relaxing with the children or feeding the ducks. More wildlife management means more wildflowers than municipal beds, more wild creatures than ornamental birds. Some are well-known venues for melas and free concerts, with a 'keep on the grass' attitude.

England's parks received more than 296 million visits each year at the end of the last century. New attitudes are emerging, councils are recognising that open space is not for car parking but vital to the quality of life of ordinary families and workers. Now millions of pounds are being spent to restore parks betrayed by the mean measures of the 1980s.

See also ALLOTMENTS, AVENUES, BANDSTANDS, FOOTBALL, FOOTPATHS, GARDENS, LAKES, LAWN, MELAS, NURSERIES, ORCHARDS, PIERS, PONDS, PROMENADES, SCULPTURES, SPAS.

P A V E M E N T S

Locally typical pavements form an integral part of the street scene; the materials – paving stones, kerbstones, cobbles and setts – traditionally came from nearby and were laid with skill.

Granite has long been used in parts of Devon and Cornwall, Ketton stone around Stamford, Lincolnshire and sandstone in Yorkshire. London had no good stone and began to import it quite early; slabs of Purbeck limestone were sent by ship from Swanage, Dorset for use in the City. Stone flags found on the more affluent streets came from quarries in west Yorkshire. This sandstone from the Coal Measures is ideal for paving because, although it splits fairly easily, it is hard but not brittle. The size of the York stones corresponded with the importance of the place. Carboniferous sandstone was also quarried in the Forest of Dean, Derbyshire, Lancashire and Northumberland for paving stones.

Barry Joyce, Derbyshire's principal conservation officer, believes the county's old causeys, the local name for pavements, are under threat. He wrote: *'As with roofing and walling, each area had its own tradition of paving, based on locally available materials. Clay paving bricks are to be found in the south of the county; limestone and gritstone setts in the centre and north-west; and sandstone setts and paving slabs in the north-east. What survives is a little regarded but important part of the county's heritage.'*

People enjoy the quality and variety in stone pavements, and the patina achieved by decades of feet is now much sought after. One London taxi driver confessed that the removal of the paving stones from his street was the last straw – he felt as if he had been robbed, and this insidious loss of detail and spread of 'anywhere' street furniture triggered his decision to move. The sadness is that the stone was probably sold back to the council for laying in a conservation area.

Once these heavy materials were liberated by rail and canal they began to wander, but they epitomised quality. We take our pavements for granted, and poor, unattractive surfaces are replacing good, old causeways. Concrete paving slabs are now found everywhere. They come in different shapes, colours and sizes, but seldom look attractive or at home. Most are not even permeable to help reduce excessive run-off. Pedestrianisation seems to degrade streets faster than anything else, with a convergence of poor design and cheap materials.

See also ALLEYS, BOLLARDS, COBBLES, FOOTPATHS, HIGH STREETS, KENNELS, KERBSTONES, MANHOLE COVERS, QUARRIES, RAISED PAVEMENTS.

P E A R S

Pear trees can live three hundred years and more. An Abbess of Shaftesbury chose to mark the border of the lands given to her by Ethelred with pear trees. About a thousand years ago churches were built by the trees and became known as pear tree churches. St Mary's at Limpley Stoke, Wiltshire is the only one that remains. To recall the tradition a pear tree has now been planted in the churchyard.

Pear trees make a significant contribution to the landscape, especially the majestic perry pear, which is grown in Gloucestershire, Herefordshire and Worcestershire, reaching sixty feet in height, planted sixty feet apart, and under-grazed by stock.

There are more than a hundred perry pear varieties worthy of note in Gloucestershire alone, and some are so particular that they will not grow more than five miles from where they arose. Almost every parish produced its own characteristic single-variety perry. The small, astringent fruit is too sour to eat, but contains varying amounts of tannins and acidity, which give complexity to the fermented juice. Some varieties had a wider distribution and have remained popular for three hundred years, such as Arlingham Squash and Taynton Squash, Barland, Green Horse and Red Huffcap; irreverently named varieties include Lumberskull, Merrylegs and Stinking Bishop. To the south of May Hill, Gloucestershire, on the old red sandstone, 56 varieties were commonly grown. Peak production was in the mid-seventeenth to mid-eighteenth centuries, when war with France meant that its wines were in short supply. In London perry was considered better than European wine.

In addition to their stature, beautiful white blossom and attractive fruit, perry pear trees can be very productive. An extraordinary tree at Holme Lacy on the banks of the river Wye in Herefordshire covered three-quarters of an acre in the 1790s by digging its elbows in the soil, layering its branches to form new trees. At its most prolific it produced five to seven tons of fruit annually. Parts of it still grow here.

The last wave of planting was in the 1850s. Remnants of these magnificent orchards can be seen in Gloucestershire around Dymock, along the river Severn at Weir Green and around Elton and Chaxhill.

A national collection of perry pears has been planted at the Three Counties Showground in Malvern, with 59 varieties so far. The old orchards are in danger, but there has been a resurgence of interest in perry making, with thirty or so craft producers making a high-quality drink for a niche market. In Hartpury (hard pear tree) in Gloucestershire they are planting the Hartpury Green, first recorded in 1691. After almost becoming extinct, it is thriving in and around the parish once more.

Worcester city council has given a Black Worcester pear to each school for the children to plant; incorporated in the arms of the city are 'three pears sable'. The trees, recognised by their distinctive tall, narrow shape, characteristic fine, square-patterned bark, white blossom and dark fruit, can still be found scattered over the county on the windward side of old orchards, hedgerows and gardens. Worcestershire county council has for some years been offering the Black Worcester and perry pears at reduced cost; more than four hundred have been planted.

Of the dessert pears the most reliable cropper, now representing more than three-quarters of the home market, is the Conference. Raised by Thomas Rivers, it was introduced to commercial cultivation in 1894, having been exhibited at and named after the National Pear Conference in Chiswick in 1885. Williams's Bon Chrétien was raised by schoolmaster John Stair in Aldermaston in 1770 and described by Edward Bunyard as *quite the best of early Pears, and should be gathered when still green and ripened in the fruit-room*. It was eventually named after the nurseryman Richard Williams of Turnham Green, who propagated it for sale.

The largest collection of pears in northern England is kept at Cannon Hall Museum near Barnsley in south Yorkshire, where 48 trees of thirty different varieties grow in an old walled garden.

See also ANCIENT TREES, APPLES, CHERRIES, CIDER & CIDER ORCHARDS, COBNUTS, CRINKLE-CRANKLE WALLS, DAMSONS, ORCHARDS, PLUMS.

P E A T

Peat was for centuries a keenly exploited local fuel from Somerset and East Anglia to Yorkshire and Northumberland. The workings could be substantial: the Norfolk Broads resulted from the flooded workings of a huge, medieval peat extraction industry.

A commoner's right to cut turfs or turves, known as turbary, was highly prized and carefully regulated. Widespread deposits of blanket peat on the Pennine moors provided ample supplies, while much rarer patches in the Cumbrian mountains were strictly policed by the late seventeenth century, sometimes by special officers called mossmen, mossgraves or mosslookers.

In the Yorkshire Dales every hamlet had designated tracks, called turf ways, turf gates or peat gates, leading to its turf pit or peat pot, and each dale had its distinctive peat spades. Turves were stored in drystone huts called peat scales, or peat cotes in the Lake District – their ruins remain, perched on valley sides in Eskdale, Langdale, Bampton, Barton, Dunnerdale and Longsleddale. Tenants also cut vegetation-covered turves, known as flaws, flax, flakes or flaughts, to make field banks (binckes) and as roofing material, or to serve as dry platforms for beehives, corn or hay mows.

Formed from decomposed plant remains during the ten thousand years since the Ice Age was at its peak, the nature of peat varies. Sedge peat is found where fresh-water or brackish swamps once flourished; the Fens of East Anglia and the Somerset Levels are prime examples. But the largest areas of sphagnum peat have developed inland, in bogs in river valleys, lake basins and upland hollows dominated by bog mosses. So-called blanket bogs develop as peat layers swell above low-lying pockets, and become raised bogs when the mossy mass traps enough water to raise the water table above the surrounding land.

The composition of the peat can change with depth. In the Somerset Levels, over six millennia, wetland evolved from estuary to swamp, fenwood and finally raised bog. Peat diggers call the last, massive layers 'best black peat' and 'light peat'. At about AD 400 climatic changes halted further formation of peat, making it a non-renewable resource.

In Somerset in 1870 commercial working began for burning. A century later peat producers found a new market: the horticultural industry. Mechanisation – the first peat-cutting machine appeared in the Levels in 1963 – and cheap transport fuelled exploitation on an industrial scale. At the 1980 extraction rate of one hundred thousand tons a year, the peat of the Somerset Levels would have been completely destroyed by 2030. In an effort to safeguard at least part of this unique region English Nature and the Somerset Wildlife Trust now manage nature reserves at Shapwick Heath and Westhay. No areas of undamaged raised mire remain, but one section at Westhay Moor comes closest. Old peat cuttings nearby are collecting water and being planted with reeds in an attempt to re-create the watery landscape that disappeared several centuries ago.

Magnificent raised mires of south Yorkshire, such as Thorne Waste and Hatfield Chase (or Hatfield Moors) near Doncaster, have been extensively damaged by peat extraction in recent years. Fisons bought Thorne Moor in the 1960s and has by now removed most of its peat, built up over thousands of years. In 2002 a leading supplier of peat, the Scotts Company, agreed to sell land to English Nature, which will attempt to restore traditional water levels and with them some safety from volatile floodwaters.

See also BEE BOLES, BOWLING GREENS, BROADS, CATTLE, CHURCHES, FENS, GRAZING MARSHES, GREEN LANES, INGS, LEVELS, MOORLAND, MOSSES, MOSSLAND, RIVERS, SALT MARSHES, SHEEP, TIDES.

PELE TOWERS

The pele towers of Northumberland and Durham emerged, as did the towered villages of Mani in Greece and the towered hill towns of Italy, as places of refuge. In Cumberland, churches at Burgh by Sands and Newton Arlosh have fortified pele towers, too. Reiving – medieval territorial feuds and opportunistic raiding – made the borders between Scotland and England a dangerous place to live, as Richard Sim describes: 'The terrible violence of this time has left its mark, not only on the English language, with some of the most sinister words in our vocabulary, but also on the border landscape in the form of a series of fortified towers and defensible houses. Words and phrases handed down from that time include "bereave" (from to reive), "blackmail" (black rent – illegal rent, the equivalent of modern protection money) and red-handed (caught "in the deede doinge").'

He continues: 'The towers of medieval times primarily reflected the need of the local gentry to defend themselves

against cross-border raiders. Such pele towers were built of stone with massive thick walls. Typically the only entrance was through a double door at ground level, one being an outer iron grating and the other of oak reinforced with iron. The bottom floor was used as a store room and the floors above were reached via a narrow, circular staircase. The upper floors were the living quarters and at the very top there would be a beacon to summon help or give warning of an impending attack. The pele was normally a chief's house.'

Dating from the fourteenth to sixteenth centuries, these square towers with a barrel-vaulted ground floor and living quarters of three or four storeys above were for refuge in times of harassment and were generally in a corner of the farmstead. Willimontswick, on the south side of the Tyne, has a battlemented square tower. Almost every village in Northumberland had one or more fortified towers. In Corbridge there are remnants of two pele towers, one in the churchyard.

See also BASTLES, CASTLES, CHURCHES, FARMS & FARMSTEADS, LANDMARKS, VILLAGES.

PENNY HEDGE

Also known as Horngarth, Kightly believed that this could be 'the oldest surviving manorial custom in Britain'. It involves the Hutton family, who rent farm land at Fylingdales near Whitby, Yorkshire, in an annual custom extraordinary in its persistence.

Complaints about excesses of wood being sold in 1315 seem to have led to the ritual, but by the time of the Dissolution abbots seem to have concocted a story, as Kightly wrote, 'to explain a custom whose real origin was forgotten, but whose performance would secure tenants' lands under the new regime'. Now the bailiff represents the Lord of the Manor of Whitby, and only one family takes part.

At 9am on the eve of Ascension Day they drive stakes with an ancient mallet into the foreshore below the high tide mark near Boyes Staithe in Whitby harbour. They then weave osiers among them to form a 'hedge' strong enough

Kentmere Hall, Westmorland.

to withstand three tides. This done, the bailiff of the Court Leet of Fyling blows the horn and shouts '*out upon ye, out upon ye*'. The penance 'hedge' is a token, but if they fail to make it, or the hedge is swept away by the tides, the tenancy will be lost, so the story goes . . .

See also HEDGES, OSIERS, TIDES.

P I E R S

Extending a practical function (to act as landing stages for steam ships full of holidaymakers), the first 'pleasure pier' was built on the Isle of Wight, at Ryde in 1814, as the gentry began to flock to the fashionable new resorts. From Clevedon pier in Somerset the occasional pleasure cruise can still be taken, but at its peak in the early 1900s it served four different steamer companies and, as late as 1939, was playing host to at least twenty ships a week. The same was true of the other piers – nearly sixty in total – dotted along the English coast. Their elegance and variety speaks of cast iron and concrete, colour and restraint, tranquillity and boisterousness.

Factory shut-downs, bank holidays, an extended railway network and the first glimmerings of disposable income opened up the coast to workers and city dwellers. Where city fathers saw opportunity to attract them, piers were built. The National Piers Society's figures show that in the 1860s and 1870s, on average, two piers were opening every year.

People were beginning to enjoy piers in their own right. A dramatic walk out over the waves, as John Betjeman put it, '*to walk on the sea without the disadvantage of being sick*'; a new perspective of the resort and coastline; the healthy sea air – all came together to increase piers' appeal. When the steamers' popularity waned and there was no longer any need for a landing station, the pier became an amusement arcade or a cafeteria, a ballroom or a theatre, or somewhere simply to fish or look longingly out to sea.

Decay began in the 1930s. The inter-war years were no time for holidays or for the already struggling steamers.

Storm, flame and accident often proved fatal during these austerities. Many piers were breached to prevent their use by invaders. To survive, many 'moved with the times' and became gaudy money pits. Others suffered the ignominy of slow erosion.

The West Pier at Brighton, designed by pier engineer *par excellence* Eugenius Birch and opened in 1866, was closed in 1975. After a quarter of a century of decline, with discussions well advanced for its restoration and redevelopment, it was almost destroyed in two suspicious fires in 2003. Then, in 2004, it suffered storm damage sufficient to cause English Heritage to withdraw support. This is a multiple tragedy, as the pier was much favoured by starlings, who, dispossessed after the hurricanes of 1987, had taken to roosting there. Fifty thousand wheeling birds may be lost to the evening sky and will no doubt be persecuted wherever they try to gather.

But the end-of-the-pier show has not happened. Since the 1960s popular interest has grown, some communities banding together to recover their piers. Clevedon – '*the most beautiful in England*', in Betjeman's opinion – collapsed while being load-tested for insurance in 1970, and lay neglected. The district council applied to demolish it in 1979, but was defeated at a public inquiry. The enthusiasm, hard work and fundraising efforts of the Clevedon Pier Preservation Trust saw that it was re-opened within ten years of the application, and by 1995 it had already been visited by half a million people. Southwold pier in Suffolk opened in 2001, the first pier built since the 1950s.

See also BEACHES, BEACH HUTS, BOATS, COASTS, FOOD, FUNICULAR RAILWAYS, LANDMARKS, PROMENADES, STARLINGS.

323

P I E S

When Simple Simon met that pie man going to the fair, he sampled perhaps something from Dorothy Hartley's mouth-watering litany: '*the Turnover, the Pastie, the Crowthie, the Fruit-between-two-skins, the Checky Pig, the*

Puff, the Cornet, the Open Tart, the Gable Tart, the Lattice (and all the varieties of the pie-plate tart), the Proper Pie, the Plate Pie, the Raised Pie, the Mould Pie, the Shell Pie (Scotch and most early English in design), and the Cottage Pie.'

The distinctive English savoury pie – the one that football supporters would accuse portly players of having eaten ('*Who ate all the pies?*') – has a double crust made from short-crust pastry. Meat pies have come in many varieties, but most of us now get by without our rabbit pie (especially the one Mr McGregor had planned for Peter Rabbit). Cornwall's Stargazy is also an acquired taste, proudly displaying the rows of baleful eyes of its whole pilchards. The Sussex churdle combined bacon, liver and vegetables beneath a cheese topping. Denby Dale in Yorkshire has an eponymous meat and potato pie, made once a generation during a time of celebration, each time larger than its predecessors.

From the Midlands came the Fidget or Fitchett pie, possibly so-called from an original 'fitched' (five-sided) shape. It is a harvest-time pie of ham, pork, vegetables and apples, with Shropshire associations. The South West had a similar dish in the Devonshire Squab.

When it comes to pork pies Melton Mowbray in Leicestershire is the place, although local producers are fighting to have it awarded Protected Geographical Indication status to curb the use of the town's name on inferior products made elsewhere. Its pork pie, its fresh meat grey rather than the ubiquitous pink, is, as the original television chef Philip Harben said in 1953, '*a very English thing and a very fine thing*', its pastry '*fashioned by hand, as a potter shapes his clay*'. It gained its pre-eminence as Melton Mowbray became a significant cheese-producing area, resulting in plentiful excess whey that supported great numbers of pigs.

Steak and kidney pies became a staple for workers in London and the bigger cities from the end of the Victorian era. Pie and mash is closely associated with London and the docks. Goddard's in Greenwich has been serving pies for five generations (poor students have superseded poor dockers as the clientele); they are the original fast food – cheap and filling. The pies once contained eels, but now many different meat and vegetarian pies are sold, the 'special' made of minced beef and served with a green 'liquor' made to a secret recipe. Pie maker Kane Goddard summed up the hardened pie-and-mash veteran in a radio broadcast in 2004: '*He'll want his pies turned upside-down, because the crispy top he wants upside-down, and when you pour the liquor on top, it softens the top of the pie, and that's how they like it, they dig their fork and spoon in, break it open, and they whack the vinegar and the pepper on, and you know they've been eating pie and mash for years.*'

See also CHEESE, FOOD, HARVEST FESTIVALS, PIGS, POTATOES, PUDDINGS, STILTON.

PIGEON LOFTS

It was once commonplace to find oneself sitting by cooing baskets on a station platform; the world of pigeon racing expanded with the railways. Now you might occasionally see a lorry full of racing pigeons heading for a far-off corner of the country, from where they will be released for the long haul home. With the disposal of allotments, the closing of the pits, the statutory protection given to the enemy (the hawk), and the competition for young men's attention, the 'Fancy' is dying and racing enthusiasts themselves are endangered. The Royal Pigeon Racing Association, whose number one member is the Queen, has a falling membership, although, in a sport so long dominated by men there are now some women's clubs.

April marks the start of the season, September the end. Saturdays are flying days, and the birds are usually home by nightfall. Having been shown the hen bird for a few minutes, the male wings it at sixty to 95 miles an hour to get back to her (pigeons mate for life). Even a seven-hundred-mile race from mainland Europe will see them home in two days. Through the summer, repeated releases of perhaps ten thousand birds occur from Official British Liberation Sites, such as the Hereford racecourse, Shap 'by the village' in Westmorland, Beachy Head car park at Eastbourne, Sussex and Melplash Showground at West Bay, Dorset. The whoosh of the birds as they circle to get their bearings before making a magical beeline for home is one of the sounds of the summer.

Most recent research shows that following the line of motorways and big roads helps them in their homing. But fanciers fear that one of the problems faced by the birds is the proliferation of microwave radiation from phone masts, which is interfering with the intricate and only partially fathomed magnetic navigation the birds use. Whatever it is, birds are getting lost in numbers, which, since some are worth tens of thousands of pounds, is an economic as well as an emotional worry.

While pigeon fanciers can be found across the country, the stronghold is in the old mining areas. Travelling in the

North East you become aware of the sheds gaining coherence of colour, brightness and form. Allotments become 'suburbs' of duotone sheds, topped with wooden crenellations on one-sided roofs in white and black, bright yellow or green, for it is here that handsome pigeon lofts are found in some profusion still.

In Derbyshire the Bonsall and District Homing Society had thirteen flying members at the end of the 1990s. The village's design statement reads: '*Lofts are ideally built to take advantage of valley sides and longer hours of sunshine, but locations here are idiosyncratic. They are located throughout the village . . . and add to Bonsall's distinctive character.*'

In County Durham a pigeon house is a cree, further north it may be a loft. Duckets and doocuts tend to be for 'doos', doves as opposed to pigeons. Betting drives the Fancy, but it should come as no surprise that men who spent hours in the dark should yearn for the sky and the heartbeat of life over the dead, black stone.

While John, on the stock-loft roof, waves the frantic fantail.
'Come on!' he yells to the open sky: 'Howway!'
And the white wings beat at the end of his outstretched fingers,
As if he too was ready to fly away.

Katrina Porteous, from 'The Pigeon Men'

See also ALLOTMENTS, BEACH HUTS, COAL MINING, CORRUGATED IRON, DAGS, DOVECOTES, LEEKS, ROADS.

Distinctive English breeds are less than two hundred years old, but regional differences emerged much earlier because pigs, notoriously difficult to herd, rarely travelled far from home. Pigs '*won't be druv*', it was said, an expression adopted by Sussex country folk, who proudly described themselves as 'pigheaded' in their resistance to change. Elsewhere, however, pigs were shod in little leather boots to trot to market.

Lowland woodlands in autumn have for centuries nourished herds of domesticated swine, themselves descended from the fierce wild boars once common in the very same woods but hunted to extinction in the sixteenth century.

In medieval times peasants kept small, bristly, prick-eared pigs that were allowed to forage in woods – a common right known as pannage – from 29 August to 31 December. Tended by swineherds, the pigs grew fat on acorns, beech nuts (mast) and bracken roots, exploiting foods that humans rarely used. The tradition survives in a few places, such as the New Forest in Hampshire.

The pig of the open forest gradually grew large and stolid, mostly confined to a household pen. Leicestershire and Northamptonshire were among the chief pig-producing regions; from there, swine fattened on peas and beans (and milk whey around Melton Mowbray, Leicestershire) were sent for victualling the Navy. Large breweries in

325

Tamworth.

Berkshire.

Hampshire.

Gloucester Old Spot.

Wandsworth, Vauxhall and Battersea, London also kept pigs, fed on distillers' waste. Dairying regions in Wiltshire and Gloucestershire fattened thousands of Welsh pigs on whey from cheese making, with the bacon, regarded as the best in the country, destined for London meat markets. Bakers made lardy cakes, associated with Wiltshire, Oxfordshire and Berkshire.

By the middle of the eighteenth century English pigs underwent a dramatic change as Chinese, Siamese and Neapolitan pigs were imported and bred with native stock. These newcomers brought the dished face now common in almost all breeds; the original native stock had a long, straight nose like the wild boar's. During the past two centuries distinctive breeds have gradually emerged through generations of convoluted crossings.

The Berkshire today is prick-eared, black with scatterings of white; it matures early, reflecting its Chinese ancestors. Once widely admired for its pork, it has greatly influenced the world's pig population.

The Wessex Saddleback, black with a white saddle, was reputed to be linked to the free-ranging pigs of the New Forest; it was merged with the Essex Saddleback to create the British Saddleback in 1967. These hardy pigs still do well outdoors on well-drained land in the South. On the Wiltshire/Oxfordshire border Helen Browning produces organic pork from Saddleback sows under the Eastbrook Farm label.

The Large White, prick-eared and long-bodied, still known abroad as the Yorkshire, is the most widely distributed breed of pig in the world.

The origins of the Tamworth, with its glorious golden ginger coat, are mysterious, but this breed had achieved a definite identity by 1860. Said to be a talkative pig of considerable character, the Tamworth is late maturing and has a long, straight snout, lean body and strong, shapely legs. Once famed for its bacon, it is now a rarity. In 1998 a pair of the breed gained fame and freedom as the 'Tamworth Two' when they escaped from an abattoir at Malmesbury, Wiltshire.

The Gloucester Old Spot, white with at least one black spot on each side, is good for both pork and bacon. Known as the 'orchard pig', the breed was traditionally fed on windfall apples from cider and perry-pear orchards in the Berkeley Vale. Local folklore has it that the spots are bruises from the falling fruit.

The Rare Breeds Survival Trust monitors numbers and works to keep minority breeds from further decline. On the critical list are the Large Black, the Middle White, the Tamworth and the British Lop. The Berkshire, the British Saddleback and the Gloucester Old Spot are listed as endangered.

See also CATTLE, COMMONS, DROVE ROADS, FERAL ANIMALS, GRAFFITI, NICKNAMES, ORCHARDS, PARKLAND, PIES, ROYAL FORESTS, SHEEP, WOODS.

PILLBOXES

Skulking in bushes beside rivers or brazenly lounging on the beach, pillboxes are a reminder of the peril felt during 1940 that invasion might come from the sea or up the valleys, as indeed had happened during the so-called Dark Ages.

Many were simple circular or pentagonal flat-topped structures made from reinforced concrete (fifteen inches or more thick), reminiscent of the faceted boxes used by pharmacists to dispense pills in the early twentieth century. The horizontal slits for guns enabled a 360-degree field of fire. Perhaps six thousand of the original 28,000 survive in Britain, a few from the First World War. The most intact line of 280 pillboxes and machine-gun nests can be found from Seaton in south Devon to Bridgwater in north Somerset. Pillboxes followed railways and canals, as well as roads and rivers. To the roof of the Art Deco Bishopstone Station in Sussex a double-layer octagonal pillbox was added.

In Northumberland, between Cresswell and Widdrington, Druridge Bay is watched over by a ruined bothie; it was built to disguise its function as defensive emplacement. At Alnmouth a stone building of uncertain origin, locally held to be a guano import shed from the nineteenth century, was refashioned with twenty gun slits by 1940. On the Yorkshire coast some pillboxes have ears, with room for a machine gun, on each side; at Fraisthorpe near Bridlington one is now stranded on the beach.

A small cylinder of concrete with slits at Kimmeridge Bay, Dorset bears the ridges of its corrugated-iron mould. Tilting precariously, it awaits its fate at the hands of the sea. Heavily undermined by the water, one of a group of low pillboxes clad in beach cobbles at Porlock Bay, Somerset is wonderfully disguised. Wavy edges to the concrete roof, a Devonian idiosyncrasy, are visible at Torcross. Some of these memorials to Churchill's promise that '*we shall fight on the beaches*' are now being listed as ancient monuments. On Burgh Island, Devon a restored pillbox was on sale for £70,000 in 2004, advertised with a view to die for.

See also BASTLES, BRIDGES, BUILDING STONES, CASTLES, COASTS, COBBLES, DRAGONS, EARTHWORKS, FORTIFICATIONS, GAPS, HILL-FORTS, MARTELLO TOWERS, PELE TOWERS, RUINS, SEA FORTS.

Kimmeridge beach, Dorset.

P I N F O L D S

Wandering animals were the bane of village and town life; vital crops in the open fields and vegetable plots could be ruined in a few minutes. Every settlement had its pound or pinfold (a term used more in the North and East), in which to corral maverick beasts and use at legitimate moments of round up. Often they were beside the smithy. The animals were impounded until a fine had been paid, something like the fate of a wrongly parked car today. Throughout feudal times this was the responsibility of the pinder. John Clare wrote of the pinder of Helpston in Northamptonshire:

> *The Pinder on the Sabbath Day*
> *Soon as the darkness waxes grey*
> *Goes round the folds at early morn*
> *To see what ſtock are in the corn*
> *There like a fox upon the watch*
> *He in the morning tries to catch*
> *And drive them to the pound for pay*
> *Careless about the Sabbath Day.*

From *The Shepherd's Calendar*

Perhaps only a ghost lingers on old maps or in names, such as Pinfold Lane or Pound House, but folds that remain tell us something of local building materials and practices, even if they have been absorbed into garden or garage. Usually they are square or round, with walls made from local stone or brick and a single gate. On the Isle of Portland, Dorset one pound has a fine stone lintel, while in Saffron Walden, Essex the gateway has an arch of brick. Generally, however, these were workaday structures. A high, brick, hexagonal pinfold survives at Raskelf, north Yorkshire. The Forest of Dean in Gloucestershire still has its pound, and in the New Forest, Hampshire an extensive new timber pound at Beaulieu Road Station is used when the pony drifts take place. There are fewer reliſt pinfolds on the eastern side of the country, but this may be because they were made of wood.

In Laxton, Nottinghamshire, where they still work an open field system, they continue to appoint a pinder to take care of stray beasts, and the pinfold is in use, helpfully just beside the Dovecote Inn. Throughout the county's villages twenty pinfolds survive; at least twelve are listed buildings.

See also CAIRNS, CATTLE, DRYSTONE WALLS, FIELDS, FORGES, NEW FOREST PONIES, PIGS, SHEEP, SHEEP-FOLDS, SHEEP-WASHES.

P I T   T I P S

At Underwood, Nottinghamshire small conical hillocks covered with conifers speak of a flurry of beautification that took place long before planting trees as carbon sinks became the talk of global warming. Only by scrambling up the steep slopes do you realise, after studying your fingernails, that they are made of shaly coal.

'Along the ridge of the great pit-hill crawled a little group in silhouette againſt the sky, a horse, a small truck, and a man. They climbed the incline againſt the heavens. At the end the man tipped the waggon. There was an enormous rattle as the waſte fell down the sheer slope of the enormous bank', D.H. Lawrence wrote in *Sons and Lovers*. Later in the twentieth century small collieries getting rid of coal spoil would deliver it from a high moving belt. Both methods created steep slopes and rounded or long hills, which punſtuate the horizons of so many northern villages and towns. Many are now part of the loved landscape, naturally regenerated or planted. Local people know what they are, a memory of the hard work of many grandfathers and some grandmothers.

It was not unusual in the 1950s to see pit heaps smoking, spontaneous combustion leaving them burning dangerously for years. Tales spoke of children lost while innocently playing on the thin crust above a fiery inferno. As the M1 was cut through Nottinghamshire and Yorkshire, many tips – long quiet, cooled and colonised by grasses and birch scrub – were suddenly quarried for burnt shale for road stone; bright red-orange scars appeared and then were gone, whole hills removed.

Nationalisation, post-war economics and new technologies began to encourage greater output from fewer men and fewer mines. Collieries closed and men started to commute to deeper mines further away, where their underground journey might take them a further five to ten miles (under the North Sea in the case of County Durham). Huge spoil heaps began to rise on the flanks of hills, out of valleys. A hill the size of Silbury, Wiltshire could be created in a few shifts, but we are speaking of years of dumping. The bulldozers shifting and grading the massive whalebacks take away the horizon altogether. Travelling along the M1 in south Yorkshire one watches the changes. Giant earthworks, some now covered in grass with cattle grazing (after much experiment), unsettle the seasoned eye – neither fish

327

East Markham, Nottinghamshire.

nor fowl, not natural, not simply functional, but a rude attempt to make things fit in.

While unseemly haste in removing all traces of a mine's existence has worsened the blow for many whose lives were bound up with the pits, there are times and places to agree with Fred Reed's '*Hurrah! They've teun the blot away.*' For more than a hundred years a walk along the beaches between Hartlepool and Sunderland on the north-east coast was like trudging through Hades. While aerial conveyors ceaselessly tipped spoil over the cliffs into the thick, black tide, sea-coalers, with expert eye, filled bags with slack worth burning. After so much for so long, a new geological formation called minestone consolidated feet thick along Blast Beach – a terrible midden.

But since the last pit closed in 1993 locals and professionals have worked to bring twelve miles of coastline back into their lives. More than a million tons of spoil have been removed and the underworld has been redeemed to the extent of achieving Heritage Coast status in 2001; golden sand to black beach and back again in a hundred years.

> *. . . The sea*
> *Has swallowed all the evidence*
> *Of yesterday, its brilliance*
> *Itself a kind of alchemy.*

Katrina Porteous, from *Turning the Tide*

See also BLUE JOHN, BRASS BANDS, COAL MINING, DENES, DIALECTS, FLASHES, GASHOLDERS, INDUSTRIAL CHIMNEYS, INGS, IRONSTONE, JET, LANDMARKS, LEAD MINES, LIMESTONE, QUARRIES.

PLACE-NAMES

The earliest place-names in England were convenient descriptions of locality. People lived by the tongue-shaped pool (Tangmere, Sussex), on the hill with the cuckoos (Yagdon, Shropshire) or by watch bushes (Warboys, Huntingdonshire). But languages evolve and are supplanted, and the forms of words shift and transform through centuries of repetition and mishearing. Place-names became representational labels, their original meanings forgotten, and irrelevant. They survive as garbled fragments of languages that once dominated everyday speech – rich archaeology to the place-name enthusiast.

Before the first century AD the Celts gave us Dover (Dubras, water) and the beginnings of Manchester (Mammucion, the place on breast-shaped hills). The Romans latinised the native names, bringing with them castra (forts) and porta (ports). The post-Roman Celts forced out by Saxon settlers took their language to Wales and Cornwall, where pen (hill) and tre (farm) remain common. Sometimes languages collided where peoples mixed: both elements of 'river Avon' mean the same thing, in Old French and Celtic. Welsh names linger in Herefordshire, Shropshire and Cheshire.

The Anglo-Saxons occupied the land from the fifth century AD. Their tribal groupings were called ingas and they might live in ham (homesteads) or on tun (farmsteads). Deornoth's group had a farm in the future County Durham – Deornoth-ingas-tun – which contracted over the centuries to Darlington. Similarly the homestead of Beornmund's people in Warwickshire became Birmingham. They were subsistence farmers and needed to know if a valley was long and narrow or short and broad, whether a hill was pointed, or low and reasonably level. So they used numerous words for naming places, many of which seem synonymous in their modern forms but originally had specific resonances: cumb (coombe), denu (dean), pic (pike) and dun (down) are a small selection. '*Many topographical words would convey not just an image of a place but also a wealth of information about the likely size, status and pattern of farming practised by the community living there*', Margaret Gelling says.

The Celts, Romans and Saxons occupied the whole country, so regional name differences came from diverse landscapes rather than the manner of description. In the 800s, after relentless attacks from Norse armies, the country was divided along a politically negotiated line roughly from the Wirral in Cheshire to London. The Saxons kept to the south and west. The Norsemen were on the other side, their lands known as Danelaw and the place-names taking a sharper, Scandinavian tone. From Yorkshire to Suffolk farms were denoted by the suffix 'by' rather than tun, homesteads by toft rather than 'ham' – Ulceby, Grimsby, Lowestoft.

From the eleventh century Norman family names were appended to communities they lorded over – such as Ashby de la Zouch and Melton Mowbray in Leicestershire – and their estates – Beaulieu, Belvoir, Richmond, Beaufort.

Naming continues, but the need for description has declined. Since the eighteenth century new communities have adopted the name of the nearest estate (Crewe, Cheshire) or village (Milton Keynes, Buckinghamshire), or have been given names to celebrate the founder (Saltaire, Yorkshire) or the industry that made it possible (Coalville, Leicestershire). In the twentieth century new residential developments took on new allusions. Anzac-on-Sea in Sussex was named in tribute to the antipodean armies during the Second World War; later it became the less-bellicose Peacehaven.

See also DIALECTS, FAMILY NAMES, FIELD NAMES, HOUSE NAMES, NICKNAMES, PUB SIGNS, RAILWAYS, RIVER NAMES.

328

P L U M S

The season for English plums starts in July, with the Early Laxton and Rivers's Early Prolific, and finishes with the September gages. Most plums do not keep long, so they have fallen from favour and may only be found in farm shops, PYO farms, WI markets and local greengrocers. In most supermarkets you will be lucky to find anything other than imported varieties, even when the Victoria is in season – our best-known and most successful plum, discovered as a chance seedling in a garden in Alderton, Sussex in 1840.

During the Second World War forty to fifty thousand tons of plums were grown every year for jam in the traditional plum-growing areas: the Vale of Evesham in Worcestershire, parts of Warwickshire, East Anglia – especially around Wisbech and the Isle of Ely, Cambridgeshire, Norfolk and Huntingdon – and Kent. Since then demand has declined drastically and we are losing valuable local and commercial varieties.

'*The Blaisdon Red is a plum grown within a five-mile radius of Blaisdon in west Gloucestershire. In this district it flourishes with the health and vigour of a weed, but with very few exceptions it does not thrive elsewhere*', wrote Humphrey Phelps, a local grower. It was a popular plum for jam making and canning, and heavy crops were picked from late August by Forest of Dean miners during their holidays. Even though most of the orchards have gone, Blaisdon celebrates the plum on the Sunday before the August bank holiday.

The Kea plum grows in rambling orchards on the Fal estuary in Cornwall and even on the beach, unaffected by the salt-laden sou'westerlies. It is a jamming plum, too tart to eat fresh, and, with a glut only every third year, it typically satisfied only local consumption. However, during the past few years a number of Cornish producers and cider makers have been diversifying into commercial Kea jam, ice-cream and wine production.

The first and second weeks of August are the time to be along the river Dart in Devon, where the Dittisham Ploughman or Small Red still grows in the sheltered valleys. At one time this juicy, rich plum was sold in Dartmouth and Torquay for flavouring ice-cream. Most of the orchards have been ousted by houses, but enough trees grow in local gardens to supply Bramley and Gage, which makes fruit liqueurs. The fresh plums are sold in Dittisham post office in season. Another, much rarer, Devon plum is the Landkey Yellow, a sweet variety from north Devon, which is being propagated by suckers and planted in local community orchards and mazzard greens to save it from extinction.

The Aylesbury Prune is associated with the upper Greensand at the foot of the Chilterns between Weston Turville in Buckinghamshire and Totternhoe in Bedfordshire. In Worcestershire the Pershore Yellow Egg was found in Tiddesley Wood in 1827 by George Crooke, who saw its potential and brought it into cultivation. What remains of the Worcestershire plum industry can be seen on the Vale of Evesham Blossom Route and Cycle Trail devised by Wychavon district council around Pershore and Evesham. The plum blossom comes out first in March, followed by pear in April, then apple. On Pershore Plum Day, every August bank holiday since 1996, many varieties are for sale, including the Pershore Yellow Egg, Pershore Purple and Pershore Emblem, introduced by a local grower in 2000, as well as chutneys, wines and juices.

Gloucestershire is taking its fruit heritage seriously. A mother orchard containing the county's fruit trees is being developed by the county council, and Charles Martell's collection of Gloucester plums includes Blaisdon Plum, Bristol Plum, Dymock Red, Old Pruin and Shit Smock.

The most honeyed and succulent flavours are found in the green and yellow gages, which originally came to us from Armenia via Greece and Italy in the 1680s. The Cambridge Gage was grown by smallholders in Cambridgeshire and is now cultivated by Wilkin and Sons of Tiptree, Essex for delicious greengage jam.

The plum family has its wild relations in the hedgerows – bullaces, sloes and damsons. The small, round bullace is common in East Anglia and Hertfordshire, the damson in Shropshire and Kent. Cherry-plum frequents Oxford and Cambridge, and in Hertfordshire it is known as 'melly-bellies' – Francesca Greenoak thought this might be a corruption of its alternative name, myrobalan. It is still used as a hedging plant; the Rothschilds planted pure hedges of it around their estates in the Chilterns and Vale of Aylesbury.

See also DAMSONS, GREENSAND, HEDGES, NURSERIES, ORCHARDS.

329

P O I N T T O P O I N T

On Boxing Day in the New Forest, Hampshire the only real point-to-point race is run. Competitors, mainly on indigenous ponies, ride across the open forest, unaware, until the day before, where they will ride. In 2002 the three-mile race began at the Weirs and the one-and-a-half-mile race started at the Whitemoor car park at Brockenhurst; the finish was at Spy Holmes near Burley. In 2003 they finished at Brackley Plain near Stoney Cross.

Once, cross-country horse races were run literally from point to ascribed point in the parish (or across parishes from steeple to steeple); these events are now ridden over standard fences around a defined course. They are amateur events

Warwickshire Drooper.

with beginnings in the Worcestershire Hunt in the early 1800s, organised by the hunt or a local group, but patronised by a much wider clientele. The riders often sport their own colours and ride their own horses, which have qualified to run by attending a number of hunting days over the winter. This is one of the few sports that has allowed women to compete with men, although between 1929 and 1967 women were confined to ladies' races; since 1976 competition has been open.

Despite coming under Jockey Club rules in 1969, point to point still offers a wilder experience for rider and onlooker, especially over those courses set out through fields. Used but a couple of times between January and June, the well-defined jumps give the game away throughout the year.

Of the hundred and more courses, one of the most attractive must be Badbury Rings in Dorset. In the shadow of ancient earthworks, al fresco bookies with deep leather bags stand by their easels, deftly exchanging notes for notes, as the crowds, relaxed among other people's Land Rovers, watch the action both far and near over the falling chalk downs.

See also EARTHWORKS, HILL-FORTS, HORSES & PONIES, RACECOURSES, RED FOXES.

330 **P O N D S**

Glacial exploits account for some of our ponds, but most have a different story to tell, an origin in human need. The mysterious abode of Jenny Greenteeth, Will o' the Wisp and Jack o' Lantern, no pond is quite like any other other. Dew ponds watered upland sheep; mill-ponds drove waterwheels; fulling pools degreased wool; lint holes fostered the retting of flax and hemp.

In Surrey the Waggoners' Wells, three large ponds hidden in a deep, wooded valley, are relics of the Wealden iron industry. These 'hammer ponds' – created by damming streams of the river Wey – once powered the bellows and hammers of the forge.

In places ponds were focal points of ancient settlements, for example at Ashmore, north Dorset – its Saxon name means the pond of the ash tree – on a high chalk ridge. Medieval monasteries kept well-stocked fish-ponds, and everywhere ponds were good for swimming and ice skating, fire-fighting, wildfowling, watering cattle and rehydrating wooden cartwheels – pictured in Constable's *Haywain*. Ornamental ponds on great estates improved the view and supplied drinking water for deer.

Cheshire retains a pond-rich landscape beloved of great crested newts, ponds dug as marl pits, to fertilise soils, and some the result of subsidence. The golden age of ponds began in the 1750s, as enclosure spurred farmers to dig field ponds to water their fenced-in stock. The Industrial

Revolution, too, promoted a pock-marked countryside, as clay, sand and gravel were scooped out of the land. A cluster of ponds at the old clay pits of Orton Brickworks in Peterborough supports eight species of pollution-sensitive aquatic plants, the stoneworts. The least-polluted ponds are among the very best natural habitats, sheltering a greater diversity of freshwater species than even the grandest lakes or rivers, including dragonflies, fairy shrimp and water spiders. There are more species of pond-living water beetle in England than there are resident birds. Some old ponds are the ancestral homes of hundreds of generations of frogs, toads and newts.

Three-quarters of our ponds have been lost since the Second World War. But as community groups adopt their local duck pond or create new wetlands to encourage wildlife, these small, liminal places are undergoing a renaissance. At Mayford Green, a busy commuter village near Woking, Surrey, locals say you can '*forget where you are*' sitting by the new pond established on a triangle of old common land that had become a featureless patch of council green. A pond creation scheme at Pinkhill Meadow, between the Thames and Farmoor Reservoir near Oxford, has resulted in a mosaic of some forty ponds and pools of varying size and permanence. Dug in the early 1990s but left to colonise naturally, the new wetland now hosts breeding lapwings, tufted ducks and reed warblers.

See also BOUNDARIES, BRICKS, BROADS, COAL MINING, DEW PONDS, DRAGONS, FENS, FIELDS, FLASHES, GRAVEL PITS, GRAZING MARSHES, HERONRIES, ICE SKATING IN THE OPEN AIR, INGS, LAGOONS, LAKES, MINES, MOATS, MONASTERIES, MOSSES, MOSSLAND, PEAT, RESERVOIRS, RIVERS, SALT MARSHES, SWIMMING PLACES, VILLAGE GREENS, WATER-MEADOWS, WILDFLOWERS.

P O P L A R

It is not the fault of the poplar that it has been used injudiciously – often in rows as screening and bleak wind-breaks. Tall but deciduous, unlike the ubiquitous leylandii, they were chosen because they are fast-growing. The Lombardy poplar, brought here in 1758, can grow sixty to eighty feet in thirty years. Other species, such as the Western Balsam poplar and the Black Italian poplar, are planted to screen water-towers and factories.

In the 1950s grants were given to farmers to plant blocks of hybrid poplars and aspens in wet, damp places to supply matchsticks or for fruit punnets. A second role was to drain odd bits of land that would have been better left for nature. The formal plantings of these 'matchstick poplars' have always looked out of place.

Populus tremula describes the native aspen, with its characteristic sound and sight of white-backed leaves, which colour to a pale yellow in autumn. It is more common in the North, while in the southern counties, particularly Kent and Sussex, it is regarded by many as a weed because of the success of its suckers.

See also ALDER, ANCIENT TREES, ASH, BEECH, BIRCH, BLACK POPLAR, ELM, FIELD MAPLE, HAZEL, HOLLY, HOLM OAK, HORNBEAM, HORSE CHESTNUT, LANDMARK TREES, LIME, LONDON PLANE, MARKET GARDENS, MONKEY-PUZZLE, OAK, ORCHARDS, PEARS, POPLAR, ROWAN, ROYAL FORESTS, SCOTS PINE, SWEET CHESTNUT, SYCAMORE, WALNUT, WHITEBEAM, WILLOW, WOODS, YEW.

PORTLAND LERRETS

The lerret is a 'double ender', said to get its name from the first of its kind, *Lady of Loretto*. Its unique home is Chesil Bank in Dorset; its shape, similar to that of Norse longships, enabled it to land on the steep, shifting shingle and launch into often ferocious seas. Up to seventeen feet long and six feet wide, lerrets were used for mackerel fishing with seine nets; latterly with six oars, now with four, strong arms rowed them through the surf. Landing was just as tricky as launching and was done swiftly by a beach crew to prevent the boat being overwhelmed by the waves. Once ashore, the boat was hauled up the beach over the oars. Its shape was adopted for most ships' lifeboats, as Eric McKee wrote, adding: *'What appears to be a simple canoe form is a successful compromise between buoyancy and power.'*

See also BEACHES, BOATS, COASTS, COBLES, CORNISH GIGS, FLATNERS, HARBOURS, NOBBIES, NORFOLK WHERRIES, PIERS, SEA FISH, SEA TRACTOR, SHINGLE, THAMES SAILING BARGES, TIDES.

POST OFFICES

For more than a century the post office has been at the heart of a place. With the introduction of the Penny Post in 1840, the volume of mail began inexorably to increase and post offices began to appear in cities. Village post offices were established, often in a room in a house or shop, with 'detached counters' for the postal service.

Nunney post office in Somerset has the recognisable red sign above the post-box in the whitewashed wall, together with the signs for '*News*', '*Tobacco*' and '*Confectionery*'. Blankney post office in Lincolnshire is in the back room of an estate house on the corner of Sleaford Road and Metheringham Road. Postmen no longer collect from St

Michael's Mount in Cornwall by rowing boat, but drive at low tide. Port Sunlight model village in Cheshire had a purpose-built general store that became a post office, a corner building in the half-timbered style of the village. Heage in Derbyshire lost its post office in 2003, but the Windmill Inn on Park Road now hosts the service and a general store in one of its rooms.

Town and city post offices are more likely to have been purpose-built. Henry Tanner of the Office of Works designed many post office buildings in the 1890s, including Halifax's former post office, in local sandstone, and Hammersmith's former post office on Blythe Road, whose tall, square, red-brick chimney provides one of London's landmarks. The style, termed 'Post Office Georgian', was popular until the 1930s. Many pre-war buildings were considered too grand for their purpose, or perhaps a useful means of raising money, and were sold off for flats, offices and shops. The high aspirations for civic buildings were beginning to crumble.

In 2004 in the UK there were around 580 post offices and 16,500 sub-post offices run by private agents. They are decreasing. The importance of the sub-post office is deeply underestimated. So much of its role is invisible and unquantifiable in maintaining the viability of the sole shop in a village or suburb and the consequent vitality of the community, which seeks advice, leaves messages and passes news through these informal hubs of local life.

See also HIGH STREETS, LANDMARKS, SHOPS, VILLAGES.

331

POTATOES

Since potatoes arrived from South America in the seventeenth century, varied soils and breeding have led to differentiation. By 1836, 136 varieties were cultivated; today we have around one hundred English varieties. Cambridgeshire had its Ox Noble and Red Nosed Kidney, Lancashire the Fortyfold and the Fluke. Robert Fenn of Sulhamstead, Berkshire named many strains after the county town – Reading Abbey, Reading Ruby, Reading Russet.

The North was kept supplied by Cheshire, Lancashire and Yorkshire. London had the potato fields of north Kent, with its light loams, the Thanet sands and chalk, and East Anglia. Potatoes are still the most significant crop in the Fens, in the fertile and easily worked peat soil. Some are delicately flowered for a brief time; they '*make*

Maris Piper.

the potato fields, for a short period in July, almost as striking as the spring bulb fields', H.J. Mason wrote. There they are stored in 'dickie pies', which encase them in sheeting and straw. Elsewhere soil and straw are used to make 'clamps' to protect them against frost. Early potatoes are grown in the South West, such as the Cornish Early, a distinctive sweet new potato ready by the end of April.

A 1987 survey suggested that the main criteria for choosing a potato were colour and size, with the South preferring a waxy texture and the North a floury one. The pale-skinned King Edward remains the favourite; it has come a long way from its origins as a Northumbrian seedling called Fellside Hero in 1902. After the Second World War a state-assisted breeding programme, based at Maris Lane in Cambridge, developed a number of new varieties, including the ubiquitous Maris Piper.

The food writer Rose Prince urges us to seek out the less common varieties, exclaiming '*this is an area of horticulture where the lack of diversity is virtually criminal*'. Varieties that are recovering against the dominance of the Cara, Estima, King Edward and Maris Piper marketed by superstores include Epicure, developed in Christchurch, Hampshire in 1897, and Sharpe's Express, from Sleaford in Lincolnshire in 1901. About the oldest variety gaining favour once more is the long, knobbly Pink Fir Apple, which has been with us since around 1850. We owe much to the campaigning of Lawrence D. Hills and the Henry Doubleday Research Association, and their *Good Potato Guide*.

The popularity of potatoes has led farmers to plough up green pastures to cultivate them. Herefordshire is one green county that has suffered such 'browning'. In the early 2000s, low carbohydrate diets knocked a hole in potato sales, although the industry did try to fight back in 2004 with what seemed like a contradiction in terms – a low-carb potato.

See also APPLE DAY, APPLES, APRICOTS, ASPARAGUS, AVALON, CATTLE, CHERRIES, COBNUTS, DAMSONS, EASTER CUSTOMS, FENS, FIELDS, FISH & CHIPS, FOOD, FROST & FROST HOLLOWS, GARDENS, GOOSEBERRIES, HONEY & BEES, LIQUORICE, NURSERIES, PEARS, PLUMS, RHUBARB.

332

P O T T E R Y

In prehistory, pottery has always marked the movement and settlement of peoples. The best clays provided goods that were traded so widely that the names of archaeological types, taken from where a fragment was first found, often bear little relation to where they originated.

Hembury ware, discovered at and associated with the Devon village, was made on Cornwall's Lizard peninsula. Neolithic Peterborough ware is widespread, although there are three distinct types: Ebbsfleet (Kent), Mortlake (Surrey) and Fengate (Northamptonshire). The Iron-Age potteries of the Malverns in Worcestershire, and the post-

Roman ones at Hunsbury, Northamptonshire and along the Severn valley in Somerset and Gloucestershire, are just a handful of those that made their mark over the centuries. In the Middle Ages, regional differences continued. Pottery from Mill Green, Essex was typified by green glaze on red earthenware; Cistercian ware from the abbeys of Yorkshire by its dark brown glaze over brick-red clay. Pottery from Scarborough, Yorkshire was popular here and abroad.

Country potteries produced cheap and robust domestic earthenware for centuries until factory production swamped the market. Many potteries, such as Verwood in Dorset, had become bustling concerns by the 1700s. Fremington in Devon added sand from the river Torridge to increase heat resistance. Conversely, at Soil Hill, Yorkshire, natural sand had to be removed for finer goods.

Barnstaple and other places in north Devon are unique in making (still) double-fired 'sgraffito' ware, the coloured surface scratched away in strong patterns to show the underlying clay. Originating in the eastern Mediterranean, with passage via Italy, northern France and the Low Countries, probably with the Huguenots, it is also found in New England and Chesapeake Bay in the US.

When the Industrial Revolution took hold in the eighteenth century the Coal Measures clays began to be more seriously exploited. Burslem, Tunstall, Hanley, Stoke-on-Trent, Fenton and Longton in Staffordshire, along the river Trent and the Trent and Mersey canal, became the world's capital for mass-production – The Potteries. Historic companies, such as Wedgwood and Middleport, emerged. Spode introduced bone china and was an early advocate of porcelain. Its blue and white design came of necessity, cobalt blue being the only pigment that withstood firing. Caughley in Shropshire pioneered its serendipitous use for Chinese willow-pattern designs. Elsewhere, Royal Worcester and Crown Derby began to appear.

Few of the beautiful brick bottle kilns remain in the north Staffordshire Potteries. Old photographs show rows and clusters of seven or so, like enormous sculptures, rising above the roofs of terraced houses. There may have been as

Sgraffito ware, Devon; kiln, Staffordshire.

many as four thousand kilns at one time, with two thousand surviving into the 1950s. The Potteries Preservation Trust calculated that there were just 47 bottle and calcining kilns in 2001. They appear in unexpected places, such as Liverton, Devon, where a curvaceous bottle kiln gives new houses something of character to cluster around.

See also CANALS, FAIRS & FAIRGROUNDS, GORSE, GRAFFITI, HEATHLAND, LANDMARKS, RIVERS, SOILS, SPRINGS.

P O U L T R Y

In every farmyard and orchard hens once scavenged among the ricks and byres, clearing up spilt corn and plucking worms and pests out of muckheaps and soil. Eggs and birds, both live and dead, were sold at local markets; indeed, many back gardens in mid-twentieth-century towns had their own chicken shed.

Prized in orchards, they kept the codlin caterpillars on the run. Cockerels were especially valued for their fighting prowess – the sport was banned here in 1849 – and prized game birds added their character to the domestic fowl stock. Descended from the wild jungle fowl of the Far East, our domestic breeds are cosmopolitan. Large Asiatic birds imported in the mid-nineteenth century laid brown eggs, virtually unknown in Europe until then; Queen Victoria's Cochin Chinas caused a sensation. Among British breeds, the robust Dorking is reckoned by some to be the breed of fowl kept by Iron-Age Britons; the Surrey town has a fine specimen as its town emblem. The Sussex fowl is another old English breed and may once have been found throughout the South East; three varieties, the Light, the Speckled and the Red, were standardised in 1903. Both the Dorking and the Sussex are big, all-purpose breeds with white skins, bred for the London meat market.

The Orpington, in Black, White, Buff and Blue, was first bred in Kent in the 1880s by farmer William Cook. The Old English Pheasant Fowl in Yorkshire and the Derbyshire Redcap, with red earlobes and large combs, are typical of northern breeds. Both are good layers with lively temperaments and a penchant for roosting in trees. The Ixworth is a newcomer, bred in the Suffolk village in 1932.

Intensive poultry units now rely on hybrids. Egg layers with a North American Leghorn ancestry and broilers bred from Plymouth Rocks are incarcerated in long, low sheds with lights on at all hours, the smell carried on breezes that are never felt by the birds. They pay for our cheap food, confined in shaming conditions in dense monocultures, prone to disease that should frighten us.

The foremost domestic duck is the Aylesbury – the Buckinghamshire town was famed in the nineteenth century as the source of fine white ducks for the table,

although most Aylesburys today are hybrid broiler ducks with substantial Chinese ancestry.

Domestic geese, descended from wild greylags, are hardy grazing birds that resist intensive rearing. Allowed to run loose in an orchard or paddock, they keep pests down and clear up after the harvest. Substantial flocks walked from the East Anglian Fens to London or the Nottingham Goose Fair, with the soles of their feet tarred to save them from wear.

See also ALLOTMENTS, CATTLE, EAST, FAIRS & FAIRGROUNDS, FARMS & FARMSTEADS, GARDENS, ORCHARDS, PONDS, SHEEP, WEATHER-VANES.

P R E F A B S

Arcon, Orlit, Phoenix, Spooner, Tarran, Uni-Seco, Universal, Weir Paragon – these 'brand names' touch the hearts of those who have ever lived in a prefab. The name 'temps' never appealed, yet the aspiration was that these single-storey, quick-built, prefabricated dwelling units would be gone in a decade or so. After sixty years some still linger, although they are going fast and, almost like pets, are remembered with nostalgic warmth. Less so the prefabricated tower blocks that came later.

In 1945 housing was just one in a heap of problems. But Churchill had an understanding of the history of the dangerous years after the First World War, when Homes for Heroes, a pacifying promise to Bolshy boys returning radicalised from the fronts, failed to materialise. Nissen huts would not do, they were too ingrained in forces' memories as inadequate. The Temporary Housing Programme might, as a title, buy some time, but people still wanted solidity, electricity, plumbing.

The task was huge. In Coventry alone tens of thousands had been bombed out of house and home. And nationally the marriage rate was soaring, as men re-entered civvy street

333

and women, pushed out of wartime jobs, were encouraged to settle down and home-make.

Enter prefabs – palaces for the people. Characterised by flat or low-pitched, corrugated-iron or asbestos roofs and concrete or aluminium walls, simple, single-storey, two-bed, detached bungalows began to appear in droves around and in cities and towns; acres, sometimes, of single-storey white blocks. There were surprises; anyone who travels the A303 through Somerset will know, not far from the bakery that puts its loaf out on a table by the highway, the landmark group of four red-roofed, semi-detached, two-storey wonders that stands curvaceously down the hill at West Camel.

They outlasted many a younger tower block, but most have now gone. Their ghosts are pointed out, and fights have been won to save the aluminium bungalows on Dolphin Road in Redditch, Worcestershire. The row of Phoenix prefabs at Wake Green Road in Moseley, Birmingham has been listed Grade II; an estate of Uni-Secos stands proud in a conservation area in Catford, some of the three hundred out of London's ten thousand that cling on. In Bristol and Avonmouth four estates of seven hundred prefabs began to disappear in 2003, while the Peabody Trust commissioned Yorkon to make 61 new dwellings for Raines Dairy in Stoke Newington, London, in four- and six-storey buildings made from container-like prefabricated units.

See also BUNGALOWS, CORRUGATED IRON, TOWER BLOCKS.

PRIDDY SHEEP FAIR

This is one of few authentic surviving fairs. It is held on the Wednesday nearest to 21 August, on the triangular green around which a scatter of farms and houses make up the former lead-mining village of Priddy on the Mendips in Somerset.

The fair is more than six hundred years old and has maintained a veracity born of commerce without modern commercialism. All year round the sheep hurdles are stacked under a thatched rick on the green; its maintenance by the villagers is a condition of the fair's survival, according to local superstition.

Under the shade of a line of ash trees perhaps a hundred coloured horses and foals are tied up, scrutinised by groups of men and, if fancied, taken away for a trot. The sheep pens are set up in the centre of the green; the packed sheep pant for lack of shade. The auctioneers stand in a truck and trundle along the line of pens, starting with the lambs, moving on to ewes with lambs, then rams and wethers. All around is horse tackle, fast food and simple fairground activity. Stalls sell Romany paintings of *vardos*, lurchers and horses, as well as mugs, plates and rows of soft tigers. A narrow booth, flanked by very big fellows, sells gold jewellery.

Up the hill by the church, rows of old agricultural implements, shoe lasts and other paraphernalia lie strewn on the grass for inspection, waiting for the auctioneer.

See also BARROWS, CAVES, FAIRS & FAIRGROUNDS, GYPSIES, HORSES & PONIES, LEAD MINES, LIMESTONE, SHEEP, VILLAGE GREENS.

PROMENADES

Promenading under avenues of trees became popular in the seventeenth and eighteenth centuries; any town with pretensions to gentility had its parade, walk or promenade. The fashion for strolling, being seen, observing and taking tea began to extend to the seaside, with promenades describing polite society as well as the edge of the land.

The development of coastal resorts began at Scarborough, Yorkshire in 1700, where the first Spa House by the sea was built as it became fashionable to walk or promenade along the beach as well as taking the waters. Esplanades, or sea-side promenades, were built partly as sea defences, but the trend for social walking meant that they offered a wider attraction. The first was developed at Weymouth, Dorset in the 1770s, after the construction of the earliest resort building to face the sea.

Genteel Sidmouth in Devon has less than a mile of esplanade tucked between the red rocks of the bay; it was built in 1837 after the railway arrived, and featured a library, which sold books and roll-out panoramas of the sea front. On the Wirral in Cheshire New Brighton's wide Marine

Promenade, built on sand-dunes by a speculator in the 1830s, offered a destination for Liverpool's day trippers on a ferry across the Mersey.

I do like to stroll along the prom, prom, prom,
Where the brass bands play
Tiddly-om-pom-pom

Promenades are bordered by decorative iron-work railings, lamps, seats and Victorian shelters, intended for winter use as well as breezy summer days. The Golden Mile in Blackpool, Lancashire, with its wide, busy promenade and tramways, has ornate nineteenth-century wind shelters, piers, rides and the 518-foot-high Tower, which opened in 1894. As part of the rebuilding of the sea defences on the south shore, three new wind shelters, a striking and graceful design by Ian McChesney, rotate with the prevailing wind. The accepted health benefits of sea air and the sea resorts that established themselves during the last two centuries have left an enduring association with rest and recuperation as well as the bright lights and bustle of the resorts. Skegness is still *'so bracing!'*, as the Great Northern Railway poster of 1923-47 proclaimed, and a walk on the prom proves it.

See also AVENUES, BANDSTANDS, BEACHES, BRASS BANDS, COASTLINE, COASTS, FERRIES, FLOODS, HOTELS, LIBRARIES, PARKS, PIERS, PUNCH AND JUDY, SAND-DUNES, SHINGLE, SPAS.

P U B   G A M E S

Games played in inns and taverns are a hangover from a partially idealised past, where a warm fire and cheap ale was a traveller's boon and villagers spent evenings at talk and sports. Pubs struggle to retain their position as community centres in the twenty-first century, when it is easier and cheaper for people to stay at home; pub games might draw them back.

Darts has weathered the storms. Its regionality is revealed by the type of board: the predominant London, or trebles, board evolved from a combination of local standards from Yorkshire, Lincoln, Burton upon Trent and Ireland. The Waterman's Arms in east London is one place where East End darts, or Fives, is still played, its board segments scoring multiples of five. *'Players in the south Manchester darts league traditionally play with a Log-end dart board'*, Linda Neilson from Droylsden tells us. The Manchester, or Lancashire, board is still used in the Log-end leagues in and around the city. The board is made from a section of elm tree, dyed black. It must be kept in water when not in use to prevent splitting. The numbers are arranged differently and there is no trebles ring.

There are table games, such as Euchre, a card game popular west of Bristol, and dominoes, which can be very different depending on where you are. Double sixes are the most widely played, but *'dominoes in Chorley or Blackpool can have more spots'*, Aiden Turner-Bishop says, necessary when Lancashire plays up to double fifteens. Double twelves are favoured in Staffordshire and double nines around Wigan, Lancashire.

For the slightly more active there is skittles. The basic version is Oxfordshire's Aunt Sally, with sticks thrown at a solitary 'dolly'. The Old English, or London, game has a 'cheese' thrown against truncheon-shaped skittles without first hitting the floor. The east Midlands has Long-Alley skittles. In the West Country players sometimes do the 'Dorset flop', launching themselves to propel the ball with both hands. Gloucester's pins are barrel-shaped; Bristol's and Devon's have bulges in the middle. In Hertfordshire's Rolly Polly, or Half-Bowl, the ball passes the pins, hitting them on the rebound. The list of differences seems nearly endless, table skittles in the east Midlands becoming

335

Hood skittles in Northamptonshire, Leicestershire and Bedfordshire and Daddlums in Kent.

Ringing the Bull involves swinging a ring on a rope to hoop over a wall-mounted horn or hook. The game has been played for so many centuries in The Trip to Jerusalem in Nottingham that the swing line has scored a trench in the sandstone wall. In Sussex you might play Toad in the Hole; in East Anglia the same game might be called Pitch Penny, Penny Slot, Tossing the Penny or Penny in a Hole. Shove Ha'penny (Push-penny around Stamford in Lincolnshire) remains popular, despite decimal coinage.

Marbles, too, has its champions. The Greyhound at Tinsley Green in Sussex has hosted the International Marbles Championship since the 1930s. Good Friday was once Marble Day, marking the end of the marble season; it was one of the few games permitted during Lent.

See also BEER, CIDER & CIDER ORCHARDS, ELM, GAMES, HORSE CHESTNUT, INNS, PUBS, QUOITS I, SHROVETIDE GAMES.

P U B S

With roots in monastic hospices for pilgrims, inns evolved to offer bed and food, while pubs grew into taverns for casual drinking and talk. Pubs long carried a reputation for being at the heart of community life, although they had developed two front doors – one leading to a public bar for the workers and the other to a more comfortable, slightly more expensive lounge for ladies and gentlemen.

Steeple Claydon in Buckinghamshire had a rhyme – 'The Black Horse kicked the Crown/then drunk the Fountain dry./The Sportsman shot the Prince of Wales/and made the Phoenix fly' – a litany of the village's pubs. The Prince of Wales, The Fountain and The Phoenix have outlived the others, but many villages have lost their only pub as wrong-headed alterations have driven the regulars away.

The mirrored and tiled Victorian bar with its billiard room, such as The Assembly Rooms in Kentish Town, London, is a contrast with the flag floor, log fire and quiet of the tiny country pub. But most local pubs are neither, and some have survived at the expense of their traditions, games, fabric and atmosphere. City pubs may have staked all on the big screen and the big games. Country pubs have to attract drivers, specialising in food rather than beer and welcoming families. The worst attempts to attract tourists by contriving fake 'olde worldeness' involve exotic materials, poor craftsmanship, bizarre memorabilia and brass pumps serving insipid corporate beers.

Authenticity is about outside and inside. The way a pub is extended, painted, advertised, lit and how the car park is organised may jar with the street or village. The Campaign for Real Ale, which has done so much to support publicans'

and punters' interest in real ale and real cider, also believes in the 'real' pub. A *National Inventory of Pub Interiors of Outstanding Heritage Interest* has been established, but as few as 250 out of sixty thousand pubs qualify for inclusion. Birmingham's Three Magpies ('1930s "Moderne"') and the Victorian Turf Tavern in Bloxwich, Staffordshire are among them, the Midlands having a particularly high proportion of survivors.

See also ALBION, ASPARAGUS, BEER, BLACK DOGS, BRICKS, BUILDING STONES, CAFÉS, CIDER & CIDER ORCHARDS, DAMSONS, DROVE ROADS, FOOTBALL, GAMES, GREEN MAN, HARE PIE SCRAMBLE, HAXEY HOOD GAME, INNS, MORRIS DANCING, MUMMING PLAYS, PEARS, PLUMS, PUB GAMES, PUB SIGNS, SHROVETIDE GAMES, TAR BARREL ROLLING, VILLAGES, WASSAILING.

P U B   S I G N S

History runs through it: an original Roman sign for a place where drinks could be taken depicted two slaves with an amphora slung between them, a sign so similar to the typical Two Brewers running with a barrel that it must be related. Before literacy was commonplace, visual cues were used to indicate where ale could be drunk. From the Romans we caught the habit of hanging ivy or other evergreens around a pole – The Bush is recognised as an early name derived from this, with cousins such as The Holly Bush in Hampstead, London, a tavern since the early 1800s, and The Furze Bush on Hatt Common at Ball Hill in Berkshire. Occasionally we still see three-dimensional pub signs, as at The Eight Bells in Bolney, Sussex. Suns and moons must be among the oldest simple signs. The Sun in Splendour in Notting Hill, London could never be eclipsed by The Electric Inn in Birmingham, although it reflects the power of progress.

Inns and pubs had several origins: they grew out of religious houses giving shelter to travellers and pilgrims, or to masons and builders (The Cross Keys, The Masons' Arms); from ale houses created by landowners in city or country for workers and to add to estate income (The Duke of Devonshire at Beeley, Derbyshire); or from simple homes selling beer in the front room.

Some names mark time. The self-proclaimed oldest inn in England, The Trip to Jerusalem, which emerges out of the Castle Rock in Nottingham, and The Man in Space at Hilltop, just nine miles away, span eight centuries. The Trip, opened in 1189, recalls those journeying to the crusades, while the twentieth-century Eastwood pub took as its founding event a short walk but a longer journey – the sign shows an umbilically connected space walker.

Some signs tell stories. The Dam Busters are remembered in their Lancaster Bombers on the sign of The Ladybower at Ashopton, Derbyshire, close by the reservoir where they did their dry runs. Traumatic local events must

be referenced in The Bull i' th' Thorn at Hurdlow, also in the Peak District, which houses an old wooden carving of a beast entwined in a hedge (Bulithornes Field in Derbyshire dates from 1373). The Bull in the Oak is found near Market Bosworth in Leicestershire, and the home of the famous song, The Old Bull and Bush, is in Golders Green, north London.

The Snowdrop Inn in Lewes, Sussex is a reminder of an exceptional snow, which claimed eight lives in 1836. The Coble at Newbiggin-by-the-Sea in Northumberland and The Yorkshire Coble at Redcar, Yorkshire both refer to fishing boats, luggers with flat bottoms specific to the North East. The Plate of Elvers at Longney, Gloucestershire celebrates the nearby Severn, renowned for its eel fishing. In the early 1990s The Cob Tree at Ightham in Kent renewed its sign after being taken over by a chain, but after local agitation the horse (a Welsh Cob) standing under a tree was exchanged for a sparkling new sign with catkins, hazelnuts and branches – a cob in Kent is a hazel tree. The pub has gone the way of many, now a private residence.

The George Eliot at Nuneaton, close to Mary Ann Evans's birthplace in Arbury, Warwickshire, commemorates one of very few women, apart from dignitaries, referred to in pub names. The sign for The Quiet Woman usually offers a less than kind reference, while The Long Bow in Tunbridge Wells surprises, being named in 1938 after Mrs Nettleton, the world archery champion.

In Knaresborough, north Yorkshire Mother Shipton, the sixteenth-century soothsayer, foretold that the third time that the bridge over the Nidd fell it would be the end of the world. The World's End now sports a sign with a vehicle plunging into the river. Another memorable crone gave her name to The Old Mother Red Cap, a country

pub in the seventeenth century, later engulfed by Camden Town, London. It lost its name as late as the 1980s to become The World's End.

Many pubs have been taken over by chains and have had their names and signs altered to reflect the fact. The loss to locality can be measured in the demise of local stories, names and events, as well as intriguing inn signs, but it is not a new or simple phenomenon.

See also ABBEYS, ALMSHOUSES, BEER, BELLS & BELL-RINGING, BLACK & WHITE BUILDINGS, BREWERIES, CAVES, COBLES, EELS, GAMES, GREEN MAN, HAZEL, HOPS, HOP-GARDENS & HOP-YARDS, HOTELS, INNS, LANDSLIPS, PLACE-NAMES, PUBS, SPRINGS.

PUDDINGS

The English muse is at its inventive best where the devising of comforting, sweet puddings is concerned. Made with eggs and milk, baked or steamed in a basin, full of custard, treacle, jams or jellies, fresh or dried apples, cherries or rhubarb, puddings are enormously diverse – a state of affairs, as always, ignored by the bland superstore shelves. Who would choose a frozen supermarket sponge over the delights of Oldbury tarts from Gloucestershire – stuffed with gooseberries – or the spicy, fruity, steamed Helston pudding from Cornwall, or Kent's Tunbridge fried cherry batter, served over baked cherries?

Some specialities continue to be associated with special occasions: the Helston Furry Dance in May; the Cotswold games at Whitsun in Oldbury. Likewise the Wilfra tart is made for an annual procession to Ripon Cathedral in Yorkshire, celebrating St Wilfrid. Bridgwater Carnival has its own pudding, a baked trifle with ice-cream, sherry or rum, topped with meringue. Treacle tarts made with dried fruit, apple, spices, breadcrumbs and syrup – more like Christmas mince pies – were made for Wareham's Cuckoo Fair in Dorset. Norfolk's treacle tart was originally made with black treacle and flavoured with lemon.

Some have grown out of practicality. Bread puddings were a tasty way of using up stale bread, as with Newcastle's steamed bread pudding, flavoured with lemon zest and served with lemon sauce, or Manchester pudding, combining crumbs with eggs, milk, layers of jam and sometimes meringue topping. In Norfolk, Nelson slices add dried fruit, lemon rind, rum and marmalade to the bread.

There were concoctions, such as Sussex pond pudding, a suet case with a whole lemon inside. Leominster in Herefordshire had its custard pie, Cambridge its burnt cream. So many places have – or had – their own special pudding or tart that it is a positive scandal that they are so little known: Cheltenham in Gloucestershire, Canterbury in Kent, Gloucester, Tadcaster in Yorkshire, Chester, Chichester in Sussex and Deptford in Kent all

337

had unique offerings. Reviving such local recipes could only have a positive impact on local fruit growing, and the freshest ingredients would enhance such mouth-watering treats as Banbury apple pie from Oxfordshire, Malvern apple pudding from Worcestershire, Lancashire fruit braid, Fen country apple cake, Dorset dumplings, Norfolk apple jacks and Nottingham batter and apple pudding (cored apples, stuffed with sugar and spices, cooked standing in batter).

See also APPLE DAY, APPLES, APRICOTS, BAKEWELL PUDDING, CARNIVALS, CHERRIES, CIDER & CIDER ORCHARDS, CUCKOOS & CUCKOO POUNDS, DAMSONS, FAIRS & FAIRGROUNDS, FOOD, GOOSEBERRIES, HONEY & BEES, ORCHARDS, PEARS, PIES, PLUMS.

PUDDINGSTONE

A strange stone stands under the oak at the heart of Standon in Hertfordshire. Glacial conglomerate doesn't have the same ring as its local name of plum pudding stone. Dropped by a passing ice sheet, boulders made up from a compaction of pebbles cemented by silica have long been prized in the county. They have a reputation for protection from the evil eye and from witchcraft, and are often found in churchyards, gateways and busy corners. They might find work as church foundation or cottage wall stone.

Their other name is mother stone, since it is believed that cobbles are growing within them. Near the ford at St Michael's, by St Albans, Hertfordshire, a blob of yellowish quartzite full of baby brown and pink flints stands three feet high by five feet long. After a main course of glacial debris perhaps you might like to try a 'recipe' for this natural concrete, which dates from 1820:

> *To Make Puddingstone*
> *To vary your dishes, and shun any waste,*
> *Should you have any left of the very same paste,*
> *You may make a plum-pudding; but then do not stint*
> *The quantum of Pebbles – Chert, Jasper, or Flint.*

John Scafe, from 'A Geological Primer in Verse'

See also FOLKTALES, FORDS, OAK, ROCKS.

PUNCH AND JUDY

Every May a surfeit of Punches and Judys gathers at London's Covent Garden. They celebrate Samuel Pepys, who wrote in 1662 about seeing Punchinello from Italy. Puppets were already popular in Tudor England, associated with the fair, but these characters have outlasted them all as popular open-air entertainment. With the railways and

rising interest in taking the sea air, the puppet booth found a new habitat and took on the stripes of the seaside.

The plot atrophied in the 1820s after being written down by a journalist, yet every show has its own script and the making of the 'swazzle' is personal – this metal mouth-part changes the voice to the characteristic high, vibrating tone of Mr Punch. Somehow the Punch and Judy show embodies the wild aspects of popular culture, shifting, offensive, anarchic.

See also BEACHES, BLACKPOOL ROCK, BRASS BANDS, COASTS, FAIRS & FAIRGROUNDS.

338

QR

Raleigh Medium/Demi, Robert Norton, 1978.

QUAKER MEETING-HOUSES

Believing that all men and women were equal in the sight of God, that there was no need for clergy and that no place was more sacred than any other, the Society of Friends emerged in a time of religious dissent. George Fox was its founder, and Pulpit Rock in Sedbergh, Yorkshire marks the place of the first gathering in 1652 with a plaque. *'Tremble at the word of the Lord'*, they were advised; consequently they were nicknamed Quakers.

Among Christian places of worship, even nonconformist chapels, Friends meeting-houses are distinguished by simplicity. Friends originally gathered in homes. Some meetings were held outside, perhaps in burial grounds, such as at Idle, Yorkshire. Meeting-houses were discreetly tucked away in country backwaters, out of persecution's reach, until the Declaration of Indulgence in 1688 enabled them to multiply unhindered.

The meeting-house at Jordans, near Chalfont St Giles in Buckinghamshire, among orchards of apples and cherries, cruelly burnt down in 2005; it had remained unchanged since 1688. Hertford's dates from 1670. Superficially it blends in with its surroundings, but inside it is unusually large to accommodate the local congregation. Come-to-Good in Kea, Cornwall is a thatched, whitewashed cottage, built in 1710, almost hidden under trees. At Alton, Hampshire the building is whitewashed with a tiled roof, matching nearby houses.

This domestic style signals the difference between unconsecrated meeting-houses and churches. Hubert Lidbetter wrote of early meeting-houses in 1935, noticing how they retained architectural integrity over centuries, an advantage of choosing the *'simple and beautiful'*. No paraphernalia of liturgy and ritual is required for the contemplative silence that dominates meetings, only benches and perhaps a platform for elders. Windows in early examples were usually set high to discourage distraction from the world outside. This simplicity of use reinforces and echoes the atmosphere of calm that permeates these *'truthful buildings'*, as Lidbetter described them.

Larger-scale meeting-houses, lacking the intimacy of the earlier ones, followed the Industrial Revolution, which swelled the Society's urban ranks. The façade of Mount Street, Manchester, built in 1830,

is a classical portico of pilasters and pediment with steps up to the entrance. The portico became a common feature in the eighteenth century; York, Darlington in County Durham (both now gone) and Peckham and Stoke Newington in London all followed the fashion. Street names remember their presence in Friends Road and Quaker Lane in London. The Rusland valley in the Lake District has a Quaker Wood.

See also BUILDING STONES, CEMETERIES, CHAPELS, CHURCHES, CHURCHYARDS, CORRUGATED IRON, CROSSROADS, MOSQUES, ROUND-TOWERED CHURCHES, SYNAGOGUES, TEMPLES, TIN TABERNACLES.

QUARRIES

Open pits from which stone or minerals are won make for dramatic landscapes. Vast and extending faces of limestone follow the A515 south of Buxton and the looping edge of the Peak District National Park, whose boundaries, in 1951, were drawn blatantly not to protect but to ensure a future for quarrying. Here, and around Castleton and Wirksworth in Derbyshire, the trees and fields used to be white with lime dust.

Visible for miles, the little church of Breedon on the Hill in north Leicestershire stands defiantly above a quarry that gnaws at its foundations. Delabole Quarry in Cornwall has been in production since medieval times and, at six hundred feet deep and a mile wide, is one of our biggest holes. Tony Foster painted the disused granite quarries of Luxulyan, Cornwall as part of his Parish Map. Luxullianite, with its black tourmaline and contrasting pink feldspar, was much prized; it was used in the Duke of Wellington's tomb at St Paul's, London.

From the fell quarries of Cumberland horses carried slate in panniers down to the sea; one route, called Moses Trod, runs for thirteen miles

341

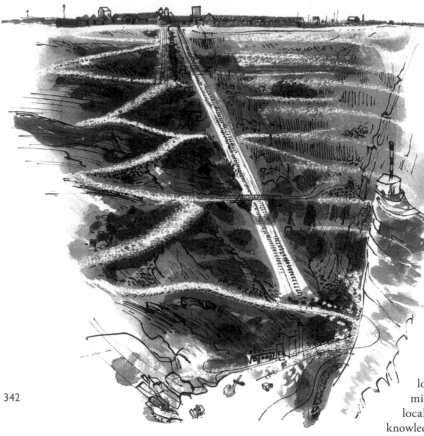

masters. Many old quarries have disappeared under the weight of our waste, often earning as much money for rubbish dumping as they did when producing stone. They have become our middens; future archaeology will have much to do.

Scale is everything. Massive workings, often for aggregates and road stone, and proposals for industrial extensions bring big protests, as in the Mendips, Somerset. The impact in terms of change of scene, never mind the noise and transport generated, can change a place forever.

On the other hand, small quarries serving local needs are vital if local distinctiveness is to be maintained. Decisions must be taken carefully. Instead of a multinational company devouring mountains for uses far away, small quarries could be re-opened close to home. This would mean that new buildings and repairs could be made from local material, the knowledge of how to mine and work the stone, and its attendant local language, would flourish, and working knowledge and pride would be riveted back into local culture.

The Herefordshire Stone Tile project, a local initiative grant-aided by English Heritage, is raising awareness and promoting the use of new stone slates and training in how to cut and dress them. In less than a year new slates from local 'delves' for the restoration of Dore Abbey were being supplied in 2002: *A significant reason for the popular support for this project is that delving is very much a small, handcrafted operation . . . production is small . . . and seen as an important source of income for local farmers.'*

See also BRICKS, BRIDGES, BUILDING STONES, CAIRNS, CASTLES, CHALK, CHURCHES, CORRUGATED IRON, DRYSTONE WALLS, FLINT, GRANITE, GRAVESTONES, GREENSAND, HIGH STREETS, IRONSTONE, KERBSTONES, LIGHTHOUSES, LIME-KILNS, LIMESTONE, MILLSTONE GRIT, PAVEMENTS, PLACE-NAMES, PUDDINGSTONE, SANDSTONES, SCULPTURES, SHINERS, TUNNELS, UNLUCKY WORDS, VACCARY WALLS, VILLAGES.

QUARTERS

Chichester, Sussex is divided by North, East, South and West thoroughfares, a physical memory of the Roman Empire. Latin quarters they are not, but increasingly we use 'quarter' to relate to neighbourhoods with recognisable identities, especially when 'regeneration' is in the air.

from Honister Hause to Ravenglass. No doubt, in the long future, stories of giants making steps, the better to climb mountains, will evolve to explain the relict quarries in different states of reclamation by nature.

Collyweston stone from Northamptonshire was mined, the blocks of stone kept underground until winter, when they were brought to the surface to allow the frost to help in splitting for roofing. The stone mines around Corsham, Wiltshire housed the Central Ammunition Depot during the Second World War, as well as providing a wartime repository for national art treasures and, later, a nuclear bunker. Chilmark quarries, also in Wiltshire, which produced the stone for Salisbury Cathedral, continue in production from underground.

Some quarries are tourist destinations, the sole source of income now that the economy of stone has gone global. Beer stone mine in Devon receives more than twenty thousand visitors a year to its man-made caves. In Cumberland Cowraik Quarry is a local nature reserve, with red squirrels amid the red sandstone; archaic dunes visible in the quarry face excite geologists and support green tiger beetles. On the much-quarried Isle of Portland in Dorset, the old workings at Tout Quarry are full of limestone sculptures, two decades of work by students and

It has become *de rigueur* to contemplate the revival of parts of cities in terms of social or working 'quarters', usually based around old street patterns and buildings of character that cry out for new uses. In its *City Centre Strategy* of 1994, Sheffield identified eleven quarters. The Cathedral Quarter characteristically has steep lanes. Derelict warehouses taken on by Yorkshire ArtSpace, which created a draw that brought artists, musicians and film makers together in the 1980s, is dulled with the title of Cultural Industries Quarter. The street layout is based on that of the eighteenth century, when small businesses set up with impressive façades in front of workshops, frequently rented by the so-called Little Mesters, self-employed cutlery makers.

Artists are often at the heart of unplanned re-creation of belief in an area. Spike Island in Bristol and, in east London, Wapping, then Hackney, then Hoxton owe much to the willingness of artists to create communities in cheap and interesting, run-down parts of town. Their inevitable displacement by 'risk-taking' developers is the greatest irony.

Authenticity can be elusive, but spearheaded by Birmingham's Irish Community Forum, Digbeth has become the city's Irish Quarter, centred on the culverted river Rea, an area settled long ago by the navvies who built the canals and much of the Victorian city. Bradford's Victorian warehousing area, centred on the now demolished Exchange Station, was known as Little Germany because of the resident family businesses.

Birmingham has been busy restoring buildings in the Jewellery Quarter. Hull's Museums Quarter embraces four museums in the High Street, including Wilberforce House. These are a far cry from the vibrancy of London's cosmopolitan Soho or Pakistani, Sikh and Sri Lankan Southall, which speak of identity being generated spontaneously as opposed to being manufactured and marketed.

See also ARTISTS' COLONIES & SCHOOLS, CANALS, CHINATOWNS, MUSEUMS, WAREHOUSES.

Q U I C K S A N D

Stories of old grey mares being sucked under the quicksand and of people being overtaken by tides roaring in 'swifter than a galloping horse' should put anyone off crossing the vast sand expanses of Morecambe Bay or the Solway Firth, where safe ways across the sand are called waths.

In Lancashire, North of the Sands, the milestone at Cartmel offers the siren call '*Lancaster over sands 15 miles/ Ulverston over sands 7 miles*', saving ten and four miles respectively. Before the building of the railway in 1857 from Hest Bank to Kents Bank, many did not make it across this treacherous terrain, where the Kent and Keer disgorge their water through shifting patterns of silt. The river Keer has dangerous 'poos', or rivulets, with quicksand on the inside

of meanders, and the channels are always on the move. Deep freshwater springs also bring problems.

Travellers were tempted by the short cuts, but only fools would go without a guide. Indeed so important was the task that in the sixteenth century King John made it a royal appointment. The current Queen's Guide to the Sands of Morecambe Bay, Cedric Robinson, tests the cross-sands walk in his bare feet to really feel the texture and micro-movement of the sand. Only then will he lead walkers in summer across the eight to twelve miles to Grange-over-Sands. When people get into trouble, the Arnside fire engine may come to the rescue, and Bay Hovercraft Rescue has built two amphibious vehicles, now on constant standby.

See also BEACHES, BELLS & BELL-RINGING, ESTUARIES, FOOTPATHS, RIVERS, SHELLFISH, TIDES.

Q U O I T S   I

Perhaps for a thousand years around mining communities metal rings have been thrown across a pitch to encircle a pin or hob embedded in soft clay.

In Ford and Etal in Northumberland the game is still played in the summer, each player having two rings of twelve pounds to throw from each end over the metal pin. In Beadnell old quoits were used to weight down salmon nets. With current rules published in 1881, the Northern Game, with an eleven-yard pitch, persists in Cumberland, Northumberland and Westmorland, with pockets in Durham and Yorkshire (the rules may differ). The North Tyne and Redesdale Agricultural Society runs an Open Quoits Competition at the annual Bellingham Show.

A version of the Long Game is played in East Anglia, especially in pubs in and around Rougham in Suffolk, where an eighteen-yard pitch is used with eleven-pound quoits of about nine inches diameter (nearly twice that of the Northern Game).

See also AGRICULTURAL SHOWS, DEVIL, GAMES, INNS, MINES, PUB GAMES, PUBS, PUB SIGNS.

343

Q U O I T S   I I

Quoit is a Cornish term for a neolithic communal burial chamber. They are most prevalent in Cornwall and the fringes of Dartmoor, but are also found in Kent. Outside England they occur in Portugal, Brittany, Ireland, Scotland and Wales. Originally covered with earth, their bare stone structures comprise enormous horizontal capstones supported by large upright stones or stone slabs, some reaching ten to fifteen feet in height. Some quoits are also known as portal dolmens, because two of the upright stones act as the entrance to the burial chamber.

The moorland of south-west Cornwall is the heartland of these megalithic tombs, and a number survive in varying stages of disintegration. Lanyon Quoit, perhaps the most well-known and resembling a giant's table, was rebuilt in 1824 following its collapse in a storm; now it is supported only on three 'legs', after the fourth broke during reconstruction. A few miles away Chun Quoit survives more or less unaltered, apart from the removal of its earth covering. It is an example of the closed-box type of quoit, with no stone doorway, looking rather like a huge stone toadstool. Mulfra, Trethevy and Zennor Quoits also enrich the West Penwith landscape.

It is more of a surprise suddenly to come across Spinsters' Rock near the Dartmoor village of Drewsteignton, in the domestic setting of a pasture. Also rebuilt in the 1800s, Spinsters' Rock is named after three legendary women – wool-spinners, or spinsters – who are said to have built the quoit for fun on their journey to deliver their spun wool. Three uprights carry a capstone weighing about sixteen tons.

Kit's Coty House, caged behind iron railings in a field near Aylesford in Kent, was described by Samuel Pepys: '*Three great Stones Standing upright and a great round one lying on them, of great bigness, although not so big as those on Salisbury Plain. But certainly it is a thing of great antiquity, and I am mightily glad to see it.*' The tomb has lost one of its great stones, apparently blown up in 1867, and its large covering of earth, which extended 180 feet in length.

See also BARROWS, CEMETERIES, CHURCHYARDS, EARTHWORKS, FOLKTALES, GIANTS, RIVERS, STANDING STONES.

Q U O M P S

Local to the borders of Hampshire and Dorset, a quomp, as Mr Hodges of Christchurch, Hampshire notes, '*is an onomatopoeic name for places built on swamps, because when you walked on them they made a hollow sound. There are areas called The Quomps by the quay at Christchurch, and further up the river Stour near the Moors river.*' Bob Gibbons adds: '*There is a road called The Quomp in Ringwood. Maybe it's a corruption of swamp, as they are always in wet places.*'

See also BANDSTANDS, BEACHES, COASTS, FENS, FLOODS, GRAZING MARSHES, INGS, MOSSLAND, OSIERS, OTTERS, PEAT, SALT MARSHES, WILLOW.

344

R A C E C O U R S E S

Testing horses against one another is an ancient practice, revealing stamina, speed and the skills of both rider and horse, and settling a wager or two.

In Derbyshire, north of Eyam, the quality of horses used to be determined on the long, straight road known locally as the Bretton racecourse. The oldest flat race in England, traced from 1519 and annually since 1618, the Kiplingcotes Derby is run over four miles of lanes and tracks in east Yorkshire. On the third Thursday in March it starts at Etton and ends at a white post at Londesborough Wold Farm in the parish of Middleton-on-the-Wolds.

The July Course at Newmarket runs parallel with the ancient Devil's Dyke, where horses have been tested for centuries, although no one seems to know how many.

Many races seem to have their origins on common land and '*Racedays were general holidays for all classes, except a few who thought racing was sinful*', according to Edward Goldsworthy in his *Recollections of Old Taunton Racecourse*.

Many racecourses were turned into airfields during the Second World War. Some faded away, but at Easton on the Hill, near Stamford in Lincolnshire, a field fifty yards wide and about half a mile in length is a remnant of the town racecourse.

Brighton's left-handed big dipper of a track flanks the Sussex Downs. Salisbury's course in Wiltshire perches '*upon the doune*', way above the Cathedral. Beverley racecourse spans part of a great chalk wold common, which looks down over town and Minster and across the boulder clay lowlands of Holderness in east Yorkshire.

Epsom on the downs, south of London, hosts one of the most colourful gatherings of travelling people, toffs and punters. Named after the twelfth Earl of Derby in 1780, the classic flat race was run on the first Wednesday of June. It was moved to Saturday at the end of the twentieth century when we lost our sense of occasion and continuity to commercial and media pressures. But the antique tradition of being able to see the races for free persists on this common land. It is a spectacular and unique event, with open-topped double deckers, funny hats, bands, Pearly Kings and Queens, south Indian foods, marquees, fairs and stalls, busy bookies from the length of the land, hundreds of thousands of people bent on a great day out, and, of course, the horses, their colourful jockeys and the sound of pounding hooves and roars from the crowds.

Cheltenham Races moved to Prestbury Park in 1902 after much oscillation, from the original figure-of-eight course high on the contested common land of Cleeve Hill, where it had been established in 1818, rising and falling in fortune with Cheltenham's spa-town aspirations. It shifted from flat racing to make its mark as *the* gathering

Lanyon Quoit, Cornwall.

for steeplechases around the Cheltenham Gold Cup in March, long attracting Irish and English punters who drink their way through gallons of Guinness. No vestiges of the hilltop grandstand remain, but thoroughbreds still train on the tops, the former hay warden regulating the gallops on 1,330 acres of common land.

Another favoured place for race-tracks is beside rivers: Nottingham by the Trent, Worcester by the Severn, Windsor by the Thames, Newton Abbot by the Teign. Chester racecourse and its nearby stables are an integral part of the city, minutes from the centre. The Roodee draws a virtual circle of one mile and 73 yards, overlooked on the east by the old Roman walls and enclosed by a meander of the river Dee. Run left-handed, races have been held on the floodplain here since at least 1540.

The tracks used for steeplechasing, or hurdles, have a different personality from flat-race tracks, punctuated with manicured brushwood and water jumps. The sound of races varies, too, until you reach the final furlongs.

Grandstands stand forlorn much of the year, but they can enliven their landscapes: the elegant wrought-iron grandstand at Ludlow, Shropshire; the new white 'tents' of Goodwood, Sussex; the simple stands at Fontwell, Sussex; the variety at Carlisle, Cumberland; the mix of old and new at Wetherby, Yorkshire. But the abiding memory is of the rails white and stark against the green turf, straight or curving away over the horizon.

See also COMMONS, DOWNLAND, EARTHWORKS, GALLOPS, HORSES & PONIES, POINT TO POINT, RIVERS.

R A I L I N G S

At the turn of the nineteenth century elegant cast- and wrought-iron railings, as well as balconies and verandahs, were being made for the new terraces, squares and crescents in London and the burgeoning spa and seaside towns, such as Bath, Cheltenham and Brighton. Despite the proliferation of catalogues and pattern books, a great variety of styles emerged.

Although railings had become rather unpopular by the mid-1800s, many Victorian and Edwardian front gardens were, and still are, bounded by decorative wrought-iron railings mounted on a low stone or brick wall. Designs differ subtly from place to place, according to the talents and tastes of the local blacksmith and commissioners. Many of these, together with scrap metal, were needlessly taken for the 'war effort' during the Second World War – misguidedly to boost morale, but apparently secretly dumped in the Thames estuary, an inadvertent updating of offering gifts to the river gods.

In south Devon '*the older gates, railings and bollards of Kingsbridge have a distinct style characteristic of Lidstones, the local foundry*', Jane Fitzgerald writes. In Derbyshire fine ironwork can be attributed to two excellent blacksmiths – Robert Bakewell and his apprentice Benjamin Yates. The simple, beaten, spear-topped railings outside West End House in Wirksworth are by Yates.

Now railings are at the forefront of urban regeneration, and public art agencies are commissioning artists to design them, at places such as Derby Station and along the canal in Coventry.

See also BANDSTANDS, CHESHIRE RAILINGS, PIERS, PROMENADES, RAISED PAVEMENTS, RIVERS, SQUARES, TERRACED HOUSES.

345

R A I L W A Y S

Despite attempts by I.K. Brunel to popularise a seven-foot railway gauge (hence some of the wide track beds on the London to Bristol route), the width between rails was standardised at four feet, eight and a half inches, perpetuating the Roman wagon gauge. Around nineteen thousand miles of rail had been laid by 1900, perhaps some built by the mythical engineer Blind Jack of Knaresborough.

As the network spread across the country 'railway towns' grew up around or emerged from station yards or railway works. Some, including Derby and Darlington, County

346 Durham were already industrialised, but developed a significant railway presence. Places such as Peterborough in Northamptonshire, Carnforth in Lancashire and Rugby in Warwickshire, however, were transformed from sleepy market towns to major centres. Swindon in Wiltshire continued to grow, but still has its 'railway village', streets of distinctive terraces built for employees of the enormous Great Western Railway works. Crewe in Cheshire appeared practically from nowhere. In 1840 a railway works was built in Monks Coppenhall, a village of about two hundred people near Crewe Hall. By 1910 Crewe was a town of fifty thousand.

Until 1948 the railways were operated by small companies, coming together into four larger groupings in the 1920s: GWR, LNER, LMS and Southern. People were loyal to their local networks, which used corporate styles that developed linear liveries. Signal boxes had overhanging hipped roofs on the London, Brighton and South Coast railway, and decorative barge-boards on the Great Northern. The lines developed nicknames and mythologies. Polegate to Eridge in Sussex was the Cuckoo Line, after the local tradition that the first cuckoo of spring is let loose at Heathfield Fair. The Great Eastern was known as The Swedey due to its agricultural traffic. The Watercress Line fed the London markets. Sidings on the GWR picked up names such as Ran-tan, New Found Out and The Straight.

Railway architecture provided new habitats for wildlife. Clinkers used in track beds emulated the Italian volcanic environment, encouraging ragwort to spread outwards from Oxford. When the lines began to close after 'restructuring' (a euphemism for mass closure and redundancy) in the 1960s, many plants and animals returned to the abandoned track beds, from slow-worms and toads to butterflies, birds and bats. Preston Junction is one of many old lines that are now nature reserves.

Around ten thousand miles of rail routes closed between the 1920s and 1990, and more since, but much – nearly a tenth – has been given over to leisure, whether as footpaths or part of the National Cycle Network. In the Forest of Dean, Gloucestershire the numerous disused routes include a sculpture trail called The Iron Road, beginning near Parkend.

See also BRIDGES, BUSES, CUCKOOS & CUCKOO POUNDS, CYCLING, DAGS, FOOTPATHS, SCULPTURES, STATIONS, TUNNELS, WATERCRESS BEDS.

RAISED PAVEMENTS

Built in part to protect pedestrians from road traffic, raised pavements, a form of terracing, are more frequently found in hilly places.

They are often the most attractive part of a street scene, due to the disposition of road, steps, pavement and houses, with elegant iron or other kinds of handrails adding further particularity. Bath, Somerset has exquisite raised flagstone walkways, not only in the city centre.

The simple stone curve six steps up along the churchyard wall of Main Street in Forest Hill, Oxfordshire could not be

more different from the five stone steps leading to the flags in front of houses in Hastings High Street, Sussex, edged with fine, black, iron railings, or the many high pavements of Lewes, Sussex, with their flint and brick walls.

See also FOOTPATHS, HIGH STREETS, KERBSTONES, PAVEMENTS, QUARRIES, RAILINGS.

R A M S O N S

As successful and invasive plants, ramsons are often undervalued, but wild garlic has formidable champions in Geoffrey Grigson – *'in blossom or leaf Ramsons is one of the most beautiful floorings'* – and Richard Mabey – *'A large stand of wild garlic in full odour is, for a couple of months a year, an impressive and unmistakable landmark.'* Indeed, places are named because of them: Ramsbottom in Lancashire, Ramsden in Essex, Ramsholt in Suffolk. The plant itself has some colourful names, including gypsy's gibbles and gypsy's onions in Somerset, ramps in Lancashire and Cumberland, rommy and roms in Yorkshire and stink plant in Lincolnshire.

In spring in the Mendips the roadside verges and woodland floors are covered with ramsons, which are as impressive as bluebells for their sheer extent and exuberance, their fresh green and white froth and, of course, the incredible smell. Ramsons can be found in shady spots throughout the country and are indicators of ancient woodland in about twenty English counties.

All parts of the plant are edible, with similar beneficial properties to those of cultivated garlic.

See also BLUEBELLS, GREEN LANES, GYPSIES, VERGES, WOODS.

R E D   F O X E S

The red fox is one of our most successful and adaptable wild creatures. Also one of the most beautiful, it can be found throughout England, including the centre of some cities, having first ventured into the suburbs in the 1930s and 1940s. This *'peculiarly British phenomenon'*, says the London Wildlife Trust, was perhaps driven by the lack of rabbits in the countryside due to myxomatosis. Their catholic diet, which includes earthworms, slugs, mice, rats, rabbits, berries, fruit and now scraps, is one reason for their survival, despite relentless persecution.

They have been closely studied in London and Bristol, where initial population increases have been savaged by the spread of sarcoptic mange; between 1994 and 1996 ninety per cent of Bristol's foxes died from this mite-borne disease. Richard Atkinson observes them often in London: *'Where I live, near Clapham Common, you often see foxes confidently trotting around after dark. Several houses in the street have recently had builders in, and I've been woken by foxes dislodging rubble and debris stacked in skips, while chewed soft toys, packaging and other random items mysteriously appear outside the back door. A family has its earth at the end of the garden, where there's a patch of brambly no-man's-land. One morning, while editing this book at the kitchen table, a fox looked me in the eye through the window, then rolled about on the grass for several minutes.'* You are most likely to see them at dawn or dusk, but if you are lucky you may also see them sunbathing on an embankment from the train window or frolicking in your garden in the moonlight.

During the Civil War, one of the results of the destruction of park pales by the Roundheads was the loss of deer, central to the royal and aristocratic sport of hunting. The patterns of land ownership began to shift and, after 1660, despite the Restoration of Charles II, Parliament was dominated by the new elite. Hunting began to take a new turn, and foxes, previously uninteresting vermin, became the main quarry. Dogs began to be bred and trained for chasing them, and adjacent landowners colluded in the wider landscape to create 'countries' across which they could hunt.

By the 1840s in east Yorkshire *'new coverts, many of which included gorse, were planted at strategic sites in the countries of the different hunts'*, A. Harris wrote. Elsewhere, most estates provided cover where foxes might live, the easier to find and hunt them. The famous Quorn hunt, which straddles Nottinghamshire and Leicestershire, owns many coverts with the name Gorse, although it is now planting these with trees. Strange round and square copses of trees spread

347

across the chalk landscape of Wiltshire were made expressly for hunting, whether of birds or foxes.

Before the Hunting Act 2004 made illegal '*the unspeakable in pursuit of the inedible*', as Oscar Wilde put it, there were more than 180 hound packs. The hunts own hounds, kennels, horses, paddocks and sometimes land. Some have their own slaughterhouses and incinerators, and house some of their workers in tied accommodation. Each pack is active between November to March. Large packs may meet five or six times a week, most just once or twice, but the traditional meet on Boxing Day attracts most supporters and seasonal visitors. Others follow on foot or by car.

The Master, huntsmen and whippers-in wear eighteenth-century hunting dress – hunting pink, a jacket named after Thomas Pink, the tailor of the infamous huntsman John Peel. This is usually red, but for the Heythrop Hunt in Oxfordshire and Gloucestershire, for example, it is traditionally green. Thirty to forty hounds, numbered in 'couples', are put to flushing the fox (chasing and killing are no longer legal). In the Lakeland mountains small 'fell packs' hunt on foot because of the difficult terrain.

'Charlie' fox has been the fulcrum across which ancient schisms and modern sensibilities have been see-sawing at the turn of the millennium. Tradition keeps kicking against cultural change. It remains to be seen if the social and visual glamour of the hunt can survive without the 'vermin' to chase. But there are already hunts that enjoy the freedom and exhilaration of cross-country hue and cry with the hounds following aniseed trails while the red fox watches from a safe distance.

See also GORSE, HARES, HORSES & PONIES, HOUNDS, HOUND TRAILING, TERRIERS.

R E D   K I T E S

Soaring above the M40, where the road cuts through the Chilterns, red kites have become a familiar landmark for those who drive between junctions 4 and 8. The great wingspan, distinctive spread of the flight feathers and forked tail marks the triumphant return of a bird persecuted to near extinction.

Common in towns and cities in medieval times, they were welcomed as scavengers, eating dead rats and carrion. But as towns became cleaner the kites moved out into the countryside, only to be persecuted by gamekeepers, who wrongly thought they would take live game birds. By 1900 they were extinct in England, leaving a small relict population in central Wales.

English Nature and the Royal Society for the Protection of Birds embarked on an ambitious programme to reintroduce them in 1989, releasing young kites from Spain in the Chilterns, with later releases in Northamptonshire

and Yorkshire. Spread is slow, since they tend to stay within two to three miles of their nests, but the success is palpable. Despite poisoning from illegal baits put out for crows and foxes, or from rats poisoned with anticoagulant rodenticides on sporting estates, the population in the Chilterns is now the densest in Europe, with 142 pairs in 2003.

Found objects, such as handkerchiefs and items of underwear, decorate their nests. English Nature recounts that '*two halves from the same unfortunate individual [teddy bear] were found in a Chilterns nest and a bear's head was found in a Yorkshire nest in 2000*'. Unusually for birds of prey they form communal roosts in winter; in the Chilterns up to two hundred may gather.

See also HERONRIES, ROADS, ROOKERIES.

R E D   S Q U I R R E L S

In the 1950s the pine woods around Branksome Chine in Poole, Dorset were home to large numbers of native red squirrels, which were taken for granted. As introduced grey squirrels expanded, the reds slowly melted away. Isolated pockets hold on in the South on Brownsea, Green and Furzey islands in Poole Harbour and on the Isle of Wight. There are discrete populations in the coniferous forest at Thetford, East Anglia, in Cannock Chase, Staffordshire and on the Lancashire coast at Ainsdale.

Most of England's thirty thousand red squirrels are found in Cumberland, Westmorland, Durham, Northumberland and north Lancashire. They are specialist seed eaters and can hold their own against greys better in conifer forests, where their preferred foods – conifer and

M40 near Watlington, Oxfordshire.

small tree seeds, hazelnuts, berries and mushrooms – are in greater supply than in broadleaved woods, which grey squirrels anyway prefer. Some people believe there is no direct competition between reds and greys, but plans are being made to prevent greys from expanding north – a red squirrel reserve in Whinfell Forest, Westmorland has already been created.

The grey is much loved in city parks, but the forester hates it, and Oliver Rackham drew attention to the threat to hazel trees whose nuts are taken early. The vitriol now poured on the unfortunate greys (which were introduced towards the end of the nineteenth century from North America) was once meted out to reds. Stefan Buczacki describes the Boxing Day, Good Friday and St Andrew's Day squirrel hunts, in which tens of thousands were killed. Their image improved with the publication of Beatrix Potter's *The Tale of Squirrel Nutkin* in 1903 – the illustration of a line of squirrels on tiny rafts heading out to an island, using their bushy tails as sails, stays in the mind. But foresters were never enamoured of this cuddly portrayal and, until they became rare, they were regarded as just another pest.

See also FERAL ANIMALS, HAZEL, ISLANDS, WOODS.

R E E D   B E D S

Common reed, the tallest of our native grasses, can reach a height of three metres. It grows in dense clumps in fens and along wet ditches, streams and slow-flowing rivers.

Reed beds traditionally were grown as cover for duck shoots and to protect mud-flats from tidal erosion, but their main use was for thatch. As thatching declined and drainage and scrub encroachment have spread, they have became one of our rarest habitats – up to forty per cent were lost between 1949 and 1990 in the UK.

The largest area of reed beds is in the Norfolk and Suffolk Broads, but even here, they have declined, perhaps because the polluted, nitrogen-rich water weakens the stems. Conservation groups are working to extend the acreage and revive their management. More than a thousand acres of new reed beds are being planned at the working gravel pits at Needingworth Quarry, along the river Ouse in Huntingdonshire, by the Royal Society for the Protection of Birds and Hanson, who will remove 28 million tons of gravel over thirty years.

Thatchers currently use all the reeds they can find locally. They prefer the thicker, longer stems of reed cut every two years, known as double wale (as opposed to single wale) – biannual harvesting is also less disruptive to wildlife. Most reed cutting is done mechanically between November and March, although there are still a few cutters who use a scythe.

Forty species rely solely upon reed beds, including bitterns and marsh harriers; a host of insects provides a rich food supply. Filsham reed beds, between Bexhill and Hastings – the largest reed bed in Sussex – is an important stopping-off point for thousands of migrating swallows and warblers. Other birds heavily dependent on reeds breed here, including reed warblers (a favourite host for cuckoos' eggs), the bearded tit (also known as the reedling) and the shy, skulking water rail (which sings only at night). Specialist moths, such as the wainscots, also thrive, alongside frog bit, water violet and the insect-eating bladderwort. The harvest mouse can be found climbing among the stems; deer, water voles, water shrews and otters also enjoy them for shelter and food.

Along the Suffolk coast shy bitterns are brilliantly camouflaged among the reeds at Minsmere. The male's distinctive booming call has earned him many local names, including butter bump, bogle, bitter-bum and bog-bumper. Many warblers also enjoy life here, including reed, sedge, grasshopper and Cetti's. At Leighton Moss in Lancashire extensive reed beds, created this century, now proudly provide a home for bitterns and bearded tits, which first arrived there in 1973. Starlings often use reed beds as winter roosts. On the Somerset Levels, at Westhay, half a million or so were seen one year, temporarily flattening the reeds.

Impressive as the reeds visibly are, under water there is even more going on. Forests of ramifying rhizomes provide a perennial and almost immortal foundation, enabling the colony to regenerate after cutting, frost or fire and produce new shoots and growth year after year, perhaps over centuries. Even the dead, hollow stems have a purpose: they enable oxygen to diffuse down into the rhizome. Reed beds have been heralded as natural composters, able to hasten the decomposition of sewage waste, and increasingly are being planted as part of eco-friendly building schemes. Because of their extensive root systems, which harbour beneficial bacteria, they can act like gigantic septic tanks, absorbing nutrients and breaking down toxins.

See also BROADS, CUCKOOS & CUCKOO POUNDS, ESTUARIES, FENS, LAKES, LEVELS, MOSSLAND, RHYNES, RIVERS, STARLINGS, THATCH.

R E S E R V O I R S

The landscape is filled with the relics of working with water, from fish-ponds to buddles – used to dam water for lead processing. Small reservoirs were made to serve canals or industries, and mill-ponds are reservoirs of sorts. Now really large-scale reservoirs dot the countryside, as water authorities stockpile against times of drought in addition to recharging aquifers.

When it was first proposed to dam the upper Tees to supply Teeside, 95 miles away, conservationists fought, but failed, to save a herb-rich grassland famous for its remarkable arctic-alpine flora overlying the special 'sugar' limestone. Cow Green reservoir was completed in the 1970s. At the same time, to the north, Kielder Water, at seven miles long the largest man-made reservoir in western Europe, was flooding almost three thousand acres of Northumberland. Of the same generation, Rutland Water stores 27,300 million gallons. It is now a training ground for the Olympic sailing team and, stocked with brown and rainbow trout, it attracts thousands of anglers each year, who compete with passing ospreys. Proposals for a new generation of water stores will prove controversial despite the potential for recreational use, for all local memory is erased. Whole villages, as well as farms, have been lost to the making of the big reservoirs.

The movement of a boat through a lock on a canal sees the flowing downstream of 150,000 litres of water. The Tring reservoirs were among those made to provide the top-up – now a national nature reserve, they draw migrant birds on their way through Hertfordshire.

In Essex eighty thousand swifts, swallows and martins swoop over Hanningfield reservoir to feed at peak fly hatches in summer. It also hosts a wide range of waterfowl, including large breeding populations of gadwall, tufted duck and pochard, as well as coot. Abberton reservoir, south-west of Colchester, is an internationally renowned wetland, important as a haven for wild duck, swans and other water birds, including many thousands of each of the top seven species – wigeon, teal, mallard, pochard, tufted duck, coot and black-headed gull – as well as hundreds of shovelers, gadwalls, golden eye pintails and great crested grebes. Since 1981, when they suddenly arrived, some thirty pairs of cormorants have nested in trees around the reservoir.

Tittesworth reservoir draws the weekend crowds from Staffordshire towns. The Welsh Harp in Hendon is a magnet for London sailors, and the many city reservoirs of the Lee valley, with their attendant waterworks and filter beds, also feed the urban birds and bats. At Barn Elms, on the other side of the metropolis, the Wildfowl and Wetlands Trust has created an accessible city nature reserve from the old reservoirs by the Thames.

See also AQUEDUCTS, BELLS & BELL-RINGING, BOUNDARIES, BROADS, CANALS, DEW PONDS, GRAVEL PITS, LAKES, LEVELS, LIMESTONE, LOST VILLAGES, MOATS, PONDS, REED BEDS, TARNS.

R H U B A R B

The idea of 'forcing' was discovered by chance two centuries ago, when a gardener accidentally left earth covering his rhubarb and noticed that '*it was sprouting pink shoots out of season, having been kept warm and dark under the soil*'.

A stretch of Yorkshire between Wakefield, Leeds and Morley, known as the pink triangle, is where nine-tenths of the world's forced rhubarb is grown. In its heyday '*you could look out from a bridge in Leeds and see seven miles of rhubarb in every direction*', grower Janet Oldroyd-Hulme said. There were about 190 growers, with pickers on day and night shifts. A special train – the Pink Express or Rhubarb Special – left for London every night in season.

Imported for its medicinal value from Siberia via Russia in the fifteenth century, rhubarb has become more popular here than anywhere. We take our rhubarb pie and tart very seriously. Forced rhubarb is more tender, less acidic and sells at a premium. It has been grown commercially for more than a century for the post-Christmas market. Rhubarb grown in the fields is harvested later, at the end of March and early April; 150 varieties exist.

The vegetable grows well in the heavy clay soil around Carlton, and needs the early cold winters. Originally the coalfields provided cheap coal to warm forcing sheds; shoddy from wool mills, high in nitrogen, was used as a fertiliser, together with potash from steel furnaces.

Competition from air-freighted tropical fruit has seen a fall to a dozen growers, but there has been a big revival in demand during the past few years, driven by the new annual Wakefield Rhubarb Festival. Taking place around the end of January, it is now such a success that it lasts for nine days. One of the most popular events is the tour of the forcing sheds, with more than two thousand visitors a season – people love to peer into the dark, ten-thousand-square-foot, candle-lit spaces and hear the eerie sound of the growing stems. There are floral, cooking and wine-making demonstrations, a five-course rhubarb dinner, brunches, talks and a rhubarb farmers' market, selling new products, such as Ruby Gold cheese and Tusky (rhubarb) sausage.

Heading towards its century, on the second Saturday of February the Leeds and District Market Gardeners' Association hold its annual Rhubarb Show at Crigglestone.

See also AGRICULTURAL SHOWS, APPLE DAY, APPLES, APRICOTS, ASPARAGUS, CHERRIES, COTTAGE GARDENS, CRAB FAIR, FAIRS & FAIRGROUNDS, FOOD, GOOSEBERRIES, LIQUORICE, MARKET GARDENS, NURSERIES, PUDDINGS, STRAWBERRIES.

R H Y N E S

Locally pronounced 'reens' and sometimes spelt rhines, rhynes are the long, ruler-straight ditches that drain the Somerset Levels, carrying surface water off to the rivers. Such drains in west Sussex are called rifes, as in Pagham Rife, Aldingbourne Rife and Ryebank Rife.

Rhynes carve up the wetland into a dense chequer-board of small, rectangular fields of about five to ten acres, providing 'wet fences' and drinking water for grazing cattle.

Gates flanked by small wing fences stand isolated at bridge points. In summer, or drought, the water is 'penned' to keep the ditches full, while in winter, or flood, water levels are reduced to ease the drainage of winter rain.

Rhynes were first dug as the moors, once open commons, were enclosed between 1770 and 1833. In places the pattern of rhynes is extremely intricate, reflecting the diversity of competing claims of the former commoners as the land was enclosed. Tiny, narrow plots cover districts where turbary (turf-cutting) rights added further complications, for instance at Catcott, Shapwick and Meare Heaths. Practical concerns also influenced where the ditches were dug: if fields were too large they would be slow to drain, but too many ditches would waste productive land.

Often lined with pollarded willows that strengthen the banks and provide roosting and nesting places for barn owls, little owls and wild bees, rhynes harbour a wide variety of aquatic plants, including yellow flag iris, frog bit, water violet, bladderwort, rushes, sedges, great water dock and marsh horsetail. '*Each shelters a particular world of butterbur or kingcup, of water mint or a great wedding-show of irises*', Adam Nicolson wrote. Before the Second World War most ditches were dredged by hand, using a hay knife to cut the vegetation and a crook to haul it onto the bank. Now machines scour the rhynes, usually every three to five years. Wildlife is better maintained by rotating the clearance.

> *A subtle sheet that contours*
> *each sunken fallow field*
> *Each level segment of sedge*
> *marooned moor, caught and held fast*
> *Rhyne by rhyne*
> *silent and sullen*
> *The chain linked and lined*
> *long wavering regiments*
> *Reeds and bulrushes*
> *slender lances that pierce the ice shadow . . .*

James Crowden, from 'Muchelney Abbey'

See also BOATS, CATTLE, FENS, GRAZING MARSHES, GREEN LANES, INGS, LEVELS, MOSSLAND, PEAT, RIVER NAMES, RIVERS, SALT MARSHES, TIDES.

R I A S

The coastline of the South has some spectacular indentations. Examples include Pagham and Chichester harbours in Sussex; Portsmouth harbour and Southampton Water in Hampshire, etched into the low-lying coastal plain; and in Devon and Cornwall complex creek systems embedded in steep valleys. Since the Ice Age southern England has been tilting into the sea, which has also been rising and has

invaded low-lying land. The drowned valleys, or rias, provide welcome havens, making these places the best for watching birds and boats in the South.

They form a particular and beautiful feature of the South West. For those on land the rias create long diversions, but ferries and a high population of boats reduce isolation. In Devon and Cornwall the water is deep and excellent for shipping and sailing. The cross-profiles of the valleys are steeply plunging, and woodland that frequently comes down to the water's edge makes the smaller rias intimate and sheltered. In the South Hams of Devon the Erme is barely serpentine, but narrow and secluded; the high tide kisses the trees. The Dart is long and winding, the Kingsbridge estuary has a handful of side creeks. Villages cling to the steep slopes, as at Noss Mayo on the Yealm, which is full of moored yachts and fishing boats. Remote creeks and scattered marshes attract otters, wildfowl and waders, including the golden plover and black-tailed godwit.

Plymouth and Saltash share the giant estuary of the Tamar and Tavy, providing an important harbour for naval vessels. In Cornwall the Fowey estuary runs straight to the north between steep slopes, offering a deep harbour capable of taking ships loading one and a half million tons of china clay. The Fal estuary is very broad across the Carrick Roads; Falmouth is an industrial port, the docks vying with marinas. This is the largest, most westerly sheltered haven on the south coast.

See also BEACONS (COASTAL), BECKS, BORES, BOUNDARIES, BOURNES, BROOKS, BURNS, ESTUARIES, FERRIES, FOOTBRIDGES, FORDS, GHYLLS, HARBOURS, RHYNES, RIVER NAMES, SEA FISH, SOUGHS, STEPPING-STONES.

R I D G E & F U R R O W

Extended waves in the land with crests just eleven human paces apart cast fine and complicated shadows and create beautiful patterns in the snow. Although the name later became associated with their length of 220 yards, these strips or ridges, gathered together, made a furlong (although

351

going against the grain really can slow down a horse at a gallop). The sinuous undulations were made by oxen and horses pulling ploughs in medieval and later times. The memory of ploughing medieval-style also persists in field shapes, as around Castleton in Derbyshire, where later parallel stone walls describe a mirror 'S' shape, a sure sign that plough teams once working the land prepared themselves for turning at the headland.

Ridge and furrow often follows this shape, although that of a later date may lie straight, with more undulations at right angles. The remains of strips amplified by ploughing, the glorious corrugations criss-crossed by later hedgerows, were part of the everyday landscape in Bedfordshire, north Buckinghamshire, west Cambridgeshire, Leicestershire, Northamptonshire, north Oxfordshire, Rutland and Warwickshire. But in the heartland in 1999 just six places were found to retain forty per cent or more of their original open-field remnants.

David Hall confirmed *'what has long been suspected anecdotally – that ridge and furrow, which was once a most characteristic and commonplace sight in the east Midlands, is now very rare and becoming rarer year by year . . . If ridge and furrow is rare and threatened in its primary area, then its survival as a significant component of the national heritage must be in some question.'* These dwindling examples are the best, in European terms, of a pattern of tenure that dominated the north of the continent for a millennium. We have let something ordinary become hard to find.

Recent aerial photographs of the fields around Clipston in Northamptonshire, Ludgershall in Buckinghamshire, Hungarton in Leicestershire, Denchworth in Berkshire and Upper and Lower Shuckburgh in Warwickshire simply take the breath away. David Hall pointed out that *'Midland fields are believed to originate at the end of the Middle Saxon period, say, the ninth century. They continued in many areas well into the nineteenth century . . . Physical diversities occur in several ways. Regions with undulating topography have small furlongs and lands change direction frequently to maintain natural drainage across the contours. In flatter areas, furlongs are large and lie with lands lying in the same direction.'*

East Anglia, south Devon and most of Cornwall seem not ever to have undergone this kind of ploughing, but from north Devon to Northumberland traces can be found. Half a century ago very gentle ridge and furrow, just a few inches high, was even evident on much chalk downland in the South. It is thought that the low level of the ridges indicates that the activity did not go on for long. In the Yorkshire Wolds aerial photographs reveal lost gentle ridges eleven hundred yards in length, typical still in northern Europe.

In Cheshire nineteenth-century ridge and furrow is commonly as narrow as three yards. In Somerset orchard trees are sometimes found on ridges made for the purpose.

But old patterns of ridge and furrow often survive in parkland, for example at Wimpole in Cambridgeshire and Boughton House, Northamptonshire, adding further interest to the many layers in the landscape.

At Tissington in Derbyshire ridge and furrow is still found on the heavy clays, where the soggy furrows and the drier tops maintain different flora. At Laxton in north Nottinghamshire the open-field system is still worked, but use of the modern plough has flattened the ridge and furrow. The irony is that the ridge and furrow that is still evident has survived because ploughing ceased.

See *also* BOUNDARIES, DESERTED VILLAGES, DOWNLAND, DRYSTONE WALLS, FENCES, FIELD NAMES, FIELD PATTERNS, FIELDS, GATES, HEDGES, INGS, LYNCHETS, PARKLAND, WILDFLOWERS.

RIVER NAMES

The richness of our long cultural relationship with rivers is evident in the names we know them by. Across England we have all but forgotten that many old languages jostle with modern English. Stratford-upon-Avon recalls a common river name. It is still recognisable as the Welsh word *afon*, and when we say river Avon we are simply saying river River, demonstrating that the newcomers did not understand the indigenous language.

Our ancestors described significance and captured meaning in names. The names of many rivers are descriptive: Thames means dark; Cam, Croome, Wellow – winding; Aire, Taw, Tern – strong/swift; Stour – strong/powerful; Leadon, Lydden – broad; Kyle, Coly – narrow; Cray – pure, clear; Derwent, Darent, Dart – oak-lined; Iwerne – possibly yew-lined, and so on.

At the turn of the river the language changes,
a different babble, even a different name
for the same river . . .

Carol Ann Duffy, from 'River'

Somewhere between Wellingborough and Thrapston, in Northamptonshire, the river Nene changes its pronunciation – to the south it is said 'nen' or 'nairn', to the north 'neen'. The Tarrant, a small tributary of the Dorset Stour, has stamped identity onto the villages in its catchment, giving its name to Tarrant Gunville, Tarrant Hinton, Tarrant Launceston, Tarrant Monkton, Tarrant Rawston, Tarrant Rushton and Tarrant Keyneston. The Tarrant is a winterbourne, and it is suggested that its name means 'trespasser', since it reminds everyone after prolonged rain that this is its valley and the road its bed.

Many place-names show the importance of water, reflecting the presence of springs (Fonthill, Teffont – *fontana* is a fountain or spring, from the Latin); wells (Sadler's Wells, Southwell, Chigwell); and fords – the most numerous descriptive name relating to water (Oxford, Fordingbridge). Bridges are commonly represented (Trowbridge – tree bridge, Bristol – meeting place at the bridge, Bridgnorth, Brigg); as are weirs (Ware – place by a weir, Edgware – Ecgi's weir); ferrys (Rock Ferry, North and South Ferriby); and places by mill streams (Melbourne, Millom).

We have many words for streams. Sike or sick, a name used in the north of England for a runnel or trickle of water, has its equivalent, sitch, in the South. Becks, ghylls or gills, burns, winterbournes, gipseys, nailbournes, lavants, rhynes and rifes have their place.

Wharves, docks, landings, hards, beaches – navigable rivers have names for everything, just as does a street. Indeed, the Humber estuary has stretches known as Hull Roads and Paull Roads; the estuary of the Fal in Cornwall has Carrick Roads and Cross Roads. The water and the riverbed are known by reach, pool, island and sand bank, and, at a different scale, the same is true of rivers that are fished. In the Thames, T.S. Eliot's '*Strong brown god*', the reaches tend to describe themselves by the littoral settlements – Limehouse, Woolwich, Barking, Erith and Gravesend Reach. Halfway Reach (known as the Guzzard into the nineteenth century) tells you how much further to the Pool of London. The bridges continue the accumulation of names, together with Temple Stair, Old Swan Pier, Nicholson's Steam Packet Wharf, Cast Iron Wharf, Puddle Dock and Old Jamaica Wharf.

See also BEACHES, BECKS, BOAT RACE, BOURNES, BRIDGES, BROOKS, BURNS, CHALK STREAMS, DIALECTS, EYOTS, FOOTBRIDGES, FORDS, GHYLLS, HARDS, KENNELS, RHYNES, RIVERS, SOUGHS, STAIRS, STEPPING-STONES, WATERFALLS, WINTERBOURNES.

R I V E R S

Seeing a man sitting quietly cross-legged with flowers and fruit spread out before him on the city banks of the river Tyne is to glimpse quiet communion with nature. Increasingly rivers in England are standing in for sacred rivers on other continents. For Hindus and Sikhs the Ganga is the most sacred of rivers, but to scatter the ashes of loved ones is difficult if you live and die in England. Water from the Ganga has been brought to the rivers Thames, Wye and Soar to bless them as places for ritual. Between Barrow upon Soar and Mountsorrel in Leicestershire families gather to scatter flowers, powder, tulsi grass and holy leaves. Amid chanting and the ringing of bells, the ashes of the dead are committed to the river, which runs to the sea, transporting them to the next life.

Ancient votive offerings of swords and gold have been found in many of our rivers. Stories, legends and myths

still cling. The spirit Peg o' Nell took one life in seven in the Yorkshire Ribble; the Dart in Devon was said to claim one life a year – '*Dart, Dart, cruel Dart/Every year thou claim'st a heart*' – and the Trent, in Nottinghamshire and Lincolnshire, three. The Tweed is appeased by the casting of salt over water and nets. These stories are likely to be very old, and worth the retelling for that alone, but they also give us hints of who has settled here and their preoccupations, and what persistence the old gods still have.

A river catchment is united by the water within it – groundwater, springs, streams and rivers. If you tamper with one part it has repercussions on the rest. Because of demands on the groundwater in the Chilterns, the river Misbourne in Buckinghamshire is now dry along part of its length.

In the north of its catchment the Dorset Stour betrays the intricate branching typical of tributaries on clay, whereas, lower down, the simpler feeder streams speak of chalk. The patterns that rivers make tell their story. The steep and narrow yet winding course of the Wye tells us of rising land. Neither land nor sea stays still, and the river ruled by gravity never runs straight. Ruskin captured this: '*All rivers, small or large, agree in one character, they like to lean a little on one side: they cannot bear to have their channels deepest in the middle, but will always, if they can, have one bank to sun themselves upon, and another to get cool under.*' A river left to its own devices reinvents itself all the time,

353

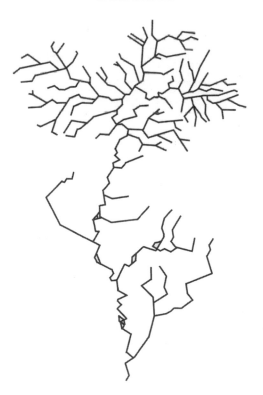

Catchment of the river Stour, Wiltshire, Somerset, Dorset, Hampshire.

---

through meanders, pools, waterfalls, ox bows, backwaters, cliffs, islands and long linear edges that juxtapose two very different worlds, each of which enriches the other.

The interface between water and land offers a great range of the richest habitats of all: one-third of our indigenous plants, about six hundred species, according to English Nature, are found in or by rivers. The assemblages of fish vary in different parts of a river and between catchments. The vegetation fringing riverbanks is crucially important for wildlife, providing safe staging and living places for birds, water voles and otters.

But few rivers have been allowed to remain 'natural'. Straight, featureless drains are deserts. This recognised, farmers increasingly are encouraged to leave wide riparian buffer strips, which also minimise the risk of fertilisers and pollutants reaching watercourses. Field names that imply wetness are a good place to start restoration planning: Drunken Field (waterlogged land), Feggy Leasow (marshy land), Flaggy Doles (land on which marsh plants grow), Mizzey (muddy land), Plashets (marshy place), The Orles (land on which alders grow). Each river has a propensity towards difference.

Rivers arise; whether thou be the Son
Of utmost Tweed, or Oose, or gulphie Dun,
Or Trent, who like some earth-born Giant spreads
His thirty Armes along the indented Meads,
Or sullen Mole that runneth underneath,
Or Severn swift, guilty of Maidens death,
Or Rockie Avon, or of Sedgie Lee,
Or Coaly Tine, or ancient hallowd Dee,
Or Humber loud that keeps the Scythians Name,
Or Medway smooth, or Royal Towred Thame.

John Milton, from 'Rivers arise; whether thou be the Son'

See also AEGIRS, BARROWS, BECKS, BOAT RACE, BORES, BOUNDARIES, BOURNES, BRIDGES, BROOKS, BURNS, CHALK STREAMS, DIALECTS, EELS, ESTUARIES, EYOTS, FERRIES, FLOODS, FOOD, FOOTBRIDGES, FORDS, FRESHWATER FISH, GHYLLS, HARBOURS, KENNELS, OTTERS, REED BEDS, RHYNES, RIAS, RIVER NAMES, SOUGHS, SPRINGS, STEPPING-STONES, SWAN UPPING, SWIMMING PLACES, WATERFALLS, WELL DRESSING, WINTERBOURNES.

R O A D S

Layer upon layer of tracks have led to the 186,383 miles of roads crossing England (2001). Movement has been a preoccupation for as long as people have needed to find food, pasture or minerals or wanted to trade or fight.

The Sweet Track offers a trace of a wooden neolithic path preserved by the swamps of Somerset. Much easier and safer were the great ridgeways. Some of the straight roads of the Romans remain in use, such as parts of the A5 and much of the Fosse Way. The settlements along them were 'on the street': Stretton, Stratford, Street. But, as Geoffrey Grigson wrote, it is *'not in human nature to walk that way [straight] between two points'*. The result, in G.K. Chesterton's memorable line, is *'A reeling road, a rolling road, that rambles round the shires'*.

The Anglo-Saxons, who prevailed from the sixth century, had *weg* – ways – rather than roads, hence highways and byways, wayfarers, rights of way. They might develop for specific needs, such as for pilgrims, drovers, pack trains or the lych way – corpse way – to the graveyard.

From the 1600s post roads began to convey the nation's letters. Parishes mostly had gravel pits from which to maintain passable surfaces. To pay for better quality roads, toll roads developed, known as turnpikes after the spiked barrier for entry and exit. In 140 years 23,000 miles of road were 'turnpiked'. At the beginning of the twenty-first century, road charging is once more seen as an option. Enclosure brought straight roads with sudden dog-legs around field corners.

The requirements of manufacturers and the ingenuity of engineers during the Industrial Revolution laid the foundations of our modern road system and created the first 'main roads' (a phrase first recorded in 1820). Thomas Telford and John McAdam devised means of creating stable road surfaces; the latter's 'Macadam' system being first tried in Bristol in 1816. Road dust remained a problem. Several roadside water pumps survive between London and Marlborough, Wiltshire, part of an attempt to keep it down. Tar was the solution, first used in Nottingham in 1845 but more widespread after 1907.

Tarred roads opened the country to motor vehicles. The familiar A, B and C road classification and numbering began in 1923. Primary roads continue until they meet another one, or arrive at the sea, hence the A2 to Dover, Kent, the A3 to Portsmouth, Hampshire and the A5 to Holyhead, North Wales. Motorways were to follow them; the first stretch – the Preston bypass in Lancashire – was opened in 1958.

See also BLACK DOGS, BOUNDARIES, BRIDGES, BUSES, DROVE ROADS, FIELDS, FINGERPOSTS, FOOTPATHS, GRAVEL PITS, GREEN LANES, GYPSIES, HAUNTED PLACES, HILL-FORTS, HOLLOW WAYS, INNS, MILESTONES, MONASTERIES, RAILWAYS, ROUNDABOUTS, SCOTS PINE, TIDES, TOLL-HOUSES, WAYSIDE & BOUNDARY CROSSES.

R O B I N   H O O D

Robin Hood is one of England's great gifts to the world. He personifies fairness and bravery in the face of corruption and greed; a purveyor of hope, he is rebellious and heroic but with his feet on the ground. He had no supernatural powers, although his prowess with a longbow was remarkable.

354

We remake him for every age, a popular hero '*feared by the bad, loved by the good*', who, as we now know him, robbed the rich to give to the poor – redistributing with elegant lightness of touch, inspiring despite tough times.

In the stories Robin and his merry men were banished to the greenwood – Sherwood Forest – and his consistent foe was the Sheriff of Nottingham. This places the story. Or does it?

Seekers after origins offer contrasting histories and geographies. An early written reference appears in *Piers Plowman* by William Langland in 1377, wherein a priest claims '*I kan [know] rymes of Robyn Hood*', implying that already legendary status had settled around the man. The first of many ballads appears in 1450, 'The talkyng of the munke and Robyn Hode':

> *In somer, when the shawes be sheyne*
> *And leves be large and long,*
> *Hit is full mery in feyre foreste*
> *To here the foulys song;*
> *To se the dere draw to the dale*
> *And leve the hilles hee,*
> *And shadow hem in the leves grene*
> *Under the gren-wode tre . . .*

Scholars point out that, while the written tales of King Arthur and his Knights showed literary eloquence, the Robin Hood ballads are less sophisticated. They were clearly for popular consumption. Robin Hood plays were performed

in different parts as a way of raising parochial money. The tales were embellished as they went until the 1520s, when pageantry involving Robin Hood waned, having tended to riot and excess. Ronald Hutton reported a revival of Robin Hood plays during the Reformation, '*from Cornwall and Devon up to the Midlands and as far north as Manchester*', and wrote that, after the accession of Elizabeth in 1558, '*Robin Hood puts in an appearance . . . in parish feasts. Three in Devon villages, such as Braunton among the sandhills of the north coast where the outlaw was given a special coat and had a "company" of attendants.*' Associations with Robin Hood cover the country, from Barnsdale and Robin Hood's Bay in Yorkshire to the Cumberland coast at Robin Hood's Chair. In Derbyshire he has a Cross, Picking Rods, Stoup, Stride and Well; in Verwood in Dorset, Butts; in Nottinghamshire, an Acre, Cave, Hills, Larder, Oak and Well; in Shropshire, another Chair, on the Stiper Stones; in Yorkshire, a Bower, Hill, Stone, Wells and more.

We may never know where Robin Hood came from – he may be an amalgamation of folk, he may have spent his early years simply in our forbears' imaginations. The point is that he evolves, stimulates and teaches. For now he brings together humanity and imagination, the two great foundations of progressive thought. And legend or real, his name and deeds have lived for more than seven hundred years, attached to many parts of the land.

355

See also ABBEYS, ALBION, ANCIENT TREES, BIRCH, CASTLETON GARLAND DAY, CATHEDRALS, CHURCHES, COAL MINING, FAIRS & FAIRGROUNDS, FOLKTALES, GREEN MAN, HEATHLAND, MAY DAY, MIDSUMMER DAY, MORRIS DANCING, MUMMING PLAYS, OAK, 'OBBY 'OSSES, PARKLAND, PUB SIGNS, ROYAL FORESTS, SAINTS.

R O B I N S

The robin is the gardener's inquisitive friend. With its attractive demeanour, orange-red breast, bold personality, haunting song and complicated roles in our folk history, it holds our affection. William Blake understood this: '*A Robin Redbreast in a Cage/Puts all Heaven in a Rage.*' Not surprisingly, people have chosen it as Britain's national bird.

Some of our old tales portray the robin and his 'wife', the wren, as sacred birds, hence the rhyme '*The robin redbreast and the wren/Are God Almighty's cock and hen*'. The bird's popular place on our Christmas cards since their inception in the 1870s may have something to do with the red-waistcoated Victorian postmen, who were nicknamed red-breasts or robins. But, more importantly, the seasonal association must still carry an echo of ancient tales of the New Year Robin killing his father, the Wren, on the Feast of Stephen, symbolising the death and resurrection of the year.

Part of a Twelfth-Night wassail song from Carhampton in Somerset goes:

*A poor little robin sits up in the tree
And all the day long so merry sings he.
A-widdling and twiddling to keep himself warm,
And a little more cider won't do us no harm . . .*

David Lack's seminal 1943 book, *The Life of the Robin*, described by Peter Lack as '*the first monograph on a bird in the modern era of science*', became one of the most famous ornithological books of all time. Observing around Dartington Hall in Devon, Lack found the robin to be '*a very aggressive and pugnacious bird*', with frequent fights, often to the death. He documented the importance of the singing. Both sexes defend their territories in autumn with a sad, restrained and thinner version of the spring song. Conor Jameson describes it as '*almost a requiem*', and, according to Chris Mead, '*it has a less bravura strain to it than the male's spring song – softer, more watery and generally a little suppressed and introverted*'.

Research by Dr Lance Workman in 1993 revealed that the robin's song varies in different places, with dialects as marked as those of Geordies and Cockneys. He used a sonograph to 'visualise' the pitch and duration of songs of birds in Mid-Glamorgan, Sussex and north Staffordshire. Subtly evident in their songs are trills and pitch changes that differ from place to place.

The spring song of the courting male is a longer and more complex version of the winter song, rivalling the blackbird's in its beauty. In fact the night songs of a robin from under a street lamp have often been confused with those of a nightingale, and are often the last of the evening – it sometimes sings in complete darkness.

See also DAWN CHORUS, DIALECTS, DOG ROSES, FOLKTALES, GARDENS, WASSAILING.

R O C K S

On the wall of Stone Farm at Blaxhall, Suffolk is a sign: '*THE BLAXHALL STONE: Said to have been ploughed up in the 19th century when no bigger than two fists, thrown down by the ploughman where it now stands, it has been growing ever since.*' Stories surface here and there of fields growing stones and of stones themselves expanding or mothering pebbles.

Huge rocks naturally out of place have sometimes been deposited by ice. The War Stone sits on a plinth in Warstone Lane in central Birmingham; a glacial erratic, it was used as a hoar stone, or boundary marker, from which its name drifted, in the process naming a cemetery and a brewery. In the Forest of Bowland in Yorkshire and Lancashire many erratic boulders have been used for boundary markers; the most extraordinary is the Great Stone of Fourstones on Tatham Fells. Where the other three have gone hardly seems to matter, this one is so huge – it has a hewn staircase of fourteen or fifteen steps to the top, like a double-decker bus for the Flintstones. Too far south for an ice sheet, the Giant's Rock on a rocky sea ledge at Porthleven, Cornwall is thought to have been dropped by a giant or an iceberg.

Rocks are named all around the coast, no doubt by mariners with a keen eye for danger and a need for landmarks. In Northumberland, where Old Norse words are in everyday use, *car(r)* and *bus* appear frequently, as in Oxcar, Jenny Bells Carr and the Bus of the Burn. Ancient peoples here felt the presence of rocks so keenly that they carved many of them remarkably; some five hundred examples of concentric and cup-and-ring patterns still exist. Northumberland has the definitive collection of five-thousand-year-old low-relief rock carvings, from a boulder in Powburn Quarry to the whaleback of sandstone near Roughting Linn waterfall, Milfield.

Hidden in the Forest of Dean, near Staunton, lies the Suck Stone, a massive wedge of rock sixty feet across, perhaps fourteen hundred tons. On the Derbyshire gritstone there are some great residual blocks, such as the Cat Stone and the Andle Stone on Stanton Moor; the Cork Stone has hand and foot holds for anyone with no tendency to vertigo. There is a characteristic look about millstone grit, amplified in the gritstone of Brimham Rocks in Nidderdale, Yorkshire, where rocks covering sixty acres stand proud in a labyrinthine group rather than spread along an edge. With

Brimham Rocks, Nidderdale, Yorkshire.

names such as Dancing Bear, the Yoke of Oxen, Eagle and the Devil's Anvil, they have been variously described as '*indescribable*' in their '*multiform singularity*' and as '*the most outlandish assemblage of rugged curiosities*'. Here you can read the edge of an ancient sea where coarse sand was dropped at angles according to the flow of currents. After eons of burial and compaction the rock found itself naked before the sand-filled winds of a cold desert, which helped to etch the bedding planes and joints. In an animistic culture this would be a natural sacred place.

Natural 'logging' or logan stones had long been held in awe because they could be rocked. Occasional perched blocks transported by ice have this property, but more are the result of differential erosion of naturally stacking rock, found particularly in the gritstone of the Pennines and on the granite tors of Devon and Cornwall. Sadly for the vandals of today, many were unseated by Victorian visitors. The Logan Rock near Porthcurno in Cornwall was pushed so hard that it actually fell onto the beach below in 1824. Its importance in attracting visitors was so great that the locals insisted that it be replaced by the naval officer whose overzealousness had caused it to fall. He is remembered in the local pub sign.

See also BOUNDARIES, DEVIL, DRAGONS, FOLKTALES, FORDS, FORTIFICATIONS, GIANTS, LANDSLIPS, PUB SIGNS, PUDDINGSTONE, QUOITS II, STANDING STONES, TORS, TURF MAZES, TURNING THE DEVIL'S STONE.

ROOKERIES

Rookeries can be centuries old. The large, bulky nests high in the tree-tops are renewed by the same birds year after year. There may be only twenty or so nests, but there can be as many as several thousand. Rookeries are most welcome landmarks; near Stockbridge in Hampshire they occupy the tops of an avenue leading to a country house – there is a saying that rooks breed only where there is money.

Since the demise of the elm, their preferred tree, they have successfully moved to oak and ash, and sometimes sycamore, beech, limes, horse chestnut and Scots and Monterey pines. They have even been seen nesting at the top of a pylon near the M5 motorway junction at Warndon, Worcestershire.

Ranmoor Cliffe rookery, in the leafy western suburbs of Sheffield, has been recorded by the Sheffield Bird Study Group for the past forty years. It is a thriving colony with about two hundred nests in pine and broad-leaved trees growing on the slope of an old quarry, and is unusual to be situated in such a built-up area. Chris Stride's website records the following: '*The spectacle that draws most attention to the rookery is the flocking, visible (and audible) at dusk and dawn. This behaviour is most frequently observed during the summer evenings as the rooks fly in from a day spent feeding in the fields of the Mayfield valley. Some gather first in the tall tree on Gladstone Road, opposite the entrance to Graham Road, others on lamp-posts in the area, rather than returning directly to the rookery. Then they take to the air, begin to circle, and are soon joined by others to form a large and noisy black cloud. Every so often one breaks from the formation and dives from the air before resuming its swirling flight path. For country folk, these displays (known as tompoking, or making pancheons)*

357

used to indicate the onset of bad weather.' Local people are appreciative: '*We absolutely love having the rooks around. From our dining table we can see them on summer evenings returning to the rookery and wheeling round – a wonderful sight. They really make you feel that you are somewhere other than in the suburb of a large city.*'

Mark Cocker, the closest and most lyrical of all rook watchers, describes their daily journeys in Norfolk, from their feeding places to their roosts, which can be as far as 27 miles away. '*As they stream towards me across the Yare floodplain there is the usual rich, plangent, drawn-out cawing, which echoes in this vast space . . . But mingled with these notes is a far wider range of soft, sometimes gull-like mewing sounds that rise on occasion into an almost yodelling sweetness. Then the jackdaws chip in with their snipped, dog-like yapping. It is a wonderful cacophony and it continues for about thirty minutes, as the birds stream to their regular roost in oak stands near the hamlet of Buckenham. During that time I count about three thousand birds heading north across the river.*'

There are a number of place- and field names associated with rooks, but far more common is the name Rookery Farm. Mark Cocker has discovered more of these around Topcroft in East Anglia than in any other part of the country.

The Rooks, Lewes's football team, was called after the town's many rookeries. John Chaplin, chairman of the Lewes Tree Group, told us that '*the loss of elms, and we had many in the town, has caused the main rookery at Elm Grove, Southover High Street, to move along the street into sycamore and younger elm in front of Southover House. In that rookery there are now 25 active nests, over half of which have to be rebuilt each year.*' In Eastgate Street there are seventeen nests in a two-hundred-year-old horse chestnut.

Rooks are widespread, often confused with their black corvid cousins, crows. The expression 'as the crow flies' really refers to rooks, which tend to fly in straight lines. Crows are more solitary, and rooks have a white patch around their beaks, which is the easiest way to distinguish them. They suffered from the effects of agricultural intensification and pesticide use in the 1960s and 1970s. They are now making a good recovery, but have not reached their pre-war numbers, and they continue to decline in the South East and Greater Manchester.

358

> . . . when the last rook
> Beat its straight path along the dusky air
> Homewards, I blest it!

Samuel Taylor Coleridge,
from 'This Lime-tree Bower My Prison'

See also AVENUES, BADGERS, DAWN CHORUS, ELM, HERONRIES, SYCAMORE, WOODS.

ROUNDABOUTS

In the early years of the twentieth century the team developing Ebenezer Howard's plans for the first garden city took inspiration from the Place de l'Étoile in Paris and put a roundabout in Letchworth, Hertfordshire. Sollershott Circus opened for traffic in 1910, with a diameter of 104 feet, circling around a central green of 55 feet – they were 'greens' then, rather than 'islands'. London followed in the 1920s, with roundabouts at Parliament Square, Hyde Park Corner and Marble Arch.

The Ministry of Transport and the Town Planning Institute together recommended that '*spaces should be provided for traffic to circulate on the "roundabout" system*', and there, in *MoT Circular* no. 302, 1929, the word appears written down for the first time. Since then the country has seen its crossroads and T-junctions disappear under the relentless march of four-arm, six-arm, scissors-type, small-island, hollow-island, double, multiple, ring-junction, false, two-level, dumb-bell, diamond, half-cloverleaf, two-bridge, three-level and free-flow interchanges.

Mini roundabouts came in the 1970s, although in the US, New York, which designed the first roundabouts, had 'dummy cops' sixty years earlier. England now has perhaps three and a half thousand roundabouts. The Groundwell Road system in Swindon, Wiltshire has a central roundabout surrounded by five minis. It quickly picked up the laconic appellation 'Magic Roundabout', first popularly, then officially. Yet there is an even more magic one, in Hemel Hempstead, Hertfordshire – it has six minis. How many driving tests have foundered in these uncongenial places? So often sponsors' signs for Britain in Bloom signal landscape at its saddest.

In stark contrast, the old bridge found and left in the roundabout at Trent Bridge, Nottingham and the heather roundabout on Canford Heath outside Poole in Dorset offer a sense of real specificity. Roundabouts have their own cult: BB Print Digital in Worcestershire created the splendid *Roundabouts of Redditch* calendar of 2002, which is now a collector's item.

See also BRIDGES, CROSSROADS, HEATHLAND, ROADS, VILLAGE GREENS.

ROUND-TOWERED CHURCHES

Round-towered churches are peculiar to Norfolk, which has upwards of 120, and Suffolk, with around forty. Essex, Cambridge and Sussex also have a handful. Some are in ruins; one, at Cockley Cley in Norfolk, fell in 1991. These churches were built in the hundred years after 1050 and tend to be a little way from the village.

One story tells that following a great flood the land level fell, revealing the old, lined wells. Wasting nothing, local people filled them with bells and added aisles. Not only the tale, but also the widely believed prosaic explanations, appear to be inventions. In East Anglia people will tell you that the towers are round because the lack of building stones inspired the resourceful use of naturally knobbly flint, which, although strong, creates all kinds of problems if you try to build corners.

Caroline Davison, who works in building conservation, explains the original work of colleague Stephen Heywood at Norfolk county council. *'The paucity of building stone theory has been largely discounted by recent research. In fact, many of the church naves, which often pre-date the round towers, use flints as perfectly adequate quoins for square corners. In addition, many of the round towers are partially built from an indigenous stone called ferruginous conglomerate, which is also perfectly adequate for making square corners – but the builders chose not to use it that way.*

'We believe now that the towers were built round for cultural reasons – when the round towers were being built the county had stronger links with the coastal communities around the Baltic and North Seas than with the rest of England. There were strong trading links, and a shared Scandinavian legacy. In fact, the idea of building round-towered churches seems to have spread from north Germany
along trade routes. There are very similar round towers in the north German regions of Lower Saxony and Schleswig Holstein, the former Danish region of Skane (now Southern Sweden), Norway and the Orkney Isles.

'Round towers were first seen in East Anglia at Bury St Edmunds Abbey and Norwich Cathedral, and then the idea seems to have filtered down to parish churches, along with other characteristic features, such as double-splayed windows.

'At Great Leighs in Essex there is a plait motif used around the church door, which is exactly replicated in a Danish church at Neukirchen, proving the direct link with this region and Scandinavia.'

See also BROADS, CATHEDRALS, CHURCHES, FENS, FLINT, THATCH.

ROWAN

This tree has been endowed with magical qualities, its orange-red berries warding off evil. Grown in graveyards in Yorkshire, it was thought to prevent *'the dead from rising'*, Geoffrey Grigson said; planted beside houses, it protects from witches.

More common in the uplands and the North, its pinnate leaves resemble those of ash – mountain ash is its other name – but it is a smaller and more delicate tree. It grows in woods, but is most often admired as a solitary tree, precarious on a bleak hillside, its bright berries hanging in clusters. Rowan and its many cultivars are widely planted in parks and gardens. Along streets it does not have the gravitas of larger trees, but it may be a godsend for the blackbirds.

See also ALDER, ANCIENT TREES, ASH, BEECH, BIRCH, BLACK POPLAR, BLACKTHORN, ELM, FIELD MAPLE, HAWTHORN, HAZEL, HOLLY, HOLM OAK, HORNBEAM, HORSE CHESTNUT, JUNIPER, LANDMARK TREES, LIME, LONDON PLANE, MONKEY-PUZZLE, OAK, ORCHARDS, PEARS, POPLAR, ROYAL FORESTS, SCOTS PINE, SWEET CHESTNUT, SYCAMORE, WALNUT, WHITEBEAM, WILLOW, WOODS, YEW.

ROYAL FORESTS

The Norman kings designated huge tracts of land as their private hunting estates. In these man-made islands harsh laws protected the interests of the royal chase; 'forest' referred to the law, not to continuous woodland.

Hatfield Forest in Essex, the remnant of a royal forest, was said by Oliver Rackham to be *'the only place where you can step into the Middle Ages to see, with only a small effort of the imagination, what a forest looked like in use'*. Elaborate banks and ditches, once crowned with timber paling and designed to keep deer in, can still be traced there and around parts of Ashdown Forest in Sussex.

359

William the Conquerer built a castle in Windsor Forest, still royal parkland.

Under the Normans vast stretches of open moorland became royal or seigneurial forests: the Pennine forests of Macclesfield, Peak and Bowland, as well as the Cumberland Forest of Inglewood and the Bishop of Durham's Forest of Weardale. In medieval times much of the North York Moors belonged to the royal Forest of Pickering. In Devon the Duchy of Cornwall claimed jurisdiction over the whole of Dartmoor; Exmoor, forty miles away, was a royal forest, too. By the twelfth century a quarter of the land may have been royal forest, Sherwood in Nottinghamshire perhaps the best-known example.

As the Middle Ages wore on, land began to pass into the hands of the nobility, and with it the right to hunt deer; forest law gave way to common law. H.L. Edlin explained: '*A Royal Forest that passed into private ownership became a CHASE, while private land adjoining a Royal Forest was called a PURLIEU. Either type of land might eventually be enclosed to form a PARK, where deer were kept, or a WARREN, for coneys and such small beasts.*' Many chases and royal forests had been 'disafforested' by the eighteenth century, releasing more land into farming. During this time foxhunting began to emerge.

Where there has been continuity of ownership, ancient wood pasture may have persisted in parkland, and unique assemblages of flora and fauna survive among the ancient trees. The culture of using woodland may still be read in the landscape. The Cranborne Chase crosses the Dorset/Wiltshire border; here one of the largest areas of worked hazel coppice, with oak, ash and maple, is still in use. But piecemeal enclosure gradually destroyed most forests. Famous lawsuits fought by the commoners of Ashdown and Epping Forests kept their forests largely intact. Here, and in the New Forest, Hampshire and the Forest of Dean,

360

Gloucestershire, echoes of medieval forest administration persist. Of all the English forests, '*the Dean is the one where a visitor seems not just to arrive among trees, but to move into a piece of ancient and foreign country*', Thomas Hinde wrote. Its inhabitants, said to be independent, lawless folk, earned their living from iron, charcoal and coal, giving this remote forest a special character, despite its present status as Forestry Commission land.

See also ANCIENT TREES, BOUNDARIES, COAL MINING, COMMONS, LANDMARK TREES, LAWN, NEW FOREST PONIES, PARKLAND, POINT TO POINT, ROBIN HOOD, WARRENS, WOODS.

R U I N S

Our view of ruins tends to be mediated by layers of time, romantic poetry, ironic melancholy, movie glamour and local tales, rather than direct memory of events. But wartime Coventry, Hull, Liverpool, Plymouth and London during the Blitz are still vivid for those who lived through it. Domestic remnants, pillboxes, airfields and the odd, wild bomb-site or gaunt church wall spark the retelling of stories; the tide of fireweed and buddleia and the colonisation by the black redstart (it mistook rubble for Alpine scree) are living memorials to that time.

Warehouses, factories, mills and docks lie waiting for new uses. In the hills there are isolated remains of houses and barns, slate and stone stolen, and in County Durham no one wants the villages abandoned after mine closures.

What did our ancestors make of abandoned places? The stones of many a walled town and dissolved abbey built the local high street, leaving us but foundations to interpret. Around some ruins stories linger. Pendragon Castle near Mallerstang in Westmorland is a collection of stacks of stones keeping the company of trees on a considerable

mound. '*Let Uter-Pendragon do what he can/The River Eden will run as it ran*', the local rhyme goes. King Arthur's father is reputed to have tried to fortify the castle with water, but the river would not comply. Other (perhaps later) tales insist that he died here, defending it from the Saxons.

Beeston Castle in Cheshire, built between 1220 and 1330 overlooking a gap to the Cheshire Plain, retains some of its outer walls and turrets and a fine set of angular and rotund walls, crowning the very top of the hill. Leland saw it as a ruin in the time of Henry VIII, but there is sufficient massive walling remaining to spark serious childhood fantasy. The paths that thread across the hill among bracken and trees demonstrate the affection in which it is held.

Indeed castles are enjoyed as repositories of our ideas of heroic history and great works. The dramatic presence of Chepstow Castle in Monmouthshire is amplified by its position on the cliffs above the river Wye. Begun in 1067, it was the first to demonstrate the full intent of William the Conqueror – it has been variously in England, last in 1974, and is currently in Wales. It is a powerful place, imposing and beautiful in its function and form. On a domestic scale, Nunney Castle in Somerset sits in a watery moat, four tall towers at each corner of a simple rectangle that remains elegant, although one wall was wrecked by cannon fire in 1645 by Oliver Cromwell. Its grace and serenity fill the village that huddles around it.

Norfolk is known for its ruined churches. In Breckland the tower of Foulden fell in the eighteenth century; at Beechamwell one of three churches lies in pieces. Olive Cook noted fifty years ago that '*No artificial ruin, no relic of former magnificence carefully preserved by the State could be as moving as the fissured tower, the fallen arches and the roofless, overgrown nave of solitary Roudham . . . enough of the tower survives to show that it must once have been extremely graceful.*'

Gravity takes its tithe. Ivy clings, jackdaws watch, the winds enter and leave through windows. The Gothic atmosphere is enjoyed in daylight – few hanker after night-time visits unless the scene is to be the setting for a concert or drama: Gregorian chants in a floodlit Fountains Abbey, Yorkshire; *Henry IV* at Haughmond, Shropshire; or the *Mysteries* in the remains of Coventry Cathedral, bombed in 1940. Culture, heritage and tourism are big business – the walls of York and Chester are worth their upkeep. But finding ruins, confronting mutability, is a luxury, especially in suburban England.

Painters and poets from the Renaissance onwards have repeatedly returned to ruins as metaphor. Wordsworth used them to rehearse his view of the decaying condition of the nation. Ruins, and their absence, have much to tell us. As David Lowenthal wrote: '*Remembering the past is crucial for our sense of identity . . . to know what we were confirms that we are.*'

See also ABBEYS, CASTLES, CEMETERIES, CHIMNEYS, CHURCHES, CHURCH-YARDS, COAL MINING, CORRUGATED IRON, DESERTED VILLAGES, DRYSTONE WALLS, EARTHQUAKES, ENGINE HOUSES, FIELDS, FOLKTALES, FOLLIES, FORTIFICATIONS, GAPS, GIN HOUSES, HAUNTED PLACES, HENGES & STONE CIRCLES, LANDSLIPS, LEAD MINES, LOST VILLAGES, MOATS, MONASTERIES, PILLBOXES, PREFABS, WALLFLOWERS.

R U S H - B E A R I N G

For hundreds of years rushes, hay or straw have been ceremonially strewn on the floors of churches (and houses) to make them warmer underfoot, to sweeten the air and to muffle the sound of heavy boots. Mixing the prosaic and the symbolic, rush-bearing ceremonies once took place all over the country, but maintained greater significance in the North West on the local saint's day or wakes week.

Rushes, sedges and reeds have been of great importance historically, especially in the North West, where the seats of the traditional ladder and spindle-back chairs were woven from club-rush. Stretches of riverbanks and blocks of fen were rented out to reed/sedge cutters for thatching; rushes were cut for basketwork, plaited to make seats for chairs and used for paper-making. Dipped in wax or mutton fat, they were also used as tapers or rushlights.

Club-rush '*is one of the species that gave the ceremony of "rush-bearing" its title*', Richard Mabey wrote in *Flora Britannica*. He added that sweet-flag, a water plant valued for the citrus scent of its crushed leaves, was one of the plants, together with scented herbs, that was used for '*disposable carpeting*' in churches, and was grown in the Norfolk fens for this purpose. There are accounts of people collecting '*small rushes known as "sieves", that grow on the fells*' near Grasmere, Westmorland.

Of the Cumberland and Westmorland rush-bearings, the largest, at Grasmere, is held on the nearest Saturday to 5 August, St Oswald's Day. Bearings – rushes woven locally in the shapes of crosses, hearts and wreaths – are attached to frames, mounted on poles and carried by children. Traditional bearings – the large, permanent pieces, such as the Serpent, St Oswald and the Hand of St Oswald – are brought out to lead the procession, following the Gold Cross and St Oswald's Banner. Inside the church the floor is covered with fresh green rushes. After the service the children are given special rush-bearing gingerbread stamped with 'Saint Oswald'. Two days later bearings are collected from the church, and sports, such as wrestling and fell running, take place, followed by a feast.

In the valleys of industrial Lancashire and Yorkshire the rush cart is the focus. In the Pennine village of Saddleworth the rush cart may be pulled by up to one hundred morris men, with forty acting as brakes. Phil Taylor tells us that it '*is always the second weekend after 12 August; if the twelfth falls on a Saturday, it's the second weekend after that. This used to be the old Saddleworth wakes, when mills and factories had their annual week's holiday.*' At Sowerby Bridge the cart is pulled by sixty local men wearing Panama hats, white shirts, black trousers and clogs, and young women take it in turns to ride on top. The cart is accompanied by music and six teams of morris dancers. From mid-August a team of ten to fifteen people cut rushes from Warley Moor, and a complex 'thatched' cart is created with a space for a person to sit.

By all accounts things became too rowdy in Rochdale, Lancashire. In the 1820s James Kay-Shuttleworth wrote: '*The rushcarts assembled in the street opposite the Butts, each with its band in front . . . in side streets were stalls with Eccles cakes, Everton toffee and Ormskirk gingerbread. Conjurers stood on stages, mountebanks and clowns were ready to perform.*' With twenty thousand spectators already in 1827, and rivalry between different groups becoming highly competitive, it was banned in the 1880s.

Many of the hay strewings that were distinctive aspects of Petertide in eastern and midland counties, including Rutland, Huntingdonshire and Bedfordshire, have disappeared – whether the tradition or the meadows were first to demise is not clear. By contrast, revival has happened in Bishop's Castle, Shropshire. Since 1975 rushes have been collected from a local lake and a rush cart made to process with morris teams and the town band. John Kirkpatrick, a folk singer and morris man, was approached to write a patronal hymn, now sung each year as part of the service.

The oldest rush-bearing ceremony (initiated in 1493) still takes place at St Mary Redcliffe, Bristol, where a Rush Sunday service is held on Whit Sunday each year and rushes gathered from Somerset are strewn.

The plaiting of rushes to make bearings and the thatching of the rush carts are some of the last vestiges of rush-gathering. That reed beds still thrive in these places says something about the intimacy of connection between nature and culture.

See also BISCUITS, BRASS BANDS, CHURCHES, FAIRS & FAIRGROUNDS, FELL RUNNING, HAY MEADOWS, MORRIS DANCING, REED BEDS, THATCH, WINDSOR & COUNTRY CHAIRS, WRESTLING.

Sassoon Primary, Rosemary Sassoon, 1995.

S A I N T S

The stories of the Saints have all the magic and wonder of the best fairytales. Saints' days were celebrated with vigour until anti-Catholicism and a zeal for work reduced them. The word 'saint' associates godliness with a special kind of mortal, singled out to do God's work. Early saints were proclaimed as such by their congregations; later, formal 'canonisation' became the charge of the Pope in Rome and continues today. Anglican and Protestant churches abandoned canonisation but are not averse to celebrating a few of the well-established and popular saints.

Saints have taken hold of our places from the earliest Christian times (some may be Christianised pagan deities, or the places of long sanctity). John Vince, writing in 1968, listed 84 who were featured in place-names, more than half of them in Cornwall. At the top of the tree are St George in England and St Piran in Cornwall.

St Piran's Day is 5 March, a day of celebration in Cornwall. He was a Celtic monk, and his oratory and hermitage at Perranporth (named for him) were once buried in the sands. They have been rediscovered and excavated, but are now beneath an unimposing concrete marker.

Nothing is known of St George except that he was martyred, possibly in Palestine, possibly in the early fourth century AD. In stories of the thirteenth century he became a Roman soldier from Turkey, who killed a dragon in Libya. His chivalrous tales returned with the crusaders, coinciding with a cultural trend for knightly romance. By 1415 his feast day, 23 April, was England's most important of the year. England shares him as a patron saint with Georgia, Portugal, Venice and many more.

Home-grown saints abound. St Alban was our first martyr, around AD 304. St Edmund was an East Anglian king killed by Danish invaders around 870. He is depicted pierced with arrows from Yorkshire to Buckinghamshire. In the cathedral of his name-town, Bury St Edmunds in Suffolk, a statue of his head is held by the wolf that recovered it.

Many other places have their own 'special' saints: Malmesbury, Wiltshire has St Aldhelm; Hexham, Northumberland St Wilfrid. East Anglia's fens, especially around Crowland, Lincolnshire, show allegiance to the hermit St Guthlac, whereas St Dunstan has links in Glastonbury, Somerset.

In mainland Europe saints' days are a time for local celebration; perhaps we could invent a new generation of local holidays here, since every parish church has its patronal saint and the parish festivities are often held on the saint's day.

See also AMMONITES, CHURCHES, COASTS, DRAGONS, GARGOYLES & GROTESQUES, HILLS, SPRINGS.

S A L T   M A R S H E S

On coastal salt marshes pioneering, salt-loving plants gain a foothold on the land just above inter-tidal mud-flats. These marshes, regularly washed by the tide, are among the most dynamic habitats on the planet. They form only in a few sheltered places, in estuaries, saline lagoons, behind barrier islands and on beach plains. At the cutting edge, nearest the sea, grows the brave glasswort salicornia, or marsh samphire (sometimes sold as 'sandfire'), that withstands soaking by six hundred tides a year. On the quieter, landward edge grow plants able to cope with only occasional inundation: sea and salt marsh rushes, golden samphire, shrubby sea blite and sea wormwood. In the middle reaches of the marsh, sea purslane, sea lavender, sea plantain, thrift and greater sea spurrey and salt marsh grass find a home.

365

Most of our eighty thousand acres of salt marsh are concentrated in four areas: the Thames estuary, the Essex coast, Liverpool and Morecambe Bay and the Wash. Each has a characteristic flora, on fine sediments on the east coast, on a sandy base on the west.

Salt marshes are famously productive. The annual growth of salt marsh grass and cord grass rivals the output of a tropical rainforest – up to eighty ounces of green vegetation per square yard in a year. Much of this organic wealth flows back into the estuary to support fish and invertebrates, including oysters, mussels and cockles, which thrive in the calm, nutrient-rich waters and are in turn eaten by birds.

In Essex the Blackwater estuary supports up to sixteen thousand wildfowl and thirty thousand waders. Redshank may even nest on the marsh, their eggs surviving the odd brush with the tide. The salt marshes of the Solway Firth in Cumberland regularly host more than 120,000 wintering wildfowl and are internationally important for wintering geese, including the entire breeding population of the Spitzbergen barnacle goose. Along this coast sheep and cattle are grazed on rich common marshes regulated by a committee, which works out the stints (numbers of animals shared out according to the carrying capacity of the land), and watched over by marsh wardens.

These areas hide reminders of our past activities, sparring or working with the sea, for example winning salt, as at Salt Cotes and Crosscanonby in Cumberland. Now scale is the problem – large coastal developments, such as the Felixstowe dock extension in Suffolk and the Thames Gateway development, threaten and destroy these unique places. Agriculture takes its toll, too: in the Wash around two thousand acres of salt marsh were converted to farming between 1970 and 1980. The sinking of south-east England – by about two millimetres a year – and rising sea levels linked to global warming are squeezing salt marshes against sea walls, which prevent their migration inland. As the marsh disappears, the waves begin to erode the sea walls themselves. 'Managed realignment' – including allowing the sea to flow onto land behind existing sea walls – offers a better prospect for the future. In 2002 controlled breaches were made in the sea wall at Abbotts Hall, a historic coastal farm eight miles south of Colchester, as the first step in re-creating protective salt marshes along the Essex coast.

See also BOWLING GREENS, CATTLE, COASTLINE, COASTS, COMMONS, ESTUARIES, FENS, GRAZING MARSHES, GREEN LANES, LEVELS, LINKS, LOST VILLAGES, MOSSLAND, PEAT, SAND-DUNES, SHEEP, SHELLFISH, TIDES.

S A N D - D U N E S

366

Paradise for children and lovers (although not at the same time), sand-dunes are miniature, soft mountain ranges by the sea. England boasts nearly thirty thousand acres of sand-dunes, concentrated on the coasts of Northumberland, Lincolnshire, Norfolk, Kent, Dorset, Devon, Cornwall, Lancashire, Westmorland and Cumberland. Behind the beach, accumulations of wind-blown sand develop into low hills of bare, shifting sand, joined by semi-stable larger

dunes, sometimes rising up to one hundred feet and held by tenacious marram grass. It may be joined by sea holly, sea spurges and scores of other distinctive flowering plants, as well as mosses and lichens. Terns, shelducks, oystercatchers and more find nesting places among the dunes, as do sand wasps and mining bees. The Lancashire dunes at Ainsdale famously play host to some two thousand natterjack toads.

These magnificent coastal landscapes are highly mobile, precariously balanced between the erosion and deposition of sand, and need to be able to migrate inland. The construction of sea defences or the stabilisation of dunes for golf-courses, housing developments and holiday resorts can seriously disrupt movement; more than half of the 121 dune sites are now eroding away as a result.

See also ASPARAGUS, BEACHCOMBING, BEACHES, COASTS, GOLF-COURSES, LINKS, NATTERJACK TOADS, WILLOW.

S A N D S T O N E S

With experience down the pit, Sid Chaplin describes the Carboniferous sandstones, constant partner of coal seams, as the '*baked sands of carboniferous shores, once fused in a fiery furnace, then torn from cliff-faces by unimaginable storms, wrenched, riven, scattered, then gathered sands, overlaid in huge beds by great masses and pressures*'. Elsewhere the Old Red Sandstone that makes Devon red, the New Red Sandstone of Nottinghamshire, the Bagshot Sands of Surrey and the cross-bedded sandstones of Penrith, Cumberland offer diverse examples of one of our common rocks. Their colours and varied hardnesses make all the difference to our hills, valleys and buildings.

See also BUILDING STONES, CAVES, CHALK, COAL MINING, GRANITE, GREENSAND, LIMESTONE, MILLSTONE GRIT, ROCKS, STANDING STONES.

S C A R E C R O W S

We have made and used scarecrows for more than five hundred years. They were used alongside, and then instead of, children, who were paid little or nothing to work long days shouting in the fields with their wooden rattles and clappers. William Cobbett was a child bird-scarer or shoy-hoy (a southern name, after the cries). Scarecrows have many local names: mawkins in Norfolk; hodmadod/hodmedod in Berkshire and the Isle of Wight; mammet in Yorkshire/Lancashire; murmet in Devon; mommet in Somerset, Warwickshire and Worcestershire. In the North those standing in potato fields are known as tattie-bogie/bogle.

Intricate, expensive machines, such as automatic gas bird-scarers, have largely replaced the familiar models attached to wooden frames, dressed in old clothes or torn fertiliser bags. However, much smarter versions are now made for agricultural shows and scarecrow festivals, such as at Wray Fair in north Lancashire and Urchfont, Wiltshire.

See also BONFIRE NIGHT, FIELDS, ORCHARDS, POTATOES, ROOKERIES, SPARROWS, STARLINGS.

S C O T S   P I N E

Our only native coniferous softwood, the Scots pine can be recognised by its scaly, reddish bark and small, evergreen needles and cones – known as deal apples or dealies in Suffolk. Planted as nurse trees on country estates in the eighteenth and nineteenth centuries, they also made landmark clumps on the tops of hills – such as May Hill,

Gloucestershire – and waymarks along droves. Beside an inn, they were a sign that drovers and their animals were welcome.

They were also used for wind-breaks – the most distinctive being the 'pine line' hedges on the Brecklands of East Anglia (locally known as deal rows) planted at the turn of the 1800s to prevent the erosion of the sandy soil. Monterey pine was used as shelter-belts on the east Devon coastal plateau; Scots and Corsican pines were ill-advisedly planted on sand-dunes to stabilise them, or for afforestation – at Sefton in Lancashire, for example. As the Victorians planned Bournemouth they planted maritime and Scots pines in parks, along the roads and cliff tops, and down the chines; the trees, and their resinous smell, now distinguish this town.

Since 1918 the Forestry Commission has carpeted the country with conifer forests, such as in Thetford Chase, Norfolk and Kielder Forest, Northumberland. Meanwhile, on the neglected heathlands of Dorset, Hampshire and west Sussex, once grazed and managed with fires to keep the pines and birch at bay, Scots pines quietly flourish.

See also ALDER, ANCIENT TREES, ASH, BEECH, BIRCH, BLACK POPLAR, BLACKTHORN, CHINES, CLUMPS, DROVE ROADS, ELM, FIELD MAPLE, HAWTHORN, HAZEL, HEATHLAND, HEDGES, HOLLY, HOLM OAK, HORNBEAM, HORSE CHESTNUT, INNS, LANDMARK TREES, LIME, LONDON PLANE, MONKEY-PUZZLE, OAK, ORCHARDS, PEARS, POPLAR, RED SQUIRRELS, ROWAN, ROYAL FORESTS, SAND-DUNES, SWEET CHESTNUT, SYCAMORE, WALNUT, WHITEBEAM, WILLOW, WOODS, YEW.

367

S C U L P T U R E S

Queen Victoria was one of the few women to sit on plinths in our cities. Most public works of art were extensions of classical sculpture – men/gods on high. During the past two decades things have really changed. There has been a recognition that art can be and do much more radical things, helping us better to know and enjoy our surroundings and adding to the identity of places. Elisabeth Frink brought us horses on the ground at Piccadilly, London and martyrs walking among us in Dorchester. In the centre of Birmingham the fountains, steps and scattered sculptures offer the feeling of being in an open-air art gallery.

Around Drewsteignton in Devon subtle sculptures surprise along walks across the fields and hills. Peter Randall-Page worked to draw our gaze into the heart of a granite boulder, to the workings of a spring, to the simplicity of a drystone wall. Antony Gormley's sculptures work on both monumental and intimate scales. His 'Angel of the North', 65 feet high by the A1, marks the entrance to Tyneside, celebrates local engineering skills and has offered itself as an icon for the North East; in the crypt of Winchester Cathedral, Hampshire a contemplative man

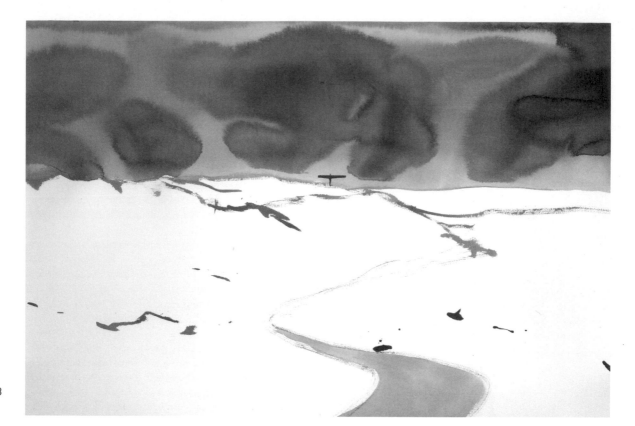

368

stands unexpectedly up to his knees in water. 'Willow Man' by Serena de la Hey is a large figure running on the Somerset Levels near the M5, who tells of the culture of osier growing in a completely new form.

Early experiments by the Forestry Commission in giving young sculptors a massive canvas and endless materials in the Grizedale Forest, Lancashire began with David Nash creating 'Running Table'. Like the Forest of Dean in Gloucestershire, which followed its lead, it draws thousands of visitors willing to wander in search of art, perchancing on the wonders of the forest as they do.

Not at first seeming like an artistic endeavour, Andy Goldsworthy has been rebuilding sheep-folds in Cumberland and Westmorland. At Mungrisdale the land was cleared of great boulders, which now crowd around and hide the drystone sheep-fold as if pressing to get in. Drystone cones have been made for pinfolds in Bolton, Brough, Crosby, Outhgill, Raisbeck and Warcop, as guardians, each using the stone of the place. At Casterton sixteen small, square folds, following the Fellfoot Drove, each holds a large boulder. At Underbarrow near Kendal two folds encircle boulders through which planted rowan trees are growing – a memorial for the farmers who had to cope with the outbreak of foot-and-mouth disease. When the trees were planted late in 2001, Andy Goldsworthy said: '*The planting of any tree is a gesture of optimism and renewal – growing out of stone in the protective embrace of a sheep-fold will I hope give that gesture a potent mix of feelings – hardship, struggle, renewal, fragility, precariousness and strength. I could think of no better work on my part that could articulate the emotional struggle that has taken place for those living in badly affected areas during this intensely difficult time.*'

Plymouth city council charged Gordon Young with the task of giving identity to a ten-mile coast path to '*stop people getting lost, and we want it a bit interesting!*' So, from little fishes in the pavement to Brunel's Spanner, lettered railings to telegraph code words, a cross-section of the Eddystone lighthouse to a float bench – a red-and-white-striped old metal float with a seat hung along its side – you make your way round the edge of the city through artefacts and quotations, which offer glimpses of the composting of history in this place, much of it offered by local people. This and his wordy Cursing Stone and Reiver Pavement in the middle of Carlisle, Cumberland show how imagination, collaboration and quality can transform the feel of a place: they speak volumes.

See also BASTLES, CAIRNS, CYCLING, DRYSTONE WALLS, FOOTPATHS, JACK AND JILL, MONUMENTS, NEW MILESTONES, PELE TOWERS, PINFOLDS, SHEEP-FOLDS.

SEA CAVES

Once you have seen wave upon wave bearing down on the Atlantic coast of Cornwall, it becomes obvious that any slight weakness in the hardest of rock faces will be excavated without mercy. The sea cave is one result. Kynance Cove on the Lizard peninsula, with its white sand and colourful beached-whale rocks, hides caves in the polished serpentine rock, exciting despite their prosaic names – the Kitchen, the Parlour and the Ladies' Bathing Pool. Tennyson ruminated in one of the caves here, 'watching wave rainbows'. We may catch a glimpse once again of the chough, that shining black bird with the handsome red beak, which makes its nest in caves and rock fissures.

Dark caves, light caves, dripping, dropping – despite their clear dangers we are drawn to explore them. Enticing and alarming us with associations of past and present smuggling and ancient tales, the presence of a cave on the headland or at the back of the beach makes a difference, intensifies the experience, often makes a sacred place. Merlin's Cave at Tintagel in Cornwall offers both natural grandeur and all the mystery of Arthurian legend. Walking into darkness and then discovering that the cave is cut right through to meet the sea on the other side heightens the power of the place.

Lundy, the Scillies and the Farne Islands have caves of note, while whole coastal counties have few or none, such as Cumberland, Lancashire, Cheshire and the east coast, from Essex up to north Yorkshire. Where there are awesome cliffs many caves are visible only from the sea. Secret and often unapproachable they remain one of the few parts of these islands fairly untouched by human activity, a boon to the sea birds and seals. The fretted cliffs around Flamborough Head, Yorkshire offer tall clefts, or geos, and chalk caves of all kinds, only viewable from boats leaving North Landing. Robin Lyth Cave is named after a fictitious smuggler from R.D. Blackmore's *Mary Anerley*. Big caves are explorable in Thornwick Bay at low tide. Blackhall Rocks in County Durham is famous for its dramatic sea caves and stacks in the soft magnesian limestone.

The Chelsea Speleological Society made an important discovery while surveying Canterbury Cave in St Margaret's Bay, Kent in 1975. Assuming it to have been etched by the sea, despite its name not appearing on maps before 1960, they found an extensive network of caves in the chalk. Mostly above the high-water mark, it proved to be a relict system formed by an underground stream, revealed when the sea cut back the face of the cliff.

Beachy Head Cave in Sussex is the longest in chalk; so far explored are 1,160 feet of passages, some inhabited by spiders, flies and moths. Although changed by rockfalls, the main cave entrance lies fourteen feet above the high-water mark; again, this must have been worn by a stream flowing above a flint layer.

For a perfect line of little caves from which to understand the processes, a visit to Durdle Cove in Dorset will reveal a honeycomb line just above the high-water mark, picking out weakness where rock has sheared against rock.

See also ARCHES, AVALON, CAVES, CHALK, CLIFFS, COASTS, COVES, FERNS, FLINT, LIMESTONE, QUARRIES, WHITE CLIFFS.

SEA FISH

The North Sea has increased in temperature by one degree Celsius in just 25 years. Eighteen species of fish, including haddock and cod, have moved northwards, some by more than seventy miles; others have sought deeper waters. Changing seas driven by climatic shifts have also brought tuna, new kinds of shark and sea-horses to our coasts. Occasional sub-tropical fish are turning up in nets, and sardines, anchovies, John Dory and red mullet are becoming more common.

Our staple sea fish have been suffering decline after a century of overfishing. Salmon are scarce, and the once-ubiquitous cod and skate are on the way to becoming rare delicacies. This, coupled with international legislation – and the availability of easier work in other trades – has turned an industry that provided the main employment in many coastal towns into a white dwarf.

The fishermen's intimate knowledge and the fish that were their livelihood are beginning to slip from the everyday. For a lifetime the harbours of East Anglia and the North East were driven by herrings; Yarmouth, Norfolk was where, until as late as the 1960s, Scots and Northumbrian girls known as 'herring lasses' would travel each year to work on fish processing. Yarmouth still has herrings on its coat of arms; the town was famous for its smoked, or 'bloated', herrings – bloaters. Now herrings are imported from Norway, having been fished out from around the east coast of England.

The fish of the North Sea were plentiful. Berwick-upon-Tweed in Northumberland still crowns a Salmon Queen each July. In the North East there were mackerel between July and October, salmon and trout from March to September and haddock from November, as well as turbot (locally called brat), whiting, sole (dab), plaice on Dogger Bank, cod, lamprey (soocker) and skate (ginny). Fish were the lifeblood of Seahouses, Boulmer and North Shields in Northumberland and South Shields in County Durham. Now the fish quay at North Shields is better known for an annual music festival.

In Yorkshire Hull and the Humber were alive with fishing boats until the end of the 1970s; the city now boasts a visitor centre called The Deep. Across the estuary in

369

Lincolnshire, Grimsby, with its football club The Mariners, was once 'Home of the Haddock'. Now it is the home of the National Fishing Heritage Centre, but still one of the country's top fish markets.

Dover sole had some geographical allegiance; to the fishermen around Kent and Sussex soles were slips, dogfish were bone dogs or bull-huss, flounders were eyeballers. Sea bass can still be found in the Essex estuaries of the Colne and Blackwater, but warmer seas are spreading their range. The Channel and the Solent held skate, mackerel, whiting, cod, plaice and pilchard. Occasionally Royal Sturgeon would appear at Mudeford and Christchurch in Hampshire, but Poole in Dorset and Beer and Sidmouth in Devon were the main centres of industry on the south coast. Plymouth Sound in Devon has the country's only Steven's goby. Weymouth, Dorset was famed for red mullet (which is now being found in the Thames estuary and beyond). The seaside rock pools of Devon, Dorset and Cornwall still have their shannies and blennies.

On the flat Somerset coast around the mouth of the Parrett the last of the mud-horse fishermen are still working. James Crowden explained: *'their method of fishing has changed little since neolithic times. Nets strung out on poles . . . The mud-horse is a sledge with a curved front which is pushed out [across the mud] and then brought back to help carry the catch.'* Haaf nets still cross the bays around Silloth and Maryport in Cumberland, as they have since the Danes arrived eleven hundred years ago. Liverpool and Fleetwood, Lancashire were the heart of the Irish Sea fishing business. Morecambe Bay, with its ferocious tides, is where whitefish and flatfish are found, the latter known as 'flukes' in Flookburgh, Lancashire, perhaps the origin of the place-name.

Pilchards made the familiar stereotype of the 'Cornish fishing village' and filled many a Stargazy pie. Huer's houses were built as lookout towers to scan for the shoals; one survives near Newquay. Fresh fish is still landed and traded across Cornwall, but, although Newlyn and Padstow stand out, like Brixham in Devon, with thriving fish markets, the future is uncertain.

See also BASKING SHARKS, BEACHES, BOATS, CHINES, COASTS, COBLES, CORNISH GIGS, EELS, ESTUARIES, FISH & CHIPS, FOOD, FRESHWATER FISH, HARBOURS, NOBBIES, PIERS, PORTLAND LERRETS, SHELLFISH, STARFISH, TIDES.

S E A   F O R T S

For centuries England guarded against sea attack with land-based defences. In the mid-1800s Lord Palmerston went one step further, placing forts on islands in estuaries to attack invading navies before they got within range of land. In the Medway estuary in Kent artist Stephen Turner worked on Hoo Island in 1998. To him, Darnet and Hoo

forts *'stand like Scylla and Charybdis down river from the former Royal Navy Dockyard at Chatham. They exist today as wonderful overgrown and derelict follies, home to all manner of wildlife.'*

Bull Sand fort was built in 1915 on a sandbank near Spurn Head, Yorkshire to protect the Humber, together with Haile Sand fort, a mile off the coast, which is visible from the sea front at Humberston, Lincolnshire. Both are armour-plated over concrete and look grim yet vulnerable, like floating islands.

Sailing out of Portsmouth harbour in Hampshire, Spit Bank, Horse Sands and No Man's Land forts erupt out of the Solent like forbidding props from a James Bond film. The mechanisation of warfare in the twentieth century pressed existing forts into new action as gun emplacements, magazines and bases. A few new ones appeared.

Off Whitstable in Kent, Redsand fort's extraordinary array of seven towers (now without linking walkways), each raised high above the sea on stilts, looks rather like a gathering of box cameras on legs. Guy Maunsell designed similar sea forts for the Mersey, the Humber and the Thames during the Second World War. After being abandoned in 1956 their ambiguous legal status proved ideal for the unlicensed pirate radio stations of the 1960s. Screaming Lord Sutch, for example, used Shivering Sands, seven miles off Herne Bay in Kent, as the base for Sutch Radio, later Radio City. Roughs Tower, off Essex, had perhaps the most unusual change of fortunes. Paddy Roy Bates and his family moved there in 1967 and continue in residence, having successfully claimed sovereignty. They are now the royal family of the Principality of Sealand.

See also BRIDGES, CASTLES, ESTUARIES, FILM LOCATIONS, FORTIFICATIONS, HILL-FORTS, ISLANDS, MARTELLO TOWERS, PELE TOWERS, PILLBOXES.

S E A - M A R K S

The singular chapel on St Aldhelm's Head, just 35 feet square, may have been used by mariners since the twelfth century as a landmark or sea-mark to guide them around the dangerous cliffs and rocks of the Isle of Purbeck, Dorset. Around the coast, church steeples were often used as navigational aids, some perhaps having beacon fires on the towers.

Day marks were erected to aid daylight approach to harbours if conspicuous rocks, natural features or buildings could not be used. Turner's Cornish painting *The Entrance to Fowey Harbour*, with its tempestuous sea and sky, gives ample reason for the presence of Gribbin Beacon; the red and white tower, more than eighty feet high, on Gribbin Head is prominent from every sea direction and denotes the otherwise cryptic way to shelter in the Fowey estuary.

Rodney Legg described lining up to enter Portland Harbour in Dorset, where '*two slender concrete faced pyramids, twenty feet high . . . stand on the grassy slopes above West Bottom at about 510 feet and 540 feet above sea level. They are set as sea-marks, which, when lined up, show the safe approach from the south. The passage they pinpoint is from south-by-south-west to north-by-north-east, charting a course between the perilous ledges off Portland Bill and the parlous offshore Shambles sandbank.*'

Vessels would pick up a red light from the 54-foot-high east light if they were approaching on an unsafe bearing towards Whitby harbour in Yorkshire; now a red light for the same purpose shines out from the steep steps up to St Mary's Church.

See also BEACON FIRES, BEACONS (COASTAL), CHURCHES, COASTLINE, COASTS, ESTUARIES, INDUSTRIAL CHIMNEYS, ISLANDS, LANDMARKS, LIGHT-HOUSES, STACKS, WHITE CLIFFS.

SEA TRACTOR

If you want to catch the South Sands Ferry at Salcombe in Devon, '*a unique motorised landing stage*' will drive you precariously but high above the water to the boat.

But at Burgh Island, further west in Devon, an unmatched creature thrills children and grizzled skippers when the tide is in. Sea Tractor III, commissioned by the island's owners as an all-tide conveyance, sporting the Royal Ensign, stands quiet by the Pilchard Inn at the end of the sands that link the island with Bigbury-on-Sea. When the tide is out one can walk across the isthmus to appreciate island life for a few hours. But when the tide is in, the Sea Tractor crawls carefully across the sand, diversifying its quarter-mile route to deliver its slightly scared passengers back and forth.

It is like a piece of the Forth Bridge gone feral: heavy tubes form the chassis, a high platform six feet up is contained by wooden planking, and open, but roofed, seating rolls on big, soft tyres.

See also BEACHES, FERRIES, FORDS, ISLANDS, SHELLFISH, TIDES.

SHEEP

The medieval and Elizabethan endowment of sheep can be seen in the glorious churches of East Anglia, the beautiful barns of the Cotswolds, the walls of Wensleydale, Yorkshire. The importance of sheep that can look after themselves on the fells and hills, that know their place, may be less obvious. Hill sheep are taught by their elders in the herd where to eat in the morning in May, where to seek shelter from frost, where to find water. Intimate knowledge of a territory, a daily round, shifting with season and weather, is passed down through the flock, and the shepherds. Hefting is one name given to this, the equivalent of a London taxi driver 'doing The Knowledge'. Flocks of sheep of the same breed make up hefted herds, which, all together on a mountain, make up the hirsel. It is illegal to remove the entire hirsel. The loss of animals to disease and economic volatility is a disaster for the culture of the sheep, as well as the people, because it takes generations for knowledge to be relearned.

The other great legacy is the extraordinary range of breeds, each originally developed by human as well as natural selection to survive well and produce most under conditions specific to the Dorset Downs, or the Cheviots, or Romney Marsh in Kent. Despite two centuries of convergent breeding, 65 named breeds still exist in Britain, for wool or meat or milk, and some are being used for conservation grazing. Many have such an intimacy with their sheep-walks that the quality of their meat and milk reflects this. The earliest sheep were shepherded here in neolithic times; the Vikings brought their own, as did some of the medieval monks. The Limestone breed was described by Robert Wallace as having evolved '*from time immemorial*' on the dry, precipitous slopes, from the Westmorland limestones to the White Peak in Derbyshire;

371

Blue Faced Leicester.

Cheviot.

Clun Forest.

Derbyshire Gritstone.

Devon Longwool.

Herdwick.

Wensleydale.

Dorset Horn.

it did poorly on boggy land. Close by, and in contrast, the Derbyshire Gritstone has survived. It was named as a breed on 15 October 1906, having been bred pure for the previous hundred years as the Dale o' Goyt (the Goyt valley runs towards Manchester).

One of our hardiest sheep, the Herdwick is native to the Fells of north Lancashire, Westmorland and Cumberland. So called because flocks were 'let' to a herdsman in lieu of wages, one story asserts that a wrecked ship from the Armada let some of its forbears ashore; another suggests that a Norwegian ship brought people and sheep from the north. There is variety within the Herdwicks themselves. In the lower lands the sheep are larger, with more and softer wool. The smallest, hardiest and healthiest survive on the fells, with scant eating and a real knowledge of the weather – they are said to foresee the approach of snow. Tall walls are a feature of their landscape, since they can easily jump six feet.

The *Shepherd's Guides*, started in the early nineteenth century, show the 'lug' or ear identifications. Caz Graham says: '*The guides are basically pictures of rather stylised sheep, with huge ears showing the individual marks that are cut out of each ear by different farmers. Each flock has its own mark, so that if sheep go missing on the fells . . . they'll get back to their rightful owner . . . The guides are updated every twenty years or so and the new one for the Lake District is going to have the new Defra flock numbers included and it's also going to be on the internet.*'

Ancient grazing rights exist in different landscapes; in the Forest of Dean, Gloucestershire the 'sheep badgers', who have rights to run sheep in the forest, are fighting to maintain their traditions.

Creative farmers and producers of organic meat, sheep's milk and cheese are driving patches of resurgence, despite complex problems in the aftermath of overstocking and foot-and-mouth disease, and in the face of global markets. The endangered sheep breeds have their champions, but there needs to be a wider recognition of the importance of maintaining their genetic variegation and sustaining the culture, the everyday working knowledge, of the people who keep them.

See also CHEESE, CHURCHES, DROVE ROADS, DRYSTONE WALLS, EARTH PIGMENTS, FAIRS & FAIRGROUNDS, FELLS, MARKETS, PINFOLDS, PRIDDY SHEEP FAIR, SALT MARSHES, SHEEP-DOGS, SHEEP-FOLDS, SHEEP-WASHES, WEATHER, YAN TAN TETHERA.

SHEEP-DOGS

'*Just as terriers varied in style in different parts of Britain, so too did the pastoral dogs – the sheep and cattle herders, drovers' dogs and shepherds' assistants*', David Hancock wrote. '*The modern list of Kennel Club recognised pedigree*

breeds bears no relation to the rich heritage of local variety once found in British pastoral dogs.' We still have the Border collie, bearded collie, Lancashire heeler and the old English sheep-dog (a dying breed), but we have lost '*the leggy short-coated Lakeland . . . the Black and Tan . . . the Blue Heelers used at ports, the Wheaten Norfolk Heeler, the huge and fierce Sussex Bobtail, the dainty black and tan Yorkshire Heeler, the Smithfield (Sheepdog) and the Drover's Cur (a distinct breed)*'.

Heelers, small herding dogs, were also known as curs, meaning dwarf dogs; there were types particular to each county. Bred to herd cattle by nipping at their heels (in the same way that Welsh corgis do), heelers were common in the 1600s to 1800s, but the advent of the railways brought the decline of droving and their usefulness diminished; the Lancashire is the only heeler to survive.

Drovers' dogs, described by Hancock as '*often huge and fierce, with the vast bobtailed sheepdogs from Sussex and Dorset having particularly fearsome reputations*', moved sheep, cattle and geese from farms to markets along wide drove roads. They could drive as many as six thousand sheep from Yorkshire to London, keeping them on course and protecting them from theft. Shepherds knew each dog by its bark and could locate trouble in the darkness. Many dogs had to find their own way home from the markets, such as Smithfield in London or Norwich, even to places as far away as Scotland. They stopped and were fed at the inns or farms where the drove had rested, and the drovers would pay for the food on their journeys south the following year.

Now he sends the dog aroond the sheep
wi' a cry o' 'gan oot wide'
Then whistles wi' a note sae shrill the dog drops in his stride
'Come bye here Moss, doon in the bit aal tan yer dusty hide.'

These lines from a well-known Northumbrian song, 'The Canny Shepherd Laddie o' the Hills', refers to the black-and-white border collies used in the area. 'Moss' is a very common name for the breed, once known as 'colleys'. An old breed that dominates herding now, it can recognise its own herd's distinctive smell and retrieve strays that get mixed with others.

See also AGRICULTURAL SHOWS, BLACK DOGS, CAIRNS, DOGS, DROVE ROADS, FAIRS & FAIRGROUNDS, GUN DOGS, HOUNDS, HOUND TRAILING, INNS, MARKETS, PRIDDY SHEEP FAIR, TERRIERS.

SHEEP-FOLDS

Cot is a local name for a sheep enclosure needed during hard winters in the limestone hills of Gloucestershire – such was their proliferation that they gave their name to the Cotswolds. In the mountains of Cumberland and Westmorland rumpled evidence of summer dwellings, or 'scales', date from Viking times. Shiels and shielings here and in Northumberland follow a similar, although later, Scottish pattern: people moving their animals up to take advantage of the summer growth and at the same time making cheese for winter use.

Alongside the ruined cottages are relict folds, for gathering and protecting animals from wolves and neighbours. These circular or angular stone enclosures persisted for many centuries, through the border raiding and after transhumance ceased at the end of the eighteenth century. Some may date back to the medieval monastic expansion of sheep farming. Circular stells – some 45 feet wide with six-foot walls – and angular bields are open enclosures for protection against the weather, carefully situated so that snow will not overwhelm them.

In the 1990s Andy Goldsworthy began an extensive art project in Cumberland and Westmorland, *'to locate the remains of one hundred sheep-folds from maps and rebuild them in such a way that they became a piece or contained a piece of sculpture'*, he explained. *'I would like it to be seen as a monument to agriculture.'* These border counties have a long tradition of running and droving sheep, but the failing pinfolds and sheep-folds reflect the difficulties faced by farming. These works, with a different cultural emphasis, are now drawing people to walk the villages and hills, adding welcome vitality to the local economy.

See also BASTLES, CAIRNS, CATTLE, COMMONS, DRYSTONE WALLS, FELLS, FIELDS, MONUMENTS, MOORLAND, NEW FOREST PONIES, PELE TOWERS, PIGS, PINFOLDS, SCULPTURES, SHEEP, SHEEP-WASHES.

SHEEP-WASHES

At Ashford in the Water, Derbyshire the neat stone parapet of the bridge extends to form a curvaceous enclosure with an opening onto the river Wye. This is where sheep were collected before being pushed into the river, where they swam and then waded across to the other side, washing the dust and grime from their fleeces before shearing.

The old packhorse bridge is known as Sheepwash Bridge after this annual practice.

A similar, horn-shaped, two-hundred-year-old rough stone sheep-wash was restored in 1997 by a farmer at Shap, Westmorland. His sheep have to leap from a five-foot raised stone platform into the river Lowther and swim across. *'As soon as the first few jumped in, the rest followed'*, Greg Neale wrote.

Wash folds, washes, wash pools, dips – are all names for the places where sheep have been immersed in water that is deep enough to give their wool a good soak in preparation for shearing. Men with long-handled poles that ended with a short, curved 'T' kept them submerged in the water. They would be brought out onto clean meadows nearby, where they could dry out and be sheared. Hazel hurdles were erected to keep them from straying, and as holding pens.

Sheep-washes were used well into the twentieth century in some places – until the 1960s in Cumberland – but now fleeces are washed after shearing. Sheep-dipping as we know it today, done to prevent sheep mite and scab, uses toxic chemicals in tanks and should be done far away from vulnerable watercourses.

Where the popular breed of Cotswold sheep brought great wealth to the area, a survey has found that many of the surviving sheep-washes were located by rivers and close to tracks or paths to which carts had access. If there were no suitable places along rivers, private constructions were made near where the sheep grazed. These were often rectangular and perhaps of dressed stone, and included leats and ramps. The survey found concentrations of sheep-washes in the *'valleys of the Coln and Leach and clusters especially around Northleach, Abingdon and Andoversford . . . then around Tetbury and Kingscote, with a lesser concentration around Cirencester'*.

On the commons of Cumberland provision was made for a public wash fold, which was supported through rates, during the last enclosure award for Mungrisdale Low Common in 1893. A century ago Portland sheep were washed in the tidal waters of the Mere at Chiswell on the Isle of Portland, Dorset.

See also BRIDGES, DEW PONDS, HAZEL, PARISH MAPS, PINFOLDS, RIVERS, SALT MARSHES, SHEEP, SHEEP-FOLDS.

374

S H E L L F I S H

Our inshore waters have provided some our most fascinating food: Morecambe Bay shrimps, Stiffkey cockles, Cromer crabs, Whitstable oysters, Brancaster mussels.

From Norfolk, Stiffkey blues range from '*pale lavender to a dark grey-blue*', according to Laura Mason and Catherine Brown. At one time they were called bluestones, the colour coming from the local mud and sand, where they live a few inches below the surface in large congregations. In the 1880s the cockles were collected at low tide by local women, using short-handled, broad rakes and nets. They were steamed and used in soups and pies and sold at seaside stalls, eaten (boiled) with vinegar and pepper. In addition to these places around the Wash, the other main shellfish-gathering area is the Thames estuary.

They are still a favourite food along the Thames and Essex coast. Carol Donaldson writes: '*While many East End traditions have died away, the displaced Cockneys of Havering [Essex] are still busy winkle picking and whelk swallowing and this peculiarity is not just the preserve of the old. Young, shaven-headed lads are dousing their cockles in vinegar at a weekend and ordering jellied eels by the pint. Maybe it's our proximity to the Thames and its seafood centres of Leigh-on-Sea and Southend that gives us a love of these unappetising creatures. The ex-Cockneys keep business brisk among the cockle sheds lining the front at Leigh, which trades in five thousand tonnes of cockles a year.*'

Despite this local trade, many lost their appetite when some cockle beds were closed due to contamination by algal toxins. Morecambe Bay in Lancashire has gained notoriety for the exploitation of collectors and shellfish, following the drownings of foreign workers unused to the ferocious tides. In 2005 the Morecambe Bay cockle beds were closed to allow the diminishing stocks to recover. On the Solway Firth, Cumberland and other estuaries conservationists are worried that suction dredging has replaced raking, depleting not only the cockles but a whole host of marine invertebrates, and disturbing and removing the food of wading birds such as oystercatchers, which are adept at opening the hard cockle shells, and herring gulls. The latter, finding the shells difficult to prise apart, have resorted to taking them to shore and dropping them from a fair height onto a hard surface. Today most cockles are sent to Spain, France and Holland.

Mussels anchor themselves to rocks and piers. Most mussel fisheries are on the east, south and west coasts. They have been farmed at Brancaster Staithe in north Norfolk for more than a century. One-year-old mussels are collected and moved to the lays – beds – in tidal creeks, where they are left to grow for a couple of years before harvesting. Brancaster fishermen used to collect whelks as well, but all that remains are the whelk sheds, where now mussels and oysters are purified. These days whelks – marine snails – once so popular with Londoners, find their main market in South Korea. They are collected from baited buckets dropped into the sea off places such as Beer in Devon, and transported to Fleetwood in Lancashire, where they are pressure cooked, processed and frozen for air freighting.

Norfolk's Cromer crabs thrive in the chalk reefs that run out from the coast, producing the country's sweetest crustaceans. About a dozen boats look after around two

375

hundred crab pots. Edible crabs are caught in many places, such as Start Point near Salcombe in Devon, Scarborough in Yorkshire and the Solway Firth, where they appear on the menus of local restaurants. Lobster pots are piled high on beaches and quays from Hastings, Sussex to St Ives, Cornwall. Willow lobster pots are still made, although largely they have been replaced by plastic and steel.

Shrimps have been netted at Morecambe Bay since the late 1700s, caught in shallow waters from nobbies, or from the shore using horses or tractors and long nets. They are cooked in Flookburgh within half an hour of being landed. In 2000 thirteen million pots of Bob Baxter's Morecambe Bay shrimps were sold by mail order.

See also BEACHES, BOATS, COASTS, ESTUARIES, FRESHWATER FISH, NOBBIES, OYSTERS, QUICKSAND, TIDES.

S H I N E R S

On the southern tip of the South Hams in Devon great slabs of shining, greeny red rock edge the fields. Where these stone fences are not covered with lichen the easily cleft mica-schist reflects and plays with the sun. Nearby they hold up hedge banks and make stiles. In Kingsbridge leats are lined with and bridged by them. But in the fields this locally quarried, slate-like material lends itself to making and marking boundaries; some uses may be as old as the Iron Age.

See also BOUNDARIES, CATTLE, DRYSTONE WALLS, SHEEP, SLATES, STILES, VACCARY WALLS.

S H I N G L E

Almost a third of the English coastline is shingle, coated in coarse pebbles, often flint eroded from chalk cliffs or carried to the beach by rivers and glaciers. Sound clues alone identify these beaches – the word shingle is thought to derive from the strange, shimmering clinking of the pebbles as they are raked by the waves. Hastings, Brighton and Worthing in Sussex are fine examples, thronging with swimmers and sunbathers in summer. At Chesil in Dorset the fishermen landing on the shingle bank at night or in fog can judge their position by the size of the pebbles. Up the road the prehistoric inhabitants of Maiden Castle amassed vast hordes of sling stones taken from the beach.

Shingle is notoriously challenging to walk along. Fishermen and their families living on Dungeness in Kent wore wooden flip-flops called baxters or backstays over their shoes, which worked like a kind of snow-shoe.

The bleak, wind-swept spit of shingle at Orford Ness in Suffolk is our largest vegetated shingled spit; it houses a now-derelict military base, where radar was invented.

The largest shingle beach by far is the great triangle of Dungeness, covering nearly four thousand acres and formed where the Channel and North Sea waters meet. At places the shingle is more than fifty feet thick, formed into ridges and hollows by the waves. During the twentieth century this unique place has been much damaged by military training, the construction of a nuclear power station and shingle extraction – half of Dungeness now lies under railways and motorways elsewhere. The spit supports an astonishing array of plants, ranging from yellow-horned poppy and sea pea, sea campion and shepherd's cress, to hollies, mosses and lichens that have lived on the beach for hundreds of years.

See also AMMONITES, BEACHCOMBING, BEACHES, BEACONS (COASTAL), BOATS, CLIFFS, COASTLINE, COASTS, ESTUARIES, FERRIES, FLINT, FOG & MIST, GARDENS, HARBOURS, HOLLY, HOTELS, ISLANDS, LICHENS, LIGHTHOUSES, LOST VILLAGES, MARTELLO TOWERS, MOSSES, PIERS, PROMENADES, RIAS, SALT MARSHES, SAND-DUNES, SEA FISH, SHELLFISH, SMELLS, STACKS, SWIMMING PLACES, TIDES, WHITE CLIFFS.

S H I N G L E S

The roofs of many buildings were covered with wooden tiles from Roman times to the Middle Ages, when clay tiles replaced them. Shingled church spires are most commonly found in Sussex – Alfriston, Playden and West Grinstead have fine examples. Oak shingles have a life span of eighty to a hundred years, and specialist building conservation firms can supply them, although until recently cedar was being used to replace old shingles, losing the wonderful silver sheen of weathered oak.

See also CHURCHES, OAK, PANTILES, SLATES, TILES, WEATHER-BOARDING.

376

The distribution of coastal shingle.

SHIPPING FORECAST

'There are warnings of gales in Sole; Lundy; Fastnet . . .' The litany of the area forecasts for shipping lulls listeners to BBC Radio 4 just after midnight and wakes them at 05.36 GMT, a daily reminder of our island state. But, warm and snug, it is hard to muster the idea that those same reassuring tones convey harsh realities aboard ship or smack out there in Rockall, Dogger or Trafalgar.

The more intimate waters to twelve miles off coast have their own shorthand listings immediately after the Shipping Forecast, each area enunciated before a brief run-down of conditions to be met heading out or home. From the Wash to North Foreland, for example: *'north becoming variable or northeast 3 or 4; fair; moderate or good'*. Twenty-four hours of wind, weather, visibility and sea state are each followed by the next day's outlook, and a general three-day outlook concludes the broadcast.

Authentic found poems every one.

See also ALBION, BOATS, BOUNDARIES, THE CHANNEL, CLOUDS, COASTLINE, COASTS, DEVIL, EAST, ESTUARIES, FLOODS, FOG & MIST, FRETS, HARBOURS, ISLANDS, LIGHTHOUSES, LOST VILLAGES, NORTH, SURFING, TIDES, WEATHER, WEATHER-VANES, WHITE CLIFFS, WIND FARMS, WINDMILLS, WINDS, ZAWNS.

SHIRE HORSES

The heartland of the Shire is the Midlands and Lincolnshire. But there are now more of these fine horses in America and in Europe than in England. Just about the biggest horse in the world, standing more than nineteen hands and weighing at least nineteen hundredweight, the Shire can get through two pairs of shoes in three weeks pulling up to twice its own weight.

Originally called the Great Horse, it traces its ancestry back through the great war-horse of medieval times, being refined during the eighteenth and nineteenth centuries for heavy farming work. Draft work of all kinds took one and a half million to their deaths in the First World War. More than a million Shires worked the land and the streets in the 1920s, but by 1960 there were a few thousand left. Now, with the number of mares dropping by a third in the ten years to 2004, the breed is endangered here.

While all kinds of vehicles have replaced them, a diminishing number of breweries, including Thwaites in Lancashire and Wadworth and Company in Devizes, Wiltshire, keep teams of working and show animals; their white, feathered legs and gentle faces always win the crowds. The Shire Horse Show held at Alwalton, Huntingdonshire

377

Shipping forecast and inshore waters areas.

in March is the heaviest in the world. The Royal Show, Bath and West Show, Bakewell Show in Derbyshire and county and local agricultural shows have classes to exhibit the paces and beauty of the regional breeds. The Shire is a favourite for ploughing matches and, increasingly, for driving competitions in the South. In France the breed would be subsidised and safeguarded as a national treasure through the national stud system, but here the Shire Horse Society struggles to encourage hard-pushed owners not to sell abroad.

See also AGRICULTURAL SHOWS, BREWERIES, EXMOOR PONIES, FELL PONIES, HORSES & PONIES, LONDON TAXIS, NEW FOREST PONIES, POINT TO POINT, SUFFOLK PUNCHES.

S H O P S

In places clever enough to have valued the quality of old shop fronts and the patterns of land holdings of earlier times, good workmanship and care continue to feed the eye. The mix of old and new can be one of a town centre's joys. Chester's thirteenth-century Rows offer a covered walkway of first-floor shops, with sympathetic new lighting. The Shambles in York gives a glimpse of the intimacy of a medieval street, although its over-restoration has dented its authenticity; it feels more like a stage set.

Shopkeepers' ancient rights of encroachment onto the pavement led to bays of small panes jutting into the street, the forerunner of the modern shop window. Cast-iron frontages appeared, like the ornate, three-storey façade of 37 Tubwell Row, Darlington, County Durham. Saltburn, on the north Yorkshire coast, has several beautiful examples of corner shops with elegant pavement canopies, more common now in Sydney, Australia. Colonnaded rows of shops, such as those in Ludlow, Shropshire, on the Market Square in Nottingham and some seaside towns, brought elegance. Butchers and dairies used hygienic white and coloured tiles. In London, notably Camden Town, single-storey shops stretched out over front gardens.

The twentieth century was the age first of the department store and then the superstore, each carving out a territory – Co-operative Stores in the North, Sainsbury's in the South – before going national and, in some cases, global. Department stores, such as Jolly's in Bath and Bentalls in Kingston upon Thames, Surrey, developed from large drapers. Many were absorbed into chains but maintained their independent personalities, at least for a while.

Second World War bombing provided the opportunity for comprehensive redevelopment. Southampton, Hull, Plymouth and Coventry were a few of the places pioneering new 'precincts', later embraced in other towns. Birmingham's Bull Ring was a shopper's fairyland in the 1960s, when municipal thinking flattened old town centres. Windows expanded to dominate the street. For some shops, such as Fenwick's in Newcastle, the Christmas display is an event – often kitsch, always ingenious.

Ubiquitous flat, plastic fascias replaced hand-crafted signs. But the conservation of quality and the importance of different ages of buildings along the high street is increasingly recognised. Continuing threat comes from powerful superstores, almost always bland in their buildings, with a gigantism that economically and culturally corrupts and depresses town centres. In the countryside the picture is as bleak; where once villages might have had every amenity, from butcher and baker to farrier and dairyman, now they are losing even their post offices and general stores.

See also ALLEYS, ARCADES, CAFÉS, CLOCKS, HIGH STREETS, KENNELS, MARKETS, PAVEMENTS, POST OFFICES, SPAS.

S H R O V E T I D E   G A M E S

Many of our mass-participation street games occur around Shrove Tuesday, when people ate, drank and played before the long abstinence of Lent. Many were prohibited or moved to the fields because they became so disruptive, since any number of people can take part. There are no boundaries and few rules, although they generally involve two teams or factions from neighbouring villages or different parts of town. Rough football is the most popular. Usually the aim is to get a ball to a goal, sometimes over distances through hedges, streams, rivers and woods.

At Atherstone in Warwickshire and Leicestershire the Ball Game has been played for eight centuries across Watling Street, the Roman road that runs through the town. This is border country between Dane and Anglo-Saxon, and local legend tells that the game developed from hostilities that involved kicking the severed head of a Dane. Others believe it to derive from an inter-county fight for a bag of gold during the reign of King John. At three o'clock in the afternoon a large leather ball with colourful ribbons, filled with water, is thrown out of the upstairs window of a

bank in Long Street (previously it was The Three Tuns) and the free-for-all begins. Hundreds of people take part and windows are boarded up. Teams no longer compete, nor is there any goal; the object is to have possession of the ball at five o'clock, when the klaxon sounds. The winner keeps the ball and gets a prize.

At Sedgefield in County Durham, where the game has been played for more than nine hundred years, two teams of townies and farmers try to get the ball to their goals, a stream and a pond five hundred yards apart. In Alnwick, Northumberland the goals are called hales and are on either side of a quarter-mile-long 'pitch'.

Workington in Cumbria has its Uppies and Doonies Football Game, now played on Good Friday and Easter Tuesday and the following Saturday. The Uppies, from the upper part of town (originally colliers), have to carry the ball to Curwen Castle to make a goal or hail, whereas the Downies, from the docks (originally dockers), have to reach a quayside capstan.

In Ashbourne, Derbyshire the teams comprise the Upp'ards and the Down'ards, who were born north and south of the Henmore Brook, which divides the town. The Royal Shrovetide Football Game used to be played in the streets and Market Square; now in the fields, the goals are two miles apart. A hand-painted ball is 'turned up' at two o'clock and the match goes on until after dark. Although the ball can be kicked or run with, it usually moves slowly by a series of 'hugs', some of which inevitably take place in the stream.

Hurling the Silver Ball is the equivalent in west Cornwall. Now it is played only at St Columb Major. A cricket-sized ball made of apple wood and coated with sterling silver is cast up by the winner of the previous year's game from a ladder in the Market Square to hundreds of people waiting beneath. The two teams, representing country and town, try

to get the ball 'to the place assigned' – two stone troughs a mile away in opposite directions or over the parish boundary. The ball can be carried, thrown or scrummed, but not kicked. The person who achieves this is carried shoulder high back to the Market Square and thence to the pubs in the town, where he dips the ball in jugs of beer to transform it into 'silver beer'.

Until the Second World War Shrovetide and Easter skipping was popular all over the country. In Sussex, Good Friday skipping on Long Rope Day was prevalent along the coast and was accompanied with chanting songs or rhymes, such as *'Jam, jam, strawberry jam/Tell me the name of my young man/A, B, C, etc'*. The heavy ropes were turned by fishermen or farm labourers, allowing six or more young men, women and children to run in and out and skip at the same time. Shrovetide skipping has recently been revived at Alciston and Piddinghoe in Sussex, and is still practised in Scarborough, Yorkshire, where mass skipping with long ropes takes place on the Foreshore Road.

See also GAMES, HARE PIE SCRAMBLE, HAXEY HOOD GAME, PANCAKE DAY, PUB GAMES.

S K Y L A R K S

In every field they mount and sing
The song of Nature and of Spring.

John Clare, from 'Larks and Spring'

379

The song of the skylark stands for summer. Normally seen only as a speck, this small, brown bird has inspired unrivalled poetry and music. From *'his watch-tower in the skies'* (Milton) his song is delivered as he ascends, hovers and descends from *'heaven, or near it'* (Shelley). He can sing for five minutes without a pause. Bird-song expert Walter Garstang described the skylark's song as *'the flawless expression of pure serenity'*. W.H. Hudson believed that on a windless day the skylark's highest notes could be heard three miles away. He eulogised about its *'mysterious beautiful music . . . like the heavenly sunshine translated into sound; subtle, insistent, filling the world and the soul, yet always at a vast distance, falling, falling like a lucid rain'*.

The skylark was once the most widespread of our breeding birds, found in most country parishes. But in just 25 years its numbers have reduced by three-quarters and its demise has caused much sorrow and consternation. The decline is most likely due to agricultural intensification and changes in farming practice. The loss of winter stubble, due to the sowing of wheat and barley in the autumn, leaves fields bereft of grain and weed seeds for the birds to feed on during the winter. By the spring the crop is too high to enable the birds to see predators approaching the nest. Recent research by the Royal Society for the Protection of Birds and British Trust for Ornithology has found that providing skylark scrapes – small unplanted areas within the crop – improves their breeding success considerably.

See also HALF-YEAR BIRDS, HERONRIES, ROBINS, ROOKERIES, SPARROWS, STARLINGS.

S L A T E S

The old thackstone roofs of Halifax, Yorkshire (Coal Measures sandstone) are low in pitch (35 degrees) and short in gable because the stones used are large and heavy, being up to one and a half inches thick. Cotswold stone slates are much thinner and smaller and are overlapped less, requiring a steeper roof (55 degrees) to keep out the wet; this gives a taller gable.

Some sedimentary rocks are fissile and can be hand-riven along narrow bedding planes to give good roofing material. These may be known as flags, thackstones, slats, flatstones, stone slates or tilestones. They range from Collyweston and Cotswold stone to slatt from the Portland Beds in Dorset. In Derbyshire alone eight types make for visually different roofs. Their heaviness dictated that the slates became smaller towards the roofline to lower the weight; in the Cotswolds different sizes are called muffities, wivetts, tants and cussems. Alan Garner describes them in north Cheshire: '*The stone slates had been sent down and stacked by size, Princesses, Duchesses, Small Countesses, Ladies, Wide Doubles and the neat Jenny-go-lightlies from under the ridge.*' The effect of the thick, diminishing courses is quietly dramatic, the colour, texture and detail being much missed in new roofing.

Some rocks, which have undergone a degree of pressure and metamorphosis, cleave easily – the French *esclater*, to split, gives us 'slate'. True slate is found among our oldest rocks. In the pre-Cambrian rocks of the Charnwood Forest in Leicestershire houses are roofed in the dark blues, purples and greens of Swithland slate. It is also found in the county town and in many villages, on houses and as gravestones, as in St Mary de Castro churchyard.

Westmorland green slates of Ordovician age vary from silver to olive green. Silurian Burlington slate found around Kirkby-in-Furness is grey-blue; Brathay slate is of a very dark blue. Cornwall Delabole slate offers a range of greys varying from green to blue, dating from the Devonian. On the Isles of Scilly scantle slate is a description of the pattern in which the small Delabole slates, or peggies, were often arranged. In Ashburton, Tavistock and Totnes, rusty grey Devonian slate is wall hung, like fish-scales, and sometimes highly patterned, giving the houses a full waterproof cladding. In the North West and in Cornwall these are sometimes covered with a further waterproofing colour-wash.

Welsh slate spread out through Cheshire and Shropshire in medieval times. It coasted its way to London and other cities and by the end of the eighteenth century was found in Georgian buildings across the country. Cheap, thin, light and robust, it quickly extended with the rise of the industrial and seafaring cities. Replacing most other materials, the homogeneous colour, shape and size has taken some of the heart out of roofs, but has given row upon row of Victorian terraces their unity. Despite the transport expenses, firms are now finding it cheaper to import slate from Brazil, ignoring the energy waste and cost to local distinctiveness.

See also BANK BARNS, BRICKS, BUILDING STONES, CHALK, CHURCHES, CORRUGATED IRON, DRYSTONE WALLS, FIELD BARNS, FLINT, GABLES, GRAVESTONES, GREENSAND, HIGH STREETS, KERBSTONES, PANTILES, PAVEMENTS, PLACE-NAMES, QUARRIES, SHINERS, THATCH, TUNNELS, UNLUCKY WORDS, VACCARY WALLS.

S M E L L S

'*Even blindfold, I'd have known where we were by the smell of the different streets – reek of rotten fruit: Spitalfields; scent of tobacco warehouses: Commercial Street; the suffocating airless stench of the Cambridge Picture Palace; Hanbury Street and the pungency of beer from Charrington's Brewery.*' Emanuel Litvinoff vividly recalled his childhood in Bethnal Green, London.

Smells provoke memories. Tobacco will jog thoughts in people from Nottingham and Bristol; similarly the sickly sweetness of Crawford's old biscuit factory in Liverpool, the spices in the warehouses along the Deptford side of the Thames in south London, the stench of the Bedfordshire brickfields. Clive Brooks remembers '*the "lino" – one specific memory, the smell of the linoleum factory in Staines, Middlesex*'. Good and bad, these memorable signifiers of place are gone, but the odorous character of Bournville in Warwickshire owes much to chocolate, Bury St Edmunds in Suffolk to sugar, the summer fields around Pershore in Worcestershire to the tang of spring onions, Bournemouth in Hampshire to pine trees.

Marcus King says: '*I feel that the single experience that makes Norfolk is the smell of the hawthorn hedges and trees on a warm breeze.*' For Clive Simmonds, London is '*the electricity-and-people smell of the Tube. (The subway in Glasgow, and the metros of Vienna, Paris, Madrid and Barcelona, all have their own distinctive smells.)*' In a recipe involving other ingredients Janet Thorning attributes her love of the Wirral, Cheshire to '*the tang of salt on the air*'; likewise Sue Carling adds '*the smell of salty sea air*' to her evocation of Cornwall.

See also BEER, BISCUITS, BLUEBELLS, BOUNDARIES, BREAD, BRUSSELS SPROUTS, CONFECTIONERY, FAIRS & FAIRGROUNDS, GORSE, LIME, RAMSONS, SCOTS PINE, WINDS.

380

S O I L S

Our land is coloured by soils; they vary with the geology under the ambient forces of nature. The sumptuous red land of the Devon hills, the white plough of the Wiltshire Downs, the chocolate fields of Herefordshire, the dark soils of the Coal Measures in south Yorkshire, the sun-devouring black peat in the flatnesses of the Lincolnshire Fens – these are the extremes that surprise. And, while most of our soils are of brown earth, even a single field may display a range when the plough makes its pass.

The delicacy of soil structure has been much taken for granted in mechanised and intensive farming. In pursuit of high crop yields, soils have been compacted by heavy machinery and drenched with fertilisers, herbicides, pesticides and heavy metals, rendering the sustaining micro-organisms incapable of activity. At the same time as damaging our soils, we have created such uncompromising conditions that we have lost our wildflowers, together with the butterflies, bees and insects they maintain.

Runnels erode soil, rivers become silt laden. Strong winds seek out the light, sandy soils of the overworked expanses of East Anglia, leaving small sand drifts beside the infrequent hedgerows and squandering topsoil that has taken long to develop.

Low intensity, organic, attuned farming is rising in popularity as counterpoint. The soils of ancient wood pasture, parkland and woodland that have never been ploughed are among the richest of habitats, and it is to them that scientists are turning to learn how to help our over-exploited soils to recover, a process that may take many decades.

See also CATTLE, CHALK, CHALK STREAMS, COB, CROPS, DOWNLAND, EARTH PIGMENTS, FENS, FIELD NAMES, FIELD PATTERNS, FRITILLARY MEADOWS, HAY MEADOWS, HEATHLAND, HEDGES, INGS, IRONSTONE, LEVELS, LIME-KILNS, LYNCHETS, MINES, PARGETING, PARKLAND, PIT TIPS, RIDGE & FURROW, RIVERS, SHEEP, SPRINGS, WATER-MEADOWS, WILDFLOWERS.

S O U G H S

The problem of water was so great in the lead mines of limestone Derbyshire that extraordinary and expensive systems of levels, or soughs, were driven through solid rock, some before the advent of gunpowder. Falling a gentle ten feet along a mile, they often met surprise caves, or shacks, and sometimes 'swallows', already full of water.

Hillcarr sough is four miles long and lined with beautifully arched stone. Magpie sough, completed in 1881, was big enough at six to seven feet high and more than four feet broad for boats to carry out the ore. Small soughs, perhaps two feet wide and three feet high, were filled with water once dug – some were so well lined with stone that they are still in full flow two hundred years later. Water disgorges at the 'tail', either into a stream, a goit (open drain) or a bolt (covered drain). The natural movement of groundwater, unpredictable anyway through the limestone, has been completely altered over wide areas; for many villages this provided piped water.

Bagshaws Directory of 1846 describes Meerbrook sough, begun in 1772 '*by a company of adventurers. It is now in the hands of four hundred shareholders of £50 each . . . it has already cost £70,000, and is estimated to cost £8,000 more.*' About four feet wide and six feet high, it runs for two and a half miles, its length doubled by contributing soughs. It drains most of the Wirksworth mines into the Derwent near Whatstandwell. Stone cairns mark its path on the surface (ventilation was always a problem during construction) and 'breathe' steam in frosty weather – its water holds a steady 15.3 degrees Celsius, having tapped a thermal supply.

See also BECKS, BOURNES, BURNS, DIALECTS, FORDS, FROST & FROST HOLLOWS, LEAD MINES, LIMESTONE, MINES, RHYNES, RIVER NAMES, RIVERS, WINTERBOURNES.

S O U N D   M I R R O R S

Known in Kent as 'listening ears', these huge concrete acoustic discs can be found on the coasts of Kent, County Durham and Yorkshire. Sound amplifiers were developed from 1914 by a Professor Mather, to locate and give early warning of enemy aircraft. His first experiment was a sixteen-foot-diameter disc cut out of a chalk cliff at Binbury Manor Farm, between Sittingbourne and Maidstone, Kent; he claimed he could detect a Zeppelin twenty miles away.

During the First World War sound mirrors were being constructed along the east coast. A large, freestanding structure with a fifteen-foot-diameter concrete dish (looking rather like an open mouth) was built at Kilnsea, Spurn Head in Yorkshire; others were positioned at Hartlepool and Redcar on either side of the Tees estuary, and at Boulby, Yorkshire, on top of the cliff, facing out to sea. The plaque on the sound mirror at Redcar reads: '*The sound of approaching*

Denge, Kent.

aircraft was reflected off the concave "mirror" surface and received into a trumpet mounted on a steel column. The trumpet was connected to a stethoscope used by the operator or "listener", and the part of the dish that produced the most sound indicated the direction of the approaching aircraft.'

Research continued between the wars and by 1923 a twenty-foot-diameter sound mirror, with new electric microphones and an improved receiving trumpet, had been built into a bank backed by a solid slab of concrete at The Roughs in Hythe, Kent, able to detect aircraft twelve miles away. Dr W.S. Tucker, appointed Director of Acoustical Research in 1925, planned to build 'a chain of twenty-foot sound mirrors along the south coast'. Two were built in 1928, one perched on top of Abbot's Cliff at Lydden Spout in Dover, Kent, which now looks like a modern sculpture – a concrete bowl cut out of a square, flat surface, supported by triangular slabs at either side – and the other at Great Stone, Denge, on the Dungeness peninsula in Kent. This was the first of three sound mirrors at Denge, which have been scheduled by English Heritage because they 'form a unique collection' showing a progression of designs. They have been made unstable by gravel extraction, but are now being repaired and underpinned.

By 1939, due to the development of radar, the Acoustical Research Station had been closed down and the sound mirrors abandoned. Some have been lost to coastal erosion or demolished. But the remaining structures have inspired Danish artist Lise Autogena to create her own benign Channel Communication Amplifiers. Placed at Folkestone, Kent and Sangatte, France, they will, according to the Arts Council, 'be perfectly aligned to receive and transmit not only the sounds of the sea, but also the human voice across 45 kilometres of water'.

See also COASTS, SCULPTURES.

S P A R R O W S

A sparrow's life's as sweet as ours.
Hardy clowns! Grudge not the wheat
Which hunger forces birds to eat;
Your blinded eyes, worst foes to you,
Can't see the good which sparrows do.

John Clare, from 'Summer Evening'

Dog walker Sybil Macdonald has likened the loud chirping from inside the hedge down the lane in Shaftesbury, Dorset to the unfathomable babble at a cocktail party. This colony of twenty to fifty house sparrows is kept happy with bird seed all year, thick hedges to nest and take refuge in and a lane with sandy patches for dust baths and puddles to bathe in. But elsewhere the picture is less rosy.

Once the commonest of all birds, the house sparrow is now protected. It was placed on the Red List of endangered birds in 2002 following a catastrophic decline in numbers – 59 per cent between 1994 and 2000, followed by a 25 per cent drop between 2000 and 2001, according to the British Trust for Ornithology. We have ten million fewer than thirty years ago.

The loss is felt particularly in London and by those who took the cheeky 'Cockney sparrer' for their own. The reasons for their decline seem complex and are still being investigated. Why have they virtually disappeared from Kensington Gardens, where sparrows should be commonplace? Only eight were counted in 2000, compared with more than two and a half thousand in 1925. No doubt the change from horse-drawn transport resulted in a loss of food; then the growth of weed-killers and pesticides since the Second World War and the recent trend towards over-tidy gardens may have been the final straw.

At the moment sparrows are faring best in the rural gardens of southern and central-eastern England. Between ten and twenty per cent of English farms have lost all their sparrows in the past two decades; it is hard to believe that in the eighteenth and nineteenth centuries sparrow clubs were formed to kill thousands of sparrows and steal their eggs.

Not only are we not prepared to share our crops with wildlife, we seem no longer willing to accommodate it in our houses. Thatch is often covered in wire netting, and modern buildings leave no roof gaps. A building in Bath was recorded as having sparrow-cotes – niches in the walls for sparrows to nest in – to prevent damage to the roof. Perhaps builders of the future could do something similar to ensure that our spadgers stay with us – otherwise there will be no more 'singing' hedges.

See also HEDGES, STRAW, THATCH.

S P A S

Spas developed around natural springs as health resorts in the eighteenth century. The waters had local reputations for curative powers and, in gaining national recognition, generated wealth for local inhabitants. The first Spa House was built in Scarborough, Yorkshire in 1700, when it became fashionable to take the medicinal spring waters and walk along the beach.

At Malvern Wells in Worcestershire the Foley Arms was built in 1810, with the Pump Room added in 1819. It still has its cast-iron balcony, its name in an arched sign and the Teck coat of arms (given by Queen Elizabeth II's grandmother). Royal patronage popularised water cures and gave impetus to the creation of hydropathic hotels in Victorian times.

The Imperial Hydro at Blackpool, Lancashire had hot and cold, rain and sea water, Turkish and Russian baths to cater for all tastes. The Clifton Grand Spa Hydro in Bristol (now the Avon Gorge Hotel) was built in 1898, aided by a new cliff railway service to Clifton Down Station. The Hydro in Matlock, Derbyshire was built by the mill owner John Smedley – in the form of a factory, it was rudely said, in case his hotel business failed. Hotel architecture was being invented; the imposing building now houses Derbyshire county council. In Tenbury Wells, Worcestershire the diminutive but startling pumphouse and its medicinal springs never quite drew the masses.

Bath, Buxton, Clifton (Hotwells), Malvern, Matlock Bath, Scarborough and Harrogate in Yorkshire, Leamington in Warwickshire and Tunbridge Wells in Kent all have fair claim to mineral-rich and sometimes warm waters. Cheltenham Spa did not see the future; during the 1930s and the war years 42 of the town's hotels closed.

All of these towns have a certain air, with municipal gardens and fine buildings receiving more care. A new lease of life may be bubbling with rising interest in healthy living. The success of bottled water tells a story in parallel with the attraction of saunas, spas and bathing across Europe and Japan. People are once more looking to take the waters, as Bath opens the doors of the Thermae Bath Spa and Buxton welcomes a new spa hotel.

See also FILM LOCATIONS, FOOD, HOTELS, INNS, PROMENADES, PUB SIGNS, SPRINGS, WELLS.

S P R I N G S

Down in the Blackmore Vale in Dorset/Somerset the villages are strung out on '*the upper greensand where the springs arise*', Ralph Whitman wrote. Early settlements trace the line of these reliable supplies of water, after which they were often named – Teffont Magna, Mottisfont, Springhead.

Water is ruled by gravity. Springs seem to contradict this, often bubbling upwards. To find water emerging forcefully from the ground is to know that there is an impediment to the downward movement of groundwater – a change in the geology, some impermeable barrier, perhaps a fault line or clay, or just more water. Forced by the weight of water above, it makes its escape, forming a spring line.

Water in the ground is dependent on rainfall and the rate at which we take from rivers and boreholes. Because the water-table has been lowered in so many places owing to

over-abstraction, many springs have disappeared, migrated downhill or become undependable. There are further repercussions: in Buckinghamshire the river Misbourne is now dry along part of its length. In London, on the other hand, because of falling industrial demand, concern is increasing about rising groundwater levels; cellars are no longer dry.

At Sutton Poyntz in south Dorset the pub sign for The Springhead shows horses hauling a giant pipe. When the Great Eastern, Brunel's first ocean liner, was broken up around 1890, the Weymouth Water Company bought one of its five huge funnels and installed it in the spring above the village, where it still collects millions of gallons a day.

The temperature of spring water remains constant winter and summer. Around some springs in Devon, stone, shelved structures, known as cream wells, were made to keep cream and butter cool.

Special springs have brought wealth to whole towns. In the 1920s the *Official Handbook* of the British Spas Federation recorded 88 springs in Harrogate, Yorkshire, with names such as the Old Sulphur Well, Crescent Spring and Pure Chalybeate. In Matlock Bath, Derbyshire the warm mineralised springs that drew an aching clientele in Victorian times include a tufa-rich spring, which will encrust with lime any object left in the water – this spring that really does turn things to stone proved an asset from the earliest days of tourism. Bath, Somerset is certainly reinvesting in its Roman heritage.

Springs, sources, spouts, risings, fountains, issues, seepages and wells, especially those by the roadside, are often marked by stone troughs or shallow bowls to allow animals to quench their thirst, and many used to have a chained cup for the traveller; small reminders of our deep understanding of the most basic need.

See also CHALK, FIELD NAMES, HOTELS, LIMESTONE, PANTS, RIVERS, SPAS, WELL DRESSING, WELLS.

383

S Q U A R E S

Leaving or creating space for market squares and village greens had long been part of the organic growth of settlements. But when Inigo Jones was retained by the Duke of Bedford to build outside the City of London on the old convent garden just off The Strand, he experimented with French and Italian ideas, creating what became the piazza of Covent Garden. No one followed his lead.

Three decades later, in 1662, overcrowding in the City for the well-to-do propelled into fashion the notion of the square. Bloomsbury and St James's Squares were built to set off fine houses. To deter the spontaneous arrival of costermongers and the like, wooden rails contained the central gravelled area, where people could promenade. With Soho Square a new idea developed: an enclosed garden was made (around a statue of Charles II) for the exclusive use of the surrounding residents, who had keys to the gate. This pattern was copied from here on. The estates of the nobility were speculatively developed north of the river to house gentry and professionals as well as themselves. Bloomsbury became a model of grid-plan streets, with first- and second-rate houses facing elegant squares, and mews behind. Iron railings were first erected around St James's Square in 1728 and soon became a distinguishing feature of garden squares; many were removed in 1941 and have yet to be replaced.

By the end of the seventeenth century Bristol, England's second city, was trying its hand, with Queen Square and St James's Square, later followed by developments in Clifton. John Wood's Queen Square and The Circus in Bath, Somerset, were built from 1729-58. The crescents were to follow, designed by his son, with naturalistic, pasture-like foregrounds and expansive views across the valley of the Avon, much like the contemporary landscaping in country estates. The Royal Crescent, built by 1775, offering elegance and healthy air with views of nature, simply took people's breath away. It still does.

Other spa towns, such as Cheltenham in Gloucestershire, Brighton in Sussex and Buxton in Derbyshire, replicated the 'health-giving' and desirable garden squares in the 1820s. As they expanded, Liverpool, Newcastle, Birmingham and Plymouth, Devon were beguiled into offering their own versions. Small towns, too, such as stone Stamford, Lincolnshire and brick Wisbech, Cambridgeshire, offered fine, small-scale squares and crescents.

Across London the idea gained momentum, for example in Hackney, around Camden Town, across Barnsbury and in Kensington, including the Ladbroke estate, where on the old Hippodrome racecourse Ladbroke Square is surrounded by streets clustered with their backs to fifteen private communal gardens.

Berkeley Square and those in Bloomsbury have majestic London plane trees that are among the finest trees in the land. Most squares in the commercial districts of London are open to the public and many private squares open on London Garden Squares Day in June. Garden Squares are particular to the British Isles and, with around six hundred in London, 461 of which are protected, they are a special feature of the capital, combining fine architecture and green oases.

See also BRICKS, BUILDING STONES, LONDON PLANE, MANHOLE COVERS, MARKETS, MEWS, PAVEMENTS, PIERS, RAILINGS, TERRACED HOUSES, VILLAGE GREENS.

384

S T A C K S

They may be echoes of beautiful arches or treacherous cracks, but detachment is the aspiration of sea stacks, to become rock pillars uniquely sculpted by the sea.

The Needles have become icons well beyond the Isle of Wight, Hampshire; they tell a story of chalk, crumpling and constant harrying. We know them as molar-like rocks, but charts of the early seventeenth century show a group of pencils to the north and Lot's Wife, or Cleopatra's Needle, in between – this was the last to fall in 1764. Frenchman's Cellar, Old Pepper, Roe Hall and Wedge survive as dangerous sentinels, pointing across the bay to Old Harry ('*his Satanic majesty*') and his crumbling Wife, who sacrifice themselves for the Isle of Purbeck. This great headland seems to spawn stacks. In aerial view or from the sea it looks as if great bites have been taken out of the chalk; you sense a production line of tough little promontories bravely standing up, better than the miniature coves, to the gnawing of the waves.

From Flamborough Head to Bempton in Yorkshire bays carved between high chalk headlands have bookends, such as Adam and Eve pinnacles and the King and Queen. The Parson and Clerk are fashioned from the brown red sandstone of Dawlish in Devon; they trudge like pilgrims, their robes heavy with the sea, although their story is one of blasphemy and dining with the devil.

Like all and sundry gathering for a parish moot, the varied stacks at Bedruthan Steps in Cornwall stand with their feet in the sand, disturbing the progress of the tide. Bedruthan was a Celtic giant, who found these stepping-stones useful. One of the rocks recalled for some the profile of Queen Bess; another, Samaritan Rock, reminds of a ship wrecked in the 1840s, allowing serious beachcombing to supplement a poor living.

We marvel at their endurance, their shapes and forms, the refuge they give to seabirds, but stacks are anthropomorphised and satanised for good reason. These recognisable rocks have always given seamen and fishermen a way of knowing where they are; the stories attached to them help to embed the shape, position and danger in the mind.

See also ALBION, ARCHES, BEACHES, CHALK, CHOUGHS, CLIFFS, COASTS, COVES, DEVIL, FLINT, LIGHTHOUSES, WHITE CLIFFS.

STAFFORDSHIRE OATCAKES

Oatcakes, with thicker variations in west Yorkshire and Lancashire known as Havercakes (perhaps from *hafre*, the Norse for oats), may be found as far south as Warwickshire. But in Staffordshire, especially the Potteries, oatcake shops demonstrate their local popularity, and everyone has their own recipe, which varies around:

8 ounces fine oatmeal
8 ounces plain flour
2 teaspoons salt
¾ pint milk (warm, not hot)
¾ pint water (warm)
½ ounce fresh yeast

After beating and half-an-hour rising, the batter is dropped onto a hot, greased griddle or pan to spread and bubble, then turned to finish as big as a floppy, golden plate. Rolled with bacon and eggs, cheese or like a sweet pancake with butter, honey or fruit, this makes a serious winter breakfast or tea.

See also BAKEWELL PUDDING, BISCUITS, BREAD, CAKES, CHEDDAR CHEESE, CHEESE, CHEESE ROLLING, CORNISH PASTIES, CREAM TEAS, DOUBLE GLOUCESTER, ECCLES CAKES, FISH & CHIPS, FOOD, PANCAKE DAY, PUDDINGSTONE, STILTON, WENSLEYDALE CHEESE.

STAIRS

Gainsborough in Lincolnshire had stairs down to the river Trent, but such was the speed of the incoming tide that drownings were frequent. Recent restoration work has built over these and established a wall along the quays.

Access to the busy foreshores of rivers, such as the Thames, was by stair. Watermen and fishermen, as well as beachcombers and amblers, would use these slippery, green, tidally washed rights of way. Irongate Stair, Pickle Herring Stair . . . many are now closed, often in disrepair, and some have been built over. We need to reclaim these intimate, historic alleys to the waterside:

385

I am the ghost of Shadwell Stair.
Along the wharves by the water-house,
And through the dripping slaughter-house,
I am the shadow that walks there.

Wilfred Owen, from 'Shadwell Stair'

See also AEGIRS, ALLEYS, BOAT RACE, BORES, FOOTPATHS, HARDS, RIVERS, TIDES.

STANDING STONES

Beside a smooth, flattened stone, 25 feet and nine inches high, a church was built at Rudston in the Yorkshire Wolds. The village name means stone cross, but the stone pre-dates the church by millennia. The suggested date for its erection is the late neolithic or early Bronze Age, 2,500 to 1,200 years before Christ was born. The choice of gritstone (from Cornelian or Cayton Bay) was fortuitous – the stone has weathered but withstood the years well. A smaller stone also crouches in the churchyard, and the area around has many contemporary burial mounds and also more than one cursus – relict banks that might have contained processional ways. The stone stands close to where the river makes the second of two right-angle turns – the Gypsey Race gives its name to other rivers in the Yorkshire Wolds that disappear for part of the year (in the chalklands of Dorset they are called winterbournes). The sacredness of the stone drew the church to it; this early, opportunistic Christianising strategy has been applied to other megaliths.

The Devil's Arrows have stood the test of time without such protection. To the west near Boroughbridge, Yorkshire, by the river Ure, three menhirs form a line (a fourth is mentioned in the sixteenth century). They vary between eighteen and 22 feet high, with a narrowing appearance, and the gritstone has been either worked or weathered at the top into deep flutings.

Such effort must have gone into shaping, moving and turning such stones that their purpose is felt to be for ritual ceremony, marking territory, meeting places, burials or as objects of worship. On Exmoor, Devon the Culborne Stone, re-erected in the 1940s, is unworked but has a cross within a wheel carved upon it, as has one of its near neighbours, part of a row. These could have been carved later when the stones were pressed into use to mark the parish boundary.

In terms of distribution, standing stones are widespread – the North York Moors, Cumberland, Westmorland and Derbyshire have a large share, and the most densely populated area we currently know is the South West. The Isles of Scilly have more than four hundred standing stones and holed stones, including the Old Man of Gugh. Cornwall has many examples, together with stone circles and rows. The Pipers make a pair, but some stand singly in the centre of small fields, welcomed by cattle as scratching posts.

In Gloucestershire the Longstone stands in Hampton Fields, south of Minchinhampton; a mile away stands the Tingle Stone, and the area is rich in barrows. The Longstone stands about eight feet high; it is of oolitic limestone and has suffered honeycomb erosion, but it is the more notable for having two holes, reputedly with healing powers. As in Cornwall, an affected limb, even a child, and certainly cloths were passed through the hole. Near Shap in Westmorland stands the Thunderstone, a glacial erratic. Close by, the remains of an avenue of stones, one and a half miles long, was orientated towards a barrow called Skellaw, the hill of skulls; it was overtaken by the town in the nineteenth century.

The Black Stone, Giant's Staff, Hangman's Stone, Hell Stone, Hele Stone, Hurl Stone, King Stone, Long Stone, Pedlar's Stone, Tingle Stone, White Stone and Whittle Stone are just some of the names accrued over ages that perhaps offer a story, a description, a secret.

See also ALBION, BARROWS, BOUNDARIES, CAIRNS, DEVIL, DRAGONS, EARTHWORKS, FOLKTALES, FORDS, GIANTS, HAUNTED PLACES, HENGES & STONE CIRCLES, HILLS, MILLSTONE GRIT, PUDDINGSTONE, RIVERS, ROCKS, TORS, TURNING THE DEVIL'S STONE, WAYSIDE & BOUNDARY CROSSES, WINTERBOURNES.

STARFISH

Starfish come in many forms, from the commonest five-pointed kind to bright red, twelve-legged varieties that look more like sunbursts. Fishermen despise them for their light-fingered prowess in decimating shellfish. They have a lot of names for them: in 1970 Willy Elmer gathered words for starfish from fishermen all around the coast, as part of his doctorate on English Dialect – the Terminology of Fishing.

See also BEACHCOMBING, BEACHES, BOATS, COASTS, ESTUARIES, OYSTERS, QUICKSAND, SEA FISH, SHELLFISH, SHIPPING FORECAST, SUNBURSTS, TIDES.

Rudston churchyard, Yorkshire. From top left, clockwise: sand star; common starfish; common sunstar; cushion star.

S T A R L I N G S

This cheeky bird, with its iridescent plumage, provides us with one of the most spectacular occurrences in nature – murmurations of starlings wheeling like shape-shifting clouds in the evening sky. Twenty years ago these winter aerial displays would have comprised millions of birds, but today we are fortunate to see groups of fifty thousand, such as those that drew crowds on Brighton's seafront before roosting on the West Pier – the largest regular roosting place in Sussex before its collapse in 2004.

In the 1980s we used to look forward to the winter return of the starlings to Leicester Square in London. But complaints of noise and droppings brought bird scarers and netting to drive them away. They would arrive in waves, filling the sky, landing among the neon lights full of chatter and business, negotiating to find a good perch. When the large Christmas tree was erected in Trafalgar Square, they thought it was for them, and quickly moved in. Now West Enders are deprived of a source of joy at the rhythms of nature.

Coniferous forests are starlings' preferred roosting places in winter; in summer they opt for deciduous woods. They also use reed beds, such as Leighton Moss in Lancashire, Slapton Ley in Devon and Westhay Moor in Somerset. Urban roosts may still include Huddersfield Station and Bradford City Hall in Yorkshire and the Runcorn to Widnes road bridge on the Cheshire/Lancashire boundary, where Nick Baker observed that a 'roost has been recorded for two hundred years'.

Fewer people witness the spectacular dispersal from winter roosts. Starling expert Christopher Feare described the phenomenon seen on radar: '*spots develop into expanding concentric circles, like slowly moving ripples on a pond. In radar parlance these patterns are called "ring angels". Some small roosts evacuate in only one ring but large roosts may produce up to twenty.*' Starlings travel up to twenty miles to feed in dispersed groups, prodding the earth for leather-jackets and other insects in grassy fields and picking ticks from the backs of sheep. These groups gather at 'moots' before flying back.

In 2002 starlings were added to the Red List of conservation concern because their numbers had fallen by seventy per cent since 1979. The reasons for this are thought to be associated with fewer leather-jackets and other insects in fields and a reduction in the acreage of permanent pasture. Starlings are probably suffering because of decreased nesting and roosting places, too, with local authorities increasingly discouraging them in city centres, modern houses being less bird friendly and old trees being cut down.

The de-intensification of agriculture is one obvious solution, and perhaps more nesting and roosting sites could be provided by emulating the starling towers that Charles Waterton constructed at Walton Hall near Wakefield, Yorkshire in the early nineteenth century. On stone pedestals to make them rat-proof, they had about sixty nesting chambers. In his biography Julia Blackburn recorded that '*The birds rewarded Waterton by coming every day in huge noisy gatherings, and feeding on the lawn in front of the house.*' We need new follies with a conservation purpose. At the very least it should be required that nesting chambers are attached to all new agricultural barns, sheds and conversions.

387

Unless we make an effort we could lose our local starlings and all the good they do in fields and gardens. We will miss their quickness to imitate mobile phones and police car sirens from the chimney pots, whistling and chattering and flapping their wings with sheer exuberance.

See also ANCIENT TREES, BRIDGES, CHIMNEYS, FIELDS, FOLLIES, HERONRIES, PIERS, REED BEDS, ROOKERIES, SPARROWS.

STATIONS

You will find in a railway station much of the quietude and consolation of a cathedral. It has many of the characteristics of a grand ecclesiastical building; it has vast arches, void spaces, coloured lights, and above all, it has recurrence of ritual. It is dedicated to the celebration of water and fire, the two prime elements of all human ceremonial.

G.K. Chesterton, from *Tremendous Trifles*

Stations were invented here, and the great Victorian buildings – where they remain – still resonate with grandeur. John Betjeman said: '*Railway stations are most important in giving places an identity*', but this was one of many key considerations ignored by the infamous Beeching report, which recommended the closure of vast swathes of railway line and their stations from the 1960s. More than four thousand have gone, and with them an indefinable 'connected-ness' – Sturminster Newton in Dorset lost its station and consequently its market, and for many decades there was a gaping physical and economic hole in the town.

The earliest stations were modelled on the coaching inns they had superseded, but in the nineteenth century they combined traditional styles – Gothic in Richmond, Surrey, classical in Huddersfield, Yorkshire, baroque

in Newmarket, Suffolk – with modern techniques and materials. The names shared the drama: Hull Paragon in Yorkshire; Carlisle Citadel in Cumberland. Corporate identity coupled with economy to create familiar standards in the fashionable architecture of the time: Italianate between Portsmouth, Hampshire and Hastings, Sussex; French renaissance on the Great Western, which also had pagoda-roofed, corrugated-iron halts, as at Appleton, Berkshire. Downham Market in Norfolk has curved gables, recalling the close historic links between the Netherlands and the Fens. Bournville in Birmingham became associated with Cadbury's and is painted in chocolate-wrapper colours.

Local materials were used both to show off the qualities of a place and to optimise resources: blue brick in Staffordshire, Accrington brick in Lancashire, Broseley tiles in Worcester. Nottinghamshire red brick makes London St Pancras stand out – it was the end of the line from that county. '*St George for England, St Pancras for Scotland*'; the station was architect Sir George Gilbert Scott's Gothic revenge for having been obliged to design the Foreign Office building in London in an Italianate style.

The impetus was lost in the twentieth century. As Richards and Mackenzie wrote, '*it tells us a good deal about the relative values of the nineteenth and twentieth centuries that where the Victorians modelled their stations on cathedrals and palaces, Modern Man models his on shopping centres and office blocks*'.

See also BRICKS, CATHEDRALS, CORRUGATED IRON, DAGS, RAILWAYS, THE UNDERGROUND.

STEPPING-STONES

Strategically placed boulders to enable foot travellers to stay dry, stepping-stones are such practical things. Yet to come across them brings great pleasure, especially when they have been worn by centuries of boots. Known as hipping

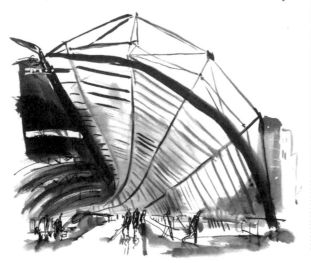

International terminal, Waterloo Station, London; York Station.

stones in the North, the sturdy, rectangular stones over the Ribble at Stainforth, Yorkshire display this hollowing, as does the more random line that challenges the river Wharfe by Bolton Abbey. Also in Yorkshire, at Gargrave, beside an old ford across the river Aire, the stepping-stones, round and fresh, are a magnet for children. Masham town council commissioned Alan Ayers to make sculptures along the footpaths around town; only when crossing a fluctuating stream do you become aware that the stones are carved. Across the stream behind the main streets in Bruton, Somerset uneven stones offer short cuts.

See also BRIDGES, FLOODS, FOOTBRIDGES, FOOTPATHS, FORDS, NEW MILESTONES, RIVERS, SCULPTURES.

S T I L E S

Took a walk in the fields saw an old wood stile taken away from a favourite spot which it had occupied all my life the posts were overgrown with ivy and it seemed so akin to nature and the spot where it stood as tho it had taken it on lease for an undisturbed existence it hurt me to see it was gone for my affections claim a friendship with such things.

John Clare, from his journal, September 1824

The most practical of artefacts attract our ingenuity and our affections. All over the country stiles of innumerable variations were and are still being devised to allow people to climb over hedges and walls into fields without letting sheep, cattle or even motorbikes follow them. The availability of stone, wood and metal reinforces the differences, but so does use and age, idiosyncrasy and tradition.

Some of the oldest are found in Cornwall, especially in West Penwith, where small fields are enclosed by huge, ancient hedge banks of earth and granite boulders, often topped by bushes. There is a sense of accumulation over generations and that many makeshift repairs have been made. Between 1997 and 2000 the Gerrans and Porthscatho Old Cornwall Society surveyed the old stiles in the parishes of St Gerrans, Philleigh and St Just and found three main types: the cattle stile, sheep stile and coffin stile, and variations.

The cattle stile through the hedge bank is the most simple and common, the airy gap spanned by a thin high stone (the shape of a lintel) with one or more stones as steps to it on either side; alternatively the stone steps lead up to a solid slab. One, at Treloan Farm, has a locally typical cart axle across the top; it is Grade II-listed.

The sheep or step stile involves a number of stones projecting from the face of a stone hedge, rising up and over each side. A granite slab sits on top of the 'hedge', which can be as wide as four feet. Where the coursing is of vertical slate, large granite steps can look rather ungainly.

The coffin stile is an early form of cattle grid, with deep stone slats or 'treads' sometimes placed over a shallow pit, and was used to replace gates into a churchyard. One at St Just has a shelf for the coffin to rest on at both sides.

If in Cornwall you have to be nimble, in Derbyshire and the Yorkshire Dales you need to be slender to get through the squeeze stiles. At their simplest just two large slabs of stone make a V shape through the stone wall, the gap narrow enough to deter sheep and cattle. Sometimes the stone slabs are roughly hewn, but they can also be beautifully tooled, as at Callow and Kirk Ireton in Derbyshire and Flockton Moor, Yorkshire. In Derbyshire the curvaceous profiles of limestone stoops or slabs in Monyash give more space for feet; there is even more elaborate keyhole shaping in the sandstone stoops at Newhaven.

389

Sometimes the stones are offset to allow a shuffle through, with one squared or wedge-shaped stone in front of the other, as at Twiston, Lancashire. Other variations include step-over squeezers and straight-sided stiles, with or without steps. Quite different are the elegant steps made from over-long throughstones protruding either side to allow escalation over walls, which are typical of parts of the Yorkshire moors and Dales; some may date from the seventeenth century, as at Malham.

Occasional mounting-block-type stiles lead into a churchyard; elsewhere, for example at Ribchester, Lancashire, elaborately wide steps might lead up and over a low, vertical, gravestone-like slab. In Somerset, at Farrington Gurney, two thinly cut stones elegantly curve away from each other like angel's wings and, just beyond, a vertical iron bar topped with a curly ended 'T' stops small animals getting through.

Cornish grid stile; wooden stile; squeeze stile, Great Longstone, Derbyshire; stone steps, Cleveland, Yorkshire.

Simple, wooden step-over stiles predominate in hedged country. Near Burwash in Sussex a charming, curved, wooden 'V', with a piece of wood nailed as a cross-bar and a step on short posts, acts as a makeshift squeezer stile and has probably been there for years. At Coombes in Sussex and Lacock in Wiltshire wood has been shaped to resemble stone slabs for squeezer stiles. Tall, wooden ladder stiles have spread across the Pennines and the Lake District in recent decades to help walkers climb over the high walls.

Stiles made in metal are among the most elegant, but may say little of locality save that here was an estate or park. Iron fence steps, ladders and kissing gates were available from Victorian catalogues. Iron ladders with a great circle for handrails are good for clearing high deer fences, for example at Horton, Lancashire, or lower, metal estate fencing, at Dubwath, Cumberland. Inverted bottled-shaped metal squeeze stiles are *typical of those found around the Bath area. It is called "The Fat Man's Agony"*', according to Michael Roberts. Those made from iron pipes for the water authority at Monkton Combe, Somerset have a workaday appropriateness. A metal scissor stile into the churchyard at Duntisbourne Rouse, Gloucestershire neatly folds to one side to let the walker through. Mechanical turnstiles persist in a few locations, as on Lindisfarne, Northumberland.

Along the river Parrett in Somerset Keith Rand has made wineglass-shaped oak squeeze stiles, demonstrating that sculptors and craftspeople have creative ideas to offer, at their best when the brief demands a new and subtle look at local distinctiveness.

See also ALLEYS, DRYSTONE WALLS, FENCES, FOOTPATHS, GATES, GORSE, HEDGES, NEW MILESTONES, WALLS.

STILTON

The Blue Bell Inn at Stilton, Huntingdonshire, on the Great North Road – one of the great post-horse and coaching routes between London and Scotland – had long sold this seasonal treat before it first appeared by name as Stilton cheese in 1722. With bread and beer, it gained fame among travellers and coachmen as the perfect fast food. The Angel and The George (now called the Stilton Cheese) joined in the bonanza until the railways bypassed the town. It is named after the place where it was sold, but has never been made there. It hails from Wymondham in Leicestershire, near Melton Mowbray, where great cheese fairs were held at the turn of the nineteenth century.

This top hat of a cheese, seriously crusty, becomes extensively blue veined as it ages. Stilton was defined in 1910 and its name protected in 1969 so that its integrity and specificity has been safeguarded. Blue and White Stilton, which now have Protected Designation of Origin status, are made in

seven creameries, from Cropwell Bishop, Nottinghamshire to Hartington, Derbyshire, using milk from Leicestershire, Rutland, Nottinghamshire and Derbyshire.

See also BLUE VINNEY, CHEDDAR CHEESE, CHEESE, DOUBLE GLOUCESTER, FOOD, INNS, WENSLEYDALE CHEESE.

STRAW

Straw is not as apparent in the fields as it once was. We no longer see the stooks left out to dry, unless thatching straw is being grown, or the thatched ricks in the fields or rickyards. Until the late 1800s some wheat varieties had stalks that approached six feet in height, which were good for thatching and many other jobs. Straw was a valuable by-product of grain production, but became the victim of mechanisation in the 1950s. The new reaper-binders and threshing machines could only tackle cereals with shorter stems, so gradually varieties were bred to produce smaller stems and bigger grains. This was good for the baker but disastrous for the thatcher, who, for the first time, had to have old varieties grown specially for him.

Wheat for thatching is cut when it is still green, and left to ripen in ricks before it is threshed and combed – providing wonderful sources of winter food for seed-eating birds. Once the grains have been threshed, the dried stalks of wheat, barley and oats have been put to a wide variety of uses. For hundreds of years straw has been used not only for thatching but also for packing breakable goods, such as pottery and fruit, as bedding for horses and livestock, for stuffing horse collars, scarecrows and mattresses, as cheeses for cider making, and some for animal feed.

The modern combine harvester leaves fields with short stubble of reduced value. In the 1960s there was a vogue for

A303, between Wincanton and Sparkford, Somerset.

burning it in an attempt to put back a little goodness into the soil. But this scorched-earth practice was banned in the 1990s, owing to the enormous amount of damage to hedges, trees and wildlife and the amount of air pollution it caused. Now straw is increasingly used for (biomass) heating, and straw bales have found a renaissance as building blocks with built-in insulation properties.

The trend towards sowing winter wheat soon after harvest has left fewer seeds and weeds among which birds can forage, and vegetation that is too high at nesting time for birds, such as skylarks. Fields of stubble in which birds can feed over winter are being encouraged once more by conservation bodies.

Straw has other uses: when we travel on the A303 between Wincanton and Sparkford in Somerset we always look out for the latest manifestations of a farmer's art. Cheddar cheese maker Archie Montgomery's straw-bale sculptures stand in one of his roadside fields. They are often accompanied by pithy slogans, such as *'Can you afford the view? We can't and we made it.'* In 2004 a giant owl became a landmark.

See *also* BREAD, CHEDDAR CHEESE, CIDER & CIDER ORCHARDS, CORN DOLLIES, CROPS, FIELDS, SCARECROWS, SCULPTURES, SKYLARKS, STRAW BEAR DAY, THATCH.

S T R A W   B E A R   D A Y

On Straw Bear Tuesday, the day after Plough Monday in the Fenland villages and towns on the borders of Cambridgeshire and Huntingdonshire, and around Grimsby in Lincolnshire, a man decked from head to toe in straw was led from house to house in the evening, dancing to music. This was banned in Whittlesey in 1909, and in other places, as a form of begging.

In 1980 folklore enthusiast Brian Kell revived the custom with the help of the Whittlesey Society. Now it takes place on the Saturday before Plough Monday. The

focus of the day is the parade of the straw bear, whose role is divided between two men because the straw costume is so cumbersome, weighing five stones. Visiting and dancing outside local pubs, he is accompanied by dancers, musicians, performers and a straw bear from Walldürn, near Frankfurt in Germany, which has its own festival. The following day the costume is ceremonially burnt.

See *also* MAY DAY, MUMMING PLAYS, 'OBBY 'OSSES, STRAW.

S T R A W B E R R I E S

The All England Lawn Tennis and Croquet Club at Wimbledon, south London may be the centre of strawberry consumption – around 23 tons are eaten during the two-week championships – but not far away, in the early 1800s, Isleworth was the hotbed of strawberry growing. It was here that some of the most important developments in their cultivation were made.

In the 1870s, after the abolition of the sugar tax, demand for jam boosted the growing of strawberries, especially in Kent around St Mary Cray and Swanley, which were close to the London markets. Some growers started to make jam themselves, for example around Cambridge, in Impington and Histon, where Chivers started. During the First World War jam for the troops left only the strawberries picked and sold on Saturdays for the public.

Places prospered where early strawberries could be grown. In the Strawberry Belt along the south-facing slopes of the Mendips, between Axbridge and Rodney Stoke in Somerset, smallholdings of one to five acres were boosted by the Cheddar Valley railway line – the Strawberry Line – which once connected the area with Bristol and London. The area was described in 1998 as *'cluttered with roadside sales points, sheds and polythene tunnels'*, which do *'little to enhance the still attractive landscape'*, by the Countryside Agency. There is an annual Strawberry Fair at Draycott, where a competition for the best fruit is judged and a Strawberry Queen is crowned.

Smallholdings on fertile fenland soil around Wisbech, Cambridgeshire were soon supplying the towns and cities of the Midlands and the North with fresh produce and strawberries for processing; the area continues to be a large producer of fruit.

Wimbledon's strawberries are grown outside near Mereworth in Kent. The variety is Elsanta, which now accounts for three-quarters of all strawberries sold nationwide and is chosen more for reliability and shelf-life than taste. Elsanta is also the preferred variety for growing in polytunnels – much resented by people who live near them – because superstores demand perfect fruit. Monty Don, who lives in Herefordshire, where polytunnels have been allowed to proliferate without the need for planning

391

permission, is passionately opposed to the sheer scale of the monoculture: 'this is the rape and pillage of the English countryside for strawberries'.

Meanwhile, back at Cheddar, a smallholder with seven acres grows seven different varieties to prolong the season and, although he uses some polytunnels, he has a flock of chickens to keep down the vine weevils. Another Somerset grower near Ham Hill grows all of his strawberries outside on raised beds, which are rotated every three years. An organic grower on the Welsh border uses polytunnels but employs hedgehogs from animal sanctuaries to eat his pests.

See also FOOD, GOOSEBERRIES, MARKET GARDENS, ORCHARDS, RHUBARB.

SUFFOLK PUNCHES

This horse almost died out in the 1960s, its job pulling the plough having been taken over by the tractor. In 1989 just 75 mares and forty foals were registered, and the breed is still rated critical by the Rare Breeds Survival Trust. In the first half of 2003 31 foals were registered with the Suffolk Horse Society.

The Suffolk Punch is immediately recognisable, with a big barrel of a body, huge quarters and shortish legs; it is notable for having little hair around the fetlocks. Reaching a height of sixteen to seventeen hands, the taller stallions may weigh up to a ton. Its colouring is important. Chris Miller says that 'chesnut is the usual spelling when referring to the colour of a Suffolk Punch – sorrel was also used earlier to define the colour. Volume I of the Suffolk Stud Book of 1880 says "There are seven shades – the dark, at times approaching a brown-black, mahogany or liver colour; the dull dark chesnut; the light mealy chesnut; the red; the golden; the lemon and the bright chesnut and the most standing colour is the last named".*

The author, Herman Biddell, then describes each particular colour with more detail.' In the fifteenth century there were horses fitting this description, and all current Suffolks have a common ancestor in Crisp's Horse of Ufford, a stallion born in 1768. The remoteness and conservatism of East Anglia reinforced the close breeding and identification with the county.

In the show ring the Suffolk stands out in a leather head collar and bit, or in an East Anglian harness with specially braided mane and tail. In Woodbridge there is a museum dedicated to the Suffolk Horse, and the largest stud now is based at Hollesley Bay Prison, which began as a training establishment for farmers before they migrated to Australia.

See also AGRICULTURAL SHOWS, CATTLE, THE CHANNEL, DOWNLAND, EXMOOR PONIES, FELL PONIES, FELLS, FERAL ANIMALS, GALLOPS, HORSE FAIRS, HORSES & PONIES, HOUNDS, LONDON TAXIS, MOORLAND, NEW FOREST PONIES, PIGS, POINT TO POINT, POULTRY, RACECOURSES, SHEEP, SHIRE HORSES, WHITE HORSES.

SUNBURSTS

That moment when, from behind a cloud, the sun's light is fractured into a fan of bright beams is one of the spectacles of nature. Constable captured these often crepuscular rays in many of his Hampstead Heath paintings. Christian religious iconography repeatedly uses the sunburst – the extravagant golden halo dominating the head of Christ as he appears above the altar in All Souls Church, by Broadcasting House in London's Langham Place, is an arresting example. We can trace this back at least to the tombs of the Pharaohs. Across Europe the spoked wheel was a recurrent prehistoric symbol of the sun. Ornamentation on buildings kept resurfacing, from Georgian fanlights to inn signs.

During the inter-war years people sought healthier living, moving to the expanding suburbs and indulging in the new excitement of sunbathing. The golden tomb of Tutankhamun had just been discovered. Solar observance was in fashion. It should not surprise us, then, that cinema façades, shop windows, neon signs, bay windows, fanlights, leaded front doors and wooden front gates burst into a song for the sun.

See also CHURCHES, CINEMAS, CLOUDS, EAST, HOUSE NAMES, PUB SIGNS, WEATHER-VANES.

S U R F I N G

On boards made by local coffin makers, the early surfers were inspired by stories from their Anzac and South African comrades during the First World War.

The best surfing beaches in Cornwall rely on great swells to hit the coast from the low pressure weather systems in the Atlantic; the best come in the autumn and winter months. Perranporth is said to have seen the first surfing in Britain. Fistral Bay is the best beach for surf, and the possibility of the local council selling part of it provoked worries about restricted access. Watergate Bay lures beginners and those who wish to experiment with kite surfing.

Newquay attracts a hundred thousand people to the World Rip Curl Boardmasters Festival. The Cribber, a legendary thirty-foot wave named after the reef half a mile off Newquay at the north end of Towan Head, has attracted attention since 1966, when it was ridden by three visiting Australian surfers, rarely achieved since. Artificial surfing reefs are mooted off Tolcarne at Newquay and Bournemouth, Hampshire.

There are long-established surfing beaches in Devon and off Cayton Bay, near Scarborough, Yorkshire. Newcastle has Long Sands, north of Tynemouth, and the mouth of the river between the harbour piers, where the Black Middens rocks create a reef break.

All beaches, though, have their points of interest, known intimately by regulars: the best part of the tide, local weather, dangerous rips and rocks below the surface. Surfers Against Sewage, based in Cornwall, campaigns imaginatively for clean seas for all of us.

See also BEACHES, BORES, COASTS, COVES, SAND-DUNES, SHIPPING FORECAST, TIDES, WEATHER, WINDS.

S W A N   U P P I N G

Their meat much prized for festive occasions, mute swans were claimed by the Crown in the fourteenth century. Later Edward IV gave swan rights to medieval freeholders, who marked their swans with special nicks on their beaks to denote ownership. A swan roll dated 1500 shows 99 different types of beak mark in the Norfolk and Suffolk Broads alone.

The ancient custom of swan upping is to mark the cygnets belonging to two London guilds, the Vintners and the Dyers, which are the last to retain their swan rights, apart from the Swannery at Abbotsbury, Dorset (all other, unmarked, swans belong to the Crown). It takes place on the third week in July between Sunbury, Middlesex and Abingdon Bridge at Pangbourne, Berkshire, and has been practised on the river Thames for four centuries. For this colourful ceremony, held with the gravity and demeanour that fits such a graceful and elegant bird, the paraphernalia of tradition is worn.

The cry '*all up*' is heard when a family of swans is spotted, and boats encircle the birds, 'upping' each out of the water. The cygnets are marked: those belonging to the Worshipful Company of Dyers are given a nick on one side of the mandible, whereas the Vintners' birds receive a nick on each side of the beak. The journey up-river takes five days, and as it approaches Windsor Castle a toast is made to the Queen, as seigneur of swans.

Each cygnet is ringed, weighed and measured by the Queen's Swan Warden from Oxford University, and the number and state of the swan population is assessed. It was this annual census that first alerted conservationists in the 1970s to the disappearance along the Thames of '*the large urban flocks, which were characteristic of the 1960s*', the Nature Conservancy Council reported. The biggest cause was found to be poisoning by lead fishing weights, used by anglers, which were banned in 1987.

The Swannery at Abbotsbury holds the largest managed colony of mute swans in the world, and it is ancient – it

393

is likely that swans were living here before the monastic establishment of the eleventh century. They graze on sea-grasses and algae in the shallow lagoon of the Fleet behind Chesil Beach.

The native mute swan is the largest of the British swans; Bewick's and whooper swans are winter visitors, eagerly awaited at places such as Slimbridge, Gloucestershire and Welney in Norfolk. Mute swans are common on lowland rivers, lakes, reservoirs, canals and coastal marshes, and often congregate in towns, where people enjoy feeding them. In winter swans gather, sometimes in their hundreds, to graze wet meadows.

Unlike the whooper swan, the mute swan does not have a far-carrying call; its distinctive 'voice' comes from the sonorous wheezing of its wings in flight.

See also BEACHES, BOATS, ESTUARIES, GRAZING MARSHES, HALF-YEAR BIRDS, LAGOONS, RIVERS, SHINGLE.

SWEET CHESTNUT

Introduced by the Romans so they could make flour from the nuts, the sweet chestnut is most at home in the South East, where it grows in old woods. Plantations of coppiced trees in Essex, Kent and Sussex were made for hop poles and, now, for chestnut paling. Oliver Rackham thinks their nuts superior in flavour to imported ones, especially after they have been frosted, and Richard Mabey believes there is huge scope for planting chestnut woods and hazel plats for their nut protein. Roasted chestnuts may have been one of the first fast foods sold in the streets of London; their smell is certainly one of the most evocative of winter.

The sweet, or Spanish, chestnut was often planted as a parkland tree to attract deer, and is easily distinguishable by its twisted trunk and mushroom-shaped canopy, browsed underneath to a straight line.

The Tortworth Chestnut in Gloucestershire is one of England's oldest and biggest living plants, yet the description 'plant' almost does a disservice to this giant organism, which has been allowed to do what most trees would, given the chance – to spread outwards, its leaning limbs taking root and growing into tall trees, and so on, forming its own copse of seventeen or more trunks; this

way conceivably it could live forever. Perhaps planted as a nut by King Egbert in 800, it was said in the 1760s to be the oldest in the country, measuring 52 feet in diameter. It is now protected from grazing animals by a wooden fence and is looked after by the Tortworth estate. Close by the church, surrounded by other magnificent parkland trees, it is well worth a pilgrimage; an ideal place to ponder the mortality of the human race and our relationship with nature.

Another landmark chestnut spreads over a quarter of an acre at Bewdley in Worcestershire. Croft Castle near Leominster, Herefordshire has an avenue of pollarded chestnuts, and there is a collection of old characters at Canford School in Dorset, which includes the largest in the country.

See also ALDER, ANCIENT TREES, ASH, AVENUES, BEECH, BIRCH, BLACK POPLAR, BLACKTHORN, ELM, FENCES, FIELD MAPLE, HAWTHORN, HAZEL, HOLLY, HOLM OAK, HOPS, HOP-GARDENS & HOP-YARDS, HORNBEAM, HORSE CHESTNUT, JUNIPER, LANDMARK TREES, LIME, LONDON PLANE, MONKEY-PUZZLE, OAK, ORCHARDS, PARKLAND, PEARS, POPLAR, ROWAN, ROYAL FORESTS, SCOTS PINE, SYCAMORE, WALNUT, WHITEBEAM, WILLOW, WOODS, YEW.

SWIMMING PLACES

Oh, many a time have I, a five years' child,
In a small mill-race severed from his stream,
Made one long bathing of a summer's day;
Basked in the sun, and plunged and basked again
Alternate, all a summer's day . . .

William Wordsworth, from 'Bathing'

Most rivers have their special spots – deep pools or old mill-ponds known to locals, where farmers turn a blind eye to benign play. Wild swimming, as Roger Deakin calls it, clings on: *'Often there's a shingle river beach near a bridge or in the elbow of an oxbow bend, or a deep pool with a submerged ladder in the bank. And the classic sign known to all unofficial bathers: a dangling, knotted rope for swinging out like Tarzan, and letting go.'*

People have been swimming in the river Frome, Wiltshire at Farleigh Weir since at least the 1500s, and from the 1930s Farleigh Swimming Club, with seventeen hundred members, has enjoyed bathing here in a pool by a tree-lined water-meadow.

Yet no rivers are designated bathing waters under the European Bathing Water Directive. When asked why, the Environment Agency replied: *'The Agency does not encourage informal swimming in rivers by members of the general public.'* But the aspiration should be that all rivers are clean enough to swim in, simple streams safe to play in and springs proudly cared for by all of us.

394

'Today's swimmers . . . are herded into chemically treated pools that simulate nature but have the wildness carefully filtered out, the "real thing" is treated with shameless disrespect', writes Deakin, whose book *Waterlog* is about not just 'our profound disconnection from natural waters' but our insidious distancing from nature, which compounds ignorance, disrespect and bad decision-making. The suggested closing, by the Corporation of London, of the three swimming ponds on London's Hampstead Heath to the Hampstead Heath Winter Swimming Club was for some the final straw, and successfully challenged in the High Court. Local people hold dear the free right to swim at their own risk in daylight hours in soft, untainted water all year, in the spring-fed men's, ladies' and mixed ponds, among kingfishers, swans and ducklings.

Some hardy people swim every day, some join in at the challenging moment of Christmas or New Year's Day, as in Suffolk with the Walberswick Shiverers – 'a group of friends who exercise their right to insanity by plunging into the North Sea each Christmas Day'. The Christmas Day race is the highlight for members of the Serpentine Swimming Club (formed in 1864) in Hyde Park, London, most of whom take a pre-work swim here daily.

See also BEACHES, BEACH HUTS, BOUNDARIES, LAKES, LIDOS, MOATS, PONDS, RIVERS.

SWORD DANCING

Sword dances on Christmas Day or Plough Monday (the Monday following Twelfth Night) were originally performances with dance and characters – the fox-skin-clad Fool, cross-dressing Bessy and sometimes Robin Hood and Maid Marian. Some, as at Grenoside in Yorkshire and Monkseaton in Northumberland, still feature characters, but mumming has largely subsumed the play element and left the dances as independent spectacles.

Long Sword dancing is particular to Yorkshire and Durham, performed by up to eight dancers in a chain, their intricate figures ending with a plait of swords being raised into a star, nut or lock. A militaristic flavour is matched in many teams' costumes, but, in Yorkshire, the members of Flamborough Long Sword side wear fishermen's smocks and hold wooden laths, perhaps to represent the weaving and mending of nets.

The Rapper Dances of Northumberland and Durham are named after the flexible, short swords which have handles at both ends. The dances are more energetic, some involving somersaulting over the rappers. Rapper teams favour white shirts, sashes or cummerbunds, clogs and breeches, or hoggers, once a pit man's Sunday best. Mining communities, such as Winlaton, Earsdon and High Spen, have had sides since the nineteenth century. The industry's subsequent

decline took with it identity and friendly local rivalries, but both Long Sword and Rapper traditions are regaining popularity among established teams and newcomers.

See also BOUNDARIES, BRITANNIA COCO-NUT DANCERS, FURRY DANCE, MINES, MORRIS DANCING, MUMMING PLAYS, ROBIN HOOD.

SYCAMORE

Wind-worn crescents of sycamore trees shelter many isolated farmsteads in the Lake District, the Pennines and Cornwall. Like the buildings, they probably date from the improvements of the eighteenth century.

It is a native of central and south highland Europe, and just possibly of Wales and northern England. Despite long-held belief that it was introduced in Tudor times, H.L. Edlin thought sycamore came with the Romans and Ted Green believes it may be native. Plantings were mature enough by the end of the seventeenth century to invoke John Evelyn's raucous dislike: he deemed its shade short lived, its droppings messy and its wood useless in his influential book *Sylva* of 1664.

Despite the planting of the 'great maple' around the houses of the nobility, prejudice persists. Now the tree is disliked because of its success, its ability to spread in gardens and its out-shading, for a while, of native trees in ash and beech woods. Because the sycamore aphid produces a dripping honeydew, the tree also antagonises car owners – it does well in the city, where the bane of its leaves, the black spot fungus, is subdued by pollution.

But the sycamore is a beautiful tree and its resilience to wind and sea spray has proved invaluable. In Shaftesbury, standing seven hundred feet up on a hill with its prow into the west wind, a sycamore-shaded walk was planted by a far-sighted philanthropist in the 1750s as a promenade from which to view thirty miles south and west across Dorset. Most of the trees were lost after a giant storm in the 1950s, but a few remain.

395

Serious woodland scientists, such as George Peterken, prefer to describe sycamore as 'a naturalised introduction that should be treated as a de facto native in most woods'. Peter Marren adds that 'the value of sycamore transcends its origins. Well-grown sycamores are lovely things – in their cumular roundness are they the nearest things to our lost elms? As a village or town tree, surely its proportions, history and place in the culture matter more than what it was doing in the Bronze Age.' Up to two hundred species of lichens and mosses are supported by older trees, and, with a heavier crop of aphids and other biomass than oak or ash, sycamore is important to tits, house martins, bats and other aerial feeders; its blossom and nectar, leaf litter, decaying wood and mycorrhizal fungi are all ecologically significant. Together with oak and hazel it is also the favourite tree of dormice.

From blasted sycamores on the Brontës' Yorkshire moors to the single tree at the summit of Oker Hill near Matlock, Derbyshire, sycamores are cultural as well as natural assets. The great sycamore at Tolpuddle, Dorset, planted where three roads meet, must have had stature in 1834, when farm labourers the Loveless brothers, James Hammett, James Brine and father and son Standfield stood together for a fair day's pay in hard times and stirred the ire of the arrogant and corrupt local aristocracy and bureaucracy. Fear of unrest and contempt for their plight led to their transportation to Australia, which made martyrs of them.

These events fuelled the trade union movement, and today the Trades Union Congress and National Trust look after this living monument, now known to date from 1685. Over time the Martyrs' Tree has been filled with vermiculite, bound with iron and pollarded. But something has worked because, after looking sick for a decade or two, the tree has revived and was looking fine in 2005, passing on its stories of 'the Victims of Whiggery', as they were described in a pamphlet by George Loveless, to thousands of trade union pilgrims and to one of its young, planted on the same triangle of grass about ten yards away.

See also ALDER, ANCIENT TREES, ASH, AVENUES, BEECH, BIRCH, BLACK POPLAR, BLACKTHORN, COTTAGES, ELM, FARMS & FARMSTEADS, FIELD MAPLE, FURRY DANCE, GRASSY TRIANGLES, HALF-YEAR BIRDS, HAWTHORN, HAZEL, HOLLY, HOLM OAK, HORNBEAM, HORSE CHESTNUT, LANDMARK TREES, LIME, LONDON PLANE, MONKEY-PUZZLE, MOORLAND, OAK, ORCHARDS, OTTERS, PEARS, POPLAR, RIVERS, ROWAN, ROYAL FORESTS, SCOTS PINE, SWEET CHESTNUT, WALNUT, WHITEBEAM, WILLOW, WOODS, YEW.

SYNAGOGUES

The earliest synagogues were discreet, as prohibition prevented them from facing onto public streets, and are identified only from remains, such as the ritual baths Mikveh or Mikvah. Jacob's Well in Bristol was long thought to be our only medieval Mikveh (now it is thought to be a burial cleansing house, a bet tohorah), but another was uncovered in London in 2001.

Styles vary. Bevis Marks is the oldest synagogue still in use. Out of sight in London's East End, it was designed in 1701 by a Quaker (with references to nonconformism and the Great Amsterdam Synagogue) for Sephardi Jews, who had fled persecution in Spain, Portugal and then Holland. The South Manchester Synagogue inclines to the Byzantine styles introduced for Ashkenazi Jews from eastern Europe, who first established a community in 1690. Manchester's Spanish and Portuguese Synagogue is now the city's Jewish Museum.

By the nineteenth century synagogues were more conspicuous, although anti-Semitism raised its head again before the century was out. Liverpool's Prince's Road Synagogue, facing the street, has turrets and a huge rose window. The Congregation of Jacob Synagogue on Commercial Road, east London dates from 1903; it was the last synagogue here in the intimate folk art style.

As Jewish communities dispersed from city centres to suburbs, redundant synagogues, which have no need for deconsecration, were converted. In east London the building with arched windows on the corner of Fournier Street and Brick Lane, which was built in the 1740s as a Huguenot chapel (they, too, sought asylum), became a nonconformist chapel (they were also excluded), then a synagogue, and is now a mosque. Mile End and Bow Synagogue became a Sikh Gurdwara.

Sharman Kadish is sanguine in her speculations, feeling that the loss of synagogues is 'linked with the perennial Jewish feeling that maybe some day we will have to move on'. She goes on to explain that the practical response of not developing strong links to a place ensures that worship can 'flourish quite independently of its physical surroundings'. Out of concern for the losses, a survey of England's Jewish built heritage began in 1997.

See also BOUNDARIES, CATHEDRALS, CEMETERIES, CHAPELS, CHURCHES, MOSQUES, QUAKER MEETING-HOUSES, QUARTERS, ROUND-TOWERED CHURCHES, TEMPLES.

Tolpuddle, Dorset.

Times New Roman Bold/Italic, Stanley Morison, 1932.

TAR BARREL ROLLING

Guisers carrying blazing 'kits' to light a Baal fire to burn the old year out are part of a singular Northumbrian festival. Geoff Noble explains: '*The Allendale tar barrel parade takes place on New Year's Eve. The flaming half-barrels, carried on the heads of forty local-born males in costume ("guisers"), process through the little town in front of the band and encircle a giant wood stack in the market place. On a given signal at about twenty minutes to midnight, the barrels are thrown forward to light the bonfire, and when the church bells strike, the crowd (often three or four thousand strong) sings "Auld Lang Syne". When the visitors head back to Tyneside, the pubs gradually re-open and the guisers are allowed their first drink of the night (and the New Year). My relatives in Allendale still claim the best year was the winter of 1962/3, when the roads were cut off by snow, food and animal fodder was dropped in by helicopter and the tar barrel party was for the locals only.*'

Now on a Saturday but originally on the Wednesday after 5 November in Hatherleigh in Devon, sledges of flaming tar barrels are pulled down the street at five o'clock in the morning, preceded by a bell-ringer, who makes a clamour to scare away evil spirits. The tar barrels are used to light a bonfire in the cattle market. In the evening a torch-lit procession with the Hatherleigh silver band leads the carnival floats around the town and is followed by a second run of flaming barrels on sledges, dragged at full pelt by up to forty local men and then taken to re-fuel the bonfire.

Bridgwater, Somerset gave up its tar barrels but now has the most spectacular carnival on the 'Guy Fawkes Circuit' of the West Country, including Bridgwater Squibs.

In Ottery St Mary, Devon something altogether more wild happens on 5 November; perhaps an ancient memory of Samhain, the Celtic New Year. This unassuming small town changes its personality altogether on an extraordinary day, beginning at half past five in the morning with loud

thuds all around town. Men discharge hand-held 'cannons' – short, bent pipes, rammed with powder and then hit on a percussive cap to set off flash and charge – often in enclosed squares, which compound the sound with echo. Anywhere else, arrests would ensue – and this is the town that took down its medieval weathercock for whistling.

In the afternoon thousands of people begin to gather – word of mouth brings students from Exeter, film crews from Japan, tradition collectors from far and wide, yet people within a few miles may know nothing. The fair glints its busy colours across the river until it is eclipsed by the great bonfire, lit at half past six in the evening, with the 'guy' sitting in puritanical top hat astride a chair on a pole six feet above the 35-foot bonfire.

The crowds head back into the centre of town, where big signs urge '*Beware of Burning Tar Barrels*' and '*You are here at your own risk*'. By half past seven people are really packed into streets and side alleys. Starting at known points around the town – Mill Street, The Institute, the Mason's Arms, the Five Bells, the Plume of Feathers, the Factory and in and out of the Square – the barrels are fired up by straw and paper, rocked into flame on the ground and, with a great shout, lifted by a man, hands clad in hessian pads, onto his shoulders. He heads off, crying 'uppard' or 'downard', perhaps as clues to his trajectory.

Through the street he runs, with tar barrel blazing. The massive crowds, packed tighter than a shoal of fish, part fluidly from fear as burning danger heads straight for them. This is no show for visitors, nothing is put on or sanitised; this is live tradition, wild and free. Old shoulder-holey pullovers or family-coloured rugby shirts are all that mark out the participants. Careful, attentive followers run, at the ready to help, and 'rollers' (carriers) run alongside to take the effort from one to another as they tire.

The right to carry barrels is often passed on within families; it does not come easy. There are seventeen barrels to be carried from four until midnight, starting with boys, then youths, then women, until the men begin with the full-size barrels; the biggest, at midnight, is a hogshead, which requires a man's full wingspan. This attentiveness, this serious community participation, is perhaps the closest we have to the Palio horse race in Siena, Italy or the running of the bulls in Pamplona, Spain, yet it is not, on the face of it, competitive.

It feels ancient, certainly older than the seventeenth century, as some claims suggest. It hits a primeval chord with its excitement and terrifying freedom of expression, as an astonishing display of anciently conceived prowess, a rite of passage, an assertion of territory, a memory of who knows what. But you feel history on the ground, a shard of deep tradition.

See also BONFIRE NIGHT, BURNING BARTLE, CARNIVALS, HALLOWE'EN, SHROVETIDE GAMES, WASSAILING, WEATHER-VANES.

399

T A R N S

The Norse name for these small mountain lakes has been handed down from the people who settled in the Lakes and the west of Yorkshire more than a thousand years ago. Water sits in hollows sculpted during the Ice Age as glaciers on the fringes of summit peaks bit into the fells. One of the characteristics of Lakeland tarns is their darkness; like the surrounding hills, often they seem to absorb light, to the extent of appearing deep and lifeless.

But A. Harry Griffin, 'Country Diary' writer for the *Guardian*, saw them differently. He often wrote about these '*pools high in the hills that reflect the sky*' and bring it '*down just in front of you, or perhaps, into the middle distance*'. His friend, the artist William Heaton Cooper, loved painting tarns, and thought of them as the '*eyes of the mountain*'. The one he found '*the most completely satisfying of all the tarns of Lakeland*' was Sprinkling Tarn, under the crags of Great End and near the track to Esk Hause.

Griffin found it difficult to choose a favourite, and shortlisted at least a dozen, including Hard Tarn, below Helvellyn, where he experienced his coldest-ever bathe. Another was Lanty's Tarn, '*nestling among Scots pines just across the trough of Grisedale*'. Near the pool lies a ruined ice house, where blocks cut from the frozen tarn in winter were stored before being carted down in summer to Patterdale Hall in Grisedale. Controversy reigns over which tarn is the highest, although one contender is the Red Tarn below Helvellyn, 2,356 feet above sea level – '*an unattractive sheet of water but not without merit on a hot day*', Alfred Wainwright opined. He described Angle Tarn as '*a dark and sinister sheet of water in the shadow of the crags of Hanging Knotts but a welcome and refreshing halting place often frequented by naked bathers*'.

Few creatures can live in these cold, clear pools lying on top of hard, insoluble rocks, but some are a good habitat for water lobelia and quillwort. At Tindale Tarn in the northern Pennines whooper swans visit in winter.

In the Yorkshire Dales lies lonely Malham Tarn, in a shallow hollow gouged by ice through the limestone to impermeable Silurian slate, enabling England's only alkaline lake to perch at twelve hundred feet above sea level. Here,

the cold and wet combines to lure ramsons into flower only in June; elsewhere in the region they come out in May. The bottle sedge has colonised the open water, forming a belt of low reed swamp. With the surrounding raised bog, carr, calcareous fen, woodland and limestone pasture, this is a superlative place for studying nature.

See also ALDER, FELLS, HILLS, LAKES, PEAT, PONDS, RAMSONS, WILDFLOWERS.

T A R T A N

Long pieces of checked cloth, or plaid, woven with undyed wool from black and white sheep, were wrapped around shoulders and waists by shepherds working in the borders as early as the fifteenth century. The distinctive pattern became known as the Shepherd's check, Shepherd's plaid, Border tartan/plaid or Northumberland tartan.

Shepherds who moved north to work following the Highland Clearances took the cloth with them, and soon Scottish estates began to introduce their own single-coloured strands to the black-and-white plaid – these were the precursors of the well-known, colourful clan tartans.

The Duke of Northumberland chose the Shepherd's check for his piper in 1760; now it is often worn by Northumbrian pipers on ceremonial occasions. The Shepherd families – descended from the original sheep herders – '*wear it proudly*'. It is Northumberland's official tartan, and is still made by weavers today. Now Newcastle and Northumberland unite behind simpler black-and-white stripes – the football strip of the Magpies.

See also BESTIARY, FAMILY NAMES, FLAGS, FOOTBALL, NORTHUMBRIAN SMALLPIPES, SHEEP.

T E M P L E S

City skylines are enriched by curved silhouettes and elegant towers. As places of worship temples have a long history. Traditions from different corners of the world have been part of the English scene for many centuries, but only in the past fifty years have they begun to spread.

Hindu temples, mandirs, are built to face the rising sun. Respectful harmony of land and building is essential and architectural geometry links the building with the universe. The holy Lord Shri Swaminarayan's nineteenth-century mandirs in Gujarat were models for Hindu architecture. Many here are dedicated to him. The mandir in Neasden, opened in 1995, is the largest outside India. Its ornate limestone and marble domes (ghummats) and crowning pinnacles (sikhars) sparkle over suburban London day and night. This work of devotion of the whole community, involving traditional craftsmen (fifteen hundred sculptors

in India alone) and modern technical know-how (five hundred cars are parked somewhere), are a gift to the capital. Hindu communities have also converted existing buildings, often disused chapels, such as on Lee Street in Oldham, Lancashire. The Shri Ram Mandir in Sparkbrook, Birmingham was a cinema.

Sikh temples are Gurdwara, the house or door of the Guru. Like Hindus, English Sikhs have adapted many older buildings, but where they are purpose-built their design derives from fortresses from times of persecution. The Guru Nanak Nishkam Sewak Jatha in Handsworth, Birmingham and Sri Guru Singh Sabha Gurdwara in Southall, London are typical in having large onion domes to mark them out as holy places, and many smaller flanking ones.

Thailand's government and people funded England's first Buddhist temple, Wat Buddhapadipa in Wimbledon, London, in 1976. Others have their architectural roots in Sri Lanka, China, Korea, Japan, South-East Asia and Tibet. The Manjushri Mahayana Buddhist Centre in Ulverston, Cumbria, converted in 1975 from the Conishead Priory, was a twelfth-century hospital founded by Augustinian monks, a residence after the Dissolution, a miners' hospital, then wartime hospital, before falling into disrepair. Its temple is made of local limestone based on a mandala, the powerfully symbolic circular design.

See also CATHEDRALS, CHAPELS, CHURCHES, DIWALI, FOLLIES, MELAS, MOSQUES, OAK, QUARTERS, ROUND-TOWERED CHURCHES, SYNAGOGUES.

Houses sharing walls, built in lines, crescents and squares, developed early here; having gained political stability by the sixteenth century, we were able to escape the town walls long before our continental neighbours, and there was some move to live and work in separate places. Rows of variegated buildings had evolved organically in village and town, but the terrace was built as an entity, often planned around grid-plan streets.

Speculative and standardised building began in the seventeenth century in London. The nobility initiated development of their town and country estates, originally for houses for the expanding professional and middle classes. The houses were built to a standard single or double width, but varied much in depth. Building lines and party walls were stipulated in the great squares and rows of the classical and Georgian estates in London, Bristol/Clifton, Bath in Somerset and Buxton in Derbyshire.

The forms and feelings of terraces have diverged greatly since then, adaptability allowing many different plans (squares, crescents, endless rows or short runs), sizes and standards of quality.

Industrial momentum demanded workers. Houses began to multiply. Back-to-back houses were a feature of many industrial towns, from Birmingham to Sheffield; they demanded least land and fewer bricks. Only a handful remain, since they gained a reputation for offering unhealthy

as well as cramped conditions. In Sunderland single-storey terraces continued to be built into the twentieth century, their only equivalents in the long rows of miners' houses across County Durham and Northumberland, including in Darlington and Jarrow. On Tyneside flats developed, perhaps a result of steep slopes and Scottish influence.

More generally, nine-inch bricks built two-storey houses with front onto the street and, at the back, yard, wash house, privy and lane. In Eastwood, Nottinghamshire The Buildings, as they were known, were erected for miners in a grid plan of simple two-up-two-down brick terraces with entries (shared, private alleys) down the slope overlooking Brinsley colliery. In the Yorkshire and Lancashire Pennines, growing mill towns were distinguished by steep, cobbled streets with 'houses on top of houses' cascading down the hills.

Endless terraces of two-up-two-down houses were packed tight around mills and factories. Manchester and Salford still have some, familiar as Coronation Street, despite massive redevelopment in the 1960s. Elsewhere the terrace took on new forms. In the mid-nineteenth century the bowed elegance of the Ramsgate lawns (a local name for terraces) in Kent contrasted with Cambridge's Jesus Terrace and de Beauvoir Town in Hackney. Edwardian terraces

402

tumble down Muswell Hill in north London and fill seaside towns. Style and ornament, materials and moment make a difference.

Fashion began fleeing the terrace in the 1840s but it refused to fade away. Instead it continued to mutate until the quest for the suburban semi overtook it in the early twentieth century. Wholesale post-war redevelopment and replacement with tower blocks in the cities caused chaos in the social fabric of communities that were used to their own front and back doors on the ground. Currently hundreds of terraced houses (mainly in the North West) are boarded up, awaiting demolition, while others (mainly in the South) are sought after. English Heritage and local people, such as the Bangladeshi and Pakistani communities in Nelson, Lancashire, continue to campaign for their retention. And the terrace is in resurgence as the most energy-efficient form of housing.

See also ALLEYS, ALMSHOUSES, BACK LANES, BRICKS, BUILDING STONES, COAL MINING, COTTAGES, GARDENS, MEWS, SQUARES, TEXTILE MILLS, TOWER BLOCKS, TOWN GATES.

T E R R I E R S

Terriers are unique to Britain – all the terrier breeds originate here. Their name derives from *terra*, earth, and they have been bred since the 1650s to pursue animals that live underground – which 'go to earth' when chased. Many counties had their own breed of terrier, each with practical working skills.

In Cumberland the *'square-built'* fell or Lakeland type of terrier was bred to accompany foot followers and, according to D. Brian Plummer, *'put to ground to kill a fox'*, rather than flush it out, when the fox was seen simply as vermin with no potential for 'sport'.

Airedales are thought to have been the result of mating bull terriers with otter hounds to produce a large ratting (and otter-hunting) terrier capable of working the banks of the river Aire in Yorkshire. In the 1800s John Hulme from Manchester crossed a terrier derived from the old English black-and-tan type with a whippet to improve its ratting and rabbiting skills. The result was the handsome, smooth-haired black-and-tan terrier, later known as the Manchester terrier. It is now becoming rare.

The Bedlington terrier, formerly Rothbury terrier, which was bred by Gypsies and miners from Rothbury Forest, Northumberland, is a combination of lurcher and a terrier brought by nail-makers from the South. Once called the Gypsy dog, used to hunt badgers, rabbits and otters, it was the poacher's favourite, and miners used it down the pit to kill rats. In someone's arms it looks remarkably like a curly-coated lamb with Roman nose and drooping ears. Yet on their own feet they are distinguished

Eastwood, Nottinghamshire; Wallsend, Northumberland.

Airedale.

Bedlington.

Border.

Lakeland.

Manchester.

Norwich.

by a roached back and hanging tail, perhaps a little like hairy whippets; meeting seven of them – the Rotherview and Toffset Bedlingtons, fashionably clipped – on the beach at Exmouth, Devon on the day before the Paignton Show confirmed that they look like nothing else.

The plucky Border terrier was formerly known as the Reedwater or Coquetdale terrier. Described by Veronica Heath as the '*canine aristocrats of the north east*', with their small, otter-shaped heads and wiry coats, they were bred to join the hunt for foxes in the border country between Scotland and England. The Scottish borders have also been the home, for four hundred years, of the good-natured, long-haired, long-backed and short-legged Dandie Dinmont terrier, or tinker's dog, which was bred for killing stoats and rats.

The short-legged, wiry coated Norfolk and Norwich terriers differ slightly: the Norwich has prick ears and the Norfolk's are dropped. The Norwich was popular with hunt-loving students at Cambridge in the late 1800s, but now is becoming rare.

'*Each English county once had its own fox terrier*', Dr Bruce Fogle wrote, '*the genes of the extinct White Cheshire and Shropshire Terrier are probably still present in this breed, together with those of the Beagle.*' The smooth-haired and the more popular wire-haired terriers, with their thicker legs and dense whiskers, were bred for flushing foxes.

The vicar of Swimbridge and Landkey in north Devon, Reverend Jack Russell, spent most of his time from 1832 to 1884 trying to '*improve the working Fox terrier*' for hunting. In other words, making it '*steady from riot*' and not tempted to chase other quarry. He produced a type of white, wire-haired terrier with legs long enough to enable it to keep up with the horses – the Parson Jack Russell. The more numerous and more variable Jack Russell, the most popular of all terriers, has slightly shorter legs and can be smooth or wire-haired.

The sturdy Staffordshire bull terrier has shorter legs than the bull terrier and a different-shaped head, coming from an English White terrier and bulldog cross. It was originally bred for bull baiting and dog fighting, which was popular in the Walsall and Bloxwich areas of the west Midlands.

The popularity of the terrier is confirmed by the variety of breeds, which number more than any other type of dog. The first terrier show, organised by Charles Cruft in 1886, was so successful that it was later enlarged to include other breeds.

During the past few years some of the old breeds have begun to lose their popularity, such as the Sealyham. Registrations with the Kennel Club for the diminutive Yorkshire terrier, which was once stuffed into the pockets of West Riding miners for ratting work, declined by more than sixty per cent between 1993 and 2002. Two

of the original breeds – the black and tan and the white English terrier – together with the Cheshire, Devonshire, Shropshire and Suffolk terriers and other localised breeds, such as the Redesdale, have been absorbed into other breeds or become extinct.

See also BLACK DOGS, CAIRNS, DOGS, DROVE ROADS, GUN DOGS, HOUNDS, HOUND TRAILING, SHEEP-DOGS.

TEXTILE MILLS

The Industrial Revolution in England changed the world – for better or worse – and the imposing mill complexes indicative of the textile industries of Yorkshire, Lancashire and Derbyshire are increasingly being reappraised and rejuvenated. Tall, monolithic complexes with boiler houses, chimneys, factory and administration buildings, these were significant centres, dominating communities.

In the mid-1900s a disused mill in a state of decay might have been swept away for new, frequently inferior, buildings. Now their sordid histories – fuelled by slavery elsewhere and atrocious conditions here, injurious to people and environments – are scrutinised, and in the buildings the hard work and skills of those who built and laboured are remembered. Their sheer quality and presence marks them out for reuse and restoration; their scale offers potential for residential conversion or public buildings, such as museums and arts centres. Impressive and historic mill landscapes of Bradford and the Derwent valley, Derbyshire have been designated UNESCO World Heritage Sites. Sometimes 'model' villages sought to better the living and social conditions of the workers, as at Titus Salt's Saltaire in Yorkshire, a dramatic expression of Victorian paternalism mixed with egotism.

Masson Mill, Matlock, Derbyshire.

In the damp air of the Pennines mills flung themselves up wherever the conditions offered potential, increasingly with monosyllabic names that would stand out on chimneys and towers: Elk, Owl, Bee, Orb, Gem. Exotic trends in architecture crept into the designs: Italian at John Lombe's silk-throwing mill in Derby, Tower Works in Leeds and Manningham in Bradford, Yorkshire; Egyptian at the office building of Temple Mill in Leeds.

They are not just in the North – early fulling-mill buildings persist from the pre-industrial wool trade of the South. In the Cotswolds many stone-built mills of the Golden Valley, around Chalford and Stroud in Gloucestershire, are now converted to flats, but some are still working, producing felt for snooker tables and tennis balls rather than Stroudwater Scarlet, a material once used in military uniforms.

See also BRICKS, BUILDING STONES, INDUSTRIAL CHIMNEYS, RIVERS, TERRACED HOUSES, WAREHOUSES, WATER-MILLS.

THAMES SAILING BARGES

Following a pattern used by the Dutch in the Middle Ages, flat-bottomed barges were worked from the seventeenth to the twentieth centuries along the shallow creeks and rivers of the 'barge coast' of Suffolk, Essex and north Kent. The Kent brick-makers Eastwoods built up a fleet of seventy barges – 'brickies' – with their own livery in the last half of the nineteenth century. Spurred by competition from steam trains, Henry Dodd started the annual Sailing Barge Matches in 1863; this inspired refinements, resulting in faster boats that proved a match for the railways.

The versatility of the Thames sailing barge was extraordinary. Its flat bottom allowed it to go far upstream and

settle steadily on the mud as the tide dropped. Its masts and complex rigging could be dramatically dropped for 'shooting' the bridges, and rapidly re-erected by a crew of just two plus a 'huffler' (an extra hand). Into London they might carry bricks and cement from Milton Creek in Kent, or hay and root crops from Suffolk, returning with horse manure for the fields. They could even sail empty, despite their lack of a keel, since a leeboard could be lowered when sailing to windward.

The showy red-brown sails of the Thames barge were dressed with fish oils, horse urine and red ochre to lengthen their lives. The flamboyance of a large sprit sail, foresail, topsail, mizzen and bowsprit jib standing above a wide, twenty-by-eighty-foot wooden hull still turns heads along their home river and neighbouring Medway and Blackwater estuaries. Numbers have dropped from eight thousand to just thirty since 1900, but they remain much loved and respected as the biggest boat to be sailed by just two people before the advent of new technology. They gather for racing from Solent to Swale to Colne throughout the summer, and can usually be seen at St Katharine's Dock in London, Maldon Quay in Essex (where there is a Sailing Barge Heritage Centre) and at Standard Quay in Faversham, Kent.

See also BOATS, BRICKS, COBLES, CORNISH GIGS, FLATNERS, NOBBIES, NORFOLK WHERRIES, PORTLAND LERRETS.

405

T H A T C H

From being the most common roofing material almost everywhere, thatch has gradually been replaced by tile or slate. Thatching materials include heather, gorse, broom, flax, reed, rye and wheat straw. These light materials were particularly appropriate in places where buildings were made of cob, chalk cob (wychert) or clunch, less able to carry the weight of stone, tile or slate. It is not surprising that Devon, which has the most cob buildings, also has the most thatch. Eaves with no gutterings far overhang the wall to drop water well away.

The materials were local and cheap. They were also efficient: '*The insulation of an average tile roof with 100mm (4in) insulating quilt is fifty per cent less than a roof with 300mm (12in) Long Straw thatch*', according to Hertfordshire county council. Of the three main forms of thatching, long straw was the most widespread – in the South, Midlands and inland East Anglia – and most frequently used. As a by-product of grain production it was readily available. It produces the shaggiest and thickest of the thatched roofs and can be identified by the hazel rodding that forms a hem around the gables and eaves. Long straw is shaken, gathered any way up and collected into compact bundles, known as yealms, which are fastened onto the existing base layer of

Mosses favour wheat straw: one endangered species of moss is confined to thatched roofs and as many as 32 mosses and liverworts have been found on one old thatched roof on Exmoor, Devon.

Water reed's heartland is in East Anglia, the Norfolk Broads in particular, and it produces thinner, more angular roofs. Reed is not pliable enough for ridging, so saw-sedge is used – about three thousand bundles are produced annually at Wicken Fen, Cambridgeshire. The lower edges of the sedge are often decorated with ornamental patterns, such as scallops, and with rods and hazel spars. Reed has been grown in small quantities in other coastal areas, such as Abbotsbury (Abbotsbury Spear) and Radipole in Dorset and Slapton Ley and Dartmouth in Devon, serving local needs.

Heather roofing was common on heathland, such as in Dorset and the New Forest, Hampshire, and among the upland moors. In Northumberland it is known as black thatch because it darkens with age. A farmhouse with heather thatch in Northumberland was found to have turf sods underneath the heather. The long-stemmed ling, complete with its flower-heads, was placed in chunks in overlapping layers with the roots at the top, held in place by iron sways hammered through the turf into the rafters. A few thatchers still work with ling, sourcing their materials from Scotland or National Trust land.

Thatchers display individual traits and styles. Jo Cox and John R.L. Thorp, for their book *Devon Thatch*, interviewed John Rodgers from Modbury, who '*came from a family that produced sixteen thatchers in five generations*'. Each family or individual has his own signature. This is often expressed in the treatment of ridges, dormers, eaves and gables.

As early as 1212 (in London) cities and towns started enacting bylaws prohibiting the construction of new buildings with thatch because of the fire risk. In the 1950s and 1960s the introduction of shorter-stemmed wheat varieties began to replace the traditional thatching varieties, such as Red Standard, a Devonshire favourite, Maris Widgeon and Maris Huntsman. These new varieties were useless for thatching, and the combine harvester was geared to short-stemmed wheat, so for the first time thatching wheat had to be grown specially.

The distribution of thatching styles became severed from locally grown materials. The Rural Industries Bureau, founded to revivify rural industries after the war, set about boosting the craft of thatching. Problems had arisen with the longevity of long-straw thatch, perhaps as a consequence of the over-use of fertilisers, which made the stems brittle. As a result, the Bureau promoted combed straw and tried to extend its use further east into traditional long-straw country. The Devon farmers who still grew thatching wheat found it more profitable to sell it to the richer counties beyond the South West; this resulted in a shortage of combed straw in Devon, where they began to use reed instead.

straw. Strips are gradually added from the eave to the ridge and held down with U-shaped willow or hazel spars. The eaves are cut and held into position with hazel liggers in varying patterns, and the whole roof is covered with wire netting to keep birds out.

In the wetter dairying country of Devon, west Dorset, the Blackmore Vale in Somerset/Dorset and parts of Cornwall, combed-straw (also known as combed wheat-reed) thatching evolved. Here the ears and leaves are removed by a reed comber. The straw is made into bundles (nitches) with the stems all facing the same way. The new straw is loosened from its bundles and laid over the old coat in horizontal courses with the sharp stalk ends facing downwards, neatly knocked into position with a leggatt and held down with crooks; the eaves are cut by hand. Combed-straw thatching produces neat, homely, ample cottage roofs. In Devon characteristic cone shapes protect the porches. The pitches are generally steep, to shed rain, but in Devon the roof pitches are said to be 'slack' or shallow, lower than those in East Anglia.

Combed wheat-straw thatch, Ashmore, Dorset; long-straw thatch, Cottered, Hertfordshire; water-reed thatch, Norfolk.

In 1960 the Bureau published *The Thatcher's Craft*, which contained a longevity table of the three types of thatch: water reed – fifty to sixty years; combed straw – 25 to forty years; long straw – ten to twenty years. Water reed was pronounced as the thatch that, despite its higher initial costs, represented the best value. This might be true in the drier, eastern part of the country, but in the South West, with roofs of lower pitches and more rain, reed may have a much shorter life span. Culture, long knowledge and appropriateness were over-ridden. Water reed still replaces the locally distinctive combed-straw thatch of the South West; perhaps three-quarters of thatching in Devon was water reed in 2000.

There were other problems. Reed roofs are stripped down to the rafters for re-thatching, but with combed straw and long straw only the damaged material is removed and a new layer of straw placed over it. Reed thatchers working on combed-straw roofs began uncovering smoke-blackened thatch and wattle work, caused by fires in the open halls of buildings built before 1550. Its importance cannot be overstated: '*Here we have an extraordinary stock of actual crops – albeit rather dried out and dusty – that were growing in the fields from the medieval period*', John Lowe wrote. '*This is the largest resource of the study of historic plant remains – archaeo-botany – left in Europe . . . The thatched roofs of Devon farmhouses are libraries of unwritten information about the farming past . . . complete with all the wild flowers which grew there 500 years ago.*'

Ways of 'over-coating' combed straw with reed have now been perfected, and it is often hard to tell the difference between water reed and combed straw. But, as Cox and Thorp point out, '*What undoubtedly has been lost in the replacement of straw with imported water reed is not only the long Devon tradition of combed straw, but also the old mutuality between Devon farming and Devon thatching, and the vernacular good sense of using a locally available material on local buildings.*'

They argue that changes since the Second World War obscured the picture of what was really 'traditional' in many places, that in the 1950s the concept of local distinctiveness was not valued as it is today. The first sign of revolt came from conservation officers in Northamptonshire, who were worried that their long-straw tradition was being lost to combed straw and water reed advocated by the Bureau, and gave listed building consent only for re-thatching with long straw. Other local authorities followed suit (except Devon) and many disputes ensued. In 2000 English Heritage produced guidance notes that reinforced the need to conserve local and regional thatching styles and techniques. Some thatchers felt the choice should be left to them and the householders. It is ironic that a kind of roofing whose success was assured because it came from local materials is now largely dependent on water reed flown in from Turkey, Hungary and the Danube delta – about one and a half million bundles annually.

Thatch has been used on most buildings, from humble cottage to manor house, farm buildings, including large tithe barns, such as at Tisbury, Wiltshire, to churches – Alec Clifton-Taylor mentions fifty to sixty in Norfolk and about twenty in Suffolk. Thatched cob walls are particularly attractive (and were much sought after for the early *I-Spy* books). Thatching is beginning to appear on new buildings and people are again working to reconnect with local sources to complete the circle.

See also BANDSTANDS, BUNS, CHIMNEYS, CHURCHES, COB, CORRUGATED IRON, COTTAGES, FARMS & FARMSTEADS, HAZEL, HEATHLAND, MOSS, PANTILES, REED BEDS, SHINGLES, SPARROWS, STRAW, TILES, WILLOW.

THREE HARES

A recurring symbol in churches, although not nearly as frequent as the Green Man, is that of the Three Hares. Usually found as wooden roof bosses, Three Hares can be seen chasing each other endlessly in a circle; they share but three ears, although each creature seems to have two. The ears form an eternal triangle.

They abound in Devon, north and east of Dartmoor, in churches such as Throwleigh, Chagford, Spreyton and South Tawton. They are found outside churches as well: examples include a 1974 stained glass at the Castle Inn, Lydford and on plaster ceilings of sixteenth- and seventeenth-century houses. They have been found in disparate places, including St Hubert's Church in Corfe Mullen, Dorset, in a medieval stained-glass window in Holy Trinity Church in Long Melford, Suffolk and on floor tiles in Chester Cathedral.

Recent research by the Three Hares Project has revealed that this is far from a parochial image – it occurs in differing forms in Europe, Iran and as far east as China, where paintings have been found on the ceilings of cave temples at Dunhuang from the Sui dynasty of AD 581-618. Textiles containing these images may have travelled back and forth along the Silk Road, exciting and influencing medieval artists and craftsmen along the route.

The symbolism of the Three Hares is not understood, although the hare has long been associated with the Anglo-Saxon goddess Eostre and with dawn, rebirth, fertility and the moon. Each time it appears, culture and religion will have imbued the symbol with its own meanings – perhaps trinity, unity and eternity.

See also CHURCHES, EASTER CUSTOMS, GREEN MAN, HARES, MOON.

407

T I D E   M I L L S

Of the five thousand or so mills mentioned in the Domesday Book, about nine hundred were built on the coast. The tide mill at Woodbridge quay, recently restored, lies on the river Deben in Suffolk, but most were located in the South, especially Hampshire, west Sussex and on the Tamar and Fal estuaries in Devon and Cornwall.

Eling tide mill at Totton near Southampton, on the edge of the New Forest, is the only surviving tide mill in the world producing flour daily using traditional methods. First built more than nine hundred years ago, it has been rebuilt and renovated many times since, most recently in the eighteenth century. The mill fell into disuse in the 1940s, but was restored over five years to re-open in 1980 as a working mill and museum.

It sits on a causeway, a toll road that links Brokenford to Eling, near the mouth of Bartley Water, which runs into the river Test. At its back the mill-pond contains the tidal water impounded by means of sea hatches with flaps, which are pushed open by the incoming tide and closed as the tide tries to run out. Under control of the miller the water is released through an internal hatch to feed the Poncelet waterwheel (there used to be two), allowing about four hours' milling. At its front was a thriving small harbour, where the mill had its own wharf.

The oldest and largest tide mill in England stands imposingly across the river Lea at Bromley-by-Bow in east London. Built in 1776, it contained three big waterwheels, but they are no longer running. Surviving tide mills are still found at Pomphlett in Devon, Emsworth, Beaulieu and Eling in Hampshire, Birdham in west Sussex, Thorrington and Stambridge in Essex and Woodbridge in Suffolk.

See also ESTUARIES, PONDS, RIVERS, TEXTILE MILLS, TIDES, WATER-MILLS.

T I D E S

Twice every day the Thames reveals and then conceals the stairs, beaches and tributaries through the centre of London. The flow of the river is as nothing against the rhythm of the tide, whose mean vertical rise and fall between 21½ and fifteen feet at London Bridge ensures that the tide reaches Teddington, Middlesex, where a weir and lock stop its natural progress. Ships, as well as baby flatfish, take a free ride up-river with the tide; in May young flounder (the size of two fifty-pence pieces) dig into the sand to wait for the next help upstream, just one of 115 fish species that inhabit the tidal Thames.

A bell is rung by the changing tide on the Wandle, a right-bank tributary of the Thames, which takes its name from Wandsworth (not the other way around). The Mersey advances and retreats through Liverpool, the Tyne through Newcastle, and small-town harbours lift and drop their boats onto sand and mud from Polperro, Cornwall to Staithes, Yorkshire. Around England the height of the tide is generally six to sixteen feet, but it can reach 47 feet in the Bristol Channel – one of the highest tidal ranges in the world.

On a quiet day at the coast you can hear the sound change as the tide turns. Tim Baber, musing from his beach hut at Mudeford, Hampshire, embellishes an explanation from *ThreeSixty*, the magazine for surfers: '*The tide is basically the longest wave on earth, responding to planetary forces, with a wavelength of half way around the world. With small local variations, it's a wave that comes twice a day, every day and one that dominates our activities, mood and view.*'

Datum is measured locally from a line on the harbour wall or a mark on the pier; the deviation from this gives the tidal range, and it usually relates to safe passage out of the harbour. In Yarmouth, Isle of Wight, for example, tidal gauges are visible on the pier as you enter and on the 'dolphin' as you leave.

Southampton Water in Hampshire is known for double high waters, resulting from the complications of water running round the Isle of Wight, and these are more accentuated in the harbours at Christchurch, Hampshire and Poole, Dorset, where there are long stands of tide (half-day high tide). In Weymouth harbour the Gulder brings a further echo of this; it is a small flood about 45 minutes after the first low water.

The tide extends to its highest and lowest range at spring tides and varies least at neap tides, each of which occurs twice a month according to the closeness of the moon, which pulls the wandering water a little higher and lower when it is full or new. The highest of the highs and the lowest of the lows occur in March and September around the equinox, again according to the moon, with the help of the sun.

Sea level is rising because of the melting of ice caps and glaciers, a contemporary sign of global warming. But in the south of England the land is also pivoting into the sea as Scotland continues to rebound since shedding its weight of frozen water after the Ice Age. So we shall never see such low tides again, and whenever the chance arises to visit the furthest foreshore we should celebrate Low Tide Days and enjoy archaeological as well as ecological explorations.

The foreshore is a miracle of life chances and life-styles. Different plants and creatures cling to different zones according to their capacity to deal with desiccation, inundation and crashing waves, as well as the local conditions of rock, mud or sand. Acorn barnacles dare no further up the rocks than mean high water of neap tides; sea anemones prefer rock pools; in sand and mud creatures dig in while the tide is out. This littoral zone is where many make their home as part of a life cycle of helpless drifting. It is here, too, that we lose ourselves when the tide is out, focusing on the tiny world of the rock pool, seaweeds, starfish, shells, rippled sand, noisy birds and strange finds.

More than a hundred square miles of sand is exposed in Morecambe Bay, Lancashire at low water. The place's worst reputation is for the rapid return of the tide, which speeds at a jogging pace on its way to high water mark. Working out when it is best to walk over the sands, venture round the point, go beachcombing and leave harbour all require local knowledge and the *Tide Tables*.

For centuries visitors to St Michael's Mount in Cornwall and Lindisfarne in Northumberland have contended with the tides. The causeway to Lindisfarne was part-built in 1954 and completed in 1966, but it is not passable for five hours around each high tide and is still lined by poles for the late or daring pilgrim. When the tide is out a river called the Low is revealed. Before the causeway there were two routes across the sands, lined by poles, and on the three-mile track from Beal shore to Chare Ends there were refuge boxes for those caught short by the sea.

When King Canute, sitting on his throne on the beach, commanded that the tide should not come, he intended to demonstrate to others his limitations, his lack of omnipotence. Although popularly remembered differently, the tale offers wisdom still.

See also AEGIRS, ALLEYS, BEACHCOMBING, BEACHES, BEACH HUTS, BORES, BOWLING GREENS, BRIDGES, EYOTS, HARBOURS, HARDS, HENGES & STONE CIRCLES, ISLANDS, PIERS, QUICKSAND, SAND-DUNES, SEA TRACTOR, SHELLFISH, SHIPPING FORECAST, STAIRS, STARFISH, TIDE MILLS.

TILES

Plain tiles and pantiles share the same territory as brick. The heart of plain tile country is the South East, extending into the Home Counties (excluding the limestone belt), the Isle of Wight, Midlands, Cheshire and Lancashire. The South East is renowned for tiles of warm red-orange. The Gault around Cambridge produces pale yellow or dun colours, whereas, according to Alec Clifton-Taylor, '*a speciality of Huntingdonshire and the western part of Cambridgeshire is the roof of variegated colours: yellows, browns, reds, pinks, greys – all in rather soft, pale shades*'. By contrast, dark purple-blue tiles can be found on roofs in south Derbyshire and east Staffordshire, produced from the Etruria marl in Stoke-on-Trent.

Early tiles are thought to resemble wooden shingles in size and shape, and began to replace them from the twelfth century. The standard size now is 265 by 165 by twelve millimetres. Plain tiles need to be laid two deep to keep out the rain, making them heavy and requiring a steeper-pitched roof than pantiles.

In the South East the perfect marriage is made between timber-framed buildings and the rambling hipped, half-hipped and cat-slide roofs that reach almost down to the ground. The valleys of roofs and angles of hipped roofs also had special tiles made for them – the latter are known as saddle-backs or bonnets. Gertrude Jekyll found '*a special charm about the fine old saddle-shaped, locally-made hip-tiles, with their saw-edged profile telling well against the sky, just as there is a charm, and the satisfying conviction of a thing being exactly right, about all the building details that are of local tradition and form the local style*'.

Special tiles were made for the ridges, but some of the serrated terracotta ridge tiles made by the Victorians were dismissed by Alec Clifton-Taylor as '*fussy cresting*'. He commented, too, on the use of tiles away from their traditional areas: '*Tiles harmonize less well in the landscape where stone and slate are the material below the soil.*' Machine-made tiles, such as 'rosemaries', were '*produced in zillions*', John Woodford wrote, and transported by canal and railway all over the country from Shropshire, Staffordshire and elsewhere. Although concrete tiles now dominate, following the housing boom of the 1950s, their standardised appearance and fading colours are losing popularity at last as clay tiles make a comeback. Hand-made tiles have a slight curve in them, making them more watertight when laid and adding texture.

409

Tiles hung on the walls of buildings first appeared towards the end of the seventeenth century in south-west Kent, Sussex (except for the south-west corner) and south-east Surrey. For weatherproofing they are often hung on the exposed sides or on the gable ends. Sometimes they are confined to the upper storeys, with weather-boarding or brick below. They tend to be brighter in colour than the roof tiles, attracting fewer lichens and impurities. Many are laid with decorative shapes, such as the '*fish-tail, the beaver-tail, the hammer-head, the scallop*', in alternate patterns, Alec Clifton-Taylor wrote.

Mathematical tiles or weather tiles reached the height of their popularity between 1784 and 1850; hung vertically, they were used to make timber houses look like brick. A feature of the South East, fine examples can be seen in towns such as Rye, Canterbury and Tenterden in Kent and, in Sussex, Brighton and Lewes, where more than sixty buildings are faced with them. Red mathematical tiles were followed by glazed blue-black ones to protect buildings from salt spray. White (actually cream) clay from the Gault produced stone-coloured tiles to match yellow bricks.

See also BRICKS, BUILDING STONES, BUNGALOWS, COTTAGES, PANTILES, SLATES, TERRACED HOUSES, THATCH, WEATHER-BOARDING.

410 TIN TABERNACLES

Here and there elegant little corrugated-iron buildings, clearly used or once used for ecclesiastical purposes, grace villages and cities. The variety of 'tin tabernacles' still in use is surprising, and includes the black-and-white church at Draycott in the Clay, Staffordshire, the Italian Pentecostal church in Gorsebrook Road, Wolverhampton and the white iron chapel at Maesbury, near Oswestry, Shropshire, built in 1906 in three days.

All were chosen from catalogues and constructed from parts. Peter Beacham explains: '*In the nineteenth century*

the detractors of corrugated iron inevitably included the ecclesiastical establishment who mocked the catalogue chapels of nonconformity as "tin tabernacles". Methodism soon shattered such presumption by demonstrating how humble temporary buildings could serve the spiritual needs of ever changing mining communities in the far south west better than the ancient parish churches stranded by their medieval geography in the wrong place. In the wastes, noise and dirt of the mining areas the "tin tent" of the chapel must indeed have seemed like a sanctuary in the wilderness. Anyone caught out in the worst of weathers will have known at least faint echoes of such experience when refuge is sought under the roof of a field barn and the rain drums deafeningly on the tin and a loose sheet bangs in the wind; we have been offered all we needed, no more and no less. That is what corrugated iron has always offered. It has entered the soul of the countryside in countless different guises and has long since proved it belongs there.*'

Norman Emery, who studied them in County Durham, found '*55 churches and chapels (and associated halls) out of 65 "tin" buildings*'; the others were '*five schools, three institutes or miners' union halls, and two theatres. Corrugated iron buildings were durable, fairly easy to erect, and, if necessary, they could be dismantled and re-erected elsewhere. They were also comparatively cheap. Basic buildings to seat 150 to 200 people cost around £200 ... At New Silksworth, where there were 800 worshippers, the cost was equivalent to £1 per head. The large, elaborate parish hall at Greenside colliery cost £1,000 in 1906.*'

Gary Green's research for Tees Archaeology in north Yorkshire reveals that, in addition to the Pentecostal church in North Skelton, '*Public buildings of this type, while relatively common in neighbouring County Durham, appear to have been less widespread in Cleveland, with only three other known examples.*'

See also CHAPELS, CHURCHES, CORRUGATED IRON, MOSQUES, QUAKER MEETING-HOUSES, SYNAGOGUES, TEMPLES, VILLAGE HALLS.

TITHE BARNS

A favourite building of Mies van der Rohe was the Great Barn at Great Coxwell in Berkshire. This, the finest of medieval tithe barns, like the architect's own buildings attempted to create sheltered volume without load-bearing walls. The intention here was to fill 152 by 44 by 48 feet with grain, wool and other produce taken as tax by the church. It is an astonishing survival, with wooden posts and beams so elegantly and carefully framed, making a kind of pillared nave with aisles, that they have carried the weight and resisted the thrust of the huge stone tile roof for more than seven hundred years. It is made of Cotswold stone as well as timber and orientated unusually north–south because of the lie of the land.

Romany Church in the Wood, Bramdean Common, Hampshire.

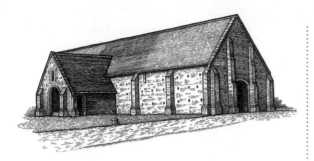

Most tithe barns were built east–west, to aid ventilation from the prevailing winds, and the oldest and biggest look a little like blind churches, well built and laying foundations for the local vernacular. Bigger than its neighbour, the church, the tithe barn at Lenham in Kent has an expanse of neat tiles sweeping tent-like towards the ground with but a person's height of wooden cladding seeming to hold it down. A long, buttressed and thatched barn forms one side of the yard at Place Farm in Tisbury, Wiltshire, which is entered through an arch. It has a distinctly ecclesiastical feel, echoes of its role as a grange outpost of Shaftesbury Abbey.

After 1836, and the substitution of tithes in kind by rent, the need for great storage houses dwindled, as did the tradition of aisled barns; this may reach back more than two thousand years, from Wessex across the southern counties and up the eastern side of the country to Yorkshire.

See also BANK BARNS, BARNS, BRICKS, BUILDING STONES, CHALK, CHURCHES, COB, CORRUGATED IRON, DRYSTONE WALLS, FIELD BARNS, FLINT, GIN HOUSES, GREENSAND, SLATES, THATCH.

T O L L - H O U S E S

Toll-houses were built at the gates or bars where tolls were collected by the turnpike trusts between 1707 and 1836. Most are modest and, as with water-mills and park gate lodges, easily recognised for what they are. Unfortunately road widening has destroyed many; the remainder are increasingly valued.

The buildings, of one or two storeys, adjacent to the road or slightly set back, are often octagonal or with a bay or three-sided front; they had many windows so the collector or pikeman could see in all directions.

Early toll-houses were built in the vernacular. Patrick Taylor enlarges: '*Toll-houses were almost universally built of what was locally available and remain to this day useful pointers to local distinctiveness and the nature of the geology thereabouts. Thus in Plymouth we find the local Devonian limestone used, in Bath an Oolitic limestone . . . and at Todmorden in the Pennines, Millstone Grit. As eighteenth century buildings, where stone was not available, brick was usually the order of the day, so that in Cambridge we find white Gault bricks, whilst in Essex red brick and tile from the London Clay.*'

He finds that some trusts had standard designs along their routes. Four surviving examples by the Truro Trust are single-storey shale and granite with a traditional linhay or lean-to section behind. Yet in the next county, Devon, John Kanefsky found in 1976 that no two of the 83 remaining toll-houses (out of about four hundred) were the same.

Fashion crept in to style the later ones. Gothic windows are a common feature – as in the Old Toll-house near Yealmpton in Devon and Marshfield in Gloucestershire. Cottage orné toll-houses appeared – Umbrella Cottage in Lyme Regis, Dorset and at Stanton Drew, Somerset – thatched with whitewashed walls. Some resemble miniature castles, such as Barber Fields Cupola toll-house on a road junction at Ringinglow near Sheffield, Yorkshire – being octagonal and three storeys high, it dwarfs the surrounding terraced cottages.

Robert Haynes and Ivor Slocombe reckon there were about two hundred toll-houses in Wiltshire, of which fifty remained in 2004, nineteen of which are listed. Most surviving toll-houses have been converted into dwellings – some so unsympathetically it would seem the owners were ashamed of their previous use. Conversely, at The Bar in Paythorne, Yorkshire, a replica of the original polygonal toll-house was added behind.

See also COTTAGES, MILESTONES, PARK GATE LODGES, ROADS, WATER-MILLS.

411

T O P I A R Y

The wonderfully knobbly giant yew and box hedge at Audley End House in Essex and the outlines of animals or trains popping up from front garden hedges are examples of the art of clipping evergreen shrubs and trees. One example belongs to the big house and the formal garden, the other to the cottage garden and suburbia.

Topiary has a long history, reaching back at least to the Romans, who fashioned ships and hunting scenes from cypresses. We imported the idea of knot gardens and parterres – low 'hedges' of dwarf box, rosemary and myrtle, forming intricate patterns – in Tudor times from Holland, the centre of the world of topiary. Out of these grew hedge mazes and puzzle walkways, the most celebrated of which is at Hampton Court, London, commissioned by William of Orange in 1690. From Holland also came the idea of pruning trees into the shapes of animals along avenues in deer parks.

Formal gardens with obelisks, cones, cubes and pyramids trimmed out of cypress, yew and box, which look like giant chess pieces, reached their apotheosis in the reign of William and Mary before falling out of fashion with the advent of the more naturalistic form of gardening advocated by Capability Brown. Extraordinary examples of this period can be seen in the garden created in 1688 at Levens Hall in Westmorland, where clipped shapes of box and yew have taken on personalities of their own, such as the Bellingham Lion, Jugs of Morocco and Judge's Wig.

Sculptor David Nash, describing the Twmps at Powis Castle, captures the humour of the ancient topiary, part wild, part tame, all history. '*Their size and age compel us to sustain them. The amount of human time and thought that has been lavished on them creates an animated quality. They seem to float or drift about the garden like green clouds; they seem to slide down the slopes to sit on walls to enjoy the view.*'

412

The taste for topiary was revived by the Arts and Crafts movement. At the turn of the twentieth century clipped hedges were used to divide gardens into compartments, or 'rooms', of informal planting, as at Lawrence Johnston's garden at Hidcote Manor in Gloucestershire and Vita Sackville-West's Sissinghurst in Kent.

Cottage gardeners liberated topiary, fashioning quick-growing privet into the shapes of everyday objects and creatures. Roadside topiaries become local landmarks. A clipped horse looking over a garden hedge near Trumpet was memorable on journeys to Hereford in the 1980s. Charles

Sapperton, Gloucestershire.

Carey from Peckham, London, writes about his 25-year-old, seven-foot-high topiary, which has been vandalised twice and had its head chopped off. '*I saw this pathetic little tree on the pavement, which had been thrown out from the house opposite, so I planted it and it started growing . . . I thought I would clip it as an ape, the big Egyptian ape in the British Museum, so I sketched it, but then decided it would be too much hard work. So I thought I'd do a peacock. I tied wood against the vertical branch and then espaliered the branches on either side. It looked like an old-fashioned sailing ship. Then I tied the branches to more wooden stakes and hung lead weights onto the end. Eventually, as I clipped it and adjusted its shape, it started to look like a peacock. It's quite famous now. My nephew got a taxi from the city and said "Holly Grove, please", and the taxi driver said, "Would that be the house with the peacock?" Lots of people stop and ask me about it. One woman shouted from her car, "I think that's hideous, I wouldn't want it in my garden!"*'

See also COTTAGE GARDENS, HEDGES, HOLLY, PARKLAND, SCULPTURES, TURF MAZES, YEW.

T O R S

Rocky peaks take the name tor from the Celtic *twr*, which came to mean tower. They are of hard rock and are especially associated with granite exposed by weathering. The great granite bosses of Devon and Cornwall are the more memorable for the curious silhouettes that erupt from the softer moorland. Dartmoor has about 170 named tors, including Haytor, Bowerman's Nose, Vixen Tor and Hound Tor. Arthur Conan Doyle captured their foreboding aspect in *The Hound of the Baskervilles*.

Angela and Paul Brassley live near Haytor, which they recall '*always seems to have somebody standing on top, and presumably this desire goes back, because the steps cut into it and the iron handholds have clearly been there for some time*'. For them, '*probably the most significant are Haytor and Saddletor, which welcome us home after a long journey*'. Birds and butterflies also use these upstanding natural landmarks on their migrations.

For John Betjeman, '*No tor on Dartmoor is quite so impressive as the granite strewn slopes of Rough Tor [on Bodmin Moor, Cornwall] on whose summit are traces of a Christian chapel and on whose slopes are iron age hut circles and barrows and in whose neighbourhood is Stannor Stone Circle*.' He described the Cheesewring, also on Bodmin, as '*flat weather rounded boulders balanced on top of one another in such an unnatural way as to look like gigantic nodding mushrooms which will soon collapse*'.

The irregular outlines of Dartmoor's peaks differ from those of Bodmin Moor, which tend to be more compact. On the Isles of Scilly coarse-grained granite, which occurs on

the outer edges of the inland islands, has been weathered into spectacular shapes, such as Pulpit Rock at Peninnis Head on St Mary's.

The name tor is used in Derbyshire, perhaps carried here by tin miners from the South West; Mam Tor is the most prominent. In Northumberland the word crag is often substituted by torr in the granite Cheviots.

See also ARCHES, GRANITE, HEATHLAND, HILLS, KAOLIN, LANDMARKS, LANDSLIPS, LETTERBOXING, MOORLAND.

TOWER BLOCKS

Tower blocks were seen by post-war architects and planners as a solution to the urgent demand for housing and a chance to rid cities of slums. Few then questioned the impact of disrupting communities, severing old and young from the ground, destroying all trace of earlier attachments and creating wide open spaces that became windswept and soul destroying. The developments fell foul of cost-cutting and sometimes low-quality building. The collapse of Ronan Point in Canning Town, east London in 1968, and the increasing social problems that clustered around dysfunctional buildings, generated serious rethinking.

Many towers were 'system-built' and only a few were purposefully placed in their surroundings, such as the Alton Estate in Roehampton, London and Derwent Tower, known as the Dunston Rocket, in Gateshead, County Durham. Park Hill Estate in Sheffield, Yorkshire was designed to include almost a thousand flats, with pubs, shops and a community centre; much lauded by designers, it is in the process of privatisation. The Rotunda in Birmingham, built in the 1960s, a simple cylinder with clean lines and pale mosaic exterior, was designed as a landmark, as was Sheffield University's Library and Arts Tower. The notable silhouette of Goldfinger's Trellick Tower in north Kensington, London, built in 1972, has a separate lift tower linked by walkways to the main block of 31 storeys. A favourite of architects, Trellick Tower's bad reputation is changing as the residents'

association encourages improvements and accepts only people who positively want to move there.

Centre Point, an office block at the east end of Oxford Street, London, built in 1959, gained notoriety by standing empty to gather value. In London staunch defence of the skyline, especially around St Paul's Cathedral, stopped much high-rise building until the last decade of the twentieth century. The bombing of the NatWest Tower and the aftermath of the traumatic attacks on New York's World Trade Center have not stopped the commercial pressure to build high. Foster and Shuttleworth's 'Gherkin' in London has marked a sea change in popular acceptability of tall buildings, partly because of its curved shape, breaking away from the cube. New and stylish buildings, as well as thinly disguised moneymakers, are pressing for positions along the Thames.

As landmarks some have been lost without regret, but others have grown to be part of their place and would leave a hole in the skyline.

See also COMMUNICATION & RADIO MASTS, COUNCIL HOUSES, LANDMARKS, WATER-TOWERS.

413

TOWN GATES

The ways in and out of medieval towns were guarded portals in the town wall. As towns and cities expanded beyond the imagination of their medieval occupants, these gates have more often than not become ruinous remains in the town centre, as in Totnes, Devon. Traffic is diverted around Winchester's medieval West Gate in Hampshire, standing at the top of the high street. As they marked important routes, suburbs grew out from them, as in Bristol, where St John's Gateway survives. So, too, does Tower Lane, one of the lanes that followed the inside of the wall, connecting the main roads. Towns founded by the Danes around the ninth and tenth centuries might have streets called gates, but this is a distinction of language, 'gate' coming from the Old Norse *gata*, meaning road.

414

York's medieval city walls are remarkably intact, built on Viking earthen ramparts above the north and east walls of the Roman fortress. Many gates remain: the Red Tower, brick-built in the late fifteenth century; the Walmgate Bar, with its twelfth-century arch, barbican, portcullis, inner oak gates and wicket; the Micklegate Bar, meaning 'great street bar', marking the road to London, still used by vehicles.

In Northumberland Alnwick's fifteenth-century gate commemorates Harry 'Hotspur' of the influential local Percy family, and has proved an obstacle to traffic for centuries, even before the 1800s, when the Duke of Northumberland had to prevent its removal by disgruntled townsfolk.

A stretch of medieval town wall and gate survive along Hartlepool's waterfront at Fish Sands, Yorkshire, where it is more than eight feet thick. The Sandwell Gate, named after a chalybeate spring and flanked by triangular 'abutments' like breakwaters, still allows access to the beach.

London's gates have famous names: Aldgate, Bishopsgate, Cripplegate. Not one of them survived the eighteenth century. Newgate was synonymous with the notorious prison, originally housed in the gate itself. On its site stands London's Central Criminal Court – the Old Bailey. The only surviving city gate is Temple Bar, which spent a century at Theobald's Park in Hertfordshire before being returned to the city in 2004.

See also CATHEDRALS, FORTIFICATIONS, HIGH STREETS, MARKETS, SHOPS, SPRINGS, TERRACED HOUSES, TOWN HALLS & GUILD-HALLS, WALLS.

TOWN HALLS & GUILD-HALLS

At a time when 'fair value' was the ethos and quality the goal, the wealth and influence of medieval trade guilds and companies enabled them to play an important role in municipal life, not least by creating imposing buildings for their meetings and functions – Guild-halls. The half-timbered Guild-hall at Lavenham, Suffolk, now a National Trust property, was built for the Wool Guild, whose influence was strong here. Cutlers' Hall in Sheffield still grants trademarks for cutlery and plate. In London the guilds became livery companies; many still exist, as do their livery halls, ancient and modern – Apothecaries', Goldsmiths', Mercers'. The City's Guildhall was the only secular building to survive the Great Fire of 1666; its origins are uncertain and now it houses the Corporation of the City of London.

Such was the power of these organisations that they could act as local government. When elected town councils first appeared after reforms in the 1830s, they often comprised the same people who had been influential in the companies. Consequently many Guild-halls transferred their allegiance to the new authorities and became town halls, such as the striking chequered flint building of 1421 in King's Lynn, Norfolk, still the town's civic, legal and social focus.

Purpose-built town halls appeared from the seventeenth century; Abingdon's impressive town hall was built in 1678; it was then the county town of Berkshire. The new corporations sometimes called on private money: a maltster in Saffron Walden, Essex; a linoleum maker in Lancaster. Smaller towns took civic pride in their halls, as the little Gothic hall in Congleton, Cheshire shows.

Otherwise, the nineteenth century was the era of classical grandeur and the high Gothic. The great Northern town (often becoming city) halls, such as Leeds, Manchester, Bradford, Preston and Bolton, rose proudly on industrial wealth. The hall became a public place for edification and

improvement. Both Liverpool and Birmingham town halls were built essentially as venues for concerts and public meetings, with the council's business relegated to other municipal buildings. Leeds's was the first town hall to integrate both roles.

New civic identities were forged by town halls as they competed with commercial monoliths in a spirit of domineering monumentality. As Gothic faded, new influences arose: Norwich connected with Scandinavia by basing its 1930s town hall on that of Stockholm, Sweden. Its clock tower stands like a beacon and the classical portico opens onto the market square.

See also BRICKS, CLOCKS, MARKETS.

TREE DRESSING DAY

The decorating of trees is prevalent in many cultures throughout the world. Here, on and around the first weekend in December, trees in towns and villages are offered winter plumage. Tree Dressing Day is a recent addition to the calendar, challenging people to share their traditions to invent a festival in which young and old, professional and amateur can share in a social celebration of the trees in the street or on the green. This multicultural community expression for everyday nature already includes music, dance, poetry and storytelling, as well as the hanging of ribbons, shapes, shining lights – anything that draws attention to the trees we take for granted.

It began in 1990, when, to show that 'every tree counts', 150 large, cut-out numbers were hung, with the help of tree surgeons, on a group of three London plane trees at the junction of Shaftesbury Avenue and High Holborn in Covent Garden, London. This launched Common Ground's Tree Dressing Day; since then local communities, authorities, schools, colleges, arts groups, hotels, parks departments, health centres, theatres and sheltered homes have taken part, organising colourful hangings or simply gathering to read with candles under their favourite trees in the public domain.

See also ALDER, ANCIENT TREES, ARBOR DAY, ASH, BAWMING THE THORN, BEECH, BIRCH, BLACK POPLAR, ELM, FIELD MAPLE, GREEN MAN, GROVELY RIGHTS DAY, HAZEL, HOLLY, HOLM OAK, HORNBEAM, HORSE CHESTNUT, LANDMARK TREES, LIME, LONDON PLANE, MONKEY-PUZZLE, OAK, ORCHARDS, PEARS, POPLAR, ROWAN, ROYAL FORESTS, SCOTS PINE, SWEET CHESTNUT, SYCAMORE, WALNUT, WASSAILING, WELLS, WHITEBEAM, WILLOW, WOODS, YEW.

TUNNELS

Many towns have stories of underground labyrinths and secret passages, most uncorroborated. In some cases, as at Frome in Somerset, their history, purpose and even extent are unknown. Many are thought to be refuges and escapes, from priest holes to smugglers' ways. In Nottingham, through pre-Conquest caves, medieval cellars, fish tanks, conduits and tunnels in the sandstone, it is said you might make your way from below the castle in the south to the north side of the city.

Brunel's straight railway tunnel at Box, Wiltshire was for some time the longest in the world at one mile, 452 yards; the sun is said to shine through its east end on Brunel's birthday. Box also has miles of former underground quarry workings turned into a mysterious tunnel complex of military stores, strongholds for national treasures and nuclear bolt-holes for government and monarchy. Portsdown in Hampshire and Dover in Kent have similarly clandestine underground establishments, but, as they have become tourist attractions, we can only surmise that there are yet others, which remain sternly classified. Many redundant tunnels have become vital roosts for bats.

To plunge into darkness is a pleasant surprise on country lanes, as on William Beckford's former estate near Fonthill Bishop, Wiltshire, where the woodland continues overhead. But it seems a long and dripping haul through the foot tunnels beneath the Thames at Greenwich and Woolwich in south-east London, which are marked by characteristic circular, brick light wells at their shaft heads. At least one isn't upside down, walking the roof, as the old canal navigators had to do. Some roads cross below rivers, as under the Tyne near South Shields, County Durham and

415

the Mersey at Queensway and Kingsway in Liverpool. After a century of plans for a Channel tunnel, Folkestone was eventually linked with mainland Europe in 1990, a feat of engineering drawing on the knowledge of its predecessors great and small.

See also BUILDING STONES, CANALS, CAVES, THE CHANNEL, FORTIFICATIONS, LEAD MINES, QUARRIES, RHUBARB, ROADS, SEA CAVES, SOUGHS, THE UNDERGROUND, WELLS.

TURF MAZES

Turf mazes (labyrinths with but one route to the centre) are peculiar to England. Their single, convoluted path stands up by a few inches in the turf, with earth or chalk shining white, in between.

Out of some sixty known, only eight have survived, for example at Alkborough (Julian's Bower) in Lincolnshire, Dalby near York, Wing in Rutland, Troy Farm in Oxfordshire, Breamore – with its miz maze – in Hampshire and Hilton village green in Cambridge. The maze at Saffron Walden common in Essex, 114 feet across and nearly five thousand feet to the middle, dates from at least the seventeenth century.

St Agnes, one of the Isles of Scilly in Cornwall, has a pebble maze, similar to ones found in Scandinavia. There are also labyrinthine floor patterns near some Roman remains, as at Oldcotes in Nottinghamshire and Harpham in east Yorkshire.

The name Troy or Troy Town is suggestive of their presence. Examples include the settlements of Troy, south of Leeds-Bradford airport in Yorkshire, and Troy Town in Kent, as well as the farm name off the A35, south of Puddletown in Dorset, and a street name off Peckham Rye

in south-east London. Reference is made to New Troy (in the twelfth century, by the fanciful Geoffrey of Monmouth) as a very early name for London.

See also AEGIRS, ALBION, CHALK, GIANTS, HILL FIGURES, ISLANDS, MORRIS DANCING, SCULPTURES, TOPIARY.

TURNING THE DEVIL'S STONE

On 5 November the bell-ringers of Shebbear in Devon make a real mess of ringing the church bells; they then emerge from St Michael's and, taking crowbars, literally turn over a great boulder beneath an old oak just beyond the east side of the churchyard. This secures safety for the village during the coming year. Perhaps the custom has shifted from Hallowe'en, when evil is at its closest, for the stories suggest that the stone belongs to the devil, that he lies beneath it, or that he dropped it, or that it kept being moved here when they were trying to build the foundations of a nearby church.

At about three feet high, four broad and six long, the Devil's Stone is of exotic, quartz-rich conglomerate. How it came to this place no one knows (ice never reached here), but the building of the church and its dedication to St Michael, traditionally the great adversary of the devil, suggests it has long been a powerful pagan presence here. The church bells and the turning of the stone seem to work. Only once, during the First World War, was the ceremony omitted, and malevolence stalked the parish for the year.

See also BELLS & BELL-RINGING, BONFIRE NIGHT, CHURCHES, DEVIL, HALLOWE'EN, STANDING STONES.

Wing, Rutland.

Vegas, David Quay, 1984.

THE UNDERGROUND

Birmingham's New Street Station has subterranean depths, and the stretches of the Tyne and Wear Metro extended under Newcastle and Gateshead city centres in the 1970s negotiated abandoned mine workings. Underground railways in England, though, are almost entirely associated with London and its historic network. The cut-and-cover lines that rattle under the streets began with the Metropolitan in 1863. Later came the deep 'tubes', the earliest now part of the Northern line, the second the Waterloo and City, known as The Drain. The East London line has a longer history, being partially constructed in Marc Brunel's pedestrian tunnel under the Thames of 1843.

Tube building boomed in the early twentieth century and had a resurgence with the Victoria line in the late 1960s and the Jubilee line from 1979 to 1999. In its early days, and again more recently, the London Underground has used high-quality design to establish itself as one of London's – and, by extension, England's – most enduring icons.

The references are manifold: the famous red logo, the 'roundel' with its horizontal bar, based on the spiked wheel of the London General Bus Company and introduced to stations in 1908; Edward Johnston's Underground font of 1916, designed in collaboration with Eric Gill; Harry Beck's iconic map of 1933, the basis of metro maps the world over and embarkation point for countless souvenirs and even art works (Simon Patterson's *The Great Bear*, 1997).

The stations stand out even if disused, particularly Leslie W. Green's ox-blood tile façades, with their characteristic arches, from 1905 to 1906. Or Charles Holden's Art Deco work of the 1920s and 1930s, on the Northern line from Clapham Common to Morden (of Portland stone) and the Piccadilly line through Southgate, Arnos Grove and Sudbury Town. The quality of the tile work and the choice of different colours for the stations, to be 'read' by people who were illiterate, were all part of the early vision, which was institutionally vandalised in the 1980s, beautiful tiled walls being drilled to hang cheap signs and cladding that soon deteriorated. A new generation of stations on the Jubilee line has once more lifted quality, as at Canary Wharf and Westminster.

Places are known by their tube station – Mornington Crescent has taken centre stage of late. Hampstead has the deepest station at 192 feet, no fun when the lifts break down – and they do. The age of the Northern line is showing; we know it as the Misery line. It has further excuse, carrying more than 660,000 passengers on the average weekday in 2004 through its 36 miles and fifty stations. The Tube system carries three million passengers on a normal weekday.

See *also* BUSES, RAILWAYS, TUNNELS.

419

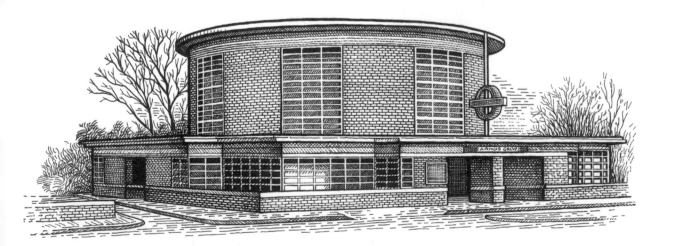

Russell Square, London; Arnos Grove, London.

U N L U C K Y   W O R D S

The Isle of Portland has the feel of an ancient and introspective place, but it shares a strange secret. The word ra**it
is never used by indigenous people. Portland stories suggest
that conies abandoning the warrens behind Chesil Beach,
set up by monks in the twelfth century, were forecasting
inundation by the sea – until recently a terrifying prospect
for Chiswell. Preferred terms are furry creatures and underground mutton (fear does not extend to eating them: a
butcher from Fortuneswell started the Portland Ra**it
Club during the Second World War). Since the islanders do
so much quarrying, another explanation hinges on animals
portending danger of rockfalls.

But fishermen in Craster and some families in other
Northumbrian villages have the same problem. Is this an
ancient prejudice – fear and superstition carried coastwise
from far away? Katrina Porteous, working as a visiting poet
on Shetland, found the same avoidance, and Robert Graves
mentioned the fisher folk of the Scottish islands steering
clear of the word. He pointed out that the two sacred and
tabooed beasts mentioned in Leviticus and native here are
the hare and the pig.

Although the hare may be indigenous and carries with
it much folklore and superstition, the ra**it was brought
here by the Romans. Around Flamborough in Yorkshire
mention of either word would have put paid to the day's
fishing in the nineteenth century.

Across Europe the word p*g carries much ill luck;
anciently it was held to presage thunder, lightning and
big winds. One can understand, then, how mention of its
name at sea would be an ill omen. In the North East alternative names include grunt, article, minister, gadgy ('old
man', Holy Island), John Alec (Seahouses), guffy or grice
(Beadnell) and gissie (Newcastle). Ra**its, too, are avoided
in Beadnell, where they are called caldies.

Fishing, quarrying and mining demand that men
(women are unlucky, too) risk their lives every day in ways
most of us cannot imagine, providing good reason to be
alert, to have fears. These are among the oldest of activities
– do they also share some history, trading culture across
land and sea?

See also BESTIARY, BUNS, DIALECTS, HARES, MINES, PIGS, QUARRIES, SEA
FISH, WARRENS.

V A C C A R Y   W A L L S

From the Latin for cow, vaccary walls were made from stones
vertically placed, useful for keeping less agile animals at
bay. They are found where the geology affords easy clefting
of big slabs, such as around Ambleside, Westmorland and
Hawkshead, Lancashire, where the fields look as though

they are edged with ranks of handsome gravestones. Brathay
flags are often used like this in the Lake District.

Testimony to heavy work and local knowledge, this
'shard walling' possibly dates from monastic times (shard
here may derive from the Old Frisian *skerd*, meaning a cut
or notch). In this area the slaty slabs, standing three feet
high, are bevelled at the top and embedded in the earth with
the edges notched together, whereas elsewhere in the Lake
District, and in north Cornwall, wire is sometimes used to
secure the tops to one another.

See also CATTLE, DRYSTONE WALLS, SHEEP, SHINERS.

V E R G E S

The green estate alongside Britain's roads covers some
523,000 acres – the size of Surrey. In pre-enclosure England
highways and their verges were part of the common land of
the manor, forming a valuable resource – sheep still graze
along the unfenced roadsides of the uplands. Along droves,
verges sustained livestock on their way to market; in south-
east Norfolk 'narrow' or 'street' commons and greens are
visible remnants of a linear network of grazing verges. Road
verges might be wide for other reasons, too: in the clay-
rich areas ways grew wider as travellers struggled to avoid
the ruts. Early nineteenth-century estate maps show cigar-
shaped fields lining the roads, as enterprising small farmers
claimed bits of the verge for themselves.

Traditionally cut for hay, grazed, or scythed by parish
'lengthmen', verges are now refuges for ancient hay-meadow
flowers, such as dyer's greenwood and spiny restharrow
– both are more likely to be found by a road than in their
original home in the fields – as well as cowslip, knapweed,
rockrose and hay-rattle. Primrose banks are eagerly watched
out for, orchid verges jealously guarded. When cow-parsley
blooms, motorists know that summer has arrived.

V

Across the chalklands of the South, roads are edged with downland refugees; in the Weald ancient sunken lanes through steep sandstone banks shelter a rich woodland flora of delicate mosses and ferns. Eroded over hundreds of years by generations of feet, hooves, cartwheels and water, these hollow ways have acquired strong characters. On the Surrey greensand their verges carry some of the county's rarest hawkweeds and orchids. Quiet Herefordshire lanes sport primrose, stitchwort, bluebell, red campion and, later, perhaps harebells. Devon lanes add bastard balm; those in Gloucestershire's Severn vale support lady's smock. Fovant, Wiltshire is memorable for its lupins.

On the Lizard Peninsula in Cornwall trackways with hedge banks harbour wild madder, navelwort and three-cornered leek. Puddles in cart-tracks across the Cornish moorland support a rare and tiny rush – its life cycle depends upon a vehicle using the ancient track just once or twice a year. Perennial flax is a good sign of a Roman road on chalk or limestone verges; it grows along Ermine Street and the A11, just north of Stump Cross, a 'Romanised' stretch of the Icknield Way marking the Essex/Cambridgeshire boundary.

Not long ago the Highways Agency routinely seeded new road verges with imported 'wildflower mixtures' – a practised eye can still spot the bold ox-eye daisies from eastern Europe along many a town bypass. In recent years, however, the best road schemes have been 'greened' with locally sourced stock. In places, more enlightened regimes are also replacing weed-killer spraying or mechanical mowing at the wrong times of year. In east Sussex sixteen miles of road verge are marked with special 'wildlife verge' posts, monitored by volunteers and managed for birds, butterflies and bumblebees; three such verges harbour spiked rampion, found almost nowhere else in the country.

See also ALEXANDERS, CHALK, COMMONS, DROVE ROADS, FERNS, GRASSY TRIANGLES, GREEN LANES, GREENSAND, GYPSIES, HOLLOW WAYS, MOSSES, ROADS, WILDFLOWERS.

VIADUCTS

Canals used aqueducts; railways, with a similar dislike of gradients, use viaducts – dramatic stone or brick arched ways over valleys and combes. Yorkshire's Ribblehead on the Settle to Carlisle line is perhaps the most famous, its 24 arches typically looking more impressive to the remote observer.

The closure of many rail lines, especially since the 1960s, has resulted in redundant viaducts. Many have gone, such as the extended brick arches across the Erewash valley on the Nottinghamshire/Derbyshire border. Despite the expense, some have been sold into private hands, others left to deteriorate. The affection that they now inspire contrasts with the protests that accompanied their original building. The Rowsley Viaduct in Derbyshire is now part of the Monsal Trail, much loved by walkers and cyclists. When it was built in 1863 John Ruskin famously declared that the valley was 'gone': 'and now, every fool in Buxton can be at Bakewell in half-an-hour, and every fool in Bakewell at Buxton; which you think a lucrative process of exchange – you Fools everywhere'.

421

Ribblehead Viaduct, Yorkshire.

Lowry's painting of Stockport viaduct in Cheshire reminds us of the domineering impact of a structure 110 feet high and 22 arches long in the centre of town. In the city lower arches usually find working uses, as behind London's King's Cross and St Pancras Stations.

Roads also use viaducts to cross valleys and marshy basins. One carries the A36 across the valley of the Midford brook at Limpley Stoke, Wiltshire, giving its name to the pub at its northern end. The railway at Kingskerswell, Devon is itself crossed by a viaduct, designed by Brunel.

The flat lands of the East have no need of viaducts; their speciality is level crossings.

See also AQUEDUCTS, BRICKS, BUILDING STONES, CANALS, CYCLING, FOOTPATHS, LANDMARKS, RAILWAYS, ROADS, STATIONS.

VILLAGE GREENS

Parking, lighting, road widening, building, playgrounds and more lie in wait for the unsuspecting village green. And yet this tranquil, social place should belong to everyone, locally at least, as it has for perhaps fifteen hundred years for '*lawful sports and pastimes*'. Many greens are commons and may technically be in the hands of the lord of the manor or the local authority, with rights shared to some degree.

The quintessential English village scene involves sunshine, pub and cricket on the green. And, given that greens are more common in the East and South, this is often the case. About a third of our village greens are in Bedfordshire, Berkshire, Buckinghamshire, Essex, Hertfordshire, Middlesex and Surrey. Some seem to have originated as clearings in the woods, but in the last two centuries many have been swallowed by extending cities and towns.

Hertfordshire sports more than a hundred greens, often triangular, as at Cottered and Northaw. The names 'green' and 'end' appear frequently, as at Potterne End, Peter's Green and Perry Green. Sandon had nine greens. Sarratt's green has a pond, useful on Bonfire Night.

Hampshire's greens are often large. Hartley Wintney once had eleven; those remaining, some with enormous oak trees, have room for everything, including Cricketers Green and Phoenix Green, which extends to 65 acres. Mellis Green in Suffolk is a mile long and runs to 174 acres.

Around the Broads, the Fens, east Lincolnshire and east Yorkshire they are infrequent. But large numbers are found further north. The many village greens of County Durham are rectangular and of great size, and most are aligned east–west; both suggest a north European origin. Cumberland had 86 greens in 1961, Northumberland 42. In the North York Moors the Quaker village of Hutton-le-Hole is a classic calendar village, with scattered cottages overlooking the slopes and stream of the white-fenced common. By contrast, Milburn in Westmorland is formally

gathered around a rectangle of green, perhaps to offer refuge for animals against weather or wolves.

Sometimes the blacksmith's shop was built on the green; churches situated away from the green suggest their younger age. Maybe a pond or two are kept puddled for grazing animals (as at Frampton on Severn in Gloucestershire). The village pump or pant often still stands, and also the pub, hard by for drink after tug o' war, May Day celebrations, gala, fête or local sports.

See also ANCIENT TREES, BACK LANES, BONFIRE NIGHT, BUTTS, CHURCHES, COTTAGE GARDENS, COTTAGES, CRICKET, GAMES, MAY DAY, PANTS, PARISH MAPS, PARKLAND, PLACE-NAMES, PONDS, ROADS, SPRINGS, VILLAGE HALLS, VILLAGES.

VILLAGE HALLS

Almost nine thousand village halls are used for public meetings, pantomimes, yoga classes, wedding receptions, horticultural shows, band practice, play groups, church services and itinerant doctor's surgeries. They are often the cultural heart of a community, and the most interesting demonstrate a pride in being where they are.

Reading rooms and village rooms were often the gift of generous benefactors and reflect high-quality craftsmanship and local materials. In Teesdale, County Durham, Eggleston village hall was built in 1887 (by the London Lead Company) as a Mechanics' Institute reading and lecture room; Copley's as a Literary Institute in 1898; Hamsterley's converted from an 1822 school in 1967. But inexpensive buildings can take on local pride and personality – off-the-peg corrugated-iron halls, for example, continue to attract local respect and care in some places, such as the green ex-fever hospital, now the village hall, at Wolverley, Worcestershire. Alderholt's reading room in Hampshire, overhung by trees, looks down at heel and vulnerable, yet its very unpretentiousness is the reason to value it.

Many village halls were built or converted as part of the local response to national celebrations. Land was perhaps gifted with money or loans from local notables and much fundraising activity from the wider community. Norton-in-Hales, Shropshire opened its first village hall in 1926; it cost

Crookham, Hampshire.

£72 plus construction as a recycled corrugated-iron hut. In 1979 this was replaced by the brick Jubilee Hall.

After the First and Second World Wars many villages chose to remember their dead by building new halls. Crookham War Memorial Hall in Hampshire has a distinctive curved roof, built after 1945 with an almost military look; the village neighbours the barracks of Nissen huts used latterly by the Gurkha regiment. The Gurkhas have gone now and the land has been sold to housing developers, leaving the hall's future uncertain.

In the 1980s and 1990s large grants were made available to parish and town councils to build new village halls. But opportunities were missed to refurbish an existing building or to aspire to designs that reinforce local distinctiveness.

The simple but charming 1930s wooden village hall at Fifehead Magdalen in Dorset contrasts much with some of the new impositions, which could be anywhere and seem to be all car park. Fontmell Magna in Dorset, however, has a handsome new hall in local stone with fine facilities.

Some are taking a social and environmental lead: Woolfardisworthy sports and community hall in Devon is built to be energy efficient, using natural materials, non-toxic paints and varnishes, with rain-water collection, water-saving devices and recycling facilities. North Moor Village Hall in Oxfordshire has solar panels and feeds its surplus electricity into the national grid. ACRE (Action with Communities in Rural England) provides a village hall information service and helps raise awareness of their value.

See also BRICKS, BUILDING STONES, CORRUGATED IRON, THATCH, TOWN HALLS & GUILD-HALLS, VILLAGE GREENS.

V I L L A G E S

What we love about villages was captured by H.J. Massingham during his sojourn through *English Downland*: 'How effortlessly each of them preserves a particular identity of its own! The smaller they are, the more isolated, the more isolated the flintier. The richer they are in little undemonstrative mannerisms of tile-hanging and weather-boarding, and the readier to avail themselves of the immemorial material of the chalk at their doors, the more vital is their personality . . . They are as true to their downs as are the ringed citadels of those hill-people slaughtered by their founders.'

Villages seem old, by virtue of their materials, which are 'true' to their place, and because of the way they sit in the land and have done for perhaps hundreds of years. Capitals of their parishes, villages are small settlements, generally with church, perhaps with pub, shop and chapel, although increasingly these have become residences.

They have many origins, rooted in economic and cultural activities as well as physical fortune. The reasons for their existence may be long gone, perhaps even the spring or ford,

mineral wealth, agriculture, fishing, certainly the garrison, are lost. Some cling on despite being overwhelmed by a major road or being enmeshed in development; some, on the other hand, revel in being seen as villages in the city – Dulwich, Greenwich and Hampstead, for example, in London.

Villages are typical of the lower lands; in the old open field areas of the Midlands, especially, nucleated villages predominate. In the uplands the patterns tend towards hamlets and scattered farms. Many village settlements are probably older even than their names suggest, and most carry names from Anglo-Saxon or Romano-British times. Observers continue to mine the names, situations and shapes for clues. Their morphology is infinitely varied, but broad patterns can be seen: long, thin street villages, nucleated villages, square or green villages gathered around small or large commons, and all manner of squatted or loosely scattered settlements.

Ashmore, high on the chalk in Dorset, may be a Romano-British settlement still clustered round its pond. Long Melford in Suffolk states its case, but Combe Martin, Devon claims to be the longest village in England on its Parish Map. It has extended down the narrow valley for more than a mile to the sea. Straggling villages along Norfolk rivers are the result of each house needing a long, thin holding to link the transport potential of both watercourse and street.

Estate villages comprise buildings eerily of the same moment – sanitised, unreal visions of the picturesque. Some were the result of clearing the view. Milton Abbas village in Dorset replaced the market town of more than a hundred houses that was removed out of sight of the manor by Baron Milton in the late eighteenth century. Its detached and semi-detached white, thatched houses formally front a single street with open lawns. Edensor, Derbyshire, with its elaborately chimneyed and strangely diverse villas, was designed by Paxton to leave Chatsworth House an open prospect.

Villages serving single industries spontaneously grew around mine, pottery or brick works, as along the Medway in Kent. Some were planned and orderly, as at Ironville in Derbyshire. Villages notable for houses with extensive upper windows speak of home weavers, as at Golcar, Yorkshire, and frame knitters, in Ockbrook, Derbyshire.

Model villages emerged to offer better living conditions first for agricultural and then industrial workers. Paternalism and philanthropy made for tied workers but better living conditions, too. Enlightened industrialists, especially Quakers, made their utopian ideals a reality. In Worcestershire Cadbury's model village of Bournville, with its low-density detached housing, gardens and greens, influenced Joseph Rowntree of York to build New Earswick in 1902/3. He sought to address the social and physical problems of poverty, offering independence as well as health, air and light. Reckitt created his Garden Village in Hull; Lever Port Sunlight on the Wirral; Crittall made Silver

423

End in Essex and Vickers built Vickerstown in Barrow-in-Furness, Lancashire.

New villages now appear out of desperate national housing policies and pressure from house builders, few of which work hard to add to quality and local distinctiveness. A growing movement interested in self-build, community making and/or eco-credentials is inventing new aesthetics and dynamics, from the Lightmoor self-build community in Shropshire to BedZed (architect Bill Dunster) in Sutton, Surrey, which provides housing, work space and community facilities for a hundred people.

'Real' villages evolve, adapt, change, reinvent vitality. The challenge we now face is ensuring that places are neither coated in aspic nor overwhelmed, their authenticity eroded by tidiness, absence or housing targets.

See also BRICKS, BRIDGES, BUILDING STONES, CHALK, CHURCHES, COB, COTTAGE GARDENS, COTTAGES, DESERTED VILLAGES, DOWNLAND, FIELDS, FLINT, FORDS, HILL-FORTS, LOST VILLAGES, PARISH MAPS, PARKLAND, PLACE-NAMES, PUBS, ROADS, SPRINGS, TERRACED HOUSES, THATCH, VILLAGE GREENS, VILLAGE HALLS.

V I L L A G E   S I G N S

The first decorative village signs were commissioned in 1912 for four villages on the Sandringham estate in Norfolk. After the Second World War the Women's Institutes in Norfolk took up the cause and raised funds for the design and production of permanent signs that depict some memorable event, legend, person or landmark. Harry Carter, a woodcarver from Swaffham, made more than two hundred village and town signs in Norfolk between the 1950s and 1970s, and some for neighbouring counties as well.

There are now more than a thousand village signs across the country, most in East Anglia. The designs and subject matter are varied, many documented by Ken Savage, a founder member of the Village Sign Society. Some are

carved in wood, some cut out of metal. Everthorpe in east Yorkshire has three stone signs on each of the main roads entering the village, carved in bas-relief by sculptor Fiona Bowley. Pulham St Mary, Norfolk has a metal sign depicting the R33 airship below some large, white fluffy clouds. Barges, wherries, the Suffolk Punch and round-towered churches also feature in East Anglian signs. Milden in Suffolk has a six-foot-high cast-iron reproduction of a fat hen plant, which gave the settlement its name – *melde* in Old English.

Signs are sometimes there for the using. The name-plate from the old Southern region railway station at Paddock Wood in Kent has been affixed to an old sleeper and used as the village sign; it comes with a built-in history.

See also BISCUITS, EASTER CUSTOMS, FINGERPOSTS, MILESTONES, ROUND-TOWERED CHURCHES, SUFFOLK PUNCHES, VILLAGE GREENS, VILLAGES.

V I N E Y A R D S

Geology and climate shape the fortunes of England's vineyards. Ancient and modern, most lie south east of a line from the Humber to the Severn. Romans' grapes thrived in Lincolnshire, but the colder temperatures of the Little Ice Age in the fourteenth century confined viticulture to the South East, where a few struggled to produce drinkable wines. In recent decades, however, warmer summers have fostered a renaissance.

Slopes facing east of south capture the most sunlight in the crucial October days of final ripening, and offer the best shelter from the prevailing westerly winds. Vineyards are best planted half-way up a slope in the 'thermal zone', avoiding both cold winds and frost hollows. Dry valleys in chalk downland are particularly favoured – Breaky Bottom in Sussex is a fine example, offering competition for Champagne. At Painshill Park in Cobham, Surrey an artificial lake below the vineyard reflects sunshine up the well-drained slope, warming the vines, which were first planted here in 1738.

Today England boasts some 250 vineyards, including Mount Pleasant in Lancashire. The river terraces of the Thames and the southern shores of the Severn estuary have been recolonised. At Pilton, Somerset, along the southern slopes of the Mendip Hills, a region favoured since late Saxon times is producing wine once again. New wine lands have appeared, too, notably the Weald – now the heartland of the modern wine industry – and sheltered slopes in Devon and Cornwall. If global warming continues, within a few decades the Derbyshire Peak District may produce wines akin to Greek vintages. Vineyards may yet appear on the shores of Wast Water and Ullswater in Cumberland and Westmorland, with vines on south-easterly slopes warmed by the lakes below.

See also DOWNLAND, FROST & FROST HOLLOWS, HILLS, ORCHARDS.

Kimberley, Norfolk; Mildenhall, Suffolk.

W

W

Waterloo Bold, Alan Meeks, 1987.

WALLFLOWERS

True to their name, wallflowers – particularly the wild forms, which are yellow and deep orange – are a feature of old walls, ruins and buildings, such as the high, buttressed walls of Gold Hill in Shaftesbury, Dorset. Originally they were brought from the eastern Mediterranean in the Middle Ages, perhaps together with Caen stone. According to Oliver Gilbert, it can take forty to eighty years for flowering plants to appear on the tops of cement-mortared walls – less time in the West, where conditions are more favourable. Wallflowers prefer limestone walls or *wall-tops where a shallow mortar-rich soil is developing. Once established, their seeds are dispersed by ants*, he wrote.

Wallflowers have always been prized for their delicious fragrance; Richard Mabey delighted in the story that they were deliberately planted into the walls of castles and manor houses in the hope that their scent would drift indoors.

See also ABBEYS, CASTLES, COTTAGE GARDENS, FERNS, LIMESTONE, WALLS.

WALLS

Boundary walls of brick or stone provide a structural and unifying form to gardens and streets. They reveal the local geology – or used to, before the arrival of dull composition stone, concrete screen blocks and imported brick.

England's climate is *conducive to the development of a luxuriant wall flora*, Oliver Gilbert wrote, north-facing aspects producing more plants than the south sides. Plants that colonise these difficult vertical habitats include yellow corydalis and various spleenworts, but, according to Gilbert, *no two towns have an identical range of plants*. Suburban walls built until about 1870 were constructed with lime mortar, softer and more readily colonised by wallflowers and others than the hard cement that replaced it. Navelwort insinuates itself into walls in the wetter West, with the more flamboyant red valerian and ferns, such as rusty back and common spleenwort, many lichens and mosses.

Village design guides and Parish Maps invariably pay homage to walls, exhort their retention and suggest that new ones are constructed using local materials. Yet garden walls, indeed front gardens, are under constant threat from car-parking, and, even where they knit together the town or village, few are listed. The importance of the detail is understood locally. We let people speak for themselves:

'Essential to the village character . . . are the many garden and field walls built up around the buildings. In places these define the winding edges of the lanes in a manner special to Wiveton. They are built in the main with coursed beach flints

and have simple flint copings. Where age has weathered them and allowed native plants to grow between the joints they symbolise perfectly the balance between the built and natural world, which is the special feature of Wiveton's character.'* Wiveton, north Norfolk.

'Great Bowden is well known for its old brick walls (many still exist, built of local Bowden bricks). These walls come in a variety of heights, and many still have the traditional (rounded) coping.' Great Bowden Village Design Statement, Leicestershire.

'Irregular stone walls form edges to gardens and building boundaries, usually topped by a distinctive "cock and hen" random stone capping, or occasionally stone copings with wrought-iron railings above. The grander the building, the more elaborate the boundary treatment. The walls around St Mary's Church are topped with unusual black slag block copings, a by-product of the eighteenth-century brass industry around Bristol.' Parish of Olveston Design Statement, south Gloucestershire.

'Blue lias . . . is common to all the old walls . . . there is considerable variety in their height, type of coping and style of gate pier . . . The majority have the traditional "cock and hen" coping, which often required considerable skill, employing as it did very fine joints and stones of consistent size and shape – detailing not often found in modern attempts at this type of construction.' Design Statement for the Parish of Charlton Mackrell, Somerset.

In the South West walls of cob roofed in thatch are not uncommon; these and tile-topped walls indicate the need to protect the walling material. E.G. Meadows wrote of Haddenham in Buckinghamshire: *'The place is noted for walls of wichert, marl with water and chopped straw built up in layers on a stone base and rendered when dry. Garden walls were capped with thatch or tiles.'*

See also BUILDING STONES, CHALK, COB, DRYSTONE WALLS, FENCES, FERNS, FORTIFICATIONS, LICHENS, MOSSES, PAVEMENTS, QUARRIES, RAILINGS, STRAW, THATCH, TILES, WALLFLOWERS.

WALNUT

The new sign in Kempston Town, Bedfordshire depicts a walnut tree, which is strange, since most were lost in a storm in the 1900s. Their significance was marked: in the 1880s the football team was called the Walnut Boys. Not many places are associated with the common walnut, brought here by the Romans (*wealh* – foreign) together with the sweet chestnut.

427

The Romans valued 'the mast of Jove' for its nuts and the topaz oil it produced. Later, walnut trees were planted in monastery gardens, farmhouse gardens, orchards and the parks and gardens of large houses. By 1664 known plantings in the North Downs of Surrey had been cut down, leading John Evelyn to champion walnuts in his book, *Sylva*. He set a good example by planting many on his family estates around Godstone, probably later felled for use as a veneer in cabinet making, marquetry and for the butts and stocks of rifles and guns used in the Napoleonic Wars.

Walnut trees are a feature of the vales of Dunster and Porlock on Exmoor, especially in the villages of Allerford and Bossington. Planted in the eighteenth century, they are no doubt orchard and parkland remnants.

Until recently there was only one known walnut plantation, seventeen acres on a farm near Colchester, Essex, the last of the experimental plantings of the 1920s. There has recently been a resurgence of interest in growing walnuts for their timber, oil and nuts – which are enjoyed green (wet), dried and pickled – from the Forestry Commission and others. The Northmoor Trust near Abingdon, Oxfordshire and the Walnut Club are promoting its conservation and growing. The largest walnut grove has been planted for the car maker Jaguar at Lount, Leicestershire, in the National Forest.

The walnut is a handsome, long-lived tree, which can grow to between eighty and a hundred feet. Nuts taken and dropped by rooks may account for some of the unusual locations of this tree in the South.

See also ALDER, ANCIENT TREES, ASH, BEECH, BIRCH, BLACK POPLAR, BLACKTHORN, COBNUTS, ELM, FIELD MAPLE, FOOTBALL, FROST & FROST HOLLOWS, HAWTHORN, HAZEL, HOLLY, HOLM OAK, HORNBEAM, HORSE CHESTNUT, JUNIPER, LANDMARK TREES, LIME, LONDON PLANE, MONKEY-PUZZLE, OAK, ORCHARDS, PARKLAND, PEARS, POPLAR, ROOKERIES, ROWAN, ROYAL FORESTS, SCOTS PINE, SWEET CHESTNUT, SYCAMORE, WHITEBEAM, WILLOW, WINDSOR & COUNTRY CHAIRS, WOODS, XANADU, YEW.

WAREHOUSES

Mills, factories and warehouses were buildings of stature in the eighteenth and nineteenth centuries. They are increasingly finding favour for new uses, being attractive and well built, embedded and understood, as well as embodying local memories. Warehouses keep company with docks, canals and railways and Victorian industrial towns, and are particularly fine in the textile towns of Lancashire and Yorkshire, such as Manchester, Leeds, Bradford, Dewsbury and Batley. Many have been lost to fire, bombed or demolished.

Manchester's imposing brick warehouses were not just store-rooms, but places where buyers came to look at and buy goods. From the 1840s they were often built in a grand style known as Italian palazzo, which was later replicated in other parts of the country. In Yorkshire, Bradford's limestone warehouses served its wool-textile industry. Many were demolished in the 1960s and 1970s, but some survive in Little Germany, the twenty-acre quarter inhabited by German wool merchants in the nineteenth century, and are undergoing regeneration. The grand façades of Batley, designed to greet buyers, created, as Mark Girouard said, *'a city of palaces even if the palaces have fallen on hard days'*.

Liverpool's docks and warehouses were built to serve its position as a pre-eminent trading city, the tall brick warehouses storing a wide variety of goods, from tea, sugar, spices and rice to silks, cotton, wool and tobacco. The early warehouses were three to six storeys high and built of mud-brown brick, with distinctive, inset central loading doors and overhanging timber hoist beams below the roof. With timber floors and stanchions, many succumbed to fire, so iron began to replace wood in vulnerable places.

Anthony Lyster's fourteen-storey tobacco warehouse on Stanley Dock, built between 1897 and 1901 with hydraulic lifts, was reputed at the time to be the largest in the world. Also enormous were the bonded fire-proof warehouses

Butlers Wharf, London.

428

built by Jesse Hartley around Albert, Stanley and Wapping Docks. These monuments to trade were recognised with Liverpool's designation as a World Heritage City in 2004, which should help to conserve its industrial heritage and buildings. Many of the surviving 150 or so warehouses need to be refurbished and new uses found for them, without destroying their distinctive characters.

Dutch and Flemish styles are visible in warehouses lining Great Yarmouth's Hall Quay and South Quay in Norfolk, at the confluence of the rivers Yare, Bure and Waveney. In the West Country 'Bristol Byzantine' was coined to describe the north Italian influence on this city's nineteenth-century warehouses. Fifteen tall, yellow-brick warehouses surround the canal basin at Gloucester docks; built to store grain and iron, they are now being redeveloped into antiques emporia, apartments, cafés and shops.

The Thames and the London docks were lined with warehouses. They were usually less impressive than in the northern cities, and many were lost to wartime bombing and post-war redevelopment. Narrow lanes that squeeze between tall, utilitarian buildings are typified by Clink Street and Shad Thames in Southwark and by Wapping Wall on the north bank of the river. Elsewhere city enclaves, such as Clerkenwell and Smithfield, notable for their surviving warehouses, are much sought after for the personality that their age, quality and density brings. The area to the north of the Piazza in Covent Garden was full of fruit and vegetable warehouses. Some were demolished, but, following enormous local and national effort, much of the area was saved from comprehensive redevelopment in the 1970s. In all these examples the buildings and narrow streets have proved adaptable for large and small lofts, flats, studios, offices, galleries, cafés and shops. Many still flaunt their original names, owners or functions.

See also CANALS, FACTORIES, HARBOURS, QUARTERS, TEXTILE MILLS.

W A R R E N S

Since the Romans introduced it, the rabbit, or coney, has been important in our economy and culture. It has fluctuated in people's esteem and affections, from being a valuable source of protein and fur, especially in winter, to an agricultural pest, loveable pet, hero of children's books and bringer of good or bad luck. The map of England is covered in names such as Warren Knoll, Conger Hill, Sharpenhoe Clappers (Bedfordshire), Coneyhurst (Sussex) and Coney Green (Lincolnshire).

The first recorded warrens were on the Isles of Scilly in 1176. Lundy and the Farne Islands also contained them; on some islands rabbits play a vital role in providing puffins and Manx shearwaters with burrows in which to nest. Coastal sites were popular; some were constructed using ready-made boundary banks on old earthworks, such as at Danebury, Hampshire and Trowlesworthy warren, Devon. Warrens were established by monks and by the landed gentry in deer parks. In time they spread to all parts of the country, especially on heathland. The extent was staggering: they covered eleven per cent of the Breckland in Norfolk in the early 1800s, where, as Oliver Rackham described, '*a dozen or more adjoined each other for mile after mile*'. A warren of 2,226 acres, surrounded by a ditch and bank more than ten miles long, was established on Lakenheath common, Suffolk by the Bishop of Ely in the twelfth century and continued until the Second World War.

The boundaries of warrens differed from place to place. On Dartmoor, Devon there were granite walls; in Driffield, Yorkshire they were of wooden palings. The cheapest were grass sods laid face down on top of one another to make a wall, two sods wide and six feet high, capped by a thick line of blackthorn or furze. Within the boundaries clusters of one to forty small earthworks or pillow mounds were made for the rabbits to burrow into. Some had built-in stone tunnels and chambers for the rabbits to nest in.

Warrens were extremely profitable. In the mid-1800s Richard Jefferies wrote: '*Rabbit-warrens were formerly looked upon as a legitimate investment, and certain to produce a good income. In more than one case large fortunes are said to have been realized in this manner.*' The key to their success was the fecundity of the rabbit. Jefferies noted that warrens '*were in full prosperity*' until the outbreak of the French wars with Napoleon, after which the value of corn rose steeply and every available scrap of land, including many warrens, was ploughed up for wheat cultivation.

The grey rabbit was most common, but different colours were reared, including black rabbits for fur for hats and clothing – Kent was known for its black conies. A few black rabbits still survive on Lundy. 'Muel' rabbits were associated with the Breckland; silver-grey with Lincolnshire and Thetford warren in Norfolk.

429

By the late 1700s escaped rabbits had become established in the wild, and in the 1800s their numbers increased dramatically due to the availability of winter fodder crops grown for cattle, and ruthless gamekeeping, which kept down their predators (stoats, weasels, polecats, badgers, foxes and buzzards). Thousands of rabbits were shot each year on estates, and many poached for the pot. By the 1950s their numbers had reached sixty to a hundred million, but in 1953/4 the most despicable form of population control was perpetrated with the introduction of myxomatosis from France, which, within two years, gave 99 per cent of rabbits a lingering death. Since then their numbers have gradually recovered to about 38 million, although the viral disease recurs.

Hares were also kept in warrens, but for sport, and there is perhaps some cross-over with their ancient stories, for there are many superstitions about rabbits, too. Even speaking their name is unlucky around some fishermen and quarrymen. Olive Cook related how '*They take on fantastic shapes and it is not difficult now to believe in the spectre known as the White Rabbit which is said to haunt the warrens near Thetford. It has large, flaming eyes and runs with such speed that it can never be caught. Many people have seen it and it always bodes ill.*' Black rabbits, however, are said to bring good fortune. In the 1960s and 1970s Northumberland farmers refused to shoot black rabbits in case it brought them bad luck.

Rabbits have an important grazing role on downs, heaths and sand-dunes, especially where they create and maintain more plant diversity and habitats (although juniper does not do well in their presence). The large blue butterfly died out when rabbits were hit by myxomatosis. One large warren on Dunstable Downs in Bedfordshire is now an ancient monument, and aided reversion to rabbit warrens is occurring on some of Norfolk's Breckland.

See also DOGS, DOVECOTES, EARTHWORKS, EASTER CUSTOMS, GORSE, HARES, HEATHLAND, HILL-FORTS, JUNIPER, LAWN, PARKLAND, UNLUCKY WORDS.

WASSAILING

Here's to thee, old apple tree
Whence thou may'st bud and whence thou may'st blow,
And whence thou may'st bear apples enow.
Hats full, Caps full, Bushel, Bushel, Bushel Sacks full,
And my pockets full too!
Huzza!

The traditional song varies, as does the custom of wassailing. It reflects the importance of cider making and drinking, much more widely than in the traditional cider counties of Somerset, Devon, Gloucestershire and Herefordshire. It is said that most villages had their own wassailing song. With the revival of interest in traditional orchards and the growth of community orchards, wassailing has become a part of the calendar once again.

'Wassail' comes from the Anglo-Saxon *waes haeil* – to be healthy, so wassailing apple trees was a way of encouraging a good crop in the following season. It usually took place after dark on Old Twelfth Night, 17 January, but could also occur on other days around Christmas and the New Year.

Often farm workers and villagers carrying lanterns, a pail and pitcher full of cider, shotguns and horns, walk to their local orchard, which is sometimes lit by bonfires, and gather round the largest or most prolific tree. This tree is known as the Apple Tree Man and is fêted as the guardian of the orchard. Cider or beer is poured on its roots and pieces of soaked toast or cake put in the branches for the robins – guardian spirits of the trees. Often the tips of the lowest branches are drawn down and dipped into the pail of cider.

The wassailers fill their earthenware cups with cider and toss it into the branches. Then they refill their cups and drink and sing a toast to the tree (such as the one above). In Carhampton, Somerset they sing:

Old apple tree, we wassail thee, and hoping thou wilt bear
For the Lord doth know where we shall be, till apples come
another year
To bear well and bloom well so merry let us be
Let every man take off his hat and shout to the old apple tree
[Chorus, shouted:]
Old apple tree, we wassail thee, and hoping thou wilt bear,
Hat-fulls cap-fulls, three-bushel bagfulls
And a little heap under the stairs
Hip! Hip! Hooray!

To drive away evil spirits and wake up the sleeping trees, cow horns are blown, trays and buckets beaten and shotguns fired into the upper branches – as much noise as possible is made. At Walton in Somerset a special wassail cup with three handles, big enough for three quarts, was filled with a mixture of hot cider, gin and ginger by the local pub and passed round at the orchard. A beautiful, three-handled mug holding three and a half pints, made by the Somerset potter John Leach in 1999, has been inscribed with a new wassail poem by James Crowden.

The wassail bowl went round from house to house in the evenings during the Twelve Days of Christmas and often in the last weeks of Advent. A mixture of hot ale, spices, sugar and roasted apples, sometimes with eggs and thick cream floating on it, was known as Lamb's Wool in Gloucestershire, and was also drunk on St Catherine's Day, 25 November. The bowl was made from turned ash or maple, often elaborately carved and kept for the purpose.

430

Wassailing the apple trees has continued in some places, such as Carhampton, for centuries, while in other areas it is undergoing a revival, as at the Brandy Wharf Cider Centre on the river Ancholme. This temple to cider in the north Lincolnshire Fens has planted its own orchard, which is enthusiastically wassailed each year. Continuity of tradition, however, does not mean that customs go unchanged. The wassail ceremony at the Stoke Gabriel Community Orchard in Devon in 2003 was joined by the Churchwarden Morris Men, the Bovey Tracey Mummers and the Global Harmony folk singers, together with a barbecue.

See also APPLES, CAROLS, CIDER & CIDER ORCHARDS, MUSIC, ORCHARDS.

WATERCRESS BEDS

Once so characteristic of the heads of chalk streams in the South, watercress beds have fallen into disuse, been devoured by just two big growers or converted into trout farms.

Watercress sandwiches were a favourite breakfast meal for workmen in London in the early 1800s, and their popularity led to the creation of watercress beds along the rivers Itchen, Bourne and other chalk streams. The railways helped develop a thriving trade between Hampshire and London. By the time Henry Mayhew wrote *London Labour and the London Poor* in 1851, nearly a thousand sellers bought from the busy watercress market in Farringdon for resale on the streets '*in time for the mechanic's breakfast*'. The railway from Alresford soon became known as the Watercress Line. The line closed in 1973, but part of it has been bought by a preservation society and it is still possible to take excursions from Alresford on the *Watercress Belle*.

London wasn't the only destination for this peppery hydroponic delicacy. In the early 1900s newly built watercress beds at Spetisbury near Blandford Forum, Dorset were supplying the wholesale fruit and vegetable market in Manchester via the Somerset and Dorset railway. Throughout the Chilterns almost all the villages had watercress beds for sales to the Midlands.

Watercress beds first dwindled in number because of contamination by liver fluke (a gut parasite that we share with sheep). Now water direct from springs or boreholes must feed the shallow, concrete, gravel-bottomed compartments to ensure purity.

Working watercress beds used to provide important habitats for wetland birds, such as the redshank, water pipit, water rail, snipe and green sandpipers, as well as water shrews and our native crayfish, but intensification and the use of zinc to control crook root has led to their decline. Small and organic watercress beds, such as that at Longbridge Deverill in Wiltshire, as well as the overgrown remains of domestic beds, still attract pied and grey wagtails, swans (usually unwelcome) and, near estuaries in the South, a recent newcomer – the egret.

At Ewelme in Oxfordshire watercress beds stretch for three-quarters of a mile along the stream that follows the main street, covering six and a half acres and dropping through 39 levels. It ceased production in 1988 but is being restored by the Friends of the Ewelme Watercress Beds with the Chiltern Society, bringing great benefits to wildlife.

See also CHALK STREAMS, DOWNLAND, FOOD, RIVERS.

WATERFALLS

In 1809 Robert Southey wrote to his brother about the Lake District's spectacular Lodore Falls, which has a main drop of ninety feet: '*Tell people how the water comes down at Lodore? Why, it comes thundering and floundering, and thumping and plumbing and bumping and jumping and hissing and whizzing and dripping and skipping and grumbling and rumbling and tumbling and falling and brawling, dashing and splashing, and purring and roaring and whirling and curling, and leaping and creeping, and sounding and bounding, and clattering and chattering, with a dreadful uproar.*' He wrote a long, onomatopoeic poem in the same vein eleven years later called *The Cataract of Lodore*.

Snouts and spouts, forces, falls, ferns, cataracts, steps, rapids, eas and linns – all describe falling water. Linn from the Celtic is in currency in Northumberland. In Yorkshire force is common, from the Old Norse *fors* or *foss*, hence Fossdale, meaning waterfall valley. Thornton Force flows over a celebrated geological unconformity. Rivers repeat endlessly the wearing down of rock. Hundreds of water-

431

falls mark the dales and moors of Yorkshire, some falling into the darkness of swallow holes, as at Alum Pot.

Below the confluence of Fossdale Gill and Hearne Beck at the head of Wensleydale, Hardraw Force, where you can get behind the curtain of water, drops 98 feet into a large plunge pool on land belonging to the Green Dragon Inn. The entrance to the waterfall is through the pub's premises at a small fee. Brass bands take advantage of the acoustics of the gorge carved out by Hardraw Scaur and hold their contests there. John William Sharples recalls: 'There was one day in the year when the valley below the Scaur was "black wi folks". That was when the band contests were held, attracting brass bands and choirs from all parts of the North. The musicians arrived at Hawes railway station and usually played through the main street before journeying on to Hardraw. Wagonettes had a busy time transporting the bands, choirs and the hundreds of people who were drawn to Wensleydale on the great day.' In 1883 Charles Blondin crossed the amphitheatre on a tightrope and cooked an omelette half-way.

In Cornwall, Pentargon waterfall plunges a hundred feet from Beeny Cliff, and Pistol Ogo shoots over the cliff at Kynance Cove. The coast between Boscastle, Cornwall and Lynton, Devon is celebrated for its waterfalls. The flat-topped, often vertical cliffs produce wonderful cascades, such as the 75-foot drop of Litter Water. J.A. Seers counted 77 streams in this stretch, 33 of which ended their journey by leaping over the cliffs. More brave still, the Fell Beck, gathering water from the southern flanks of Ingleborough in Yorkshire, plunges into the darkness of Gaping Ghyll and freefalls more than three hundred feet (twice the height of Niagara Falls in Canada).

The smallest of waterfalls brings delight: dippers nest behind the six-foot falls along the little stream at Cusop Dingle above Hay-on-Wye, Brecon/Herefordshire, and endless pleasure is had by children on Kimmeridge beach in Dorset below a twenty-foot natural shower.

See also BEACHES, BECKS, BRASS BANDS, CLIFFS, COASTS, FRESHWATER FISH, GHYLLS, GORGES, LAKES, LIMESTONE, MOORLAND, MOSSES, RIVERS, WEIRS, XANADU.

WATER-MEADOWS

Water-meadows are a particular feature of chalk valleys, although they are not exclusive to these landscapes. They are the relic of a system, started here in the late 1500s, of encouraging the premature growth of grass to provide stock with an early bite. High labour costs meant that they became uneconomical to maintain; few are still operational, such as the Britford Water-Meadows near Salisbury in Wiltshire, a Site of Special Scientific Interest.

Water was used to keep the ground warm, diverted from the river by means of high ditches or carriers to flood or float the meadow. Floating was controlled by a series of sluices, which diverted the water through narrow head mains, over the meadow and into the wider drains. Hay could be taken in the summer, after which the meadow could be floated again to encourage grass growth for late grazing.

With their rumples, carriers and sluices, water-meadows are significant historic features, and important habitats for wildlife. Some are being restored, such as the Maiden Newton water-meadows on the river Frome in Dorset. Only four per cent of the once-common water-meadows along the valleys of the Avon, Test, Itchen, Meon, Wey, Loddon and Wallington in Hampshire are regarded as being 'well preserved'; at Ovington, on the river Itchen near Alresford, volunteers regularly dig out the ditches to keep the channels open. Water-meadows make good habitats for young trout, grass snakes, adders and wading birds and provide a refuge for the beleaguered water vole. The swallows seem to gather here, and painters, too. In Salisbury much effort is going into reviving the Harnham water-meadows that Constable painted in front of the Cathedral.

See also CHALK STREAMS, EELS, FIELDS, HALF-YEAR BIRDS, HAY MEADOWS, RIDGE & FURROW, RIVERS, SHEEP, WILDFLOWERS, WINTERBOURNES.

WATER-MILLS

In just a mile the Stirchel, or little Stour, in Dorset powered Melbury Mill, Spraggs Mill, Cann Mill, French Mill and Gears Mill. Between Croydon and the Thames the river Wandle has seen the ebb and flow of more than two hundred mills. Free energy powered mills for grinding corn, fulling

cloth, working forge hammers and saws and making paper and silk, needles and gunpowder. Long leats contoured their way from upstream to deliver a head of water, or sluices were constructed to increase the flow of water to the wheel.

Adapted over centuries to role and place, mills, with their associated weirs, waterworks and ponds, were once ubiquitous. Five thousand at the time of Domesday had risen and then fallen to fifteen thousand by 1900. Many burnt down, explosive flour dust and whirring wooden equipment proving a volatile mix. Millers worked together, or not, to control the flow of the streams and rivers for mutual benefit.

There may be only sixty mills now working commercially in the UK; stone-ground flour is still produced at Cann Mill near Shaftesbury in Dorset. Tourism provides an income for some, as at Winchester in Hampshire, Thetford in Norfolk and Constable's Flatford in Suffolk. Mills may now be homes, factories, pubs, hotels or offices, but their characteristic shape, positions and familiarity with water give them away. There are other subtle indicators of lost buildings: perhaps soapwort (used as a natural soaping agent in fulling mills) growing along the stream, or lime-loving hart's-tongue ferns in proliferation. The village name Abinger Hammer in Surrey recalls the loss of tranquillity suffered along the Tillingbourne, famous for its gunpowder mills.

The mills themselves vary endlessly within regional families. In Oxfordshire and Warwickshire they tend to be of brick with their waterwheels inside. Suffolk mills, often weather-boarded, can be very large with ten or twelve pairs of millstones. East Yorkshire's mills are of brick and pantile, Cornwall's of stone and slate. Along the Monnow, which divides Herefordshire from Monmouthshire, the solid mills are of stone.

In south Somerset wheels and turbines first used in the nineteenth century are giving way to state-of-the-art micro-hydropower, as ten historic mills reclaim their capacity to generate electricity, this time for domestic use and the national grid. They will produce six hundred thousand kilowatt hours a year, reducing carbon emissions by 260 tons.

See also DEVIL, FERNS, MILLSTONE GRIT, RIVERS, TEXTILE MILLS, TIDE MILLS, WEIRS.

WATER-TOWERS

Since water demand and supply fluctuate, short-term storage proves necessary. A high reservoir can make use of gravity to distribute the water. Where this cannot be achieved on the ground, especially in the flatter parts of the country, water-towers have increased in number and sophistication. In the late 1990s nearly a thousand were recorded across Britain, and more keep being discovered. Metal boxes on stilts (typical of many Second World War airfields); concrete mushrooms dominating hillsides (as at Colerne, Wiltshire); cylindrical drums on arched legs (Mursley, Buckinghamshire); elegant brick structures (near Fordham in Cambridgeshire) – their forms are many and varied.

Water-towers often have a scale and presence that makes them an important and well-loved feature of the skyline. In Essex the Balkerne tower is a grand, monumental building, all Gothic-classical arches with a pagoda-like roof and observation turret. Its proportions have gained it the nickname Jumbo, attempts to turn it into executive apartments being fought by the Save Jumbo for Colchester campaign.

There are just such conversions at Potterhanworth in Lincolnshire, Munstead in Surrey and Dunnington in Yorkshire. Other towers have diverse lives, whether summerhouses (Steyning, Sussex) or incinerators (Hornsea, Yorkshire). Many host mobile telephone aerials, which sadly changes their lines from clean-cut to hirsute.

433

They can be folly-like, as the mock-medieval castle on the Sandringham estate at Appleton, Norfolk, or the archetype of a science-fiction rocket ship (Chilton Foliat, Wiltshire). They are almost always landmarks: the 1885 lighthouse-like Rockwell tower at Wellington, Somerset; Rimswell water-tower in Yorkshire – a tank on elegant, square-sectioned pillars above a classical lodge (the Hull to Withernsea bus stops by it); the 1974 tower in Baydon, Wiltshire, like a giant thistle with angular supporting struts enclosing the central shaft and cupping the tank. York University's 'wineglass' is more like a mushroom than many of the similarly Swedish-design-inspired towers of the 1960s and 1970s. Where the spherical tanks more familiar from American films appear, there is usually an American connection, such as an air-force base, as at Chicksands, Bedfordshire.

See also AIRFIELDS, COOLING TOWERS, DEW PONDS, LANDMARKS, RESERVOIRS.

WAYSIDE & BOUNDARY CROSSES

Wild moors and stone crosses keep company with one another. Striding across Dartmoor, medieval granite crosses link the abbeys of Buckland, Buckfast and Tavistock that fringe the moor. Horn's Cross, Mount Misery Cross and Siward's (or Nun's) Cross are just three waymarks along the Monk's Path. Some of the 150 or so crosses are reckoned to be more than a thousand years old; many have been lost and some found again. Mark stones were often put up to guide travellers across difficult and remote terrain. Others are boundary markers or more recently erected memorials or commemorative stones.

Of the many remnants and simple crosses, such as Old Ralph and Fat Betty, on the Yorkshire Moors, one of the finest is Lilla Cross on Fylingdales Moor, believed to stand over the grave of the chief minister who died for his king, Edwin of Northumbria, in AD 625.

Cornwall is known for its ancient granite crosses. More than four hundred complete crosses have been recorded, and perhaps two hundred bits and bases. Most of the wayside crosses and boundary crosses are on the West Penwith and Bodmin moors. Wayside crosses mark the footpaths and tracks to parish churches, monasteries, chapels, holy wells and pilgrim routes. On coffin paths crosses were erected at the places where coffin bearers rested. At St Clether on Bodmin Moor a round or wheel-headed cross shows where it is safe to ford the river Inny.

Boundary crosses demarcate parish glebe land and perhaps monastic boundaries and church sanctuaries. The Cross in Hand on Tregonetha Downs marks the place where three parish boundaries meet. The parish of St Buryan in West Penwith, with a sanctuary extending beyond the walls of the churchyard, contains the greatest number of old crosses in the county. Most of the wayside and boundary crosses are wheel-headed, some carved with the figure of Christ; some have a Latin cross in relief painted with limewash. Holed wheel crosses are found throughout the Cornish moorlands; many have lost their base stones and shafts.

Some crosses have been found in hedge banks, with shafts used as gateposts. A number have been found by researching field names: two fields called Cross Park revealed previously undiscovered stones.

Upton Beacon, Yorkshire. From top left, clockwise: Chapel Amble Cross, St Kew, Cornwall; Bennet's Cross, Dartmoor, Devon; Malo Cross, Saltergate, Yorkshire.

434

Most of the crosses are dated between the ninth and thirteenth centuries. The Longcross in the parish of St Endellion is one of four very early Christian inscribed stones in Cornwall that display the chi-rho monogram. It also has an inscription in Latin and Ogham.

See also CHURCHYARDS, ELEANOR CROSSES, FOOTPATHS, GREEN LANES, HOLLOW WAYS, MARKET CROSSES, STANDING STONES, VILLAGE GREENS.

W E A T H E R

There is a Nottinghamshire expression that needs to be said with feeling: *'It's black over Bill's mothers.'* Similar sentiments are echoed, in Cheshire, for example: *'"By heck youth," he said, "it's a thin wind aback of Polly Norbury's"'* (Alan Garner, *The Stone Book Quartet*). *'Lovely day!'*; *'Ooh, it's cold again'*; *'Parky, i'n' it?'*; *'If I leave my umbrella at home, it's bound to rain'.* We love it, don't we, at least talking about it.

The national stereotype is well founded and, given our quixotic weather, why not? Thousands of slightly varied predictive rhymes are trotted out. Perhaps the most commonly known, *'Red sky at night, shepherd/sailor's delight, red sky in the morning, shepherd/sailor's warning'*, has been around for a long time.

It makes sense that people working on the land and on the sea would gather knowledge and wisdom to help them survive constantly changing weather. Katrina Porteous, while talking with fishermen from Holy Island to Boulmer in Northumberland, found many observations on the subject of foretelling weather, for instance from Ralph Wilson: *'If ye look from here and ye see the Farne Islands standing as if ye were looking at a mirage – standing out of the water, so they don't look as if they're connected – I would guarantee that rain's within 24 hours.'*

Climate is a more abstract thing. The average annual patterns are set by the long-term wars between warm, wet air travelling over the Atlantic Ocean and dry air, cold or hot, from the mighty landmass of Eurasia. The Lake District receives an annual rainfall of more than eighty inches, with some parts exceeding this (Sty Head has 170 inches); the Pennines and the high moors of the South West are not quite so wet. These are also the areas of least sunshine and highest snowfall. Topography makes all the difference, interfering as it does with the whims of the winds on both a grand and a very local scale. The driest areas, where less than 25 inches falls on average, run from the rain-shadow areas of Yorkshire, through Nottinghamshire and Lincolnshire, to the Essex coast (St Osyth receives twenty inches), London and the northern edge of Kent, and most of Suffolk and south-east Norfolk. Around the coast temperature is tempered by the sea and snowfall is rare.

Our awareness of the increasing unpredictability of weather is underlined by the scientific consensus that climate is shifting and very quickly. What impact will that have on the micro-climate and local conditions from day to day? Extreme weather is one result.

Occasional extremes are not new, as Daniel Defoe's writing about the Great Storm of 1703 testifies. In Stratton Strawless, Norfolk, Robert Marsham wrote of the iron earth in 1740, perhaps the most terrible long winter England had ever known (until 1962/3). The song thrush did not sing until March, hawthorn did not flower until June. He kept a diary of 'Indications of Spring', which, amazingly, his family has continued until the present day, giving us a unique glimpse of changes over 250 years. Now some of the birds he awaited in spring are overwintering here; some plants have completed their flowering before he recorded their beginning.

Today we grace the spotting of the recurrence of things in nature, such as birds' arrival and flowering dates in spring, with the name phenology. Amateur observers are now demonstrating earlier arrival of birds that were recorded by Gilbert White in the *Natural History and Antiquities of Selborne* in the eighteenth century: *'swallows – 13 April, swifts – 27 April and flycatcher – 12 May'*.

In Camden Square, north London in 1858 George Symons began to record rainfall in his garden and to collect rainfall records from other enthusiasts. It was the summer of the Great Stink – the drought was causing all manner of engineering as well as ambient problems across the capital. From this work grew a network of rainfall recorders across the country. It is now possible to show that the Oval gets significantly less rain than Lord's cricket ground five miles away in London. The rain gauge in Astwick, Bedfordshire, in the garden where the weather forecaster John Kettley used to live, showed a fluctuation in annual rainfall of 16½ to 33 inches between 1990 and 2004; the average – 24 inches – is dry. To the north and to the south it is wetter – the village is in the rain shadow of the Chilterns.

Competitive amateur claims recording hours of sunshine in the 1920s and 1930s led to many speculative bungalow developments between Hastings and Bognor Regis in Sussex. Bognor remains the sunniest place in England. Every big settlement warms its atmosphere from the storage-heater effect of concrete and Tarmac, but the heat island central London generates is a significant two degrees Celsius warmer than its green belt.

Pea soupers are no longer part of the language. The yellow, acrid fogs that lent mystery to the London docks for Sherlock Holmes disappeared with the Clean Air Acts and the fall in the domestic burning of coal. Smog has turned back into fog in the Trent valley, too, although it remains one of the foggiest lowland areas, as drivers on the M1 will know. But Great Dun Fell in Westmorland

435

suffered 233 days of fog per year between 1963 and 1976, compared with six days in Carlisle.

Front-page weather is usually acute: the fearsome floods devastating Lynmouth, Devon in 1952 and Boscastle, Cornwall in August 2004; tornadoes in Torbay, Devon; thunderstorms; the 1962/3 freeze; the closure of the Snake Pass in Derbyshire and the M62 by blizzards. Climate change is seen through the little egret colonising southern estuaries, the black cap and chiffchaff staying over winter, the comma butterfly flitting through Northumberland, telling us that winters and summers are notably warmer the length of the country. Gardeners are getting used to the survival of tender plants over winter and vineyards are producing better wine.

The weather in the warmer, wetter west, the drier, colder east, the really wet, really cold northern mountains and the temperate, sea-washed coastline hides many pockets of extreme or surprising aspects of daily difference, whether the cat is washing behind its ears or not.

See also BUNGALOWS, CIDER & CIDER ORCHARDS, CLOUDS, CRICKET, EAST, FLOODS, FOG & MIST, FRETS, FROST & FROST HOLLOWS, NORTH, SHIPPING FORECAST, TIDES, VINEYARDS, WASSAILING, WEATHER-VANES, WINDS.

WEATHER-BOARDING

436

Weather-boarding is characteristic of east Sussex, Kent and Essex, particularly of the Weald of Kent, where wood was plentiful. It also occurs in Suffolk, east Surrey, Middlesex, Hertfordshire and Buckinghamshire.

In the 1600s elm or oak boards were applied horizontally to the outsides of farm buildings as cladding. They were attached in different ways – overlapped, feather edged, tongue and grooved. In the eighteenth and nineteenth centuries weather-boarding became more widespread with the growing availability of softwoods and the mechanisation of sawmills.

There are many examples of magnificent weather-boarded wind- and water-mills, barns and granaries. Cranbrook in Kent has a high street of white-painted, weather-boarded buildings overlooked by a magnificent weather-boarded windmill with white sails. In the lower Rother valley the weather-boarding is often painted in soft, pastel shades, the window frames picked out in dark colours.

Domestic buildings weather-boarded with oak and elm are usually left unpainted; farm buildings and those that are near the sea are often painted black or tarred, like the deezes of Hastings, Sussex. Black is the traditional colour for weather-boarded buildings in Essex, under red tiles, although white is ousting it. The Essex and Hertfordshire border is traditional weather-board country; in Hertfordshire some plastered buildings may have a black weather-board plinth. From this area the style emigrated

to New England and evolved into the vernacular of the north American north-east coast.

See also BARNS, BEACH HUTS, BLACK & WHITE BUILDINGS, BOATS, CHURCHES, DEEZES, ELM, FARMS & FARMSTEADS, OAK, WATER-MILLS, WINDMILLS.

WEATHER-VANES

'*I am puff-breasted, proud-crested . . . And I stick it all out/For I cannot change the chance that made me.*' This Anglo-Saxon riddle is about a wind catcher, moved by heaven's breath. By the ninth century Pope Nicholas had decreed that weathercocks should be placed on all abbeys and churches to remind Christians that they must guard against sin. The cockerel – Shakespeare's '*trumpet to the morn*', that awakes '*the god of day*' – would have been recognised in the Middle Ages for its roles as pagan and Christian symbol, as a greeter of the sun and dispeller of evil spirits, and the vigilant bird that crowed when St Peter betrayed Christ.

On top of the spire of the north tower of Ottery St Mary's church in Devon stands a whistling cockerel that is '*thought to date from about 1340, and is reputed to be the oldest one in Europe that is still functioning*', the Reverend W.E. Wright relates. '*In 1908 our spire was rebuilt . . . This gave an opportunity to examine the cock, and the trumpet-like tubes passing through it. Each tube was found to have a tongue, so that in high winds a considerable noise was produced. At the same time the bird was given a new tail, as the old one was found to have a number of holes in it. It is thought that these resulted from soldiers of Cromwell's army, who were billeted in the town one winter, using the weathercock for target practice with their muskets . . . Unfortunately, when the cock was put back on the steeple, it would "crow" even in a moderate breeze. People nearby objected to their sleep being disturbed by this tiresome bird, so the tubes were blocked, and the cock crows no more.'*

The Victorians brought the cockerel back into fashion. The plump, handsome, golden cockerel that surmounts the church tower at Baltonsborough, Somerset, made by a local blacksmith in the nineteenth century, is one of hundreds to greet the dawn.

Representational and heraldic weather-vanes became popular in Tudor times. They evolved from the pennons attached to the lances of medieval knights – the word vane is derived from the Old English *fane*, meaning flag or banner. One of the earliest heraldic church weather-vanes can be seen on Etchingham church, Sussex, where Sir William Etchyngham erected a copper replica of his banner in about 1360.

Gilded metal banners with royal arms and crown finials, made in about 1669, surmount the four towers on the Tower of London. Pennants are the second most common variety of weather-vane. They come in many forms – stiff, square or rectangular, with forked or swallow tails, the balance usually a simple or elaborate arrow.

Fish, full of Christian symbolism, are also bringers of good luck. A golden salmon catches the sun from the dizzy heights of Christchurch Priory's tower, which stands at the confluence of the Hampshire Avon and the Dorset Stour. Sadly it has had to overlook the demise of the river's native salmon, slipping out of our lives owing to human greed and ineptitude. *'Heaven's golden salmon high above/Forever swimming against the wind's tide'*, wrote James Crowden for the libretto of 'Silver Messenger', Karen Wimhurst's new music to celebrate the Stour.

Another symbol of luck is the ship, heralding the sailor's safe journey home. The six-foot-long, four-foot-high Golden Barque was erected on the cupola of Portsmouth Cathedral's tower by the churchwardens in 1710. Every time the Barque was brought down for repair mothers would place their babies in it to offer protection from drowning. Too fragile now, the Barque can be seen in the Cathedral; a replica graces the tower.

In Bungay, Suffolk the story of the black dog, Old Shuck, is remembered in a weather-vane on a lamp-post in the market square, made as the result of a competition in 1933. More recently, in 1955, Hampshire county council reinforced its identity with a gilded copper weather-vane, featuring a Hampshire hog on a wheat sheaf, above its offices in Winchester. A new Old Father Time sends mixed messages to the bowlers at Lord's cricket ground in London.

See also BLACK DOGS, CATHEDRALS, CHIMNEYS, CHURCHES, DRAGONS, EAST, FLAGS, FRESHWATER FISH, GARGOYLES & GROTESQUES, MARKET CROSSES, NICKNAMES, NORTH, POULTRY, PUB SIGNS, SAINTS, SHIPPING FORECAST, TOWN HALLS & GUILD-HALLS, WEATHER, WINDMILLS, WINDS.

WEIRS

Weirs were constructed to control the flow of a river or stream. At their simplest they are an obstruction that causes water to back up and then fall over a sloping face. Ware in Hertfordshire means place by a weir, and has been known as such since at least 1200; it was pronounced 'weir' until the past fifty years.

The smallest of streams may demonstrate the manifold ways in which water has been pushed around for a variety of purposes, perhaps the most common being to power a mill. Weirs were the first point of diversion for a contouring leat taken off to power a downstream wheel, and many exist beside mills or mark ancient mill sites.

In Belper, Derbyshire the beautiful Horseshoe Weir is Grade II* listed; its walls and sluices were built by Jedediah Strutt to power the West Mill at the end of the eighteenth century. The Derwent valley is filled with innovative structures, many by Richard Arkwright, built to force water to work in the birthplace of the Industrial Revolution.

The elegant, curved cascade in Bath, Somerset by Pulteney Bridge allows water to be diverted to a lock for the passage of boats. The unusual tumbling weir in Ottery St Mary, Devon is a circular hole down which water pours, originally to power a Georgian factory.

Teddington Weir and lock in Middlesex mark the tidal reach of the Thames, and the limit of jurisdiction of the Port of London Authority. Bargemen and fishermen opposed its building in 1811.

Where river engineering works have made rivers uniform, other artificial structures have been introduced to vary flows and habitats. Weirs may be used to create pools by the concentration of flow; groynes deflect the current in slow-moving rivers to introduce diversity.

Swimming, sliding, boating and fishing are some of the consequent uses of mill-ponds and weirs. In 1999

437

Margaret Elsworth composed a song with Tim Laycock about her childhood memories of West Stour in the Blackmore Vale, Dorset:

We'd cross the lip of the rolling bay
Like watery tightrope walkers
And the bravest slid right down the weir
And into the foaming waters
We used to play and play
Down by the rolling bay.

See also CANALS, MUSIC, RIVERS, TEXTILE MILLS, WATER-MILLS.

WELL DRESSING

We are rarely obliged to carry water; for our forbears a local supply was vital. In the limestone area of Derbyshire a constant source was celebrated. During the summer, village and town wells are still dressed with pictorial tableaux of flowers. This custom may be very old, perhaps pre-dating the Romans, who at Fontinalia would scatter flowers into the fountains. In Genzano, south of Rome, an Italian tradition of making a patterned carpet of flowers down the main street also survives.

Tissington, it is said, was fortunate to have flowing water throughout the drought of 1615 and thereafter celebrated its six wells on Ascension Day. Another story tells that its well dressings began in 1348/9, when the villagers escaped the Black Death and credited their sweet water. In other villages the tradition of creating floral pictures around the wells may be a Victorian creation. Certainly the dressing of taps in Wirksworth and Youlgreave is traced to the first piped water supplies in the 1820s. In Eyam the custom was restored or created for the Festival of Britain in 1951.

The tableaux are made by local people, working fervently in garage or marquee. They impress petals and seeds, overlapping like fish scales, into wet clay on soaked wooden board. Most call this petalling, but in Holymoorside they call it flowering and use whole flower-heads. It may take a week of work, and interest is now so high that the process itself attracts visitors. The scenes created may be biblical, celebrate a local anniversary or refer to themes ranging from VE Day to nature conservation. Local lichens are much used since they keep their colour, especially golden lichen, which is known in some villages as bronze moss. Some use alder cones, called 'blacks', to make the outlines; others use hogweed, bark or rhubarb seeds. We look forward to the day when the local verges and fields are so full of wildflowers that they can again be used.

Well dressing must have been widespread. In Bristol conduits were decorated in the Middle Ages. Primroses were placed on the Virgin's Well in Tortworth on May morning.

Bisley in Gloucestershire has dressed its wells since the 1860s; in the 1980s Huntingdonshire tried its hand, Longstanton learning from Holywell near St Ives. In nature, of course, upwellings would dress themselves with wildflowers . . .

See also ALDER, BEER, CHALK, DRAGONS, GIN, HAUNTED PLACES, HOTELS, LICHENS, LIMESTONE, PANTS, RHUBARB, RIVERS, SPAS, SPRINGS, VERGES, WELLS, WILDFLOWERS.

WELLS

Vertical holes dug down to the water-table, lined in brick or stone, from which water was winched or pumped, are draw wells. But 'well' originally suggested a natural upwelling. The Fountain, a pub at the base of Shaftesbury's steep greensand hill, recollects the force of the flow and the dependence of the hilltop town on the village of Enmore Green, the source of its pure water and the basis of the strange Byzant Ceremony, a ritual of exchange. The town had many 'blind' wells, which stored rain-water from roofs – a practice that should once more be fostered.

Sadler's Wells, Clerkenwell and Well Walk mark just a few memories of formerly important public water supplies in London. In Soho the pub sign for the John Snow recalls the doctor who documented the spread of cholera in 1854, deducing from his mapping of incidences that it was spread by water, contaminated by sewage, from the pump in Broadwick Street.

But many upwellings were thought to be health-giving, and people who came to take the water often left in return bits of clothing on an adjacent tree. In Somerset it was believed that the springs facing east were able to cure eye problems. Sore Eyes Well in Shipley Glen, Yorkshire was a rag or clootie well; a rowan still stands beside it, but now so does a sewage outfall. Many wells have disappeared into undergrowth, under buildings or simply dried up because of groundwater exploitation.

Yet the reverence for water is easily understood, especially where it bubbles purely from the rock, the life force springing from the ground. We still throw coins into wells and make wishes, as our ancestors more seriously threw in offerings for the deity of the well – life, health and prosperity depended directly upon it. Golden Roman pins and earlier items are sometimes found. St Mary's Well at Portishead in Somerset is an example of a pin or pen well; people still dropped bent pins here in the 1960s.

Holy wells abound, together with tales of miracles. Many used to have elegant structures and troughs, which add further particularity to their symbolic power of purity and life. In Cornwall many survive as beautiful, small-roofed and arched well houses, some with doors, cared for and revered by someone. Madron Holy Well feeds a baptistery in the ruined chapel; beside it rags are still placed

438

on the trees. In Sancreed (St Euny's Well) and in Kenwyn churchyard the wells are walled, with steps leading down, a pattern found elsewhere, as at St Augustine's Well in Cerne Abbas, Dorset and on the green in Foolow, Derbyshire.

The high altar of Winchester Cathedral is built directly over a spring, which floods the crypt. In Kirkoswald, Cumberland the church is built over St Oswald's Well, the water from which runs under the length of the nave and emerges outside, where a chained cup and stone plaque celebrate its purity.

The city of Wells beside the Mendips in Somerset owes its name and existence to its springs. Five large and many smaller ones are known collectively as St Andrew's Well, once the Bottomless Well. They emerge from an underground, limestone-bound river beside the Cathedral, sometimes erupting through the lawns. Through moats and high-street gutters, conduits and sluices the water of Wells bathes every corner of the place.

Prophecy is one of the noted powers of wells: Marvel Sike spring at Brampton, Northamptonshire predicted trouble by running over; the Drumming Well at Oundle in Northamptonshire is said to have foretold the death of Charles II. Drumhill Spring in Stowey Sutton, Somerset amplifies sound as water and air is forced through the rock.

The rise and rise of bottled water is placing ever more demands on springs and wells. Malvern springs is where the enterprising Mr Schweppes began his business supplying the Great Exhibition in 1851. The most famous brand in the world now owns these holdings and can take forty million litres per year to bottle as Malvern Water. The Pewtriss Well (the company prefers to call it Primeswell) yields more than half, but its owners seek to exploit Walm's Well and others. The Malvern Spa Association, which protects more than twenty wells, feels the groundwater will be dried out by this major player. Local people, cyclists, walkers and tourists take their own bottles to fill up, as they do at St Anne's Well in Buxton, Derbyshire. Water used to be free.

See also BEER, CHALK, DRAGONS, GIN, HAUNTED PLACES, HOTELS, KENNELS, LIMESTONE, PANTS, RIVERS, SPAS, SPRINGS, VILLAGE GREENS, WELL DRESSING.

WEM SWEET PEA SHOW

Here are sweet peas, on tiptoe for a flight:
With wings of gentle flush o'er delicate white

John Keats, from 'I stood tip-toe upon a little hill'

This is a festival for eye and nose: the waft of sweet-scented blooms that hits you as you enter the cosy town hall is followed by the stunning spectacle of rows of green metal vases overflowing with pink, lavender, mauve, purple,

blue, white, cream, maroon and red. The Wem Sweet Pea Show in Shropshire was started in 1988 as the two-day Henry Eckford Centenary Show, to commemorate the beginning of this Victorian's sweet pea enterprise in the town. It aimed '*to encourage the growing and saving of some of the varieties of the old-fashioned sweet peas, many of which Mr Eckford bred himself*', Val Good says.

Eckford saw the potential of raising new varieties of sweet peas through cross-fertilisation. In 1888 he left his employment in Gloucestershire to devote his time to growing them at his nursery in Wem. At the bi-centenary Sweet Pea Exhibition at Crystal Palace to commemorate the sending of the first sweet-pea seeds from a Sicilian monk to Dr Uvedale in England in 1699, 115 of the 264 varieties exhibited had been raised by Henry Eckford. Until his intervention sweet peas were sweet smelling, but produced only a few small flowers on each weak stem. He managed to produce a larger range of colours and slightly larger flowers – known as grandiflora-type or old-fashioned sweet peas. Subsequent plant breeders went on to produce increasingly larger-flowered sweet peas, but neglected their wonderful scent.

The first show at Wem was so successful, attracting more than four thousand people, that the newly formed Eckford Sweet Pea Society of Wem and the National Sweet Pea Society were persuaded to make it an annual event. It is now extended over two days on the third Saturday and Sunday in July. The town revels in its connections. Street signs have small sweet-pea motifs on them, and while the show is being held cafés, pubs and shops in the

439

high street, from baker to electrical supplier, competitively display sweet peas in their windows. Garden after garden has intricate constructions, some carefully guarded, full of glorious colour.

See also AGRICULTURAL SHOWS, COTTAGE GARDENS, GARDENS, GOOSEBERRIES, LEEKS, SMELLS.

WENSLEYDALE CHEESE

On its home turf a wedge of Wensleydale might be eaten with fruit cake or apple pie. This mild cheese was almost lost to its Yorkshire dale, the name carried off by big business. The Hawes factory buy-out in 1992 kept the integrity of the name in its place and milk is now supplied only by cows grazed on the limestone pastures of the valley.

From its Cistercian beginnings as a sheep cheese, through transformation due to the use of shorthorn cows' milk, the older cheeses assumed a natural blue. Flat cheeses were made in spring and before the autumn frosts, with tall truckles in between. Positive feedback may take us all the way to seasonal cheeses reflecting calving and new grass, and see the return of a full complement of wildflowers and creatures to the dale, so that we can all agree with Wallace: '*Nice bit of Wensleydale, Gromit.*'

See also BLUE VINNEY, CATTLE, CHEDDAR CHEESE, CHEESE, DOUBLE GLOUCESTER, FAIRS & FAIRGROUNDS, FIELDS, SHEEP, STILTON.

440

WHALES, DOLPHINS & PORPOISES

In March 2004 a fifteen-ton sperm whale was stranded in shallow waters off the Wash, proving that large whales are not confined to far-flung places – some feed off our shores and pass through on migration from feeding to breeding grounds. But there is more chance of spotting some of the smaller cetaceans, including dolphins and porpoises. Of the 28 species that have been recorded in our territorial waters, ten are annual visitors or residents, including the common, bottlenose, Risso's and white-beaked dolphins, harbour porpoise and minke whale.

We have changed from being a whaling nation to a whale-watching one. Whaling was encouraged by the British government with bounty incentives, and the main whaling ports of Hull and Whitby in Yorkshire, Newcastle upon Tyne, Liverpool and London prospered from the Greenland whale fishery. By 1818, 64 ships were sailing from Hull, and two years later 688 whales were caught, producing eight thousand tons of whalebone. From here and the whaling stations established on the island of South Georgia, according to Friends of the Earth, '*Britain helped to kill off the Blue Whales of the Antarctic and North Atlantic and the North Atlantic Right Whale*'.

Popular opinion has become increasingly appalled at our treatment of these intelligent mammals. In 1972 the British government signed a United Nations resolution for a ten-year moratorium on all commercial whaling, but it was not imposed by the International Whaling Commission until the 1985/6 season. It continues to be extended, despite opposition from Japan, Norway and Iceland.

Now whales and dolphins are protected in British territorial waters. It seems ironic that as we have discovered an affection for our coastal cetaceans they are rapidly being killed by fishing fleets. Hundreds of dolphins are inadvertently caught in the nets of pair-trawlers (nets as large as two football pitches dragged between two boats) and are found washed up on the beaches of Devon and Cornwall. Discerning restaurants refuse to cook with bass caught by pair-trawlers. UK boats are banned from pair-trawling within twelve miles of the coast in our territorial waters, but not within our two-hundred-mile offshore area, which includes the continental shelf.

Harbour porpoises appear to be declining in number, no doubt for the same reason, especially in the southern North Sea and English Channel. But they can be seen off the coast of Northumberland and from Flamborough Head and Spurn Head in Yorkshire from July to September.

Today bottlenose dolphins are the species most frequently seen in small groups off the Northumberland coast in summer, especially around the Farne Islands. They sometimes venture up east-coast estuaries, such as the Blackwater, Crouch and Thames, and are spotted from south, south-west and north-west coasts in summer.

The common dolphin enjoys bow-riding with boats off the south-west coast, and Risso's dolphin might take a look at you if you are on the ferry between Portsmouth and Bilbao, Spain in winter or sailing off the west coasts between May and September. During 2004 Risso's were seen in unprecedented numbers in the North Sea, thought to be following squid northwards as waters grow warmer. Killer whales (orcas) have been seen off Cornwall and the Isles of Scilly during May.

The sighting of a whale was always a big occasion. In his diary John Evelyn wrote of a 58-foot baleen whale in the river Thames: '*A large whale was taken betwixt my land abutting on the Thames and Greenwich, which drew an infinite concourse to see it, by water, horse, coach, and on foot, from London, and all parts.*' Nevertheless it was killed with a 'harping iron'. We have different sensibilities now. In January 2006, thousands of Londoners watched an eighteen-foot northern bottlenose whale that had strayed far from her Atlantic Ocean feeding grounds make her way slowly up the Thames to Battersea Bridge, and were saddened by her death as rescuers tried to move her to deeper waters.

The closest that most of us will get to a whale is in the Oxford University Museum of Natural History or the

Natural History Museum in London. The life-sized model of a blue whale never fails to amaze. The last dolphinarium closed in 1993, opinion popularly agreeing that confinement for these creatures has no place in a civilised society.

See also BASKING SHARKS, BEACHES, BOATS, COASTS, ESTUARIES, SEA FISH.

W H I T E B E A M

Reaching sixty feet, whitebeam (*Sorbus aria*) is characteristic of chalk and limestone soils, particularly among scrub, woodland edges and remote crags and gorges. It is distinguished by the white, downy underside to its oval, serrated leaves, which are said to predict rain when they are slightly upturned and the glimpses of silver showing. Its creamy white flowers bloom in May and June and turn to scarlet berries in September. They become edible for humans as they begin to rot – that is, if the blackbirds haven't got there first.

Its wood, which is very hard, is used by wood engravers and was sought after for cogs for machine wheels before the invention of cast iron. A number of cultivars and the Swedish whitebeam have been used for many years as street trees across the country.

Whitebeam is peculiar for its ability to produce distinct local endemic species – some of which number only a few tens of trees – each with subtle differences of leaf, petal and fruit. These are found in isolated places, such as the Wye valley, Avon Gorge, the valleys of Westmorland and the coastal woodlands of Exmoor. Micro-species include *Sorbus devoniensis*, locally called French Ales (confusingly *alise* is the French name for wild service tree), which is limited even in Devon, and *Sorbus subcuneata*, confined to Exmoor.

A unique whitebeam growing beside a car park on Exmoor, while awaiting taxonomic definition, has been given the name Sorbus no-parkingii.

See also ALDER, ANCIENT TREES, ASH, BEECH, BIRCH, BLACK POPLAR, BLACKTHORN, CHALK, DAMSONS, ELM, FIELD MAPLE, GORGES, HAWTHORN, HAZEL, HOLLY, HOLM OAK, HORNBEAM, HORSE CHESTNUT, JUNIPER, LANDMARK TREES, LIME, LIMESTONE, LONDON PLANE, MONKEY-PUZZLE, OAK, ORCHARDS, PEARS, POPLAR, ROWAN, ROYAL FORESTS, SCOTS PINE, SWEET CHESTNUT, SYCAMORE, WALNUT, WILLOW, WOODS, YEW.

W H I T E   C L I F F S

The whiteness of our southern cliffs may be the source of the ancient name Albion. The whiteness is chalk – pure, lime-rich rock made up of billions upon billions of '*coccoliths secreted by algae*' (Richard Fortey). The White Cliffs of Dover are emblems of England.

*. . . on the French coast the light
Gleams and is gone; the cliffs of England stand,
Glimmering and vast, out in the tranquil bay.*

Matthew Arnold, from 'Dover Beach'

Developments and sea defences now protect the base of the cliffs, so rockfalls are less common and this stretch of cliffs is green with growth.

In *King Lear* (Act IV, scene vi) Edgar's description of what is now called Shakespeare Cliff in Kent captures the scale and power:

441

*How fearful
And dizzy 'tis to cast one's eyes so low!
The crows and choughs that wing the mid-way air
Show scarce so gross as beetles. Half-way down
Hangs one that gathers samphire – dreadful trade!
Methinks he seems no bigger than his head.
The fishermen that walk upon the beach
Appear like mice.*

Often soft enough to bite and chew to assuage your indigestion, chalk is structurally capable of standing up to the elements. It can form the highest of cliffs: at Beachy Head and the Seven Sisters in Sussex the cliffs reach more than five hundred feet and they are topped by some of the richest chalk grassland. Continual undercutting by the sea causes constant rockfalls, which keeps these bastions glistening white and beautiful.

England has almost sixty per cent of the chalk coast of Europe and many of its best habitats. Its softness supports shells and sponges that bore, as well as green seaweeds, all peculiar to the chalk.

Great sweeping cliffs along the Dorset coast are edged by golden sand, with Durdle Door and Bat's Head demonstrating the formation of arches. The contortions of the chalk, so folded as the Alps were rising, are apparent in the thin line of chalk that makes spectacular sea stacks: Old Harry and his Wife on the Purbeck side and the Needles by the Isle of Wight. At Freshwater Bay, Isle of Wight the lines of flints show the chalk has been turned almost vertical from its horizontal bedding.

As far west as Devon at Beer Head the chalk appears again, high, proud and slightly green; around the corner landslips contort the Hooken Cliffs, but pinnacles of chalk peer out to sea.

In Norfolk a surprise awaits: the sixty-foot cliffs at Hunstanton are of red chalk, full of iron compounds, topped with white chalk.

The great north-facing cliffs at Speeton and Bempton in Yorkshire, with the cliffs and promontory of Flamborough Head, are different again: calcium carbonate has fortified the chalk, giving it greater resistance and a sugary look. But the weaknesses are relentlessly sought out by the sea, as witnessed by the deep coves, arches, stacks and caves. On the shore there are seaweeds and invertebrates found nowhere else in England. Bempton Cliffs reach four hundred feet, and among the 33 species of seabird, vulnerable now to the changing fortunes of the North Sea, are gannets, guillemots, kittiwakes and puffins (known locally as mackerel gant, scout, petrel and Flamborough Head pilot), which gather in unparalleled colonies here from April to mid-August.

See also ALBION, ARCHES, CHALK, CHOUGHS, CLIFFS, COASTS, COVES, DEVIL, FLINT, LANDMARKS, SHIPPING FORECAST, STACKS.

W H I T E   H O R S E S

Hill figures are unique to England. They are simply cut out of the turf to reveal the rock below. Almost all are confined to the chalk.

One above all bears immense age with considerable grace. The White Horse is visible across the wide Oxford vale that carries its name. It imparts identity to an area much beyond Uffington. Was it a landmark, territorial marker, totem, emblem of victory, celebration or monument? To Morris Marples 'the Uffington horse is a work of art, being in that respect far ahead of any of the other white horses, whatever their other merits may be.'

Some say it is a dragon. Above is Uffington Castle, a big hill-fort, a long barrow and a round barrow and, below, a small, deeply scooped valley edged by a steep, flat-topped spur. This – Dragon Hill – reinforces one legend that associates St George and the killing of the dragon with these parts. But Thomas Hughes, author of *Tom Brown's Schooldays*, weaves a question: what if it were Pendragon Hill – the word referring to the chief of kings to the ancient Britons, father of Arthur?

In the fourteenth century the White Horse was worth a detour, offered as a great monument, second only to Stonehenge as recorded in *Tractatus de Mirabilibus Britanniae*. In 1738 the Reverend Francis Wise popularised the idea that origins lay with King Alfred, but G.K. Chesterton, in his 'Ballad of the White Horse', had Alfred endowing the horse with great antiquity:

> *Before the gods that made the gods*
> *Had seen their sunrise pass,*
> *The White Horse of the White Horse Vale*
> *Was cut out of the grass.*

Chesterton noted that turf crawls as men sleep and that to keep the horse white people must intervene. Thomas Hughes agreed to be chronicler to the White Horse in 1857 at the time of its re-whiting, and wrote a fictional book, *The Scouring of the White Horse*, filled with real observations of the hard work and hard revelling on 17 and 18 September. Shape and outline may, therefore, change over time; once aerial warfare began hill figures were turfed over to prevent their use as landmarks by enemy pilots.

The Uffington White Horse is an awesome 2,890 to 3,230 years old. David Miles and Simon Palmer's definitive estimation was achieved out of archaeological work and

442

Kilburn Hill, Yorkshire.

Optical Stimulated Luminescence Dating (analysis of the soil's last exposure to sunlight). They argued that the body of the beast has thinned no more than a metre from that time. Early Iron-Age coins show representations of similar beasts, facing to the right, as does the Uffington horse.

Wiltshire claims most white horses. Over time it has run to twelve or more; eight are still extant all along the downs through the centre of the county. Some are naïvely drawn and may be standing or running, short- or long-tailed, most have an eye and all face to the left, bar the one cut in 2000 at Devizes. They include Alton Barnes (1812), Broad Town (1864), Cherhill (1780), Hackpen (1838), Ham Hill, Marlborough (1804), Rockley and Tan Hill. Devizes had two (1845, lost, and 2000), as did Pewsey (1785, lost, and 1937). At Westbury (1778) there was an older horse; local stories link it to King Alfred's victory at Edington (Ethandun) in 878. In 1957 and 1995 it was filled in with cement instead of chalk – the nearby cement factory, with its lone, high chimney, adds to the landmarks of this corner of the county. In 2001 pressure hoses were used to clean it.

Chalk makes the dramatic underlay to most of these equines. But in north Yorkshire, at Roulston Scar in the Hambleton Hills, the white horse is cut in limestone and limewashed, inspired by the festivities at Uffington in 1857. One Christmas the horse turned into a zebra, a prank unlikely to have been perpetrated by the Kilburn White Horse Association, which maintains it.

At Tysoe in Warwickshire people have been turning up many kinds of evidence in search of the creature that gave its name to the Vale of the Red Horse, referred to by the cartographer John Speed in 1606. County Durham, Surrey, Sussex, Buckinghamshire and Hampshire all have

their own memories or existing white horses. It is odd that Kent, with its Saxon emblem of the white horse (Invicta), had none present in the Downs until 2003, when a new one was cut at Folkestone above the exit from the Channel Tunnel.

Early marketing perhaps gave us the largest white horse at Osmington in Dorset. It is the only one with a rider – George III – and was cut to flaunt royal patronage of Weymouth. It must be at its best seen from the sea, and one story says that it was cut by engineers stationed there during fears of invasion by the French. Thomas Hardy in *The Trumpet Major* suggests that the horse is a memorial to the Battle of Trafalgar.

Many public houses and inns reflect the signs of the times, allegiance shifting from the Royal Oak of the Stuarts to the White Horse, emblem of the House of Hanover, when George I ascended the throne. The white horse of Osmington cleverly carried on the flattery.

History rides with us, shapes us and depends upon us. Whatever meanings we endow the white horse with today, it has proved a robust emblem.

See also ALBION, BARROWS, CHALK, CHALK STREAMS, COB, DOWNLAND, FLINT, GALLOPS, HILL FIGURES, HILL-FORTS, HORSES & PONIES, INDUSTRIAL CHIMNEYS, INNS, LANDMARKS, 'OBBY 'OSSES, PUB SIGNS, RACECOURSES, TURF MAZES.

443

WILDFLOWERS

Our passive appreciation of wild plants lies in deep contrast to our forbears' practical, everyday knowledge and need of them. Working wisdom about plants was mixed with superstitions and inherited associations with magic and special powers. A culture of plant lore flourished, some of which persists, from using feverfew against headaches to not taking hawthorn blossom into the house because it brings bad luck.

Formal knowledge took a step forward in 1551 when William Turner from Morpeth, Northumberland wrote the first part of his *New Herball*. Woodcuts borrowed from Bavarian physician Leonhard Fuchs provided accurate portrayals of the plants to aid identification. Katrina Porteous says: '*This book was a landmark in botany and medicine. For the first time, physicians were able to read in their own language, English, an original study of the plants vital to their profession.*' He was criticised: '*Now . . . every man, nay every old wife, will presume, not without the murder of many, to practise Physik*', one detractor claimed. In 1597 John Gerard's more famous *Herball* was published and many others followed.

The first *Flora of the British Isles* and the initial County Flora – of Cambridgeshire – were compiled by John Ray in 1660. Distinguished amateur and professional botanists, including many Victorian clergymen, have since compiled comprehensive County Floras. We have also produced some fine botanical illustrators, such as the Reverend William Keeble Martin, who have given us a good picture of the treasury of wild plants we had. H.C. Watson pioneered a more systematic method of cataloguing plants, with distribution maps, in *Cybele Britannica* (1847) and *Topographical Botany* (1883). Now we have the technology to map precisely what plants we have left, but not the will, it seems, to conserve them.

In *The Englishman's Flora* (1958) the writer and poet Geoffrey Grigson explored our cultural relationship with plants, including local and vernacular names that give clues to their uses and our attitudes towards them. For example, one of the field poppy's local names, headache, refers to people's fears that smelling a poppy would bring one on. This connects with other names – thunderbolt, thunderflower and thundercup warned children that picking the flower may presage a storm.

Grigson's work has been importantly amplified by *Flora Britannica*, Richard Mabey's *tour de force*, which brings together contemporary botany with continuing everyday familiarity with plants, incorporating information sent by hundreds of local correspondents and using colour photographs instead of botanical illustrations.

The geological and topographical complexity of England is mirrored by an intricate distribution of wild plants. Even within a single parish the range of habitats offers many niches – from wet valley bottoms to exposed hilltops, from coast to heath and woodland, even from the south to the north side of a wall.

That wildflowers thrive in thin, unpromising soils and in difficult conditions is their virtue and their undoing. Put down fertiliser and the plants are soon crowded out by vigorous grasses and crops; herbicides complete the affront. Yet man and nature had worked together for hundreds of years, giving us rich flora in arable fields and continuous grassland. One old hay meadow can contain as many as 150 different plants. The unnatural, mono-tonal green of the fields signals not only the loss of richness but also the loss of variegation, the failure of the local patois of the wild.

Brutal forms of intensive agriculture have eliminated most wildflowers from the hay meadows, water-meadows and arable fields. The so-called arable 'weeds', hay rattle, corn cockle and corn marigold, are now very rare. Wetland plants continue to disappear fast, owing to widespread land-drainage schemes. Meadows of fritillaries used to be commonplace in river valleys of the South and East,

444

now a handful remain. Even the resilient buttercups are becoming a less familiar spring spectacle.

Arguments for benign farming fell on deaf ears. The Department of the Environment's 'Countryside Survey 1993' reported that even the traditional reservoirs of wild plants, such as hedgerows, riverbanks and road verges, had suffered a loss in diversity even when not physically damaged. By 2004 a survey found that nearly a third of native British plants had significantly decreased in forty years, and in 2005 it was stated that one in five of our wildflowers is threatened with extinction.

The strategy of conservationists has been to safeguard key sites, both for research and so that plants can recolonise the surrounding areas when conditions improve. But there is danger in this approach. In some places these reserves have become vulnerable, isolated islands, surrounded by one crop and little else. Nothing can replace the familiar plants in their everyday landscapes, for us or for the security of the species. Parish Floras give us the scale on which to sense gain or loss, and are where real conservation should begin.

In Devon residents made a poster of the Flora of Chagford. It has beautiful illustrations of one hundred species found in the parish, from navelwort on the granite walls, tansy and cuckoo flower in the hedgerows, bilberry on the moors, ragged robin in the marshy places, water crowfoot in the river and dog's mercury in the woods, to self-heal, catsear, devil's bit and field scabious in the meadows. While researching their Parish Map project they discovered a meadow that has never been ploughed or sprayed, which contains 46 species of flowering plant.

The Parish Mappers of Elham, Kent also discovered the richness of their chalk flora; in addition to their eight-by-four-foot painted Parish Map they have made a floral map, and they are now tackling the hard job of conserving what they have and creating the right conditions to enable wildflowers to return.

It is the common, not the rare, plants that characterise places and tell the seasons: snowdrops along Wiltshire streams, lesser celandine ('spring messenger') along the road verges, carpets of bluebells in Derbyshire's Derwent woods, white ramsons in Hampshire hedge bottoms, stretches of gorse across the Bagshot sands in Surrey, bilberry on the Pennine moors, the patriotic mix of red campion, stitchwort and bluebells along the deep lanes of Herefordshire, thrift along the Cornish coast – things we hope our grandchildren will take for granted.

See also ALEXANDERS, ANTY-TUMPS, BARROWS, BEACHES, BLUEBELLS, BROADS, CHALK, CHINES, CHURCHYARDS, COBNUTS, COTTAGE GARDENS, CROPS, DAFFODILS, DOG ROSES, DOWNLAND, DRYSTONE WALLS, EARTHWORKS, EASTER CUSTOMS, FELLS, FENS, FERNS, FIELD NAMES, FIELDS, FRITILLARY MEADOWS, GARDENS, GOLF-COURSES, GORGES, GORSE, GRASSY TRIANGLES, GRAZING MARSHES, GREEN LANES, GRUFFY GROUND, HAY

MEADOWS, HEATHLAND, HEDGES, HOLLOW WAYS, HONEY & BEES, INGS, LANDSLIPS, LAWN, LIMESTONE, LINKS, MAY DAY, MIDSUMMER DAY, MISTLETOE, MOORLAND, MOSSES, MOSSLAND, OLD MAN'S BEARD, ORCHARDS, OSIERS, PARISH MAPS, PONDS, RAMSONS, REED BEDS, RHYNES, ROYAL FORESTS, RUSH-BEARING, SALT MARSHES, SAND-DUNES, SHINGLE, SOILS, STRAW, THATCH, VERGES, VILLAGE GREENS, WALLFLOWERS, WALLS, WATER-MEADOWS, WELL DRESSING, WOODS.

W I L L O W

Pollarded willows line the rhynes of the Somerset Levels and the tributaries of the Thames; weeping willows fringe the lawns along the Cam in Cambridge. Coppiced osiers are found in West Sedgemoor, Somerset, while cricket-bat willows grow straight in some river valleys in Essex. Willow wood has found many uses.

Crack willow, called snap willow in Kent, gets its name from its brittle twigs. It is planted along rivers to help stabilise the banks, pollarded every five to ten years or so to provide straight poles and pliable wands for baskets. Left unpollarded, it can grow to eighty feet.

The white willow, also known as saugh or saugh tree, and sometimes as popple, can be recognised by the silvery white underside of its elegant, long, thin, olive-coloured leaves. Up to a hundred feet high, it is found by rivers and streams, generally becoming less common towards the West. It pollards well.

A weeping form of white willow, hybridised with the true weeping willow from China, is the familiar tree of parks and gardens, riverside pubs and hotels, where willows hang over the river, leaves almost touching the water. The bay willow is a bushy tree that grows north of the Midlands, so-called because its leaves are similar to that of the bay tree.

Sallow is the name given to the smaller, bushier species of willow, of which the goat, pussy willow or sally is the most common, found all over the country in hedgerows and scrubby places. John Clare captured them in 'The March Nightingale': *Now sallow catkins once all downy white/Turn like the sunshine into golden light'*. The goat willow also has the name of palm willow in Leicestershire, palmer in Dorset and palm tree in Wiltshire, Oxfordshire and Yorkshire, because its branches are used for Palm Sunday church decorations.

The finest cricket bats in the world have been made from a specific variety of willow since the 1790s. Cricket-bat willow makes wood that is light, strong and shock absorbent. Its tough, light timber also made early artificial limbs, as well as polo balls. Particularity is lent to corners of Norfolk, Suffolk and Essex, especially the Till and Blackwater valleys, which nurture this fast-growing tree in plantations along ditches. The young trees are planted thirty feet apart and the shoots on the lower eight feet of trunk are continuously removed, so that no knots form. They are felled when they reach a circumference of four feet and eight inches – every twelve to fifteen years.

Apart from the watery places evoked in *The Wind in the Willows* these trees thrive in a wide range of habitats. Creeping willow inhabits dune slacks all round the country, readily hybridising with other species. Twenty-three forms of willow grow on the Sefton coast in Lancashire, of which thirteen are hybrids, three of them quite rare.

See also ALDER, ASH, BEECH, BIRCH, BLACK POPLAR, BLACKTHORN, CRICKET, DAMSONS, EASTER CUSTOMS, ELM, FIELD MAPLE, GORGES, HAWTHORN, HAZEL, HOLLY, HOLM OAK, HORNBEAM, HORSE CHESTNUT, JUNIPER, LIME, LIMESTONE, LONDON PLANE, MONKEY-PUZZLE, OAK, OSIERS, POPLAR, RHYNES, RIVERS, ROWAN, SCOTS PINE, STRAWBERRIES, SWEET CHESTNUT, SYCAMORE, WALNUT, WHITEBEAM, YEW.

445

W I N D   F A R M S

Since 1991 enormous, pale, sleek turbine towers with two or three wind-catching blades have been raised across Cornwall, Northumberland, County Durham, Cumberland, Yorkshire and less likely settings, including Gloucestershire (Lynch Knoll), Hertfordshire (Kings Langley), Essex (Dagenham) and Norfolk (Somerton and Swaffham). Wherever they are proposed, opinion becomes highly charged. To some they are elegant and graceful symbols of a cleaner future. To others they are landscape-blighting eyesores. At between 82 and 260 feet high in necessarily exposed places these machines cannot be hidden. Other worrying issues have to be faced – bird and bat deaths, noise and sunlight flicker.

Pollarded willows, Frampton on Severn, Gloucestershire. Near Barnsley, Yorkshire.

Delabole in Cornwall has the earliest dairy farm turned wind farm. The electricity it produces is used by the community, improving the local supply quality and illustrating how a place can use its own resources to advantage. Residents, surveyed six months after its completion, were overwhelmingly supportive, as are visitors.

There were 42 farms across England and Cornwall at the end of 2004, with more planned. Several are offshore, including Blyth in Northumberland and Scroby Sands in Norfolk. The government is committed to producing ten per cent of the country's energy by renewable means by 2010, and wind turbines are a favoured means to this end. But there are fears of landscapes being 'industrialised', even alongside the nuclear power plant at Hinkley Point in Somerset. In treacherous times the benign decentralising of production would seem to make sense. Wind farms may or may not prove to be the best solution. But we must face up to the impact of our insatiable demands for energy, and having literally to live with its production might set us thinking. Small wind turbines on our houses, with small-scale community wind farms to help power towns, would encourage self-sufficiency.

See also CLOUDS, SHIPPING FORECAST, TIDE MILLS, WATER-MILLS, WEATHER, WEATHER-VANES, WINDMILLS, WINDS.

446

W I N D M I L L S

It may be that windmill technology came back from the East with crusading knights. Amberley in Sussex and Weedley in Yorkshire have the earliest recorded examples of windmills here, from the tail-end of the twelfth century.

The post mill was the first incarnation, a vertical post with a wooden construction on top, containing the mechanism, which could be turned to face the sails into the wind. But they had a tendency to blow over, so tower mills – masonry or brick cones with swivelling wooden caps – were developed in response. Burton Dassett in Warwickshire has perhaps the earliest survivor.

Many places still have Windmill Hills. Mills had become a part of everyday life. They ground corn and powered sawmills, as at Buckland, Surrey. In East Anglia, where the population of windmills was most dense, they operated drainage pumps. Here the influence of Dutch engineers led to the introduction of 'smock' mills – timber towers, often octagonal in plan. Although many appear in Norwich School paintings of the eighteenth century, only one remains – in Herringfleet, Suffolk – and it is from a later era. The other survivors are mostly brick tower mills with boat-like caps, unique to Norfolk. Advances enabled their height to increase, the conical form changing to a more cylindrical one, such as Morse's Mill at Thurne Dyke, Norfolk. The tallest on the Broads remains Berney Arms High Mill, built in the 1860s.

Lincolnshire has distinctive mills, in Heapham, Waltham and Lincoln itself, with white, ogee-curved caps and an exposed wind-shaft beam (Dutch influenced, again). Alford is a fine example, with five sails rather than the usual four (Heage in Derbyshire has six).

Mills continued to develop, with common sails (cloth over a wood frame) giving way to timber shuttered sails. Smaller models evolved, such as the skeletal 'trestle' mills and hollow-post mills, which exist at How Hill in Norfolk. Many farms also had wind-driven water pumps standing in the fields, their metallic squeaks at variance with the deep creaks of the big wooden mills.

Wind power, though, became subordinated to the petrol engine and electricity, and windmills declined – the energy may have been free, but it could not be turned on.

The Society for the Protection of Ancient Buildings created a mills group in 1931. It has connected enthusiasts, leading to conservation and renovation. Some windmills are now houses. Others are open to the public, including Bursledon in Hampshire and the white, weather-boarded Union Mill in Cranbrook, Kent, the tallest smock mill at seventy feet.

Where they still stand, working or not, windmills command the surrounding landscape, not only by their shape and mobility but simply because the situation was chosen for exposure.

See also ARTISTS' COLONIES & SCHOOLS, CLOUDS, MILLSTONE GRIT, NORFOLK WHERRIES, RIVERS, SHIPPING FORECAST, TEXTILE MILLS, TIDE MILLS, WATER-MILLS, WEATHER-BOARDING, WIND FARMS, WINDS.

W I N D S

The wind tantalises us with its invisible power – in many cultures this is the breath of god, the founding mystery. It is a source of violence, gentleness and miracles.

East Anglia and the South suffer between twenty and sixty tornadoes a year. The Parish Map of Selsey in Sussex shows a little whirlwind gathering in the sea, dated 1998. This stretch of country seems to attract spirals of wind that can do significant damage to roofs and trees.

On 8 December 1954 a tornado streaked from Chiswick to Southgate – nine miles – across London at 212 miles per hour, devastating a strip up to four hundred yards wide. People saw cars lifted fifteen feet in the air. When a tornado that was centred on Small Heath, Birmingham took the roofs off tens of houses and uprooted hundreds of trees on 28 July 2005, someone reported seeing a lucky ten-year-old boy fly through the air, as though playing Quidditch, and land back on the ground.

Wind is measured on the Beaufort scale. It runs from Force 0, with a wind speed of less than one mile per hour, through Gale Force 8 (30-35mph) to Hurricane Force 12 (60-100mph). Hearing Storm Force 11 carefully spelled out on the Shipping Forecast is not unusual and, rarely, hurricanes come this way. Camden told how Albion was surrounded by terrible northern winds and unpassable seas and that 'some are for placing the nativity of the winds hereabouts, as if they had been all generated here, and the confluence of matter had made this island its general rendezvous'. Certainly history tells stories of Julius Caesar, the Spanish Armada and other miscreants being scattered by the winds – it seems they have sometimes served us well.

On fine days the coast also enjoys sea breezes, which flow inland from a cool sea to hotter land when opposite winds are not too strong. At night this situation is reversed, giving rise to an offshore 'land breeze'. Fishermen know and use these well. On the peninsula of Devon and Cornwall sea breezes from north and south converge, producing eastward-marching bands of cumulus cloud; glider pilots learn to beware of the 'sea breeze bottleneck', where the land narrows north of Lyme Bay, which must be crossed during flights to the west. East Anglian farmers south of the Wash curse the sea breeze when it blows in bean aphids or contaminating pollen from wild sugar beet near the coast.

It is from the west that our prevailing winds help the Gulf Stream to keep us warmer than our latitude would suggest. They bring rain and are lured to drop it by westerly hills and the Pennines. Shelley's 'Ode to the West Wind' opines: 'Wild Spirit, which art moving everywhere;/Destroyer and Preserver; hear, O hear!' He ends with the optimistic lines: 'if Winter comes, can Spring be far behind?' It is the north wind that brings us winter, and the east wind that consolidates it, blowing from the 'wastes of Siberia'. In summer an easterly wind brings the heat and dryness of the great continental landmass. Winds from the south help our winged migrants to reach us – red admirals, swallows – flying from Africa via Europe. The south wind also brings occasional 'blood rains', sand carried from the Sahara high in the atmosphere for 1,600 miles. On 1 July 1968 people all the way from Liphook in Hampshire to the Midlands had to clear layers of red dust from their cars and homes after a dry wind.

Most cultures have names for particular winds. We have but one: the feared easterly Helm Wind, which blows down into Cumberland from the Pennines. It is astonishingly local, blasting the villages that lie in the shadow of the Cross Fell range in the Eden valley – Gamblesby, Kirkland, Melmerby, Milburn and Ousby – but said never to cross the Eden. Whenever the wind blows, telltale cloud formations appear, known as the Helm Cloud and the Helm Bar. Locals dread its onset in spring and autumn, for it can roar like a train for days on end when the conditions are right. It scorches vegetation, knocks sheep and people off their feet, rips slates from roofs, even makes farm gates impossible to open. John Ruskin regarded it as one of the 'Plague Winds' of the world. Gail Vines explains what Gordon Manley, a twentieth-century geographer, discovered: 'The secret of the helm wind lies in the unique ramp-shape of the Pennine Ridge: a gentle upward sloping approach on the east, a solid, unbroken ridge crest and a steep but very long, smooth descent on the western, lee side. Once air has passed over the ridge, it becomes warmer, drier and faster. With no obstacles to slow its progress on the downward slope, the wind acquires tremendous force.'

Other places have a reputation: Windwhistle Hill, near Chard in Somerset, Windhill in west Yorkshire and Windle in Lancashire are all descriptive names. The tower of St Botolph's, or the Boston Stump, in Lincolnshire attracts the breezes; it is said that the piety of the prospective saint so disturbed the devil that he huffed and puffed strongly enough that the wind never leaves. A strong gust of wind in Cheshire might be called Whittle, following a grisly incident in the wind in the sixteenth century, involving a dropped coffin bearing a Captain of the same name. A puff of wind in Cornwall may get noted as a waddy. Meg Amsden reports that in the Norfolk/Suffolk Broads sudden winds are known as Rogers – they have been known to drive boats up the banks and to strip windmills of their sails.

The people who gather on Parliament Hill in north London to fly their kites, and participants in Kite Festivals, for example on Barbury Castle near Swindon, Wiltshire, make visible the unseeable. So do the billowing sails of the dinghies on Hornsea Mere in Yorkshire and the wind

447

Hawthorn.

surfers' movements in Chichester and Langstone harbours in Hampshire. The sport was invented by Peter Chilvers off Hayling Island in the late 1950s.

Even though you cannot see the wind, the sheltering sycamores around Pennine farms, the sculpted forms of the beeches across Exmoor in Devon, the shapes and orientations of harbours, the floating presence of the buzzard and the flight path of planes landing at Manchester airport all tell of its dominance and direction.

See also ALBION, CLOUDS, COOLING TOWERS, CROP CIRCLES, DEVIL, EAST, FOG & MIST, FRETS, FROST & FROST HOLLOWS, HALF-YEAR BIRDS, HARBOURS, NORTH, SHIPPING FORECAST, WEATHER, WEATHER-VANES, WIND FARMS, WINDMILLS.

WINDSOR & COUNTRY CHAIRS

English vernacular furniture is all too often overlooked in favour of the work of the great cabinet makers – Chippendale, Hepplewhite and Sheraton. But there is a rich tradition of regional and local variety found in 'country' furniture, especially the Windsor and the rush-seated ladder- and spindle-back chairs, which kept our woodland in good heart.

Chair making proliferated in the late eighteenth and nineteenth centuries to supply local needs. As people became more affluent, chair-making centres developed in places such as High Wycombe in Buckinghamshire, Macclesfield in Cheshire, Worksop in Nottinghamshire, Spilsby in Lincolnshire, Todmorden in Yorkshire, Yealmpton and Cullompton in Devon and Axbridge in Somerset.

Bernard Cotton explained: 'Windsor chairs were distinguished from other turned chairs in having a shaped wooden seat into which the legs and back support spindles and splats were morticed.' This basic framework has been embellished and spontaneously interpreted in myriad ways by chair makers all over the country, who used wood from local sources to make Windsor arm, high-backed, side, kitchen and rocking chairs.

Different 'Windsor' chairs were made in Cornwall, Devon, Somerset, Nottinghamshire, Lincolnshire, south Yorkshire and Durham. But the main centre of production was the Chilterns and Thames valley, centred on High Wycombe. Windsor, Berkshire was the place from which the chairs were dispatched to London. Surrounded by beech woods and close to the city, it was in an ideal position for the trade to develop; it also served the South, Midlands and East Anglia.

At the beginning of the season self-employed wood-workers in the Chilterns bought standing trees from the estates and turned them into chair parts to be sold on to the chair manufacturers. The beech woods would have been alive with activity: craftsmen turning beech wood on their pole lathes into chair legs; working in saw-pits to make elm planks for the seats; in temporary shelters creating seat bottoms with an adze; immersing yew branches in steaming tanks and bending them to make an arm or top bow. In among the trees there would be stacks of turned chair legs drying; in the village of Radnage they stuffed the legs into hedges to air.

The four chair makers in High Wycombe in 1790 grew to nearly a hundred factories in 1877, producing 4,700 chairs a day. Over the years they manufactured a wide variety, from comb-back (armed) chairs with turned or cabriole legs and high-hoop-back arm and side chairs with wheel-motif fretted splats, to square and scroll-back side chairs with various kinds of cross splats, and one of the most popular kinds of all – the lath-back Windsor side chair, which is still made today.

By contrast, chair makers in the North West – Cheshire, Lancashire, Cumberland and Westmorland – produced turned, rush-seated chairs with ladder and spindle backs. These simple, elegant seats were made mainly of ash and alder, but birch, beech, cherry, elm, sycamore, walnut and yew were also used. Alder was seldom employed elsewhere for chair making, but was reasonably common along rivers, where it was planted to stabilise the banks. Its main attraction was that it could be made to resemble mahogany in grain and colour.

The Macclesfield ladder-back chairs, with their distinctive, round stay rails with barrel-shaped ends, may have been borrowed from a device used in the silk industry called a 'picking stick'. The family firm of Leicester, which was in business between 1814 and 1881, was responsible for many of these fine chairs. The seats were made by outworkers who specialised in weaving rush or willow. Club-rush and sea club-rush were cut from lakes, fens, riverbanks and estuaries in early July and dried. They were also used in the annual rush-bearings, where rush carts piled high with bundles of shaved rushes were constructed with great skill; Bernard Cotton suggested that these rushes were sold to the seat makers after the ceremonies.

The Dales rush-seated chairs of about 1800 to 1870 are characterised by the single row of spindles that decorate the backs. Variation was achieved in the many different designs of turned spindles for the backs and front stretchers. Rush-seated ladder-back chairs were also a feature of the Lincolnshire towns of Spilsby, Louth and Alford in the north and Boston and Spalding in the south.

The Mendlesham chair, attributed to Richard Day of Mendlesham, Suffolk, is representative of the East Anglian

High back Windsor chair.

classical chair, with its flat-top and formal back splays and turned buttons, and its curved and shaped arms (side chairs are rare); it embraced some aspects of the Windsor chair, such as the turned legs and shaped seat. Made with fruit-wood and elm or sycamore seats, these chairs were probably made for special occasions.

See also ALDER, ASH, BEECH, ELM, OAK, RUSH-BEARING, SYCAMORE, WALNUT, WOODS.

WINTERBOURNES

Winterbourne is a descriptive name found in the southern chalklands for a stream that flows only when the water-table is high, usually in winter. Because the water flow is unreliable, it makes conditions difficult for wildlife, but a number of species, especially some small invertebrates, have adapted to cope with long periods without flowing water.

Many villages adjacent to these sporadic streams have been named after them, such as Winterbourne Stoke on the river Till and Winterbourne Bassett on the Kennet in Wiltshire, Winterborne Monkton and Winterborne Came on the South Winterborne in Dorset.

After the rivers Nailbourne, Lavant and Gypsey Race seasonal streams are called nailbournes in Kent, lavants in Hampshire and gipseys (hard 'g') in the Yorkshire Wolds. From medieval times death was said to follow the appearance of the Gypsey Race, and later all manner of disaster.

See also BECKS, BOURNES, BROOKS, BURNS, CHALK STREAMS, DIALECTS, FORDS, RHYNES, RIVERS, SOUGHS, STANDING STONES.

WOODS

We have no wilderness, no expanses of wildwood, no great forests on the scale of northern Europe. What we do have are ancient woods, and they are the more precious because, as Oliver Rackham writes, '*For a thousand years England, at least, has had less woodland than most European countries and has taken correspondingly more care of its woods. By the thirteenth century AD woodland management was a fully-developed art with conservation as its chief objective.*' We and our woods have learned to live and work together, although there have been aberrations: voracious coniferisation and the loss of woodland skills in the twentieth century, for example.

This was predominantly a wooded land, and the remnants of ancient woodland present the richest of all habitats, from the flora, fauna and mycorrhizal fungi of their soils to the range of lichens, ferns, insects, birds and animals they support and the shrubs and flowers beneath them. We also have patches of wood pasture in parkland, where grazing with occasional trees has been the regime for hundreds of years.

Trees rarely gather as a single species, as in the yew wood of Kingley Vale in Sussex. Most enjoy one another's company, different assemblages typifying different ecological and conservation conditions. Oliver Rackham suggests at least 31 types of ancient woodland in England; George Peterken offered 58 ancient and semi-natural woodland types. They multiply within the broader groupings of ash-wych elm, ash-maple, hazel-ash, ash-lime, oak-lime, chestnut, birch-oak, alder, beech, hornbeam and elm.

Oaks are our most common woodland trees; sessile oak (*Quercus petraea*) predominates in the North and West uplands and pedunculate oak (*Quercus robur*) in the South and East. Birch now pops up anywhere; it is a hardy pioneer, enjoying the company of oak. Ash seeks out the limestones, from the Mendips in Somerset to the magnesian limestone in County Durham. Beech prefers chalk downs and wolds and the oolitic limestone of the Cotswolds; under its dark shadow little will grow, making it one of the most open woodlands in which to walk. Hornbeam is most comfortable in the Home Counties, and sweet chestnut sticks to the South on acid soils. Alder enjoys plashy places; it still dominates the Broads and wet parts of Breckland in Norfolk and, together with willow, borders the Cheshire meres. Wych elm makes for mixed woodland, especially in the North. Lime woods are found in Lincolnshire, but rarely elsewhere (although six thousand years ago lime was *the* lowland tree). Beneath the oaks and beech of the New Forest holly muscles in. Among the colours of the Wye valley in spring the white blossom of the wild cherry stands out. Box hangs on where it is dry and warm, as at Box Hill in Surrey, and the sparely scattered wild service tree usually indicates lime or clay.

To visit a favourite bluebell wood in spring or to explore the wood close by every day is a luxury with real benefits:

> *Who hath not felt the influence that so calms*
> *The weary mind in summers sultry hours*
> *When wandering thickest woods beneath the arms*
> *Of ancient oaks and brushing nameless flowers*

John Clare, from 'Wood Rides'

Woods make places. The abundance of woodland in Kent and Sussex is unexpected, so densely peopled are they. In Dorset the absence of woodland is equally surprising.

449

The Forestry Commission is changing its emphasis on discordant evergreens, which have dominated planting for three-quarters of a century, diminishing the personality and ecology of so much of our uplands and heaths. Over the next century it will 'persecute the conifer' in favour of hardwood, carbon fixing, nature conservation, recreation and landscape.

Woods are always changing: expanding as grazing diminishes in the uplands, failing to regenerate as abundant deer eat saplings, contracting as development presses, degenerating as craft skills are lost. Lack of disturbance is important – ancient woodland and semi-natural woods may contain varieties of common species that have adapted to local conditions. But, as climate warms, droughts come more often, diseases proliferate and storms threaten. The debate is on. Should we be planting other varieties of oak and chestnut, and species such as walnut, and finally allowing that the sycamore is worth having? We all need to be involved, it is our places that will be changing. And we must actively work the patches of woodland around us, as well as planting more, for, as W.H. Auden said, 'a culture is no better than its woods'.

See also ALBION, ALDER, ANCIENT TREES, ASH, BEECH, BIRCH, BLACK DOGS, BLACK POPLAR, BLACKTHORN, BLUEBELLS, CROSSROADS, DAFFODILS, ELM, FERNS, FOLKTALES, GREEN MAN, GROVELY RIGHTS DAY, HAWTHORN, HENGES & STONE CIRCLES, HOLLY, HOLM OAK, HORNBEAM, HORSE CHESTNUT, LANDMARK TREES, LICHENS, LIME, LONDON PLANE, MIDSUMMER DAY, MISTLETOE, MONKEY-PUZZLE, OAK, ORCHARDS, PARKLAND, RAMSONS, ROBIN HOOD, ROWAN, ROYAL FORESTS, SCOTS PINE, SWEET CHESTNUT, SYCAMORE, WALNUT, WILLOW, YEW.

450

W R E S T L I N G

'To give a Cornish hug is a proverbial expression', Joseph Strutt wrote in the early nineteenth century, claiming that 'the inhabitants of Cornwall and Devon have, we are well assured, from time immemorial, been celebrated for their expertness in this pastime, and are universally said to be the best wrestlers in the kingdom'. Champions ran in families, such as the Menadues from Penryn, but sons have other aspirations now. Today, with small numbers and audience, 'razzlin' just clings on. Perhaps it is a victim, for the moment, of its own truth – nothing commercial here, no acting, just gentlemanly holding to gwarry wheag yu gwarry teag (fair play is good play).

Although intensely physical, the effort in the 'hug' seems static, more like Japanese sumo wrestling but less gross. Strict Cornish rules forbid kicking (unlike Devon); the object is to lift and throw one's opponent onto his or her back – when three points of shoulders and hips are touching the ground. Bouts are judged by three Sticklers, matching 'unthrown men' by elimination until the tournament is won. Celtic sports gatherings are reinforcing old links with Brittany and with Spain, Iceland, Scotland and northern England.

Cumberland and Westmorland wrestling retains an authenticity and identification with place rare in contemporary sport. It is also practised in Lancashire, Northumberland and County Durham. Farming families dominate, as they have for centuries, and the place for combat is the grass at a local gala or show. Fighting at different weights, men or boys clad in white ('stripped into their dublets and hosen, and untrussed', Strutt described), clench fists behind each other's backs:

The wrestling starts, late; a wide ring of people; then cars;
Then trees; then pale sky. Two young men in acrobats' tights
And embroidered trunks hug each other; rock over the grass
Stiff legged, in a two-man scrum. One falls: they shake hands

Philip Larkin, from 'Show Saturday'

The sport has moved with the times but it retains its local popularity. With up to seventy events in the year it also draws increasing numbers of visitors to Lakeland sports, galas and agricultural shows, such as Ribblehead Sheep Show.

In the Midlands Sikh and Indian wrestling are growing in popularity, and in London Turkish wrestling has a following.

See also AGRICULTURAL SHOWS, FELL RUNNING, PUB GAMES.

Cumberland and Westmorland wrestling, Alwinton Show, Northumberland.

You Can Read Me, Phil Baines, 1995.

X A N A D U

The way we see our surroundings is a cultural phenomenon that shifts and changes. The seventeenth century brought revolutions in scientific and technological thought, which led to the expansion of industry, the growth of cities and the drift to a mass society. In the eighteenth century a ripple of reaction grew into a flood through the poets and artists of the Romantic movement.

They began to express how they valued Nature for its spiritual power rather than simple utility, in what Alasdair Clayre described as *the new genius that broke through at this moment, in the description of the landscape, in the sense of communion with nature and in the feeling of close relationship with all other living beings*. They explored their sensibilities through emotion and morality, expressing nostalgia for the loss of innocence and beauty.

Some of our greatest poets, including William Blake, Lord Byron, John Clare, Samuel Taylor Coleridge, John Keats, Percy Bysshe Shelley and William Wordsworth, added to the momentum.

The great poetic outburst of Romanticism, hardly vanquished by T.S. Eliot and twentieth-century poetry, has influenced us all. Just as Columbus did not 'discover' America, neither did the eighteenth-century thinkers 'discover' beauty, or even 'the sublime' in the mountains, nor for the first time see *a World in a Grain of Sand*, but their words shifted our cultural vision, sizing the canvas for others, including Turner and Constable – *Painting is but another word for feeling*.

Coleridge spent much time in the West Country, exploring the importance of the Imagination and pioneering the transference of the experience of walking in the hills, in weather or by the sea into poetry. Exchanging visits with his good friends Dorothy and William Wordsworth in the Lake District, his own role was eclipsed by the work he influenced in William Wordsworth – the seminal poetry of *The Prelude*.

The vital role of detail and the particular to the poetic mind is nowhere more poignantly told than in this cautionary tale. Depressed and tired, Coleridge one day went for a long walk on his own, from his house at Nether Stowey in the Quantock Hills in Somerset. He had been reading *The Pilgrimage* – 'In Xanada did Cublai Can build a stately Pallace' – by Samuel Purchas (1614), which clearly echoed in his mind. He was not well and stopped on the way, probably at the isolated Ash Farm.

Here, *in a sort of Reverie brought on by two grains of Opium, taken to check a dysentery*, he began to compose a poem in his head:

In Xannadù did Cubla Khan
a stately Pleasure Dome decree;
Where ALPH, the sacred River, ran
Thro caverns measureless to Man
Down to a sunless Sea.

His dreaming was broken by a knock at the door. Punctuation so profound that we shall never know what more Coleridge had to say, since later he could retrieve but 54 lines – the *person on business from Porlock* had interrupted the Muse. This fragment of poetry, exotic in inception as well as content, has nevertheless been tied by Richard Holmes to the *erotic, magical geography of Culborne Combe seen from Ash Farm*.

See also ARTISTS' COLONIES & SCHOOLS, LAKES, MUSIC, SCULPTURES, WATERFALLS.

Y A N   T A N   T E T H E R A

Believed to be derived from Ancient British, the language of counting sheep had many local forms into the twentieth century. The count went to twenty, each twenty being marked by a stone or on a stick to keep 'score'.

453

	Yorkshire (Wensleydale)	Cumberland	Cornwall	Suffolk
One	Yain	Yan	Onan	Hant
Two	Tain	Tyan	Dyw	Tant
Three	Eddero	Tethera	Tyr	Tethery
Four	Peddero	Methera	Pedyr	Futhery
Five	Pitts	Pimp	Pymp	Fant
Six	Tayter	Sethera	Whe	Sarny
Seven	Later	Lethera	Seyth	Darny
Eight	Overro	Othera	Eath	Dorny
Nine	Coverro	Dothera	Nau	Downy
Ten	Disc	Deek	Dek	Dick
Eleven	Yain disc			
Twelve	Tain disc			
Thirteen	Eddero disc			
Fourteen	Peddero disc			
Fifteen	Bumfitt			
Sixteen	Yan a bum			
Seventeen	Tean a bum			
Eighteen	Tethera bum			
Nineteen	Methera bum			
Twenty	Jiggit			

See also ACCENTS, ALLEYS, DIALECTS, DRYSTONE WALLS, SHEEP.

Y E W

The autumn of 2003 was an excellent one for snottygogs in the south of England, reminding one that some yews are female (red, scrunchy, slithery berries underneath) and some are male (eerily tidy underfoot). The Sussex word for the seeds, contained in translucent sticky red arils (berries), compares with snodder gills in Hampshire, snat berries in Northampton and snottle berries in Yorkshire.

Of all our trees the yew has kept its Ancient British name. This suggests early power and enduring significance emerging from the venerability it emanates, the indestructibility of its wood and the fact that it is evergreen – what better symbols of eternal life?

Sunless, tangled woods of yew darken the white chalkland at Hambledon Hill in Dorset and Kingley Bottom in west Sussex, north of Chichester (this is the finest stand of yew, ancient and young, in Europe). Still following the chalk they trace antique routes, such as the Pilgrims' Way in Surrey and Kent. Further west individual yews, so prevalent along old drove roads, such as the line of the A30 near Stockbridge, are known as the Hampshire weed. Around Bristol they dominate some woods, as at Bourton Combe. In Dorset and Wiltshire they were planted to protect houses. In the North yews commune with ash on limestone, as at Whitbarrow and Witherslack in Westmorland, but are also found on other rocks.

There was a fashion for yew hedges and topiary in Tudor times, following the French. In Norfolk, at Blickling Hall, a hedge of a hundred yards in length reaches seventeen feet high, and at Melbourne in Derbyshire there is a tunnel of more than a hundred yards in three-hundred-year-old yews. The 99 yews of Painswick churchyard in Gloucestershire have voluptuously melted into one another with countless clippings. The avenues of upright, fastigiate Irish yews found in cemeteries seem rigidly forlorn in comparison with the undisciplined, hollow, spreading English yews found close to the parish church.

The prime association of the yew is with the churchyard, as Tennyson reminds us in 'In Memoriam': *'Old Yew, which graspest at the stones/That name the under-lying dead'*. The yew (with the willow) certainly used to stand in for the palm in the church year, but most commonplace explanations are contested. The churchyard keeps them separate from animals, but cattle only die from poisoning if they gorge on the leaves. It offers easy access for the making of bows, but yew from Spain was much in demand for this in the Middle Ages. Folklorist Jennifer Westwood thinks these are relatively recent fancies. She believes that the detail revolves around ecclesiastical history, with the planting of yew trees in churchyards growing out of Roman practice later reinforced by the Normans.

Yew will outlast iron: a spear made of yew found at Clacton, Essex has been dated to more than a quarter of a million years ago, the oldest wooden artefact known. The yew's most profound role as a symbol of immortality has been revisited many times through antiquity and it persists. English custom was to strew yew branches in the grave; people continued to do this in early nineteenth-century Suffolk. But in Victorian times came the switch from everlasting life to associations with death and mourning. Now the yew offers increasing hope – the clippings are harvested for use in anti-cancer drugs.

Allen Meredith believes that the enormous yew on an island in the Thames at Ankerwyke, Buckinghamshire is an *axis mundi*, the sacred centre of tribal territory. He has placed the signing of the *Magna Carta* under its branches, rather than at the park marked Runnymede across the river – Rune mede was where the Saxons met to consult the runes. With a girth of more than 31 feet it is thought that the Ankerwyke yew would have been big even then; it is perhaps two and a half thousand years old.

Trees at Clun in Shropshire and Darley Dale in Derbyshire are both 33 feet in girth and reckoned to be three thousand years old. The yew at Darley Dale stands well above the ground and is surrounded by stones. At Ashbrittle in Somerset the 38-foot-girth tree stands high on an ancient mound. They are youngsters in comparison with the yew at Crowhurst in Surrey, which has its own door and may be four thousand years old.

See also ALDER, ANCIENT TREES, ASH, BEECH, BIRCH, BLACK POPLAR, BLACKTHORN, CHURCHYARDS, CLIPPING THE CHURCH, EASTER CUSTOMS, ELM, FIELD MAPLE, HAWTHORN, HAZEL, HOLLY, HOLM OAK, HORNBEAM,

HORSE CHESTNUT, JUNIPER, LANDMARK TREES, LIME, LONDON PLANE, MONKEY-PUZZLE, OAK, ORCHARDS, PEARS, POPLAR, ROWAN, ROYAL FORESTS, SCOTS PINE, SWEET CHESTNUT, SYCAMORE, TOPIARY, WALNUT, WHITEBEAM, WILLOW, WOODS.

Z A W N S

The coast of Cornwall is intricately carved by the waves. Its hard rocks notwithstanding, many narrow clefts have been etched by the sea; in the west Cornish dialect these are called zawns. Softer minerals in the Permian granite, including tin and also copper – staining the rocks with bright verdigris (turret-roof green) – have succumbed to marine erosion along the veins, often leaving vertical cliffs on all sides. Sometimes these have been further accentuated by mining.

Zawn a Bal means mine cleft. At Barrett's Zawn a tunnel, now fallen in, was made to move slate to the sea. Botallack Loe Warren Zawn offers more than 23 minerals, including copper, cuprite and malachite and also botallackite. Nearby Stamps and Jowl Zawn offers twelve minerals (the misheard *stampez an jowl* means the devil's stamping mill). Zawn Buzz and Gen is the English attempt to make sense of *bos an gean* – the giant's home. Only too often language and dialect are flattened by surveyors.

Chough Zawn embodies both avian history and hope. This proud, black, red-billed bird is the emblem of Cornwall; perhaps its aerial acrobatics will once more be seen here. Climbers love these challenging cliff faces. Great Zawn offers magnificent granite climbing, exposed to the westerly elements and above the ocean swells, with 220 feet of multi-pitch routes, including Desolation Row, Xanadu, Dream and Liberator.

On the granite Isle of Lundy Big Zawn, Grand Falls Zawn and Arch Zawn are known as good climbs. In Wales and on the Isle of Portland in Dorset the word re-emerges; in Breton the word *saon* means valley. Back in Penwith, Cornwall a walk around the coastal path will introduce you to at least 35 zawns in the granite between Newlyn and St Ives.

See also CHOUGHS, CLIFFS, COASTLINE, DEVIL, ENGINE HOUSES, GRANITE, MINES, SHIPPING FORECAST, XANADU.

Z I G Z A G S

Gilbert White, father of natural history, created a formal path through the beech trees from Selborne in the eighteenth century, as recounted by Richard Mabey: '*he built the famous zig zag up the Hanger, and at the top a hermitage in which to hold summer picnics*'.

But it was the Victorians who popularised the idea of the promenade, and with it the proliferation of paths negotiating steep slopes for the sheer enjoyment of finding a view. Londoners flocked to Box Hill in Surrey by railway in the nineteenth century and took pleasure in walking up the chalk Zig Zag. With the dominance of the car this has become a metalled road and is enjoyed as a challenge by drivers, as is Zig-Zag Hill in Dorset, which climbs thrillingly through ever-tightening chicanes up the chalk edge towards Ashmore.

Many seaside towns boast fine promenades overlooked by hotels and encouraging bracing walks in view of the sea. Bournemouth, a Victorian invention, masses its hotels along the cliff top, with winding walks and wind-blown pine trees. There is also a remarkable promenade along the undercliff, with beach huts, booths and breakwaters disappearing in perspective along the strand. Linking the upper walks and lower promenade are the chines and an array of zigzag paths, the bane of parents in search of leisure, the joy of little legs. The views are at each turn spectacular, with the Needles glistening from the Isle of Wight and Old Harry from the Isle of Purbeck.

Folkestone also has a high promenade, the Leas, the place to be seen in Edwardian times, backed by hotels, lawns and bandstand. From here you can drop straight down in the funicular Leas Lift, or via tortuous paths through fantastic artificial tunnels and caves, catching your breath on the way up in tucked-in shelters with fine views.

See also BANDSTANDS, BEACHES, CHINES, CLIFFS, COVES, DROVE ROADS, FUNICULAR RAILWAYS, HOLLOW WAYS, PROMENADES, STACKS, WHITE CLIFFS.

455

Celebrating Local Distinctiveness
Bachelard, Gaston. *The Poetics of Space*. Beacon Books, 1958/1969.
Clifford, Sue and King, Angela (eds.). *Local Distinctiveness: Place, Particularity and Identity*. Conference Papers. Common Ground, 1993.
Gould, Stephen J. *Eight Little Piggies*. Jonathan Cape, 1993.
Mandelbrot, Benoît. *The Fractal Geometry of Nature*. Freeman, 1977.

A

Abbeys
Aston, M. *Monasteries in the Landscape*. Tempus, 2000.
Raistrick, A. *The Pennine Dales*. Arrow, 1972.
Abbots Bromley Horn Dance
Abbots Bromley Parish Council. Abbots Bromley Map. 2000.
Hole, Christina. *British Folk Customs*. Hutchinson, 1976.
Kightly, Charles. *The Customs and Ceremonies of Britain*. Thames & Hudson, 1996.
Accents
Caxton, William. *Eneydos* (Preface). 1490.
Claibourne, Robert. *The Life and Times of the English Language*. Bloomsbury, 1990.
Crystal, David. *The Cambridge Encyclopedia of Language*. CUP, 1987.
Orwell, George. *Politics and the English Language*. Typophiles, 1947.
Trudgill, Peter. *The Dialects of England*. Basil Blackwell, 1990.
Turner-Bishop, Aiden. Email, 27 April 2004.
Aegirs
Environment Agency. 'The Severn Bore and Trent Aegir Predictions' 2003, 4, 5.
Hole, Christina. *English Folklore*. Batsford, 1940.
Agricultural Shows
Larkin, Philip. 'Show Saturday'. *Collected Poems*, Faber & Faber, 1988.
North Tyne and Redesdale Agricultural Society. Bellingham Show Catalogues 2003, 2004.
Riddle, C. 'So Useful an Undertaking': A History of the Royal Cornwall Show 1793-1993. Royal Cornwall Agricultural Association, 1993.
Airfields
Bannerman, Kenneth P. *A Towering Control: The Story of Britain's Airfields*. IS Enterprises, 2001.
Bowdler, Roger. 'Aerodromes and Air Force buildings', *Deserted Bastions: Historic Naval and Military Architecture*. SAVE, 1993.
Foot, William. 'Landscape of War', *British Archaeology*. August 2000.
Lake, Jeremy. 'Historic airfields: evaluation and conservation', *Materiel Culture: The Archaeology of Twentieth-century Conflict*, Schofield, J. et al (eds.). Routledge, 2002.

'Historic Military Aviation Sites', *English Heritage Conservation Bulletin*, Issue 44. June 2003.
English Heritage Conservation Bulletin, Issue 41. September 2001.
Albion
Ackroyd, Peter. *Albion*. Chatto & Windus, 2002.
Collins, Roger and McClure, Judith (eds.). *Bede: The Ecclesiastical History of the English People*. OUP, 1969/1994.
Ekwall, E. *Dictionary of English Place Names*. OUP, 1936.
Evans, Ivor H. (revised by). *Brewer's Dictionary of Phrase and Fable*. Cassell, 1990.
Geoffrey of Monmouth. *The History of the Kings of Britain*. Penguin Classic, 1966/1984.
Nennius. 'British History and The Welsh Annals'. *Arthurian Period Sources*, vol. 8. Phillimore, 1980.
Radice, Betty (ed.). *Bede: The Ecclesiastical History of the English People*. Penguin Classic, 1955/1990.
Westwood, Jennifer. *Albion: A Guide to Legendary Britain*. Grafton, 1985.
Wood, Michael. *In Search of England*. Viking, 1999/Penguin, 2000.
'Gildas'. *Period Sources*, vol. 7. Phillimore, 1978.
Alder
Cotton, Bernard D. *The English Regional Chair*. Antique Collectors' Club, 1990.
Edlin, H.L. *Trees, Woods and Man*. Collins, 1956/1978.
Edlin, H.L. *Woodland Crafts in Britain*. David & Charles, 1949/1973.
Fraser, Andrew J.L. Letter, 1993.
Tansley, A.G. *The British Isles and their Vegetation*. CUP, 1965.
Alexanders
Grey-Wilson, Christopher and Blamey, Marjorie. *The Illustrated Flora of Britain and Northern Europe*. Hodder & Stoughton, 1989.
Grigson, G. *The Englishman's Flora*. Paladin, 1975.
Mabey, R. *Flora Britannica*. Chatto & Windus, 1996.
Vickery, A. *A Dictionary of Plant Lore*. OUP, 1995.
Alleys
Addison, W. *The Old Roads of England*. Batsford, 1980.
Barton, Richard. Email, 15 March 2004.
Bebbington, G. *Street Names of London*. Batsford, 1972.
Cross, Rosie. Emails, 2003.
Jones, Mark W. *A Walk around the Snickleways of York*. William Sessions, 1983.
Room, A. *The Street Names of England*. Paul Watkins, 1992.
Slade, Chris. Email, 6 August 2003.
Somerville, Margaret. Conversation, September 2004.
Taplin, Kim. *The English Path*. The Boydell Press, 1979.

Whitworth, A. *The A–Z of Whitby Yards*. Culva House, 2003.
Geographers' A–Z London Atlas.
Allotments
Crouch, David and Ward, C. *The Allotment*. Faber & Faber, 1988.
Deakin, Roger. *Ten Rod Plot*. Albion Television, 1992.
Friends of the Earth Allotments Manual, 1976.
Thompson, Elspeth. *Urban Gardener*. Sunday Telegraph, 1999.
Almshouses
Bailey, B. *Almshouses*. Robert Hale, 1988.
Betjeman, J. *Cornwall: A Shell Guide*. Faber & Faber, 1964.
Cockburn, E.O. *The Almshouses of Dorset*. Friary Press, 1970.
Ammonites
Bassett, Michael G. 'Formed Stones', Folklore and Fossils. National Museum of Wales, 1982.
Middlemiss, F.A. *Fossils*. David & Charles, 1969.
British Mesozoic Fossils. British Museum (Natural History), 1967.
Ancient Trees
Green, Ted. Meeting, 6 January 2004.
Johnson, O. (ed.). *Champion Trees, The Tree Register*. Whittet Books, 2003.
Mitchell, A. *A Field Guide to the Trees of Britain and Northern Europe*. Collins, 1974.
Rackham, Oliver. *Ancient Woodland: Its History, Vegetation and Uses in England*. Edward Arnold, 1980/Castlepoint Press, 2003.
Rackham, Oliver. *History of British Countryside*. Dent, 1986.
Rackham, Oliver. *Trees and Woodland in the English Landscape*. Dent, 1976.
'Veteran Trees'. *Nature in Avon: The Proceedings of the Bristol Naturalists Society*, vol. 61, 2001.
Anty-tumps
Buczacki, Stefan. *Fauna Britannica*. Hamlyn, 2002.
Chinery, Michael. *The Natural History of the Garden*. Fontana/Collins, 1977.
Duffey et al. *Grassland Ecology and Wildlife Management*. Chapman & Hall, 1974.
King, T.J. 'The Plant Ecology of Ant-Hills in calcareous Grasslands. (1) Patterns of Species in Relation to Ant-hills in Southern England. (2) Succession in the Mounds'. *Journal of Ecology* 65, 1977.
Knight, Maxwell. *Be a Nature Detective*. Frederick Warne, 1968.
Smith, C.J. *The Ecology of the English Chalk*. Academic Press, 1980.
Thomas, Jeremy, illustrated by Lewington, Richard. *The Butterflies of Britain and Ireland*. Dorling Kindersley/National Trust, 1991.

Wildlife and Archaeology of Porton Down. MOD.
Apple Day
The Apple Map. Common Ground, 1993.
The Apple Broadcast. Common Ground, 1994.
The Common Ground Book of Orchards. Common Ground, 2000.
Apples
Morgan, Joan and Richards, Alison. *The New Book of Apples*. Ebury Press, 2002.
Smith, Muriel. *The National Apple Register of the United Kingdom*. Ministry of Agriculture, Fisheries and Food, 1971.
Ward, Ruth. Conversations, 1992.
Apple Games and Customs. Common Ground, 2005.
The Common Ground Book of Orchards. Common Ground, 2000.
Apricots
Davenport, Philippa. 'Golden Wonders'. *Country Living*, June 1995.
Greenoak, Francesca. *Forgotten Fruit: The English Orchard and Fruit Garden*. Andre Deutsch, 1983.
Grigson, Jane. *Fruit Book*. Penguin, 1982.
Roach, F.A. *Cultivated Fruits of Britain: Their Origin and History*. Blackwell, 1985.
Ward, Ruth. 'Apricot Villages'. May 1992.
Aqueducts
Brabbs, Derry. *England's Heritage*. Weidenfeld & Nicolson, 2003.
Burton, Anthony. *Daily Telegraph Guide to Britain's Working Past*. Aurum Press, 2002.
Ruddock, Ted. *Arch Bridges and their Builders 1735-1835*. CUP, 1979.
Sealey, Anthony. *Bridges and Aqueducts*. Hugh Evelyn, 1976.
Smith, Peter L. *Canal Architecture*. Shire, 1997.
'Bricks and Canals'. British Brick Society, Information 85, October 2001.
The Cromford Canal, Walking Britain's Heritage. Amber Valley Borough Council, 2000.
Arbor Day
Box, John. 'Dressing the Arbor Tree'. *Folklore* 114, April 2003.
Arcades
Cathcart Borer, M. *The Story of Covent Garden*. Robert Hale, 1984.
Dixon, R. and Muthesius, S. *Victorian Architecture*. Thames & Hudson, 1985.
Lloyd, David W. *The Making of English Towns*. Gollancz, 1984.
Arches
Hodge, Pol and Clarke, Matthew. Emails, 9 and 21 September 2003, via Cornish Dictionary online.
Perkins, J.W. *Geology Explained in Dorset*. David & Charles, 1977.

Steers, J.A. *The Coastline of England and Wales.* CUP, 1964.

Artists' Colonies & Schools
Cross, T. *Painting the Warmth of the Sun: The St Ives Artists 1939-1975.* Lutterworth, 1995.
Dakers, C. *The Holland Park Circle: Artists and Victorian Society.* Yale UP, 1999.
Jacobs, M. and Warner, M. *The Phaidon Companion to Art and Artists in the British Isles.* Phaidon, 1980.
Mallalieu, H.L. *The Norwich School: Crome, Cotman and their Followers.* Academy Editions, 1974.
Moore, A. *The Norwich School of Artists.* HMSO, 1995.

Ash
Edlin, H.L. *Trees, Woods and Man.* Collins, 1956/1978.
Rackham, Oliver. *Ancient Woodland.* Castlepoint Press, 2003.
Rackham, Oliver. *The History of the British Countryside.* Dent, 1980.
Rackham, Oliver. *The Last Forest.* Dent, 1989.
Rackham, Oliver. *Trees and Woodland in the English Landscape.* Dent, 1990.

Asparagus
Hargreaves, John. *Harvests and Harvesters: Fruit and Vegetable Growing in Britain.* Gollancz, 1987.
Mabey, Richard. *Flora Britannica.* Chatto & Windus, 1996.
Smith, Philip H. 'The Sefton Coast sand dunes, Merseyside'. *British Wildlife,* October 2000.
Yorke, Reg. Email, 19 August 2005.

Avalon
Evans, Ivor, H. (revised by). *Brewer's Dictionary of Phrase and Fable, 14th edition.* Cassell, 1990.
Hawkins, Desmond. *Avalon and Sedgemoor.* David & Charles, 1973.
Westwood, Jennifer. *Albion: A Guide to Legendary Britain.* Grafton, 1985.
Wood, Michael. *In Search of England.* Viking, 1999/Penguin, 2000.

Avenues
Grigson, Geoffrey. *Geoffrey Grigson's Countryside.* Ebury Press, 1982.
Lasdun, Susan. *The English Park: Royal, Private and Public.* Andre Deutsch, 1991.
Legg, Rodney. *The Stour Valley: From Stourhead to Christchurch.* Halsgrove, 2003.
Thomas, Keith. *Man and the Natural World: Changing Attitudes in England 1500-1800.* Allen Lane, 1983.

B

Badgers
Neal, Ernest. *The Natural History of Badgers.* Guild Publishing, 1986.

Harris, Stephen; Morris, Pat; Wray, Stephanie; Yalden, Derek. *A Review of British Mammals.* Joint Nature Conservation Committee, 1995.
Thomas, Edward. 'The Combe', from *The Collected Poems of Edward Thomas.* OUP, 1978.

Bakewell Pudding
Harben, P. *Traditional Dishes of Britain.* Bodley Head, 1953.
Mason, Laura with Brown, Catherine. *Traditional Foods of Britain: An Inventory.* Prospect Books, 1999.

Bandstands
Girouard, Mark. *The English Town.* Yale University Press, 1990.
Weir, Christopher. *Village and Town Bands.* Shire, 1981.

Bank Barns
Brunskill R.W. *Traditional Farm Buildings of Britain.* Gollancz, 1999.
Brunskill R.W. *Vernacular Architecture of the Lake Counties.* Faber & Faber, 1974.
Child, P. 'Farm Buildings' in *Devon Building* (Beacham, Peter, ed.). Devon Books, 1990.

Barns
Brunskill, R.W. *Traditional Farm Buildings of Britain and their Conservation.* Gollancz, 1998.
Brunskill R.W. *Vernacular Architecture of the Lake Counties.* Faber & Faber, 1974.
Child, P. 'Farm Buildings' in *Devon Building* (Beacham, Peter, ed.). Devon Books, 1990.
Harris, R. *Traditional Farm Buildings.* Arts Council, nd.
Lawson, Anne. Letter, 18 November 2002.
Wingfield Gibbons, David et al. *The New Atlas of Breeding Birds in Britain and Ireland: 1988-1991.* BTO/T. & A.D. Poyser, 1993.

Barrows
Ashbee, Paul. 'Barrows, cairns and a few impostors'. *British Archaeology,* no. 32, March 1998.
Bender, Barbara. Email, 2004.
Bender, Barbara. *Stonehenge.* Berg, 1998.
Harte, J. *Cuckoo Pounds and Singing Barrows.* Dorset Natural History and Archaeological Society, 1986.

Basking Sharks
Brassley, Angela and Paul. Conversation, 31 May 2003.
Brown, Paul. 'Push by Britain to save basking shark'. *Guardian,* 8 November 2002.
McCarthy, Michael. 'Trophy hunters put the future of the basking shark at risk'. *Independent,* 8 November 2002.
'Fish of the day'. *BBC Wildlife Magazine,* May 2004.

Bastles
Brown, R.J. *English Farmhouses.* Robert Hale, 1993.

Herdman, Mary. Conversation, 14 January 2004.
Mercer, Eric. *English Vernacular Houses.* The Stationery Office Books, 1975.
Ryder, Peter F. *Bastles and Towers in the Northumberland National Park.* Unpublished report, 1990.
Sim, Richard. Email, 4 December 2003.

Battlefields
Beckensall, Stan. *Northumberland: The Power of Place.* Tempus Publishing, 2001.
Burne, A.H. *The Battlefields of England.* Penguin, 1950/1996.
Williams, D.T. *The Battle of Bosworth Field.* Bosworth Publications, Leicestershire.
English Heritage Register of Historic Battlefields. HMSO, 1995. County Council, 1996.

Bawming the Thorn
Gittins, John. *Acorn.* Cheshire Landscape Trust. Various dates.
Kightly, Charles. *Customs and Ceremonies of Britain.* Thames & Hudson, 1986.
Stuart Smith, Elizabeth. Conversations, various dates.

Beachcombing
Ferris, L.C. *Pebbles on Cornwall's Beaches.* Tor Mark Press, nd.
Gates, Phil. 'Country Diary'. *Guardian,* 7 November 2002.
Conchological Society of Great Britain and Ireland.
Crown Estate.
Society of Thames Mudlarks.

Beaches
Hudson, S. *Islomania.* AGRE Books, 2000.
Pye, K. and French, P.W. 'Targets for Coastal Habitat Recreation no. 13'. English Nature Science, 1993.
The Good Beach Guide. Marine Conservation Society.

Beach Huts
Baber, Tim. Conversations and emails, 22 August 2002 and 5 December 2005.
Ferry, Kathryn. *Sheds on the Seashore: From Bathing Machines to Beach Huts* (book forthcoming).
Ferry, Kathryn. Email, 18 September 2003.
Gershlick, Janet. *Southwold Beach Huts.* Hair-Raising Publications, 2003.

Beacon Fires
Bromwich, Margaret. Letter, 27 August 2004.
Grigson, Geoffrey. *Geoffrey Grigson's Countryside.* Ebury Press, 1982.
Harte, Jeremy. *Cuckoo Pounds and Singing Barrows.* Dorset Natural History and Archaeological Society, 1986.

Beacons (Coastal)
Craster, E. *The Craster papers, Beadnell in the Eighteenth Century.* Northumberland County Record Office, nd.
Somerville, Christopher. *English Harbours and Coastal Villages.* Weidenfeld & Nicolson, 1989.

Woodman, Richard and Wilson, Jane. *The Lighthouses of Trinity House.* Thomas Reed, 2002.

Beating the Bounds
Hodgson's *History of Northumberland.* 1758.
Kightly, Charles. *The Customs and Ceremonies of Britain.* Thames & Hudson, 1986.
Aveton Gifford Parish Map. 1992.

Becks
Ekwall, E. *English River Names.* OUP, 1928.
Nicholson, Norman. 'Beck'. *Collected Poems.* Faber & Faber, 1994.

Bee Boles
Foster, A.M. *Bee Boles and Houses.* Shire Publications, 1988.
Francis, Sally. Emails, 2004.
Walker, Penelope and Crane, Eva. 'Bee Shelters and Bee Boles in Cumbria'. *Transactions of Cumberland and Westmorland Archaeological Society,* vol. xci, 1991.
Bee Boles. Dry Stone Walling Association of Great Britain.

Beech
Cobham Resource Consultants. *The Lincolnshire Wolds Landscape.* Countryside Commission, 1993.
Cotton, B.D. *The English Regional Chair.* Antique Collectors Club, 1990.
Edlin, H.L. *Trees, Woods and Man.* Collins, 1956/1978.
Edlin, H.L. *Woodland Crafts in Britain.* David & Charles, 1949/1973.
Land Use Consultants. *The Quantock Hills Landscape.* Countryside Agency, 2003.
Ratcliffe, D.A. (ed.). *A Nature Conservation Review.* CUP, 1977.
Tansley, Sir A.G. *The British Isles and their Vegetation.* CUP, 1965.
Corporation of London.

Beer
Atkins, Ronald. *Collins Gem: Beer.* HarperCollins, 1997.
McGill, Angus (ed.). *Pub: A Celebration.* Longmans, Green & Co. Ltd, 1969.
Owen, C.C. 'History of Brewing in Burton Upon Trent'. *Journal Institute of Brewing,* January-February, 1987.
Protz, Roger and Sharples, Steve. *Country Ales and Breweries.* Weidenfeld & Nicolson, 1999.
Smith, Philip G. *Water, water, water!* 1999.
Wheeler, Graham. *Home Brewing.* CAMRA, 1993.
CAMRA.

Bells & Bell-ringing
Baker, Mary. *Folklore and Customs of Rural England.* David & Charles, 1974.
Berryman, Adrian. Email, 3 May 2002.
Camp, John. *In Praise of Bells.* Hale, 1988.

Corbin, Alain. *Village Bells: Sound and Meaning in the Nineteenth-century French Countryside.* Columbia University Press, 1998.

Ingram, Tom. *Bells in England.* Frederick Muller, 1954.

Major, Bob (Reginald Harrison). *Bells of the Isle.* John Crowther, nd.

Strutt, Joseph. *The Sports and Pastimes of the People of England.* Thomas Tegg, 1838.

Westwood, J. and Simpson, J. *The Lore of the Land.* Penguin, 2005.

Dartmoor Changes (CD). Aune Head Arts, 2005.

The Towers and Bells Handbook. The Towers and Belfries Committee of the Central Council of Church Bell Ringers, 1973.

Bestiary

Carroll, Lewis. *Alice in Wonderland.* Macmillan, 1865.

Hartley, Dorothy. *Food in England.* Futura, 1954.

Jenkins, Simon. *England's Thousand Best Churches.* Penguin, 1999.

Mason, Peter. *The Brown Dog Affair.* Two Sevens Publishing, 1997.

Birch

Edlin, H.L. *Woodland Crafts in Britain.* David & Charles, 1949/1973.

Rackham, Oliver. *Ancient Woodland.* Castlepoint Press, 2003.

Biscuits

Baldock, Dorothy. *Favourite Norfolk Recipes.* Salmon Books, 1996.

Duff, Julie. *Cakes Regional and Traditional.* Grub Street, 2003.

Francis, Sally. Email, 8 May 2004.

Mason, Laura with Brown, Catherine. *Traditional Foods of Britain: An Inventory.* Prospect Books, 1999.

Pettigrew, Jane. *The Festive Table.* Pavilion, 1990.

Rothwell, Catherine. *Lancashire Recipes Old and New.* Countryside Publications, 1979.

Sekers, Simone. *Fine Food.* Hodder & Stoughton, 1987.

Black & White Buildings

Atkinson, T.D. *Local Style in English Architecture.* Batsford, 1947.

Brunskill, R.W. *Timber Building in Britain.* Gollancz, 1994.

Clifton-Taylor, Alec. *The Pattern of English Building.* Faber & Faber, 1972.

Black Dogs

Briggs, K.M. *A Dictionary of British Folk Tales.* Routledge & Kegan Paul, 1971/1991.

Bromwich, Margaret. Letter, August 2004.

Hole, Christina. *English Folklore.* Batsford, 1940.

Westwood, Jennifer. *Albion: A Guide to Legendary Britain.* Grafton, 1985.

Blackpool Rock

Mason, Laura with Brown, Catherine. *Traditional Foods of Britain: An Inventory.* Prospect Books, 1999.

Race, Margaret. *The Story of Blackpool Rock.* 1990.

Black Poplar

Cooper, Fiona. *The Black Poplar: Ecology, History & Conservation.* Windgather Press, 2006.

Cooper, Fiona. 'The Black Poplar'. *Tree News,* Spring/Summer 2003.

Cooper, Fiona. Email, 26 October 2003.

Miles, Archie. *Silva: The Tree in Britain.* Ebury Press, 1999.

Mitchell, Alan. *A Field Guide to the Trees of Britain and Northern Europe.* Collins, 1974.

Peterken, George. 'The Black Poplar'. *Tree News,* Autumn/Winter 2001.

Rackham, Oliver. *The History of the Countryside.* Dent, 1986.

Blackthorn

Cobbett, William. *Rural Rides.* 1830.

Grigson, Geoffrey. *The Englishman's Flora.* Paladin, 1975.

Marren, Peter. *Britain's Ancient Woodland Heritage.* David & Charles, 1990.

Pollard, E., Hooper, M.D. and Moore, N.W. *Hedges.* Collins, 1974.

Snow, Barbara and David. *Birds and Berries.* T. & A.D. Poyser, 1988.

Blow Holes

Craster, J. *The Natural History of Dunstanburgh.* Castle Point/MPBW, 1963.

Graham, F. *Bamburgh: The Farnes.* Butler Publications, 1991.

Hammond, Reginald J.W. (ed.). *West Cornwall.* Ward Lock, 1971.

Robinson, Adrian and Millward, Roy. *The Shell Book of the British Coast.* David & Charles, 1983.

Bluebells

Gibbons, Bob. 'Britain's top ten bluebell sites'. *Plantlife,* Spring 2004.

Gilmour, John and Walters, Max. *Wild Flowers.* Collins New Naturalist, 1954.

Grigson, Geoffrey. *The Englishman's Flora.* Paladin, 1975.

Marren, Peter. *Woodland Heritage.* David & Charles, 1990.

Rackham, Oliver. *Ancient Woodland.* Castlepoint Press, 2003.

Bluebells for Britain: a report on the 2003 Bluebells for Britain Survey. Plantlife, 2004.

Blue John

Edwards, K.C. *The Peak District.* New Naturalist, 1962/Fontana, 1973.

Innes-Smith, R. *Castleton and its Caves.* Derbyshire Countryside, 1994.

Blue Vinney

Rance, Patrick. *The Great British Cheese Book.* Macmillan, 1982.

Boat Race

Arlott, John (ed.). *The Oxford Companion to Sports and Games.* OUP, 1975.

Kightly, Charles. *The Customs and Ceremonies of Britain.* Thames & Hudson, 1986.

Boats

Elmer, W. *The Terminology of Fishing: A Survey of English and Welsh Inshore Fishing Things and Words.* The Cooper Monographs 19, English Dialect Series. Franke Verlag, 1973.

McKee, Eric. *Working Boats of Britain: Their Shape and Purpose.* Conway Maritime Press, 1983.

Porteous, K. (ed.). *The Bonny Fisher Lad: Memories of the North Northumberland Fishing Community.* The People's History, 2003.

Porteous, K. *Longshore Drift: A Radio Poem.* Jardine Press 2005.

Williamson, T. *The Norfolk Broads: A Landscape History.* Manchester UP, 1997.

Bollards

Aaron, Henry. *Street Furniture.* Shire, 1980.

Denton, Pennie. *Seaside Surrealism: Paul Nash in Swanage.* Peveril Press, 2002.

Joyce, Barry et al. *Derbyshire Detail and Character.* Alan Sutton, 1996.

Legg, R. *Swanage Encyclopaedic Guide.* Dorset Publishing Company, 1995.

Warren, Geoffrey. *Vanishing Street Furniture.* David & Charles, 1978.

Dartmoor National Park Design Guide. 1979.

Street Furniture from Design Index 1968/69 (Third Edition). Council of Industrial Design, January 1968.

Bonfire Night

Crowden, James and Rook, Pauline. *Bridgwater: The Parrett's Mouth.* AGRE Books, 2000.

Etherington, J. *Lewes Bonfire Night.* SB Publications, 1993.

Hole, Christina. *British Folk Customs.* Hutchinson, 1976.

Keys, David. 'Ancient High Spirits'. *Independent,* 3 October 1989.

Kightly, Charles. *The Customs and Ceremonies of Britain.* Thames & Hudson, 1986.

Sykes, Homer. *Once a Year: Some Traditional British Customs.* Gordon Fraser, 1977.

Bores

Fisher, Catherine. 'The Severn Bore'. *Immrama.* Seren Books, 1988.

Hole, Christina. *English Folklore.* Batsford, 1940.

Rowbotham, F.W. *The Severn Bore.* David & Charles, 1964.

Witts, C. *The Mighty Severn Bore.* River Severn Publications, 1999.

The Severn Bore and Trent Aegir Predictions. 2003, 4, 5.

Boundaries

Addison, W. *The Old Roads of England.* Batsford, 1980.

Field, J. *English Field Names.* David & Charles, 1972.

Gelling, M. *Signposts to the Past.* Phillimore, 1978.

Hall, David. *Turning the Plough.* English Heritage/ Northamptonshire County Council, 2001.

Hoskins, W.G. *The Making of the English Landscape.* Hodder & Stoughton, 1955/2005.

Hunter, John. *The Essex Landscape.* Chelmsford, 1999.

Rackham, Oliver. *The History of the Countryside.* Dent, 1980.

Sternberg, *The Dialect and Folklore of Northamptonshire.* SR Publishers, 1851 (facsimile, 1971).

Tindall, Gillian. *The Fields Beneath.* Granada, 1980.

Boundary Stones

Brian, Anthea. Letters, 9 March 1997 and 21 February 2004.

Brian, Anthea and Thomson, P. *The History and Natural History of Lugg Meadow.* Logaston Press, 2002.

Winchester, A. *Discovering Parish Boundaries.* Shire, 2000.

Bournes

Ekwall, E. *English River Names.* OUP, 1928.

Bowling Greens

Evans, R.D.C. *Bowling Greens: their history, construction and maintenance.* Sports Turf Research Institute, 1988.

Moore, Ian, *Grass and Grasslands,* Collins, 1966.

Strutt, Joseph. *The Sports and Pastimes of the People of England.* Thomas Tegg, 1838.

Brass Bands

Gammon, Vic and Sheila. 'The Musical Revolution of the Mid-nineteenth Century' from 'Repeat and Twiddle to Precision and Snap' in *The British Brass Band: A Musical and Social History* (Herbert, Trevor, ed.). OUP, 2000.

Herbert, Trevor (ed.). *The British Brass Band: A Musical and Social History.* OUP, 2000.

Moss, Phil. *Manchester's Music Makers.* Neil Richardson Publications, 1994.

Raistrick, Arthur. *The Pennine Dales.* Arrow Books, 1968.

Weir, Christopher. *Village and Town Bands.* Shire, 1981.

Bread

Ascherson, Neal. 'The Failure of the Melting Pot'. *Local Distinctiveness: Place, Particularity and Identity* (Clifford, Sue and King, Angela, eds). Common Ground, 1993.

Blythman, Joanna. *Shopped: The Shocking Power of British Supermarkets.* Fourth Estate, 2004.

Blythman, Joanna. 'A Slice of Life'. *Guardian,* 1 July 1995.

459

Hartley, Dorothy. *Food in England.* Futura, 1954.
Lawrence, Felicity. *Not on the Label.* Penguin, 2004.
National Association of Master Bakers. Letters, 1991.

Breweries
Protz, Roger (ed.). *Good Beer Guide.* CAMRA, 2004.
Protz, Roger and Sharples, Steve. *Country Ales and Breweries.* Weidenfeld & Nicolson, 1999.
Wheeler, Graham. *Home Brewing.* CAMRA, 1993.
Whitbread's Brewery incorporating The Brewer's Art. Whitbread & Co., 1951.
CAMRA.

Bricks
Berry, Penny. *Bricks: A Study of Brick Making and Building in East Anglia.* Pullet Press, 1988.
Berry, Penny. Conversations and letters, 2004.
Brian, Anthea. 'The Distribution of Brick Bonds in England up to 1800'. *Vernacular Architecture,* vol. II, 1980.
Brian, Anthea. Letter, March 1997.
Brunskill, R.W. *Brick Building in Britain.* Gollancz, 1990.
Clifton-Taylor, A. *The Pattern of English Building.* Faber & Faber, 1972.
Leslie, Kim. 'The Ashburnham Estate Brickworks 1840-1968'. *Sussex Industrial History,* One, 1970/71.
Leslie, Kim. Conversations, various dates.
Minter, P. *The Bulmer Brick and Tile Co Ltd* (leaflet).
British Brick Society News.

Bridges
Clifton-Taylor, Alec. *English Stone Building.* Gollancz, 1983.
De Mare, Eric. *The Bridges of Britain.* Batsford, 1954.
Highways Agency. *The Appearance of Bridges and other Highway Structures.* HMSO, 1996.
Jervois, E. *The Ancient Bridges of Mid and Eastern England.* Architectural Press, 1932.
Jervois, E. *The Ancient Bridges of the South of England.* Architectural Press, 1930.
Richards, J.M. *The National Trust Book of Bridges.* Jonathan Cape, 1984.
Wordsworth, William. *Guide to the Lakes.* 1810.
Bridges in Hampshire of Historic Interest. Hampshire County Council, 2000.

Britannia Coco-nut Dancers
Cass, Eddie. *The Lancashire Pace-Egg Play: A Social History.* FLS Books, 2001.
Kightly, Charles. *The Customs and Ceremonies of Britain.* Thames & Hudson, 1986.

Broads
Malster, Robert. *The Norfolk and Suffolk Broads.* Phillimore & Co., 2003.
Rackham, Oliver. *The History of the Countryside.* Dent, 1968.

Ratcliffe, D.A (ed.). *A Nature Conservation Review.* CUP, 1977.
Sterry, Paul. *Norfolk Broads.* Dial House, 1995.
Williamson, Tom. *The Norfolk Broads: A Landscape History.* Manchester University Press, 1997.
The Broads: A Review. Countryside Commission, 1983.

Brooks
Ekwall, E. *English River Names.* OUP, 1928.
Tennyson, Alfred Lord. 'The Song of the Brook' in *The River's Voice* (King, Angela and Clifford, Susan, eds.). Green Books, 2000.

Brussels Sprouts
Hargreaves, John. *Harvests and Harvesters: Fruit and Vegetable Growing in Britain.* Gollancz, 1987.

Building Stones
Arkell, W.J. and Tomkeieff, S.I. *English Rock Terms.* OUP, 1953.
Clifton-Taylor, Alec. *The Pattern of English Building.* Faber & Faber, 1972.
Gale, A.W. et al. *The Building Stones of Devon.* The Devonshire Association, 1992.
Robinson, Eric. *London Illustrated Geological Walks.* Scottish Academy Press, 1985.
Thomas, Jo. *Stone Quarrying.* Discover Dorset. Dovecote Press, 1998.
Williams, M. *The Slate Industry.* Shire, 2002.
Wright, Adela. *Craft Techniques for Traditional Buildings.* Batsford, 1991.
The Quality of Leicester. Leicester City Council, 1993.

Bungalows
Edwards, Arthur M. *The Design of Suburbia: A Critical Study in Environmental History.* Pembridge Press, 1981.
Hardy, Denis and Ward, Colin. *Arcadia for All.* Mansell, 1984.
King, Anthony D. *The Bungalow: The Production of a Global Culture.* OUP, 1995.

Buns
David, Elizabeth. *English Bread and Yeast Cookery.* Allen Lane, 1977.
Fitzgibbon, Theodora. *A Taste of the West Country.* Dent, 1972.
Hartley, Dorothy. *Food in England.* Futura, 1954.
Jones, Julia and Deer, Barbara. *Cattern Cakes and Lace: A Calendar of Feasts.* Dorling Kindersley, 1987.
Mason, Laura with Brown, Catherine. *Traditional Foods of Britain: An Inventory.* Prospect Books, 1999.

Burning Bartle
Kightly, Charles. *The Customs and Ceremonies of Britain.* Thames & Hudson, 1986.

Burns
Ekwall, E. *English River Names.* OUP, 1928.

Buses
Turner-Bishop, Aiden. Letter, 15 May 2002.

150 years of London's Buses. London Transport, 1979.

Bus Shelters
Bauman Lyons Architects

Butts
Arlott, John (ed.). *The Oxford Companion to Sports and Games.* OUP, 1975.
Bailey, Brian. *The English Village Green.* Robert Hale, 1985.
Dainton, Courtney. *Clock Jacks and Bee Boles.* Phoenix House, 1957.
Field, John. *A History of English Field-Names.* Longman, 1993.
Grigson, Geoffrey. *The Shell Country Alphabet.* Michael Joseph, 1966.

C

Cabmen's Shelters
Aaron, Henry. *Pillar to Post: Looking at Street Furniture.* Frederick Warne, 1982.
Thompson, Vance. 'The London cabby'. *Outing,* vol. 45, 1904.
Warren, Geoffrey. *Vanishing Street Furniture.* David & Charles, 1978.

Cafés
Cathcart Borer, M. *The Story of Covent Garden.* Robert Hale, 1984.
Maddox, Adrian. *Classic Cafés.* Black Dog Publishing, 2003.
Old English Coffee Houses. The Rodale Press, 1954.

Cairns
Allen, Bob. *Escape to the Dales.* Michael Joseph, 1992.
Bender, Barbara. Conversation. 18 March 2004.
Goldsworthy, Andy. *Sheepfolds.* Michael Hue-Williams Fine Art, 1996.
Wainwright, A. *Fellwalking with Wainwright.* Michael Joseph, 1984.

Cakes
Buttery, Pauline. Conversations and letters, 2003/4.
Duff, Julie. *Cakes, Regional and Traditional.* Grub Street, 2003.
Mason, Laura with Brown, Catherine. *Traditional Foods of Britain.* Prospect Books, 1999.
Tracey, Dee. 'Godcakes'. *Country Matters* (Warwickshire Rural Community Council), Autumn/Winter 1997.

Canals
Briggs, Jonathan. 'Canals – Wildlife Value and Restoration Issues'. *British Wildlife Magazine,* August 1996.
Hadfield, Charles and Boughey, Joseph. *Hadfield's British Canals.* Alan Sutton, 1998.
Harding, Bruce. *Grand Union Canal Character Guide.* British Waterways consultation draft, 14 July 1999.
Jones, Barbara. *The Unsophisticated Arts.* The Architectural Press, 1951.
Lansdell, Avril. *Canal Arts and Crafts.* Shire, 1994.

Devizes Wharf and Locks: A Story. British Waterways/ Kennet and Avon Canal Trust, c.2000.
Stratford upon Avon Canal Guide. Stratford upon Avon Canal Society, 1973.

Carnivals
Crowden, James and Rook, Pauline. *Bridgwater: The Parrett's Mouth.* AGRE Books, 2000.
Kightly, Charles. *The Customs and Ceremonies of Britain.* Thames & Hudson, 1986.
Carnival Chronicle

Carols
Callaghan, Barry. *The Sheffield Carols.* Yorkshire Folk Arts, 2003.
Court, Glyn. *Carols of the Westcountry.* Westcountry Books, 1996.
Dearmer, P.; Vaughan Williams, R.; Shaw, M. *The Oxford Book of Carols.* OUP, 1928.
Evans, Ivor H. (revised by). *Brewer's Dictionary of Phrase and Fable, 14th edition.* Cassell, 1990.
Keyte, Hugh and Parrott, Andrew (eds.). *The Shorter New Oxford Book of Carols.* OUP, 1993.
McCormick, Fred. 'Village Carols from the Royal Hotel, Dungworth', 20 December 1999, at www.mustrad.org.uk/ reviews/hark.htm
Oates, David. *Sound, sound your instruments of joy!* Troon Tales 4.
Russell, Ian. *Carols from Padstow in Cornwall.* Musical Traditions Web Services, 2003.
Russell, Ian. *A Festival of Village Carols: A First Collection of Carols from the Derbyshire Peak District.* Village Carols, 2000.
Russell, Ian (ed.). *Hark, Hark! What News, Village Carols from the Royal Hotel, Dungworth.* Village Carols, 1996.

Castles
Johnson, Paul. *The National Trust Book of British Castles.* Grafton, 1981.
Somerset Fry, Plantagenet. *Castles of Britain and Ireland.* David & Charles, 1996.
Dunstanburgh Castle, Northumberland Landscape Survey Report. English Heritage, 2003.
Market Towns: Highlighting their Assets. English Heritage.

Castleton Garland Day
Kightly, Charles. *The Customs and Ceremonies of Britain.* Thames & Hudson, 1986.

Cathedrals
Anderson, W. *The Rise of the Gothic.* Hutchinson, 1985.
Auden, W.H. from 'Here on the cropped grass of the narrow ridge I stand'. *The English Auden, poems, essays and dramatic writings* (Mendelsen, Edward, ed.). Faber & Faber, 1977.

Clifton-Taylor, Alec. *The Cathedrals of England*. Thames & Hudson, 1986.

Edwards, D.L. *Cathedrals of Britain*. Guild Publishing, 1989.

Norwich, J.J. *Britain's Heritage*. Kingfisher Books, 1983/1991.

Scott, R.A. *The Gothic Enterprise*. University of California Press, 2003.

Cattle

Alderson, L. *Rare Breeds*. Shire Album 118, 1984.

Low, A. *Domesticated Animals of the British Isles*. 1845.

Porter, V. *British Cattle*. Shire, 2001.

Tims, A.E. Letters, 27 April and 3 December 2004.

Vince, J. *Old British Livestock*. Shire Album 5, 1974.

Wallace, R. *Farm Stock of Great Britain*. Oliver & Boyd, 1907.

Passport to North Devon. Westcountry Books for the Beaford Centre, 1995.

Caves

Bahn, Paul. 'Art of the Hunters'. *British Archaeology* 72, September 2003.

Hindle, A. *Literary Visitors to Yorkshire*. Hesketh, 1981.

Taylor, John. *Part of this Summer's Travels . . . (1639)*. Reprint L93.01 in Local Studies.

Thornber, N.; Stride, A.H. and R.D.; Myers, J.O. *Britain Underground*. Dalesman Publishing Company and Blandford Press, 1953.

Ward, Colin. *Cotters and Squatters*. Five Leaves, 2002.

Kent Underground Research Group.

Cemeteries

Abney Park Trust, conversations.

Hudson, Kenneth. *Churchyards and Cemeteries*. Bodley Head Children's Books, 1984.

Loudon, J.C. 'On the Laying Out of Cemeteries'. 1843.

Worpole, Ken. *Last Landscapes: The Architecture of Cemeteries in the West*. Reaktion Books, 2003.

Paradise Preserved: an introduction to the assessment, evaluation, conservation and management of historic cemeteries. English Heritage and English Nature, 2002.

Register of Parks and Gardens: Cemeteries. English Heritage, 2003.

Chalk

Cobham Resource Consultants. *The Lincolnshire Wolds Landscape*. Countryside Commission, 1993.

Constable, F. *The England of Eric Ravilious*. Lund Humphries, 2003.

Featherstone, Neil. Emails, August 2003.

Fortey, Richard. *The Hidden Landscape*. Jonathan Cape, 1993.

Green, M. *A Landscape Revealed: 10,000 years on a Chalkland Farm*. Tempus, 2000.

Hooker, Jeremy. 'Matrix'. *Soliloquies of a Chalk Giant*. Enitharmon Press, 1974.

Naipaul, V.S. *The Enigma of Arrival*. Viking Penguin, 1987.

Wright, Adela. *Craft Techniques for Traditional Buildings*. Batsford, 1991.

Chalk Streams

English Nature and the Environment Agency. *The State of England's Chalk Rivers*. Environment Agency, 2004.

Frake, Allan and Hayes, Peter. *Report on the Millennium Chalk Streams Fly Trends Study*. Environment Agency and Wiltshire Fishery Association, 2001.

Mainstone, C.P. *Chalk Rivers: Nature Conservation and Management*. English Nature and the Environment Agency, 1999.

Millais, John Everett. 'Ophelia'. 1851/2.

River Restoration and Chalk Streams. Seminar Proceedings, River Restoration Centre, 2001.

Rivers, Rhynes and Running Brooks. Common Ground, 2000.

The Channel

Bonavia, Michael. *The Channel Tunnel Story*. David & Charles, 1987.

Mortimore, Rory. *The Chalk of Sussex and Kent*. The Geologist's Association, 1997.

Smith, Hillas. *The English Channel*. Images Publishing, 1994.

White, Mark. 'Island Britain' in Crossings: The Prehistory of the Channel Region (conference). Sussex Archaeological Society, 20 September, 2003.

Williamson, James A. *The English Channel*. Collins, 1959.

Woodcock, Andrew. 'The Archaeological Implications of Coastal Change in Sussex' in *The Archaeology of Sussex to AD 2000*. University of Sussex, 2003.

Chapels

Barton, David A. *Discovering Chapels and Meeting Houses*. Shire, 1975.

Beacham, Peter and Ravilious, James. *Down the Deep Lanes*. Devon Books, 2000.

Betjeman, John. *First and Last Loves*. John Murray, 1952.

Cornwall Archaeological Unit. *Diversity and Vitality: The Methodist and Nonconformist Chapels of Cornwall*. Cornwall County Council, 2001.

Wood, Eric S. *Historical Britain*. Harvill Press, 1997.

English Heritage Conservation Bulletin, 2002.

The Making of Dorset Chapels. Dorset Archaeological Committee, 2000.

Nonconformist Chapels and Meeting-houses, Derbyshire. RCHME, HMSO, 1986.

Nonconformist Chapels and Meeting-houses, Shropshire and Staffordshire. RCHME, HMSO, 1986.

Cheddar Cheese

Rance, Patrick. *The Great British Cheese Book*. Macmillan, 1982.

Cheese

Hartley, Dorothy. *Food in England*. Futura, 1954.

Hodgson, Randolph. Email, 2003. Neal's Yard Dairy.

McAllister, John. 'Whey Ahead'. *Guardian*, 13 March 1993.

Rance, Patrick. *The Great British Cheese Book*. Macmillan, 1982.

Trewin, Carol. Email, 19 April 2004.

Cheese Rolling

Hole, Christina. *British Folk Customs*. Hutchinson, 1976.

Kightly, Charles. *The Customs and Ceremonies of Britain*. Thames & Hudson, 1986.

Rance, Patrick. *The Great British Cheese Book*. Macmillan, 1982.

Cherries

Grubb, Norman H. *Cherries*. Crosby Lockwood & Son, 1949.

Housman, A.E. 'Loveliest of Trees'. *A Shropshire Lad*. *The Collected Works of A.E. Housman*. Jonathan Cape, 1939.

Hubbard, Rebecca. 'Soggy bags of summer bliss'. *Guardian*, 1 July 1989.

Roach, F.A. *The Cultivated Fruits of Britain: Their Origins and History*. Basil Blackwell, 1985.

Spiers, Virginia. *Burcombes, Queenies and Colloggetts*. West Brendon, 1996.

Stamp, L. Dudley. *The Land of Britain, Kent*. Geographical Publications, 1943.

The Common Ground Book of Orchards: Conservation, Culture and Community. Common Ground, 2000.

Chert

Cobham Resource Consultants. *The Blackdown Hills Landscape*. Countryside Commission, 1989.

Hind, D. *Chert Use in the Mesolithic of Northern England*. University of Sheffield, 1998.

Nicholas Pearson Associates. *Blackdown Hills AONB Countryside Design Summary*. The Blackdown Hills Rural Partnership, 1999.

Cheshire Railings

Cheshire Railings: Scheme to grant aid their refurbishment. Vale Royal Borough Council, 1990.

Chimneys

Brunskill, R.W. *Illustrated Handbook of Vernacular Architecture*. Faber & Faber, 1971.

Clifton-Taylor, Alec. *The Pattern of English Building*. Faber & Faber, 1971.

Fletcher, Valentine. *Chimney Pots and Stacks: An Introduction to their History, Variety and Identification*. Centaur Press, 1968/1994.

Wordsworth, William. *Guide to the Lakes* (edited by Ernest de Selincourt). OUP, 1906/1982 (first published in 1810).

Chinatowns

Lau, Steve. *Chinatown Britain*. Chinatown Online, 2002.

Merriman, N. (ed.). *The Peopling of London: Fifteen Thousand Years of Settlement from Overseas*. Museum of London, 1993.

Chines

Nicholas Pearson Associates. *The Isle of Wight Landscape*. Countryside Commission, 1994.

Priest, Becky. *Island Chines*. Isle of Wight Council, 1998.

The Chines of Bournemouth and Poole. Bournemouth Borough Council, nd.

Chinese New Year

McAuley, Ian. *Guide to Ethnic London*. Michael Haag, 1987.

Choughs

Buczacki, Stefan. *Fauna Britannica*. Hamlyn, 2002.

Wingfield Gibbons, David et al. *The New Atlas of Breeding Birds in Britain and Ireland 1988-1991*. BTO, 1993.

'Choughed about choughs!' *English Nature Magazine*, July 2002.

Churches

Atkinson, T.D. *Local Style in English Architecture*. Batsford, 1947.

Bettey, J.H. *Church and Parish*. Batsford, 1987.

Cox, J.C. and Ford, C.B. *The Parish Churches of England*. Batsford, 1935.

Gilbert, O. *Lichens*. HarperCollins, 2000.

Grigson, G. *The Shell Country Book*. Phoenix House, 1962.

Jenkins, Simon. *England's Thousand Best Churches*. Penguin Books, 2000.

Morris, E. *Towers and Bells of Britain*. Robert Hale, 1955.

The Quantock Hills Landscape. Countryside Agency, 2003.

Churchyards

Beacham, Peter and Ravilious, James. *Down the Deep Lanes*. Devon Books, 2000.

Fewins, Clive. *The Church Explorer's Handbook*. Canterbury Press, 2005.

Gilbert, Oliver. *Lichens*. HarperCollins, 2000.

Greenoak, Francesca. *God's Acre*. E.P. Dutton, 1985.

Grigson, Geoffrey. *Geoffrey Grigson's Countryside*. Ebury Press, 1982.

Langdon, Andrew. *Stone Crosses in North Cornwall*. Federation of Old Cornwall Societies, 1992/Andrew Langdon, 1996.

Lees, Hilary. *English Churchyard Memorials*. Tempus Publishing, 2000.

Mabey, Richard. *Flora Britannica*. Chatto & Windus, 1996.

Rackham, Oliver. *The History of the Countryside*. Dent, 1986.

Vallance, Aymer. *Old Crosses and Lychgates*. Batsford, 1920.

461

Cider & Cider Orchards
Copas, Liz. *A Somerset Pomona: The Cider Apples of Somerset.* The Dovecote Press, 2001 (reprinted in 2004 by Liz Copas).
Crowden, James. *Cider, the forgotten miracle.* Cyder Press 2, 1999.
Mabey, D. *Good Cider.* Whittet Books, 1984.
Morgan, J. and Richards, A. *The New Book of Apples* (illustrated by Elisabeth Dowle). Ebury Press, 2002.
Roach, F.A. *Cultivated Fruits of Britain.* Basil Blackwell, 1985.
Good Cider Guide. CAMRA, 2005.

Cinemas
Day, Roy. 'The Picture-Palace – its coming and going'. *Bristol Industrial Archaeology Society Journal* 18, 1985.
Eyles, Allen. *Odeon Cinemas 1: Oscar Deutsch Entertains Our Nation.* BFI, 2002.
Eyles, Allen. *Old Cinemas.* Shire, 2001.
Harwood, Elain. *Picture Palaces.* English Heritage, 1999.
Cinema Theatre Association.

Cliffs
Covey, R. and Laffoley, D.d'A. *Maritime State of Nature.* English Nature, 2002. `
Pye, K. and French, P.W. *Targets of Coastal Habitat Re-creation.* English Nature, 1993.
Ratcliffe, D.A. (ed.). *A Nature Conservation Review.* CUP, 1977.
Steers, J.A. *The Coastline of England and Wales.* CUP, 1964.
Birds, Summer 2000.

Clints & Grikes
Fortey, Richard. *The Hidden Landscape.* Jonathan Cape, 1993.
Hartley, Marie and Ingilby, Joan. *The Yorkshire Dales.* Dent, 1956.
Walters, Martin and Gibbons, Bob. *Travellers' Nature Guide to Britain.* OUP, 2003.
Nature Atlas of Great Britain. Pan Books and Ordnance Survey, 1989.

Clipping the Church
Hole, Christina. *British Folk Customs.* Hutchinson, 1976.
Kightly, Charles. *The Customs and Ceremonies of Britain.* Thames & Hudson, 1986.
Simpson, Jacqueline and Roud, Steve (eds.). *Oxford Dictionary of English Folklore.* OUP, 2000.
Sykes, Homer. *Once a Year.* Gordon Fraser, 1977.

Clocks
Beeson, C.F.C. *English Church Clocks 1280-1850.* Phillimore/ Antiquarian Horological Society, 1971.
Fleet, Simon. *Clocks.* Octopus, 1972.
Hill, Susan. *The Spirit of the Cotswolds.* Michael Joseph, 1988.

McKay, Chris. *The Turret Clock Keeper's Handbook.* Antiquarian Horological Society, 1999.

Clouds
Bosanquet, R.E. (ed.). *In Troubled Times.* Spreddon Northern Classics, 1989.
Goethe, J.W. von. 'In Honour of Howard' (translated by Hüttner, Johann Christian and Soane, George). *London Magazine and Theatrical Inquisitor IV,* July 1821.
Hamblyn, R. *The Invention of Clouds.* Picador, 2001.
Jacobson, Bernard. *Towards a New Landscape.* Bernard Jacobson Gallery, 1993.
Page, R. *Weather Forecasting the Country Way.* Penguin, 1981.
Shakespeare, W. *Hamlet.* 1603.
Shelley, Percy Bysshe. 'The Cloud'. *Prometheus Unbound: A Lyrical Drama in Four Acts, with Other Poems.* C. & J. Ollier, 1820.

Clumps
Land Use Consultants. *The North Pennines Landscape.* Countryside Commission, 1991.
Lasdun, Susan. *The English Park.* Andre Deutsch, 1991.
Mabey, Richard. *Flora Britannica.* Chatto & Windus, 1996.
Mackay, Duncan. *The Secret Thames.* Ebury Press, 1992.
Masefield, John. *Grace Before Ploughing.* Heinemann, 1966.
Miles, Archie. *Silva: The Tree in Britain.* Ebury Press, 1999.
Penn, Roger. *Portrait of Ashdown Forest.* Robert Hale, 1984.
Watkins, Alfred. *The Old Straight Track.* Abacus, 1974/1978.
The Quantock Hills Landscape: An Assessment of the AONB. Countryside Agency, 2003.

Coal Mining
Chaplin, Sid. *The Thin Seam.* Phoenix House, 1950.
Lawrence, D.H. *Sons and Lovers.* Penguin, 1913.
Rumsby, P.L. 'Pattern of Coal Production and Utilization' in *Geological Aspects of Development and Planning in Northern England* (Warren, P.T., ed.). Yorkshire Geological Society, 1970.

Coastline
Fortey, Richard. *The Hidden Landscape.* Jonathan Cape, 1993.
Pattison, Keith; Porteous, Katrina; Soden, Robert. *Turning the Tide.* District of Easington, 2001.
Raban, Jonathan. *Coasting.* Collins Harvill, 1986.

Coasts
Cooper, Andrew. *Secret Nature of the Channel Shore.* BBC Books, 1992.
Covey, R. and Laffoley, D.d'A. *State of Nature: Maritime – Getting onto an Even Keel.* English Nature, 2002.

Lindley, Kenneth. *Coastline.* Hutchinson & Co., 1967.
Rothschild, Miriam and Marren, Peter. *Rothschild's Reserves.* Harley Books, 1997.
Soothill, Eric and Thomas, Michael. *The Natural History of Britain's Coasts.* Blandford Publishing, 1987.
Soper, Tony. *A Natural History Guide to the Coasts.* Webb & Bower/National Trust, 1984.
Developing English Nature's Maritime Strategy, State of Nature one year on. English Nature, 2002.
Living with the Sea. English Nature, 2003.

Cob
Hurd, J. and Gourley, B. (eds.). *Terra Britannica.* English Heritage/ICOMOS UK, 2000.
McCann, J. *Clay and Cob Buildings.* Shire, 1983.
Wright, A. *Craft Techniques for Traditional Buildings.* Batsford, 1991.
The Cob Buildings of Devon. Devon Historic Buildings Trust, 1992.
'A View of their Parish by the People of Winkleigh'. Beaford Arts Centre, 1997.

Cobbles
Ashurst, John and Dimes, Francis. *Conservation of Building and Decorative Stone.* Butterworth-Heinemann, 1998.
Barber, Chips. *Along the Otter.* Obelisk Publications, 1996.
Clifton-Taylor, Alec. *Lewes.* Alastair Press, 1990.
Clifton-Taylor, Alec and Iveson, A.S. *English Stone Building.* Gollancz, 1983/1994.
Hawkins, Michael. *Devon Roads.* Devon Books, 1988.
Haxby, Joanna. Email, 16 November 2004.
Ostergaard, Troels and Whittow, John. *Rocks and Pebbles of Britain and Northern Europe.* Penguin Books, 1980.

Cobles
Porteous, K. (ed.). *The Bonny Fisher Lad: Memories of the North Northumberland Fishing Community.* The People's History, 2003.

Cobnuts
Game, Meg. *In a Nutshell: The Story of Kentish Cobnuts.* Chris Howkins, 1999.
The Common Ground Book of Orchards. Common Ground, 2000.

Coes
Hoskins, W.G. *One Man's England.* BBC, 1978.
Rogers, Frank. *More Curiosities of Derbyshire and the Peak District.* Derbyshire Countryside Ltd, 2000.
Bonsall Parish Map.

Commons
Clayden, Paul. *Our Common Land.* Open Spaces Society, 2003.
Cockburn, Cynthia. Letters, conversations, 2004.

Deakin, Roger. Conversations, emails and letters, 2003/4/5.
Gould, Dennis. 'Greenham Common Blues'. *Postcard Poems.* Green CND, 1982.
Stamp, D. and Hoskins, W.G. *The Common Lands of England and Wales.* Collins, 1963.
Williamson, T. and Bellamy, L. *Property and Landscape.* George Philip, 1987.
Conservation Bulletin 44, English Heritage, June 2003.
Open Space, vol. 26, no. 9, 2000.

Communication & Radio Masts
Coulson-Thomas, C.J. *Cornwall's Conquest of the Air.* Heritage, 1975.

Confectionery
Mason, Laura. *Sweets and Sweet Shops.* Shire, 1999.
Mason, Laura with Brown, Catherine. *Traditional Foods of Britain: An Inventory.* Prospect Books, 1999.
Orwell, George. *Coming Up for Air.* Gollancz, 1939.
Richardson, Tim. *Sweets: A History of Temptation.* Transworld, 2002.
Whittaker, Nicholas. *Sweet Talk: The Secret History of Confectionery.* Phoenix, 1998.

Corn Dollies
Fellows, Heulwen. *The Corn Dolly Maker.* Felcraft, 1977.
Hole, Christina. *British Folk Customs.* Hutchinson, 1976.
Lambeth, M. *Discovering Corn Dollies.* Shire, 1974.
Sandford, Lettice and Davis, Philla. *Decorative Straw Work.* Batsford, 1964.
Corn Dollies. WI Books, 1979.

Cornish Gigs
McKee, Eric. *Working Boats of Britain: Their Shape and Purpose.* Conway Maritime Press, 1983.

Cornish Pasties
Hall, Stephen. *The Cornish Pasty.* AGRE Books, 2001.
Mabey, David and Mabey, Richard. *In Search of Food: Traditional Eating and Drinking in Britain.* Macdonald & Janes, 1978.
Trewin, Carol and Woolfitt, Adam. *Gourmet Cornwall,* Alison Hodge, 2005.

Corrugated Iron
Beacham, Peter and Ravilious, James. *Down the Deep Lanes.* Devon Books, 2000.
Bevan, Bill. 'Town of Tin'. *British Archaeology* 59, June 2001.
Emery, Norman. 'Corrugated Iron Buildings in County Durham'. *Durham Archaeological Journal* 6, 1990.
Corrugated Iron Club website: www.corrugated-iron-club. info

Cottage Gardens
Brookes, John. *Planting the Country Way.* BBC Books, 1994.
Chivers, Susan and Woloszynska, Suzanne. *The Cottage Garden: Margery Fish at East Lambrook Manor.* John Murray, 1990.

462

Genders, Roy.
The Cottage Garden.
Pelham Books, 1969.
Hadfield, Miles. *A History
of British Gardening.*
Penguin Books, 1960.
Hamilton, Geoff. *Geoff
Hamilton's Cottage Gardens.*
BBC Books, 1995.
Hoyles, Martin.
The Story of Gardening.
Journeyman Press, 1991.

Cottages
Brunskill, R.W. *Houses
and Cottages of Britain.*
Gollancz, 1997.
Clifton-Taylor, Alec. *The
Pattern of English Building.*
Faber & Faber, 1972.
Evans, Tony and Lycett Green,
Candida. *English Cottages.*
Cassell, 1982.
Mason, Peter F.
Hampshire: A Sense of Place.
Hampshire Books, 1994.
Penoyre, John and Penoyre,
Jane. *Houses in the Landscape.*
Faber & Faber, 1978.
Ward, Colin. *Cotters and
Squatters: Housing's Hidden
History.* Five Leaves
Publications, 2002.
Wordsworth, William.
Guide to the Lakes. 1810.

Council Houses
Briggs, A. *A Social History of
England.* Weidenfeld &
Nicolson, 1983, 1994.
Denton, P. (ed.). *Betjeman's
London.* John Murray, 1988.
Edwards, A.M.
The Design of Suburbia.
Pembridge Press, 1981.
Stevenson, Greg. *The 1930s
Home.* Shire, 2000.
Swenarton, M.
Homes Fit For Heroes.
Heinemann, 1981.
Twentieth Century Society.

Counties
Davies, N. *The Isles: A History.*
Papermac, 2000.
Denton, P. (ed.). *Betjeman's
London.* John Murray, 1988.
Dowson, Chris S.
Email, 9 February 2004.
Dutson, Michael.
Email, 2 September 2003.
Sherdley, Steve.
Email, 24 September 2002.
Association of British Counties
website: www.abcounties.co.uk

Coves
Blyton, Enid.
Five on a Treasure Island.
Hodder & Stoughton, 1942.
Kipling, Rudyard.
'A Smuggler's Song'.
Perkins, J.W. *Geology Explained in
Dorset.* David & Charles, 1977.

Crab Fair
Kightly, Charles. *The Customs
and Ceremonies of Britain.*
Thames & Hudson, 1986.
Nicholson, Norman.
Cumberland and Westmorland.
Robert Hale, 1949.
Palmer, Geoffrey and Lloyd,
Noel. *A Year of Festivals.*
Frederick Warne, 1972.
Simpson, J. and Roud, S.
*The Oxford Dictionary of
English Folklore.* OUP, 2000.

Sykes, Homer. *Once a Year:
Some Traditional British
Customs.* Gordon Fraser, 1977.
Apple Games and Customs.
Common Ground, 1994.

Cream Teas
Davenport, Philippa. 'The
Cream of Cornish Fare'.
Financial Times, 19 July 2003.
Mason, Laura with Brown,
Catherine. *Traditional Foods
of Britain: An Inventory.*
Prospect Books, 1999.

Cricket
Arlott, John (ed.).
*The Oxford Companion to
Sports and Games.* OUP, 1975.
Bailey, Brian.
The English Village Green.
Robert Hale, 1985.
Dunkling, Leslie and Wright,
Gordon. *Pub Names of Britain.*
Dent, 1993.
Edlin, H.L. *Woodland
Crafts in Britain.*
David & Charles 1949/1973.
Meikle, R.D. *Willows and
Poplars of Great Britain and
Ireland.* BSBI, 1984.
Miles, Archie. *Silva: The Tree in
Britain.* Ebury Press, 1999.
Rice, Jonathan.
The Pavilion Book of Pavilions.
Pavilion Books, 1991.

Crinkle-crankle Walls
Brunskill, R.W. *Brick Building
in Britain.* Gollancz, 1990.
Clifton-Taylor, Alec. *The
Pattern of English Building.*
Faber & Faber, 1972.
Lasdun, Susan.
*The English Park: Royal,
Private and Public.*
Andre Deutsch, 1991.
Rodgers, Frank. *More
Curiosities of Derbyshire and
the Peak District.* Derbyshire
Countryside, 2000.

Crop Circles
Delgado, Pat and Andrews,
Colin. *Circular Evidence.*
Bloomsbury, 1989.
Feynman, Richard. *QED.*
Princeton University Press,
1985.
Goodman, Kent. *Crop Circles of
Wessex.* Wessex Books, 1996.
Noyes, Ralph (ed.).
The Crop Circle Enigma.
Gateway Books, 1990.

Crops
Davis, B.; Walker, N.;
Ball, D.; Fitter, A. *The Soil.*
Collins, 1992.
Gardiner, Vince and Matthews,
Hugh. *The Changing
Geography of the United
Kingdom.* Routledge, 2000.
Gillings, Simon. 'Confusing
cereals, baffling beet?' *BTO
News,* March-April 2004.
Grigg, David.
*English Agriculture:
An Historical Perspective.*
Basil Blackwell, 1989.
Moss Wightman, Ralph.
Green Days. Westhouse, 1947.
Russell, Sir E. John. *English
Farming.* Collins, 1941.
Shrubb, Michael. *Birds, Scythes
and Combines: A History of
Birds and Agricultural Change.*
CUP, 2003.

Thirsk, Joan. *Alternative
Agriculture: A History.*
OUP, 1997.
Arable Farming, 24 May 2004,
5 April 2004, 26 April 2004.
'Cereals 2004'. *Farmers Weekly,*
4 June 2004.
*The High Weald: Exploring
the Landscape of the Area of
Outstanding Natural Beauty.*
Countryside Commission, 1994.
State of Agriculture. Defra, 2002.
National Association of British
and Irish Millers.
SUSTAIN.

Crossroads
Grigson, Geoffrey. *The Shell
Book of Roads.* Ebury, 1964.
Halliday, Robert. 'Criminal
graves and rural crossroads'.
British Archaeology, no. 25,
June 1997.
Lopez, R.S. 'The Crossroads
Within the Wall' in
The Historian and the City
(Handlin, O. and Burchard,
J., eds.). MIT, 1963.
Robertson, Alan W.
*Post Roads, Post Towns and
Postal Rates 1635-1839.*
Privately printed, 1961.
Guide Sheet 1. Meltham Civic
Society, 1980.

Cuckoos & Cuckoo Pounds
Field, John. *A History of English
Field-Names.* Longman, 1993.
Harte, Jeremy. *Cuckoo Pounds
and Singing Barrows:
The Folklore of Ancient Sites
in Dorset.* Dorset Natural
History and Archaeological
Society, 1986.
Jordan, Kathy. *The Haunted
Landscape, Folklore, Ghosts
and Legends of Wiltshire.*
Ex Libris Press, 2000.
Legg, Rodney. *Swanage
Encyclopaedic Guide.* Dorset
Publishing Company, 1995.
Simpson, J. and Roud, S.
*Oxford Dictionary of English
Folklore.* OUP, 2000
Wenham, Chris et al (eds.).
*The Migration Atlas, Movements
of the Birds of Britain and
Ireland.* BTO, 2002.
Westwood, Jennifer. *Albion:
A Guide to Legendary Britain.*
Grafton, 1985.

Cycling
Betjeman, John.
Summoned by Bells.
The Camelot Press, 1960-84.
Cycling Touring Club.
Bexon, P. Lenton Local History
Society. Email, 15 April 2004.
Sustrans.

D

Daffodils
Jones, Joanne.
Email, 7 May 2002.
Land Use Consultants.
The Isles of Scilly.
Countryside Agency, 2002.
Lewis, Joanna. *Sovereigns,
Madams and Double Whites:
Fruit and Flower Pioneers of
the Tamar Valley.* Tamar
Valley AONB Service, 2004.
Robinson, William.
The Wild Garden. 1870.

Spiers, Virginia.
'Country Diary'.
Guardian, 9 April 2003.
Daffodil Way – Dymock-Kempley.
Windcross Public Paths
Group, nd.

Dags
Jones, Barbara.
The Unsophisticated Arts.
The Architectural Press,
1951.
Opolovnikov, A. and
Opolovnikova, Y.
*The Wooden Architecture of
Russia.* Harry N. Abrams, 1989.
Turner-Bishop, Aiden.
Email, 12 September 2003.
Wikeley, N. and Middleton, J.
*Railway Stations, Southern
Region.* Peco Publications,
1971.

Dales
Edwards, K.C. *The Peak District.*
Fontana New Naturalist,
1973.
Raistrick, A. *The Pennine Dales.*
Arrow, 1972.
Thurlow, William,
Yorkshire Place-names.
Dalesman Paperback, 1979.

Damsons
Barratt, Victoria. *A Taste of
Damsons – from jelly to gin.*
Westmorland Damson
Association, 1997.
Evans, Paul. 'Country Diary'.
Guardian, 14 April 1999.
Green, Fiona. *Orchards in
the North.* Countryside
Commission, 1993.
Roach, F.A. *The Cultivated
Fruits of Britain: Their
Origin and History.*
Blackwell, 1985.
*The Common Ground
Book of Orchards.*
Common Ground, 2000.

Dawn Chorus
Greenoak, F. *All the Birds of
the Air: The Names, Lore and
Literature of British Birds.*
Andre Deutsch, 1979.
Nicholson, E.M. and Koch, L.
Songs of Wild Birds.
Witherby, 1936.
Slabbekoorn, H. and Peet, M.
Great Tit song (University of
Leiden, Netherlands). Quoted
in *Guardian,* 17 July 2003.

Deezes
Black, John. *Odd and Unusual
England.* Spurbooks, 1974.
Peak, Steve (ed.). *Hastings
Stade, the Fishing Beach and
Maritime History.* Hastings
Borough Council, 1995.
Robinson, Adrian and
Millward, Roy. *The Shell
Book of the British Coast.*
David & Charles, 1983.

Denes
Porteous, Katrina. 'Roads'
in *Turning the Tide*
(Pattison, Keith; Porteous,
Katrina; Soden, Robert).
District of Easington, 2001.
Ratcliffe, D.A. (ed.).
A Nature Conservation Review.
CUP, 1977.
*Green spaces ... your spaces:
Newcastle's Green Space
Strategy.* Newcastle City
Council, April 2004.

463

'The Character of England: Durham Magnesian Limestone Plateau'. *Countryside Commission/English Nature*, 15, 1996.

Deserted Villages
Aston, Mick. *Monasteries in the Landscape*. Tempus, 2000.
Rowley, Trevor and Wood, John. *Deserted Villages*. Shire, 2000.
Taylor, Christopher. *Village and Farmstead*. George Philip, 1984.
Williamson, Tom and Bellamy, Liz. *Property and Landscape*. George Philip, 1987.
Wright, Patrick. *The Village that Died for England*. Jonathan Cape, 1995.

Devil
Briggs, Katherine M. *A Dictionary of British Folk-Tales in the English Language*. Routledge, 1970/71.
Simpson, J. and Roud, S. *Oxford Dictionary of English Folklore*. OUP, 2000.
Udal, J.S. *Dorsetshire Folklore* (1922). Facsimile, Dorset Books, 1989.
Westwood, Jennifer. *Gothick Hertfordshire*. Shire, 1989.
Westwood, Jennifer. *Gothick Norfolk*. Shire, 1989.

Dew Ponds
Brandon, Peter. *The South Downs*. Phillimore, 1998.
Jesse, R.H.B. *A Survey of the Agriculture of Sussex*. Royal Agricultural Society of England, 1960.
Lucas, E.V. *Highways and Byways in Sussex*. Macmillan, 1924.
Martin, Edward. *Outlines of Sussex Geology and other essays*. Archer & Co., 1932.
Powys, T.F. *Bottle's Path and other stories*. Chatto & Windus, 1946.
Pugsley, Alfred J. 'Dewponds in Fable and Fact'. *Country Life*, 1939.
Conservation Land Management, vol. 2, no. 2. English Nature, 2004.

Dialects
Bragg, Melvyn. *The Adventure of English*. Hodder & Stoughton, 2003.
Chambers, J.K. and Trudgill, P. *Dialectology*. CUP, 1980.
Clairborne, Robert. *The Life and Times of the English Language*. Bloomsbury, 1990
Crystal, David. *The Cambridge Encyclopedia of Language*. CUP, 1987.
Green, J. *Cassell's Dictionary of Slang*. Cassell & Co., 1998.
Griffiths, Bill. *North East Dialect Survey and Word List* Centre for Northern Studies. University of Northumbria, 2001.
Howard, P. *The State of the Language*. Penguin, 1986.
Reed, Fred. *The Northumberman*. Iron Press, 1999.
Sternberg, T. *The Dialect and Folklore of Northamptonshire*. 1851. SR Publishers, 1971.

Trudgill, Peter. *The Dialects of England*. Blackwell, 1990.
Upton, C. and Widdowson, J.D.A. *An Atlas of English Dialects*. OUP, 1996.

Diwali
Brown, A. *Festivals in World Religions*. Longman, 1986.
The Quality of Leicester. Leicester City Council, 1993.

Dog Roses
Gates, Phil. 'Heaven Scent'. *BBC Wildlife Magazine*, May 2003.
Grigson, Geoffrey. *The Englishman's Flora*. Paladin, 1975.
Hutchinson, John. *Common Wild Flowers*. Pelican, 1945.
Hutchinson, John. *More Common Wild Flowers*. Pelican, 1948.
Keble Martin, W. *The Concise British Flora in Colour*. Ebury Press and Michael Joseph, 1965.
Robinson, William. *The Wild Garden*. 1870. Century Hutchinson/The National Trust, 1986.
Vickery, Roy. *A Dictionary of Plant Lore*. OUP, 1995.

Dogs
Bonser, K.J. *The Drovers*. Macmillan, 1970.
Croxton Smith, A. *British Dogs*. Collins, 1945.
Cunliffe, Juliette. *History of the Whippet*. Interpret Publishing, 2000.
Fogle, Dr Bruce. *The Encyclopaedia of the Dog*. Dorling Kindersley, 1995.
Gordon, John F. *All about the Cocker Spaniel*. Pelham Books, 1976/1987.
Hancock, David. *Old Farm Dogs*. Shire, 1999.
Hart-Davis, Duff. *Fauna Britannica*. Weidenfeld & Nicolson, 2002.
Heath, Veronica. 'Brave Hearts' (Country Diary). *Guardian*, 9 November 2001.
Larkin, Dr Peter and Stockman, Mike. *The Ultimate Encyclopedia of Dog Breeds and Dog Care*. Southwater, 1997.
Plummer, D. Brian. *The Complete Book of Sight Hounds, Long Dogs and Lurchers*. Robinson Publishing, 1991.
Plummer, D. Brian. *The Sporting Terrier*. The Boydell Press, 1992.

Double Gloucester
Rance, Patrick. *The Great British Cheese Book*. Macmillan, 1982.
Double Gloucester. English Country Cheese Council.

Dovecotes
Cooke, A.O. *A Book of Dovecotes*. T.N. Foulis, 1920.
Hansell, P. and J. *Dovecotes*. Shire, 1988.

Downland
Coppock, J.T. *An Agricultural Geography of Great Britain*. Bell & Sons, 1971.
Harvey, Graham. *The Killing of the Countryside*. Jonathan Cape, 1997.

Hudson, W.H. *Nature in Downland*. Dent, 1923.
Hudson, W.H. *A Shepherd's Life*. Methuen, 1910/1933.
Jefferies, Richard. *The Open Air*. Chatto & Windus, 1885.
Massingham, H.J. *English Downland*. Batsford, 1936.
Meredith, George. 'The Lark Ascending' from *Poems and Lyrics of the Joy of Earth*. 1883.
Lowland Calcareous Grassland: A Scarce and Special Habitat. English Nature, 2001.
Species Action Plans. Butterfly Conservation.

Dragons
Attwater, Donald. *Dictionary of Saints*. Penguin, 1965/1983.
Crossley-Holland, Kevin. *British Folk Tales*. Orchard Books, 1987.
Elvidge, Heather. Emails, 29 September 2003 and 26 April 2004.
Farmer, David Hugh. *The Oxford Dictionary of Saints*. OUP, 1978/1987.
Field, John. *A History of English Field Names*. Longman, 1993.
Heaney, Seamus. *Beowulf*. Faber & Faber, 1999.
Simpson, Jacqueline. *British Dragons*. Batsford, 1980.
Unerman, Sandra. 'Dragons in Twentieth Century Fiction'. *Folklore*, vol. 113, no. 1, April 2002.
Westwood, Jennifer. *Albion: A Guide to Legendary Britain*. Grafton, 1985.
Whitlock, Ralph. *Here Be Dragons*. Allen & Unwin, 1983.

Drove Roads
Addison, Sir William. *The Old Roads of England*. Batsford, 1980.
Belsey, Valerie. *Discovering Green Lanes*. Green Books, 2001.
Belsey, Valerie. *The Green Lanes of England*. Green Books, 1998.
Bonser, K.J. *The Drovers*. Country Book Club, 1970.
Boumphrey, Geoffrey. *British Roads*. Thomas Nelson, 1939.
Hannigan, Des. *Ancient Trackways*. Pavilion, 1994.
Hey, David. *Packmen, Carriers and Packhorse Roads: Trade and Communication in North Derbyshire and South Yorkshire*. Leicester University Press, 1980.
Hindle, Brian Paul. *Roads, Tracks and their Interpretation*. Batsford, 1993.
Raistrick, Arthur. *The Pennine Dales*. Arrow 1968/1972.
Taylor, Christopher. *Roads and Tracks of Britain*. Dent, 1979.
Toulson, Shirley. *The Drovers*. Shire, 1980.
Wright, Geoffrey N. *Roads and Trackways of Wessex*. Moorland, 1988.

Drumlins
Chris Blandford Associates. *The Solway Coast Landscape*. Countryside Commission, 1995.

Field, John. *A History of English Field Names*. Longman, 1993.

Drystone Walls
Brooks, Alan; Adcock, Sean; Agate, Elizabeth. *Dry Stone Walling*. BTCV, 2003.
Hoskins, W.G. *The Making of the English Landscape*. Hodder & Stoughton, 1955/2005.
Hoskins, W.G. *One Man's England*. BBC, 1978.
Lund, Jamie. Email, 16 June 2004.
Speakman, Colin. *Yorkshire Dales*. Pevensey Press, 2001.
Withers, C.W.J. *Discovering the Cotswolds*. John Donald Publishers, 1990.
The Condition of England's Dry Stone Walls, ADAS for Countryside Commission, 1994.
Dacre Walls Walk. Dacre Parish Council, 2003.

Dudley Locusts
Fortey, Richard. *The Hidden Landscape*. Jonathan Cape, 1993.
Nature's Place. English Nature, November 2000.

E

Earth Pigments
Chris Blandford Associates. *The Mendip Hills Landscape*. Countryside Commission, 1998.
Clifton-Taylor, Alec. *The Pattern of English Building*. Faber & Faber, 1972.
Durrance, E.M. and Laming, D.J.C. *The Geology of Devon*. University of Exeter Press, 1982.
Field, John. *A History of English Field Names*. Longman, 1993.
Hardy, Thomas. *The Return of the Native*. Smith Elder & Co., 1878.
Lancaster, Michael. *Britain in View: Colour and the Landscape*. Quiller Press, 1984.
Landscape Design Associates. *The Dedham Vale Landscape*. Countryside Commission, 1997.
Penoyre, John and Penoyre, Jane. *Houses in the Landscape*. Readers Union, 1978.
Wright, Adela. *Craft Techniques for Traditional Buildings*. Batsford, 1991.
Combe Martin Parish Map.

Earthquakes
British Geological Survey.

Earth Stations
Coulson Thomas, C.J. *Cornwall's Conquest of the Air Heritage*. Tavistock, 1975.
Hoskins, W.G. *One Man's England*. BBC, 1978.
Huntingdon, Tom. 'The Whole World's Watching'. *Air and Space Magazine*, April/May 1996.

Earthworks
Cavendish, Richard. *Prehistoric England*. Artus Books, 1983/1993.
King, Angela and Clifford, Sue. *Holding Your Ground*. Wildwood House, 1987.
English Heritage.

464

East
Ratcliffe, D.A. (ed.).
A Nature Conservation Review,
vol. I. CUP, 1977.
Shakespeare, William. *Hamlet.*
1603.
Swift, Graham. *Waterland.*
Heinemann, 1983.
Walton, Izaac. *The Compleat
Angler* (1653). Everyman, 1962.

Easter Customs
Cass, Eddie. *The Lancashire
Pace-Egg Play: A Social History.*
FLS Books, 2001.
Grigson, Geoffrey.
The Englishman's Flora.
Paladin, 1958.
Hole, Christina. *British Folk
Customs.* Hutchinson, 1976.
Jones, Julia and Deer, Barbara.
*Cattern Cakes and Lace:
A Calendar of Feasts.*
Dorling Kindersley, 1987.
Kightly, Charles. *The Customs
and Ceremonies of Britain.*
Thames & Hudson, 1986.
Mabey, Richard.
Flora Britannica.
Chatto & Windus, 1996.
Pettigrew, Jane. *The Festive
Table.* Pavilion Books, 1990.
*Field Days – ideas for
Investigations and Celebrations.*
Common Ground, 1997.

Eccles Cakes
Harben, Philip.
Traditional Dishes of Britain.
Bodley Head, 1953.

Edible Dormouse
Buczacki, Stefan. *Fauna
Britannica.* Hamlyn, 2002.
Hart-Davis, Duff.
Fauna Britannica.
Weidenfeld & Nicolson, 2002.
A Review of British Mammals.
JNCC, 1995.

Eels
Crowden, James and Wright,
George. *In Time of Flood.* The
Parrett Trail Partnership, 1996.
Deakin, Roger. *Waterlog:
A Swimmer's Journey through
Britain.* Chatto & Windus,
1999/Vintage, 2000.
Field, John. *A History of English
Field-Names.* Longman, 1993.
Fort, Tom. *The Book of Eels.*
HarperCollins, 2002.
Hart-Davis, Duff.
Fauna Britannica.
Weidenfeld & Nicolson, 2002.
Hartley, Dorothy. *Food in
England.* Futura, 1954.
Malster, Robert.
The Norfolk and Suffolk Broads.
Phillimore Books, 2003.
Miller, Eric. Email, 4 May 2002.
Sutherland, Patrick and
Nicolson, Adam. *Wetland:
Life in the Somerset Levels.*
Michael Joseph, 1986.
Sly, Rex. *From Punt to Plough:
A History of the Fens.*
Alan Sutton, 2003.

Elm
Edlin, H.L. *Woodland
Crafts in Britain.*
David & Charles, 1949/1973.
Johnson, Owen. *The Sussex Tree
Book.* Pomegranite Press, 1998.
Land Use Consultants.
The Isles of Scilly.
Countryside Agency, 2002.

Lasdun, Susan. *The English Park.*
Andre Deutsch, 1991.
Mabey, R. *Flora Britannica.*
Chatto & Windus, 1996.
Rackham, O. *The History of
the Countryside.* Dent, 1986.
Richens, R.H. *Elm.* CUP, 1983.
Wilkinson, G. *Epitaph for the
Elm.* Arrow Books, 1978.
*Elms and associated places of
interest in East Sussex.*
Sussex Downs Conservation
Board, 2002.

Engine Houses
Barton, D.B. *Cornwall's Engine
Houses.* Tor Mark Press, 1989.
Burton, Anthony.
*Daily Telegraph Guide to
Britain's Working Past.*
Aurum Press, 2002.

Estuaries
Cooper, Andrew. *Secret
Nature of the Channel Shore.*
BBC Books, 1992.
Covey, R. and Laffoley, D.d'A.
*State of Nature: Maritime –
Getting onto an Even Keel.*
English Nature, 2002.
Lindley, Kenneth. *Coastline.*
Hutchinson & Co., 1967.
Rothschild, Miriam and
Marren, Peter. *Rothschild's
Reserves.* Harley Books, 1997.
Soothill, Eric and Thomas,
Michael. *The Natural History
of Britain's Coasts.* Blandford
Publishing, 1987.
Soper, Tony. *A Natural History
Guide to the Coasts.* Webb &
Bower/National Trust, 1984.
*Developing English Nature's
Maritime Strategy, State
of Nature one year on.*
English Nature, 2002.
Living with the Sea.
English Nature, 2003.

Exmoor Ponies
Hulme, Mike and Barrow,
Elaine (eds.). *Climates of the
British Isles.* Routledge, 1997.
Miles, Roger. *Forestry in
the English Landscape.*
Faber & Faber, 1967.
Rackham, Oliver. *Trees and
Woodlands in the British
Landscape.* Dent, 1990.
Exmoor Pony Society.

Eyots
Drabble, Margaret.
*A Writer's Britain:
Landscape in Literature.*
Thames & Hudson, 1979.
Grahame, Kenneth. *The Wind
in the Willows.* Methuen, 1908.
Mackay, D. *The Secret Thames.*
Ebury Press, 1992.
Ravenstein, E.G. *The Oarsman's
and Angler's Map of the
Thames.* 1893, reprinted by
Old House Books, 1991.
'A Nature Conservation Strategy
for London'. *Ecology
Handbook,* no. 4, nd.

F

Factories
Girouard, Mark.
The English Town.
Yale University Press, 1990.
Harwood, Elain. *England:
A Guide to Post-war Listed
Buildings.* Batsford, 2000.

Fairs & Fairgrounds
Aston, Mick. *Monasteries in the
Landscape.* Tempus, 2000.
Bonser, K.J. *The Drovers.*
Country Book Club, 1970.
Hole, Christina. *Traditions
and Customs of Cheshire.* SR
Publishers, 1970 (orig 1937).
Kerr Cameron, David.
The English Fair.
Alan Sutton, 1998.
Kightly, Charles. *The Customs
and Ceremonies of Britain.*
Thames & Hudson, 1986.
Mason, Laura with Brown,
Catherine. *Traditional Foods
of Britain: An Inventory.*
Prospect Books, 1999.
Pettigrew, Jane. *The Festive
Table.* Pavilion Books, 1990.
University of Sheffield National
Fairground Archive.

Family Names
Betjeman, John. *First and Last
Loves.* John Murray, 1952.
Bragg, Melvyn.
The Adventure of English.
Hodder & Stoughton, 2003.
Hoskins, W.G. *Devon.*
Collins, 1957.
Hudston, Sara. *Islomania.*
AGRE Books, 2000.
Office of National Statistics
names database.
Society of Genealogists.

Farms & Farmsteads
Brunskill, R.W. *Traditional
Farm Buildings of Britain.*
Gollancz, 1999.
Massingham, H.J. *English
Downland.* Batsford, 1936.
Mercer, Eric. *English Vernacular
Houses.* RCHM HMSO, 1975/9.
Taylor, Christopher.
Village and Farmstead.
Book Club Associates, 1983.
*English Heritage Conservation
Bulletin.* Issue 42, March
2002.

Fell Ponies
Hartley Edwards, Elwyn (ed.).
Encyclopedia of the Horse.
Bounty Books, 1985.
Rare Breeds Survival Trust.

Fell Running
Askwith, Richard.
*Feet in the Clouds: A Tale of
Fell-Running and Obsession.*
Aurum Press, 2004.
'Conserving Lakeland'. *Friends
of the Lake District Magazine,*
no. 40, Winter/Spring, 2003.
Burnsall Feast Sports.
Fell Runners Association.

Fells
Duerden, Frank.
Best Walks in the Lake District.
Constable, 1986.
Varley, Martin. *Flora of the Fells.*
Friends of the Lake District
and English Nature, 2003.
Wainwright, A.
Fellwalking with Wainwright.
Michael Joseph, 1984.
Walters, Martin and Gibbons,
Bob. *Britain, Travellers'
Nature Guides.* OUP, 2003.
Whittow, John.
Geology and Scenery in Britain.
Chapman & Hall, 1992.
Winchester, Angus. *The Harvest
of the Hills.* Edinburgh
University Press, 2002.

Fences
Edlin, H.L. *Woodland
Crafts in Britain.*
David & Charles, 1949/1973.
Jekyll, Gertrude.
Old West Surrey. Kohler &
Coombes, 1904/1978.
High Weald Design Project.
High Weald AONB, nd.

Fens
Bevis, Trevor. *Flooded Fens.*
Privately printed, 2001.
Bevis, Trevor.
*Water water everywhere:
The Draining of the Fens.*
Privately printed, 1992.
Brooks, Alan and Agate,
Elizabeth. *Waterways and
Wetlands: A Practical
Handbook.* BTCV, 1976/1997.
Gerrard, Valerie. *The Story of
the Fens.* Robert Hale, 2003.
Grigson, Geoffrey.
Shell Country Alphabet.
Ebury, 1966.
Hunter Blair, Andrew.
Great Ouse Country.
John Nickalls, 2002.
Kingsley, Charles.
Hereward the Wake.
Macmillan & Co., 1866.
Mason, H.J. *The Black Fens.*
Providence, 1984.
Meers, Nick and Seddon, Sue.
Enigmatic England.
Alan Sutton, 1990.
Sly, Rex. *From Punt to Plough:
A History of the Fens.*
Alan Sutton, 2003.
Swift, Graham. *Waterland.*
Picador, 1983.
Wood, Eric S. *Collins Field
Guide to Archaeology in
Britain.* Collins, 1968/1982.

Fen Skating
Deakin, Roger. 'Turkey, Fish
and Gutta Percha on ice'.
Independent, 13 January 2001.
Gerrard, Valerie. *The Story of
the Fens.* Robert Hale, 2003.
Page, Robin. 'An Icy blast'.
Daily Telegraph, 12 January
2002.

Feral Animals
Beckensall, Stan.
*Northumberland: The Power
of Place.* Tempus, 2001.
Buczacki, Stefan. *Fauna
Britannica.* Hamlyn, 2002.
Butler, Chris. 'Project Parakeet'
(research for doctoral thesis,
Oxford University, 2004).
Dards, Jane. 'Habitat
Utilisation by Feral Cats
in Portsmouth Dockyard,
proceedings of a symposium
held at Royal Holloway
College, University of
London'. Universities
Federation of Animal
Welfare, 1981.
Harris, Stephen et al.
A Review of British Mammals.
JNCC, 1995.
Hart-Davis, Duff.
Fauna Britannica.
Weidenfeld & Nicolson, 2002.
Macdonald, David W. and
Tattersall, Fran. *Britain's
Mammals: The Challenge
for Conservation.* People's
Trust for Endangered
Species, 2001.

465

Wingfield Gibbons, David et al. *The New Atlas of Breeding Birds in Britain and Ireland 1988-1991*. T. & A.D. Poyser, 1993.
Rare Breeds Facts and Figures. Rare Breeds Survival Trust, 1991.

Ferns
Allen, David. 'Tastes and crazes' in *Cultures of Natural History* (Jardine, N. et al, eds.). CUP, 1996.
Freethy, Ron. *British Ferns*. Crowood Press, 1987.
Martin, Rickard. 'Ferns – a case history' in *The Common Ground of Wild and Cultivated Plants* (Perry, A. Roy and Ellis, R. Gwynn, eds.). National Museum of Wales, 1994.
Page, Chris. *The Ferns of Britain and Ireland*. CUP, 1997.
Rackham, Oliver. *Ancient Woodland*. Castlepoint Press, 2003.

Ferries
Legg, Rodney. 'Chain Ferry'. *Purbeck Magazine*, Winter 2000.
Luckhurst, Colin. 'Country Diary'. *Guardian*, 16 June 2000 and 2 June 2003.
Wheatley, Keith. *National Maritime Museum Guide to Maritime Britain*. Webb & Bower, 1990.
Out and About in the South Hams. 2001.

Field Barns
Child, P. 'Farm Buildings' in *Devon Building* (Beacham, Peter, ed.). Devon Books, 1990.
Bonsall Village Design Statement.
Walls and Field Barns (leaflet). Yorkshire Dales National Park.

Field Maple
Grigson, Geoffrey. *The Englishman's Flora*. Paladin, 1975.
Hunter, John. *The Essex Landscape*. Essex County Council, 1999.
Marren, Peter. *Woodland Heritage*. David & Charles, 1990.
Miles, Archie. *Silva: The Tree in Britain*. Ebury Press, 1999.
Rackham, Oliver. *Ancient Woodland*. Castlepoint Press, 2003.
Vickery, Roy. *A Dictionary of Plant Lore*. OUP, 1995.

Field Names, Field Patterns, Fields
Field, John. *English Field Names: A Dictionary*. David & Charles 1972/ Alan Sutton 1998.
Field, John. *A History of English Field Names*. Longman, 1993.
Gurney, Ivor. 'Up There' in *Field Days* (King, Angela and Clifford, Sue, eds.). Green Books, 1998.
Hall, David. 'Turning the Plough' in *Midland Open Fields: Landscape Character and Proposals for Management*. English Heritage and Northamptonshire County Council, 2001.

Harvey, Graham. *The Forgiveness of Nature: The Story of Grass*. Jonathan Cape, 2001.
Hoskins, W.G. *The Making of the English Landscape*. Hodder & Stoughton, 1955/2005.
King, Angela and Clifford, Sue. *Field Days: A Poetry Anthology*. Green Books, 1998.
Lund, Jamie. Email, 16 June 2004.
Maxwell, Robert. *Wasdale Head: An Historic Landscape Survey*. National Trust North West Region (unpublished report).
Rackham, Oliver. *The History of the Countryside*. Dent, 1986.
Taylor, Christopher. *Fields in the English Landscape*. Alan Sutton, 1987.
Tindall, Gillian. *The Fields Beneath*. Granada, 1981.
Wood, Eric S. *Historical Britain*. Harvill Press, 1995.
Field Days – ideas for Investigations and Celebrations. Common Ground, 1997.
A Manifesto for Fields. Common Ground, 1997.

Fingerposts
Beacham, Peter and Ravilious, James. *Down the Deep Lanes*. Devon Books, 2000.
Free, Roger. 'Finger Tips'. *Dorset*, April 2004.
Hands, Stuart. *Road Signs*. Shire, 2002.
Hawkins, Michael. *Devon Roads*. Devon Books, 1988.
Osborn, George. *Dorset Curiosities*. Dovecote Press, 1986.
Porteous, Katrina. Letters, 2004/5.
Somerset into the 21st century. Somerset County Council, 1998.

Fish & Chips
Ellis, Hattie. *Eating England*. Mitchell Beazley, 2001.
Harben, Philip. *Traditional Dishes of Britain*. Bodley Head, 1953.
Mudd, Tony. 'Fish and Chips by the Sea' in *Let's Go Out*. Redwood, 2000.
Stein, Rick. 'Fish and Chips' in *British Greats*. Cassell & Co., 2000.
National Federation of Fish Friers.

Flags
Crampton, William. *The Observer's Book of Flags*. Bloomsbury, 1991.
Turner-Bishop, Aiden. Letters, 2003.
The Country Life Book of Nautical Terms under Sail. Trewin Copplestone Publishing, 1978.

Flatners
Elmer, W. *The Terminology of Fishing: A Survey of English and Welsh Inshore Fishing Things and Words*. The Cooper Monographs 19, English Dialect Series. Franke Verlag, 1973.
Hazell, M. *Sailing Barges*. Shire, 2001.

McKee, Eric. *Working Boats of Britain: Their Shape and Purpose*. Conway Maritime Press, 1983.

Flint
Behague, John. *Lucky Sussex*. Pomegranate Press, 1998.
Clifton-Taylor, Alec. *The Pattern of English Building*. Faber & Faber, 1972.
Davison, Caroline; Knight, Michael; Yates, David. Norfolk County Council. Conversations/emails, various dates.
Harding, Phil. Email, 7 April 2003.
Hart, Stephen. *Flint Architecture of East Anglia*. Giles de la Mare, 2000.
Hooker, Jeremy. *Flints, Soliloquies of a Chalk Giant*. Enitharmon Press, 1974.
Land Use Consultants. *The Chilterns Landscape*. Countryside Commission, 1992.
Linder, Gary. North Norfolk District Council. Conversation, 2003.
Orne, Bernard and Orne, Elizabeth. *Flint in Norfolk*. Running Angel, 1984.
Wright, Adela. *Craft Techniques for Traditional Buildings*. Batsford, 1991.
Chilterns Buildings Design Guide, Chilterns Flint. Chilterns AONB Conservation Board, 2003.
North Norfolk Design Guide. NNDC, 1998.
Round Towered Churches Society.

Floods
Delderfield, Eric R. *The Lynmouth Flood Disaster*. The Raleigh Press, 1953.
Mackay, Duncan. *The Secret Thames*. Ebury Press, 1992.
Environment Agency.

Fog & Mist
Dickens, Charles. *Bleak House*. 1853.
Griffiths, Bill. *NE Dialect*. University of Northumbria, 2001.
Hague, D.B. and Christie, R. *Lighthouses: Their Architecture, History and Archaeology*. Gomer Press, 1975.
Porteous, Katrina. Email, 26 September 2003.
Westwood, Jennifer. *Albion*. Grafton, 1985.
Meteorological Office.

Folktales
Betts, Henry. *English Legends*. Batsford, 1950.
Briggs, K.M. *A Dictionary of British Folk-Tales in the English Language*. Routledge, 1970.
Bromwich, Margaret. Letter, 6 May 2002.
Manwaring, Kevan. Letter, 12 January 2004.
Padel, Ruth. *British Greats*. Cassell & Co., 2000.
Westwood, Jennifer. *Albion*. Grafton, 1985.
Westwood, J. and Simpson, J. *The Lore of the Land*. Penguin, 2005.

Follies
Hatt, E.M. *Follies*. National Benzole/ Chatto & Windus, 1963.
Headley, Gwyn and Meulenkamp, Wim. *Follies, Grottoes and Garden Buildings*. Aurum, 1999.
Whitelaw, Jeffery W. *Follies*. Shire, 1982/1997.

Food
Billy Bragg and the Blokes. 'England, Half English'. Cooking Vinyl, 2002.
Gould, Stephen J. *Eight Little Piggies*. Jonathan Cape, 1993.
Hartley, Dorothy. *Food in England*. Futura, 1954.
Mason, Laura with Brown, Catherine. *Traditional Foods of Britain*. Prospect Books, 1999.

Football
Cann, Steve. Conversations, 2004.
Chitty, Gill and Wood, Jason. 'A Sporting Chance'. *English Heritage Conservation Bulletin*, October 2002.
Herman, Roger. Conversations, 2004.
Inglis, Simon. *The Football Grounds of England and Wales*. Willow, 1985.
Quiggin, Alison H. 'Games – the Myth of Play' in *Man, Myth and Magic*, 1970.
Steele, Simon. Conversations, 2004.
Williams, Tony. *The Guinness Non-League Football Fact Book*. Guinness, 1991.

Footbridges
Clifton-Taylor, Alec. *English Stone Building*. Gollancz, 1983.
De Mare, Eric. *The Bridges of Britain*. Batsford, 1954.
Hardy, Thomas. *The Mayor of Casterbridge*. 1886.
Highways Agency. *The Appearance of Bridges and other Highway Structures*. HMSO, 1996.
Jervois, E. *The Ancient Bridges of Mid and Eastern England*. Architectural Press, 1932.
Jervois, E. *The Ancient Bridges of the South of England*. Architectural Press, 1930.
Richards, J.M. *The National Trust Book of Bridges*. Jonathan Cape, 1984.
Bridges in Hampshire of Historic Interest. Hampshire County Council, 2000.

Footpaths
Hannigan, Des. *Ancient Trackways*. Pavilion, 1994.
King, Angela and Clifford, Sue. *Holding Your Ground: An Action Guide to Local Conservation*. Temple Smith, 1985.
MacColl, Ewan. 'The Manchester Rambler'. 1932.
Taplin, Kim. *The English Path*. The Boydell Press, 1979.
Thorpe, Adam. 'In the Author's Footsteps'. *Guardian*, 29 May 2004.
Wainwright, A. *Walks in Limestone Country*. Westmorland Gazette, 1970.

Bonsall Village Design Statement.
Derbyshire CC, 2002.

Fords
Cumming, Carolyn and
Grimsdale, Edward
(The Buckingham Society).
Letters, 2004.
Field, John. *A History of English
Field Names.* Longman, 1993.
Gelling, Margaret and Cole,
Ann. *The Landscape of Place-
Names.* Shaun Tyas, 2000.
Good, Ronald. *The Old Roads
of Dorset.* Longmans,
1940/Horace G. Commin
Ltd, 1966.
Grigson, Geoffrey. 'Shining
Fords' in *English Excursions.*
Country Life, 1960.
Hawkins, Michael. *Devon Roads.*
Devon Books, 1988.
Thomas, Jill.
Email, 20 June 2002.
Wood, Eric S. *Historical Britain.*
Harvill Press, 1997.

Forges
Blythe, Ronald. *Akenfield:
Portrait of an English Village.*
Pantheon Books, 1969.
Crowden, James.
Email, 7 April 2004.
Fowler, Peter. *Farms in
England: Prehistoric to Present.*
RCHM, 1983.
Porteous, Katrina. Letters,
July 2004 and April 2005.
Wood, Eric S. *Historical Britain.*
Harvill Press, 1995.
Felbridge and District History
Group.

Fortifications
Bergstrom, Theo. *Hadrian's
Wall.* Bergstom & Boyles
Books Ltd, 1975.
Brabbs, Derry.
England's Heritage.
Weidenfeld & Nicolson, 2001.
Breeze, David J. and Dobson,
Brian. *Hadrian's Wall.*
Penguin, 1976.
Palmerston Forts Society.

Freshwater Fish
Davies, Cynthia et al.
*Freshwater Fishes in Britain:
The Species and their Distribution.*
Harley Books, 2004.
Lewis, Vaughan.
*Nature Conservation and
Game Fisheries Management.*
English Nature, 1997.
Paxman, Jeremy. *Fish, Fishing
and the Meaning of Life.*
Penguin Books, 1994/5.
Scott, Jock.
Salmon and Trout Rivers.
Chorley & Pickersgill, nd.
Walton, Izaak. *The Compleat
Angler.* 1653 (Dent, 1962).
Wheetler, Alwyne. *Freshwater
Fishes of Britain and Europe.*
Rainbow Books, 1992.
Young, Barbara.
'Raising the Bar, Turning the
Tide'. Environment Agency,
Autumn 2004.
Our Nation's Fisheries.
Environment Agency, 2004.
Reader's Digest Atlas. 1965.

Frets
Houghton, D. *Weather at Sea.*
Fernhurst Books, 1998.
Porteous, Katrina.
Email, 26 September 2003.

'Staithes Song'. Composed by
Staithes villagers with Blaize.

Fritillary Meadows
Grigson, Geoffrey.
The Englishman's Flora.
Paladin, 1958.
Mabey, Richard.
Flora Britannica.
Chatto & Windus, 1996.
Local Flora Britannica.
Common Ground, 1995.

Frost & Frost Hollows
Bartlett, D. and Bartlett, K.
Signpost to the Weather.
Edward Stanford, 1949.
Brooks, C.E.P. *The English
Climate.* English Universities
Press, 1954.
Bush, Raymond. *Frost and the
Fruit Grower.* Cassell, 1946.
Crowden, James.
Cider, the Forgotten Miracle.
Cyder Press 2, 1999.
Manley, Gordon.
Climate and the British Scene.
Collins, 1952.
Shirley, David. *Hertfordshire:
A Guide to the Countryside.*
Egon Publishers, 1978.
Stirling, Robin. *The Weather of
Britain.* Giles de la Mare, 1997.

Funicular Railways
Body, Geoffrey and Eastleigh,
Robert L. *Cliff Railways of
the British Isles.*
David & Charles, 1964.
Lindley, Kenneth.
Seaside Architecture.
Hugh Evelyn, 1973.
Pearson, Lynn F. *Piers and
other Seaside Architecture.*
Shire, 2002.

Furry Dance
Dearmer, Percy; Vaughan
Williams, Ralph; Shaw,
Martin. *The Oxford Book of
Carols.* OUP, 1928.
Hole, Christina. *British Folk
Customs.* Hutchinson, 1976.
Kightly, Charles. *The Customs
and Ceremonies of Britain.*
Thames & Hudson, 1986.
Mabey, Richard.
Flora Britannica.
Chatto & Windus, 1996.
Muss, David.
Cornwall and Scilly Peculiar.
Bossiney Books, 1979.

G

Gables
Clifton-Taylor, Alec.
The Pattern of English Building.
Faber & Faber, 1972.
Garner, A. *The Stone Book
Quartet.* HarperCollins, 1992.
Joyce, Barry. Conversation,
December 2002.
Penoyre, J. and Penoyre, J.
Houses in the Landscape.
Faber & Faber, 1978.
Williams, M. *The Slate Industry.*
Shire, 2002.

Gallops
Betjeman, J. 'Upper Lambourne'
in *Trees be Company.* (King,
Angela and Clifford, Sue,
eds.) Green Books, 2001.
Gill, James.
Racecourses of Great Britain.
Barrie & Jenkins, 1973.
Wale, Lindy. Letter, 2004.

Games
Arlott, John (ed.). *The Oxford
Companion to Sports and
Games.* OUP, 1975.
Body, Geoff and Gallop, Roy.
'Somerset's Mystery Game'.
Somerset Life, March 2002.
Vallins, John. 'Silence in Court'
(Country Diary).
Guardian, 14 May 2002.
Wales, Tony. *Sussex Customs,
Curiosities and Country Lore.*
Ensign Publications, 1990.

Ganseys
Porteous, Katrina.
Letters, 2004.
Thompson, Gladys.
Guernsey and Jersey Patterns.
Batsford, 1955.
North East Fisher Gansies.
Tyne and Wear County
Council Museums, 1980.

Gaps
Hoskins, W.G. *The Making of
the English Landscape.* Hodder
& Stoughton, 1955/2005.

Garages
Berkowitz, Nina; Cross,
Andrew; Jones, Helen.
*It's a gas . . . visit seven petrol
stations by public transport.*
MTA Design/CETA Imaging
pamphlet, nd.
de Burton, Simon. 'Clear View'.
Direct Living, Autumn 2004.
Jones, Helen. 'Buildings
designed to advertise fuel'.
British Archaeology, October
1998.

Gardens
Alexander, Christopher et al.
A Pattern Language.
OUP, 1977.
Brookes, John.
Planting the Country Way.
BBC Books, 1994.
Keen, Mary. 'The Spirit of
Place: Fact or Fantasy?' in
*The National Trust Gardens
Conference 2001 Proceedings.*
National Trust, 2001.
Rackham, Oliver. *The History of
the Countryside.* Dent, 1986.
Robinson, William.
The English Flower Garden.
John Murray, 1883.
*The Art of Gentle Gardening:
Thoughts on Linking Plants,
People and Places.* Common
Ground, 1995.

Gargoyles & Grotesques
Blackwood, John and Collett,
David. *Oxford's Gargoyles and
Grotesques: A Guided Tour.*
Charon Press, 1986.
Jenkins, Simon. *England's
Thousand Best Churches.*
Penguin Books, 1999.
Kahn, John.
The Charm of the Cotswolds.
Reader's Digest, 1999.
Poyntz Wright, Peter. *Hunky
Punks: A Study in Somerset
Stone Carving.* Heart of
Albion Press, 1982/2004.
Sansom, Clive. 'Gargoyles' in
The Cathedral. Methuen, 1958.

Gasholders
Buchanan, R.A.
*Industrial Archaeology in
Britain.* Allen Lane, 1974.
Burroughs, Stuart.
Letter, September 2004.

Clarke, Jonathan.
'Volatile Heritage'.
*English Heritage Conservation
Bulletin,* March 2002.
Lancaster, Michael. *Britain in
View.* Sandtex/Quiller, 1984.
Smith, Norman. *Gas
Manufacture and Utilization.*
British Gas Council, 1945.
Warren, Geoffrey.
Vanishing Street Furniture.
David & Charles, 1978.

Gates
Barnes, William.
One Hundred Poems.
The Dorset Bookshop, 1971.
Chris Blandford Associates.
Solway Coast Landscape.
Countryside Commission,
1995.
Brian, Anthea. Letters, 2003/4.
Harrison, Bill. *Dartmoor Stone
Crosses.* Devon Books, 2001.
Moreland, T.E. 'The Field Gates
of England'. *The Countryman,*
Summer 1961.
Tanner, Robin and Tanner,
Heather. *Wiltshire Village,*
Robin Garton, 1939/1978.
Wright, Joseph. *The English
Dialect Dictionary.* 1898.
Dacre Walls Walk.
Dacre Parish Council, 2003.

Ghylls
Deakin, Roger. *Waterlog.*
Chatto & Windus, 1999/
Vintage, 2000.
Field, John. *A History of English
Field Names.* Longman, 1993.
Gelling, Margaret.
Place Names in the Landscape.
Dent, 1984.
Slade, Chris. Emails, 2004.
*Landscape of the Sussex Downs
AONB.* Countryside
Commission and Sussex
Downs Conservation Board,
1996.

Giants
Bett, Henry. *English Legends.*
Batsford, 1950.
Gee, H.L.
Folk Tales of Yorkshire.
Thomas Nelson, 1952.
Shortt, Hugh. *The Giant and
Hob-Nob.* Salisbury and
Wiltshire Museum, 1972.
Tongue, Ruth in *A Dictionary
of Folk Tales in the English
Language* (Briggs, Katherine
M.). Routledge, 1970.

Gin
Mason, Laura with Brown,
Catherine. *Traditional
Foods of Britain.*
Prospect Books, 1999.

Gin Houses
Child, P. 'Farm Buildings'
in *Devon Building*
(Beacham, Peter, ed.).
Devon Books, 1990.
Lawson, Anne. Letters, 2002.

Glastonbury Festival
O'Farrell, Kate.
Conversations, 2004.
Glastonbury Festival.

Glow-worms
Palmer, Ray. *Lamp of the
Night.* British Naturalists'
Association, nd.
Robinson, Eric and Summerfield,
Geoffrey. *John Clare Selected
Poems and Prose.* OUP, 1978.

Tyler, John. 'The Ecology and Conservation of the Glow worm, Lampyris noctiluca (L) in Britain'. *ATALA*, vols 10-12, 1982-1984 (86).

Tyler, John. *The Glow-worm*. Lakeside Printing, 2002.

South Lincolnshire Herald and Post. 3 May 1991.

UK Glow-worm survey.

Golf-courses

Eyre, K. *Sand Grown: The Lytham St Anne's Story*. Landy Publishing, 1999.

Gange, Alan C.; Lindsay, Della E.; Schofield, J. Mike. 'The Ecology of Golf Courses'. *Biologist* 50 (2), 2003.

Smith, Philip H. 'The Sefton Coast Sand-dunes, Merseyside'. *British Wildlife*, October 2000.

Nature. BBC Radio 4, January 2003.

European Golf Association Ecology Unit.

Gooseberries

Grigson, Geoffrey. *The Englishman's Flora*. Paladin, 1975.

Grigson, Jane. *Good Things*. Michael Joseph, 1971.

Jesse, R.H.B. *A Survey of the Agriculture of Sussex*. Royal Agricultural Society of England, 1960.

Mason, Laura with Brown, Catherine. *Traditional Foods of Britain*. Prospect Books, 1999.

Roach, F.A. *Cultivated Fruits of Britain*. Blackwell, 1985.

Smith, Dave. Letter, 16 March 1992.

Sykes, Homer. *Once a Year*. Gordon Fraser, 1977.

Upton, Clive and Widdowson, J.D.A. *An Atlas of English Dialects*. OUP, 1996.

Gorges

Fortey, Richard. *The Hidden Landscape*. Jonathan Cape, 1993.

Gates, Phil. 'Flotsam and Jetsam'. *Guardian*, 3 January 2002.

Humphreys, Richard. *The British Landscape through the Eyes of the Great Artists*. St Michael in association with the Tate Gallery, Octopus Publishing/Hennerwood Publishing, 1989.

Muir, R. and Muir, N. *Rivers of Britain*. Webb & Bower, 1986.

Gorse

Draper, Jo. *Pots, Brooms and Hurdles from the Heathlands*. Verwood and District Potteries Trust, 2002.

Field, John. *A History of English Field Names*. Longman, 1993.

French, Colin; Murphy, Rosaline; Atkinson, Mary. *Flora of Cornwall*. Wheal Seton Press, 1999.

Harris, A. 'Gorse in the East Riding of Yorkshire'. *Folk Life*, vol. 30, 1991-2.

Humphries, C.J. and Shaughnessy, E. *Gorse*. Shire Natural History, 1987.

Vickery, Roy. *A Dictionary of Plant Lore*. OUP, 1995.

Flora Facts and Fables. Summer 2004.

Graffiti

Ackroyd, Peter. *London: The Biography*. Chatto & Windus, 2000.

Banksy. *Banging Your Head Against a Brick Wall*. Banksy, 2001.

Sinclair, Iain. *Lights Out for the Territory*. Granta, 1997.

Williams, Heathcote. Letter (via Leana Pooley), 30 August 2004.

Granite

Clifton-Taylor, Alec. *The Pattern of English Building*. Faber & Faber, 1972/1980.

Ellis, Clarence. *The Pebbles on the Beach*. Faber & Faber, 1954.

Muir Wood, Robert. *On the Rocks: A Geology of Britain*. BBC, 1978.

Haytor Granite Tramway and Stover Canal. Devon County Council/Teignbridge District Council, 1985.

Grassy Triangles

Tracey, Dee. 'Godcakes'. *Country Matters*, no. 22, Warwickshire Rural Community Council, Autumn/Winter 1997.

Gravel Pits

Wale, Lindy. Letter, 26 November 2004.

Gravestones

Burgess, Pamela. *Churchyards*. SPCK, 1980.

Calder-Marshall, Clare. Letter, 2002.

Evans, I.M. (ed.). *Charnwood's Heritage*. Leicestershire County Council, 1976.

Gilbert, Oliver. *Lichens*. HarperCollins, 2000.

Lees, Hilary. *English Churchyard Memorials*. Tempus Publishing, 2000.

Wood, Eric S. *Historical Britain*. Harvill Press, 1995.

Grazing Marshes

Chris Blandford Associates. *The Solway Coast Landscape*. Countryside Commission, 1995.

Dickens, Charles. *Great Expectations*.

Reeves, Anne and Williamson, Tom. 'Marshes' in *Rural England: An Illustrated History of the Landscape* (Thirsk, Joan, ed.). OUP, 2002.

Williamson, Tom. *Hedges and Walls*. National Trust, 2002.

UK Biodiversity, Priority Habitats: Coastal and Floodplain Grazing Marsh. JNCC, 2001.

Green Lanes

Addison, Sir William. *The Old Roads of England*. Batsford, 1980.

Belsey, Valerie. *Discovering Green Lanes*. Green Books, 2001.

Belsey, Valerie. *The Green Lanes of England*. Green Books, 1998.

Bonser, K.J. *The Drovers*. Macmillan, 1970.

Cobham Resource Consultants. *The Lincolnshire Wolds Landscape*. Countryside Commission, 1993.

Derek Lovejoy Partnership. *The South Devon Landscape*. Countryside Commission, 1993.

Dodds, A.E. and Dodds, E.M. *Peakland Roads and Trackways*. Moorland Publishing, 1974.

Hippisley Cox, R. *The Green Roads of England*. Methuen, 1914.

Hoskins, W.G. *The Making of the English Landscape*. Hodder & Stoughton, 1955/2005.

Hunter, John. *The Essex Landscape*. Chelmsford, 1999.

Taylor, Christopher. *Roads and Tracks of Britain*. Dent, 1979.

Wainwright, Alfred. *A Bowland Sketchbook*. Michael Joseph, 1991.

Woolerton Truscott. *The Forest of Bowland Landscape*. Countryside Commission, 1992.

Green Man

Anderson, William. *Green Man*. HarperCollins, 1990.

Anderson, William. *The Rise of the Gothic*. Hutchinson, 1985.

Basford, Kathleen. *The Green Man*. D.S. Brewer, 1978.

Centerwall, Brandon S. 'The Name of the Green Man'. *Folklore* 108, 1997.

Fowles, John and Horvat, Frank. *The Tree*. Aurum Press, 1979.

Judge, Roy. *The Jack-in-the-Green*. D.S. Brewer, 1979.

Pevsner, Nikolaus. *The Leaves of Southwell*. King Penguin, 1945.

Poyntz Wright, Peter. *The Rural Bench Ends of Somerset*. Avebury, 1983.

Stone, Brian (trans.). *Sir Gawain and the Green Knight*. Penguin, 1974.

Whetstone, George. *The Second Parts of the Famous Historie of Promos and Cassandra*. 1578.

Greensand

Centre for Environmental Interpretation. *The Surrey Hills Landscape*. Countryside Commission, 1998.

Clifton-Taylor, Alec. *The Pattern of English Building*. Faber & Faber, 1972/1980.

Cobham Resource Consultants. *East Hampshire Landscape*. Countryside Commission, 1991.

Perkins, John W. *Geology Explained in Dorset*. David & Charles, 1977.

Greetings

McCrum, R.; Cran, W.; MacNeil, R. *The Story of English*. Faber & Faber, 1986.

Rawling, Tom. 'The Old Showfield' in *Field Days* (King, Angela and Clifford, Sue, eds.). Green Books, 1998.

Trudgill, Peter. *The Dialects of England*. Basil Blackwell, 1990.

Grovely Rights Day

Hole, Christina. *A Dictionary of Folk Customs*. Hutchinson, 1976.

Kightly, Charles. *The Customs and Ceremonies of Britain*. Thames & Hudson, 1986.

Ross, Lieutenant Colonel C.C.G. *The Story of Oak Apple Day in Wishford Magna*. 1987.

Sykes, Homer. *Once a Year*. Gordon Fraser, 1977.

The History of Oak Apple Day in Wishford Magna, nd.

Gruffy Ground

Allen, Bob. *Escape to the Dales*. Mermaid, 1992.

Barnatt, John and Penny, Rebecca. *The Lead Legacy*. Peak District National Park Authority, 2004.

Chris Blandford Associates. *The Mendip Hills Landscape*. Countryside Commission, 1998.

Hoskins, W.G. *One Man's England*. BBC, 1978.

Neale, F.A. 'Mendip the Fourth Dimension' in *Man and the Mendips* (Hall, W.G., ed.). Mendip Society, 1971.

Gun Dogs

Croxton Smith, Arthur. *British Dogs*. Collins, 1945.

Fogle, Dr Bruce. *The Encyclopaedia of the Dog*. Dorling Kindersley, 1995.

Gordon, John F. *All about the Cocker Spaniel*. Pelham Books, 1976/1987.

Hart-Davis, Duff. *Fauna Britannica*. Weidenfeld & Nicolson, 2002.

Larkin, Dr Peter and Stockman, Mike. *The Ultimate Encyclopaedia of Dog Breeds and Dog Care*. Southwater, 1997.

Gypsies

Bender, B. *Stonehenge*. Berg, 1998.

Cloves, Jeff. *The Official Conker Book*. Jonathan Cape, 1993.

Hancock, Ian F. 'We Are the Romani People'. *Interface*, vol. 28, 2002.

Longfellow, H.W. *The Village Blacksmith*. 1862.

Thomas, P.A. and Campbell, S. *Housing Gypsies*. Cardiff Law School, 1992.

H

Half-year Birds

Fortey, Richard. *The Hidden Landscape*. Jonathan Cape, 1993.

Greenoak, Francesca. *All the Birds of the Air*. Andre Deutsch, 1979.

Lack, Andrew and Overall, Roy. *The Museum Swifts: The Story of the Swifts in the Tower of the Oxford University Museum of Natural History*. Oxford Museum of Natural History, 2002.

Shrubb, Michael. *Birds, Scythes and Combines: A History of Birds and Agricultural Change*. CUP, 2003.

Walton, Izaac. *The Compleat Angler* (1653). Dent, 1962.

Wernham, Chris et al (eds.). *The Migration Atlas*. BTO/ T. & A.D. Poyser, 2002.

White, Gilbert. *The Natural History of Selborne* (1788-89). Penguin, 1977.

Wingfield Gibbons, David et al. *The New Atlas of Breeding Birds in Britain and Ireland: 1988-1991*. BTO/T. & A.D. Poyser, 1993.

BTO Migration Watch. Concern for Swifts. RSPB.

Hallowe'en

Deer, Brian. 'The burning issue'. *Sunday Times*, 29 October 1995.

Hole, Christina. *British Folk Customs*. Hutchinson, 1976.

Hopkins, Tony. *The Cheviot Way of Life*. Northumberland National Park, 1992.

Hutton, Ronald. *The Stations of the Sun*. OUP, 1996/2001.

Keys, David. 'Ancient high spirits'. *Independent*, 31 October 1989.

Kightly, Charles. *The Customs and Ceremonies of Britain*. Thames & Hudson, 1986.

Matthews, Caitlin. *The Celtic Tradition*. Element Books, 1989.

Simpson, J. and Roud, S. *Oxford Dictionary of English Folklore*. OUP, 2000.

Apple Games and Customs. Common Ground, 1994.

Harbours

Adlard Coles, K. *The Shell Pilot to the English Channel*. Faber & Faber, 1985.

Eddison, Jill. *Romney Marsh: Survival on a Frontier*. Tempus, 2000.

Williamson, J.A. *The English Channel*. Collins, 1959.

Hards

Chun, David. 'Hards, quays and landing spaces on the Upper Hamble'. *Hampshire Field Club and Archaeological Society Newsletter*, Autumn 1997.

Kim Wilkie Environmental Design. *Thames Landscape Strategy: Hampton to Kew*. Thames Landscape Steering Group, 1994.

Open Spaces Society. 'Hards as public open spaces'. *Open Space*, Autumn 2004.

Public Launch Points on the Hampshire Coast: A Position Paper. Hampshire County Council, 1994.

Hare Pie Scramble

Kightly, Charles. *The Customs and Ceremonies of Britain*. Thames & Hudson, 1986.

Simpson J. and Roud, S. *Oxford Dictionary of English Folklore*. OUP, 2000.

Sykes, Homer. *Once a Year*. Gordon Fraser, 1977.

Hares

Auden, W.H. and Isherwood, Christopher. *Dog Beneath the Skin*. Faber & Faber, 1935.

Blake, William. *Auguries of Innocence*. 1789.

Buczacki, Stefan. *Fauna Britannica*. Hamlyn, 2002.

Burns et al. *Final Report of the Committee of Inquiry into Hunting with Dogs in England and Wales*. HMSO, 2000.

Ewart Evans, George and Thomson, David. *The Leaping Hare*. Faber & Faber, 1972.

Gee, H.L. *Folk Tales of Yorkshire*. Thomas Nelson & Sons, 1952.

Hart-Davis, Duff. *Fauna Britannica*. Weidenfeld & Nicolson, 2002.

Hutchins, Michael R. and Harris, Stephen. *The current status of the brown hare (Lepus europaeus) in Britain*. Joint Nature Conservation Committee, 1996.

Porteous, Katrina. Emails and letters, 2003/4/5.

Harvest Festivals

Hole, Christina. *A Dictionary of British Folk Customs*. Paladin, 1978.

Kightly, Charles. *The Customs and Ceremonies of Britain*. Thames & Hudson, 1986.

Shap Calendar of Religious Festivals 1993-1994. Shap Working Party on World Religions in Education, nd.

Haunted Places

Bromwich, Margaret. Letter, 6 May 2002.

Coxhead, J.R.W. *Legends of Devon*. Western Press, 1954.

Harries, John. *Ghost Hunter's Road Book*. Letts, 1968.

Harte, Jeremy. *Cuckoo Pounds and Singing Barrows*. DNHAS, 1986.

Hole, Christina. *Haunted England*. Batsford, 1940.

Jordan, Katy. *The Haunted Landscape*. Ex Libris, 2000.

Mitchell, W.R. *Haunted Yorkshire*. Dalesman, 1994.

Tegner, H. *Ghosts of the North Country*. Frank Graham, 1974/Butler, 1991.

Walker, Ted. 'Breakwaters' in *Fox on a Barn Door*. Jonathan Cape, 1965.

Westwood, Jennifer. *Albion: A Guide to Legendary Britain*. Grafton, 1985.

Whitaker, Terence W. *Lancashire Ghosts and Legends*. Granada, 1980.

Wiltshire, Kathleen. *More Ghosts and Legends of the Wiltshire Countryside*. Venton Educational, 1984.

Hawthorn

Bradshaw, A.D. 'The Significance of Hawthorns in Hedges and Local History'. Standing Conference for Local History, National Council of Social Service, 1979.

Cornish, Vaughan. *Historic Thorn Trees in the British Isles*. Country Life, 1941.

Grigson, Geoffrey. *The Englishman's Flora*. Paladin, 1975.

Mabey, Richard. *Flora Britannica*. Chatto & Windus, 1996.

Stevens, Cindy. *Hawthorn*. Sage Press, 2001.

Vickery, Roy. *Oxford Dictionary of Plant-Lore*. OUP, 1995.

Haxey Hood Game

Hole, Christina. *British Folk Customs*. Hutchinson, 1976.

Kightly, Charles. *The Customs and Ceremonies of Britain*. Thames & Hudson, 1986.

Simpson, J. and Roud, S. *Oxford Dictionary of English Folklore*. OUP, 2000.

Sykes, Homer. *Once a Year*. Gordon Fraser, 1977.

Hay Meadows

Gates, Phil. 'Making hay while the sun shines'. *BBC Wildlife Magazine*, May 2004.

Harvey, Graham. *The Forgiveness of Nature: The Story of Grass*. Jonathan Cape, 2001.

Jefferies, Richard. *The Open Air* (1885). Wildwood, 1981.

Ratcliffe, D. (ed.). *A Nature Conservation Review*. CUP, 1977.

Hazel

Edlin, H.L. *Trees, Woods and Man*. Collins, 1956/1978.

Grigson, Geoffrey. *The Englishman's Flora*. Paladin, 1975.

Kightly, Charles. *The Perpetual Almanack of Folklore*. Thames & Hudson, 1987.

Mabey, Richard. *Flora Britannica*. Chatto & Windus, 1996.

Marren, Peter. *The Wild Wood*. David & Charles, 1992.

Marren, Peter. *Woodland Heritage*. David & Charles, 1990.

Rackham, Oliver. *Ancient Woodland*. Castlepoint Press, 2003.

Rackham, Oliver. *The History of the Countryside*. Dent, 1986.

Wilkinson, Gerald. *Trees in the Wild*. Book Club Associates, 1976.

Apple Games and Customs. Common Ground, 1994.

The Common Ground Book of Orchards. Common Ground, 2000.

Heathland

Moore, Norman. *The Bird of Time*. CUP, 1987.

Rackham, Oliver. *The History of the Countryside*. Dent, 1986.

Hedges

Bates, H.E. 'The hedge chequerwork' in *The English Countryside*. Batsford, 1939.

Blunden, Edmund. 'The Landscape' in *The Legacy of England*. Batsford, 1935.

Brooks, Alan and Agate, Elizabeth. *Hedging: A Practical Handbook*. BTCV, 2002.

Greave, Valerie. *Hedgelaying Explained*. National Hedge-laying Society, nd.

Hoskins, W.G. 'The Making of the Landscape' in *The West in English History* (Rowse, A.L., ed.). Hodder & Stoughton, 1949.

Marren, Peter. *Nature Conservation*. Collins New Naturalist, 2002.

Rackham, Oliver. *The History of the Countryside*. Dent, 1986.

Streeter, David and Richardson, Rosamond. *Discovering Hedgerows*. BBC, 1982.

Williamson, Tom. *Hedges and Walls*. National Trust, 2002.

Hedgerows of England. Countryside Agency, 2000.

Henges & Stone Circles

Bender, Barbara. *Stonehenge: Making Space*. Berg, 1998.

Cavendish, Richard. *Prehistoric England*. Artus Books, 1983.

Chippindale, Christopher. *Stonehenge Complete*. Thames & Hudson, 1983/1994.

Darvill, Tim. 'Ever Increasing Circles: the sacred geographies of Stonehenge and its landscape' in *Science and Stonehenge: Proceedings of the British Academy* (Cunliffe, Barry, ed.). 1992.

Greeves, Tom. 'Woodhenge Echoes' in *PULP!* Common Ground, 1989.

McOmish, David; Field, David; Brown, Graham. *The Field Archaeology of the Salisbury Plain Training Area*. English Heritage, 2002.

English Heritage.

Heronries

Buczacki, Stefan. *Fauna Britannica*. Hamlyn, 2002.

Gelling, Margaret and Cole, Ann. *The Landscape of Place-Names*. Shaun Tyas, 2000.

Greenoak, Francesca. *All the Birds of the Air*. Andre Deutsch, 1979.

Hart-Davis, Duff. *Fauna Britannica*. Weidenfeld & Nicolson, 2002.

London Biodiversity Partnership. 'Grey Heron Species Action Plan'. *Tree Talk*, January 2002.

Malster, Robert. *Norfolk and Suffolk Broads*. Phillimore, 2003.

Tansley, Arthur. *The British Islands and their Vegetation*. CUP, 1939/1965.

British Trust for Ornithology.

High Streets

Bebbington, Gillian. *Street Names of London*. Batsford, 1972/1988.

Hoskins, W.G. *One Man's England*. BBC, 1976/1978.

Room, Adrian. *The Street Names of England*. Paul Watkins, 1992.

English Place-Name Society.

Hill Figures

Brown, M. 'Long Man of Wilmington and the Cerne Giant: some points of comparison' in *The Cerne Giant, an Antiquity on Trial* (Darvill, T.; Barker, K.; Bender, B.; Hutton, R.; eds.). Oxbow, 1996.

Clifford, S. 'Staying Power' in *The Cerne Giant etc* (as above).

Hill-forts

Dyer, James. *Hillforts of England and Wales*. Shire, 1992.

Williams, Geoffrey. *The Iron Age Hillforts of England: A Visitor's Guide*. Horace Books, 1993.

469

Ekwall, Eilert. *Oxford Dictionary of English Place-Names.* OUP, 1936.

Francis, Sally. Email, 3 May 2004.

Gelling, Margaret and Cole, Ann. *The Landscape of Place-Names.* Shaun Tyas, 2000.

Wagstaff, Claire. Letter, 2 September 2003. English Heritage.

Hills

Ekwall, Eilert. *Oxford Dictionary of English Place-Names.* OUP, 1936.

Gelling, Margaret and Cole, Ann. *The Landscape of Place-Names.* Shaun Tyas, 2000.

Housman A.E. *A Shropshire Lad.*

Hollow Ways

Arkell, W.J. and Tomkeieff, S.I. *English Rock Terms.* OUP, 1953.

Barnatt, John and Smith, Ken. *The Peak District Landscapes Through Time.* Batsford, 2004.

Dodd, A.E. and Dodd, E.M. *Peakland Roads and Trackways.* Moorland Books, 1974.

Hoskins, W.G. *The Making of the English Landscape.* Hodder & Stoughton, 1955/2005.

Massingham, H.J. *English Downland.* Batsford, 1936.

Prudden, Hugh. *Geology and Landscape of Taunton Deane.* Taunton Deane Borough Council, 2001.

Rackham, Oliver. *The History of the Countryside.* Dent, 1986.

Thomas, Edward. *The Icknield Way.* Constable & Co., 1916.

Watkins, Alfred. *The Old Straight Track.* Methuen, 1925.

White, Gilbert. *The Natural History of Selborne, 1788-9.* Penguin, 1977.

The Landscape of the Sussex Downs AONB. Countryside Commission/Sussex Downs Conservation Board, 1996.

The Surrey Hills Landscape. Countryside Commission, 1998.

Holly

Cooper, Quentin and Sullivan, Paul. *Maypoles, Martyrs and Mayhem.* Bloomsbury, 1994.

Mabey, Richard. *Flora Britannica.* Chatto & Windus, 1996.

Marren, Peter. *Wild Woods.* Nature Conservancy Council, 1992.

Marren, Peter. *Woodland Heritage.* Nature Conservancy Council, 1990.

Milner, J. Edward. *The Tree Book.* Collins & Brown, 1992.

Rackham, Oliver. *Ancient Woodland.* Castlepoint Press, 2003.

Wilkinson, Gerald. *Trees in the Wild.* Book Club Associates, 1976.

Williamson, Tom. *Hedges and Walls.* National Trust, 2002.

Holm Oak

Francis, Sally. Email, 3 May 2004.

Marren, Peter. *The Wild Woods.* Nature Conservancy Council, 1992.

Honey & Bees

Ellis, Hattie. *Sweetness and Light.* Hodder & Stoughton, 2004.

Wilson, Bee. *The Hive.* John Murray, 2004.

Hops, Hop-gardens & Hop-yards

Filmer, Richard. *Hops and Hop Picking.* Shire, 1998.

Nicolson, Nigel. *Kent.* Weidenfeld & Nicolson, 1988.

Wraight, Ian and Dyer, Mark. *Herefordshire and Hops. Real Ale and Cider in Herefordshire: A Guide to the County and its Pubs.* CAMRA, 1985.

The High Weald AONB. Countryside Commission, 1994.

Malvern Hills Landscape AONB. Countryside Commission, 1993.

Hornbeam

Edlin, H.L. *Woodland Crafts in Britain.* David & Charles, 1949/1973.

Hunter, John. *The Essex Landscape.* Essex County Council, 1999.

Rackham, Oliver. *The Last Forest: The Story of Hatfield Forest.* Dent, 1989.

Horse Chestnut

Cloves, Jeff. *The Official Conker Book.* Jonathan Cape, 1993.

Grigson, Geoffrey. 'Monkey Puzzle and Horse Chestnut' in *Gardenage.* Routledge & Kegan Paul, 1952.

Mabey, Richard. *Flora Britannica.* Chatto & Windus, 1996.

Vickery, Roy. *Oxford Dictionary of Plant Lore.* OUP, 1995.

Horse Fairs

Kerr Cameron, David. *The English Fair.* Alan Sutton, 1998.

Kightly, Charles. *Customs and Ceremonies of Britain.* Thames & Hudson, 1986.

Horses & Ponies

Edwards, Elwyn Hartley. *The New Encyclopaedia of the Horse.* Dorling Kindersley, 2001.

British Horse Society.

English Nature.

Rare Breeds Survival Trust.

Hotels

Fowler, Peter (ed.). *Hotels and Restaurants 1830 to the Present Day.* RCHM, 1981.

Lindley, Kenneth. *Seaside Architecture.* Hugh Evelyn, 1973.

Taylor, Derek and Bush, David. *The Golden Age of British Hotels.* Northwood Publications, 1974.

Eating British. Guild of Fine Food Retailers, 2004.

Hounds

Bonser, K.J. *The Drovers.* Macmillan, 1970.

Croxton Smith, Arthur. *British Dogs.* Collins, 1945.

Cunliffe, Juliette. *History of the Whippet.* Interpret Publishing, 2000.

Fogle, Dr Bruce. *The Encyclopaedia of the Dog.* Dorling Kindersley, 1995.

Hancock, David. *Old Working Dogs.* Shire, 1998.

Hart-Davis, Duff. *Fauna Britannica.* Weidenfeld & Nicolson, 2002.

Heath, Veronica. 'Brave Hearts' (Country Diary). *Guardian,* 9 November 2001.

Heath, Veronica. 'Humane Hunting' (Country Diary). *Guardian,* nd.

King, Angela; Ottaway, John; Potter, Angela. *The Declining Otter: A Guide to its Conservation.* Friends of the Earth, 1976.

Larkin, Dr Peter and Stockman, Mike. *The Ultimate Encyclopaedia of Dog Breeds and Dog Care.* Southwater, 1997.

Plummer, D. Brian. *The Complete Book of Sight Hounds, Long Dogs and Lurchers.* Robinson Publishing, 1991.

Hound Trailing

Croxton Smith, Arthur. *British Dogs.* Collins, 1945.

Heath, Veronica. 'Humane Hunting' (Country Diary). *Guardian,* nd.

Nicholson, Norman. *Cumberland and Westmorland.* Robert Hale, 1949.

House Names

Miles, Joyce. *Owl's Hoot: How People Name their Houses.* John Murray, 2000.

I

Ice Skating in the Open Air

Bray, William (ed.). *The Diary of John Evelyn.* 1818.

Griffin, A. Harry. 'Country Diary'. *Guardian,* 14 January 2002; 21 April 2003; 15 December 2003.

Leapman, Michael. *London's River: A History of The Thames.* Pavilion Books, 1991.

Legg, Rodney. *The Stour Valley: From Stourhead to Christchurch.* Halsgrove, 2003.

Page, Robin. 'An icy blast'. *Daily Telegraph,* 12 January 2002.

Industrial Chimneys

Aspin, Chris. *The Cotton Industry.* Shire, 1981.

Aspin, Chris. *The Woollen Industry.* Shire, 1982.

Barton, D.B. *Cornwall's Engine Houses.* Tor Mark, 1989.

Bolton, John. 'The Chimney at Jenny Brown's Point (Keer to Kent, Spring 93)' in *From Keer to Kent* (Ayre, Barry, ed.). Arnside/Silverdale AONB Landscape Trust, 2001.

Brunskill, R.W. *Brick Building in Britain.* Gollancz, 1990.

Burton, Anthony. *Daily Telegraph Guide to Britain's Working Past.* Aurum, 2002.

Crocker, Gladys. *The Gunpowder Industry.* Shire, 1986.

Derwent Valley Mills Nomination Steering Panel. *Nomination of the Derwent Valley Mills for inscription on the World Heritage List.* Derwent Valley Mills Partnership, 2000.

Hall, W.G. (ed.). *Man and the Mendips.* The Mendip Society, 1971.

Willies, Lynn. *Lead and Leadmining.* Shire, 1982.

Ings

Bowler, Pete. 'Country Diary'. *Guardian,* 23 October 2004.

Brian, Anthea. 'Lammas Meadows'. *Landscape History,* vol. 15, 1984.

Ratcliffe, D.A. *A Nature Conservation Review.* CUP, 1977.

Warburton, Stephen, et al. *The Yorkshire Derwent: A Case for Conservation.* 1978.

Inns

Ashley, Peter. *Pubs and Inns: Local Heroes.* Everyman/English Heritage, 2001.

Burke, John. *The English Inn.* Batsford, 1981.

Burke, Thomas. *The English Inn.* Herbert Jenkins, 1947.

Hogg, Gerry. *The English Country Inn.* Batsford, 1974.

Luscombe, William G. *A Book of Inns.* St Catherine's Press, 1946.

Ironstone

Clifton-Taylor, Alec. *The Pattern of English Building.* Faber & Faber, 1972/1980.

Pevsner, Nikolaus. *Northamptonshire (The Buildings of England).* Yale University Press, 2003.

Sutherland, D.S. *Northamptonshire Stone.* The Dovecote Press, 2003.

North Lincolnshire Local Plan. 2003.

Islands

Blyton, Enid. *Five on a Treasure Island.* Hodder & Stoughton, 1942.

Grigson, Geoffrey. *The Scilly Isles.* Duckworth, 1977.

Hudston, Sara. *Islomania.* AGRE Books, 2000.

Kingsley, Charles. *Hereward the Wake.* Macmillan & Co., 1866.

Langham, A.F. *The Island of Lundy.* Alan Sutton, 1994.

RSPB.

J

Jack and Jill

Green, Madalyn. *The Rhyme of Banbury Cross.* Banbury Museum, nd.

Harrowven, Jean. *The Origins of Rhymes, Songs and Sayings.* Pryor Publications, 1998.

Mackenzie, Roy. *Fifteen Mendip Villages.* Roy Mackenzie, 2002.

Opie, Iona and Opie, Peter (eds.). *The Oxford Dictionary of Nursery Rhymes.* OUP, 1997.

'Notes and queries'. *Guardian,* 26 November 2003.

Banbury Hobby Horse Festival.

470

Jack of the Clocks
Neale, F. and Lovell, A.
Wells Cathedral Clock. Wells
Cathedral Publications, 1995/98.

Jet
Muller, Helen. *Jet Jewellery and
Ornaments.* Shire, 2003.

Juniper
Hudson, W.H. *Nature in
Downland.* Dent, 1923.
Mabey, Richard. *Flora Britannica.*
Chatto & Windus, 1996.
Massingham, H.J. *English
Downland.* Batsford, 1936.
Biodiversity Action Plan: Juniper
(Juniperus communis).
JNCC, 2001.
*Wildlife and Archaeology at Porton
Down.* MOD, 1990.

K

Kaolin
Barton, R.M. *An Introduction to
the Geology of Cornwall.*
D. Bradford Barton, 1964.

Kennels
Butler, Bob. Email, 5 April 2004.
Cruickshank, Dan and Burton,
Neil. *Life in the Georgian City.*
Viking, 1990.
Hawkins, Michael. *Devon Roads.*
Devon Books, 1988.
Human, Brian.
Letter, 27 June 2004.
Salmon, Arthur L. *Cornwall.*
Methuen, 1903/1925.
Warren, Derrick. *Curiosities
of East Devon.* Obelisk
Publications, 1999.

Kerbstones
Clifton-Taylor, Alec.
The Pattern of English Building.
Faber & Faber, 1972/1980.
Clifton-Taylor, Alec and Ireson,
A.S. *English Stone Building.*
Gollancz, 1983/1994.
Cruickshank, Dan and Burton,
Neil. *Life in the Georgian City.*
Viking, 1990.
Hawkins, Michael. *Devon Roads.*
Devon Books, 1988.
Joyce, Barry et al. *Derbyshire Detail
and Character.* Alan Sutton, 1996.
Mason, Roger. 'Heathen, xenoliths
and enclaves: kerbstone
petrology in Kentish Town'
in *Geology on your Doorstep*
(Bennet, Matthew R. et al, eds.).
The Geological Society, 1996.
Robinson, Eric. *London Illustrated
Geological Walks, Book Two.*
Scottish Academic Press, 1985.
Robinson, Eric. 'The Stones of
the Mile End Road: a geology
of Middlemiss country'.
*Proceedings of the Geologists'
Association, 108,* 1997.

Kippers
Grigson, Jane. *Good Things.*
Penguin Books, 1973.
Hunter, Adrienne. 'Shutting
the smokehouse door'.
Northern Echo, 29 June 1992.
Mason, Laura with Brown,
Catherine. *Traditional Foods
of Britain.* Prospect, 1999.
Robson, L. & Sons. *The Kipper
Trail* (leaflet). 1991.
Weeks, Bill. 'What Constitutes a
Canny Northumbrian Kipper'.
Northumbriana Magazine,
Winter 1990-Spring 1991.

L

Lagoons
Grigson, Geoffrey.
Geoffrey Grigson's Countryside.
Ebury Press, 1982.
Rackham, Oliver. *The History
of the Countryside.* Dent, 1986.

Lakes
Charlton, Beryl. *Upper North
Tynedale: A Northumbrian
Valley and its People.* 1978.
Dickinson, Gillian. *Rutland:
A Guide and Gazetteer.*
Barrowden Books, 1984.
Gunton, Tony. *Wild Essex.*
Lopinga Books, 2000.
Hoskins, W.G. *The Making of
the English Landscape.* Hodder
& Stoughton, 1955/2005.
Macan, T.T. and Worthington, E.B.
Life in Lakes and Rivers.
Collins New Naturalist, 1974.
Marshall, J.D. *Portrait of Cumbria.*
Robert Hale, 1981.
Mercer, Derrik. *Exploring Unspoilt
Britain.* National Trust/Reed
International, 1985.
Mitchell, W.R. *Wild Pennines.*
Robert Hale, 1976.
Pearsall, W.H. and Pennington, W.
The Lake District.
Collins New Naturalist, 1973.
Rackham, Oliver. *The History of
the Countryside.* Dent, 1986.
Rollinson, William. *A History of
Cumberland and Westmorland.*
Phillimore, 1978.
Whittow, John. *Geology and
Scenery in Britain.*
Chapman & Hall, 1992.
Wordsworth, William. *Guide to
the Lakes.* Frances Lincoln, 2004.

Landmarks
Watkins, Alfred. *The Old Straight
Track.* Methuen, 1925.

Landmark Trees
Berry, G.R. Letter, 2004.
Mabey, Richard. *Flora Britannica.*
Chatto & Windus, 1996.
Porteous, Katrina. Letters
and emails, 2003/4/5.
Stukeley, William.
Antonine Itineraries. 1723.
Watkins, Alfred. *The Old Straight
Track.* Methuen, 1925.
Wilks, J.H. *Trees of the British
Isles in History and Legend.*
Frederick Muller, 1972.
Wright, Geoffrey N.
Roads and Trackways of Wessex.
Moorland, 1988.

Landslips
Arber, M.A. 'Landslip near Lyme
Regis'. *Proceedings of the
Geologists Association,* vol. 84, 1973.
Bender, Barbara.
Email, 18 March 2004.
Hyland, P. *Wight.* Gollancz, 1985.
Wilson, Peter. 'Landslides in
Lakeland'. *Conserving Lakeland,*
Winter/Spring 2003.

Lanes
Clare, John. 'The Village Minstrel'.
1821.

Lavender
BioRegional Development Group.

Lawn
Beale, Reginald.
The Book of the Lawn. 1931.
Brautigan, Richard. *The Revenge
of the Lawn: Stories 1962-1970.*
Simon & Schuster, 1972.

Brown, Jane. *The Pursuit
of Paradise: A Social History
of Gardens and Gardening.*
HarperCollins, 1999/2000.
Fort, Tom. *The Grass is Greener:
Our Love Affair with the Lawn.*
HarperCollins, 2000.
Harvey, Graham. *The Forgiveness
of Nature: The Story of Grass.*
Jonathan Cape, 2001.
Loudon, John Claudius.
*The Suburban Gardener and
Villa Companion.* 1838.
Rackham, Oliver.
The History of the Countryside.
Dent, 1986.
Tubbs, Colin R. *The New Forest:
An Ecological History.*
David & Charles, 1968.

Lead Mines
Allen, Bob. *Escape to the Dales.*
Mermaid, 1992.
Barnatt, John and Penny, Rebecca.
The Lead Legacy. Peak District
National Park Authority, 2004.
Barnatt, John and Smith, Ken. *The
Peak District: Landscapes through
Time.* Windgather Press, 2004.
Hoskins, W.G. *One Man's England.*
BBC, 1978.
Kirkham, Nellie. *Derbyshire Lead
Mining through the centuries.*
D. Bradford Barton Ltd, 1968.
Neale, F.A. 'Mendip, the Fourth
Dimension' in *Man and the
Mendips* (Hall, W.G., ed.),
Mendip Society, 1971.
Willies, Lynn. *Lead and Lead
Mining.* Shire, 1999.
'Images from the Lead Mining
Industry and Silver Mining
in the North Pennines'.
*Northumberland County Council
Archaeology in Northumberland,*
vol. 14, 2004.

Leeks
Grigson, Jane. *Good Things.*
Michael Joseph, 1971/
Penguin, 1973.
National Vegetable Society.

Letterboxing
Swinscow, Anne.
Dartmoor Letterboxes.
Kirkford Publications, 1984.

Levels
Brandon, Peter.
The Sussex Landscape.
Hodder & Stoughton, 1974.
Coles, John. 'Prehistory in the
Somerset Levels 4000-100 BC' in
The Archaeology of Somerset (Aston,
Michael and Burrow, Ian, eds.).
Somerset County Council, 1982.
Costen, Michael. *The Origins
of Somerset.* University of
Manchester Press, 1992.
Gelling, Margaret and Cole, Ann.
The Landscape of Place-Names.
Shaun Tyas, 2000.
Gibbons, Wes. *The Weald.*
Unwin Paperbacks, 1981.
Hawkins, Desmond.
Avalon and Sedgemoor.
David & Charles, 1973.
Purseglove, Jeremy.
Taming the Flood. OUP, 1989.
Sutherland, Patrick and Nicolson,
Adam. *Wetland: Life in the
Somerset Levels.* Penguin, 1986.
Townsend Warner, Sylvia. *Somerset.*
Paul Elek, 1949.
The High Weald AONB.
Countryside Commission, 1994.

*Latest news from the Somerset Levels
and Moors partnership,* Spring
2004.
*Shapwick Heath National Nature
Reserve* (leaflet). English Nature.

Libraries
Brown, Jonathan. *The English
Market Town.* Crowood Press, 1991.
Girouard, Mark. *The English Town.*
Yale University Press, 1990.
Greenhalgh, Liz and Worpole, Ken,
with Charles Landry for
Comedia. *Libraries in a World of
Cultural Change.* UCL Press, 1995.
Thompson, Anthony. *Library
Buildings of Britain and Europe.*
Butterworth, 1963.

Lichens
Baron, George.
Understanding Lichens.
Richmond Publishing, 1999.
Broad, K. *Lichens in Southern
Woodlands.* Forestry Commission,
HMSO, 1989.
Gilbert, Oliver. *Lichens.*
HarperCollins, 2000.
Williamson, Tom. *Hedges and
Walls.* National Trust, 2002.

Lidos
Powers, Alan (ed.). *Farewell My
Lido.* Thirties Society, 1991.
Smith, Janet. *Liquid Assets:
The Lidos and Open Air
Swimming Pools of Britain.*
English Heritage, 2005.

Lighthouses
Ashley, Peter. *Guiding Lights.*
English Heritage/Everyman,
2001.
Constable, Freda.
The England of Eric Ravilious.
Lund Humphries, 2003.
Cooper, Howard. Letters,
January 2003.
Hague, Douglas B. and
Christie, Rosemary.
Lighthouses. Gomer, 1975.
Mason, Benedict. *Lighthouses
of England and Wales.*
Collins Classics CD, 1991.
Porteous, Katrina. 'Longstone
Light' in *The Lost Music.*
Bloodaxe Books, 1996.
Woodman, Richard and Wilson,
Jane. *The Lighthouses of Trinity
House.* Thomas Reed, 2002.

Lime
Abraham, Frances and Rose,
Francis. 'Large-leaved Limes
on the South Downs'.
British Wildlife, December 2000.
Edlin, H.L. *Trees, Woods and Man.*
Collins, 1956/1978.
Mabey, Richard. *Flora Britannica.*
Chatto & Windus, 1996.
Mitchell, Alan. *A Field Guide to
the Trees of Britain and Europe.*
Colllins, 1974.
Ratcliffe, Derek (ed.). *A Nature
Conservation Review.* CUP, 1997.
Thomas, Keith. *Man and
the Natural World: Changing
Attitudes in England 1500-1800.*
Allen Lane, 1983.

Lime-kilns
Appleby, Stephen K.
Letter, 17 August 2002.
Barker, Paul. 'History of local
Lime Kilns in Keer to Kent'.
A/S AONB, Spring, 1997.
Cossons, Neil. *BP Book of
Industrial Archaeology.*
David & Charles, 1975.

471

Grigson, Geoffrey.
The Shell Country Alphabet.
Shell/Rainbird, 1966.
Palmer, Marilyn. 'Post-medieval
industrial landscapes:
their interpretation and
management' in *Landscape –
the richest historical record*
(Hooke, Della, ed.). Society
for Landscape Studies, 2000.
Riley, Hazel and Wilson-North,
Robert. *The Field Archaeology
of Exmoor.* English Heritage,
2001.
Taylor, Eric.
'Limekilns in Avon'.
*Bristol Industrial Archaeology
Society Journal,* 17, 1984.
Taylor, Eric.
'Limekilns on Mendip'.
*Bristol Industrial Archaeology
Society Journal,* 18, 1985.
E.W. 'Work on Beadnell Point'.
*Archaeology in
Northumberland,* 1994-5.
Williams, Richard. *Limekilns
and Limeburning.* Shire, 1989.
Yeates, Gwyneth M.
'The Limekilns of Clevedon'.
*Bristol Industrial Archaeology
Society Journal,* 13, 1980.
Limestone
Auden, W.H. 'In Praise of
Limestone' in *Collected Poems.*
Faber & Faber, 1991.
Barnett, John and Smith, Ken.
*The Peak District Landscapes
through Time.*
Windgather Press, 2004.
Edwards, W. and Trotter, F.M.
*British Regional Geology: The
Pennines and Adjacent Areas.*
HMSO, 1954.
Fortey, Richard. *The Hidden
Landscape.* Jonathan Cape, 1993.
Withers, Charles W.J.
Discovering the Cotswolds.
John Donald Publishers, 1990.
North Pennines Landscape.
Countryside Commission, 1991.
Links
Gates, Phil. 'Home from Home'.
BBC Wildlife Magazine,
August 2004.
English Nature.
Liquorice
Campbell, W.D. 'Wychwood'
in *A Country Diary* (Page,
Jeanette, ed.). Guardian, 1994.
Hudson, B. and Van Riel, R.
Liquorice. City of Wakefield
Metropolitan District Council,
2003.
Mabey, Richard. *Flora Britannica.*
Chatto & Windus, 1996.
Mason, Laura with Brown,
Catherine. *Traditional Foods
of Britain: An Inventory.*
Prospect Books, 1999.
Richardson, Tim. *Sweets:
A Temptation.* Transworld, 2002.
Whittaker, N. *Sweet Talk.*
Phoenix, 1998.
Locks
Hadfield, Charles and Boughey,
Joseph. *Hadfield's British
Canals.* Alan Sutton, 1998.
London Plane
Mitchell, Alan.
*A Field Guide to the Trees of
Britain and Northern Europe.*
Collins, 1974.
Tree Register.

London Taxis
Bayley, Stephen. 'The London
Taxi' in *British Greats.*
Cassell & Co., 2000.
Georgano, Nick. *The London
Taxi.* Shire, 2000.
Lost Villages
O'Riordan, Tim.
Emails, 2005.
Robinson, Adrian and
Milward, Roy. *The Shell
Book of the British Coast.*
David & Charles, 1983.
Rowley, Trevor and Wood,
John. *Deserted Villages.*
Shire, 2000.
Taylor, Christopher.
Village and Farmstead.
George Philip, 1984.
Westwood, Jennifer. *Albion:
A Guide to Legendary Britain.*
Grafton, 1985.
Willson, Beccles. *Lost England:
The Story of our Submerged
Coasts.* George Newnes, 1902.
Wood, Eric S. *Historical Britain.*
Harvill Press, 1995.
Lynchets
Barratt, John and Smith, Ken.
*The Peak District: Landscapes
through Time.* Windgather
Press, 2004.
Hinton, David A. Email,
24 August 2004.
Keen, Laurence and Carreck,
Ann. *Weld: Historic Landscape
of the Weld Estate Dorset.*
Lulworth Heritage, 1987.
McOmish, David. 'Report
on the Survey of the Strip
Lynchets at Worth Matravers,
Dorset' in *Purbeck Papers*
(Hinton, David A., ed.).
University of Southampton/
Oxbow Books, 2004.
Muir, Richard and Muir, Nina.
Fields. Macmillan, 1989.
Whittington, G.
'The Distribution of Strip
Lynchets'. *Transactions
and Papers of the Institute of
British Geographers,* 1962.

M

Maltings
Wood, Eric S. *Historical Britain.*
Harvill Press, 1995.
*Whitbread's Brewery
incorporating The Brewer's Art.*
Whitbread & Co., 1951.
Manhole Covers
Aaron, Henry. *Street Furniture.*
Shire, 1980.
Ashley, Peter. *Hard Furnishings.*
English Heritage/Everyman,
2002.
Joyce, Barry; Michell, Gordon;
Williams, Mike. *Derbyshire:
Detail and Character.*
Alan Sutton, 1996.
Payne, Matthew.
'The hole story'. *New Scientist,*
25 October 2004.
Porteous, Katrina. Letters,
photographs, emails, 2005.
Market Crosses
Hogg, Garry.
Odd Aspects of England.
David & Charles, 1968.
Morrison, Kathryn A.
English Shops and Shopping.
Yale University Press, 2003.

Market Gardens
Burnham, Paul and McRae,
Stuart. *Kent: The Garden of
England.* Paul Norbury
Publications, 1978.
Galinou, Mireille (ed.).
*The Glorious History of
London's Parks and Gardens.*
Anaya Publishers, 1990.
Hargreaves, John. *Harvests
and Harvesters: Fruit and
Vegetable Growing in Britain.*
Gollancz, 1987.
Roach, F.A. *Cultivated Fruits
of Britain: Their Origin and
History.* Blackwell, 1985.
Spiers, Virginia. *Burcombes,
Queenies and Colloggetts.*
West Brendon, 1996.
Stamp, L. Dudley (ed.). *The
Land of Britain: The Report
of the Land Utilisation Survey
of Britain.* Geographical
Publications, 1943.
Unwin, A.C.B. *Commercial
Nurseries and Market Gardens.*
Twickenham Local History
Society, 1982.
Markets
Girouard, Mark.
The English Town.
Yale University Press, 1990.
Hoskins, W.G. *The Making of
the English Landscape.* Hodder
& Stoughton, 1955/2005.
Morrison, Kathryn A.
English Shops and Shopping.
Yale University Press, 2003.
Munby, Lionel M.
The Hertfordshire Landscape.
Hodder & Stoughton, 1977.
Martello Towers
Hollands, Ray and Harris, Paul.
Along the Kent Coast.
Alan Sutton, 2003.
English Heritage.
May Day
Judge, Roy. *The Jack-in-the-
Green. A May Day Custom.*
D.S. Brewer, 1979.
Kightly, Charles. *The Customs
and Ceremonies of Britain.*
Thames & Hudson, 1986.
Newton, Gordon. 'In Search of
Jack' in *The Rochester Sweeps
May Festival Programme,* 1993.
Strutt, Joseph. *The Sports
and Pastimes of the People of
England.* Thomas Tegg, 1838.
Maypoles
Bailey, Brian. *The English Village
Green.* Robert Hale, 1985.
Hole, Christina.
*A Dictionary of British Folk
Customs.* Granada, 1978.
Simpson, J. and Roud, S. *The
Oxford Dictionary of English
Folklore.* OUP, 2000.
Strutt, Joseph. *The Sports
and Pastimes of the People of
England.* Thomas Tegg, 1838.
Sykes, Homer. *Once a Year:
Some Traditional British
Customs.* Gordon Fraser, 1977.
Barwick-in-Elmet Historical
Society.
Melas
Brown, Alan (ed.). *Festivals in
World Religions.* Longman, 1986.
Mews
Girouard, Mark.
The English Town.
Yale University Press, 1990.

Rosen, Barbara and
Zuckermann, Wolfgang.
The Mews of London.
Webb & Bower, 1982.
Midsummer Day
Field, John. *A History of English
Field Names.* Longman, 1993.
Hall, Stephen. Conversations,
1990s.
Hole, Christina. *British Folk
Customs.* Hutchinson, 1976.
Hutton, Ronald.
*The Rise and Fall of Merry
England.* OUP, 1994.
Kightly, Charles. *The Customs
and Ceremonies of Britain.*
Thames & Hudson, 1986.
Noall, Cyril. *The Cornish
Midsummer Eve Bonfire
Celebrations.* Federation of
Old Cornwall Societies, 1963.
Simpson, Jacqueline. *British
Dragons.* Batsford, 1980.
Strutt, Joseph. *The Sports
and Pastimes of the People of
England.* Thomas Tegg, 1838.
Golowan Community Arts Trust.
Milestones
Addison, Sir William.
The Old Roads of England.
Batsford, 1980.
Benford, Mervyn. *Milestones.*
Shire, 2002.
Davidson, Iain. 'The Milestone
Society, Northumberland rep'.
The Northumbrian, June/July
2004.
Dodd, A.E. and Dodd, E.M.
Peakland Roads and Trackways.
Moorland Publishing, 1974.
Gow, G. and the Dorset
Countryside Treasures Team.
Dorset Milestone Survey.
Dorset County Council, 1980.
Hawkins, Michael. *Devon Roads.*
Devon Books, 1988.
Haynes, R.I.E. 'Wiltshire
Milestones'. *Leisure in
Wiltshire,* 1968.
Porteous, Katrina. Emails,
letters, photographs, 2004/5.
Thompson, Ian. 'Finger Stones
in Penwith, Cornwall'.
Milestones and Waymarkers,
the Journal of the Milestone
Society, vol. 1, 2004.
*New Milestones, Sculpture,
Community and the Land.*
Common Ground, 1988.
Millstone Grit
Barnett, John and Smith, Ken.
*The Peak District: Landscapes
through Time.* Windgather
Press, 2004.
Edwards, W. and Trotter, F.M.
*British Regional Geology: The
Pennines and Adjacent Areas.*
HMSO, 1954.
Watts, Martin. *Corn Milling.*
Shire, 1998.
The Forest of Bowland.
Countryside Commission,
1992.
The Nidderdale Landscape.
Countryside Commission,
1991.
Mines
Atkinson, Conrad. *Cleator Moor.*
1987.
Pattison, Keith; Porteous,
Katrina; Soden, Robert.
Turning the Tide.
District of Easington, 2001.

472

Mistletoe
Mabey, Richard. *Flora Britannica*. Chatto & Windus, 1996.
Snow, Barbara and Snow, David. *Birds and Berries*. T. & A.D. Poyser, 1988.
Kissing Goodbye to Mistletoe? Plantlife, 1999.

Moats
Darvill, T.C. Moats, *Monuments Protection Plan*. English Heritage, 1988.
Deakin, Roger. *Waterlog: A Swimmer's Journey through Britain*. Chatto & Windus 1999/Vintage, 2000.
Hunter, John. *The Essex Landscape*. Essex County Council, 1999.
Rackham, Oliver. *The History of the Countryside*. Dent, 1986.
Wood, Eric S. *Historical Britain*. Harvill Press, 1995.

Monasteries
Aston, Mick. *Monasteries in the Landscape*. Tempus, 2000.
Brabbs, Derry. *Abbeys and Monasteries*. Weidenfeld & Nicolson, 1999.
The Monastic Buildings and the College at Ely (leaflet). c.2000.

Monkey-puzzle
Grigson, Geoffrey. *Gardenage*. Routledge & Kegan Paul, 1952.
Meyer, Bobby. *Monkey Puzzle*. Sage Press, 2001.
Miles, Archie. *Silva: The Tree in Britain*. Ebury Press, 1999.
Exmoor National Park Local Plan. 1997.

Monuments
Mace, Rodney. *Trafalgar Square, Emblem of Empire*. Lawrence & Wishart, 1976.
Weinreb, Ben and Hibbert, Christopher. *The London Encyclopaedia*. Macmillan, 1983.

Moon
Field, John. *English Field Names*. David & Charles, 1972.
Field, John. Letters and conversations, 1996.
Grigson, Geoffrey. *The Englishman's Flora*. Paladin, 1975.
Hough, Carole and Cox, Barrie. 'Moonhill'. *Journal of the English Place-Name Society*, 28, 1995/6.
Oswald, Alice. *The Thing in the Gap-Stone Stile*. Oxford Poets, 1996.

Moorland
Hartley, Marie and Ingilby, Joan. *Life and Tradition in the Yorkshire Dales*. Dent, 1968.
Hey, David. 'Moorlands' in *Rural England* (Thirsk, Joan, ed.). OUP, 2000.
Raistrick, Arthur (ed.). *North York Moors National Park*. HMSO, 1969.
Whittow, John. *Geology and Scenery in Britain*. Chapman & Hall, 1992.
Winchester, Angus. *The Harvest of the Hills*. Edinburgh UP, 2000.

Morris Dancing
Howkins, Alun. '*Beyond the Broadcast*. Making History: Morris dancing – the disputed origins' at www.bbc.co.uk

Kightly, Charles. *The Customs and Ceremonies of Britain*. Thames & Hudson, 1986.
Peck, Arthur. *The Morris and Sword Dances of England*. 1978.
Rippon, Hugh. *Discovering English Folk Dance*. Shire, 1975/1993.

Mosques
Brown, Sarah. 'The Shah Jehan Mosque, Woking'. *English Heritage Conservation Bulletin* 46: Autumn 2004.
Frishman, Martin and Khan, Hasan-Uddin (eds.). *The Mosque: History, Architectural Development and Regional Diversity*. Thames & Hudson, 1994.
Merriman, Nick (ed.). *The Peopling of London*. Museum of London, 1993.

Mosses
Prendergast, Hew and Sanderson, Helen. *Britain's Wild Harvest*. Royal Botanic Gardens, Kew/The Countryside Agency, 2004.
Richards, Paul. *A Book of Mosses*. Penguin Books, 1950.
Secord, Anne. 'Artisan Botany' in *Cultures of Natural History* (Jardine, N., Secord, J.A. and Spary, E.C., eds.). CUP, 1996.

Mossland
Gelling, Margaret and Cole, Ann. *The Landscape of Place-Names*. Shaun Tyas, 2000.
Gibbons, Bob. 'Chartley Moss NNR Staffordshire'. *British Wildlife*, vol. 10, no. 1, October 1998.
Hargreaves, John. *Harvests and Harvesters*. Gollancz, 1987.
Woolerton Dodwell Associates. *Arnside and Silverdale Landscape*. Countryside Commission, 1997.

Mountain Hares
Macdonald, David W., and Tattersall, Fran. *Britain's Mammals: The Challenge for Conservation*. Mammals Trust UK, 2001.
Mallon, D.P. *The Mountain Hare in the Peak District*. Derbyshire Wildlife Trust, 2001.

Mumming Plays
Alford, Violet. *The Hobby Horse and other Animal Masks*. Merlin Press, 1978.
Cass, Eddie. *The Lancashire Pace-Egg Play: A Social History*. Folklore Society, 2001.
Helm, Alex. *Eight Mummers' Plays*. Ginn & Co., 1971.
Kightly, Charles. *The Customs and Ceremonies of Britain*. Thames & Hudson, 1986.
Lincolnshire Folk Department. *Plough Plays in Lincolnshire*, nd.
Simpson, J. and Roud, S. *Oxford Dictionary of English Folklore*. OUP, 2000.

Music
Burke, John. *Musical Landscapes*. Webb & Bower, 1983.
Sadie, Stanley (ed.). *The New Grove Dictionary of Music and Musicians*. Macmillan, 1980.

N

Natterjack Toads
Bridson, R.H. *The Natterjack Toad*. Nature Conservancy Council, 1978.
Buczacki, Stefan. *Fauna Britannica*. Hamlyn, 2002.
Cooke, M.C. *Our Reptiles and Batrachians*. H. Allen & Co., 1893.
Simpson, David. 'The fall and rise of Ainsdale's Natterjacks'. *British Wildlife*, February 2002.
Smith, Philip H. 'The Sefton Coast sand-dunes, Merseyside'. *British Wildlife*, October 2000.

New Forest Ponies
Hampshire County Council.
The New Forest Pony Breeding and Cattle Society.
Rare Breeds Survival Trust.

New Milestones
Clifford, Sue. 'New Milestones: sculpture, community and the land' in *Geological and Landscape Conservation* (O'Halloran, D. et al, eds.). Geological Society, 1994.
Clifford, Sue. *Places: The City and the Invisible*. Public Art Development Trust, 1993.
Cork, Richard. *A Place for Art*. PADT, 1993.
Morland, Joanna. *New Milestones, Sculpture, Community and the Land*. Common Ground, 1988.

Nicknames
Briggs, Katherine M. *A Dictionary of British Folk-Tales in the English Language*. Routledge, 1970.
Ellis, Hattie. Letter, 16 June 2004.
Green, Jonathon. *Slang*. Cassell & Co., 1998.
Greenwell, G.C. *Glossary of Terms used in the Coal Trade of Northumberland and Durham 1888* (third facsimile). Frank Graham, 1970.
Hudston, S. *Islomania*. AGRE Books, 2000.
Hyland, Paul. *Wight*. Gollancz, 1984.
Pewsey, Stephen. Email, 17 May 2002.
Porteous, Katrina. Emails and letters, 2003.
Origins of the name Geordie. Local Studies Library Factsheet no. 5, Newcastle City Council, nd.

Nobbies
Elmer, W. *The Terminology of Fishing: A Survey of English and Welsh Inshore Fishing Things and Words*. The Cooper Monographs, 19 English Dialect Series. Franke Verlag, 1973.
McKee, Eric. *Working Boats of Britain: Their Shape and Purpose*. Conway Maritime Press, 1983.

Nomansland
OS Map Explorer OL30 at 940075.

Norfolk Wherries
Hazell, M. *Sailing Barges*. Shire, 2001.

McKee, Eric. *Working Boats of Britain: Their Shape and Purpose*. Conway Maritime Press, 1983.
Malster, Robin. *The Norfolk and Suffolk Broads*. Phillimore, 2003.
Williamson, Tom. *The Broads: A Landscape History*. Manchester UP, 1997.

North
Armitage, Simon. *All Points North*. Viking, 1998.
Bragg, Melvyn. *The Adventure of English*. Hodder & Stoughton, 2003.
Davies, Norman. *The Isles: A History*. Papermac, 1999.
Dickens, Charles. *Hard Times*. 1854.
Dorling, Daniel and Thomas, Bethan. *People and Places: A 2001 Census Atlas of the UK*. The Policy Press, 2004.
Engels, Friedrich. *The Condition of the Working Class in England*. 1844/5.
Harrison, Tony. 'Facing North' in *Selected Poems*. Penguin, 1987.
McCarthy, Helen. *Self-Esteem Society Report*. Demos, 28 July 2004.
Watson-Smyth, Kate. *How you say it puts the accents on success*. UCL, nd.
Wenham, Chris et al (eds.). *The Migration Atlas*. BTO, 2002.

Northumbrian Smallpipes
Baines, Anthony. *Woodwind Instruments and their History*. Faber & Faber, 1962.
The Northumbrian Small Pipes. Topic Records, TSCD487.

Notting Hill Carnival
Merriman, Nick (ed.). *The Peopling of London*. Museum of London, 1993.
Embroiderers Guild.

Nurseries
Galinou, Mireille (ed.). *The Glorious History of London's Parks and Gardens*. Anaya Publishers, 1990.
Lasdun, Susan. *The English Park: Royal, Private and Public*. Andre Deutsch, 1991.
Morgan, Joan and Richards, Alison. *The Book of Apples*. Ebury Press, 1993.
National Council for the Conservation of Plants and Gardens Devon Group. *The Magic Tree*. Devon Books, 1989.
Roach, F.A. *Cultivated Fruits of Britain: Their Origin and History*. Blackwell, 1985.
Shewell-Cooper, W.E. 'Laxton Lineage'. *The Field*, 1948.

O

Oak
Ackroyd, Peter. *Albion: The Origins of the English Imagination*. Chatto & Windus, 2002.
Clarke, R.A. et al. *The Blasted Oak. The Oak Tree: Natural History, Art and Myth in European Culture*. Herbert Art Gallery and Museum, 1987.

473

Forman, H. Buxton (ed.). *The Poetical Works of John Keats*. Reeves & Turner, 1902.
Fowles, John and Horvat, Frank. *The Tree*. Aurum Press, 1979.
Frazer, Sir James. *The Golden Bough*. Macmillan, 1978.
Green, Ted. Conversation, 6 January 2004.
Ratcliffe, Derek (ed.). *A Nature Conservation Review*. CUP, 1977.
Shakespeare, William. *The Merry Wives of Windsor*.
Wilks, J.H. *Trees of the British Isles in History and Legend*. The Anchor Press, 1972.

Oast-houses & Kells
Brunskill, R.W. *Traditional Farm Buildings of Britain and their Conservation*. Gollancz, 1982/1999.
Filmer, Richard. *Hops and Hop Picking*. Shire, 1998.
Grigson, Geoffrey. *Geoffrey Grigson's Countryside*. Ebury Press, 1982.
Nicolson, Nigel. *Kent*. Weidenfeld & Nicolson, 1988.
Walton, Robin and Walton, Ivan. *Kentish Oasts: 16th-20th Century*. Christine Swift, 1997.

'Obby 'Osses
Alford, Violet. *The Hobby Horse and other Animal Masks*. Merlin Press, 1978.
Bennet, George. Email, 16 May 2005.
Helm, Alex. *Eight Mummers' Plays*. Ginn & Co., 1971.
Kightly, Charles. *Customs and Ceremonies of Britain*. Thames & Hudson, 1986.
Sykes, Homer. *Once a Year: Some Traditional British Customs*. Gordon Fraser, 1977.

Obelisks
Barnes, Richard. *The Obelisk: A Monumental Feature in Britain*. Frontier, 2004.
'Cranleigh Obelisk'. *The Milestone Society Newsletter*, 5 July 2003.

Old Man's Beard
Grigson, Geoffrey. *The Englishman's Flora*. Paladin, 1975.
Hudson, W.H. *Nature in Downland*. Dent, 1923/ Futura, 1981.

Onions
Hargreaves, John. *Harvests and Harvesters: Fruit and Vegetable Growing in Britain*. Gollancz, 1987.
Hills, Lawrence D. *Grow Your Own Fruit and Vegetables*. Faber & Faber, 1971.
Macdougall, Ian. *Onion Johnnies*. Tuckwell Press, 2002.
Mason, Laura with Brown, Catherine. *Traditional Foods of Britain: An Inventory*. Prospect Books, 1999.

Orchards
'Orchards and Wildlife' (conference papers). Common Ground/English Nature, 1999.
The Common Ground Book of Orchards. Common Ground, 2000.

Community Orchards. Common Ground, 1999.

Osiers
Chapman, Chris. *Secrets of the Levels*. Somerset Books, 1996.
Crowden, James. *In Time of Flood*. The Parrett Trail Partnership, 1996.
Howard, A.L. *Trees in Britain*. Collins, 1946.
Lynch, Kate. *Willow: Paintings and Drawings with Somerset Voices*. Furlong Fields Publishing, 2003.
Stott, Ken. *Cultivation and Use of Basket Willows*. The Basketmakers Association and IACR Long Ashton Research Station, 2001.
Stott, Ken. 'Willows' in *PULP!*. Common Ground, 1989.
Sutherland, Patrick and Nicolson, Adam. *Wetland: Life in the Somerset Levels*. Michael Joseph, 1986.

Otters
Ekwall, Eilert. *English River Names*. OUP, 1928.
King, Angela and Potter, Angela. *Guide to Otter Conservation for Water Authorities*. Vincent Wildlife Trust, 1980.
King, Angela; Ottaway, John; Potter, Angela. *The Declining Otter: A Guide to its Conservation*. Friends of the Earth, 1976.
Maxwell, Gavin. *Ring of Bright Water*. Penguin Books, 1963.
Porter, Helen and Hyland, Paul. *Otter: Lutra lutra on the Stour*. Common Ground, 2001.
Weir, Vincent. *The Otter*. Otter Haven Project, 1978.
Williamson, Henry. *Tarka the Otter*. Penguin Books, 1927.

Oysters
Buczacki, Stefan. *Fauna Britannica*. Hamlyn, 2002.
Ellis, Hattie. *Eating England*. Mitchell Beazley, 2001.
Kightly, Charles. *The Customs and Ceremonies of Britain*. Thames & Hudson, 1986.
Mason, Laura with Brown, Catherine. *Traditional Foods of Britain: An Inventory*. Prospect Books, 1999.
Trewin, Carol and Woolfitt, Adam. *Gourmet Cornwall*. Alison Hodge, 2005.
Younge, C.M. *Oysters*. Collins, 1960.
Native Oyster (Ostrea edulis) *Biodiversity Action Plan*. English Nature, 1999.

P

Pancake Day
Hole, Christina. *British Folk Customs*. Hutchinson, 1976.
Ingram, Tom. *Bells in England*. Frederick Muller, 1954.
Kightly, Charles. *The Customs and Ceremonies of Britain*. Thames & Hudson, 1986.
Sykes, Homer. *Once a Year*. Gordon Fraser, 1977.
Wagstaff, Claire. Email, 3 September 2003.

Pantiles
Clifton-Taylor, Alec. *The Pattern of English Building*. Faber & Faber, 1972.
Crowden, James and Rook, Pauline. *Bridgwater: The Parrett's Mouth*. AGRE Books, 2000.
Fortey, Richard. *The Hidden Landscape*. Jonathan Cape, 1993.
Penoyre, John and Penoyre, Jane. *Houses in the Landscape: A Regional Study of Vernacular Building Styles in England and Wales*. Readers Union, 1978.
North Norfolk Design Guide. North Norfolk District Council, 1998.

Pants
Bailey, Brian. *The English Village Green*. Robert Hale, 1985.
Herdman, Mary. Letter, 14 January 2004.
Public Monuments and Sculpture Association.

Pargeting
Buxbaum, Tim. *Pargeting*. Shire, 1999.
Clifton-Taylor, Alec. *The Pattern of English Building*. Faber & Faber, 1972.
Wright, Adela. *Craft Techniques for Traditional Buildings*. Batsford, 1991.
Traditional Building Materials in Essex, no. 1 Pargeting. Essex County Council, 1982.

Parish Maps
Leslie, Kim. Letters, 1998-2005.
Sadler, Helen. Letter, 1996.
From place to PLACE: maps and Parish Maps. Common Ground, 1996.

Park Gate Lodges
Ashley, Peter. *Comings and Goings*. Everyman Pocket Books/English Heritage, 2002.
Lasdun, Susan. *The English Park: Royal, Private and Public*. Andre Deutsch, 1991.
Mowl, Tim and Earnshaw, Brian. *Trumpet at a Distant Gate: The Lodge as Prelude to the Country House*. Waterstone, 1985.

Parkland
Harvey, Graham. *Parkland*. National Trust, 2002.
Lasdun, Susan. *The English Park: Royal, Private and Public*. Andre Deutsch, 1991.
Rackham, Oliver. *The History of the Countryside*. Dent, 1986.
Rackham, Oliver. *Trees, Woods in the British Landscape*. Dent, 1990.
Biodiversity Action Plan: Lowland Wood-pasture and Parkland. JNCC, 2002.
'Heritage Counts: the State of England's Historic Environment, 2005'. English Heritage, 2005.

Parks
Conway, Hazel. *Public Parks*. Shire, 1996.
Girouard, Mark. *The English Town*. Yale University Press, 1990.

Greenhalgh, Liz and Worpole, Ken. *Park Life: Urban Parks and Social Renewal*. Comedia and Demos, 1995.
Jordan, Harriet. 'Historic Public Parks'. *English Heritage Conservation Bulletin 43*, October 2002.
Nicholson-Lord, David. *Calling in the Country: Ecology, Parks and Human Need*. Comedia, 1994.

Pavements
Clifton-Taylor, Alec. *English Stone Building*. Gollancz, 1983/1994.
Clifton-Taylor, Alec. *Lewes*. The Alastair Press, 1981/1990.
Copperwheat, Cherrill. 'Shades of Grey'. *Landscape Design*, June 1995.
Hawkins, Michael. *Devon Roads*. Devon Books, 1988.
Joyce, Barry et al. *Derbyshire; Detail and Character*. Alan Sutton, 1996.
Traffic Management in Historic Areas (Traffic Advisory Leaflet). Department of Transport, January 1996.

Pears
Greenoak, Francesca. *Forgotten Fruit: The English Orchard and Fruit Garden*. Andre Deutsch, 1983.
Jordan, Katy. *The Haunted Landscape: Folklore, Ghosts and Legends of Wiltshire*. Ex Libris Press, 2000.
Mason, Laura with Brown, Catherine. *Traditional Foods of Britain*. Prospect Books, 1999.
Williams, Ray. *Perry Pears*. The National Fruit and Cider Institute, 1963.
The Churchwardens, St Mary's, Limpley Stoke (leaflet).
Worcester Black Pear (leaflet). Worcestershire County Council, nd.

Peat
Coles, John. 'Prehistory in the Somerset Levels 4000-100 BC' in *The Archaeology of Somerset* (Aston, Michael and Burrow, Ian, eds.). Somerset County Council, 1982.
Hartley, Marie and Ingilby, Joan. *Life and Tradition in the Yorkshire Dales*. Dalesman Books, 1989.
Hoskins, W.G. *The Making of the English Landscape*. Hodder & Stoughton, 1955/2005.
Ratcliffe, Derek (ed.). *A Nature Conservation Review*, vol. 2. CUP, 1977.
Winchester, Angus. *The Harvest of the Hills: Rural Life in Northern England and the Scottish Borders, 1400-1700*. Edinburgh UP, 2000.
Woodcock, Nigel. *Geology and Environment in Britain and Ireland*. UCL Press, 1994.
'Peat bogs saved for the nation'. *The Garden*, April 2002.

Pele Towers
Brabbs, Derry. *England's Heritage*. Seven Dials, 2001.

474

Chris Blandford Associates.
The Solway Coast Landscape.
Countryside Commission,
1995.
Raistrick, A. *The Pennine Dales.*
Arrow, 1968.
Ryder, Peter F. *Bastles and
Towers in the Northumberland
National Park.* 1990.
Sim, Richard.
Email, 4 December 2003.
English Heritage.
Penny Hedge
Kightly, Charles. *The Customs
and Ceremonies of Britain.*
Thames & Hudson, 1986.
Pollard, E.; Hooper, M.D.;
Moore, N.W. *Hedges.*
Collins, 1974/1977.
*Horne's Guide to Whitby and
District,* c.1975.
Piers
Coombes, Nigel. *Striding Boldly.*
Clevedon Pier Trust, 1995.
Lindley, Kenneth.
Seaside Architecture.
Hugh Evelyn, 1973.
Mickleborough, Timothy J.
Guide to British Piers.
National Piers Society,
1998.
Pearson, Lynn F. *Piers and
other Seaside Architecture.*
Shire, 2002.
Pies
Harben, Philip.
Traditional Dishes of Britain.
Bodley Head, 1953.
Hartley, Dorothy. *Food in
England.* Futura, 1954.
Hirst, Christopher.
'Market town in upper-crust
battle to give its pork pies
a slice of history'.
Independent, 31 July 2004.
McMillan, Ian.
'Who ate all the pies?' BBC
Radio 4, 28 November 2004.
Mason, Laura with
Brown, Catherine.
Traditional Foods of Britain.
Prospect Books, 1999.
Pigeon Lofts
Crouch, David and Ward,
Colin. *The Allotment.*
Faber & Faber, 1988.
Hartley, Dorothy. *The Land of
England.* Macdonald, 1979.
Porteous, Katrina. 'The Pigeon
Men' in *Turning the Tide*
(Pattison, Keith; Porteous,
Katrina; Soden, Robert).
District of Easington, 2001.
Bonsall Village Design Statement.
Royal Pigeon Racing
Association.
Pigs
Clutton-Brock, Juliet.
*A Natural History of
Domesticated Mammals.*
British Museum, 1987.
Ellis, Hattie. *Eating England.*
Mitchell Beazley, 2001.
Hall, Stephen and Clutton-
Brock, Juliet. *Two Hundred
Years of British Farm Livestock.*
British Museum, 1989.
Malcolmson, Robert and
Mastoris, Stephanos.
The English Pig: A History.
Hambledon Press, 1998.
Porter, Val. *British Pigs.*
Shire, 2002.

Tubbs, Colin. *The New Forest.*
Collins New Naturalist, 1986.
Wales, Tony. *A Sussex Garland.*
Countryside Books, 1979.
Wallis, Derek.
The Rare Breeds Handbook.
Blandford Press, 1986.
Wiseman, Julian. *The Pig:
A British History.*
Duckworth & Co., 2000.
*The Common Ground
Book of Orchards.*
Common Ground, 2000.
Pillboxes
Longstaff-Tyrrell, Peter.
*Barracks to Bunkers: 250 years
of Military Activity in Sussex.*
Alan Sutton, 2002.
Osborne, Mike. *Defending
Britain: Twentieth-century
Military Structures in the
Landscape.* Tempus, 2004.
Porteous, Katrina.
Letters, emails, conversations,
2001-2005.
British Archaeology, June 2002.
'CB, Bothie or Pillbox?' and
'Going, Going, Guano!'
*Archaeology in
Northumberland,* vol. 14, 2004.
*English Heritage Conservation
Bulletin* 44, June 2003.
Pinfolds
Goldsworthy, Andy. *Sheepfolds.*
Michael Hue-Williams Fine
Art, 1996.
Lyth, Philip. *The Pinfolds of
Nottinghamshire: A Gazetteer.*
Nottinghamshire County
Council, 1992.
English Heritage.
Pit Tips
Lawrence, D.H. *Sons and Lovers.*
Penguin, 1948.
Pattison, Keith; Porteous,
Katrina; Soden, Robert.
Turning the Tide.
District of Easington, 2001.
Reed, Fred. 'The Pit Heap'
in *The Northumberman.*
Iron Press, 1999.
Place-names
Ekwall, Eilert. *The Oxford
Dictionary of English
Place-Names.* OUP, 1936.
Field, John. *Place Names of
Britain and Ireland.*
David & Charles, 1980.
Gelling, Margaret. *Signposts to
the Past.* Phillimore, 1988.
Gelling, Margaret and Cole,
Ann. *The Landscape of Place-
Names.* Shaun Tyas, 2000.
English Place-Name Society.
Plums
Greenoak, Francesca.
*Forgotten Fruit: The English
Orchard and Fruit Garden.*
Andre Deutsch, 1983.
Mabey, Richard.
Flora Britannica.
Chatto & Windus, 1996.
Phelps, Humphrey. 'Plum
Crazy'. *The Countryman,*
Autumn 1989.
Taylor, H.V. *The Plums of
England.* Crosby Lockwood
& Son Ltd, 1949.
Landscape Ecology and Forestry
Service. *Survey of Orchards
in Southern Buckinghamshire.*
Buckinghamshire County
Council, October 1995.

*Common Ground
Book of Orchards.*
Common Ground, 2000.
Gloucestershire Orchards
Group.
Pitstone Local History Society.
Point to Point
The Jockey Club.
The New Forest Pony Breeding
and Cattle Society.
Ponds
Boothby, John (ed.). *Ponds and
Pond Landscapes of Europe:
Proceedings of the International
Conference of the Pond Life
Project.* Maastricht, 1998.
Hoskins, W.G. *The Making of
the English Landscape.* Hodder
& Stoughton, 1955/2005.
Mercer, Derrik (ed.).
Exploring Unspoilt Britain.
National Trust/Reed
International Books, 1985.
Poplar
Edlin, H.L. *Trees, Woods and
Man.* Collins, 1956/1978.
Miles, Archie. *Silva: The Tree in
Britain.* Ebury Press, 1999.
Mitchell, Alan. *A Field Guide to
the Trees of Britain and
Northern Europe.* Collins, 1974.
Rackham, Oliver.
Ancient Woodland.
Castlepoint Press, 2003.
Portland Lerrets
Elmer, W. *The Terminology
of Fishing: A Survey of
English and Welsh Inshore
Fishing Things and Words.*
The Cooper Monographs
19, English Dialect Series.
Franke Verlag, 1973.
McKee, Eric. *Working Boats
of Britain: Their Shape and
Purpose.* Conway Maritime
Press, 1983.
Williamson, T. *The Norfolk
Broads: A Landscape History.*
Manchester University Press,
1997.
Post Offices
Ashley, Peter. *Open for Business.*
English Heritage/Everyman,
2002.
Porteous, Katrina. Letters,
emails, conversations,
2001-2005.
Royal Mail. *The Post Office
since 1840,* nd.
The British Postal Museum
and Archive.
Potatoes
Hills, Lawrence D.
The Good Potato Guide.
Henry Doubleday Research
Association, 1989.
Mason, H.J. *The Black Fens.*
Providence Press, 1973/1984.
Prince, Rose. 'Savvy Shopper:
potatoes'. *Daily Telegraph,*
19 November 2005.
Stamp, L. Dudley (ed.). *The
Land of Britain: The Report
of the Land Utilisation Survey
of Britain.* Geographical
Publications, 1943.
Taylor, George M. *British Herbs
and Vegetables.* Collins, 1947.
Trewin, Carol and Woolfitt,
Adam, *Gourmet Cornwall,*
Alison Hodge, 2005.
Wilson, Alan. *The Story of the
Potato.* Alan Wilson, 1993.

Pottery
Clark, Garth. *The Potter's Art:
A Complete History of Pottery
in Britain.* Phaidon, 1995.
Grant, Alison.
*North Devon Pottery:
The Seventeenth Century.*
University of Exeter, 1983.
Laing, Lloyd. *Pottery in Britain
4000 BC-AD 1900.*
Greenlight, 2003.
McGarva, Andrew.
*Country Pottery: Traditional
Earthenware of Britain.*
A. & C. Black, 2000.
Poultry
Hams, Fred. *Old Poultry Breeds.*
Shire, 1999.
Webb, Julie. 'Keeping the
pecking order'. *The
Countryman,* December 2003.
Prefabs
Stevenson, G. *Palaces for the
People: Prefabs in Post War
Britain.* Batsford, 2003.
Priddy Sheep Fair
Hawksley, Simon.
Email, 3 May 2002.
Kerr Cameron, David.
The English Fair.
Alan Sutton, 1998.
Promenades
Lindley, Kenneth.
Seaside Architecture.
Hugh Evelyn, 1973.
Somerville, Christopher.
Britain Beside the Sea.
Grafton Books, 1989.
*Shifting Sands: Design and the
Changing Image of English
Seaside Towns.* English
Heritage and CABE, 2003.
Pub Games
Martin, Brian P. *Tales from
the Country Pub.*
David & Charles, 1998.
Neilson, Linda. Emails,
7 September and 23 October
2003.
Turner-Bishop, Aiden.
Letter, 5 September 2003.
The National Marble Museum.
Pubs
Brabbs, Derry.
English Country Pubs.
Weidenfeld & Nicolson, 1986.
Brandwood, Geoff.
'Historic Pub Interiors'.
*English Heritage Conservation
Bulletin,* 43, October 2002.
Davidson, Andrew. *Licensed to
Sell.* English Heritage, 2005.
Girouard, Mark. *Victorian Pubs.*
Studio Vista, 1975.
CAMRA.
Pub Signs
Corballis, Paul. *Pub Signs.*
Lennard Publishing, 1988.
Dunkling, Leslie and Wright,
Gordon. *Pub Names of
Great Britain.* Dent, 1994.
Haydon, Peter.
The English Pub: A History.
Robert Hale, 1994.
Puddings
Baldock, Dorothy.
Favourite Norfolk Recipes.
J. Salmon Ltd, nd.
Easlea, Kate. *Dorset Dishes.*
Paul Cave Publications,
1979/1981/1984/1990.
Hartley, Dorothy. *Food in
England.* Futura, 1954.

Mason, Laura with Brown,
Catherine. *Traditional Foods of
Britain.* Prospect Books, 1999.
Norwak, Mary.
A Taste of Norfolk. British
Food and Farming/Royal
Agricultural Society, 1989.
Persey, Amanda.
Favourite Somerset Recipes.
J. Salmon Ltd, nd.
Price, Jo and Price, Merlin.
*Traditional Gloucestershire
Recipes.* Minimax Books, 1985.
Rothwell, Catherine. *More
Lancashire Recipes.* Countryside
Publications Ltd, 1979.

Puddingstone
Hart, Stephen.
*Flint Architecture of East
Anglia.* Giles de la Mare
Publishers, 2002.
Munby, Lionel M.
The Hertfordshire Landscape.
Hodder & Stoughton, 1977.
Scafe, John. *A Geological Primer
in Verse.* Longman, Hurst,
Rees, Orme & Brown, 1820.
Westwood, Jennifer.
Gothick Hertfordshire.
C.I. Thomas & Sons, 1989.

Punch and Judy
Herbert, Trevor (ed.).
*The British Brass Band:
A Musical and Social History.*
OUP, 2000.
Simpson, J. and Roud, S.
*Oxford Dictionary of English
Folklore.* OUP, 2000.

476

Q

Quaker Meeting-houses
Botum, David A.
*Discovering Chapels and
Meeting Houses.* Shire, 1975.
Lidbetter, Hubert.
The Friends Meeting House.
Ebor Press, 1979.
Historic Chapels Trust.

Quarries
Arkell, W.J. and Tomkeieff, S.I.
English Rock Terms.
OUP, 1953.
Clifton-Taylor, Alec.
The Pattern of English Building.
Faber & Faber, 1972.
Falkener, Keith.
'Corsham Stone Mines'.
*English Heritage Conservation
Bulletin,* 44, June 2003.
Gale, A.W. et al. *The Building
Stones of Devon.* The
Devonshire Association, 1992.
Williams, M. *The Slate Industry.*
Shire, 2002.
Wood, Chris. 'Dore Abbey
Roofing Grant'. *English
Heritage Conservation Bulletin,*
43, October 2002.
Wright, Adela. *Craft Techniques
for Traditional Buildings.*
Batsford, 1991.
The Quality of Leicester.
Leicester City Council, 1993.
*The Roofs of England: Stone
Slates.* English Heritage, 1997.

Quarters
Cattell, John and Hawkins, Bob.
*The Birmingham Jewellery
Quarter: An Introduction and
Guide.* English Heritage, 2000.
Sheffield's City Centre Strategy.
Sheffield City Council, 1994.

Quicksand
Rose, Lesley. 'Take a Walk on
the West Side: The Cross
Sands Walk over Morecambe
Bay'. Letter and article, 2003.
Rose, Lesley. *Treacherous Sands.*
Video for British Video
History Trust, 1998.
Scott, Walter. *Redgauntlet.* 1824.
Timberlake, R.R. 'Crossing
the Sands' in *Keer to Kent,
a look at life in the Arnside/
Silverdale Area of Outstanding
Natural Beauty from 1986
to 2000* (Ayre, Barry, ed.).
Arnside/Silverdale Landscape
Trust, 2001.

Quoits I
Bett, Henry. *English Legends.*
Batsford, 1950.
Newbery, Elizabeth and Fecher,
Sarah. *Ford and Etal:
A Companion Guide.*
Ford and Etal Estate, 1995.
Strutt, Joseph. *The Sports
and Pastimes of the People of
England.* Thomas Tegg, 1838.
*North Tyne and Redesdale
Agricultural Society Bellingham
Show Catalogues.* 2003, 2004.

Quoits II
Bord, Janet and Bord, Colin.
*A Guide to Ancient Sites in
Britain.* Granada Publishing,
1979.
Harlech, Lord. *An Illustrated
Guide to the Ancient
Monuments Maintained
by the Department of the
Environment, Southern
England.* HMSO, 1977.
Hoskins, W.G. (ed.).
Dartmoor National Park.
HMSO, 1957.
Muir, Richard.
*Landscape Encyclopaedia:
A Reference Guide to the
Historic Landscape.*
Windgather Press, 2004.

Quomps
Gibbons, Bob.
Letter, 6 August 2003.
Hodges, Mr. Conversation,
4 August 2003.

R

Racecourses
Aldred, David H. *Cleeve Hill.*
Alan Sutton, 1990.
Davies, Hunter and Herrmann,
Frank. *Great Britain:
A Celebration.*
Hamish Hamilton, 1982.
Gill, James.
Racecourses of Great Britain.
Barrie & Jenkins Ltd, 1975.
Lasdun, Susan. *The English Park.*
Andre Deutsch, 1991.
Taylor, C. *Fields in the English
Landscape.* Dent, 1975.

Railings
Fitzgerald, Jane. *Off the Map.*
Green Books, 2000.
Joyce, Barry et al. *Derbyshire:
Detail and Character.*
Alan Sutton, 1996.
Long, Christopher. Letter to
the *Evening Standard,*
24 May 1984.
Muthesius, Stefan.
The English Terraced House.
Yale University Press, 1982.

Railways
Bonavia, Michael R.
*Historic Railway Sites in
Britain.* Robert Hale, 1987.
Boumphrey, Geoffrey.
British Roads.
Thomas Nelson, 1939.
Thomas, Simon.
'Wildlife on a branch line'.
British Wildlife, April 2003.
Vintner, Jeff.
Railway Walks: GWR and SR.
Alan Sutton, 1990.
Great Western Railway Magazine,
vol. 23, no. 5, May, 1911.
Sustrans.

Ramsons
Evans, Paul. 'May Flowers'
(Country Diary).
Guardian, 23 May 2001.
Grigson, Geoffrey.
The Englishman's Flora.
Paladin, 1975.
Mabey, Richard.
Flora Britannica.
Chatto & Windus, 1996.
Offwell Woodland and Wildlife
Trust.
Plants for a Future.

Red Foxes
Harris, A. 'Gorse in the East
Riding of Yorkshire'.
Folklife, vol. 3, 1991-2.
Hart-Davis, Duff.
Fauna Britannica.
Weidenfeld & Nicolson, 2002.
Williamson, Tom and Bellamy,
Liz. *Property and Landscape.*
George Philip, 1987.
Fox watch, Urban foxes.
London Wildlife Trust, 1983.

Red Kites
Coane, Sophie. Letter to the
Guardian, 29 December 2003.
English Nature/RSPB.
Return of the Red Kite.
English Nature, 2002.
Greenoak, Francesca.
All the Birds of the Air.
Andre Deutsch, 1979.

Red Squirrels
Buczacki, Stefan. *Fauna
Britannica.* Hamlyn, 2002.
Potter, Beatrix.
The Tale of Squirrel Nutkin.
F. Warne & Co. Ltd, 1903.
Rackham, Oliver. *The History of
the Countryside.* Dent, 1986.
*Red Squirrel Biodiversity Action
Plans.* English Nature,
1998-2004.
Species recovery programme.
English Nature, 1996.

Reed Beds
Friday, Laurie (ed.). *Wicken Fen.*
Harley Books, 1997.
Hawke, C.J. and Jose, P.V.
*Reedbed Management for
Commercial and Wildlife
Interests.* RSPB, 1996.
Preston, C.D. and Croft, J.M.
*Aquatic Plants in Britain and
Ireland.* Harley Books, 1997.
Purseglove, Jeremy.
Taming the Flood. OUP, 1989.
Tansley, A.G.
Britain's Green Mantle.
Allen & Unwin, 1968.
Walters, Martin and Gibbons,
Bob. *Britain: Travellers'
Nature Guides.* OUP, 2003.
*Sussex Wildlife Trust Nature
Reserves Guide.* 2002.

Reservoirs
British Waterways.
Friends of Tring Reservoirs.

Rhubarb
Hargreaves, John. *Harvests
and Harvesters: Fruit and
Vegetable Growing in Britain.*
Gollancz, 1987.
Mason, Laura with
Brown, Catherine.
Traditional Foods of Britain.
Prospect Books, 1999.
Walker, John. 'Dark Secret'.
NFU Countryside,
February 2003.
'Living National Treasure:
Rhubarb Grower'.
Country Life, 6 March 1997.

Rhynes
Coones, Paul and Patten, John.
*The Penguin Guide to the
Landscape of England and
Wales.* Penguin, 1986.
Crowden, James. 'Mulcheney
Abbey' in *In Time of Flood:
The Somerset Levels – the River
Parrett* (Crowden, James and
Wright, George). The Parrett
Trail Partnership, 1996.
Sutherland, Patrick and
Nicolson, Adam. *Wetland:
Life in the Somerset Levels.*
Michael Joseph, 1986.
*Enjoy the Avalon Marshes
and its Villages.*
Somerset Levels and Moors
Partnership, 2002.
*Nature Conservation and the
Management of Drainage
Channels.* NCC/ADA, 1989.
*Somerset Levels and Moors
Character Areas,* nd.

Rias
Derek Lovejoy Partnership.
The South Devon Landscape.
Countryside Commission,
1993.
King, Angela and Clifford,
Sue (eds.). *The River's Voice.*
Green Books, 2000.
*Rivers, Rhynes and
Running Brooks.*
Common Ground, 2000.

Ridge & Furrow
Field, John. *Field Names:
A Dictionary.*
David & Charles, 1972.
Hall, David. 'Medieval Fields
in their many forms'. *British
Archaeology,* 33, April 1998.
Hall, David. *Turning the
Plough. Midland Open Fields:
Landscape Character and
Proposals for Management.*
English Heritage/
Northamptonshire County
Council, 2001.
Hoskins, W.G. *The Making
of the English Landscape.*
Hodder & Stoughton,
1955/2005.
Rackham, Oliver.
The History of the Countryside.
Dent, 1986.
Taylor, Christopher. *Fields
in the English Landscape.*
Alan Sutton, 1987.
*Common Ground Manifesto
for Fields and Field Days.*
Common Ground, 1997.

River Names
Croad, Stephen. *Liquid History.*
Batsford, 2003.

Duffy, Carol Ann. 'River'. *The River's Voice* (King, Angela and Clifford, Sue, eds.). Green Books, 2000.
Ekwall, E. *English River Names*. OUP, 1928.
River, Rhynes and Running Brooks. Common Ground, 2000.

Rivers
Clifford, Sue. 'The Ducks Swim in Stone' in *River Calling*. London Rivers Association, 2002.
Hole, Christina. *English Folklore*. Batsford, 1940/1945.
Milton, John. 'Rivers arise; whether thou be the Son' in *The River's Voice* (King, Angela and Clifford, Sue, eds.). Green Books, 2000.
Ruskin, John. *The Elements of Drawing*. Smith, Elder, 1857/1973.
Rivers, Rhynes and Running Brooks. Common Ground, 2000.

Roads
Anderson, J.R.L. *The Oldest Road: An Exploration of the Ridgeway*. Wildwood House, 1975.
Bird, Graham and Mann, John. 'British Road Numbering'. *Journal of the Railway and Canal History Society*, vol. 34, part 2, no. 182, July 2002.
Boumphrey, Geoffrey. *British Roads*. Thomas Nelson, 1939.
Chesterton, G.K. *The Flying Inn*, 1914.
Grigson, Geoffrey. *The Shell Book of Roads*. Ebury/Shell Mex/BP, 1964.
Hannigan, Des. *Ancient Trackways*. Pavilion, 1994.
Hey, David. *Packmen, Carriers and Packhorse Roads: Trade and Communication in North Derbyshire and South Yorkshire*. Leicester University Press, 1980.
Hindle, Brian Paul. *Roads, Tracks and their Interpretation*. Batsford, 1993.
Robertson, Alan W. *Great Britain: Post Roads, Post Towns and Postal Rates 1635-1839*. Privately printed, 1961.
Wright, Geoffrey N. *Roads and Trackways of Wessex*. Moorland, 1988.
Regional Transport Statistics, November 2002. Department for Transport, 2002.

Robin Hood
Holt, J.C. *Robin Hood*. Thames & Hudson, 1982/1989.
Hutton, Ronald. *The Rise and Fall of Merry England*. OUP, 1994.
Padel, Ruth. 'Robin Hood' in *British Greats*. Cassell & Co., 2000.
Westwood, Jennifer. *Albion: A Guide to Legendary Britain*. Grafton, 1985.

Robins
Blake, William. 'Auguries of Innocence'.
Burton, Robert. 'Naturalist in the Garden'. *The Garden*, 1994.

Dacombe, Ursula. *Farmers Weekly*, 26 January 1951.
Graves, Robert. *The White Goddess*. Faber & Faber, 1961.
Jameson, Conor. 'A Song for all Seasons'. *Birds*, Spring 2002.
Lack, David. *The Life of the Robin*. The Fontana New Naturalist, 1970.
Lack, Peter. 'The legacy and significance of *The Life of the Robin* by David Lack.' *British Wildlife*, vol. 13, no. 2, December, 2001.
Mead, Chris. 'Robins'. *BBC Wildlife*, December 1984.
Nicholson, E.M. and Koch, Ludwig. *Songs of Wild Birds*. Witherby, 1936.
Searle-Chatterjee, Mary. 'Christmas Cards and the Construction of Social Relations in Britain Today' in *Unwrapping Christmas* (Miller, Daniel, ed.). OUP, 1993.
Simpson, J. and Roud, S. *Oxford Dictionary of English Folklore*. OUP, 2000.

Rocks
Beckensall, Stan. *Northumberland: The Power of Place*. Tempus, 2001.
Blackmore, R.D. *Lorna Doone*, 1869.
Lawrence, D.H. *Sons and Lovers*. 1913/Penguin, 1948.
Munby, Lionel M. *The Hertfordshire Landscape*. Hodder & Stoughton, 1977.
Porteous, Katrina. Email, 19 February 2003.
Rogers, Frank. *Curiosities of Derbyshire*. Derbyshire Countryside, 2000.
Westwood, Jennifer. *Gothick Hertfordshire*. C.I. Thomas & Sons, 1989.

Rookeries
Chaplin, John. Letter, 7 November 2002.
Cocker, Mark. 'Birds of a feather' ('Country Diary'). *Guardian*, 8 December 2003.
Cocker, Mark. 'Black beauties' ('Country Diary'). *Guardian*, 26 November 2001.
Cocker, Mark and Mabey, Richard. *Birds Britannica*. Chatto & Windus, 2005.
Harris, Bob. 'Modern high-rise' (letter). *Birds*, Autumn 1986.
Jefferies, Richard. *Field and Farm*. Phoenix House, 1957.
Marchant, John. 'Rooks Rally'. *BTO News*, 209, March-April 1997.
Stride, Chris. *Ranmoor Cliffe Rookery* at www.sbsg.pwp. blueyonder.co.uk/ ranmoorrooks.html UK Phenology Network.

Roundabouts
Beresford, Kevin. *Roundabouts of Great Britain*. New Holland, 2004.
Brown, Mike. *The Design of Roundabouts*. Transport Research Laboratory/ HMSO, London, 1995.
The Art of Gentle Gardening: Thoughts on Linking Plants, People and Places. Common Ground, 1995.

Round-towered Churches
Atkinson, T.D. *Local Style in English Architecture*. Batsford, 1947.
Davison, Caroline. Email, 2002.
Williamson, T. *The Norfolk Broads*. Manchester University Press, 1997.
Round Tower Churches Society.

Rowan
Grigson, Geoffrey. *The Englishman's Flora*. Paladin, 1975.
Snow, Barbara and Snow, David. *Birds and Berries*. T. & A.D. Poyser, 1988.

Royal Forests
Edlin, H.L. *Trees, Woods and Man*. Collins, 1956/1978.
Hey, David. 'Moorlands' in *Rural England* (Thirsk, Joan, ed.). OUP, 2000.
Hinde, Thomas. *Forests of Britain*. Gollancz, 1985.
Rackham, Oliver. *The Last Forest: The Story of Hatfield Forest*. Dent, 1989.

Ruins
Clifford, Sue. 'For looking at or living in? Local distinctiveness from the inside out' in *The Cultural Landscape*. ICOMOS-UK, 2001.
Cook, Olive. *Breckland*. Robert Hale, 1956.
Janowitz, Anne. *England's Ruins, Poetic Purpose and the National Landscape*. Basil Blackwell, 1990.
Jenkins, Simon. *England's Thousand Best Churches*. Penguin, 1999.
Lowenthal, David. *The Past Is a Foreign Country*. CUP, 1985.
Somerset Fry, Plantagenet. *Castles of Britain and Ireland*. David & Charles, 1996.
Westwood, Jennifer. *Albion: A Guide to Legendary Britain*. Grafton, 1985.

Rush-bearing
Cotton, Bernard D. *The English Regional Chair*. Antique Collectors' Club, 1990.
Hole, Christina. *A Dictionary of British Folk Customs*. Paladin, 1978.
Kightly, Charles. *The Customs and Ceremonies of Britain*. Thames & Hudson, 1986.
Mabey, Richard. *Flora Britannica*. Chatto & Windus, 1996.
Taylor, Phil. Email, 4 December 2004.
Local Flora Britannica. Common Ground, 1995.
The Rushbearing in Grasmere (booklet), nd.

S

Saints
Attwater, Donald. *The Penguin Dictionary of Saints*. Penguin, 1983.
Betts, Henry. *English Legends*. Batsford, 1950.
Farmer, David Hugh. *The Oxford Dictionary of Saints*. OUP, 1987.
Vince, John. *Discovering Saints in Britain*. Shire, 2001.

Salt Marshes
Chris Blandford Associates. *The Solway Coast Landscape*. Countryside Commission, 1995.
Covey, R. and Laffoley, D.d'A. *State of Nature*. English Nature, 2002.
Gunton, Tony. *Wild Essex*. Lopinga Books, 2000.
JNCC. *UK Biodiversity Priority Habitats: Coastal Salt Marsh*. 2001.
Tabor, Ray. 'Turning the tide for salt marshes'. *British Wildlife*, October 2003.

Sand-dunes
Pye, K. and French, P.W. *Targets for Coastal Habitat Re-creation*. English Nature, 1993.
Tansley, A.G. *Britain's Green Mantle*. Allen & Unwin, 1968.
Tansley, A.G. *Our Heritage of Wild Nature*. CUP, 1946.
Walters, Martin and Gibbons, Bob. *Travellers' Nature Guides, Britain*. OUP, 2003.

Sandstones
Chaplin, Sid. *The Thin Seam*. Phoenix House, 1950.
North Pennines AONB. *Good Practice in the Design, Adaptation and Maintenance of Buildings*. North Pennines Partnership, 2000.

Scarecrows
Haining, Peter. *The Scarecrow: Fact and Fable*. Robert Hale, 1986.
Simpson, J. and Roud, S. *Oxford Dictionary of English Folklore*. OUP, 2000.

Scots Pine
Edlin, H.L. *Trees, Woods and Man*. Collins, 1956/1978.
Edlin, H. L. *Woodland Crafts in Britain*. David & Charles, 1949/1973.
Grigson, Geoffrey. *The Englishman's Flora*. Paladin, 1975.
Mabey, Richard. *Flora Britannica*. Chatto & Windus, 1996.
The Devon Landscape: A Draft Strategy for Consultation. Devon County Council, 1994.

Sculptures
Randall-Page, Peter et al. *Granite Song: A Common Ground Project*. Devon Books, 1999.
Plymouth Waterfront Walk. Plymouth City Council, 2001.

Sea Caves
Davies, G.M. *The Dorset Coast*. A. & C. Black, 1956.
Perkins, J.W. *Geology Explained in Dorset*. David & Charles, 1977.
Kent Underground Research Group.

Sea Fish
Black, William. *The Land that Thyme Forgot*. Bantam Press, 2005.
Butterfield, W. Ruskin. 'Folk-names for marine fishes and other animals at Hastings'. *The Hastings and East Sussex Naturalist*, vol. 2, 1912-17.

477

Crowden, James. *In Time of Flood*. The Parrett Trail Partnership, 1996.

Duncan, Katherine. *An Introduction to England's Marine Wildlife*. English Nature, 1992.

Porteous, Katrina (ed.). *The Bonny Fisher Lad*. People's History, 2003.

Porteous, Katrina. Email, 25 June 2003.

Samuel, Olive J. *Tales of Old Mudeford*, nd.

Starkey, ed. D.; Reid, C.; Ashcroft, N. *England's Sea Fisheries*. Chatham Publishing, 2000.

Field Guide to the Water Life of Britain. Reader's Digest, 1984.

Sea Forts
Turner, Steve. Emails, 2004 and 2005.

Project Redsand.

Sea-marks
Aylard Coles, K. *The Shell Pilot to the South Coast Harbours*. Faber & Faber, 1939.

Legg, Rodney. *Durdle Door and White Nothe, Purbeck Coastal Walks*. Dorset Publishing Company, 1995.

Sea Tractor
Barber, Chips. *Around and about Burgh Island and Bigbury-on-Sea*. Obelisk Publications, 1998.

Sheep
Graham, Caz. Email, 1 May 2003.

Hartley, Dorothy. *The Land of England*. Macdonald, 1979.

Wallace, Robert. *Farm Live Stock of Great Britain*. Oliver & Boyd, 1907.

Sheep-dogs
Bonser, K.J. *The Drovers*. Macmillan, 1970.

Croxton Smith, A. *British Dogs*. Collins, 1945.

Fogle, Dr Bruce. *The Encyclopaedia of the Dog*. Dorling Kindersley, 1995.

Hancock, David. *Old Farm Dogs*. Shire, 1999.

Hancock, David. *Old Working Dogs*. Shire, 1998.

Hart-Davis, Duff. *Fauna Britannica*. Weidenfeld & Nicolson, 2002.

Heath, Veronica. 'A dog's life' (Country Diary). *Guardian*, 29 July 2005.

Hopkins, Tony. *The Cheviot Way of Life*. Northumberland National Park, nd.

Larkin, Dr Peter and Stockman, Mike. *The Ultimate Encyclopaedia of Dog Breeds and Dog Care*. Southwater, 1997.

Porteous, Katrina. Email, 28 July 2003.

Sheep-folds
Goldsworthy, Andy. *Sheepfolds*. Michael Hue-Williams Fine Art, 1996.

Rodgers, Frank. *Curiosities of Derbyshire and the Peak District*. Derbyshire Countryside Ltd, 2000.

English Heritage.

Sheep-washes
Humphries, Andrew. 'Folds in the Landscape' in *Sheepfolds* (Goldsworthy, Andy). Michael Hue-Williams Fine Art, 1996.

Hurst, Derek et al. *Sheepwashes in the Cotswolds AONB*. Cotswolds AONB Partnership, 2002.

Lawrence, Ian. *Fontmell Magna in Retrospect*. Brambledown Press, 1988.

Morris, Stuart. *Portland: An Illustrated History*. Dovecote Press, 1986.

Shellfish
Mason, Laura with Brown, Catherine. *Traditional Foods of Britain*. Prospect Books, 1999.

Robinson, Adrian and Millward, Roy. *The Shell Book of the British Coast*. David & Charles, 1983.

Stein, Rick. *Seafood Lovers' Guide*. BBC Worldwide, 2000.

Shiners
Derek Lovejoy Partnership. *The South Devon Landscape*. Countryside Commission, 1993.

Turrell, Trudy. Conversations, 2003.

Shingle
Robinson, Ged. *Dungeness: A Unique Place*. Sutton House, 1988.

Rothschild, Miriam and Marren, Peter. *Rothschild's Reserves: Time and Fragile Nature*. Balaban Publishers and Harley Books, 1997.

Shingles
Clifton-Taylor, Alec. *The Pattern of English Building*. Faber & Faber, 1972.

Fitzgerald, Jane with Turrell, Trudy. *Off the Map*. Green Books, 2000.

Jenkins, Simon. *England's Thousand Best Churches*. Penguin, 1999/2000.

Turrell, Trudy. Conversations, 2003.

Wright, Adela. *Craft Techniques for Traditional Buildings*. Batsford, 1991.

Shipping Forecast
Meteorological Office website: www.metoffice.com

Shire Horses
Rare Breeds Survival Trust. Shire Horse Society.

Shops
Morrison, Kathryn A. *English Shops and Shopping*. Yale University Press, 2003.

Powers, Alan. *Shop Fronts*. Chatto & Windus, 1989.

Shrovetide Games
Candlin, Lillian. *Tales of Old Sussex*. Countryside Books, 1985.

Hole, Christina. *British Folk Customs*. Hutchinson, 1976.

Kightly, Charles. *The Customs and Ceremonies of Britain*. Thames & Hudson, 1986.

Simpson J. and Roud, S. *Oxford Dictionary of English Folklore*. OUP, 2000.

Sykes, Homer. *Once a Year*. Gordon Fraser, 1977.

Wales, Tony. *Sussex Customs, Curiosities and Country Lore*. Ensign Publications, 1990.

Skylarks
Garstang, Walter. *Songs of Birds*. John Lane/Bodley Head, 1922.

Hudson, W.H. *Nature in Downland*. Dent, 1923.

Milton, John. 'L'allegro' in *An Exaltation of Skylarks* (Beer, Stewart). SMH Books, 1995.

Nicholson, E.M. and Koch, Ludwig. *Songs of Wild Birds*. Witherby, 1936/1943.

Porteous, Katrina. 'Skylark' in *The Lost Music*. Bloodaxe Books, 1996.

Shelley, Percy Bysshe. 'To a skylark' in *An Exaltation of Skylarks* (Beer, Stewart). SMH Books, 1995.

'SAFFIE success for skylarks'. *Fieldfare* (RSPB), 25 January 2004.

Skylark (Alauda arvensis) Species Action Plan. Joint Nature Conservation Committee, 2004.

Slates
Clifton-Taylor, Alec. *The Pattern of English Building*. Faber & Faber, 1972.

Garner, A. *The Stone Book Quartet*. HarperCollins, 1992.

Joyce, Barry. Conversation, December 2002.

Penoyre, J. and Penoyre, J. *Houses in the Landscape*. Faber & Faber, 1978.

Williams, M. *The Slate Industry*. Shire, 2002.

Wright, Adela. *Craft Techniques for Traditional Buildings*. Batsford, 1991.

Smells
Brooks, Clive. Email, 3 May 2002.

Carling, Sue. Email, 2 May 2002.

King, Marcus. Email, 8 May 2002.

Litvinoff, Emanuel. *Journey through a Small Planet*. Robin Clark, 1993.

Simmonds, Clive. Email, 7 May 2002.

Thorning, Janet. Email, 2 May 2002.

Soils
Hearn, Katherine; Jarman, Rob; Haycock, Nick. 'Soil Conservation: the ultimate test of sustainability'. *Conservation Land Management*, vol. 2, no. 2. Summer 2004.

Soughs
Barnatt, John and Penny, Rebecca. *The Lead Legacy*. Peak District National Park Authority, 2004.

Kirkham, Nellie. *Derbyshire Lead Mining through the Centuries*. D. Bradford Barton, 1968.

Willies, Lynn. *Lead and Lead Mining*. Shire, 1999.

Bagshaws Directory. 1846.

Sound Mirrors
Barrett, Claire. *Sound Mirrors, Greatstone, Kent*. The Twentieth Century Society. 2003.

Scarth, Richard N. *Echoes from the Sky*. Hythe Civic Society, 1999.

Arts Council. English Heritage.

Sparrows
Dainton, Courtney. *Clocks, Jacks and Bee Boles*. Phoenix House, 1957.

Shrubb, Michael. *Birds, Scythes and Combines: A History of Birds and Agricultural Change*. CUP, 2003.

Cirl Bunting Bulletin. Winter 2002/3.

Spas
Alderson, Frederick. *Inland Resorts and Spas of Britain*. David & Charles, 1973.

Fowler, Peter (ed.). *Hotels and Restaurants 1830 to the Present Day*. RCHM, 1981.

Lindley, Kenneth. *Seaside Architecture*. Hugh Evelyn, 1973.

Springs
Ralph, Whitman. *Portrait of Dorset*. Robert Hale, 1965.

River, Rhynes and Running Brooks. Common Ground, 2000.

Squares
Beresford, Camilla. *The Development of Garden Squares*. London Parks and Gardens Trust, 2003.

Girouard, Mark. *The English Town*. Yale University Press, 1990.

Trevelyan, G.M. *English Social History*. Longman, 1944.

English Heritage.

Stacks
Barton, R.M. *An Introduction to the Geology of Cornwall*. Pitman Press, 1964.

Bruce, Peter. *Wight Hazards*. Boldre Marine, 2001.

Haseler, Henry. *Scenery on the Southern Coast of Devonshire*. Sidmouth. J. Wallis, 1818.

Steers, J.A. *The Coastline of England and Wales*. CUP, 1964.

Stairs
Owen, Wilfred. 'Shadwell Stair' in *The Collected Poems of Wilfred Owen* (Day Lewis, C., ed.). Chatto & Windus, 1964.

River Calling. London Rivers Association, 2002.

Rivers of Meaning. London Rivers Association, 1996.

Rivers, Rhynes and Running Brooks. Common Ground, 2000.

Standing Stones
Bender, Barbara. Conversations and emails, November 2004.

Bord, Janet and Bord, Colin. *A Guide to Ancient Sites in Britain*. Paladin, 1979.

Cope, Julian. *The Modern Antiquarian*. Thorsons, 1998.

Cosgrove, Judith. 'Moor Stones give us a clue'. *Chagford Times*, 1988.

478

Land Use Consultants.
The Isles of Scilly.
Countryside Agency, 2002.
Landscape Design Associates.
The Cornish Landscape.
Countryside Commission,
1997.
Riley, Hazel and Wilson-North,
Robert. *The Field Archaeology
of Exmoor.* English Heritage,
2001.
Watkins, Alfred. *The Old
Straight Track.* Abacus, 1974.
Starfish
Barrett, John. *Life on the
Seashore.* Collins, 1974.
Elmer, W. *The Terminology
of Fishing: A Survey of
English and Welsh Inshore
Fishing Things and Words.*
The Cooper Monographs
19, English Dialect Series.
Franke Verlag, 1973.
Starlings
Blackburn, Julia.
*Charles Waterton, 1782-1865:
Conservationist and Traveller.*
Pimlico, 1991/Vintage, 1997.
Catchpole, C.K. and Slater, P.J.B.
*Bird Song: Biological Themes
and Variations.* CUP, 1995.
Cocker, Mark and Mabey,
Richard. *Birds Britannica.*
Chatto & Windus, 2005.
Feare, Christopher. *The Starling.*
Shire Natural History, 1985.
Nicholson, E.M. and Koch,
Ludwig. *Songs of Wild Birds.*
H.F. & G. Witherby Ltd, 1936.
Stations
Bonavia, Michael R.
*Historic Railway Sites in
Britain.* Robert Hale, 1987.
Chesterton, G.K. *Tremendous
Trifles.* Methuen, 1909.
Richards, Jeffrey and
Mackenzie, John M.
*The Railway Station: A Social
History.* OUP, 1986.
Wikely, N. and Middleton, J.
*Railway Stations Southern
Region.* Peco Publications,
1971.
Stepping-stones
Grigson, Geoffrey. *Geoffrey
Grigson's Countryside.*
Ebury Press, 1982
Stiles
Barry, Victor B.M.
Email, 27 December 2004.
Brooks, Alan and Adcock, Sean.
Drystone Walling.
BTCV, 1977-2002.
Lovett Jones, Gareth.
English Country Lanes.
Wildwood House, 1988.
Roberts, Michael.
Gates and Stiles.
Old Cockerel Press, 2001.
Robinson, Eric and
Summerfield, Geoffrey (eds.).
*The Selected Poems and Prose of
John Clare.* OUP, 1978.
Williamson, Tom. *Hedges and
Walls.* National Trust, 2002.
Cornish Stiles in the Roseland,
vols I and II. St Gerrans and
Porthscatho Old Cornwall
Society, 1997-2000.
Stilton
Hickman, Trevor.
The History of Stilton Cheese.
Alan Sutton, 1995.

Mason, Laura with Brown,
Catherine. *Traditional Foods
of Britain: An Inventory.*
Prospect Books, 1999.
Straw
Cox, Jo and Thorp, John R.L.
Devon Thatch.
Devon Books, 2001.
Hartley, Dorothy. *The Land of
England.* Macdonald, 1979.
Shrubb, Michael. *Birds,
Scythes and Combines.*
CUP, 2003.
Blackmore Vale Magazine,
21 August 2002.
Straw Bear Day
Hole, Christina.
British Folk Customs.
Book Club Associates, 1976.
Kightly, Charles. *The Customs
and Ceremonies of Britain.*
Thames & Hudson, 1986.
Ridgewell, Gordon.
'Straw bears'. *FLS News*,
June 2002 and February 2003.
Ryall, Janet. 'Anglia's man
of straw'. *NFU Countryside*,
January 2000.
Simpson, Jacqueline.
'Straw men'. *FLS News*,
February 2003.
Strawberries
Hargreaves, John.
*Harvests and Harvesters:
Fruit and Vegetable Growing
in Britain.* Gollancz, 1987.
Hills, Lawrence D.
The Good Fruit Guide.
HDRA, 1984.
Mason, Peter F. *Hampshire:
A Sense of Place.* Hampshire
Books, Hampshire County
Council, 1994.
Roach, F.A.
Cultivated Fruits of Britain.
Blackwell, 1985.
Unwin, A.C.B. *Commercial
Nurseries and Market Gardens.*
Twickenham Local History
Society, 1982.
The Mendip Hills Landscape.
Countryside Commission,
1998.
Suffolk Punches
Miller, Chris.
Email, 9 February 2004.
Wells, Marion.
Email, 9 February 2004.
Rare Breeds Survival Trust.
Suffolk Horse Society.
Sunbursts
Oliver, Paul; Davis, Ian;
Bentley, Ian. *Dunroamin:
The Suburban Semi and its
Enemies.* Pimlico, 1981.
Rice, Brian and Evans, Tony.
The English Sunrise. Matthews
Miller Dunbar, 1972.
Surfing
Nelson, Chris and Taylor, Demi.
Surfing Britain (Footprints
Surfing Guide). Footprint
Handbooks, 2005.
Swan Upping
Greenoak, Francesca.
All the Birds of the Air.
Andre Deutsch, 1979.
Kightly, Charles. *The Customs
and Ceremonies of Britain.*
Thames & Hudson, 1986.
*Confluence: New Music for
the River Stour.*
Common Ground, 1998-2001.

Lead Poisoning in Swans.
Report of the Nature
Conservancy Council's
Working Group, 1981.
Sweet Chestnut
Rackham, Oliver.
Ancient Woodland.
Castlepoint Press, 2003.
Swimming Places
Deakin, Roger. *Waterlog.*
Chatto & Windus, 1999/
Vintage, 2000.
Fryer, Rob. 'The Farleigh
Weir Appeal, 1999'. Farleigh
and District Swimming Club.
Gardner, Dr Simon.
Letter, 10 December 1998.
Vines, Gail. 'Wild swimmers'.
New Scientist, 17 July 1999.
Wordsworth, William.
Selections from Wordsworth.
Ginn & Co. Ltd, 1932/1958.
Sword dancing
Peck, Arthur. *The Morris and
Sword Dances of England.*
The Morris Ring, 1978.
Rippon, Hugh.
*Discovering English Folk
Dance.* Shire, 1975/1993.
Sharp, Cecil J. *The Sword
Dances of Northern England*,
part 1. Novello & Company,
1911-13.
Sycamore
Green, Ted. 'Is there a case
for "The Celtic Maple"
or the "Scot's Plane"?'.
British Wildlife, 2005.
Grigson, Geoffrey.
The Englishman's Flora.
Paladin, 1975.
Mabey, Richard. *Flora Britannica.*
Chatto & Windus, 1996.
Marren, Peter.
*Nature Conservation: A Review
of the Conservation of Wildlife
in Britain 1950-2001.*
HarperCollins, 2002.
Marren, Peter. Conversations,
2004.
Wilks, J.H. *Trees of the British
Isles in History and Legend.*
Frederick Miller, 1972.
*Tolpuddle: An Historical Account
through the Eyes of George
Loveless.* TUC, 1997.
Synagogues
Kadish, Sharman (ed.).
*Building Jerusalem: Jewish
Architecture in Britain.*
Vallentine Mitchell, 1996.
Kadish, Sharman.
'Jewish Heritage UK'.
*English Heritage Conservation
Bulletin*, issue 46, 2004.
Wigoder, Geoffrey.
The Story of the Synagogue.
Weidenfeld & Nicolson, 1986.

T

Tar Barrel Rolling
Kightly, Charles. *The Customs
and Ceremonies of Britain.*
Thames & Hudson, 1986.
Noble, Geoffrey.
Email, 1 December 2003.
Sykes, Homer. *Once a Year.*
Gordon Fraser, 1977.
Tarns
Griffin, A. Harry. 'A place to
reflect' (Country Diary).
Guardian, 11 August 2003.

Griffin, A. Harry. 'Pools'
Paradise' (Country Diary).
Guardian, 17 November 2003.
Jones, Cory. 'Malham Tarn
Nature Reserve'. *British
Wildlife*, October 2001.
Muir Wood, Robert.
*On the Rocks: A Geology of
Britain.* BBC, 1978.
Tansley, A.G.
Britain's Green Mantle.
Allen & Unwin, 1968.
Wainwright, A. and Brabbs,
Derry. *Fellwalking with
Wainwright.* Michael Joseph,
1984.
Whittow, John. *Geology
and Scenery in Britain.*
Chapman & Hall, 1992.
Tartan
Mills, T.F. 'History of Military
Tartans' at regiments.org/
tradition/tartans.htm
The Northumberland Tartan
Company.
Temples
Buddhist Society.
Jain Alliance.
Swaminarayan Hindu Mission
UK.
The World Sikh University,
London.
Terraced Houses
Cooper, Malcolm.
'Nelson, Lancashire: What
future for Mill Housing?'
*English Heritage Conservation
Bulletin*, 41, September 2001.
Lambrick, George. 'Stop
Wrecking Victorian Terraces'.
British Archaeology, June 2002.
Muthesius, Stefan.
The English Terraced House.
Yale University Press, 1982.
Terriers
Bonser, K.J. *The Drovers.*
Macmillan, 1970.
Croxton Smith, A. *British Dogs.*
Collins, 1945.
Fogle, Dr Bruce.
The Encyclopaedia of the Dog.
Dorling Kindersley, 1995.
Hancock, David. *Old Working
Dogs.* Shire, 1998.
Hart-Davis, Duff.
Fauna Britannica.
Weidenfeld & Nicolson, 2002.
Heath, Veronica. 'Brave Hearts'
(Country Diary). *Guardian*,
9 November 2001.
Larkin, Dr Peter and
Stockman, Mike. *The
Ultimate Encyclopaedia
of Dog Breeds and Dog Care.*
Southwater, 1997.
Plummer, D. Brian.
The Sporting Terrier.
The Boydell Press, 1992.
Waller, Tony and Waller,
Maureen. Conversation,
2004.
Textile Mills
Brabbs, Derry. *England's
Heritage.* English Heritage/
Cassell & Co., 2001/2003.
*Nomination of the Derwent
Valley Mills for Inscription
on the World Heritage List.*
Derwent Valley Mills
Partnership, 2000.
Thames Sailing Barges
Hazell, Martin. *Sailing Barges.*
Shire Album, 2001.

479

Society for Sailing Barge Research website: www.sailingbargeresearch.org.uk
Thatch
Clifton-Taylor, Alec. *The Pattern of English Building*. Faber & Faber, 1972.
Collins, E.J.T. (ed.). *Crafts in the English Countryside: Towards a Future*. Countryside Agency, 2004.
Cox, Jo and Thorp, John R.L. *Devon Thatch*. Devon Books, 2001.
Lowe, John. 'Dorset's Thatch Heritage'. Dorset Archaeology and Natural History Society newsletter, 1996/7.
Mercer, Ian. *Building in the Dartmoor National Park*. DNPA, 1979.
Nash, Judy. *Thatchers and Thatching*. Batsford, 1991.
Penoyre, John and Penoyre, Jane. *Houses in the Landscape: Regional Study of Vernacular Building Styles in England and Wales*. Faber & Faber, 1978.
Prendergast, Hew D.V. and Sanderson, Helen. *Britain's Wild Harvest: The Commercial Uses of Wild Plants and Fungi*. Royal Botanic Gardens, 2004.
Wright, Adela. *Craft Techniques for Traditional Buildings*. Batsford, 1991.
Thatch and thatching: a guidance note. English Heritage, 2000.
Thatch in Hertfordshire. Hertfordshire County Council, 1983.
Three Hares
Evans, George Ewart and Thompson, David. *The Leaping Hare*. Faber & Faber, 1972.
Three Hares. BBC Radio 4, 2004.
The Three Hares Project.
Tide Mills
Southgate, Michael. *The Old Tide Mill at Eling*. Eling Tide Mill Trust, nd.
Tides
Adlard Coles, K. *The Shell Pilot to the South Coast Harbours*. Faber & Faber, 1962.
Baber, Tim. *Mudeford Sandbank News*, Late Summer, 1999.
Barber, Chips. *Around and about Burgh Island and Bigbury-on-Sea*. Obelisk Publications, 1998.
Graham, Frank. *Holy Island: a short history guide*. Butler, 1987.
Rose, Lesley. 'Take a Walk on the West Side: The Cross Sands Walk over Morecambe Bay'. Letter and article, 2003.
Rose, Lesley. *Treacherous Sands*. British Video History Trust, 1998.
Tiles
Clifton-Taylor, Alec. *Lewes*. The Alastair Press, 1981.
Clifton-Taylor, Alec. *The Pattern of English Building*. Faber & Faber, 1972.
Jekyll, Gertrude. *Old West Surrey*. Kohler & Coombes, 1904/1978.

Penoyre, John and Penoyre, Jane. *Houses in the Landscape: A Regional Study of Vernacular Building Styles in England and Wales*. Faber & Faber, 1978.
Woodford, John. *Bricks to Build a House*. Routledge & Kegan Paul, 1976.
Wright, Adela. *Craft Techniques for Traditional Buildings*. Batsford, 1991.
Tin Tabernacles
Beacham, Peter and Ravilious, James. *Down the Deep Lanes*. Devon Books, 2000.
Emery, Norman. 'Corrugated Iron Buildings in County Durham'. *Durham Archaeological Journal* 6, 1990.
Green, Gary. 'Detailed Study of The Foundation Christian Fellowship Pentecostal Church Skelton, Redcar and Cleveland Unitary Authority'. Tees Archaeology, 2003. Unpublished.
Green, Gary. Email, 5 September 2003.
The Corrugated Iron Club website: www.corrugated-iron-club.info
Tithe Barns
Brunskill, R.W. *Traditional Farm Buildings of Britain and their Conservation*. Gollancz, 1987.
Harris, R. *Traditional Farm Buildings*. Arts Council, nd. National Trust.
Toll-houses
Dodd, A.E. and Dodd, E.M. *Peakland Roads and Trackways*. Moorland Publishing Company, 1974.
Freethy, Ron. *Turnpikes and Toll Houses of Lancashire*. 1987.
Hawkins, Michael. *Devon Roads*. Devon Books, 1988.
Haynes, Robert and Slocombe, Ivor. *Wiltshire Toll Houses*. The Hobnob Press, 2004.
Kanefsky, John. *Devon Tollhouses*. Exeter Industrial Archaeology Group, Department of Economic History, University of Exeter, 1984.
Rogers, Frank. *More Curiosities of Derbyshire and the Peak District*. Derbyshire Countryside, 2000.
Taylor, Patrick. *The Toll-Houses of Cornwall*. Federation of Old Cornwall Societies, 2001.
Wright, Geoffrey N. *Turnpike Roads*. Shire, 1992.
Topiary
Bryant, Ken and Giles, Roger. *Queen Camel Now and Then*. Queen Camel Playing Field Committee, 1990.
Carey, Charles. Conversation, via Leana Pooley, 16 October 2004.
Evans, Tony and Lycett Green, Candida. *English Cottages*. Cassell, 1982.
Hadfield, Miles. *A History of British Gardening*. Penguin, 1960.
Hobhouse, Penelope. *Plants in Garden History*. Pavilion Books, 1992.

Joyce, David. *Topiary and the Art of Training Plants*. Frances Lincoln, 1999.
Lasdun, Susan. *The English Park*. Andre Deutsch, 1991.
Meyer, Bobby. *Topiary for Everyone*. Search Press, 1999.
Nash, David. *Twmps*. Oriel 31 and Seren, 2001.
Tors
Betjeman, John. *Cornwall: A Shell Guide*. Faber & Faber, 1964.
Brassley, Angela and Brassley, Paul. Letter, 3 November 2003.
Durrance, E.M. and Laming, D.J.C. (eds.). *The Geology of Devon*. University of Exeter Press, 1982.
Land Use Consultants. *The Isles of Scilly*. Countryside Agency, 2002.
Loveridge, F.L. and Loveridge, E.A. *Devon*. Penguin Books, 1939.
Weller, Philip. *The Hound of the Baskervilles: Hunting the Dartmoor Legend*. Devon Books, 2001.
Young, Rob. Letter, 26 November 2002.
Tor Formation (fact sheet). Dartmoor National Park, nd.
Tower Blocks
Colquhoun, Ian. *The RIBA Book of Twentieth Century British Housing*. Architectural Press, 1999.
Commission for Architecture and the Built Environment (CABE).
Town Gates
Girouard, Mark. *The English Town*. Yale University Press, 1990.
Lloyd, David W. *The Making of English Towns* (new edition). Gollancz, 1998.
Town Halls & Guild-halls
Chamberlain, Russell. *The English County Town*. The National Trust/ Webb & Bower, 1983.
Girouard, Mark. *The English Town*. Yale University Press, 1990.
Wood, Eric S. *Historical Britain*. Harvill Press, 1995.
Tree Dressing Day
Tree Dressing Day Manual. Common Ground, 1994.
Tree Dressing Day Times. Common Ground, 1993.
Tunnels
Bonavia, Michael R. *Historic Railway Sites in Britain*. Robert Hale, 1987.
Errand, Jeremy. *Secret Passages and Hiding Places*. David & Charles, 1974.
Turf Mazes
Field, R. *Mazes Ancient and Modern*. Tarquin Publications, 1999.
Fowles, John. 'Islands' in *Wormholes*. Jonathan Cape, 1998.
Turning the Devil's Stone
Kightly, Charles. *The Customs and Ceremonies of Britain*. Thames & Hudson, 1986.

U
The Underground
James, Simon. *Mind the Gap*. HarperCollins, 2001.
Long, Christopher. 'Ghosts Beneath Our Feet'. *Mayfair Times*, November 1988.
Wolmar, Christian. *Down the Tube: The Battle for London's Underground*. Aurum Press, 2002.
London's Transport Museum.
London Underground.
Unlucky Words
Baker, M. *The Folklore of the Sea*. David & Charles, 1928/1979.
Fowles, John. *Islands*. Jonathan Cape, 1978.
Graves, Robert. *The White Goddess*. Faber & Faber, 1961.
Jones, M. and Dillon, P. *Dialect in Wiltshire*. Wiltshire County Council, 1987.
Morris, S. *Portland*. Dovecote Press, 1985.
Porteous, Katrina. Emails and conversations, 2003-2005.
Somerville, C. *Britain Beside the Sea*. Grafton Books, 1989.
Todd's Geordie Words and Phrases. Butler Publishing, 1976.

V
Vaccary Walls
Brambles, Geoff. *Kendal Building Stones* (leaflet). Cumbria RIGS, nd.
Brooks, Alan and Adcock, Sean. *Dry Stone Walling: A Practical Handbook*. BTCV, 1977/2002.
Wright, A. *Craft Techniques for Traditional Buildings*. Batsford, 1991.
Verges
Martin, Stephen. *The Long Meadow: An Historical Ecology of Roadsides in Britain*. Landscapes, 2003.
Rackham, Oliver. *The History of the Countryside*. Dent, 1986.
Road Verges for Wildlife (leaflet). East Sussex County Planning Department, nd.
Viaducts
Richards, J.M. *The National Trust Book of Bridges*. Jonathan Cape, 1984.
Images of England.
Village Greens
Bailey, Brian. *The English Village Green*. Robert Hale, 1985.
Darley, Gillian. *Villages of Vision*. Paladin, 1978.
Hoskins, W.G. *The Making of the English Landscape*. Hodder & Stoughton, 1955/2005.
Hoskins, W.G. and Stamp, L. Dudley. *The Common Lands of England and Wales*. Collins, 1963.
Sharpe, Thomas. *The Anatomy of the Village*. Penguin, 1946.
Taylor, Christopher. *Village and Farmstead*. George Philip, 1984.
Village Halls
Beaton, Louise. *Village Halls in England 1998: The Report of the 1998 Village Halls Survey*. ACRE, 1998.

480

Villages
Darley, Gillian. *Villages of Vision*. Paladin, 1978.
Hoskins, W.G. *The Making of the English Landscape*. Hodder & Stoughton, 1955/2005.
Massingham, H.J. *English Downland*. Batsford, 1936.
Mingay, G.E. (ed.). *The Victorian Countryside*, vol. 1. Routledge & Kegan Paul, 1981.
Sharpe, Thomas. *The Anatomy of the Village*. Penguin, 1946.
Taylor, Christopher. *Village and Farmstead*. George Philip, 1984.
Williamson, Tom and Bellamy, Liz. *Property and Landscape*. George Philip, 1987.
Wood, Eric S. *Historical Britain*. Harvill Press, 1995.

Village Signs
Savage, Ken. 'Village signs of Kent, Suffolk, Norfolk, Essex, Cambridgeshire' at Village Sign Society.

Vineyards
Selley, Dick. 'Geological and climatic controls on Britain's vineyards'. *Geoscientist*, vol. 14, no. 11, November 2004.

W

Wallflowers
Gilbert, Oliver. *Rooted in Stone: The Natural Flora of Urban Walls*. English Nature, 1992.
Greenoak, Francesca. *God's Acre*. E.P. Dutton, 1985.
Mabey, Richard. *Flora Britannica*. Chatto & Windus, 1996.

Walls
Gilbert, Oliver. *Rooted in Stone*. English Nature, 1992.
Meadows, E.G. *Changes in our Landscape: Aspects of Bedfordshire, Buckinghamshire and the Chilterns 1947-1992*. The Book Castle, 1992.
Design Statement for the Parish of Charlton Markell, nd.
Great Bowden Village Design Statement. 2000.
Parish of Olveston Design Statement. Doveton Press, 2004.
Wiveton Village, North Norfolk Coast, nd.

Walnut
Edlin, H.L. *Trees, Woods and Man*. Collins, 1956/1978.
Edlin, H.L. *Woodland Crafts in Britain*. David & Charles, 1949/1973.
Menear, Sarah. *Trees and Woodland on Exmoor*. Exmoor National Park Authority, 1997.
Rackham, Oliver. *Trees and Woodland in the English Landscape*. Dent, 1990.
Riley, Hazel and Wilson-North, Robert. *The Field Archaeology of Exmoor*. English Heritage, 2001.
Roach, F.A. *Cultivated Fruits of Britain: Their Origin and History*. Blackwell, 1985.

Warehouses
Giles, Colum and Hawkins, Bob. *Storehouses of Empire: Liverpool's Historic Warehouses*. English Heritage, 2004.

Girouard, Mark. *The English Town*. Yale University Press, 1990.

Warrens
Buczacki, Stefan. *Fauna Britannica*. Hamlyn, 2002.
Cook, Olive. *Breckland*. Robert Hale, 1956/1980.
Field, John. *A History of English Field-Names*. Longman, 1993.
Greeves, Tom. *The Archaeology of Dartmoor from the Air*. Dartmoor National Park/Devon Books, 1985.
Harris, A. 'Gorse in the East Riding of Yorkshire'. *Folk Life*, vol. 30, 1991-2.
Hart-Davis, Duff. *Fauna Britannica*. Weidenfeld & Nicolson, 2002.
Jefferies, Richard. *Field and Farm*. Phoenix House, 1957.
Jenkins, Simon. *England's Thousand Best Churches*. Penguin, 1999.
Macdonald, David W. and Tattersall, Fran. *Britain's Mammals: The Challenge for Conservation*. Mammals Trust UK, 2001.
Rackham, Oliver. *The History of the Countryside*. Dent, 1986.
Sheail, John. *Rabbits and their History*. David & Charles, 1971.
Simpson, J. and Roud, S. *Oxford Dictionary of English Folklore*. OUP, 2000.

Wassailing
Hole, Christina. *British Folk Customs*. Hutchinson, 1976.
Kightly, Charles. *The Customs and Ceremonies of Britain*. Thames & Hudson, 1986.
Apple Games and Customs. Common Ground, 2005.

Watercress Beds
Hunt, B. Letter, 2 April 1999.
Mayhew, Henry. *London Labour and the London Poor*. George Woodfall, 1851.

Waterfalls
Allen, Bob. *Escape to the Dales*. Michael Joseph, 1992.
Fellows, Griff J. *The Waterfalls of England*. Sigma Leisure, 2003.
Raistrick, Arthur. *The Pennine Dales*. Eyre & Spottiswoode, 1968.
Seers, J.A. *The Coastline of England and Wales*. CUP, 1964.
Thompson, D. Mark. Hardraw Force Waterfall website: www.hardrawforce.com/BCHistory.htm

Water-meadows
Harvey, Graham. *The Forgiveness of Nature*. Jonathan Cape, 2001.
Hampshire County Council, Water Meadows in Hampshire, Hampshire County Council, nd.
Rivers, Rhynes and Running Brooks. Common Ground, 2000.
English Heritage.

Water-mills
Aspin, Chris. *The Woollen Industry*. Shire, 2000.

Bush, Sarah. *The Silk Industry*. Shire, 2000.
Watts, Martin. *Water and Wind Power*. Shire, 2000.
Wenham, Peter. *Watermills*. Robert Hale, 1989.
Wood, Eric S. *Historical Britain*. Harvill Press, 1995.
Whitchurch Silk Mill (leaflet). SPAB.

Water-towers
Barton, Barry. *Water Towers of Britain*. Newcomen Society, 2003.

Wayside & Boundary Crosses
Beadle, J. Brian. *Walking to Crosses on the North York Moors*. Trailblazer Publishing, 1998.
Chapman, Chris. *Wild Goose and Riddon: The Dartmoor Photographs of Chris Chapman*. Devon Books, 2000.
Harrison, Bill. *Dartmoor Stone Crosses*. Devon Books, 2001.
Langdon, Andrew. *Stone Crosses in North Cornwall*. The Federation of Old Cornwall Societies, 1992/Andrew Langdon, 1996.
Lees, Hilary. *English Churchyard Memorials*. Tempus Publishing, 2000.
Ogilvie, Elizabeth and Sleightholme, Audrey. *The Illustrated Guide to the Crosses on the North York Moors*. The Village Green Press, 1994.
Rowe, Laura. *Granite Crosses of West Cornwall*. Bradford Barton, 1973.

Weather
Cathcart, Brian. *Rain*. Granta, 2004.
Clifford, Sue and King, Angela. *Local Distinctiveness: Place, Particularity and Identity*. Common Ground, 1993.
Cox, Evelyn. *The Great Drought of 1976*. Hutchinson, 1978.
Garner, Alan. *The Stone Book Quartet*. HarperCollins, 1992.
Moss, Stephen and Simons, Paul/Met Office. *Weather Watch*. BBC, 1992.
Porteous, Katrina (ed.). *The Bonny Fisher Lad*. The People's History, 2003.
Meteorological Office.

Weather-boarding
Brunskill, R.W. *Timber Building in Britain*. Gollancz, 1994.
Clifton-Taylor, Alec. *The Pattern of English Building*. Faber & Faber, 1972.
Penoyre, John and Penoyre, Jane. *Houses in the Landscape*. Readers Union, 1978.
Warren, Rebecca. *The High Weald*. Countryside Commission, 1994.

Weather-vanes
Crowden, James and Wimhurst, Karen. '*Silver Messenger*'. Confluence/Common Ground, 2001.
Dainton, Courtney. *Clocks, Jacks and Bee Boles*. Phoenix House, 1957.
Mockridge, Patricia and Mockridge, Philip. *Weathervanes*. Shire, 1993.

Mockridge, Patricia and Mockridge, Philip. *Weathervanes of Great Britain*. Robert Hale, 1990.
Shakespeare, William. *Hamlet*. 1603.
Watson, Lyall. *Heaven's Breath: A Natural History of the Wind*. Hodder & Stoughton, 1984.
Wright, Rev. W.E. Letter, July 2003.

Weirs
Confluence: New Music for the River Stour. Common Ground, 1998-2001.
Croad, Stephen. *Liquid History: The Thames Through Time*. English Heritage/Batsford, 2003.
Nomination of the Derwent Valley Mills for Inscription on the World Heritage List. Derbyshire County Council et al, 2000.
Rivers, Rhynes and Running Brooks. Common Ground, 2000.

Well Dressing
Porteous, Crichton. *The Well Dressing Guide*. Derbyshire Countryside, 1974.
Quinn, Phil. *The Holy Wells of Bath and Bristol Region (Monuments in the Landscape, vol. 6)*. Logaston Press, 1999.
Rivers, Rhynes and Running Brooks. Common Ground, 2000.

Wells
Bord, Janet and Bord, Colin. *Sacred Waters*. Paladin, 1986.
Quinn, Phil. *The Holy Wells of Bath and Bristol Region (Monuments in the Landscape, vol. 6)*. Logaston Press, 1999.
Shepherd, Val. *Historic Wells in and around Bradford*. Heart of Albion Press, 1994.
Stanton, W.I. 'The ancient springs, streams and underground watercourses of the City of Wells', Wells Natural History and Archaeological Society, 1987 and 1988.
Rivers, Rhynes and Running Brooks. Common Ground, 2000.
Source, The Holy Wells Journal.

Wem Sweet Pea Show
Genders, Roy. *The Cottage Garden*. Pelham Books, 1969.
Good, Val. Letter, 18 February 2002.
Hadfield, Miles. *A History of British Gardening*. Penguin Books, 1960.
National Sweet Pea Society.

Wensleydale Cheese
Hodgson, Randolf. 'Neal's Yard Dairy Cheese List' and emails, 2003-2005.
Mason, Laura with Brown, Catherine. *Traditional Foods of Britain*. Prospect Books, 1999.
Rance, Patrick. *The Great British Cheese Book*. Macmillan, 1982.

Whales, Dolphins & Porpoises
Levin, Anna. 'Seeing cetaceans'. *BBC Wildlife Magazine*, April 2002.

Hart-Davis, Duff.
  Fauna Britannica.
  Weidenfeld & Nicolson, 2002.
Macdonald, D.W. and Tattersall,
  Fran. *Britain's Mammals:
  The Challenge for Conservation*.
  PTES, 2001.
Morris, George.
  Letter, 20 August 1991.
Wainwright, Martin. 'Dolphins
  Flourish in North Sea'.
  Guardian, 2 April 2005.
Weir, Caroline R. 'Killer
  Whales in British Waters'.
  British Wildlife, December
  2002.
Horne's Guide to Whitby.
  Horne & Son, nd.
Whale Campaign Manuals,
  1 and 2. Friends of the Earth,
  1972 and 1974.
Whitebeam
  Bryan, Sarah. Conversation,
  July 2002.
  Exmoor Biodiversity Action Plan.
  Exmoor National Park, nd.
White Cliffs
  Covey, R. and Laffoley, D.d'A.
  State of Nature – Maritime.
  English Nature, 2002.
  Durrance, E.M. and Laming,
  D.J.C. *The Geology of Devon*.
  University of Exeter Press, 1982.
  Featherstone, Neil.
  Email, 18 August 2003.
  Fortey, Richard. *The Hidden
  Landscape*. Jonathan Cape, 1993.
  Robinson, A. and Millward, R.
  *The Shell Book of the British
  Coast*. David & Charles, 1983.
  Steers, J.A. *The Coastline
  of England and Wales*.
  CUP, 1964.
White Horses
  Carrdhus, K. and Miller, G.
  *The Search for Britain's
  Lost Unique Hill Figure
  (Red Horse of Tysoe)*. 1965.
  Hughes, Thomas. *The Scouring
  of the White Horse*. 1857.
  Marples, Morris. *White Horses
  and other Hill Figures*.
  1949/Alan Sutton, 1981.
  Miles, David and Palmer,
  Simon. 'White Horse Hill'.
  Current Archaeology, 142, 1995.
Wildflowers
  King, Angela. *Paradise Lost?*
  Friends of the Earth, 1980.
  Mabey, Richard. *Flora Britannica*.
  Chatto & Windus, 1996.
  Marren, Peter. 'County Floras'.
  British Wildlife, August 1999.
  Perring, F.H. and Walters, S.M.
  Atlas of the British Flora.
  Botanical Society of the
  British Isles, 1990.
  Porteous, Katrina.
  Letter, 24 May 2003.
  Vickery, Roy. *A Dictionary of
  Plant Lore*. OUP, 1995.
  Chagford Times. Chagford Parish
  Maps Project. Published by the
  residents of Chagford, 1988.
  Parish Maps. Common Ground,
  1996.
Willow
  Clare, John. 'The March
  Nightingale' in *Selected Poems
  and Prose of John Clare*
  (Robinson, Eric and
  Summerfield, Geoffrey, eds.).
  OUP, 1978/9.

Grigson, Geoffrey.
  The Englishman's Flora.
  Paladin, 1975.
Meikle, R.D. *Willows and
  Poplars of Great Britain and
  Ireland*. BSBI Handbook
  no. 4, BSBI, 1984.
Mitchell, Alan. *A Field Guide to
  Trees of Britain and Northern
  Europe*. Collins, 1974.
Wind Farms
  Bunyard, Peter. 'Wind power –
  the future of energy supply'.
  The Ecologist, 22 March 2002.
  The British Wind Energy
  Association.
  Friends of the Earth.
Windmills
  Bonwick, Luke. 'Heapham
  Windmill'. *Lincolnshire Mill
  News*, 80, July 1999.
  Hawksley, Geoff. 'Weekend
  Tour of Devon, 2004'.
  Mill News, 101, October 2004.
  Watts, Martin. *Water and Wind
  Power*. Shire, 2000.
  Williamson, Tom. *The Norfolk
  Broads: A Landscape History*.
  Manchester University Press,
  1997.
  Preserved Power.
  Hampshire County Council
  Museums Service, 1999.
  SPAB Mill News 81 (October
  1999), 87 (April 2002);
  92 (July 2002), 93 (October
  2002).
Winds
  Amsden, Meg. Email to Gail
  Vines, 16 May 2005.
  Defoe, D. 'The Storm 1704' in
  Defoe's Works, vol. v. George
  Bell & Sons, 1879.
  Manley, Gordon.
  Climate and the British Scene.
  Collins, 1952.
  Moss, Stephen and Simons,
  Paul. *Weather Watch*.
  The Met Office/BBC, 1992.
  Simpson, John E. *Sea Breeze
  and Local Wind*. CUP, 1994.
  Uttley, David.
  *The Anatomy of the Helm
  Wind*. Bookcase, 1998.
  Vines, Gail.
  'When the helm wind blows'.
  New Scientist, 14 May 2005.
  *The Macmillan Nautical Almanac
  1997*. Macmillan, 1996.
  Selsey Parish Map.
Windsor & Country Chairs
  Cotton, Bernard D. *The English
  Regional Chair*. Antique
  Collectors' Club, 1990.
Winterbournes
  Ekwall, E. *English River Names*.
  Oxford, 1928.
  Grigson, Geoffrey.
  The Shell Country Alphabet.
  Michael Joseph, 1966.
  Westwood, Jennifer. *Albion:
  A Guide to Legendary Britain*.
  Grafton, 1985.
Woods
  Marren, Peter.
  Woodland Heritage.
  David & Charles, 1990.
  Rackham, Oliver.
  Ancient Woodland.
  Castlepoint Press, 2003.
  Ratcliffe, D.A. (ed.).
  A Nature Conservation Review.
  CUP, 1977.

Wrestling
  Higgins, Mike. 'The regular
  re-invention of sporting
  tradition and identity:
  Cumberland and
  Westmorland Wrestling
  c.1800-2001', nd., at
  www2.umist.ac.uk/sport
  Larkin, Philip. 'Show Saturday'
  in *Collected Poems*.
  Faber & Faber, 1988.
  Mudd, David. *Cornwall
  and Scilly Peculiar*.
  Bossiney Books, 1979.
  Strutt, Joseph. *The Sports
  and Pastimes of the People of
  England*. Thomas Tegg, 1838.

X

Xanadu
  Clayre, Alasdair (ed.).
  Nature and Industrialization.
  Open University, 1977.
  Coleridge, Samuel Taylor.
  'In Xanadu'. 1797 (poem
  from the Crewe Manuscript,
  British Museum).
  Holmes, Richard.
  Coleridge: Early Visions.
  Hodder & Stoughton, 1989.
  Wright, David.
  Introduction to *The Penguin
  Book of English Romantic Verse*.
  Penguin Books, 1968.

Y

Yan Tan Tethera
  Birtwistle, Harrison.
  Yan Tan Tethera. 1983/4.
  Relph, Ted. 'Te deu wid sheep'
  at www.lakelanddialectsociety.
  org/counting_sheep.htm
  Whitehead, John. 'Counting
  Sheep: the traditional way'
  at www.slaidburn.org.uk/
  counting_sheep.htm
  *ABC, Common Ground Rules
  for Local Distinctiveness*.
  Common Ground, 1992.
Yew
  Artzell, H. *The Yew Tree*.
  Hulogosi, 1991.
  Bevan-Jones, R.
  The Ancient Yew.
  Windgather Press, 2002.
  Chetan, A. and Brueton, D.
  The Sacred Yew. Penguin,
  1994.
  Tennyson, Alfred Lord.
  'In Memoriam A.H.H.'
  in *The Poems of Tennyson*.
  Longman, 1969.
  Westwood, Jennifer.
  'Churchyard Yews'
  (unpublished). Email,
  17 November 2003.

Z

Zawns
  Arkell, W.J. and Tomkieieff, S.I.
  English Rock Terms. OUP, 1953.
  Steers, A.J. *The Coastline of
  England and Wales*.
  CUP, 1946/1964.
  Whittaker, David. *Zawn Lens*.
  Wavestone Press, 2003.
Zigzags
  Lindley, Kenneth.
  Seaside Architecture.
  Hugh Evelyn, 1973.

Mabey, Richard.
  Introduction to Gilbert
  White, *The Natural History of
  Selborne*. Penguin, 1977.
Perkins, John W.
  Geology Explained in Dorset.
  David & Charles, 1977.
*The Landscape of the Sussex
  Downs AONB*. Countryside
  Commission/Sussex Downs
  Conservation Board, 1996.

ACKNOWLEDGEMENTS

Common Ground is a small charity dependent upon grants and donations. We offer most grateful thanks to our funders: Defra Environmental Action Fund, Carnegie UK Trust, Cobb Trust, John Ellerman Foundation, Garfield Weston Foundation, Headley Trust, Lyndhurst Settlement, Raphael Trust, Tedworth Trust and, over a longer time frame, the Countryside Agency, English Nature, National Lottery: Arts Council of England, Esmée Fairbairn Charitable Trust and many supporters and individuals who have enabled us to experiment with ideas, to help others campaign, to research and to write.

This book is the result of years of looking, talking, gathering, learning and being enthused by people, by the land, by creatures, by stories, by connections, by the great variety show around us. Curiosity and idealism have led us along generalist pathways, seeing the possibilities in breadth yet aware of specific depths beyond our reach. Without help nothing could have found its way on to paper, but any weaknesses, mistakes and imperfections are, of course, our own.

Three people have worked directly with us in the research and writing of this book. We offer Gail Vines, Darren Giddings and Kate O'Farrell our huge thanks for their hard work, intrepid forays and flair.

Gail has lived in Aberdeenshire, Bristol, Liverpool, London, Bedfordshire, Cambridge and Lewes, Sussex, and has spent most of her holidays exploring bits of the English countryside on foot. An early fascination with the natural world led to field research on oystercatchers and magpies. In the early 1980s she moved into science journalism, writing and editing biological features for *New Scientist*. Now freelance, she also writes for *Kew* magazine, works as an editor for *Plantlife International* and aspires to write a celebration of the natural and cultural richness of a patch of downland east of Lewes.

Darren was born and lives in the West Country, although he studied the history, art and language of the early Middle Ages at Newcastle upon Tyne for a spell. He has eked out a living variously working in a record shop, writing for children's television, processing scientific research grant applications, broadcasting charity appeals on local radio and putting handles on paint tins. He has worked with Common Ground since 1998, researching, making newsletters and websites and hosting fish cabarets.

Kate grew up in Gosport, Hampshire, studied archaeology at Reading and worked with the Oxford Archaeology Unit and Wessex Archaeology, but now digs only her allotment. She joined Common Ground in 1999 as research and information officer.

Katrina Porteous has been our Northumberland correspondent and we cannot thank her enough for lifting our spirits and for her generosity in passing on all manner of detail, books, cuttings and photographs as well as wisdom and findings from her own researches. Katrina is a poet. Her work reflects knowledge, pride and affection for the working communities of the North East. From deep immersion she has given voice to the dialect of people and place in books such as *The Lost Music*, *The Wund an' the Wetter*, *The Bonny Fisher Lad* and *Turning the Tide*.

As honorary Common Grounders, she and Gail Vines have nourished us with poetry, science and local knowledge. We wish we could have done justice to the material sent, which cheered us like packets of mixed seeds through the years of writing.

Similarly, David Holmes has generously acted as our art director and mentor since the first Common Ground poster in 1985, demanding that we aim high and drawing in a fantastic array of fine illustrators, with sterling assistance from Toby and Polly.

Special thanks go to:
The Trustees and Directors of Common Ground – Barbara Bender, Roger Deakin, Robin Grove-White, Richard Mabey, Rupert Nabarro and, previously, Fraser Harrison and Robert Hutchison. Without their wisdom and constancy we should have withered in the wilderness long ago.

The people who have worked with us during the past decade and more (ideas evolve in the alchemy of the everyday) – Dan Keech, Jane Kendall, Beatrice Mayfield, John Newton, Leana Pooley, Helen Porter, Neil Sinden, Stephen Turner, Karen Wimhurst and Rachel Hyde, who voluntarily and creatively disciplined the tides of information for this book.

Our agent Vivien Green at Sheil Land (excellent grounding names), always there with wise admonishments, confident tones and careful timing.

Richard Atkinson, our publisher at Hodder & Stoughton, who pursued us and the idea for the best part of a decade. What can we say? He has given us the opportunity to write the book we have always wanted to create and the means to do it, with great enthusiasm, combining support and lightness of touch. Nicola Doherty, assistant editor at H&S, who attended, with smiles, to our well-being. Karen Geary, publicity director; Elizabeth Hallett, production director; Simon Shelmerdine. Rachael Oakden, who edited 300,000 words, tussling with our style and … er … profusiosity, more demanding than her young child. Hilary Bird, indexer, and Barbara Roby, proof-reader. Stuart Smith, Karl Shanahan and Victoria Forrest for big and small design.

Illustrators and artists. They are specifically acknowledged elsewhere, but we want to add our profound thanks for their patience and care in responding to our very specific demands. Their skills are obvious; we are fortunate to have had them journey with us.

We acknowledge our forebears and betters – and have quoted women and men from books, journals, magazines, websites, newspapers, correspondence. But many people whose names may not appear in the book are deeply implicated in generating our view of things; we offer thanks to all for their inspiration and mention just a few: Jay Appleton, W.H. Auden, Walter Benjamin, John Betjeman, Italo Calvino, John Clare, Alec Clifton Taylor, Derek Cooper, Loren Eiseley, Nan Fairbrother, Richard Fortey, Jane Grigson, Geoffrey Grigson, Dorothy Hartley, Seamus Heaney, W.G. Hoskins, Richard Jefferies, Charles Kightly, Tim Lang, Barry Lopez, Richard Mabey, Robert MacFarlane, Peter Marren, H.J. Massingham, George Monbiot, Iain Nairn, Norman Nicholson, Adam Nicolson, Oliver Rackham, Simon Schama, Will Shakespeare, Dorothy and William Wordsworth and many, many more, including map makers from John Speed to the Ordnance Survey.

Thanks to:
Our colleagues in both governmental and non-governmental organisations, who have provoked us and furthered the arguments in different ways: Action for Market Towns, Ancient Tree Forum, Black Environment Network, British Trust for Ornithology, Campaign for Real Ale, Campaign to Protect Rural England, Commission for Architecture and the Built Environment, Council for British Archaeology, Countryside Commission/Agency, English Heritage, English Nature, Environment Agency, Friends of the Earth, Greenpeace, Local Heritage Initiative, National Forest, National Trust, New Economics Foundation, Open Spaces Society, Royal Society for the Protection of Birds, Society for the Protection of Ancient Buildings, Soil Association, Sustain, Twentieth Century Society, Wildlife Trusts, Woodland Trust, officers in national agencies and local authorities from Devonshire to Derbyshire, Norfolk to Herefordshire, Northumberland to West Sussex.

The library service, especially in Shaftesbury, Dorset, for relentlessly pursuing obscure books from far-off corners. There is no substitute for a book, except the person who wrote it and the place explored, but the world-wide web helped us to check and search with phenomenal speed and reach. It is a fantastic, democratic resource base; thank you to all who make it so.

Local people who have gathered together to make Parish Maps, ABCs, Community Orchards, Apple Day events, to celebrate local distinctiveness in so many ways. Without their activities we cannot learn and help others.

People from across the world who have taken our ideas into their cultures and fed us from their own work: Helen Armstrong in Sydney and Brisbane, Australia; Jerry de Gryse in Tasmania, Australia; Dolores Hayden at Yale University and Richard Westmacott at the University of Georgia, US; Donatella Murtas, Maurizio Maggi and colleagues in the ecomusée world in Italy; Mike Flood from Powerful Information and his allies in Lithuania, Romania, Nigeria, Sierra Leone and more.

Friends and stalwarts, who never shirked out-of-the-blue demands and animated conversations, despite our long silences: Angela and Paul Brassley,

483

Fanny Charles, Michael Clifford, Cynthia Cockburn, James Crowden, Laurie Fricker, Lizzie Kessler, Kim Leslie, Duncan Mackay, David Nash, Gay Pirrie-Weir, Leana Pooley, Jane Powell, Frances Price, Eric Robinson, Carol Trewin and Jennifer Westwood. Also Alastair Anderson, Peter Andrews, Chris Baines, Kathleen Basford (the late), Peter Beacham, Susan Bell, Valerie Belsey, Jonathan Briggs, Stefan Buczacki, Bob Butler, Chris Chapman, Edward Chorlton, Ian Christie, John Cooper Hammond, Philippa Davenport, Michael Dower, Matt Dunwell, Hattie Ellis, Paul Evans, Rob Fairbanks, Graham Fairclough, Clive Fewins, Meg Game, Michael Gee, John Gittins, Andy Goldsworthy, Ted Green, Ruth Grundy, Clifford Harper, Graham Harvey, Randolph Hodgson, Danny Hughes, Gregor Hutcheon, Rose Jaijee, George Lambrick, Judy Ling Wong, John Maine, James Marsden, Robin Maynard, Ed Mayo, George Nicholson, Robin Nicholson, David Pedley, Peter Randall-Page, James Ravilious (the late), Robin Ravilious, Fiona Reynolds, Anthony Richards, Linda Ridgely, Grant Sonnex, Virginia Spiers, Martin Stott, Trudy Turrell, Humphrey Welfare, Kim Wilkie, Ken Worpole and Rob Young.

Our gratitude seems such a small offering to the selflessness shown to us by so many individuals, who contacted us with contributions and thoughts. Thank you to everyone, including those who omitted to tell us their names, and to anyone we have failed to represent:

P.J.V. Adams, Gaby Adnitt, Jess Allen, Peter Allen, Peter C. Allinson, Isabel Alonso, Daphne Anson, Stephen K. Appleby, Paul Ashbee, John Asher, Christine Ashmore, Richard Atkinson, Marigold Austin, M.I. Awde, Tim Baber, Ken Bagnall, Chris Bagshaw, Teresa Baier, Eileen Baird, David Ball, Damien Barber, Stuart Bardsley, Paul Barker, Tony Barker, Rupert Barnes, Molly Barrett, Anna Barry, Victor B.M. Barry, Roger Barstow, Richard Barton, John Baylis, John S. Beadle, Simon Bean, Simon Beavis, Penny Berry, Adrian Berryman, Paul Bexon, Henry Biggs, Philip Bodie, Chris Bray, Anthea Brian, Mike Bridgman, Linda Briggs, Allan Brigham, Margaret Bromwich, C. Brooks, Nora Brown, Teresa Brown, Roger Budgeon, Richard Bull, Wendy Bullar, Mandy Bulloch, Les Bunce, Arthur Burns, Stuart Burroughs, Grenville Burrows, Nick Burrows, Richard Burton, Simon de Burton, Richard Bush, Tim Butterworth, Pauline Buttery, Cath Byram, Patsy Caffrey, Clare Calder-Marshall, Sheelagh Callaghan, Mary Cameron, Neil Campling, Steve Cann, Charles Carey, Sue Carling, Peter Cartmell, Bridget Cass, Julian Cass, F.M. Caton, John Chaplin, Ian Cheeseman, Cathy Clark, Matthew Clarke, Frances Clayton, Jeff Cloves, Ian Coe, Sue Coe, Dominic Cole, John Collins, David G. Collyer, Tony Cooke, Fiona Cooper, Richard Cooper, Ricky Cooper, Colin Cope, Ann Couper-Johnston, Peter Cox, Nick Cracknell, Ann Creber, Benedict Critchley, Sarah J. Crofts, Arthur Cross, Rosie Cross, Joan Crump, Nick Crump, P.M. Cudmore, Rosemary Culkin, Scilla Cullen, Carolyn Cumming, Chris Currie, Bill and Lesley Cutting, Caroline Davison, Malcolm Davison, Chris Dawson, Valerie Dawson, Charissa Day, Iestyn Day, Marti Dean, Kate Dewey, Meriel Dobinson, Carol Donaldson, Sheila Donaldson, Graham Downie, Ron Duckett, Doreen Duckworth, Gerald Duke, Michael Dutson, Susan Dye, John Easterbrooke, Lesley Edleston, Nita Edwards, Jonathan Elcock, Heather Elvidge, Rose Evans, Sue Everett, Al Ferrier, Kathryn Ferry, Neil Featherstone, Mike Flowerday, David Flowers, Bob Ford, Lynn Fomison, Claire Forrest, Carol Forster, Tony Fox, Sally Francis, Andrew Fraser, Barry Freeman, Tony and Elizabeth Gentil, Bob Gibbons, Roger Glanville, Ian Goole, Michael Goormachtigh, Alistair Gordon, Dave Gorman, Pam Gough, Ros Gough, Dennis Gould, Judith Gowland, Allan Graham, Caz Graham, Damaris Graham, Ben Green, Gary Green, Tony Greenway, Chris Griffiths, Edward Grimsdale, Geraldine Hackworth Cater, David Haden, Caroline Hall, R.B. Hamilton, Anne Hardcastle, Phil Harding, Toby Hardwick, Nigel Harrison, Tim Harrold, Sahdia Hassen, Martin Haswell, Dorothy Haughton, Tom Haverly, Simon Hawksley, Robert Hawley, Joanna Haxby, Mary Herdman, Roger Herman, Rob Higgins, Neil Hillier, David A. Hinton, Nick Hirst, Chris Hobson, Pol Hodge, Mr Hodges, Christine Hodgetts, Jill Holmes, Steven J. Homewood, Caroline Hope, Ian and Gill Horsley, Leonard Horton, Jane Houghton, Peter J. Howard, Brian Human, John Hurd, Carrol Hurdle, John Hyde, Tom Ikins,

Fiona Jackson, Noel Jackson, Dan Jago, Rob Jarman, Cliff Jenkins, Peter Jenkins, Tiffany Jenkins, Paul Jeorrett, Helen Jones, Joanne Jones, Jules Jones, Mary Jones, Katy Jordan, Barry Joyce, Nicholas Keep, Yvonne Keeping, Edwina Kellock, Jayne Kendal, Jane Kendall, Debbie Kenyon-Jackson, David and Patricia Kerridge, Chris King, Marcus King, P.N. Kinston, Tony Kirby-Suttie, John Knight, Janet Landon, Meike Laurnson, Anne Lawson, Adrian Lay, Sheila Lee, Claire Leslie, Samantha Letters, Andrew I. Lewer, Peter N. Lockyer, Sally Lomax, John Lowe, Jamie Lund, Kate Lynch, Glenn Lyons, Joan and Sam Main, Kevan Manwaring, Peter Marlow, Peter Marron, Teresa Marron, Napier Marten, Steve Maskell, Jenifer Maughan, Jane MacNamee, Bernard A. McCann, Joy McCarthy, Sheila McGary, Adam McGovern, Zara McQueen, Frazer Melton, Ian Mercer, Chris Miller, Eric Miller, Hazel Miller, M.A. Miller, Jennifer Moore-Blunt, Jim Moran, Margaret Morley, Faith Moulin, Tony Mudd, Eleanor Murphy, Eileen Murton, Tim Neal, Linda Neilson, Penny Neyroud, Geoffrey Noble, Les Owen, A. Nelson Owen, David Owner, Tony Parker, Philip Parker, Anita Patchett, David Pearce, Dale Peck, Nigel Pennick, Stephen Pewsey, Margaret Phillimore, Andy Pickard, Simon Pipe, L.C. Pople, Mr Potter, Jane Powell, Katy Pritchard, Martin Prothero, Richard Purslow, Kevin Pyke, Lut Rahman, Richard Ranft, Christine Ravenscroft, Eunice Rees, Ash Reynolds, Lesley Rhodes, Chris Riddle, John Risby, Tamsin Ritchie, Lesley Ann Rose, Edna Ross, Peter Rowan, Tim Russell, Phil Ryder, Alex Ryding, Anthony Rylands, Helen Sadler, G. Sandhu, Carolyn Saunders, Derrick Scrivener, Matthew Searle, Paul Sharman, Kathryn Sherdley, Steve Sherdley, Richard Sim, Clive Simmonds, Martin Skipper, Chris Slade, Brian Sleightholm, Jan Smart, Colin Smith, Dave Smith, Harold Smith, Joke Snel, Margaret Somerville, Elaine Spencer-White, Martin Spray, Simon Steele, Kirsty Stevens, Greg Stevenson, Janet Stevenson, Sarah Stewart, David Stocker, John Tabor, Colin Taylor, Ian Taylor, Maurice Taylor, Patrick Taylor, Phil Taylor, Derek Thomas, Jill Thomas, Jo Thomas, Pete Thomas, Richard Thomas, Thebe Thomas, Dan Thompson, Irene Thompson, Jim Thompson, Peter Thompson, Janet Thorning, Ted Tims, Alison Tingley, Dee Tracey, David Turner, Stephen Turner, Aiden Turner-Bishop, Robert Turton, Gloria Tyler, Peter Ursem, Candy Verney, Marjorie Vincent, Claire Wagstaff, Bryan Waites, Lindy Wale, Charlotte Walker, Mary Walker, P. Waller, David Walton, Edward Warde, Rebecca Warren, Rob Warren, Will Watson, God Wayland, Ruth Webster, Tom Webster, Iris Wells, Marion Wells, Alan West, Derek Wetenhall, Kathryn Wheeler, Mike Wiles, Michael Wilkinson, Alice Williams, Angela Williams, Heathcote Williams, Kim Williams, Alexander Wilson, Neil Windett, Chris Wood, Tony Wood, Chris Woodley-Stewart, Nicholas Worden, W.E. Wright, Reg Yorke, Gordon Young, Rob Young. Aiden Turner-Bishop and Dennis Gould take the awards for fantastic offerings.

England's richness is protected and expressed through many societies, groups and organisations. We thank all those who selflessly work locally and nationally. Many are scattered through the book; here we mention just a few:
Association of Show and Agricultural Organisations, Austwick Cuckoo Festival, Banbury Hobby Horse Festival, Barwick Maypole Committee, Bingham Heritage Trails Association, Black Cherry Ltd (Chertsey's), Black Swan Rapper, Blaize, Bodmin Wassail, Bonsall Village Design Group, Brigg Life, The Buckinghamshire Society, Burnsall Feast Sports, Centre for Metropolitan History, Chappell Millennium Green Trust, Charlton Mackrell Village Design Statement Group, Cornish Language Fellowship, Dean Heritage Museum Trust, Drystone Wall Society, FARNE (Folk Archive Resource North East), Folk South West, Fowler's Troop Deptford Jack in the Green, Friends of Real Lancashire, Great Bowden Village Design Statement Group, The Green Shop, Guildford Society, Huntingdonshire Society, Langport Mummers, Northumberland Rapper Sword Dance, Nuneaton Carnival Committee, Olveston Parish Plan, Penrhos Trust, Rolleston on Dove Village Website, Royal Cornwall Agricultural Association, Ryburn 3 Step, St Peter's Village Tour, Wennington Village Association.

We have tried to populate the book with voices from local people, profound thinkers, graceful commentators: their plurality is an important part of our inheritance and surroundings. We thank everyone we have quoted and hope that the bibliography leads others to their published works. We are grateful to the following for specific permissions: Tim Baber, Peter Beacham, Penny Berry, J. Blades, Joanna Blythman, Carol for Pete Bowler, Billy Bragg, Angela and Paul Brassley, Anthea Brian, John Brookes, Barry Callaghan, Charles Carey, John Chaplin, Peter Child, Mark Cocker, Fiona Cooper, Liz Copas, Richard Cork, Bernard D. Cotton, James Crowden, Caroline Davison, Roger Deakin, Michael Dutson, Margaret Elsworth, Norman Emery, Chris Feare, Neil Featherstone, David Gardiner, Phil Gates, Roger Glanville, Andy Goldsworthy, Dennis Gould, Caz Graham, Gary Green, Graham Harvey, Seamus Heaney, Mary Herdman, Mr Hodges, Randolph Hodgson, Jeremy Hooker, Sara Hudston, Paul Hyland, Owen Johnson, Barry Joyce, Charles Kightly, Tim Laycock, Rodney Legg, Kim Leslie, John Lowe, David Lowenthal, Jamie Lund, Richard Mabey, Peter Marren, Charles Martell, Peter F. Mason, Eric Miller, Joan Morgan, David Nash, Adam Nicolson, Geoff Noble, Tim O'Riordan, Alice Oswald, Robin Page, George Peterken, Katrina Porteous, Rose Prince, Hugh Prudden, Oliver Rackham, Peter Randall, Eric Robinson, Helen Sadler, Steve Sherdley, Richard Sim, Clive Simmonds, Jacqueline Simpson, Virginia Spiers, Patrick Taylor, Jill Thomas, Jo Thomas, Ruth Ward, Jennifer Westwood, W.E. Wright.

We thank all of the individuals, publishers, agents, executors and trustees for their generosity. Full references are given in the bibliography. The following are reproduced by permission of: Anvil Press Poetry, for Carol Ann Duffy, 'River' from *The Other Country*, 1990. Penguin Books Ltd, for Simon Armitage, *All Points North*, Viking, 1998; Felicity Lawrence, *Not on the Label*, 2004. Robert Hale Ltd, for Brian Bailey, *The English Village Green*, 1985; Olive Cook, *Breckland*, 1956; Norman Nicholson, *Cumberland and Westmorland*, 1949. HarperCollins Publishers Ltd, for © H.L. Edlin, *Trees, Woods and Man*, 1956/1978; © Tom Fort, *The Grass is Greener*, 2000; © Tom Fort, *The Book of Eels*, 2002; © Alan Garner, *The Stone Book Quartet*, 1992. Hodder & Stoughton Ltd, for John Betjeman, *First and Last Loves*, 1952; Melvyn Bragg, *The Adventure of English*, 2003; W.G. Hoskins, *The Making of the English Landscape*, 1955 and 2005. Chrysalis Books Group plc, for Edmund Blunden, *The Landscape in the Legacy of England*, © Edmund Blunden, 1935; Christina Hole, *English Folklore*, © Christina Hole, 1940; H.J. Massingham, *English Downland*, © H.J. Massingham, 1936; Adela Wright, *Craft Techniques for Traditional Buildings*, © Adela Wright, 1991. OUP, for Trevor Herbert (ed.) *The British Brass Band*, 2000; Ronald Hutton, *Rise and Fall of Merry England*, 1994; Ronald Hutton, *Stations of the Sun*, 1996; J. Richards, J. and John Mackenzie, *The Railway Station: A Social History*, 1986. Bill Hamilton, Literary Executor of the Estate of the late Sonia Brownell Orwell, for © George Orwell. Caroline Grigson, Literary Executor of the Estate of the late Geoffrey Grigson. Sophie Grigson, Literary Executor of the Estate of the late Jane Grigson. Pollinger Limited and the proprietor, for D.H. Lawrence, *Sons and Lovers*, Penguin Books, 1913. Reader's Union, for John and Jane Penoyre, *Houses in the Landscape: A Regional Study of Vernacular Building Styles in England and Wales*, 1978. Shire Publications, for Christopher Feare, *The Starling*, 1985. The Society of Authors as the Literary Representative for A.E. Housman.

Our sincere apologies if we have missed or misrepresented anyone. Please inform us so that we might rectify this.

Picture Acknowledgements
For more than two decades Common Ground has been indebted to artists whose work has uplifted and informed our work and helped to promote our ideas.

Many illustrators and artists have given very generously of their time for this book. It has been enriched by them in ways that no words could achieve. We thank them for the deliberate and careful responses to our often exacting briefings – in a book about local distinctiveness you cannot get away with any old bridge, a somewhere-or-other café or a tree. Our admiration for your capacity to 'take lines for a walk' grows at every turn. Thank you.

Ivan Allen: 3 left, 5, 22, 26, 32, 47, 51, 62, 63, 91, 100, 133, 134, 144, 154, 182, 187, 192, 221, 227, 263, 265 right, 274, 280, 287, 326, 333 bottom, 334, 335, 337, 371, 379, 385, 412, 415, 428, 433 left, 437, 445 right, 446, 449, 450. Richard Allen: 6 right, 55, 56, 67, 72, 78, 86, 102, 126 left, 173, 176, 198, 205, 236, 245, 325, 329, 341, 348 top, 357 right, 372, 389, 420, 441, 442. David Atkinson: 45, 59, 80, 82, 83, 115, 217, 366 right, 376, 377, 386 bottom right. Richard Atkinson: 299. Grahame Baker Smith: 31, 88 bottom, 111, 153, 158, 203, 429, 432. Ian Beck: 188, 296, 370, 381, 386 left, 416, 422, 433 right, 434 left. Graham Bence: 167. Thomas Bewick: 319, 355, 360. Peter Blake: 200 top, 209 (from a photograph by Michael Clifford), 286. Ed Briant: 276, 306, 307. Mick Brownfield: 386 top right. Chloë Cheese: 39, 70, 77, 246 right, 365, 375, 410. Matthew Cook: 64. Chris Corr: 285, 345 left. Ken Cox: 126 right, 156, 157, 160, 206, 241, 242, 308, 323. Andrew Davidson: 333 top, 403. Mel DeLasti: 258, 281. Matthew Dennis: 215, 443 right. Alan Fletcher: 118, 237, 260, 318. David Gentleman: 243, 342, 384. Mickey Georgeson: 110, 300, 332 bottom. Jonathan Gibbs: 273, 345 right. Darren Giddings: 353. Andy Goldsworthy: 374 left. Glyn Goodwin: 10 left, 16, 34, 40, 53, 69, 76, 94, 107, 130, 137, 142, 148, 161, 275, 327, 366 left, 434 right. Antony Gormley: 181, 368. Mark Greenwood: 135, 421. Brian Grimwood: 10 right, 382. Paul Guest: 202. Nick Hardcastle: 44, 174, 180 top, 231, 249, 374 right, 400, 408. Clifford Harper: 3 right, 8, 15, 27, 28 left, 28 right, 41, 48, 54, 57, 68, 81, 90, 116, 119, 121, 165, 168, 200 bottom, 223, 226, 229, 230, 234, 267, 272, 290, 291, 315, 331 right, 347, 348 bottom, 359, 361, 378, 391, 411 top, 419, 443 left. Hans Helweg: 25. John Hinchcliffe: vi, 172 left, 199, 407, 448. Angela Hogg: 18, 97, 109 left, 114, 117, 128, 183, 193, 194, 196 right, 261, 262, 265 left, 277 left, 332 top, 338, 392 right, 393, 436 bottom. David Holmes: 12, 21, 89, 98, 101, 109, 180 bottom, 196 left, 282, 356 left, 356 right, 357 left, 396, 413. Toby Holmes: 42 right, 52, 75, 84 left (from a photograph by Angela King), 122 (from a photograph by Sue Clifford), 138, 145 left, 224 (after Linda Francis, from *Hedging: A Practical Handbook*, BTCV, 1998), 246 left (from a photograph by Angela King), 255 (from a photograph by Angela King), 431. David Inshaw: 143. Jayne Ivimey: 219. Colin Kennedy: 17, 266, 301, 310, 392 left. John Lawrence: 84 right, 454 left. Eric McKee: 298, 331 left. John Maine: 268. Robert Maude: 254, 316, 414 left. Francis Mosley: 131, 147, 208, 232, 247, 271 left, 271 right, 295, 399, 414 right. David Nash: 20, 93, 305, 445 left, 447, 454 right. Stuart Newman: 259, 312. Nick Orsborn: 6 left, 390. Michael O'Shaunessy: 85, 169, 248, 288, 344. Ian Pollock: 279, 358. Katrina Porteous: 104. Mark Reddy: 367. Mary Roberts-Hogan: 42 left, 125, 163, 164. Lucinda Rogers: 37, 88 top, 112, 162, 177, 191, 197, 404, 405, 406, 411 bottom, 424, 439. Karl Shanahan: 228. Charles Shearer: 170, 171, 172 right, 256, 284, 309. Jim Sillavan: 33, 324, 346, 387, 402 top. Stuart Smith: 60. Peter Till: 322, 351, 436 top. Stephen Turner: 218. Peter Ursem: 179, 184, 311. Dan Williams: 9, 87, 149, 186, 216, 277 right, 388, 394, 395, 401, 402 bottom. Sue Williams: 19, 145 right. Gordon Young: 317.

We are grateful for kind permission from: Anthea Brian to redraw maps from 'The Distribution of Brick Bonds in England up to 1800' (*Vernacular Architecture*, vol. II, 1980). BTCV and Linda Francis to redraw hedges from Brooks, Alan and Agate, Elizabeth, *Hedging: A Practical Handbook* (BTCV, 1998). Willy Elmer for use of his work on Starfish names from Elmer, W., *The Terminology of Fishing: A Survey of English and Welsh Inshore Fishing Things and Words* (The Cooper Monographs 19, English Dialect Series, Franke Verlag, 1973). Mrs Betty McKee to reproduce Eric McKee's meticulous boats from *Working Boats of Britain* (Conway Maritime Press, 1983). Jo Thomas to redraw maps of stone buildings from *Stone Quarrying* (Dovecote Press, 1998).

486

490

495

498

503

504

INDEX

511